LAROUSSE WINE

An Hachette UK Company
www.hachette.co.uk

Originally published in France by Editions Larousse as *Grand Larousse du Vin*.
First published in Great Britain in 2017 by Hamlyn, a division of Octopus Publishing Group Ltd,
Carmelite House, 50 Victoria Embankment, London EC4Y 0DZ
www.octopusbooks.co.uk | www.octopusbooksusa.com

Distributed in the US by Hachette Book Group, 1290 Avenue of the Americas, 4th and 5th Floors, New York, NY 10104

Distributed in Canada by Canadian Manda Group, 664 Annette St., Toronto, Ontario, Canada M6S 2C8

ISBN 978-0-600-63509-3

A CIP catalogue record for this book is available from the British Library

Printed and bound in China

10 9 8 7 6 5 4 3 2 1

English Edition
Group Publishing Director: Denise Bates
Translation: JMS Books LLP
Senior Editor: Pollyanna Poulter
Copy Editor: Hilary Lumsden
Junior Designer: Jack Storey
Senior Production Controller: Allison Gonsalves

French Edition 2010
Publishing Director: Isabelle Jeuge-Maynart
Editorial Director: Véronique de Finance-Cordonnier
Editorial: Aude Mantoux
Editor: Ewa Lochet, together with Élisabeth Andreani and Guillaume d'Oléac d'Ourche
Art Director: Emmanuel Chaspoul, with the help of Anna Bardon and Sylvie Sénéchal
Layout: Natacha Marmouget
Publishing systems: Marie-Noëlle Tilliette and Philippe Cazabet
Proofreader: Chantal Pagès, with the help of Madeleine Biaujeaud, Nathalie Kristy, Joëlle Narjollet, and Sylvie Porté
Index: Rupert Hasterok
Illustrations: Valérie Perrin, with the help of Josiane Martin
Vineyard maps: Laurent Blondel
Cover: Véronique Laporte
Production: Annie Botrel
Photography: See photographic credits at the back of the book

The publisher would like to thank Camille Durette, Julie-Fleur Colomer, Véronique Jean, Magali Marquet, and Adèle Rosenfeld for their invaluable help.

French Edition 2016
Publishing Directors: Isabelle Jeuge-Maynart and Ghislaine Stora
Editorial Directors: Agnès Busière and Émilie Franc
Editor: Marion Dellapina
Proofreaders: Madison Deschamps and Julien Tardif
Index: François Bernier
Designers: Maeva Lebegue and Aurore Élie
Layout: Valérie Verroye-Nacci
Cover: Véronique Laporte
Production: Donia Faiz
Photography: See photographic credits at the back of the book

The publisher would like to thank Lucie Pommet for her invaluable help.

NEW EDITION: COMPLETELY REVISED & UPDATED WITH ADDITIONAL CONTENT

LAROUSSE WINE

THE DEFINITIVE REFERENCE FOR WINE LOVERS

HOW TO UNDERSTAND & ENJOY THE WORLD'S BEST WINES

hamlyn

PREFACE

Wine is an invitation to go on a journey. This book bears witness to that trip. The road begins with discovery of the extraordinary diversity of grape varieties and *terroirs* that exist all over the world. It then introduces you to the people involved and the work they accomplish in countless vineyards and wine cellars. Finally, it takes you into the world of wine tasting and reveals the incredible variety of wines on every continent.

I am dedicated to learning about the wines of the world. I have spent a good part of my life in this pursuit, and I continue to study the development of the many, diverse vineyards with immense curiosity. Driven by a quest for new *terroirs* and grape varieties, I have visited several regions and on every occasion have learned a great deal, both on a cultural and a personal level. Today, I am aware that every continent displays a desire, even an obsession, to produce the finest wines.

There is no doubt that the traditional vineyards of Europe, represented in particular by France, but also by Italy and Spain, still occupy a leading position as a result of their history, culture, traditions, and scale. However, many of us have yet to discover the fascinating diversity of vineyards in Central and Eastern Europe. Some countries in the Middle East also show good potential, with the emergence of small, ambitious wineries. And what about all the New World wines that arrived on the shelves of our supermarkets and our wine shops starting some 25 years ago, transforming the economic landscape of wine production? There are beautiful estates to explore, whether in Chile or Argentina, and each embarked on the hunt for new *terroirs* suitable for producing ever more concentrated, balanced wines. Lastly, we watch with interest as India and China develop significant wine projects. The fact that Asia is as interested in producing wine as it is tea represents a real sea change. But wine inspires aspirations everywhere. New countries are introducing viticulture, and a huge variety of wines are out there for us to investigate.

This book will help you discover the diversity and richness of wines produced throughout the world. I also hope it will inspire you to rediscover familiar wines as well as to explore those with unexpected aromas and flavours.

Olivier Poussier
World's leading sommelier

CONTRIBUTORS

The following have contributed to this edition:

Georges Lepré, Master Sommelier, technical consultant for the entire book

and:

Guy Bonnefoit, wine expert and author of books on wine
Pierrick Bourgault, agronomist, journalist, and photographer
Jean-Moïse Braitberg, journalist and author of books on wine
David Cobbold, journalist and critic, author of articles and books on wine
Jean-Michel Deluc, Master Sommelier, international consultant, and lecturer
Michel Dovaz, oenologist, professor at the Académie du Vin in Paris
Sébastien Durand-Viel, journalist and critic, author of articles and books on wine
Benoît Grandin, wine journalist
Mathilde Hulot, journalist and author of books on wine
Egmont Labadie, journalist and author on gastronomy and wine
Valérie de Lescure, journalist and critic, author of books on wine
Evelyne Malnic, journalist and author of books on wine
Antoine Petrus, Best Young Sommelier in France 2007

The publisher is also grateful to the following for their assistance: Myriam Huet for *Vers une agriculture plus écologique* (*Toward greener wine production*), *Des techniques qui font polémique* (*Techniques that are controversial*), and *Les idées fausses autour du vin* (*False beliefs about wine*); Hélène Piot for *Sommelier, l'ambassadeur des vins* (*The Sommelier as wine ambassador*); and Véronique Raisin for *Le marché mondial du vin* (*World of wine*).

Contributors to the updated edition:

David Cobbold, co-director of the book, journalist, critic, author of articles and books on wine, co-founder of the Académie du Vin in Paris.
Sébastien Durand-Viel, co-director of the book, critic, wine tutor, author of articles and books on wine, co-founder of the Académie du Vin in Paris.
Olivier Borneuf, professional wine taster, consultant, co-founder of and tutor at the Académie du Vin in Paris.
Mohamed Boudellal, journalist and critic, has contributed to key specialized wine trade publications including La Revue du Vin de France.
Florence Kennel, journalist and writer, specializing in Burgundy, Jura, and Alsace. Author of two books on wine, she is also a wine technician and oenologist.
Hervé Lalau, French journalist working in Belgium, assistant editor-in-chief at In Vino Veritas, co-founder of the blog les5duvin, holder of the Ordre du Mérite Agricole (Order of Agricultural Merit).
Florent Leclerq, journalist, senior reporter and wine critic.
Marc Vanhellemont, independent journalist, contributor to different Belgian and French wine magazines, founder member of the blog les5du vin.
Aymone Vigière d'Anval, wine journalist for 15 years in print media.

Contents

ARBOIS

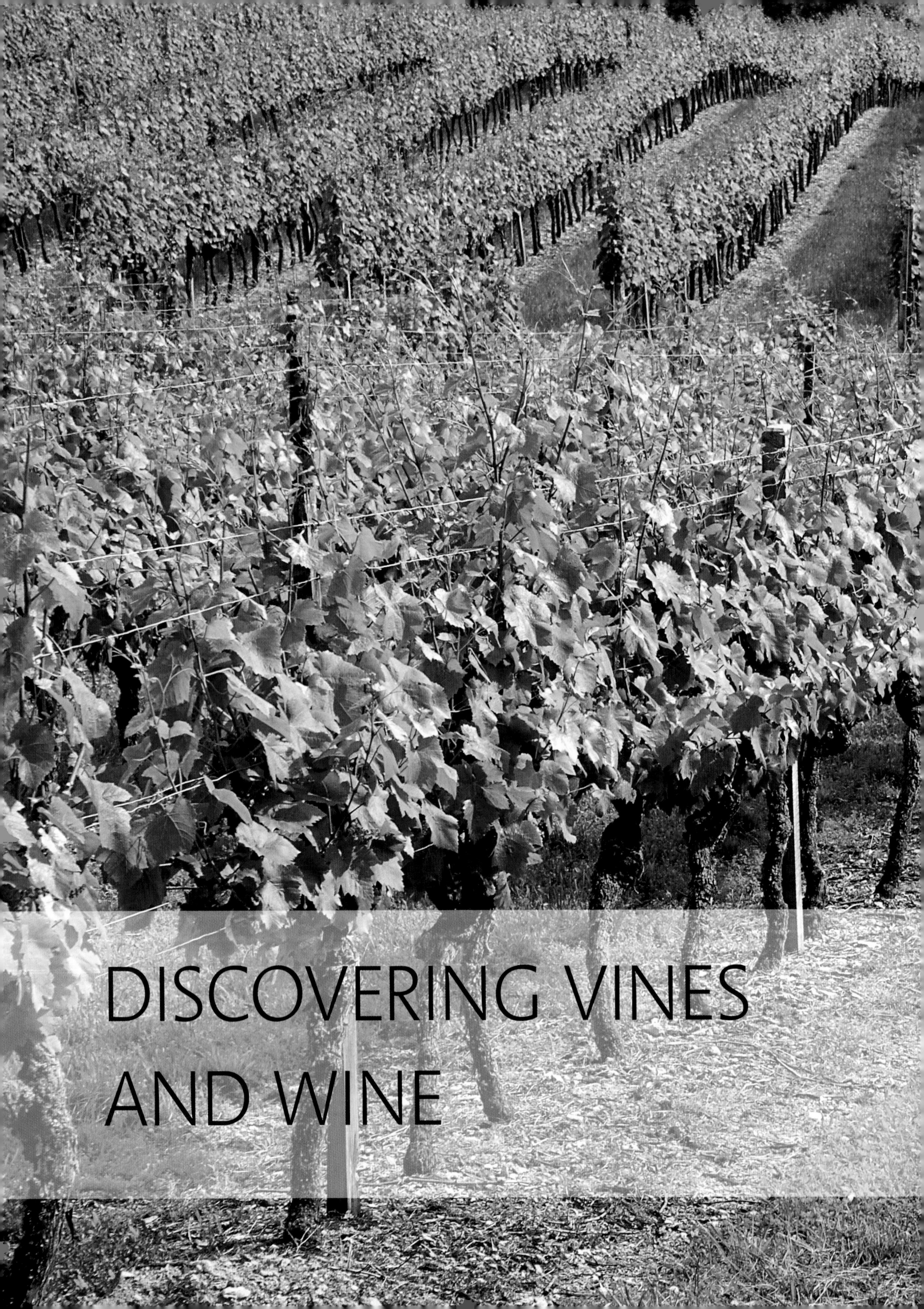

DISCOVERING VINES AND WINE

THE ORIGINS OF WINE

HOW WINE BEGAN

Who made the first wine? Where was the first vineyard located? So many questions remain unanswered. However, the fact remains that wine has been intimately linked to Western culture for 9,000 years and continues to influence it today.

The first vineyard

The accidental production of wine probably first occurred in areas where wild vines grew naturally that were also populated by humans. The next step – the deliberate cultivation of the vine – was a significant one. Archaeologists can tell whether seeds found at inhabited sites came from wild or cultivated grapes. Cultivated grape seeds have been discovered in the north of Iran. They are 9,000 years old. So the first vineyards were already in existence somewhere at this time. Certainly, in this part of the world, with both the climate and topography favourable to vines, they once grew in the wild.

The Babylonians evoked a magical vineyard made of precious stones in the epic poem of Gilgamesh (18th century BC), the earliest written work.

WINE, A MAJOR PART OF CIVILIZATION. When looking at the early period of wine's history, it is vital to take into account the increasing role it played in the daily lives of the Babylonians and Ancient Egyptians, and then the Ancient Greeks and Romans. This and, importantly, its use in religious events and rituals, made wine a major feature of early Western civilization. At the time of the Ancient Greeks, wine was also known in China, although the inhabitants did little to exploit it. Vine cultivation was also known in inhabited parts of Persia and India, but without having left any significant traces. No trace of vine cultivation has ever been found in pre-Columbian America, despite the presence of wild vines and the existence of quite sophisticated civilizations.

> Greek ceramic representing Dionysus.

Dionysus, Bacchus, and the wine of the early Christians

GREECE. The role of wine in Christian practices descends in a direct line from Ancient Greek and Roman rituals. Its use in sacramental rites has links with Judaism; but it is with the Greek cult of Dionysus, the god of wine, and of Bacchus, his Roman equivalent, that the greatest similarities are found. According to legend, Dionysus brought wine to Greece from Asia Minor, which is now Turkey. As the son of Zeus, he was born twice: once as a mortal human and once as divine. His first birth was to a simple mortal mother, Semele. He was the vine and the wine was his blood.

THE ROMAN EMPIRE. The Romans adopted the Greek gods and added them to their own pantheon. Dionysus became Bacchus, the name by which he was already known in the Greek cities of Lydia, in Asia Minor. Bacchus was transformed from the god of wine into a saviour. His cult spread among women, slaves, and the poor. The emperors tried to stamp it out, but without much success. Christianity, the development of which is inseparable from that of the Roman Empire, adopted many of the rites associated with Bacchus and attracted, in its early stages, the same categories of the faithful: women, slaves, and the poor. The significance of the Eucharist is too complex a subject to be dealt with in just a few lines, but suffice to say that the presence of wine at communion was as important to a Christian congregation as that of the priest. As a result of the vital role it played in religious practices, wine survived even during the Dark Ages of the barbarian invasions that followed the decline of Rome.

DID YOU KNOW...?

For people in the Middle Ages, wine and beer were not luxuries but necessities. *The water supply in urban areas was impure and often dangerous. The antiseptic role played by wine made it a part of the rudimentary medicine of the era. Mixed with wine, water became drinkable, if not palatable. Water was rarely consumed on its own, at least in towns. 'Water is not wholesome, sole by its self, for an Englishman,' wrote English physician Andrew Borde, in 1542.*

> Harvesting, crushing grapes, and filling barrels, represented by a miniature in a Book of Hours used in Paris.

The English fondness for Bordeaux wines

In the 14th century, considerable amounts of wine were exported to England from Bordeaux; to the extent that the average annual consumption at that time was not surpassed until 1979. King Edward II of England ordered the equivalent of more than a million bottles on the occasion of his marriage to Isabel of France in 1308. By the reign of Elizabeth I, almost three centuries later, consumption was more than 40 million bottles of wine per year, with a population of just 6.1 million.

The conquest of Northern Europe

Wine was linked to the Mediterranean way of life. North of the Alps, more sedentary activities such as winemaking were endangered by the threat of invasion. It was only the church, which needed wine and managed to maintain a continuous supply, that facilitated the survival of vineyards. So after Europe emerged from its turbulence, most vineyards were to be found near monasteries and cathedrals.

MONKS AND WINE. Monks were not content simply to make wine; literate and secure in the church's tenure of the land they also wanted to improve it. In the Middle Ages, the Cistercians of Burgundy were the first to study the climate and soil of the Côte d'Or region in order to select the best plants, experimenting with pruning and choosing the best areas to produce the ripest grapes. They built walls around the best vineyards to protect against thieves; the *clos* (walled vineyards) that remain still bear witness to these wine-producing monks. The Cistercians of Kloster Eberbach did the same in the Rhine district, which is today one of the most famous wine regions of Germany (*see* p.408). Their goal was not just to produce wine for Mass, but also for hospitality purposes and for sale. As a result, the monks played a key role in the commercial wine trade in the Middle Ages.

Trading in wine

Once life in Europe became more peaceful again, vineyards increased and trade resumed. However, wine had never wholly abandoned its role as a commercial commodity: during the High Middle Ages (circa the 5th to 10th centuries), merchant ships slipped discreetly out of Bordeaux or the mouth of the Rhine into pirate-infested western seas and headed for what is now the United Kingdom, Ireland, and further north. Even the least powerful barbarian chiefs felt obliged to celebrate festive occasions with wine, and the most remote hermitage still needed communion wine.

With the revival of trade, great fleets carrying wine appeared and hundreds of ships headed for London and the Hanseatic ports. Rivers also became important trade routes; barrels filled with wine were heavy and cumbersome, so transportation by ship was often the only option.

WINE AS PORTRAYED IN ANCIENT MINIATURES

Illuminations in several books from the Middle Ages represent the various labours undertaken in the vineyards – evidence of the presence of wine in medieval society.

1

3

2

4

5

6

1. Pruning the vines, the *Book of Hours* of Charles of Angoulême (14th century).
2. Harvesting and crushing the grapes, *Breviary d'Amor* (14th-century encyclopedia).
3. September labours, the Duke of Berry's *Très Riches Heures*, the Book of Very Rich Hours (15th century).
4. Pruning the vines in March, Roman missal used at Tours (early 16th century).
5. Scenes of trading life (14th century).
6. A treatise on hygiene (15th century).
7. Monk tasting wine, *Book of Health* (13th century).
8. The Marriage at Cana, *Très Belles Heures*, Book of Very Beautiful Hours of Notre Dame (15th century).

7

8

REVOLUTIONS IN WINE

For many centuries, wine producers and wine merchants worked to satisfy the demand for ordinary wines for 'everyday' drinking; but towards the end of the 17th century there was a new development: a wealthy public wanting to enjoy wines that produced a more intense taste experience.

Lovers of good wines

The appreciation of good wine stretches back a long way. The Ancient Romans were familiar with where the best wines in their empire were to be found, and in the Middle Ages kings and high-ranking churchmen also demanded high quality. A few centuries later, in France and, of course, England, a new development took place, the emergence of a social class equipped with both money and a sense of taste that was prepared to pay extra for good wines. In France, the Regency courtesans (1715–1723) demanded – and obtained – large quantities of the best quality, most effervescent Champagne. Meanwhile in England around the same time, or even earlier, the country's nouveau riche and most influential people began demanding the best red wines from Bordeaux, while English merchants had already created the market for sparkling wine.

It is to this generation that we owe the concept of great wines as we appreciate them today. Until that time, wine was consumed during the year in which it was made; and at the approach of the harvest the price of 'old' wine dropped. However, in 1714, a Parisian wine merchant asked his supplier in Bordeaux for 'some good wine, old, dark and velvety'. And from this point onward, ways were found to mature and improve wine. The age of quality wines had begun.

***Around 1865, the extent of French vineyards reached its peak: 6.25 million acres (2.5 million ha),** despite measures – from planting limits to actually grubbing up vineyards – undertaken by different governments over the centuries to curb wine production.*

The great Bordeaux wines

Arnaud de Pontac, president of the Bordeaux parliament around 1660, has often been credited with launching the search for quality. Owner of Château Haut-Brion, he set to producing a new type of wine, applying methods that later would become common practice: separating white and black grape varieties, small yields, careful selection, and strict attention to the winemaking process and maturation. The aim, of course, was to create a reputation that justified charging high prices. In London, Haut-Brion wines reached three times the price of other good wines. Within one generation, other estates in the Bordeaux region – Latour, Lafite, and Margaux, in particular – had followed Haut-Brion's lead. Such refinements were successful: selection of the best grape varieties, draining of the vineyards, and increasing precision in maturation and care in the cellars. Fine wines began to be made in great quantities.

> During the 18th century, wine became an essential part of a sophisticated menu.

The grandfather of oenologists

For centuries, winemaking was based on knowledge acquired through sensory experience, and hence had not been subjected to serious investigation by scientists. That was to to change in 1854, however, when Louis Pasteur made a study of three types of fermentation, that of vinegar, beer, and wine. The results of his research were not put into practice until the 20th century, and were not implemented by wineries until 1945 or even later, but it was the start of formal education in the wine industry and oenologists were trained to advise on production at single estates as well as at cooperatives. Science had finally entered the wine industry.

> Loading of casks of wine on the quays at the port of Bordeaux (around 1890).

In France, in the 18th century, the Industrial Revolution and the development of towns and cities, with their steadily increasing numbers of workers, increased the demand for cheap wine. The railroads made it possible to supply this need by shipping wine from the vast vineyards in the south.

THE NEW WINES OF THE 17TH AND 18TH CENTURIES. From the 17th century and throughout the 18th century, the development of vineyards matched that of Paris itself. Wine consumption increased and wines from the Orléans and Auxerrois regions were introduced to meet the demand. But the joint requirements of England and Paris outstripped the capacity of the merchants. So, rather than buying from the vineyards, they began to purchase grapes from growers, giving rise to a new business: wine producers who, in addition to the production of their vines, blended, bottled, and finally delivered their own wines – creating 'umbrella' brands that guaranteed a consistent quality to consumers.

DID YOU KNOW...?

Champagne was the direct result of the union between a pressure-resistant bottle and cork. *Regional wine production had stagnated during the 16th century. Effervescence was a problem when Champagne was transported long distances. It caused explosions within the barrels, the only form of container authorized by royal decree before 1728. The bottle (which the English were the first to use for the transportation of wine) and Portuguese cork came together to solve this problem and the first sparkling Champagnes were thus developed in England. Benedictine monk and Abbey of Hautvilliers cellarman, Dom Pérignon, for his part, provided Champagne's other stroke of good fortune, noting the importance of separating the varieties of grapes on the press.* (see also *pp.88–9*).

IN THE 19TH CENTURY. Members of parliament and clerks of the court drank 'bourgeois' wines that were seen as eminently acceptable at even the best tables, in Bordeaux in particular. During the 19th century, wine merchants developed their marketing methods and began selling wine in bottles; previously wine had been sold only in barrels. Wine became one of France's major industries, largely due to industrialization and the advent of railroads. In sun-drenched Languedoc-Roussillon, where high-yielding varieties are grown on the plains, vast quantities of wine are produced for everyday consumption.

TRUE OR FALSE

Banning the drinking of wine in the Islamic world goes back to the era of the prophet Muhammad.

FALSE. *The ban dates from two or three centuries later and was introduced by legal experts. It was also dictated by the threat of famine. After a series of victories, Islam was able to live on the profits of war; but eventually its resources became exhausted, and the cultivation of wheat and rice replaced that of grapes, in order to feed the people.*

The scourge of the vine

It was in 1863, in the south of France, that the most devastating scourge of the vine appeared. The hugely destructive phylloxera is a member of the aphid family. It is no larger than the head of a pin, but it slowly kills the vine by feeding on the sap of its roots. It arrived by accident from North America, when steamboats began crossing the ocean at sufficient speed for the parasite, living on imported plants, to survive the journey. The whole of Europe was affected and hardly a vine escaped. After 40 years of havoc, the solution – that of grafting vines onto American rootstocks, which were immune to the aphid – was finally found (*see* p.34).

Phylloxera, however, was not the only problem; two other cryptogamic diseases – mildew and powdery mildew – hit the vines of Europe at the same time or even earlier. In France, as in other European regions, many affected vineyards were never replanted.

THE NEW WORLD OF WINE

In many respects, it took most of the 20th century for the world of wine to recover from the phylloxera crisis. However, a more recent decade – the 1980s – heralded a key turning point in wine history. New players on the stage began to up their game and match the quality of European producers.

The French *appellations d'origine* (designations of origin)

At the end of the 19th century, the reputation of the French wine industry was in ruinous decline due to the massive and fraudulent production of large quantities of wine. Baron Leroy de Boiseaumarié, owner of Château Fortia at Châteauneuf-du-Pape, decided, along with a number of others, to pursue a different course of action. He decided to abandon mediocre grape varieties giving high yields, inadequate and ill-delineated land, excessive fertilization, etc. He advocated using certain adapted grape varieties and sought the banning of others, as well as fixing the minimum percentage of alcohol content and the maximum yield per acre. His struggle lasted almost a dozen years. Finally, in 1930, the law on *appellations d'origine* became the charter of all Châteauneuf-du-Pape wine producers. Champagne adopted it in 1935; Arbois and the Val de Loire, Bordeaux, and Burgundy in 1936; and Beaujolais in 1937. The system of *appellations* was put in place progressively as all other French regions followed suit. Today it is the basis of all legislation for wine production in Europe, with successive modifications and revisions, the last of which was passed in 2009. (*See box* p.95.)

> ***Many wine-producing areas have emerged in New World countries since the 1980s.*** *Players on the world's 'chessboard of wine' change constantly, and wines from new producers now rub shoulders with those of European vineyards at the tables of wine lovers.*

Vineyards of the world: the most closely controlled products

After 1945, science began to play an important role in viniculture, developing research programmes that studied vine cultivation, wine fermentation, and maturing in cellars. Along with new knowledge came greater control, and yields became higher and more regular.

At the same time, the consumption of wine was being transformed. In European countries where wine was produced traditionally, consumption dropped significantly while value increased. And new consumer markets developed, such as the USA, which became the world's leading market in 2013, and in China. Vineyards across the world adapted to these changes. Vines were uprooted in Europe while new plantations appeared in other countries. The best New World wines began to rival the top European wines in quality. The end of the 20th century proved a very prosperous period for producers. For wine lovers it was a golden age, with many more good wines becoming available on the market at relatively reasonable prices. The victims of these developments were the producers of cheaper wines.

Wine production on a grand scale

Vines are grown in half of the French political regions or departments. Nearly 2 million acres (806,000 ha) of vines (in 2015) yielded nearly 1.1 billion gallons (43 million hl) or around 6 billion bottles. In the league of wine producers, France ranks second to Italy (in volume of wine produced) but ahead of Spain. The US is in fourth position. The average annual consumption per capita in France was 42 gallons (160 l) in 1965, but is now down to about 11.3 gallons (43 l) per year.

> A 'map' showing the California vineyards during the 1940s.

Grape varieties in New Zealand

The hybrids dominant until the 1960s were replaced by European varieties, first German and then French. (Sauvignon Blanc in 1970 and Chardonnay in 1980). The success of Sauvignon Blanc in New Zealand has been remarkable. Today, it represents 70 per cent of production. Among the red varieties, only Cabernet Sauvignon has a long history of use in New Zealand, but it has now largely been overtaken by Merlot and Pinot Noir.

> During the period of Prohibition in America (1919–1933), banned wine was seized and poured down the drain.

In the United States

Most current North American wine producers did not exist before 1966. At least 70 per cent of California wine companies were started after this date; in New York State, at least 80 per cent were launched after 1976. During the 1970s and 1980s, new producers managed to have some local regulations modified, along with, in most states, the fiscal measures imposed at the end of Prohibition. Until the mid-1980s, wines produced in the United States were not intended for export. However, in 1991, America became the fourth-largest wine producer in the world, after Italy, France, and Spain and ahead of Argentina – a position it has retained to this day.

In South America

As the political and economic conditions of South American countries began to stabilize after the 1980s, foreign investors started to express greater interest in land that might be suitable for vineyards. At the same time, most of the local producers modernized their installations and developed new styles of wines adapted to the global market.

Since the early 1990s, Chilean wines have been unbeatable in many markets, especially those where the demand for quality is matched by that for value. Argentina embarked on this course later than its neighbour Chile, but is in a good position today. The other South American countries are not in the same category in terms of size, but Uruguay and Mexico produce some interesting wines and Brazilian production could be stimulated in the future by its internal market.

In South Africa

Following the abolition of apartheid in 1991, South Africa's isolated wine industry embarked on the conversion of its production, until then primarily devoted to brandy made from wine grapes. Farmers had previously concentrated on quantity, but now had to switch their focus to quality. Vineyards that grew grape varieties intended for bulk production and destined for distillation were now converted to 'noble varieties' (Chardonnay, Sauvignon Blanc, Cabernet Sauvignon, Merlot, Syrah, Pinotage) more adapted to international tastes. In 1991, more than 70 per cent of harvested grapes did not find their way into bottles of wine, unlike 15 years later when more than 70 per cent of the annual harvest was being made into wine. And the red grape varieties, led by Cabernet Sauvignon and Syrah/Shiraz at the head, are now gaining ground. This rapid conversion allowed South Africa to offer very good quality wines. Progress meant the export of South African wines tripled between 1998 and 2013. Greater political stability also attracted foreign investors, including the Swiss, Germans, Belgians, Italians, Americans, and the French.

Grape varieties in Australia

Forty years ago, Riesling and Semillon were the only quality white grape varieties grown in any great quantity in Australia. It was not until the beginning of the 21st century that they were overtaken by Chardonnay and then Sauvignon Blanc. Syrah (known as 'Shiraz' in Australia) was formerly used for making fortified wines. It is now extremely fashionable and forms the base of a large number of the country's most successful wines: whether as a single grape variety or blended with Cabernet, or with Grenache and Mourvèdre. It is followed by Cabernet Sauvignon, which has gained ground rapidly. Merlot serves as a blender, and Pinot Noir is used mostly in sparkling wines or is planted in cooler areas.

FALSE BELIEFS ABOUT WINE

Wine long remained the exclusive domain of connoisseurs, those who possessed specialized knowledge and did their best not to share it. In the absence of clear explanations, a new enthusiast trying to access information could sometimes come to the wrong conclusions.

The older a wine, the better it is.

‘A wine for laying down is a wine that will improve with time. It deserves to wait for a few years before it is consumed. This applies particularly to tannic red wines, which are rough on the tongue when young. With time, the tannins soften and the flavour develops; but if kept too long wine loses body and acidity dominates. One must monitor its development, since there is nothing worse than uncorking a bottle and finding that it must once have been good, but not anymore. Much better to uncork a bottle too soon than open a dozen too late!’

Rosé: a mixture of red and white wines?

‘Making rosé wine (see p.66) requires essentially red grapes as the colour is contained in the skins. The exact intensity of the colour required is achieved, either by the same process as used for red wine (leaving the juice in contact with the skins for just a few hours; known as the bleeding method) or by the process used for making white wine (the grapes are crushed lightly and then pressed to extract a little colour, and this juice with its slight colour is then fermented; called the direct pressure method). Blending red and white wine together is only permitted in France during the production of pink Champagne. On the other hand, blending black and white grapes in the fermentation tank is authorized.’

Crystals in the wine! Has the winemaker added sugar?

‘These crystals, clear in white wine, sometimes coloured in reds, are made of potassium bitartrate, or just tartrate, and tend to form more quickly in lower temperatures. To prevent this happening in the bottle, the tartrates are sometimes deliberately precipitated by cooling the wine in the tank. The tartrates in no way affect the quality of the wine. So, don’t worry if you find any of these small crystals in your wine. They have nothing to do with sugar and have no adverse effects on the taste of the wine or on your health!’

Vines must suffer to produce great wines.

'The soil of a good vineyard should never be very fertile. In fact, when grape vines are planted in rich soil, they become too vigorous and their yield too high. They produce grapes that are dilute and make wine that is too light. However, in order for the grapes to ripen, the vine must not be deprived of nutrients or suffer an imbalance. A lack of iron, for example, can prevent photosynthesis and slow the growth of the fruit. The same applies to water: when the vines are overwatered, the fruit becomes saturated, diluted, and lacking in sugar. If too dry, the vine shuts down and the grapes fail to ripen. Vines, therefore, need to be able to grow stress-free, drawing nutrients from the soil on a regular but not excessive basis.'

Tears in a wine are glycerin.

'The clear droplets that slide slowly down the side of the glass are called 'tears' (or 'legs'). They are caused by the difference in the rate of evaporation and the capillary tension between water and alcohol, and are that much larger when the alcohol content is high. The internal wall of the glass also has some bearing on the 'tears'. Glycerol is one of the alcohols contained in wine, but in a lower concentration than ethanol. The term 'glycerin' is therefore incorrect. It is often believed that tears are an indication of quality or keeping potential. This is wholly false: the tears simply give a hint of the wine's richness in alcohol (see also p.209).'

Red wines are consumed chambré!

'Drink wine chambré, perhaps, but not 'at ambient temperature', such as when a room reaches 77°F (25°C). The term dates from the end of the 19th century, when the temperature in a bedroom rarely exceeded 59°F (15°C). When bringing red wine up to temperature, care must be taken not to go above 64°F (18°C) or the alcohol comes to the fore and dominates the flavour. Don't hesitate to cool a red wine that is too warm by plunging it into a bucket of cold water, even adding a few ice cubes to lower the wine's temperature by two or three degrees. Be careful not to make it too cool. A robust red wine becomes very hard and its tannins will seem rough if it is served too cold (see also pp.186–7).'

At one time bovine blood was added to wine to colour it.

'Wine naturally contains many proteins, which form into solid matter. To remove them, an unrelated protein from an external source is added to the vat or cask. This attaches to the proteins and causes them to settle at the bottom. The wine, now clear, can then be transferred to another container. This procedure clarifies the wine. Egg albumin is used most frequently, either in the form of fresh egg white or freeze-dried powder, but bentonite is also used; this is not a protein but a type of clay with the same properties. Albumin from the blood of cattle was used at one time but has been banned since the mad cow disease crisis. In any case, these proteins were never used to colour the wine.'

THE WINE-PRODUCING *TERROIRS*

The word terroir *covers a number of factors that influence the character of the wine. While natural conditions can be modified, it is the choice of site that remains key to the final qualities of the wine.*

The concept of *terroir*

Originally conceived with reference to wine production in France, the concept of *terroir* is now universally known. It covers all the natural and climatic elements linked to a particular vineyard area. The terroir determines the character of the wine, just as the grape variety (vine variety) and the choices made by the wine-producer during viticulture and the wine-making process.

A FEW PARAMETERS. *Terroir*, contrary to commonly held beliefs, does not simply refer to the soil and what lies beneath the vines (granite, limestone, etc.). It also includes other local factors, such as the slope (hillsides or plain), altitude, exposure, environment (proximity to a forest, lake, etc.), and of course the climate. The *terroir* is the combination of all these factors and it gives each wine-producing site its unique identity.

***TERROIRS* IN OTHER PARTS OF THE WORLD.** Today, the *terroirs* of certain vineyard regions in the New World are clearly identified. They are capable of producing great quantities of wines that compare favourably with the *grands crus* of Bordeaux or top quality Spanish and Italian wines. When compared with wines such as Château Latour, Sassicaia, Vega Sicilia, and Scharzhofberger wines, they can hold their own. Opus One from the Napa Valley in California, Cuvée Almaviva from the Maipo Valley in Chile, and Hill of Grace from Henschke in Australia are just some examples of these.

Wine derives its 'nobility' from the* terroir *in which the vines are grown. *The key elements of light, temperature, and water combine with the soil to determine its quality and characteristics.*

Some areas are more favourable than others

Vines do not always produce good wine. Wet or humid regions do not suit vines; and while they will still grow in cold countries, the fruit fails to ripen properly. For the most part, the best quality wine is produced from vines grown in less fertile soil; on rich, alluvial plains their large grapes produce wine without character. In temperate climates, the best *terroirs* prove to be those with poor soil on well-drained hillsides where excess water is avoided, and the vines enjoy good exposure to sunlight in order for their fruit to ripen effectively. As a result, the best wines are often grown in gravelly, sandy or stony soil, and on a hillside rather than on a plain. In northern vineyards, they also enjoy a southeast aspect, affording lengthy exposure to the sun. These are the key characteristics and features of a quality *terroir* that encourages the growth of the vine and the production of ripe, concentrated grapes.

TRUE OR FALSE?

Vines grow well at high altitude.

TRUE. *High-altitude plateaus are much sought-after terroirs in Australia, in southern Italy, and in all regions with very hot summers. The cool nights and sunny days in such areas result in a temperature range that encourages the grapes to develop their full aromatic potential. The reverse is true of mountainous areas, where temperatures drop too low and strong winds dry out the plants.*

Good climatic conditions

Globally, the best areas for vines are generally between 35° and 50° latitude, north or south. Europe, with its temperate climates, has a privileged location.
The seasons alternate, with fairly long and dry summers, in which the grapes mature slowly, followed by long, cold winters that allow the vines to rest. These conditions are essential, even if in some cases growers can compensate for less favourable locations: for example, through irrigation in very dry climes, as in the case of Australia.

THE BASIC REQUIREMENTS. Vines require good sunlight, moderate rain (between 20 and 28 in/500 and 700 mm *per annum*) and moderate temperatures (between 50° and 77°F/10° and 25°C). If temperatures are too high or too low, growth is halted; excessive rain produces, at best, enormous grapes saturated with water and lacking sweetness and flavour (*see* p.48).

Is this the end of French distinction?

European countries, and France in particular, are very attached to the concept of *terroir*. It forms the basis of all regulations on *appellations d'origine* (*see* pp.94–5). Until the mid-20th century, wine producers the world over always felt that quality wines could only be produced in the 'traditional' countries. The increase in international trade and the opening up of many countries combined with the extraordinary economic success of the wine industry in the 1980s to encourage wine producers to produce ever greater quantities of wine and, in some cases, to make quality wines outside the usual 'recognized' areas. Today, every vineyard has the potential to produce quality wines.

> At Châteauneuf-du-Pape, pebbles help retain warmth accumulated during the day, which benefits the vines at night. These thick layers of pebbles also reduce the evaporation of water from the subsoil.

THE ROLE OF THE MESOCLIMATE. In addition to the regional climate, the natural environment can, in subtle ways, produce a more localized mesoclimate favourable to vine cultivation. A nearby forest can offer a natural barrier to wind; the presence of a body of water will mitigate changes in temperature and enhance light radiation; passing air currents will influence the ripening of the grapes by drying the atmosphere, etc. In countries like Switzerland, where one might think it would be too cold for vines, producers choose areas with beneficial mesoclimates, like the perimeters of lakes.

ANNUAL VARIATIONS. In countries with fairly stable climates, such as Chile, Australia or Roussillon, wines tend to be of a similar quality year after year. On the other hand, in certain regions of France and in other European countries, extreme climatic conditions (frost, drought, hail, torrential rain, etc.) can damage the quality of the wine in a given *terroir*. It is a good idea, therefore, to take note of vintages (or the year of the harvest) for European wines that sell at higher prices.

The effects of global warming

Studies of the consequences of climate change reveal that a rise in temperature has been globally beneficial for the quality of wine due to an improved ripeness of the grape. However, while a hot summer is often associated with a *grand millésime*, excessive warming between now and the end of the century could have detrimental effects on wine production in certain southern regions. Problems include drought, the development of disease, or the potential erosion of the soil due to repeated flooding.

NEW AREAS OF PRODUCTION AND THREATENED REGIONS. Logically, the regions most in danger are those with the hottest climates, such as southern Europe and California. By 2100, if nothing is done, only the coastal zones of the American West, cooled by the Pacific Ocean, will still be able to cultivate vines. We are already seeing vineyards above the 50th parallel, in Sweden and Denmark.

POSSIBLE SOLUTIONS? In an attempt to anticipate or counteract the effects of climate change, it has been suggested that vines should be trained low in order to retain humidity and afford grapes protection from the sun. Wine-producers can also choose north-facing exposures, try cover-planting, and manage the canopy in such a way as to limit the exposure of the grapes to the sun. The development of controlled irrigation has also been put forward as a solution. In southern hemisphere locations, such as Australia,

Water: neither too much nor too little

Generally speaking, the water content of a good *terroir* is either poor or very low; vine roots and water do not go well together. In wet climates, freely draining soil is ideal for cultivating vines, unlike very compact earth with very fine granulation that impedes the flow of water. Poor natural drainage can be improved by the laying of drains; the best *crus* in the Bordeaux region use this method. However, the vines must never be short of water or they risk becoming dormant. A constant and uninterrupted water supply is the ideal.

DID YOU KNOW...?

The same grape variety can result in a very different wine depending on the soil in which it is grown. *One such example is in the hillside vineyards of the Côte d'Or, from which Pinot Noir wines are produced. Take two vineyards in soil based on limestone rock, growing at a similar altitude with similar exposure. One has stony soil, the other a high proportion of fine clay elements. The first will give very fruity, fairly light, and supple wines; whereas those from the second will be much more tannic and less rounded.*

vineyards could be planted in cooler zones (*see box* p.473). Scientists are already working on ways of adapting the roots of certain vine varieties to support higher temperatures, while also seeking to counteract the detrimental effects of excessively high temperatures on the taste of the wine (for example, high sugar and alcohol content). And lastly, replanting grape varieties from southern regions in more northerly areas is an option under consideration, along with creating new hybrids adapted to high temperatures.

What types of soil do vines prefer?

Poor and stony soil, shale, granite, sandstone, and a variety of other forms of soil are suitable for vine cultivation. The soil must perform four key functions: to serve as a support system, to provide and manage moisture, to give warmth (different soils warm and cool at different speeds), and to feed the vines.

WHY LOW FERTILITY? The vine is one of the least demanding plants in terms of nutritive elements. Traditionally, vines were cultivated on land that was insufficiently fertile for other crops. In fact, if the land is too rich it can produce an excessive yield, and yield and quality do not generally make a happy marriage: the juice of the grapes is too diluted, the flavour less concentrated, and the wine less impressive. The vine must 'suffer,' in a sense, from the poor quality of the soil, in order to deliver a concentrated grape. Its roots go deeper in search of nutrition, resulting in wines that express their *terroir* more effectively.

PERMEABLE OR DENSE? It is not enough to define soil in terms of fertility. Each soil has its own structure. Aerated and permeable soils heat up very quickly, helping to ripen the grapes properly. Examples include the sandy soil of the St-Émilion area, the limestone soil of Champagne, or the gravelly soil in the Médoc. Others are heavy, moist, and cool, like the clay of the Alsatian plain or at the foot of the Burgundy hillsides. The best *grands crus* come from permeable soil, for example gravel on a limestone base, such as at Château Haut-Brion. Dense, moist soils, such as the marshy area in the Dordogne Valley (fertile alluvial soil) are doubly inconvenient: they encourage rot and are slow to heat up. While various factors need to be taken into account, there are still exceptions to these basic rules. The Château Paveil de Luze from the Margaux appellation produces wine from vines grown on land that is cool and allows the fruit's essential qualities to be retained.

Does a *terroir* have a taste?

A key role in the quality, aroma, and taste of wines is attributed to the soil, particularly in France. Although it may be cause for debate, this has led to the demarcation of the *appellations d'origine contrôlées* that now extend throughout all European Union countries.

A FEW EXAMPLES. According to some specialists, substances present in the subsoil are very important for the flavour of the wine. Château Pétrus, in the *terroir* of Pomerol, has a rich and concentrated taste as a result of iron in the subsoil. The Burgundy *grand cru* Chevalier-Montrachet is lighter than its neighbour Montrachet because it is grown on more stony soil. The opulence and fleshiness of Château Cheval Blanc is due to the sandy, gravelly soil on clay subsoil (but also to a higher proportion of Cabernet Franc compared with other *crus* from St-Émilion). The brown, calcareous soil of the Burgundy *grand cru* La Tâche, which is very clay-rich, gives the wine greater aromatic fullness and elegance, compared with the austere Romanée-Conti. Still, we should bear in mind that the terroir is first and foremost a delicate and complex interaction between all the elements of the natural environment, of which the soil is just one part. Besides its composition, soil regulates the intake of water and minerals which play an important role in the profile of the harvested grape.

WHAT ROLE DOES THE *TERROIR* PLAY IN THE MAKING OF A GREAT WINE?

Oliver Poussier's opinion, *as The Best Sommelier in the World in 2000, is as follows:*

'A great wine is a combination of complexity, finesse, balance, and persistence, which give enormous pleasure to those who taste it. With time, its flavour and aromas should improve. The fullness of its expression comes more from its terroir than from the grape variety or the year in which it was grown. There can be no great wine without a man who, through an intimate understanding of the terroir, knows how to reveal its very quintessence.'

In the opinion of Michel Rolland, *an oenologist from Bordeaux who offers wine advice throughout the world:*

'A great wine is the sum of a number of factors, the most important being the terroir, which gives the wine its character. Man is the vital, indispensable link in the process by which a wine's qualities are revealed, through his constant work in the vineyards and wineries adapted to their conditions and circumstances. The age of the vineyard, its balance, and yield are also important.'

1

2

3

The artists of *terroir*

The 20th and early 21st centuries saw the emergence of a generation of winemakers who changed the face of the world of wine. While earlier great names in oenology – Emile Peynaud, Pascal Ribéreau-Gayon – had focused on removing faults in the wine, the newcomers' priority was to create a style. Whereas the Bordeaux producers, including well-known oenologist Michel Rolland, favoured a concentrated, fruity style that has so often served as the modern model, other winemakers were more modest in their goals and content to focus on getting the best out of their own small vineyards. However, through their skill at revealing the quintessential nature of their particular *terroir*, they

DENIS DUBOURDIEU, MAGICIAN OF THE HAPPY MEDIUM

Oenologist, wine producer, and academic, Denis Dubourdieu's place among the great Bordeaux winemakers is secure. Owner of several estates in the Sauternes region and the Bordeaux hills, this native of Barsac built his reputation on the search for a compromise between a style accessible to a wider public and respect for the *terroir*. A great specialist in white wines, and a consultant to numerous French and other vineyards, he promoted the development of grape varieties at the northernmost limits of their cultivation. His art lay in revealing the aromas of the grapes to make fruity, fresh, and elegant wines. As Denis himself said, the Dubourdieu style rested

ANNE-CLAUDE LEFLAIVE, A BORN WINEMAKER

When dynamic, innovative, pragmatic Anne-Claude Leflaive from Burgundy took over the family estate in Puligny-Montrachet, she wanted to stamp her own style on it by venturing into organic growing. Soon convinced by conclusive results, she decided to convert all 57.5 acres (23 ha) to biodynamic cultivation to produce *grands crus* in keeping with her philosophy. Until her death in 2015, Anne-Claude did her utmost to give the vines renewed vigour in order to maximize their expression of the *terroir*. Even the most sceptical must admit that the Leflaive style, is synonymous with excellent keeping qualities and good evolution.

4

5

1. Anne-Claude Leflaive
2. Denis Dubourdieu
3. Paul-Vincent Avril
4. Paul Draper
5. Egon Müller
6. Michel Rolland

6

PAUL-VINCENT AVRIL, THE EXCELLENCE OF SIMPLICITY

The American magazine *Wine Spectator* described the 2005 Châteauneuf-du-Pape from Clos des Papes as the best wine in the world in 2007. This came as a surprise to the newly initiated, but not to those wine-lovers familiar with the excellent work achieved by Paul-Vincent Avril in his 87.5-acre (35-ha) vineyard. The small yields produced by organic methods – no more than five bunches of grapes per vine – and rigorous selection of very ripe Grenache are his apparently quite simple rules for success. However, the essence of Paul-Vincent's skill lies in the actual winemaking process, which avoids overly frequent *remontage* ('pumping over' during fermentation) and results in wines, albeit with a high alcohol content, that are supple and velvety, and further refined during a long period of ageing in the vat.

EGON MÜLLER, HEIR TO A CHARACTER

Egon Müller, owner of the Scharzhof estate in the Ruwer Valley, is the fourth to bear the name since 1887. His father, Egon Müller III, who died in 2001, took this vineyard, planted with Riesling, to the top of the league of German wines – if one is to judge by the price of his Trockenbeerenauslese (selection de grains nobles) sold at the Trèves wine auction. 'The quality of our wines is 100 per cent due to the vines, 101 per cent if we add the cellar work,' joked Egon Müller IV. Indeed, part of his recipe for success seems to be a combination of good fortune in owning an exceptional *terroir* and the use of only well-ripened,meticulously hand-picked grapes. The balance lies in his character and personal philosophy – the most secret but powerful of ingredients.

PAUL DRAPER, THE CALIFORNIA VISIONARY

Paul Draper settled at Ridge Vineyards in the Santa Cruz Mountains, southwest of San Francisco Bay, in 1967, having spent some time in Chile. Over the years, this doctor of philosophy and atypical wine producer has become one of the great visionaries of Californian winemaking, producing excellent red wines that have often been placed ahead of Bordeaux *grands crus* in blind tastings. On the one hand, his art lies in the identification of the best Cabernet Sauvignon *terroirs*, and on the other, in a collection of the oldest Zinfandel vines. The well-judged use of French and American oak barrels for the maturation process lends a final touch to his wines, which are considered exceptional, the *cuvée* Ridge Monte Bello in particular (*see also* box p.447).

THOUSANDS OF GRAPE VARIETIES

There are 6,000 to 10,000 different grape varieties in the world, but only a few dozen of them are cultivated over extensive areas. Each of these types of vine has its own distinct features, and it is these that influence the character of the wine.

What is a *cépage*?

A *cépage*, broadly speaking, is a variety of vine. However, this term is not strictly correct from a botanical point of view. A variety is technically produced from seed, which is not so in the case of vines. *Vitis vinifera*, a type of domesticated vine that originated in Asia Minor, is the species of almost all modern cultivated grape varieties. As a result of natural mutation, crossbreeding, and selection engineered by people, there are now several thousand grape varieties with names such as Cabernet, Chardonnay, Pinot, Riesling, etc. Today, just a few dozen varieties provide the bulk of wine production. Some are now famous across the globe, such as Cabernet Sauvignon and Chardonnay.

***'Lambrusque' is a form of wild vine** (liana) that grows up trees in woodland. It is the distant ancestor of cultivated vines and can still be found in a few regions of Europe and Asia: Austria, the Balkans, the Caucasus, Afghanistan.*

Each one has distinctive characteristics

There are several types of grape: those intended for eating, which produce attractive fruit; those for drying, providing us with raisins; and those intended for winemaking. Some have multiple usages. Muscat of Alexandria grapes, for instance, can be used for raisins or Muscat wine.

In botanical terms, grape varieties are distinguished by morphological characteristics (their colour, shape, number of fruit bunches, the way the leaves are notched) and by physiological features (their flowering, ripening time, susceptibility to disease, yields, etc.) The winemaker will choose a variety according to the quality of wine required and according to the *terroir* in which it is to be planted. (All grape varieties are likely to produce the best results in certain soils and/or in a particular climate.)

THE ROLE OF TASTE. Each grape variety has distinct traits that give the wine its character. For example, a given vine will produce fruit in which the sugar or tannin content is of greater or lesser significance, or with aromas of more or less pronounced intensity. A wine made from the Sauvignon Blanc grape has certain characteristic flavours – fruity, floral, or herbaceous notes – common to all Sauvignon Blanc wines the world over. However, depending on the *terroir*, the latitude, the date of the harvest, the climate, and winemaking methods used, variations may occur in their aromatic make-up as in their structure. Thus, a Sauvignon Blanc wine made in Sancerre, France, will be dry, firm, fruity, and typical of the grape; if produced in the Marlborough region in New Zealand, its substance will be more mineral, expansive, and more exotic.

> The indentation of the leaves is one of the morphological characteristics that helps in the identification of a grape variety.

DID YOU KNOW...?

***There are no fewer than 40,000 different names given to grape varieties around the world.** However, many of these refer to the same variety – the names vary according to the country and even from one region to another. Taking into account different synonyms and translations, the varieties cultivated across the planet number about 5,000. Experts are still a long way from achieving a truly accurate number.*

From ampelography to the study of the genome

Ampelography, which was developed in the 19th century, has several aims: one is the study and description of the growth cycle of grape varieties, their aptitudes, and their faults; another is the identification and listing of the different varieties. In France, the experimental estate at Vassal, run by INRA (National Institute for Agricultural Research), has a unique collection of 3,500 grape varieties (*Vitis vinifera*, wild vines, hybrids) from 47 countries.

Researchers are also trying to establish a genetic map of the vine. This, in the long run, will permit greater understanding of the physiology of the growth and ripening of grapes, and so give better control over production. It would also allow faster and more precise selection of varieties that have, for instance, sustained resistance to diseases or with a high potential for quality. The study of DNA already allows researchers to establish the genetic footprint of grape varieties and so better identify and differentiate between them. It also reveals or confirms the relationship between traditional grape varieties.

How many grape varieties in one wine?

In the early days of winemaking, it was often normal to mix two or three varieties with somewhat different characteristics: one to give colour and tannins; another for delicacy and bouquet; and a third, possibly high-yielding variety, was added to the final mix to ensure some degree of consistency in the production. Today, many wines are still a mixture of two or three grape varieties that complement each other in terms of quality and yield. However, some wines are produced from a single grape variety, and are known (in French) as *monocépages* or varietals.

SOME EXAMPLES: Chablis is made exclusively from Chardonnay; Beaujolais is made solely from Gamay; Vouvray comes from Chenin Blanc; Sancerre from Sauvignon Blanc. On the other hand, red Bordeaux wines contain, in varying proportions, Cabernet Sauvignon, Cabernet Franc, Merlot, and a few secondary varieties that give the wine many nuances. Some mixes are even more complex: Châteauneuf-du-Pape, for example, can contain as many as 13 different grape varieties.

Grape varieties: a free choice or imposed?

Over the course of time, in each region, certain varieties became dominant. This may have occurred through mutation or local selection, or when the environment was found to be favourable to imported varieties and those varieties eventually became native to that area. In most European countries, when the regulation of wine production is firmly established, the varieties were ratified and the types of wine represented by their grape varieties were sanctioned by *appellations d'origines*.

LEGISLATION INFLUENCES CHOICE IN EUROPE. Until 2009, it was not permitted to simply plant a grape variety anywhere you chose, and each region had a precise list of 'recommended' and 'authorized' varieties. Today, every member state of the European Union has an official catalogue of grape varieties that are authorized to be planted–for eating or for winemaking. In France, this covers 200 varieties for winemaking. The choice of grape varieties available for the production of specific appellation wines is set out in a precise list that distinguishes between three categories of grape variety: principal, complementary, and accessory (*see* box p.43). The regulation is more flexible in the case of an IGP wine, or a *vin de France* (wine without a GI).

AND IN THE REST OF THE WORLD? On the American continents, in Australia, and in New Zealand and South Africa, wine producers in a given region are not required to use any particular variety. The regulations allow them complete freedom in the choice of the grape variety. They have adopted the practice of naming the grape variety on the label, which is an important indicator for the consumer.

Printing the grape variety on the label

Labels of European *appellation contrôlée* (AOC) wines rarely specify the name of the grape variety from which they are made. The label on a red Burgundy, for example, does not mention that the wine is made solely from Pinot Noir. California winemakers were among the first to distribute wines under the name of their grape variety, encouraging consumers to identify, for example, Chardonnay as a wine as well as a type of vine.

In France, one drinks a Beaujolais or a Burgundy rather than a Gamay or Pinot Noir. Apart from some notable exceptions, including Alsace, the names of grape varieties do not generally appear on the main AOC wine labels, although things are changing, as in Cahors, which now capitalizes on its name as much as Malbec does, the great local variety. Listing the grape variety is, on the other hand, widespread in the case of IGP wines and *vin de France*. In general, the practice of listing the variety, whether on the front or back label, now has plenty of momentum as it enables the consumer with little knowledge of the various subtleties of the appellations to identify a wine more easily. Institute of Origin and Quality) (INAO), disapproves of this practice, and does not officially recognize *vins de cépage*, or wines bearing the name of the grape variety.

DID YOU KNOW...?

Relatively few grape varieties are used in so-called **vins de cépage**. *These are, for the most part, Cabernet Sauvignon, Merlot, Syrah, Pinot Noir (red wines), and Chardonnay, Sauvignon Blanc, Pinot Grigio (Pinot Gris), and Viognier (white wines). In France and most other countries, listing the name of the grape variety indicates that the wine contains at least 85 per cent of it. Therefore up to 15 per cent of a second variety can be introduced (which each appellation must authorize). When the names of two or more varieties are listed, 100 per cent of the wine must be from a given variety.*

International and indigenous grape varieties

The Chardonnay and Cabernet Sauvignon wines of California, Chile's wines from Merlot, and the Syrah or Shiraz wines of Australia are some of the grape varieties originally associated with classic French wines that have crossed borders. When wine production developed in the New World, winemakers naturally made use of the most prestigious European grape varieties. Some of them proved unsatisfactory, but others adapted well. Grown on vast areas of land, they produced new wines that enjoyed rapid success. Demand increased, confirming their popularity to the detriment of other, often more local varieties. That said, the greater part of world production still comes from little-known or non-classic grape varieties. These may be grown because of local tradition, for their yield, or because they are well adapted to local soils and climate. But it is not only the classic varieties that produce good wine. It has long been the tendency globally to promote a handful of grape varieties to the point of making them commonplace. They may still be popular but in many regions and countries the emphasis is now being put on local varieties, capable of producing wines that are both original and of good quality. This great new resource and wealth of new flavours should in future contribute to the general broadening of the palette of wines available to the world's consumers.

> After grafting, the part of the plant that will remain above ground is coated with a wax mixture.

The effects of the phylloxera crisis

Between 1860 and 1880, an aphid called phylloxera, accidentally introduced to Europe from the United States, wreaked havoc on European vineyards (*see* p.21). The larvae of this parasite attack the young roots of the vines, biting into the plant tissue with their projecting mouthpieces. For American varieties, their impact was very limited; but the aphids swarmed in huge quantities over the roots of the less resistant European *Vitis vinifera*. Their bites caused disruption in the cells of the plant until the circulation of the sap was finally blocked. The vines then weakened and died over the course of three to ten years.

TRUE OR FALSE?

Ungrafted vines have all disappeared.

FALSE. *Even though most of the vineyards in the world are planted with grafted vines, there are exceptions. In France, for instance, the Marionnet vineyard in Touraine contains a plot planted with vines that are 120 to 150 years old, therefore from the pre-phylloxera era. One part of that estate has also been planted* franche de pied, *which is to say with ungrafted vines, and they are still resistant to phylloxera. But it is the vineyards of Washington State in the USA and also in Chile that have the most ungrafted vines.*

GRAFTING SAVES THE DAY. Determined to save the grape varieties of *Vitis vinifera*, European growers found the solution was to graft them onto the roots of wild American vines, which were resistant to the parasite. Since then, vine stocks have been composed of a graft (the part of the plant that grows above ground) attached to a rootstock. The former is always a *Vitis vinifera*, while the rootstock is nearly always from another species.

SEVERAL TYPES OF ROOTSTOCK. The rootstock that supports the graft must fulfill a number of conditions: it must be resistant to phylloxera, suited to the *terroir* in which it is to be planted, and compatible with the graft. Also its vegetative properties must conform to the needs of the grower. These days, every member country of the European Union has a list of rootstocks recommended for grafting. (All others are banned.) In France, several dozen among those available have been selected for their resistance to drought, as well as to soil lime (which causes chlorosis, a disease resulting in yellowing of the leaves), and for their fast rate of growth. Unfortunately, the latter encourages high yields to the detriment of quality and hardiness. These rootstocks are all of American origin (*Vitis riparia*, *V. rupestris*, or *V. berlandieri*).

Constant improvement of grape varieties

The improvement of grape varieties, which aims to obtain better quality fruit and make the plants more resistant to different vine

Small differences rather than similarities

The long-term survival of vineyards presupposes the eradication of diseases and the use of clonal selection. There are, however, disadvantages to the use of clones. The quality of a wine does not, in fact, depend on the vines being exactly the same as each other, but rather on the very slight differences that exist between members of the same variety. Clonal selection, however, produces plants with one genetic identity. To remedy this, nurseries offer several cloned versions of the same variety. There are, for example, 26 registered clones of Cabernet Franc, all with slightly different characteristics.

diseases, depends essentially on two kinds of selection: massal selection and clonal selection. A number of big estates, especially in the Bordeaux region, prefer to rely on local genetic diversity and the use of massal selection. But it is perfectly possible to use both kinds of selection, actually planting vine stock selected by both processes in the vineyards of the same estate.

MASSAL SELECTION. This has been used in agriculture for centuries. It entails choosing the most appropriate plants for a given purpose: fruit appearance or taste. In the case of grape vines, plants are selected for propagation according to foliage density or the strongest wood, or for bearing the most fruit or the largest–or smallest–grapes, depending on the type of production required. Massal selection favours local genetic heritage, but offers no guarantee that the plants will be healthy.

CLONAL SELECTION. Practiced by nurseries since 1960, clonal selection responds to the potential of health deficiencies in massal selection. A particularly suitable vine plant is selected, its health is checked (through virological tests), and its characteristics are improved as required (with thermotherapy or heat treatments). The results are then approved by an authorizing agency before the nursery proceeds to make identical copies by cloning (taking cuttings or grafting) from this basic plant material for certified sale and distribution.

The creation of new varieties

Research centres in every country breed different varieties of *Vitis vinifera* to create crossbreeds. (These are not hybrids, which are the result of crossing two different *Vitis* species.) They are tested for many years before being recognized as new varieties. In France, hybrids are not used to make AOC wines.

BASIC CROSSBREEDING. The only human intervention involved in basic crossbreeding is the choice of the parent plants. A Riesling can be crossed with a Traminer a dozen times and obtain a dozen different crossbreeds, just as a man and a woman can have a dozen children who are different from each other. In the future, once the genetic code of grape varieties has been mapped, crossbreeds will no doubt be selected according to their genes.

THE GERMAN EXAMPLE. The most active centre of vine research is in Geisenheim, in the Rhine region. Its activities date back many years, including responsibility for the creation of Müller-Thurgau in 1883 (a cross between Riesling and the Madeleine Angevine), which is a widely cultivated white variety in Germany. Other, very aromatic, white varieties that have been very successful since their early- to mid-20th-century creation include the Scheurebe (Sylvaner and Riesling), the Huxelrebe (Chasselas and Muscat), and the Kerner (a cross between Trollinger and Riesling).

Recourse to genetic engineering?

Microbiologists are interested in manipulating the genetic codes of grape varieties to strengthen the vine's defences, or, more ambitiously, to obtain better-tasting fruit. French researchers, for example, have succeeded in isolating the gene responsible for the immunity of American vines against fan-leaf, a serious virus that causes degeneration of the vine. At present, if a plot of land is infected, the only remedy is to treat the soil and then wait seven years before replanting, using American vine stocks. With genetically modified vines, the alternative rootstock would no longer be needed; and it would be possible to replant immediately, even in infected soil. However, before venturing into the realm of genetically modified crops, researchers and producers must make sure that such interventions present no risks to the health of the environment and guarantee that the character of the modified grape variety will remain unchanged. At the moment, no field trials are being made of genetically modified grapes or of wine made from them.

The failure of 'direct producers'

When phylloxera destroyed European vineyards, grape growers tried to replace old vines with 'direct producers.' These plants, produced by crossing the European species (*Vitis vinifera*) with American species, were supposed to combine the qualities of French vines with the resistance to disease of the American grape varieties. The resistance to phylloxera was, indeed, excellent; but the resulting fruit was coarse. The flavour was 'foxy,' making the wines unattractive. Such crossbreeding is now banned, and hybrids of European with American species are only used as vine rootstocks.

> One of the pre-phylloxera vines preserved in the Domaine La Charmoise belonging to the Marionnet brothers.

THE GREAT RED GRAPE VARIETIES

From among the vast number of red grape varieties, some have been selected for their distinctive characteristics and some, such as Cabernet Sauvignon, Merlot, and Syrah, have become international stars. But good wine can be made entirely from less well-known varieties.

Cabernet Sauvignon

This grape variety was derived from crossbreeding a Sauvignon Blanc and a Cabernet Franc. The cross-fertilization took place three centuries ago, somewhere in the Gironde area of Bordeaux, France.

THE PRINCIPAL *TERROIRS*. This has long been a traditional grape variety in the Médoc of Bordeaux. The poor, gravelly, warm soil of this *terroir* seems to offer the ideal conditions for its cultivation in temperate climates; but it can adapt to various conditions and is planted all over the world in vineyards that receive a minimum of 1,500 hours of sunlight per year. Frequently planted in the New World, it is often found in countries in the south of Europe, North Africa, the Middle East (Lebanon, Israel), and China.

THE CHARACTERISTICS. Dark red in colour, it has aromas of black fruit (blackcurrants, black cherries) and vegetal aromas (pepper, mint...) when young. Wine made from this grape variety becomes brick red, with cedar wood aromas, as it develops. When the yield is controlled, the wine producer can draw a great wine from this grape: fine, tannic, spicy, which both can and must be aged. Cabernet Sauvignon is often blended with other Bordeaux varieties (Merlot, Cabernet Franc), where it gives structure to wines to lay down: a great red Bordeaux from a good year will continue improving for decades.

***White wine can be made from red grape varieties.** It is achieved by simply preventing the grape juice, which is colourless, from macerating with the skins. Wine colour comes from the pigment in the skins.*

Cabernet Franc

This grape variety is similar to Cabernet Sauvignon. It may not have tannic power or body but it produces very pleasant wines when it has reached a good maturity.

THE PRINCIPAL *TERROIRS*. Cabernet Franc is also grown in certain regions of the Loire Valley of France, Anjou, and Saumur. Its early maturing qualities mean it can be planted further north than Cabernet Sauvignon. It is also grown in Bordeaux where it supports Cabernet Sauvignon and especially Merlot in the vineyards of the Right Bank. Apart from northern Italy and, in smaller quantities, California, this grape variety is increasingly grown outside France.

CHARACTERISTICS. It produces wines with aromas of red fruit, sometimes vegetal when maturity is lacking. In the Bordeaux area, when blended with Merlot or Cabernet Sauvignon, this variety is almost always the minor component. On the other hand, in the wines of the Loire Valley, such as Saumur-Champigny, Bourgueil,

> Cabernet Sauvignon

> Cabernet Franc

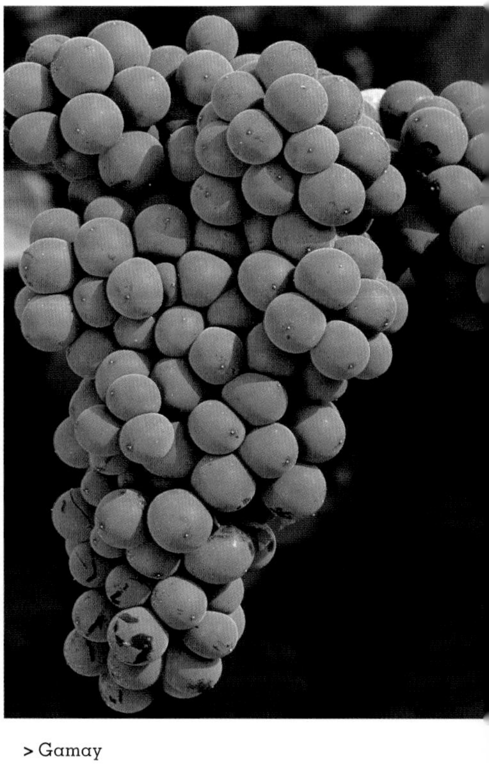

> Gamay

and Chinon, it dominates other varieties. Much of the wine is for drinking young, but some cuvées from the Loire age gracefully.

Gamay

The precise origin of this grape variety is not known, but it was undoubtedly pre-14th century and probably in the Beaujolais region of France. Gamay is principally known for its popular light and fruity red wines, but under certain conditions it is capable of producing wines that are more full bodied and structured.
THE PRINCIPAL *TERROIRS*. Gamay likes granitic soil. It is the only grape variety used in the production of red Beaujolais, though it has also been grown in the Loire Valley (particularly Touraine), in some vineyards in central France, and in Switzerland.
CHARACTERISTICS. Wine made from Gamay is light, rich in primary aromas, and has the flavour of ripe red fruit. It has little tannin and is often acidic. This grape variety became popular in the late 20th century due to the popularity of Beaujolais Nouveau. But the Beaujolais *crus* made in the traditional way give more prominence to the floral fruitiness of the grape.

Grenache

Spanish in origin and brought to France around the 14th century, this grape variety arrived in the Rhône Valley, at Châteauneuf-du-Pape, three centuries later.
THE PRINCIPAL *TERROIRS*. It is grown across southern France, from Provence through the Languedoc. It gives the best results on dry and stony soils, and in warm climates, like those of Rivesaltes or Châteauneuf-du-Pape. It is one of the main red grape varieties in Spain and is sometimes used as a complement to Syrah in Australia.
CHARACTERISTICS. Wine made with Grenache is rich in alcohol, heady, and with low acidity. Its oxidizing qualities are valuable in the production of natural sweet wines (Banyuls, Maury, and Rivesaltes). In France, Grenache is often blended with Mourvèdre and Syrah in the production of wine to lay down. In Spain, it produces supple wines in Rioja and much more concentrated ones in the Priorat region of Catalonia.

Merlot

Merlot, which possibly originated in the Bordeaux region, was only recorded in the 19th century.
THE PRINCIPAL *TERROIRS*. The *terroir* of choice for Merlot is on the right bank of the Garonne in Bordeaux, at St-Émilion and Pomerol, on a cool mix of limestone and clay, as well as in Entre-Deux-Mers. But it is also grown in the south of France, the north of Italy, California, and Chile especially.
CHARACTERISTICS. Wine made from Merlot is supple and fruity, with aromas of blackcurrant and plums. It is generally for early drinking, but when blended with other grape varieties, notably Cabernets Sauvignon or Franc, it can produce a wine that takes on a splendid complexity. Indeed, Merlot plays an essential role in such illustrious *crus* as Pétrus.

Nebbiolo

Nebbiolo was possibly already being cultivated in the Piedmont region during the Roman era. It is Italy's major contribution to the classic grape varieties.
THE PRINCIPAL *TERROIRS*. Nebbiolo is hardly grown at all outside the Piedmont region of Italy – the area that suits it best – apart from a minimal presence on the American continent.
CHARACTERISTICS. This classic Italian grape variety produces great powerful wines that are acidic, tannic, and warming at the same time, Barolo and Barbaresco. With legendary longevity, they need to spend a certain length of time in bottle to allow their bouquet to develop.

> Grenache

> Merlot

> Nebbiolo

Pinot(s)

This ancient vine almost certainly originated in Burgundy and was known in the 13th century under the name Morillon. Genetically unstable, Pinot is the origin of a large family of grape varieties, including red and white: Pinot Noir, Meunier (red), Gris or Beurot (greyish pink), white, etc.

PINOT NOIR. Fairly delicate, Pinot Noir requires temperate climates. It offers a sensitivity to the subtleties of terroir and is subject to a great genetic instability, which has given rise to the emergence of many clones.Burgundy produces very accomplished wines. In France, in *blanc de noirs,* it is used in Champagnes. Elsewhere, it gives good results in Germany and New Zealand and some regions of the USA, South Africa, and Australia.

PINOT MEUNIER. Grown mostly in Champagne. Gives supple, fruity red wines.

> Pinot Noir

Syrah

For many years, it was thought that Syrah originated in Persia, but the discovery that its genome revealed Mondeuse – a variety from Savoie, France – among its antecedents, eventually put an end to that theory. With its small yields, this grape variety makes high-class wines when grown on the *terroirs* to which it is most suited.

THE PRINCIPAL *TERROIRS*. Syrah is most notably the grape variety of the Rhône Valley and forms the base of famous great wines such as Hermitage and Côte-Rôtie. It is also cultivated in Australia, under the name Shiraz, where it produces very good results.

CHARACTERISTICS. Syrah produces a *vin noir*, a peppery, structured wine with aromas of black fruit and sometimes violets. It is used as a single variety in some of the great Côtes du Rhône wines from the northern part of that area. It is also used as an improving variety in wines from Mediterranean regions, to which it brings structure and aromas.

> Syrah

Tempranillo

Tempranillo is considered the most prestigious of the Spanish grape varieties. It owes its name to its early-ripening qualities, as *temprano* is the Spanish word for 'early.'

THE PRINCIPAL *TERROIRS*. Tempranillo is grown most notably in Spain, where it has become the leading red grape variety. It is found only in limited quantities elsewhere in the world, with Portugal and Argentina being the only places where it is grown extensively.

CHARACTERISTICS. The key grape variety of the powerful and harmonious great Spanish wines of Rioja and Ribera del Duero, lending itself well to barrel maturation. Its aroma is reminiscent of Burgundy's Pinot Noir. In Portugal, where it is called *Tinta Roriz* or *Aragones*, it is one of the five recommended varieties in the production of red port.

Zinfandel (Primitivo)

The only wine that is considered typically American is made from Zinfandel – known as 'Zin' in the United States. This grape variety of Croatian origin was introduced to the USA around 1850, almost certainly from Italy where it was grown under the name Primitivo, in the Puglia region especially.

THE PRINCIPAL *TERROIRS*. Cultivated in several Balkan countries, a little in Mexico and Australia, but the most well-known wines come from southern Italy and California.

CHARACTERISTICS. An excellent grape variety rich in sugar and fruity aromas. It is a multipurpose grape, producing white wines (from black grapes), rosé wines (called 'blush'), and table wine, as well as wines for ageing. Generally, it is used as a single variety, but it can also be blended with other reds.

Other important red grape varieties

The varieties listed below are of varying importance. Some are linked exclusively to an appellation.

BARBERA. Very widespread in Italy (Piedmont) and in California, Barbera produces generous, nicely crisp wines.

BLAUFRÄNKISCH. Called Lemberger in Germany, this Austrian grape variety produces fruity wines, full of freshness in the style of those from Beaujolais.

CARIGNAN. Most commonly grown in the south of France and in Mediterranean countries. It produces wines that are robust, full-bodied, tannic, crisp, and of variable quality.

CARMENÈRE. Originally from Bordeaux, this variety is grown especially in Chile where it can produce full-bodied, perfumed wines when harvested fully ripe. It is also grown in Veneto.
CINSAUT (OR CINSAULT). A medium-quality grape variety that is happy in hot climates, it is used for blending (in the south of France, Lebanon, and North Africa), as it brings suppleness and lightness.
GROLLEAU. Grown mostly in the Loire Valley of France, it produces light wines with low alcohol content, including rosés. It is most used in the Anjou, Touraine, and Rosé de Loire AOCs.
KADARKA. This grape variety from Eastern Europe is cultivated particularly in several regions of Hungary, including Eger and Villány. It produces fresh, spicy, and somewhat delicate red wines, and good rosés. It is also found in other countries in Eastern Europe.
LAMBRUSCO. A grape variety grown in Emilia-Romagna in Italy, it goes into making several sweet, light, and slightly sparkling wines that are produced for rapid consumption.
MALBEC (OR CÔT, OR AUXERROIS). The principal grape variety used to make Cahors AOC wines, it produces a dark, structured wine that is fresh and perfumed. It is also symbolic of Argentina where it gives ripe, sun-drenched wines.
MONDEUSE. Related to Syrah, this grape variety is most characteristic of the Savoie region of France. The wine that is produced from it is structured and tannic.
MONTEPULCIANO. One of the principal Italian varieties. Produces vigorous red wines in central Italy. Often blended with Sangiovese.
MOURVÈDRE. This variety is used for producing blends in the Rhône Valley, Languedoc, and Provence, with, in the case of the latter, Bandol at the forefront. It is also cultivated in Spain, its country of origin. It produces tannic, full-bodied, spicy wines with good keeping qualities.
NÉGRETTE. Because it is fragile, this grape variety is becoming increasingly rare. Mainly found in the Haute-Garonne of southwest France, at Fronton, it brings violet and licorice aromas to supple wines with a medium lifespan.

Rediscovered grape varieties

Grape varieties don't escape the influence of production methods. One such example is Mourvèdre. Its future seemed uncertain after the Second World War, when new grafts took badly, but it is now being grown in increasing quantities. Viognier is also a 'miracle' grape variety. Reduced to a few dozen acres in the 1950s, due to poor conditions that affected the health of the vines, its production was irregular. But today, in the Rhône and the Midi, large amounts of Viognier wines are produced and a piece of previously forgotten wine heritage is slowly being rediscovered. Wines are also made from pre-phylloxera vineyards and labeled 'Forgotten Vines.'

NIELLUCCIO. This grape variety is grown in northern Corsica, where it forms part of the blend for the Patrimonio AOC.
PETIT VERDOT. Grown in Bordeaux land elsewhere, it is used in making the AOCs Medoc and Graves. It produces rich and tannic wines that improve with age.
POULSARD. Grown especially in the Jura region of France, Poulsard produces very light-coloured wines with a particularly delicate aroma. It is often used alone in Arbois wines.
SANGIOVESE. This great grape variety from Tuscany produces fruity, balanced wines, the most famous being Chianti and Brunello di Montalcino.
TANNAT. Rich in tannin, this grape variety is the principal component of many Pyrenean wines, notably those from Béarne, France. It is also popular in Uruguay.

> Tempranillo

> Zinfandel

> Petit Verdot

THE GREAT WHITE GRAPE VARIETIES

White grape varieties, used alone or in conjunction with others, produce a wide variety of wines: dry, off-dry, aromatic, and sweet. Among the best known, Chardonnay, Riesling, Chenin Blanc, and Sauvignon Blanc are now cultivated all over the world.

Chardonnay

Chardonnay is a grape variety that has 'gone global'. Exactly when it came into being is unknown, but its 'parents' have been identified as Gouais Blanc, a mediocre variety from the Jura and Franche-Comté regions of France, and Pinot Noir.

THE PRINCIPAL *TERROIRS*. Most notably grown in Burgundy and Champagne. This prestigious variety is used in Montrachet and all the great white Burgundy appellations, as well as in the Champagne *blancs de blancs*. It is resilient and can adapt to varying soils and climates.

CHARACTERISTICS. Chardonnay is capable of producing varied aromas, an expression of the climate as much as the methods of vinification, in particular the use sometimes of wood. In hot climates the aromas of brioche, fresh butter, hazelnuts, green fruit, citrus fruit, or gunflint found in the Chardonnays of Burgundy give way to those of citrus fruits, pineapple, and exotic fruits in hotter regions. The greatest Chardonnay wines, such as white Burgundies, age well. Others, especially those not aged in wood, are intended for early consumption.

***The skins of white grapes contain very few anthocyanins, the pigment that is present in red varieties.** They are translucent, with a colour that varies from pale green to yellow-gold, and can even sometimes be slightly pink.*

Chenin Blanc

Already being cultivated by the ninth century at Glanfeuil Abbey in the Anjou district of the Loire Valley, Chenin is a very versatile grape variety.

THE PRINCIPAL *TERROIRS*. Chenin Blanc is still widespread in the Loire, from Anjou to Touraine, in appellations such as Bonnezeaux, Savennières, and Vouvray. But it is also grown widely outside France, in South Africa in particular. This all-purpose grape variety adapts well to all soils and all climates.

CHARACTERISTICS. Depending on the *terroir* and the harvest dates, Chenin can produce wines that differ greatly, from *crémant* to natural sweet wine, from dry to sweet wines, from crisp to those lacking in character, and from the very ordinary to exceptional. In the heart of Chenin territory, in the Layon Valley at Vouvray, it can produce white wines for ageing, the crispness of its youth evolving in maturity to a voluptuous sweetness. In South Africa it also reveals its versatility.

> Chardonnay

> Chenin Blanc

> Gewurztraminer

DID YOU KNOW...?

The grape variety Chardonnay goes by many different names, depending on the region. *Across France, it is called Melon Blanc in Arbois; Petite Sainte-Marie in Savoie; Rousseau or Roussot in the Yonne; Beaunois near to Tonnerre in the Côte d'Or; Luisant at Besançon; Auvergnat Blanc in the Loiret; Arnoison in Touraine... to mention just a few examples. Chardonnay is not the only grape variety that goes by many different names; far from it. Every grape variety is likely to have different names, derived from local traditions.*

Gewurztraminer

The aromatic Traminer (*gewürz* is the German word for spice,) was imported from the Palatinate, and has been grown in Alsace since 1870. Traminer, which is in fact Savagnin Blanc, a grape variety from the Jura region, is made up of two pink versions. One is not aromatic (Klevner from Heiligenstein) and the other is very much so, the Traminer Musqué or Gewurztraminer.

THE PRINCIPAL *TERROIRS*. The variety is at home growing on both sides of the Rhine, in Alsace and in southern Germany, as well as in northern Italy and in Austria. Outside the central European vineyards, it is grown with only limited success. It is nevertheless also cultivated in California.

CHARACTERISTICS. Gewurztraminer produces a wine that is very fruity, with pronounced spicy notes and an aroma of roses. Good wines from Alsace or Baden (Germany) have an intense presence on the palate, despite being almost always weak in acidity. Harvested late, this wine becomes voluptuous and rich.

Muscat(s)

Probably originally from Asia Minor, Muscat was cultivated in Ancient Greece and is one of the oldest grape varieties in the world. It constitutes a vast family of at least 200 varieties, including black, red, and white.

THE BEST KNOWN MUSCATS AND THEIR *TERROIRS*. The Muscat of Alexandria is the most extensively grown, with the Muscat Blanc à Petits Grains being judged the best. The Muscat Ottonel – a product of crossbreeding Muscat with Chasselas, which took place in the Loire during the 19th century and was carried out by Moreau-Robert – found refuge in Alsace, Austria, and Eastern Europe. Aleatico, a black Muscat grape cultivated in many regions of Italy, is probably a parent of the Muscats.

CHARACTERISTICS. Anyone who has tasted a Muscat grape will have no difficulty in recognizing a wine made from this variety. The wines are very varied and range from a sparkling white to the rich, dense, fortified wines of Australia. Dry wines are made from Muscats in Alsace. There are very aromatic, naturally sweet and heady wines at Frontignan, as well as sparkling wine at Die, and so on.

Riesling

This ancient grape variety is of German origin.

THE PRINCIPAL *TERROIRS*. For some oenophiles, Riesling rivals Chardonnay in quality. But it doesn't have the same resilience and is restricted to shale and the limestone clay soils in northern Europe, on well-exposed hillsides. Widespread in Germany, where it occupies the finest *terroirs*, it is also grown in Austria and northern Italy, and also in France (in Alsace only). In the New World, it produces good results in Australia notably where it retains its legendary acidity, even in hot climates. The crisp acidity of the German Rieslings can, however, be lacking when this variety is cultivated in hotter climates.

> Muscat de Beaumes-de-Venise

> Muscat de Frontignan

> Riesling

CHARACTERISTICS. Riesling produces wines with a good balance of acidity and sweetness. They can be dry, fine, elegant, lemony, and for early drinking. But this grape variety also makes great sweet wines and wines to lay down; vigorous and complex, they will keep for decades. Generally speaking, the French wines are drier and higher in alcohol than the German ones.

Sauvignon Blanc

Grown for centuries in the Loire and Bordeaux regions of France, this grape variety is now cultivated all over the world.

THE PRINCIPAL *TERROIRS*. Sauvignon Blanc likes the limestone soil and cool climate it finds in the Loire and Bordeaux regions; it loses its vigour and interest in hot climates. It is nevertheless cultivated in many countries and especially in New Zealand where it produces a wine of note that is very intensely perfumed.

CHARACTERISTICS. This grape variety produces a dry white wine for early drinking. It is direct and distinctive, sometimes simple, with aromas of citrus fruit, green fruit, and marked vegetal notes without the addition of other grape varieties. It secures the reputation of the wines of Sancerre, Pouilly, and Quincy, all in the Loire Valley. In the Bordeaux region, it is often blended with Sémillon, whether in dry or sweet wines, and is used in the making of white Graves and Sauternes.

> Sauvignon Blanc

> Sémillon

Sémillon

Sémillon is subtle and restrained, needing time to assert itself, and is therefore not a very fashionable wine.

THE PRINCIPAL *TERROIRS*. Apart from the Gironde of Bordeaux, the *terroir* in which it thrives best, it is mainly in the Hunter Valley of Australia that this grape variety has made a name for itself. Despite this, there are plantings of Sémillon in Chile, Argentina, and South Africa.

CHARACTERISTICS. Sémillon takes on *pourriture noble* (botrytis, or 'noble rot') well and gives fleshiness and body to sweet wines, particularly Sauternes. It is also used in blends for dry white wines and is present, notably, in the great white Graves. The Australians use Sémillon on its own to produce superb dry wines for ageing.

Other important white grape varieties

The following grape varieties are of varying importance. Some are exclusively linked to an appellation.

ALBARIÑO. This Spanish grape variety produces interesting dry white wines, including Rías Baixas, which is a DO (*denominación de origin* – equivalent to the French *appellation d'origine*).

ALIGOTÉ. This variety produces the dry, fairly crisp, white AOCs Bourgogne Aligoté and Bouzeron.

BOURBOULENC. Grown in Provence and Languedoc, this grape forms part of many AOCs (Bandol, Cassis, Minervois, etc.).

CATARRATTO. This Sicilian grape variety goes into the production of Marsala, and also table wines.

CHASSELAS. Both a dessert and a wine grape variety, it is used in winemaking at Pouilly-sur-Loire, in Alsace, in Savoie, in Germany (Gutedel), and especially in Switzerland. It produces a supple and delicate wine.

CLAIRETTE. An ancient grape variety from the Midi, where it is used to make a dry, floral, slightly flabby wine.

COLOMBARD. A native of southwest France, it is also grown in California and South Africa. The wines produced from it are fresh and perfumed. It is also used in the production of brandy.

FOLLE BLANCHE. These grapes are used to make Gros-Plant and the finest Armagnac brandies.

FRIULANO. The principal grape variety in northwest Italy, Friulano produces a straw-coloured wine with almond aromas.

FURMINT. A great Hungarian grape variety, it is the basis of the sweet, very aromatic wine Tokaji.

JACQUÈRE. Mainly cultivated in Savoie, this variety produces a wine that is low in alcohol, lively, floral, and light.

MACCABEU. As Viara, widely grown in Spain for white Rioja, and in Penedès for sparkling Cava.

MALVASIA. A name given to a number of vines, mostly unrelated. Cultivated in Italy, Greece, and Portugal, notably, it has given its name to some of the sweetest Madeiras.

MARSANNE. From the northern Rhône region, this grape variety is similar to a Roussanne, but produces a more supple wine with less finesse and perfume.

The grape varieties benefiting from a wine *appellation d'origine* in France

The specifications for French *appellation d'origine* wines restrict the choice of grape varieties in order to preserve the traditional character or typicity of regional wines. Included is a hierarchy that distinguishes between the 'main' grape variety, which is an obligatory component of the wine, always used in sizeable proportions; the 'complementary' varieties, present in lesser amounts; and the 'accessory' varieties, which must not exceed 10 per cent of the whole. Any modification to the mix of grape varieties in an appellation wine is subjected to prior experimentation. Each new grape variety that is accepted will have the status of 'accessory' variety.

MAUZAC. This grows mostly in Limoux (Blanquette de Limoux) and in Gaillac in southwestern France, where it produces dry and sweet wines, sparkling and still.

MELON DE BOURGOGNE. Called Muscadet in the Nantes region, it produces a dry, easy-to-drink wine.

MÜLLER-THURGAU. Grown in Germany and elsewhere, this grape variety produces a robust, slightly musky wine.

MUSCADELLE. This fragile grape variety brings an aromatic touch to some of the sweet wines of southwest France.

PALOMINO. This produces a neutral white wine that forms the basis of sherry (fino, manzanilla, and amontillado). Outside Spain, it is grown in California, Australia, and South Africa.

PEDRO XIMÉNEZ. This very sweet white grape variety is used to make sherry and Montilla-Moriles.

PETIT MANSENG. This variety from Gascony, France, is intense, structured, and aromatic and is used to make Jurançon.

PINOTS. Pinot Gris (pink to bluish-grey fruit) is used in the rich, fleshy, white wines of Alsace and has been favoured by German wine-producers for several years. In Italy and the New World, under the name Pinot Grigio, it produces rather light wines. Pinot Blanc is grown in Alsace and northeastern Italy for a supple and fruity wine. It is very much in vogue in Germany and progress in New Zealand.

ROUSSANNE. An aromatic variety from the northern Rhône region and Savoie, it produces a fine, balanced wine to lay down.

SAVAGNIN. A grape variety from the Jura region of France, it is made into Vin Jaune or sometimes a very distinctive white wine. Blended with other grape varieties, it brings to the wine an element of quality and a capacity for ageing.

SEYVAL BLANC. This hybrid, very crisp grape produces a neutral, dry white wine in the state of New York and in Canada.

SYLVANER. Widely planted in Alsatian and German vineyards, this high-yielding grape is made into simple, floral, and vigorous wines.

TORRONTÉS. One of the most interesting white grape varieties grown in Argentina, giving wines that are heady and aromatic, sometimes musky.

UGNI BLANC (TREBBIANO). Used to make Cognac brandy, this also goes into the making of crisp, fairly neutral white wines from Provence and Languedoc. In Italy it is known as Trebbiano.

VERDEJO. Considered one of the best white grape varieties of Castille-León, Spain, it is a notable presence in Rueda.

VERDELHO. Known as one of the principal grape varieties that go into the making of Madeira wines, it is also part of the blend used in several Australian whites.

VIOGNIER. Grown in the south of France and in the Pyrénées-Orientales at Vaucluse, it can produce full-bodied and aromatic wines of great quality (Condrieu and Château-Grillet AOCs). It is being increasingly planted in the New World.

WELSCHRIESLING. This grape variety is made into light, fruity wines in Austria, northern Italy, and southeastern Europe.

> Riesling vines in the Schoenenbourg *terroir*, a *grand cru* of Alsace (Domaine Hugel & Fils).

GRAPE VARIETIES AND *TERROIRS*: FAMOUS COMBINATIONS

The combination of terroir *and grape variety strongly influences a wine's personality. In some vineyards, the factors affecting quality – climate, exposure, soil – combine to transform the 'expression' of the grape variety and result in a unique wine.*

Cabernet Sauvignon in Bordeaux

A classic or noble red grape variety, Cabernet Sauvignon is harvested late. It is resistant to rot and is completely happy in poor soil, so long as it is well drained.

The Cabernet Sauvignon grape is grown all over the world, but the Bordeaux region provides the ideal *terroir*. This is especially so on the left bank of the Gironde, where the majority of the soil is a stony and gravelly mix and where the ocean climate dominates.

In this region, where the vineyards of Haut-Médoc and Graves are found, it is the dominant grape variety of the *grands crus classés* or great growth wines, blended with Cabernet Franc and Merlot. Cabernet Sauvignon produces wines with a tight tannic fabric, especially in a young wine, which ensures a longevity that is sometimes exceptional. As they age, they take on the body, elegance, and finesse of a great wine.

The grape grower can improve the wines that a terroir produces by making the right choices, *such as choosing an appropriate grape variety or the best way to manage the vines. The grapes must be able to ripen satisfactorily and express their original, characteristic features.*

Syrah in Cornas

Syrah is a tannic red grape variety that produces wines that age well. It grows best in granitic terrain. It is particularly found in the north of the Rhône Valley and notably in the prestigious appellations of Côte-Rôtie, Hermitage, and Cornas.

In a semi-continental climate, Cornas is grown on very sunny southern and south-eastern slopes, steep terraces of silty soil supported by retaining walls.In the northern Rhône Valley, this appellation is the first to be harvested. Syrah is the only grape variety to be grown there, and it produces a fine, powerful wine, dark red in colour. The aromas are of soft red fruit along with touches of spice and violets. As it ages it evolves toward aromas of truffle, leather, licorice, and cooked fruits.

> Cabernet Sauvignon grapes in Graves, Bordeaux.

Viognier in Condrieu

Viognier is a capricious and fragile white grape variety that gives only low yields. It is the exclusive variety used in two French AOC wines, Château-Grillet and Condrieu. The latter appellation, with a moderate continental climate, extends over steep hillsides arranged in terraces on pebbly sand or granitic soil. This is where Viognier produces its best results: a superb white wine, pale yellow in colour with golden glints, and generous aromas, both floral (violet, iris, wild flowers) and fruity (white peach, apricot). A supple, unctuous, and heady mouth feel is matched with great freshness and good length on the palate. It is a rare, expensive, and sought-after wine for early drinking. The use of casks for fermentation and maturation provokes debate, disputed by some, approved of by others.

Chardonnay in Puligny-Montrachet

A white grape variety of quality when held to a low yield, Chardonnay produces fine wines that age well. While it is grown more or less everywhere in the world, with good results, in Burgundy it produces the greatest dry white wines in France.

In the climate of Burgundy, Chardonnay produces the best results on stony, limestone clay soils that grow wines of great concentration and finesse. This is the case in the appellation of Puligny-Montrachet, in Côte de Beaune. The climate is temperate, tending toward continental. The soil lies in banks of marly limestone clay; and the exposure is east-southeast, giving the perfect amount of sunshine. Grown in this *terroir*, Chardonnay produces fairly small grapes. Their sugar content can reach high levels, while still retaining a significant acidity, resulting in particularly well-balanced, powerful, pleasant wines. They are mouth filling and fleshy, notably with regard to the four *grands crus* (Montrachet, Chevalier-Montrachet, Bienvenues-Bâtard-Montrachet, and Bâtard-Montrachet) that are found in Puligny.

Tempranillo in Rioja

Tempranillo is the Spanish answer to Cabernet Sauvignon. Its name is derived from *temprano*, the Spanish word for 'early,' since it is an early-ripening variety. The fact that it ripens quickly enables it to be successful in continental climates. It produces the best results in Rioja, in northern Spain. This is particularly true west of the town of Logroño in Rioja Alta, the highest part of the region (between 1,300 and 1,600 ft [400 and 500 m]), open to the Atlantic. It prospers on arid and stony soil, made up of solidified sediments and rocks that centuries of erosion have uncovered. The resulting wines are reputed for their finesse, structure, and their excellent ageing properties.

> Viognier grapes in France's Condrieu vineyards.

Sangiovese in Chianti

Seventy to 80 per cent or more of the grapes grown in the Chianti appellation are of this Italian red variety. Sensitive to variations in the soil and the climate, it ripens at different rhythms in different vineyards. Grown in the sandy clay of the Colli Aretini, the wines are tender; while in the limestone clay of the Rufina crus, they become full-bodied; and they are rich and strong from the Colli Senesi but the most renowned come from the Classico area between Sienna and Florence. Under a generous sun, ripening is often tempered by the proximity to the cool sea and the general whims of the climate. To favour the balance of the grapes, they are often harvested as late as the end of October, as for other Italian grape varieties. In the best versions, Chianti is a firm wine with good acidity, vigorous tanins, and aromas of cherry and tea.

> A Tempranillo vine in Rioja, Spain.

Qualified specialists in *terroir*

Claude and Lydia Bourguignon have been studying soils for more than 25 years; not only their physical and chemical composition but also their microbiological properties. They have discovered the role played by small creatures, from insects to microorganisms, which enable the plant successfully to assimilate the soil's mineral elements and help develop the expression of a *terroir* in the wine. They also demonstrated that clay plays a vital role in storing these elements. Thanks to these studies, the Bourguignons have been able to draw up a register classifying the soil's capacity to produce great wines.

FROM VINE TO BOTTLE

THE GROWTH CYCLE OF THE VINE

The vine is both a hardy perennial and a fruit tree. Hence it has an annual cycle of fruit production and its own particular life cycle: grown from a cutting, it becomes a young vine before reaching full maturity and maximum production.

The needs of the vine

Vines need light above all. However, direct sunlight is not essential; daylight alone is adequate. The average temperatures required are quite specific, however: 50°F to 77°F (10°C to 25°C). Above 82°F (28°C), the vine's water content evaporates and its leaves wither. Growth also stops when it becomes too cold. It only requires water intermittently and does not need an excessive amount (20 to 27.5 inches or 500 to 700 mm per year). If the climate is too wet, the vine may be attacked by diseases or produce berries that contain far too much water, causing the skin to burst. Wind and rain can also have a negative effect, especially during flowering.

***In vineyards all over the world, the vine's growth cycle resumes in the same way.** Dormant at the beginning of winter, the vine starts to grow in the spring to produce ripe clusters in autumn. That is, if the climate is mild, and the wine-producer is careful...*

The vine and vine leaf

THE VINE. The fruiting branches or arms of the vine grow on a sizeable wooden stem or trunk. The branches consist of a succession of internodes, lengths of branch separated by swellings or nodes from which the leaves, buds, tendrils and inflorescences emerge. During the summer, a branch matures and its colour changes from green to brown. This is known as lignification, and at this stage the branch becomes a cane.

VINE LEAVES. Attached alternately at the nodes, the leaves have five main veins, but the wide variation in the rest of the leaf – lobes, serrations, villosity (presence of a surface fuzz), and pigmentation – is a reminder that the leaves are a key element in differentiating grape varieties.

Flower buds

BUDDING. This stage in the vine's growth cycle is when the buds open in spring (March to April in the northern hemisphere and September to October in the southern hemisphere). After a long period of dormancy in winter, branches and leaves grow and the sap begins to flow.

THE PROMPT BUD AND LATENT BUD. The prompt bud grows in the same year in which it develops, unlike the latent bud beside it, which grows into a shoot only in the year after it begins to develop. The prompt bud produces only short secondary shoots, which sometimes produce small clusters of grapes. (These small bunches are almost never harvested.) In contrast, the latent bud develops the following year into branches that will bear fruit. Thus the quantity of the harvest for a particular year is in part dependent on the growth of the plant during the previous year.

> Budding

> Flower buds

> Flowers

Pests that damage vines

Fungi: Powdery mildew develops on green parts of the vine from budding and then attacks the skin of the berries. Mildew also affects the green parts of the plant. The grapes turn brown and shrivel. But *Botrytis cinerea* (see box p.54) is harmful, but can also be beneficial, depending on the type of wine.

Parasites: Besides phylloxera (see p.21 and p.34), grape worms and mites (which cause *Colomerus vitis* and *Caleptrimerus vitis*) are harmful to vines, along with red or yellow spider mites.

Viruses: Transmitted by grafting, short-leaf and coil viruses, for example, are detrimental to the yield, longevity, and sugar content of the berries.

> Having reached their maximum size, the clusters soak up the sun to reach full maturity.

FLOWERING. The inflorescences, which later become the clusters of grapes, lie at the base of branches on the opposite side to the leaves. There may be anything between zero and four per branch. Tendrils, located on higher nodes, are modified inflorescences that develop into slender stems. Depending on variety and environmental conditions, the number of flowers that make up the inflorescences can vary from a hundred to several thousand. Flowering depends on the variety and especially on the weather. It takes place between five and ten weeks after budding (May to June for the northern hemisphere and November to December in the southern hemisphere).

From flowers to grapes

FRUIT SETTING. This stage of the cycle of the vine is when the ovaries of pollinated flowers develop into tiny berries: the inflorescences became clusters. The phenomenon of fruit setting occurs in early summer. This is the most crucial moment in the growth cycle of the vine, because it largely determines the size of the harvest.

BERRY GROWTH. This takes place in four distinct phases. The first slow growth lasts about 20 days, then it accelerates for a similar period, only to slow sharply again until *véraison*.

VERAISON. This refers to the physiological process during which the sugars in the berries begin to intensify. The berries of red grapes begin to acquire their colour. It is in essence the actual beginning of the maturation of the grapes (in August for the northern hemisphere, and February in the southern). The degree of maturity, which determines the harvest date, is decided according to the type of wine required.

DORMANCY. In autumn, falling leaves indicate the end of the annual growth cycle and the beginning of winter dormancy.

> Fruit setting

> Berries growing

> Véraison

WORK IN THE VINEYARD DURING THE YEAR

Current wine production combines the expertize of centuries gone by with science and the most advanced modern techniques.

Human intervention

PREPARATION OF THE GROUND. In many prestigious vineyards, traditional methods of cultivating the soil continue to be used: banking up the earth in autumn (to protect the vines from excessive cold and damp), ploughing back the earth in the spring (to open up the base of the vines), de-earthing (removal of soil from between the vines), and hoeing. Wine-growers who follow the non-cultivation method replace these tasks with the use of herbicides instead, while other producers use cover-crop planting to combat soil erosion (*see also* p.58).

***Despite advances in technology, the work of the wine producer has not changed:** his task is to manage growth; to control weeds, insects, and grapevine diseases; and to harvest at the right time. The schedule of work on the vine is still the same.*

FERTILIZATION. Manure may be added, along with other fertilizers and various additives (organic or inorganic substances to make the soil more fertile).

TREATMENTS. Bordeaux mixture (*see* box on the following page) and other preventative pesticide treatments are applied repeatedly to the graft, stem, and branches.

PRUNING. Between December and March (in the northern hemisphere), while the sap is down, the vines undergo winter pruning (*see* p.52) using techniques specific to each individual region in order to reduce growth. Summer pruning, which consists of several operations – trimming, topping, thinning, etc. (*see* p.52) – helps to retain the sap for the berries, to aerate the vine, and to optimize the amount of sun received.

> Winter pruning

> Burning of clippings after pruning

> Tying pruned vine shoots

> Mechanical ploughing

> Thinning

> Harvest

Bordeaux mixture

Mildew is a disease caused by a fungus attacking the vine leaves and grape clusters. The traditional remedy is known as Bordeaux mixture. This blue-coloured fungicide is prepared with copper sulphate and slaked lime, and is sprayed on the vines. The Bordeaux mixture used today is less toxic and degrades more readily than the version used decades ago. However, the use of copper, which accumulates in the soil, has been criticized to the point that a directive was passed by the European Union in 2002 to limit its use and decrease the amount permitted every year. Laboratories are testing replacement products.

> Harvest at Château Reynon, in Bordeaux.

Work in the vineyard, month by month (for the northern hemisphere)

JANUARY. The vines are pruned by hand. This delicate work is still little mechanized, although mechanical hedge trimmers are sometimes used to reduce costs. The vine cuttings that have been removed are burned.
FEBRUARY. Pruning of the vines continues.
MARCH. The vine awakes from its winter dormancy. With many regions having given up on tilling the soil, unwanted plant growth is removed either with herbicides or, more and more frequently, by grassing over the strips between the rows of vines. We are also seeing the return of ploughing, advocated by those in favour of organic and sustainable viticulture.
APRIL. This is when new buds appear (budding). At the same time, young vines are planted and trellising takes place (repairing the posts, the wires, and then attaching the plant).
MAY. Spring frosts are a concern at this time. The plants are treated against disease (mildew, powdery mildew, grey rot) and animal pests (grape worms, spider mites, etc.), and these treatments continue until mid-September. They must cease between 15 days and three weeks before harvest. A second ploughing is carried out. Organic wine producers do not weed.
JUNE. The vine flowers. New branches are trellised. Treatments continue.
JULY. Another ploughing. Further treatments, if necessary. The vine is cut back. Branches that are too long are pollarded. If the vine grows too extensively, a 'green harvest' can be carried out, a thinning in which some of the young clusters are removed in order to limit the yield.
AUGUST. Second thinning. Preventative treatment, if necessary.
SEPTEMBER. Harvest begins. Harvesting machines often replace human grape pickers, except for expensive wines and in certain specific cases. In vineyards in hot climates, it is common to harvest at night to take advantage of the cooler temperature.
OCTOBER. Harvesting ends. The soil is enriched with fertilizer, manure, or organic waste.
NOVEMBER. If the year is a good one, the last few grapes are harvested; this is the late harvest. The large shoots are pruned. Anti-mildew treatment is applied. Ploughing takes place. If appropriate, old vines are uprooted.
DECEMBER. The drains are cleared. Roads, terraces, and walls are repaired. Pruning work begins.

DID YOU KNOW...?

Using a horse-drawn plough, a practice that had been abandoned for many years, *is back in fashion, used by wine-growers who follow biodynamic and organic farming methods. Mechanized ploughing still takes place, but heavy tractors compact the earth. Horses, by contrast, can plough more lightly. And if the vines are being grown on steep slopes, they are easier to plough with a horse rather than with a machine.*

PRUNING AND YIELD OF THE VINE

Since the beginning of viticulture, growers have found that when vines are pruned – when they are prevented from achieving full natural growth – they yield better quality fruit and thus better wine.

The principles of pruning

The wine producers of Europe and the New World sometimes use different methods of pruning, although all have the same aim. In addition, the rules for AOP classified wines often demand specific pruning methods. The object of the exercise in all cases is both to regulate the function of the vine to obtain sufficient quantities of the best grapes and to shape the plant to make it easier to tend.

IN EUROPE. European wine producers prune their vines in winter to control the growth of the plant and reduce yields: the shorter the vine is cut, the fewer the grapes. In summer, the vine develops its foliage at the expense of the fruit. So, in order to encourage cluster ripening, the vines are trimmed laterally and vertically. This ancient practice of maintaining a balance between the volume of leaves and fruit must be carried out so that the grapes ripen under the best possible conditions, with the leaves acting as a 'lung' for the vine via photosynthesis, and the grapes ripening thanks to the effects of sunlight on the foliage.

***Pruning allows the vines to be shaped as required.** Even today, it is the least mechanized of all the tasks performed in a vineyard.*

IN THE NEW WORLD. Pruning methods have had to be adapted to suit the vineyards of the New World, where the vines are sometimes planted in more fertile soil and in a warmer climate and European techniques might produce abundant but low quality wines. Californian and Australian winemakers now employ 'canopy management,' which involves shaping the leaf mass to reduce yields and thus ensure better concentration of juice in the grape. In addition, since the late 1980s in California and Australia, new vineyards are planted in locations at higher altitude, on less fertile land.

A technique for every season

WINTER PRUNING. Winter pruning shapes the vine (*i.e.* determining the growth path it takes), which will maintain its shape through the years, and stabilizes production. In the first two or three years, the structure is pruned. Then the pruning is just of the fruit-bearing parts, intended to leave on the vine a number of fruit-bearing buds compatible with the desired output and the plant's capabilities. This concerns only the shoots (the shoots of that year). Short pruning means leaving only the shoot bases with a very small number of eyes. The short shoots are designated by different terms: *court-bois*, *coursons*, *cots*, etc. When fruiting branches of a certain length are left on the stock, this is called long pruning. The vine shoots are then called *longs-bois*, *baguettes*, or *astes* in France.

> Winter pruning at the Champagne Roederer estate in France.

SPRING PRUNING. In the spring, barren branches, called suckers, which have developed at the base or the trunk of the vines, are removed.

SUMMER PRUNING. During the summer, leaf stripping (which is leaf removal near the cluster to expose it to sunlight), the topping of branches (the removal of the top of the branches), and thinning (trimming of summer growth) are carried out. The parts of the plant that have grown are identified and trained to the trellising system (the supporting set of posts and wires). Depending on whether this is done prudently or too severely, this thinning process will have a positive or negative effect on the quality of the harvest.

> Summer pruning at the Michel Juillot estate in Côte Chalonnaise, France.

Yield

To produce quality wines, it is essential to limit the yield of vines.

IN THE PAST. The old methods of viticulture were laborious and often doomed to failure: rot, mildew, insects, rain, wind, hail, and frost damaged the grapes and man could not prevent this effectively. Those who could afford it sent workers to remove the insects by hand, but others lost their crops. A wet summer meant the grapes rotted because there were no anti-rot treatments. However, traditional methods produced low yields per acre of vines, so the grape juice was concentrated and had good flavour potential.

TODAY. One acre (0.4 ha) of vines may contain 1,500 to 12,000 vines, rarely more. Each vine can produce a single grape cluster or a full basket of them. These choices fall to the wine producer, who is constrained by any regulations governing the vineyards. French and Italian laws, for example, are based on a maximum yield of a certain volume of wine per acre. Germany sets no upper limit to production, but requires a classification of wines according to the amount of sugar in the musts. As for the New World, they have no regulations and do not impose restrictions on yields. But the best vineyards limit their yields in the same way as in Europe.

WHAT WORK NEEDS TO BE DONE? Minimal enrichment is required, but other work is needed. Winter pruning can control the growth of the plant. Summer pruning promotes the concentration and maturity of the grapes. Similarly, de-budding, de-suckering (removing unwanted young shoots) at the end of spring, and the 'green harvest' (removing some of the clusters) during the summer contribute to reduction of the yield.

Different ways of guiding vine growth

Goblet: The 'cup' resembles a small tree with a rather short trunk and arms heading in opposite directions, each terminated by a spur with two eyes.

Cordon: Cordon trellising involves bending the trunk and placing it horizontally at the desired height along a wire.

Guyot: Guyot trellising comprises a vertical trunk and one or two very short arms. During pruning, the long fruit-bearing branches and a spur are kept. The latter offers a shoot to be retained for the next year.

Two worlds, two schools of thought

Although both Europe and the New World produce low and high yield wines, the wine authorities of Europe believe that low yields are good. In which case it should follow that vines whose yields are limited because of poor soil, high planting density, hard pruning, and minimal soil enrichment produce a better wine. But in the New World, as elsewhere, it is possible to produce extremely high quality wines from larger yields; everything depends on conditions, the behaviour of the vines and the end product they intend to achieve.

TRUE OR FALSE?

The lower the yield, the better the wine.

FALSE. A vine has to be healthy and have the correct supply of moisture to produce grapes capable of creating a good wine, and planting density varies widely depending on the availability of water, so the equation is more complex than this.

A level of 3.5 tons per acre (50 hl/ha) would appear to be a reasonable yield for grands vins (2,670 bottles per acre, or 6,600 bottles per hectare), in most cases if the plants are healthy, But local conditions and climates especially can affect these figures. In a year when the weather is perfect, a yield of 4 tons per acre (70 hl/ha) could provide an excellent wine; but in a tough year, even a yield of 2 tons per acre (35 hl/ha) may produce mediocre wines.

THE HARVEST

Harvest is the vital link that connects the work in the vineyard to the production of wine. This is an opportunity for growers to see their efforts rewarded in the quality of the crop. Each cluster contains a record of the past year within its berries.

A perfect grape

The decision to begin the harvest, by assessing exactly when the grapes are at their optimum level of maturity, is always difficult. Different varieties reach their respective maturity at different times. In addition, grapes from the same variety that are planted in different positions don't necessarily ripen at the same time.

PHYSIOLOGICAL MATURITY. When grapes ripen, sugar builds up in the berries. During maturation, the sugar level rises steadily. At the same time, the acidity of the grapes gradually decreases. At that stage the grapes are ripe, and this is called 'alcoholic maturity.' Measurement of maturity, based on the sugar/acid ratio, may be taken by state laboratories – especially in Europe. The wine producer also takes individual measurements. After pressing the first berries that have been picked, the juice or must is measured using a hydrometer (to check its sugar content) or a refractometer (to measure the potential alcohol content).

PHENOLIC MATURITY. This is another test of maturity for red or black grapes, which takes into consideration the colour of the skins and taste of the seeds. A good level of phenolic maturity allows production of red wines with ripe and pleasant tannins, as opposed to herbaceous and rough ones. The faults of the latter are excused by saying that they were 'picked too soon.'

***In a week, a single machine can do the same amount of work as 50 people in three weeks.** Mechanization of harvesting has reduced the operating costs of many vineyards.*

Unknowns in the harvest

THE SHORT YEARS. Wine producers sometimes bring forward the harvest date, either by choice or because they have been forced to do so. In the event of deteriorating berry health or disastrous weather conditions, they will opt for less than perfect maturity, rather than losing their crop. This will be a 'short year.' Similarly, in the case of a very hot year, if the acidity of white grapes, which is essential for the balance of the wine, is falling too quickly, it may be necessary to harvest earlier than expected.

SELECTIVE HARVESTING. On the other hand, if production of a sweet white wine is being considered, their over-ripeness, or their transformation resulting from the action of the botrytis, is desired. To this end, skilled grape pickers gather only clusters or berries that have reached the necessary stage. They must make several passes around the vineyard, and this is called selective harvesting.

> The ripe grapes can be harvested individually in several passes.

Botrytis cinerea and grey rot

Botrytis cinerea is a fungus that grows on grape skins that have swollen during maturation. This condition is responsible for the grey rot that changes the colour of the wine and gives it a musty taste. One particular form of *Botrytis cinerea* leads to the formation of brown rot, or so-called 'noble rot.' In this case, the fungus attacks the berry and changes its flavours. Gradually the grapes shrivel and have high concentrations of sugar and acidity. This botrytis is sought for the sweet white wines of Bordeaux and southwest France (Sauternes, Monbazillac), the sweet wines from the Loire Valley (Vouvray, for example) and from Alsace, as well as for some wines from Germany, Austria, and Hungary (Tokay).

> Manual harvesting in the vineyards of the Médoc.

Manual harvesting

HARVESTING THE GRAPES. There are generally two grape pickers, or cutters, and they pick the grapes on each side of the row. Pruning knives have been replaced by pruning shears with straight blades and shears with curved blades, and sometimes by a pair of scissors with rounded points.

TRANSPORTING THE GRAPES. The harvested grapes used to be placed in wicker or wooden containers. Today, they are mainly placed in plastic boxes, with a similar capacity of 13–22 lbs (6–10 kg), which are easy to wash.

REMOVING THEM FROM THE ROWS. Baskets or buckets are emptied into larger containers supported by carriers. They take their load to the edge of the vineyard where they tip it into a bin or transport container. There are three to five cutters for each carrier, depending on the harvest in the particular vineyard.

PROTECTING THE GRAPES. Some wine producers prefer wooden or plastic boxes, which serve to transport the grapes as well as pick them. This reduces handling, keeping the grapes whole and intact until they reach the place where the wine will be produced.

DID YOU KNOW...?

The harvest is an occasion for many festivals. *The proclamation of the harvest, the earliest legal date on which it is permitted to harvest (in Europe), is often announced in a solemn fashion. But the grape harvest begins and ends with festivities ranging from a simple banquet to large traditional festivals. The custom of holding a banquet was once very common, with La Paulée in Burgundy and Gerber in southwest France among those that have survived to the present day. Some festivals, such as Les Acabailles in Graves and Sauternes, include a floral procession. Finally, there is a French tradition on the last day of the harvest that the grape pickers accompany the last cart to the place where the wine is to be produced.*

TRUE OR FALSE?

Mechanical harvesting alters the taste of the wine.

FALSE. Mechanized harvesting has been on the increase since the 1970s. The berries are harvested by shaking, and the leaves are removed by a fan. With these advances in technology, it is virtually impossible to distinguish between wines that have been manually or mechanically harvested, at least in years when the climate has been mild. Even so, harvesting in prestigious vineyards is mostly done by hand.

Mechanical harvesting

Today, virtually all vineyard regions use mechanized harvesting, except where the terrain is very rough or steep. The rows of vines must be accessible regardless of weather conditions, which implies chemical weeding or the more eco-friendly mowing of grass. To produce a quality wine, the vineyard must be in perfect health at the time of harvesting. The development of rot, for example, causes significant losses from the heavy release of juice during picking and during the transfer of the crop. Two types of machine exist: self-propelled and towed. In most cases, picking the berries from the stalk is done via a series of alternate crosswise movements.

TOWARDS GREENER WINE PRODUCTION

It was during the 1960s that the use of weedkillers and other artificial aids became commonplace in agriculture, in order to make work easier and reduce production costs. Since the turn of the millennium, more concern is being shown for the impact of this method on the environment.

Sustainable agriculture

This form of agriculture uses all products at its disposal to combat pests and diseases. It is sustainable in that it acts with a sense of proportion, using treatments only when appropriate.
To qualify as sustainable, an estate must meet many specific criteria, consisting of 'good practices that are objectively environmentally friendly,' including those specific to viticulture. Some certifying bodies specify allowing grass to grow in the vineyard to combat soil erosion, and maintaining hedges and ditches in order to preserve fauna and flora.

Today, France is the third-largest consumer of pesticides; *its vineyards, which occupy only 4 per cent of agricultural land, account for the consumption of more than 14 per cent of these chemicals, according to French biodynamic agriculture association, F.*

Organic farming

According to statistics from Agence Bio, a public interest group responsible for the promotion of organic farming, organic wine production in France has increased from fewer than 500 estates on 11,775 acres (4,765 ha) in 1998 to more than 4,500 on 158,080 acres (64,000 ha) in 2013. Although this represents only 8 per cent of French vineyards, the area of land used has increased thirteenfold in 15 years! Spain is at the forefront of organic viticulture in Europe, followed by Italy and France.
Proponents of organic farming refuse to use synthetic chemical products, relying instead on natural treatments or the prevention of disease through better maintenance of the vineyard. Since 2012, European regulations on organic farming that concern only winegrowing techniques, have included organic wine-making, authorizing fewer additives than in conventional wine-making, with much lower maximum doses and a ban on GM.
NO PESTICIDES. Not using pesticides preserves life in the soil, allowing it to develop, transform, and regenerate. All pesticides are banned to safeguard biodiversity. Sulphur and copper are used to combat diseases, while seaweed is used to repair the damage caused by botrytis. There are also modern techniques of biological control, such as sexual confusion, which can reduce the number of insects attacking the grape cluster. However, organic agriculture does not have a solution for everything, and it still has not found a way to combat serious diseases that cause vine death.
NO ARTIFICIAL CHEMICAL FERTILIZERS. Organic

'Natural' wines?

Some wine producers choose to ban the use of any additives, such as selected yeasts, sugar (chaptalization), and even sulphur dioxide, an antioxidant and antibacterial agent that prevents the wine from turning into vinegar or oxidizing. This method of wine-making and bottling without using sulphur requires scrupulous hygiene and very strict storage conditions.
A 'natural wine' (for which there is no official definition) may hold some surprises (flavours of straw, bruised apples, even of compost), and there is always a chance of the undesired presence of gas masking what was being sought at the outset: the pure expression of *terroir.*

> Horse-drawn ploughing at a vineyard on the Coulée de Serrant estate, in the Loire Valley.

Preparations that harness energy

Biodynamic preparations are supposed to stimulate the life forces at work inside the plant.

Horn manure: A cow horn is filled with cow dung and buried in the soil between the time of the autumn equinox and spring, so that the dung virtually turns into humus. Its main action is to help the vine roots penetrate deeper into the soil, resulting in a greater resistance to drought.

Horn silica: Composed of finely ground quartz combined with a little water, the mixture is placed in a cow horn, and buried between early summer and Christmas, and subsequently exposed to the sun. It is used to stimulate the development of fruit.

Dung compost: This consists primarily of cow dung, silica, limestone, and various preparations made from plants (yarrow, camomile, nettle, oak bark, dandelion). These composts, which are rich in bacteria, enhance the decomposition process of organic matter and help depleted soil to recover its vitality.

> Agriculture that respects the natural environment and encourages biodiversity in the vineyard.

viticulture does not look to feed the plant directly other than with organic substances, often in the form of compost or green manure. The aim is to sustain soil fertility by maintaining its biological activity.

NO WEEDKILLERS. Weeds are removed by ploughing, or cover planting is practised, mowing these plants when required.

Biodynamics

In 1924, Rudolf Steiner, the Austrian esoteric philosopher and scientist, produced guidelines for this discipline, which studies the link between humans, plants, the earth, and the entire universe. Regarded as a branch of organic farming, biodynamics goes much further than simply excluding the use of artificial chemicals. It uses 'fundamental' products (*see* box above), based on silica from cow dung or plants.

THE PRINCIPLE OF HOMEOPATHY. The preparations are diluted in water, according to the principle of homeopathy, then 'energized' by mixing, first in one direction, then the other, for a set period of time. Next, the energized solution is spread in droplets on the ground, in place of dung and compost, or on leaves, instead of silica. Plants, such as nettles, valerian, horsetail, or cedar are also used in the form of homeopathic tinctures or dilutions, to avoid disease.

THE CALENDAR. Implementing biodynamics requires a knowledge of the position of the stars and constellations on a daily basis. Exponents believe that plant growth depends on cosmic influences that act in a certain pattern, directly linked to the positions of the Moon and the Sun in relation to the constellations of the zodiac. Hence, depending on the day, the plant stimulates its roots, leaves, flowers, or fruit. Work and treatment on the vines are governed by this timetable. Consequently, it is best to plant during 'root days' or 'fruit days.' To improve the quality of the grapes, cultivation and treatment should take place on 'fruit days.'

AN IRRATIONAL APPROACH? This may seem strange to rational minds. Steiner, who never farmed and was teetotal, however, asked that his theories be scientifically tested. Today, this method does not lack effectiveness. Is this due to the degree of care taken by wine producers or to the actual preparations used? Biodynamic wine producers are convinced by this method. Although some practitioners are 'non-believers,' results are often seen.

FERMENTATION

It is through alcoholic fermentation that grape juice becomes wine. This fermentation is the conversion of natural sugars (glucose and fructose) into alcohol, under the action of yeasts (tiny microorganisms). Carbon dioxide is also produced. A second process (malolactic fermentation), generally follows and gives the wine softness.

Alcoholic fermentation

Fermentation is a complex chemical reaction and a totally natural process. The grapes ferment once the skin of the berries is broken: the sugars inside the ripe fruit then come into contact with the yeasts introduced or already present in the winery environment, and fermentation begins if the temperature is favourable. The wine producer simply crushes the grapes and provides the container (a vat) that holds the juice.

THE PROCESS. Under the action of the yeasts (microscopic organisms), fermentation produces first carbon dioxide and then ethanol, which is the alcohol in wine. Other substances result from the fermentation process: glycerol, which makes the wine rich; esters or aromatic compounds; higher alcohols used as flavour carriers; aldehydes; and acids. By-products from the fermentation contribute significantly to the flavour of the wine and are particularly responsible for so-called 'secondary' aromas (*see* p.211).

***Fermentation is a perfectly natural phenomenon.** People have used this process from the earliest times to create wine to quench thirst and provide the greatest possible pleasure.*

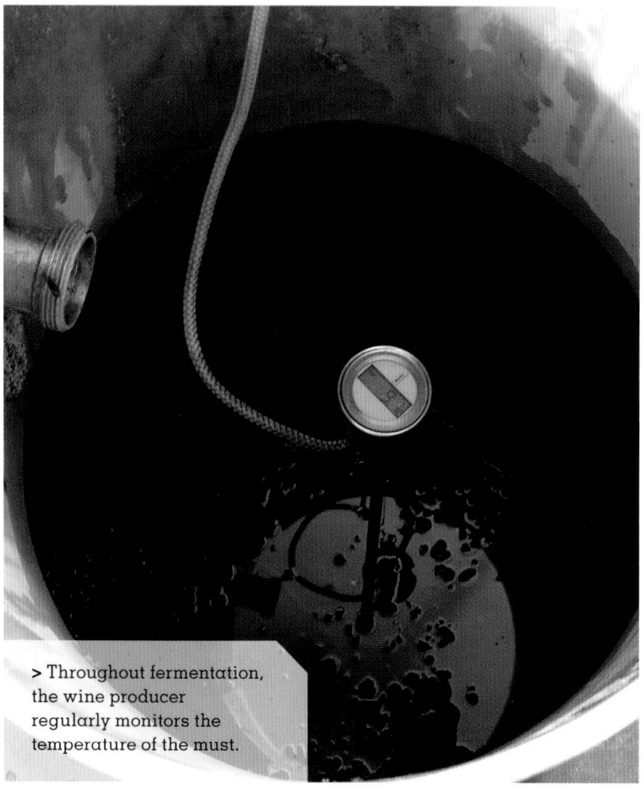

> Throughout fermentation, the wine producer regularly monitors the temperature of the must.

Young wine

When the yeast has converted all of the sugar into alcohol, fermentation stops. Sometimes the sugar content is so high that the alcohol reaches a level that inhibits the action of the yeast: it produces a powerful yet sweet wine, still containing residual (unfermented) sugar. Also, if the ambient temperature is insufficient, the yeast may stop working before the sugar has been transformed: the wine will thus have an alcohol content lower than would have been possible in terms of the maturity of the grapes. Alcoholic fermentation usually ends after one to three weeks. The young wine is then very cloudy, because of the lees (dead yeast cells), pulp, and seeds in the vat.

Yeasts

Fermentation is caused by the action of yeasts present on the skin of the grapes or in the air, or on the cellar equipment. Among the many types, *Saccharomyces cerevisiae* is the dominant yeast in wine fermentation. Each yeast has special features as regards the production of alcohol, resistance to alcohol and temperature, and functional temperature range, the formation of flavouring substances, and the rate of fermentation.

NATURAL OR SELECTED YEASTS. To better control fermentation, some wine producers prefer to employ selected

DID YOU KNOW...?

*Vinification **differs for red and white wines.** For red wines (see pp.68–9), the crushed grapes and juice are placed in a vat and we wait for fermentation to start. The length of time that this takes varies. For white wine (see pp.64–6), the grapes are first pressed to extract the juice, which is then fermented on its own in vats or barrels. Hence, the difference in colour, taste, and structure between reds and whites. Only red wines are fermented with their skins and seeds; these pass on not only colour but also tannins and additional ingredients that provide flavour. After fermentation comes the maturation phase (see pp.76–9).*

Chaptalization and reverse osmosis

Described in 1801 by Jean-Antoine Chaptal in his *Treatise on making wines*, chaptalization is the adding of sugar to a must to increase the alcoholic strength. Adding 2.27 oz of sugar per gallon of must (17 g/l) produces an extra one per cent of alcohol. Enrichment with sugar is carefully controlled in France. Banned in the south, it is allowed in the north to a limited extent, but must not add more than two per cent of alcohol to the wine. It does not add any quality to the wine in terms of taste or bouquet. The novelty of chaptalization lies in the possibility of measuring the amount of sugar added (*see also* p.63). Chaptalization is sometimes replaced by self-enrichment techniques, the most common of which is reverse osmosis. This involves subtracting a certain amount of water from the must (*see also* p.62), which results in an increase in the concentration of other ingredients (including sugar). The addition of concentrated must is also permitted in place of sugar.

> *Cuvier* is the French word for the place where winemaking vats are located in a winery.

yeasts (or yeast cultures). For safety reasons, this technique is most often used for wines produced in large quantities. Small-scale wine producers tend to prefer native yeasts as a way of standing out from the competition.

Temperature control

When the temperature exceeds 54°F (12°C), the must begins to ferment. Once engaged, the process generates heat and proceeds automatically. The must warms and fermentation starts bubbling under the action of the carbon dioxide. Around 95–99°F (35–37°C), yeasts will be killed by the heat and fermentation stops. Today, steel tanks are equipped with a system for cooling and, if necessary, heating the must. Regulating the temperature of the tanks is one of the great advances in wine production. The gain in quality is important, and the deterioration caused by breaks during fermentation is avoided.

Malolactic fermentation

Malic acid, which can exist in high concentrations in grapes, has a distinctive green-apple taste. After fermentation, the action of lactic bacteria transforms malic acid into lactic acid and carbon dioxide (thus a malolactic or secondary fermentation). Lactic acid (with a more rounded taste) is less bitter than malic acid, so the wine becomes softer. This degradation of malic acid into lactic acid is always sought in a quality red wine (and in some white wines). For it to take place, a specific temperature (68°F/20°C) is required. The winery is heated if necessary, or hot water is circulated through the pipes used for cooling the tanks. Sometimes it is necessary to resort to culturing (adding lactic bacteria).

TRUE OR FALSE?

Wine cannot be sweetened.

FALSE. In Germany, for the QmP category of wine (*see* p.98), as in Italy too, a method of adding unfermented must is used. It must come from the same vineyard and be of the same expected level of quality as the wine. It is added after fermentation, and before bottling, to produce a sweeter style.

TECHNIQUES THAT ARE CONTROVERSIAL

Scientific research has helped to improve wine quality. Yet some oenological practices may worry the consumer, who does not always understand what they involve.

CRYOEXTRACTION OR EXTRACTION USING COLD TEMPERATURES

‘Sweet wines are generally made from grapes concentrated by botrytis or by over-ripening. With cryoextraction, grapes that are insufficient in sugar are enriched by freezing them. The grapes are placed in cold storage at a temperature between 23°F and 18°F (-5°C to -8°C) for 20 or more hours. During pressing, which takes place soon after, only the sweetest (not frozen) grapes have their juice extracted.

• **FOR.** Cryoextraction may be regarded as a system of selection, since it eliminates the insufficiently concentrated grapes. It can also remove water from a recent rainfall.

• **AGAINST.** Using these methods makes things artificially easier, say many wine producers. To make a great sweet wine means accepting the restrictions imposed by nature.’

REVERSE OSMOSIS OR CROSS-FLOW FILTRATION

‘Another way to concentrate the must is to eliminate some of the water from the grapes by very fine filtration carried out at high pressure. The filter lets the water through, but not other substances whose molecules are larger.

• **FOR.** In difficult years, this may be a solution that saves the wine.

• **AGAINST.** Concentrating the must will never replace true levels of ripeness. It is even more shocking that these devices, which are very expensive, are sometimes used by those producers classified as *grands crus*.’

OAK SHAVINGS TO REPLACE BARRELS

‘Oak shavings come in the form of chips that are cut, dried and heated in the oven. In the fermenting wine, they produce flavours of coconut, toast, or smoke, depending on the extent to which they are heated. They are used in vats as a kind of infusion. In South America, they have been used since the 1980s; the European Union has authorized their use since 2006.

• **FOR.** Oak flavours without any disadvantages: this technique is much cheaper and much easier to use! A Bordeaux barrel of 59 gal. (225 l), used for three years, costs $3.65 per gal. (€74 per hl) of wine produced. The shavings, used at a dose of 0.67 oz per gal. (5 g/l), cost just 25 cents per gal. (€5 per hl).

• **AGAINST.** The flavour produced by this technique does not compare to the complexity of barrel ageing.’

THE USE OF SULPHUR

‘Sulphur dioxide (SO_2) is used to protect the must and wine against oxidation. It also has an antiseptic role against microorganisms. At low doses, it is put into the must before fermentation starts, as it prevents the development of bacteria for a short time, while allowing the growth of the yeast. Another dose is added after fermentation to stabilize the wine, then at bottling. Part of this sulphur evaporates (*see also* p.65 and p.78).

- **FOR.** An oxidized wine is not good; a vinegary wine is not good either. The doses of sulphur dioxide are now very low and are no longer likely to cause any much-maligned headaches!
- **AGAINST.** Some brave souls produce wine without sulphur dioxide. Those who manage to avoid faults (oxidation, fermentation problems, bacterial invasions) produce wines with exceptional purity of fruit. The rest produce wine with significant faults. Is it worth doing?’

CHAPTALIZATION OR ADDING SUGAR

‘When the grapes are not ripe enough, you can add sugar to the must at the start of fermentation. This is called chaptalization. Using 2.27 oz of sugar per gal. (17 g/l) of must produces one degree of additional alcohol. In France, the doses added must be less than two degrees, in other words 4.54 oz per gal. (34 g/l). In southern French regions, this method is not allowed; but you can enrich the must with rectified must concentrate, solutions of almost pure sugar obtained from grapes (*see also* p.61).

- **FOR.** Used in moderate doses and to correct a slight lack of maturity due to weather conditions, chaptalization can improve the balance of the wine. In addition, nuclear magnetic resonance can now accurately measure the added sugar in the must and prevent any harm being done.
- **AGAINST.** Used excessively, it produces poor wines, unbalanced by too much alcohol. Furthermore, with reasonable yields and well-maintained vineyards, chaptalization is not necessary except in cold and rainy years!’

THE ADDITION OF YEASTS DURING FERMENTATION

‘Even if fermentation is a spontaneous phenomenon, it is sometimes slow to start and it is hard to finish with musts that are very high in sugar. Hence, the wine producer adds dehydrated, commercially purchased yeasts to the must (*see also* p.61).

- **FOR.** Some strains of yeast, selected for their resistance to high levels of alcohol, are very useful when fermentation is difficult to complete. The addition of yeast also helps prevent the development of certain organisms naturally present on the skin of berries or in the winery, which can be harmful (*e.g.* Brettanomyces produces a rustic odour reminiscent of horse sweat).
- **AGAINST.** More and more growers, particularly those who practice organic farming, refuse to use these yeasts because they are afraid of standardization. They prefer indigenous yeasts, as they feel that these are better able to retain the character of the *terroir*. It should be noted that flavoured yeast strains were misused in the 1980s, producing many flavours such as banana or pear drop, resulting in many similar young wines.

PRODUCING WHITE AND ROSÉ WINES

Despite its many variants, the production of white wine is still based on the fermentation of the grape juice alone. Making rosé wine follows the same principle, though sometimes the juice must first be coloured by keeping it in brief contact with the skins.

Which grapes for which wine?

The type of wine produced (white, rosé, or red) is determined by two factors: the nature of the grape (the presence or absence of colourants) and the duration of maceration (contact between the juice, known as the must, and the solids, including the skin).

WHITE GRAPES. If the grapes are white, with a colourless pulp, they are almost always used to produce white wine. In this case, it is important that only the must, separated from the solid parts of the cluster (skin, seeds, etc.), is used for fermentation, without any maceration (*see* below).

RED GRAPES WITH COLOURLESS PULP. If the grapes are red, with a coloured skin or film and a colourless pulp, it is possible to make a white, rosé, or red wine. If there is no contact with the skin, white wine is produced. If the contact is brief, it will be a rosé wine (*see* p.66). If it is prolonged, red wine will result (*see* pp.68–9).

RED GRAPES WITH COLOURED PULP. If the grapes are red, with a coloured pulp and film, only red wine may be produced, whether or not maceration takes place. These grapes, called teinturiers, are rarely used alone, but may serve to accentuate the colour intensity of the wine.

***Vinification, or winemaking, is the phase between the completion of the harvest and the end of alcoholic fermentation.** It involves different stages, depending on the wine that the winemaker wants to produce.*

From vine to wine press

For white wine production, it is essential that the grapes reach the winery with their skin intact, not broken, so that the yeasts on the skin do not come into contact with the pulp. The clusters are picked whole, preferably by hand if the grower is seeking optimal conditions. In the same vein, the preferred means of transportation for the grapes is in boxes rather than in large containers where they would be crushed.

CRUSHING OR DE-STEMMING. Sometimes the grapes are pressed whole. This is the case for Champagnes and sparkling wines. But they can also be pre-crushed and de-stemmed – two operations that help facilitate the extraction of the must. The crushing is done to break the berries, without crushing the seeds. De-stemming separates the berries from the stems (the skeleton of the cluster). In both cases, once the operation is complete, the grapes are immediately transferred into the wine press by pumping. In terms of maceration, it is important to avoid the presence of stems as they give the grape juice a bitter taste.

Cold soak

In most cases, the white winemaking process does not involve maceration. But sometimes the winemaker seeks flavours present in the skins of grapes, especially for the Sémillon, Sauvignon Blanc, Muscat, Riesling, and sometimes Chardonnay varieties. To this end, a brief 'cold soak' or maceration is carried out before pressing: the grapes, which have already been de-stemmed and crushed, are put in a vat for a few hours. This technique, also called 'pre-fermentation maceration,' may yield a deeper wine colour after a few years in bottle.

> When they reach the winery, the grapes are poured into a container equipped with an endless screw or worm gear.

Different wine presses

There are many kinds of wine press, with capacities ranging from a few hundred pounds to several tons of grapes. Modern presses are completely automated, and the most common type of press is horizontal. Among them, the pneumatic press, which has an inner membrane that is inflated to press the grapes, has the gentlest action. Some winemakers prefer traditional vertical presses, however: for moderate pressure over a large area, they give a clearer juice, which is less difficult to settle.

> During de-stemming, the stalks are separated from the berries.

PRESSING. Pressing aims to extract all the juice from the grapes. This task takes a relatively short time, yet is one of the most delicate stages in white wine production because the quality of the wine depends upon it. (Also, the mass of semi-liquid pulp must be maintained at low temperature to avoid fermentation starting early. This can only take place between 54°F and 75°F [12°C to 24°C].) If the pressing is done in appropriate conditions, it results in a clear juice without crushing the seeds. If they were crushed, the wine might taste grassy. As well, this process must be done quickly to avoid oxidation.

Clarifying the must

SETTLING. After it has come from the wine press, the must can be rather cloudy. It contains solids or sedimentary material that can make wine taste bad, and must be removed. To do this, the juice may be moved to the centrifugal extractor, which is quick and efficient, although some allege that this reduces the quality of the resulting wine. This technique is mostly used by producers of very large volumes of *vin ordinaire*. The other method, stabilization by cold (at almost 32°F or 0°C) is better, as the juice is prevented from starting fermentation while the sediment naturally falls to the bottom of the tank.

ADDING SULPHUR. Whatever the method used for settling, sulphur is added at this stage. This means adding sulphur dioxide (SO_2) to the juice to prevent oxidation and to neutralize development of any microorganisms. The doses depend on the health of the juice and the ambient temperature. Used in excess, sulphur dioxide can mask all the wine's flavours. Dosage is tightly regulated and adjusted for each wine (*see also* p.78).

Alcoholic fermentation

The juice is then poured into vats where it will ferment slowly for one to four weeks. Fermentation can be stimulated by an injection of cultured yeasts or by inoculation with fermenting juice from another vat. The temperature determines the extent of fermentation and hence the style of wine desired. The lower the temperature, the more time the wines will take to ferment. This enables more sediment to be extracted and results in higher quality wines. The higher the temperature, the quicker the fermentation, but also often lower quality and an increased possibility of an inferior taste, that is to say, a 'cooked' flavour.

FERMENTATION VATS. To make wine, the wine producer can choose vats made of wood, stainless steel, concrete, terracotta, or plastic. Each has its advantages and drawbacks. Stainless steel is very common, as it is easier to clean and cool. But temperature can also be regulated in other types of vats. A wooden vat has a thermal inertia that steel lacks. To make great wine for ageing,

TRUE OR FALSE?

Additives used are always mentioned on the label.

FALSE. In France, several consumer groups, and some winemakers, would like the label to list any additives that are not from the grape. Only sulphur dioxide has to be mentioned right now. If used in excessive quantities, this is likely to cause headaches for some people.

Wine produced in barrels

Throughout history, the Burgundians made great white wines, including Chardonnay, in casks designed for long ageing. The capacity of the cask, about 60 gal. (228 l), is ideal for white wine production without temperature control: the liquid rises to 77°F (25°C) and is maintained at this level through fermentation. The wine acquires a special flavour, related to its contact with the wood. Finally, the wine remains in contact with its lees (the deposit resulting from fermentation), which protects it from oxidation and enriches it at the same time. The winemaker mixes the lees into the wine regularly using a stick, in order to make it complex and rich. That is what we call *batonnage* (*see also* p.77).

Burgundian winemakers use oak barrels (*see* box above). More generally, many great châteaux have reverted to wooden vats after embracing the modern trend of stainless steel.

Final stages

NO MALOLACTIC FERMENTATION. Naturally occurring after alcoholic fermentation, malolactic fermentation (*see* p.61) helps to round out acidic wines, but it may degrade fruity wines from warm regions that lack acidity. In general, the white winemaker seeks to prevent 'malo' and treat the wine to remove the bacteria that can cause it. Doing so calls for dosing the wine slightly with sulfite again, passing it through a centrifuge, or using microfiltration followed by bottling under sterile conditions.
DECANTING. Fermentation and wine production are now complete. Yet the wine still needs to be clarified. It contains sediment, a deposit consisting primarily of yeast that has completed its task. The wine is therefore carefully poured out of the vat while the sediment remains at the bottom. This operation is called racking. It will be repeated several times during the maturation process (*see* p.76). For the development of certain wines, such as Muscadet in Nantes, France, the sediment is left in the wine until it is bottled, which results in certain flavour characteristics, such as the presence of gas bubbles that give the wine extra freshness.

The case of sweet wines

Sweet wines are made from grapes so sweet that fermentation cannot transform all the sugar into alcohol. For sweet wines, wine producers leave the grapes on the vine until they are too ripe, hoping that *Botrytis cinerea* (or 'noble rot') will appear. The fungus dries the grapes, whose already sweet juice is concentrated into very rich droplets. The wine will then go through the same production as for dry white wines. However, in an environment high in sugar, yeast works more slowly and is exhausted after a few days. Fermentation stops and some of the sugar will not be transformed into alcohol, hence the sweet taste. This applies to wines such as Sauternes in France, Trockenbeerenauslese in Germany, Tokaj aszú in Hungary, and several New World wines. We may also use desiccated grapes, that is to say, grapes dried on racks. This is the case for *vin de paille* in France (*see* box below) or Italian Vin Santo.

Rosé wine production

There are three ways to produce rosé wines: pressing, *saignée* ('bleeding'), and blending (which, among AOP wines, applies only to Champagne). Direct pressing results in pale and subtle wines, while *saignée* produces more 'winey' and full-bodied ones. With rare exceptions, a rosé is always consumed in a year or two of bottling. Its aromas and flavours are most often richer versions of white wines.
PRESSING. Some rosés, made from grapes that are deep in colouration and sufficiently ripe, can be obtained by direct pressing. This is the case with the rosés of Provence in France. The must is then processed with techniques used for producing white wine. A slight maceration before pressing is often necessary to imbue the wine with a deep colour. White wines are produced in the same way but using grapes with little or no colour, like Grenache Gris. In those instances, even if you leave the skins to soak in the juice, there is very little change in colour.
SAIGNÉE. This involves draining off a certain proportion of juice from a red wine vat after only a few hours of maceration (and before filling the vat again). The majority of the rosé wines from Tavel in France are produced in this way. The must that is 'bled,' and which has not yet begun to ferment, is made into wine in accordance with the principles of white winemaking.
BLENDING. Permitted only in Champagne in France, it involves adding to white wine, before its second, sparkling fermentation, a percentage of red wine from Champagne grapes. About 95 per cent of rosé Champagnes are produced in this way.

TRUE OR FALSE?

Rosé wine can be produced by mixing red and white wine.

TRUE. But in EU countries, only Champagne can blend wines in this way (*see* below). In other countries, blending is allowed to produce table wines.

DID YOU KNOW...?

Producing* vin de paille *can take up to four years. *A product of Jura, France, this very special wine is made from grapes left on a bed of straw (now more often on racks) from October to January, which results in desiccation of the berries to produce a richer and more concentrated juice. While 220 lbs (100 kg) of grapes normally produces 18–20 gal. (70–75 l) of must, the equivalent volume for* vin de paille *is no more than 5 or 6 gal. (20–25 l). Fermentation in small casks is very slow and may take up to four years. Produced in limited quantities, this wine has an amber colour and a rich flavour with a hint of nuts.*

41

MAKING RED WINE

It may be easier to make red wine than white wine. The work of the winemaker is to oversee the development of a natural process that is very simple in principle. However, the production of red wines still requires careful handling and a great deal of skill.

Basic principles

As with white wines, winemaking involves transforming the sugary must into alcohol. The distinctive feature of making red wine is its maceration. During this infusion stage, the colouring matter, tannins, and aromatic compounds contained in the solid parts of the grape (skin and pulp) are dissolved in the juice, giving the wine its colour and character. The techniques employed all follow the same principle, although they vary depending on the grape variety, climate, and local traditions.

> ***A long period of maceration gives the wine its colour*** *and tannic structure, but any excessive extraction of substances in the solids may yield vegetal or bitter flavours that are sometimes unpleasant.*

Classic maceration

The maceration process described here is broadly used in France and around the world. Red grapes are first crushed and de-stemmed. They are burst, releasing their juices, and detached from the skeleton of the cluster (the stalk). Then the must, the juicy mass of crushed grapes, is transferred into thermo-regulated stainless steel or wooden vats. The duration of fermentation, involving maceration and fermentation, can range from a few days to three weeks, depending on the style of wine.

CAP FORMATION. Once in the tank, the solids of the berries rise to the top and come together to form the 'cap.' Gradually, the colourants and all the constituent parts of the cap will transfer to the juice. This operation, called 'extraction,' is encouraged by the heat of fermentation, with the winemaker restricting the temperature to around 86°F (30°C).

PUNCHING DOWN, *REMONTAGE*, OR USE OF A ROTARY VAT. Some techniques can facilitate the extraction process. Punching down involves pushing the cap into the must with a stirrer, a wooden paddle, hydraulic cylinders, or even feet.

Remontage, or 'pumping over,' is immersing the cap by pumping the juice gently from the bottom of the vat to soak over it.

There also are vats equipped with rotary blades that re-suspend the solids in the liquid. Whatever method is used, the operation is delicate, because the goal is to extract the colours and flavours, but not to excess.

LENGTH OF MACERATION. For the production of many wines, only a very partial extraction from the solids is required because the emphasis is on primary flavours (*see* p.211). The time spent in a maceration vat is therefore relatively short. However, for a wine like Chinon from the Loire Valley, berries can be macerated for a month or more to extract the maximum character. The wine will be rich in tannins and so will be aged for some time before drinking.

TRUE OR FALSE?

The winemaker constantly checks the thermometer.

TRUE. Monitoring the temperature during fermentation is critical. The must should be kept in a desired temperature range and, if necessary, a cooling system used. Fruit flavour and finesse are extracted via fermentation at a relatively low temperature of around 75°F (24°C). With higher temperatures, 86–97°F (30–36°C), even for a very short period of time, maximum colour and intensity of flavour are produced.

> Crushing grapes at Château Lascombes in Margaux, France.

Carbonic maceration

The greatest difference between carbonic maceration and the previous method is the use of uncrushed grapes. Fairly widespread in Beaujolais, France, this technique places whole berries in a closed vessel, which is filled with carbon dioxide. Under the effect of this gas, a peculiar phenomenon called 'intracellular fermentation' occurs. It leads, inside each berry,

> Racking the wine during wine production.

> Wine is also racked during the maturation stage.

to the formation of a small amount of alcohol and malic acid degradation. This fermentation-in-a-berry is accompanied by the production of bright, primary flavours. A short fermentation period of four to six days produces a very floral wine, with an immediate softness. Subsequently, carbon dioxide is released and the fermentation continues normally. Carbonic maceration is well established for wines produced from Gamay grapes and sold young, like much Beaujolais. It is also now widely applied to certain varieties, where a portion is blended with wines made using traditional maceration to produce a softer result, especially in Mediterranean regions.

Running off and pressing

Whatever the method of maceration, it is necessary at some point to drain the liquid in the vat. When the winemaker considers the optimal maceration time complete, whether alcoholic fermentation is complete or not, the wine is 'run off.' A valve is opened at the bottom of the tank to flush out the liquid, permanently separating it from the solids. This completes the maceration phase.

FREE-RUN WINE AND PRESS WINE. The juice that is run off, which is of the finest and highest quality, is called free-run. Next, the grape skins and lees (solids still containing liquid) are pressed to extract any remaining juice – called 'press wine.' This represents 8 to 15 per cent of the total volume of a tank. At a later stage, possible blending of the free-run and press wine will depend on various criteria.

FINAL FERMENTATION. The free-run and press wines are then placed in separate tanks. At this stage, winemakers conduct a comprehensive analysis, including the alcohol and acidity levels. Fermenting of the juice then will be completed if the process was not completed at the time of running off. Following alcoholic fermentation, malolactic fermentation will take place in all cases (see p.61). The wine is then clarified during the maturation phase (see p.76).

Vins de garage

The term *vins de garage* is not an official one, and the vogue is now largely over. It relates to small vats that could fit into the garage of a private home. This style of wine is produced from small vineyards with a deliberately reduced yield of fully ripened grapes. Setting aside the hype that has made their prices soar, *vins de garage* are excellent wines, often from St-Émilion in Bordeaux, although neighbouring Médoc and other regions also produce these wines. Making the wine requires extreme care: removal of the stalks by hand, followed by long maceration in stainless steel vats, punching down the must, placing in new oak barrels for malolactic fermentation, and ageing for 18–24 months.

MAKING SPARKLING WINES

All fermentation produces carbon dioxide gas that escapes into the open air. If trapped in a pressure-resistant container, the gas creates a sparkling wine. Champagnes and sparkling wines are produced on the basis of this principle, with some variations.

Basic principles

THE ANCESTRAL METHOD. Historically, sparkling wines were produced using what we call the 'ancestral' method, also known as the 'rural,' 'Dioise,' or 'Gaillacoise' method. This method is still practised by some producers in the French regions of Die, Limoux, and Gaillac. It involves putting the wine into bottles during fermentation, before all the sugar has been transformed into alcohol. The method is tricky, and sometimes the bottles explode under the pressure of the gas after being sealed. Following a year in the cellar, they are ready for sale. The wines produced in this way in France are generally AOP. They are – from Die: Clairette de Die Tradition (Muscat-based); from Limoux, wines produced by the Blanquette traditional method; and from Gaillac (the Gaillac Method), both the latter based on Mauzac.

***Production of sparkling wines always follows the same principle,** which is to allow the wine to ferment in a closed bottle (or sometimes a closed vat), so that the carbon dioxide produced by fermentation cannot escape and is dissolved into the wine.*

THE CHAMPAGNE METHOD. Later, producers in Champagne developed what is called the Champagne method, also known as the traditional method. Safer than the ancestral approach, it was the first to let the must ferment in vats to produce a still wine between 9 and 9.5 per cent alcohol. Then a second fermentation is generated in sealed bottles, by adding sugar and yeast at the bottling stage. This technique is now used in many areas of France: in the Loire (Vouvray, Saumur, Crémant de Loire), in Burgundy (Crémant de Bourgogne), in Bordeaux (Crémant de Bordeaux), in Alsace (Crémant d'Alsace), in the Rhône (Clairette de Die, sparkling Saint-Péray), in the South (Crémant de Limoux), etc. Around the globe, among the best-known sparkling wines, Spanish Cava and the best sparkling wines of the New World are also prepared in this way. German Sekt and Italian Prosecco use the closed tank method, with secondary fermentation in a pressurized tank.

> Traditional presses at the Louis Roederer house at Aÿ in Champagne.

DID YOU KNOW...?

Dom Pérignon, a monk from the Abbey of Hautvillers, *did not 'invent' sparkling Champagne, although he did realize the advantages of separating white and red grapes in the wine press to refine the (still) wines that he made.*

> Mechanical *remuage* of bottles (*gyropalettes*) at Château Moncontour in the Loire Valley.

Harvesting for blending

The complex stages involved in the production of Champagne – each 'maison' or producer has its own secrets – make it a highly distinctive wine. The selection of grapes is essential. These consist of red grapes (Pinot Noir and Pinot Meunier) and white (Chardonnay, but also Arban, Petit Meslier, and Pinot Blanc), grown in a named and clearly defined area, with the maximum authorized yield.

PRESSING AND FERMENTATION. Soon after picking the grapes, pressing is carefully performed in order to obtain clear juice, whose brief contact with the skin of the berry has resulted in only a little tannin and no colour. The first fermentation takes place in wooden vats or, more often, stainless steel tanks.

BLENDING. Blending then takes place: at each stage of the operation officials taste wines from each vintage, and generally from different terroirs, grape varieties, and plots. The goal is to assemble a wine that reflects the style of the house and achieves the same character and quality from one year to the next. Wines from previous years, so-called reserve wines, may form part of the blending of a non-vintage wine.

Second fermentation

THE PRISE DE MOUSSE ('formation of bubbles'). Once the blending of the wine is complete, a mixture of sugar and yeast – the *liqueur de tirage* – is added during bottling. The whole mixture is then bottled into thick glass bottles, sealed with metal caps, or, more rarely, cork stoppers. The bottles are stored horizontally in the darkest and coolest cellars. Second fermentation starts, including the production of carbon dioxide to form the bubbles or *prise de mousse*. This takes about a month.

REMUAGE. The wine is then stored in the cool cellars that are typical of the Champagne region or in air-conditioned warehouses. Ageing here, which has a legal minimum term of at least 15 months after bottling (three years for vintage wines), leaves a deposit of dead yeast. To remove this deposit, as is traditional, the bottles are placed on special tilted racks called *pupitres*. For two or three months, the tilt of the bottles is progressively increased. The bottles are manoeuvered or 'riddled,' two by two, by experienced cellar workers (*remuers*). Today the majority of Champagne bottles are riddled mechanically in large cages called *gyropalettes*.

From disgorgement to corking

The next step, disgorgement, involves removing the residue that has been deposited in the neck of the bottles. This is accomplished by soaking the bottle neck in a liquid refrigerant that freezes the sediment in an ice cube. Then the bottle is opened and, under pressure from the gas inside, the ice is ejected with the deposit. It is quickly replaced by *liqueur d'expédition*, a mixture of Champagne and sugar cane. This stage, called *dosage*, determines the future character of the Champagne: brut, extra dry, sec, demi-sec, or doux/sweet. At corking, the bottles are closed with cork stoppers, held in place by a metal wire cage. Generally, they are not sold immediately, but stored for a few weeks by the producer so that this dosage can blend with the wine. 'Zero-dosage' Champagnes are those where no sugar is added at the final stage.

Charmat method and gasification

Other sparkling wines are produced by different methods. With the Charmat process, the second fermentation, following the addition of the *liqueur de tirage*, takes place not in the bottle but in a closed tank. The wine is then cooled, filtered, and transferred under pressure into a second tank, possibly sweetened with *liqueur d'expédition*, and bottled. This process is more economic. Gasification is a simple method in which carbon dioxide is injected into the wine before bottling. No appellations are authorized for sparkling wines produced in this way.

207
SM
212

MAKING FORTIFIED WINE

Fortified wines are often rich in sugar, but always full of flavour and alcohol. Making wine of this kind involves the addition of alcohol, called mutage or fortification. If this process takes place during fermentation, the action of the yeast is stopped, thus preserving some of the sugar from the grapes. If it takes place after, the fortified wine is dry.

The basic principles

Fortified wines are produced in the same way as other wines, the difference being the addition of alcohol in the form of rectified spirit or *eau-de-vie*. Sherry, port, and Madeira from the Iberian peninsular nations, French *vins doux naturels*, such as Rivesaltes and Banyuls, Marsala from Sicily, and Muscats from Australia, are all examples of fortified wine. They differ in terms of the grape varieties from which they are made, the point the alcohol is added, the amount of alcohol involved, and the method of ageing. There are two methods of fortification: during fermentation (port, for example) or after (sherry). Historically, wine was fortified so that it could be shipped elsewhere without spoilage. When the processes of fermentation were poorly understood, it often restarted in wine casks and damaged the wine during transport. Over time, this practice became established to the point of constituting an entire family of wines.

Fortification can highlight the specific flavours of the grapes from which the wines are made. *Depending on the alcohol used, the type of maturation, and the ageing time, very different styles can be produced.*

Port

Port is produced in the Douro Valley in northern Portugal. Most port is made using modern techniques. After being separated from the cluster and crushed, the berries are poured into vats where the fermentation will start. Giant drums or other containers use rotation or mechnical punching down to mix the juice and skins. The aim of this is to extract the maximum pigments and flavours from the skin surrounding the berry. As with traditional methods, including crushing the grapes by trampling on them, the winemaker stops the fermentation by adding alcohol.

THE ADDITION OF *EAU-DE-VIE*. When fermentation has reached the required level of alcohol (about 9% ABV), the new wine is poured into tanks and an *aguardiente* (grape brandy) is added. The amount of alcohol corresponds to 25 per cent of the volume of wine, which brings the level of alcohol in the port to about 18–20 per cent volume, depending on the extent to which the action of the yeast is neutralized. The sugar not converted into alcohol remains. The result, at least initially and for red ports, is a dark red colour and a pleasant sweetness with a strong taste of alcohol. White ports also exist. Ports then need time for the alcohol to blend into the wine. During the first spring, the winemaker tastes the wine and classifies it according to its qualities, deciding which ageing method to apply since there are different styles of port.

> At cellars in Oporto, the winemaker takes a sample using a pipette.

Sherry

Hailing from Andalusia in Spain, this is a white wine that is fortified at the end of its fermentation. Made from the Palomino grape variety, the new wine is poured into wooden barrels that are not completely filled. A few months later, a special yeast called *flor* appears in some barrels. (A similar procedure is followed in the Jura, in France, to produce ***vin jaune***, but without the addition of alcohol.) The sherry is then fortified with grape brandy depending on its style: a small amount for *finos* (up to about 15.5 per cent alcohol) affected by the *flor*, more for *olorosos* (up 18 per cent), which

> Barrels of sherry in the Bodega González Byass cellars, in Jerez, Spain.

DID YOU KNOW...?

The grapes for some ports are still crushed by being foot trampled. *After being crushed and removed from the cluster, the grapes are put into large open stone containers, called* lagares, *where they are trampled under foot. Although laborious, this traditional method is considered the best way to extract the colour of grapes without the risk of crushing the seeds. The juice then ferments in the* lagares *for between 24 and 36 hours before the addition of* eau-de-vie *distilled from grapes. The cost of labour, however, means that these techniques are used to produce only the very best wines in Oporto, Portugal.*

come from barrels where *flor* has not developed. The wines are then aged in *soleras*, rows of barrels laid out at three or four different heights, with the oldest wines on the lowest level (*see also* p.77). It is the blending of wines of different vintages and the ageing of sherry that gives it its complexity, with each bottle containing wine from different barrels and of different ages. There are also categories of sweet sherry and these are blended using very sweet wines made with Pedro Ximenez (PX) grapes.

Vins doux naturels

France's *Vins doux naturels* exist in different colours and are also aged in different ways, resulting in a range of styles (*see* pp.160–1). Produced mainly in Roussillon and Languedoc (Banyuls, Rivesaltes, Maury, Roussillon, Muscat de Mireval, de Rivesaltes, de St-Jean-de-Minervois, de Lunel, and de Frontignan), and a to a lesser extent in the Rhône Valley (Muscat de Beaumes-de-Venise, Rasteau), and also in Corsica (Muscat du Cap Corse), they are fortified with a 96 per cent alcohol spirit, amounting to 5 to 10 per cent of the volume of the must during fermentation. This produces, in general, wines of between 15.2 and 17 per cent ABV.

For red wines, a short maceration (two or three days) is followed by adding the alcohol to the fermenting juice. However, in some cases, in Banyuls and Maury especially, fortification is practised on the marc, that is to say, the solid parts of the grape (skin, seeds, etc.). The marc-alcohol mixture is then macerated for 10 to 15 days, which produces wines that are rich in colour, tannin, and flavours. Whites and Muscats are produced in the way of regular white wines, with the fortification also taking place during fermentation.

Vins de liqueur

Production of *vins de liqueur* is much more limited than for *vins doux naturels*. Their alcohol content is between 16 and 22 per cent. These wines are made by mixing grape juice prior to fermentation with neutral alcohol (brandy distilled from wine, grape must concentrate, or a mixture). This is the case, for example, with Pineau des Charentes, a blend of Cognac and grape juice from the same area; Floc de Gascogne, which is fortified with Armagnac; and Macvin du Jura, which is fortified with marc.

Finos and olorosos, two families of sherry

Sherry has a range of styles, from dry (*manzanilla*) to sweet (cream). It is divided into two families: *finos*, which are dry and light; and *olorosos*, which are deep-coloured and powerful. *Fino* should be drunk very young and not aged in bottle. *Manzanilla* is the driest and lightest style of all, with a slightly iodized taste; *amontillados* are more amber and are aged in cask for at least eight years. *Olorosos* are often aged for longer still. These are dry, rich, and concentrated wines.

> Some wines such as Maury are aged outdoors in demijohns.

THE ART OF MATURATION

Vinification, in the strict sense of the term, is complete when the must has been transformed into wine by fermentation. Maturation then begins, and comes to an end at the point of bottling.

The aims and duration of maturation

The term 'maturation' describes the slow work required to refine and develop the qualities of a wine. When maturing a wine, a winemaker has two objectives. The first aim is technical, namely to clarify the wine. The second is sensory, to allow the wine to develop perfectly and acquire complex flavours.

The maturation period can be very short for simple wines, a few weeksor even days, though for most wines it is no more than a few months. On the other hand, maturation for non-vintage Champagnes takes at least 18 months and 3 years or more for vintage Champagnes. Red or white *grands vins* for laying down (*grand crus* from Bordeaux, Burgundy, or the Rhône, for example, are often matured for 12 to 18 months), while for some ports and sherries it can take 5 years or much longer. Depending on the type of wine that the winemaker expects, maturation can take place on a large scale in tanks, large oak casks of various capacities, or in bottle. In recent decades, the use of barrel ageing has increased considerably, sometimes using new barrels, especially for fine wines (*see* pp.80–1).

The length of time for maturation varies according to the type of wine being produced. *Young wines are bottled immediately after being made, while red* vins de garde *are aged for 6 to 18 months, sometimes up to 24 months.*

> New barrels in a Bordeaux barrel cellar.

Clarifying the wine

After the wine has been made, it still has tiny particles of grape material, yeast, and bacteria suspended in the liquid. These lees, which would likely produce a second fermentation on contact with any residual sugars, are generally removed in part or totally. If racking, fining, and filtering are the most common methods used, there are also other practices such as centrifuging (where the wine is placed in a rotating drum which spins the solids toward the edge) or pasteurization (in which the wine is briefly heated to very high temperatures).

RACKING. This is the most common method. It is generally used for quality wines, and is completed by filtration before bottling. Racking means separating the wine from the lees by carefully pouring it from one container to another. This operation eliminates the lees that had settled naturally at the bottom of the tank or barrel and, optionally, oxygenates and softens the wine (*see also* p.66). It also releases residual carbon dioxide produced during fermentation. When the wine must be stored in tanks or barrels for a long time, racking is done two to four times per year. But this frequency may greatly increase when the maturation period is short or after fining.

FINING. This method is often used before bottling, whether or not racking has already taken place. It takes advantage of colloid flocculation. The fining agent, once in contact with the wine, forms sediment by binding with any microscopic impurities. All that remains is to eliminate, by successive rackings, the sediment that has precipitated to the bottom. The best agent for red wines is beaten egg white (six eggs per barrel), while for white wines casein is best. Another popular material is bentonite clay. After fining, red wines lose some of the roughness caused by tannins, and gain softness and finesse.

FILTERING. This sometimes complements the racking carried out during maturation. But more often it takes place before bottling. The plate or membrane filters used here have smaller or larger pores. When they are tiny (less than one thousandth of a millimetre), the wine not only has the lees removed, but is also sterilized because bacteria too are unable to pass through the very tiny holes.

Maturation *sur lie*

When the lees are retained during the wine's development, it is called maturation *sur lie* (on the lees). Some Muscadets in the Pays Nantais of France are matured in this way, and the wine retains a little residual carbon dioxide, which brings a certain sensation of freshness. Similarly, some Bordeaux wines (red *vins*

> The Château de Beaune winery in Burgundy is home to the prestigious wines of Bouchard Père & Fils.

de garage, *see* p.69; Pessac-Leognan whites) or white *grands vins* from Burgundy are matured on the lees. In the latter case, the lees (sediments) may be stirred, causing the lees that have settled to the bottom of the barrel or tank to be re-suspended in the wine. They are stirred with a stick, or by machine in the case of large volumes. The aim is to increase interaction between the solids and the liquid so that the wine becomes more complex, soft, and rich. Fining and a light filtration are often carried out before bottling.

Hygiene issues

In the past, many wines were spoiled as a result of poor hygiene, since the mechanisms of oxidation and proliferation of bacteria were little known. Today, wine producers pay special attention to the cleanliness of their cellars and equipment. Tanks, for example, must be cleaned and scaled regularly to avoid bacteria. For barrels, the perfect hygienic solution would be for the container always to be full; otherwise the most frequently adopted solution is 'wicking,' which involves burning sulphur in the empty barrel before sealing it tightly.

Blending, an optional step

Blending is a difficult technique involving the combining of wines from a single (or otherwise) estate, produced from one or several grape varieties. These wines therefore have different characteristics. In Bordeaux, for example, wines from a number of vats from various vineyards are combined, often from different grape varieties, from vines of different ages and harvested at different times. In regions where ageing in barrels is normal practice, the decision involves selecting various barrels for final blending, depending on the appellation criteria (grape varieties, geographic location).

AT WHAT STAGE? For many white or red wines, including some fortified wines, blending can occur throughout the maturation process up to the final bottling. For Champagne, blending is done before maturation, just after fermentation, sometimes involving up to 50 or 60 selected vats. In Bordeaux, part of the blending takes place between November and March, according to the harvest, but a final adjustment or blending may be made just before bottling.

THE CASE OF SHERRY. Sherry is aged in *solera*. A *solera* is a system of traditional blending in which wine is drawn for bottling from the oldest stage, the *solera*, and replaced with wine from the next-oldest. The young wine goes into one first stage called the *criadera*. Because of this unique method of fractional blending, each bottle contains wine from several *soleras*, but also wines of different ages from within a single *solera*.

TRUE OR FALSE?

The period of maturation continues until the wine is consumed.

FALSE. Also known as 'bringing up' the wine, maturation takes place between the end of fermentation and bottling. It is done in steel tank or a wooden container (or barrel). Once the wine is bottled, ageing takes over.

> Piping

> Racking

> Stirring

Aerating the wine, but avoiding oxidation

In general, red wines, but also some white wines, need aeration when starting to mature. This is ensured either by the racking, by the very slow diffusion of oxygen through the seams of the barrel and the bung hole, or by micro-oxygenation or *microbullage* (*see* box below). But the amount of oxygen should remain minimal. Except in rare cases, such as wines fortified with alcohol, the producer always avoids any direct and prolonged contact between the wine and air. Oxygen promotes the growth of bacteria such as acetobacter, which can turn the alcohol into vinegar. It also alters the colour and taste of wine. To avoid all these pitfalls, the wine producer generally adds sulphur and/or carries out 'topping up' or filling barrels.

Microbullage

Exposing wine to oxygen requires much skill. Even the use of 'natural' micro-oxygenation, by simply maturing wine in barrels, has risks. To achieve an ideal level of micro-oxygenation, and not leave it to chance, Patrick Ducournau, a winemaker in Madiran (Gascony), has introduced a new device: a *microbullage* generator installed at the bottom of a neutral tank. It is a small piece of equipment common in laboratories, and the amount of bubbles produced can be adjusted. This system works well, and it has been approved for use by European wine authorities.

TOPPING UP. To avoid oxidation, containers of wine must be filled completely,so that no air pockets are present. Some evaporation occurs naturally in the tanks or barrels used for maturation. The speed at which the wine evaporates varies, depending on the humidity and temperature of the winery, but to compensate, the container must be topped up regularly using a large pipette called an *ouillette*. For an appellation wine, the quality of wine used for the topping up must be equivalent to that of the wine being aged, and from the same source. In France, only the *vin jaune* of Jura (*see also* p.307) and some *vins doux naturels* are aged without topping up. The wine is therefore reduced by evaporation and a thin film of yeast known as a *voile*, forms on its surface. The slow subsequent oxidation produces distinct flavours.

ADDING SULPHUR. Sulphur, in the form of sulphurous anhydride (or sulphur dioxide), is used during the production and maturation of wine. In the correct doses, it is, with its antioxidant and antibacterial properties, extremely effective, protecting the wine and combatting certain problems. But unfortunately it also has many disadvantages: it helps cause ferric and copper casse disorders, it is responsible for various defects (reduced mercaptan odour, *see* box next page), and in particular it can cause discomfort and headaches in some people, especially if the dose is not correct and the minimum possible. Its use is restricted by French and European regulations, and chemists are looking for alternatives. To date, nothing has been found to replace it, although various products or practices (rigorous hygiene, filtering, etc.) have reduced its use. Some producers are trying to make wine without sulphur, but very few manage to produce on a regular basis bottles that do not contain some faults (*see* p.58).

> Topping up

> Taking a sample

> Barrels in the winery

Faults in wine

With the knowledge that wine-makers now possess, few wines have faults.

MINOR FAULTS. There may be a slight smell of staleness, fermentation gas, or sulphur. In most cases, these defects disappear with time. If they are present, it is possible to oxygenate the wine by pouring it into a carafe, or 'decanting' as it is known, when it is about to be drunk (see p.193). The stale smell is the result of prolonged deprivation of oxygen. Aerating the wine before bottling should prevent the smell of fermentation gas. As for the smell of sulphur, which is caused by a dosing error, this lingers mostly in white wines, which are very sensitive to oxidation and protected by more sulphur anhydride, although this fault is becoming increasingly rare. Potential animal odours should also be mentioned, which can arise due to the action of a strain of yeast known as Brettanomyces. Such smells can be highly unpleasant and contamination of this kind is impossible to rectify.

MAJOR FAULTS. Serious faults – mercaptan, oxidation, or acetification – are both unacceptable and irreparable. Mercaptan, caused by a reaction of the fermentation yeast with sulphur in the lees, produces an unpleasant smell of rotten eggs. Oxidation, resulting in a deterioration of the bouquet, is caused by prolonged contact with air and an insufficient dosage of sulphur dioxide during ageing. Acetification, or acetic spoilage, is caused by a bacterium (acetobacter) and produces an 'acetic' wine (which tastes of vinegar). The sale of such wine is prohibited once such volatile acidity exceeds a certain level.

DID YOU KNOW...?

***Even organic wines may contain sulphur.** However, the specifications followed by organic wine producers impose much lower levels of sulphur anhydride than in conventional viticulture. Some producers have banned its use totally. This is not without its risks because there are two potential dangers with an untreated wine: either premature ageing, even maderization (this is especially the case for white wines, displaying a yellow colour and taste similar to Madeira); or an instability making them unsuitable for shipping, exposure to light, and heat. This can lead to re-fermentation or the serious fault in wine called acetification.*

The maturation of *vins doux naturels*

During maturation especially, the specific characteristics of fortified wines become clear. There are two categories of *vins doux naturels*.

MUSCATS. These must be protected from oxidation to preserve their fruity flavours.

OTHER WINES. Rivesaltes, Maury, Banyuls, and Rasteau reach their peak after an ageing process in which oxidation plays an important part. They mature mostly in demijohns or in wood. Gradual oxidation alters them completely and gives them hints of cocoa, plum, and coffee. These wines, when they are very old, have a flavour known as *rancio*, which means 'rancid' in Spanish. They have an amber colour with green hues and distinctive flavours of walnuts, raisins, and prunes.

THE ROLE OF BARREL AGEING

In Bordeaux and Burgundy, as in other French regions, new oak barrels are used in making red wines and, to a lesser extent, white wines, from Chardonnay, for example. The wine gains spicy and toasted or grilled flavours from the casks. But there could be other reasons for barrel ageing...

Not such a recent fashion

Maturation in oak barrels is common for wines that need to be aged for a long period. In the great châteaux of Bordeaux (Latour, Haut-Brion, etc.), the wine was once sold in barrel to *négociants* who were responsible for its maturation. It was only in the 20th century that the idea of wine being 'estate bottled' developed. The use of new wood first became widespread in the 1970s, although it is recorded as early as the 18th century. 'Oaky' wine, or more accurately oaky flavours, became fashionable. This wood flavouring, which is what it essentially is, became even more marked once the famous American critic Robert Parker began to appreciate and popularize it. There are other reasons, however, that can make the wine producer decide to age wine in cask (*see* below).

***Today, it would be difficult to find a wine region where no producer ages at least part of their wine in new** oak barrels, including Australia, New Zealand, and California, even if the trend is on the wane.*

The size and age of the barrels

The word 'barrel' is a generic term for all wooden containers used to house wine. The best-known today are the Bordeaux barrel, containing 59 gal. (225 l), and the Burgundy barrel, which holds 60 gal. (228 l). The latter is also known as a *pièce*.

THE STANDARD SIZE. The ideal size for a barrel was gradually determined by trial and error. Without detailed discussion, an average capacity of between 53 and 61 gal. (200 and 230 l) became accepted. The Bordeaux barrel has become a standard, and is thought to provide the most suitable surface area of wood to enrich the wine with its aromas. Smaller barrels provide a proportionally greater ratio of contact area between the wine and the wood, but they are less economical. Larger barrels, which can hold 79/105 or 158 gal. (300/400 or 600 l), reduce the ratio of contact area between the wood and the wine.

THE IMPORTANCE OF NEW BARRELS. A new wooden barrel will provide the wine with the most aroma and flavour. When used for the first time, tannins and other substances are transferred to the wine, and tartar crystals, even a portion of wine, are deposited into the wood. Year after year, fewer constituent elements are exchanged back and forth: the thicker the tartaric layer, the less effect the wood will have.

THE USE OF OLDER BARRELS. A barrel that is no longer new (a barrel that has held several vintages of wine) does not provide the wine with wood tannins, but just a slow oxygenation. Air enters via the bunghole and some seams (not through the pores of the wood). This slow oxygenation is very favourable to the development of the wine, helping to blend the flavours and soften the tannins. For some fortified wines such as Banyuls, port, and Maury, maturation of this kind produces so-called *rancio* flavours.

DID YOU KNOW...?

***A wine with oak-like flavours has not always been aged in wooden barrels.** It is possible to obtain such flavours with oak chips placed into stainless steel vats of wine. To reduce production costs and compete with overseas producers, France has allowed the use of oak chips since 2006. Indeed, some estates in the New World (Chile, Australia, etc.) have been using this technique for a long time. Similarly, the famous Greek Retsina has a resiny flavour because small pieces of Aleppo pine resin are added to the must* *(see box p.427).*

> Carved stopper in a barrel from Alsace.

How long in the barrel?

The length of time a wine matures in barrel varies from 6 to 18 months for wines from Bordeaux or Burgundy to more than two years for Spanish Gran Reservas. It depends mainly on the constitution of wine, its ability to 'take the wood' and resist drying out. All wines would end up 'dried out' and lose their richness if they remain in a wooden container for too long. Some experts believe that we can assist the contact between the wine and wood by filtering the wine before putting it into barrels, thereby preventing the lees from being deposited on the sides of the barrel.

> At the Michel Juillot estate in Mercurey (France), Clos des Barraults wine spends 18 months in barrels.

Oak flavours

Although some (rare) barrels are made of chestnut or acacia, oak is universally appreciated for its physical properties and flavour contributions. Its wood is rich in components that enhance the flavour of wine. To date, more than 60 polyphenols have been identified in its cells, including 18 different phenols – the most significant being vanillin. Depending on the origin of the wood and its preparation, wine tasters can distinguish other aromas: coconut, pepper, carnations, smoke, etc. The oak also provides the wine with types of tannin other than those transmitted by the skin and stalks of the grapes (so-called 'vegetable' tannins).

CHOOSING A SUITABLE OAK. When choosing a barrel, winemakers always consider the source and ageing of the wood. Oak of the Limousin forest of France, which has a 'coarse grain' from a wide tree, produces a strong, firm wood, with powerful tannins that are well suited to *eaux-de-vie* such as Cognac. Patraean (sessile) oak generally provides a 'fine grained' wood and softer tannins, but the way the trees are cultivated is more important than their geographical provenance. A long drying period for the wood in the open air and heating the barrel while it is being assembled also influence the end result.

TRUE OR FALSE?

An ordinary wine will gain character by being aged in oak barrels.

FALSE. Maturation in new oak is not a universal panacea. The belief that a meagre wine can be rescued by 'improving' it with a rich wood is an illusion, and even an error. Experience shows that for a successful interaction between the wood and the wine, the wine must be able to integrate the wood; it must be substantial, or have a strong 'body.' Far from hiding the characteristics of the wine, the wood must actually play a modest part and only increase its complexity of flavour.

Oak trees for wine barrels

It takes more than 100 years for an oak tree to mature sufficiently to be commercialized. To meet the ever-increasing needs of the coopers, who export worldwide, French oak is no longer sufficient. Supplies now come from diverse sources: oaks from Poland, Slovenia, Croatia, and Russia, all of high quality, are also used. American oak provides complementary flavours approaching coconut. American oak barrels are cheaper to produce and are valued for certain types of wine.

MAKING A BARREL

An age-old practice, the sequence of tasks undertaken by the cooper has barely changed through the centuries. Some parts of the job are now carried out using machines, but making barrels remains a skilled craft.

The key steps

A barrel consists of pieces of wood called staves, held together by iron or chestnut hoops, with a circular 'head' at either end. To make a barrel the cooper must: take measurements; produce the staves; shape and assemble them; arch them over fire; trim; prepare and produce the ends; drill and bind the barrel together; then finish off and test its strength.

MANUFACTURE. The cooper begins by making the wooden staves (28 to 32 on average) and head pieces (12 to 16). This was traditionally done by hand, but nowadays is usually done using a machine.

SHAPING. The cooper then creates the shape of the barrel for the first time, by assembling the staves together one by one in a rough circle. They are then gradually tightened and balanced.

***A cooper can give a new lease of life to an old barrel.** He takes it apart, planes the staves, then reassembles the whole thing. The newly revealed surface of the wood will now have qualities similar to those of new oak.*

ARCHING OVER FIRE. This is generally done over a wood fire placed inside the assembled staves. This operation in particular determines how long the barrel will last. If this heating process is not carried out properly, the staves may break at the bilge (the widest part of the barrel) after a few years of use, because of constant play in the wood.

FROM TRIMMING TO BINDING. Trimming is to prepare the heads of the barrel in order to embed the two lids (sinking). Once these are in place, it only remains to make the final hoop.

FINISHING TOUCHES. Once the barrel has been assembled, finishing touches include sanding the heads and bevels; piercing the bunghole; recording the origins of the wood, the degree of heating, and the name of the manufacturer. Then there is a final check that everything looks and feels good before the barrels are sold.

> Preparing the staves

> Assembling the staves roughly in a circle

> Arching over a fire

> Bordeaux barrels made at the Darnajou cooperage.

SIGNATURE. Every barrel that is ready for use is signed off by the craftsman on the two heads. This signature indicates their expertize and provides information about the origin of the barrel.

The effect of heat on the barrel

Arching over a fire, a crucial step in manufacturing a barrel, has the effect of toasting its inner walls. Experience has shown that the degree of toasting results in appreciable differences in the wine being matured. A high level of toast carbonizes the barrel and produces a charcoal layer between the wine and the wood: it generates strong flavours and a wide variety of phenolic compounds. (When the grilled or smoked character of a wine is pronounced, we say that it is 'toasted.') A gentle toast, by contrast, will better display those components of the wood with slightly more nuance.

TRUE OR FALSE?

The barrel was invented by the Gauls.

FALSE. Though the Gauls actually made barrels as we know them today, historians believe that the origins of the barrel are much older. The first wooden containers, from around 2000 BC, were probably composed of slats held together by links, and the whole thing was coated with a resinous substance. They were first used to contain solids, before being improved, much later, so that they could also hold liquids.

DID YOU KNOW...?

The best oak trees are often said to come from the French forest of Tronçais in the département of Nièvre. *Jean-Baptiste Colbert, Louis XIV's busy minister, who planted this forest, never imagined that he would contribute to the production of the finest wines. His aim was to have a source of the oak for the construction of royal ships to fight the English fleet.*

> Final binding using a press

> Smoothing off with a plane

> Stamped signature

SOME BEAUTIFUL BARRELS

Cask, barrel, vat... These wooden containers, made of oak or chestnut, are used to age or to store wines. Sometimes they are also works of art.

1

2

3

4

5

6

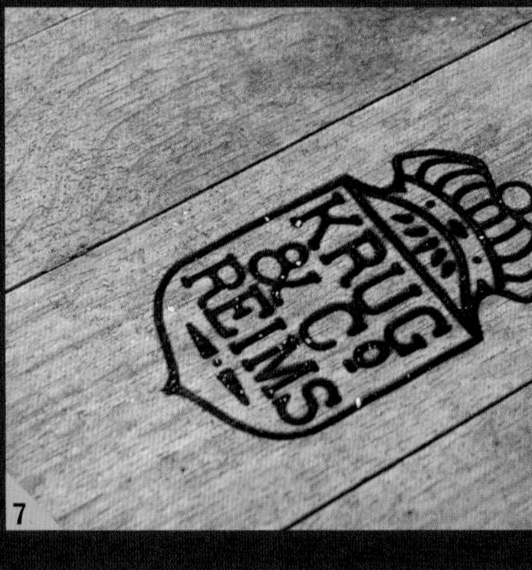

7

8

9

10

11

12

1. Barrel with stamp (Bouchard Père & Fils, Beaune).
2. Carved stopper on a vat (Domaine Marcel Deiss, Bergheim).
3. and 4. Carved stoppers (Domaine Hugel & Fils, Riquewihr).
5. Carved stopper on a barrel (Château de Pommard).
6. A die stamp with Château Latour emblem (Pauillac).
7. Krug estate stamp (Reims).
8. and 12. Carved vats (Louis Roederer, Reims).
9. and 10. Painted vats (Château de Pommard).
11. Carved vat (Domaine Hugel & Fils, Riquewihr).

BOTTLING

It is impossible to discuss wine without mentioning its inseparable companion, the bottle. When ageing is complete, the wine is bottled – a complex and difficult task. Once in its glass container, the wine leaves the estate or the cellar of the négociant *to be offered to the consumer.*

Preparing the wine

FINAL PROCEDURES. Most wine lovers will not tolerate particles or deposits in a bottle. In most cases, the producer completely clarifies the wine before it is bottled. This involves two procedures before bottling: fining and filtration (*see* p.76). They may be combined, but they can also affect the flavour of wine.

A CONTROLLED ENVIRONMENT. At this stage, the wine, which is perfectly clear and stable, must be bottled. Again, careful attention to detail and cleanliness are required because poor bottling can jeopardize the quality of the wine. There is a significant risk of contamination by the bottling equipment and glass. In addition, aeration of the wine, if too extensive, can cause oxidation. Finally, care must be taken to ensure an effective closure.

***Ultimate legal responsibility for a wine rests with whoever bottled it,** be it the estate owner, merchant, a cooperative, or a bottling company.*

The choice of the bottle

Glass remains the ideal material for storing and ageing wine. The international standard bottle is 750 ml. Almost all of the great wines of the world are sold in bottles of this capacity or a multiple of this volume.

THE COLOUR OF THE GLASS. The colour of glass used for the bottle is far from irrelevant. It varies according to region and wine, but must be dark enough to protect the wine from light. It has been found that the wine develops faster in a clear bottle, even if the wine cellar is dark.

PREPARATION OF THE BOTTLE. The cleanliness of the bottles is essential. The method most often used to clean new bottles is injecting hot water or steam. Using second-hand bottles is risky, even if the cleaning is carried out meticulously. The bottles are immersed in hot water with detergent added, brushed, and rinsed under pressure.

Bottling

BOTTLING THE WINE. One challenge of bottling is to fill the bottle with a specific volume of wine, while leaving enough room for the closure and making allowances for increased volume due to changes in the temperature of the liquid. That is why bottling machines have become increasingly efficient. Larger-scale producers have their own plants while smaller wine-makers will sub-contract the job to specialists who use portable machinery.

SEALING THE BOTTLE. Adding the traditional bottle closure is carried out by a method based on a simple principle. The cork (*see also* pp.88–9), which is new, of good quality, and of a 'relaxed' composition, is compressed by 'jaws' or 'clamps' in order to be smaller than the bottle neck, and then rapidly pushed into it by a vertical piston.

Capacity of bottles

Major wine regions offer many traditional sizes other than the standard 750 ml. In Champagne, a magnum contains 1.5 litres (or 2 bottles), a Jeroboam 3 litres (or 4 bottles), a Rehoboam 4.5 litres (6 bottles), a Methuselah 6 litres (8 bottles), a Salmanazar 9 litres (12 bottles), a Balthazar 12 litres (16 bottles), and a Nebuchadnezzar contains 15 litres (20 bottles). Sweet 'late harvest' wines or wines made from grapes that have been dried on the vine (Sauternes, *vin de paille*, Italian Recioto della Valpolicella) are often sold in 37.5 or 50 cl bottles.

'Bordeaux'

'Burgundy'

> Today the bottling process at wineries is very often completely automated.

Bottles and their shapes

Different regions or countries have adopted specific bottle shapes to distinguish their wines. The shapes have become conventions but are rarely compulsory, except in certain cases – in France, these are in Alsace and the Jura.

THE THREE MOST COMMON SHAPES. These are the 'Bordeaux,' the 'Burgundy,' and the 'flute.' The Bordeaux is straight with a high 'shoulder.' It is coloured green or brown for red wines and dry white wines, and semi-clear for sweet wines. It is often also used for many wines from outside Bordeaux and elsewhere. The Burgundy is the main bottle for those French regions between Chablis and Lyon, as well as in the Rhône Valley and part of Languedoc. Almost all red wines and white wines from Burgundy are bottled in bottles of this type, as well as some Chardonnays and Pinot Noirs from other countries. The main colour is a muted green. The third format commonly used is the tall 'flute' of the Rhine and Mosel of Germany. Rhine flutes are made of brown glass, while those from the Mosel and Alsace (France) are green.

TRADITIONAL SHAPES. These are less universally used, but restricted to wines produced in certain areas, whether in France or elsewhere. Jura has a special shape and size for *vin jaune*: a 1.3 pint (62 cl) *clavelin* is used to show what is left of a litre after six years of evaporation in barrel. Champagnes and other sparkling wines are housed in thick glass bottles that can withstand the pressure of carbon dioxide, but whose shapes can vary. Other bottle shapes include the *quille* used in Provence and a similar bottle for Verdicchio in Italy. The Franconia region of Germany uses a *bocksbeutel*, a bulging and flattened bottle. Vintage port comes in a straight bottle with a tall shoulder and a slight swelling at the neck.

BOTTLES FOR MARKETING PURPOSES. Today, the size and shape of bottles are increasingly seen as marketing vehicles. Some wines are noteworthy for their heavy and expensive glass as well as original shapes and colours. However, heavy bottles have been criticized for the expense and the extra carbon footprint in transportation that their weight entails.

TRUE OR FALSE?

Wine in bulk and estate-bottled wine are the same quality.

FALSE. The expression 'estate wine' denotes one made from vines belonging to the winery – produced, blended, aged, and bottled there. The distinction between estate-bottled wine and wine sold in bulk is crucial for the owner, since one is the finished product, while the other is simply a raw material.

'Flute' from Alsace

'Quille' from Provence

'Clavelin'

'Champagne'

CLOSURES

Choosing the bottle stopper is a complex task that is very important for the longevity of wine. Although new materials are increasingly being used, cork still dominates in the manufacture of bottle stoppers.

The bark of the cork oak

A UNIQUE MATERIAL. Cork has unique physical properties and has long been considered the perfect material for sealing a glass bottle. Its cells form microscopic 'suckers' that grip the bottle neck. It is more or less inert and in principle impervious to liquids. It degrades slowly in contact with wine and humidity, and it has been estimated that a cork closure should be renewed every 25 to 30 years. But, despite all the efforts of the cork producers, it is not completely reliable and occasionally some bottles have a 'corked' or tainted aroma and flavour. Its impermeability varies from one bottle to the next, as becomes especially apparent in wine for laying down.

A UNIQUE TREE. The cork oak (*Quercus suber*) grows mainly in the western Mediterranean and Portugal. A cork oak is stripped – they call it 'extracted' – of bark every 12 years; but only the fourth, fifth, and sixth extractions provide highest quality cork. You can expect yields a quarter of the time across the lifetime of a tree (from 150 to 200 years).

***If well kept in the cellar, a good cork can protect a wine for several decades;** but to be safe, the leading estates re-cork their wines every 25 years.*

Preparation of the cork

DRYING. Planks of cork bark are removed from the tree, stacked, and dried in the open air. They must be exposed to the sun, rain, and cold for two winters and one summer before they can be used to make stoppers. During this drying process, the cork loses its sap and its tissues tighten.

BOILING. After drying, the planks are boiled in water at 212°F (100°C) for 30 to 60 minutes. The cork then expands by about 20 per cent and acquires its maximum elasticity. The planks emerging from this process are now sterile and can be smoothed out. They are then rested for two or three weeks before being cut. At this stage, an initial selection takes place on the basis of two criteria: thickness and quality. This is made easier by straightening the four sides of the raw plank.

Production of corks

CUTTING. When the planks have an ideal level of moisture, they are cut into strips of the same width as the length of the corks they will become. To produce a cork just under an inch (24 mm) in diameter, which is the most common size, you need planks with a thickness of 1.1 to 1.2 inches (28 to 30 mm). The strips are then passed onto a punch. This work is done manually – so as to avoid defects, many of which can occur – to produce a good percentage of quality corks. The final yield is about 33–55 lbs of stoppers (15–25 kg) per 220 lbs (100 kg) of raw cork.

SHAPING. The plugs cut from the punch are sanded with emery to obtain a regular and smooth surface and cross-section. They are then washed to remove the dust and residue in the lenticels (as the small holes visible on the surface are called). Often, their appearance is improved by passing them through a dye bath.

FINAL SELECTION. There then follows a second screening stage. This sorting can be partially automated with machines capable of counting the number of lenticels flush with the surface of the cork. It is, however, carried out largely by hand because green spots, dry cork, or cracks might not be spotted by mechanical processing.

FINISHING TOUCHES. Sometimes the lenticel pores are clogged with powdered cork paste, which improves the mechanical properties of the cork.

Other closures

Some wine producers are considering abandoning cork in favour of plastic, aluminium, or glass. Manufacturers are using aluminium screwcaps, glass stoppers,and plastic corks that look like traditional corks. In the case of plastic, the benefits have only been proven for wine to drink young (young reds, whites, and rosés to drink within 3 years). After that time, they have, for the moment, the tendancy to allow air in, oxidizing the wine. Screwcaps and glass stoppers don't have this problem.

A closure for every kind of wine

There are several types of closure, each designed for different wines. From a standard diameter of just under an inch (24 mm), they are compressed

DID YOU KNOW...?

The cork stopper in its present form was discovered in England in the 17th century thanks to the country's trade with Portugal. *It arrived with the introduction of more solid glass bottles, thanks to the carbon-fired furnaces that could reach a higher temperature than wood-burning ones. Previously, wine had been shipped in barrels and then drawn off into carafes to be served, but the cork and bottle would go on to conquer the continent. Closures made of cork and other materials were used by the Greeks and Romans to seal amphorae, but cork was then abandoned and had been forgotten by the Middle Ages.*

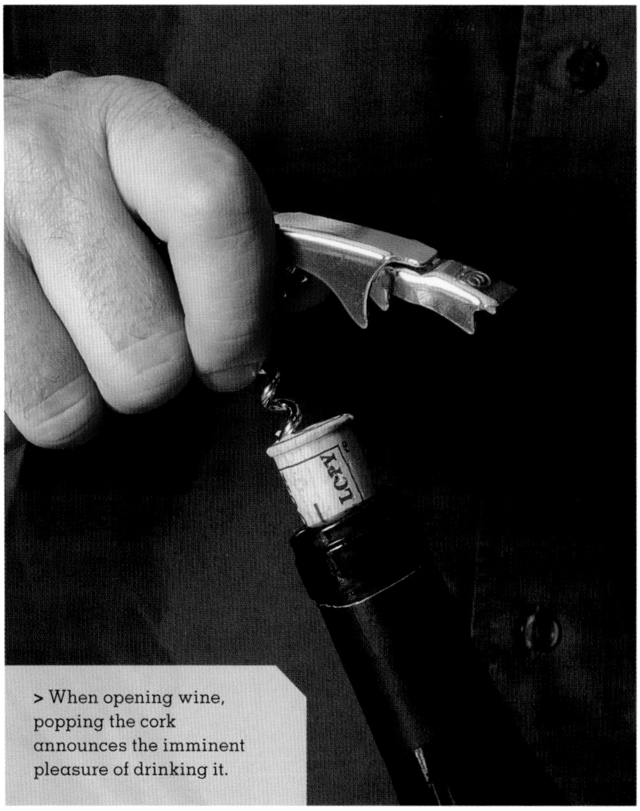

> When opening wine, popping the cork announces the imminent pleasure of drinking it.

by a machine into a 0.73 inch (18.5 mm) neck. Champagne corks, which are wider, at 1.2 inches (31 mm), are compressed even more, because they must withstand pressurized carbon dioxide. Except in the case of Champagne, labelling corks is not compulsory in France. When done, it generally includes the vintage, the place of bottling, and the name of the producer or wine.

LONG CORKS. Estates generally use these closures to protect their high quality wines as they age over decades; their reserve wines may be re-corked every 25 years.

SHORT CORKS. These are made of cork and are used for wines with a shorter lifespan.

AGGLOMERATED CORKS. Made of amalgamated cork granules, and treated to eliminate the risk of contamination that can result in 'cork taint', they are used for an increasing number of wines and for most Champagnes.

SYNTHETIC CORKS. Plastic foam or coloured closures, these are suitable for wine that needs to be kept for a short time, and are being increasingly used for this purpose.

CHAMPAGNE CORKS. Agglomerated cork onto which one to three layers of solid cork are adhered. They are driven halfway into the bottle, so only the part driven into the bottle is compressed (hence the mushroom shape). They must be labelled with the word 'Champagne' and the relevant vintage, if applicable.

SCREWCAPS. These have been accepted by some wine professionals and by a growing number of wine-growing countries, but have had difficulty finding favour with consumers in traditional wine-drinking regions. The screwcap eliminates the danger of odour pollution from molecules that might get trapped in a cork and prevents the risk of premature oxidation, which can vary from bottle to bottle. Screwcaps are used in the majority of cases in certain countries (Switzerland, New Zealand, Australia, South Africa, and Chile) and are gaining ground elsewhere.

GLASS STOPPERS. A fairly recent invention from the Czech Republic, this kind of closure is relatively expensive but has all the advantages of a screwcap with additional aesthetic appeal. They are similar in appearance to the closures on some carafes and are rendered waterproof with a neoprene ring that makes it very easy to open and reseal. These closures are being used on ever greater numbers of Austrian and German wines and have started to turn up in France.

A restricted area of cork production

The area in which the cork oak tree will grow is limited: the Iberian peninsula, southern France, southern Italy, Corsica, Sardinia, and North Africa. Portugal is by far the greatest producer. The increasing number of bottles that use cork closures has stretched the production chain and made the quality of corks more of a gamble, which in turn has accelerated the adoption of alternative systems.

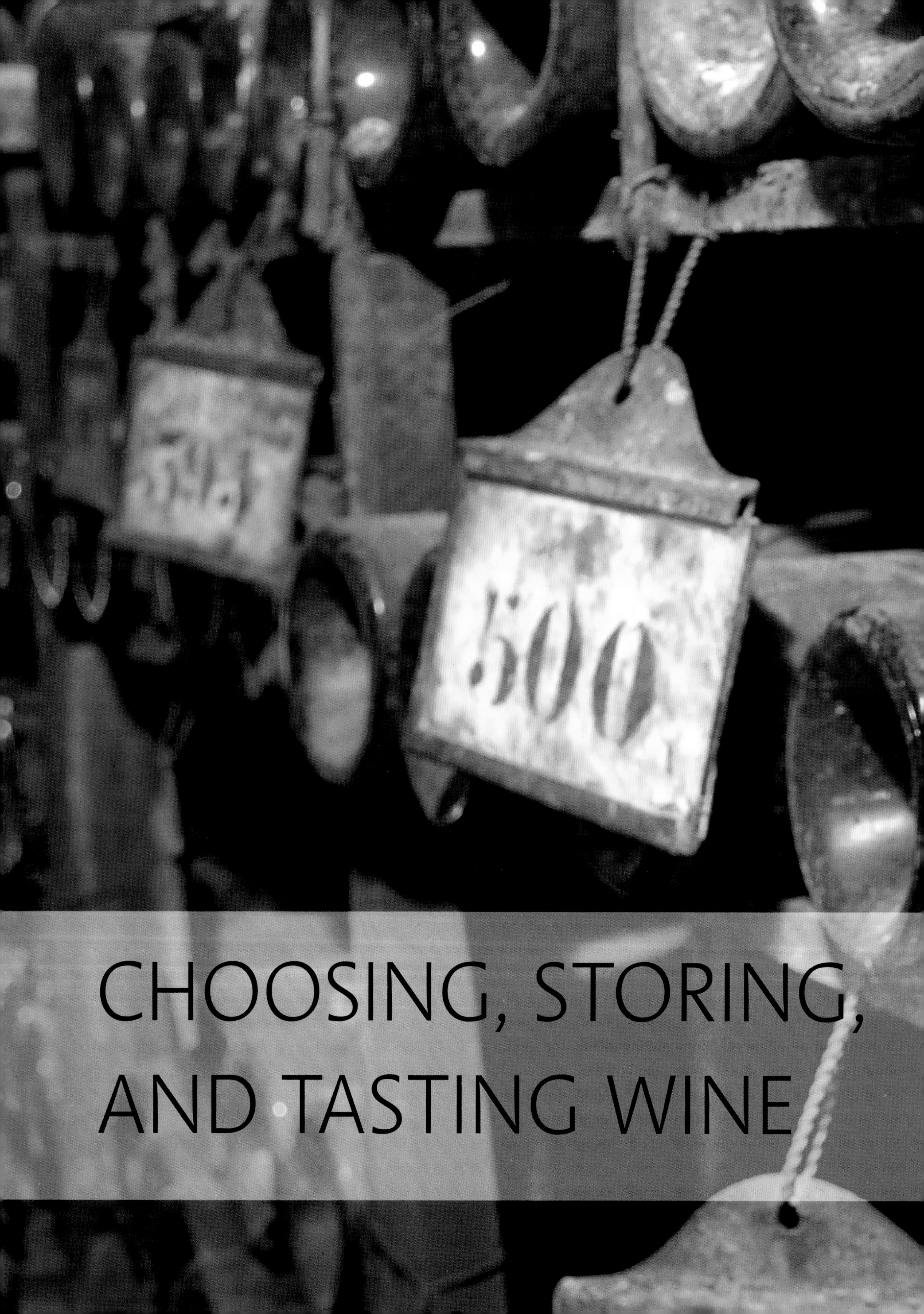

CHOOSING, STORING, AND TASTING WINE

579

PRODUCE OF FRANCE
GRAND VIN
DE
HATEAU LATOUR
PREMIER GRAND CRU CLASSE
PAUILLAC
1990
APPELLATION PAUILLAC CONTRÔLÉE

HOW CAN YOU IDENTIFY A WINE?

APPELLATION SYSTEMS

*Supervised in France by the INAO (*Institut National de l'Origine et de la Qualité*) and by similar organizations in other European countries, through strict production regulations the aim of the appellation system is to guarantee the source of wines and how typical they are in terms of regional characteristics.*

Appellations in Europe

Every bottle of European wine carries a label indicating its geographic provenance, guaranteeing its source and its compliance with specific production regulations. The system was developed in France during the first half of the 20th century, and its broad principles have been adopted by a number of countries. Since 2009, the European Union has harmonized the designation systems. There are now two main categories of wines, sometimes with sub-categories, each with its own rules for production and labelling. Each EU member country retains some traditional descriptions, but all adopt a similar approach. European countries that are not members of the EU, such as Switzerland, follow their own rules.

***One of the tasks that the European Union's new system of appellations** has set itself in the face of competition from the New World is to make wine classification clearer.*

AOP and IGP

The simplest and most accessible category is wine without geographic indication (in French VSIG, *vins sans indication géographique*). In France these wines are marked Vin de France, but each country has its own designation (*see* table on page 99). The next category up in the rankings in terms of status and quality consists of wines with a geographical indication (in French IG, *indication géographique*). This group of wines, which is supervised by the INAO in France, has two sub-categories with more restrictive specifications that vary individually by region and appellation: IGP and AOP.

IGP Wines with a Protected Geographical Indication (in French IGP, *indication géographique protégée*) correspond, in France, to the former designation Vin de Pays. Their production area can be regional, departmental, or local, with variants depending on the country. For these wines, the rules of production are more flexible than for the AOP category and the list of authorized grape varieties is more extensive.

AOP Wines with a Protected Designation of Origin (in French AOP, *appellation d'origine protégée*) correspond, in France, to the old AOC designation, which can still be used. Whilst

Why are there now more AOC wines?

The number of French AOC wines has increased over the last four decades, but not always having taken the same route. Some villages in the Rhône Valley, for example, have been able to add their name to the Côtes-du-Rhône regional appellation. These specified areas have then achieved independence later, such as Vinsobres, Beaumes-de-Venise (for red), and recently Cairanne, which became AOC wines in their own right. Viré-Clessé in the Mâconnais sub-region has undergone a similar process. Elsewhere, the name of a cru has been systematically added to a regional appellation; in Alsace, the AOC Alsace Grand Cru includes 51 separate designations. In Languedoc, the number of AOCs has multiplied: the old AOC Coteaux-du-Languedoc followed by a local geographical indication has disappeared, and these have either become AOCs in their own right (Terrasses du Larzac, La Clape…) or designations (AOC Languedoc followed by the name of an area) as a stage to becoming fully fledged AOCs.

> The 124 acres (50 ha) that produce the Burgundy *grand cru* of Clos de Vougeot are shared by more than 70 owners.

New European regulations

The reformed appellation regulations introduced in August 2009 provide for two categories of wine.

Wines without geographic designation: This category corresponds to the *vins de France* and is now allowed to indicate grape variety and year. The wine is also allowed to contain up to 15 per cent of another vintage. Yields are not limited and certain winemaking techniques such as adding aroma through wood shavings or producing low alcohol variants are permitted.

Wines with geographic designation: These correspond to the French Appellation d'Origine Protégée (AOP) and *Indication Géographique Protégée* (IGP) classifications. AOP wine specifications were drawn up by the Organisme de Défense et de Gestion (ODG) representing the wine trade. They are subject to controls on production and the wines themselves carried out by an independent inspection body of wine professionals (known as the OI). IGP wines are also are obliged to institute similar specifications under inspection by an independent organization approved by the INAO. The addition to a given blend of 15 per cent from another year or grape variety will be permitted, unless the specifications of the AOP do not allow this.

> The Schlumberger estate at Guebwiller produces Alsace and Alsace Grand Cru wines.

production constraints (yields, grape varieties, etc.) are more restrictive than for IGP wines, each appellation sets its own specifications, which must then be approved by a regulatory body, in France the INAO. Each country of the European Union retains the right to use its traditional terms (DOC and DOCG in Italy, DOC and DOCa in Spain).

French AOP Wines

The INAO recognizes nearly 440 IGP and AOP designations. Initially established in the 1930s, AOPs have proliferated and now account for just under half of total production. Originally defined according to the 'local, loyal, and continuous usage' of a region, they guarantee both the source of a wine (a specific geographical area) and compliance with rules of production.

THE GEOGRAPHIC AREA. This may be regional – Burgundy, Alsace, Bordeaux – or tied to a local community or commune – St-Estèphe in Bordeaux, Gigondas in the Rhône Valley, Morgon in Beaujolais. It may even cover only a very small location – a *cru*, or a *grand cru* vineyard, such as Zinnkoepfléin Alsace, or cover a few hundred thousand acres (Côtes du Rhône, Bordeaux). In Burgundy, there is a complex and precise hierarchical system of appellations that stack up snugly like Russian dolls: a regional appellation (Burgundy), a commune appellation (Gevrey-Chambertin), a *premier cru* commune appellation (Gevrey-Chambertin *premier cru* Cazetiers), and a *grand cru* appellation (Le Chambertin). Specific descriptions such as *cru bourgeois* do not fall under AOP regulation – their attribution is overseen by the *Bureau Veritas*, an independent organization, at the request of the trade – nor does the description *cru classé* found in Bordeaux and Provence fall under these regulations. On the other hand, an appellation such as Saint-Emilion Grand Cru depends on it. There are even some appellations that cover only a single estate or vineyard, such as Château-Grillet in the Rhône Valley or Romanée-Conti (see pp.288–9) in Burgundy, for example.

GRAPE VARIETY. The grape variety or varieties authorized for a given appellation are strictly defined in Europe. It might be a single grape per wine – Gamay for Beaujolais – or a blend of varieties – Cabernet Sauvignon, Cabernet Franc, and Merlot for Bordeaux reds, for example (*see also* pp.32–5).

YIELD. Each AOC has a set maximum yield expressed in hectolitres of wine per hectare (hl/ha) or tons per acre (tons/acre), or by weight of grapes in Champagne. This amount varies widely: 4.8 tons per acre (80 hl/ha) in Alsace, 1.8 tons per acre (30 hl/ha) for Banyuls wines.

TECHNIQUES. Regulations even control the number of vines per acre, harvesting methods, pruning techniques, chaptalization, vinification, the date it goes to market, and the amounts to be sold. Controlling this last point causes the authorities the most trouble, even though every quantity produced is registered and checks are made to ensure that this corresponds with the yield of the wine producer who has made it. In certain regions, the production methods are actually part of the AOC designation: in Champagne, for example, there are strict rules governing the processes of *cueillette* (picking by hand), grape-pressing, and maturing the wine.

Vins de France and IGP

Created in 2009, the *vins de France* have replaced the old *vins de table*. Although they do not have a geographical indication, they can and do mention both the vintage and the grape variety on their labels. IGPs, sometimes referred to as *vins de pays*, are more strictly regulated: the geographical area, yields, techniques, and grape varieties are the subject of legislation, although this is more flexible and less restrictive than for AOPs.

Italian regulations

Wines are divided into two categories depending on whether they are with or without a geographical indication. The latter include simple *vini,* with no indication of region, variety, or vintage. Ranked above these are *vini varietali (*varietal wines) produced from at least 85% of one or two specific grape varieties on a restricted list. The variety or varieties used may be indicated on the label as well as the vintage, but not the region of origin.
THE HIERARCHY OF QUALITY. Wines with geographical indications fall into three categories, theoretically reflecting a hierarchy of quality. IGT (Indicazione Geografica Tipica) is the equivalent of the IGP in France. These wines must come from a specific area named on the label, use authorized grape varieties, and follow production and labelling regulations. Above these are the DOP (Denominazione di Origine Protetta) wines, which are divided into two subcategories: DOC and DOCG. In the second category, which is in theory more prestigious, the term Garantita is added to Controllata and indicates that the wines have been tasted and approved. The areas of these appellations are often more restricted than those for IGT wines and have a more established reputation. A DOC may request to be upgraded to DOCG status after at least 10 years of existence, providing it accepts a series of stricter controls, including on its average selling price.
SPECIFIC DESCRIPTIONS. In the DOP category, and for some of the most extensive appellations, a wine called Classico comes from the historic heart of the appellation area, generally the place with the greatest potential. A wine described as Superiore contains 0.5% more alcohol than a wine of the same name without this description. This is the logical consequence of a further requirement to lower the maximum yield per acre. Some appellations allow the description Riserva to be used for wines that have been matured for a longer period than that required by the appellation.

Spanish regulations

Production is organized around the two categories defined by the European Union: wines without a geographical indication (simply described as vino), and wines with a geographical indication. For the latter, Spanish legislation recognizes a hierarchy of five quality levels.

> An advertisement for Tio Pepe, a sherry produced by Gonzáles Byass in Spain.

Wine age on Spanish labels

Vino joven (young wine): wine bottled as soon as possible after clarification; also known as vino del año (this year's wine).

Vino de crianza (matured wine): wine that has been matured for at least two years, with a minimum of six months in barricas (oak barrels).

Reserva: red wine with three years maturation in a bodega (cellar), of which at least one year is in barricas. Rosé and white wine must have two years, with six months in barrels.

Gran reserva: red wine that has matured for five years, with a minimum of 18 months in barrels. There are few whites or rosés in this category, but these require four years of maturation, of which six months must be in barrels.

vigneti
FONTANAFREDDA
PROVINCIA
DIVIETO
di CACCIA
RIFUGIO FAUNISTICO

THE FIVE QUALITY LEVELS.
- *Vinos de la tierra* are wines with a protected geographical indication, the equivalent of French IGP wines. The legislation dealing with these is more flexible than for those of higher quality.
- Vinos de Calidad con Indicació Geográfica (VCIG). This is an intermediate stage prior to qualifying for the main DO subcategory described below. For a VCIG area to achieve DO status, it must have been in existence for at least five years. The name of the region must be on the label.
- Denominaciónes de Origen (DO). These wines come from a specific wine-producing area where production is regulated by an organization which ensures that the regulations established for each DO are respected, whether in terms of grape varieties, yields, vinification methods, or ageing. The term Denominación de Origen appears on the label, followed by the name of the appellation.
- Denominaciónes de Origen Calificada (DOCa). This subcategory is now limited to two appellations, Rioja and Priorat, and has stricter production regulations than DO wines.
- Vinos de Pago (DO/DOCaPago) is a sub-category specific to Spain for designating remarkable wine-producing locations which, although outside areas with DO or DOCa status, are considered to be of equivalent or higher quality. They determine their own production requirements, which must be even more demanding than those for a DO or a DOCa.

German regulations

While conforming to new European regulations, the German system retains its own classification with respect to white wines, based on geographical origins, quality, and sugar content of the grape juice.

THE FOUR QUALITY LEVELS. Wines with no geographical indication are simply labelled *Deutscher Wein* (German wine). Wines with a geographical indication include *Landwein*, the equivalent of *vin de pays*, but these make up only a fraction of total production. Ranked above these are QbA (*qualitätswein bestimmter anbaugebiete*), quality wines produced in one of the 13 specific regions and, at the highest level, the *prädikatswein*, meaning 'wines of distinction.'

CLASSIFICATION BY SUGAR CONTENT. *Prädikatswein* is made from grapes with a sugar content sufficient to require no chaptalization. Such wines are further divided into six subcategories according to the sugar content of the original must. These are, in ascending order: *kabinett* (the basic QmP wine), *spätlese* (a sweet or dry wine), *auslese* (an more powerful sweet or dry wine), *beerenauslese* (a sweet wine made from selected grapes), *trockenbeerenauslese* (TBA; a very sweet wine, made from shrivelled botrytized grapes), and *eiswein* ('ice wine' made from an extremely concentrated must where the grapes have been subject to frost on the vine). This official classification might be misleading for non-German wine lovers, but it reflects a desire to produce quality wines with the emphasis on the ripest grapes. The sugar content of the must should not be confused with the residual sugar content of the finished wine. Hence a *kabinett* can be sweet, and, conversely, a *spätlese* perfectly dry in taste. Alcohol levels are usually a reflection of this: a *kabinett* with residual sugar will contain less alcohol than a dry *kabinett*, for example.

DID YOU KNOW...?

Austria has the strictest wine laws of any European country.

As in Germany, wine quality is determined by the maturity of the grapes. In 2003, however, the category of DAC (Districtus Austriae Controllatus) *was created. It guarantees the distinctive character of certain wines made from selected grape varieties, much like AOC, thus allowing each regional wine producer's association to choose a type of wine that is typical for that area. There are now 9 DACs in Austria and others could be created in the future.*

> A decorative signpost surrounded by vines in Baden, Germany.

A comparative table of European appellations

The European Union has now harmonized legislation around common categories (IGP, AOP) but each country can retain its traditional terms: this table shows how to draw a parallel between the different categories, with up to four grades in each country .

	TABLE WINE (WINE WITHOUT GEOGRAPHIC DESIGNATION)	QUALITY WINES PRODUCED IN SPECIFIED REGIONS	
	Wine without geographic indication/ Vins sans indication géographique(VSIG)	Protected geographic indication (IGP	Protected geographic appellation/ Appellation d'origine protégée (AOP)
France	*Vin de France*	*Vin de pays*	*Appellation d'origine contrôlée* (AOC)
Italy	*Vino, Vino varietale*	*Indicazione geografica tipica (IGT)*	*Denominazione di origine controllata* (DOC) *Denominazione di origine controllata e garantita* (DOCG)
Germany	*Deutscher Wein*	*Landwein*	*Qualitätswein bestimmter anbaugebiete* (QbA) *Prädikatswein (1)*
Spain	*Vino*	*Vino de la tierra*	*Vinos de calidad con indicación geográfica (VCIG)* *Denominación de origen (DO)* *Denominación de origen calificada (DOCa)* *Vino de Pago calificado*
Portugal	*Vinho*	*Vinho regional*	*Indicação de proveniencia regulamentada (IPR)* *Denominação de origem controlada (DOC)*
Great Britain	Table wine	Regional wine	English/Welsh vineyards quality wine
Hungary	*Asztali bor*	*Tájbor*	*Minöségi bor* *Védett eredetű bor*
Greece	*Epitrapezios oinos*	*Topikos oinos* *Oenoi onomasias kata paradosi*	*Oenoi Onomasia Proeléfseos Anotréras Piotitos (OPAP)* *Oenoi Onomasia Proeléfseos Eleghomeni (OPE)*
Austria	*Wein*	*Landwein*	*Qualitätswein* *Prädikatswein (2)* *Districtus Austriae Controllatus (DAC)*

1. *Prädikat* (distinction) includes six grades of maturation and quality: *kabinett, spätlese, auslese, beerenauslese, trockenbeerenauslese, eiswein.*
2. *Prädikat* (distinction) recognizes seven grades of maturity and quality: *spätlese, auslese, beerenauslese, ausbruch, trockenbeerenauslese, eiswein, strohwein.*

APPELLATIONS FROM OTHER COUNTRIES

The countries of the New World grade their wines more by grape variety and brand than by provenance. The idea of appellation as it is understood in Europe is nonetheless gaining ground.

Fewer restrictions than Europe

Many New World countries – in the southern hemisphere and the United States, for example – are more concerned with factors other than geography, looking to grape variety and brand (or the name of the wine producer) to guide consumer choice, rather than place of origin. All these countries have an established regulatory system and comply with international agreements, and the old European practice of using appellation names (like Chablis or Champagne, for example) is dying out. Most of the countries of the New World have since begun to regulate geographic designations, but with far fewer constraints than in Europe.

Wine production rules in New World countries are extremely relaxed. *If they include the idea of* terroir *(local character), this is often interpreted liberally – a wine from one region may be made in part with grapes from another region.*

America

The United States has been using an appellation system known as AVA (American viticultural area) since the 1980s. This legislation only applies to the origins of the wine and does not regulate the wine sector's methods or practices; grape varieties, yields and choice of production techniques are thus left to the producers. All that is required is to identify concentrically arranged production zones – the state, the county, and then the actual AVA, which is a more specific region still (*see also* p. 435).

REGULATION. When a wine bears the name of a state (California, Texas, etc.) or county, at least 75 per cent of the grapes used to produce that wine must have been cultivated in the stated region. If the bottle is labelled as an AVA, the proportion of those grapes has to be at least 85 per cent; certain states, such as Oregon, are even stricter. Mention of a vintage on the bottle indicates that at least 95 per cent of the wine is from that year. AVAs are defined according to natural climatic frontiers, topographic regions, or specific soil types, but the defined areas are very variable. Some are very localized and homogenous, such as

> Entry sign at the Fetzer Vineyards in Mendocino County, California.

Grape varieties in the New World

If a wine contains a certain percentage of a grape variety, that variety may be mentioned on the label; for wines exported to the European Union, the content must be at least 85 per cent. If two varieties feature on the label, they together must make up 100 per cent of the blend. The rules are sometimes more flexible for wines intended for domestic consumption. In New Zealand, Argentina, Australia, South Africa, and the United States (with the exception of Oregon, which has a stricter regime), it is enough for the wine to consist of between 75 and 85 per cent of the variety mentioned on the label.

Sonoma Valley
Vintners & Growers Alliance
BLACKSTONE WINERY
ARROWOOD
B.R. COHN WINERY
WELLINGTON
KUNDE
FAMILY WINERIES
SL CELLARS
BENZIGER
LANDMARK
LEDSON
2 MI
ST FRANCIS
VJB VINEYARDS & CELLARS
1 MILES
KENWOOD VINEYARDS
SCHUG
Valley of the Moon
MAYO FAMILY WINERY
CASTLE

> The Errazuriz estate in Aconcagua, Chile.

Napa Valley, while others are more spread out, such as Central Coast, which extends from San Francisco to Santa Barbara. The regulations are more fluid; however, 'estate-bottled' on the label means that 100 per cent of the wine came from vineyards owned or controlled by the winery in the same viticultural area. Labels might also say 'grown, produced and bottled by'.

Canada

Regulations here vary by region. The Vintners' Quality Alliance (VQA) bases its requirements on the French appellation system; these apply only in British Columbia and Ontario, but almost all Canadian wine is produced there. VQA wines are evaluated by an independent jury, who judge their style and quality. Approved wines receive a black VQA stamp; wines scoring more than 15 out of a possible 20 points receive a superior appellation and a gold stamp.

TWO CATEGORIES. VQA requirements state that wines must come from grape varieties cultivated in their own province and they must be bottled there. With the exception of several wines made with *Vitis labrusca* grapes (which were once in the majority), the wine produced cannot claim to be of VQA standard. The two provinces have been divided into regions and sub-regions, all with well-defined characteristics and each with their own regulations. Wines are given a 'regional' appellation when at least 85 per cent of the wine comes from the area indicated. This proportion has be 100 per cent for sub-regions in Ontario. The grape variety listed on the label should make up at least 85 per cent of the contents of the bottle, as well as the mention of the year. The label must be stamped 'product of Ontario' or 'product of British Columbia'.

Chile

The DO (*denominación de origen*) designation has been in existence here only since 2002. Five large regions have been recognized, divided into sub-regions that correspond to particular valleys. While many of the wines are made with blends sourced from different regions, there are some that have nonetheless built up a solid reputation, such as Colchagua and Casablanca. The idea of named places of origin or specific areas as an index of wine style is making headway, as can be seen from the appearance of the 'Costa', 'Andes' and 'Entre Cordilleras' labels, signifying a greater sensitivity to the effect of terroir.

Argentina

Argentina produced national wine legislation in 1999 and again in 2004 to regulate production under the supervision of the *Instituto nacional de vitivinicultura*. Even bearing in mind the considerable economic clout wielded by the large companies that dominate national wine production, the system is extremely flexible and subject to few restrictions – there are no regulations limiting yield, for example. Three kinds of origin may appear on the label: *indicación de procedencia* (indication of provenance); *indicación geografica* (geographic designation) for wines vinified and bottled in a region; *denominación de origen controlada* (a denomination corresponding to France's AOC) theoretically for wines of superior quality. An indication of origin may be included on the label if 100 per cent of the wine originates from the place mentioned. Grape variety may be indicated if this represents at least 85 per cent of the wine produced. Vintages are required to contain 85 per cent wine from the year in question.

Australia

Most Australian wines indicate the name of the grape variety, and the wine's geographical provenance. Blending on an industrial scale is a widespread practice in Australia, and while it is principally confined to entry-level wines, some of the country's greatest wines (such as Grange) are made this way. Australia has operated a regulatory system of Geographical Indications (GI) since 1993; this divides the wine-making areas into zones, regions and sub-regions and the latter, the most localized specification, are more logically arranged according to terroir. *See also* the chart on page 473.

DID YOU KNOW...?

***The illicit use of names such as Chablis and Champagne was common practice** in the 1970s in North America, Australia, and elsewhere. Regulatory bodies such as the INAO in France and the European Union have since put a stop to it. In the first instance, such agreements covered only wines intended for export, but they were extended to include the domestic market. Australia totally banned the use of the names Champagne and Burgundy; but in the United States there are still several American brands of sparkling wine that use the name Champagne. The term* champaña *has been generally suppressed in Argentina, and you now are much more likely to see* méthode champenoise *or* méthode traditionelle *printed on the labels.*

ON THE LABEL Producers are now obliged to include their address on the label, but are not required to reveal the origins of the grapes; if they choose to do so, 85 per cent of the grapes must come from the place indicated. The same is true of the grape variety. If several regions or varieties are indicated, they must be listed in descending order of importance.

New Zealand

New Zealand producers have used French and German names to identify their style of wines for many years. Today, listing the grape variety remains common practice but mentioning the region of production is becoming the rule rather than the exception, not least as certain regions, such as Marlborough, have made quite a name for themselves. An appellation system, the Geographical Indication Registration Act, was initiated in 2006, but is yet to achieve compliance within the industry, and more than anything else, the labelling rules can be thought of as the legislation governing the wines. If a grape variety, a year or a region is indicated, an 85 per cent rule has applied since 2007. The district of Wairapara, including the town of Martinborough, which has imposed its own rules, features a small adhesive label detailing '100% Martinborough Terrace Appellation Committee', certifying that the wine is 100 per cent from that region.

South Africa

The 'Wine of Origin' system (WO) introduced in 1973 divides the vineyards into four different production zones: the largest being the geographical area that crosses several regions (Western Cape is the best known by far), followed by the regions, sub-regions (districts), and areas (wards), in decreasing order of size (*see also* p.467). The delimitation of the zones is determined by geographic, topologic, and geologic factors. Any winery wishing to benefit from a WO appellation must subject wines to constant sensory tests and chemical analysis from harvesting to bottling, thanks to organoleptic and chemical analysis, and a tasting for certification. The WO also regulates labelling: the 85 per cent rule applies if a grape variety or year is mentioned, with a 100 per cent rule in operation if a zone of production is indicated. The number of wines submitting to these checks is growing all the time.

> Vines belonging to Drayton's Family Wines in the Hunter Valley, Australia.

HOW TO 'DECODE' A WINE LABEL

Reading a wine label is like looking at its passport or identity card. For the producer, the label should tempt someone to buy the bottle as well as provide a certain amount of information required by law. For the consumer, the label should provide enough information to make an informed choice.

A wine's passport

Wine labelling is subject to strict regulation by public authorities working in conjunction with professional bodies, and addresses one chief concern: providing the consumer with the best information possible about the product's origins and its principal characteristics. Some of the details included also serve to provide the authorities with data for fiscal use.

The label's first duty is to certify the authenticity of the wine, ensuring that it was produced according to the winemaking regulations in force for a given producer and category of wine. In France, the *direction générale de la concurrence, de la consommation et de la répression des fraudes* (DGCCRF, dealing with competition, consumer information, and fraud) and the customs and excise authorities are entitled to check whether a wine matches the details provided on its label, and if the label itself conforms to regulations.

The label 'speaks' to the buyer, who is often faced with multiple shelves of bottles. *It guarantees the authenticity of the wine and allows government authorities to check its conformity with current regulations.*

Useful information

The information given on the front label, and the rear label where present (*see* p.109), provides the consumer with certain information. Apart from the origins of the wine, it may provide details of the year of harvest. It also will show the name of the producer or bottler, or whether it comes from a cooperative, etc. It is worth remembering that only certain phrases, such as *mis en bouteille au château* (estate-bottled), are legally protected. Others, such as *vieilles vignes* (old vines), are terms specific to the producer who made the wine and are really no more than marketing devices.

Regulations governing wine labels are in a constant state of flux, as demonstrated by recent declarations of the European Union with respect to appellations (*see* p.95) and regulations for organic farming (see p.58).

The capsule and the cork

Most bottles carry a capsule, also known as a 'foil'. In France, they are marked with an excise stamp indicating the registered winemaker and region of production, and confirming that the wine is licensed for distribution by the excise authorities. French bottles without a capsule must feature a paper excise stamp (see p.127). To combat fraud, a number of winemakers have resorted to stamping their corks, detailing the origins of the wine (either the name of the winery or appellation) and the year. Sparkling appellation wines such as Champagne and the crémants are obliged to include their appellation on the cork. Some countries (South Africa, Austria, and Portugal) feature a 'ribbon' supplied by the government, which is attached over the cork or capsule.

> The capsule, known as the *capsule représentative des droits* (CRD) in France, proves that the wine may be legally distributed.

DID YOU KNOW...?

The name, business name, or address of the bottler must be encoded if it includes all or part of the name of an appellation. *A French wine or an IGP wine, bottled and sold by a merchant in a region whose name is also an appellation may mention the place of bottling only as a postal code,* e.g. IGP Pays d'Oc, bottled by ... in 33000 *instead of* bottled in Bordeaux.

> Wine labels can be plain or creative and even signed works of art, and form the object of many collections.

Mandatory details

CATEGORY. In France, wine belongs to one of two categories: wine without geographic designation, in other words *vins de France*, and wine produced in specified regions, *i.e.* IGP wines and protected appellations (AOP; *see also* p.95).

In the case of wine with no geographic designation, the label features either '*vin de France*' or '*vin de la communauté européenne*' (European Community wine). IGP wines are indicated by 'IGP ou vin de pays' followed by the name of the geographical area (e.g. IGP Atlantique). AOP wines must include their appellation on their labels; it may be a region, such as Alsace or Champagne, or a more specific area. In Burgundy, the appellations first list the region, then the villages located within the region, and then, like the last in a series of Russian dolls, the individual estate, which may be very small indeed (*see* p.276). In such cases, the consumer is expected to know that Échézeaux, for example, is a small but prestigious estate in Burgundy.

BOTTLER'S NAME AND ADDRESS. The label generally shows if the wine was bottled where it was made; in such cases it is legally entitled to bear the inscription *mis en bouteille à* (or *de*) *la propriété* (or possibly either *au/du domaine* or *au/du château*), all of which mean the same thing. It is worth bearing in mind that French law considers a cooperative as an extension of a producer; if an individual producer's wine is made individually but bottled by a local cooperative, the producer will still have the right to print *mis en bouteille à la propriété* on the label. If a wine is bottled outside the estate by a third party, the label must bear the inscription *mis en bouteille par...* (bottled by...) followed by the bottler's name and postal code. Inscriptions such as *mis en bouteille dans nos chais* (or *par nos soins*) generally indicate that it is a wine blended from multiple sources.

NOMINAL VOLUME. Detailed in litres, centilitres, or millilitres. The most common value is 750 ml, although the half-bottle (375 ml) and the magnum (1.5 litres) are found. Sweet wines (straw wines, late-harvested wines, etc.) are sometimes sold in 330 ml or 500 ml bottles. The *clavelin* (620 ml) is used only for Jura *vin jaune* ('yellow wine', *see* p.307). Bordeaux and Champagne wines are also to be found in bottles sizes up to 15 litres, known in Champagne as a 'nebuchadnezzar' (*see also* box on p.86).

ALCOHOLIC STRENGTH. Expressed in percentage of alcohol by volume (ABV). Most wines have an alcohol content of between 11 and 14% ABV, but some may have a lower strength, such as Italy's Moscato d'Asti at 6% ABV, or be considerably more potent, such as natural sweet wines. (Banyuls can be more than 20% ABV.)

THE COUNTRY OF PRODUCTION, *e.g.* 'Product of France'. This category was once reserved for wines intended for export, but is now obligatory for all wines.

HEALTH WARNINGS. An indication of the presence of sulphites, *i.e.* sulphur compounds used as preservatives, was initially required on labels of bottles destined for English-speaking

> Château Le Bon Pasteur is a Pomerol made by Michel Rolland, a leading winery consultant.

countries, but is now required on the front or rear label of all wine sold in Europe. The presence of residue from milk-or egg-based products which can be used to clarify wine must also be indicated. Similarly, a graphic warns against consumption of alcohol for pregnant women.

LOT NUMBER. Added to the label or printed directly onto the bottle as required by the producer or the merchant to make the specific bottle identifiable and traceable.

The main optional items

Optional details allow producers to include additional information about the nature of the wine, making the consumer's choice easier.

VINTAGE. Inclusion of the year of production, which sometimes features on a collar around the neck of the bottle, is optional for both AOC wines and IGP wines, but almost all producers mention it. Including the year for *vin de table* was not permitted for many years in France, but is now legal. If the vintage is specified, at least 85 per cent of the wine, whatever its category, must come from the year indicated.

TRADEMARK. This may be a simple logo (a proper name followed by the ® sign, for example) or something more complex (winery name and location, such as *Domaine* X, *Château* Y, etc.). The terms *château*, *clos*, and *abbaye* may be used only for AOP wines and must refer to an actual place that exists on a survey map. The terms *domaine* and *mas* cannot be applied to *vins de France*. Only the phrase *mis en bouteille au château* or its various equivalents will guarantee that the wine is estate-produced.

TRADITIONAL EXPRESSIONS. Terms such as *cru classé*, *premier cru*, *grand cru*, and *cru* are traditional monikers associated with a limited number of wines and defined by appropriate legislation. Bordeaux *crus classés* refer to a hierarchical grading of estates (*see* pp.250–1). Burgundy's *premiers crus* and *grands crus*, much like the *grand crus* of Alsace, denote a classification by place and local character (*see* pp.279 and 305). In Champagne, the monikers refer to the villages (*see* box, p.298). Provence's *crus classés* date back to the 1950s when they were instituted by the Côtes-de-Provence appellation (see p.348).

GRAPE VARIETY. The inclusion of grape variety for AOC wines in France varies by appellation. Always included in Alsace, it appears on rare occasions in Bordeaux (for wines made with Sauvignon Blanc) and occasionally in Burgundy (for wines made with Pinot Noir). At least 85 per cent of an IGP wine must be made from the grape variety indicated on the label. If it is a blend, the various varieties used are generally listed on the back label. Inclusion of grape variety is also optional for *vins de France*. In the great majority of the world's wine-producing countries, more emphasis is often placed on the name of the grape or grapes than on the appellation, and this features systematically on the label. Legislation in European countries prescribes a minimum percentage (between 85 and 100 per cent of the grape variety indicated).

VINEYARD TERMS. Words such as 'owner', 'grower' etc. may optionally be included (for Champagne, *see* box on p.301).

What is 'retreat'?

In order to benefit from a registered appellation of origin in France, a wine must combine certain recognized qualities when tasted and analyzed. If it fails to live up to the appellation's criteria, but is wine of a 'sound and sellable' quality, the producer may request for the wine to *replier* (literally, to 'retreat') into a larger and less demanding appellation in the same area. A Pauillac, for example, may 'retreat' to a Médoc or a Bordeaux, and a Chablis to a Burgundy. This said, surplus wine that exceeds authorized yields is never subjected to such a 'retreat' and so-called *déclassé* (declassified) wine is best avoided since it is never what it claims to be.

PRODUCTION METHODS. When a wine has been produced organically, the winemaker may indicate this on the label (in France) with the European logo (*see* image above). In such cases, it is also required to detail the name of the certificating organization (usually Ecocert in France). Terms such as *agriculture raisonnée* or *vin naturel* are merely terms from the producer. Agriculture conforming to biodynamic standards may be certified by an organization (Demeter, Biodyvin); but, in contrast to organic farming, such certification is not compulsory and the term 'biodynamic' is not protected.

Other optional details

VENDANGES MANUELLES (handpicked). To include this on the label, the winemaker must have had the wine grapes harvested manually.

CUVÉE NON FILTRÉE (unfiltered). This term means that the wine has been fined, but not filtered (*see* p.76). The larger deposit thrown by an unfiltered wine is never detrimental to its taste.

ÉLEVAGE SUR LIES (or similar; matured on the lees). In regions such as Nantes in the Loire Valley, the lees are not removed (by racking). Instead, the wine is left 'on the lees' until it is bottled (*see* p.76). The wine thus retains residual carbon dioxide created during fermentation, which accentuates its lively texture.

VIEILLI EN FÛT (DE CHÊNE). Aged in (oak) casks; these are usually *vins de garde* (wines for laying down). This maturation produces vanilla, woody or toasted notes, especially if new casks have been used. Often more expensive, such wines are not always of a better quality, as the notes introduced by the wood can 'drown out' other aromas.

OFFICIAL DISTINCTIONS. If a wine has won awards or competitions, these distinctions may legally be recorded on the label, although the wine should be from the vintage recognized. Such distinctions are reserved in France for appellation wines and IGP wines. For the merit of such awards, *see* p.121.

ILLUSTRATION ON THE LABEL. In France, the image of an estate building or the residence of the proprietor featured on a label must be of an actual structure, even if it is a reproduction of a work of art. In either case, a representation of any *château* other than the one whose name the wine bears is not permitted.

RESIDUAL SUGAR LEVEL. Inclusion of terms such as *sec*, *demi-sec*, *moelleux*, or *liquoreux* (dry, medium dry, medium sweet, sweet) is not obligatory. This can lead to occasional surprises, notably with Alsace wines in which sugar content is never certain, except when identified as botrytized or late harvest. Nonetheless, if the term is mentioned on the label, it must correspond to a precise residual sugar level defined in regulations.

> A wine's vintage may be listed on a label placed on the shoulder of the wine bottle.

> Bugey-Cerdon wines are *pétillant*, and they are often rosé.

AOC Champagne

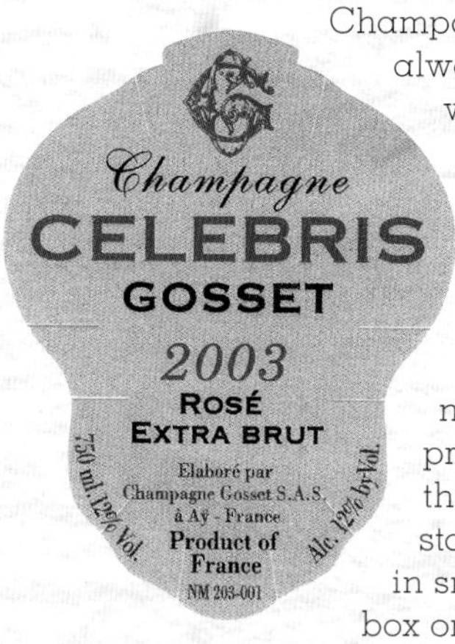

Champagne is always an AOC wine, even if not stated on the label. The brand and the name (or business name) of the producer and the appropriate status (generally in small type; see box on p.301) must always be accurately displayed. Terms such as *cuvée réservée* and *tête de cuvée* are more commercial than official in nature. Vintage-dated wines are required to be from the year indicated and to have been aged for at least three years. The label may also feature *blanc de blancs* when the Champagne has been made exclusively from Chardonnay grapes, or *blanc de noirs* when made from Pinot Noir, Pinot Meunier, or a blend of these two varieties.

Non-regulated features

These are details that convey information the authority of which is based on nothing beyond the good faith of the claimant.

VIEILLES VIGNES (old vines). Old vines generally yield a more concentrated wine in that it is made from a smaller, and thus better, yield. But since the consumer is unable to determine the age of the vines, such a detail is of no real use.

***CUVÉE SPÉCIALE, RÉSERVE EXCEPTIONNELLE, GRANDE CUVÉE*, ETC.** These terms imply that the wine represents the best quality (and highest price) from a given producer, either because the wine is from an exceptional location or from especially mature vines. In either case, such assertions are founded only on the good faith of the winery.

CRÈME DE TÊTE. This term is applied to Sauternes wines made using the first selection of fruit from the harvest. The wines are made only with overripe grapes and are extremely sweet.

GRAND VIN DE (followed by the name of a region). Such claims are largely advertising. This should not to be confused with a *grand vin* of a *cru classé* Bordeaux château, which denotes a wine of great quality. In such cases, the phrase *grand vin* must be followed by the name of the region concerned, *e.g.* *Grand Vin de Bordeaux*.

SERIAL NUMBER. Its presence on the label implies a certain rarity for the wine, but this may be relative.

Sparkling wines

The term 'sparkling wine' denotes a wine containing carbon dioxide under pressure, which is released and effervesces when the wine is opened. French sparkling wines are divided into *vins perlants*, *vins pétillants*, and *vins mousseux*, in ascending order of effervescence. The lattermost category includes Champagnes

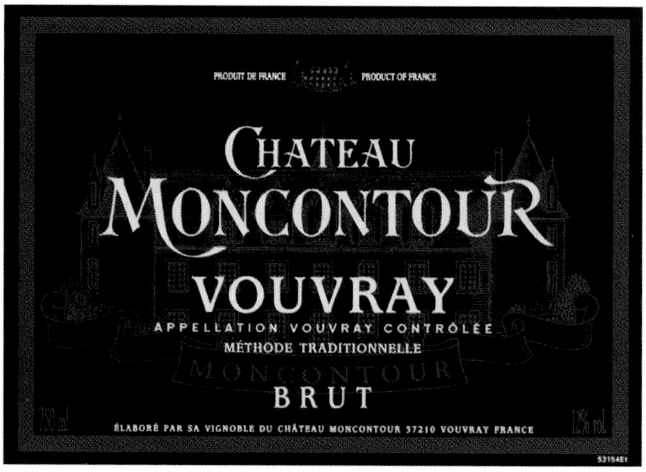

> The label for a sparkling Vouvray.

Classification varies by country

The information contained on wine labels produced in most countries is now more or less the same: appellation name, nominal container volume, grape variety, the name of the producer or seller, the alcohol content by volume, any health warnings, and country of origin. That said, while European regulations – even those determining the size of the lettering on the labels – are gradually converging, the hierarchy of the information detailed on the label is very different from country to country. On Spanish, Portuguese, and Greek labels, for example, the name of the seller or of the individual wine may feature more prominently than the appellation. In most New World countries, the appellation often takes second place to the grape variety.

and other *crémant* styles. The labels of *vins perlants* and *vins pétillants* are not subject to any particular regulations.

DOSAGE. This term refers to the residual sugar level (expressed in grams per litre). In other words, it is the sucrose content of the sugar mixture that is added after disgorgement that gives the wines a more or less sweet taste. Depending on the residual sugar level, the wine may be classified as: *doux* (more than 50 g/l), *demi-sec* (between 33 and 50 g/l), *sec* (between 17 and 35 g/l), *extra-dry* (between 12 and 20 g/l), *brut* (less than 15 g/l), or *extra-brut* (less than 6 g/l). Levels of less than 3 g/l may be classified as *brut nature*, *non dosé*, or *dosage zéro* (all meaning 'no added sugar').

PRODUCTION METHOD. The vast majority of quality sparkling wines are produced using the secondary fermentation method first used in Champagne. The label may thus read *méthode traditionnelle*, a term that has replaced *méthode champenoise*. Some French wine regions, such as Gaillac, Limoux (Blanquette), and Savoie prefer another method that achieves sweeter wine with fewer bubbles: young wines are bottled before all the residual sugar has turned into alcohol, and fermentation continues in the bottle, releasing carbon dioxide. Labels here may mention *méthode ancestrale* or *méthode rurale*. A slight variation on this method is used for Clairette de Die sparkling wine from the Rhône, and has become known as the *méthode dioise*.

CRÉMANT. First applied to semi-sparkling (*demi-mousse*) Champagne, the term *crémant* has been used since 1992 in France to identify sparkling wines with a geographic appellation and a traditional production method. The foremost French appellations are the *crémants* de Bourgogne, d'Alsace, du Jura, de Bordeaux, de Die, de Limoux, and de Savoie. Further afield in Europe you will also find Crémant du Luxembourg, Cava in Spain, Sekt in Germany, and various wines labelled *metodo classico* in Italy.

Rear label

Although it is not a compulsory feature, the label on the back of the bottle is often the wine's true passport, with the label on the front serving more as a simple business card. Positioned on the opposite side of the bottle, and sometimes even larger than the front label, it conveys information as varied as the grape variety, the characteristics of the parcel of land from which the wine was sourced, the manner and length of its maturation, the ideal serving temperature, and even some serving suggestions for food that the wine will complement. The rear label is extremely common in English-speaking countries and is catching on more and more in France.

TRUE OR FALSE?

No obligatory or optional details are included on the rear label.

FALSE. Some winemakers use the rear label to include both required and optional information, while the front label is used to attract consumer attention with an image such as a reproduction of a painting or a branded wine name. This approach is also used for basic table wine in order to hide its modest origins or its perceived poor image.

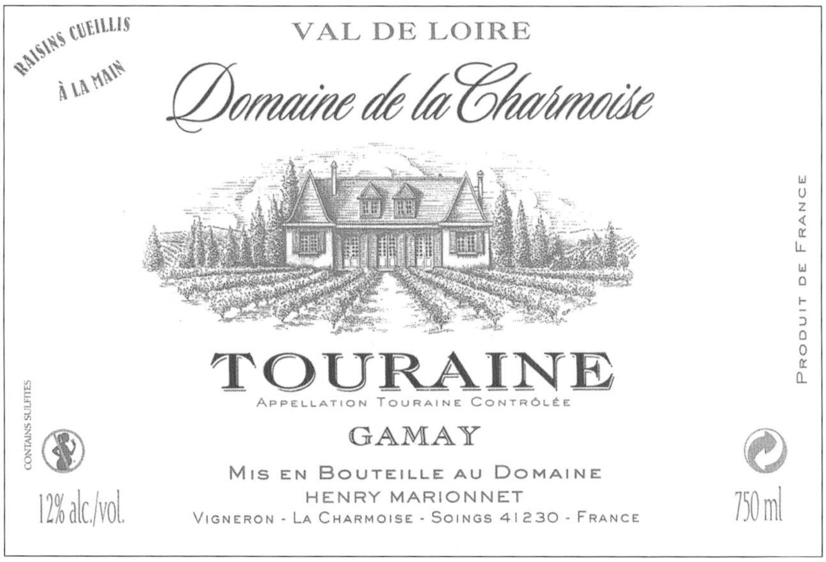

> The label...

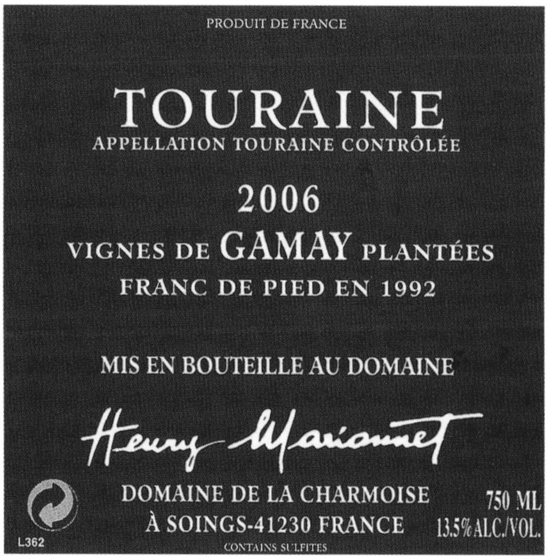

> ... and the back label.

SOME EXAMPLES OF DIFFERENT LABELS

As a wine's passport, the label has evolved in significant ways. After the inclusion of required information, optional details – which are nevertheless regulated – and statements and terms that amount to little more than marketing, there is little room left on the classic label. As a result, many bottles now have a label on the back too, featuring even more information aimed at promotion or helping the consumer understand the product.

BORDEAUX WINE

BURGUNDY

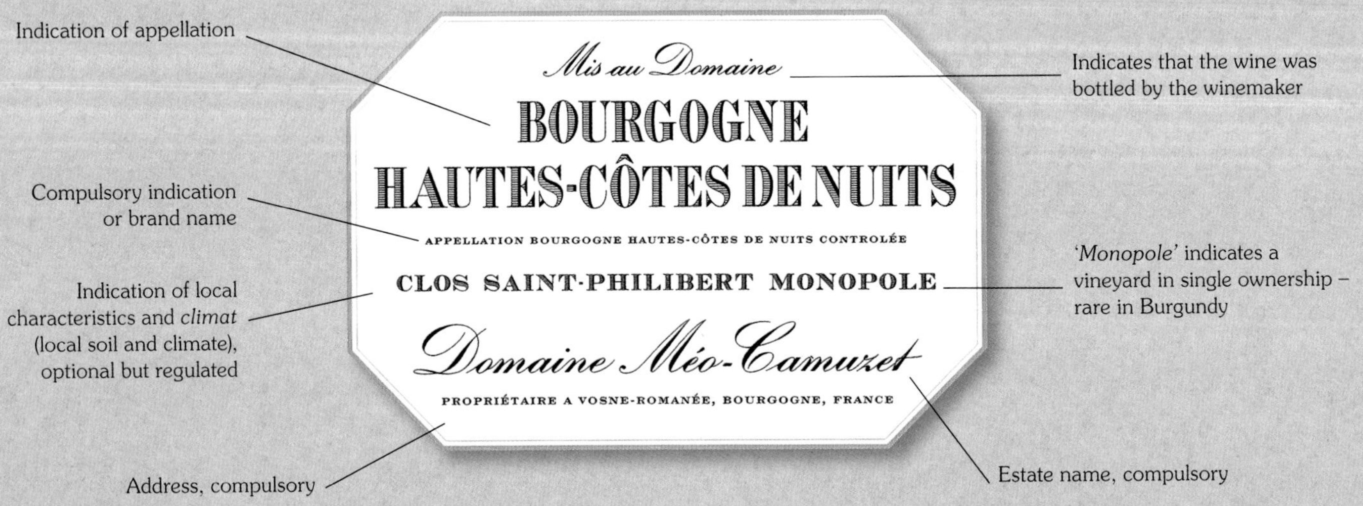

CHAMPAGNE

ALSACE

All other compulsory details appear on the back label.

VIN DE PAYS
(Indication géographique protégée)

Label

Back label

SPANISH WINE

Optional design

Name of the wine

Appellation, compulsory

Regulated, indicating that the wine is at least three years old, of which 12 months were spent in barrel

Denominación de origen calificada, compulsory, indicating that the wine corresponds in category to an AOC

Trademark, producer or brand name

Regulated, indicating that the wine was made, matured, and bottled at the estate (even if the grapes may have come from other estates)

All other compulsory details are included on the back label

ITALIAN WINE

Optional design; should generally represent an existing building or site

Name of a line of wines, regulated

Indication of origin, regulated, must be followed by *Denominazione di origine controllata et garantita* (DOCG). 'Classico' indicates that the wine is from the appellation's historic heartland

Optional but regulated; generally indicates that the wine has been matured for two years, of which three months were in the bottle (this period may vary by appellation)

Producer's name, compulsory, and also the brand name, optional

All other compulsory details are included on the back label

GERMAN WINE

AUSTRALIAN WINE

All other compulsory details feature on the back label

CHILEAN WINE

AMERICAN WINE

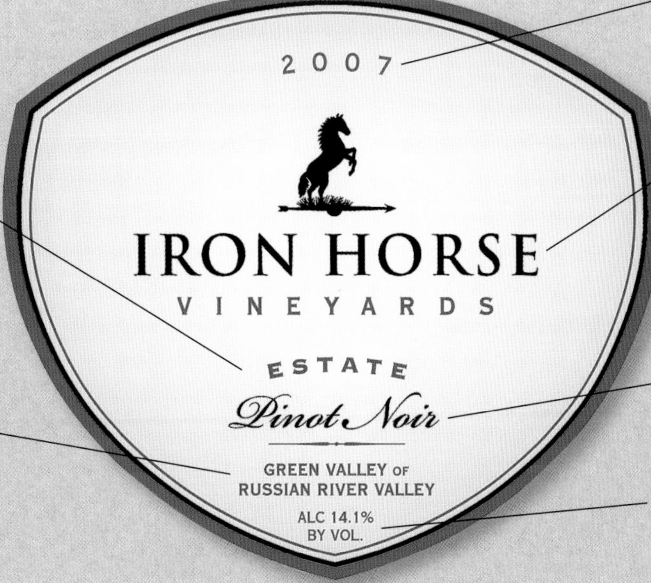

All other compulsory details are featured on the back label

LABELS OLD AND NEW

Understated or eyecatching, classic or modern, original labels are as diverse as the wines they represent. Some of the most beautiful examples are even collector's items.

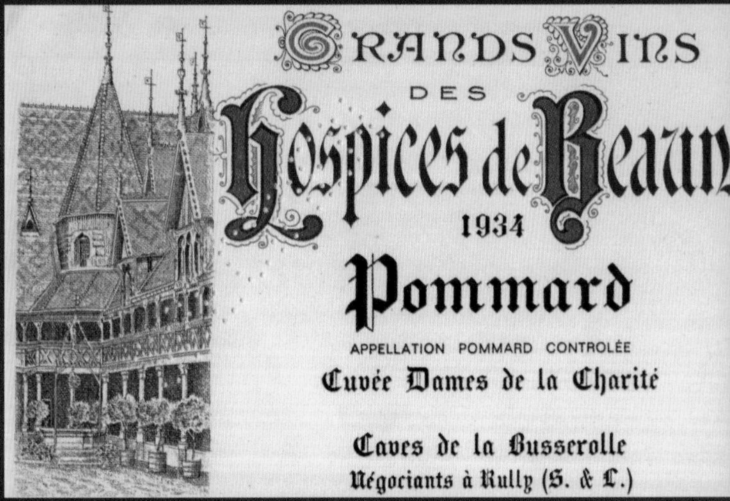

Château
Leyritz Moncassin
Rosé
Vincent DELMOTTE
Propriétaire
SCEA SOVIMON
47700 LEYRITZ MONCASSIN
FRANCE
BUZET
APPELLATION BUZET CONTROLÉE
12% vol.
MIS EN BOUTEILLE AU CHATEAU
750 ml
PRODUIT DE FRANCE
CONTAINS SULPHITES

Cuvée du Poilu
CÔTES DU RHÔNE
APPELLATION CONTRÔLÉE
1918
1988
MIS EN BOUTEILLE PAR LES PRODUCTEURS RÉUNIS A F 26790-357
CAVE LA ROMAINE
75cl
12,5 % Vol.
84110 VAISON - LA - ROMAINE
PRODUIT DE FRANCE

CUVÉE SAINT-VALENTIN
SAINT-AMOUR
APPELLATION SAINT-AMOUR CONTRÔLÉE
MIS EN BOUTEILLE PAR
LOUIS TÊTE À 69430 BEAUJEU - FRANCE
PRODUIT DE FRANCE
13% vol 75 cl

VIN des AMPHORES
SYRAH
VIN DE PAYS D'OC
Les Coteaux de Saint-Cyr
MIS EN BOUTEILLE
PAR LA S.C.V. SALLELES D'AUDE
PRODUIT DE FRANCE
12%vol.
75 cl

CUVÉE
PASTEUR
ARBOIS
APPELLATION ARBOIS CONTRÔLÉE
12,5%Vol.
75cl.e
PRODUIT ET MIS EN BOUTEILLE PAR
HENRI MAIRE AU CHATEAU BOICHAILLES 39600 ARBOIS JURA FRANCE

LOIRE
VALLÉE DU RHÔNE
SUD-OUEST

HOW TO BUY WINE

TOOLS FOR BUYING WINE

In order to choose from the huge range of wines available, wine enthusiasts may turn to expert media and buying guides. While these are useful, remember that, ultimately, the opinions presented depend on the writers' own preferences.

Buying guides

Every year, buying guides are published with a view to helping consumers find the best value for their money, or simply the best in a particular category. Some aim to outline the best estates or the best wines for each appellation or *terroir*, others focus on low-priced wines or wines available in supermarkets. The guides differ primarily in their presentation. For some, it is the tasting notes of a given vintage that are a priority, while others focus on regions and producers as a whole. One guide may be based on the opinions of famous critics, while another relies on a panel of experts. To be credible, the tastings need to be carried out blind.

Are their recommendations reliable?

All guides judge samples that they receive from producers, which leaves the door open to potential variability in that producers will be sure to send only their best wines. In general, the tastings are taken very seriously and the experts judge the wine sent to them objectively, particularly given their level of experience. But the fact remains that any assessment of a wine involves the subjective element of a taster's personal preferences, which reflect the taster's gustatory habits. In addition, no general review can claim to be exhaustive. If a wine is not listed in relevant guides, this does not necessarily mean that it is of poor quality. However, it is rare for an excellent wine to remain unnoticed for long.

Accepting these reservations, buying guides remain valuable tools for the variety that they offer and the practical information that they provide. They also are a useful indicator of general trends in prices and other developments in the wine world, such as the emergence of interesting new producers, or changes in fashions or winemaking practices that affect the styles of wines in a particular area.

Wines that have been praised as being excellent value often disappear quickly from winery inventories. *Enthusiasts may be able to find them at wine retailers or in restaurants, but in the latter case the price will be different.*

Some leading wine guides

ANDREA ROBINSON'S WINE BUYING GUIDE FOR EVERYONE (Andrea Robinson). This reference title from a high-profile master sommelier and television host offers lively, practical advice on successful wine buying and food pairing. Learn more at her fun, constantly updated website: Andreawine.com.

EXPLORING WINE (Steven Kolpan, et al.). The wine textbook for the prestigious Culinary Institute of America. It's a weighty tome with all the basics, but also amazing reference material on the art and science of matching food and wine.

HUGH JOHNSON'S POCKET WINE BOOK (Hugh Johnson, et al.) The world's most popular quick reference for wine has been published annually for 40 years. A stable of top contributors

The mainstream press and the wine press

In France, there is now an annual publishing ritual. Every autumn, when the supermarkets run big wine promotions, most mainstream weekly and monthly reviews and magazines devote special issues to wine. Since they are aimed at the general public, the articles are usually written for novices. Serious wine enthusiasts are likely to prefer the specialized wine press, even though the authors of the mainstream articles and issues are frequently the same as those who write for the specialized press.

> A wine that you don't like is too expensive, no matter what its price. But there are good wines in every price category.

DID YOU KNOW...?

A competition medal is not always a guarantee of quality. *There are some very serious competitions, both at an international level (the Brussels International Wine Competition, Vinalies, IWC, Decanter), the San Francisco Chronicle Wine Competition) and at a regional level. But among the 80 competitions held each year in France, there is a lack of rigour in some – especially the regional events. In addition, there is no guarantee that when a medal is awarded to a winery, it will appear only on the label of the particular wine that won at the tasting, although the best competitions do exercise controls.*

> Tasting wines regularly allows you to define your own preferences and so to make better purchases.

from around the planet makes it authoritative and up-to-date with definitions, vintage ratings, and more.
OLDMAN'S GUIDE TO OUTSMARTING WINE (Mark Oldman). This very popular title presents wine know-how in just over 100 very short chapters. While full of solid information, it's also presented in a fun, lighthearted style – with 'cheat sheet' summaries, recommendations, and pronunciations.
THE OXFORD COMPANION TO WINE (Jancis Robinson). More than 800 pages of erudite entries covering everything from fundamentals to esoterica, this is widely regarded as the leading encyclopedia on wine. An essential reference for members of the trade studying for advanced qualifications.
SECRETS OF THE SOMMELIERS (Raj Parr and Jordan Mackay). Industry experts Parr and Mackay employ anecdotes and stories to weave together practical advice on wine from the realm of elite sommeliers. As the subtitle indicates, they show readers how to think and drink like a pro.
WINDOWS ON THE WORLD COMPLETE WINE COURSE (Kevin Zraly). A 25-year bestseller developed from 35 years of teaching at New York City's number-one wine school. Beyond the expected basics, Zraly's work on interpreting labels is particularly helpful, and a series of end-of-chapter quizzes help readers retain what they learn.
THE WINE BIBLE (Karen MacNeil). Journalist, television host, and educator MacNeil has assembled nearly 1,000 pages of comprehensive yet readable wine reference material on all key topics for both novice and expert alike. Skillfully done: very clear and appealing.
WINE FOR DUMMIES (Ed McCarthy and Mary Ewing-Mulligan). Master of Wine Ewing-Mulligan and her husband apply the wildly popular 'Dummies' format to demystify wine for the masses. Twenty quick chapters bring even the most nervous newbie up to speed.
WORLD ATLAS OF WINE (Hugh Johnson and Jancis Robinson). Dozens of colourful maps detailing the world's leading wine regions are accompanied by statistics on local terroir – latitudes, elevations, annual rainfall, etc – and excellent explanatory comments. Another top resource for serious students of wine.

The merits of tasting

To 'understand' a wine, nothing beats tasting (*see* pp.203–25). It is very difficult to obtain an accurate idea of the style of a wine purely from its description. We therefore cannot recommend enough that enthusiasts take advantage of the many opportunities that are available for tasting.
WHERE CAN WINES BE TASTED? Tasting events are organized across the country by regional wine associations and promotional bodies. Plus, there are several great events produced by leading wine publications. Tastings are also offered by wine retailers, and there are wine clubs that provide beginners with a general introduction or serious wine lovers with a deeper understanding of specific wines. Tastings at producers can be an excellent education. But while they are a good opportunity to sample a wine you tend to feel ill at ease if you don't make a purchase. In which case, it's a good idea to buy just a few bottles and to taste them again at home before making a more substantial purchase. Get into the habit of making notes during each tasting: this will enable you to gain maximum benefit from the many recommendations.

Some simple criteria for choosing wine

Wine enthusiasts need to choose on the basis of their own criteria, from the vast number of wines listed in guides. What types and styles of wine capture their interest (see pp.154–61)? In what price range? Are they looking for a wine to drink immediately, as part of their regular consumption? Or is it a wine to lay down in the cellar, which will be saved for a special occasion? Taking these factors into account will help considerably in making a choice.

THE PRICE OF WINE

While the price of a bottle is on the whole supposed to reflect the quality of the wine, it also depends on its reputation, reviews in guides and, ultimately, supply and demand.

The wine hierarchy

A theoretical hierarchy is applied to wine across Europe, which in France starts with *vins de France,* wines with no indication of specific origin, and goes right up to the prestigious French appellations and estates, with wines that can demand hundreds of euros, or even more. Generally, a long-standing reputation equates to a higher price. While the *vins de France* and IGP categories are in theory less expensive than the AOP/AOC wines, because yields are higher, some wines in these categories renowned for their quality are sold at prices equal or superior to some wines with protected appellation status.

The value of an appellation

Each European appellation, or wine-producing area, has a benchmark price set by demand. This is the price per barrel or hectolitre (approximately 26 gallons) at which transactions between producers and *négociants* are carried out. The system is particularly relevant in regions in which production is high (such as Bordeaux, Languedoc, and the Rhône Valley) and where a substantial proportion of the wine is bought and marketed through *négociants* or cooperative cellars. It is less important in areas where most of the production is sold in bottles at the estate, such as in Alsace. Displayed in the local newspaper, an appellation's average price is based on its reputation, its previous prices, the quantity of wine available, the quality of the vintage, and demand.

Various other factors also contribute to determining the retail prices of wines, such as the vagaries of fashion and the wine producer's reputation. Lastly, the price of a wine can depend on the way it is sold (direct, via supermarkets, specialist merchants, etc.).

Prices by wine-producing area

The following table offers guideline prices for a range of appellations in France and other countries, arranged by 'wine family' (*see* pp.154–61). These prices are for single bottles sold at the estate. These prices have been converted from the native currency into US dollars and pounds Sterling, but please note that prices will fluctuate according to exchange rates.

LIGHT, FRUITY RED WINES					
Coteaux-du-Lyonnais	< $7 (£4)	Vin de Savoie (except Mondeuse)	< $14 (£9)	Arbois	< $20 (£14)
Beaujolais	< $14 (£9)	Hautes-Côtes-de-Beaune	< $17 (£10)	Alsace Pinot Noir	< $20 (£14)
Touraine Gamay	< $20 (£14)	Côtes-du-Jura	< $18 (£11)	Hautes-Côtes-de-Nuits	< $20 (£14)
Bardolino	< $14 (£9)	Dôle (Switzerland)	< $18 (£11)	Burgundy	< $28 (£17)
Valpolicella	< $14 (£9)	Bourgueil	< $17 (£10)	Mâcon	< $28 (£17)
FULL-BODIED, FRUITY RED WINES					
Chianti	< $14 (£9)	Côtes-du-Rhône-Villages	< $17 (£10)	Saumur-Champigny	< $19 (£12)
Bordeaux, Bordeaux Supérieur	< $20 (£14)	Gaillac	< $17 (£10)	Languedoc	< $20 (£14)
		Bergerac	< $20 (£14)	Saint-Émilion	< $28 (£17)
Buzet	< $14 (£9)	Graves	< $20 (£14)	Crozes-Hermitage	< $28 (£17)
Fronton	< $14 (£9)	Pinotage (South Africa)	< $11 (£7)	Saint-Joseph	< $28 (£17)
Barbera d'Alba	< $14 (£9)	Bierzo	< $14 (£9)	Primitivo (Italy)	< $28 (£17)
Rioja (joven)	< $14 (£9)	St-Nicolas-de-Bourgueil	< $18 (£11)	Chilean Merlot	> $28 (£17)
GENEROUS, POWERFUL, COMPLEX RED WINES					
Pomerol	> $7 (£4)	Rioja (reserva)	< $28 (£17)	Saint-Émilion Grand Cru	< $40 (£25)
Côtes-du-Roussillon-Villages	< $14 (£9)	Californian Zinfandel (Sonoma, Napa Valley)	< $20 (£14)	Valpolicella Amarone	> $20 (£14)
Toro (Spain)	< $17 (£10)			Shiraz (Barossa Valley, Australia)	< $35 (£22)
Cahors	< $7 (£4)	Madiran	< $20 (£14)		
Minervois-la-Livinière	< $18 (£11)	Pécharmant	< $28 (£17)	Châteauneuf-du-Pape	> $28 (£17)
Corbières-Boutenac	< $20 (£14)	Priorat	< $28 (£17)	Malbec from Mendoza (top of the range)	> $40 (£25)
Douro	< $20 (£14)	Gigondas	< $35 (£22)		
SLEEK, TANNIC, COMPLEX RED WINES					
Bordeaux blends from Stellenbosch (South Arica)	< $14 (£9)	Cornas	> $17 (£10)	Saint-Julien	> $19 (£12)
		Pauillac	> $17 (£10)	Côte-Rôtie	> $28 (£17)
Chianti Classico	< $28 (£17)	Pessac-Léognan	> $17 (£10)	Hermitage	> $28 (£17)
Haut-Médoc	< $28 (£17)	Saint-Estèphe	> $17 (£10)	Brunello di Montalcino	< $55 (£35)
Bandol	> $14 (£9)	Saint-Émilion Grand Cru Classé	> $18 (£11)		
Margaux	> $14 (£9)	Barbaresco, Barolo	< $28 (£17)		

SLEEK, ELEGANT, COMPLEX RED WINES					
Mercurey	< $28 (£17)	Vosne-Romanée	> $35 (£22)	Gevrey-Chambertin	> $40 (£25)
Pommard	> $20 (£14)	Corton	> $40 (£25)	Great reds from Ribera del Duero	> $55 (£35)
Volnay	> $20 (£14)	Great reds based on Cabernet-Sauvignon from the Napa Valley	> $40 (£25)	Bolgheri Sassicaia	> $140 (£90)
Chambolle-Musigny	> $35 (£22)				
FRUITY, LIVELY ROSÉ WINES					
Luberon	< $14 (£9)	Côtes-de-Provence	< $8 (£5)	Bordeaux	< $10 (£6)
Rosé de Loire	< $7 (£4)	Corsica	< $14 (£9)	Coteaux-d'Aix-en-Provence	< $17 (£10)
Irouléguy	< $14 (£9)	Coteaux-Varois	< $17 (£10)	Fronton	< $20 (£14)
STRONGER, FULL-BODIED ROSÉ WINES					
Corbières	< $7 (£4)	Languedoc	< $14 (£9)	Tavel	< $20 (£14)
Côtes-du-Rhône	< $7 (£4)	Lirac	< $14 (£9)	Bandol	< $28 (£17)
Bordeaux Clairet	< $14 (£9)	Marsannay	< $17 (£10)	Rosé des Riceys	< $28 (£17)
LIVELY, LIGHT, DRY WHITE WINES					
Gros-Plant	< $11 (£7)	Bourgogne Aligoté	< $14 (£9)	Vin de Savoie (jacquère base)	< $14 (£9)
Bergerac	< $14 (£9)	Cour-Cheverny	< $14 (£9)	Petit Chablis	< $17 (£10)
Entre-Deux-Mers	< $14 (£9)	Touraine Sauvignon	< $14 (£9)	Vinho Verde	< $8 (£5)
Muscadet	< $7 (£4)	Côtes de Gascogne IGP	< $14 (£9)	Fendant and Chasselas (Switz.)	< $17 (£10)
Picpoul de Pinet	> $7 (£4)	Alsace Sylvaner	< $14 (£9)	Mâcon	> $14 (£9)
FRUITY, SUPPLE, DRY WHITE WINES					
Rueda	< $14 (£9)	Corsican wines	< $17 (£10)	Jurançon Sec	< $20 (£14)
Gaillac	< $14 (£9)	Arbois (Chardonnay or Sauvignon)	< $17 (£10)	Sancerre	< $20 (£14)
Côtes-de-Provence	< $14 (£9)	Graves	< $17 (£10)	Soave Classico	< $20 (£14)
Casablanca Sauvignon Blanc (Chile)	< $17 (£10)	Saumur	< $20 (£14)	Chablis	< $28 (£17)
		Dry Montlouis	< $20 (£14)	Pouilly-Fumé	< $28 (£17)
Penedès dry white	< $14 (£9)	Quincy	< $17 (£10)	New Zealand Sauvignon Blanc	< $28 (£17)
	–	Vin de Savoie Chignin Bergeron	< $20 (£14)	Rías Baixas	< $35 (£22)
SLEEK, FULL-BODIED, DRY WHITE WINES					
Grüner Veltliner from Wachau and Kamptal (Smaragd)	> $35 (£22)	Pessac-Léognan	> $17 (£10)	Chassagne-Montrachet	> $28 (£17)
		Napa Valley Chardonnay	< $35 (£22)	Hermitage	> $28 (£17)
Savennières	< $20 (£14)	Châteauneuf-du-Pape	> $20 (£14)	Pouilly-Fuissé	> $35 (£22)
Vouvray	< $28 (£17)	Meursault	> $20 (£14)	Puligny-Montrachet	> $40 (£25)
Chablis Premier Cru	< $28 (£17)	Chablis Grand Cru	> $28 (£17)	Montrachet	> $55 (£35)
VERY AROMATIC DRY WHITE WINES					
Alsace Muscat	< $14 (£9)	Alsace Gewurztraminer	< $20 (£14)	Condrieu	> $28 (£17)
Alsace Pinot Gris	< $14 (£9)	Fino or Manzanilla sherry	< $20 (£14)	Vin Jaune from the Jura	> $28 (£17)
Alsace Riesling	< $14 (£9)	Château-Chalon	> $28 (£17)	Argentinian Torrontès	< $17 (£10)
SEMI-DRY AND SWEET WHITE WINES					
Pacherenc-du-Vic-Bilh	< $14 (£9)	Cérons	< $28 (£17)	Riesling SGN	> $28 (£17)
Cadillac	< $17 (£10)	Vouvray Moelleux	< $28 (£17)	Sauternes	> $28 (£17)
Coteaux-du-Layon	< $28 (£17)	Late Harvest Riesling (VT)	< $35 (£22)	Hungarian Tokaji	> $28 (£17)
Jurançon	< $28 (£17)	Passito de Pantelleria	< $55 (£35)	Gewurztraminer SGN	> $35 (£22)
Monbazillac	< $28 (£17)	Barsac	> $28 (£17)	Pinot Gris SGN	> $35 (£22)
Montlouis Moelleux	< $28 (£17)	Gewurztraminer (VT)	> $28 (£17)	German Riesling Beerenauslese and Trockenbeerenauslese (Mosel, Rheingau)	> $70 (£45)
Ste-Croix-du-Mont	< $28 (£17)	Quarts-de-Chaume	> $28 (£17)		
NATURAL SWEET WINES AND FORTIFIED WINES					
Mireval Muscat	< $14 (£9)	Banyuls	> $14 (£9)	Muscat de Beaumes-de-Venise	< $28 (£17)
Muscat de Rivesaltes	< $14 (£9)	Rivesaltes	> $14 (£9)	Muscat de Frontignan	< $28 (£17)
Pineau des Charentes	< $20 (£14)	Macvin du Jura	< $28 (£17)	Rasteau	< $28 (£17)
Port	< $20 (£14)	Maury	< $28 (£17)		
SPARKLING WINES					
Lambrusco	< $10 (£6)	Vouvray	< $28 (£17)	Montlouis, Saumur	< $14 (£9)
Clairette de Die	< $14 (£9)	Blanquette de Limoux	< $14 (£9)	Crémant du Jura	< $14 (£9)
Crémant de Bordeaux	< $14 (£9)	Crémant d'Alsace	< $14 (£9)	Cava	< $17 (£10)
Gaillac	< $14 (£9)	Crémant de Bourgogne	< $14 (£9)	Champagne	> $18 (£11)
Prosecco	< $14 (£9)	Deutscher Sekt	< $17 (£10)	Moscato d'Asti	< $17 (£10)

BUYING FROM WINE SHOPS AND SUPERMARKETS

Most wines consumed at home today are bought in supermarkets. While the choice and prices are often attractive, information may be lacking, except for rare stores with dedicated wine department staff. A good wine retailer will offer sound advice and wines that are not available in supermarkets, although the prices are higher than in supermarkets.

Supermarkets

STRENGTHS. Price is, of course, their main strength. Due to centralized buying and low logistical costs, supermarkets offer very competitive prices in all wine categories. They are often lower than those of wine retailers, and sometimes even lower than those available at the winery itself. Faced with the growing demand for good wines, some supermarkets have hired highly qualified, specialized buyers. Others have entered into contracts with big wineries or even wine-producing regions in order to develop a good quality brand of their own. Progress has also been made regarding the display and storage of wines, especially in superstores. Bottles spend less time on the shelves exposed to light, but the policy can vary from one store to another in the same chain. Some supermarkets have even created fine wine 'cellar' areas where the wines are stored away from light at the correct temperature.

WEAKNESSES. Supermarkets receive the most criticism from wine producers. In order to get their wines stocked, they are forced not only to commit to large quantities, but also to commercial terms that could place the producer at risk financially in a difficult year. The large-scale distribution market therefore favours the bigger producers and *négociants*, and wine regions with high production volumes. Supermarkets may also be criticized for the way wine is displayed on the shelves without any real respect for region. Availability can also be an issue; a customer might find a good wine one week, and then learn that it is not available a few weeks later. Finally, in the absence of a salesperson to provide advice, you are left on your own to make sense of labels, armed with a good guide (*see* pp.104–15).

Today's market offers thousands of wines from all around the world. *Most purchases are made in supermarkets, where prices are usually the most competitive. Wine retailers offer specialized selections and valuable advice.*

Wine fairs and festivals at big retailers

Wine fairs or festivals organized by large retailers annually or bi-annually present some excellent opportunities. While there will always be both good and some less impressive wines on offer, genuine bargains can be found with a little searching. If in doubt, a wine from a good producer in a less good vintage will be a better buy than the reverse. It is a good idea to visit these events during their first few days of opening, as the best bargains tend to disappear very quickly. Take along a guidebook, wine supplement, a wine magazine (some of the leading magazines are *Wine Spectator*, *Wine Enthusiast*, *Wine & Spirits*, Robert Parker's *The Wine Advocate*, *Decanter*, and *The World of Fine Wine*), or an internet-enabled smart phone. They can all prove to be very useful.

> Wine retailers should always be able to help you discover interesting new wines.

> A wine merchant's shop in St-Émilion, France.

IN CONCLUSION. Most supermarkets today offer consumers a huge range of wines at very competitive prices. However, do not expect to discover some wonderful gem of a wine, since many producers choose, for image reasons, not to be represented in this segment of the market.

The independent wine retailer

For many wines, the wine retailer remains the main link between the producer and consumer. Some merchants have professional qualifications, although not all are officially recognized. A good wine retailer will impress with their accessibility, and their love and knowledge of wine. They may travel to individual wine regions and attend trade tastings regularly to find new and great value wines to offer their customers. Their range will include the classics, little-known wines, older vintages, seasonal wines, easy-drinking bottles, and wines to lay down. A wine merchant should be able to advise both the occasional buyer and the serious enthusiast.
VALUABLE ADVICE. Like a sommelier, the wine retailer's job is to help customers find the right balance between quality, price, and good food-pairing combinations. Like a personal adviser, they can help the neophyte with the mysteries of wine and offer regular tastings at their store. The services of a good wine merchant warrant slightly higher prices (between 10 and 20 per cent on average) than those of the supermarkets. However, not all wine merchants possess this ideal profile.

Wine retail chains

Halfway between the independent wine retailer and the supermarket, wine chain stores (such as Binny's in Illinois and Crown in Florida) attempt to combine the services of the former with the competitive prices of the latter. While prices are kept low by centralized purchasing, the service that you receive will depend on the manager and their team. Chains are found around many large cities and offer a good selection of all styles of wine in a wide range of prices.
ADDITIONAL SERVICES. Most chains organize tastings, sales promotions, and wine fairs. Some also offer detailed catalogues and special services such as the possibility of buying 'futures' or *en primeur* (*see* pp.128–9) wines for laying down (sometimes at prices lower than those available at the estate), home delivery, or express shipping of a bottle or case to friends.

DID YOU KNOW...?

Retailers often have their own brands. *To meet growing demand, many large retailers have created their own labels. These are wines from various sources, produced by cooperatives or négociants and bottled directly on behalf of a retailer. The quality of certain wines is often praised by critics. But the quality can also be variable and is often limited by the perceived need for low prices.*

BUYING FROM WINERIES

Direct purchasing has several advantages: in addition to possible discounts, it can offer an opportunity to discover little-known wines and to build a special relationship with a winemaker or a member of staff. But there are drawbacks.

Buying at the property

Buying at the property is sometimes a good way to obtain good wines that are not widely distributed, or possibly not distributed at all. In addition, establishing an ongoing relationship with staff at the property can sometimes lead to access to older vintages or special-edition bottlings.

THE RIGHT CONDITIONS. Visiting a winery offers the chance to learn how it is run. If you can take a tour, seeing a clean, well-organized cellar is a good sign. For a successful tasting, always make an appointment, especially around harvest time. If you like the wine, you will probably be happy to buy a few bottles. If you don't, you should not feel obliged to buy.

As it can be difficult to make an immediate decision, it is a good idea to sample a selection of wines from the same region at home before you visit, and before placing a big order.

Otherwise, wines that seemed enjoyable when tasted at the vineyard or cellar may subsequently reveal themselves to be quite ordinary. Knowing you made the right choice will be worth the effort made in advance.

SOME PRECAUTIONS. Visitors to French wine regions are advised not to buy wine without an invoice. All bottles should be clearly labelled and have a '*capsule-congé*,' a capsule with the government seal on it, showing that the relevant tax has been paid. Alternatively, they should be accompanied by an official document called a '*congé*' (*see* box). Do not let yourself be taken in by an offer of 'declassified wine,' which has no real meaning, since any wine that does not comply with the appellation regulations must be thrown out. If your purchases were to be officially inspected on your trip, you would be likely to receive a heavy fine.

WINE TASTINGS. Regional tasting events for the general public offer the chance to sample a wide range of wines. The friendly atmosphere makes them a convenient and enjoyable way to meet producers, and to taste a lot of wines in comparatively little time.

***Wine tourism is booming.** Wine trails are becoming more established across the world. They provide guidance on exploring a wine region, over a weekend or longer. Check out promotional websites for your favourite wine regions for more information.*

Buying from a cooperative

There are more than half a million grape growers in France, and millions across Europe. Not all market their own wine; some sell their grapes to a cooperative. Cooperatives offer a service to growers without much land or without the equipment to make and store wine. They will market the grower's entire production, either by delivering it in bulk to merchants or by selling the bottled wine themselves. They generally produce wines that offer good value. The best cooperatives pay the growers according to grape quality and encourage the planting of noble grape varieties, thereby contributing to improving a region's reputation for good quality wines.

Some growers are members of a cooperative that gives them a share of their production in the form of wine bottled with their own labels, which they can then sell. This practice is very common in Champagne, where many wines that are associated with a particular 'producer' are in fact produced by a cooperative, as the latter is legally considered

> Keeping notes and tasting wines several times helps you to make an informed choice.

Proof of 'congé' (clearance) is a legal requirement in France

Transporting wine in France is strictly regulated. A *'capsule-congé'* with a tax stamp must be affixed to the top of each bottle, to show that duties have been paid. Wine bought in bulk or in bottles without capsules must be accompanied by a *'congé'* (clearance certificate), issued by the wine producer or by the nearest tax office. This document should include the name of the vendor and the wine, the volume and number of containers, the consignee, and the method and duration of transportation. Transporting wine in France without clearance constitutes tax fraud and is punishable by a fine.

to be an extension of the property. In such cases, it is best to go directly to the cooperative where the prices are likely to be lower for an equivalent wine.

In bottles or in bulk?

The purchase of wine 'in bulk' (*i.e.* not in bottles) is now changing, not only for everyday drinking but also for some higher quality wines, and the Bag-in-Box system has replaced the old European 'Cubitainer' (a rigid plastic box), which can hold 3, 5, or 10 litres (between around 6 and 21 pints). The wine is prevented from coming into contact with air as the bag inside the box, which is equipped with a tap, gradually contracts as the wine is consumed. This ensures the wine keeps well, even for two weeks or more, providing the ambient temperature is reasonable (not more than 59°F (15°C). This packaging is now used by some wine producers, merchants, and cooperatives, as well as supermarkets. If you do still buy European wine in the older Cubitainer format, it should be consumed quickly. Buying in bulk generally gives you around 25 to 33 per cent more wine for the same price as bottled wine.

TRUE OR FALSE?

Buying from a winery is always less expensive.

FALSE. Buying directly from a winery, especially in large quantities, remains one of the most popular ways of obtaining good wine at an attractive price. However, not all producers discount like this, and some even discourage it by aligning their prices with those at wine retailers, in order to avoid unfair competition. On the other hand, the cost of transporting an order of a dozen bottles can have consequences on the price.

Transporting wine

Whatever colour it is, white, rosé or red, sudden changes in temperature should be avoided. When moving wine or taking delivery of wine, it is best to avoid periods of extreme heat or cold. Furthermore, wine is heavy: a case of 12 bottles weighs about 35 lbs (16 kg) – more if the cases are made of wood or if the winery uses heavier grade bottles. (Sparkling wine bottles are the heaviest.) If you are a serious shopper, it's a good idea to check your vehicle's loading capacity before filling your car, to avoid damaging the suspension.

Once the wine has safely arrived at its destination, the bottles should be checked and then placed directly in a cool, dark spot. Letting the wine rest for one to two weeks before drinking is recommended, or for several months for old vintages of fine wines. The above precautions also apply if you have the wine delivered, but the cost will be higher (*see* box, p.131).

> Traveling around a wine region and visiting wineries is a great way to learn about wine.

DID YOU KNOW...?

***Some European producers** sell a portion of their wine at depots on the outskirts of large towns. Bottles are simply displayed on pallets or in crates, and prices are often great. However, these big discount stores require a degree of caution from the wine enthusiast. It is important to pay attention to aspects such as the origin, packaging, and vintage of the wines, as well as the reputation of the producer. The words* 'mise en bouteilles à la propriété' *('bottled at the property') represent a guarantee of authenticity, but not quality.*

1

2

Buying wine futures or *en primeur*

Buying wine futures or *en primeur* is the purchase of wine – usually a top Bordeaux but also some Burgundies – before it has been released to the market. It is becoming less and less advantageous due to its speculative nature, with the risk that prices may not increase, or may even decrease.

THE PRINCIPLE

Wines of the most recent vintage, still being matured and not yet bottled, are sold by subscription on a preview basis. The prices can be lower than those listed when the wines finally become available on the open market around 18 months later. For example, a wine purchased *en primeur* in 2016 that will have been made from the 2015 harvest, will not be available to be supplied in bottles until end 2017. One could say that the *en primeur* system functions on a *quid pro quo* basis. The producer receives advance payment, and in return the purchaser *may* receive a discount on the future price of the wine. The procedure is straightforward: you agree to buy a certain quantity of the latest vintage while it is still in barrels at a fixed price per bottle. You pay half or the entire value of the order immediately, less VAT, and receive a certificate of reservation. The balance, with VAT, then becomes due on delivery. The terms of sale (quantity, possibility of split orders, delivery dates, etc.) depend on the producers or any intermediaries. Subscriptions usually open during the spring or, at the latest, during the summer following the harvest, for a certain proportion of the wine and for a limited period of two to three months. In the case of Bordeaux, prices are established at tastings in spring, which attract thousands of professionals from all over the world (wine merchants, sommeliers, cellarmen, journalists). The tastings are covered by the specialist media (***Wine Spectator***, ***Revue du Vin de France***, ***Bettane & Desseauve***, etc.). It is advisable to read their reports carefully before approaching producers or wine merchants. The prices of the wines vary every year depending on the quality of the vintage, the volumes produced, demand and the state of the world markets.

WHICH WINES ARE INVOLVED?

Traditionally, the *en primeur* system operates in Bordeaux; but, in recent years,

3

4

1. Vines at Château Lynch-Bages in Pauillac, one of the classified growths that may be purchased *en primeur*.
2. A cellar in Burgundy.
3. Sampling in the winery at Château Bon Pasteur in Pomerol.
4 and 5. In the spring, wine professionals taste wines that have just been made, so as to form an idea of their potential.

5

it has gained popularity in other wine regions such as Burgundy, the Rhône Valley, Alsace, and even Languedoc. In Bordeaux, some 200 wines (the classified growths, the *cru bourgeois, and others*) are involved. The most speculative investments are to be found towards the top of the price range, and these wines have seen their prices shoot up in value, encouraged by demand from the export markets led by the USA and China.

MANY ADVANTAGES

There can be advantages to this type of purchase, providing first of all, that you are dealing with an honest and reliable vendor. Buying *en primeur* is often the best way of obtaining a wine below its market price once bottled. It is possible to see savings of 20 to 30 per cent on the final sale price, depending on the year. Buying this way ensures that you obtain a wine that may later become very hard to find. For some rare wines it can even be the only opportunity to purchase. But patience is required – you need enough storage space and must not always expect to make substantial gains.

...BUT ALSO A FEW RISKS

There are risks involved in buying *en primeur* wines, both in terms of price and quality, or if you have the misfortune to deal with someone dishonest. If prices collapse, the final market price may be less than the subscription price. The wine that is delivered may turn out to be not as good as you expected. Judging a wine's potential by tasting it in its extreme youth is a difficult exercise, particularly as the final proportions of the grape varieties and vineyard plots may not have been determined, and it is not always easy to predict how a wine will evolve. This speculative market is a constant attraction for the less scrupulous in particular; never buy from a merchant or website that doesn't provide comprehensive warranties, especially guaranteed delivery.

You should also check the clauses describing shipping costs and VAT to calculate how much your wine will cost. Ultimately, any particular year's wine is rarely all good or all bad; your choices will therefore be based on trustworthy reviews, so it is preferable to seek out a variety of opinions for your information.

WHERE TO BUY *EN PRIMEUR*

Formerly the sole preserve of wine merchants, the *en primeur* market is now accessible through a variety of channels including wine shops, mail order companies, the internet (*see* next page), and producers themselves.

BUYING THROUGH OTHER CHANNELS

The sale of wine by mail order has largely been replaced by sale through the internet. Reputable sites – it is absolutely essential to choose a good one – represent a good source and their services and information content can often help the amateur to make purchases. Auctions are also of increasing interest to informed enthusiasts in search of old vintages.

Buying online

Today, buying by mail order is almost exclusively carried out online via virtual wine merchants who in some cases also have physical outlets. There are two kinds of online wine merchants. Those who have little or no stock and operate on a 'just-in-time' basis. They buy their wines according to demand, while others hold a large inventory of stock and can offer both *en primeur* wines (*see* pp.128–9) and older vintages. Finally, many producers also sell their wines via the internet.

HOW TO CHOOSE A WEBSITE. There are hundreds, if not thousands, of websites that sell wines online. The most interesting are those that also provide information and advice about their products, such as food-pairing suggestions, etc. When using online services, it is essential to compare offers and terms of sale, *i.e.* the quality and range of wines available; the price per bottle, which may or may not include tax; the minimum quantity that may be purchased per wine; shipping costs, which can be very high; and the after-sales service in the event of a complaint. When an order is placed, specify the exact date of delivery; if it is a grouped order (*see* box on following page), decide where the bottles can be stored, and check the merchandise for errors or breakages on arrival.

> A few rare bottles of fortified wine sold at auction at Sotheby's in London

Reliable sites for buying wine online

www.bbr.com Britain's oldest wine and spirit merchant, having traded from the same shop for over 300 years. The website offers an extensive and eclectic wine list and also offers *en primeur* wines.

www.brownderby.com Lots of great California wines at this mid-America retailer, with some hard-to-find gems and always low mark-ups.

www.chambersstwines.com Impressively esoteric selections by this New York merchant, with plenty from around the world.

www.directwine.co.uk An independent wine merchant located in Belfast, this website offers a comprehensive range of high quality wines. It also offers *en primeur* wines.

www.jean-merlaut.com Operated by a large family of wine producers and wine merchants, this French site offers some of the best value for wine on the internet, particularly in the Bordeaux *en primeur* market.

www.klwines.com A serious California wine retailer for more than 30 years. Wines from around the world, and real-time inventory shown on the website.

www.laithwaites.co.uk Large independent UK merchant. Laithwaites offers a broad selection of wines and also offers *en primeur* wines.

www.wine.com The largest internet wine commerce site in America. It offers a broad selection of wines and competitive prices.

www.wineandco.com A French site that has established itself as a serious contender in terms of choice, deliveries, and providing information.

www.1855.com This French site has a simple, straightforward style, and offers a selection of more than 500 wines, with a wide variety of Bordeaux classified growths, frequently at attractive prices. Single bottle purchases are possible.

Payment and shipping

Shipping costs for wines purchased online vary from one site to another. Some sites offer free shipping for orders above a certain amount. Make sure you find out in advance. Secure online payment by credit card is almost always available. Wines tend to be delivered within 5 to 10 business days, or sometimes more quickly. For all such sites, it is advisable to call before ordering in order to be sure of the terms of payment and delivery.

> Bids by candlelight at the Hospices de Beaune.

Through wine clubs

Wine clubs, like that run by *The Wall Street Journal* or other publications, used to dominate the mail order scene but have adapted and now have a solid online presence. They continue to offer other services to their members via their sales outlets, such as at themed tastings. You can buy on the spot, or have the wine delivered, and order by phone or online. In general, wines of generic appellations are sold at higher prices than in the supermarkets. However, wine enthusiasts can find *grand cru* wines and wines from very good estates at prices below those charged by wine merchants.

Auctions

Auctions are not just for very expensive, rare bottles of famous wines. They may provide an opportunity for a collector to find wines from the vintage of their birth year, for example. The informed wine enthusiast, assuming they can control the urge to indulge in a wild bidding spree, can acquire a case of wine from a good vintage, which may or may not be famous, but may be secured at a good price.

It is possible to participate in an auction without being present, *simply by communicating your maximum bid to the auctioneer at least 24 hours in advance, or by bidding by telephone, or even via the internet.*

WHAT TYPES OF WINE? Most wines sold at auction are ready to drink, or soon will be; so it should not be necessary to age them in a cellar. Bargains are found by avoiding very prestigious wines and reading up on the history of the lot, and especially the storage conditions. Only reputable vendors, such as Artcurial, provide this information systematically. To identify interesting lots, enthusiasts with as yet little experience would be well-advised to seek the help of an expert, in the form of a friend or a wine merchant. To avoid paying over the odds, it is also worth obtaining a price list for fine wines from various years compiled by experts and to limit the amount bid to the market value, less the fees payable by the purchaser.

PRACTICAL INFORMATION. Information on auctions in France can be found in the *Gazette Drouot*, available from newsstands, which lists all the upcoming auctions in Paris and other areas. You can then contact the auctioneers to request a detailed catalogue of the lots and their estimated value, and information on the condition of the bottles, such as the label and the cork, the level of the wine in the bottle neck (*see also* pp.142–3), whether it is in the original case, and how it was stored. In addition to the auction price, there is usually commission, taxes, and shipping and insurance costs, which can add up to 20 per cent to the basic price.

DID YOU KNOW...?

Organizing a group purchase can be worthwhile in order to qualify for prices that are usually available only to trade customers. *This can be done through a wine club, or simply among friends, but in all cases it's worth taking great care in the preparation and delivery of the order (the quantities of each wine, collection of payment upon ordering, where the wines will be stored, etc.). Group purchases usually enable savings on shipping costs, and are also a good option when buying* en primeur *(see pp.128–9).*

1924
1923
1912
1899
1896
1920

HOW SHOULD WINE BE STORED?

THE IDEAL ENVIRONMENT FOR STORING WINE

Although it is a romantic image, an old cellar lit by candlelight is not necessarily the best place to store wine. If a wine is to achieve optimal ageing, then some basic rules need to be observed.

Temperature: cool and unchanging

THE EFFECT OF TEMPERATURE. Wine should be kept at a fairly constant temperature between 46 and 61°F (8–16°C), the ideal being between 50 and 54°F (10–12°C). Below these temperatures, wine will not develop, even though it may still remain drinkable for a long time.

High temperatures, above 68°F (20°C), are more harmful because the wine will age prematurely, and, particularly damaging, it will also loseits colour and fresh flavours. But it is primarily sudden changes in temperature that should be avoided: a gradual increase in cellar temperature from 50°F (10°C) in the winter to 64°F (18°C) in the summer will do little harm. However, the same variation in one day – or even one week – could result in problems. As the wine expands and contracts in the bottle, unwelcome pressure is applied to the cork. Eventually, the wine seeps out around the cork, leaving a sticky deposit on the capsule. The bottle has begun to 'weep,' meaning that air can enter, causing the wine to oxidize prematurely.

If wine is to be kept for more than a few weeks, *it should be stored in correct conditions. For this, a good cellar should be ventilated, dark, clean, quiet, and fairly humid.*

CONTROLLING THE ENVIRONMENT. When choosing a storage area, record the maximum and minimum temperatures in various locations in the area in order to identify the coolest places (ideally, do this over a year). If possible, locate any sources of heat and reduce their effect, for example by insulating hot water pipes. Block out any sources of very cold air, but still allow air to circulate. Insulate doors leading to heated parts of the house with extruded polystyrene ('Styrofoam'). The goal is to obtain as constant a temperature as possible.

Wine should not be exposed to light

Light damages wine, especially white wines and sparkling wines, and eventually gives it a taste of rotten egg. Make sure your storage area is dark and screen any sources of direct outside light. Install a low-power light source (25 watts) so that you can move around,

> A spacious cellar can be made into a special place to enjoy wines with friends.

> Wine needs a cool, dark, quiet environment to mature in peace.

but avoid fluorescent and halogen lamps. Make sure you always turn the light off when leaving.

High humidity

The ideal humidity in a cellar is 75 to 80 per cent. Too much humidity can cause labels to peel off, and mould to grow on corks. But a lack of moisture is even more dangerous, causing corks to dry out (*see* p.142).

If your storage area is very dry, the humidity can be increased by covering the floor with a layer of gravel, and then sprinkling it with water on a regular basis. However, in much of the UK, the natural humidity is generally sufficient. In very damp cellars, the use of dehumidifiers can prevent excessive moisture. But they can be expensive, and may be worth installing only in very large cellars. In a small storage area, the ventilation could be improved instead and any specific sources of moisture insulated.

Good ventilation but no drafts

Air circulation is essential, even though it can raise the temperature. A good storage area should have air vents or fans to draw in and circulate air from outside. However, it should also be possible to seal off air inlets during very cold or very hot weather. If the cellar is north–south oriented, place fans as low as possible on the north side and as high as possible on the south side. Convection will cause warm air to exit through the high vents on the south side. This will then be replaced by cool air entering from the north side.

Hygiene: beware of bad smells!

Clean the area thoroughly before storing any wine. Use a disinfectant, preferably an odourless one, to remove mould and grime. Apply whitewash, a porous paint that will not impede natural ventilation, to brick or stone walls. Avoid storing bottles next to paint or fuel, as these can generate fumes that will affect the wine, even through the cork. Vegetables, or any plant or food products stored nearby, can result in the development of fungi and the appearance of insect pests.

A quiet environment: avoid vibrations

Frequent, strong vibrations can have a damaging effect on wine, whether from inside (from a household appliance, for example) or outside (from a road that is used by heavy vehicles, or a nearby subway or rail line). Strong vibration cause wines to age more quickly and in an unbalanced manner.

The ideal storage area

An appropriate wine storage area should have the following conditions:

- A north-facing orientation;
- Ventilation via a door and/or small north-facing air inlet near the ground, and a south-facing static or mechanical outlet near the ceiling;
- High humidity (75 to 80 per cent);
- A constant temperature, between 46 and 61°F (8–16°C);
- Darkness;
- Clean, with no odours;
- Calm (no vibration);
- Damp, gravel floor;
- Stone or brick walls.

CREATING A CELLAR

When creating an area to store or age wine, take into account the number of bottles and type of wine to be stored, and also – more importantly – the space available. Whether you live in a town or in the country, there are options and solutions for every situation and budget.

Before starting

DEFINE THE PROJECT. It is a good idea to spend some time planning your cellar before embarking upon its creation. Poor design can result in exorbitant costs, out of all proportion to the value of the wines to be stored, or a failure to fulfill the cellar's primary purpose of providing the best conditions in which to age your wines. Make an estimate of the number and type of bottles of wine to be stored. A hundred bottles of the same type of wine will need a different amount of space from 10 batches of wines from different wine-producing areas, for example. Will the cellar be purely for storing wine, or will it also be used for tasting?

DECIDE UPON THE LOCATION. Check that the proposed space (basement, garage, shed, etc.) meets the requirements of a good cellar (*see* pp.134–5). The use of an unsuitable space could involve the installation of expensive equipment (*e.g.* air conditioning to maintain the cellar at the right temperature) and increase your electricity bill. Unless you use a cellar-installation specialist, it is best to draw up a precise specification, which should then be scrupulously respected by the person or contractor who undertakes the work.

***Once stored, a wine should not be handled.** You should not have to move one bottle to reach another. Avoid rigid layouts that cannot easily be changed.*

> A prefabricated underground cellar.

PROTECT YOUR INVESTMENT. A large cellar should be protected in the event of a flood, fire, or burglary, especially if it is in the basement of an apartment building. Such protection can be very expensive (reinforced doors, insurance, etc.), so it may be preferable to purchase a wine storage cabinet or to rent cellar space elsewhere, rather than to leave your cellar vulnerable to theft.

Turnkey cellars

There are a number of things to consider when creating a cellar (the nature of the site, choice of materials, etc.) if it is to function correctly. If you are not a diy enthusiast, it may make sense to use a specialized contractor to install either a prefabricated cellar – an underground vaulted or Spiral Cellar that is sunk in the ground – or a custom-built cellar in a garage, a basement, or even inside an apartment.

Prices for prefabricated cellars start at around $16,000 (£12,000) for a small cellar that can store about 600 bottles. A Spiral Cellar with capacity for 1,000 bottles should cost from $30,000 (£20,000) complete with stairs and concrete compartments. For a larger cellar, with room for 2,000 bottles, expect to spend around $65,000 (£50,000). Model 'show' cellars can be viewed at manufacturers' showrooms; it is essential to visit them before making a purchase.

Renting a cellar

If you live in a large city, you may be able to rent storage space. Depending on the service, the wine is stored lockers or in walk-in rooms. Current rates may be about $25 (£15) per month for a 12-case locker. Security is excellent, but renting such a space requires working around certain business hours for retrieving or depositing bottles. A short-term cellar at home is therefore advisable, where wine can be stored for a few days or longer in appropriate conditions.

> To be completely stable, metal racks should be attached to the floor and wall.

Converting a space into a cellar

As long as the project is researched thoroughly before work starts, the conversion of an existing space into a cellar can be an economical and convenient solution.

BASEMENT CELLARS. It is essential to check the temperature and humidity at different times of the year and ensure good ventilation (via air vents). In there is insufficient humidity, the floor can be covered with gravel or even sand (*see* p.135). Hot water and heating pipes should be insulated. Poor thermal insulation can be improved by building a cavity wall, a brick wall separated from the existing wall with a space between them. The installation of an air conditioner may be necessary.

GARAGE CELLARS. Whether occupying all or part of a garage, this type of cellar generally requires very good insulation. To separate off a corner to create a cellar, it's advisable to build a concrete block wall. The walls and door will need to be insulated with extruded polystyrene ('Styrofoam'), and the ceiling with a double layer of the same material or fibreglass. In the absence of an air vent, it may be necessary to equip the space with an air conditioner and a humidifier.

Wine 'fridge'

If space for a suitably protected cellar is not available, then a wine cabinet or 'fridge' may prove to be the best solution, especially for modest quantities of wine (less than 200 bottles). There is a wide range of models of all sizes (starting at around $1,000/£800 for 30 bottles). The simplest enable wines to be stored but not to be aged, while more sophisticated models offer two or three temperature zones, with different compartments for storing, chilling, and bringing wines up to temperature, the largest models can hold up to 200 bottles and cost around $3,000–$5,000 (£1,800–£3,000).

Wine cabinets may be equipped with a simple cooling system or a dual system that also provides warmth if the cabinet is placed in an area that is not heated in the winter. Make sure that any model you consider is equipped with an anti-vibration system. Also, in the event of a malfunction, a good model should ensure very gradual warming or cooling.

DID YOU KNOW...?

You can install a cellar in your apartment. *A north- or east-facing room can be used as a cellar, provided the wine can be protected from light and the right conditions in terms of temperature and ventilation can be maintained. These can be difficult to achieve, and often require the installation of an air conditioner, making it an expensive operation. It would be better to use this kind of cellar to store wine intended for consumption in the near future (a year at most), as it will not age very well, or to install one or two wine cabinets instead. The same applies to smaller spaces, even if they are well insulated, such as a cupboard under the stairs, or a closet in a bedroom. Take care to avoid vibrations, light, heat, and poor ventilation.*

Four different wine collections

Classic or eclectic, simple or sophisticated, a wine collection reflects its owner's preferences. The choice will depend on the storage space available and how much money they are willing to spend but above all it will depend upon their taste. To buy a number of bottles in one style of wine on a modest budget, for example, sparkling wines, a less prestigious appellation (Crémant de Bourgogne or Cava, for example) could be selected. But if not limited by price, a top quality vintage Champagne could be chosen instead. Here are four examples of a well-balanced collection based on four different budgets.

The simple cellar

STYLE	NO.	NAME OF WINE
Light or fruity dry white wines	6	Bourgogne Aligoté, Cheverny, Touraine, Anjou Blanc, Bordeaux Blanc, Entre-Deux-Mers, Pinot Blanc d'Alsace.
Sleek, full-bodied, dry white wines	10	Chablis Premier Cru, Saint Aubin, Givry, Savennières, Vouvray, Riesling d'Alsace.
Sweet white wines	4	Ste-Croix-du-Mont, Cérons, Coteaux-de-l'Aubance, Monbazillac.
Fruity red wines	15	Beaujolais, Red Burgundy, Red Anjou, Côtes-de-Forez, Coteaux-du-Lyonnais, Bourgueil, Saint-Nicolas-de-Bourgueil, Bordeaux, Côtes-du-Rhône-Villages, Vins de Pays d'Oc.
Complex red wines	10	Bordeaux Supérieur, Haut-Médoc, Côtes de Castillon, Graves, Cahors, Buzet, Minervois, Corbières, Pécharmant, Côtes de Nuits Villages.
Rosé wines	4	Côtes-de-Provence, Côteaux d'Aix, Luberon, Tavel, Languedoc, Fronton, Bordeaux rosé.
Sparkling wines	6	Blanquette de Limoux, Clairette de Die, Gaillac, Saumur, Vouvray, Crémant de Bourgogne, Crémant d'Alsace, Crémant de Jura.

The convivial cellar

STYLE	NO.	NAME OF WINE
Light or fruity dry white wines	12	Muscadet, Entre-Deux-Mers, Bordeaux, Petit Chablis, Bourgogne blanc, Sylvaner d'Alsace.
Sleek, full-bodied, dry white wines	12	Pessac-Léognan, Graves, Chablis Premier Cru, Meursault, Puligny-Montrachet, Crozes Hermitage.
Sweet white wines	6	Loupiac, Ste-Croix-du-Mont, Coteaux-du-Layon, Montlouis, Late Harvest Alsace Pinot Gris, Late Harvest Alsace Riesling, Jurançon.
Fruity red wines	12	Bordeaux, Bordeaux Supérieur, Red Burgundy, Beaujolais Villages, Beaujolais, Hautes-Côtes-de-Nuits, Saumur-Champigny, Bourgueil, Vin de Savoie, Côtes-du-Rhône-Villages.
Complex red wines	12	Haut-Médoc, Médoc, Pauillac, St-Estèphe, St-Julien, St-Émilion, Pessac-Léognan, Volnay, Vosne-Romanée, Crozes-Hermitage, St-Joseph, Bandol.
Rosé wines	6	Bordeaux Clairet, Marsannay, Languedoc, Irouléguy, Palette.
Sparkling wines	6	Dry non-vintage Champagne.
Natural sweet wines	4	Banyuls, Muscat de Rivesaltes, Muscat de Beaumes-de-Venise, Port.

The refined cellar

STYLE	NO.	NAME OF WINE
Light or fruity dry white wines	12	Premières-Côtes-de-Blaye, White Bordeaux, Graves, Bandol, Bellet, Cassis, Coteaux-d'Aix, St-Véran, Macon Villages, Pouilly Fumé, Sancerre, Roussette de Savoie, Jurançon sec.
Sleek, full-bodied, dry white wines	18	Pessac-Léognan, Puligny-Montrachet, Chassagne-Montrachet, Meursault, Chablis Grand Cru, Savennières, Vouvray, Château-Châlon, Condrieu, Riesling d'Alsace Grand Cru.
Sweet white wines	12	Sauternes Crus Classés, Bonnezeaux, Gewurztraminer Sélection de Grains Nobles, Riesling Sélection de Grains Nobles, Vouvray, Tokaji.
	3	Loupiac, Ste-Croix-du-Mont, Coteaux-du-Layon, Montlouis, Jurançon.
Fruity red wines	12	Bordeaux, Crus du Beaujolais, Red Burgundy, Beaujolais Villages, Crus du Beaujolais, Hautes-Côtes-de-Nuits, Saumur-Champigny, Bourgueil, St-Nicolas-de-Bourgueil, Vin de Savoie, Côtes-du-Rhône-Villages.
Complex red wines	18	Haut-Médoc, Margaux, Saint Julien, Pauillac, St-Émilion Grand Cru, Pomerol, Pommard, Volnay, Chambolle-Musigny, Gevrey-Chambertin, Côte-Rôtie, Hermitage, Cornas, Bandol.
Rosé wines	6	Bordeaux Clairet, Marsannay, Coteaux-du-Languedoc, Irouléguy, Palette, Côtes-de-Provence.
Sparkling wines	6	Top brand Champagnes, vintage Champagnes.
	6	Saumur, Vouvray, Clairette de Die, Crémants.
Natural sweet wines	5	Port, Rivesaltes, Banyuls, Maury, Rasteau.

The prestige cellar

STYLE	NO.	NAME OF WINE
Light or fruity dry white wines	24	Premières-Côtes-de-Blaye, White Bordeaux, Graves, Bandol, Bellet, Cassis, Coteaux-d'Aix-en-Provence, White Burgundy, White Beaujolais, Macon Villages, St-Véran, Sancerre, Roussette de Savoie, Jurançon sec.
Sleek, full-bodied, dry white wines	24	Pessac-Léognan, Puligny-Montrachet, Chassagne-Montrachet, Meursault, Chablis Grand Cru, Savennières, Vouvray, Château-Châlon, Condrieu, Riesling d'Alsace Grand Cru.
Sweet white wines	12	Sauternes Crus Classés, Bonnezeaux, Gewurztraminer Sélection de Grains Nobles, Riesling Sélection de Grains Nobles, Vouvray, Tokaj.
	6	Loupiac, Ste-Croix-du-Mont, Coteaux-du-Layon, Montlouis, Jurançon.
Fruity red wines	24	Bordeaux Supérieur, Crus du Beaujolais, Hautes-Côtes-de-Nuits, Saumur-Champigny, Bourgueil, St-Nicolas-de-Bourgueil, Vin de Savoie, Côtes-du-Rhône-Villages.
Complex red wines	30	Haut-Médoc, Médoc Crus Classés, St-Émilion Grand Cru, Pomerol, Pommard, Volnay, Chambolle-Musigny, Gevrey-Chambertin, Côte-Rôtie, Hermitage, Cornas, Côte Rôtie, Bandol.
Rosé wines	12	Bordeaux Clairet, Marsannay, Languedoc, Irouléguy, Palette, Côtes-de-Provence, Coteaux d'Aix.
Sparkling wines	12	Top brand Champagnes, vintage Champagnes.
	6	Saumur, Vouvray, Montlouis, Crémants.
Natural sweet wines	5	Port, Rivesaltes, Banyuls, Maury, Rasteau.

IN THE SILENCE OF THE CELLAR

Wine is fragile and needs to be treated with care in order to age properly and realize its full potential. Within the dark coolness of the cellar a silent alchemy occurs.

1

2

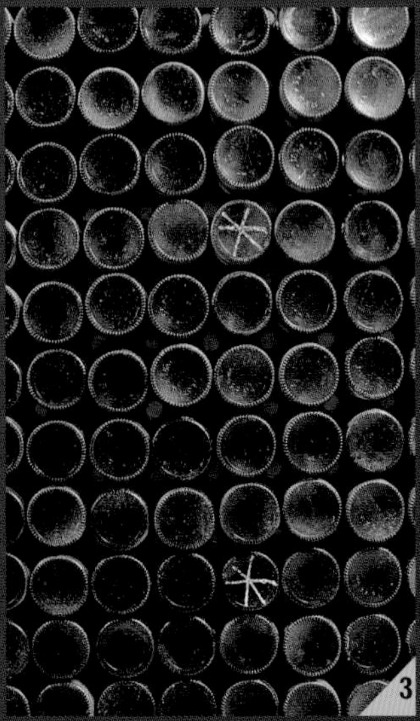
3

4

5

6

7

8

1. Domaine Trimbach (Alsace).
2. Domaine Michel Juillot (Burgundy).
3. Domaine Hugel & Fils (Alsace).
4 and 8. Private cellars.
5. Louis Roederer Champagne.
6. Domaine Bouchard Père & Fils (Burgundy).
7. Domaine Jean-Maurice Raffault (Loire Valley).
9. Château Lascombes (Bordeaux).
10. Château Angélus (Bordeaux).

9

10

ORGANIZING AND MANAGING YOUR CELLAR

When all the conditions for good storage have been met, the next stage is to plan the layout. Wine needs to be arranged so that it can age in the best conditions, and, most importantly, so that you can find bottles with ease when the time comes to drink them.

Storing bottles

POSITION AND LOCATION OF BOTTLES. With the exception of brandies, some fortified wines and *vins de liqueur*, or wines closed with screwcaps or glass stoppers, bottles should be laid horizontally (so that the wine stays in contact with the cork). You can stagger the rows, if you choose, or stack them, but all the bottles should be easily identifiable to avoid unnecessary handling. The air is cooler near the ground, so it is recommended that the wine is organized by style as follows, from bottom to top: sparkling wines, dry white wines, sweet wines, rosés, red wines for short- to medium-term drinking and, finally, prestigious red wines for long-term drinking. A well-maintained cellar book (*see* below), or cellar management software, will enable the ageing and consumption of wines to be monitored.

Managing a cellar requires discipline, time and some basic knowledge. *To reap maximum benefit, it is important to check the levels of the wines and the state of the corks...and to drink the wines at the right time.*

STORAGE STRUCTURES. Compartments and shelves should be stable and easily accessible. They can be made of stainless steel or wood (treated against insects and moisture), stone, brick or concrete. When batches are small (fewer than six bottles), individual cell style storage is preferable, since it protects the wine against thermal shock, humidity, and vibrations. Cardboard boxes should be avoided: they soon deteriorate due to humidity and release odours that can harm the wine. Beware of tissue paper: it can stick to labels and stain them. It is possible to leave bottles in their original wooden crate, as long as the lid is removed to let them breathe, and the crate is raised off the floor. However, wooden crates encourage insects and parasites, and make a thief's work much easier.

LABELS. Orient labels to allow different batches to be located easily. Alternatively, tags can be attached to the necks of the bottles or the cases can be labelled. To preserve wine labels, bottles can be covered in plastic wrap or the labels can be covered in boat varnish. Labels may also be removed from empty bottles by using wide transparent tape, specially made for this purpose. Alternatively, fill the bottle with cold water and then immerse it in hot water.

> Wooden cases must be treated to protect against humidity and insects.

Monitor the level of the wine in the bottles

Unfortunately, it is inevitable that as it ages a little wine will evaporate through the cork, but the amount will vary from one bottle to another, since cork is by nature a variable material. So the 'level' of the bottle becomes important. Being aware of the level when buying at auction is crucial. When a wine is young, the level should still be high in the neck. After several years in the cellar, it sometimes descends to the base of the neck. A level at the top of the 'shoulder' of the bottle is possibly acceptable for wines more than 20 years old but increases the risk of oxidation. A mid-shoulder level is typical for wines more than 30 years old; in younger wines, it would suggest a problem linked to a bad quality cork or if a general problem, excessive heat or insufficient humidity. Bottles are sometimes said to 'weep.' When the level reaches the bottom of the shoulder, there is real cause for concern about the wine's condition. It certainly will have lost some of its resale value. As for below mid-shoulder level, this almost always indicates that the wine has become undrinkable.

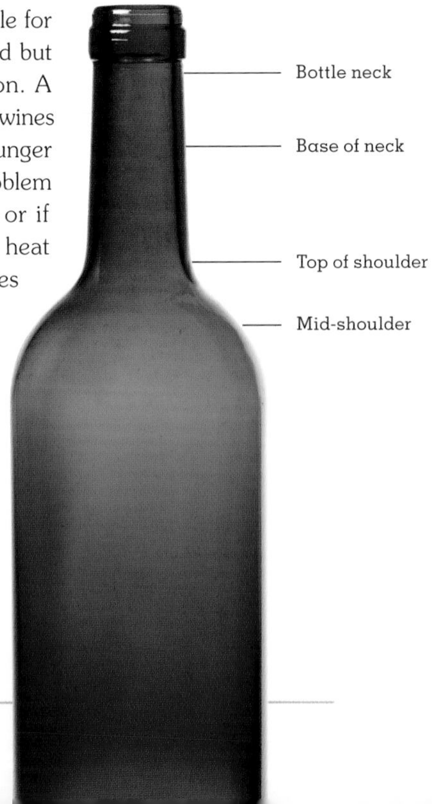

> In a large cellar, it is essential to label the batches carefully.

EXAMPLE OF A CELLAR RECORD

IDENTIFICATION	
WINERY NAME	Château Sociando-Mallet
APPELLATION	Médoc
REGION	Bordeaux
COLOUR	Red
VINTAGE	2010
PURCHASE	en primeur the Internet
DATE	May 2011 (delivery June 2012)
PRICE	35
MERCHANT	Jean Gautreau
ADDRESS	(only en primeur purchase)
MANAGEMENT OF BOTTLES STORED	
NUMBER OF BOTTLES	one case of 12 bottles
REMAINING	10
DRINK BEFORE	2025-2040
TASTING NOTES	

SERVED AT CHRISTMAS 2015: One bottle (with Michael, Sandra, Andy, and Bill). Still a little closed, tannins very noticeable, lots of power. Intense and very long in the mouth. Promising, needs more time.

SERVED MARCH 30, 2016: One bottle with Eric and Sandra. Decanted one hour before the meal. Lots of substance, beginning to open up, subtle tannins and woodiness. Still very promising. Superb, showing incredible youth. Perfect with the duck breast.

The cellar book

A cellar book where you can record wine purchased and consumed will help you to keep your cellar up to date. However, it can be time-consuming if you have a lot of single bottles or wines in small quantities.

PRESENTATION. Use a special notebook or software to record the wines you have purchased by the case and/or those that you plan to keep for a long time (see table above). A good cellar book will keep track not only of incoming and outgoing wines, but also of your tasting notes, helping you to monitor your wines as they age and to plan future purchases.

USE IN THE CELLAR. If helpful, make a sketch of the cellar layout in your cellar book. Label the racks and compartments. For the bottles, use individual labels or plastic tags. If wine is stored in wooden cases, be sure to leave the side of the case with the wine's name visible, so that you do not have to move it.

TRUE OR FALSE?

Bottle sizes affect the wine.

TRUE. Different bottle sizes are not just a matter of varying volumes of wine: they also affect the ageing process. Wine matures more slowly in large bottles – a fact that should be remembered when making a purchase. This is due to the effect of the increased mass, and the oxidation-reduction phenomena in the maturing process, as well as a slower rate of sedimentation. Many wine enthusiasts believe that a magnum (1.5 litres or two bottles) is the optimal size for ageing.

Storing wine in wooden cases

Wines may be stored in their original wooden cases or crates, despite a slight risk of dry rot. Place the boxes on strips of wood rather than directly on the floor. Cardboard boxes should only be used for temporary storage, as the humidity will cause them to become mouldy and develop odours. Remember to keep the original wooden cases if you plan to sell the wine later: they are reassuring for buyers at auctions and increase the value of the wine. This is particularly true for magnums and expensive wines.

STORING WINE: A FEW TIPS

At one time or another, most wine lovers have some questions about the storage of the wines in their cellar. The answers are generally a matter of common sense, but these tips will help you make the right choices.

Should wine be stored upright or lying down?

‘There is no doubt that to store and age most wines in the best possible conditions, bottles should be kept in a horizontal position – at least if the closures are made of real cork, which is still usually the case. However, this is not an issue for synthetic closures or aluminium caps because they do not dry out and so the bottles may be stored upright. Precautions need to be taken when transporting older bottles, and an upright position means they will be less disturbed.

My cellar has flooded. Will the wine be OK?

‘In theory, your wine will be alright. The capsule and cork should be sufficient protection for a bottle, in the event that it spends a few days under water. However, you may lose the labels. If this is a risk, when organizing your wine make sure that you could identify any bottles that had lost their ‘identity card’. If your bottles were stored in wooden cases, it’s best to get rid of them, as they could start to rot after being soaked and then give the wine a bad taste.’

How can I protect my labels?

‘There may be an air of romance around a mouldy, indecipherable label, but it could prevent you from identifying the wine. The best way of protecting labels is partially to cover the bottles with plastic wrap. This will protect labels from humidity for a while, but the plastic will need to be replaced after two or three years. A water-resistant varnish would be another solution.

How can I avoid unwanted flavours?

‘A good wine cellar has no odours. While a little mould might seem part of the charm of some grand old cellars, the musty, fungal odour sometimes found in fine wines may have been transmitted by mould. If you have a damp basement, it is best to clean and aerate it regularly. But avoid the use of any chemical products that could remain in the atmosphere and harm the wine. And it is well known that while cheese and wine go well together at the table, they are poor company when stored in the same cellar.’

Do I need to worry about noise?

'As a rule, wine likes peace and quiet. Being subject to movement and vibration will cause it to age more quickly and can cause certain problems. Avoid storing wine near a rail line or a road where heavy trucks pass. Continuous vibrations can stimulate certain bacteria and reactivate malolactic fermentation in unstable wines. This problem can be avoided by placing rubber spacers – pieces of tyre, for example – under the racks, if they are mobile, which will absorb the vibrations.'

I am bottling some wine. What type of cork should I use?

'We now know that the air that slowly passes through traditional corks is not essential for the ageing process. On the other hand, these corks can spoil excellent wines by giving them a 'corked' taste. To avoid this problem, use synthetic corks. The air in the space between the cork and the wine – about half of the neck – is sufficient for the wine to "breathe".'

How long should I wait to drink a wine that has just been shipped?

'Generally speaking, once wine is in bottle it should not be shaken. So after wine has been transported, it is important to allow it a period of rest. The length of time that it is allowed to rest varies. For a young red, or any white wine, three or four days are usually enough. If the wine was bottled less than two months ago, it is best to wait a good week. If the wine is more than five years old, and especially if it is red, it would be advisable to wait eight to 10 days. For a fine red wine more than 10 years old, allowing it to rest for at least two weeks is recommended.'

How long can I keep wine purchased in bulk?

'As little time as possible, if you intend to bottle a wine that is in a Cubitainer. Allowing the wine to rest for 24 hours in a cool place is a good idea, but then bottling should not be delayed. Once bottled, it is advisable to wait a week before opening the first one. A boxed wine for everyday consumption can wait three to four months before being opened. Since no air can enter as the bag inside empties, it can be kept for a few weeks in a cool place.'

KEEPING AND AGEING WINES

Some wines improve over the course of a slow maturation process, while others are intended to be enjoyed in their youth. Knowing the principles of how wines change as they age offers a better understanding of when they are at their peak and the best time to drink them.

Early wines were consumed young

The quality of a great wine is often gauged by its capacity to age; but this was not always the case. For centuries, it was thought best to drink wine when it was young. Before the use of sulphur and the bottling of wine became widespread, there was considerable risk that a wine would quickly turn into vinegar. With the help of today's scientific analyses, we now understand why wine is an unstable liquid. The presence of oxygen can cause the wine to oxidize badly, even transforming alcohol into acetic acid, or vinegar, due to the bacteria *Acetobacter aceti*. In the past, fermentation was a rather random process that took place in barrels or vats that were relatively clean, but left the wine exposed to the air. For a long time, the only way of compensating for the poor production conditions was to make wines with a high alcohol or sugar content.

How wine ages is determined in part by the winemaker, but it depends mainly on the grape variety, the nature and age of the vines, the microclimate and soil (or terroir), and the weather during a particular year.

Wines that improve with age

It is only thanks to the development of certain techniques over the last few centuries that we are now able to keep wine for any length of time. They include fortification (the addition of alcohol during fermentation), the use of sulphur dioxide to combat bacterial growth, and *ouillage* (ullage, the regular topping up of the barrels with more wine to compensate for evaporation and prevent the wine from coming into contact with air). To which must be added the arrival of the glass bottle. Prior to this, once the wine was drawn from the barrel, it had to be consumed. The glass bottle and cork, which first enabled wine to be kept at home in appropriate conditions, did not appear until the late 18th century. Before their arrival, wine was aged in barrels stored by wine merchants or in taverns.

These new techniques also enabled certain wines that were considered undrinkable just after they had been made (because they were so tannic, acidic, and concentrated) to be kept until they softened and reached their peak – the stage at which a wine's various flavours open up – and its components (tannins, acidity, etc.) became balanced. The notion of keeping wines to let them improve was born.

> The longevity of a wine depends on many factors, including the *terroir*, the type of grapes, and the winemaking processes.

Wines evolve in bottle

OXIDATION. The work of Louis Pasteur during the 19th century showed that wine deteriorates through oxidation or exposure to air. Oxidation causes red and white wines to become brown, much like an apple that has been peeled. But why does wine oxidize in the bottle, given that the cork lets in little or no air? The oxygen dissolved in the wine continues to cause slow reactions, and not all corks are perfectly waterproof. It is recommended that the corks of wines for long-term keeping should be changed every 30 years.
CHEMICAL REACTIONS. Research has helped to explain certain changes in colours and flavours. Tannins and flavour components that come mainly from grape skins (and give wines their colour), and also from the grape stalks and wooden barrels, undergo changes over time. They combine with each other

(polymerization) and fall to the bottom of the bottle (sedimentation). A wine with a purplish colour will gradually become ruby red and then lighten to an orangey brick red. The astringent acidity of young fruit will soften. The aggressiveness of an immature wine disappears, giving way to generosity and smoothness, expressed through complex flavours. All wines move through this ageing process, but very light wines or those lacking body don't benefit from it.

> Truly great wines, capable of lasting decades, are rare. To drink such a wine is a privilege and a special occasion.

What is a wine 'for laying down'?

Each type of wine develops at its own pace. Some, like Beaujolais and many white wines, should be consumed young: they quickly reach their peak and then rapidly decline. Others, like the great wines of Bordeaux, Burgundy, and the Rhône Valley, take longer to reach their peak, where they remain for a long time, before declining slowly. These are wines for laying down (*vins de garde*).

GRAPE VARIETIES SUITED TO AGEING. Grape varieties are a key factor in the longevity of wines. Those made from noble, austere Cabernet Sauvignon, and powerful, smooth Merlot grapes (in Bordeaux), or Pinot Noir (in Burgundy) and Syrah (in the Rhône) are much more concentrated than the light, fruity wines produced from the Gamay grape (in Beaujolais). Among reds, wines suitable for laying down include: Cabernet Franc, Grenache, Mourvèdre, Tannat (Madiran), Malbec (Cahors) Petit Verdot, Carignan, Tempranillo from Spain, and Nebbiolo and Sangiovese from Italy and others that are less well known. Among white wines, there are: Gewurztraminer, Riesling, Roussanne, Chardonnay, Grenache Blanc, Chenin, Sémillon, and Muscadelle (the last three having exceptional ageing potential when they are used to make sweet wines).

VINIFICATION AND MATURATION. The potential of a wine to improve with age also depends on how it is made. For red wines, the winemaker's goal is to extract plenty of tannins by grape skin maceration before pressing (*see* p.68) and after fermentation, in order to give the wine the structure necessary for gradual ageing. The balance between free-run wine and press wine has a major impact on the final texture. Maturing wine in new barrels is another significant factor in ageing potential. With white wines, the key is to obtain a good level of acidity. For those that are not made from a grape variety with high acidity, barrel ageing also helps ageing potential a little.

TRUE OR FALSE?

A wine's development can only be monitored by tasting.

TRUE. To know when a wine has reached its peak, it is not advisable to rely on the suggestions made by the producer or wine merchant at the time of purchase, since storage conditions, which can vary from one place to another, will affect its development. The best method is to open a bottle from time to time and taste it.

DID YOU KNOW...?

Whether a wine is humble or a grand cru, its life cycle in the bottle remains the same. *After what is known as 'bottling sickness', wines slowly regain their original flavours, then lose the 'rough' character of their early youth: fermentation- and maturation-related characters gradually fade, allowing the primary flavours of the fruit to come through. The ageing process then begins, often characterized by a short period of the wine being mute or 'closed'. Finally, the wine enters its peak period: its texture becomes softer, and its complex bouquet blends notes of fruit with spice or herbal aromas. This period can last several decades for some grand crus before they begin to decline.*

Average wine longevity

While some wines should be consumed young, others need to be kept for a few years before being enjoyed once they have fully matured. Each wine should be opened within a certain period of time, depending on the wine region, the type of wine produced, and also the quality of the vintage in question. The best wines are generally the best wines to lay down. These vintages may be rated from 1 to 10 (see pp. 624–163).

Key:
- good vintages are ready to drink (meaning vintages scoring 6 to 7 out of 10)
- great vintages are ready to drink (scores of 8 to 9)
- exceptional vintages are ready to drink (scores of 10 out of 10)

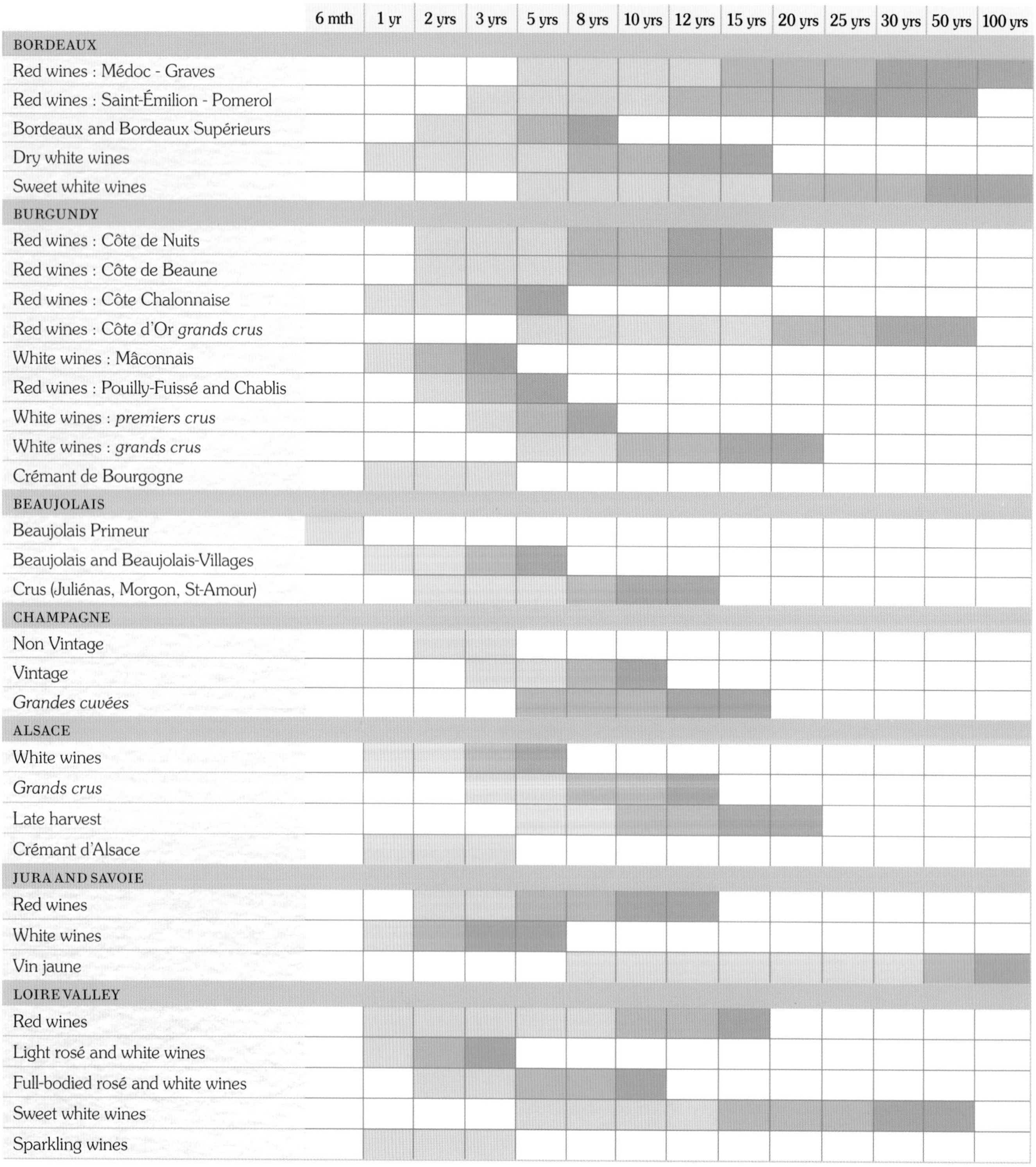

	6 mth	1 yr	2 yrs	3 yrs	5 yrs	8 yrs	10 yrs	12 yrs	15 yrs	20 yrs	25 yrs	30 yrs	50 yrs	100 yrs
RHÔNE VALLEY														
Red wines														
White wines														
Rosé wines														
LANGUEDOC AND ROUSSILLON														
Red wines														
White wines														
Natural sweet wines														
PROVENCE														
Red wines														
White and rosé wines														
CORSICA														
Red wines														
White and rosé wines														
Sweet white wines														
SOUTHWEST FRANCE														
Red wines														
Dry white wines														
Sweet white wines														
ITALY: Piedmont and Tuscany														
Barolo and Brunello di Montalcino														
SPAIN														
Rioja and Ribera del Duero red wines														
Fino sherry														
PORTUGAL														
Vintage port														
GERMANY: Mosel and Rhine regions														
Dry white wines														
Sweet white wines														
Ice wines														
SWITZERLAND, AUSTRIA, AND HUNGARY														
Red wines														
Dry white wines														
Sweet white wines														
MEDITERRANEAN COUNTRIES AND NORTH AFRICA														
Red wines														
Rosé wines														
UNITED STATES: California														
Red wines														
White wines														
CHILE														
Red wines														
White wines														
ARGENTINA														
Red wines														
White wines														
SOUTH AFRICA														
Red wines														
White wines														
AUSTRALIA														
Red wines														
White wines														
NEW ZEALAND														
Red wines														
White wines														

COLLECTING AND INVESTING IN WINES FOR YOUR CELLAR

At the top end of the market, wine can become not only a passion but also an investment opportunity. Purchasing these wines is complex and can be risky, but they will develop and add value to a fine collection.

Collecting wines

Some wine enthusiasts regard their cellar as a 'formal' collection. It might contain a wide variety of wines from several countries or regions, or a collection from a single region, all the vintages from one great château, or all the châteaux from a certain vintage.

APPROPRIATE STORAGE CONDITIONS. Collectors have to take extra care regarding storage conditions, since some very old wines are fragile. Labels and wooden cases should also be looked after – some may be kept, along with the bottles, as souvenirs after the wine has been consumed, or they may add value in the event of resale.

BOTTLE SIZES. Unlike an ordinary cellar, a formal wine collection may include several magnums or even larger bottles that will not fit into standard racks and will need appropriate storage space. Very large bottles are often kept in their original boxes.

One of the finest collections of rare wines in the world belongs to Michel Chasseuil. *Now retired, he patiently assembled 20,000 bottles of fine wines throughout his working life.*

Collection strategies

Wine collectors, unlike investors, are not limited to buying 'safe' wines that can easily be resold. They may adopt different strategies, depending on their approach. They might, for example, collect all the Pauillac classified growths of the year of their birth, or systematically buy all the vintages of one château *en primeur* (*see also* pp.128–9), or all the labels produced by a small but prestigious appellation in Burgundy, such as Clos de Vougeot. They will buy only perfect bottles, and, if wines are not available *en primeur*, will source them from cellars where the storage conditions are known to be reliable. Finally, every collector hopes that when the time comes to drink the wine, or to sell it, the source – their own cellar – will enhance its reputation.

How much wine should one buy?

How many bottles of wine should be kept in a cellar? The answer is simple: as many as possible depending on the objectives of the collection. If you feel that your collection has become too large, or you want to expand or change it, then it is always possible to sell bottles at auctions or on internet sites.

THEORY. To collect fine wines that will not reach their peak for at least a decade, you will need a large cellar.

DID YOU KNOW...?

French government institutions such as the Elysée Palace, the National Assembly, and most of the ministries have their own wine cellars, *often managed by a sommelier. These cellars represent significant assets, and their collections vary depending on the origin of the wines and the tastes of the incumbent. For a long time, the best cellar was said to be that of the Hotel de Lassay, the official residence of the president of the National Assembly. The Elysée Palace cellar, which holds the French president's wines, has had its ups and downs, but still contains treasures that are reserved for important state dinners.*

> Bottles of Château Latour, Grand Cru Classé.

> The collector Michel Chasseuil and his vintages of Pétrus.

If they are consumed at a rate of two or three bottles per year, or are being kept as a long-term investment, the quantity will inevitably multiply over time. For example, if you buy 36 bottles of a top Bordeaux every year for 10 years, and drink just two a year, you will have 340 bottles at the end of that period. A collection for drinking and a collection for investment purposes should be approached quite differently. In the first scenario, you may as well store the wines in your own cellar, especially if you have friends who share your passion. In the second scenario, it can be preferable to rent secure storage with a professional company.
REALITY. In practice, this difficult choice rarely comes to pass. Most collectors, unless they have an unlimited budget or are planning a career as a wine merchant, are wine enthusiasts who very often succumb to the urge to share their prized bottles with friends, rather than taking the risk of pursuing the speculative approach to its logical conclusion of selling the wine. Furthermore, unless you plan to leave an inheritance for your descendants, it should be kept in mind that – once you yourself have reached a certain age – you may not be around to enjoy a great wine at its peak. So there is a balance to be struck between collecting two types of wine: those that one can be sure of drinking in the medium term, and great wines that will be consumed much later or which will be sold to raise funds for the collection's renewal.

Insuring a cellar

Like all property, a cellar can be covered by a home insurance policy. However, its existence must be declared and it contents' value assessed in order to receive compensation in the event of a claim. Unless stipulated in a policy, there is no specific coverage for the contents of a cellar. In other words, if your policy does not state a precise amount for the value of the wine stored, you will be covered only for a fixed sum that depends on the type of insurance. It is strongly recommended that all possible proof of wine purchases (invoices, photographs, etc.) be carefully preserved, and that your policy is based on the wine's current valuation.

Wine as an investment

When purchasing wine for speculative purposes, it is advisable to be familiar with the market and to buy at the best possible price.
WHICH WINES SHOULD I BUY? Wines that are bought as an investment include the *grands crus* of Bordeaux, the top Burgundies and some of the wines from the Rhône Valley. Wines that start out as being expensive generally generate the highest margins, with a few exceptions. There is one golden rule: you should only buy wine with money from your savings, or, if you are a collector, from the profits from sales of other wines.
HOW SHOULD I BUY WINES? It's also necessary to be sure that you are buying a good vintage. This is why buying *en primeur* is often the best way of obtaining a good deal; regional wine fairs in Europe are another possibility.
WHAT RETURN CAN I EXPECT? Investing in wine can be very profitable. This was the case over the last 20 years of the 20th century for anyone who has invested in some of the great vintages of Bordeaux (1985, 1986, 1989, 1990, 1995, and 2000), whose prices have sometimes increased threefold, or more. However, as a rule, do not expect to achieve an overall gross margin of more than 50 per cent in less than 10 years. You can monitor your investment's development on relevant investment websites; but, when you choose to sell, whether it is through an auction room or online, it is best to consult an expert.

1983
Les Grands Vins du Jura
ARBOIS
APPELLATION ARBOIS CONTROLÉE
cuvée sélectionnée par

HOW TO CHOOSE WINE

WINE STYLES

An inexperienced wine enthusiast may be daunted by the task of choosing from the huge variety of wines available from supermarkets or wine merchants. It helps to bear in mind the wine's style or family. Here are 14 wine styles, classified according to their sensory qualities and principal grape varieties. For each style, the most representative appellations are listed, as well as the dishes with which they pair best, and the ideal temperatures at which they should be served.

Light, lively, and fruity reds

These wines are essentially for immediate consumption and can be classified as fruity wines for 'easy drinking.' Typically, they have expressive aromas of soft fruits or flowers, and their light tannic structure is compensated by a pleasant crispness, with a simple and thirst-quenching finish. Not all wines from this category necessarily belong to this family as the production methods influence the result a great deal.

GRAPE VARIETIES. These include Cabernet Franc, Gamay, Pinot Noir, Poulsard, Tempranillo, Trousseau, Corvina (Italy) and Mencía (Spain). These wines deliver a spectrum of aromatic expressions with essentially fruity and floral primary aromas .

APPELLATIONS. A few examples in this category include, from France: Anjou, Beaujolais, Beaujolais Villages, Bourgueil and St-Nicolas de Bourgeuil, Chinon, Saumur Champigny, Sancerre rouge, Côtes-du-Jura, Coteaux-du-Lyonnais, Bourgogne, Hautes-Côtes-de-Beaune, Hautes-Côtes-de-Nuits, Pinot Noir d'Alsace; Italian wines include Valpolicella, Spanish include Bierzo; California has Zinfandel; Switzerland has Pinot Noir from the Valais.

FOOD PAIRING. These light and fruity red wines are best with simple foods and summer dishes. They go well with charcuterie, quiches, pizzas, savoury pastries, terrines, and poultry dishes; and are especially good with hard and semi-hard cheeses (cow's or sheep's milk).

SERVING. Serve these wines lightly chilled, between 54 and 57°F (12–14°C); they are best when consumed young, within two years of bottling or three at most.

***It's easier to choose a bottle** if you keep in mind that wines can be classified according to their style, their colour, and their tasting personality, e.g. complex, classy reds or firm, light whites, and so on.*

Medium-bodied, fruity reds

These are often simple wines, but they differ from the lighter reds in their heavier mouth-feel and sometimes more perceptible, though unaggressive, tannins, and some wines have increased alcohol. In general, they are not matured in new wood and they retain their fruity character. These wines will develop a bouquet reminiscent of red or black fruits, often with spicy undertones in certain cases.

GRAPE VARIETIES. Cabernet Franc, Carignan, Grenache, Merlot, Mondeuse, Pinot Noir, Syrah, and Sangiovese are the most common grape varieties used in making these wines.

APPELLATIONS. These fruity wines include the French appellations Bergerac, Bordeaux Supérieur, Buzet, Chinon, Castillon-Côtes-de-Bordeaux, Côte Chalonnaise, Côtes-de-Provence, Coteaux d'Aix, Côtes-du-Rhône, Côtes-du-Rhône-Villages, Fronton, Saint-Joseph, Crozes-Hermitage. In Italy, there is Chianti, and in Spain Penedès, Somontano and some Riojas, for example.

FOOD PAIRING. These wines go well with game birds, savoury meat pies, white meat and grills, as well as pressed, uncooked cheeses such as Tomme.

SERVING. These wines are best consumed after ageing for one or two years in the bottle; they should be served at a temperature between 59 and 63°F (15–17°C).

DID YOU KNOW...?

***The colour of a red wine can offer some clue to its identity.** The palette of young reds ranges from very light ruby to darkest purple. A wine with an intense, dark appearance (or colour) is associated with – rightly or wrongly – concentration. On the other hand, a paler wine suggests a more fluid, lighter, less tannic palate. But there are plenty of exceptions.*

Full-bodied, fruity reds

> A selection of full-bodied, fruity reds.

These wines are more pronounced and powerful, with a soft texture based on high alcohol content and plenty of tannins that will need some time to integrate. They are generally matured in oak barrels or vats and develop a complex bouquet with woody or even spicy notes often associated with ripe, dark fruits. Initial tasting reveals a full-bodied impression, whether they are hot, sunny-climate wines (from Mediterranean-type climates) or more classic appellations such as those of the Libourne region of Bordeaux. The finish is complex and long. Wines containing a high percentage of Merlot, such as those from Pomerol and St-Émilion (*see* pp.267 and 268), are particularly smooth and are also often the most expensive in this category.

GRAPE VARIETIES. These red wines often come from varieties such as Malbec, Cabernet Sauvignon, Grenache, Merlot, Mourvèdre, Syrah, Tannat, Tempranillo, and Zinfandel.

APPELLATIONS. These include the following French designations: Cahors, Châteauneuf-du-Pape, Corbières, Côtes-du-Roussillon-Villages, AOCs from Languedoc, Fronsac, Gigondas, Madiran, Minervois, Pomerol, and St-Émilion Grand Cru. Outside France, there are the Rioja and Ribera del Duero wines of Spain, Merlots from Chile, Zinfandels from California, and Shiraz from Australia.

FOOD PAIRING. These complex, powerful, and generous wines demand richly flavoured, fatty dishes such as cassoulet, duck confit, mushrooms (especially truffles), foie gras escalope, dishes in red wine sauce (daubes), grilled or roasted red meat, game, and pressed, uncooked cheeses such as Tomme or Cantal.

SERVING. These wines need to be left for at least three years in bottle. If consumed young, they will benefit from being decanted and served at a temperature of 59–63°F (15–17°C).

Complex, tannic, austere reds

These reds, which can be classy and distinguished, are often found in the higher price brackets. They deserve attention when tasted, and will mature in bottle for several years. Due to their significant tannin content, they will often taste rather austere when young. But over time the tannins will soften, yielding a firm, elegant, dense body with a finer texture. Usually matured in casks, much of it in new barrels, they develop toasty, spicy notes and soft red and black fruit aromas. It is on their maturity in particular that they reveal their complex aromas. They are distinguished by their long, classy finish.

GRAPE VARIETIES. These wines are made from grapes such as Cabernet Sauvignon, Mourvèdre, Syrah, Nebbiolo (Italy), and Tempranillo (Spain).

APPELLATIONS. French appellations include Bandol, Cornas, Côte-Rôtie, Graves, Haut-Médoc, Hermitage, Margaux, Pauillac, Pessac-Léognan, St-Estèphe, and St-Julien. In Italy, there is Barolo and in Spain some Riojas, Ribera del Duero, and Toro; in California, Chile, Australia, and South Africa, there is Cabernet Sauvignon.

FOOD PAIRING. These complex, tannic, 'thoroughbred' reds go best with full-flavoured but not over-fatty dishes such as truffles, game, duck, pigeon, and roast meat such as lamb; they are also good with pressed, uncooked cheeses such as Cantal or St-Nectaire.

SERVING. These wines are best consumed no earlier than five years after bottling; they should be decanted and served at a temperature between 59 and 63°F (15–17°C).

Complex, elegant, and fine reds

This category comprises essentially the best wines made from Pinot Noir in the world, such as the *premier* and *grand cru* wines of Burgundy, but also the best Pinot Noir from Alsace, Germany, Switzerland, Austria, the USA, South Africa, Australia, and New

Zealand. These red wines are characterized by the finesse of their aromas of red berries or flowers, which, over time can transform into notes of undergrowth. They are also distinguished by their smooth, silky texture and long-lasting finish.

GRAPE VARIETIES. Pinot Noir is the principal grape variety of this category, but you can sometimes find other varieties sharing its profile, such as Mencía from Galicia in Spain, the best Gamays (*crus* from Beaujolais), or even Nebbiolos from Piedmont in Italy.

APPELLATIONS. In Burgundy, the appellations are essentially Côte de Nuits, Côte de Beaune, and Côte Chalonnaise. The USA has Pinot Noir from Oregon, Central Otago comes from New Zealand, Mornington Peninsula from Australia, and Walker Bay from South Africa.

FOOD PAIRING. These elegant reds go well with refined dishes that are not overpowering in taste: such as those based on poultry, white meat, and game birds. Avoid spicy dishes or those with heavy sauces to showcase the refinement of the wine.

SERVING. Depending on the concentration of the wine, it should be laid down for 2 to 10 years in the cellar and served at a temperature between 59° and 63°F (15° and 17°C).

Fresh and fruity rosés

These easy-drinking wines should be enjoyed young. They are very refreshing, slightly crisp, with an expression of aromatic fruit. They are either made using the direct pressing method with red grapes, or the *saignée* method with a vat of red grapes (which can also contain some white grapes in certain cases).

GRAPE VARIETIES. The chief varieties include Cinsault, Grenache, Gamay, Pinot Noir, Merlot, and Cabernet Franc, as well as Zinfandel in California.

APPELLATIONS. These lively, fruity wines come from many French appellations, the most well-known of which are Coteaux-d'Aix-en-Provence, Coteaux Varois, Luberon, Côtes-de-Provence, Bordeaux,along with an increasing number of other appellations and regions.

FOOD PAIRING. These wines are the perfect accompaniment to light summer cooking, especially crudités, pasta with vegetables, mixed salads, grilled or steamed fish, vegetable tarts, tapenade, pizzas, and cheese.

SERVING. These wines are best consumed in their first year and should be served at 46–50°F (8–10°C). They should not be

> Some complex, elegant, 'thoroughbred' reds.

> Several fresh and fruity rosés.

over-chilled, since this will limit their fruity, floral bouquet.

Round, full-bodied rosés

While retaining rosé's refreshing quality, these wines are less crisp and offer a soft-fruit or sometimes a little spicy bouquet. They have a rounder, grapey mouth-feel and a light tannic structure. They are deeper in colour than the wines above and are essentially made by the *saignée* method (*see* p.66).

GRAPE VARIETIES. Carignan, Grenache, Merlot, Cabernet Sauvignon, Mourvèdre, Négrette, Pinot Noir, Syrah.

APPELLATIONS. The rosés from the following French appellations are good examples of this category: Bandol, Bordeaux clairet, Coteaux-du-Languedoc, Côtes-du-Rhône, Lirac, Marsannay, Rosé des Riceys, and Tavel. There also are the rosés of Italy, Spain, and all around the Mediterranean basin.

FOOD PAIRING. These full-bodied, round rosés go well with full-flavoured summer dishes that involve olive oil, vegetables, and fish, such as aïoli, bouillabaisse, tian of aubergine, ratatouille, and red mullet. They are also good with grills and cheeses, as well as Middle Eastern or Asian dishes.

SERVING. These wines should be served chilled, between 46 and 50°F (8–10°C) and should generally be consumed within two or three years of bottling,but some can mature for a longer time.

> A selection of light, firm, dry whites.

Light, firm, dry whites

These lively, easy-drinking, refreshing wines develop uncomplicated flowery and fruity bouquets.

GRAPE VARIETIES. The most commonly used French varieties are Aligoté, Chasselas, Chardonnay, Jacquère, Melon de Bourgogne (Muscadet), Pinot Blanc, Sauvignon Blanc, and Sylvaner. In Italy there is Trebbiano and Pinot Grigio, in Spain Palomino and Airén, and in Germany Müller-Thurgau.

APPELLATIONS. The appellations that best illustrate this family are Bourgogne Aligoté, Cheverny, Crépy, Entre-Deux-Mers, Mâcon-Villages, Muscadet, Petit Chablis, Alsace Pinot Blanc, Alsace Sylvaner, and Apremont. Also included are Switzerland's Fendant, Portugal's Vinho Verde, the Sauvignon Blanc or Pinot Grigio of Friuli (Italy), and the modern whites of La Mancha (Spain).

FOOD PAIRING. These firm, light wines are best with simple cuisine and unadorned flavours and often go well with fatty dishes, seafood such as oysters and mussels, raw or cooked vegetables, grilled and fried fish, charcuterie, and cheeses.

SERVING. Drink these wines quite young (less than two years in bottle) and chilled to around 46°F (8°C).

Supple, fruity, dry whites

These wines are soft-bodied, with a very fruity bouquet. They often have a touch of citrus and white fruit, and are pleasantly fresh.

GRAPE VARIETIES. These whites are produced from varieties such as Altesse, Chardonnay, Chenin, Clairette, Gros Manseng, Mauzac, Rolle/Vermentino, Sauvignon Blanc and Sémillon. In

DID YOU KNOW...?

Rosé is the oldest of the wine styles. *It was not until the end of the 17th century that black and white grapes were separated on the vines and in the vats. The wines of centuries ago were therefore either white, when the skins were removed on the press, or rosé when everything went into the vat. There are still echos of this time in the UK where Bordeaux is known as 'claret', an anglicized version of the term* clairet.

Refreshingly crisp white wines

White wines are made using white grapes, or from some red grapes without macerating the skins. (This results in an absence of tannins, which makes the wine thirst-quenching.) An often very refreshing crispness means that white wines are particularly good partners for seafood as well as for cheese. They are also a pleasant aperitif and go equally well with many dishes – not just seafood.

Spain there is Albariño, Maccabeo, Verdejo; in Italy Garganega, Fiano and Verdicchio; and in Austria Grüner Veltliner.
APPELLATIONS. French AOCs: Bandol, Bellet, Cassis, Chablis, Côtes-de-Blaye, Coteaux-d'Aix-en-Provence, Côtes-de-Provence, Gaillac, Graves, Jurançon sec, Pouilly-Fumé, Pouilly-Fuissé, Montlouis, Roussette de Savoie, Saint-Véran, Sancerre and Corsican wines. In Spain: Rías Baixas and Monterrei, Rueda and Somontano. In Italy: Soave, Verdicchio de Castelli di Jesi and whites from Sicily and Sardinia.
FOOD PAIRING. These wines go well with a variety of dishes, whether simple or more elaborate, including raw or cooked shellfish, seafood pasta, fish mousse, raw or grilled fish, charcuterie, and a wide range of cheeses.
SERVING. These white wines can be consumed up to three years after bottling, or even longer for the best wines. They should be served chilled, between 46 and 50°F (8–10°C).

Full-bodied, classy, dry whites

More complex than the preceding whites, these wines are notable for rich, sometimes fleshy, mouth-filling structure. They also have a pleasant crispness that makes them very refreshing. The finish is long and perfectly balanced. Often matured or vinified in oak barrels, these wines mingle toasty notes with a touch of vanilla creaminess. Aromas include ripe orchard fruit, aromatic herbs, and white flowers.
GRAPE VARIETIES. These distinguished whites are made with varieties such as Chardonnay, Chenin Blanc, Marsanne, Riesling, Roussanne, Sauvignon Blanc, Sémillon, Grüner Veltliner, Petite Arvine.
APPELLATIONS. These include, among others, Burgundy's greatest white wine appellations, such as Chablis Premier and Grand Cru, Corton-Charlemagne, Meursault, Chassagne-Montrachet, Puligny-Montrachet, and Montrachet; also Loire Valley appellations including Montlouis, Savennières, and Vouvray. As well, there is the Bordeaux appellation Pessac-Léognan, and many wines from California, Chile, New Zealand, and South Africa also come from these varieties.
FOOD PAIRING. These wines naturally accompany fine dining. They are good with Coquilles Saint-Jacques, lobster, turbot, and also with pan-fried foie gras, wild mushrooms, white meats in cream sauces, creamy cheeses such as St-Félicien or St-Marcellin, and mature goat's cheeses like Picodon.

SERVING. The full amplitude of these wines is revealed after three to five years in bottle, or even longer for some; above all, they should not be served too cold. Somewhere between 50 and 54°F (10–12°C) is best.

Aromatic, dry whites

These wines are notable for their exuberant flavours and big personalities. Typically, their characteristic aromas often make it possible to identify the grape variety simply by scent.
GRAPE VARIETIES. Such is the case with Gewurztraminer, with its notes of exotic fruits such as lychee, and Viognier, with its scents of peach or apricot, and Muscat with its aromas of fresh grapes; the smoky, spicy, honeyed notes of Pinot Gris; or Riesling, the mineral or floral tones of which are sometimes reminiscent of petroleum. The same can be said of some wines matured in such a way as to give marked notes of *rancio* such as: *vin jaune* from Jura, sherry from Spain and other oxidative wines such as tawny port and *vins doux naturels* from Roussillon.
APPELLATIONS. The most famous French appellations are the *vin jaune* from Jura, and Condrieu and Château-Grillet from the Rhône Valley. In Alsace, they simply follow the German approach, displaying the name of the grape variety, whether Gewurztraminer, Muscat, Riesling, or Pinot Gris, citing the localities for the *grands crus*. In Spain, the best-

> A full-bodied, classy, dry white.

known appellation is fino or amontillado sherry from the larger family of sherries (*see vins doux naturels*, pp.160–1).

FOOD PAIRING. These distinctive wines require special treatment; those made with Savagnin or Palomino grapes go best with aromatic dishes flavoured with spices or herbs, such as meat, fish or seafood curries, chicken with cream and morels, lobster in tomato and tarragon sauce. Rieslings and Pinots Gris are good with salmon with dill, and also with smoked fish. In terms of cheese, pressed, cooked cheeses such as Beaufort and Comté, or those with a pronounced taste like Munster, complement them particularly well.

SERVING. The fino sherries and wines made from Muscat and Viognier grapes should be consumed fairly young and between 46 and 50°F (8–10°C); the rest need three to five years in bottle and should be served between 50 and 54°F (10–12°C).

> Some rich, medium-dry and sweet whites.

Rich, medium-dry and sweet whites

The chief characteristic of these wines is the proportion of residual sugar naturally contained in the grape juice that has not been transformed into alcohol. This can be obtained either by supermaturation (leaving the grapes to ripen longer to reduce their moisture content), which means that they are harvested late to give a very concentrated juice, or by the action of a microorganism, *Botrytis cinerea*, on the grapes (*see* box p.54). In the first case, the wines will be medium-dry or rich; in the second they are described as sweet as they are packed with sugars. These wines are defined by their soft, almost viscous body, balanced by good acidity (crispness) and a rich, complex bouquet of fruits and honey. They also have a long, lasting finish.

GRAPE VARIETIES. Only certain varieties are suitable for these wines. The best-known are Chenin Blanc from the Loire Valley; Petit Manseng, Sauvignon Blanc, Sémillon, and Muscadelle in southwest France; Muscat, Gewurztraminer, Riesling, and Pinot Gris in Alsace and in Germany, and Furmint in Hungary. Many of these grape varieties are also used to make wine in this way in other parts of the world.

APPELLATIONS. The principal appellations include: in Alsace, Gewurztraminer *vendanges tardives* and *sélection de grains nobles*, Pinot Gris *vendanges tardives* and *sélection de grains nobles*, and Riesling *vendanges tardives* and *sélection de grains nobles*; in the Loire region, Bonnezeaux, Coteaux-de-l'Aubance, Coteaux-du-Layon, Quarts-de-Chaume, Montlouis, and Vouvray. Additionally, Barsac, Cérons, Jurançon, Monbazillac, Sainte-Croix-du-Mont, and Sauternes in southwest France; and the icewines of Germany (*eiswein*) and Canada, Beerenauslese and Trockenbeerenauslese in Germany and Austria, and late-harvest and noble rot wines in the New World.

FOOD PAIRING. As well as being splendid on their own, these white wines are traditional partners for rich dishes such as foie gras, chicken à la crème, duck à l'orange, blue cheeses like Roquefort, tarts made with yellow fruit, and cream-based desserts (sabayon, crème brûlée). Not too sugary, they also go very well with more exotic, spicy cuisine, and they match salty with sweet.

SERVING. These wines are best appreciated after three to five years in bottle, except for the great wines in this category which will keep for a long time. They should be served chilled but not iced, around 46–54°F (8–12°C).

TRUE OR FALSE?

White wines don't keep.

FALSE. Great sweet whites can remain drinkable for several centuries! The secret of a long life is the combination of three elements: sugar, alcohol, and acidity. These wines come from often acidic grape varieties, such as Sémillon or Sauvignon Blanc (for Sauternes), Chenin Blanc (for Vouvray), Riesling in Alsace and Germany, Furmint (Hungarian Tokaji), for example).

Sparkling wines

Quintessential party drinks, sparkling wines constitute a large family in which Champagne is the most illustrious representative. However, practically all the wine-producing regions of the world produce this type of wine. Significant levels of carbon dioxide and good acidity give them a light and lively feel that makes them very refreshing. In terms of dryness, they can be zero-dosage, *extra-brut*, *brut*, *sec*, *demi-sec* or *doux*. Sparkling wines have delicate flavours of fruit, flowers, and sometimes bread or pastries.

GRAPE VARIETIES. The principal varieties are Chardonnay, Chenin Blanc, Clairette, Mauzac, Muscat, Pinot Blanc, Pinot Noir, Pinot Meunier, Sauvignon Blanc, Savagnin, as well as Glera in Italy for Prosecco, Xarel-lo, Parellada and Maccabeu in Spain for cava.

APPELLATIONS. While Champagne gets top honours, other regions produce great sparkling wines, too. Some are crafted according to the same method of secondary fermentation in the bottle, such as the *crémants* from Alsace, Burgundy, Jura, Savoie, Bordeaux, and the Loire, as well as Crément de Limoux from the Midi, Saumur and Vouvray in the Loire Valley, and cava in Spain. Other appellations are produced using a different method, such as Clairette de Die, traditionally produced Blanquette de Limoux, and some sparkling wines from Gaillac. Some of these sparkling wines are often lighter and sometimes fruitier than Champagne. Moscato d'Asti, Asti Spumante, and Italian Prosecco are examples, as well as Germany's Sekt.

FOOD PAIRING. While appreciated as an aperitif, sparkling wines can also be served throughout a meal. The *brut* varieties go well with seafood; fish terrine; or fish that is grilled, smoked, or served in a light cream sauce. They are also good with semi-soft cheeses with a crust such as Camembert. *Sec* and *demi-sec* sparkling wines also go with the same cheeses, and with fruit desserts (if not too sweet), meringues, and dishes with a light custard sauce (*crème anglaise*).

SERVING. Sparkling wines should be generally be consumed when young and must be served chilled, at a temperature between 46 and 50°F (8–10°C).

> Several sparkling wines.

Vins doux naturels (VDN) and fortified wines

This family groups together fortified wines, strongly aromatic with a high alcohol and sometimes a sugar content. They are developed by regionally specific methods.

Vins doux naturels (VDN) and fortified wines are produced by mutage, the process of adding neutral alcohol during or at the end of fermentation in order to retain (for the sweet versions) some of the grapes' natural sugars while increasing the final alcoholic strength to 15–20% ABV. These wines are produced in warm regions such as Languedoc, Roussillon, the southern Rhône Valley, Corsica, Spain, Italy and, Portugal, and also in California, South Africa, and Australia. All have a silky, sumptuous mouth-feel with a long, aromatic finish. *Vins de liqueur* (VDL) are a blend of grape juice, very slightly fermented or not at all, with eau-de-vie (neutral spirits). Alcohol strength ranges from 16 to 22% ABV, and they have a particularly fruity flavour.

GRAPE VARIETIES. The principal varieties used in the making of French *vins doux naturels* are, for reds, mainly Grenache Gris or Noir and Maccabeu; the whites are made with Grenache Blanc, Maccabeu or Muscat. The main varieties for port are

DID YOU KNOW...?

To keep a sparkling wine from overflowing when uncorked, *ensure that all of the wine in the bottle is at the same low temperature. Just leave it in the bottom of the refrigerator for three hours. A Champagne bucket can then be used to keep the wine chilled throughout the meal. Remember that most great white wines should be served at a temperature between 52 and 54°F (11–12°C).*

Tinta Roriz, Tinto Cao, Touriga Franca, and Touriga Nacional. *Vins de liqueur* are chiefly made using Folle Blanche, Colombard, and Ugni Blanc for whites; Merlot, Cabernet Sauvignon, and Cabernet Franc for the rosés and reds. Macvin uses grape varieties from the Jura region of France.

APPELLATIONS. Port in Portugal. In France, Banyuls, Rivesaltes, Maury, Rasteau, Muscat de Beaumes-de-Venise, Muscat du Cap-Corse, Muscat de Frontignan, Muscat de Mireval, and Muscat de Rivesaltes. Sherry, Madeira, Malaga, and Marsala also belong to this category of fortified wines, despite significant differences in the way they are made. Among the VDLs, Pineau des Charentes, Floc de Gascogne, and Macvin du Jura hold an AOC. Others include Ratafia from Champagne.

FOOD PAIRING. VDNs are excellent on their own; but they also have a place at the table, especially at the end of a meal. Depending on how they are made (*see* box below), they call for different dishes. The whites made in an oxidative style (open to air), go well with foie gras, whether fresh or in a terrine. The other whites are best with fruit desserts such as apricot tart and also with blue cheeses like Roquefort. Because of their tannic strength and fruitiness, the reds that have been exposed to the open air – such as Banyuls Rimage and vintage ports – make good partners for game and sweet-savoury dishes such as duck cooked with figs or cherries, or even Peking Duck. They are also good with blue cheeses, and work well with plain chocolate. This is especially true of Banyuls Rimage and vintage port. The oxidative reds make good partners for chocolate desserts.Because of their high sugar and alcohol content, VDLs are best served as aperitifs, although they can also be served with pan-fried foie gras.

SERVING. Muscat-based VDNs should be consumed while young and fruity, as should the *vins de liqueur*. However, oxidative white and red VDNs may be consumed young but also improve with keeping. The rest of these wines are worth keeping three to five years in bottle to allow their full qualities to come to the fore.

> A few *vins doux naturels* and *vins de liqueur*.

Vins doux naturels: flavours and colours!

Depending on how they are made, the colour and flavour personality of these wines varies. Wines produced with no exposure to air and bottled early retain their primary aromas of fruits and flowers and, for reds, their full tannic strength. Examples include the Muscats from Beaumes-de-Venise and Frontignan in France, which have a lovely golden colour and delicious notes of apricot, melon, honey, flowers and fresh mint. The same goes for Rivesaltes wines, which retain a clear appearance and aromas of white flowers and honey. On the other hand, contact with air, or oxidation, develops deep colours and a maderized or *rancio* bouquet in these wines. So, for example, Rivesaltes, when matured in an oxidative environment, takes on dark tones ranging from slight brick-red to intense amber. They also have pronounced notes of almonds, walnuts, hazelnuts and candied citrus fruits.

1

2

3

4

Legendary wines

Known as 'dream wines' because they seem almost unattainable, they are very rare and – of course – expensive. These wines are more talked about than consumed.

PÉTRUS 1945

Although it was not among the *grands crus* classified in Bordeaux in 1855, Pétrus has become a legend; and its 1945 vintage a legend within a legend. Why? Because 1945 was when Edmonde Loubat gained a controlling interest in Pétrus, and lifted her vineyard to the ranks of greatness thanks to a savvy alliance with the wine merchant Jean-Pierre Moueix. Enjoyed by Britain's Queen Elizabeth as well as the late President Kennedy, Pétrus boomed during the 1960s. It's a cult wine, and a bottle of Pétrus 1945 is valued at $11,700 (£9,000).

CHEVAL BLANC 1947

Classified as an A-list *premier grand cru*, the wine from Château Cheval Blanc, owned by Bernard Arnault and Albert Frère, has been established since the 19th century as one of the greatest St-Émilions. It is distinguished by a 91-acre (37-ha) vineyard planted with an unusually high proportion of Cabernet Franc grapes, in an area where Merlot is king. The legendary year of 1947 made its mark as an exceptional vintage. The wine has a still-astonishing youthfulness and jammy, spicy, coffee aromas reminiscent of a great vintage port. Estimate: $8,000–$19,3500 (£6,000–£15,000) per bottle.

MOUTON-ROTHSCHILD 1945

Owned by the Rothschild family since 1853, this 208-acre (84-ha) domaine in the Pauillac appellation of Bordeaux was classified as *second cru* in 1855. Then Baron Philippe de Rothschild secured its elevation to *premier cru* in 1973. Considered legendary by many, the 1945 vintage bears a label showing V for wartime victory, the first in a long series of labels designed by artists. Appreciated as much for its quality as for its symbolism, on September 28, 2006, Mouton-Rothschild 1945 became the world's most expensive wine at an auction organized by Christie's: a lot of 12 bottles was sold for a total of $311,000 (£190,000) or almost $30,000 (£19,000) per bottle.

CHÂTEAU D'YQUEM 2001

At the time it was classified in 1855 as *premier grand cru exceptionnel*, this 247-acre (100-ha) Sauternes estate

1. Pétrus (Bordeaux).
2. Château Mouton-Rothschild (Bordeaux).
3. Château Cheval Blanc (Bordeaux).
4. Château d'Yquem (Bordeaux).
5. Romanée-Conti (Burgundy).
6. Scharzhofberger (Mosel).
7. Tokaj maturing in barrel.
8. Château Rayas (Châteauneuf-du-Pape).

was already much appreciated by the American president Thomas Jefferson, and by many of the crowned heads of Europe. Owned since the 18th century by the Lur-Saluces family, the domaine passed into the control of the LVMH luxury group in 1999. Two years later it produced one of its most famous vintages, acclaimed by all critics as exceptional and equal to the great years 1811 and 1847. Its price? Around $520 (£400) per bottle.

ROMANÉE-CONTI 1990

Covering only 4.5 acres (1.80 ha), this Burgundy 'monopole' (i.e. land exclusive to a sole proprietor) produces fewer bottles than the smallest châteaux of the Bordeaux region. The critics are unanimous in considering this wine close to perfection, most notably the 1990 vintage, and describe it as the quintessence of Pinot Noir. The price of a bottle is around $22,000 (£17,000) per bottle, which makes Romanée-Conti 1990 one of the world's most expensive wines.

CHÂTEAU RAYAS 1978

Discreet, if not secret, this famous Châteauneuf-du-Pape *cru* stands out by being produced exclusively from old Grenache vines. By contrast, the reputation of this great appellations rests on the blending of many varieties. Château Rayas was taken over by Jacques Reynaud in 1978. His trial run was a masterstroke, and the 1978 vintage took the US by storm. Celebrated for its concentration and finesse, this wine – characterized by spicy, leathery overtones – requires lengthy laying down. At auction a bottle will go for more than $1,950 (£1,500).

TBA SCHARZHOFBERGER 1976

In Germany's Saar Valley, Egon Müller is the heir of a family whose name is associated with great Riesling. Ripening by 'noble rot' produces outstanding sweet wine, thanks to the concentration of sugars and acidity. It also does not exceed 6% ABV. A Trockenbeerenauslese (TBA), the equivalent of a French 'Sélection de Grains Nobles', from the Scharzhofberger vineyard is a remarkable wine. The 1976 vintage, considered one of the best ever, is estimated to sell for more than $1,300 (£800) per half-bottle.

TOKAJ DISZNOKÖ 6 PUTTONYOS 1993

The rebirth of the prestigious Tokaj region in eastern Hungary was marked by the arrival of Western investors. Disznokö, the 'boar's rock', whose *terroir* was classified as *grand cru* in 1772, is owned by the AXA insurance company, which has entirely restructured it. In the Aszú category (sweet wines made from individually picked grapes), the 1993 vintage signalled the true revival of the domaine.

Recent vintages

Rating the quality of each vintage (from 1 to 10) serves as an indication for a whole wine-producing region. It helps to judge a wine's keeping potential, but bear in mind that it is an estimate only. In fact, appreciable differences are found within the same vintage, depending on the grape varieties, appellations, *crus*, and vineyard plots.

Key: Average year Good year Great year Exceptional year

ND: data unavailable. Regarding port, the years for which there is no information were not officially declared as 'vintage.' For other regions (South Africa, Argentina, Chile, Switzerland), the absence of evaluation signifies that there were no wines worth laying down.

	2015	2014	2013	2012	2011	2010	2009	2008	2007	2006	2005	2004	2003	2002	2001	2000	1999	1998	1997	1996	1995	1994
Bordeaux Reds	10	7	5	7	8	9	10	8	7	7	10	7	8	7	7	10	7	8	6	8	8	7
Bordeaux Dry whites	7	8	6	7	7	9	9	7	7	8	9	8	6	8	7	8	6	7	6	8	8	8
Bordeaux Sweet whites	9	9	7	6	9	10	9	8	7	8	8	5	9	9	8	6	8	8	9	9	9	7
Burgundy Reds	9	7	8	8	8	8	9	6	8	7	10	7	8	8	7	7	6	8	7	8	7	7
Burgundy Whites	8	8	7	8	8	8	8	7	7	8	10	8	10	8	8	8	6	8	8	10	8	8
Champagne (Vintage)	9	7	7	7	8	7	8	8	7	8	7	8	7	9	5	8	8	7	8	10	8	5
Alsace	8	7	6	7	8	8	8	7	7	7	7	7	6	5	6	6	5	7	7	6	6	6
Jura, Savoie	9	7	7	7	8	8	9	7	7	8	9	7	8	7	5	7	7	7	7	8	7	6
Loire Valley	9	8	5	7	7	8	9	7	7	6	9	6	8	6	7	8	6	7	8	9	8	6
Rhône Valley	8	6	7	7	8	9	9	6	7	7	9	7	7	5	8	8	8	9	7	7	8	6
Languedoc-Roussillon	9	8	6	8	9	8	9	7	8	7	7	7	7	5	8	8	6	7	6	6	7	5
Provence	9	9	6	7	7	8	8	6	7	8	6	8	6	5	7	7	8	8	7	7	8	5
Corsica	9	8	6	8	8	8	9	7	8	8	7	8	8	5	8	8	8	8	5	6	6	6
Italy Piedmont	9	5	8	7	7	7	8	9	6	8	6	8	8	7	8	7	8	10	10	10	7	7
Italy Tuscany	9	5	7	7	8	8	9	9	7	9	7	8	9	7	8	10	9	8	10	10	10	8

	2015	2014	2013	2012	2011	2010	2009	2008	2007	2006	2005	2004	2003	2002	2001	2000	1999	1998	1997	1996	1995	1994
Spain Rioja	9	7	6	7	8	8	9	10	7	8	8	7	8	6	8	8	7	8	7	8	10	9
Portugal Vintage port	9	5	7	8	9	8	7	8	7	8	10	9	9	7	8	10	–	8	9	7	–	10
Germany Mosel	10	6	6	8	7	8	9	7	8	8	7	7	7	8	7	6	7	8	8	6	7	8
Germany Rhine	10	6	6	8	7	8	9	7	8	7	8	7	8	8	8	7	7	7	7	7	7	7
Switzerland	7	7	–	7	8	8	9	9	9	8	9	9	10	8	8	9	8	10	–	–	–	–
Austria	10	6	8	7	7	8	8	7	8	9	8	8	7	9	8	8	10	8	10	9	9	8
Hungary Tokaj	6	7	9	nd	7	8	9	8	8	7	8	6	9	5	9	10	8	5	4	5	6	4
United States California	7	8	9	8	7	9	9	8	9	7	7	7	8	9	8	7	8	7	10	8	9	9
Chile	7	9	7	8	8	8	8	8	9	9	8	9	8	9	9	8	9	–	–	–	–	–
Argentina	6	7	9	8	9	8	9	8	9	9	9	8	8	9	8	8	9	–	–	–	–	–
South Africa	7	5	8	8	8	9	10	8	8	9	9	8	9	8	9	9	8	–	–	–	–	–
Australia	9	7	6	8	7	8	9	8	7	9	10	9	9	9	9	8	8	9	8	9	8	9
New Zealand	9	8	8	7	8	8	8	8	7	9	8	8	7	8	7	9	8	9	8	8	8	8

For red Bordeaux, the following great past vintages must be mentioned : 1990, 1989, 1985, 1982, 1978, 1970, 1961,1959, 1955, 1953, 1947 and 1945.

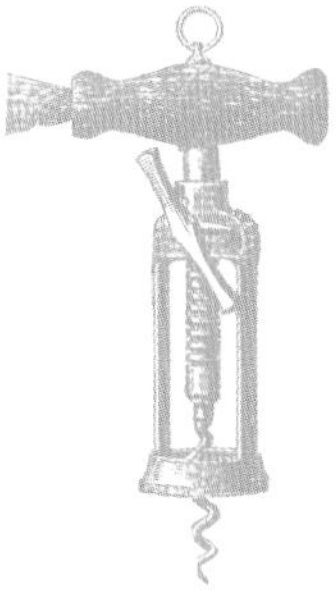

LOIRE
SUD-OUEST
SAINT-JOSEPH
2006
CÔTE-RÔTIE
2006
CÔTE-RÔTIE
VIN JAUNE
Côtes du Jura
ARBOIS
ARBOIS

LANGUEDOC
LANGUEDOC
VINS ÉTRANGERS
LE ROC DES ANGES
CLOS DES ROQUES
CAMAS
AQUILAE
CANTAGALLO
MICHEL JODOIN
HENRY OF PELHAM
CHARDONNAY
ETCHART
ESPIGA
TARAPACA

PRINCIPLES FOR MATCHING FOOD WITH WINES

A modest wine is an agreeable accompaniment to an unpretentious meal. However, when the cuisine is more elaborate or the ingredients rather special, a fine wine is more appropriate. Here is some advice on matching wines to dishes, depending on circumstances and on particular flavours.

Choose according to circumstances

Wine is not always consumed with every meal in everyday life and for a simple meal, a simple, modest wine without the accolade of a famous appellation is quite suitable. However, the pleasure of more elaborate cuisine is enhanced if it is accompanied by high quality wine, which is generally more expensive. Here are some suggestions, which can be adapted according to your budget, knowing that you can find real flavour experiences across a wide range of prices.

A SINGLE DISH. Simplicity is normally the name of the game, along with a little thoughtful planning, when you and your friends gather to share a single, convivial dish. For a chilli, some spaghetti, or a paella, a fresh and fruity red will go down well, such as a Beaujolais-Villages, a Côtes-du-Rhône or a light red from the Loire. For a paella made with fish or shellfish, try a reasonably powerful white wine from southern France. A rosé from Provence, Languedoc or the south-west of France will also complement any of the three dishes below left.

***Among the terms typically used to describe the delicate match** of food and wine are marriage, alliance, and harmony. For a successful pairing, it's important to take into account the texture and flavour characteristics of both.*

A FAMILY GATHERING. For family feasts, several wines from well-known appellations or estates might be suggested. In order to suit everyone, it's best to opt for 'consensus' wines. Among French whites, the wines of Alsace, Entre-Deux-Mers, Muscadet, Mâcon Villages, Saint-Véran, Sancerre, and Pouilly-Fumé should be mentioned. Several choices are possible for red wine. If opting for a roast: think of *crus* from Beaujolais, Côtes-de-Bourg, Gigondas, Madiran, Minervois, Bandol, Cornas, Bourgueil, St-Nicolas-de-Bourgueil.

A GOURMET MENU. The more refined the cuisine the more important it is that the accompanying wines should be of indisputable quality. Among the white wines, you might consider one of the Côte de Beaune *crus* or a Saint-Joseph or a Hermitage, Pessac-Léognan, Savennières, Condrieu, Château-Chalon, an Alsace *grand cru* or Jura. Good red wines are legion, although sometimes high-priced. Worthy choices are the grand families of Pomerol or Saint-Émilion, the classified *crus* of Médoc or Graves, Côte-Rôtie and the *premiers* and *grands crus* of Burgundy.

SUNDAY MENU

Chicken liver terrine
> ***Pouilly-Fuissé***

Roast guinea-fowl with mushrooms
> ***Cahors***

Strawberry tart
> ***Sainte-Croix-du-Mont***

While not too expensive, the wines suggested to serve with this Sunday meal are of reasonable quality and sufficient flexibility to go well with the classic dishes. The pungent white wine will match the richness of the first course, while a Cahors will flatten the earthy flavours of the mushrooms. Strawberry tart cries out for a sweet wine such as Sainte-Croix-du-Mont from Bordeaux.

In what order?

AS AN APERITIF. Cocktails or spirits actually do nothing to help prepare the palate to appreciate delicious cuisine and accompanying wines. Before embarking on a good meal, the simplest option is to serve a white wine that will also go with the first course. The most elegant choice would be a glass of Champagne.

WITH THE FIRST COURSE. The aim is to stimulate the taste buds without overwhelming them. For example, you could choose a lively, fruity Muscadet-type wine or one made from grapes such as Sauvignon Blanc, Sylvaner, Aligoté, or Chardonnay; these wines can also be served as an aperitif.

WITH THE MAIN COURSE. It is important to select one or more wines that will not clash with the preceding one. In general it's advisable to serve dry white wine before red, the lightest wine before a more full-bodied one, and the simplest wine before the most complex.

WITH CHEESE. Cheese's naturally salty, lactic character goes better with white wines, dry or sweet, than with reds. At any

Wines for snacks

Here are some ideas for enjoying wine with just a snack. A Beaujolais, Beaujolais-Villages, Côte-Roannaise, Côtes-du-Forez, or a Coteaux-du-Lyonnais or a Gamay from Touraine go well with all kinds of charcuterie, due to their natural crispness, while lively whites also work well. The same goes for good Chianti Classico and many Rhône-style blends from the New World. A *vin jaune* from the Jura goes well with Comté cheese; a dry amontillado sherry works with a few shelled walnuts; an oxidative Banyuls pairs nicely with a good sheep's-milk cheese accompanied by a spoonful of black-cherry jam; a Gewurztraminer can be enjoyed with a mature Munster served with country bread. Partner Clairette de Die with a simple brioche and serve gourmet biscuits with *demi-sec* Champagne or off-dry sparkling wine.

> A chilled, crisp white wine is the perfect choice to prime the appetite.

rate, avoid serving find red wine with a plate of cheese, blue cheeese or goat's cheese in particular. *See also* p.172.

WITH DESSERT. You could opt for a sweet wine or for a white *vin doux naturel* (such as a French Muscat from Mireval, Rivesaltes, or Beaumes-de-Venise) or a red VDN (such as Rasteau, Rivesaltes, Banyuls, or port). These whites go particularly well with fruit-based desserts, while the reds are good with chocolate in all its various forms.

Choosing according to the season

Our food preferences are influenced, to some degree, by the weather. In cold weather, everyone appreciates rich, warming dishes; while summer heat sparks a desire for vegetables and fresh fruit. Likewise, the pleasure experienced from drinking this or that wine varies according to the seasons and the dishes featured on the menu.

TRUE OR FALSE?

Sweet wines can be served as an aperitif.

TRUE. Although sweet wines are perfect dessert wines, they can also be enjoyed as an aperitif, especially if foie gras is to follow as a first course. For a holiday feast, choose Cérons, Coteaux-du-Layon, Jurançon, Sainte-Croix-du-Mont, or Monbazillac. For a gastronomic blowout, or for really special occasions, serve a late-harvest wine such as sweet Sauternes or rich Vouvray.

TRADITIONAL MENU

Oysters
> ***Chablis (or unoaked, cool-climate Chardonnay)***

Roast duck with baby vegetables
> ***Saint-Émilion Grand Cru (or fine, structured Merlot)***

Roquefort
Gâteau Saint-Honoré
> ***Muscat de Beaumes-de-Venise (or any late-harvest Muscat)***

Down-to-earth, country cooking calls for the Chablis (or steely Chardonnay) served with the oysters, the comforting St-Émilion Grand Cru (or high-end Merlot) with the roast duck, and a great harmony of flavours with the perfect combination of Roquefort cheese and Muscat de Beaumes-de-Venise, which will remain on the table for the Gâteau Saint-Honoré.

GASTRONOMIC MENU

Chilled duck foie gras
> ***Sauternes***

Roast leg of lamb with ceps
***Médoc* cru classé**

Chocolate gâteau
> ***Banyuls Rimage or Maury Vintage***

This elegant menu for ten guests is one you can serve without worrying about pairing mistakes. The subtle food-wine matches are perfect: foie gras with a sweet white wine is a classic; the lamb with mushrooms seems to have been made for great Médoc. As for the chocolate cake, which everyone will enjoy, it has few wine affinities except with a vin doux naturel, *such as the Banyuls or red Maury.*

CHILLED REDS AND SUMMER ROSÉS. In warm weather, lively, fruity wines are often best. The liveliness is conveyed by a sense of freshness, due to perceptible acidity and a delicate touch of soft tannins. These quaffable reds can be served at a temperature around 57°F (14°C); they include French Beaujolais, Côtes-du-Forez, Coteaux-du-Lyonnais, Côte-Roannaise, Alsace Pinot Noir, Anjou, Bourgueil, Bordeaux, and Bordeaux Supérieur. Italian Dolcetto and Spanish Garnacha can also fit the bill.

THIRST-QUENCHING WHITES. If you want a snappy white, try a French Bourgogne Aligoté, Cheverny, Crépy, Entre-Deux-Mers, Mâcon-Villages, Saint-Pourçain, Alsace Sylvaner, or a Vin de Savoie. If serving more sophisticated dishes, it's best to opt for the 'blancs de blancs,' whether Champagne, Pouilly-Fumé, Sancerre, Menetou-Salon, Chablis, Graves, or Alsace Riesling. Outside France, Sauvignon Blanc is generally a safe bet.

WINES FOR WINTER. Long winter evenings are made for rich, well-structured wines. The whites will be full-bodied and fleshy. To serve with good quality fish, shellfish, and white meats, try Beaune, Corton-Charlemagne, Meursault, Puligny-Montrachet, Savennières, Alsace Pinot Gris, white Châteauneuf-du-Pape, or Chardonnays from California or elsewhere. Red wines should be robust and structured with fruit and tannins. There's no better accompaniment for roasted or sauced red meat, game stew, or other slow-cooked dishes than a red from Cahors, Madiran, Pauillac, Gevrey-Chambertin, Vacqueyras, Rioja, or Chilean Cabernet Sauvignon and Malbecs from Argentina.

DID YOU KNOW...?

A strong, characterful wine is necessary to accompany a powerfully flavoured dish.
If you match a delicate dish with a really powerful wine, you risk killing the flavours of the food with those of the wine. For instance, a fish mousse should be accompanied by a dry, light wine, with good acidity, such as Muscadet or Sancerre; and a fish in sauce is best paired with a supple wine with subtle aromas, such as a Savennières or white Pessac-Léognan; while fish in meunière *sauce calls for an Alsace Riesling or a Mâcon Clessé or another Mâcon* cru; *finally, a delicate red such as a Pinot Noir or Sancerre is a good choice for* ris de veau *(veal sweetbreads).*

Match the dominant flavour of a dish

Taste buds are receptive to four basic flavours: sweet, salty, sour, and bitter, and in addition, umami, which is found in several kinds of dishes. In food, these elements are perceived to varying degrees. In wine, it is accepted that 'salty' hardly exists. For successful pairings of food and wine, it is advisable to not partner wines with dishes that have an excess of one of the four basic flavours.

WITH SALTY DISHES. Avoid overuse of salt (in cured meat, charcuterie, salty fish, etc.). It will detract from the appreciation of complex, old, mellow wines, whether red or white. With rather salty meat dishes, it's best to serve a young and tannic red as the salt softens the tannins and enhances the wine's

> Seafood's iodized flavour goes well with a simple white wine.

fruity flavours. With salty fish dishes, serve a lively and reasonably powerful white wine.

WITH SWEET DISHES. The basic rule of thumb is sugar with sugar. Most sugary dishes will over-intensify dry wines. They make reds too astringent and whites too bitter. These dishes need very fruity wines that are soft and aromatic or very powerful. For dishes like the famous duck à l'orange, which is sweet and sour, a pairing is hard to find. A fortified wine like Banyuls or a port can do the trick.

WITH ACIDIC DISHES. Acidity is a threat to every tannic or mature wine. With a vinaigrette, for example, water is the only possible accompaniment. With a lightly acidic dish, serve a very young, simple white or rosé wine rather than a red, especially one that is very tannic and has been patiently aged. Otherwise a double offence will have been committed, against the wine and the dish!

WITH BITTER DISHES. Bitterness, along with umami, can be hidden in many ingredients, especially certain vegetables such as artichokes, asparagus, endives (chicory), and spinach. Coffee, tea, and chocolate are also bitter. Wines do not go well with bitter foods, which turn them hard and astringent. There are a few exceptions: Alsace Muscat, *vin jaune*, and sherry can be served with bitter vegetables (so long as these are not seasoned with a vinaigrette); red VDNs are fine with bitter chocolate, but in rare cases, you could also try a dry and tannic red wine.

> A country terrine is a delicious reason for a wine tasting without having to serve a meal.

Harmonize textures and aromas

Lovers of fine food don't just appreciate a dish for its flavours, but also for its textures and aromas. In the context of a good meal, these elements should also be considered when choosing the wine.

TEXTURES. There are smooth wines (Beaujolais, Muscadet), fleshy wines (Burgundy, Côtes-du-Rhône), and astringent wines (wines from southwest France, Bordeaux). These characteristics can complement certain dishes. For instance, a beef stew is well matched with a fruity, lively Beaujolais-Villages that will soften the fibrous texture of the beef and the pungent flavour of the sauce. Likewise, the cuisine of southwestern France is perfect with the well-structured wines of that region (Madiran, Cahors, Tursan, Côtes-du-Brulhois), with the tannins softened by the fleshy, salty, full-flavoured dishes. In general, dishes with a soft consistency are associated with light, low-tannin wines, while rich dishes with a fuller texture are best with a rounder wine.

AROMAS. Sometimes the food can enhance the wine, although this is not easy to achieve. Some partnerships are nevertheless well known: duck with cherries or figs intensifies the red and black fruit flavours of a Banyuls Rimage; a dish made with truffles is sublime with a mature Hermitage or a Pomerol; an orange or lemon tart enhances the bitter-orange taste of an old Sauternes. The important thing to bear in mind is that the flavour of the wine should not overpower that of the dish, or vice versa.

Difficult pairings

Vinaigrettes and bitter vegetables (artichokes, asparagus, endives, spinach) kill the flavour of most good wines. Also, the natural sweetness of petits pois and carrots can blunt the taste of tannic reds. Eggs are difficult to pair with wine, not least because their slick texture coats the palate and prevents the tastebuds accessing the wine. In the case of meats and fish, there is less chance that they will alter the taste of wine; nevertheless, take care with very spicy dishes (east Asian ones, for example) and with sweet-and-sour flavours (including Chinese). In general, this type of cuisine goes only with highly structured, aromatic white wines like Gewurztraminer, Riesling, and Pinot Gris, or rosés such as Tavel or Côtes-de-Provence, and also with sweet wines. Few reds will suit them.

TRUE OR FALSE?

Wine suffers more from cold than heat.

FALSE. It is heat rather than cold at the point of service that can ruin the quality of a wine. White wines, rosés, and very young reds, above all, should be served chilled. It's interesting to note that a low temperature accentuates the sharper or tannic characters of these wines, enabling them to counterbalance the heaviness of certain dishes.

Proven partnerships

From a wide range of possibilities, some pairings of foods and wines have proven their worth and contributed to fine gastronomy.

WITH SEAFOOD. In the case of shellfish, the choices range from Muscadet through Entre-Deux-Mers, Sancerre, Cassis, St-Véran, or perhaps a Bouzeron, for example. For good quality fish served in sauce or with shellfish, it's better to go for the white *premiers* or *grands crus* from Burgundy or one of the rare white Hermitages. Riesling from Alsace, a region where great dry or sweet white wines proliferate, deserves fine seafood dishes or even caviar. Outside France, consider Italian Vermentino and Spanish Rueda.

WITH MEAT DISHES. There's nothing better for a grand occasion than a red Bordeaux, or a Cahors or Madiran, with roast lamb. The most appropriate choices to serve with game birds are found among the great red Burgundies, but for other small game head towards a Côte-Rôtie, Madiran, Châteauneuf-du-Pape or a Bandol. With a casserole, the preferred partner is a Côtes-du-Rhône-Villages or a Cahors. For a creamy chicken dish, the unctuous flavour of a white Burgundy such as Meursault makes a good choice. With grilled meat, a Médoc or a red wine from the Côte de Nuits is preferable. In the New World, good red options are Washington State Syrah, Oregon Pinot Noir, and Argentinian Malbec.

REGIONAL ALLIANCES. Many traditional European dishes have a natural affinity with the wines produced in their region. Cahors and Madiran are good partners for the rich cassoulets of southwest France. Switzerland's dry white wines are a splendid accompaniment to a fondue. In Spain, the dry white wines of Rías Baixas, made from the local Albariño grape, are served with Galician shellfish, while further inland classic red Riojas are traditionally served with roasted or grilled meat.

TRUE OR FALSE?

The wine used to cook should be served at table.

TRUE. Wine features as an ingredient in many recipes. The traditional French *coq au vin* was originally made with wine from Chanturgues; it became *coq au vin jaune* in Jura, *coq au Chambertin* in Burgundy, and *coq au Riesling* in Alsace. Throughout Europe, meat is slow-cooked in wine, whether in a French *daube*, a Greek *stifado*, or an Italian *stufato*. These dishes should be served with a bottle of the same wine that was used to make them.

Wine and cheese: a delicate match

Making good partners with wine and cheese is not immediately obvious: cheese is salty, often with a pronounced flavour and a fairly dense, creamy texture.

WITH RED WINES. Reds generally go less well with cheese than do white wines, as their tannins are accentuated through umami and the milky texture. The custom of serving a mature red wine with cheese is often a mistake, because the subtle taste of the wine will be masked by the cheese's stronger flavour. There are a few exceptions, though: hard and semi-hard cheeses from the Pyrenees that are not too strong, such as Ossau Iraty, work with red wine that is not too tannic. Likewise, pressed, uncooked cheeses (Cantal, Gouda, Mimolette [Edam], St-Nectaire) make good partners for great, aged Bordeaux wines where the tannins have softened (Médoc, Pomerol, St-Émilion, Pessac-Léognan). In the New World, look for drier, lighter, aged styles of Pinot Noir and Merlot.

WITH WHITE WINES. Whether dry or somewhat sweeter, white wines are the easiest pairing with cheese. Their sharpness brings a necessary freshness and their fruitiness counterbalances the cheese's strong flavour personality. The absence of tannins in white wines also explains this alliance. Tannin, especially in young red wines, is firmly accentuated by the cheeses.

EXCEPTIONAL WINE CALLS FOR EXCEPTIONAL FOOD

With a top* cru classé *from Bordeaux. *To do a grand vin justice, dishes sometimes need a little adaptation. The many noble or fine tannins in a great Bordeaux do not go well with desserts, except, possibly, for the one suggested here, where the wine can reveal its full complexity. Avoid putting too much garlic in the lamb and don't make the dessert too sweet.*

GASTRONOMIC MENU

Quail stew

Roast leg of lamb

Pommes forestière

Aged Mimolette (or Edam)

Fresh fruits macerated in Bordeaux wine

GASTRONOMIC MENU

Foie gras

Roast duck with peaches and spices

Roquefort

Puff pastries

With a Sauternes. *An opulent, fleshy, dominant wine, Sauternes calls for savoury, rich, spicy dishes. Its classic partners are foie gras, Roquefort, or puff pastries. In this menu, duck (which goes very well with fruit) is accompanied by peaches. Together with the Sauternes, it's a perfect partnership.*

With a Banyuls. *An opulent, powerful, rich wine that goes well with savoury, spicy, strong flavoured dishes. Its high alcohol content is balanced by cool ingredients and fruit. The menu suggested here presents no problem.*

GASTRONOMIC MENU

Duck foie gras

Tajine of pigeon with almonds and raisins

Stilton

Gâteau Opéra

GASTRONOMIC MENU

Terrine of scallops

Free-range chicken in cream and chanterelles

Creamy Chaource

Peach Melba

With a vintage Champagne. *A 'white' menu will highlight this great Champagne. The seafood, the lightness of the chicken, the cream, chanterelles, cheese, and Peach Melba all make splendid partners for this festive wine. Colours and textures come together in perfect harmony.*

With a* vin jaune *from Jura, France. *The unusual aromas (walnuts, spices, warm bread) and the dominating, persistent flavour of* vin jaune *will harmonize perfectly with each of the dishes suggested here; although it might be helpful to alert your guests to this wine's distinct character.*

GASTRONOMIC MENU

Asparagus in sauce *mousseline*

Coq au vin jaune

Comté

Walnut gâteau

Successful food and wine partnerships

The following table lists some classic and more regional partnerships of foods and wines. It also suggests more surprising matches that have been discovered during tastings. However, these suggestions are only a guide; there are no fixed rules for pairings. Personal taste and culture strongly influence the appreciation of different flavours.

APPETIZERS	
Anchovies, fresh	Chablis, white Banyuls, white Châteauneuf-du-Pape, Collioure rosé, Coteaux-d'Aix rosé, Spanish rosé, fino sherry.
Artichokes, stuffed (with bacon, mushroom, onion)	Lirac rosé, Tavel, dry Alsace Muscat, Spanish rosé.
Asparagus, green	Viognier, dry Muscat, Alsace Muscat, Collioure Blanc, fino sherry.
Asparagus, white	Pinot Blanc, Alsace Muscat.
Avocado	Côtes-de-Provence rosé, Mâcon-Villages, Sancerre.
Caviar	*Blanc de blancs* Champagne, dry Alsace or German Riesling (or iced vodka!).
Chicory (endive) and walnut salad	Savagnin-based Jura wines: Arbois, Côtes-du-Jura, L' Étoile.
Eggs Mimosa (or devilled eggs)	Chinon rosé, Spanish rosé, white Côtes-de-Provence, Mâcon-Villages.
Foie gras terrine	Sweet wines such as Sauternes, Coteaux-du-Layon, Jurançon moelleux, Monbazillac, Pinot Gris *sélection de grains nobles*, Gewurztraminer *sélection de grains nobles*, or a fortified wine such as Banyuls or port.
Gazpacho	Spanish rosé, Collioure rosé, Côtes-du-Rhône rosé, Tavel.
Guacamole	Sweet wine if spicy, otherwise see Avocado.
Melon	*Vins doux naturels*: Muscat de Beaumes-de-Venise, Muscat de Rivesaltes, Banyuls, Rivesaltes; ruby port; sercial or bual Madeira.
Salad Auvergnate (mixed salad with sausage, and potatoes)	Beaujolais-Villages, Côtes-d'Auvergne, Côtes-du-Forez.
Salade niçoise (mixed salad with olives, tuna, anchovies)	Bandol rosé, white Bellet, white Cassis, Coteaux-d'Aix rosé.
Taramasalata	Pouilly Fumé, Alsace Riesling, or New World Sauvignon Blanc.

HOT FIRST COURSES	
Bacon quiche	Pinot Blanc, Pinot Gris, white wines from Savoie or light red wines (Beaujolais, Alsace Pinot Noir, red Sancerre).
Cheese soufflé	Jura wine made with Savagnin grapes, Arbois, Côtes-du-Jura, Château-Chalon.
Escargots à la bourguignonne (snails)	Bourgogne Aligoté, white Beaujolais, Chablis, Mâcon-Villages, or unoaked Chardonnay.
Fish soufflé	Chablis, white Graves, white Pessac-Léognan, Pouilly Fumé, California Fumé Blanc.
French onion soup	Beaujolais-Villages, Entre-Deux-Mers, Mâcon-Villages, New World Chardonnay.
Fresh foie gras, warm	A rich, sweet wine such as Banyuls Rimage or Sauternes; full-bodied red wines (Madiran, Cahors, St-Emilion).
Frogs' legs	Bourgogne Aligoté, Petit Chablis, Mâcon-Villages, Alsace Riesling, Alsace Sylvaner.
Garbure (stew with cabbage, beans, salted duck or pork, etc.)	Cahors, Irouléguy, Madiran, or New World Malbec or Tannat.
Onion tart	Pinot Blanc or Sylvaner.
Petits farcis provençaux (courgettes or other stuffed vegetables Provençal-style)	Bandol rosé, white or rosé Bellet, red Côtes-du-Rhône-Villages, Tavel, or New World Grenache.
Pike quenelles	Chablis, Pouilly-Fuissé, Saint-Véran, Roussette de Savoie, lightly oaked Chardonnay.
Pizza	Coteaux-d'Aix-en-Provence red or rosé, Luberon red or rosé, Chianti, Valpolicella, Barbera.
Vol-au-vent	Jura *vin jaune*, a great Chardonnay (Corton-Charlemagne, Meursault, Montrachet, Sonoma Chardonnay).

CHARCUTERIE	
Andouille (chitterlings)	Mâcon-Villages, Sancerre, Savennières, South African Chenin Blanc.
Boudin noir (black pudding)	Chinon, Crozes-Hermitage, Saint-Joseph, Saumur-Champigny, and good New World Cabernet Franc or Syrah.
Chicken liver mousse	Beaujolais *crus*, white Beaune, white Ladoix-Serrigny, Meursault, or full-bodied New World Chardonnay.
Chorizo (spicy)	Cahors, Irouléguy, Rioja, Grenache, Zinfandel.
Country pâté	Beaujolais, Chinon, Coteaux-du-Lyonnais, Côtes-du-Rhône-Villages, Crozes-Hermitage, Saint-Joseph, Saumur-Champigny, and New World Cabernet Franc or Syrah.
Dried sausage or salami	Crozes-Hermitage, Burgundy Hautes-Côtes-de-Beaune, Burgundy Hautes-Côtes-de-Nuits, Sancerre rouge, and Sonoma Pinot Noir or Washington State Syrah.
Game terrine	Bergerac, Châteauneuf-du-Pape, Mercurey, Gevrey-Chambertin, Pomerol, St-Émilion, Vacqueyras, Garrafeira from central Portugal, and many good American Rhône-style blends.
Ham, cooked	Beaujolais-Villages or Beaujolais *crus*, Mercurey, Mâcon-Villages.
Ham, cured	Collioure, Irouléguy, Pinot Grigio from Italy's Alto Adige, Soave Classico, Rheingau Riesling trocken (dry), fino or manzanilla sherry, and many young Spanish red wines.
Ham, smoked	Riesling – French *vendange tardive* style, German *spätlese* style, or New York State off-dry style.
Jambon persillé (cold ham in parsleyed gelatin)	White or red Beaujolais, Chablis, white Mercurey, Pouilly-Fuissé, white Saint-Romain, and many good unoaked Chardonnays.
Pork sausage	Buzet, Côtes-du-Rhône, Gigondas, Italian Dolcetto d'Alba, Washington State Merlot, and Spanish Rioja.
Rabbit terrine	Bourgueil, Cheverny, Cour-Cheverny, St-Nicolas-de-Bourgueil, Morgon, Moulin-à-Vent, and good New World Cabernet Franc.
Rillettes	Montlouis, Sancerre, Vouvray, as well as New World Chenin Blanc and Sauvignon Blanc.
Salami	Irouléguy, Tavel, Vin de Corse rosé; red or rosé from Spain's Navarra; red from Italy's Barbera, Chianti Classico, Montepulciano d'Abruzzo, Rosso Conero; or dry amontillado sherry.

EGGS	
Eggs in gelatin	Young, fruity wines from the Côte de Beaune (Santenay, Maranges).
Eggs poached in red wine	Beaujolais *crus*, red Mâcon, Pinot Noir from the Côte de Beaune and Côte Chalonnaise, as well as basic Pinot Noir from Oregon.
Omelette, cheese	Chardonnays and Savagnin from Jura, France; and unoaked New World Chardonnay.
Salmon eggs (red caviar)	Chablis, Alsace Riesling, Vouvray; and good South African Chenin Blanc.
Scrambled eggs	Light and fruity red wines (Beaujolais or unoaked New World Gamay).
Scrambled eggs with truffles	White Hermitage, Montrachet, and Sonoma Chardonnay.

SHELLFISH	
Crab	White Cassis, Chablis, Entre-Deux-Mers, Muscadet, New Zealand Sauvignon Blanc, and good American Chardonnay.
Crayfish, poached in wine or broth	Condrieu, white Châteauneuf-du-Pape, dry Riesling.
Crayfish, grilled	Chablis Premier or Grand Cru, white Hermitage, Pessac-Léognan, Riesling.
Lobster in a tomato and tarragon sauce	Good Pinot Gris, Jura *vin jaune*, medium-dry Vouvray or Chenin Blanc.
Lobster, grilled	Corton-Charlemagne, white Hermitage, Pessac-Léognan, Meursault, Alsace Riesling, Savennières, Verdicchio dei Castelli di Jesi, good Washington State or Sonoma Chardonnay.
Mussels in cream sauce	White Bergerac, white Côtes-de-Blaye, Pouilly-Fuissé, white Rully, and crisp New World Chardonnay.
Mussels in white wine	Entre-Deux-Mers, Muscadet, Sauvignon Blanc, Albariño.
Oysters	Chablis, Entre-Deux-Mers, Muscadet, Picpoul-de-Pinet, young Riesling.
Oysters, cooked	*Blanc de blancs* Champagne, white Graves, rich Riesling, Savennières, Vouvray, and good New World Chenin Blanc.
Paella	White Yecla (Spain), dry rosé, and generally any dry aromatic white wine, such as Sauvignon Blanc.
Prawns/langoustines in mayonnaise	Pouilly Fumé and Sancerre, or any good Sauvignon Blanc; as well as Chablis or any good unoaked Chardonnay.
Scallops	*Blanc de blancs* Champagne, white Châteauneuf-du-Pape, white Hermitage, Pessac-Léognan, good dry Riesling.
Shrimps	White Bergerac, white Cassis, Petit Chablis, Entre-Deux-Mers, Muscadet, Picpoul-de-Pinet, and most crisp, unoaked whites from around the world.
Shrimp in sweet and sour sauce	Pinot Gris, Alsace Muscat, Tavel, Bellet rosé.

FISH	
Bouillabaisse	Bandol rosé, Cassis, Coteaux-d'Aix-en-Provence rosé, Tavel, as well as Spanish rosé.
Cod, salted, with aïoli	White or rosé Bandol, Cassis, white or rosé Côtes-de-Provence, rosé Collioure, Irouléguy rosé, as well as Spanish rosé.
Cod, salted, in purée	Cassis, white Hermitage, white Saint-Joseph, and good Roussanne.
Eel in Bordelaise sauce	Red Bergerac, red Bordeaux supérieur, Graves, satellite appellations of St-Émilion, and good New World Cabernet Franc.
Fish pie (with cream sauce)	Mâcon-Villages, Pouilly-Fuissé, Oregon Pinot Gris, Bianco di Custoza, Pfälz (Germany) Sylvaner, Nahe (Germany) Müller-Thurgau, and Napa Valley Chardonnay.
Fish, plain	White wines of a varying degree of crispness, depending on how fatty the fish and its garnish are: from Chilean Chardonnay to one of the *grands crus* of Burgundy or Alsace. Red wines, if not too tannic (such as Cabernet Franc, Gamay, or Pinot Noir).
Fish terrine	Bouzeron Aligoté, Chablis, white Graves, Mâcon-Villages, Muscadet, Sancerre, Alsace Silvaner, and lightly oaked New World Chardonnay.
Freshwater fish	Chablis, Swiss Chasselas, white Graves, white Mercurey, Montlouis, white Rully, Sancerre, Vouvray, and good New World Pinot Gris and Pinot Blanc.
Fried fish	Beaujolais, Entre-Deux-Mers, Gamay, Muscadet, Roussette de Savoie, Chardonnay- or Savagnin-based whites from the Jura, Pinot Grigio from Friuli (Italy), Frascati Superiore (Italy), and good Sauvignon Blanc.
Hake, cold with mayonnaise	Mâcon-Villages, Pinot Blanc, white Vin de Savoie, and Sylvaner.
Oily fish (swordfish, herring, mackerel, sardines, tuna)	Bourgogne Aligoté, Muscadet, Sancerre, Sauvignon Blanc from South Africa and New Zealand, Sylvaner, white Dão (Portugal), Vinho Verde (Portugal).
Raw fish	Chablis Premier Cru, Meursault, white Graves, New Zealand Chardonnay.
Red mullet	Red Bandol or Bandol rosé, Collioure, red or white Côtes-de-Provence.
Salmon in sorrel sauce	Condrieu, white Châteauneuf-du-Pape, and good Viognier.
Salmon, poached	Whites: white Burgundy, Sancerre, Savennières, dry Vouvray, Sicilian white wine, and good Chenin Blanc. Reds: Beaujolais-Villages, Bourgueil, and Oregon Pinot Noir.
Salmon, smoked	*Blanc de blancs* Champagne, good dry Riesling, Sancerre (or a peaty single-malt whisky).
Sardines, grilled	Côtes-de-Provence, white Côtes-du-Rhône-Villages, white Coteaux-du-Languedoc.
Sea bass (Bass), grilled	White Bellet, white Châteauneuf-du-Pape, white Côtes-de-Provence, Chablis Premier or Grand Cru, and good American Chardonnay.
Smoked fish	Chablis Premier Cru, *blanc de blancs* Champagne, Pouilly-Fumé, Sancerre, off-dry Riesling, and Pinot Gris.
Sole meunière	White Bellet, Chablis Premier or Grand Cru, Sancerre or other good Sauvignon Blanc, and Riesling.
Sushi	Mâcon, Muscadet, St-Véran, Menetou-Salon, New Zealand Sauvignon Blanc.
Tuna Basque-style (with ham and tomatoes)	Red or rosé Collioure, red or rosé Coteaux-du-Languedoc, red Côtes-du-Rhône-Villages, Irouléguy rosé, Tavel, and Spanish rosé.
Turbot in hollandaise sauce	Corton-Charlemagne, white Hermitage, Meursault, Pessac-Léognan, and good Sonoma or Washington State Chardonnay.
White fish in *beurre blanc*	*Blanc de blancs* Champagne, dry or medium-dry Vouvray, Meursault, Pessac-Léognan, Puligny-Montrachet, Savennières, Mosel (Germany) Rieslings, and good Sonoma or Washington State Chardonnay.
White fish, grilled	A dry white *grand cru*, white Coteaux-d'Aix-en-Provence, Soave (Italy), Verdicchio (Italy), white Vin de Corse, and oaked dry Sémillon.
Whitebait, fried	Bourgogne Aligoté, Mâcon, Muscadet, Vinho Verde (Portugal).

LAMB	
Lamb couscous	Cahors, Côtes-du-Rhône-Villages, Madiran, Gigondas, and good New World Grenache and Rhône-style blends.
Lamb curry	Bergerac, Castillon-Côtes-de-Bordeaux, Francs-Côtes-de-Bordeaux, Lalande-de-Pomerol. (Also, good beer!)
Lamb sautéed Provence-style	Red Coteaux-d'Aix-en-Provence, red Côtes-de-Provence, Côtes-du-Rhône-Villages, and good New World Grenache and Rhône-style blends.
Lamb stew	Pinot Noir from Côte de Beaune, Côte Chalonnaise, Oregon, and New Zealand, as well as Beaujolais *crus*.
Leg of lamb with herbs and/or garlic	Generous, powerful red wines (Bandol, Châteauneuf-du-Pape, Côtes-du-Roussillon-Villages, Coteaux-du-Languedoc, St-Chinian, Vacqueyras, and good New World Syrah and Rhône-style blends).
Mechoui (spit-roasted lamb)	Red Coteaux-du-Languedoc, Bandol, red Coteaux-de-Mascara (Algeria), and good New World Syrah and Grenache.
Rack of lamb	Graves, Médoc, Pauillac, Pessac-Léognan, St-Julien, as well as California, Washington State, and Chilean Cabernet Sauvignon.
Roast lamb	Classy, complex red wines like the Bordelais *crus* (Graves, Margaux, Pauillac, Pomerol, St-Émilion), a good vintage Bandol; Spanish Rioja Reserva and Ribera del Duero; California, Washington State, Chilean Cabernet Sauvignon.
Roast shoulder of lamb	Haut-Médoc, Médoc, and California, Washington State, or Chilean Cabernet Sauvignon
Saddle of lamb	Côte-Rôtie, Hermitage, Médoc, Pomerol, St-Émilion, and good New World Cabernet, Merlot, or Syrah.
Tajine of lamb with apricots	Bonnezeaux, Coteaux-de-l'Aubance, Coteaux-du-Layon, Quarts-de-Chaume, Montlouis Moelleux, Vouvray Moelleux. Also good Oregon Pinot Gris or Pinot Blanc.
Whole leg of lamb, spit-roasted	Pinot Noir from Côte de Beaune or from Oregon; Cabernet Franc from Bourgueil, Chinon, St-Nicolas-de-Bourgueil, or Washington State.

1998
"HUGEL"
HOMMAGE A JEAN HUGEL
ALSACE
APPELLATION ALSACE CONTRÔLÉE
HJH
HJH
TOKAY PINOT GRIS
"HUGEL"
GEWURZTRAMINER
"HUGEL"
RIESLING

BEEF	
Beef casserole	Cahors, Corbières, Côtes-du-Rhône-Villages, Côtes-du-Roussillon-Villages, Madiran, and a broad range of New World Malbec, Syrah and Rhône-style blends.
Beef Wellington	Reds from Bordeaux (Médoc or the Libournais) and Burgundy. Also good New World Cabernet Sauvignon and Pinot Noir.
Bœuf bourguignon	Chinon, Corbières, Côtes-du-Rhône-Villages, Mercurey, Minervois, Rully, St-Amour, red Saumur. Also good New World Cabernet Franc and Pinot Noir.
Carpaccio	Reds from the Côte Chalonnaise; Chianti Classico or Chianti Rufina; good New World Sangiovese.
Chateaubriand	Gevrey-Chambertin, Graves, Pomerol, Pommard, St-Émilion. Also good New World Merlot and Pinot Noir.
Chili con carne	Argentinian Malbec; California Zinfandel; St-Chinian, Cahors.
Couscous with meatballs	Gris de Boulaouane (Morocco), Fitou, red Coteaux-de-Mascara (Algeria), Côtes-du-Rhône, New World Rhône-style blends, Cairanne rosé, and, in general, lively, fruity or full-bodied rosés.
Entrecôte à la bordelaise	Bergerac, Bordeaux supérieur, Côtes-de-Blaye, Castillon-Côtes-de-Bordeaux, Fronsac, Graves, and good New World Cabernet France and Merlot.
Entrecôte, grilled	Cabernet Sauvignon-based wines from around the world, including a recent vintage Médoc. Also, young, generous Rhône-style blends (including Châteauneuf-du-Pape, Cornas, Gigondas, Vacqueyras).
Pot-au-feu (beef stew)	Red Anjou, Bourgueil, Côtes-de-Bordeaux, Saumur-Champigny, Pinot d'Alsace, red Sancerre. Also, New World Cabernet Franc and Pinot Noir.
Roast beef	Powerful, well-structured, generous red wines (from the Côte de Nuits, Margaux, Pauillac, Pomerol, and St-Émilion to Washington State Merlot and Oregon Pinot Noir).
Steak tartare	Buzet, Cahors, Crozes-Hermitage, Chilean Merlot, Australian Shiraz.
Steak with pepper sauce	Red Côtes-du-Rhône, Fronton, California Zinfandel, Australian Shiraz.
Steak, grilled	Chénas, Fronton, Cornas, Moulin-à-Vent, Chianti Classico Riserva, as well as Washington State Syrah and Argentinian Malbec.

PORK	
Andouillette à la crème (sausage made with pork chitterlings in cream sauce)	White Beaujolais, Chablis, Pouilly-Fuissé, white Rully, Saint-Véran, and good, rich, New World Chardonnay.
Andouillette, grilled	Light red wines (red Anjou, Beaujolais-Villages, Gamay, Pinot Noir, red Sancerre); dry, fruity white wines (Chablis, Gaillac, white Saumur, good New World Chardonnay).
Choucroute (dressed sauer-kraut/white cabbage)	Alsace Pinot Gris, Alsace Riesling, Alsace Sylvaner.
Curried pork	Pinot Gris, Gewurztraminer, white Lirac, white Hermitage, and, in general, fragrant, dry, white wines.
Pork grill	Full-bodied, fruity wines: Bergerac, Crozes-Hermitage, Saint-Joseph, Saumur-Champigny, and good New World Cabernet Franc and Syrah.
Pork shoulder	Light white wines (white Anjou, Mâcon-Villages, Pinot Blanc, Sylvaner, dry Riesling) and light, fruity red wines (Beaujolais, Mâcon-Villages, young Pinot Noir).
Potée au chou (pork and cab-bage soup/stew)	Brouilly, Mâcon-Villages, red Sancerre, and good young Pinot Noir.
Roast pork	Crozes-Hermitage, Côte-de-Beaune, Côtes-du-Rhône-Villages, Saint-Joseph, and New World Rhône-style blends.

VEAL	
Blanquette de veau (creamy veal stew)	Beaujolais-Villages, Mâcon-Villages, white Mercurey, white Givry, red Sancerre, and good, rich New World Chardonnay.
Calf's head	Beaujolais *crus*, Pouilly-Fuissé, Sancerre rosé, Tavel and other good, dry rosé.
Escalope Normande (with mushrooms, calvados, and cream sauce)	White Burgundy, Chardonnay- or Savagnin-based Jura wine, California Chardonnay, Washington State Chardonnay.
Escalope, fried	Beaujolais *crus*, red wines from Côte de Beaune, red Graves. Also Oregon and New Zealand Pinot Noir.
Osso-buco	Barbera, Barbaresco, Chianti Classico, Valpolicella.
Pan-fried veal kidneys in mustard sauce	Full-bodied, fairly young red wine (Pomerol, Saint-Émilion); Chinon, Morgon, St-Amour, Côte Chalonnaise Pinot Noir. Also good New World Cabernet Franc and Merlot.
Roast veal	Beaujolais *crus*, Côte de Beaune Pinot Noir, Oregon and New Zealand Pinot Noir.
Rolled veal	Beaujolais *crus*, Bourgueil, St-Nicolas-de-Bourgueil, New World Cabernet Franc, Burgundy Pinot Noir, Oregon and New Zealand Pinot Noir.

Veal chop	Médoc *grands crus* (Pauillac, St-Estèphe), *crus* from the Côte de Nuits (Gevrey-Chambertin, Chambolle-Musigny). Also, fine California Cabernet and Oregon Pinot Noir.
Veal liver	Chinon, Pomerol, St-Émilion, red Sancerre. Also, good New World Cabernet Franc and Merlot.
Veal Marengo (with mushrooms and red wine)	Côtes-du-Rhône-Villages, Costières-de-Nîmes, Ventoux, red wine from Dão (Portugal). Also, good New World Grenache and Rhône-style blends.
Veal Orloff (braised with mushrooms and béchamel sauce)	A great white Burgundy such as Chassagne-Montrachet, Corton-Charlemagne, Meursault; also deep, fruity red wines, *e.g.* a Burgundy from the Côte de Beaune. From the New World, try Sonoma Chardonnay or Oregon Pinot Noir.
Veal sweetbreads in cream sauce	A great white Burgundy such as Corton-Charlemagne, Meursault, Montrachet, Château-Chalon; Jura *vin jaune*, Alsace Pinot Gris, medium-dry Vouvray. Also, rich New World Chardonnay or Pinot Gris.

DUCK, GOOSE, PIGEON	
Cassoulet	Cahors, Côtes-du-Brulhois, Madiran. Also New World Malbec and Rhône-style red blends.
Duck à l'orange	Young sweet wines: Cérons, Loupiac, Monbazillac, Sauternes, Jura *vin jaune*. Also, late-harvest Sémillon.
Duck confit	Bergerac, Buzet, Cahors, Châteauneuf-du-Pape, Madiran, Pécharmant. Also, New World Malbec and Rhône-style red blends.
Duck with figs or cherries	Rich, powerful wines (Bandol, Châteauneuf-du-Pape, Rhône-style red blends); young fortified wines (Banyuls, Maury, Rivesaltes).
Duck with olives	Côtes-du-Rhône-Villages, Gigondas, Vacqueyras, and New World Rhône-style blends.
Peking duck	Gewurztraminer or Pinot Gris, and Arbois, Château-Chalon, or Jura *vin jaune*.
Magret (duck breast)	Good Bordeaux vintages (Médoc and Libournais). Also good Cabernet and Merlot.
Pigeon pastilla (savoury game bird pie)	Rioja or good New World Tempranillo. Also, a fortified wine (Banyuls, Muscat de Beaumes-de-Venise, Muscat de Rivesaltes, or Muscat du Cap-Corse); red Costières-de-Nîmes; Alsace Muscat; Gris de Boulaouane (Morocco).
Roast duck	Merlot-based wines: Lalande-de-Pomerol, Pomerol, Saint-Émilion; also good Pinot Noir such as *crus* from the Côte de Nuits.
Roast goose	Mature red wines from Côte-Rôtie (or Syrah), Côte-de-Nuits (or Pinot Noir), Madiran (or Tannat), Margaux (or Cabernet), St-Émilion (or Merlot), and even late-harvest Pinot Gris.
Roast pigeon	A good vintage Cabernet or Merlot from Médoc or the Libournais; or a Bandol, Châteauneuf-du-Pape, or Hermitage. Even a Chilean Merlot.
Salmis de palombes (slow-cooked pigeon breast)	Pomerol, Saint-Émilion, Chilean Merlot, Washington State Merlot.

POULTRY	
Chicken Basque-style (chicken fricassee-style dish with tomatoes, peppers, and ham)	Bordeaux supérieur, Corbières, Coteaux-du-Languedoc, Fronton. Also good New World Merlot and Grenache.
Chicken with cream and mushrooms	Arbois, Château-Chalon, Jura *vin jaune*, good Pinot Noir or Chardonnay from Côte de Beaune, Sonoma, or Oregon.
Chicken with ginger	White wines that are medium-dry and rich, or sweet such as Jurançon, late-harvest Gewurztraminer, and late-harvest Pinot Gris.
Chicken with truffles	Great Chardonnays (Corton-Charlemagne, Meursault, Montrachet, Russian River from California); white Hermitage, Arbois, Château-Chalon, Jura *vin jaune*.
Chicken vinaigrette	Anjou-Villages, Bourgueil, Chinon, St-Nicolas-de-Bourgueil, Saumur-Champigny, and good New World Cabernet Franc.
Chicken, roast	Good Pinot Noir from France (Côte de Beaune, Côte Chalonnaise), New Zealand, or the USA. Also Gamay (Moulin-à-Vent).
Chicken, stewed	Beaujolais, white Mâcon, Pouilly-Fuissé, white Rully, and generally good Chardonnay.
Coq au vin	Burgundy, New Zealand, or Oregon Pinot Noir. Also Gamay (Moulin-à-Vent).
Turkey with chestnuts	Côte Chalonnaise Pinot Noir (Mercurey, Givry) or Côte de Beaune (Savigny-les-Beaune, Volnay). Also New Zealand or American Pinot Noir.
Turkey, stuffed	Full-bodied wines such as Châteauneuf-du-Pape, Hermitage, Pomerol, Madiran, St-Émilion, and Washington State or Chilean Merlot. Also good Oregon or Sonoma Pinot Noir.

RABBIT	
Rabbit in mustard sauce	Chénas, Chinon, Mercurey, red Sancerre, St-Joseph. Also a broad spectrum of good New World Cabernet Franc, Pinot Noir, and Syrah.
Rabbit stew	Beaujolais-Villages, Bourgueil, Côte Chalonnaise, Saumur-Champigny. Also, good New World Cabernet Franc.

Rabbit with prunes	Bergerac, Buzet, Côtes-de-St-Mont, red Gaillac, Pécharmant. Also, good New World Malbec.
Roast rabbit with thyme	Les Baux-de-Provence, Coteaux-d'Aix-en-Provence, Palette, red Vin de Corse. Also, good New World Rhone-style red blends.

GAME	
Game generally	In principle, serve the best red vintages at their peak: *grands crus* from Burgundy, Bordeaux, or the Rhône Valley. Also, top New World Pinot Noir, Cabernet, and Syrah.
Game, marinaded	Cahors, Châteauneuf-du-Pape, Madiran, Gigondas, Vacqueyras. Also good New World Rhone-style red blends.
Haunch of venison with hunts-man's sauce	Côte-Rôtie, Hermitage, Corton, Châteauneuf-du-Pape. Also, good New World Syrah.
Jugged hare	Bandol from a great year, Côte-Rôtie, *grands crus* from Côte de Nuits, Châteauneuf-du-Pape, Hermitage, Pomerol, St-Émilion. Also, good New Zealand Pinot Noir and Washington State Merlot or Syrah.
Roast haunch of boar	Châteauneuf-du-Pape, Côtes-du-Roussillon-Villages, Corbières, St-Chinian, and good New World Rhône-style red blends.
Small feathered game (wood-cock, pheasant, partridge)	Pinot Noir from Côte de Beaune, Côte de Nuits, New Zealand, Oregon, and Sonoma.
Small furred game (wild rabbit, hare)	Côte Chalonnaise Pinot Noir, Médoc, St-Émilion. Also good New World Pinot Noir and Merlot.

VEGETABLES (SEE ALSO APPETIZERS)	
Cabbage, stuffed	Beaujolais-Villages, Gamay, South African Pinotage.
Cauliflower	Luberon, Dolcetto, Sauvignon Blanc.
Eggplant	Red Coteaux-d'Aix-en-Provence, Coteaux-du-Languedoc, and red Côtes-de-Provence; also Greek red wines (Xinomavro, Naoussa).
French green beans	White Sancerre or Sancerre rosé, Coteaux-d'Aix-en-Provence rosé, white Côtes-de-Provence. Also, good New Zealand Sauvignon Blanc.
Gratin dauphinois (gratin potatoes)	Chardonnay- or Savagnin-based white wines from the Jura, *e.g.* white Arbois; white Roussette-based wines from Savoie; good Sonoma Chardonnay.
Mushrooms	Merlot- or Pinot Noir-based wines at their peak, such as reds from the Libournais (Bordeaux) and Burgundy, or Washington State and Oregon.
Pasta	Light white, rosé, or red wines depending on the ingredients in the sauce.
Pasta with tomato and basil	Good rosés, including from Côtes-du-Rhône-Villages, Lirac, or Coteaux-d Aix-en-Provence.
Pasta with meat sauce	Beaujolais-Villages, Bourgueil, Coteaux-du-Tricastin, Mâcon-Villages, Chianti Classico, Valpolicella, and Zinfandel.
Seafood pasta	Chablis, Mâcon-Villages, Sancerre, Sauvignon Blanc, dry whites from Italy.
Raw vegetables	Dry white wines, Bourgogne Aligoté, Petit Chablis, Sauvignon Blanc, or light Gamay-based reds.
Risotto	Dry, fruity Italian white wines (Pinot Grigio, Bianco di Custoza, Trebbiano d'Abruzzo), Italian red wines (Chianti Classico), or Spanish reds (Rioja or La Mancha).
Truffles	Good Merlots such as Pomerol and St-Émilion *grands crus*; also good Syrah such as from the north Rhône Valley (Côte-Rôtie, Hermitage); and good Barolo (Italy).

DESSERTS	
Chocolate-based desserts	Fortified red wines (Banyuls, Maury, Malaga, port, Rivesaltes).
Crème brûlée	Muscat-based *vins doux naturels* (Muscat de Rivesaltes, Muscat de St-Jean-de-Minervois), Jurançon, Pacherenc-du-Vic-Bilh.
Desserts with spices	Aromatic, sweet wines (late harvest Pinot Gris or Pinot Gris *sélection de grains nobles*, and Jurançon).
Entremets (between courses – palate cleanser)	Dry or medium-dry Champagne; Clairette de Die, Muscat-based *vins doux naturels*.
Floating islands (meringue with vanilla custard)	Medium-dry rosé Champagne, Muscat-based *vins doux naturels*.
Fruit Charlotte	Medium-dry Champagne, Muscat-based *vins doux naturels* (Muscat de Beaumes-de-Venise, Muscat de Rivesaltes, Moscatel de Valencia).
Fruit Sabayon	Sweet, Sauternes-type wines, late harvest Pinot Gris and Gewurztraminer *sélection de grains nobles*.
Lemon tart	Sweet wines (Cérons, Jurançon, Ste-Croix-du-Mont, Sauternes).
Red berry tart	Dry or medium-dry rosé Champagne, Clairette de Die, sparkling Gaillac, Muscat-based *vins doux naturels*.
Tarte Tatin (caramelized apple tart)	Rich Loire Valley wines such as Bonnezeaux, Coteaux-du-Layon, Coteaux-de-l'Aubance, Montlouis moel-leux, Quarts-de-Chaume. Also, late-harvest Sémillon.

Château
Le Bon Pasteur
PRODUIT DE FRANCE
POMEROL
APPELLATION POMEROL CONTROLEE
2005
14%vol.
750 ml
S.C.E.A. des Domaines ROLLAND
POMEROL - GIRONDE - FRANCE
GRAND VIN DE BORDEAUX
MIS EN BOUTEILLE AU CHATEAU

Pairing cheeses with wines

The table below lists the seven great cheese categories with their chief characteristics, the best-known examples of each category, and their classic wine pairings.

The table on page 183 presents, in alphabetical order, a selection of cheeses together with the wines that suit them best.

GREAT CHEESE CATEGORIES AND WINE MATCHES	
FROMAGE FRAIS AND WHITE CHEESES	
Examples	All fromage frais and white cheeses made with cows' or goats' milk, *e.g.* Fontainebleau, Petit-Suisse.
Characteristics	Soft consistency, strong milky taste, more or less salty, perceptibly sharp.
Complementary wines	If serving the cheese with sugar or, better still, honey, select sugar-rich wines such as Muscat-based VDNs (Muscat de Rivesaltes, Muscat de Mireval) or soft, aromatic wines (late-harvest Gewurztraminer, late-harvest Pinot Gris, Jurançon); if they are served with herbs, salt, and pepper, choose a dry, aromatic white wine (Condrieu, Pinot Gris, Viognier).
GOATS' MILK AND SHEEPS' MILK CHEESE	
Examples	Broccio, Chabichou, Charolais, Crottin de Chavignol, Pélardon, Pouligny-Saint-Pierre, Saint-Félicien, Saint-Marcellin, Selles-sur-Cher, Valençay.
Characteristics	The density of the cheese depends on how long it has been matured: whether it is fresh, semi-dry, or dry. The drier the cheese, the stronger and saltier it will taste.
Complementary wines	Select soft, fruity, dry white wines (Chablis, dry Jurançon, Pouilly-Fuissé, dry Vouvray) and lean toward Sauvignon Blanc-based wines (Sancerre and Pouilly-Fumé); alternatives are medium-dry white Chenin Blancs (Vouvrays or Montlouis) and light, low-tannic reds made from Gamay grapes (Beaujolais), Cabernet Franc (Bourgueil, St-Nicolas-de-Bourgueil), or even Pinot Noir (Hautes-Côtes-de-Beaune, Hautes-Côtes-de-Nuits, Oregon or Sonoma Pinot Noir).
SEMI-SOFT CHEESE WITH SURFACE CRUST	
Examples	Brie, Brillat-savarin, Camembert, Chaource, Coulommiers.
Characteristics	Smooth cheeses with a taste ranging from sweet and creamy to powerful or strong.
Complementary wines	Avoid young and tannic reds; it's best to go for reds that are fruity and have very little oak influence (Pinot Noir such as Burgundy from Côte Chalonnaise and Côte de Beaune, Coteaux Champenois, red Sancerre; red Côtes-du-Rhône; Pomerol, St-Émilion); also young *blanc des blancs* Champagnes.
SEMI-SOFT CHEESE WITH WASHED RIND	
Examples	Époisses, Livarot, Pont-l'Évêque, Langres, Maroilles, Mont d'Or, Munster, Reblochon, Vacherin.
Characteristics	Creamy cheeses with a pronounced, often powerful, flavours.
Complementary wines	Avoid powerful, full-bodied reds; choose aromatic white wines (Gewurztraminer, dry or late harvest; peak-condition Meursault; mature Riesling; Jura *vin jaune*; and mature Champagnes).
BLUE CHEESE	
Examples	Bleu d'Auvergne, Bleu de Bresse, Fourme d'Ambert, Roquefort, Stilton.
Characteristics	Creamy, often fatty, cheeses with a strong, salty taste.
Complementary wines	Choose sugar-rich wines such as white or red VDNs (Muscat de Beaumes-de-Venise, Banyuls, Rivesaltes), and sweet wines (Coteaux-du-Layon, Quarts-de-Chaume, Cérons, Sauternes).
PRESSED, UNCOOKED CHEESE	
Examples	Cantal, Edam, Gouda, Mimolette, Morbier, St-Nectaire, Tomme de Savoie.
Characteristics	These are often formed into balls or wheels; some have a creamy texture, others a denser body.
Complementary wines	Select mature Bordeaux or similar red wines (Médoc, Pauillac, Pomerol, St-Émilion, good New World Cabernet or Merlot) and also white wines from Jura or Savoie.
PRESSED, COOKED CHEESE	
Examples	Appenzell, Comté, Emmental, Fribourg, Gruyère.
Characteristics	Hard, rather salty cheeses, often with a strong taste.
Complementary wines	Best with rather aromatic, dry, white wines, preferably from Savagnin grapes like the Jura *vin jaune*; also opulent, mature, white wines such as Meursault and Sonoma Chardonnay.

CHEESE FROM A TO Z WITH BEST WINE PAIRINGS

CHEESE	WINES
Abbaye de Cîteaux	Beaujolais-Villages, Côte Chalonnaise, Fleurie, Gamay.
Appenzell	Château-Chalon, Jura *vin jaune*.
Banon	Red Côtes-du-Rhône-Villages, good New World Grenache, white Côtes-de-Provence.
Basque or Corsican sheeps' milk cheese	Dry Jurançon, Muscat du Cap-Corse.
Beaufort	Château-Chalon, Jura *vin jaune*.
Bleu d'Auvergne	Loupiac, Maury, Sainte-Croix-du-Mont, young Sauternes.
Bleu de Bresse	Monbazillac, white Rivesaltes.
Bleu des Causses	Banyuls Vintage, Barsac.
Bleu de Gex	Cérons, Maury, Loupiac.
Boursault	Bouzy, Coteaux Champenois, red Mâcon, Rosé des Riceys.
Bouton-de-Culotte	Beaujolais, white or red Hautes-Côtes-de-Beaune or Mâcon, good Oregon Pinot Noir.
Brie de Meaux or de Melun	Champagne, Pomerol, St-Émilion, red Sancerre, Merlot.
Brillat-Savarin	*Blanc de blancs* Champagne.
Brin-d'Amour	Red Vin de Corse, white or red Côtes-de-Provence.
Broccio de Corse	Dry Corsican white wines or Muscat.
Camembert	Sweet cider, Champagne, Coteaux Champenois.
Cantal	Red Côtes-d'Auvergne, Mercurey, Pomerol, St-Émilion, Merlot.
Chabichou	White Menetou-Salon, white Sancerre, Sauvignon Blanc.
Chaource	Rosé Champagne, Coteaux Champenois.
Charolais	Chablis, Mâcon-Villages, Saint-Véran, unoaked or lighly oaked Chardonnay.
Chèvre, mature	Beaujolais, Mâcon-Villages, Pouilly-Fuissé, unoaked or lightly oaked Chardonnay.
Comté	Château-Chalon, mature Meursault, good Sonoma Chardonnay, Jura *vin jaune*.
Coulommiers	Young *blanc de blancs* Champagne, Coteaux Champenois.
Crottin de Chavignol	Pouilly Fumé, white Sancerre, Sauvignon Blanc.
Edam	Chinon, Médoc, Pauillac, Cabernet Franc, Cabernet Sauvignon.
Emmental	Roussette de Savoie, white Vin de Savoie.
Époisses	Red Bandol, full-bodied Gewurztraminer.
Fontainebleau	Muscat de Beaumes-de-Venise, Muscat de Mireval.
Fourme d'Ambert	Banyuls, Rivesaltes, port.
Fribourg	Château-Chalon, mature Meursault, good Sonoma Chardonnay, Jura *vin jaune*.
Gouda	Médoc, Madiran, St-Estèphe, Cabernet Sauvignon.
Gruyère	Mature Swiss Chasselas, Roussette de Savoie, Roussette du Bugey.
Laguiole	Red Bergerac, Fronton, Cabernet Franc.
Langres	Fairly mature Champagne, Marc de Champagne.

CHEESE	WINES
Livarot	Late-harvest Gewurztraminer, late-harvest Pinot Gris.
Maroilles	Full-bodied Gewurztraminer, late-harvest Pinot Gris.
Mimolette, aged	Graves, Médoc, Pomerol, St-Émilion, good New World Cabernet Sauvignon and Merlot.
Mont-d'Or	Mature Swiss Chasselas (Dézaley), Mâcon-Villages, Roussette de Savoie.
Morbier	White wine from Savoie.
Munster	Dry or late-harvest Gewurztraminer.
Neufchâtel	Hard cider, Champagne, Coteaux Champenois.
Ossau-Iraty	Jurançon, white Irouléguy.
Pélardon	Red or white Châteauneuf-du-Pape, Condrieu, Viognier-based whites.
Pérail de Brebis	Corbières, Coteaux-du-Languedoc, Côtes-du-Roussillon, Faugères, St-Chinian, Rhône-style red blends.
Picodon	Red Côtes-du-Rhône-Villages, red or white St-Joseph, good New World Grenache.
Pont-l'Évêque	Chassagne-Montrachet, Meursault, good New World Chardonnay, mature Riesling.
Pouligny-Saint-Pierre	Cheverny, white Reuilly, white Sancerre, Sauvignon Blanc.
Reblochon	Pouilly-Fuissé, Crépy, Roussette de Savoie.
Rocamadour	Dry Jurançon, sherry.
Roquefort	Banyuls Rimage, port, Rivesaltes *rancio*, Sauternes.
Saint-Félicien	Red or white Beaujolais, white St-Joseph, Roussanne.
Saint-Marcellin	Red Beaujolais, white Châteauneuf-du-Pape, white St-Joseph, Roussanne.
Saint-Nectaire	Chinon, Médoc, Pauillac, good New World Cabernet Sauvignon or Cabernet Franc.
Sainte-Maure	Dry or medium-dry Vouvray or Monlouis.
Salers	Red Côtes-du-Rhône-Villages, Mercurey, Pomerol, St-Émilion, good Merlot.
Selles-sur-Cher	Pouilly-Fumé, white Sancerre, Sauvignon Blanc.
Stilton	Banyuls, Maury, vintage or LBV port, tawny port, 10, 20 or 30 years old.
Tomme d'Abondance	Swiss Chasselas, Roussette de Savoie, white St-Joseph, Roussanne.
Tomme d'Auvergne	Côtes-d'Auvergne, red Côtes-du-Rhône-Villages, Mâcon-Villages.
Tomme des Pyrénées	Mature Madiran or Tannat.
Tomme de Savoie	Bourgueil, Chinon, red and white wines from Savoie including Roussette de Savoie, good Cabernet Franc.
Vacherin	Mature Swiss Chasselas (Dézaley), mature Meursault, Roussette de Savoie, good Sonoma Chardonnay.
Valençay	Quincy, white or rosé Reuilly, white Sancerre, Sauvignon Blanc.
Vieux-Gris de Lille	Good ale, gin.
Vieux-Pané	Red Anjou, St-Nicolas-de-Bourgueil, red Touraine, good New World Cabernet Franc.

HOW TO SERVE WINE

SERVING TEMPERATURE

To get the most from the tasting experience, it is important to serve wines at the temperature that suits them best. A wine that is too warm or too cold cannot be fully appreciated.

Regulating the temperature

CHILLING WINE. An ice bucket is the quickest and best way to chill wine. It is important to add water to the ice and to immerse as much of the bottle as possible so that all of the wine is at the same temperature. It will take 10–15 minutes for the temperature to drop from 68 down to 46°F (20 to 8°C). A refrigerator will take between 1.5 and 2 hours to achieve the same result, maybe more in warm weather. The time taken to cool the wine is an important factor: too short and the contents of the bottle may not all be of the same temperature, too long and the wine will be too cold. Likewise, a wine chiller sleeve may not always achieve an even cooling of the wine.

Never put a bottle of wine in the freezer or in the chill cabinet of a refrigerator, which is far too cold; the bottle may also burst if it's forgotten.

When the wine has reached the correct temperature for serving, simply add a few ice cubes to the ice bucket to maintain its cool temperature, bearing in mind that it is important not to over-chill. The same principles apply when using a wine cooler or an insulated thermal bag. Sparkling wines are treated in the same way.

WARMING A WINE. Ideally, the bottle should be left for 2–3 hours in a room where the temperature is at around 64°F (18°C). Never place wine near a source of heat such as a fireplace, radiator, or oven; this risks giving it 'heat stroke' and will adversely affect the flavours. Red wines should be treated with particular care – especially old, rare vintages, since these are most susceptible to extremes of temperature. Once taken from the cellar, give them time to warm up gradually in a temperate room.

The temperature at which wine should be served depends not only on its colour, *but also on its character, the season, and the temperature of the room where it is to be enjoyed.*

Every wine style has its own temperature

How does temperature affect the taste of wine? Warmth causes aromatic components to evaporate, which simply means that it allows the wine's pleasant bouquet to come to the fore. As aromas vary from one wine to another, different wines are at their best at different temperatures.

WHITE WINES COOLER THAN REDS. This is the general principle, but the range of temperatures is wide in both cases. The rule of 'white wine at refrigerator temperature and red wine at room temperature' is rather perfunctory. It tends to encourage serving white wines too cold and red ones too warm. In reality, each style of white wine requires a different temperature, and many reds – if not all – should be served a few degrees below room temperature.

NOT TOO COLD, NOT TOO WARM. Wine suffers far more from heat (which may bring out any possible flaws) than from cold.

Is a wine thermometer necessary?

It may be helpful to use a thermometer to determine if a wine is at the correct temperature. But one or two degrees more or less won't spoil a wine. You could check the temperature of a wine you are tasting with a thermometer two or three times to get a sense of what a bottle chilled to, say, 50°F (10°C) tastes like, then put the thermometer in a drawer and trust your senses.

> To warm an over-chilled bottle of wine, just leave it for a while in a temperate room.

A great red wine may become completely unbalanced if served at 72°F (22°C). As heat accentuates the presence of alcohol, white wines should, in general, be served well chilled to modify the alcohol. When the bottle is chilled, the wine's acidity blends with its fruitiness, making it pleasantly refreshing, as should be expected from all white wines. However, it's a mistake to serve great white wine too cold, as their particular qualities – on the nose as well as in the mouth – may be enhanced if they are just cool. In warm weather, wines should be served slightly cooler than normal, in order to prevent the bottle from warming up too quickly. Conversely, in cold weather (even if the room is well heated), wines (whites or young reds) should not be over-cooled, even if they are supposed to be tasted chilled.

IT ALL DEPENDS ON THE CHARACTER OF THE WINE. A straightforward, supple wine should be served cooler to accentuate its slight acidity. Likewise, an alcohol-rich wine should also be served cooler. On the other hand, a very crisp or tannic wine should not be over-chilled as cold accentuates any bitter, acidic characters.

TRUE OR FALSE?

It's better to serve a wine too cold than too warm.

TRUE. The wine's aromas will be revealed as the temperature rises. If the wine is served too warm, the aromas will be masked by the alcohol.

WINES AND SERVING TEMPERATURES

WINE TYPE	EXAMPLES	TEMPERATURE
SPARKLING WINES		
Dry sparkling wines	Cava, *crémant*, Saumur, Champagne	43–46°F (6–8°C)
Sweet sparkling wines	Medium-dry Champagne, Moscato d'Asti	43–46°F (6–8°C)
Special selections	Vintage Champagne	46–50°F (8–10°C)
WHITE WINES		
Ordinary off-dry whites	White Anjou, Loupiac, Muscat	45–48°F (7–9°C)
Medium-dry whites	Medium-dry Vouvray, Riesling Spätlese, Soave	45–48°F (7–9°C)
Sweet whites	Sauternes, Tokaji, Vin Santo, Muscat du Cap-Corse	45–54°F (7–10°C)
Ordinary dry whites	Muscadet, Sancerre, Pinot Gris, dry Riesling, Sauvignon Blanc	50–54°F (10–12°C)
Full-bodied dry whites	Burgundy, Graves, Sémillon, Viognier, Chardonnay, Chenin	50–54°F (10–12°C)
Classy dry whites	Burgundy, Pessac-Léognan, Savennières	54°F (12°C)
ROSÉ WINES		
	Ordinary rosés are served as for dry white wines	50–54°F (10–12°C)
RED WINES		
Young, fresh reds	Loire wines, Beaujolais, Côtes-du-Rhône, Valpolicella, Cabernet Franc, Grenache	57°F (14°C)
Ordinary reds	Bordeaux, Burgundy, Cabernet Sauvignon, Chianti Classico, Merlot, Pinot Noir, Sangiovese, Syrah, Tempranillo	61°F (16°C)
Great reds	Bordeaux, Côte-Rôtie, Gevrey-Chambertin, Corton, Vino Nobile de Montepulciano, Barolo	63–64°F (17–18°C)
FORTIFIED WINES		
	French *vins doux naturels* (whites)	46–50°F (8–10°C)
	Fino and manzanilla sherry	50–54°F (10–12°C)
	Amontillado sherry, sercial madeira, French *vins doux naturels* (red)	54°F (12°C)
	Oloroso or cream sherry, bual madeira	57°F (14°C)
	Ruby port	57°F (14°C)
	Tawny port	61°F (16°C)
	Vintage port	61–64°F (16–18°C)

OPENING THE BOTTLE

Serving wine should not be hasty and improvised; each part of the process contributes to the pleasure of tasting. The host should therefore be versed in all aspects of serving wine, including the essential stage of opening a bottle of wine with ease.

The corkscrew

There are two criteria for choosing a good-quality corkscrew. First, the part that penetrates the closure (cork) should be of the right shape. A helix (sometimes called 'the worm') that is sufficiently long and wide, and with a good point, is essential for providing a solid grip without the danger of the closure crumbling or breaking. The traction mechanism is also important. The most basic corkscrews with a T-shaped handle require too much effort from the arm and shoulder muscles: a tight closure is resistant. It's better to choose a corkscrew with a lever system that wedges itself against the neck of the bottle. There is a wide range of models available, from the 'waiter's friend' to the corkscrew with a counter-screw mechanism or the 'Screwpull,' which works on the boring/digging principle (*see* pp.190–1). Finally, devices powered by gas or air should be used with caution; the pressure of the gas could spoil the wine and if the bottle has a manufacturing defect, there's a danger that it may shatter or explode when being opened.

> ***Opening a bottle of wine is a great moment, and should not be rushed.*** *Having been enclosed in the bottle after the various production processes, the wine now comes into contact with the air and is ready to reveal all its qualities.*

Opening a still wine

The closure should be extracted without having to resort to force and without being torn, since the wine is susceptible to abrupt changes in pressure.
ACTIONS. Any difficulties experienced in opening a bottle of wine depend on the type of corkscrew used, but the process is always the same. First, the foil wrapper on the neck should be

OPENING A STILL WINE

Troublesome closures

Sometimes cork or plastic closures stubbornly resist extraction. Here are some solutions.

The closure is sticking. Warm the neck of the bottle by running hot water over it – but keep the closure dry. This will moisten and expand the glass. Alternatively, hold the corkscrew at a slight angle while turning it.

The closure is broken. Hold the corkscrew at a slight angle and turn it carefully into the remaining closure. If this doesn't work, push the closure into the bottle. When pouring the first glass, use the corkscrew's worm to keep the closure away from the neck; it will then float on the surface of the wine.

A few pieces of closure in the wine will not affect its taste. If there are more, the wine can be decanted (*see* p.193) into a clean bottle, carafe, or pitcher.

cut and (at least the upper part) removed; this ensures that the wine will not come into contact with the foil. If the wine is to be decanted (*see* p.193), the whole of the wrapper should be removed to give a better view of the wine. Next, wipe the neck and top with a clean cloth, then drive the worm of the corkscrew through the centre of the closure, taking care not to split it. Finally, extract the closure in a single smooth movement. Of course, this procedure assumes the bottle is not sealed with a screwcap.

SHOULD A BOTTLE BE OPENED IN ADVANCE? In general, simple red, white, or rosé wines such as Beaujolais or Côtes-de-Provence rosé are opened at the last moment, unless they are required to be decanted. Fuller-bodied, but still young, white wines may be opened 1–2 hours in advance; they also can be poured into a carafe or decanter half an hour before serving. Still-young but distinguished red wines will benefit from being opened 2–4 hours before being served, or decanted 1–2 hours in advance. As for old wines, they should not be opened too early; if they are first left standing upright, any sediment will drop to the bottom.

EXCEPTIONS. Some cork closures, especially those of mature Bordeaux wines, are very long and often fragile and so must be opened with care. When the worm of the corkscrew has penetrated the closure fully, draw it up by a fraction of an inch, give it an extra twist inward (taking care that the worm does not go right through the closure), and then extract the whole closure. 'Waiter's friend' corkscrews are often effective in dealing with very old closures.

Particular care is also required with a delicate bottle of wine, such as an old Burgundy. When it is being transported from storage to where it is to be served, it should be kept lying on its side. (Carrying it in a basket may be a good idea.) The slightest abrupt movement should be avoided throughout the whole process, including when the bottle is being opened.

Opening sparkling wines

A bottle of sparkling wine is always opened in front of the guests. But never do this directly in front of anyone or towards a window: turn the bottle towards a wall.

PRECAUTIONS. Since the wine is under pressure, opening a bottle clumsily or quickly may force the closure out violently. You will lose a lot of *mousse* (and wine), not to mention whatever damage the closure might do as it shoots out of the bottle. Therefore start by chilling the wine, and avoid shaking the bottle so as not to increase the pressure of the gas. The wine should be cooled to between 43–48°F (6–9°C). So avoid leaving it in the refrigerator too long. Once it has left the cellar, it is preferable to chill it for a while in a bucket containing a mixture of water and ice; accelerated chilling can only damage the wine.

ACTIONS. First, remove the foil wrapper, in order to access the wire cage and the closure. Gently untwist the wire, keeping your thumb on top of the cork, then take off the wire cage and its cap. The secret of successful opening consists of holding the bottle at a slight angle, and keeping the cork closure well supported with one hand while with the other gently turning the bottle (not the closure). You will feel the closure rising, pushed up by the pressure of the gas. Use your thumb to lever the closure out gently as soon as it begins to move up the neck.

OPENING A SPARKLING WINE

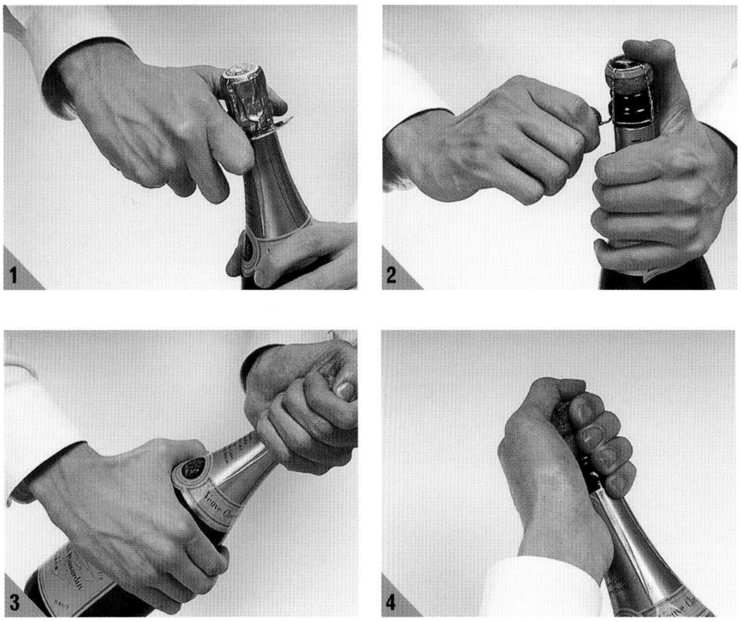

CORKSCREWS

Although they are made for a very specific task, many corkscrews are attractive objects in their own right as well as being a pleasure to use and are often collected.

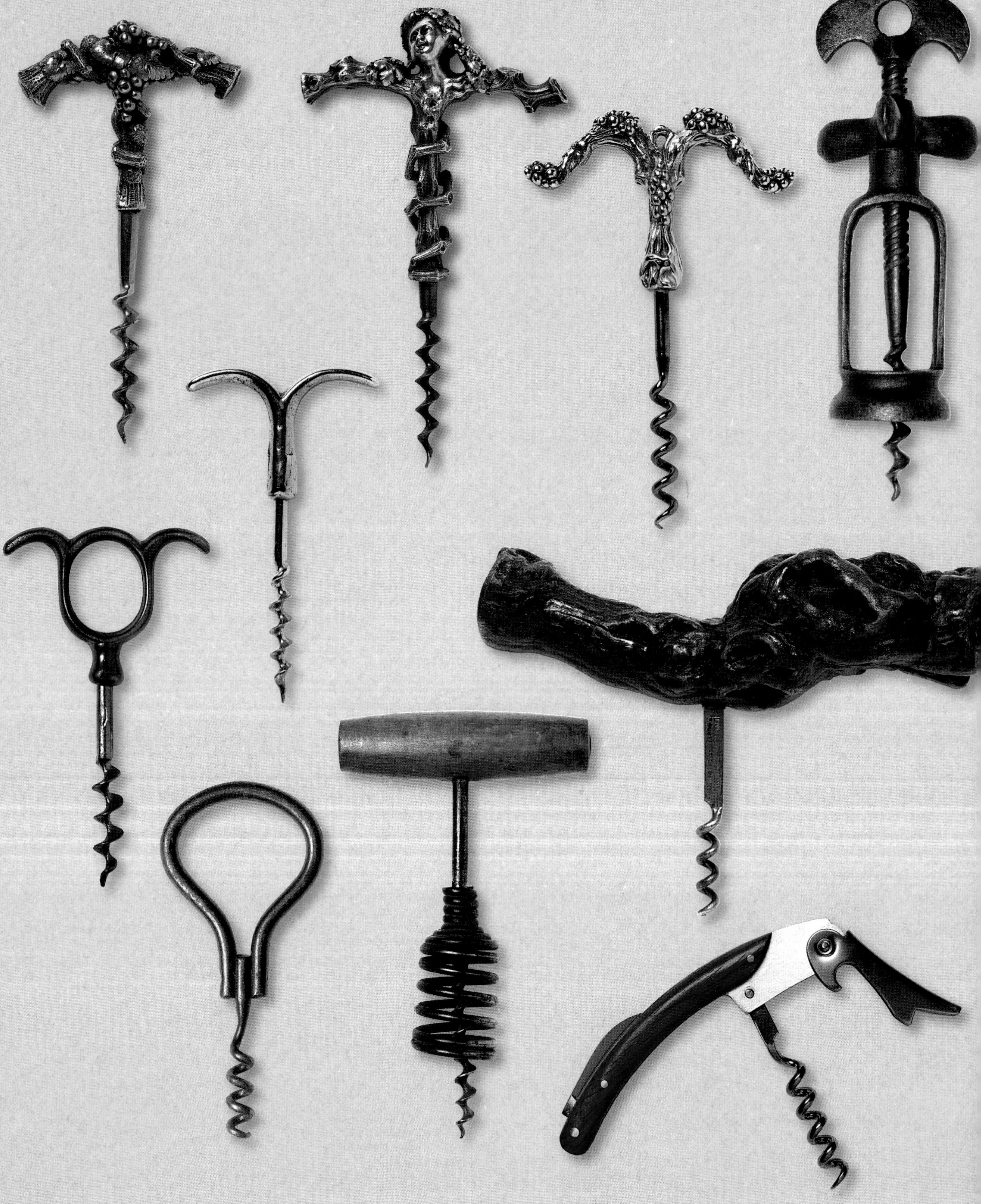

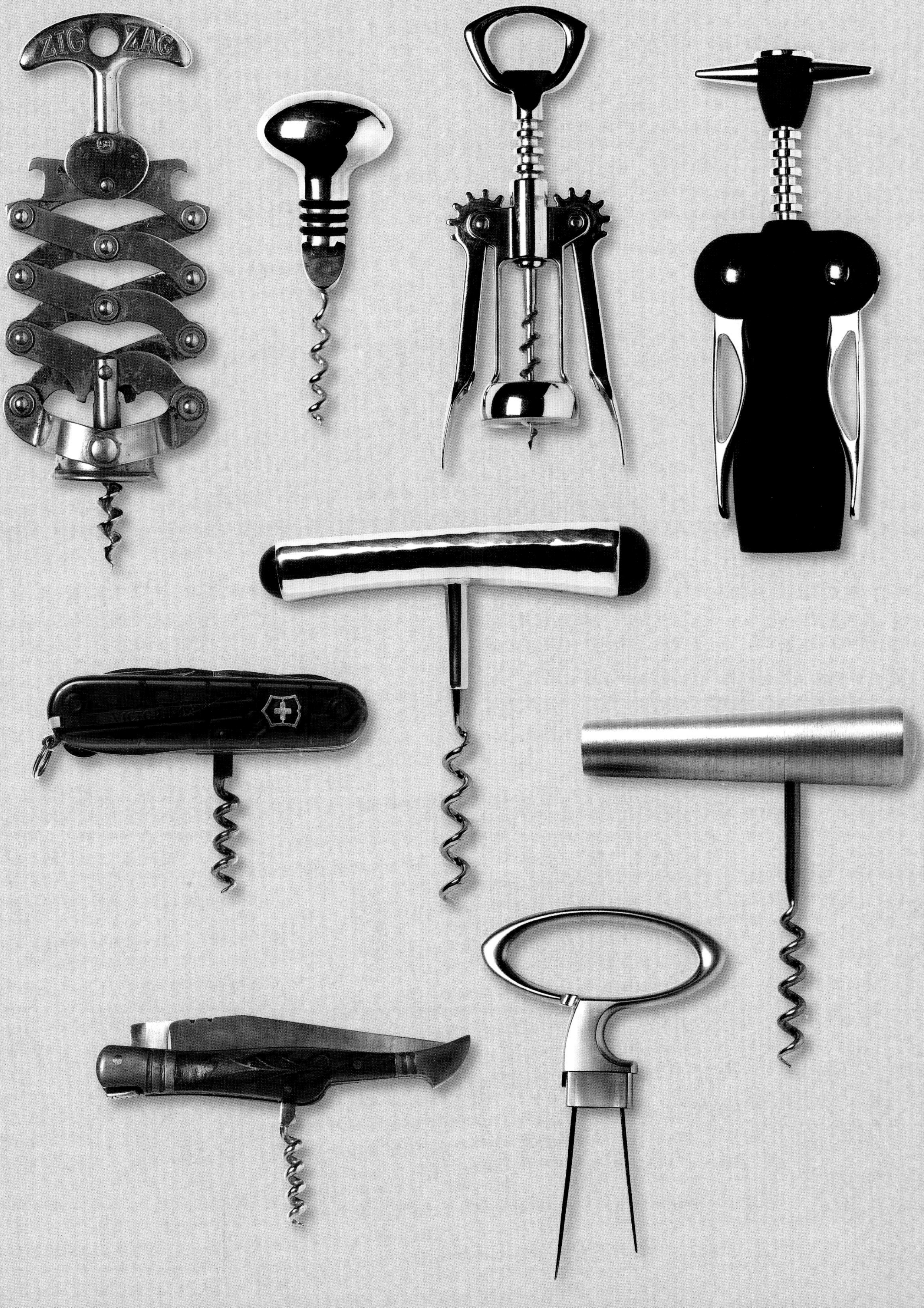
ZIG ZAG

DECANTING THE WINE

A delicate operation that requires a degree of skill, there are three reasons to decant a wine: to separate any sediment from the wine, to aerate it, and to modify its temperature.

Advantages and disadvantages

Most wines can be served directly from the bottle, but some benefit from being decanted into a carafe or a pitcher. In many cases, where the wine shows traces of sediment, it should be decanted. For other wines, it depends on their age and the time they will remain in a decanter (*see* box below).

Advocates of decanting assert that young wine that has been decanted for one or even several hours will become more aromatic and round, and generally more pleasurable to taste. However, if left too long in a decanter, it may lose its freshness and vitality. Decanting can invigorate vintage wines, but it can also harden them and dissipate their precious aromas.

Do not forget that wine continues to aerate when passing from the decanter to the glass, and also when gently swirled in the glass. Before decanting, therefore, take the precaution of tasting the wine.

***Decanting can improve a wine in two ways:** it removes any sediment (or even pieces of cork closure), and it aerates the wine, which may enhance the drinking experience.*

Sediment: quality or defect?

CRYSTALS. Some young, light, white wines occasionally show deposits of crystals. These are caused by the crystallization of potassium bitartrate following a sudden drop in temperature. Despite their appearance, these crystals present no danger to health and will not affect the taste of the wine. Stand the bottle upright and the deposit will collect on the base in a few seconds. They can be avoided by careful pouring.

COLOURED SEDIMENT. Older red wines produce natural sediment from precipitation of colour and tannin molecules. This is a fairly light sediment and requires careful handling of the bottle in order to avoid it. Decanting is necessary unless the wine has become too fragile (*e.g.* old wines from Burgundy). The decision should be made immediately after the bottle is opened and the wine has been tasted initially: an immature, slightly hard wine will benefit from decanting, but a delicious wine in full bloom does not require it.

What wines should be decanted?

RED WINES WITH SEDIMENT

Bordeaux: *premiers crus, grands crus*, classified growths, St-Émilion *grands crus*, great Pomerols.

Rhône Valley: Hermitage and other wines from the northern valley, as well as Châteauneuf-du-Pape in the south.

Other French wines: the best wines from Provence, Madiran.

Italy: Barolo, Brunello di Montalcino, Sassicaia, Ornellaia.

Spain: Vega-Sicilia, Pingus, and the better wines of Penedès. Also, some Riojas tend towards sedimentation.

Portugal: vintage and crusted ports. Late bottled and tawny ports do not need to be decanted.

New World: Cabernet Sauvignons and Syrah/Shiraz from California, Washington State, Australia, and Chile.

YOUNG RED WINES

Bordeaux: good vintage wines from the smaller châteaux of Bordeaux. Also, many good Cabernet Sauvignon wines from elsewhere in the world.

Burgundy: the Beaujolais *crus* and the communal appellations of the Côte d'Or. Also, many good Pinot Noir wines from elsewhere in the world.

Rhône Valley: all the reds. Also, many Syrah and Rhône-style blends from elsewhere in the world.

Other French wines: Cahors, red Bandol, Chinon, Faugères, and those wines with good acidity and tannin content when young; or all traditionally vinified, highly concentrated wines. In Italy, Barolo, Barbaresco, and Brunello.

WHITE WINES

Some white wines improve if decanted just before serving: young Loire wines, white Graves, Alsace *vendanges tardives*, great Rhine and Mosel wines from Germany, white oak-aged Riojas from Spain. Others do not benefit: very mature white Bordeaux and Burgundies, mature white wines except for the ones cited above, most young white wines, Champagne, and other sparkling wines.

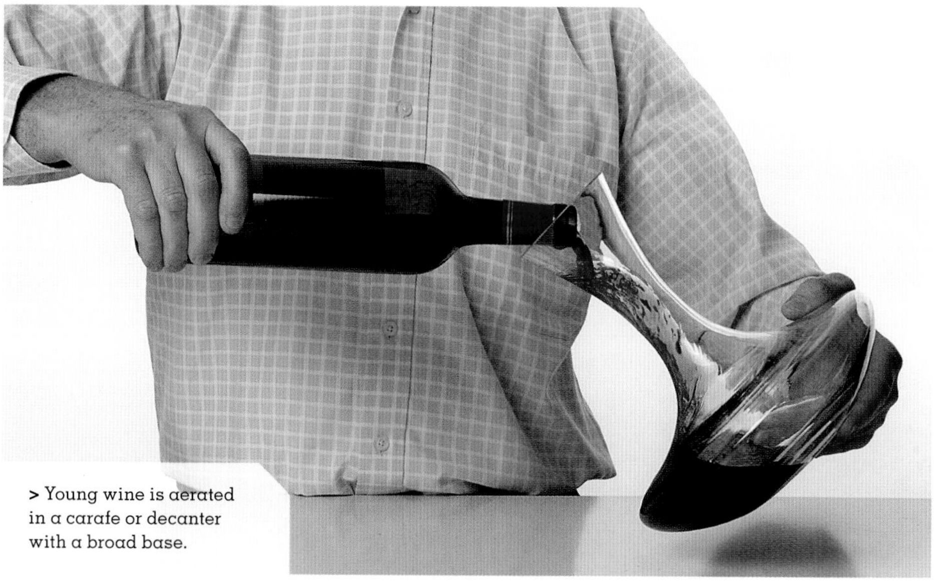

> Young wine is aerated in a carafe or decanter with a broad base.

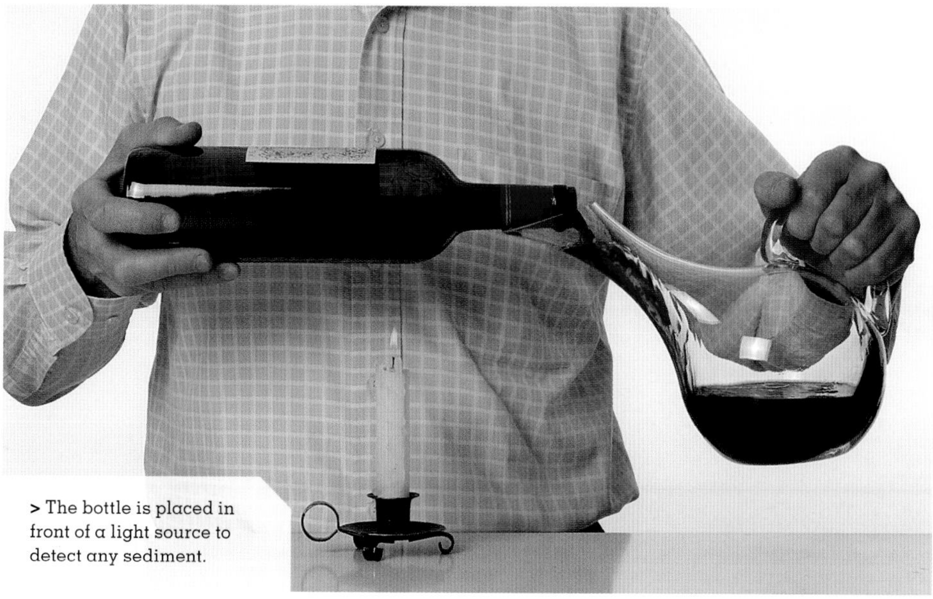

> The bottle is placed in front of a light source to detect any sediment.

How to decant

WHAT CONTAINER? Wine can be decanted into a carafe, a jug, or a decanter. However, the shape and size of the vessel play an important role, as this dictates how much of the surface area of the wine is exposed to the air. After the initial 'shock' of aeration to a wine that has until then been in a closed environment, its aromas will expand more or less rapidly depending on the decanter's shape. So, for young, good quality wines, a flat decanter with a very broad base best facilitates the interaction of the wine with air; for older wines, it's better to choose a decanter that exposes only a small amount of the wine's surface area to the air. Once filled, be sure to replace the stopper afterwards. Always, rinse and drain the decanter before use; and if using a funnel or a fabric filter, wash them beforehand. When pouring the wine into the decanter, make sure you are well balanced and do not hold the bottle at arm's length.

DECANTING A YOUNG WINE. The aim is to aerate the wine and allow it to soften and reveal its bouquet. Simply open the bottle and pour it into a clean carafe. The wine may be poured fairly quickly: if it splashes near the top of the carafe, it will simply aerate better. It is best to allow the wine to rest for at least an hour before drinking, with the open decanter in the room where it will be served. This will allow it to reach room temperature gradually.

DECANTING A MATURE WINE. Due to the fragility of the wine, this is a delicate operation requiring patience and dexterity. It is done just before serving the wine, and the decanter should be stoppered.

Stand the bottle upright in a cellar for about two days beforehand and the sediment will collect at the bottom. If the bottle is left lying down, the sediment will collect on the side; in the latter case, transport it from the cellar in a wine cradle. When the closure has been pulled, the wine should be poured very slowly (but steadily, to avoid any swirling) into a decanter. A light source such as a candle or flashlight positioned under the neck of the bottle will show when the first sediment comes to the top. As soon as sediment reaches the neck, stop pouring and set the bottle upright.

Caring for decanters

Decanters should be clean and washed with the same care as glasses, using plenty of hot water to rinse them as much as possible. To dry a decanter, first wipe the outside with a clean cloth, then turn the decanter upside down to let any remaining water flow out. The best way to drain a decanter is to place it on a well-anchored rack, to ensure stability, and leave it in a well-aired environment. It should not be kept enclosed and empty for too long and should always be rinsed well with hot water before every use.

If your decanter shows traces of previously decanted wines, use unrefined sea salt and wine vinegar to clean it, shaking until all traces have disappeared. Rinse well in clean, hot water.

GLASSES

Faced with an enormous range of choices, it is important to select glasses that will enhance the appreciation of wine and that also reflect your own taste. The aesthetic factor should not be neglected, as it often enhances the pleasure of tasting.

Choosing glasses

For the best tasting experience, the glass should satisfy the demands of the the eye, the nose, and the mouth. Wine tastes different, and better, when consumed from the appropriate glass. Points to bear in mind when choosing glasses are, in order of importance: shape, size, and what they are made from.

SHAPE. The bowl of a wine glass should be in the shape of a semi-closed tulip. The rim of the bowl should curve slightly inward to capture the wine's aromas and channel them toward the nose. A glass with a shallow bowl creates more wine surface area to expose to air and will not retain the aromas. The stem of the glass should be sufficiently long to hold without the fingers touching the bowl. A glass of chilled white wine will warm up rapidly when in contact with the hand.

SIZE. The glass should be big enough to hold an adequate amount of wine without being more than a quarter or one-third full. If the glass is too small or too full, the wine cannot be swirled to release its aromas, nor can the glass be tilted to examine the wine. A normal serving of wine is around 3 oz (90 ml); ideally, the capacity of a glass should be at least 9.5 oz (280 ml). Some restaurants use much bigger glasses; avoid this at home to spare yourself the disagreeable impression of having just a drop of wine in the bottom of your glass. In any case, these glasses have a special purpose as the large surface area helps to volatilize the aromas of a young wine; they should not be used for old, delicate wines. On the other hand, a large glass, with a capacity of 12 oz (350 ml), is preferable for the best red wines when served at their peak.

MATERIAL. The glass should be transparent, smooth, and without facets. Heavy glasses in cut crystal or gilded are certainly beautiful, but they detract from the appreciation of wine and the pleasure of tasting. Coloured glasses make it impossible to admire the wine's colour and intensity. The ideal material is fine crystal, which provides optimal clarity and quality for an unimpeded view of the contents of the glass. Experts who have carried our comparative tastings are convinced that the quality of the glass contributes to tasting pleasure. All the same, the material is of less importance than the shape or size of the glass.

The same wine consumed from different shaped glasses will not taste the same. *A classic wine glass should have the same qualities as a tasting glass, as well as being both attractive and hardwearing.*

A glass for every wine?

In addition to standard wine glasses, others are available – traditional glasses (*see* box) or those specially designed to enhance a particular type of wine. After years of research, great crystal manufacturers such as Riedel and Spiegelau have created ranges of glasses designed to optimize tasting of the world's great wines. However, it is by no means essential to have a different wine glass for every appellation or style; though it is accepted that white wine glasses are smaller than those for red wine. The tulip shape of the glass is the chief consideration, but for sparkling

> Water glass

> Burgundy glass

> Bordeaux glass

> White wine glass

Traditional glasses

Most wine-producing regions have developed a glass considered ideal for tasting local wine. Having evolved from regional traditions, these glasses have great charm. In general, their chief purpose is to celebrate easy-drinking wines with no pretensions. The most famous example is the Alsace wine glass: a small balloon set on a long, green-tinted stem. The purpose is to reflect a light colour into the white wine, while also highlighting the freshness of the wine served. Obviously, the high quality wines of Alsace don't need such a prop.

wines, a flute is the preferred shape. To these classic glasses, a Burgundy glass may possibly be added and another for port, sherry, and liqueurs. The only glass that is free from any any dictates in terms of shape and material is the water glass.

Specialized or technical wine-tasting glasses are also available, such as the INAO-type glasses (*Institut National des Appellations d'Origine*) or the 'Les Impitoyables' tasting range. Used by professional tasters, these high-specification glasses are designed to reveal any defects in a wine (*see also* p.204.).

> The bowls of wine glasses should be tulip-shaped to retain aromas.

Caring for wine glasses

Many wine tastings are ruined by dirty glasses. But the 'dirt' isn't always visible: detergents or rinsing products can leave a film that may be undetectable by sight or smell when the glass is empty, but react when in contact with wine (or water), giving it a bad taste.

Glasses attract and retain odours, which may come from the washing or drying processes, or from how they are stored. However, they are all easy to avoid. It's best not to put wine glasses in the dishwasher, but to wash them by hand in plenty of hot water. If necessary, use just a little gentle detergent or soap. While still warm and damp, they should be wiped and polished with a clean cotton or linen cloth, which itself has been rinsed after washing to remove any smell of detergent or fabric conditioner. Avoid using new cloths, which might leave fluff or threads on the glasses.

Store the glasses in a closed cupboard, preferably not in the kitchen. Stand them upright or slip the bases (foot) into glass-holders. If stored upside-down, they will absorb the smell of the cupboard. Finally, take them out well beforehand so that you can check they are clean and air them before arranging on the table.

> Port glass

> Flute

What glass for bubbles?

The Champagne *coupe* has long been associated with this wine. Though, from a formal tasting point of view, it's useless. The wide bowl immediately dissipates the wine's bouquet and instantly disperses the *mousse*, not to mention the stream of bubbles. For Champagne and, in general, for all sparkling wines, the flute is the best choice. The wine should be poured to fill the tall glass three-quarters full. The height of the bowl means that bubbles will form easily and last longer; the narrow rim will ensure that none of the bouquet is lost. The tulip glass is an acceptable alternative to the flute.

DINING WITH WINE

Ever since the first grape harvest took place in a vineyard somewhere in the ancient world, wine was destined to end its journey in a glass at a table, as part of a meal. And yet, sometimes even a tiny mistake in serving the wine is enough to spoil the pleasure of tasting it: every detail matters and brings tangible reality to the pleasure of tasting.

Choosing and preparing the wines

It is accepted that wines to be served with a meal should be chosen according to the occasion and the foods that make up that meal (*see* pp.168–83). Expect to serve at least one 750ml bottle of wine for every three or four guests. The selected wines should be checked and handled with great care, from the moment they are taken from storage to when they are consumed; attention to details is important. Although wines for immediate drinking, including rosé wines, can be opened and consumed with no delay, other – certainly mature red – wines require more care due to their style and their age.

INSPECT THE BOTTLES. If possible, choose mature wines to serve at a meal about two days beforehand. Check the bottles in storage; ideally they will be have been stored lying down, with the label uppermost. This way, you can be sure that the sediment settles in one place, on the opposite side from the main label. Handle the bottles gently, with no sudden movements. Keep them oriented as they were laid, and use a good flashlight to check the clarity of the wine and the amount of the sediment.

BRING TO THE CORRECT TEMPERATURE AND NEUTRALIZE THE SEDIMENT. Young, dry white wines can be chilled a few hours before serving. Mature white wines showing some sediment should be stood upright the evening before they are to be chilled and served. Young red wines generally have very little sediment and so can simply be placed upright the morning before the evening that they are to be served. Mature red wines with sediment should be gently set upright two days in advance, before being decanted if necessary.

The order in which wines are served follows a few simple rules: *dry white wine should be served before red wine; young red wine before mature red; lighter wines before fuller-bodied ones; simplest wines before the most complex.*

How many wines should be served?

A single wine can be consumed throughout a meal, or a different wine can be served with every course. (Or no wine at all needs be served.) The number of wines served also varies according to the occasion and time of day – lunch or dinner, a family meal, or a gourmet meal for food lovers (*see also* p.168).

FAMILY OR FRIENDS. A meal for family or friends implies simplicity. A single, well-made, unpretentious wine is fine; and the colour is a matter of choice. A Sunday meal or a meal with friends is an occasion where a choice of wines adapted to the menu is welcome. In addition to the aperitif – which may be the wine planned for the first course – three or four wines may reasonably be expected to follow: a white wine for the first course, a red wine for the main course, another wine for the cheeses, and finally a dessert wine.

AMONG CONNOISSEURS. If the meal has been specially planned as 'fine dining,' the wine selection may be doubled; but remember that all these wines will be swallowed rather than tasted and spat out, so there is potential for over-imbibing throughout the course of a meal.

Setting

About two hours before the guests arrive, it's a good idea to attend to final preparations. Anticipating some details in this way will help the service go smoothly at the table.

OPENING THE BOTTLES. Except for sparkling wines, which should be opened in front of guests, all bottles can be opened and the wines tasted quietly in advance in order to check their condition (*see also* the box on p.197). White wines should then be resealed and returned to the refrigerator. Any red wines requiring decanting should be decanted into carafes (*see* p.193). These should be stoppered afterwards, and kept at optimum temperature. It is pointless to reseal red wines that have not been decanted. Finally, in case more wine is required, it's good to have an unopened bottle of each wine in reserve.

POINTS TO REMEMBER. Don't forget to have a napkin handy in order to wipe the neck of the bottle (or a damp bottle) while you are serving. Chill several bottles of mineral water, both still and sparkling.

PLACING THE GLASSES. At each place setting, the glasses are arranged in order of serving, from left to right facing the plate. To avoid laborious manipulations during the meal, it's best to set out all the necessary glassware right away. The water glass should be placed behind the wine glasses. If it happens that

several bottles of the same memorable great wine are served during the meal, the possibility of having to change glasses with each bottle opened should be catered for, as there can be great differences from one bottle to another.

Always taste before serving

As soon as the selected bottles have been opened, it's time to check the wine. First, check each closure (if natural cork) by sniffing it in order to detect possible defects. Then proceed to a 'control' tasting. Some musty smells disappear quickly; but 'corky' smells are more serious. If a musty smell is very light, the first glass may be the only one affected, and simple aeration is often enough to clear it. If it persists, it's best to open another bottle. If in doubt, do not hesitate to change. Once checked, each bottle can be decanted (just in case), and then served.

Table service: be as attentive as a waiter

THE HOST'S ROLE. Throughout the meal, the host generally plays the role of wine waiter and shoulders the responsibility of serving the wine. As a courtesy, the host will taste each bottle before pouring, and make sure that wines remain (as much as possible) at the right serving temperature. They also see that each glass is filled to one-third of capacity throughout the meal.

THE CORRECT TEMPERATURE. Sparkling and white wines should be kept sufficiently chilled by standing them in a bucket containing water and some ice cubes. It is a good idea to serve red wines one or two degrees colder than prescribed: as soon as they are poured into a glass they warm up by a degree or so.

TRUE OR FALSE?

Dry Champagne goes well with desserts.

FALSE. Contact with sugar hardens the taste of dry Champagne. For desserts, therefore, make a point of choosing those wines made to accompany them, known collectively as 'dessert wines.' Examples are late-harvest Muscat or Sémillon. Dry Champagne is ideal as an aperitif or served throughout a meal. For dessert, it's best to serve a medium-dry Champagne.

WINE IN A RESTAURANT

A restaurant is chosen for the quality of its food, its decor, its wine selection, and its price bracket. It's not always easy to navigate your way through a long, impressive wine list; but a quick glance can establish a fairly good idea of its range and prices. Additionally, you can ask the sommelier (or wine waiter) for advice.

Choosing wine

A quick glance at the wine list will help the customer get an idea of the amount of attention the restaurant pays to wine. A short and well-chosen selection is better than a long list of famous appellations, the service of which is not always to be trusted. The wine list should also reflect the style of the restaurant's cuisine; so it's interesting to note the influence on the list of certain wine-producing regions. The presence of a sommelier confirms that real attention is paid to wine selection and service.

FOOD/WINE HARMONY. Good waiters will never be offended if asked both for the menu and the wine list. This shows the customer cares about both aspects of the meal. On a first visit to a restaurant, it is hard to know whether the food should be ordered first, followed by the wines, or vice versa. Creative cuisine should be explained, and a simple listing of the ingredients may guide the choice of wines. If it's impossible to resist a dish whose composition might alter the wine, it's best to ask the sommelier's advice. Conversely, if a particular wine attracts your attention, the waiter or sommelier will be able to recommend the best dish to complement it.

***The sommelier is simultaneously wine waiter, oenophile, psychologist, jurist,and food lover.** He or she presides over the wine 'ceremony' and is a skilled guide to the subtle relationships between the wines and the foods on the menu.*

Wine lists

PRESENTATION. Restaurant efficiency is reflected in the simplicity of the wine list. It should be laid out clearly so that the client can navigate their way through it easily. The wines should be classified by colour, then by a combination of varietals, countries, regions, or appellations. Additionally, a good list will show wines by vintage, and maybe even by sub-appellation. And, obviously, they should always show the price clearly – by the glass (for some wines) and by the bottle (for all wines). However it is presented, the information given in the list should be consistent. The best restaurants should show (as appropriate) each wine's village, site, *clos*, proprietor's name, and the vintage. When a 'house wine' is listed, it generally means a simple wine selected to complement the restaurant's style of cuisine, but it will never be a truly great wine.

USEFUL SPECIFICS. A sommelier will be able to provide useful additional information, such as the quality of a vintage, the grape varieties, production techniques, the exact location of the estate, etc. Learn from your sommelier, but do not monopolize them indefinitely. Their role is to look after all the tables in a restaurant, preparing the glasses and bottles, and serving the wine.

DID YOU KNOW...?

***The profession of sommelier is more than 4,000 years old.** In fact, it goes back to the time of the Pharaohs, when the sommelier was responsible for preparing drinks for the country's kings and nobles, making and serving both beer and wine. Until the middle of the 20th century, the sommelier also bottled the wine in the cellar of the restaurant where he worked. When it became customary to bottle wine at estates, sommeliers began working on the restaurant floor* (see also *pp.200–1*).

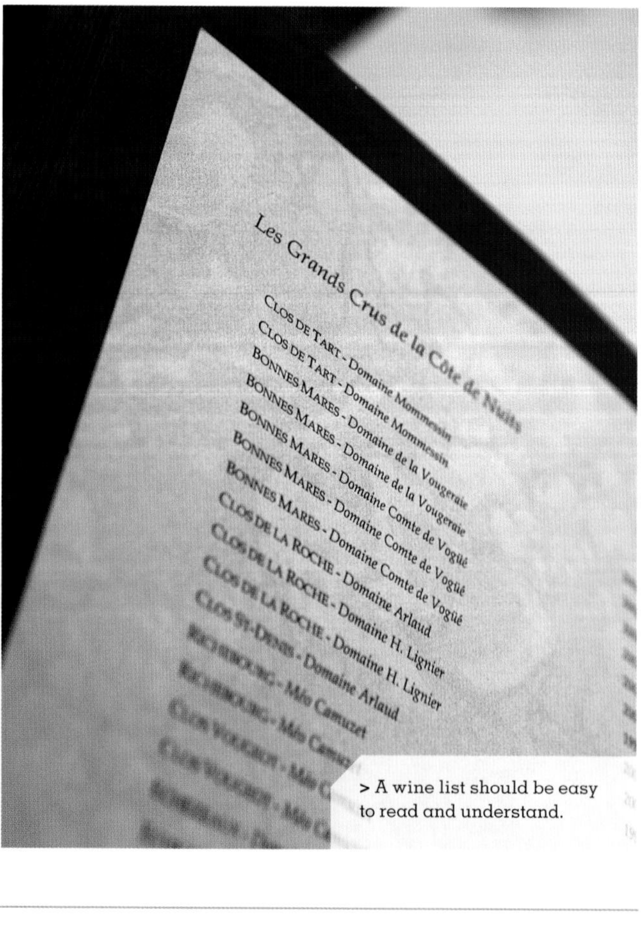

> A wine list should be easy to read and understand.

What if there's something wrong with the wine?

The wine served is defective: it may be musty, maderized, oxididated, flat, 'corked,' etc. Defects should be noted by the waiter serving the wine or the sommelier when they first taste the wine, in which case the bottle should be changed. If there is even the slightest doubt, it is the customer's prerogative to ask for another bottle. However, some restaurants may warn you that rare bottles or those from an old vintage are ordered at your own risk and will be charged whatever happens.

You don't like the wine. There's nothing wrong with the wine, which has been warmly recommended by the waiter or the sommelier, but for whatever reason you do not like it. You should mention this, and the staff should make another suggestion to suit your taste. Having taken the risk, it's incumbent on the restaurant to behave both nobly and with modesty.

> When the person who has ordered the wine approves it, the sommelier will fill the glasses.

Sommeliers

When bewildered by pages and pages of *crus* from different regions and varying prices, the customer can turn for advice to a helpful professional. Although bringing up the price can be a delicate matter, a talented sommelier will pick up small hints as to just how much a customer would like to spend. There should be no need for embarrassment if a suggestion is unsuitable; just ask for another, being as precise as possible about what you like. And while the sommelier's suggestion is almost always a good one, the final decision remains with the customer. The sommelier will be familiar with the wines they suggests, but that counts for less than the customer's preference and the etiquette of service.

Serving the wine

Once the order has been taken, the sommelier prepares the appropriate glasses and gets the selected bottles. The service, as it is properly called, then begins. Each bottle is presented to the client so that she or he can check and agree that the appellation, vintage, and producer are just as ordered. The sommelier then opens the bottles, sniffing closures and often tasting each wine. If necessary, they will decant the wine and keep it at the correct temperature.

In top restaurants, the signal to serve a wine is given by the person who has ordered it. The sommelier will serve them first, so that they can taste the wine. This enables the host to check the wine's intrinsic quality and its temperature. If approved by the customer, the service continues in order of precedence, not forgetting to refill the glass of whoever has tasted first. Drinks should be served from the right, giving each guest the opportunity, if they want, to glance at the label while the sommelier may discreetly murmur the wine's name and vintage. The sommelier will fill the glasses to one-third and will be vigilant to ensure no guest is without wine. The sommelier will also serve any bottled water. A sommelier will respond to the customer's demands at all times. If the customer cannot find a wine they like – or notes a defect in quality, such as the wine being 'corked' or having a temperature problem – they are within their rights to point it out and to ask for another bottle.

1

WORLD'S BEST SOMMELIERS

2016 Arvid Rosengren (Sweden)
2013 Paolo Basso (Italy)
2010 Gerard Basset (UK)
2008 Andreas Larsson (Sweden)
2004 Enrico Bernardo (Italy)
2000 Olivier Poussier (France)
1998 Markus Del Monego (Germany)
1995 Shinya Tasaki (Japan)
1992 Philippe Faure-Brac (France)
1989 Serge Dubs (France)
1986 Jean-Claude Jambon (France)

FRANCE'S BEST SOMMELIERS

2014 Jonathan Bauer-Monneret (Le Spring, Paris)
2012 Romain Iltis (L'Arnsbourg, Baerenthal)
2010 Benjamin Roffet (Le Trianon, Versailles)
2008 Manuel Peyrondet (Hôtel Bristol, Paris)
2006 Pascal Leonetti (Auberge de l'Ill, Illhaeusern)
2004 Dominique Laporte (Le Phare, Palavas-les-Flots)
2002 David Biraud (Hôtel Crillon, Paris)
2000 Franck Thomas (consultant)

Sommelier as wine ambassador

The working environment of the sommelier is one of contrasts, sometimes within the confines of a shadowy cellar, and sometimes in the full glare of the spotlight, advising customers in a restaurant.

CONNOISSEUR AND MANAGER

Away from the limelight, the sommelier is always topping up his or her knowledge throughout their career. This involves visits to vineyard regions to become familiar with wines and wineries and to learn about each new vintage. The sommelier never stops learning, never ceasing to seek out those wines best suited to the cuisine and clientele of the restaurant. There are two key criteria: the style of the wine and, obviously, its price. The sommelier is first and foremost a manager: he or she has overall responsibility for the cellar – for its correct maintenance, controlling inventory, developing the wine list, and establishing prices in agreement with supervisors. In well-known restaurants that can afford to acquire and store very expensive bottles of wine, the sommelier must also be able to forecast the wines' potential and decide whether to serve or save them. Finally, the sommelier establishes the daily inventory, ensuring the wines are stored at service temperature to meet the restaurant's immediate requirements.

ON STAGE

This is where the sommelier steps int the limelight. The uniform is timeless black apron, matching jacket, anc gold lapel pin in the shape of a cluste of grapes. The tools are at the ready corkscrew, white napkin, decanter, anc small dish in which to lay the closure, i necessary. The tasks are unchanging advise the customer, bearing in minc the food selected; present the wines anc spirits; and serve them. 'It's a comple scenario,' emphasizes Philippe Faure Brac, World's Best Sommelier in 1992 'The script and the partners change a every meal. You need to have a sens of who you are dealing with: wine lover novice, business executive wanting t

1. Recording wines taken from the cellar.
2. Opening: sure, precise actions.
3. Checking the wine before serving.
4. Insignia of a master sommelier.

impress guests, lovers, the affluent or not...'

SOMMELIER COMPETITIONS...

To prepare for this often twice-daily performance, increasing numbers of sommeliers enter various competitions organized by their trade associations. They compete for the title of best regional sommelier, best sommelier in France, or in Europe, or in the world. Theres also a competition for best student sommelier, and one for the best young (under 24) working sommelier. The basic elements are usually the same, but the competitions vary difficulty in terms of the the questions and the level of skill required. The theory section involves questions on regional history and the geography of vineyards and wineries, as well as oenology, technology, legislation, the organization of a wine list, the spelling of wines and appellations, cellar management, a knowledge of spirits, coffees, teas, mineral waters, cigars – nothing is left out.

The best candidates go on to undergo a series of practical tests: serving wine, wine and food pairings, taking an order in a foreign language, correcting an inaccurate wine list (for example, a white wine slipped in among the reds, a non-existent vintage, faulty spellings, an incorrect price).

Jean-Luc Jamrozik, sommelier of the Hôtel Baltimore in Paris, is a member of the Union of French Sommellerie (UDSF and regularly prepares candidates for various competitions. 'I get to play difficult clients,' he explains with a gently sadistic smile. 'The kind who want red wine with fish or white with game, or who say they are allergic to sulphur, or who play at being blasé and demand to be surprised...'

Apart from the prestige of being singled out from among their peers, the winner generally does not receive money but a far more appropriate prize: distinguished bottles of wine, a trip to vineyard regions around the world, a chance to meet the great names in the profession, meals in the best Michelin-starred restaurants, the opportunity to develop new wines, etc. These competitions are becoming increasingly popular, with more women becoming involved, although the number of women in the profession is still deplorably low, as is sadly shown in the list of winners of the most prestigious contests. But change is on the menu!

HOW TO TASTE WINE

THE BASICS OF SUCCESSFUL TASTING

The colour, the aromas, the flavours, and the texture all speak volumes to our senses when we taste wine. However, the enthusiastic amateur often lacks the vocabulary to describe these sensations adequately, being unable to 'decode' the different elements making up the wine, and needs advice on how to taste it.

The art of tasting

Tasting is essentially a technical exercise which takes place in three stages and involves three of our senses in turn: sight, smell, and taste. Although there are tasting events open to the general public, wine lovers often organize private tasting events with friends. It is something everyone can do, requiring just a little attention to detail and respecting a few important conditions.

Choosing a venue

Choosing the right room is important. It should be bright, with sufficient daylight or neutral lighting (but no strip lighting or coloured lamps). The air should not be 'polluted' with cooking smells, flowers, tobacco, or perfume. The ideal room temperature is somewhere between 64°F and 68°F (18°C–20°C), as this will enable your wine to show its best. (The idea of allowing the wine to stand in a room for a few hours so that it warms up from cellar temperature and tastes better dates back to a time before central heating.) The table should be covered with a white cloth, or, in the absence of one, the glasses should be placed on a piece of white paper, which will allow people to judge the colour of the wine objectively.

***Tasting will help you learn about wine.** Tasting wine regularly sharpens the senses and gradually improves the specific vocabulary required to communicate wine-related opinions clearly.*

Selecting your equipment

GLASSES. Choosing glasses is important because they influence the appearance and aroma of the wine. Avoid using coloured glasses. A tulip-shaped glass with a transparent stem, sometimes known in France as an *Angoulême*, is a great choice. The tasting glass created by professionals some 30 years ago and known as the INAO glass is also still recommended.

With its semi-elliptic form, the mouth is narrower than its curved bowl, allowing it to concentrate aromas and to avoid spills when the wine is swirled in the glass. INAO-type glasses are available from department stores and any good wine merchant. A taster should smell their glass before using it to make sure there are no residual odours (from the box or from detergent). The glass may be rinsed with water or, better still, moistened with the first wine to be tasted. The ideal approach is to provide a fresh glass with every wine. If this is not possible, provide a minimum of two glasses per taster so that wines may be compared.

SPITTOONS. These are indispensable accessories, allowing tasters both to spit out a tasted wine and to empty their glasses (*see* box p.205). However, other containers can also be used, such as a deep bowl, vase, or Champagne bucket.

Getting wine ready

The wines, which will have been stored horizontally in a cellar, should be placed upright 24 hours before the tasting so that any sediment will settle at the bottom of the bottle. They should be opened an hour before the tasting and, if necessary, be decanted into a carafe. The whites should be placed on ice or refrigerated for a few hours and then taken out half an hour before tasting to reach the right temperature; they should be opened just before being tasted.

What is blind tasting?

This is a completely objective method of tasting wines without knowing their identity. The bottle is covered with paper or some kind of sleeve – whatever the taster's level of expertise, there is always the danger of being influenced by the label. A wine with a great reputation will always raise expectations and the reverse can also be true. In blind tasting, the intrinsic quality of the wine is left to speak for itself, which may well lead to some surprises.

> Bottles disguised with paper sleeves at a blind tasting.

Appropriate physical conditions

A taster should be fresh and rested, and in good health. Fatigue will affect judgment, and colds in particular are a considerable handicap to taking in the aromas and flavours of the wine. The best time for wine tasting is in the morning, when the senses are sharpest and concentration is at a maximum. But wine lovers generally prefer to get together at the beginning of an evening before dinner, when the agenda is about friends and fun. Tasting after a meal should be avoided; the senses are 'saturated' and the body is digesting the food.

Before tasting, avoid drinking coffee or smoking cigarettes, since this will 'spoil' the palate. By the same token, bread – a neutral foodstuff – is preferable to cheese or salty crackers to 'cleanse' the palate between wines that are particularly tannic or acidic.

A few simple rules for successful tasting

When tasting, it is best to observe at least a degree of silence in order to encourage concentration. As fascinating as it is to share your thoughts, there will be time for this later. The person leading the tasting may therefore suggest a summary of the wines tasted, after sampling a set number of bottles. Each guest will keep notes of their observations on a tasting sheet provided for this purpose (for a few examples, *see* pp.222–5). This is an invaluable exercise for reinforcing a taster's judgment. The notes will provide a starting point as your tasting ability develops, and you trace the evolution of wines. Tasting is an exercise in memory as well – the more you taste, noting colours, aromas, and flavours in your 'reference library' of experience, the more you will be in a position to identify a wine's sensory characteristics and, by comparing many, to assess its qualities.

Equally important are honesty, modesty, and respect for the opinions of others: virtues for life, too! There actually is no such thing as 'good' or 'bad' in tasting – everyone has their own ideas and may defend these in discussion, always preserving respect for others.

DID YOU KNOW...?

Spitting out a wine is normal at tastings.
For a beginner, spitting out wine might seem odd and a bit disgusting, not to mention frustrating, but it is a necessity. Formal tastings do not take place at mealtimes, and so wine is being sampled on its own. Even if the quantity is not sufficient to actually cause drunkenness, it may well dull the senses or cause you to lose concentration. In addition, swallowing the wine is not actually neccessary to assess it, as all the 'tasting' takes place between the nose and the mouth. So people spit out wine in order to be able to appreciate the aroma and the body of several wines more keenly.

APPEARANCE

The first contact with a wine is visual – the eye perceives the wine's colour and depth of colour as soon as it is served. For an observant taster, wine begins to tell its story while it is still in the glass. Looking at what is known in French as the wine's robe *('dress') – its hue, brilliance, surface, and its 'legs' – allows a taster to uncover many valuable clues as to the wine's origins, age, personality, and indeed its quality.*

Noting the appearance

A taster begins by trying to define a wine's colour: its hue, its intensity, and its clarity. To see these clearly, the wine should be held – in good lighting – in front of a neutral background (a white tablecloth, for example) or placed on any white surface.

HUE. The colour of a wine is evaluated according to two criteria: hue and its intensity. The terms used to describe the first stem from the world of precious stones (ruby, topaz), metals (gold, copper), flowers (rose, violet), and fruits (lemon, cherry). *See also* box below.

INTENSITY. Since there are so many different shades of colour, it is important to define the hue by its intensity. This varies between 'pale' and 'very dark', moving through 'light', 'dark', 'deep', 'intense' and 'profound'. Some of the vocabulary used, such as 'poor', 'soft' and 'weak', are already indications of quality.

CLARITY. This should be perfect and not compromised by any foreign particles in suspension in the wine, such as dust, flakes or any residue from finings or dead yeast that may float around in the liquid. If it is not clear, it may be described as 'cloudy', 'hazy' or 'opalescent'. These are all signs of poor winemaking or contamination of the wine, generally making it unfit to drink. As wine production techniques advance, however, these faults are less and less likely to occur. Nevertheless, wines that are deliberately unfiltered or unfined can be slightly hazy in appearance, without actually being faulty.

***Visually inspecting a wine is the first step in waking the senses.** It prepares and conditions the mind and the other senses for tasting the wine.*

What does the appearance of a wine tell us?

A wine's colour not only tells us its type – white, red or rosé – but it can also reveal details about the age of the vines, the yield, the year, the age of the wine and even the manner of its maturation.

VARIETIES AND VINTAGES. The substances that lend a wine its colour originate with pigments contained in grape skins. There are few of these to be found in white grapes, but they are very prevalent in red grapes, with different intensities according to the variety and maceration time. A wine made with Gamay grapes has a pretty ruby colour, unlike one made with Cabernet Sauvignon, which is a deep garnet. The gradual development of the vines partially determines the maturity of the grape pigments, although the colour intensity of a wine is more predicated on actual vintage quality. Thus a 1994 Médoc will have a less intense

> To inspect a wine's appearance, it should be placed above a white surface.

The palette of colours

Red wines: peony, light ruby, dark ruby, vermilion, garnet, deep garnet, carmine, deep purple. When aged: brick red, russet, chestnut, mahogany, coffee.

Rosés: pale grey, very light rose, pink, raspberry, carnation, strawberry, cherry, salmon pink. When older, they become: salmon, orange, brick, copper, onion skin.

White wines: pale yellow with a hint of green, pale yellow, lemon, pale gold, golden yellow, straw gold. After several years of maturing: old gold, bronze, copper, amber, mahogany, coffee.

hue than the more concentrated 1996, which was a hotter year. In the same way, white wines will have a deeper colour when the grapes were harvested in hotter years, which encourages slight over-maturity.

VINE YIELD. The colour intensity is also a function of the yield that the winemaker has obtained from the vines. The higher the yield, the less concentrated the grapes and the lighter the resulting liquid. By contrast, the lower the yield, the more the wine will gain in intensity. This is often the case with old vines, which bear fewer grapes and which almost always produce a wine with a pronounced colouration.

CONDITION OF THE GRAPES. The health of grape clusters is also a factor that influences a wine's appearance. If made with a spoiled lot of grapes, the wine will have less colour intensity, whatever the variety or yield.

WINE AGE. The colour of a white wine intensifies with age, while that of a red wine fades. As a result, the colour of a wine can allow you to assess its age. When very young, reds (and some rosés) have a slight blue tinge that often lends a purple

DID YOU KNOW...?

A wine 'throwing a deposit' or looking cloudy is not necessarily a bad sign. *If unfiltered or only partially filtered, some young wines will display a slight haze, arising from fine lees in suspension that will go on to form an entirely normal deposit. By the same token, it is entirely normal to find deposits in old wines or small crystals resulting from a precipitation of tartaric acid, one of the ingredients of wine, the latter being the result of a sudden change in temperature.*

Sparkling wines

Much like still wines, sparkling wines are judged on their colour, clarity, and brilliance.

In addition, the wine's foam (bubbles) should also be examined. The best shape of glass is a tall 'flute,' which is preferable to a standard 'cup' glass, which can spoil the wine's effervescence. The taster first looks at the foam that forms spontaneously in the glass when the wine is poured, noting the size, duration, and the size of the bubbles. A good foam is of a reasonable size, long-lasting, and made up of small bubbles. Once this has subsided, it leaves behind the *cordon*, a ring of bubbles adhering to the side of the glass. These bubbles, which should be small, will rise regularly from the bottom of the glass to the ring at the top in columns known in French as the *cheminée*. Large bubbles that burst immediately at the surface, the absence of a ring of bubbles, or minimal effervescence do not suggest a high quality wine. But note that the serving temperature and the choice of glass both play a role in the formation of bubbles and froth – cold inhibits effervescence and heat encourages it.

> The stream of bubbles rising to form a *cheminée* replenishes the ring of froth that forms at the edge of the glass.

hue to their overall appearance. In time, they will acquire shades of deep orange as the pigments and tannins start to yellow. As whites contain few tannins, their colour develops much more slowly, from shades of green and yellow to gold.

VINIFICATION. This too plays a role in wine colour. For reds, a long maceration allows more of the pigmented substances to be extracted (*see* p.68). For rosés, the different methods of production, either by crushing or by *saignée* ('bleeding' of the vats, *see* p.66), result in different shades of wine: rather pale in the case of the former method, and darker in the latter. A new barrel will intensify wine hue as it boosts the combination of the substances causing colouration. Whether white or red, a wine will have a darker shade when matured in barrels than the same wine that has been stored in steel tanks.

The surface and the meniscus

THE SURFACE (the topmost view of a wine). To observe the surface accurately, tasters first place themselves directly above the glass – the top view – and then hold the wine up to light – the side view. The surface is judged according to the brilliance of its appearance and by the way it catches the light. Observing the surface should confirm the clarity of the colour. A wine with clarity issues will also present a surface with the same problems; and a suspect will be described as 'matte', 'dull', 'flat' and 'lustreless'. More positively, the wine's surface might be described as 'brilliant', 'lustrous', 'luminous' or 'intense'. For white wines and rosés, lustre is an important and fundamental index of quality. For red wines, such a quality should be considered in light of the recent winery trend to avoid filtration, an operation otherwise carried out just before bottling and intended to increase the clarity and brilliance of a wine (*see* p.76). Without filtration, a wine will lose in brilliance but gain in colour intensity.

THE MENISCUS (OR RIM). When inspecting the surface of red wines, and to a lesser extent rosés, tasters will pay special attention to its outside edge, known as the 'meniscus.' Because the wine is at its thinnest here, the wine's true colour will be most apparent. If there is a touch of blue, it suggests that the wine is still very young; if it reveals more shades of terracotta and brick red, it will be an older wine. This development of colour, a result of pigments taking on an orange or brick-red tint with time due to the ageing of tannins, is of varying significance and meaning for different wines. Thus, hints of purple or a bold red are appropriate for wines that are enjoyed young; by the time these have taken on an orange meniscus, they are no longer fresh. Orange and ochre go in tandem with a more developed

Common visual faults

The most common faults encountered today are a lack of colour intensity and, in the case of red wines, a colour that has turned prematurely to a brown brick-red; this is usually the result of a spoiled harvest or insufficiently matured grapes. It could also be an indication of too high a yield, winemaking that was rushed or badly carried out, or premature oxidation.

wine, which has some age. Shades of brown and garnet, however, are acceptable only in wines capable of very long ageing. For wines that do not have sufficient physical or aromatic capabilities for long ageing, these are signs of decrepitude. Much like the wine's colour, the meniscus should be in proportion to the year printed on the label. Thus, if the label suggests that the wine is still young but the meniscus already shows signs of age, it is not likely to be a wine of good quality. The colour then will be described as 'old', 'tired' or 'impaired'. In the reverse case (an old wine with a less well developed meniscus), the taster will note the youth of its colour.

The 'legs'

WHAT EXACTLY ARE LEGS? By placing the glass up to light and swirling the wine, or rotating it to slide up the sides of the glass, tasters will be able to see traces of a transparent liquid that slips down more slowly than the rest of the wine. These are the 'legs', and inspecting them is the last stage of a visual examination of wine. They are the result of twin phenomena arising from physical tension between water and alcohol and from the mixture of alcohol, sugars, and glycerols in the wine. The legs display the body of a wine – its viscosity or tactile thickness. Well-defined, viscous legs that flow gently down the glass are a sign of wine rich in residual sugars and/or alcohol. By contrast, a less rich wine will have fewer, finer, and more fluid legs that move more quickly. The phenomenon is described in terms of the wine's fluidity or viscosity, using words like 'watery', 'liquid' and 'fluid' for a wine with a low alcohol or sugar content and 'thick', 'syrupy' and 'unctuous' in the opposite case.

HOW SHOULD LEGS BE INTERPRETED? 'Legs' are rarely considered a sign of good or bad quality in a wine. Instead, they provide more information about its personality or categorization in the great wine families (*see* pp.154–61). For white wines, abundant 'legs' with a certain viscosity suggest a sweet or medium-sweet style of wine, rich in sugars (a Sauternes or Jurançon, for example) rather than a dry wine. In blind tastings, where the wine's identity is unknown, inspecting such details will yield helpful clues for tasters.

> Inspecting a wine's 'legs' will give you an idea of the its alcohol and/or sugar content.

IF WINE IS LUSTROUS, IT IS ALIVE

Jean-Michel Deluc, Master Sommelier.

'The brilliance of a wine is a visual expression of its acidity. A young wine, whether it is red, white, rosé, sparkling, sweet, or dry, will have a brilliance from undiminished acidity. This acidity beds down and softens with age, and the wine loses its lustre. Acidity is the life of a wine, and as long as it remains, the wine will have a shine. A wine that has lost this has reached the end of its time.

The oldest wine I have ever tasted was an 1834 Pedro Ximenez sherry. It was a coffee colour, with a sweet texture. Its density had made it opaque, and yet it still had a shine, a surprise that bowled me over!'

Tastevin

An accessory popular with Old World cellar masters, the tastevin is a shallow, round metal receptacle resembling a small cup. It is not really possible to 'nose' a wine with a tastevin because of its low profile; it is primarily used to judge the fine detail and intensity of a wine's appearance and clarity, thus helping to estimate the general state of the wine more objectively.

Professional winemakers are thus able to follow the development of the different wines held in their cellars.

WINE AROMA OR 'NOSE'

Sniffing a glass of wine, identifying the different aromas, and investigating its complexity and subtlety is one of the great pleasures of tasting. Nonetheless, this exercise is one that often frustrates novice tasters, who have trouble telling aromas apart. A short refresher course will be useful in reawakening your olfactory memory.

Analyzing the 'nose' of a wine

A wine's aroma delivers about 70 per cent of all information about that wine. For the best results in analyzing the aroma of a wine, tasters should choose a tulip-shaped glass and fill it to only about a third of its capacity. They will also monitor the serving temperature of the wine – somewhere between 46 and 64°F (8–18°C) depending on wine colour and origin (*see* p.186–7) – which influences the volatility of the aromatic ingredients of the wine. If it is too cold, the aromas will not be able to vaporize easily; if it is too hot, they will evaporate too quickly and be overpowered by alcohol fumes.

The best advice is to sniff the glass several times without inhaling too hard, in order to avoid saturating your senses. Also, wait a little between each inhalation. Analyzing the aroma of a wine splits into three stages.

FIRST NOSING. For the initial olfactory contact with a wine, tasters will angle their glasses and lightly breathe in the wine aromas. They make sure, on the one hand, that the wine is not tainted with undesirable smells and, on the other, that they capture the delicate, volatile scents of the wine (those present in the upper part of the glass). The latter soon disappear after serving.

SECOND NOSING. This stage is intended to identify the wine's aromatic personality. Tasters will grasp the glass by its base and rotate it to swirl the wine and oxygenate it. This will accelerate the vaporization of the various aromatic compounds. (To make this easier, feel free to keep the glass on the table while swirling it.) They will then inhale a few times, dipping their noses into the glass for several seconds, in order to assess the strength, the intensity, and the richness of the nose, while trying to identify the different aromas of which it is composed.

THIRD NOSING. This shows the wine's character after a long period of oxygenation in the glass. Once the wine is in contact with the air, its various aromatic compounds develop at different rates according to their volatility. So it's an interesting exercise to dip your nose back into the glass (without swirling its contents) after leaving the wine to stand for a while. Tasters often note the development of new aromas and changes in intensity.

***The term 'nose' describes the collection of scents that characterize a wine.** One might use the term 'aroma' to designate the fresh and fruity scents of young wines, and 'bouquet' to express the aromatic richness of a wine at the height of its powers or in its old age.*

> Giving the wine a gentle swirl in its glass will oxygenate it.

DID YOU KNOW...?

***Smell is the most active of our senses and yet, paradoxically, the least educated.** Although smell is the most developed sense among newborns, as adults we just react to odours in an instinctive and primary manner, accepting or rejecting them but rarely analyzing them. This often causes problems for tasters called upon to identify the characteristic aromas of a wine. To help, good tasters attempt to smell everything around them that produces a scent (flowers, fruits, spices, as well as the scents of the countryside, the kitchen, the bakery, etc.), hoping to capture and catalogue them in each of the family groups of smells. It's not a difficult exercise and certainly not an unpleasant one – tasting is a little like 'dusting off' our memory, diving into our life history to bring up memories associated with particular smells.*

Nasal and retronasal passages

The sense of smell is called upon not only during the sniffing stage, but also during the actual tasting itself. Aromatic molecules in a vaporized state will rise toward the back of the nasal cavity along two routes: the nasal passage, which passes directly through the nostrils when we breathe in, and the less direct retronasal passage, which links the mouth to the nose via the throat when we breathe out.

It's therefore only at the moment of drinking that tasters complete their olfactory analysis of the wine, by uncovering the aromas that are not directly accessible to the nose. Indeed, because of their low volatility, some scents need to be warmed in the mouth in order to pass from a liquid state to a gaseous one. Only at that moment do flavours and aromas mix and juxtapose themselves. What we recognize, for example, as the taste of strawberries is in fact the smell of strawberries; the 'taste' is thus the sum total of sensations that are as much olfactory (aromas) as they are gustatory (flavours).

> Analyzing the nose of a wine requires concentration and an effort of memory from a taster.

Describing the bouquet of a wine

The best way to describe the aromas or bouquet of a wine is in stages, starting with an overall impression before pointing out the different scents and aromas you find in the wine.

AROMATIC CHARACTERISTICS. At first, tasters will try to describe the wine's aromatic features in a general way, assessing intensity in terms of 'strong' or 'weak' or the various gradations between them. The vocabulary used might include terms such as 'expressive', 'intense', 'powerful', 'generous' and 'exuberant'. By contrast, there is 'inexpressive', 'weak', 'poor' and 'limp'. In certain circumstances, the wine does not develop any clear aroma in the glass, such as when it has just been poured or when served too cold; the bouquet is then said to be 'closed.' This objective and descriptive vocabulary is often augmented with more subjective thoughts such as 'pleasing', 'agreeable', 'elegant' or 'classy'. As well, there is 'banal', 'ordinary', 'simplistic' or 'vulgar'.

IDENTIFYING DIFFERENT AROMAS. The next level of analysis may be a more difficult exercise. Rather than trying to identify a specific aroma, it is often easier to identify the 'family' of scents to which it belongs, referring to such groups as floral, fruity, vegetal, mineral, spicy, balsamic, toasted or chemical aromas (*see* table on p.214).

Aromas may also be distinguished according to the origins, age and production methods of the wine, as some of these groups of scents overlap with others.

PRIMARY AROMAS. These show the fruit characteristics of the grape variety (or varieties) that comprise the wine. They may be floral, fruity, vegetal, mineral or spicy, according to the grape varieties. They are at their strongest when the wine is young, especially if it has been matured exclusively in vats.

SECONDARY AROMAS. These are the result of fermentation, the process that transforms grapes into wine. Consequently, they often are called 'fermentation aromas'. They are determined by the nature of the yeast and the style of winemaking, and are part of the 'chemical' family of aromas: amylic (bananas or nail varnish), fermentative (yeast, soft bread) or lactic (butter, milk, cream). These aromas are associated with young wines and disappear after a couple of years of bottle age. Secondary aromas are also introduced by maturing the wine in barrels, and these are spicy scents (pepper, vanilla, cinnamon) or toasted (grilled, roasted, smoked).

TERTIARY AROMAS. These aromas develop when wine is matured in vats or barrels and then in bottle. They are linked to the redox (reduction-oxidation) reaction that depends on the container – an inert vat, barrel or bottle. Relatively short ageing in new barrels produces spicy notes (pepper, vanilla, cinnamon) or burnt aromas (grilled, toasted, roasted, smoked) whereas long maturing over several years in old barrels produces *rancio*-type oxidative notes. During ageing in bottle, in the absence of oxygen the aromas develop slowly, adding musky and vegetal notes to the aromatic framework.

196
REBOUCHE

What can the nose of a wine tell you?

Just like its appearance, the nose of a wine reveals important information about its personality and its quality. Pleasant intensity and a large palette of aromas are signs of high quality and will excite a taster who encounters them. The primary and secondary aromas are usually the dominant scents, providing valuable information about the grape variety, the age of the wine, the production methods, indeed even the year and the yield.

FRUIT RIPENESS. To a large extent, the quality of the aromas contained in the glass depends on the ripeness of the grapes. A less ripe, dilute Sauvignon Blanc will give off an unsophisticated grassy scent with just a hint of citrus fruits. When more mature and made from a low yield, it will reveal complex aromas of pineapple or grapefruit zest.

WINE ORIGIN. A Chardonnay produced in Chablis will have a fresh bouquet with mineral and white flower notes, very different from one made in Meursault, which will be more opulent with hints of almond and hazelnut. Furthermore, a wine created beneath the Languedoc sun is even heavier, with potent notes of ripe fruit.

WINE AGE. A wine best expresses its complexity with time; the different perfumes of a wine – the primary, secondary, and tertiary aromas – evolve while the wine is being matured in a tank or a barrel, and then later as it ages in the bottle. In the best examples, and for wines to lay down, a wine captures the scents from its whole history, expressing the quintessence of the land where it was made and yet always retaining the memory of the original fruit. It is important, nevertheless, not to lose sight of the fact that most wines gain nothing from ageing and are produced instead to be enjoyed with their youthful aromas.

DID YOU KNOW...?

A wine's bouquet is never exactly the same twice. *It varies according to the distance travelled by the bottle, the breathing time, the temperature of the venue and of the bottle, atmospheric conditions (humidity, air pressure), and the shape of the glass. This last point is influential in olfactory research; indeed, the same wine, tasted in three glasses of different shapes, will have three distinct aromatic profiles. Wine is alive and subject to moods and whims in much the same way that the judgment of a taster may alter with changes in their physical and mental state.*

CONFIRMATION OF VISUAL INSPECTION. A wine's bouquet should back up its visual appearance. A wine with a young appearance should thus have young, fruity notes; a great red wine that has been laid down and reached its peak will have more complex aromas. If this is not the case, the wine will suffer from an imbalance and disharmony that tasting will only confirm (*see* pp.216–8). To sum up, tasters will note the complexity or simplicity of the bouquet offered by the wine, its rusticity or sophistication, its coherence or dissonance, its youth or maturity, using terms such as 'elegant', 'vigorous' or 'distinguished', or, in the opposite case, 'banal', 'ordinary', 'simple', 'lacking harmony,' 'undistinguished'.

Olfactory flaws

The most common faults in wine are those resulting from its production methods. Poor hygiene in the winery can leave a taint of mould or mildew. A wine that has not been oxygenated will have a reduced, 'closed' nose; on the other hand, too much oxygen is harmful to wine and results in an oxidized odour. Inappropriate addition of sulphur can also have a detrimental effect. In too great a quantity, sulphur has an acrid and penetrating smell. When poorly integrated, it has a rotten egg odour known as 'mercaptan'. A fault in the wine's aroma may also be caused by an external factor such as a bad cork or certain wood treatment products used in the framework of the barrels or the storage pallets, which can leave a 'corky' smell.

Aroma families

This table outlines the various aroma families (floral, herbaceous, fruit, mineral, etc.) by colour and by category (primary aromas: *i.e.* stemming from each grape variety; secondary, resulting from fermentation; tertiary, from maturation and ageing).

AROMA FAMILY	RED WINES AND ROSÉS
FLORAL GROUP	
Primary aromas	Iris, peony, rose, violet.
Tertiary aromas	Dried flowers, pressed roses.
FRUIT GROUP	
Primary aromas	Small red and black fruits (blackcurrant, cherry, strawberry, raspberry, Morello cherry, redcurrant, blackberries), fruit jams, black olives, prunes.
Secondary aromas	Bananas, licorice.
Tertiary aromas	Cooked fruits, fruit liqueurs.
HERBACEOUS GROUP	
Primary aromas	Blackcurrant stems, humus, black pepper, green tomato.
Tertiary aromas	Mushroom, humus, forest floor, truffle.
MINERAL GROUP	
Primary aromas	Chalk, clay, flint.
SPICE GROUP	
Primary aromas	*Garrigue*, bay leaf, pepper, thyme.
Secondary aromas	Cloves, licorice.
CHEMICAL GROUP	
Secondary aromas	Acetone, banana, yeast, sulphur, nail varnish.
MUSK GROUP	
Tertiary aromas	Leather, fur, game, meat juices, venison.
BALSAMIC GROUP	
Secondary aromas	New wood, oak, pine, resin, turpentine, vanilla.
TOASTED GROUP	
Secondary aromas	Cocoa, cigars, smoke, tar, grilling, roasting, tobacco, soot, tea, warm bread.

AROMA FAMILY	WHITE WINES
FLORAL GROUP	
Primary aromas	Acacia, hawthorn, orange flower, geranium, rose, lime blossom.
Tertiary aromas	Camomile, dried flowers.
FRUIT GROUP	
Primary aromas	Apricot, citrus fruits (lemon, orange, grapefruit), pineapple, banana, quince, fig, fruit candies, exotic fruits (lychee, mango, papaya), nuts (almond, hazelnut), melon, peach, pear, green apple, cooked apple.
Secondary aromas	Pineapple.
Tertiary aromas	Dried fruits, honey.
HERBACEOUS GROUP	
Primary aromas	Blackcurrant stems, boxwood, mushroom, fennel, fern, hay, fresh-cut grass, fresh mint, straw, 'cat's pee'.
Tertiary aromas	Rare or non-existent.
MINERAL GROUP	
Primary aromas	Chalk, iodine, gasoline, flint, silica.
SPICE GROUP	
Primary aromas	White pepper.
Secondary aromas	Cinnamon, cloves, vanilla.
CHEMICAL GROUP	
Secondary aromas	Fresh butter, *brioche*, cream, milk, yeast, bread, sulphur.
MUSK GROUP	
Tertiary aromas	Rare or non-existent.
BALSAMIC GROUP	
Tertiary aromas	New wood, oak, pine, resin, turpentine, vanilla.
TOASTED GROUP	
Secondary aromas	Grilling, *brioche*, mocha, tea, warm bread, roasting.

1945
ANNÉE DE LA VICTOIRE
TOUTE LA RÉCOLTE MISE EN BOUTEILLES AU CHATEAU
1945
Cette récolte a produit
24 jéroboams numérotés de A à Y.
1475 magnums numér. de M.1 à M.1475
74422 bout. & ½ bout. numér. de 1 à 74422
2000 "Réserve du Château" marquées R.C.
Cette bouteille porte le No 60,255
Philippe de Rothschild
Château Mouton Rothschild
APPELLATION PAUILLAC CONTROLÉE

TASTE

The third and final stage is the tasting itself! The wine reveals its complete personality, including flavours, texture, structure, and balance. But thanks to the information they have gathered so far, tasters now have some idea about what they are about to sample. Tasting should confirm and add to the previous observations, and, in the best instances, deliver total satisfaction.

Tasting: no easy task

Tasters at work can present quite a spectacle: grimacing and gurgling, swirling the wine around their mouths before spitting it out again, with a look of total concentration on their faces.

However, it is all far from being just for show; the whole procedure is essential for the proper appreciation of a wine. It is not just the tongue that is involved – although this is sensitive to the four principal flavours – the whole mouth plays a part in tasting, including the gums, the inside of the cheeks, and the palate, registering sensations such as temperature and texture, and the wine's chemical qualities such as astringency or effervescence, where present. A wine taster's facial contortions are merely an attempt to get the most from their sensory organs.

Although the actual technique is simple, the tasting itself turns out to be more difficult. In a comparatively short space of time (less than a minute), a taster has to assess the various individual sensations that combine to form the whole tasting experience in the mouth, which is not an easy task. They must consider each element of the tasting separately: the structure, balance, harmony, and complexity of the wine's flavours.

Everyone can try a tasting, all that is needed is a little concentration. *With practice, it is possible for wine lovers eager to satisfy their curiosity about wine to become almost as competent as a professional.*

The three stages of tasting

While the tasting itself is carried out in one action, the analysis is split into three successive stages.

ATTACK PHASE. The attack phase is the first impression felt on the tongue when the taster takes a small sip of wine. They will immediately note the temperature and the presence of any gas, and will also form an idea of the wine's overall personality. The attack phase of a quality wine will be open, clean, and precise, but may also be generous, aromatic, and fruity. If this first contact with the wine does not make much of an impression, the attack is said to be 'weak', fleeting' or 'watery;' or it may be described as 'aggressive' if it elicits a strong or unpleasant taste sensation.

MID-PALATE STAGE. The 'evolution' stage corresponds to the development of the wine in the mouth. Tasters roll a sip of wine around their mouths for a few seconds, giving the impression of 'chewing', and then breathe in a column of air through the mouth in order to accelerate the flow of aromatic particles to the olfactory bulb – an organ at the back of the nasal cavity – via the retronasal passage (*see* box on p.211). These olfactory sensations, tactile and thermal, combine to deliver an overall impression. The taster's task is therefore to try to differentiate between them in turn before analyzing and assessing the balance of the wine.

FINISH. The last stage deals with the length of flavour of the wine 'in the mouth' once it has been swallowed (or spat out). This gives an idea of the 'size' of a wine. The longer the finish, the higher the quality and the greater the wine's potential for laying down. The finish is measured in seconds (a unit of time known as a *caudalie* by French tasters, from the Latin *cauda*, 'tail'). The finish is described as 'long' or 'lingering' – in the very finest cases, the French compare it to a 'peacock's tail' – while a less substantial finish is referred to as 'short', 'brief', 'fleeting' or even 'non-existent'. The difficulty lies in not confusing the flavour length with the sensations elicited by the acidity, alcohol, or tannins – burning, warmth, or astringency – which tend to obscure it. The taster concentrates on the most dominant flavour and then, having swallowed (or spat out) the wine, focuses on what remains of it until it has disappeared.

Flaws in flavour

Some olfactory faults (see p.213) become more apparent during tasting. Dirty or musty smells are revealed as a 'bad taste', comparable to the smell of rotting vegetation or a stable. A wine with too much sulphur has an unbalanced flavour reminiscent of garlic, rubber, or rotten eggs (mercaptan). An oxidized wine will have an acidulated flavour in the case of whites, and a sweet-and-sour taint sometimes called *rancio* in the case of reds. A wine with a 'corky' aroma will taste like the smell of cardboard. Other faults are inherent in a poorly balanced wine and are not always perceptible in the wine's aroma.

A burning sensation indicates an excess of alcohol or acidity. A large dose of sugar, unbalanced by alcohol and appropriate acidity, delivers a cloying, heavy sensation, lacking in finesse. Poorly ripened tannins in a young wine produce a strong acrid sensation, and in an older wine dryness.

> Once the wine has been analyzed in the mouth, it can be swallowed or spat out.

Each tasting requires a conclusion, and tasters sum up their experience succinctly, giving a verdict on the wine's quality not only at the time of tasting, but also on its future. (Is it ready to be enjoyed right away, for example, or does it require more ageing, or has it passed its best?) Here, of course, is where tasters can give free rein to their own tastes!

Analyzing flavours and aromas

A wine's flavours are derived from its different components. Acidity comes from various acidulating elements; sweetness comes from any residual sugar as well as from alcohol; bitterness is linked with the presence of tannins; saltiness is rare, present only in very small amounts and deriving from various saline elements. All these flavours combine during tasting as juxtapositions, sometimes cancelling each another out (*see* box, p.218), but almost always complementing the aromas. The latter, which will have already been partly identified after analyzing the wine's 'nose', are confirmed at the tasting stage.

So a red wine whose bouquet has notes of very ripe red fruits should also 'taste' of red fruits. Backed up by a sweet flavour, that character will be all the more apparent. By contrast, a dominant acidic flavour will point towards an imbalance between flavour and aroma, which does not say much for the wine's quality. However, in a dry white wine with prominent citrus aromas

Tannins

Mostly found in red grape varieties, tannins are extracted from the skins during maceration or may develop during storage in barrels (as 'noble' tannins). The level and quality of tannins is determined by various factors: the maturity of the fruit, the duration of maceration, and even the grape variety (Gamay is less tannic than Cabernet Sauvignon). Tannins are responsible for the structure of the wine and play an essential role in ageing.

In the mouth, they are perceptible as a sensation of astringency (or dryness), which gives a 'chewiness' to the wine and how pronounced this is depends on the wine's origins, its quality, and age. Tannins are described (in decreasing amounts) as being 'rough', 'bitter', 'firm', 'round' and 'fine'. In time, tannins evolve from harsh to soft, and from heavy to fine, and never the other way around.

Wine texture

Texture reflects a combination of tactile sensations in the mouth and is one of the first elements of tasting that can be appreciated by an amateur, even before any analysis of the balance. The texture depends on the relationship between the principal constituents of a wine: alcohol, acidity, tannins, and sugars. The terms used to describe it are often the same as those used to describe fabrics: a texture is said to be 'supple', 'caressing', 'satiny', 'velvety', 'silky', or by contrast, 'grainy', 'coarse', 'rough' or 'rustic'. Comparisons are frequently made with the human body, hence the 'body' of a wine may be 'fleshy', 'full-bodied', 'robust' or conversely 'thin', 'lean' or 'sinewy'. Other terms, such as 'suave', 'unctuous', 'viscous', 'creamy' and 'syrupy', are commonly used to describe the texture of white wines that are rich in residual sugars.

The quality of the texture may also be understood within the context of the appellation – a Médoc wine, made predominantly from Cabernet Sauvignon grapes and rich in tannins, will not have the same velvety feel as a Pomerol, where Merlot, rich in alcohol and often lower in tannins, reigns supreme.

> In red wines, astringency reinforces the sensation of acidity.

(lemon, grapefruit), a fresh tang of acidity should predominate in the mouth. The perception of the harmonious interaction of flavours in the mouth and the aromas detected in the nose of a wine are therefore essential elements that allow a taster to assess a wine's quality and balance.

Analyzing tactile sensations

In addition to the aromatic and olfactory sensations it generates, a wine generates different tactile sensations in the mouth as a whole, and especially in its mucous membranes:

SOFTNESS. The sensation of softness is evoked by alcohol, which has a soft and slightly sweet character; this is reinforced by the possible presence of any residual sugars. Alcohol is what gives dry white wines their softness and, in the case of reds, provides an idea of the wine's richness.

ACIDITY. The sensation of acidity is provided by various acidic elements in the wine. Although these can be less apparent in red wines, they come more to the fore in white wines and in rosés as their acidity encourages salivation and thus a sensation of freshness.

ASTRINGENCY. A sensation of dryness in the mouth, induced by tannins (*see* box, previous page), is most often encountered in red wines; but it's also a feature of rosés made using the *saignée* (bleeding) production method. Along with acidity and alcohol, tannins are one of the elements that make up the framework or 'skeleton' of a wine.

Each of these sensations can be analyzed and assessed separately, although in most cases they combine to form a composite experience. In a sweet or dry white wine, and in some rosés, the wine's tactile personality is defined by the pairing of acidity and softness; for reds and other rosés, the defining factors are acidity, softness, and astringency. There are as many combinations possible as there are wines, but the result must be balanced. It should not produce any unpleasant sensations from an excess of one of the components. Examples include a 'burn' from excess of alcohol or acidity, or a dryness and harshness caused by insufficiently ripened tannins, or by a lack of softness in the wine (*see* pp. 220–1). An appreciation of the texture of the wine derives from all these tactile sensations combined, and is known as the 'body' or 'fullness' of the wine.

DID YOU KNOW...?

We recognize four basic tastes: sweetness, saltiness, sourness, and bitterness. *Contrary to belief, the tongue's tastebuds are not more sensitive to one flavour or the other; all our tastebuds can detect the entire range of flavours. During tasting, the flavours interact with one another, forming partnerships or cancelling out their opposites: saltiness reduces bitterness, sweetness dominates saltiness but diminishes the perception of acidity and slows the perception of bitterness. It is therefore important to assess the balance of flavours in general – or, more precisely, the balance of sugars on the one hand with acidic and bitter elements on the other, which indicate the balance of a wine (see pp.220–1). Each individual has a personal sensitivity or threshold of perception for each taste component.*

RAS
RIESLING
Engelgarten

THE SYNTHESIS OF TASTING

It is now time to put everything together and assess the quality of the wine, summing it up in three words: balance, harmony, and pleasure. Balance many be appreciated directly during tasting, and harmony is a synthesis of all the data gathered – tastes, aromas, and visual impression, while pleasure is the preserve of the taster.

Balance and harmony

When judging the overall quality of a wine, two criteria are usually applied: balance and harmony.

BALANCE. A wine is said to be balanced when the various tasting components – acidity and sweetness in white wines; tannins, acidity, softness in reds – combine in a satisfactory manner, creating a subjective impression of balance. Judged as structural and quantitative, balance should be distinguished from harmony, which is aesthetic and qualitative.

HARMONY. A wine is considered harmonious when its constituents combine but do not all tell the same story. Each element taken individually should have no disagreeable quality (such as bitter tannins, piercing acidity, or a softness that is too alcoholic); and when taken as a whole, each of them should work well with the others, producing an overall pleasing impression.

This is usually achieved by a combination of varying levels of the three tasting components rather than their presence in equal amounts. However, the notion of harmony in terms of wine varies from one country to another, according to education and different cultural practices.

> ***Tasting a wine involves being able to distinguish between each of its aspects.*** *To be a good taster you just need an open and enquiring mind and the ability to be a little discerning with your senses, but above all you need a good memory.*

Balance in dry whites

The balance of dry white wines depends on the relationship between their acidity and alcohol content. The former gives the wine freshness and vivacity, while the latter produces sweetness and softness – in other words, part of its body. In the mouth, the two sensations should be balanced. To understand how they are related, imagine two straight lines at ninety degrees (*see* diagram). The nearer the wine is to the point where the lines cross, the more it is judged to be balanced. A wine with strong acidity and little alcohol and body is revealed as aggressive, thin, and insubstantial, while one with weak acidity and a normal alcohol level is described as *nerveux* or 'nervous.'

In the same way, higher alcohol levels with the same acidity lead to suppleness, roundness, and body, or even to a heaviness experienced as an unpleasant sensation of warmth in the mouth.

Nuances exist within this balance and define the different styles of wine. An Alsace Riesling can be distinguished by its 'nervousness,' while a Meursault should reveal certain opulence. Despite these differences, neither wine would be considered imbalanced. The combination of flavours and aromas also plays a role in the balance of the wine by reinforcing or dulling tactile sensations.

BALANCE IN DRY WHITES

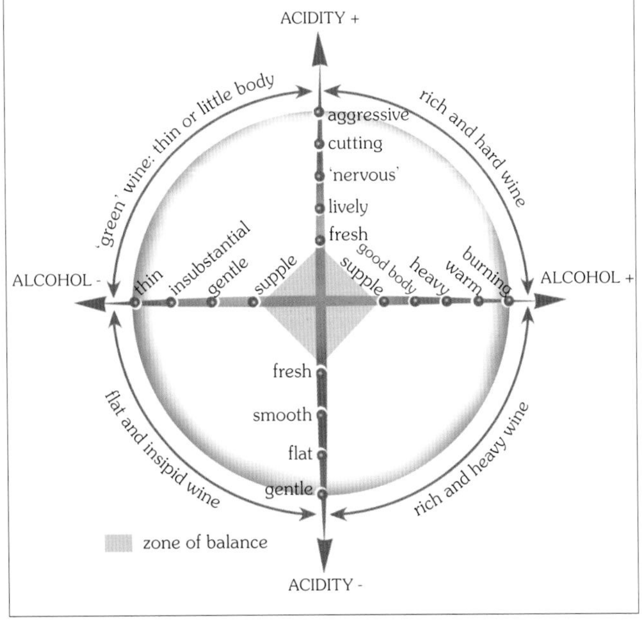

The balance of sweet whites

To the acidity and alcohol present in all white wines are added the residual sugars specific to sweet and very sweet wines (*see* diagram). These reinforce the tactile sensation of softness created in the mouth by alcohol. Balance is achieved when no single one of the characteristics is allowed to dominate the other two.

The secret of harmonious wines lies in two important rules of thumb: the richer a wine is in sugars, the higher its alcohol content, while the higher the sugar and alcohol, the more the wine's acidity should pull the whole back towards the centre, representing the ideal balance. A degree of insufficiency in any one of the constituents will immediately cause imbalance. When dominated by sugars, for example, a wine will be syrupy.

Even within this balance there are nuances in texture – a

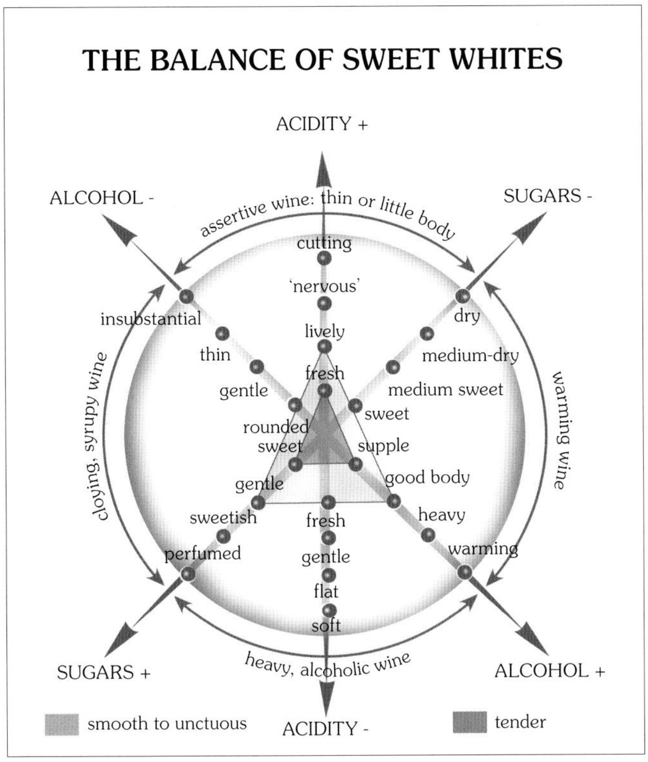

wine may be tender, supple, unctuous – which will define the wine's richness as well as its style. By the same token, some sweet wines have a considerable acidity that, far from being aggressive, brings a pleasant 'nervousness' to the wine. This is the case for sweet wines from the Loire Valley such as Coteaux-du-Layon and Vouvray. During tasting, the amateur taster should also bear in mind the power of the aromas and flavours, which should back up and confirm the richness of the wine.

The balance of reds

Assessing the balance of red wines is made more difficult by the presence of tannins. In the diagram (right), the ideal balance is at the centre of three lines representing alcohol, acidity, and tannins. In this case, possible nuances dictated by the style of wine include a solidity of structure if the tannins somewhat dominate the alcohol and acidity, or more rounded and integrated in the opposite case. The further away from the centre of the diagram a wine travels, the more robust an example of its style it will be, until reaching a point where the harmony is upset as one or two of the dominant characteristics are sidelined. The more tannin a wine possesses, the greater the astringency, which can be perceived as unpleasant if it is not compensated by acidity and alcohol at a proportional level. From being described as tannic, a wine then becomes harsh, rough, bitter, and astringent. When dominated by tannins and acidity, a wine gains in firmness to the point where, as the sensation of softness is obscured, it feels austere, rigid, and biting. This can be seen in wines made with Cabernet Sauvignon grapes that are rich in tannins. When ripe, they display a certain austerity that dulls with age. When less ripe, they can be more 'angular', eliciting an unpleasant sensation that is a mixture of astringency and bitterness.

DID YOU KNOW...?

Red wines are sometimes sorted into 'feminine' and 'masculine' categories. *A feminine style includes very supple wines where, along with the coupling of tannins and alcohol, there is a perceptible lessening of acidity and a dominant sweetness. With 'masculine' wines, by contrast, astringency carries the day and consolidates the structure of the wine.*

The balance of sparkling wines

The family of sparkling wines is large because of the diversity of grape varieties that can be used to make them (both reds and whites) and the different production methods used (*see* pp.70–1). Nonetheless, effervescence apart, they are similar to white wines in structure.

Sparkling wines are balanced by two components: acidity and sweetness. Effervescence is then added to the mix, to reinforce or attenuate the sensation of acidity. The bubbles are assessed during the attack phase according to their quantity and fineness or size. This gives the 'tone' of the wine, the degree to which it is aggressive or subtle. A wine that foams excessively in the mouth is a bad sign. Sparkling wines often display a higher level of acidity than dry white wines; this guarantees vivacity, but in excess produces a disagreeable biting sensation. The bubbles should mellow the acidity, and do the same for the sweetness, without making the wine insipid. The finish should be fresh and aromatic, without retaining the burning sensation caused by acidity or the sweetish flavour of a poorly balanced *dosage* (sugars added during production).

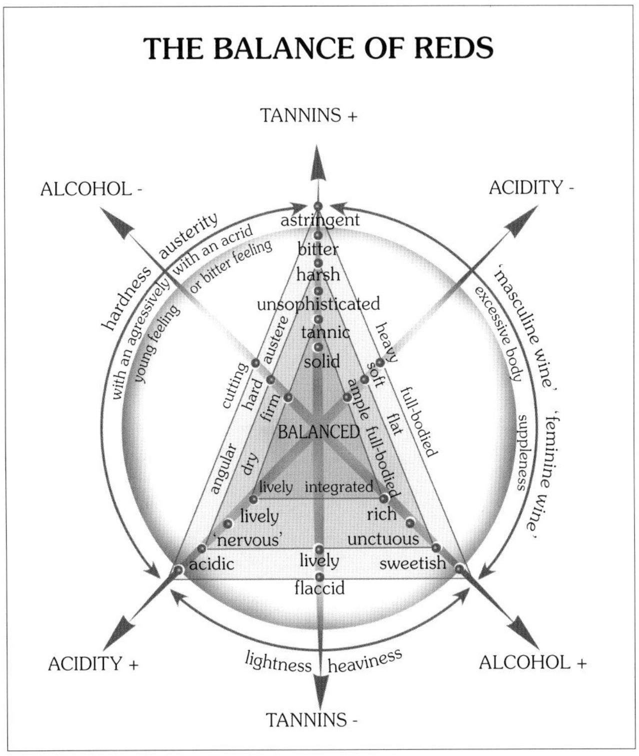

Some sample tasting notes

Judging the quality of a wine is not just to do with taste; the professional taster makes use of their considerable knowledge and wide range of tasting experiences, so the more knowledge and experience an amateur can accumulate, the better they will be able to understand wine and to evaluate its qualities and faults.

What's the point of tasting notes?

As well as the perception of its aromas and flavours, tasting involves making an overall judgement on a wine, reflecting the pleasure (or lack of) experienced. Technical tastings judge the quality of a wine, and make detailed analyses of the sensations detected according to a precise set of criteria, but they also call upon the taster's knowledge of wine and winemaking.

While tasting sheets for professionals are available as precise pre-printed documents, amateurs might simply jot down their impressions in a notebook or cellar book (*see* p.143).

FOR THE PROFESSIONAL. Professional tasters are looking, above all, for any flaws in the wine: imbalance, weakness, lack of local character, lack of fruit, bitterness, etc. They examine the appearance, nose, and mouth-feel of a wine to gain an overall impression. They assess the wine's qualities, its potential for laying down, and the period when it will be at its peak (when the wine will taste its best). They note the purchase price and potential price changes with age and suggest serving conditions (temperature, decanting.). They may also suggest potential foods to accompany it. The wine is scored out of 100, 20, 10, or even 5 points, a ranking that is sometimes expressed as stars.

FOR THE AMATEUR. Amateur tasters follow the same tasting ritual, and attempt to assess the harmony of the wine. They may suggest thoughts on its evolution, and perhaps note potential food-pairing suggestions. They may also include notes from various wine guides or magazine articles. Tasting notes also allow collectors to follow the development of the wines in their cellars; and where a wine has been passed on, tasting notes will allow the recipients to get to know the wines.

TASTING NOTES Wine no. 1	
Date:	January 2013
PROVENANCE	
Region:	Bordeaux
Appellation:	Pauillac
Producer:	La Rose Pauillac
Year:	2005
VISUAL APPEARANCE	
Colour:	Ruby with hints of garnet.
Intensity:	Sparkling and glistening.
Concentration:	Full and rich.
BOUQUET	
Intensity:	Good intensity.
Quality:	Elegant, subtle, and complex.
Aromas:	Red and black fruit aromas, a little stewed fruit, soft spicy and smokey notes with undergrowth, showing good development.
TASTING	
Attack:	Open, creamy, and velvety.
Mid-palate:	Rich and ample mouth-feel with plenty of suppleness that combines freshness with vinosity. Harmonious, softly woody, tannins well integrated.
Finish:	Good flavourful length.
Balance:	Very well balanced.
CONCLUSION	
Quality:	An excellent Pauillac at an age to drink.
Drinking notes:	May be enjoyed now, drink from now on. Open the bottle an hour before serving. Can be kept until 2020. Serve with red meat or duck.

TASTING NOTES
Wine no. 2

Date:	January 2014
PROVENANCE	
Region:	Burgundy
Appellation:	Savigny-lès-Beaune, Cuvée de Réserve
Producer:	Maison Aegerter
Year:	2004
VISUAL APPEARANCE	
Colour:	Ruby colouration with hints of garnet.
Intensity:	Sparkling and velvety.
Concentration:	Fluid.
BOUQUET	
Intensity:	Good intensity.
Quality:	Elegant, aromatic, and developed.
Aromas:	At maturity, slight jammy fruit (cherry) notes, with elegant aromas of leather, soft spice, and faded flowers.
TASTING	
Attack:	Open and perfumed.
Mid-palate:	Smooth mouth-feel, silky texture with softened tannins. Delicate flavours and nicely develped, with a finish of leather and spices.
Finish:	Long and flavourful finish.
Balance:	Very well balanced.
CONCLUSION	
Quality:	A delicate wine at maturity.
Drinking notes:	May be enjoyed now, drink within two years, with roasted white meat. Open the bottle an hour before serving.

TASTING NOTES
Wine no. 3

Date:	November 2013
PROVENANCE	
Region:	Alsace
Appellation:	Gewurztraminer Fronholtz late harvest
Producer:	Domaine Ostertag
Year:	2011
VISUAL APPEARANCE	
Colour:	Lovely intense golden colour, good clarity.
Intensity:	Scintillating.
Concentration:	Plenty of nice substantial legs.
BOUQUET	
Intensity:	Intense, opens well.
Quality:	Elegant, nuanced.
Aromas:	Charming rose notes with a hint of spices, mango and peach, and notes of honey.
TASTING	
Attack:	Supple and sweet.
Mid-palate:	Smooth body, coats the mouth well. A sugary character is apparent but not overpowering, with plenty of freshness, nice weight, aroma of roses clearly there.
Finish:	Long and flavourful finish.
Balance:	Very good balance with no heaviness; sugars well integrated.
CONCLUSION	
Quality:	A very attractive wine with perfect balance, showing subtle delicacy.
Drinking notes:	Too young for the moment, needs another three years to best express its potential. Will age well in ten years. Decant into a carafe if it is to be enjoyed in its first three years.

TASTING NOTES Wine no. 4	
Date:	May 2014
PROVENANCE	
Region:	Languedoc
Appellation:	Corbières rosé
Producer:	Domaine deu Grand Arc cuvée 'La Tour Fabienne'
Year:	2013
VISUAL APPEARANCE	
Colour:	Reasonably soft rosé, with a raspberry colour with good clarity.
Intensity:	Scintillating.
Concentration:	Nice flowing legs, but few in number.
BOUQUET	
Intensity:	Expressive
Quality:	Appealing fruit notes.
Aromas:	Pronounced red fruits – strawberries, raspberries, redcurrant jelly, and intense peppery aromas and a delicate floral hint of Reseda.
TASTING	
Attack:	Good attack, with plenty of suppleness and slightly sparkling.
Mid-palate:	Ample and generous; a rounded mouth-feel with bold fruit and spicy flavours.
Finish:	Average length; aromatic, with a hint of agreeable bitterness.
Balance:	Alcohol and acidity in perfect balance.
CONCLUSION	
Quality:	A vinous rosé with a generous body, but not out of balance.
Drinking notes:	Drink chilled within two years. Should be served with grills or white meat.

TASTING NOTES Wine no. 5	
Date:	January 2012
PROVENANCE	
Region:	Spain
Appellation:	Rioja Reservar
Producer:	Contino
Year:	2004
VISUAL APPEARANCE	
Colour:	Clear ruby-red, still fresh and clear.
Intensity:	Just beginning to mature with a slight brick-red rim.
Concentration:	Fine, flowing legs.
BOUQUET	
Intensity:	Good intensity.
Quality:	Elegant, sophisticated with some charming hints of maturity.
Aromas:	Slightly fleshy notes linked with more integrated woody, toasted notes. When aerated, cooked fruit notes and spices become apparent.
TASTING	
Attack:	Supple, quite soft.
Mid-palate:	Average mouth-feel, underlined by fine, well-integrated tannins. Bold fruit character, with notes of stewed stone fruit.
Finish:	Good aromatic length, but with a slightly alcohol note at the finish.
Balance:	Balance correct.
CONCLUSION	
Quality:	A wine that has developed very well, a great exampe of Spanish winemaking.
Drinking notes:	Having reached its peak, the wine is drinkable now and within tdwo or three years. Decanting recommended just before service to best bring out its fruit aromas.

TASTING NOTES
Wine no. 6

Date:	September 2012
PROVENANCE	
Region:	Champagne
Appellation:	Champagne
Producer:	Veuve Cliquote Ponsardin Cuvée 'La Grande Dame'
Year:	2004
VISUAL APPEARANCE	
Colour:	Golden with hints of pale green.
Intensity:	First mousee is fine and airy. Presence of cordon.
Concentration:	Very fine bubbles, showing a cheminée rising to the cordon. Effervescence continues in the glass.
BOUQUET	
Intensity:	Good intensity.
Quality:	Elegant, fresh, and complex.
Aromas:	Floral notes (white floweer) mingle with notes of ripe white fruit (peach) and touches of citrus (grapefruit zest). Followed by slight notes of toasted almonds, brioche, nougat, and dried fruit.
TASTING	
Attack:	Fresh and creamy.
Mid-palate:	Ample mouth-feel, supple, combining freshness and vinosity. Fruity flavours dominate, against toasty and roasted background.
Finish:	Very long and flavourful.
Balance:	Very well balanced.
CONCLUSION	
Quality:	A very great wine from this fine vintage, both ripe and fresh.
Drinking notes:	Drink among like-minded friends from today, as an aperitif with amuse-gueules flavoured with paprika and parmesan. Also worth keeping for two to three years in a good cellar.

TASTING NOTES
Wine no. 7

Date:	January 2014
PROVENANCE	
Region:	Argentina
Appellation:	Mendoza, Finca El Portillo, Malbec
Producer:	Bodegas Salentein
Year:	2012
VISUAL APPEARANCE	
Colour:	Intense ruby appearance, going over into a bluish-black with purple at the rim.
Intensity:	Scintillating and profound.
Concentration:	Average
BOUQUET	
Intensity:	Intense and deep.
Quality:	Elegant, powerful, and spicy.
Aromas:	Interplay of power and character. Shades of fruit couli sauce (blackcurrants, blackberries, myrtle), spice notes (pepper, cinnamon, vanilla), and liquorice. Toast and cocoa notes.
TASTING	
Attack:	Full-bodied and flavourful.
Mid-palate:	Structured wine with acidity and tannins integrating with warm, ripe fruit.
Finish:	Average length with hints of liquorice and pepper.
Balance:	Again rests on the strength of its structure.
CONCLUSION	
Quality:	Excellent Malbec, mature and intense, with good structure.
Drinking notes:	Ready for drinking now or for laying down in a cellar until 2017.

BOUCHARD PÈRE
CHARD PÈRE & FILS
2000
CHEVALIER-MONTRACHET
BOUCHARD PÈRE & FILS
2003
ORTON-CHARLEMAGNE
GRAND VIN D
APPELLATION
VIGNE DE L

BOUCHARD PÈRE & FILS
1998
CORTON
GRAND CRU
& FILS

DESCRIBING WINE

Once the techniques of tasting have been mastered, the amateur needs to be able to describe the sensations felt. To understand the vocabulary used by professional tasters, bear in mind that it is based on some simple basic principles.

Tasting vocabulary

There is no official lexicon of tasting terminology, but a certain number of basic terms are commonly used; they are set out on the following pages in alphabetical order, along with their definition. These terms have become established through use. Many clearly work by analogy: the aromas of a wine are described in terms of familiar scents (fruits, spices, etc.); the texture (the tactile sensation experienced of wine in the mouth) is described by referring to the quality of a fabric, for example; and its structure is often compared to the human body. The personality of a wine is described in much the same way: it may be 'simple', 'complex', 'unsophisticated' or 'elegant'. Given all these terms, the taster has an almost infinite vocabulary at their disposal to describe and analyze sensations.

The terms associated with the formal tasting of wine are complementary to the technical vocabulary connected with winemaking contained in the glossary (pp.494–503) and the chapter 'From the vine to the bottle'.

A

ACACIA The charming scent of acacia flowers often features in the aroma of young Chardonnay and Chasselas wines, when their acidity is tempered.

ACERBIC Of a rather sharp nature; used where perceptible acidity is accentuated by the presence of unripe tannins.

ACIDITY Sensed by the tongue, but also through the secretion of saliva, which it promotes through the sharp sensation it leaves on the mucous membranes. Acidity plays a fundamental role in the mouth-feel of a wine and the general balance of its flavours. *See also*, CRISP.

ACRID Said of a wine with unpleasant bitterness, often due to tannins that are very pungent.

AGGRESSIVE Characteristic of a wine producing an attack of excess acidity or astringency on the mucous membranes.

ALCOHOL Alcohol is the principal constituent of wine after water. It eventually loses its burning and dehydrating character (as encountered in brandies), and instead takes on a distinctly sweet taste, which is a major contributor to softness in dry wines.

ALMOND, ALMOND BLOSSOM A flavour of almond blossom is sometimes detected in Sauvignon Blanc and Sylvaner white wines. The aroma of dried almonds, which is similar to vanillin, is often found in Chardonnays as they age. Notes of bitter almonds are a feature of many very young white wines, and are also an element of the muted, nutty taste found in some old red wines. The aroma of toasted almonds is part of the attraction and the distinction of white wines of a certain age.

AMBER Of great distinction, the subtle scent of amber is sometimes found in the finest Chardonnay wines (Champagne, Chablis, Côte d'Or) and certain sweet wines from southwestern France.

AMBERING Ambering is a feature of sweet wines of a certain age, but is also found in dry or low-sugar white wines from good vintages that are apt to age without oxidation or becoming excessively dry.

AMIABLE Characteristic attributed to a pleasing wine without pretension.

AMPLE The term applied to wines that 'fill the mouth' without a sense of heaviness.

ANISEED Aroma found as a trace element in the bouquet of certain white wines that have reached a good age.

APPEARANCE The colour, brilliance, and overall visual impression of a wine.

APPLE The various varieties of apples each have their own flavours, and each are found in different concentrations in a number of white wines (Muscadet, Sauvignon Blanc, Riesling, etc.).

APRICOT Aroma characteristic of certain white wines, particularly in the Rhône Valley; associated with the Viognier grape variety when very ripe.

ASTRINGENCY A sense of dehydration resulting from tannins, notably those present in red wines. As wine ages, astringency mellows as the tannins are 'used up' and lose intensity, sharpness, and general presence.

ATTACK The first impression felt when wine enters the mouth.

AUSTERE The term applied to red wines whose tannins and acidity are most prominent and where a bouquet that might make this more agreeable is absent.

B

BALANCE Quality found in wine where the various flavour groups (alcohol, acidity, and sweetness in white wines; alcohol, tannins, acidity, and softness in red wines) play off one another in a satisfactory manner, without any single one dominating or underperforming.

BALSAMIC More or less resinous odours (pine, cedar, juniper, wood, etc.) found in young wines matured in new barrels. Also a feature of ripeness in great red wines.

BANANA Aroma frequently occurring in wines meant for early drinking, especially in batches made using carbonic maceration. It should be tempered with other floral and fruit aromas, as in Beaujolais or white Mâcon wines; otherwise the nose will be reminiscent of nail polish.

BAY LEAF Spicy aroma characteristic of certain grape varieties originally found in the South of France, such as Syrah and Grenache.

BEER An aroma similar to that of beer is sometimes found in the white Chasselas wines of Switzerland as they begin to lose their freshness.

BERGAMOT The extremely pleasant odour of this essential oil is found in aromatic wines at a certain stage of their bottle ageing.

BILBERRIES Aroma very often associated with WILD BLACKBERRIES (*see* under BLACKBERRIES below) and found under the same conditions.

BITTER Bitterness is not a feature of good wine, except perhaps in a few reds as a mild and transitory state. It is an anomaly when found elsewhere.

BLACKBERRIES, WILD Aroma often referred to in red wines of some maturity with rich and varied fruit notes.

BLACKCURRANTS The aroma of blackcurrant fruit or juice is invariably an element of the bouquet of Cabernet Sauvignon, irrespective of the country where it was harvested. It is sometimes found in the fruit scents of a large number of red varieties (Merlot, Syrah, Mourvèdre, etc.) when they reach their tasting peak.

BODY Terms such as 'body', 'full-bodied,' and so on are used of wines where the joint dominance of tannins and sweetness is perceptible and imply a certain alcoholic fullness.

BOUQUET The entirety of the aromatic impressions conveyed by a mature wine in the sense that they combine to form a coherent and homogeneous whole. Various subtle notes alternate and intertwine in a subtle and agreeable ensemble.

BOUQUET GARNI Term used to describe the scents of aromatic dried herbs often found in Mediterranean red wines.

BRETTANOMYCES Spoilage yeast imparting bad aromas or flavours (mustiness, acetic spoilage, or mould) to a wine; a fault arising during the storage of empty barrels.

BRICK RED Colour found in mature red wines, where the brownish hue is reminiscent of old tiles or bricks.

BRILLIANCE Term qualifying the luminosity of a wine, *i.e.* its ability to reflect light. A lack of brilliance – dullness – is considered a flaw.

BROOM The yellow flowers of Spanish broom have a pleasant and penetrating odour, reminiscent of wallflowers, which forms part of the aroma of some Chardonnay and sweet wines.

BURNED *see* EMPYREUMATIC

BUTTER An aromatic nuance sometimes found in very ripe batches of white wine, when low in acid and high in richness. Also attributed to maturation in new oak barrels.

C

CARAMEL An aroma common in white wines that are past their best, oxidized, or maderized.

CARNATION Aroma often referenced for some red wines with a slightly austere bouquet.

CAUDALIE French term for a unit of 'length' (*see* LENGTH) after swallowing. One *caudalie* = one second.

CHERRY Various aromas of different varieties of cherries are often found as constituents of the bouquet in many red wines.

CHERRY PLUM Aroma found in white wines from very ripe years, with an overall richness that imparts an extremely enticing appeal to the bouquet.

CINNAMON Aroma sometimes found in fine examples of sweet (Jurançon, Sauternes) or dry (Pouilly-Fuissé, Corton-Charlemagne) white wines.

CIVET Fairly pronounced musky scent, not always unpleasant, and reminiscent of game meats. A feature of older red wines such as Burgundy's Pinot Noirs.

CLARITY The transparency of a wine's appearance, which may be: crystalline, brilliant, limpid, veiled, hazy, troubled, or opaque.

CLEAN Said of a wine whose aromas and flavours are upfront and precise, without ambiguity.

CLOSED A term referring to a wine with a 'mute' or undeveloped bouquet.

CLOSURE Generic term for a wine bottle stopper, whether natural cork, synthetic or screwcap.

CLOVES Scent found in Rhône Valley reds after a few years of ageing.

CLOYING Said of slightly thick wines whose heaviness is exacerbated by lack of acidity.

COCOA Aroma sometimes found in wines with a fruity and spicy nose when they reach great maturity. Also attributed to maturation in new oak barrels.

COFFEE Aroma that develops in the bouquet of good quality old wines. Also attributed to maturation in new oak barrels.

CORKED Unpleasant smell of damp and rotten cork or cardboard, arising either from a fault in the closure itself or a lack of hygiene in the cellar.

CRISPNESS Sensation of freshness attributed to the action of acidity on the tongue. *See also* ACIDITY.

CUT HAY Scent typical of wines most often encountered as they pass from a phase of fermentation aromas to those of maturity.

D

DELICATE Said of wines with a subtle structure, but not lacking in charm or character.

DRY Wines are called dry where any sweetness is subtle or masked, without this harming the balance of the whole.

E

EASY-GOING Said of a wine that offers immediate pleasure, with few tannins and a good balance of sweetness and acidity.

EGLANTINE Rose-like aroma sometimes found in light and very subtle wines.

ELEGANT Description implying a certain class and an absence of heaviness.

EMACIATED Said of a wine that has lost its 'body' or its softness, due to too much or faulty ageing.

EMPYREUMATIC Referring to a category of aromas including tar, soot, burned wood, caramel, singed bread, and also, in a more attenuated manner, tea, coffee, cocoa, tobacco, biscuits, etc. Such aromas are often spoken of as 'smoky', 'toasted', 'roasted' or 'burned.'

F

FADED A faded wine has lost its brilliance, its best aromas, and its freshness.

FENNEL An aroma sometimes found in very ripe dry white wines.

FERMENTATION Fermentation as a type of scent is not well known, and comes from the decomposition of yeasts when the wine is on the lees.

FERN-LIKE Aromatic characteristic found in white wines of great quality, and which gives them an airy bouquet.

FIG The aroma of dried figs, often combined with that of stewed or preserved strawberries, is a typical feature of soft red port or Banyuls wines, and also of dry red wines from very ripe vintages after some age.

FILLED OUT Said of a red wine with sufficient – but not excess – tannin and flavour, giving a good impression of body.

FIRM Typical of a young red wine; equates to a slight dominance of tannins and acidity.

FLINTY Aroma found in some lively, light white wines (Sauvignon Blanc, Muscadet, Burgundy made with Aligoté grapes).

FLORAL Wine bouquet where the aroma of flowers is dominant.

FRESH Term used to refer to aromas such as mint and citronella, which evoke sensations associated with coolness or refreshment.

FRUIT First stage of a wine's bouquet, after alcoholic fermentation, where the dominant aromas are of fresh fruit. The term is more often applied to reds and rosés, although white wines may possess pronounced fruit aromas such as apple, lemon, banana, and others.

FULL Said of a wine that seems to fill the mouth with a substantial and balanced richness, or an impression of abundance.

FULL-BODIED Term describing the tactile sensation of softness in a wine, when it is rich in alcohol and/or sugar.

FUR Nuance in the musky group of aromas, found in some red wines with some age.

G

GAMEY Animal aromas that may feature to a greater or lesser degree in the bouquet of old red wines. At its slightest, it is the scent of prepared fur; when more obtrusive, it is the smell of wildfowl – or of 'fox' in old Pinot Noirs. Some develop into more varied venison aromas, while others take on a repellent nature known in French as *ventre de lièvre* or 'hare belly'.

GENEROUS Term most often applied to wines rich in alcohol.

GLUGGABLE Said of a wine that is easy to drink, due to a lack of astringency and to having the correct proportion of fresh acidity and sweetness (without heaviness).

GRAPEFRUIT Aroma often perceived in very crisp sparkling white wines, can be reminiscent of pink or white grapefruit. Also recognized in some naturally high-acid white varietals and in some rosés.

GRASSY Aromas or flavours reminiscent of freshly mown lawns or vegetal shoots. Generally considered disagreeable.

GREEN Used in reference to under-ripe fruit characters in a white, red, or rosé wine that is very crisp, where excess of acidity comes through.

GRENADINE An aroma typical of Côtes du Rhône and Provence rosés.

H

HARD Describes red wines with a synergy of tannins and acidity that provide astringency and also aggressiveness. Lack of any soft fruit characters in the wine reinforces this characteristic still further.

HARMONIOUS Quality ascribed to well-made wines, where each group of flavours (alcohol, acidity, and sweetness in white wines; alcohol, tannins, acidity, and softness in red wines) melds pleasantly with the others to create a charming whole.

HARSH Excessive astringency, where tannins 'grate' on the mucous membranes of the mouth with real intensity and insistence.

HAVANA Scent of green tobacco leaves features as a trace element in very fine red wines.

HAWTHORN Aromatic characteristic found in young, dry, and slightly green white wines.

HAZELNUT Aroma often found in high quality white wines after several years of ageing (Chardonnay).

HEADY Characteristic of wines where rich body is accompanied by an elevated alcohol content.

HEAVY Characteristic of a wine lacking any lightness, suppleness, or freshness.

HONEY Aroma typical of lightly sweet to very sweet wines.

HONEYSUCKLE Aroma found in some Chardonnay and Sauvignon Blanc white wines, as well as other gently aromatic grape varieties.

HUMUS Aroma reminiscent of the forest floor or dead leaves, encountered in fairly good quality red wines that have aged.

HYACINTH Floral aroma often encountered with aromatic white grape varieties after a few years of bottle age (Sauvignon Blanc, Rhine varieties, fine Muscats).

I

IN BLOOM Said of a wine that has reached its peak and where its full personality comes to the fore, both in taste and aroma.

INTEGRATED Said of a wine where all flavour sensations express themselves in unity.

IODINE Term applied to wines whose aromas evoke the seaside.

IVY Ivy leaf aromas are often referenced in many Cabernet wines, when their bouquet is first forming.

J

JAMMY Used in tasting to express an aroma or taste that is reminiscent of jam or cooked fruit.

JUNIPER Aroma often encountered in some highly perfumed wines.

L

LACTIC Aroma arising from faulty malolactic fermentation or from an indeterminate combination of circumstances, more or less resulting in the odour of *fromage frais* or fermented cheese.

LEATHER Leather aromas of various kinds are often encountered in certain red wines after a few years of ageing (Bandol, Châteauneuf-du-Pape, Madiran, Corton, Hermitage, Chambertin, etc.).

LEGS Transparent streams of liquid that run down the inside walls of the glass when the wine has been agitated. Indicates a wine's richness in alcohol or residual sugar.

LEMON (CITRONELLA) Quite a common aroma in young, crisp, and light white wines.

LEMON BALM An aroma found in young white wines. Close to that of lemon zest, but more rarefied and less acidic.

LENGTH Duration of a wine's flavour in the mouth after swallowing. *See also* CAUDALIE.

LICHEN Herbal aroma present in certain red wines.

LICORICE Aroma and flavour often found at the finish of certain red wines.

LIGHT-BODIED Said of wines with a distinct lack of richness or structure.

LIME (BLOSSOM) Aroma found in certain white wines with very subtle bouquets.

LONG Said of a wine with considerable length of aroma or flavour after swallowing.

M

MADERIZATION Oxidation in a white wine to the point of browning its colour and giving it the taste of Madeira; a serious flaw.

MEDIUM SWEET Descriptor for wines lightly dosed with residual sugar, where sweetness provides more suppleness than an overtly sugary sensation.

MERCAPTAN Very strong, unpleasant sulphurous odour. Reminiscent of rotten eggs. A chemically faulty wine.

MINT Two separate aromas should be distinguished here: those of peppermint and fresh mint. Both are found as trace notes in certain white wines, and create the freshness and vivacity of the bouquet.

MOUTH-FEEL Term designating the entirety of the sensations felt in the mouth.

MUSHROOM Pleasant aroma, similar to Portobello mushrooms, often found in mature wines. It can be unpleasant and resemble mildew if the wine has been made with botrytized grapes.

MUSK Aroma reminiscent of animals. It is slightly fetid in a state of reduction, but extremely pleasant when aerated. Often referred to in various high quality wines of a certain age.

MUSKY Generic term designating a family of animal-related smells (fur, game, leather, etc.) that feature in older red wines. When encountered in young wines, such odours are often unpleasant but will disappear with aeration.

N

NERVOUS Physical character attributed particularly to white wines, and sometimes to reds, where the interplay of high acidity and sweetness create an impression of opposition or tension.

NOSE The overall olfactory characteristics of a wine.

NUTMEG Aromatic spice often referred to in very sweet white wines of a certain age, and in some red wines.

O

ONION Aroma caused by chemical reduction and occasionally found in very old red wines.

ORANGE (FLOWER) Aroma found in the bouquet of some Sauvignon Blancs and other aromatic white grape varieties.

ORANGE (ZEST) References are often made to orange zest characters in respect to young white wines made from extremely ripe harvests. Also present in some fortified wines.

P

PEACH Flavours and aromas of white or yellow peaches are often found in aromatic white wines (Viognier and Pinot Gris) as well as in some Côtes du Rhône reds and Beaujolais wines.

PEACH (BLOSSOM) Very delicate aroma, similar to pistachio or bitter almonds, sometimes found in young and fresh aromatic white wines.

MEDOC
MIS EN BOUTEILLES
AU CHATEAU

PEAR Aroma very often encountered in young unoaked white wines, and in some high quality red wines – in the most evanescent and subtle phase of the nose and in the final phase of the palate.

PEONY The slightly peppery aroma of this flower is also found in wines that share its colour.

PEPPERS (GREEN) Aroma and flavour perceptible in red wines that are rich in tannins and whose fruit flavours are less than ideally ripe.

PINE Resinous or medicinal aroma referred to in some red wines.

PINEAPPLE Aromatic quality found in a large number of white wines made from very ripe grapes.

PISTACHIO Very subtle aroma, similar to bitter almonds but more delicate. Sometimes found in red wines with sophisticated bouquets.

PRUNES Aroma defined by hints of stewed fruits such as prunes. Usually a sign of overripeness. Typical of port and old red wines, but considered a flaw in young red wines.

PUNGENCY Describes a juxtaposition of astringency and tartness, combined with a certain roughness that is more or less repellent.

Q

QUINCE Aroma found in rich and sweet white wines, linked with other aromas of very ripe or candied fruit.

R

RANCIO Aromas (prunes, tobacco, leather, Madeira) that develop with age, typical of naturally soft old wines, port, mature red wines, and old brandies.

RASPBERRIES Common constituent scent of Pinot Noir, Grenache, and numerous other red wines (including Beaujolais).

REDCURRANT Aromatic feature found in light red wines and reds intended for early drinking.

RESIN Balsamic-like aroma that features in the bouquets of certain red wines.

ROSE Primary aroma in Gewurztraminer and various varieties of Muscat. A delicate note of faded roses is found in some high quality, old red wines.

ROUGH High levels of astringency.

ROUNDED Term applied to wines with no angularity, in other words where softness and suppleness dominate without heaviness.

S

SAPPY Professional term used to express an expansiveness of aromas and abundance of flavours as the wine passes through the mouth.

SEVERE A wine under the joint dominance of tannin and acidity, accompanied by austere aromas. Not appealing.

SHARP Describes a wine with marginally dominant acidity and tannin, giving a slightly aggressive edge. Not appealing.

SILKY Term expressing the sheer feel of a wine in the mouth. Very appealing.

SMOKY Aroma evoking a wood fire. Almost a given in Pessac-Léognan reds and some Côte de Nuits wines. Also attributed to maturation in new oak barrels. *See also* EMPYREUMATIC.

SMOOTH Physical characteristic of a wine with high viscosity, a result of a judicious balance of tannin and acidity and no shortage of softness.

SOFT Name given to the overall effect of various sweet constituents in a wine (alcohol, glycerol, sugar), especially in red wines, and in particular when this group of substances dominates and is enhanced by a lack of hard sensations.

SOFTNESS Characteristic of wines lacking acidity relative to their tannin content, which is normal.

SOLID Said of wines possessing a good, sound framework of tannins on a balanced base of fruit and acidity.

SOURNESS Characteristic most often associated with a wine that is beginning to spoil.

SPICES Considerable number of aromas. Includes the full range of spices used in cooking and baking. Sometimes found in various white and red wines that have reached some maturity.

STALE Characteristic odour of wines that have been left open without a stopper, and generally accompanied by the loss of any expected aromas in the wine.

STALKY A disagreeable, acerbic character with a more or less herbaceous character. Caused by prolonged maceration with shredded grape stems during vinification.

STAR ANISE Similar aroma to aniseed, but more intense.

STRAWBERRY Aroma of wild strawberries is common in young red wines intended for early drinking. Stewed or preserved strawberry aromas are often found in tandem with those of dried figs in soft red wines and old, dry red wines.

SUCROSITY Neologism used in tasting to express the level of a wine's apparent sugar content, which may be, in ascending order: fruity, medium-sweet, sweet, or syrupy.

SUPPLE Texture displayed by restrained tannin and acidity, allowing the natural softness of the wine to shine through.

SWEET White wines and rosés are called sweet when a perceptible amount of sugar remains in the wine, imparting a soft feel and sweet taste.

T

TANNIN Substance extracted from grape skins giving red wines their structure and some character.

THICK Said of red wines with such soft tannins that subtlety or harmony is lost.

THIN Term applied to wine of a weak consistency, where all of its constituent elements are generally lacking.

THOROUGHBRED Said of a wine of incomparable elegance and distinction.

THYME Aroma found fairly frequently in certain white wines from the south of France and Haute-Provence.

TIRED Said of a wine that has lost its coherence and its tone.

TOASTED A note of toasted or 'grilled bread' is found in some red wines, and 'toasted almonds' is an aroma encountered in fine white wines as they begin a phase of reduction in the bottle. Also attributed to maturation in new oak barrels.

TOBACCO Notes of green tobacco leaves, associated with the hints of Havana beloved of *parfumiers*, are sometimes found in very fine red wines.

TRUFFLE Very distinguished aroma found in high quality, old red wines. White truffle is sometimes encountered in certain vintages of aged white or sweet wines.

V

VANILLA Aromatic element of numerous white and red wines. It develops naturally in the woody part of the grape stem or (more frequently) in the oak of the wooden vats or barrels for wine production.

VEGETAL Aromas reminiscent of the plant world. Also said of tannins that supply a certain astringency due to a lack of maturation or robust extraction.

VELVETY Said of a wine whose mouth-feel evokes velvet.

VENISON *see* GAMEY

VINOUS Said of a wine whose richness in alcohol is clearly apparent. Also known as alcoholic.

W

WALLFLOWER Small ornamental plant whose aroma is often compared with the finest Chardonnays and Chenin Blancs.

WARMING Term expressing the sensation of warmth in the mouth, under the influence of a certain richness in alcohol.

WAX The aroma of wax is common in some great expressions of Chardonnay and Sémillon, especially some sweet wines from the Loire Valley.

WEAK Implies, on the one hand, a certain lack of alcohol and, on the other, a shortfall in constitution – indicating potential fragility and difficulties in storage.

WOODY One of the balsamic group of aromas, found in wines aged in new barrels.

Y

YOUNG A wine is considered young if it has retained a good portion of its initial fruit aromas and flavours.

GREAT WINE REGIONS OF THE WORLD

2003
DISZNÓKŐ
TOKAJI ASZÚ
5 PUTTONYOS
2001
GUERROUANE
Appellation d'Origine Garantie
VIN DU MAROC
LES VINS DU MONDE
Afrique du Sud
2008
Pinotage

Château
Le Bon Pasteur
PRODUIT DE FRANCE
OMEROL
ON POMEROL CONTROLEE
2004
Domaines ROLLA
GIRONDE
2004

Summary of main areas

KEY WINE REGIONS

North Sea
UK
NETHERLANDS
GERMANY
Elbe
RUSSIA
BELGIUM
Rhine
LUXEMBOURG
Moselle
Atlantic Ocean
Champagne
CZECH REPUBLIC
Loire
Danube
SLOVAKIA
UKRAINE
FRANCE
MOLDAVIA
Dnieper
SWITZERLAND
AUSTRIA
HUNGARY
GEORGIA
Burgundy
Crimea
SLOVENIA
ROMANIA
Bordeaux
Piedmont
Po
CROATIA
Black Sea
Rhône
Danube
Rioja
Ebro
SERBIA
Tuscany
BULGARIA
PORTUGAL
SPAIN
Corsica
ITALY
MACEDONIA
TURKEY
Sardinia
Balearic Islands
Jerez
GREECE
SYRIA
Sicily
CYPRUS
LEBANON
MOROCCO
ALGERIA
TUNISIA
Mediterranean Sea
Crete
ISRAEL
KAZAKHSTAN
40° N
AZERBAIJAN
JAPAN
CHINA
ARMENIA
30° N
PAKISTAN
EGYPT
Pacific Ocean
INDIA
ETHIOPIA
0°
Indian Ocean
ZIMBABWE
AMIBIA
AUSTRALIA
SOUTH AFRICA
30° S
40° S
NEW ZEALAND

WORLD OF WINE

Vines are found on every continent of the world, although their distribution is anything but equal. While Europe still largely leads the field in terms of total land area devoted to vineyards, the two Americas, Asia, and especially Australia and New Zealand are witnessing expansion in their respective grape-growing regions. Even so, real changes are occurring in the areas of consumption and production.

Global vineyards

LARGEST VINEYARDS. According to figures supplied for 2014 by the International Organization of the Vine and Wine (OIV), the vineyards of the world cover 18.5 million acres (7.5 million hectares). In descending order, the largest vine-growing nations by surface area are: Spain, France, Italy, the USA, Portugal, and Argentina. These figures are often adjusted (with the exception of those relating to the vineyards of Turkey, China, Iran, and Romania) since the data gathered by the OIV includes the total surface area of planted vines, without distinguishing between grapes for eating, winemaking, and distilling.

Italy is now the number one wine producer by volume, *outpacing France, Spain, the USA, Argentina, and Australia. Global wine production in 2014 amounted to about 2.9 billion cases (270 million hectolitres).*

GLOBAL TRENDS. Vineyard plantings worldwide have been on the increase since 2011, after a long downward trend. European growing areas remain the largest, with more than 60 per cent of total world production, followed by Asia, America, Africa, and Oceania (Australia, New Zealand). Setting aside the difficulty of measuring the portion of vineyards just for wine production in some countries (China, for example).

CONSUMPTION STABILIZED. America became the world's largest consumer of wine in 2009, and global consumption has tended to stablilize after this date – the decline recorded in 2009 in the European countries that have traditionally been the largest producers and consumers (France, Italy, Spain, and Germany), being compensated by the USA and China especially. China's meteoric rise has been spectacular. In 2014 it became the seventh largest consumer of wine in the world.

Europe in long decline

The Old World has witnessed a year-on-year reduction in its wine-producing area, most notably from official policy to tear out vines in European countries; more grubbing-up plans, as seen in France; or a restructuring of vineyards in the countries that have recently joined the EU. Nevertheless, the decline has now slowed significantly and new laws on plantation rights in 2015 could well make a difference. The wine-producing regions of the EU (of which there are 28) amounted to 8.4 million acres (3.4 million hectares) in 2014. Depending on the particular harvest, France and Italy take turns in holding the title of largest global producer; but Spain devotes the most actual land to wine production.

The New World situation

South America and Oceania have seen their grape plantings grow dramatically during the past 20 years; and Argentinian, Brazilian, and, to a lesser extent, Chilean vineyards are still expanding. As far as production is concerned, the slight drop witnessed in Argentina over the past few years has been balanced out by Chile's performance, so in 2013 and 2014 wine production in South America remained at a high level. Australian production has remained the same for several years while New Zealand has seen a strong growth since 2011.

New wine-producing countries

Asia continues to be a focal point for growth among the world's wine producers. Chinese growers have experienced a rapid rise since 1998, reaching nearly 2 milllion acres (800,000 ha) by 2015 – the second largest vineyard area in the world. China is, without doubt, the principal force behind growth in the wine market in Asia. Production in Africa has stabilized. In South Africa, the largest African producer and ranked 7th in the world, the industry has been stimulated by exports that drive production forward and has been increasing slightly since 2011.

India – promising but restricted

The Indian market is an exceptional case, since the country's population is very young (three-quarters of its citizens are under 35 years of age). Wine consumption – estimated at an annual 1.6 million cases (15 million litres), of which 20 per cent is imported – should grow steadily in the next few years. India also can now claim more than 70 wine producers distributed between three areas of wine production: Nasik and Sangli, both in Maharashtra, and Bangalore in Karnataka. Even if India remains a large consumer of beer and spirits (especially whisky), the national market is promising for wine and its economic weight should not be underestimated. The actual buying market is approaching 30 million inhabitants – meaning consumers who for the most part live in three states: Maharashtra, Karnataka, and Delhi, and who belong to the most leisured classes. These three states alone account for 75 per cent of India's entire wine consumption.

China, the top wine consumer in Asia

In 2014, China accounted for 6.5 per cent of the world's wine consumption, placing it in fifth position in the global rankings. In the same year it became the leading market for red wine, a trend set to continue in the coming years, stimulated in particular by the increase in its domestic production and in the number of Chinese vineyards (up by 25 per cent since 2011). France still remains the principal supplier to the Asian countries, followed by the USA, Italy, Australia, and Chile. Finally, it's worth noting that Hong Kong is now the key market through which quality wines are funnelled into all of East Asia.

International changes

After a pause and a slight decline during the crisis years of 2008 and 2009, international trade has taken off again both in terms of value and volume, increasing by 100 per cent and 60 per cent respectively on 2000 figures. However, the trends vary greatly. France, the previous market leader, has seen a decline in some areas of the market while remaining the biggest exporter in terms of value, ahead of Italy. In the long term the decrease in the volume of French exports is due to the rise of the New World market and the increase in exports from Italy and from Spain in particular, which was the world's biggest exporter of wine in terms of volume in 2014. The New World has risen to the export challenge and, with the exception of the USA, wines have seen a rapid increase in global markets for the last 20 years, a momentum that continues and is not under question despite recent trends revealing contrasting developments: Australia and Argentina have seen export figures stagnate while those of Chile and New Zealand continue to grow. The six leading importers (Germany, UK, USA, France, Russia, and China) account for almost 50 per cent of total imports. The wine market is becoming an increasingly global sector. Ten years ago 27 per cent of wine consumed was imported whereas today that figure is over 43 per cent.

WINE-PRODUCING COUNTRIES

COUNTRY	SURFACE AREA (thousands of acres/hectares)	PRODUCTION (millions of gallons/thousands of hectolitres)
WESTERN AND CENTRAL EUROPEAN ZONE		
Austria	111/45	59.4/2,250
Bulgaria	158/64	1.97/747
Czech Republic	42/17(*)	1.71/650 (*)
France	1,957/792	1,236/46,804
Germany	252/102	243.5/9,209
Greece	284/110	76.6/2,900
Hungary	160/65	67.5/2,555
Italy	1,705/690	1,168.4/44,229
Portugal	553/224	162.7/6,195
Romania	474/192	108.1/4,093
Croatia	86/35 (*)	53.9/2,044 (*)
Slovenia	39/16(*)	13.9/527 (*)
Spain	2,523/1,021	1,009.4/38,211
Switzerland	37/15	24.6/933

Figures for 2014 (OIV), 2011 where marked (*). There are other wine-producing countries in this zone in addition to those mentioned above, but their yield is either very low or the most recent figures are unreliable or unavailable. These include (in probable order of size): Slovakia, Republic of Macedonia, Cyprus, Bosnia, Luxembourg, the UK, and Malta.

COUNTRY	SURFACE AREA (thousands of acres/hectares)	PRODUCTION (millions of gallons/thousands of hectolitres)
EASTERN EUROPEAN ZONE – EAST ASIA – MIDDLE EAST		
Georgia	140/57	42.1/1,596
Israel	22/9	2.36/895
Lebanon	35/14	25.7/975
Moldova	353/143	157.1/5,948
Russia	156/63	108.9/4,124
Turkey	1,255/508	1,134.9/42,964
Ukraine	208/84	137.8/5,219

– Figures for 2011 (OIV). Turkey and Lebanon devote a large part of their production to grapes for eating.
– Grape-producing countries that do not feature in this table include: Afghanistan, Armenia, Azerbaijan, Iran, Iraq, Jordan, Kazakhstan, Kyrgyzstan, Syria, Tajikistan, Turkmenistan, Uzbekistan, Yemen.

COUNTRY	SURFACE AREA (thousands of acres/hectares)	PRODUCTION (millions of gallons/thousands of hectolitres)
AMERICAN ZONE		
Argentina	561/227	401.4/15,197
Brazil	220/89	72.1/2,732
Chile	494/211	260.5/10,050
United States	1,050/425	544.5/22,300

Figures for 2014 (OIV) Several other countries in this zone produce wine. These are, in order of output: Mexico, Uruguay, Canada, Peru, Bolivia, Venezuela.

COUNTRY	SURFACE AREA (thousands of acres/hectares)	PRODUCTION (millions of gallons/thousands of hectolitres)
AFRICAN ZONE		
Morocco	119/48 (*)	(100.8/3,819 (*)
South Africa	326/132	298/11,316
Tunisia	54/22 (*)	(39.5/1,496 (*)

Figures for 2014 (OIV), 2011 where marked (*).

COUNTRY	SURFACE AREA (thousands of acres/hectares)	PRODUCTION (millions of gallons/thousands of hectolitres)
OCEANIC ZONE		
Australia	376/152	317/12,000
New Zealand	94/38	84.6/3,204
ASIAN ZONE		
China	1,974/799	295.2/11,178
India	(294/119	0.4/170
Japan	50/19 (*)	45.5/1,726 (*)

Figures for 2014 (OIV), except Japan (2011).
China and India devote a large part of their production to grapes for eating.

FRANCE

Lille
Somme
Rouen
Oise
Seine
Caen
Reims
Épernay
Marne
Paris
Meuse
Nancy
Strasbourg
Moselle
Rhine
Aube
Seine
Les Riceys
Rennes
Vilaine
Sarthe
Loir
Orléans
Auxerre
Chablis
Colmar
Angers
Loire
Tours
Cher
Yonne
Dijon
Saône
Doubs
Nantes
Bourges
Beaune
Arbois
Poitiers
Vienne
Creuse
Loire
Mâcon
La Rochelle
Atlantic Ocean
Roanne
Rhône
Clermont-Ferrand
Lyon
Chambéry
Cognac
Allier
Rhône
Isère
Grenoble
Bordeaux
Dordogne
Valence
Cahors
Lot
Agen
Orange
Durance
Gaillac
Tarn
Avignon
Auch
Nimes
Nice
Toulouse
Montpellier
Aix-en-Provence
Pau
Marseille
Garonne
Carcassonne
Toulon
Narbonne
Bastia
Aude
Perpignan
Mediterranean Sea
Ajaccio
N
Wine-producing regions
Alsace and Lorraine
Champagne
Loire Valley
Jura
Savoie
Rhône Valley
Southwest France
Provence
Languedoc-Roussillon
0
125 miles (200 km)

BORDEAUX

Bordeaux is synonymous with wine all over the world. It has come to symbolize exceptional vineyards and legendary châteaux and is home to some of the greatest wines on earth. Their excellence has inspired wineries in other countries, from Italy to Australia to California in the USA.

Long-standing reputation

ORIGINS. Wine production began in the Bordeaux region early in the 1st century with the arrival of the Roman legions. Its wines soon became famous – by the 4th century the poet Ausonius was already singing their praises. However, the region's wines did not really flourish until the 12th century, with the marriage in 1152 of Eleanor of Aquitaine to the future Plantagenet King Henry II of England. This marked the beginning of significant wine trade between Bordeaux and England.

FROM THE 17TH TO 19TH CENTURIES. A new era of trade began in the 17th century with the arrival of the Dutch, who bought wine for distillation. This was also the period when the great châteaux, such as Haut-Brion, were built. In the 18th century, wine began to sell in bottles, and exports increased. London society developed a taste for the wines of Bordeaux, particularly red wines of the Médoc, which the English called the new French clarets. Meanwhile, new vine-growing practices developed in the Médoc. The 'Place de Bordeaux' (a marketing system) started to play, and still plays, a key role. It was supported by the emergence of new winemaking and storage techniques, and the influence of new wine merchants, who were largely responsible for the distribution of the wines (as they are today: merchants sells around 75 per cent of the Gironde's production and 95 per cent of the *grands crus*). The 19th century was a golden age for Bordeaux vineyards. It saw, among other things, the establishment of a hierarchy among the wineries of the left bank of the Garonne, with the 1855 classification of the Médoc *grand crus*. Then, at the end of the 19th century, the vineyards suffered devastating attacks of phylloxera and mildew. Then came the First World War, global economic crisis, and then war again.

FROM THE 20TH CENTURY TO TODAY. It was not until the 1950s that the vineyards recovered. New classifications – of Graves, St Émilion, and the *crus bourgeois* – were created. With the exception of the *crus bourgeois* classification, which was annulled in 2007, these continue to reflect the excellence of Bordeaux's wines. There have been a few scandals (involving fraud) and increasingly serious challenges to its supremacy from foreign competition. But Bordeaux appears to have armed itself with the means of continuing its success. Bordeaux's *en primeur* sales continue to constitute the major event of the year in the wine world. Vinexpo, the biennial international trade fair, and 'open days' throughout the vineyards, attract many thousands of visitors. Anxious to improve their image, become more competitive, and provide greater transparency, producers have created unions and other groups. One is Sweet Bordeaux (an association of producers of sweet wines, *see also* p.271), another is the Côtes-de-Bordeaux appellation, introduced in 2008 – a real force representing one-sixth of Bordeaux's output, with a total

BORDEAUX STATISTICS (AOC)

Vineyard area: 276,758 acres (112,000 ha)

Production: 58.8 million cases (5,300,000 hl)

Red and rosé: 88%

White: 12%

(CIVB)

> Château de Monbadon in the Libourne region.

DID YOU KNOW...?

The oldest wine property in Bordeaux is Château Pape Clément, *which dates from the late 13th century. When Bertrand de Goth was made archbishop of Bordeaux in 1299, he received this estate in Pessac from his elder brother. Six years later, he became pope (Clément V) and gave his name to the château. Since that time it has consistently produced wines that rank among Bordeaux's finest.*

area of 27,000 acres (11,000 ha) and producing 5.6 million cases (500,000 hl).

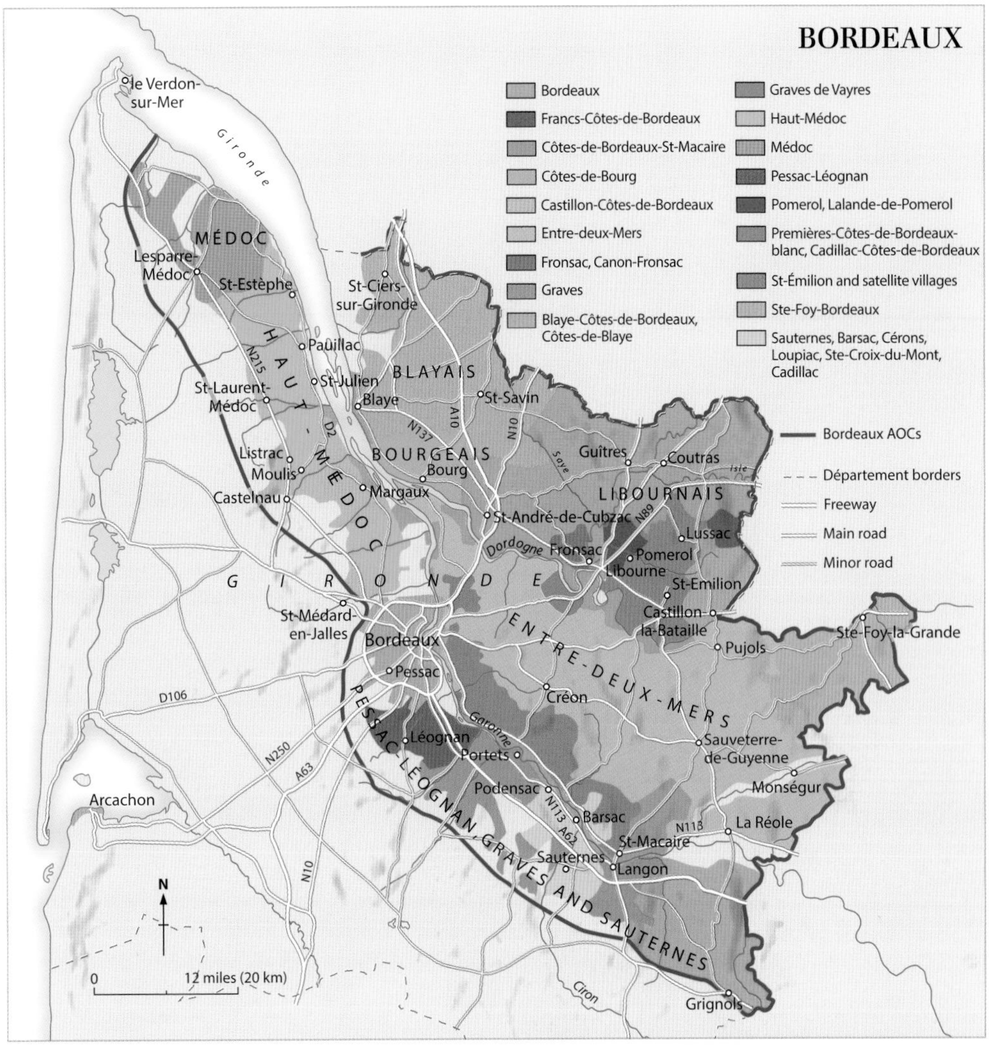

Climate

Bordeaux's vineyards enjoy a temperate, maritime climate. The large Landes forest forms a shield to protect the vines from westerly winds and regulates area temperatures. But the proximity of the ocean is an important factor. Mild, wet winters are followed by early springs (which are prone to hailstorms and cold rain) and then hot, dry summers. Finally, sunny weather blesses the fall, with mists that are ideal for the development of the noble rot (*Botrytis cinerea*) that is necessary for the production of great sweet wines.

Vineyard landscape

Bordeaux's vineyards occupy the entire *département* of the Gironde. Three generic appellations – Bordeaux, Bordeaux Supérieur, and Crémant de Bordeaux – are produced throughout the region. The other appellations are grouped into three broad geographical areas.

THE LEFT BANK AND THE CITY OF BORDEAUX. This area covers the Médoc (northwestern Bordeaux), Graves, and Sauternes (southeastern Bordeaux). The soil is composed mainly of various types of gravel. Pebbles of uneven sizes are mixed with clay, alluvial deposits, or sand, with some areas of clay-limestone. This base produces red wines and both dry and sweet white wines. The Médoc is itself divided into two regional appellations: the Médoc and the Haut-Médoc. The latter contains well-known appellations at the level of the communes (in alphabetical order: Listrac, Margaux, Moulis, Pauillac, St-Estèphe, and St-Julien). The Left Bank is home to some very fine wines and some of the most famous châteaux in the world, such as Château Lafite-Rothschild, Château Margaux, Château Léoville-Las-Cases, and Château Cos d'Estournel in the Médoc; Château Haut-Brion in Graves; Château d'Yquem, Château Climens, and Château Rieussec in Sauternes.

THE RIGHT BANK AND THE PORT OF LIBOURNE. This area encompasses the vineyards of Blaye and Bourg to the north; Libourne at the centre, with St-Émilion, Pomerol, and Fronsac; and Castillon to the east. The soils are mostly clay and limestone (Fronsac, St-Émilion) or made up of clay (Pomerol). The Right Bank also has several world-famous châteaux, with Pétrus and Château L'Église-Clinet in Pomerol, and Château Ausone and Château Cheval-Blanc in St-Émilion.

Bordeaux stars

There is an elite group of about ten prestigious *grands crus* that are the stuff of dreams. They are never far from the minds of serious wine lovers, collectors, and investors. Each of these properties has a unique personality, a soul. Their names? Château Margaux (Margaux), the jewel of the Médoc; Château d'Yquem (Sauternes), the only wine in Bordeaux to be awarded the special rank of *premier cru supérieur*, the 'best of the best' of sweet white wines; Château Haut-Brion (Pessac-Léognan), which did so much for the reputation of Bordeaux wines in Britain; Pétrus (Pomerol), a cult wine; Château Latour (Pauillac), the ultimate expression of Cabernet Sauvignon; Château Cheval-Blanc and Château Ausone, Château Angélus, Château Pavie (the four *premiers grands classés* at St-Émilion), among the rarest wines in the world; Château Lafite-Rothschild, the first of the first growths (*premier des premiers crus*) in 1855; and Château Mouton-Rothschild (Pauillac), which was made a *premier cru* in 1973, and is famous not only for the quality of its wines but also for its labels by well-known artists.

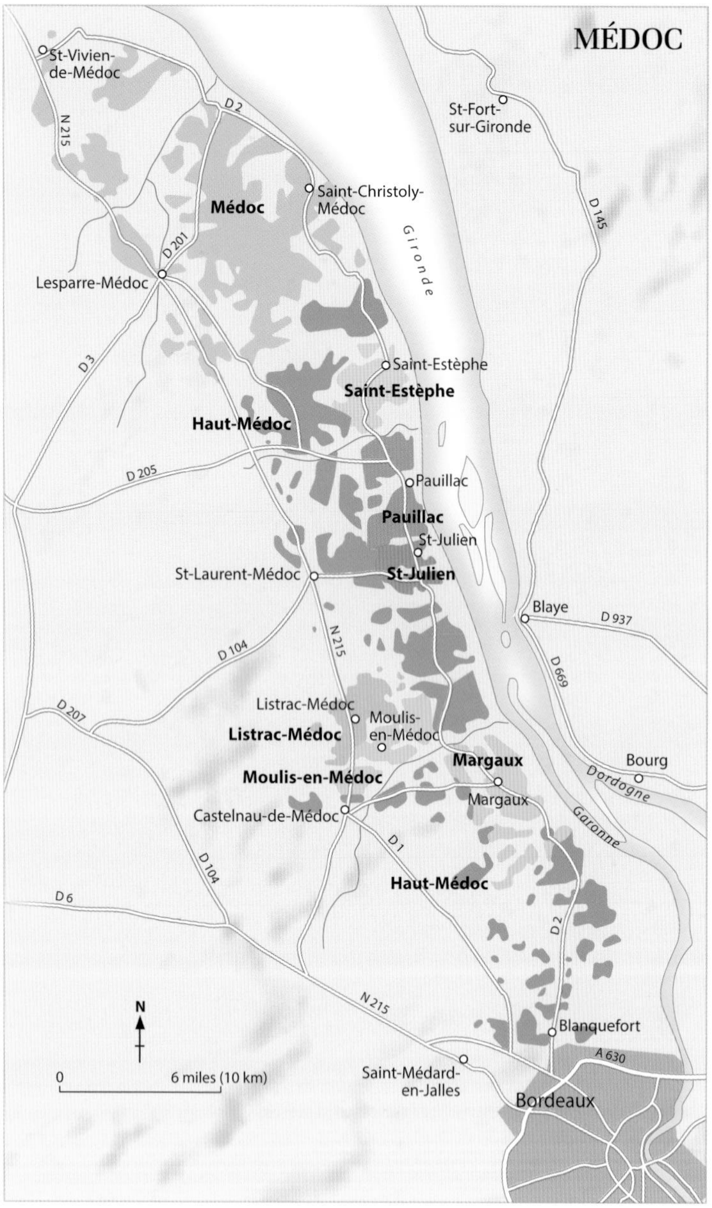

BETWEEN THE GARONNE AND THE DORDOGNE. This region consists mainly of vineyards in the Entre-Deux-Mers appellation. It produces dry and sweet white wines, as well as full-bodied reds (primarily with Merlot). The soil is made up of clay and gravel. The AOCs of Ste-Croix-du-Mont, Loupiac, and Cadillac, which produce sweet wines, are located along the right bank of the Garonne River.

Bordeaux grape varieties

Eight grape varieties are used to create the blends that make up Bordeaux's wines.

MERLOT. References to Merlot in St-Émilion date back to the 18th century. It is the most widely grown red wine grape in Bordeaux, dominating the appellations of St-Émilion, Pomerol, Côtes-de-Bordeaux, Bordeaux Rouge, and Bordeaux Supérieur. Ripening early, it produces full-bodied, fruity wines that are simultaneously supple and elegant.

CABERNET SAUVIGNON. This is Bordeaux's star red wine grape, and the main variety grown in the Médoc and Graves. Harvested when fully ripe, it produces fine, dark, distinguished, extremely complex wines known for their exceptional length on the palate, tannic structure, and capacity for ageing. It is also an important element in blends, appearing in the wines of the Bordeaux Supérieur, Haut-Médoc, and Côtes-de-Bordeaux appellations.

CABERNET FRANC. A popular red wine grape in the Libourne area, where it competes with Merlot, it can produce wines that, even after 50 years in the cellar, still show incredible youth. It is grown almost everywhere in the Gironde.

PETIT VERDOT. This red variety has a long history and is used in several wines of the Médoc, bringing colour, tannin, and spicy notes.

MALBEC (ALSO KNOWN AS AUXERROIS AND CÔT). This great red variety of the Cahors region is used in many blends in Bordeaux, bringing fruity flavours and structure.

SÉMILLON. This white grape is the king of Sauternes, and of all the sweet wines produced in the Gironde (and in neighbouring Monbazillac). Offering high yields, it is also widespread in Graves and the Entre-Deux-Mers region. Sémillon's fruit and finesse enable the production of truly great white wines, both dry and sweet. It partners particularly well with Sauvignon Blanc.

SAUVIGNON BLANC. The other great white grape of the Bordeaux region. Its yields are low, but it is prized for structure, freshness, and length on the palate. It produces very flavourful dry white wines with pronounced herbaceous notes (Bordeaux, Pessac-Léognan, Blaye, Entre-Deux-Mers) that develop great complexity with age. It is also used in sweet wine blends.

MUSCADELLE. A traditional Bordeaux white grape variety, Muscadelle gives wines a pleasant floral aroma. But it is now in danger of disappearing due to its extreme sensitivity to disease.

TRUE OR FALSE?

Bordeaux's grands crus can age for more than 50 years.

TRUE. Although they are now enjoyable in their relative youth, as fruity, fresh wines, the wines of Bordeaux have the potential to improve with age and should be kept for five to 15, or even 20 years. However, only wines from great vintages – the most recent being 2009, 2010, and 2015 – from Médoc, St-Émilion, Pomerol, and Graves, and the best appellations (Pauillac, Margaux, St-Julien) can be kept for 50 years without a few wrinkles developing.

Bordeaux and branded wines

In 1930, Baron Philippe de Rothschild had the idea of selling his second wine under the brand name 'Mouton Cadet' with a different label from that of his prestigious property, Château Mouton-Rothschild (Pauillac). Success quickly followed. Today, Mouton Cadet, a blend of different wines from the Bordeaux region, is the leading brand of Bordeaux wine in the world. Other brand names followed. Among the largest, there are: Baron de Lestac, Malesan, Blaissac, Cellier d'Yvecourt, Croix d'Austéran, Batiste de Vignac.

'Châteaux'

Bordeaux has more than 6,000 wine-producing châteaux. One would think that any label mentioning a château is referring to a 'real' château. This is not the case. Often, the only château is the one in the name – and these are no more than ordinary houses, farm buildings, or winemaking facilities. There are, of course, some authentic châteaux; but they are rare. Indeed, in Bordeaux, the term 'château' is simply applied to wine-producing properties and has nothing to do with architecture. For example, there is no château associated with the legendary estates of Pétrus, Latour, or Mouton. However, not everyone can claim the term: a château implies a vineyard owned by a sole proprietor cultivating their own vines and making their own wine.

> The *terroirs* of the vineyards in Bordeaux offer the best expressions of Cabernet Sauvignon.

Bordeaux blends

The wines of Bordeaux are made by blending different components. This solid tradition has developed over many years, and it has become a real art. Bordeaux's wines, whether they are a generic appellation or a *grand cru classé*, are generally a combination of several grape varieties from various parcels or *terroirs*. The proportions of each will vary depending on the vintage, the winemaker, and the main grape varieties specified for that appellation. The goal is to obtain the best balance and the best expression of the *terroir*. As a rule, there are at least two grape varieties involved in each wine, often three, and sometimes four.

Style of wines

The wines of Bordeaux are defined by their immense diversity. The region produces red, rosé, dry white, sweet white, and sparkling wines. Plus, their styles can be very different, even within an appellation. While there is comparative unity in terms of grape varieties and winemaking techniques, there are huge variations in the soil, microclimates, and the composition of the blends.

RED. These wines may be light, for drinking when they are young and fruity (Bordeaux); full-bodied with a fine tannic structure, for consumption within five years (Bordeaux Supérieur); full-bodied and supple with good ageing potential (St-Émilion, Pomerol, Fronsac); or finally, complex and tannic when young, but with a huge capacity to age (Pauillac, St-Julien, etc.).

ROSÉ. Produced all over the Gironde department under two appellations, Bordeaux rosé and Bordeaux clairet, these are fruity wines that should be consumed young.

DRY WHITE. Produced all across the department of the Gironde, these are lively and pleasant to drink (Entre-Deux-Mers, Côtes-de-Bordeaux-Blaye, and the vast Bordeaux appellation); but they also can be more robust and powerful with good ageing potential (Pessac-Léognan, Graves).

SWEET WHITE. Lead by Sauternes and Château d'Yquem, these wines are made primarily in the appellations of Sauternes, Cérons, Cadillac, Ste-Croix-du-Mont, Barsac, and Loupiac, totalling around 7,400 acres (3,000 ha). They are also produced in a few other areas such as Graves Supérieur and Côtes-de-Bordeaux-St-Macaire. Some of these wines may be kept for a remarkably long time.

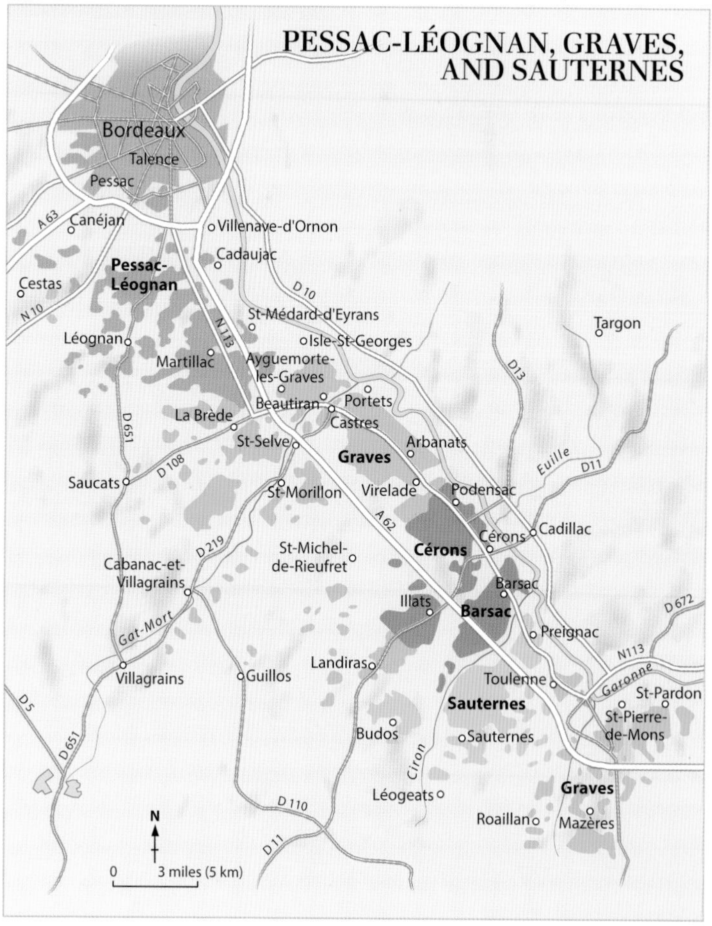

> Barrels in the cellar of Château Lascombes in the Margaux appellation.

SPARKLING. White and rosé sparkling wines are produced throughout the Bordeaux region, and are currently very popular.

Classifying Bordeaux wines

The first classifications of the region's wines appeared at the end of the 17th century; but the most famous is the 1855 classification, which established rankings for the red wines of the Médoc. Over time, it was followed by several others. Bordeaux now has a total of 171 classified growths (*crus classés*), corresponding to approximately 13,000 acres (5,300 ha) of vines.

THE 1855 CLASSIFICATION (OF THE WINES OF THE MÉDOC). This hierarchy consists of 61 wines divided into five categories, from first to fifth growth. It has been revised just once, in 1973, when Château Mouton-Rothschild was promoted from second to first growth.

CLASSIFICATION OF THE WINES OF SAUTERNES AND BARSAC. This also dates from 1855. Château d'Yquem stands alone as the only superior first growth (*premier cru supérieur*) and is followed by 11 first growths and 14 second growths.

CLASSIFICATION OF GRAVES. The first classification of Graves was in 1956, with a revision in 1959. It contains 16 estates representing 13 red wines and nine white wines.

CLASSIFICATION OF ST-ÉMILION. None of the *grands crus* of St-Émilion were included in the 1855 classification. The wine union (*syndicat viticole*) therefore established its own classification, which is reviewed every ten years. The first classification took place in 1954.

CRUS ARTISANS. This group existed for over a century and a half, disappeared in the 1930s, and was restored in the 1990s. In 1994, the word 'artisan' was recognized by the European Union and a classification took place in 2002. 'Cru Artisan' implies a family-scale operation that is responsible for the growing of the grapes and the making and selling of the wines. The classification recognizes 44 *crus artisans* covering 840 acres (340 ha), mainly in the Médoc and Haut-Médoc.

CRU BOURGEOIS. The term *cru bourgeois* appeared in the 19th century in the Médoc, as an intermediate ranking between the *crus classés* and the *crus artisans*. The first official list, which dates from 1932, records 490. The classification was gradually forgotten, but then regained popularity in the 1980s. In 2003, a new, very official list was drawn up; but it was immediately challenged in court. Annulled in 2007, *cru bourgeois* returned in 2009 in a new form. The

TRUE OR FALSE?

The legendary wine of Pétrus is a grand cru classé.

FALSE. There is no classification in Pomerol. Despite its rarity, prestige and quality, Pétrus does not appear in any of the official classifications (*see also* p.267).

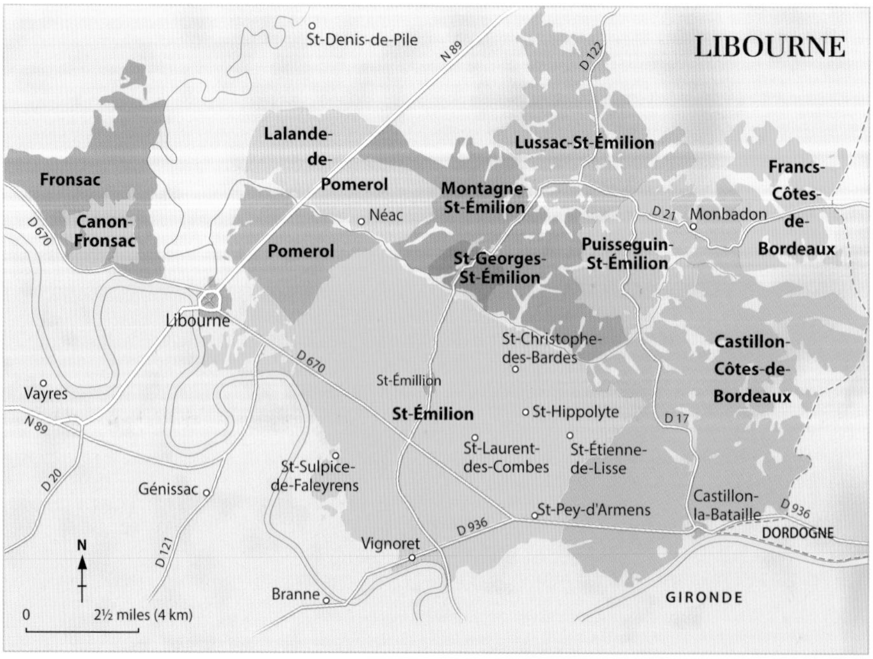

term was authorized for use on bottles from 2008 onward. Rather than a classification, it is now a type of certification, awarded every year by an independent body on the basis of certain criteria. The certification applies to a specific vintage and is granted two years after the harvest.

'Second' wines

To make their *grand vins*, the châteaux of Bordeaux use the best possible blending components. Anything that does not qualify for the '*premier*' (or '*grand*') wine is used to produce a '*second*' wine (and sometimes even a '*third*' and a '*fourth*'). These are sold under a different label, and generally offer excellent quality at lower prices. Sometimes the second wine is as good as the first wine. This should not come as a surprise: both are the product of an excellent *terroir*.

> Less concentrated than the *grand vin*, a 'second' wine is ready for drinking when it is younger.

Selected 'second' wines

Château Ausone: Chapelle d'Ausone

Château Beychevelle: Amiral de Beychevelle

Château Brane-Cantenac : Baron de Brane

Château Cheval-Blanc: Le Petit Cheval

Château Cos d'Estournel: Pagodes de Cos

Château Haut-Brion: Clarence de Haut-Brion

Château Lafite-Rothschild: Les Carruades

Château Lascombes: Chevalier de Lascombes

Château Latour: Les Forts de Latour

Château Léoville-Las-Cases: Clos du Marquis

Château Léoville-Poyferré: Pavillon de Léoville-Poyferré

Château Margaux: Pavillon Rouge du Château Margaux

Château Montrose: La Dame de Montrose

Château Mouton-Rothschild: Le Petit Mouton

Château Pavie-Macquin: Les Chênes de Macquin

Château Pichon-Longueville Comtesse de Lalande: La Réserve de la Comtesse

Château Pontet-Canet: Les Hauts de Pontet-Canet

Château Sociando-Mallet: La Demoiselle de Sociando-Mallet

Bordeaux AOCs

REGIONAL AND GENERIC APPELLATIONS
- Bordeaux
- Bordeaux clairet
- Bordeaux rosé
- Bordeaux sec
- Bordeaux supérieur
- Côtes-de-Bordeaux
- Crémant de Bordeaux

LEFT BANK
- Barsac
- Cérons
- Graves
- Graves supérieur
- Haut-Médoc
- Listrac-Médoc
- Médoc
- Moulis-en-Médoc
- Margaux
- Pauillac
- Pessac-Léognan
- St-Estèphe
- St-Julien
- Sauternes

RIGHT BANK
- Côtes-de-Bourg
- Côtes-de-Blaye
- Blaye
- Blaye-Côtes-de-Bordeaux
- Canon-Fronsac
- Castillon-Côtes-de-Bordeaux
- Francs-Côtes-de-Bordeaux
- Fronsac
- Lalande-de-Pomerol
- Lussac-St-Émilion
- Montagne-St-Émilion
- Pomerol
- Puisseguin-St-Émilion
- St-Émilion
- St-Émilion Grand Cru
- St-Georges-St-Émilion

ENTRE-DEUX-MERS
- Cadillac
- Cadillac-Côtes-de-Bordeaux
- Côtes-de-Bordeaux-St-Macaire
- Entre-Deux-Mers
- Entre-Deux-Mers-Haut-Benauge
- Loupiac
- Ste-Croix-du-Mont
- Ste-Foy-Bordeaux

Bordeaux's classified growths (*crus classés*)

CLASSIFICATION OF THE WINES OF THE MÉDOC (1855)

First Growths (*Premiers Crus*)
- Château Haut-Brion, Pessac
- Château Lafite-Rothschild, Pauillac
- Château Latour, Pauillac
- Château Margaux, Margaux
- Château Mouton-Rothschild, Pauillac (added in 1973)

Second Growths (*Seconds Crus*)
- Château Brane-Cantenac, Cantenac
- Château Cos d'Estournel, St-Estèphe
- Château Ducru-Beaucaillou, St-Julien-Beychevelle
- Château Durfort-Vivens, Margaux
- Château Gruaud-Larose, St-Julien-Beychevelle
- Château Lascombes, Margaux
- Château Léoville-Barton, St-Julien-Beychevelle
- Château Léoville-Las-Cases, St-Julien-Beychevelle
- Château Léoville-Poyferré, St-Julien-Beychevelle
- Château Montrose, St-Estèphe
- Château Pichon-Longueville, Baron de Pichon, Pauillac
- Château Pichon-Longueville, Comtesse de Lalande, Pauillac
- Château Rauzan-Ségla, Margaux
- Château Rauzan-Gassies, Margaux

Third Growths (*Troisièmes Crus*)
- Château Boyd-Cantenac, Cantenac
- Château Calon-Ségur, St-Estèphe
- Château Cantenac-Brown, Cantenac
- Château Desmirail, Margaux
- Château Ferrière, Margaux
- Château Giscours, Labarde
- Château d'Issan, Cantenac
- Château Kirwan, Cantenac
- Château Lagrange, St-Julien-Beychevelle
- Château La Lagune, Ludon
- Château Langoa-Barton, St-Julien-Beychevelle
- Château Malescot-St-Exupéry, Margaux
- Château Marquis d'Alesme-Becker, Margaux
- Château Palmer, Cantenac

Fourth Growths (*Quatrièmes Crus*)
- Château Beychevelle, St-Julien-Beychevelle
- Château Branaire-Ducru, St-Julien-Beychevelle
- Château Duhart-Milon, Pauillac
- Château Lafon-Rochet, St-Estèphe
- Château Marquis de Terme, Margaux
- Château Pouget, Cantenac
- Château Prieuré-Lichine, Cantenac
- Château St-Pierre, St-Julien-Beychevelle
- Château Talbot, St-Julien-Beychevelle
- Château La Tour-Carnet, St-Laurent-en-Médoc

Fifth Growths (*Cinquièmes Crus*)
- Château d'Armailhac, Pauillac
- Château Batailley, Pauillac
- Château Belgrave, St-Laurent-Médoc
- Château Camensac, St-Laurent-Médoc
- Château Cantemerle, Macau-en-Médoc
- Château Clerc-Milon, Pauillac
- Château Cos Labory, St-Estèphe
- Château Croizet-Bages, Pauillac
- Château Dauzac, Labarde
- Château Grand-Puy-Ducasse, Pauillac
- Château Grand-Puy-Lacoste, Pauillac
- Château Haut-Bages-Libéral, Pauillac
- Château Haut-Batailley, Pauillac
- Château Lynch-Bages, Pauillac
- Château Lynch-Moussas, Pauillac
- Château Pédesclaux, Pauillac
- Château Pontet-Canet, Pauillac
- Château du Tertre, Arsac

CLASSIFICATION OF THE SWEET WHITE WINES OF SAUTERNES AND BARSAC (1855)

Superior First Growth (*Premier Cru Supérieur*)
- Château d'Yquem, Sauternes

First Growths (*Premiers Crus*)
- Château Climens, Barsac
- Château Clos Haut-Peyraguey, Bommes
- Château Coutet, Barsac
- Château Guiraud, Sauternes
- Château Lafaurie-Peyraguey, Bommes
- Château Rabaud-Promis, Bommes
- Château de Rayne-Vigneau, Bommes
- Château Rieussec, Fargues-de-Langon
- Château Sigalas-Rabaud, Bommes
- Château Suduiraut, Preignac
- Château La Tour Blanche, Bommes

Second Growths (*Seconds Crus*)
- Château d'Arche, Sauternes
- Château Broustet, Barsac
- Château Caillou, Barsac
- Château Doisy-Daëne, Barsac
- Château Doisy-Dubroca, Barsac
- Château Doisy-Védrines, Barsac
- Château Filhot, Sauternes
- Château Lamothe, Sauternes
- Château Lamothe-Guignard, Sauternes
- Château de Malle, Preignac
- Château de Myrat, Barsac
- Château Nairac, Barsac
- Château Romer du Hayot, Fargues-de-Langon
- Château Suau, Barsac

CLASSIFICATION OF THE WINES OF GRAVES (1959)

Premier Grand Cru

- Château Haut-Brion (red), Pessac

Crus classés

- Château Bouscaut (red and white), Cadaujac
- Château Carbonnieux (red and white), Léognan
- Domaine de Chevalier (red and white), Léognan
- Château Couhins (white), Villenave-d'Ornon
- Château Couhins-Lurton (white), Villenave-d'Ornon
- Château Fieuzal (red), Léognan
- Château Haut-Bailly (red), Léognan
- Château Laville-Haut-Brion (white), Talence
- Château Malartic-Lagravière (red and white), Léognan
- Château La Mission-Haut-Brion (red), Talence
- Château Olivier (red and white), Léognan
- Château Pape Clément (red), Pessac
- Château Smith-Haut-Lafitte (red), Martillac
- Château La Tour-Haut-Brion (red and white), Talence
- Château La Tour-Martillac (red and white), Martillac

CLASSIFICATION OF THE RED WINES OF ST-ÉMILION (2012)

PREMIERS GRANDS CRUS

Premiers Grands Crus classés A

- Château Angélus, Saint-Émilion
- Château Ausone, Saint-Émilion
- Château Cheval-Blanc, Saint-Émilion
- Château Pavie, Saint-Émilion

Premiers Grands Crus classés B

- Château Beau-Séjour-Bécot, Saint-Émilion
- Château Beauséjour (Duffau-Lagarrosse), Saint-Émilion
- Château Belair-Monange, Saint-Émilion
- Château Canon, Saint-Émilion
- Château Canon-la-Gaffelière, Saint-Émilion
- Château Figeac, Saint-Émilion
- Château La Gaffelière, Saint-Émilion
- Château Larcis-Ducasse, Saint-Laurent-des-Combes
- Château Pavie-Macquin, Saint-Émilion
- Château Troplong-Mondot, Saint-Émilion
- Château Trottevieille, Saint-Émilion
- Château Valandraud, Saint-Émilion
- Clos Fourtet, Saint-Émilion
- La Mondotte, Saint-Émilion

GRANDS CRUS CLASSÉS

- Château Balestard La Tonnelle, Saint-Émilion
- Château Barde-Haut, Saint-Christophe-des-Bardes
- Château Bellefont-Belcier, Saint-Laurent-des-Combes
- Château Bellevue, Saint-Émilion
- Château Berliquet, Saint-Émilion
- Château Cadet-Bon, Saint-Émilion
- Château Cap de Mourlin, Saint-Émilion
- Château Chauvin, Saint-Émilion
- Château Clos de Sarpe, Saint-Christophe-des-Bardes
- Château Corbin, Saint-Émilion
- Château Côte de Baleau, Saint-Émilion
- Château Dassault, Saint-Émilion
- Château Destieux, Saint-Hippolyte
- Château Faugères, Saint-Étienne-de-Lisse
- Château Faurie de Souchard, Saint-Émilion
- Château de Ferrand, Saint-Hippolyte
- Château Fleur Cardinale, Saint-Étienne-de-Lisse
- Château Fombrauge, Saint-Christophe-des-Bardes
- Château Fonplégade, Saint-Émilion
- Château Fonroque, Saint-Émilion
- Château Franc-Mayne, Saint-Émilion
- Château Grand Corbin, Saint-Émilion
- Château Grand Corbin-Despagne, Saint-Émilion
- Château Grand Mayne, Saint-Émilion
- Château Grand Pontet, Saint-Émilion
- Château Guadet, Saint-Émilion
- Château Haut-Sarpe, Saint-Christophe-des-Bardes
- Château Jean Faure, Saint-Émilion
- Château L'Arrosée, Saint-Émilion
- Château La Clotte, Saint-Émilion
- Château La Commanderie, Saint-Émilion
- Château La Couspaude, Saint-Émilion
- Château La Dominique, Saint-Émilion
- Château La Fleur Morange, Saint-Pey-d'Armens
- Château La Marzelle, Saint-Émilion
- Château La Serre, Saint-Émilion
- Château La Tour-Figeac, Saint-Émilion
- Château Laniote, Saint-Émilion
- Château Larmande, Saint-Émilion
- Château Laroque, Saint-Christophe-des-Bardes
- Château Laroze, Saint-Émilion
- Château Le Châtelet, Saint-Émilion
- Château Le Prieuré, Saint-Émilion
- Château Les Grandes Murailles, Saint-Émilion
- Château Montbousquet, Saint-Sulpice-de-Faleyrens
- Château Moulin du Cadet, Saint-Émilion
- Château Pavie-Decesse, Saint-Émilion
- Château Peby-Faugères, Saint-Étienne-de-Lisse
- Château de Pressac, Saint-Étienne-de-Lisse
- Château Petit-Faurie-de-Soutard, Saint-Émilion
- Château Quinault-l'Enclos, Libourne
- Château Ripeau, Saint-Émilion
- Château Rochebelle, Saint-Laurent-des-Combes
- Château Saint-Georges Côte Pavie, Saint-Émilion
- Château Sansonnet, Saint-Émilion
- Château Soutard, Saint-Émilion
- Château Tertre Daugay, Saint-Émilion
- Château Villemaurine, Saint-Émilion
- Château Yon-Figeac, Saint-Émilion
- Clos de l'Oratoire, Saint-Émilion
- Clos des Jacobins, Saint-Émilion
- Clos La Madeleine, Saint-Émilion
- Clos Saint-Martin, Saint-Émilion
- Couvent des Jacobins, Saint-Émilion

Bordeaux's most famous wines

Bordeaux abounds with great wines and prestigious appellations. We have chosen the following order in which to present these appellations: first, the generics – those produced throughout the département *of the Gironde; then the appellations on the Left Bank of the Gironde estuary and the Garonne River; followed by those on the Right Bank; and finally, those that lie between the Dordogne and Garonne rivers (or Entre-Deux-Mers).*

BORDEAUX AOC

THE WHOLE REGION

This is the largest appellation in the Gironde: it covers the entire department (109,000 acres or 44,000 ha). It sits alongside the Atlantic Ocean, divided into two sub-regions separated by the Gironde estuary and the Garonne River. The AOC produces about 24.4 million cases (2.2 million hectolitres) of wine, mostly red, but also some dry whites. It is hard to find any common characteristics that unify these wines. They vary so much due to the different *terroirs* and the dominant grapes (Merlot or Cabernet Sauvignon). In general, they are harmonious, pleasant, and for drinking relatively young.

> **GRAPE VARIETIES** Merlot, Cabernet Franc, Cabernet Sauvignon, Malbec, and Petit Verdot for the red wines; Sémillon, Sauvignon Blanc, and Muscadelle for the white wines.

> **SOIL** Alluvial deposits, gravel, clay-and-limestone, silica-clay-sand.

> **STYLE** Along with their classic colour, the red wines present, depending on the blend, a bouquet dominated by red and dark fruit (raspberries, strawberries, blackcurrants), flowers (violets), and pepper embellished with hints of spice. The palate is well-structured, fruity, round, supple, and not very full-bodied. The whites typically have a pale golden colour with hints of green. The nose develops aromas of fruit (citrus, peach) and white flowers, underscored with occasional notes of sweet spices. In the mouth, they are supple, rounded, fruity, with some body.

Colour:
Red and white.

Serving temperature:
About 50°F (10°C) for the white wines; 59 to 61°F (15 to 16°C) for the reds.

Ageing potential:
2 to 3 years for the whites; 2 to 5 years for the reds.

BORDEAUX SUPÉRIEUR AOC

THE WHOLE REGION

Produced across the same area as Bordeaux AOC, Bordeaux Supérieur wines are subject to more stringent production conditions – with more limited yields and a maturation period of at least 12 months (increasingly in oak barrels). They also generally have a higher alcohol content. The vast majority of the appellation's production is red wine, but some sweet white wines are also produced, unlike in the standard Bordeaux appellation.

> **GRAPE VARIETIES** Merlot, Cabernet Franc, Cabernet Sauvignon, Malbec, and Petit Verdot for the red wines; Sémillon, Sauvignon Blanc, Muscadelle for the white wines, with Ugni Blanc, Merlot Blanc, and Colombard.

> **SOIL** Identical to those for Bordeaux AOC: alluvial deposits, gravel, clay-and-limestone, silica-clay-sand.

> **STYLE** The red wines are deeply coloured. The nose is more concentrated and more complex than for Bordeaux AOC, with aromas of red and dark fruit, notes of vegetation, and hints of spice and vanilla. The palate is generous, smooth, fruity, and structured, and supported by powerful, firm tannins that need a little time to soften. The finish is fruity and refreshing. The sweet white wines have a golden colour; a rich, complex nose; and a fruity palate, with a good balance of fruit, alcohol, and acidity.

Colour:
Red and white.

Serving temperature:
46 to 50°F (8 to 10°C) for the white wines; 59 to 61°F (15 to 16°C) for the reds.

Ageing potential:
3 to 5 years for the whites; 5 to 10 years for the reds.

CRÉMANT DE BORDEAUX AOC

THE WHOLE REGION

This recent appellation (1990) upholds a long-standing Bordeaux tradition and provides a regulatory framework for sparkling wines. They may be produced anywhere in the Gironde department, through the method of second fermentation in bottle. *Crémant* is mostly white (about 333,000 cases or 30,000 hl), but there is also some rosé.

> **GRAPE VARIETIES** Sémillon, Sauvignon Blanc, Muscadelle, Ugni Blanc, Colombard for white crémant; Cabernet Sauvignon, Cabernet Franc, Merlot, Malbec, and Petit Verdot for the rosé.

> **SOIL** Gravel, clay-and-limestone, silica-clay-sand, alluvial deposits.

> **STYLE** Pleasantly flavourful, Crémant de Bordeaux has a pale golden colour and fine bubbles. The nose is fresh and fruity with floral notes (white flowers) and hints of citrus and hazelnut. The palate is well-constructed, with a good balance between well-integrated acidity and flavour complexity. A generally elegant wine. Rosé crémant has a pleasant bouquet of small red berries.

Colour: *White and rosé.*

Serving temperature: *42 to 46°F (6 to 8°C).*

Ageing potential: *Drink within a year.*

BORDEAUX ROSÉ AOC

THE WHOLE REGION

This is the only regional appellation that produces exclusively rosé wines. Charming and easy to drink, there are about 2.8 million cases (260,000 hl) produced every year; and, like all rosés in France, it is very popular.

> **SOIL** Sand, gravel, clay-and-limestone, silica-clay-sand.

> **STYLE** Bordeaux rosé has a pure, clear colour – in all shades of pink. It develops delicate flavours of small red berries (strawberries) and flowers, accompanied by hints of spice. The palate is supple, well balanced between freshness and fruit, with a fine tannin structure and a long, fruity finish.

Colour: *Rosé.*

Serving temperature: *About 46°F (8°C).*

Ageing potential: *Drink within a year.*

Superior Bordeaux Supérieur!

In 2001, Dominique Méneret, a former fine wine merchant working in the 'place de Bordeaux,' bought a 156-acre (63-ha) property near Castillon, 67 acres (27 ha)of which were planted with Merlot. Since then, he has gone to great lengths to obtain expert advice, including that of Stéphane Derenoncourt. His desire is to make great wine, like the ones that he used to sell. It seems he has achieved his ambition. At the 2007 *en primeur* tastings, his Château de Courteillac delighted the American critic Robert Parker, who awarded it a score of 89–91 out of 100. Some *grands crus classés* would be very happy with such a result! Other châteaux shine in this category thanks to their superior quality and consistency of their wines, for example St-Barbe, Lauduc, La Verrière, and Penin.

BORDEAUX CLAIRET AOC

THE WHOLE REGION

Historically the first style of wine produced in Bordeaux, *clairet* is the same light red that the French were exporting to England in the Middle Ages. Due to its delicate colour the English called it 'French claret.' The name remained to describe wines with a colour somewhere between rosé and red – which is obtained by a light maceration of red grapes. This rather small appellation consists of 2,300 acres (925 ha) spread throughout the Gironde, and it produces about 355,000 cases (32,000 hl) per year.

> **GRAPE VARIETIES** Merlot (dominant), Cabernet Sauvignon, Cabernet Franc, Malbec.

> **SOIL** Sand, gravel, clay-and-limestone, silica-clay-sand.

> **STYLE** Light, fresh, and delicate, Bordeaux Clairet has a bright, pale red colour. The bouquet expresses aromas of strawberries, redcurrants, and flowers. The palate is fresh and full-bodied for a rosé highlighted by a fine tannin structure.

Colour:
Red.

Serving temperature:
42 to 46°F (6 to 8°C).

Ageing potential:
2 years.

MÉDOC AOC

LEFT BANK (MÉDOC)

In Latin, 'Médoc' means 'in the middle of the water.' And this sub-region is shaped like a peninsula, bordered to the west by the ocean and to the east by the Gironde estuary. The appellation covers 14,100 acres (5,700 ha) and benefits from an exceptional geographical location. A distinction is made between the 'Haut-Médoc' (at the south), which contains the grands *crus classés*, and the 'Bas-Médoc' (at the north end of the peninsula), which corresponds to the actual Médoc appellation. Production is large, with 38 million bottles of red wine only on average. There are no *crus classés*.

> **GRAPE VARIETIES** Cabernet Sauvignon, Merlot, Cabernet Franc, Malbec, Petit Verdot.

> **SOIL** Gravel.

> **STYLE** Appealing and balanced, Médoc wines have a deep colour and a bouquet with a fine range of aromas: dark and red fruit, notes of pepper, licorice and even, when the wine is young, a suggestion of mushrooms and undergrowth. The palate is well-structured and generous,with well-defined, delicious tannins. With age, the flavours soften with roasted, gamey notes.

Colour:
Red.

Serving temperature:
59 to 63°F (15 to 17°C).

Ageing potential:
Drink from the second year onward; it will keep 5–10 years.

Selected Médoc and Haut-Médoc producers

MÉDOC

- **Château Bournac (Civrac-en-Médoc).** Lots of class, with good capacity to age. Reliable wines for this appellation.
- **Château Fontis (Ordonnac).** Elegant, balanced, refined wines.
- **Château La Tour de By (Bégadan).** Very fine, delightfully supple wines capable of ageing for a very long time.
- **Château Les Ormes-Sorbet (Couquèques).** A deep, balanced, elegant, refined Médoc with excellent potential for ageing.

HAUT-MÉDOC

- **Château Camensac (St-Laurent-du-Médoc).** Top quality wine.
- **Château Carone Ste-Gemme (St-Laurent-du-Medoc).** Distinguished, deep, tannic wine, with great potential to improve with age.
- **Château Clément-Pichon (Parempuyre).** Very elegant, refined wine. Also, the second wine: Château de Conques.
- **Château Preuillac (Lesparre).** Excellent wine, well-structured and fruity: typical of the appellation.

HAUT-MÉDOC AOC

LEFT BANK (MÉDOC)

This appellation consists of the vineyards located at the south end of the Médoc peninsula *(see* Médoc AOC), upstream of the Garonne. It covers 11,780 acres (4,765 ha), and produces exclusively red wines (32 million bottles on average). The Haut-Médoc is where many of Bordeaux's best wines are found, including five of the 1855 classified growths. The same region contains the prestigious single-commune appellations of Pauillac, St-Julien, St-Estèphe, Margaux, Listrac, and Moulis.

> **GRAPE VARIETIES** Cabernet Sauvignon, Merlot, Cabernet Franc, Malbec, Petit Vefrdot.

> **SOIL** Gravel, clay, and limestone.

> **STYLE** The wines are more full-bodied than those of Médoc AOC. Deep red garnet in colour, the wines of the Haut-Médoc develop a delightful bouquet expressing ripe red fruit, dark fruit (blackcurrants), hints of sweet spices, vanilla, and roasted notes. The palate is full-bodied and generous with all the same characters as the nose, supported by a fine tannin structure, and a long finish.

Colour: *Red.*

Serving temperature: *62 to 64°F (17 to 18°C).*

Ageing potential: *7 to 16 years.*

ST-ESTÈPHE AOC

LEFT BANK (MÉDOC)

St-Estèphe is the northernmost of the six Médoc appellations. The vineyards were planted during the Roman conquest and are located around the commune of the same name, forming an enclave with Pauillac to the south and the Haut-Médoc wrapping around. The appellation covers about 3,000 acres (1,200 ha) and produces 778,000 cases (70,000 hl) of earthy, austere, robust wines (exclusively red). The St-Estèphe appellation contains five of the 1855 classified growths.

> **GRAPE VARIETIES** Cabernet Sauvignon, Merlot, Cabernet Franc.

> **SOIL** Clay-gravel.

> **STYLE** Virile, powerful, and well-structured, the wines of St-Estèphe have a concentrated colour and a bouquet, when young, that expresses aromas of lilies, red and dark fruit, sweet spices, and violets. With age, there are tertiary notes of game and undergrowth. The palate is harmonious, powerful, and well-structured with fine, closely textured, distinguished tannins that need time to soften; the finish is very fresh and distinctive. This is an excellent wine for laying down.

Colour: *Red.*

Serving temperature: *62 to 64°F (16 to 18°C).*

Ageing potential: *15 to 25 years, or more for certain grands crus.*

ST-JULIEN AOC

LEFT BANK (MÉDOC)

Located between Pauillac and Margaux, St-Julien is the smallest appellation in the Médoc (2,273 acres or 920 ha), but it is one of the most prestigious in terms of its châteaux. The vineyards, which cover the communes of St-Julien and Beychevelle, produce about 511,000 cases (46,000 hl) of exclusively red wine. The appellation contains 11 classified growths, which include five second growths. The style of the wines varies considerably depending on the château, but with one common characteristic: the wines are all powerful and concentrated.

> **GRAPE VARIETIES** Cabernet Sauvignon, Merlot, Cabernet Franc.

> **SOIL** Gravel, marl, pebbles.

> **STYLE** The wines are potent, harmonious, and refined, with a typically dense, dark purple colour. The delicate bouquet offers distinctive aromas of dark fruit (blueberry, blackcurrant, blackberry) with notes of plum, licorice, tobacco, a slight smokiness, and a hint of game. The palate is full-bodied, rich, beautifully structured, balanced, and sappy, supported by fine tannins that are close-knit, yet velvety and elegant. The finish is long, spicy, and fruity.

Colour: *Red.*

Serving temperature: *62 to 64°F (16 to 18°C).*

Ageing potential: *15 to 25 years, or more for certain grands crus.*

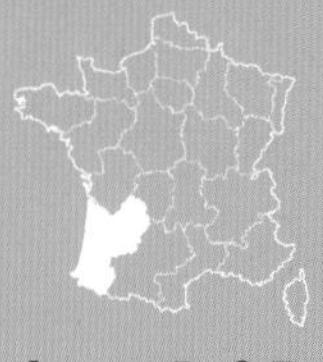

Bordeaux, Left Bank

CHÂTEAU *HAUT-BRION*

If Haut-Brion has anything to thank for a reputation that goes back several centuries, it is principally its location atop two exceptional gravel hillsides, looking out over a maze of streams and rivulets; documents from the Middle Ages attest that its value has been recognized since ancient times.

> Jean-Philippe Delmas an
Prince Robert of Luxembou

CHÂTEAU HAUT-BRION

135, avenue Jean-Jaurès
33608 Pessac Cedex

Area: *133 acres (54 ha)*
Production: *153,000 bottles p.a.*
Appellation: *Pessac-Léognan*
Red grape varieties: *Cabernet Sauvignon, Merlot, Cabernet Franc, Petit Verdot*
White grape varieties: *Sémillon, Sauvignon Blanc*

The doyen of Bordeaux

Jean de Pontac, a leading light in the Bordeaux parliament, acquired the estate through marriage in 1525 and was the first to give it the full attention it deserved. He patiently extended the vineyards and in 1549 built the château that is featured on modern labels. A cellar ledger from 1660 attests that its wine was served at the table of the king of England, and the château was the first to appear under its own estate name ('Ho-Bryen', in its English version), as noted by an English writer of the period. Haut-Brion passed from family to family – always by marriage – until the French Revolution, and Thomas Jefferson, the future president of the United States, recommended it to relatives and friends in America in 1787. Talleyrand, Napoleon's Minister of Foreign Affairs and the owner of the estate between 1801 and 1804, served its finest wines to his royal guests.

1855 and the exception made for Haut-Brion

The estate then passed through several hands before becoming the property of Joseph-Eugène Larrieu, a Parisian banker, under whose ownership it flourished. In 1855, it was the only château in the Graves region to retain its classification, ranking with the *premier cru*, furthermore, of the big names of the Médoc (Margaux, Lafite Rothschild, and Latour). Three generations were to follow, replanting the vineyards, modernizing the cellars, and refining the wine-making techniques, before another period of uncertainty between the wars. It was at this point that Clarence Dillon, a Francophile American banker, bought up Château Haut-Brion, devoting part of his wealth to it and saving it from being divided up, as eventually happened to a number of its neighbours. The vineyards now stand at Pessac, less than 1.25 miles (2 km) from the heart of Bordeaux, whose urban climate encourages early ripening of the grapes.

The Dillon family

The Dillon family made it a point of honour to plough all the profits back into the wine-making company and entrusted generations of the Delmas family to run the vineyards, with Jean-Bernard Delmas taking over from his father in 1961 for the 'vintage of the century,' a special vintage to commemorate a centenary of production. He then found himself entrusted with managing the entire estate in 1975 when Joan Dillon, Duchesse de Mouchy and Clarence's granddaughter, took over responsibility for the company, and this meticulous and passionate duo took Haut-Brion to new heights of excellence. Their 1989 vintage is a legendary wine, and both the 2000 and the 2010 followed in its footsteps. Prince Robert of Luxembourg (Joan Dillon's oldest son, from her marriage to Prince Charles of Luxembourg) and Jean-Philippe Delmas, now hold the reins as they have done for the last 12 years.

This smooth succession only reinforced the impressive uniformity of this *premier cru classé*; there are no 'junior' wines at Haut-Brion. The estate sticks rigidly to several essential principles applied unfailingly to the vines, of which just under half are Merlot, with 40% Cabernet Sauvignon, 10% Cabernet Franc, and 1% Petit Verdot. Much of this is down to Delmas the elder, who opted for short fermentation periods and long, slow maturation – Haut-Brion is often the last of the *grands crus* to bottle a particular year's wine. Above all, he conducted research and carried out sophisticated experiments to select the best clones, and for 30 years has advocated a clear reduction in yields, based on limiting the number of clusters per plant and rigorous selection during the grape harvest. He thus began to set aside a not insignificant portion of the harvest, making it possible both to tighten the focus on the *grand vin* and to bring out a celebrated second wine, Le Clarence de Haut-Brion. The Dillon estates now produce a remarkable range of *grands crus* and, more than 30 years ago, bought up La Mission Haut-Brion, their neighbours and only real competitors in the area. In addition, they make small quantities of a dry white wine with the best reputation in Bordeaux; it is based on Sémillon and Sauvignon grapes but made in an opulent, rich, and unctuous style with a minerality slightly reminiscent of the best Burgundies.

CHÂTEAU HAUT-BRION, PREMIER GRAND CRU CLASSÉ, PESSAC-LÉOGNAN

The most outstanding Château Haut-Brion wines make a striking impression, with aromatic intensity that evolves into silky strength. Their great complexity, combining a succession of black fruit, cherries, and tobacco with an oaky or roast coffee finish, is astonishingly drawn out with a beautiful freshness, a hint of minerality, soft, flavoursome tannins, and a bewitching smoky note, the calling card of the best wines from Pessac-Léognan. For many wine-lovers, Haut-Brion is the epitome of elegance among the greatest of the *grands crus*, whose seductive charm, lying deep in the heart of the wine, is as irresistible as it is profound.

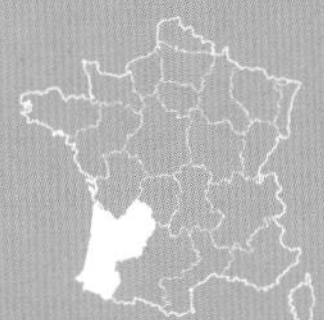

Bordeaux, Left Bank

CHÂTEAU *MARGAUX*

The history, reputation, architecture, and incomparable charm of the wines of Château Margaux all combine to make this Médoc institution the epitome of Bordeaux prestige and elegance.

CHÂTEAU MARGAUX

33460 Margaux

Area: *232 acres (94 ha)*
Production: *400,000 bottles p.a.*
Appellation: *Margaux*
Red grape varieties: *Cabernet Sauvignon, Merlot, Cabernet Franc, Petit Verdot*
White grape variety: *Sauvignon Blanc*

The silky nectar of the Médoc

It is the most famous of the Médoc *premiers crus*, and has been called 'the most feminine' – is it really all about seduction? 'Margaux' was the name given by the great Ernest Hemingway to his beautiful and statuesque granddaughter, who became a model and an actress. As with the beauty of an exquisite woman, there is no mistaking the grace of this *premier cru*. Its best years exhibit a perfect harmony between all the ingredients, beginning with the incomparable mellowness of its tannins. It comes from a terroir known as La Mothe de Margaux, which looks out from gentle hills over the surrounding countryside of the Gironde below and has been known for centuries for the great wines it produces. The estate acquired its current location and dimensions at the end of the 16th century through the ministrations of Pierre de Lestonnac, and is noted for its fine, deep, gravelly soil, laid down millennia ago.

The birth of Margaux

The first to discover the unequalled quality of the wines produced here was an estate manager named Berlon at the beginning of the 17th century, who separated growths of white and red grapes and identified the best plots of land – and Margaux was born. Under the name 'Margose', by the 18th century it had already become one of the great Bordeaux wines on sale to rich wine-lovers in London, and is featured in a Christie's sale catalogue from 1771. Thomas Jefferson, the future president of the United States and American ambassador to France at the time, ordered bottles of the 1784 and, having tasted it, wrote that it 'was not possible to find a better bottle in Bordeaux'. After the upheaval of the French Revolution, Margaux became the property of Bertrand Douat, Marquis de la Colonilla, a Basque entrepreneur who had acquired his title and fortune in Spain. At the turn of the 19th century, he had the old fort torn down, the moat filled in, and a new château built in a neo-Palladian style with an imposing colonnade, designed by the architect Louis Combes. The banker Alexandre Aguedo, who followed him in 1830, helped Margaux takes its place among the five *premiers crus* in the 1855 classification; and in 1879 its new owner, the Count of Pillet-Will, took it to still greater heights, notably creating the 'Pavillon Rouge' (the precursor to its second wines) and helping the vineyard to recover after phylloxera, aided by the Grangerous, a father-and-son team of cellar masters.

The standard-bearer for the appellation

The Margaux appellation, named for the local area and the château, was created in 1954. It was inspired by the excellence the wine had epitomized over the centuries and immediately became one of the beacon vineyards of the Médoc; but the economic crisis of the 1970s forced the Ginestets, a family of Bordeaux merchants, to part company with an estate that was then in decline. The astronomical price did not deter André Mentzelopoulos, a Greek émigré, founder of the Félix Potin grocery group, and a pioneer of supermarket chains; following the advice of Émile Peynaud, the renowned oenologist, he organized the restoration of Margaux and went on to expand the estate considerably. Although he was to die only three years later, his daughter Corinne took up the reins and was fortunate enough to recruit Paul Pontallier, who arrived in 1983 and was appointed general manager seven years later. Through a combination of rigour and inspiration, this two-person team took the estate to its pinnacle. Legendary vintage followed legendary vintage: 1982, 1986, 1990, 1996, 2000, 2005, 2009, 2010.... These wines were the result of merciless grape selection, with barely 40% of the harvest chosen to make the *grand vin*. Of these, 90% are in turn taken from the best Cabernet Sauvignon vineyards, which are planted on fine or medium gravelly soils with a rise of 32 feet (10m). Merlot, which covers a fifth of the estate, is used more for the Pavillon Rouge, which has recently had the benefit of more stringent grape selection. The 30 acres (12 ha) of Sauvignon Blanc are used to make the 'Pavillon Blanc', which is labelled as a Bordeaux supérieur and reputed to be the best white wine in the Médoc.

CHÂTEAU MARGAUX, PREMIER GRAND CRU CLASSÉ, MARGAUX

Its ruby-red appearance is shot through with purple and its nose, of incomparable richness, is bursting with red fruit, white flowers, licorice, and toasted aromas. This well-structured wine develops in stages in the mouth, with integrity, purity, opulence, and extraordinary length. On the subject of the 2000 vintage, to which he gave the highest possible marks, Robert Parker concluded that 'it communicates its terroir perfectly, embodying a perfect alliance of strength and elegance'. The smoothness of its tannins and the purity of its fruit, coming from Cabernet Sauvignon grapes harvested at perfect ripeness, turn it into a wine that can almost be appreciated in its youth, but truly gives up its secrets in its maturity, with exceptional aromatic refinement, a silky texture, and infinite length...

> Owner and manager Corinne Mentzelopoulos.

PAULLAC AOC

LEFT BANK (MÉDOC)

Pauillac is the wine capital of the Médoc; it has excellent soil, a superb climate, and centuries-old expertise in winemaking, uniting truly exceptional conditions for the production of extremely fine wines. Furthermore, it is home to three of the five 1855 first growths (*premiers grands crus classés*) – Lafite, Latour, and Mouton – along with a plethora of other wines. Perched on superb gravel hilltops, the vineyards stretch over 3,007 acres (1,217 ha) and produce 716,000 cases (64,500 hl) of exclusively red wine, with very few exceptions (such as Mouton-Rothschild, which also makes a white wine). The red wines vary enormously, ranging from the austerity of Château Latour to the suppleness of Château Lafite-Rothschild.

> **GRAPE VARIETIES** Cabernet Sauvignon (dominant), Merlot, Petit Verdot, Malbec.

> **SOIL** Gravelly hilltops.

> **STYLE** Rich, dense, and profound, the wines of Pauillac have a deep ruby colour. The bouquet is delicate, elegant, and complex, evoking dark fruit (Morello cherries, blackcurrants) and flowers (roses, irises), mixed with roasted notes and hints of cedar, smoke, leather, and incense. The rich, full-bodied, smooth palate is highlighted by a fine framework of powerful, tight tannins that need time to soften. The finish is long, with lots of fruit. These wines have an exceptional capacity to improve with age; you somehow just have to manage to wait for them.

Colour: *Red.*

Serving temperature: *61 to 64°F (16 to 18°C).*

Ageing potential: *15 to 25 years, or more for some grands crus.*

Château Cordeillan-Bages

The name of this Pauillac estate may not ring any bells. However, the château's restaurant is run by Michelin-starred chef Jean-Luc Rocha. The wine is a match for such great cuisine: an opulent Cabernet Sauvignon (80 per cent) grown and produced by Château Lynch-Bages, a fifth growth. This magnificent wine has a beautiful, dark red colour and a delicate, complex bouquet that offers a delightful combination of ripe fruit and hints of spice (vanilla, cinnamon) with toasted notes. The full-bodied, smooth palate is supported by delicious, refined tannins. Complex, powerful, and distinguished, this is a wine that ages very well.

LISTRAC-MÉDOC AOC

LEFT BANK (MÉDOC)

Initially famous during the 18th century, the commune of Listrac became popular again in the early 20th century. In 1913, it was one of the largest wine-producing communes of the Médoc peninsula, with 3,410 acres (1,380 ha) of vines. However, all of this changed during the economic crisis of the 1930s. In 1957, Listrac was granted AOC status and became one of the six single commune appellations of the Médoc. Spread across three terraces on the edge of the Haut-Médoc, the vineyards (1,399 acres or 566 ha) are protected from the prevailing winds by a vast pine forest, enabling slow and steady ripening of the grapes. It produces about 420,000 cases (37,580 hl) of exclusively red wine.

> **GRAPE VARIETIES** Merlot (dominant), Cabernet Sauvignon, Cabernet Franc, Petit Verdot.

> **SOIL** Gravel, clay-and-limestone.

> **STYLE** Listrac-Médoc has a dark colour with hints of deep purple. The nose is intense, with aromas of red fruit, balsamic notes, and hints of spice with vanilla and toast. The palate is powerful and harmonious – with good volume and fine, powerful tannins that, over time, soften to yield a generous, elegant wine.

Colour: *Red.*

Serving temperature: *62 to 64°F (16 to 18°C).*

Ageing potential: *8 to 12 years.*

Listrac – a touch of white in the heart of Médoc

- **Listrac** This small appellation in the north of Médoc is undergoing a renaissance. Less well known than some, its red wines include a significant amount of Merlot and are increasingly smooth and elegant, offering exceptionally good value for money. Following the example set by its leading producer, Château Clarke, several other châteaux have embraced the idea of reviving small-scale production of white wines, something for which it was renowned in the 19th century.
- **Château Clarke (Rothschild family)** The key producer in the appellation. It owes its revival to Baron Edmond de Rothschild, who bought it in 1973 and completely modernized its operations with the help of oenologist Michel Rolland. After the death of the baron, who so loved the property that he asked to be buried there, his son Benjamin took over. The wines produced by its talented technical director, Yann Buchwalter, fulfill all ambitions: they are powerful and elegant, with good potential for ageing. The château also continues to produce a high-quality white wine, Le Merle Blanc, vinified in barrels, from a 7.5 acre (3 ha) plot planted with Sauvignon Blanc, Sémillon, and Muscadelle. Other highly recommended producers of the appellation have followed their lead, including Château Fonreaud and Château Saransot-Dupré, and more recently Château Fourcas Dupré, Château Fourcas Hosten, and Château Lestage.

MOULIS-EN-MÉDOC AOC

LEFT BANK (MÉDOC)

In existence since the 13th century, Moulis covers 1,507 acres (610 ha) and produces 386,000 cases (34,750 hl) of wine. It owes its name to the numerous windmills (*moulins*) that used to exist in the commune. The appellation stretches away from the Gironde, to the west of Margaux, along a narrow strip 7.5 miles (12 km) long. Now sheltered from winds by a pine forest, the microclimate is well suited to ripening grapes. It produces exclusively red wines and contains no classified growths.

> **GRAPE VARIETIES** Cabernet Sauvignon, Merlot.
> **SOIL** Gravel, alluvial deposits, limestone.
> **STYLE** Refined, powerful, and complex, the wines of Moulis have a deep ruby colour with dark glints. The fine, rich bouquet presents aromas of stewed and ripe red fruit mixed with notes of toast, licorice, and hints of violet, humus, and undergrowth. The palate is harmonious and elegant, with plump, silky tannins.

Colour: *Red.*

Serving temperature: *61 to 63°F (16 to 17°C).*

Ageing potential: *5 to 15 years.*

MARGAUX AOC

LEFT BANK (MÉDOC)

Château Margaux, the legendary first growth, is famous all over the world. However, the Margaux appellation has many other very fine châteaux, with a total of 21 in the 1855 classification. The vineyards enjoy very favourable conditions for the ripening of grapes: good soil, excellent natural drainage, and proximity to the Gironde estuary. The appellation lies at the south end of the Médoc, encompassing 3,677 acres (1,488 ha) and five communes: Margaux, Cantenac, Labarde, Soussans, and Arsac. The appellation produces about 867,000 cases (78,000 hl) of exclusively red wine, with the exception of Château Margaux's white wine, Pavillon Blanc.

> **GRAPE VARIETIES** Cabernet Sauvignon, Merlot, Cabernet Franc, Malbec, Petit Verdot.
> **SOIL** Gravel hilltops.
> **STYLE** Refined and elegant, the wines of Margaux have a dense ruby colour that becomes tinged with garnet as they mature. The very delicate, complex nose is full of finesse – with aromas of red and dark fruit, flowers mixed with roasted notes, wood, truffle, and vanilla, underscored with hints of tobacco, violets, cinnamon, and prunes. With age, they evolve into aromas of undergrowth and mushrooms. The palate is harmonious and full-bodied, supported by finely textured, delicate, delicious tannins. The finish continues with total harmony and elegance.

Colour: *Red.*

Serving temperature: *61 to 63°F (16 to 17°C); decanting is essential.*

Ageing potential: *Drink from the third year onward, up to 20 years.*

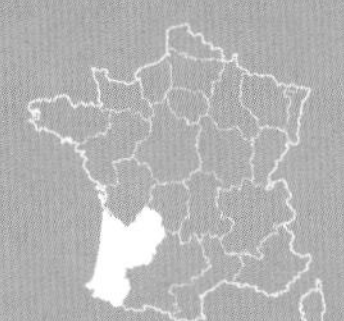

Bordeaux, Left Bank

CHÂTEAU *D'YQUEM*

The miracle has repeated itself almost every year since the 18th century: from rotten grapes fertilized with horse dung, the people of Yquem conjure a golden wine of refulgent intensity, with never-ending flavour. The product of patience and rigour, a wealth of experience accumulated over generations and traditions kept alive over years, this is considered the greatest sweet wine in the world. What's more, it tastes better after 25, 50, or even 100 years in bottle.

CHÂTEAU D'YQUEM

33210 Sauternes

Area: *247 acres (100 ha)*
Production: *100,000 bottles p.a.*
Appellation: *Sauternes*
White grape varieties: *Sémillon, Sauvignon Blanc*

A beneficial fungus

The wine-growers' greatest ally here is *Botrytis cinerea*, a fungus that attacks the grapes. Elsewhere, it can often appear as an enemy of wine-making, but in Sauternes, where it has become a friend to viticulture, it is known as 'noble rot.' It attacks the skins of the individual Sémillon grapes, Sauternes' greatest variety, withering them and concentrating the juices and the sugar as it develops its fabulous aromas. In Yquem, perhaps more than on any other estate, *botrytis* has chanced upon conditions that are ideal for accomplishing this miracle of nature: the clay limestone soil is as suitable for it as the location of the vines – the top of a hill, at whose feet flows the Ciron. As autumn comes, the river envelops the vines with its morning mists, promoting the growth of the *botrytis* fungus, before the water vapour is dissipated by sun and wind, encouraging the grapes towards extra maturity. The harvesters make numerous passes through the vines, picking only bunches – indeed, even individual grapes – that have been properly infected with noble rot. These selections, which can be repeated six to ten times, are known in French as '*tres*' and can extend into December.

The labours of the Lur-Saluces

It took the local people some time to appreciate the 'nobility' of *botrytis*. The château, now listed as a historic monument, was built in the 16th century by the Sauvages, a prominent Bordeaux family. At the time, the lords of the Yquem estate were making a mellow white wine that was not so intensely sweet, and it was not until the 18th century that they began to harvest rotten grapes to produce juice that was rich and complex, with an incredible potential for laying down. It captivated Thomas Jefferson, the ambassador and future president of the newly founded United States of America, who sang its praises in his own country. Françoise-Joséphine Sauvage d'Yquem, the wife – and soon to be widow – of Louis-Amédée de Lur-Saluces, managed the estate for the entire first half of the 19th century, making constant improvements throughout the period. In 1855, it was the only Sauternes wine to be classified *premier cru supérieur*. The Marquises de Lur-Saluces were to continue to look after the estate assiduously for a century and a half, increasing the planted area to 320 acres (130 ha), with 80% Sémillon and 20% Sauvignon, and with about 100 in active production, and installing 62 miles (100 km) of irrigation canals to drain it. The furrows were maintained with a draught horse whose dung was used as fertilizer.

CHÂTEAU D'YQUEM, PREMIER CRU SUPÉRIEUR, SAUTERNES

Tasting a glass of Château d'Yquem is a fantastic experience, whatever the vintage. Over the course of decades, the wine passes from a pale gold to amber, gaining in richness over time without ever losing its unique balance, in which softness, strength and freshness dance a thrilling waltz without a trace of heaviness or a wrong note. As it slowly breathes, the wine offers new aromas and surprising flavours every time it is revisited – you will notice complex and subtle fruity notes, such as orange marmalade, apricot jam, roasted pineapple, and the like. The French expression *faire la queue de paon* ('to make a peacock's tail'), which describes how the rich sensations of a flavour spread across and intoxicate your whole palate, could have been invented for it. And the older it becomes, the more subtle it is – which cannot be said of everyone….

Rigorous grape selection

The yield was just over half a ton per acre (10 hl/ha). Alexandre, the last of the Lur-Saluces to manage Yquem and who perfected it, said that 'each vine stock produces a single glass of wine.' The grape selection process was merciless and there have even been years without an Yquem, such as 1992 and 2012, as the wine produced was judged too average to bear the name. In the cellar, its excellence is a matter of patience: the grapes selected are subject to a series of precise pressings and the juice is vinified in barrels with infinite care, then aged for three years before blending and racking.

Château d'Yquem came into the hands of Bernard Arnaud at the end of the last century, and the boss of LVMH made some changes: he astutely entrusted management of the estate to Pierre Lurton, who was also running Château Cheval Blanc in Saint-Émilion. It is humbling to encounter a wine that is capable of improving for 50 years and still be dazzling at the end of a century.

> Vines growing at Château Larrivet Haut-Brion, in the appellation of Pessac-Léognan.

PESSAC-LÉOGNAN AOC

LEFT BANK (GRAVES)

This appellation was created when the AOC of Graves was divided in 1987. The *Graves de Bordeaux* region has long been known for its superb vineyards, concentrated in two main areas: Pessac and Léognan. Located on the southern and southwestern outskirts of Bordeaux, the appellation covers 10 communes (Cadaujac, Canéjan, Gradignan, Léognan, Martillac, Mérignac, Pessac, Saint-Médard-d'Eyrans, Talence, and Villenave d'Ornon), and contains all of the Graves *grands crus classés*, including the legendary Château Haut-Brion. It mainly produces red wines (3,200 acres or 1,300 ha, yielding 744,000 cases or 67,000 hl), with some dry white wines (655 acres or 265 ha, yielding 167,000 cases or 15,000 hl).

> **GRAPE VARIETIES** Merlot, Cabernet Sauvignon, Cabernet Franc, Malbec, and Petit Verdot for the red wines; Sauvignon Blanc (at least 25 per cent), Sémillon, and Muscadelle for the white wines.

> **SOIL** Gravel, rounded pebbles.

> **STYLE** Rich and elegant, the reds have a cherry colour tinged with black. The nose develops intense aromas of very ripe red fruit and flowers (violets), underscored by mingling notes of toasted almonds, resin, and smoke. The palate is full-bodied and well-structured, with closely knit tannins and a long, fruity finish with hints of licorice. The dry whites are a light golden colour that deepens with age. The intense, complex nose exudes aromas of stone fruit (peaches, nectarines), citrus, and flowers, with hints of hazelnut and beeswax. The palate balances acidity and fruit with smoothness and strength. The lingering finish returns to all the flavours of the bouquet.

Colour: *Red and white.*

Serving temperature: *46 to 50°F (8 to 10°C) for the white wines; 61 to 63°F (16 to 17°C) for the reds (which may require decanting).*

Ageing potential: *3 to 8 years for the white wines; 10 to 15 years for the red wines.*

Château de France

This château's buildings date from the 17th century and are part of the history of Bordeaux. Château de France – developed in turn by Taffard, a member of the Guyenne parliament, and then Jean-Henri Lacoste, a fabric merchant – was acquired by Bernard Thomassin in 1971, who elevated it to new heights. Advised by Michel Rolland and currently managed by Arnaud Thomassin, Château de France is a member of the Union des Grands Crus de Bordeaux and produces red wines made primarily from Cabernet Sauvignon (60 per cent) and Merlot (40 per cent) – called Château de France, Château Coquillas, and Le Bec en Sabot – as well as whites made from Sauvignon Blanc, namely Château de France and Château Coquillas. Its wines are among the best in the Pessac-Léognan appellation.

GRAVES AOC

LEFT BANK (GRAVES)

Graves is the only appellation in France to be named after a type of soil: *graves de Bordeaux* (Bordeaux gravel). The vineyards, located along the left bank of the Garonne, to the south of Bordeaux, cover 8,649 acres (3,500 ha) in a 30-mile long (50-km) strip. As a result, they are very diverse. Production is largely red wines, with less than a third devoted to fine white wines, both sweet and dry. The sweet white wines are sold under the Graves Supérieur appellation.

> **GRAPE VARIETIES** Merlot (dominant), Cabernet Sauvignon, Cabernet Franc for the reds; Sauvignon Blanc, Sémillon, and Muscadelle for the whites.

> **SOIL** Gravel.

> **STYLE** Elegant and sensual, the red wines have a deep garnet colour. The nose is fragrant and complex, combining aromas of red and dark fruit, floral notes, hints of spice and vanilla, and roasted, smoked notes. The palate is well-structured, with a long, generous finish. With age, these wines develop richness and complex flavours. The dry white wines are fresh with an attractive, bright, gold-green colour. The nose is refreshing with aromas of white fruit, citrus, floral notes, and hints of spice and beeswax. The palate balances acidity with smoothness and richness. The finish lingers with fruit, freshness, and warmth. Deep yellow in colour, the sweet white wines have a very aromatic nose (white fruit, citrus, notes of acacia); the palate is generous and structured, with a long fruity finish.

Colour: *Red and white.*

Serving temperature: *46 to 50°F (8 to 10°C) for the dry and the sweet white wines; 61 to 63°F (16 to 17°C) for the reds.*

Ageing potential: *2 to 3 years for the dry white wines; 5 to 10 years for the sweet white wines; up to 8 years for the reds.*

The Women of Graves

In 1991, the *Syndicat des Graves* was the first union of wine producers in France to elect a woman, Françoise Lévêque, as its president. She remained president until 1997. Today, quite a number of wines in the Graves region are made by women. After pursuing very different paths – some were born into winemaking families, others come from various backgrounds – they are all passionate about producing their wines with a feminine touch. Though they refuse to say that these are 'wines made by women'. We cannot list them all, so here is a small selection.

- **Catherine Gachet, Château La Tour des Remparts (Preignac).** Superb Graves.
- **Isabelle Labarthe, Château d'Arricaud (Landiras).** Lively, fruity wines.
- **Marie-Hélène Yung-Théron, Château de Portets (Portets).** Good success with two colours of wines.
- **Catherine Martin-Larrue, Château Haut-Pommarède (Portets).** Very personal red Graves of excellent quality.

CÉRONS AOC

LEFT BANK (SAUTERNES REGION)

Northwest of Barsac, Cérons is named after the Ciron river, which runs through it and which is responsible for the nocturnal mists that help the development of *Botrytis cinerea*. With only 94 acres (38 ha) producing 14,400 cases (1,300 hl), this sweet white wine is not widely available. It has the distinction of being either *moelleux* or *liquoreux* (the latter has a higher level of residual sugar) depending on the year and weather conditions.

> **GRAPE VARIETIES** Sémillon (dominant), Sauvignon Blanc, Muscadelle.

> **SOIL** Gravel, sand, limestone.

> **STYLE** Golden in colour, the wines present an intense bouquet with aromas of fruit (citrus, exotic, and crystallized) as well as hints of honey, caramel, vanilla, and acacia flowers. The palate is very fragrant, full-bodied, smooth, and voluptuous, with a remarkably long, aromatic finish.

Colour: *White.*

Serving temperature: *About 46°F (8°C).*

Ageing potential: *10 years or more.*

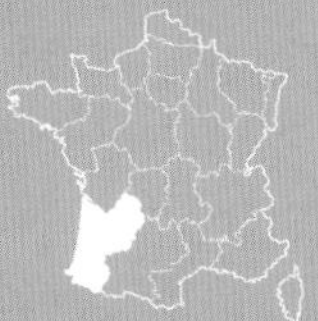

Bordeaux,
Left Bank

LÉOVILLE BARTON AND *LANGOA BARTON*

Hailing originally from Ireland, the Barton family established itself in Bordeaux centuries ago, acquiring the pretty Léoville château and beautiful Langoa estate, to which they added their family's name, nearly 200 years ago.

CHÂTEAU LÉOVILLE BARTON

33250 Saint-Julien

Area: *126 acres (51 ha)*
Production: *200,000 bottles p.a.*
Appellation: *Saint-Julien*
Red grape varieties: *Cabernet Sauvignon, Merlot, Cabernet Franc*

CHÂTEAU LANGOA BARTON

33250 Saint-Julien

Area: *42 acres (17 ha)*
Production: *80,000 bottles p.a.*
Appellation: *Saint-Julien*
Red grape varieties: *Cabernet Sauvignon, Merlot, Cabernet Franc*

Guardians of tradition

Over time (and despite the vagaries of history, economic upheaval, and disputes over succession), Langoa Barton has become the Bordeaux wine-making estate that has been owned longest by the same family – a rare example of enduring affection and loyalty. This has also influenced the choices made by successive generations of Bartons in running their estate. They have always favoured the classic model of Médoc *grands crus*, which helped them stand out in the famous 1855 classification and brought them the prestigious rating of *deuxième cru* ('second growth'), just behind the three first growths. They have thus retained a large preponderance of Cabernet Sauvignon grapes among their vines, not giving in to the fashion for Merlot, and have continued to produce wines that are tannic, dense, rich, and deep, matured slowly in barrels and likely to improve after being laid down for a long time.

Accessible excellence

The family stayed true to these principles when it purchased a large parcel of Léoville land, which has since been shared between Léoville Barton, Léoville Las Cases, and Léoville Poyferré. Under the enlightened, sincere, and enthusiastic management since 1985 of Anthony Barton (who is now aided by his daughter Lilian), the first of these has become one of the greatest *grands vins* of its appellation and of the Médoc in general, regularly aspiring to the standards of the *premiers crus* while remaining at a relatively reasonable price point compared to its peers – a Bordeaux bargain for oenophiles in search of very great wines.

Sovereign elegance

The vineyards at Léoville Barton cover 126 acres (51 ha) and are made up of 72% Cabernet Sauvignon, 20% Merlot, and 8% Cabernet Franc. Maturation is carried out in the traditional manner over 18 to 20 months, in barrels of which half are renewed each year. The fantastic success enjoyed by the wines of recent years is due to the fact that, thanks to their age and incredibly careful management, the vines have achieved a fantastic balance, with the grapes reaching the picking stage when they are perfectly ripe and concentrated, and Anthony Barton has had the skill to adapt and refine his wine-making methods to extract their very essence. This painstaking task is made possible through patience and the quality of the maturation process, with the result that Léoville Barton has a bouquet of rare complexity and great subtlety. It has plenty of strength and body in the mouth without ever losing touch with its sovereign elegance. Langoa Barton, a vineyard of only 42 acres (17 ha), has raised itself practically to the same heights as its neighbour, but with none of the concentration, and less richness. Anthony Barton nonetheless devotes the same care to it and has made it just as great a success.

CHÂTEAU LÉOVILLE BARTON, CRU CLASSÉ, SAINT-JULIEN

With its inky appearance of deepest purple, Léoville Barton reveals itself to be packed full of aromas, density, and appeal from the very outset, with a texture that is mature and creamy. Temptation must be resisted, however, and the wine should be allowed to mature sumptuously as it ages; it will then bloom and show its grandiose side, with fruits, spices, and its characteristic aromas of cedar, crowned with the charm of a Saint and the strength of a Pauillac – Langoa Barton is entirely in the same tradition, although it may sometimes come off slightly worse in the inevitable comparison.

> Anthony Barton.

Bordeaux, Left Bank

DOMAINE *DE CHEVALIER*

Like very few others in Bordeaux, Domaine de Chevalier – never classified as a château – located on the edges of the Landes forest in the Graves region produces excellent wine of both colours.

DOMAINE DE CHEVALIER

102, chemin Mignoy 33850 Léognan

Area: *111 acres (45 ha)*
Production: *120,000 bottles p.a.*
Appellation: *Pessac-Léognan*
White grape varieties: *Sauvignon Blanc, Sémillon*
Red grape varieties: *Cabernet Sauvignon, Merlot, Petit Verdot, Cabernet Franc*

A sense of moderation

The Graves region stretches out south of Bordeaux, tucked in between the Garonne and the Landes forest. Uniquely in Bordeaux, its name is derived from its gravelly soils, made up of rock granules, gravel chips, and pebbles deposited by the river during its long geological history. The deposits in these gravelly hillsides, with their beneficial properties for vine stock (improved drainage and weather resistance), are particularly deep in the northern part of the region, which has enjoyed its own appellation since 1987: Pessac-Léognan. Its name comes from two of the local communities: the commune of Pessac, and Léognan, which is out in the country and whose estates are more or less carved out of the Landes forest. The Domaine de Chevalier is just such a one; planted along the edge of the pine forest, the estate cultivates vines, a sense of moderation, and good taste in equal measure – both of its low, white stone buildings, whose sober architecture melts into the countryside, and of its wines, an archetypical version of Bordeaux elegance. The wine-making aspirations of this estate, originally known by its Gascon name of Chivaley ('Chevalier'), first saw the light of day in the mid-19th century and there have been only three owners since then: Jean Ricard, with whom it all began; Claude Ricard, who won the estate its first honours, including the title of 'classified growth' in 1953; and Olivier Bernard, the incumbent since 1983, who has lifted the estate to the very pinnacle of the appellation. This last – and energetic – owner has turned the estate (which is also his home) into a place cut from the same cloth as himself, at once convivial and refined. Over the last 30 years he has reimagined the estate, investing great sums and endowing it with the powerful new tool of a cellar that is as spectacular as it is functional, to complement the regenerated (largely replanted) vineyards, which are serenely approaching maturity.

Haute couture wines

While there may be something to the old saying that there are no *grands vins* without great terroir, the ground still has to be understood and properly tended. At the Domaine de Chevalier, you need only stroll around the vineyards, which are tended like a garden, to be aware of the obsessive care that is lavished on the vines. The closeness of the forest is just a part of the surroundings, creating an enclosed space that accentuates the effects of the climate as it heats and cools. While spring frosts are to be feared, a smaller crop may ripen more easily. The 111 acres (45 ha) of vineyards are arranged contiguously around the buildings, with 99 acres (40 ha) planted with red grapes and 5 acres (2 ha) with white, all rooted in the same thin soil of black sand and fine white gravel on a clay limestone base with ideal drainage. With meticulous harvests, stringent grape selection, high-precision vinification, sophisticated maturation techniques, and star consultants (the likes of Denis Dubourdieu and Stéphane Derenoncourt), Olivier Bernard has allowed himself every means at his disposal to maintain the exceptional standards of both colours of wine. While the estate's name may have been made with its small output of white wines, whose fullness and refinement are matched by very few, its red wines, which age with a grace and charm entirely typical of Bordeaux, are absolutely up to the mark.

DOMAINE DE CHEVALIER RED, CRU CLASSÉ, PESSAC-LÉOGNAN

The estate's *grand vin* is matured in barrel for between 14 and 24 months, with a proportion of oak that varies between 40 and 60%, depending on the particular wine's potential. The estate's red wine, under the dominance of its Cabernet Sauvignon, has an elegant style, with a dense, deep purple appearance and a subtly perfumed nose (black fruit with smoky and oaky notes), a fleshy body that retains a velvety texture, fine tannins, and a beautiful freshness – a composition both classic in its balance and modern in the quality of its fruit, and never outspoken, instead remaining subtle, refined, and accessible from an early age.

DOMAINE DE CHEVALIER WHITE, CRU CLASSÉ, PESSAC-LÉOGNAN

Fermented and matured in barrel, the white wine is a blend of the two great Bordeaux white grape varieties, with 75% Sauvignon Blanc and 25% Sémillon. Its extremely delicate and pure aromas of soft spices mixed with white and yellow fruit infuse it with an unctuous fullness that is broad and concentrated, and yet paradoxically leaves a feeling of lightness in the mouth. Dense and yet airy, this gauzy wine, which derives its energy from its crystalline acidity, can stretch itself to attain a considerable length and will age happily.

BARSAC AOC

LEFT BANK (SAUTERNES REGION)

This appellation is located on the left bank of the Garonne, northwest of Sauternes, from which it is separated by just a small river (the Ciron). The climate in Barsac is rather special: in the fall, misty mornings are often followed by direct afternoon sunshine, creating favourable conditions for the growth of *Botrytis cinerea* or 'noble rot,' the fungus that produces the greatest sweet white wines. The wines, renowned for their complexity (the AOC contains 10 1855 classified growths), may be sold under the Barsac or the Sauternes appellation – but the same does not apply to the wines of Sauternes.

> **GRAPE VARIETIES** Sémillon (dominant), Sauvignon Blanc, Muscadelle.

> **SOIL** Clay, limestone, or gravel.

> **STYLE** Refined, sleek, and elegant, the wines have a golden colour that evolves with age to shades of amber. The nose is intense with a mixture of stone fruit (peaches), exotic fruit, notes of honey, hazelnuts, and dried apricots with hints of crystallized orange peel, vanilla, and brioche. This intensity reappears on the palate, which is full-bodied and perfectly balanced with smoothness and freshness. The finish is long and lingering.

Colour: *White.*

Serving temperature: *About 46°F (8°C).*

Ageing potential: *20 years or more.*

SAUTERNES AOC

LEFT BANK (SAUTERNES REGION)

This is the most famous of Bordeaux's sweet wine appellations, and it includes the iconic Château d'Yquem (*see* pp.264–5), one of the greatest sweet wines in the world. The vineyards of Sauternes cover 4,366 acres (1,767 ha), about 25 miles (40 km) south of Bordeaux. They are spread over five communes, including Barsac (which has its own AOC), and enjoy excellent conditions: protection from bad weather by the pine forests to the west, night mists owing to the proximity of the Garonne, and plenty of sunshine in the fall, encouraging the development of the famous noble rot – vital for the production of great sweet wines. The appellation produces exclusively sweet white wines. The method of producing these nectars, appreciated all over the world, are rigorous – with manual harvesting of overripe grapes, berry by berry, in a series of selective pickings. The best *terroirs* are on the high ground furthest from the river. This is where most of the classified growths are located.

> **GRAPE VARIETIES** Sémillon (dominant), Sauvignon Blanc, Muscadelle.

> **SOIL** Gravel, clay-and-limestone, limestone.

> **STYLE** The wines have a sumptuous 'old gold' colour that evolves with age to a warm amber. The Sauternes bouquet is typically very complex and intense, exploding with an exuberant symphony of fruit, floral notes, hints of honey, spices, almond paste, and beeswax, all delicately combined. The palate is full-bodied, powerful, smooth, refined, and elegant, with a perfect balance between fullness and acidity, and a very long finish.

Colour: *White.*

Serving temperature: *42 to 46°F (6 to 8°C).*

Ageing potential: *Enjoyable when young, but will keep for up to 100 years.*

Selected Sauternes

Other than Chateau d'Yquem, there are some extremely fine sweet wines.

- **Cru Barréjats (Pujols-sur-Ciron).** A tiny vineyard, but huge in terms of finesse, purity of flavour, and depth.
- **Château Climens (Barsac).** Perhaps the finest and most *liquoreux* (having high residual sugar) of Sauternes wines.
- **Château de Fargues (Fargues).** Superb; worthy of a *premier cru*.
- **Château La Tour Blanche (Bommes).** Harmonious Sauternes with a superb bouquet.
- **Château Rieussec (Fargues-de-Langon).** A powerful *premier cru* with enormous personality.
- **Château Sigalas-Rabaud (Bommes).** Unparalleled finesse.

- **Château Suduiraut (Preignac).** A rich, deep, elegant *grand cru* with exceptional longevity.

BLAYE-CÔTES-DE-BORDEAUX AOC

RIGHT BANK (BLAYE REGION)

Vines were planted in the Blaye region well before they were in neighbouring Médoc. Wine estates here developed along the estuary, taking advantage of the dynamic, flourishing shipping industry. The vineyards, located to the north of Bordeaux, across from the Médoc, cover about 13,590 acres (5,500 ha) and produce mostly red wines.

> **GRAPE VARIETIES** Merlot (70 per cent), Cabernet Sauvignon, Cabernet Franc, Malbec for the reds; Sauvignon Blanc, Sémillon, and Muscadelle for the whites.

> **SOIL** Clay-and-limestone.

> **STYLE** These wines have an intense ruby colour; the bouquet is powerful and fruity (red and dark fruit), embellished with hints of spice. The palate is supple and harmonious, with well-integrated tannins and a long finish returning to the flavours of the bouquet. The white wines are pale yellow in colour, tinged with green, and present aromas of yellow fruit, citrus notes, and hints of juniper. The palate is well-balanced between acidity and fruit, which linger on the finish.

Colour:
Red and white.

Serving temperature:
61 to 64°F (16 to 18°C). (Grands crus should be decanted two hours before serving.)

Ageing potential:
7 to 20 years (and up to 25 years for the grands crus).

BLAYE AOC

RIGHT BANK (BLAYE REGION)

On the right bank of the Gironde – north of Bordeaux and near the town of Blaye, with its citadel built by Vauban – the vineyards are planted on hills and in small valleys, and receive lots of sunshine. This appellation produces red wines only under more restricted conditions than for Blaye Côtes de Bordeaux (planting density, yield). The production remains very modest in volume, but as a result the wines are concentrated and powerful.

> **GRAPE VARIETIES** Merlot, Cabernet Franc, Cabernet Sauvignon, Malbec, Petit Verdot for the red wines.

> **SOIL** Clay-and-limestone, gravel.

> **STYLE** The red wines have a deep, but bright, colour. The nose offers notes of red and dark fruit (raspberries, strawberries, cherries, blackberries, blackcurrants), underscored with hints of flowers (peppery rose, violet), vegetal aromas (mint, pepper), spices, chocolate, and wood. The palate is supple, rounded, and well-balanced, with beautifully textured, fine, silky tannins and a long, fruity finish. Very full-flavoured, the white wines are deep yellow in colour; the nose offers a delightful range of citrus notes (lemon, grapefruit, tangerine) and stone fruit, with hints of toasted almonds; the palate is well-structured and intense, well-balanced with an elegant framework of silky tanins and a long fruity finish.

Colour:
Red and white.

Serving temperature:
50 to 54°F (10 to 12°C) for the white wines; 61 to 63°F (16 to 17°C) for the reds.

Ageing potential:
Drink within a year; white wines keep for 2 to 3 years; reds for 3 to 7 years.

> The underground cellars at Château Bertinerie (Blaye-Cotes-de-Bordeaux AOC).

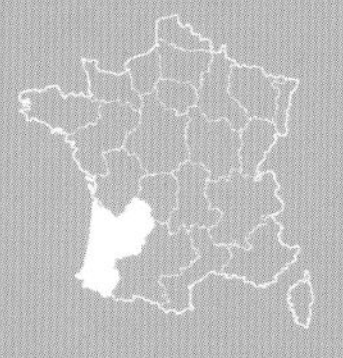

Bordeaux, Left Bank

CHÂTEAU *LATOUR*

An understated label, a simple name, a strong, reassuring image, and immense prestige: this is Château Latour. For centuries, its very mention has conjured up notions of magnificence and longevity – its story is long and complex, fraught with passion and yet still entirely up-to-date.

Ancient prestige

While the site of the château at Latour was of amazing importance from a strategic point of view during the Hundred Years' War, its wine-making history only truly begins in 1718, when the Marquis Nicolas-Alexandre de Ségur planted the first vineyard. The reputation of its wines was soon to spread beyond the borders of France: in 1787, Thomas Jefferson, then the ambassador of the newly created United States of America, records the name of the château in his travel journal and buys several small bottles of its wine; even at this point, Latour wine cost 20 times as much as normal Bordeaux. Château Latour was definitively granted its letters patent in 1855, with the classification decreed by Napoléon III that granted it the title of *premier cru*, an honour shared with only three other châteaux in the Médoc and Graves.

Thirty years of British presence

Château Latour was sold to a British group in 1963, with no harm at all to the wine's prestige as the consistency of the cru remained unaffected. François Pinault, a businessman and great wine-lover, purchased the property in 1993 and, after 30 years of good and faithful service on the part of the British, the château was once again French.

Ideal terroir

The Latour terroir, located in the Pauillac AOC, fulfils every criterion required for excellence. The vines are planted over 198 acres (80 ha) but l'Enclos, a plot of 116 acres surrounding the château, takes pride of place; it is the only one to produce Château Latour's *grand vin*. The stony ground would be too poor for any other crop, but it has proven ideal for vines, with a hillside of gravelly soil that promotes perfect drainage of rainwater down towards the river. The gentle incline of its three slopes allows for constant exposure to the sun. Vines grow here effortlessly, whatever the vagaries of the weather and the sustenance and water it requires. What is more, the closeness of the Gironde protects the vineyard from extremes of temperature.

Grape varieties

The Cabernet Sauvignon that covers 75 per cent of the cultivated area is king here, providing the wine with its tannic structure, colour, and concentration. It also guarantees slow and harmonious ageing, so the wines can be laid down for long periods. Merlot, which accounts for 23 per cent of the vineyard, is less forceful, softer, and more aromatic, and provides a delicate complement; Cabernet Franc and Petit Verdot, which cover up to 2 per cent, are included where necessary in the final blend.

Extremely well-tended vines

To keep the average age of the vines as high as possible, each vine stock is allowed to die a natural death before being replaced with a new plant. When the moment for harvesting comes, a choice is made among the vines of those worthy to provide grapes to make a Latour. To ensure there are never more than eight bunches of grapes per vine stock, there is a 'green harvest' in July; by sacrificing a portion of the grape bunches, they achieve greater concentration of juices and other substances in the individual grapes. After the grapes have been scrupulously hand-picked, there follows closely monitored vinification, ageing for 18 months in barrel, and meticulous bottling, so the high quality of the wine, its remarkable capacity to age beautifully, and its unimpeachable consistency – whatever the vintage – should come as little wonder.

The taste of Latour

Château Latour's *grand vin* bears all the hallmarks of an exceptional wine. While undeniably austere in its young years, from the age of 12 this *premier cru classé* displays all the accomplishments of an unalloyed masterpiece. Over time, the compact essence of the wine combines with the tannins of a great dynasty to attain perfect harmony. Structured, succulent, persistent, and forceful, the wine also has a natural capacity for ageing magnificently over 30, 40, or even 50 years, and much more besides for the great vintages. It needs to be decanted so that its bouquet can develop completely. Served at 64°F (18°C), it will go with Pauillac lamb, red meat, and game. Mention should also be made of Les Forts de Latour, the château's 'second wine', which has enjoyed an entirely deserved reputation for some little time; it has unimpeachable style and, while it may not scale the heights achieved by its big brother, it has all the flavour and charm of a Médoc second growth. It ages extremely well (15 years) and should also be decanted.

CÔTES-DE-BOURG AOC

RIGHT BANK (BOURG REGION)

The Côtes de Bourg has some of the oldest vineyards in Bordeaux; their wines have competed with those of the Médoc since the 19th century. Located south of the town of Blaye, across from Margaux, this appellation covers 15 communes on hillsides overlooking the Gironde estuary. The 9,760 acres (3,950 ha) of vineyards, known as the 'Little Switzerland of the Gironde', produce about 1.9 million cases (180,000 hl) of mostly red wines that are very pleasant and full-bodied, and age well.

> **GRAPE VARIETIES** Merlot (dominant), Cabernet Sauvignon, Cabernet Franc, Malbec for the reds; Sémillon, Sauvignon Blanc, Muscadelle, and Colombard for the whites.

> **SOIL** Alluvial deposits, sandy-clay, and limestone.

> **STYLE** Rustic and charming, the reds have a deep colour and an intense nose of fresh and stewed dark fruit and spices. With age, they develop notes of mushroom, humus, and venison. The palate is generous, powerful, and wellstructured with fine, silky tannins, and a long, flavourful finish. Dry and fruity, the white wines have a pale colour, and a very aromatic nose of flowers and white fruit; the palate is harmonious, smooth,and well balanced between fruit and freshness.

Colour:	Serving temperature:	Ageing potential:
Red and white.	*About 50°F (10°C) for the white wines; 61 to 63°F (16 to 17°C) for the reds.*	*2 to 3 years for the whites; 3 to 8 years for the reds.*

FRONSAC AOC

RIGHT BANK (LIBOURNE REGION)

Bordered by the Dordogne and Isle rivers, these very old vineyards enjoyed a golden period in the 17th century under Richelieu, the Duke of Fronsac, who built a villa in the area to host sumptuousparties. The appellation extends to the gates of Libourne, covering about 2,076 acres (840 ha) and producing around 489,000 cases (44,000 hl) of exclusively red wine. The winesproduced in the communes of Fronsac and St-Michel-de-Fronsac may also be sold under the Canon-Fronsac appellation. There is no official classification in Fronsac.

> **GRAPE VARIETIES** Merlot, Cabernet Sauvignon, Cabernet Franc, Malbec.

> **SOIL** Alluvial deposits (Fronsac *molasse*), clay-and-limestone.

> **STYLE** Charming and full-bodied, the wines of Fronsac have a concentrated ruby colour. The nose develops intense aromas of mainly red fruit mixed with spicy notes (pepper) with touches of undergrowth. The balanced, robust, rich, full palate is supported by solid, flavourful tannins that require several years to settle down.

Colour:	Serving temperature:	Ageing potential:
Red.	*61 to 63°F (16 to 17°C). (Decant, if possible.)*	*5 to 10 years.*

Châteaux Vrai Canon Bouché and Le Tertre de Canon

In 2005, Philip Haseth-Möller bought 30 acres (12 ha) of land on the high plateau near the village of Fronsac. Self-taught, he engaged the services of Stéphane Derenoncourt, a consultant who advises many of the vineyards in St-Émilion (Pavie-Macquin and Canon-la-Gaffelière among others), and of the renowned agrobiologist Claude Bourguignon, who specializes in matching grape varieties with soil types. The result was two very fine wines (with Merlot as the dominant grape): Vrai Canon Bouché and Le Tertre de Canon, both excellent expressions of the *terroir*.

POMEROL AND LALANDE-DE-POMEROL AOCS

RIGHT BANK (LIBOURNE REGION)

One of the jewels of Bordeaux, the Pomerol appellation contains the equally famous Pétrus, one of the rarest and most expensive wines in the world. Paradoxically, it is one of the few appellations that does not have a classification system for its wines. The vineyards of Pomerol, a commune that does not have a village, date back to Roman times. It is located about 30 miles (50 km) east of Bordeaux, near the town of Libourne. The vineyards are spread over 2,009 acres (813 ha) of terraces above the Isle River and produce 344,000 cases (31,000 hl) of exclusively red wine. In the same region as Pomerol, separated from the prestigious appellation by a stream called the Barbanne, the Lalande-de-Pomerol appellation covers two communes, Lalande-de-Pomerol and Néac. It produces, from the same grape varieties, wines that are similar to those of its prestigious neighbour – even, in some cases, managing to rival them.

> **GRAPE VARIETIES** Merlot (80 per cent to 100 per cent), Cabernet Franc, Cabernet Sauvignon, Malbec.

> **SOIL** Clay-gravel.

> **STYLE** Powerful, rounded, and supple with a very deep, dense colour, the wines of Pomerol develop full, complex aromas of red and dark fruit, spices, and hints of violet. They are underscored with hints of tobacco, licorice, truffle, and game, which become more complex with age. The palate is full, smooth, and fleshy, steeped in fruit flavours with a powerful structure of silky, dense tannins. The lingering finish is long and fragrant. The wines of Lalande-de-Pomerol are deep red and powerful, with a fine bouquet and elegant, well-integrated tannins.

Colour:
Red.

Serving temperature:
61 to 64°F (16 to 18°C). (Decant several hours before drinking.)

Ageing potential:
3 to 15 or 20 years.

Selected Pomerol producers

After Pétrus, the 'king' of the appellation, and other famous châteaux such as L'Évangile, La Conseillante, or Vieux Château Certan, there are some very good wines to be found in Pomerol:

- **Château Belle-Brise (Libourne).** Pomerol elegance and class.
- **Château Bellegrave (Pomerol).** A very typical Pomerol with great finesse and concentration.
- **Château Gombaude-Guillot (Pomerol).** Both of the property's wines (Clos Prince and Château Gombaude-Guillot) are organic; well-balanced and harmonious, they combine power and great elegance.
- **Château La Ganne (Libourne).** Very good value.

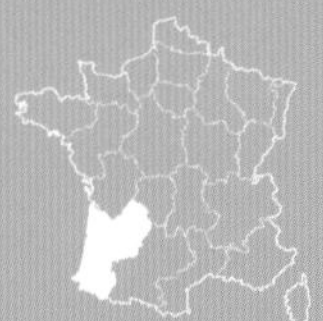

Bordeaux, Right Bank

CHÂTEAU *AUSONE*

Under the aegis of the Vauthier family, the famed Saint-Émilion estate, Ausone, is ploughing its own furrow, maintaining a close link with its terroir, and pushing the demand for perfection as far as it will go.

CHÂTEAU AUSONE

Lieu-dit Ausone
33330 Saint-Émilion

Area: *17 acres (6.9 ha)*
Production: *20,000 bottles p.a.*
Appellation: *Saint-Émilion*
Red grape varieties: *Cabernet Franc, Merlot*
NB: Saint-Émilion *premier grand cru classé* (A)

Going down in legend

Château Ausone had the honour of leading the first official Saint-Émilion classification in 1955, and connoisseurs who have had the rare privilege of tasting Ausone wines that have been laid down for more than a century say they still display incredible quality. The famous American critic Robert Parker has suggested drinking the current great vintages after 40 to 50 years of ageing to appreciate all their lavishness. There are now four estates in Saint-Émilion that have been classified as *premiers grands crus*, but a number of experts place Château Ausone ahead of the others; it has come back from the brink, however.

A disputed estate

During the 1960s and 1970s, the property was owned by two seemingly close-knit families; in fact, they disagreed on almost everything, in particular the way the vines should be managed and the wines made. The results came under heavy criticism from the experts, and even though the estate's status saved it from falling out of favour, it did not spare it an embarrassing controversy. The upshot was that one of the families took over the whole of the estate in 1995 and Alain Vauthier, its principal partner, took over the reins. Since the 1998 vintage, Château Ausone has regained its special place on the Mount Olympus of the great Bordeaux *grands crus*.

Manufacturing secrets

With its consistency and small size, the château at Ausone has a strong link to its terroir in the Burgundian sense of the word. Alain Vauthier is a stalwart defender of the estate, explaining that the great terroirs always have their roots in history and put up a good fight against the slings and arrows of history, economics, and the climate. For him, the job of its human stewards is to refine our understanding of the soil – in other words, to adapt the grape varieties and techniques used to get the very best out of it. Château Ausone enjoys the best location possible in what is undoubtedly the best-known appellation: its 17 acres (6.9 ha) are fully exposed to the sun halfway up the hill at Saint-Émilion, on a sort of limestone hillock covered with a thin layer of gravel. It has been planted with equal amounts of Merlot and Cabernet Franc. The latter, often of great age and always the product of 'massal selection', (*i.e.* exclusively taken from original vines), exhibits exceptional quality. Alain Vauthier decided to favour Cabernet Franc from the outset – the grape regularly has a 55% share in the final blend – and also to remove the young vines, which have since been used to make La Chapelle d'Ausone, a second wine. He has drastically reduced yields and pushed the demand for perfection to great lengths, for example by carrying out malolactic fermentation not in tanks but in small casks. Pauline, Vauthier's daughter, has been working with him for about 12 years, quietly suggesting several alterations to increase the brilliance of the fruit in the grape juice still further, and the proportion of new barrels used during ageing has thus changed from 100 to 85%. We should also mention that La Chapelle d'Ausone is one of the Saint-Émilion second wines closest and most faithful to the *grand cru* from which it is taken.

CHÂTEAU AUSONE, PREMIER GRAND CRU CLASSÉ (A), SAINT-ÉMILION

The results are flabbergasting… but impossible to find. Château Ausone remains less well known and (a little) less expensive than Château Petrus, but is much rarer, with an average output of only 20,000 bottles, rising to 24,000 in good years. Matured in barrel (with 85% new oak), this magnificent creation draws its originality from its 60% Cabernet Franc content, which produces a signature aroma and a singular crispness, even in young wines. Only the luckiest among us will have had an opportunity to taste the sublime mellowness of its tannins, the rich palette of its perfumes and its subtle, never-ending mineral notes, the hallmark of an exceptional terroir. This magical trio of flavour advantages, each an enhancement of the others, is the unique, envied signature style of Ausone.

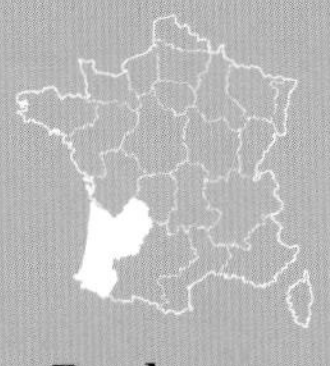

Bordeaux,
Right Bank

THE LITTLE PRINCE OF *SAINT-ÉMILION*

Self-made man and self-proclaimed autodidact Jean-Luc Thunevin saved Bordeaux in the 1990s with Château Valandraud, his vin de garage that was classified as a Premier Grand Cru in 2012.

CHÂTEAU VALANDRAUD

6, rue Guadet 33330 Saint-Émilion

Area: *22 acres (8.9 ha)*
Production: *35,000 bottles p.a.*
Appellation: *Saint-Émilion*
Red grape varieties: *Merlot, Cabernet Franc, Cabernet Sauvignon, Malbec, Carmenère*

The story doesn't start until 1989

Jean-Luc Thunevin, a Saint-Émilion restaurateur and wine merchant, and Murielle Arnaud, his wife, wanted to make wine their way, but owned no vines; in 1989, however, they were to chance upon an acre and a half (0.6 ha) of land in the Fongaban Valley that was in a bad state and unwanted by the neighbours.

Resuscitated vines

Murielle worked night and day to revive the vines to ensure a good harvest, while Jean-Luc put in the hours on wine-making techniques far removed from those common in Bordeaux, to make a wine that was both full and open. Their first vintage, released in 1991, was a triumph. Sour grapes and controversy followed almost immediately from some quarters – Château Valandraud was decried as *vin de garage* ('garage wine'), produced using methods entirely inappropriate for great estates like those in the Médoc, and destined for trading on the international market. 'The critics haven't got time to waste on pointless squabbling,' notes Thunevin with amusement, 'what they're interested in is what ends up in the glass, and they are still as excited about our bottles as ever.'

Spying out the land

Valandraud is hard to come by and expensive, with the result that its two indefatigable creators have been able to expand their vineyards, as they acquired a series of small parcels of land spread out over the Saint-Étienne-de-Lisse area. 'Good wine-growing land – it has nothing to do with garages,' remarks this smiling and happy proprietor of an estate that now extends over almost 22 acres (8.9 ha). This expansion of the estate has not been to the detriment of the wine quality, however – anything but, and the efforts of this quality-obsessed couple were crowned with success in 2012, when Château Valandraud was classified as a Saint-Émilion *premier grand cru classé*. The market sealed this triumph by making one of its wines the most sought-after in the appellation. Bordeaux has never known a success of such completeness and speed, which of course attracted a certain amount of envy. 'We were extremely lucky to arrive here at this point in time,' asserts Jean-Luc Thunevin, before getting down to details: 'There's not a lot of movement in Bordeaux – people are happy to make wine the old way, with the exception of a few estates, such as Lynch-Bages or Le Pin, and a few people like Émile Peynaud or Michel Rolland.'

Challenging convention

Having set out 'without a cent', but having had the good fortune to get their hands on this little parcel of land and being able to borrow some money, this couple threw themselves into the work with one overriding idea: 'small yields make great wines'. They achieved this with 'green harvests' to limit the number of bunches per vine stock and merciless grape selection of the picked grapes, so that only the best quality was retained. As Thunevin says with a smile: 'we invented grape-by-grape selection, and even made a machine to grade the grapes'.

His other challenge to received wisdom that paid off was to harvest extremely ripe grapes and extract plenty of colour, substance, and flavour from them with regular *pigéage* ('punching down', when the caps of the grapes float to the top of the wine vat) during vinification, before patiently finishing fermentation in barrel and maturing in new casks. The outcome was a full wine that retained plenty of charm, which he achieved by choosing Merlot as the principal grape. Production remains modest, of course, with an average of around 15,000 bottles. The estate has also branched out with a wine christened 'Virginie de Valandraud', which is less dense and more affordable. Jean-Luc Thunevin's advice is now much sought-after and has benefited numerous estates in the immediate area. With a mischievous smile, but no hint of boasting, he can certainly say: 'I woke up Bordeaux.'

CHÂTEAU VALANDRAUD, PREMIER GRAND CRU CLASSÉ (B), SAINT-ÉMILION

The wines are matured in new casks and then left in barrel for between 18 and 30 months, depending on the potential of the particular year. No fining or filtration is undertaken before bottling. Its tenebrous, deep-purple appearance promises very ripe black fruits (blackcurrants and blackberries) on the nose. These are accompanied by mocha notes and a subtle oakiness that never dominates. Highly concentrated and velvety, it nonetheless reveals a beautiful freshness that lends elegance and length in the mouth-feel and betokens a potential for laying down. Its luxuriant richness cheerfully comes to the fore in successive waves, based on melting, flavoursome tannins that further underscore the fruit and maturity of this extremely fine wine.

> Jean-Luc Thunevin and Murielle Arnaud, the estate managers.

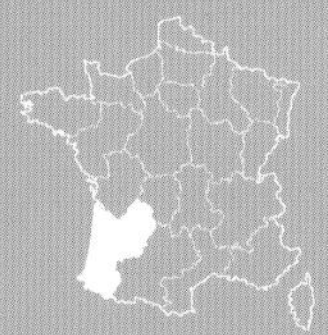

Bordeaux, Right Bank

PETRUS

Although anonymous immediately after the war, the little Pomerol estate, Petrus, has, in just a few decades, become one of the most famous and popular wines of Bordeaux – a rise that can clearly be attributed to its unique terroir, but also to a confluence of extraordinary talents.

PETRUS

3, route de Lussac
33500 Pomerol

Area: *28 acres (11.3 ha)*
Production: *30,000 bottles p.a.*
Appellation: *Pomerol*
Grape varieties: *Merlot, Cabernet Franc*

The birth of a legend

With no imposing buildings, no renowned cellar, no signpost, not even a mention of a château associated with its name, Petrus cultivates discretion – even though this star Pomerol estate stands at the very pinnacle of the Bordeaux hierarchy. The name is known to wine expert and peon alike and has a power that is the stuff of legends: it exudes exclusivity, excellence, luxury, and rarity. Although completely unknown at the end of the war, Petrus needed no more than a few decades to skyrocket into the Bordeaux firmament. At the time, Pomerol was an understated appellation – a sort of 'anti-Médoc' – with no reputation to speak of, made up of small family estates, of which Petrus was just one. The foundations were laid in the 19th century by the Arnaud family, who gave the name of the first pope to an estate of 30 acres (12 ha or so) located at the highest point of the appellation. Edmonde Loubat, who ran an upmarket hotel opposite the station at Libourne, took a close interest in the estate, acquiring parts of it in 1925, and it was this businesswoman – described as energetic, tenacious, and intuitive – who spotted the extraordinary potential of the vineyard. She worked tirelessly for 20 years to promote its wines, constantly on the move and getting her foot in every door – including at Buckingham Palace, where Petrus was introduced to the English gentry at the then Princess Elizabeth's wedding in 1947. Two years later it was to become associated with another visionary, Jean-Pierre Moueix, a young man from Corrèze with a great future before him, who had founded a wine merchant's at Libourne in 1937. Both shared the same conviction: Petrus could grow to equal the great estates of the Left Bank.

The hand of the Berrouets

After Great Britain, the next to succumb to the charms of this unclassified wine with no name to speak of was the United States, with Kennedy its first ambassador. Jean-Pierre Moueix did not content himself merely with establishing a solid network of international business connections; he took over control of the estate and proved his mettle as a winemaker before calling in Jean-Claude Berrouet in 1963, an exceptional wine expert and the last piece in the puzzle. Despite the occasional crisis and protracted wrangling over succession of ownership, the next 50 years have definitively established Petrus at the summit, surpassing even the most exalted Médocs at auction, where it achieves astronomical prices. The estate has had a new cellar since 2014, a functional and attractive structure that has been integrated into the landscape, maintaining the discretion so dear to its owners. The generations have rung the changes, with Jean-François and Jean Moueix, the son and grandson of Jean-Pierre Moueix, now heading up Petrus' holding company, and Olivier Berrouet has taken over from his father, preserving a style born equally of a very particular terroir and a passion that has never put a foot wrong.

PETRUS, POMEROL

Petrus' style is primarily about the impeccable ripeness of its grapes, which is perfected in the cellar with tailor-made maturation. A young Petrus, invariably deeply coloured, reveals its charms in its velvety texture, its depth, its tannins that are both powerful and yet subtle, and accents of fruit that are often blended with floral notes. It cannot be accused of exuberance, and is sometimes austere in its young years, but time will strip away this beautiful superstructure little by little, refining the tannins and the bouquet, which with age will turn to aromas of spices and truffles. A legendary wine for which you must expect to wait ten years, and often more.

Secret clay

It is said that clay is required for a good terroir, but there are few great terroirs that are fundamentally clay soils. Here, however, they talk of a 'miracle clay', with fine particles that act like a sponge, draining away water or holding on to it to return it, drop by drop, to the plant as it needs it. Petrus has exactly 28.5 acres (11.5 ha) of vineyards, located on a well-aerated hillside rising to an elevation of 130 feet (40m), and its surface black clays with red clays shot through with ferruginous sandstone beneath are planted almost exclusively with Merlot (95% of the total planted area), a variety known for its body and which here achieves a fullness and subtlety of expression that is unique. Every precaution is taken to pick the grapes at full ripeness, after which it is all about sensitivity and the human touch – from the Berrouets, father then son, who have refined a technique that is at once appealing and sophisticated, with no histrionics, overconcentration, or ostentatious oaky notes, and intentionally constructed to be laid down.

ivier Berrouet,
ologist and general
ager since 2008.

AOC ST-ÉMILION

RIGHT BANK (LIBOURNE REGION)

St-Émilion is the first wine-producing area to be included in Unesco's World Heritage List as a 'cultural landscape', It is also one of the most famous in the world. The vineyards enjoy a temperate climate thanks to the nearby Dordogne river. They cover 13,300 acres (5,400 ha) and eight communes, producing exclusively red wine. Depending on the soil, exposure, and age of the vines, as well as the concentration of the grapes, wine producers may sell their wines under two appellations: St-Émilion and St-Émilion Grand Cru *(see* below). In 1955, a classification was drawn up for the *grands crus*, with the proviso that it be updated every 10 years.

> **GRAPE VARIETIES** Merlot (dominant), Cabernet Franc, Cabernet Sauvignon.

> **SOIL** Limestone, clay-alluvial deposits (Fronsac *molasse*), gravel alluvium, sand.

> **STYLE** With the passing of time, the dark colour of the wines of St-Émilion quickly becomes a beautiful garnet, tinged with brown and orange. The complex nose offers ripe, stewed red and dark fruit, with notes of leather, sweet spices, and woody-smokiness. With age, aromas of undergrowth and humus develop, with notes of game. The palate is full, fleshy, well-structured, and supported by delicate, silky tannins. A beautiful finish offers fruit, spice, and smoky notes.

Colour: *Red.*

Serving temperature: *61 to 63°F (16 to 17°C). (Decant if possible.)*

Ageing potential: *3 to 8 or 10 years, or more.*

ST-ÉMILION GRAND CRU AOC

RIGHT BANK (LIBOURNE REGION)

This appellation covers the same area as that of St-Émilion *(see above)*. To be described as *grand cru*, wines must meet certain quality criteria (yields limited to 2.4 tons/acre (40 hl/ha), maturation in barrels for 12 months). The appellation has four *grands crus classés A*, namely Château Ausone, Château Cheval-Blanc, Pavie and Château Angelus, and 15 *grands crus classés B*.

> **GRAPE VARIETIES** Merlot (dominant), Cabernet Franc, Cabernet Sauvignon.

> **SOIL** Limestone, clay-alluvial deposits (Fronsac *molasse*), gravel alluvium, sand.

> **STYLE** The wines of St-Émilion Grand Cru have a purple colour and present a very fragrant, concentrated, complex nose – mingling ripe, dark fruit and flowers, with notes of prunes, hints of spice, vanilla, and toasted almonds. The palate is full-bodied, fleshy, and well structured, with good quality, fine, closely knit tannins that need time to soften. The finish is long, fresh, and full-flavoured.

Colour: *Red.*

Serving temperature: *61 to 64°F (16 to 18°C). (Decant if possible.)*

Ageing potential: *7 to 20 years, or more for the* crus classés.

Grand crus and organic farming

The number is still few, but the list of St-Émilion Grand Cru properties that have adopted organic or biodynamic methods does become longer every year. Among the main names are: Château Barrail des Graves (Gérard Descrambe, St-Sulpice-de-Faleyrens), one of the very first; Châteaux Fonroque and Moulin du Cadet (Moueix, St-Émilion and Libourne); Château Franc-Pourret, Domaine du Haut-Patarabet, Clos Chante l'Alouette (Vignobles Ouzoulias, St-Émilion); and Château Trapaud (Trapaud family, St-Etienne de Lisse), Château Moulin de Lagnet (Chatenet family, Saint Christophe des Bardes), Château Croque-Michotte (Geoffrion family, Saint-Émilion).

THE ST-ÉMILION 'SATELLITES'

RIGHT BANK (LIBOURNE REGION)

Four communes neighbouring St-Émilion are permitted to add that name to their own. To the far north is Lussac-St-Émilion (3,558 acres or 1,440 ha). Following on from the vineyards of Pomerol and St-Émilion to the north is Montagne-St-Émilion (4,000 acres or 1,600 ha), and St-Georges-St-Émilion (494 acres or 200 ha). Facing the St-Émilion plateau lies Puisseguin-St-Émilion (1,840 acres or 745 ha). Using the same grapes as St-Émilion AOC, these appellations offer wines with personality and represent excellent value.

> **GRAPE VARIETIES** Merlot (dominant, sometimes up to 90 per cent), Cabernet Franc, Cabernet Sauvignon, Malbec.

> **SOIL** Clay and limestone. Lussac's soil is varied: clay-gravel in the valleys, sandy clay on the plateaus, and clay-limestone on the hillsides.

> **STYLE** The wines of Lussac are elegant and well-structured; Montagne's are classy, generous, and distinguished; St-Georges' are full-bodied and powerful; Puisseguin's are full-bodied and fleshy.

Colour:
Red.

Serving temperature:
59 to 63°F (15 to 17°C).

Ageing potential:
5 to 9 years

FRANCS-CÔTES-DE-BORDEAUX AOC

RIGHT BANK OF THE DORDOGNE

The name 'Côtes de Francs' dates back to the 6th century. After the battle of Vouillé in 507, Clovis, the king of the Franks, defeated the Visigoths and seized Aquitaine. The place where a detachment of the Frankish army established itself was called *Ad Francos*, which later became 'Francs.' Located about 30 miles (50 km) northeast of Bordeaux, this appellation is one of the smallest and the most easterly. The vineyards cover 1,235 acres (500 ha) spread over the three communes of Francs, Saint-Cibard, and Tayac. It produces about 177,600 cases (16,000 hl) of red wine and a small quantity of white wine, both dry and sweet.

> **GRAPE VARIETIES** For the red wines: Merlot (dominant), Cabernet Sauvignon, and Cabernet Franc; for the white wines: Sémillon (dominant), Muscadelle, and Sauvignon Blanc.

> **SOIL** Limestone covered with Agen *molasse* (to the south), and limestone with Fronsac*molasse*.

> **STYLE** The red wines have a very dark colour. The nose offers aromas of very ripe red and dark fruit with spicy notes. The palate combines smoothness and volume with a tannin structure that needs time to soften. The whites develop a citrus and exotic fruit bouquet, with hints of honey. The palate is full and well-balanced.

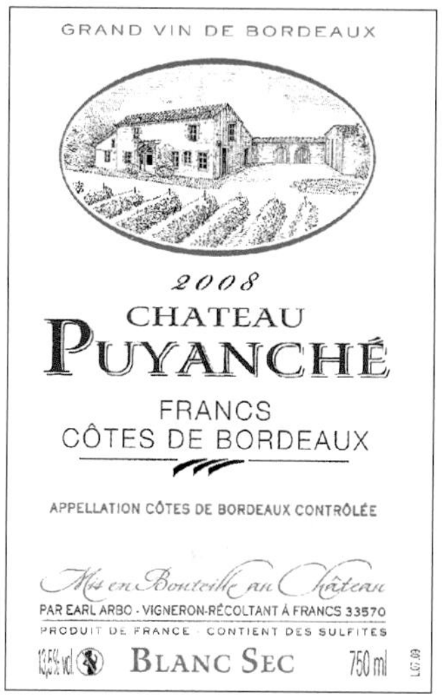

Colour:
Red and white.

Serving temperature:
46 to 50°F (8 to 10°C) for the whites; 57 to 61°F (14 to 16°C) for the reds.

Ageing potential:
1 to 3 years for the whites; 3 to 5 years for the reds.

CASTILLON-CÔTES-DE-BORDEAUX AOC

RIGHT BANK OF THE DORDOGNE

This is a land steeped in history – the battle of Castillon in 1453 ended the Hundred Years War. The appellation covers 5,683 acres (2,300 ha) on the right bank of the Gironde, to the east of St-Émilion. It produces 1.1 million cases (100,000 hl) of full-bodied, generous, exclusively red wines.

> **GRAPE VARIETIES** Merlot, Cabernet Franc, Cabernet Sauvignon.

> **SOIL** Clay-and-limestone, gravel.

> **STYLE** The wines have a dark ruby colour. The nose is expressive and complex, with aromas of ripe red fruit and prunes. It is underscored with notes of vegetation and spices. The palate is fruity and well-structured, with generous tannins.

Colour:
Red.

Serving temperature:
61 to 64°F (16 to 18°C).

Ageing potential:
5 to 10 years.

ENTRE-DEUX-MERS AOC

ENTRE-DEUX-MERS

This region consists of a plateau crisscrossed with valleys, and it takes its name from a location between two rivers, the Dordogne and the Garonne – forming its borders to the north and south. This vast appellation stretches over 3,707 acres (1,500 ha) and produces an average of 854,700 cases (77,000 hl) per year of dry white wines. Nine communes (Arbis, Cantois, Escoussans, Gornac, Ladaux, Mourens, Soulignac, St-Pierre-de-Bat, and Targon), located in the same area, are entitled to the appellation Entre-Deux-Mers-Haut-Benauge.

> **GRAPE VARIETIES** Sauvignon Blanc (dominant), Sémillon, Muscadelle.

> **SOIL** Limestone, silica, gravel, alluvial deposits.

> **STYLE** Entre-Deux-Mers wines have a brilliant golden colour with hints of green; they are lively, fruity, supple, and very fresh tasting. The nose presents notes of lemon, blackcurrant buds, and just a hint of iodine. The finish is relatively long and full-flavoured with citrus notes.

Colour: *White.*

Serving temperature: *About 46°F (8°C).*

Ageing potential: *2 to 3 years.*

STE-FOY-BORDEAUX AOC

ENTRE-DEUX-MERS

Located between Bordeaux, Perigord, and Agen, this ancient medieval zone lies on the eastern boundary of the Bordeaux wine-producing region. Containing 19 villages, it follows a series of hills and plateaus that overlook the Dordogne River. With only about 741 acres (300 ha), Ste-Foy-Bordeaux's production is limited; but it is highly appreciated by connoisseurs. It mainly produces red wines, plus a few rare dry and sweet white wines.

> **GRAPE VARIETIES** Cabernet Sauvignon, Cabernet Franc, Merlot for the red wines; Sauvignon Blanc, Sémillon, Muscadelle, Sauvignon Gris for the whites.

> **SOIL** Gravel, sand.

> **STYLE** Opulent and powerful, the red wines have a magnificent bouquet of red fruit, dominated by cherries, mixed with delicate notes of leather and undergrowth. The palate is fleshy, full-bodied, and powerful, with a solid tannin structure that needs time to soften. The finish is long and flavourful. The sweet white wines have a beautiful warm golden colour. Their delicate nose expresses aromas of white flowers and honey with a subtle hint of musk. The palate is rounded, full, and smooth, and is highlighted by a superb freshness. The finish is very long and fragrant. The dry white wines have a pale yellow colour, and a lively, fruity bouquet (citrus); the palate is well-balanced between fruit, acidity, and smoothness.

Colour: *Red and white.*

Serving temperature: *46 to 50°F (8 to 10°C) for the dry and the sweet white wines; 61 to 63°F (16 to 17°C) for the reds.*

Ageing potential: *2 to 3 years for the dry whites; 3 to 6 years for the reds; 4 to 7 years for the sweet whites.*

CADILLAC AOC

ENTRE-DEUX-MERS

Overlooked by Cadillac's château in that beautiful 17th-century walled town, the appellation extends along the right bank of the Garonne River, 19 miles (30 km) southeast of Bordeaux. The microclimate in the vineyards is suitable for the development of noble rot. Some 22 communes have the right to the appellation. Representing excellent value, the wines of Cadillac are well worth exploring. This appellation should not be confused with Cadillac-Côtes-de-Bordeaux AOC, which produces only red wines.

> **GRAPE VARIETIES** Sémillon, Sauvignon Blanc, Muscadelle.

> **SOIL** Clay-and-limestone, gravel.

> **STYLE** The wines of Cadillac have a golden colour with hints of topaz; the bouquet typically offers aromas of honey, acacia, honeysuckle, and crystallized fruit. The smooth, flavourful palate has plenty of substance, with some roasted notes that linger on the finish.

Colour: *White.*

Serving temperature: *About 46°F (8°C).*

Ageing potential: *10 to 15 years, or more.*

'Sweet Bordeaux'

In the Gironde, 15 sweet wine appellations – Sauternes, Barsac, Loupiac, Ste-Croix-du-Mont, Premières-Côtes-de-Bordeaux, Graves supérieur, Graves de Vayre, Cadillac, Cérons, sparkling Bordeaux, Bordeaux supérieur, Bordeaux Haut-Benauge, Côtes-de-Bordeaux-St-Macaire, Franc-Côtes de Bordeaux, and Ste-Foy-Bordeaux – have joined together to form 'Sweet Bordeaux', a group that shares tastings and celebrates a 'sweet attitude' with a view to conquering new markets: 'sweet hours', 'sweet music', and 'sweet parties' are organized in an attempt to attract a younger clientele and show that these wines can be enjoyed with a wide range of foods, and not only the traditional *foie gras*. Here are some of the Sweet Bordeaux wines.

- **Château Haura**, Barsac (Cérons AOC). High in residual sugar, this is a delicious, full-bodied, complex wine with excellent balance.
- **Château La Grave**, Ste-Croix-du-Mont (Ste-Croix-du-Mont). This offers a 'Sentiers d'Automne', a powerful, full-bodied, smooth wine.
- **Château Petit Clos Jean**, Cérons (Loupiac AOC). The Cuvée Prestige is full of charm, elegance, and power.
- **Château Peyruchet**, Loupiac (Loupiac AOC). The *liquoreux* (high residual sugar) wines represent the appellation.

LOUPIAC AOC

ENTRE-DEUX-MERS

Located on small hills 25 miles (40 km) south of Bordeaux, the vineyards of Loupiac (850 acres or 344 ha) enjoy excellent sunshine, very good natural drainage, and mists in the fall that – with the presence of the Garonne – create ideal conditions for the growth of *Botrytis cinerea*, the noble rot necessary for the production of sweet wines.

> **GRAPE VARIETIES** Sémillon (dominant), Sauvignon Blanc, Muscadelle.

> **SOIL** Clay, gravel.

> **STYLE** A beautiful yellow colour with hints of gold, the wines of Loupiac are generous and very refined. Elegant and complex, the nose presents aromas of crystallized fruit, exotic fruit, and figs, with notes of spiced bread, yellow flowers, honey, acacia, currants, and prunes. The palate is full and creamy, with an elegant structure supported by good acidity. The finish is long and flavourful.

Colour: *White.*

Serving temperature: *About 46°F (8°C).*

Ageing potential: *As much as 100 years, or more.*

STE-CROIX-DU-MONT AOC

ENTRE-DEUX-MERS

This slightly unusual appellation is located to the southeast of Bordeaux, across from Sauternes, and covers 941 acres (381 ha) of steep hills in the commune of the same name. The vineyards of this appellation enjoy a microclimate that favours the development of *Botrytis cinerea*, with mild weather in the fall and humidity at night. Ste-Croix-du-Mont produces exclusively sweet white wine.

> **GRAPE VARIETIES** Sémillon, Sauvignon Blanc, Muscadelle.

> **SOIL** Clay-and-limestone, limestone.

> **STYLE** The wines of Ste-Croix-du-Mont have a charming, intense golden colour; the nose offers aromas of jam (peach, apricot), citrus, and exotic fruit, mixed with notes of raisins and figs, and underscored with hints of honeysuckle, acacia, and honey. The palate is full-bodied, creamy, and very flavourful with a long, smooth finish that lingers with the same fruit flavours as the nose.

Colour: *White.*

Serving temperature: *46 to 50°F (8 to 10°C).*

Ageing potential: *Up to 10 years, or more.*

BURGUNDY

A highly symbolic wine region, Burgundy today covers the same area as the medieval province. It produces some of the greatest wines of France (and the world), both white and red. While the complex layout of its estates and its diverse hierarchical structure is part of its charm, it can also make navigating their way around its wines difficult for the layman.

Monks, *clos*, and complicated classifications

The region of Burgundy bridges the north and south, not only of France but also Europe. This central location has long contributed to the awareness and dissemination of its wines.

FROM THE FOUNDATION OF THE ABBEYS TO THE FRENCH REVOLUTION. Vines are believed to have been growing in the Beaunois region as early as 200 AD. Yet the real boom in Burgundy wine production is linked to Christianity, not only due to the demand for sacramental wine (communion was given in bread and wine until the 13th century, and the faithful often received it daily), but also due to the location of monasteries in the Middle Ages, where the vineyards were often handed down by important local leaders, and served as a means of raising money. The monks, who enjoyed a good standard of living, patiently selected the plots (or '*climats*') that would produce the best wines, which could be sold at the highest prices (*see also* p.17). They were even supposed to have tasted the earth in order to evaluate a particular location! It is more likely that they marked out plots by tasting wines for the payment of tithes in kind. To protect the most precious locations (and avoid disputes with their neighbours), they built stone walls and created the famous Burgundy *clos*, or enclosed vineyard.

FROM THE REVOLUTION TO THE FIRST CLASSIFICATIONS. The French Revolution was an opportunity for winemakers in Burgundy to take revenge on the

VINEYARD STATISTICS (AOC)

BURGUNDY

Vineyard area: 69,190 acres (28,000 ha)
Production: 15.5 million cases (1,400,000 hl)
Reds and rosés: 29%
Whites: 61%
Crémants: 10%

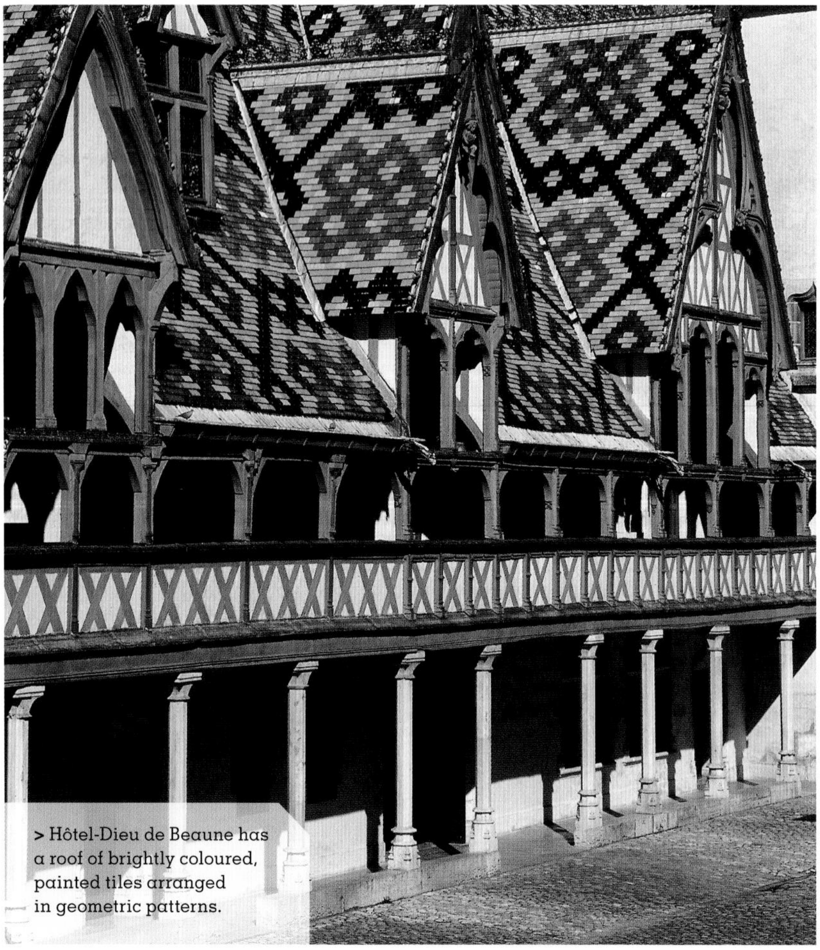

> Hôtel-Dieu de Beaune has a roof of brightly coloured, painted tiles arranged in geometric patterns.

Hospices de Beaune Auction

Founded in 1452 by Nicolas Rolin and Guigone Salins to rescue and care for the poor, the Hospices de Beaune owns a vast inherited estate of more than 148 acres (60 ha), which produces plenty of *premiers crus* and *grands crus*. Each year, the estate's wines are sold in *pièces* (the name for 60-gallon (228 l) Burgundian barrels) on the third Sunday of November at the largest sale of wine in the world. Organized since 2005 by the great British auction house Christie's, the sale is held by candlelight. The proceeds from this sale (€10 million in 2015) are still used to finance the Hôtel-Dieu, which also has a regional health centre. The prices received during the auction serve as an indicator to determine the average price for Burgundy wines of that vintage.

> Harvest in a village in Burgundy.

aristocratic and monastic estates. The fragmentation of estates there began in 1791 with a selling off of national assets, such as those of Clos de Vougeot (*see also* p.283). This sale of property notably profited the local bourgeoise and the first trading houses were created in the 18th century. By 1861, a classification of the 'Agricultural Committee of the District of Beaune' prefigured the modern system of *appellation contrôlée*. They could already distinguish very fine wines or *têtes de cuvée*, which included Romanée-Conti, Clos de Vougeot, and Chambertin *grands crus*

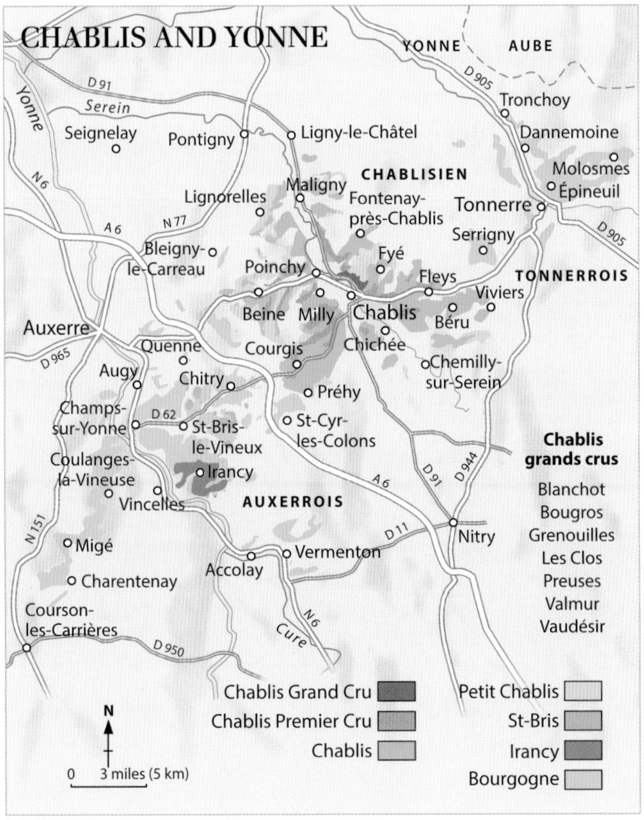

and *premiers crus*. This classification has been simplified (somewhat) by the National Institute of Appellations of Origin (INAO), which removed the highest classification, retaining only the *grands crus* and *premiers crus*. The appellation regulations started to appear in 1936, and the first were for the *grands crus*, followed quickly by local appellations.

Chablis and Yonne vineyards

Chablis is the hallmark of fine, dry, white wine, where the balance between freshness, provided by acidity, and fruit character results in wines that are quite similar to the great whites of the Côte d'Or, but more vigorous. However, making wine in the Chablis region is not easy, since it is located at the northernmost limit of commercial viticulture. The great enemy here is frost, so much so that growers must sometimes, in winter, install vineyard heaters (a kind of oil-fired brazier) or sprinkle water on the vines to form a protective coating around the plant.

Chardonnay, here called 'Beaune', grows especially well on the marl and limestone soils of the Yonne district. The *premiers crus* sites of Chablis (*see* p.281), and even more so the *grands crus*, rival the great whites of the Côte d'Or, with greater minerality and lesser richness. The *grands crus* are all concentrated around the town of Chablis itself, between the villages of Fyé and Poinchy.

In other vineyards around Yonne, Auxerre, and Tonnerre, there are good-quality red wines such as Bourgogne Côte-Saint-Jacques (formerly Coteaux de Joigny) or Bourgogne Vézelay, but in a style that is much lighter than their prestigious neighbours further south in the rest of Burgundy.

Côte d'Or

Côte d'Or stretches from Dijon in the north to Santenay in the south, via Beaune. The wines produced here are more complex, more expensive, and more lasting than elsewhere in Burgundy. They come from famous villages such as Gevrey-Chambertin

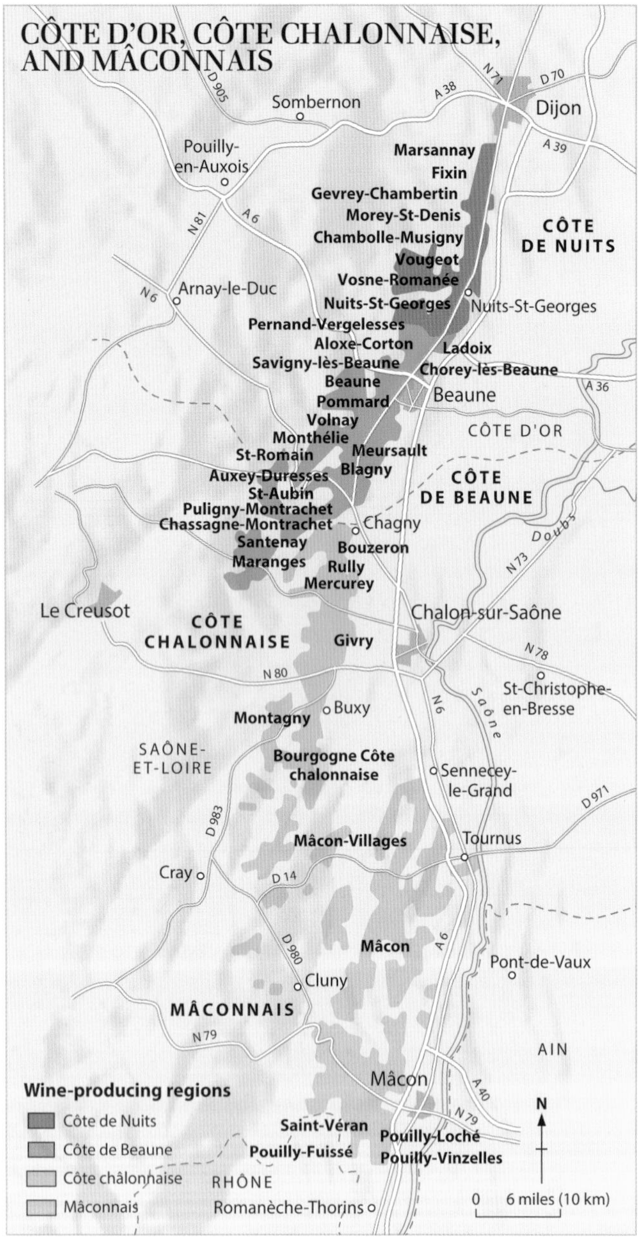

Vosne-Romanée, Pommard, Meursault, and Puligny-Montrachet. They often have these appellations of origin, as well as *'climats'*, of which the most notable are classified as *premier cru* and *grand cru*. In 2015, the *climats* of the Côte d'Or have been granted Unesco world heritage status. The region is divided into two parts, Côte de Nuits to the north and Côte de Beaune to the south. The first produces almost exclusively red wine, the second both reds and whites. Côte d'Or takes its name from the Orient: the vines face east to make the most of often limited sunlight. As with Chablis, this area marks the northern limit of viticulture, with long, severe winters and hot, dry summers, which explains the differences between the vintages. The vineyards are located on steep slopes, which are composed of marl and limestone. The altitude varies between 500 and 1,300 ft (150 and 400 m), and the best wines are almost always mid-slope. The local village itself is generally located lower down.

Côte Chalonnaise

This region is the continuation of the last villages of the Côte d'Or to the south. Its geology is similar to the Côte d'Or, with outcrops of limestone and marl, and some steep sites are very exposed; but the clear line of the Côte d'Or here breaks down into a succession of hills and valleys. Apart from the generic or regional appellations of Burgundy such as the AOC Bourgogne Côte Chalonnaise, the region has five communal appellations: Bouzeron, Rully, Mercurey, Givry, and Montagny. Red, white, and sparkling wines are produced.

Mâconnais

This vast vineyard area, comprising 17,100 acres (6,920 ha) south of the Côte Chalonnaise, produces AOC Mâcon red and white wines. Several villages are allowed to use their own name; and some, like Pouilly, have acquired an excellent reputation. There are also many limestone hills, perfect for Chardonnay, as well as areas of granite rock with sandy soil, more suitable for Gamay. Near Viré, Clessé, and Lugny, the soil is favourable for light white wines. The highest hills and best slopes are located toward the south of the region. This is where well-known villages develop good white Chardonnays, such as Pouilly-Fuissé and Saint-Véran.

Beaujolais

At 37,065 acres (15,000 ha), this is the largest and southernmost vine-growing area in the whole of Burgundy. Beaujolais extends from south of Mâcon to the suburbs of Lyon. It has little in common with the rest of Burgundy, apart from the business network and geographic proximity. Limestone, while dominant elsewhere, gives way here to the granite and igneous rocks of a mountain range separating the Loire River, to the west, from the Saône. Here, the Gamay grape dominates. The region is often considered an appellation producing just 'thirst-quenching wines' designed to accompany snacks in the bars of Lyon. But it also develops high quality wines, particularly within the 10 Beaujolais *crus*, some of which are capable of being aged for several years. Hence the description 'drinkable', which generally describes a refreshing, supple, and fruity wine and is often used to describe the wines of this region, but does not do justice to

DID YOU KNOW...?

Gamay, the main grape of Beaujolais, was at one time banned on the Côte d'Or. *In 1395, Philip the Bold banned from the Côte d'Or (and ordered uprooting of) the 'very bad and foul Gamay vine, a plant that produces a great abundance of wine [...] which is of the sort that is very harmful to human beings... because it is full of great and terrible bitterness.' Nevertheless, Gamay can make great wines when its yields are controlled, as in Beaujolais!*

the diversity of the wines produced here. The production of white is small-scale, but often of good quality.

Burgundy grape varieties

The three main varieties of Burgundy are well known: two are red, Pinot Noir and Gamay, and one is white, Chardonnay. While Pinot Noir and Chardonnay exist worldwide, Gamay is rarely cultivated elsewhere, except in the Loire Valley and Switzerland. Other grape varieties exist, including Aligoté and Sauvignon Blanc (Saint-Bris), and, on anecdotal evidence, Pinot Blanc and César.

PINOT NOIR. This delicate variety is difficult to cultivate. And Burgundy represents the northern limit of its cultivation in France, as in Champagne and Jura. Yet here it produces the best results, particularly in Côte d'Or, where the red *grands crus* are among the greatest wines in the world.

> Vines around the hill of Vieille Morte, near the village of Rivolet in Beaujolais.

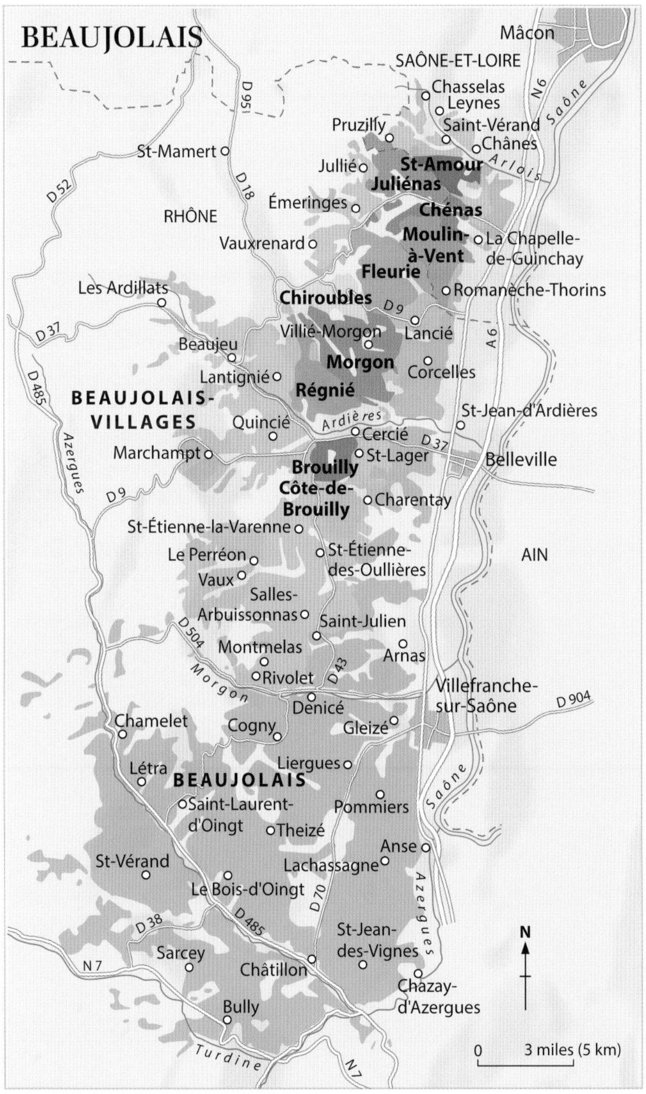

GAMAY. This grape could have a bad reputation because of overproduction. It is true that, if badly cultivated, it provides diluted and bland wines, where only carbonic maceration (*see next page*) reveals a few flavours. But this does not take into account the fact that if the harvest is restricted, Gamay is able to produce wines that are delicious, fresh and light. Plus, the best Beaujolais wines can come, with ageing, to closely resemble their neighbours from Côte d'Or. The issue today is how to diversify the grape variety by introducing others such as Syrah and Marselan (a cross between Gamay and Reichensteiner).

CHARDONNAY. Which variety seems most closely linked to Burgundy? And yet, if there is a truly international grape, it is Chardonnay. It is particularly fond of limestone, found extensively in Burgundy. It can vary enormously in its flavour profile, depending on the winemaking and soil. For example, Chardonnays from Burgundy aged in wood contain particular notes of butter and toast.

ALIGOTÉ. A simple grape variety, this is intended to produce thirst-quenching, lively, refreshing, but not too complex, wines. They do, however, have a little more depth and complexity around the village of Bouzeron, a communal AOC dedicated to this variety.

SAUVIGNON BLANC. Present in the Yonne notably, this grape variety, originally from the Loire and also used in Bordeaux, produces lively, aromatic whites at St-Bris.

Burgundy wine production

RED BURGUNDY. Pinot Noir requires a delicate balance in its maturity, and this needs to be correctly extracted by the wine producer: harvested too early or during cool years, it will result in vegetal flavours and a light wine with excessive acidity; harvested too late or subjected to excessive extraction, it will yield a heavy, alcoholic wine that lacks finesse. Traditionally, portions of the stems (the 'skeletons' of the grape clusters) were retained, as these were supposed to give the wine tannic structure; but this practice is no longer common. Oak ageing is now more popular than ever, especially for grands vins; but new oak is used less frequently than in Bordeaux. As little wine as possible is extracted from the barrels to avoid any contact with air during maturation. Filtration is also less prevalent than in other regions, such as Bordeaux, for example.

WHITE BURGUNDY. The whites may be less demanding in their development. If it is a *premier* or *grand cru* from the Côte d'Or or Chablis, the wine is produced in small oak barrels. If it is a generic Chablis or Mâcon wine, stainless steel or cement tanks are used to preserve freshness, lightness, and a simple and pleasant fruitiness. This fermentation is sometimes followed by ageing in oak barrels, until the end of malolactic, in order to add some complexity. The wine then remains on its lees, with fining and filtering kept to a minimum. The *grands crus* generally benefit from stirring (mixing of lees with a stick placed in the barrel), which adds complexity, richness, and depth.

THE CASE OF BEAUJOLAIS. In order to preserve the fresh and delicate aromas of the Gamay, the winemakers use an original technique known as 'semi-carbonic maceration' (*see also* p.68). This involves fermenting the destemmed but uncrushed grapes in a sealed vat. Two processes take place simultaneously: at the bottom of the vat the squashed grapes release juice and then ferment, emitting carbon dioxide. At the top of the vat, now saturated with carbon dioxide, an 'intracellular' transformation takes place within the whole berries, with the appearance of preliminary aromas. The free-run wine is then drained and the solid parts pressed, after which the two types of juice are put together to finish the fermentation, before being matured in tanks or barrels. This type of vinification intensifies the fruity aromas of the grape. As for the structure, it will depend on the maceration time in tank, which may vary from 3 to more than 15 days. Another version of this technique (carbonic maceration), used in particular to produce Beaujolais Nouveau, consists in depositing the whole clusters in a large sealed vat filled with carbon dioxide. Within a few days, this optimizes the intracellular transformation process, resulting in the quite intense release of fruity aromas and slight extraction of the tannins.

Beaujolais Nouveau

Following the development of *vins de primeur* in 1951, Beaujolais Nouveau has been arriving on tables after the third Thursday of November each year (since 1985). This is a fruity and refreshing young wine, which has no pretensions and brightens up the late autumn. It has a bright, purplish, sometimes fluorescent colour, and its flavours of exotic fruits and fresh grapes (when it is successful and has little or no chaptalization) go very well with the cooked meats and various other nibbles served up at bars in Lyon or Paris.

> Clos des Barraults (red) and Vignes de Maillonge (white), two Mercureys from the Juillot estate.

Appellations and *crus*: a complex system

At the bottom of the scale are regional appellations, followed by village or local appellations, then *premiers crus,* and finally *grands crus.*

REGIONAL APPELLATIONS. These cover wines from many vineyards in Burgundy (*e.g.* Bourgogne Passetoutgrains) or wines from a large sub-region (*e.g.* Bourgogne Hautes-Côtes-de-Nuits).

VILLAGE WINE. These are local appellations attached to the *terroir* around a specific Chambertin commune has the words *'Appellation Gevrey-Chambertin Contrôlée'* written on it. However, some 'village' AOCs overlap with nearby villages. Thus, an AOC Nuits-Saint-Georges wine can come from Premeaux, a nearby village.

TRUE OR FALSE?

All Burgundy wines are made from a single grape variety.

FALSE. Bourgogne Passetoutgrains is one-third Pinot Noir with the rest Gamay, and generic white Burgundy and Crémant de Bourgogne can include Chardonnay, Pinot Blanc, Aligoté, and Melon de Bourgogne (as well as Sacy in Yonne).

PREMIERS CRUS. This name distinguishes certain plots among the villages of the Côte d'Or, the Côte Chalonnaise, and Chablis. The label offers the name of the village and the specific plot, for example Gevrey-Chambertin Clos St. Jacques. A *premier cru* wine can come from a single site, for example Beaune-Grèves, or be a blend of *premiers crus* from different great sites (such as Beaune Premier Cru without any further indication).

299
500
594
20
450

Brotherhood of the Knights of Tastevin

While the name of this famous brotherhood evokes the Middle Ages, it is actually a relatively recent creation. Founded in 1934 by Georges Faiveley and Camille Rodier, its goal was to restore the reputation of Burgundy wines, which had been battered by the crisis of 1929. The Brotherhood owns the famous Château du Clos de Vougeot (but not the vineyards), in which it holds its 'chapters', during which new members are inducted. (They now have almost 12,000 worldwide.) It brings together statesmen and men of letters, famous people and enthusiasts – all with the aim of making them ambassadors for Burgundy wines. Since 1950, it has organized selections of Burgundy wines under the name 'Tastevinage'. This labelling process is rigorous and contemporary in its outlook despite the somewhat old-fashioned logo on the bottles!

GRANDS CRUS. These are small, but famous appellations; and on labels their name is always followed by the words 'Appellation Grand Cru Contrôlée.' For example, the *grand cru* Romanée-Saint-Vivant is labelled 'Romanée-Saint-Vivant, Appellation Grand Cru Contrôlée'. A *grand cru* can straddle several villages; for example, Grand Cru Corton is produced from certain plots in the Aloxe-Corton, Ladoix-Serrigny, and Pernand-Vergelesses districts.

Here is a trick to figure out Burgundy: the shorter the name, the more prestigious the wine. Thus, Musigny (*grand cru*) is more prestigious than Chambolle-Musigny (a village appellation); Chambertin (*grand cru*) is superior to Gevrey-Chambertin (a village appellation), and so on. But this rule does have many exceptions.

Main market players

As in many other regions, wine production is divided among independent producers, *négociants*, and cooperatives, but with specific features and important differences.

INDEPENDENT WINE PRODUCERS. The great wines of Burgundy have traditionally been expensive, and the prices achieved in recent years have done nothing to change that tradition. Côte d'Or is the home of small independent producers. This is reflected in small lots of handcrafted wines, the fragmentation of the *climats*, and the complexity of appellations. Bottling in-house has grown significantly since the 1970s. But the small size of plots and the great demand mean that the producers, apart from a few major estates (Leroy, Prieur, and De Vogüé, for example), rarely have older wines for sale. In fact, they may have nothing to offer apart from the most recent harvest. It is the size of the plots that explains the extreme diversity of wines within the same appellation: a small producer is not generally free to blend several plots to counteract a bad or less favourable vintage. Good and bad sit side by side and the consumer sometimes finds it difficult to find a way through the maze of names and appellations, as fascinating they are sometimes discouraging. Prices also act as a reliable guide, and a wine priced significantly lower than its neighbours must be treated carefully and with circumspection. Accordingly, wines from elite wine producers (Chandon de Briailles, Coche-Dury, Comtes Lafon, or Méo-Camuzet, for example) are often expensive and sold mainly abroad and for major events.

BURGUNDY *NÉGOCIANTS*. In Burgundy, wine merchants are not content, as elsewhere, to simply sell wines made by others. We can distinguish ordinary *négociants* from *négociants* who buy grapes, make wine, blend, age, and put it on the market. They have often been criticized for the uniformity of their wines and some poor vintages. But the quantity of wine they produce enables them precisely to control the blending, and erase the imperfections of a wine-producing area as fragmented and capricious as Burgundy. They often have an estate themselves, producing *premiers crus* and *grands crus*, including wines to rival those of elite independent wine producers. But such high standards have a price! Above all, like the estates in Champagne, Burgundy *négociants* provide the bulk of exports.

COOPERATIVES. It would be wrong to think that the independent or individual nature of the wine producers in Burgundy would make them reject cooperatives as a means of production. But they are definitely more important on the periphery, in Chablis, Hautes Côtes, Mâconnais, and Beaujolais, than in Côte d'Or. Some are excellent, such as La Chablisienne or the Buxy cooperative, and the Vignerons des Terres Secrètes (Mâconnais) or Bailly Lapierre (Yonne), which produce wines of good quality. They now have state-of-the-art facilities (which are often lacking in independent wine producers) and encourage their members to produce the best possible grapes.

DID YOU KNOW...?

During the late 19th century, several villages in the Côte d'Or were awarded the right to add to their name the name(s) of the* grands crus *produced in their locality. *Thus, in 1882, Chambolle took the name Chambolle-Musigny, Gevrey became Gevrey-Chambertin, both Puligny and Chassagne villages share the name of their* grand cru, *the famous Montrachet. Aloxe added the name Corton, although this wine is also produced in the villages of Pernand-Vergelesses and Ladoix, while Vosne has naturally benefited from the reputation of Romanée.*

Burgundy AOCS

** *grand cru* * general appellation including *premiers crus*

REGIONAL AND GENERIC APPELLATIONS (produced throughout Burgundy)
- Bourgogne Aligoté
- Bourgogne Coteaux Bourguignons
- Bourgogne Passetoutgrains
- Crémant de Bourgogne

CHABLIS
- Petit Chablis
- Chablis *
- Chablis Grand Cru **
- Bourgogne Côte-de-St-Jacques

AUXERRE, TONNERROIS, AND VÉZELIEN
- Bourgogne Chitry
- Bourgogne Côtes d'Auxerre
- Bourgogne Coulanges-La-Vineuse
- Bourgogne Épineuil
- Bourgogne Vézelay
- Bourgogne Tonnerre
- Irancy
- St-Bris

CÔTE DE NUITS
- Bonnes-Mares **
- Bourgogne Hautes-Côtes-de-Nuits
- Bourgogne La Chapelle-Notre-Dame
- Bourgogne Le Chapitre
- Bourgogne Montrecul
- Chambertin **
- Chambertin-Clos de Bèze **
- Chambolle-Musigny *
- Chapelle-Chambertin **
- Charmes-Chambertin **
- Clos de la Roche **
- Clos de Tart **
- Clos de Vougeot **
- Clos des Lambrays **
- Clos St-Denis **
- Côte-de-Nuits-Villages
- Échezeaux **
- Fixin *
- Gevrey-Chambertin *
- Grands Échezeaux **
- Griotte-Chambertin **
- La Grande Rue **
- La Romanée **
- La Tâche **
- Latricières-Chambertin **
- Marsannay
- Mazis-Chambertin **
- Mazoyères-Chambertin **
- Morey-Saint-Denis *
- Musigny **
- Nuits-Saint-Georges or Nuits *
- Richebourg **
- Romanée-Conti **
- Romanée-Saint-Vivant **
- Ruchottes-Chambertin **
- Vosne-Romanée *
- Vougeot *

CÔTE DE BEAUNE
- Aloxe-Corton *
- Auxey-Duresses *
- Bâtard-Montrachet **
- Beaune *
- Bienvenues-Bâtard-Montrachet **
- Blagny *
- Bourgogne Hautes-Côtes de Beaune
- Chassagne-Montrachet *
- Chevalier-Montrachet **
- Chorey-lès-Beaune or Chorey
- Corton **
- Corton-Charlemagne and Charlemagne **
- Côte-de-Beaune
- Côte-de-Beaune-Villages
- Criots-Bâtard-Montrachet **
- Ladoix-Serrigny or Ladoix *
- Maranges *
- Meursault *
- Monthélie *
- Montrachet **
- Pernand-Vergelesses *
- Pommard *
- Puligny-Montrachet *
- St-Aubin *
- St-Romain
- Santenay *
- Savigny-lès-Beaune or Savigny *
- Volnay *

CÔTE CHALONNAISE
- Bourgogne Côte Chalonnaise
- Bourgogne Côtes-du-Couchois
- Bouzeron
- Givry *
- Mercurey *
- Montagny *
- Rully *

MÂCONNAIS
- Mâcon
- Mâcon followed by a village name
- Mâcon Supérieur
- Mâcon-Villages
- Pouilly-Fuissé
- Pouilly-Loché
- Pouilly-Vinzelles
- Saint-Véran
- Viré-Clessé

BEAUJOLAIS
- Beaujolais
- Beaujolais-Villages
- Beaujolais Supérieur
- Brouilly
- Chénas
- Chiroubles
- Côte-de-Brouilly
- Fleurie
- Juliénas
- Morgon
- Moulin-à-Vent
- Régnié
- St-Amour

Best-known wines of Burgundy

Wines from Burgundy are fairly consistent in terms of style, with the exception of red Beaujolais wines. Whites are drier and with greater minerality in the north, richer and more aromatic in Côte d'Or. They are mostly Chardonnay, which gives them, if not an exact likeness, at least a family resemblance. The reds have a greater diversity: there is little in common between a Passetoutgrains and a fine Côte de Nuits.

CRÉMANT DE BOURGOGNE AOC

THE WHOLE REGION

In Burgundy, sparkling wines have been produced since the 19th century; but since 1975 they have been entitled to the appellation Crémant de Bourgogne (if they are produced from wines that undergo a second fermentation in bottle). Without the reputation of their neighbours in Champagne, they generally offer good value for money.

> **GRAPE VARIETIES** Pinot Noir and Gamay (20 per cent maximum) for rosés; Chardonnay (30 per cent minimum) with the addition of Aligoté, Melon, or Sacy.

> **SOIL** All Burgundy *terroirs* are suitable, with a preference for calcareous marl, chalky soil as in Champagne, or granite to the south.

> **STYLE** The *blanc de blancs* shows white flowers, citrus, and green apple flavours that evolve with time towards note of white orchard fruit and toast. The *blanc de noirs* presents aromas of berry fruit (cherry, blackcurrant, or raspberry). It is a powerful wine on the palate, long and persistent. Keeping it results in a little more roundness and warmth, with dried fruit flavours that are sometimes honeyed or spicy. The rosé (Pinot Noir, with or without Gamay) is a delicate wine with subtle red fruit flavours.

Colour:
White and rosé.

Serving temperature:
39 to 48°F (4 to 9°C) depending on the occasion (as an aperitif or with a meal).

Ageing potential:
3 to 5 years maximum.

BOURGOGNE PASSETOUTGRAINS AOC

THE WHOLE REGION

This appellation (which is also written 'Passe-tout-grains'), established in 1937, applies to red or rosé wines from all over Burgundy. It is produced from up to two-thirds Gamay and one-third Pinot Noir. The grapes are blended in the tank, not as finished wines. In a region that history has led to focus on single-variety wines, it is a sufficiently original trait to be worth noting. Rosé wines, which are less common, must be produced by fermenting grapes, whether crushed or not, without pressing them before fermentation.

> **GRAPE VARIETIES** Pinot Noir and Gamay.

> **SOIL** Pinot Noir is found almost everywhere in Burgundy, Gamay particularly in Mâconnais on siliceous, clay, sandy, or granite soil.

> **STYLE** For red wines, the style varies according to the proportion of Gamay and Pinot, but these are usually fruity, light, 'thirst-quenching wines'. They can assume a purplish, almost fuchsia hue, and they are full of light in their youth. The rosés are a little more intense in colour, with a slight hint of orange; their fruity, delicious flavours evoke gooseberries.

Colour:
Red and rosé.

Serving temperature:
54°F (12°C) for both reds and rosés.

Ageing potential:
3 to 5 years maximum.

CHABLIS AND PETIT CHABLIS AOC

CHABLIS AND YONNE

Before the onset of phylloxera, the Chablis region produced one-third of all Burgundy wines. It is centred round the small town of Chablis, whose dry whites have been well known since the 9th century. This vineyard, the most northerly in Burgundy, is particularly vulnerable to spring frosts. Worldwide, Chablis is synonymous with dry, mineral-laced white wine. Its name has been stolen again and again for anything similar. Petit Chablis AOC, less well known, produces wines that are lighter, with fewer flavours than Chablis… but it's cheaper!

> **GRAPE VARIETY** Chardonnay.

> **SOIL** Slopes of Kimmeridgian calcareous clay and the Portlandian limestone plateau. > **STYLE** Chablis used to be produced and aged in oak barrels, but these were seldom new. The use of stainless steel tanks for vinification has opened up new horizons. Petit Chablis wines are lively, fruity and direct. Chablis wines have body and roundness, with fruit (green fruit, citrus fruit), floral, and mineral notes, with a firm and refreshing acidity. If left to age three or four years, the wine acquires complexity and richness.

Colour:
White.

Serving temperature:
50 to 52°F (10 to 11°C).

Ageing potential:
3 to 6 years for Chablis;
3 years at most for Petit Chablis.

CHABLIS GRAND CRU AND CHABLIS PREMIER CRU AOC

CHABLIS AND YONNE

The *grands* and *premiers crus* from Chablis are among the finest white wines of Burgundy. The grands crus come from seven *'climats'*, and their names come after the words Chablis Grand Cru: Blanchot, Bougros, Les Clos, Grenouilles, Preuses, Valmur, and Vaudésir. More affordable than their counterparts from the Côte de Beaune, they can age longer than regular Chablis irrespective of *cru*, and they gain complexity and richness as they mature. The *premiers crus* are more numerous. Among the best known are Fourchaume, Montée de Tonnerre, Mont de Milieu, Montmains, and Vaucoupin.

> **GRAPE VARIETY** Chardonnay.

> **SOIL** Kimmeridgian calcareous clay in which there are still deposits of tiny oysters from the time when a shallow, warm sea covered Burgundy.

STYLE The various *crus* are not always easy to recognize, since their differences are as much based on style of cultivation and wine production as from different *terroirs*. After at least five years in the cellar, a *premier* or *grand cru* from Chablis is a complex yet open wine, where flavours of flint and stone give way to hints of lime, dried fruit, and sometimes of mushrooms.

Colour:
White.

Serving temperature:
54 to 57°F (12 to 14°C).

Ageing potential:
10 years for premiers crus; *10 to 15 years (and sometimes more) for* grands crus.

Selected Chablis producers

- **La Chablisienne.** This excellent cooperative is responsible for about a third of the production of Chablis. Its wines are often impeccable, and include a selection of the oldest vineyards classed as *premier cru*. Its finest wine is the Château Grenouilles (*grand cru*), which is very rare and much sought after.

- **Domaine Garnier** Domaine Garnier. Two young brothers full of passion run this estate of 59 acres (24 ha), and its entire range of wines are highly recommended. They are produced in vats or barrels and comprise Chablis, Petit Chablis, and Chablis Grand Cru. There is an excellent late-harvest Chablis Grains Dorés, which is powerful and full bodied.

- **William Fèvre.** This *négociant*, a subsidiary of the Beaune estate Bouchard Père & Fils, has the largest area of *grands crus* from this appellation. It is known for its very pure, direct wines that are good for laying down.

- **Domaine Vincent Dauvissat.** This estate is a Chablis icon under the masterful hand of Vincent Dauvissat. Its 30 acres (12 ha) are cultivated with great precision and care to produce wines of a purity and intensity that has few rivals. Its *grands crus* (Les CLos, Les Preuses), are produed in very small quantities and are much sought after.

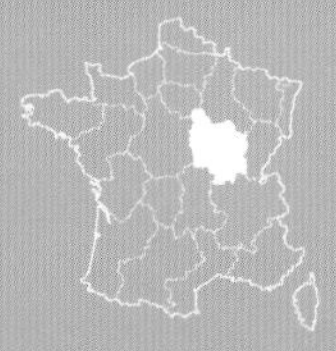

Burgundy

LA CHABLISIENNE

With its monopoly grand cru and its high-end positioning, the La Chablisienne cellar cooperative is the exception rather than the rule in France.

LA CHABLISIENNE

8, boulevard Pasteur
89800 Chablis

Founded: *1923*
Area: *2,965 acres (1,200 ha)*
Production: *N/A*
Appellation: *Chablis*
White grape variety: *Chardonnay*

A co-op at the top

With 300 members and 2,965 acres (1,200 ha) under cultivation, La Chablisienne is the largest cooperative in Burgundy (from a commercial point of view) and the most famous to boot. It thus includes Chablis, one of the largest appellations in Burgundy at 8,150 acres (3,298 ha), 15 *premiers crus* and six *grands crus*, of which one (Château Grenouilles) is a monopoly – all unheard of for a wine collective. 'It was really a political choice to allocate Château Grenouilles to us,' emphasizes Damien Leclerc, the current cellar manager. Seventeen acres (6.8 ha) of *grand cru* from a single occupant – no one can afford that in Chablis. But thanks to the goodwill of their bankers and the government authorities, the cooperative members were to enter the exalted ranks of owners of *grands crus* in 2003. This accolade also marked the logical outcome of another strategic decision, taken ten years previously, to bottle the entire output of the cellar for sale to individuals, instead of selling more than three-quarters in bulk to wine merchants. At the time (in 1992), the Gulf War had just finished, the stock market was wavering... and the market had 'forgotten' to keep its side of the bargain, leaving the small producers, whose unsold stock was about to go off in the cellar, in the lurch; they came to the La Chablisienne manager's office to tell him their tales of woe, even though he had taken just as much of a hit as they had. In declaring its commercial independence, the cooperative thus became an entirely separate brand. It has jealously guarded its credibility as such ever since, disdaining large-scale distribution, and you will never see its label in a supermarket.

Famine...

It has been quite a journey for this little cellar, which was founded in 1923 thanks to the tireless work of Abbé Balitrand, who created the Union of Chablis wine-growers; even then, wine merchants were choking the life out of small producers by laying down the law to them. Initially, the Chablisienne group included the villages on the outskirts of Chablis (those without any stake in the great terroirs of Chablis), who felt spurned by the wine-makers of the main town – who in turn were deaf to the claims of their appellation, as it was located beyond the confines of their town. United in their poverty, the cooperative members were first and foremost mixed farmers, although at the time no one was making any money to speak of, even in Chablis; the unyielding hillsides were producing very little, essentially, and in three years out of five, the few grapes that escaped mildew and rot ended up ravaged by the frosts of spring – so it made more financial sense to be a farmer and grow wheat.

In the years 1945–50, Blanchot, now a *grand cru*, was fallow land or just little groves of vines, and children would sled down the slopes of the Les Clos *grand cru*, which was planted with alfalfa for horses at the summit and cereals halfway down, as it froze every year. People were selling off their *premier cru* vineyards so they were no longer obliged to pay the taxes on them. The children of the nursery owner who refused the 74 acres (30 ha) at Fourchaume that were offered to him for next to nothing must be kicking themselves today: Fourchaume is now one of the most popular *premiers crus* in Chablis.... In the 1950s and '60s, however, the lucky ones were those surrounding Saint-Bris-le-Vineux, a village of flourishing cherry trees.

LA CHABLISIENNE, CHÂTEAU GRENOUILLES, CHABLIS GRAND CRU GRENOUILLES

As documented on old postcards, the area was once known as 'le chalet des Grenouilles'. The flattering title of 'château', which was better for sales, was conferred in 1960 by Philippe Testut, the former owner. Before World War II, the Les Clos and Grenouilles *grands crus* had only been planted in the most accessible parts of their respective areas, while the parts susceptible to frost, as recounted by the historian Henri Cannard, were left as pasture into the 1950s. Grenouilles is the smallest of the *grands crus* (along with Moutonne) but has the benefit of good exposure to the south-southwest on an extremely sunny hillside. Its wines are said to be full, perhaps even massive, and less elegant than some, but extremely expressive in their young years.

... and feast

Such poverty is difficult to imagine, given the current prosperity of today's wine-growers. The Eureka moment came in the 1960s with the advent of heaters – hallelujah! At dawn on May mornings, they would either burn fuel or spray water, creating a cloud of sooty smoke or a sheet of ice on several of the hillsides that were most susceptible to freezing over, and either of which was enough to save the budding vines from the frost. The process was expensive, but the harvest was saved, at least in part. However, the lake at Beine, once the reservoir supplying the water on these frozen May mornings, is now used only for canoeing.

Since the 1980s, it has thus been more profitable to be a wine-grower than a farmer, and the vines have seen off the cows. Nowadays, there are even some who say that it would be more profitable to bottle your wine at your own estate than to send the grapes (in the form of freshly pressed juice) to La Chablisienne, whose little tankers tirelessly ply the village roads to collect the grape-must as soon as it is harvested. However, to 73-year-old Roland Bourcey, a former cooperative administrator, who has been a wine-grower in the area all his life, this seems a bit pretentious: 'Having my name on a label – with my 64 acres (26 ha)? I'd rather be someone producing nine million bottles,' he exclaims. But the cooperative is about more than margins or clientele – it's about a spirit; as Bourcey says, '"La Chab" is my second family.'

FIXIN AOC

CÔTE DE NUITS

This little village, the most northerly of the Côte de Nuits, produces mainly high quality red wines. Though little known to wine lovers, some of them are reminiscent of Gevrey-Chambertin in terms of their character. The appellation includes several *premiers crus*, including Les Hervelets, La Perrière, Le Clos du Chapitre, and Le Clos Napoléon.

> **GRAPE VARIETY** Pinot Noir.

> **SOIL** Brown calcareous soil, fairly homogeneous for the *premiers crus*, with marl in some places (*e.g.* Les Hervelets), as well as a combination of limestone and marl elsewhere.

> **STYLE** The wines are powerful yet delicate, with good tannic structure, but without being too aggressive. They are rather deep in colour and suggest aromas that are typical of Pinot Noir (violet, blackcurrant, cherry), developing after a few years to more gamey and spicy notes.

Colour: *Red.*

Serving temperature: *55 to 59°F (13 to 15°C).*

Ageing potential: *10 to 15 years.*

GEVREY-CHAMBERTIN AOC

CÔTE DE NUITS

This extensive appellation is one of the most famous in Côte de Nuits, and also one of the most understandable! Here, no *grand cru* has a name that is completely different from the main village. The nine *grands crus*–Chambertin, Charmes-Chambertin, Chambertin-Clos de Bèze, Chapelle-Chambertin, Griotte-Chambertin, Latricières-Chambertin, Mazis-Chambertin, Mazoyères-Chambertin, and Ruchottes-Chambertin total 215 acres (87 ha), more than from any other village. Napoleon was reputed to drink only Clos de Bèze wines – diluted, they say, with water. There also are no fewer than 26 *premiers crus*.

> **GRAPE VARIETY** Pinot Noir.

> **SOIL** Hard rock, covered with a thin layer of brown silt on top. Marl and limestone are on the slopes.

> **STYLE** The best Gevrey-Chambertins are powerful, fruity, and tannic, with a structure that will last. The wines have a bright colour when young, ranging from dark red to black cherry. On the nose, notes of cassis, cherry, and raspberry evolve over time into cocoa, coffee, and hints of damp woodlands. In the mouth, full and fleshy textures dominate. The *grands crus* here rarely disappoint, but fragmentation sometimes leads to variable quality. Some *premiers crus*, including the famous Clos-St-Jacques, can compete with *grands crus*.

Colour: *Red.*

Serving temperature: *57 to 61°F (14 to 16°C).*

Ageing potential: *10 to 30 years.*

MOREY-ST-DENIS AOC

CÔTE DE NUITS

This small village rests between two famous neighbours (Gevrey-Chambertin and Chambolle-Musigny). The vineyards lie on a limestone hill that runs from Gevrey to Vougeot. Two of the *grands crus* around the village are from old walled monastery cloisters that are typical of Burgundy: Clos de Tart (which is a monopole) and Clos St-Denis, as well as the Clos de la Bussiere Premier Cru. The other *grands crus* are the Clos de la Roche and Clos des Lambrays, and part of Bonnes-Mares (the other part being on Chambolle-Musigny). Morey-St-Denis Burgundy develops red wines that are to be laid down in the classic, solid, and well-structured style of Côte de Nuits. Because it is not well known by the general public, this appellation represents good value for money, at least in comparison to its prestigious neighbours.

> **GRAPE VARIETY** Pinot Noir.

> **SOIL** Clay-and-limestone.

> **STYLE** Depending on their origin, the red wines of Morey derive their full-bodied nature from Gevrey-Chambertin in some cases, while others gain their delicacy from Chambolle. Overall, these are wines with class and power, including a rich bouquet of violets and strawberry, which sometimes also is reminiscent of truffles.

Colour: *Red.*

Serving temperature: *57 to 61°F (14 to 16°C).*

Ageing potential: *10 to 30 years.*

CHAMBOLLE-MUSIGNY AOC

CÔTE DE NUITS

In 1878, only the commune of Chambolle was allowed to append its name to that of its most famous *climat*, Musigny, which overlooks the Clos de Vougeot. A former stronghold of Cîteaux Abbey, Chambolle-Musigny has two *grands crus*: Bonnes-Mares (shared with Morey-St-Denis) and Musigny. Lighter than the Chambertins, the red wines of Chambolle-Musigny have an admirable bouquet and sweetness; and they are usually considered the finest, most delicate, and most elegant of the Côte de Nuits. The very timbre of the name of the village conjures up a sense of elegance and lightness when you say it. The *premier crus* are also top quality, the best being Les Amoureuses, located below the plots of Musigny. White Musigny is found only occasionally.

> **GRAPE VARIETY** Pinot Noir.

> **SOIL** Limestone, often mixed with clay marl.

> **STYLE** Restrained power, combined with elegance: this is the hallmark of the best wines of the village, which are some of the greatest reds from Burgundy. They are less tannic and less structured than the wines of Morey-St-Denis and Gevrey-Chambertin. They have a potent violet and red berry nose in their early years, giving way with age to riper, spicier, more gamey aromas (such as prunes, truffles, and damp woodland).

Colour:
Red.

Serving temperature:
57 to 61°F (14 to 16°C).

Ageing potential:
10 to 20 years.

VOUGEOT AOC

CÔTE DE NUITS

Clos de Vougeot is probably the most famous or the flagship Burgundy wine, although its dispersal among multiple owners with small plots (80 owners across 124 acres/50 ha) can result in very different wines depending on their location on the hillside and the work of the producer. But the appellation, which owes its name to the Vouge, a small local river, is more than just that famous Clos, owned by Cîteaux Abbey from the 12th century, whose medieval castle is the headquarters of the Brotherhood of Knights Tastevin of Burgundy (*see box* p.294). It develops a small amount of white wine, too – in particular the Clos Blanc Premier Cru (sometimes called Vigne Blanche), which is quite rare in Côte de Nuits.

> **GRAPE VARIETIES** Pinot Noir for red; Chardonnay for white.

> **SOIL** Brown, calcareous, rather thin soils at the top of the hills; marl clay and limestone lower down on the hills.

> **STYLE** Vougeot reds have a dark colour, almost purple when young, as well as a powerful, rich, almost sweet flavour at that age, enhanced by a bouquet of violets and berries (blackcurrant). This distinct combination, elements of which are present in other wines, albeit less systematically, enables them to be recognized. While not the most subtle Burgundy wines, they are full-bodied and generous in the mouth and have a velvety texture. The white wines are rather dry, with a floral bouquet (of hawthorn and acacia) enhanced with notes of toast. The mouth can be quite mineral, similar to Aloxe-Corton wines, in a lighter style than the great whites of the Côte de Beaune. It develops a more spicy and full-bodied flavour after a few years.

Colour:
Red and white.

Serving temperature:
54 to 55°F (12 to 13°C) for the whites; 57 to 61°F (14 to 16°C) for the reds.

Ageing potential:
5 to 10 years for the whites; 10 to 20 years for the reds.

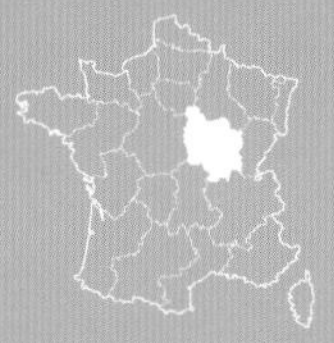

Burgundy, Côtes de Nuits

DOMAINE *DUGAT-PY*

Bernard and his son Loïc – patient tillers of the soil – tend their vines with love and incredible attention to detail at the Dugat-Py estate in Gevrey-Chambertin.

DOMAINE DUGAT-PY

Cour de L'Aumônerie
rue Planteligone
21220 Gevrey-Chambertin

Founded: as Domaine Dugat in 1923, rechristened Dugat-Py in 1994
Area: *25 acres (10 ha)*
Production: *35,000 bottles p.a.*
Appellation: *Gevrey-Chambertin*
Red grape variety: *Pinot Noir*
White grape variety: *Chardonnay*

Gevrey-Chambertin, the soul of Pinot Noir

With 1,011 acres (409 ha) of appellation to its name (of which 198 acres/80 ha are *premiers crus*), Gevrey-Chambertin is the largest of the villages on the Côte de Nuits and the proud possessor of nine of the 24 *grands crus*. The slopes of Vosne-Romanée, which boasts no fewer than six of these, are the most famous incarnation of Burgundian Pinot Noir. The history of winemaking at Gevrey begins with the Romans and was of course continued by monks, so it comes as no surprise that the Dugat family, who can trace their roots back more than 300 years, now work in a high-ceilinged vaulted cellar from the late 17th century whose slender architectural lines echo the early Gothic period. This clerical building, which is in fact a monastery cellar that came into the family's hands after the French Revolution, turned out to be a good place to be and to live, as if some gentle influence could be felt there and the monks had been able to detect it.

Bernard Dugat, an old-school winemaker

The first thing that strikes you about the Dugat courtyard is that it is empty – there are no gleaming straddle tractors or imposing caterpillar-tracked vehicles or new-look soil pulverizers; there's only the winemaker coming to welcome you. With his pickaxe in his hand, he might perhaps be a little annoyed at interrupting a day of hoeing that had started at 7am that morning. The old spring practice of hoeing out the weeds at the base of the vine stock has been continued by Bernard, his son Loïc, and their five employees for each of the 11,000 vines on the 27 acres (11 ha) of the estate. After hoeing, there is pruning – but not with electric trimmers, a modern tool that cuts more efficiently but doesn't allow you to get close enough to the branching points of the vine shoots. His colleagues smile as they see the Dugats wielding a saw and gardening secateurs, but only these allow them to control their cuts and feel the toughness of the wood, so they work more accurately and cleanly. Ploughing is next, using a horse (as M. Dugat the elder used to do), then hoeing, then a severe trimming of the buds and cutting back foliage – but with shears, not machinery. Anyone can raise their arms for ten minutes to trim the top of a vine stock five or six feet (1.8m) off the ground, but keeping them raised over 27 acres (11 ha) is another matter…. 'Even so', exclaims Bernard Dugat, 'I'm not going to do it by machine – and compress the soil I had just taken the trouble to plough and hoe a minute before?'

Burgundian to the bone

These are not just vineyards, they are gardens, although they can sometimes have 32,000 plants per acre (13,000 plants per hectare). Bernard, Loïc, and Jocelyne (née Py), the mother of the family, treat each of the plants, which include many old vines, like gnarled, arthritic old friends that need looking after. They haven't torn out a vine for 20 years, and when they replant new growth, it is always in the same place (or very nearly), as the old vines fight ferociously to choke out the young ones and prevent them from taking hold. The yields from these venerable and long-standing ancestral vines are necessarily low: the estate produced an average of 1.3 to 1.4 tons per acre (22 to 23 hl/hectare) in 2014, about half that of others. And while the wines are certainly expensive, when measured against the hours of work devoted to the vines…. As Bernard Dugat points out: 'I have swung a pickaxe with both my grandfather and my father,' and Loïc too is following in the family tradition. The old folk in this farming family don't retire when they turn 67, and they are folk who have always worked hard. After World War I, the family had to fall back on growing blackcurrants and running a vine nursery, but the Dugats have always been winemakers, hard-working and modest, with a nice trade in their wines (and the barrels that went to the Leroys, the family of Lalou Bize-Leroy). They started bottling their wine at the estate in the 1970s, using a 'double spigot', an old manual system that is attached to each barrel. They witnessed the first journalists turning up in their courtyard, with mutual astonishment, and Bernard has been to New York only once in his life to sell his wines, a record as exceptional as he is. Burgundian to the bone, he doesn't talk about his hectares, he talks about his 'heritage'.

DOMAINE DUGAT-PY, GRAND CRU CHARMES-CHAMBERTIN

None of the Chambertin owners date back beyond 1900, although with the Dugats, Charmes has been in the family since the 17th century (thanks to an inheritance on the Bollenot side of their grandmother's family). The vines are located in 'proper Charmes', *i.e.* in its historic heart, near Chambertin (the king of the Gevrey *grands crus*), as opposed to the modern boundaries that have generously increased the Charmes label in the less renowned area of Mazoyères. Two-thirds of the wine is made from a little plot of 98-year-old vines, yielding a wild and spicy wine, with a round mouth-feel that is velvety, concentrated, and silky. The wine is fermented in barrel for 18 to 19 months and 40% is made with whole grapes that have not been destemmed.

Tasting the stalk

Nowadays, this preserver of traditions, who has been organically certified since 2003, has been overtaken by the nostalgic and yet worldly trend of the 'artisan winemaker with clogs and an iPhone' – but he doesn't care. When harvest comes, he tastes his grapes in order to work out the right date for picking. Everybody does this on the Côte, but the Dugats go one better than testing the grape flesh and the pips; they put the stalk in their mouths. Who would have hit upon the idea of tasting the green stems of the grape bunches? 'Some years it is sugary, like menthol, it's crunchy. And then it's good – it must not have had the time to go brown and turn into wood', explains Bernard. A simple procedure, but rarely carried out, and it is efficient: in 2003, the Dugats were not caught out by the heatwave and accelerated maturation of the vines. 'We had seen that something was up since April, with new growth 8 inches (20 cm) higher than usual, so we booked the refrigerator lorry well in advance. We and Lalou Bize-Leroy were the only ones to have one at harvest, as all the other trucks had been requisitioned by the hospitals. And when you taste our 2003 wine, it's not overcooked, it hasn't turned into jam.'

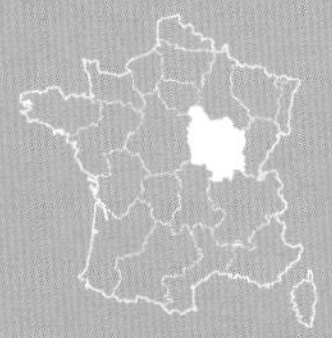

Burgundy,
Côte de Nuits

LA ROMANÉE-*CONTI*

This modest parcel of land – 4.5 acres (1.8 ha) in the heart of the Côte de Nuits – has a global reputation; the red wine produced by La Romanée-Conti has long since achieved legendary status, although it is true that it is more talked about than drunk.

A history going back centuries

The Romans were the first to recognize the extraordinary potential of this region's *terroir*, followed a little later by Cistercian monks who were to confirm their observations, and the boundaries of the winemaking area have been set since 1512. In 1760, the Prince of Conti, a born Burgundian and a counsellor to Louis XV, bought the parcel of land for an exorbitant price, although the estate was expropriated during the French Revolution and sold as a national asset in 1792; it was after this event that the establishment received its official title, La Romanée-Conti.

A terroir that makes all the difference

La Romanée-Conti wine is a demonstration of the primordial power of terroir – on this minuscule patch of land, and using the same grape variety as the rest of Burgundy, unique scents and flavours are unlocked. Accorded the same care and treated using the same methods, the closest neighbours (a stone's throw away) produce remarkable wines, certainly, but they are always different. It is a total mystery, although one that can be observed time and time again....

Facing east on a slightly inclined slope, the vineyard has ideal exposure to the sun and perfect drainage. Pinot Noir is entirely at home here and can express its characteristics completely. The owners did all they could for some time to preserve the original vines, but after the crop of 1945, the long ravages of phylloxera forced them to tear everything out and replant with rootstock that was immune to the parasite – and so there was no Romanée-Conti made between 1946 and 1951 inclusive.

From vine to cellar: a faultless progression

Aubert de Villaine and Henry-Frédéric Roch, the current co-owners of the estate, maintain their respect for the vines and take their inspiration from the principles of biodynamics. It all starts in the vineyard – to get ripe, healthy grapes, nothing is ever forced by using chemical products that might make the work easier but which exhaust the soil and the vines. The treatment the vines have to undergo remains minimal, timely, and natural, and the yields are subjected to rigorous monitoring. Each bunch of grapes is checked as it is harvested – any grape that is doubtful or not ripe enough is eliminated. The grapes are minimally destalked or not at all, depending on the case, and fermentation is carried out very simply until completion. The wine is then matured for at least 18 months in new oak casks from the Forest of Tronçais.

Once bottled – and besides 75cl bottles, they use several magnums and jeroboams – the wine spends another year in the estate's cool cellars before being made available to a select group of enthusiasts and about 100 cellar masters, who then take on responsibility for the essential slow ageing process. An unimpeachable cellar is required, as this is a demanding wine that will brook no compromise. A good year will keep for at least 20 years; a great year for 30 or 40 or even more.

A many-splendoured nectar

To appreciate this legendary wine fully, it should be served at 61°F (16°C). It does not require decanting; with older vintages that have thrown a deposit, all that is required is very slowly to place the bottle upright two days before opening and to pour it into glasses with no sudden movements. To get the best of the fabulous bouquet, the glass should be of very fine crystal and tulip-shaped.

At its peak, La Romanée-Conti wine is a unique marriage of robustness and silkiness. It has an extraordinary complexity on the nose, with notes of black fruit, preserved Morello cherries, blueberries, woodland scents, and blonde tobacco, followed by hints of oak, sweet spices, antique rose, Russian leather, truffles.... In the mouth, its richness translates into a blend of softness, finesse, and sophistication, and the wine has a long finish, never weakening, like a caress of flowers and licorice; the silence that follows Mozart is still Mozart.

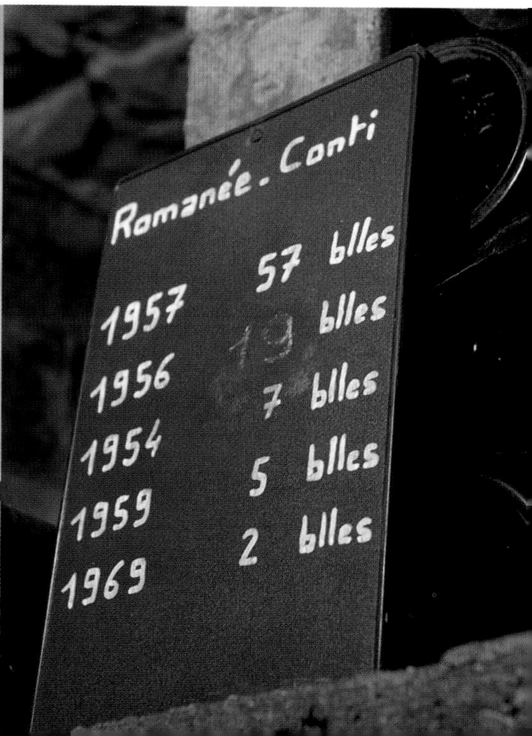

CÔTE DE NUITS

VOSNE-ROMANÉE AOC

This appellation is bordered by Nuits-St-Georges to the south, and Chambolle-Musigny and Vougeot to the north, around and above the charming villages of Vosne-Romanée and Flagey-Échezeaux. It includes no fewer than eight *grand crus*, including La Romanée-Conti (*see* pp.304–5), held as a monopole with La Tâche by the estate that bears its name. Some *grands crus* are tiny in size (La Romanée and La Grande Rue, promoted from *premier cru* status in 1992), but the others are not much larger in area (Richebourg, Romanée-St-Vivant, Échezeaux, Grands Échezeaux). However, this does not prevent them from being divided between multiple owners. The *grands crus* and *premiers crus* are grouped above the village plots. These *grands crus* achieve the highest prices for Burgundy wines, in particular those sold by Domaine de la Romanée-Conti. Fortunately, some *premiers crus*, like Les Malconsorts, Les Suchots, Les Chaumes, Aux Brûlées, and Les Beaux Monts, are excellent and produce outstanding wines that, in good years, can rival the *grands crus*.

> **GRAPE VARIETY** Pinot Noir.

> **SOIL** Calcareous soils often mixed with clay loam, with the depth varying from an inch or two to three or four feet at most.

> **STYLE** The *grands crus* are always rich, heady, and opulent, especially those of the Domaine de la Romanée-Conti. Tannic structure is a common characteristic of wines from Vosne-Romanée, as well as their richness and character, both smooth and powerful. After a few years, their tertiary bouquet develops, revealing aromas of spice, leather, damp woodlands, and violets.

Colour: *Red.*

Serving temperature: *57 to 61°F (14 to 16°C).*

Ageing potential: *10 to 30 years, and beyond for* grands crus *in the best vintages.*

Selected Côte de Nuits producers

Should we prefer wines from independent producers to those from a *négociant*? That is the dilemma facing enthusiasts intent on tracking down the great Burgundies. The former may be exceptional, but are impossible to find, while the latter are not always the most successful, nor the most affordable, although generally consistent in quality. However, as is often the case in Burgundy, there is little point in generalizing and it would be going out on a limb to rank producers according to their status. So what is the answer? Research, study, and plenty of tastings. Only with persistence come rewards.

- **Domaine Faiveley:** Les Damodes. A Nuits-St-Georges Premier Cru AOC produced in a manner that is both modern (cold maceration) and traditional, without too much new oak, is a wine with deep colour that comes from one of the best Nuits *premiers crus* (there are no *grands crus*).
- **Domaine Liger-Belair:** Richebourg Grand Cru AOC. In 2001, Thibault Liger-Belair decided to re-establish the vineyards of this estate, founded in 1720, which had previously been in a sharecropping system. He converted the estate to biodynamics after a few years, with the sole objective of elevating of its soil. Just try his wonderful Richebourg to be convinced that he has succeeded.
- **Domaine Méo-Camuzet:** Clos de Vougeot Grand Cru AOC. This beautiful family estate in Vosne-Romanée produces one of the best Vougeots, a rich, complex, and concentrated wine. The excellent location of its plot, at the top of the Clos, near the castle, makes this not at all surprising.

CÔTE DE NUITS

NUITS-ST-GEORGES AOC

The small town that gave its name to the Côte de Nuits was for a long time the rival of Beaune in the wine trade. While it still has a few large *négociants* (Faiveley, Labouré-Roi), the field today is dominated by Beaune. The vineyards are distributed from Nuits-St-Georges to Premeaux-Prissey along a 4.5-mile (7-km) strip on the hillsides, which explains their diversity. They are almost all red, predominantly from Pinot Noir (about 98 per cent). Some Chardonnays still exist (less than 2 per cent), and they provide remarkable white wines, albeit in very small numbers. There is no *grand cru* but 40 *premiers crus*. Nuits-St-Georges has its own hospice, just like Beaune. Much more modest in size, it has a beautiful vineyard of 21.7 acres (8.8 ha). Hospice wines are very good quality.

> **GRAPE VARIETIES** Pinot Noir for reds; Chardonnay for whites.

> **SOIL** This consists of alluvial scree on the north slope, with marl clay and limestone to the south, all on a limestone bedrock.

> **STYLE** Depending on whether they are from the north, near Vosne, or the south, around Premeaux, the reds have a distinct character: they are more opulent and perfumed in the north (the Premier Cru Les Damodes is from near Vosne-Romanée), and more aromatic and robust to the south, partly due to the heavier soil. Generally full-bodied, these wines are intense in colour, sometimes almost mauve. They offer red fruit, blackcurrant, and licorice flavours when young, progressing to leather and truffle as they age. Whites, which are quite rare, have a nice golden colour after a year or two, and brioche aromas that turn to white flowers.

Colour:
Red and white.

Serving temperature:
54 to 55°F (12 to 13°C) for the whites;
57 to 61°F (14 to 16°C) for the reds.

Ageing potential:
4 to 8 years for the whites;
5 to 10 years for the reds.

CÔTE DE BEAUNE

ALOXE-CORTON AOC

The village of Aloxe-Corton is dominated by the hill of Corton and its two *grands crus*: Corton (the only red *grand cru* in the Côte de Beaune, and the largest in Burgundy) and Corton-Charlemagne (whites only). It is said that the vineyard of Corton-Charlemagne was the personal property of the emperor Charlemagne, who donated it to the collegiate church at Saulieu in 775 AD. Other, more or less apocryphal, stories are reported regarding this legendary wine, the first of which claims Charlemagne must have preferred it because it would not stain his beard....

> **GRAPE VARIETIES** Pinot Noir for the reds; Chardonnay for the whites.

> **SOILS** Corton occupies the eastern slope of the hill, Corton-Charlemagne the south and southwest slopes. There is lighter soil at higher levels, with a high percentage of chalk. The bottom of the hill produces wines that are less powerful and more flexible.

> **STYLE** The reds are very tannic when young, and powerfully aromatic. They have a strong regional flavour, from which fruity and spicy notes emerge after several years in bottle. One should not drink these before they are five years old. The whites are among the best in the world, with a spicy bouquet. They are very mineral when young, but really start to open up and reveal the subtle aromas of hazelnut and spice after five years. They should be kept for 15 or 20 years.

Colour:
Red and white.

Serving temperature:
54 to 57°F (12 to 14°C) for the whites;
57 to 61°F (14 to 16°C) for the reds.

Ageing potential:
10 to 20 years for the whites;
10 to 30 years for the reds.

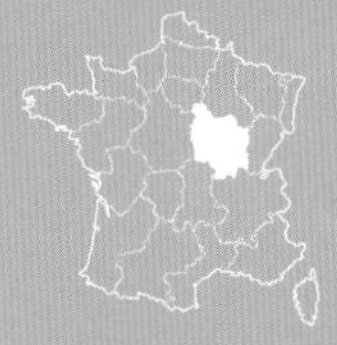

Burgundy,
Côte de Beaune

MAISON *JOSEPH DROUHIN*

Being a wine merchant in Burgundy is about more than just bottling up wine for sale; Robert Drouhin is also a major vineyard-owner and Maison Joseph Drouhin manages and tends his vines with great passion.

MAISON JOSEPH DROUHIN

7, rue d'Enfer
21200 Beaune

Founded: *1880*
Area: *193 acres (78 ha)*
Production: *N/A*
Appellation: *Beaune*
White grape variety: *Chardonnay*
Red grape variety: *Pinot Noir*

The Drouhins, a Beaune dynasty

Beaune is the capital of the Burgundy wine trade, and this prosperous town of 20,000 souls is famed for the Hospices de Beaune, an architectural jewel built in the 15th century to care for the poor, and for the auctions held at the Hospices on the third Sunday of November. Beaune is also home to a good number of the old merchant families (those with 'three tombs in the cemetery', as they say locally). The Drouhins, with their splendid house in the rue d'Enfer ('Hell Road' – perfectly located... just behind Notre-Dame basilica), are one of the dynasties of merchant-growers in Beaune – and the term 'grower' is used advisedly as, with them, a wine sale will often begin with the grapes, which are harvested, pressed, and turned into wine by the merchant. Robert Drouhin was born a Jousset, but, after being orphaned as a child, was brought up and then adopted by his uncle, Maurice Drouhin. And so in 1938 Robert was abruptly relocated to Beaune, where he put down his roots. The Drouhins were already doing very nicely at that time; Joseph, who originally hailed from the Auxois region, had established the business, married a woman from Chablis and thrown himself into wine-selling, buying up vineyards from 1918. All the work was done with horses back then, and as the animals couldn't be asked to walk too far for too long, the vineyards were all located at Beaune; it was at this point that Joseph acquired the renowned Clos des Mouches, which was to become the badge of the Drouhins. The only exception to their 'proximity rule' was a parcel of land at Clos de Vougeot, the Côte de Nuits *grand cru*, bought in 1928 'for the prestige rather than the profit', as Robert admits.

A family saga

A number of plots of land acquired in this way were lying fallow and had not been replanted since the ravages of phylloxera at the end of the 19th century, which had forced wine-growers to tear out everything, and the money flowing to the Drouhin coffers was coming from the Côtes du Rhône and Madeira, which the business had no trouble selling. The great shift upmarket was undertaken by Maurice, who took young Robert with him wherever he went. Maurice thus became the exclusive distributor of the Romanée-Conti estate for France and Belgium. But his brilliant career was interrupted by World War II, which saw him imprisoned by the Germans. Before his arrest he had had time to wall up a part of the cellar in Beaune, and Robert remembers helping him to blacken the still-fresh cement to give it a patina to match the rest of the walls. The Germans failed to get their hands on the stash, which was partly made up of gorgeous consignments of Romanée-Conti. However, Maurice's stay in prison did stop him from acquiring parts of the Romanée-Conti estate that had been put up for sale; his wife came to ask for advice through the grille in the visiting room and he responded that times were too uncertain to consider making a bid – a missed opportunity to become the co-owner of the jewel of Burgundy....

JOSEPH DROUHIN, BEAUNE PREMIER CRU, CLOS DES MOUCHES RED

Of the 193 acres (78 hectares) of land owned by the business, 91.5 acres (37 ha) are located in Côte de Nuits and Côte de Beaune, along with the majority of the *grands* and *premiers crus*. The Drouhins have turned Clos des Mouches, their Beaune *premier cru*, into an icon, but while much of the glory comes from their white, the family also produce a very stylish version in red. The land at Le Clos rises up towards Pommard, benefiting from well-drained soil with a small admixture of sand that explains the elegant character of its reds. Soft, refined, adorned with fruity, floral, and spicy notes, with a long mouthfeel and a silky texture, precise flavours, and extremely delicate tannins, it is a great Burgundy, of deliberate delicacy, that will take on a touch of velvet after a few years of being laid down.

Robert Drouhin, bespoke wine merchant

In 1957, at the age of 24, Robert succeeded his uncle. At the time, the estate was still cultivated with a horse-drawn plough and the science of wine-making was still in its infancy. Robert immersed himself in it and also had the vision to invest in land at Chablis, where the vines were still good value. Motor vehicles were developed and tractors arrived, and the Drouhin estate was subsequently extended as far as Côte de Nuits, 12 miles (20 km) north of Beaune. The science of chemistry had begun, agronomy was in full swing, and Robert remembers his pride at seeing his beautiful green vines, full of life and gorged with fertilizer... until he noticed that the wines were getting diluted in equal measure, and that each year a new molecule was being invented in the struggle against the downside of excessively vigorous growth, starting with the rot it encouraged; from 1976 onwards, he veered towards sustained cultivation. One day in 1988, as he was setting off on a fishing trip with Philippe, his eldest boy (Véronique, Frédéric, and Laurent, his three other children, also work at the wine merchants), he dug a spade into the ground to collect some earthworms: nothing. He dug in a few paces further on: nothing again – the soil is dead, Philippe said... The time had come for biodynamic farming to come to the estate and now the Drouhin plants come from vinestocks cultivated in the business's nursery, the drystone walls have been rebuilt around the Clos des Mouches (old-school, without an ounce of cement), and, when a vine is torn out, it is left fallow for at least five years – the old way as well – to kill all the nematodes that infested the old vineyard soils. This is bespoke wine-making... on the scale of a vast, 193-acre (78-hectare) stretch of land.

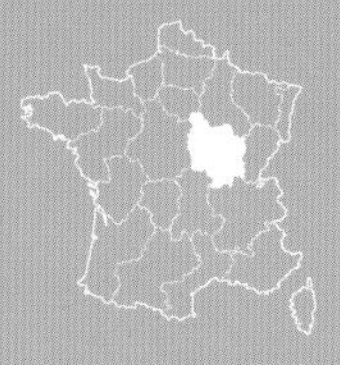

Burgundy,
Côte de Beaune

DOMAINE DES *COMTES LAFON*

Dominique Lafon was a catalyst for a dynasty of farmers and landowners,allowing his family to move completely into wine-making and climb to the top of the heap of the great producers of Meursault.

DOMAINE DES COMTES LAFON

5, rue Pierre Joigneaux
21190 Meursault

Area: *34 acres (13.8 ha)*
Production: *60,000 bottles p.a.*
Appellation: *Meursault*
Red grape variety:
Pinot Noir
White grape variety:
Chardonnay

René Lafon, the saviour

Meursault is the largest wine-making village on the Côte de Beaune, the queen of white wine – and of red as well, as the fort marks the transition point between the hill at Volnay to the north and the *grands crus* of Puligny to the south. The village has not a single *grand cru*, although it does have a rich tradition of village appellations, with 781 acres (316 ha) of classified vineyards – three times as much as at Volnay, so Meursault has always had plenty of wine for sale at the low end of the scale of Côte appellations, which starts at the village classifications and rises to the *grands crus*. Not an obvious place from which to make it big, especially when, like the Lafons, you have one foot in a solid engineering tradition and the other in a series of profitable farms – unless your heart belongs to vineyards, with a deep-seated attachment to this estate founded by Jules Lafon (b.1864), who married Marie Bloch, the daughter of a great Meursault family. Everything that old Jules built up, however, was allowed to fall apart by the next generation, and it fell to René Lafon, the grandson, to save the property from bankruptcy and sale. Working as an engineer in Paris during the week, René Lafon would turn up at 2pm on Saturdays and receive clients all weekend, tirelessly pulling corks and investing his salary in a crazy money pit of an estate in a village that, when all was said and done, was quite poor.

The agony and the ecstasy of Meursault

While it's difficult to believe now, Meursault was hanging on by its fingernails in the 1960s; the estate's 5 acres (2 ha) of

Santenots, that delightful Volnay *premier cru*, had been planted with alfalfa. In 1958, as Dominique Lafon recounts, there were 12 *ouvrées* (a little more than 12 acres/5 ha) of Meursault for sale, and one of his colleagues, a local winemaker, was tempted. His wife dissuaded him furiously: 'you never even get round to selling your own wine! The postman has a car and we don't!' So the couple went off and bought a second-hand 203 at Dijon and brought it home as a hailstorm started. The car stayed in the garage for the entire year, as there wasn't any money left to put petrol in it! Nowadays, a hectare of vineyard at Meursault starts off at a base price of €200,000 (official estimate of the Syndicat Viticole de Meursault, which is anxious to keep it modest to limit death duties), climbing to a million euro, perhaps two, for the nice parcels of land.

Even in such precarious circumstances, René Lafon succeeded in keeping the estate afloat, famously entrusting the vines to various subcontractors, so when his son Dominique turned up at the estate in 1986 to work there full-time, he found not a single pair of secateurs, let alone a tractor.

Dominique Lafon, the convert

Vines are Dominique's passion. The current Count Lafon – the fourth to bear the name – has calloused hands and a pontifical title with no 'de' conferred by the pope on his ancestor Jules for services rendered (he exempted priests from paying taxes). Despite having trained at the 'viti', the school of viticulture at Beaune, Dominique is nonetheless an outsider, having no pedigree of a long line of interrelated winemakers. He was astonished to discover the thinking of his age ('treat first, think later'), although he too initially followed the prescriptions for phytosanitary products to be sprayed onto the vines according to a calendar determined by a technical expert; in 1989, however, after he had spent three years at the estate, his wife happened to say he shouldn't go for a walk with their little girl that evening as everybody had sprayed the vines, and he understood with a shock that he was making the world unbreathable for his own daughter. The decision to move towards organic farming, followed by biodynamics, was taken, and the reborn winemaker also benefited from a sudden American interest in Meursault, which took the crimp off the profitability of the estate and allowed him to invest. Dominique Lafon has now imposed his style of elegant wines, never heavy nor too heady, and has decided that what the vines yielded him was not destined to end up camouflaged behind the toasted or hazelnut notes of a new barrel. He has become an established figure in the village and his estate serves as a kind of base camp for the young people who come to train in biodynamics and making red and white wines; he is one of the few winemakers on the Côte to prove his ease with both.

DOMAINE DES COMTES LAFON, MEURSAULT PREMIER CRU CLOS DE LA BARRE

Dominique Lafon finished salvaging all 42 acres (17 ha) of the estate in 1993 and has since converted them to organic farming. These are spread over four villages and produce 15 appellations. Clos de la Barre is located behind the house where the Lafons live, in the heart of the village; this 5-acre (2-ha) parcel of land, entirely walled in, is their monopoly and has also become the emblem of the estate. It is exposed to the east, on a thin layer of clay soil that lies directly on the rock beneath, and is a good representation of the estate's style, giving refined, slender wines with a freshness that is as astonishing as the purity of their aromas. Always more taut and nervous than the other Meursaults, the Clos wines develop beautiful citrus fruit aromas in their young years and retain the luminosity that marks out the great Meursaults.

> Dominique Lafon, director of the domaine.

CÔTE DE BEAUNE

LADOIX-SERRIGNY AOC

The most important village of the Côte de Beaune, Ladoix includes Aloxe-Corton and Pernand Vergelesses along with Corton and Corton-Charlemagne *grands crus* on its beautiful hills. Recently, the INAO elevated 11 *climats* to *premier cru* status, including Hautes-Mourottes, which produces red wine in a style reminiscent of the *premiers crus* of Aloxe. White wines are less common (20 per cent of production), but of good quality.

> **GRAPE VARIETIES** Pinot Noir for the reds; Chardonnay for the whites.

> **SOIL** Consists of gravel, limestone, and some marl.

> **STYLE** The best reds are reminiscent of Corton, without acquiring the fullness and body of that *grand cru*. They have a fleshy body and more delicate flavours – raspberry and cherry, but also spices and cocoa as the reds age. Whites can be confusing, with buttery notes and more vegetal flavours. They do not, however, have the richness and power of the great whites from closer to Beaune.

Colour:
Red and white.

Serving temperature:
52 to 54°F (11 to 12°C) for the whites;
57 to 61°F (14 to 16°C) for the reds.

Ageing potential:
5 to 10 years for the whites;
10 to 15 years for the reds.

CÔTE DE BEAUNE

BEAUNE AOC

The charming medieval town of Beaune has become wealthy as a result of the Côte d'Or wine trade over the centuries, and it shows! A tourist, as well as a cultural, attraction, it becomes the centre of the region in connection with the auction at the Hospices de Beaune on the third Sunday in November (*see* p.288). It is a large appellation of some 1,011 acres (409 ha), with many *premier crus* – some of which can almost rival *grands crus* (Clos des Mouches, Clos du Roi, and the Vigne de l'Enfant-Jésus from Bouchard Père & Fils on the *climat* of Grèves). It mainly produces reds (88 per cent). Among the rare whites, some are outstanding, such as the Joseph Drouhin Clos des Mouches.

> **GRAPE VARIETIES** Pinot Noir for the reds; Chardonnay for the whites.

> **SOIL** Between 680 and 980 ft (200 and 300 m) in altitude, the AOC has a limestone base with thin brown soils, marls interspersed with iron oxide, and clay-limestone soil at the foot of the hill.

> **STYLE** The reds are powerful and feature a rich, aromatic spectrum (black and red fruits), supported by rather elegant tannins. They evolve into typically Burgundian flavours of damp woodland and truffle accented with a touch of spice. The whites are more straightforward and easier to drink, with the exception of *premiers crus* that can sometimes, at their best, compete with their neighbours from Puligny and Chassagne.

Colour:
Red and white.

Serving temperature:
54 to 57°F (12 to 14°C) for the whites;
57 to 61°F (14 to 16°C) for the reds.

Ageing potential:
5 to 10 years for the whites;
6 to 10 years for the reds.

CÔTE DE BEAUNE

POMMARD AOC

A name that is almost synonymous with the great wines of Burgundy, this village produces exclusively red wines, but does not have a *grand cru*. The vineyards, bordered to the south by Volnay and to the north by Beaune, consist of a wide strip. The *premiers crus* (27 *climats*) are almost all around the village of Pommard, and Les Épenots and Les Rugiens are generally regarded as the best. The appellation, which was granted in 1936, was among the first in the region.

> **GRAPE VARIETY** Pinot Noir.

> **SOIL** Clay-and-limestone. Alluvial rock and stony debris with brown limestone soil, sometimes containing iron oxide.

> **STYLE** The wines are deep coloured, with intense flavours and concentration that allows them to improve. The bouquet has notes of fruit (blackcurrant, currant, cherry) and evolves with time into more gamey aromas (such as damp woodland, leather, and chocolate).

Colour:
Red.

Serving temperature:
57 to 61°F (14 to 16°C).

Ageing potential:
5 to 15 years.

VOLNAY AOC

CÔTE DE BEAUNE

The village is located high on the hillside, with the vineyards stretching from one side to the other and below. Volnay is bordered to the southwest by Meursault and Monthélie, and to the northeast by Pommard. The appellation produces only red wines (whites are entitled to the appellation Meursault). The *premiers crus* – Caillerets, Champans, Clos des Chênes, and Clos des Ducs – are renowned for a quality of wine that highlights finesse and sensitivity. Santenots, another *premier cru*, is found nearby in the commune of Meursault, although it falls within the Volnay AOC.

> **GRAPE VARIETY** Pinot Noir.

> **SOIL** Mostly limestone at the top of the hill, the soils are stonier on the mid and lower slopes.

> **STYLE** A delicate perfume of violet and strawberry emerges from Volnay when it is young; and while age brings greater complexity (with plum and spice notes) and greater softness, it does not detract from its natural elegance, even if it fades a little.

Colour: *Red.*

Serving temperature: *57 to 61°F (14 to 16°C).*

Ageing potential: *5 to 15 years.*

MONTHÉLIE AOC

CÔTE DE BEAUNE

This old village with a castle is perched on the hill at Meursault. It was long operated by the Abbey of Cluny. The Burgundians typically pronounce the name 'montli', as if they were quickly finishing a drink. It is true that until the mid-1980s, the village wines (mostly red) were regarded as rustic and unpretentious. Since then, talented winemakers have taken advantage of the potential of their plots, and the best wines have developed character, structure, and flavour, and are now sought after on account of their good value. The best known of the nine *premiers crus* from Monthélie are Sur la Velle and Les Champs Fulliot.

> **GRAPE VARIETIES** Pinot Noir for the reds; Chardonnay for the whites.

> **SOIL** A limestone base covered with marl and red clay.

> **STYLE** The reds are quite light, rather like their light relatives or neighbours from Volnay. The nose is delicate, often with notes of black and red fruits, and is sometimes accented with flowers (peony, violet). It evolves with age to damp woodland and spice notes. The tannins are mild and often supple, even when the wines are young. The whites are reminiscent of Meursault to an extent, but are lighter and less concentrated, with a more floral and less complex nose, at least when young.

Colour: *Red and white.*

Serving temperature: *50 to 54°F (10 to 12°C) for the whites; 57 to 61°F (14 to 16°C) for the reds.*

Ageing potential: *5 to 10 years for the reds and the whites.*

AUXEY-DURESSES AOC

CÔTE DE BEAUNE

Auxey-Duresses (pronounced 'ossai') is a former possession of the Abbey of Cluny, situated in a narrow valley that rises in the Hautes Côtes between Meursault (to the south), Monthélie (to the north), and St-Romain (to the west). Before the AOC establishment, wines from this small village were sometimes sold as Volnay or Pommard. The pleasant wines produced here, especially the reds (but with a significant proportion of whites), are generally sold at quite modest prices for wines from the Côte de Beaune.

> **GRAPE VARIETIES** Pinot Noir (70 per cent) for the reds; Chardonnay for the whites.

> **SOIL** On the Monthélie side, marl limestone on a stony base for the red *terroirs*; finer limestone is the soil for the whites, on the *climats* of Val and Mount Mélian.

> **STYLE** The *premiers crus*, like Les Duresses and Clos du Val, can produce fine reds with raspberry flavours, leading to a comparison with some Volnays. The best whites, with a delicious toast and hazelnut note, have no reason to envy Meursault, since they have enough body, but should be consumed younger.

Colour: *Red and white.*

Serving temperature: *54 to 57°F (12 to 14°C) for the whites; 57 to 61°F (14 to 16°C) for the reds.*

Ageing potential: *5 to 10 years for the whites and the reds.*

MEURSAULT AOC

CÔTE DE BEAUNE

This village is synonymous with rich and fleshy white wines, where Chardonnay is at its best and produces an iconic Burgundy. Meursault has no *grands crus*, but an impressive number of *premiers crus* (Les Charmes, Les Perrières, Les Gouttes d'Or, etc.), a total of 21. Production is sometimes of variable quality; so we must rely primarily on named producer (apart from the *premiers crus*). The idea of producing red wine (less than 4 per cent of the vines) would seem ridiculous were it not for the wonderful Clos de Mazeray, from Domaine Jacques Prieur. The reds are also entitled to use the appellation Blagny, after the nearby hamlet of that name. The latter may also sell its whites under the appellation Meursault or Puligny-Montrachet, depending on where they originate.

> **GRAPE VARIETIES** Pinot Noir for the reds; Chardonnay for the whites.

> **SOIL** Calcareous marls.

> **STYLE** About 96 per cent of the wines are white. The *premiers crus* produce the finest and most concentrated wines, while the *vins de village* have less character. These wines have strong and persistent flavours, and can age and improve remarkably. The bouquet is delicate when young, with floral and plant tones (ferns, lime, white flowers), but develops toward more pronounced notes of hazelnut and dried fruit, honey, and characteristic buttery notes. In the mouth, richness often dominates; but a proper Meursault can keep the balance necessary for freshness – a restrained, yet clearly crisp context. The red wines are similar to wines from Blagny and a few Volnays (in terms of smoothness), but rather unusual due to the very small quantities produced. You really have to want to make red Meursault.

Colour:
White and red.

Serving temperature:
54 to 57°F (12 to 14°C) for the whites;
57 to 61°F (14 to 16°C) for the reds.

Ageing potential:
5 to 10 years for the reds;
10 to 15 years for the whites.

PULIGNY AND CHASSAGNE AOCs

CÔTE DE BEAUNE

These two picture-postcard communes are home to the most famous white wines in Burgundy (and the world). These are the *grand crus* from Montrachet (pronounced 'mon-rah-shay'): Le Montrachet, Chevalier-Montrachet, Bienvenues-Bâtard-Montrachet, Bâtard-Montrachet, and Criots-Bâtard-Montrachet. Le Montrachet covers just under 20 acres (7.99 ha), and few owners possess more than a couple of acres of it. This shows the rarity of this wine, which has a smooth, penetrating, and haunting bouquet that very few enthusiasts can boast of ever having tasted. Only the top experts can distinguish the Chevalier-Montrachet from its fuller-bodied neighbour, and if Le Montrachet outstrips its neighbours, it is by a short head. Besides the *grands crus*, the two municipalities produce red and white *vins de village* for the Chassagne-Montrachet and Puligny-Montrachet AOCs. Curiously, Chassagne-Montrachet is better known for its reds, which are certainly worthy of note, than for its whites, which nonetheless represent 60 per cent of its production.

> **GRAPE VARIETIES** Pinot Noir for the reds; Chardonnay for the whites.

> **SOIL** A limestone base is sometimes covered with reddish marls or thin and stony soils.

> **STYLE** The white *grands crus* are powerful and need to be left to develop: it is unwise to open them before five years, and they can be enjoyed at their best after 10 years. Their bouquet is rich and heady with notes of butter, gingerbread, hazelnut, and dried fruit. A richness and creaminess are evident in the mouth, always with a nice balance from crisp acidity, which give these wines a significant freshness that you would not necessarily expect. The *premiers crus* are generally excellent; for Puligny, Les Pucelles and Les Caillerets are noteworthy; for Chassagne, En Remilly. The reds are powerful and tannic, with flavours of red or black fruit (cherry and blackcurrant). Clos Pitois, Morgeot, and La Maltroye are among the best *premiers crus* from Chassagne. They are often good value for money.

Colour:
White and red.

Serving temperature:
54 to 57°F (12 to 14°C) for the whites;
57 to 61°F (14 to 16°C) for the reds.

Ageing potential:
5 to 15 years for the reds;
10 to 30 years for the whites.

CÔTE DE BEAUNE

SANTENAY AND MARANGES AOCs

At the southern end of the Côte de Beaune, red wine dominates the landscape. There are several *premiers crus* and the wine enthusiast can obtain some good deals. Less powerful, these wine are to drink young but the best offer a certain fruity delicacy and the elegance of a very good Pinot Noir. The Santenay AOC has several towns and hamlets, and shares the appellation of Santenay with Remigny. The Maranges AOC is shared by three villages: Dezize-lès-Maranges, Sampigny-lès-Maranges, and Cheilly-lès-Maranges, and it has six *premiers crus*.

> **GRAPE VARIETIES** Pinot Noir for the reds; Chardonnay (13 per cent) for the whites.

> **SOIL** The top of the hills consist of limestone soil, while further down, this is mixed with marl.

> **STYLE** The reds combine floral characters (peony, violet) and red fruit with hints of licorice. The tannins are firm, sometimes a bit rustic, with a real fullness in the mouth. The whites are vigorous and refreshing, with mineral and floral tones developing into dried fruits and herbaceous notes.

Colour:
White and red.

Serving temperature:
50 to 54°F (10 to 12°C) for the whites; 57 to 61°F (14 to 16°C) for the reds.

Ageing potential:
5 to 10 years for the reds and whites.

Selected Côte de Beaune producers

- **Domaine Chandon de Briailles:** white Corton, Corton Grand Cru AOC. A lovely estate in Savigny, it's owned by the Nicolay family, which has very nice plots in Corton, especially in Bressandes. It produces very fine wines – very traditional. They need to be set aside to mature in order to enjoy them fully.

- **Maison Joseph Drouhin:** Clos des Mouches, Beaune Premier Cru AOC. In the 1920s, this fine producer from Beaune bought up this Beaune vineyard, plot by plot. It produces one of the best *premiers crus* of the appellation, both white and red.

- **Domaine Jacques Prieur:** Clos Santenots, Volnay Premier Cru AOC. This 52-acre (21 ha) estate, taken over in 1988 by the Labruyère family, has plots in the greatest *terroirs* of Burgundy, including a plot of Le Montrachet. Its Volnay Clos des Santenots has both balance and finesse.

- **Domaine Jadot:** Clos Malta, Santenay Premier Cru AOC. This wine, which comes from the Jadot estate, is fresh and powerful without the hardiness occasionally found in Santenays. White and red versions of this *premier cru* are available, both being very accomplished wines. Louis Jadot also distributes the Domaine du Duc de Magenta, with a good selection of *premiers crus* in Chassagne and Puligny.

- **Domaine Leflaive:** Les Pucelles, Puligny-Montrachet Premier Cru AOC. The most beautiful estate for whites in the Côte de Beaune, it is operated entirely by biodynamics under the management of Brice de La Morandière, assisted by Pierre Morey. Its *premiers crus* are almost as good as a *grand cru*, and Les Pucelles is certainly one of the most renowned. Unfortunately the prices are far from affordable.

- **Domaine Louis Latour:** Corton Grancey, Corton Grand Cru AOC. Purchased in 1749 from Count Grancey, this is the seat of the estate. The Latour family were granted the privilege of adding 'Grancey' after Corton. Corton-Charlemagne Grand Cru from the estate is also top quality.

MERCUREY AOC

CÔTE CHALONNAISE

Mercurey is one of five appellations in the Côte Chalonnaise (along with Bouzeron, Rully, Givry, and Montagny) and certainly the most prestigious. It spans two communes, Mercurey and St-Martin-sous-Montaigu. Here, reds dominate (though there are some whites) in 1,581-acre (640-ha) vineyard area: three times larger than the one in Rully, to the north. This appellation has large, well-managed estates and a number of *négociants* (Antonin Rodet is the most well-known). A Mercurey from a good producer can represent excellent value for money (for a Burgundy, that is) and can be aged for several years. Some *terroirs* have been classified as *premiers crus* by the INAO (32 *climats* have been classified *premier cru*); but others, including unclassified *climats*, have an excellent reputation. The best vineyards include Clos du Roy, Clos Voyen, Les Champs Martin, Clos des Barrault, and Clos l'Evêque.

> **GRAPE VARIETIES** Pinot Noir for red wines; Chardonnay and Aligoté for white wines.

> **SOIL** Outcrops of limestone and marl.

> **STYLE** The white wines are refreshing, with a hint of minerality as well as floral and spicy flavours. Although much more affordable than their neighbours in Côte d'Or, they are less complex and less powerful. The reds are firm but delicate when young, with flavours reminiscent of raspberry, strawberry, or cherry. With age, they develop spicy and gamey characters.

Colour:
Red and white.

Serving temperature:
50 to 54°F (10 to 12°C) for the whites; 57 to 61°F (14 to 16°C) for the reds.

Ageing potential:
3 to 6 years for the whites; 4 to 8 years for the reds.

Selected Côte Chalonnaise producers

- **Domaine Ragot: AOC Givry.** This estate in Givry covers 22 acres (9 ha), with 17 acres (7 ha) of Pinot Noir. It is run by Nicolas Ragot and boasts a delightful array of local *terroirs*. The red wines are crisply fruity, even when young, and would interest those looking for excellent value for money. The *premiers crus* are worth keeping a little longer.

- **Domaine Faiveley: La Framboisière, Mercurey AOC.** This beautiful Côte de Nuits estate also owns vineyards in Mercurey, notably among the finest *premiers crus* (Clos du Roy and Clos des Myglands). La Framboisière is aptly named, as it is a delicious wine that brings to mind raspberries and red fruit. It is typically velvety.

- **Domaine De Villaine: Aligoté-Bouzeron, Bouzeron AOC.** The manager of the Domaine de la Romanée-Conti operates this beautiful estate of approximately 50 acres (20 ha) with his wife. Two-thirds of its production is white. His Bouzeron (Aligoté) will convince even the hardest sceptic that this grape variety can produce complex wines. Mention should also be made of the precise and scintillating Rully.

- **Château de Chamirey, Mercurey AOC.** This old and large estate covers almost 99 acres (40 ha) and belongs to the Devillard family, who produce rich and full-bodied Pinot Noirs. There is a lovely series of six *premiers crus*.

- **Michel Juillot: Clos des Barraults, Mercurey Premier Cru AOC.** A beautiful family estate of nearly 79 acres (32 ha), located mainly in Mercurey. Harvesting here is carried out by hand, and the wine production process is very traditional. Within a consistent range mention should be made of the powerful and fine Mercurey Premier Cru Clos du Roi red wine.

Selected Mâconnais producers

- **Domaine Cordier: Vieilles Vignes, Pouilly-Fuissé AOC.** This wine displays a beautiful complexity of flavours – revealing hints of vanilla and white flowers leading on to honey, with just enough richness and liveliness to support it.
- **Domaine Guffens-Heynen: Mâcon-Pierreclos AOC.** A tiny but hugely successful estate, established in 1976 by a Belgian couple who apparently had not forgotten that Flanders and Burgundy were once united. The Mâcon-Pierreclos and Pouilly-Fuissé are some of the best wines of the region.
- **Domaine Jacques and Nathalie Saumaize:** Produced from a 50-year-old vineyard and aged in wood, these elegant wines have no shortage of depth, with a nice balance between richness and freshness.
- **Domaine de la Bongran: Tradition, Viré-Clessé AOC.** Jean Thévenet has demonstrated that you can harvest late in Mâconnais, which has often landed him in trouble with the AOC authorities. However, he continues to produce particularly original wines.

MÂCONNAIS

MÂCON AND MÂCON-VILLAGES AOCs

The Mâconnais is the heart of southern Burgundy. It spans some 40 miles between the end of the Côte Chalonnaise and the famous Solutré Rock. The region is further south than the Côte d'Or, and the climate is gentler. The red wines are entitled to the Mâcon AOC (or the Mâcon-Supérieur, if they have an additional degree of alcohol). They are often produced from Gamay, although Pinot Noir may be used. White should be produced from 100 per cent Chardonnay. Twenty villages have the right to include their name alongside the AOC. This is the case for Chardonnay, Lugny Prissé, Igé, Loché, La Roche-Vineuse, and Pierreclos. The Mâcon-Villages AOC is for white wines only. The Viré-Clessé appellation (689 acres/279 ha) replaced the Mâcon-Viré and Mâcon-Clessé AOC in 2002.

> **GRAPE VARIETIES** Gamay and Pinot Noir for reds; Chardonnay for whites.

> **SOIL** Pinot likes brown calcareous soils, while Gamay prefers granite soils similar to those of Beaujolais. Sandy, clay, or silica soils will be better suited to Chardonnay.

> **STYLE** The whites are quite variable, depending on whether they are aged in wood or stainless steel vats. In the first case, they gain in complexity and richness but they can lose in terms of freshness and liveliness. In the second instance, the emphasis is on fruit character and simplicity. This style is more representative of white Mâcon: pale, fresh, light, and clean. It whets the appetite without tiring it. Reds made from Pinot Noir are entitled to the appellation Bourgogne (or that of Passetoutgrains, if they contain the required proportion of Gamay). As for rosés, they are rich and lively, with subtle, slightly tart, red berry flavours.

Colour:
Red, rosé, and white.

Serving temperature:
50 to 54°F (10 to 12°C) for the whites; 57 to 59°F (14 to 15°C) for the reds.

Ageing potential:
3 to 6 years.

MÂCONNAIS

POUILLY-FUISSÉ AOC

Three appellations here begin with the name of Pouilly; but Pouilly-Fuissé produced in Fuissé, Solutré, Vergisson, and Chaintré is better known than Pouilly-Loché and Pouilly-Vinzelles, because of its larger level of production. This is where the best white wines in the Mâconnais are produced – something that has long been known by the monks of Cluny, who had many of their vineyards here.

> **GRAPE VARIETY** Chardonnay.

> **SOIL** Clay-and-limestone slopes.

> **STYLE** In the classic style of Burgundian whites, Pouilly wines are marked by a minerality and crispness well balanced by their fullness. Usually vinified in barrels, the wines are powerful and aromatic, and age gracefully, offering a bouquet reminiscent of the great Chardonnays at maturity.

Colour:
White.

Serving temperature:
50 to 54°F (10 to 12°C).

Ageing potential:
3 to 6 years.

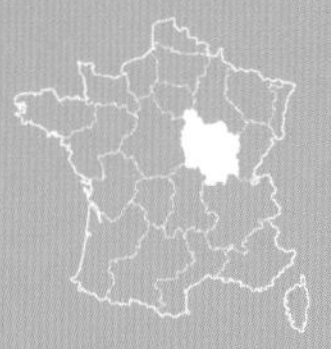

Burgundy, Mâconnais

DOMAINE *JOSEPH BURRIER*

Frédéric-Marc Burrier is the latest in a dynasty of great property owners and small winemakers with just one aim in mind – to keep the estate intact. He is now fighting to make Pouilly-Fuissé a Burgundy premier cru.

JOSEPH BURRIER

Beauregard
71960 Fuissé

Area: *109 acres (44 ha)*
Production: *N/A*
Appellation: *Pouilly-Fuissé*
Red grape varieties: *Gamay, Pinot Noir*
White grape variety: *Chardonnay*

Seventeen generations

Pouilly-Fuissé is the driving force of the Mâcon region. With 1,977 acres (800 ha) under cultivation, it is also the second largest village appellation in Burgundy after Chablis, which boasts 8,150 acres (3,298 ha). Pouilly-Fuissé comprises four villages: Fuissé (almost a third of the appellation), Solutré-Pouilly (a further scant third), Vergisson (a quarter), and Chaintré (15%). With its Roman roof tiles, cicadas, almond trees, and white stone, it hovers like a vision of the South of France at the foot of the famous escarpments known as the Rocks of Solutré and Vergisson. Lyon is just 40 miles (60 km) down the road, but the appellation also has one foot in Beaujolais, whose granite slopes reach almost as far as here.

Frédéric-Marc Burrier, the manager of the vast Château de Beauregard estate and of two other family-owned labels, with a total of 109 acres (44 ha) under cultivation, is a worthy representative of this hybrid terroir. The roots of his family tree are embedded equally in Beaujolais reds and Fuissé whites, and the Burriers have been growing vines in the Gamay region for 17 generations. In 1899, however, Marc Burrier, a descendant of a line of wine merchants, married Jeanne Deshaires, an only daughter from the Mâcon area, who was sadly to become a young widow. Jeanne and her four sons returned to her parents' house at Beauregard, the Burriers' current stronghold, a thick-walled house perched atop an outcrop of white limestone with a panoramic view across the surrounding countryside to the rocks. The following generation managed to make an advantageous match between Joseph, one of the sons, and a daughter from Château de Fuissé, a prosperous house that can be seen from Beauregard. Joseph looked good in a suit and tie but had little clue as to how to use a pickaxe, but this happy alliance saw his estate triple in size at a stroke, with 50 acres (20.2 ha) of Pouilly-Fuissé added to boot. The Burriers have made every effort to preserve this inherited land together with the tenant holdings that at the time were part and parcel of any large business of this kind.

Tenacity and ambition

The situation has grown more complicated with each passing generation, however, and Frédéric-Marc now has 17 grandchildren and heirs, although he is the only person to be entrusted with the vines, with the other family members taking a private income. Frédéric-Marc is the family's representative and depends on their goodwill; they reappoint him as head of the property every five years. He does not have the final say, however, and has to convince his shareholding cousins and siblings that lowering yields, adopting organic farming practices, and extending fallow periods are all essential moves even if it means lower profits. However, Frédéric-Marc is nothing if not tenacious, and upon his return to the family estate in 1999, following a brilliant career in Beaune working for wine merchants Louis Jadot, he put forward a bold and ambitious winemaking proposal, converting his 160 vineyard plots to organic farming.

The result in agricultural terms became evident all too soon, with a 25% drop in yield, but the shareholders survived the shock. Beauregard ploughed its land and then adopted hand pickaxes, as manual labour costs skyrocketed. Again, the shareholders accepted the consequences and supported their ambitious cousin. And now that Château de Beauregard is a safe bet, Frédéric-Marc is fighting his latest battle: recognition for some of the Pouilly-Fuissé plots as a *premier cru* – bizarrely enough, no distinction is made on the label between the splendid slopes of the famous rocky spurs at Solutré and Vergisson or the Beauregard plateau and the vineyards in the valley. It turns out to be due to World War II, during which the dotted demarcation lines went astray. Frédéric-Marc has spent months reading his appellation's archives and recounts that while the Côte d'Or, in the Occupied Zone, cheerfully classified everything as a *premier cru* so that the vineyards would escape the wartime occupying forces' taxes, Pouilly-Fuissé, in the Vichy zone, refrained from stoking jealousy between the villages by failing to send the Ministry of Agriculture the classified list of elite wine-producing villages it had requested.

A quest for premiers crus

Don't make waves: this pacifist motto is at the heart of all collaboration, but it also worked well for the wine trade, which was more than happy to find superb Chardonnays at lower prices than in the Côte region. However, since Frédéric-Marc Burrier arrived at the estate in 1999, he, along with the 50 or so estates that the appellation now includes, has consistently upturned this trend. 'I felt it was an injustice to be denied access to recognition. I started discussing it in 2007 and the application was officially lodged in 2010. But there is no collective memory of *premiers crus* here, and for the moment at least, 65% of Pouilly-Fuissé wine is sold in bulk to the trade, with no mention of the name of the vineyard.' But the new generation of vintners from Vergisson, Fuissé, and Solutré intends to continue the fight for as long as it takes. Patience is certainly a necessary virtue in a winemaker. 'My father always used to say that the soil had to rest when you tear out a vine', says Frédéric-Marc. 'He recommended leaving it fallow for seven years. A winemaker who doesn't do so and replants immediately after digging out the old vine like an annual, has no understanding of the profession. I leave a fallow period of five years, and plant the vine to last fifty. I'm just passing through.'

JOSEPH BURRIER, POUILLY-FUISSÉ, CHÂTEAU DE BEAUREGARD VERS CRAS

Frédéric-Marc Burrier heads up a portfolio of brands that include the 106 acres (43 ha) surrounding the house at Beauregard, the Joseph Burrier and Georges Burrier estates, 17 acres (6.9 ha) at Saint-Véran, and 30 acres (12 ha) in Beaujolais (Fleurie, Moulin-à-Vent, Morgon, Saint-Amour, and Chiroubles). He has also recently acquired vineyards from his neighbour at Château du Clos that have been certified organic since 2013. Les Cras has become the signature vineyard for Beauregard (which it surrounds), and for Pouilly-Fuissé in general, as it is located on a limestone outcrop that is typical of what might be expected of a Mâcon *premier cru*. While clay gives Chardonnay its power and its honey aromas, it can be heavy at times. Chalky soils lend acidity and vivacity to the wines, so they age well. Exposed slabs of limestone and old vines from 1961 and 1964, the oldest on the estate, sit happily together, making a white with excellent ageing potential: sophisticated, always ripe on the nose with a hint of cinnamon, white flowers, spice, and a concentrated mouth-feel with good definition on the finish.

BEAUJOLAIS AND BEAUJOLAIS-VILLAGES AOCs

BEAUJOLAIS

These vineyards are located in the Rhône department, except for the canton of La Chapelle-de-Guinchay, which is located in the Saône-et-Loire. The picturesque hills, where the vineyards ascend to 1,600 or even 2,000 ft (500 or 600 m), dominate the Saône Valley. Profiting from a regulatory decision in the 1950s that allowed the initial harvest to be put on sale early, the Beaujolais AOC was popularized worldwide by the Beaujolais Nouveau. This opportunity is focused on the third Thursday of November, just weeks after the harvest. But its sudden popularity, which created an image of an unambitious easy-to-drink red wine, was a double-edged sword. Its top producers would now like to be taken more seriously. It should be remembered that the best of Beaujolais are these 10 *crus*: Brouilly, Chénas, Chiroubles, Côte-de-Brouilly, Fleurie, Juliénas,Morgon, Moulin-à-Vent, Régnié, and St-Amour.

> **GRAPE VARIETIES** Gamay for reds and rosés; Chardonnay for whites.

> **SOIL** The soil in this area consists of granite alluvium from the Tertiary and Quaternary periods, which allows expression of all the fruitiness and charm in Gamay.

> **STYLE** Beaujolais Nouveau is naturally designed for fun, as it provides a refreshing and instantly pleasing accompaniment to snacks and conversation. A standard Beaujolais or a 'Villages' wine is fresh with red fruit (currants), grape, and spice flavours that enable it to be consumed over an entire meal, where it usually goes very well with meats from the deli and simple dishes. White Beaujolais (and even rosés) are produced in limited numbers, but are often very good quality. If made from Chardonnay, they can bear comparison with the wines of Mâconnais when they are well produced.

Colour:
Red, rosé, and white.

Serving temperature:
59 to 61°F (15 to 16°C) for the reds; 50 to 54°F (10 to 12°C) for the whites and rosés.

Ageing potential:
3 to 5 years.

JULIÉNAS AOC

BEAUJOLAIS

Juliénas includes some of the oldest wine-producing sites in Beaujolais. Its high and steep slopes provide excellent locations for ripening grapes. The appellation straddles the departments of Saône-et-Loire and the Rhône, facing south to the valley of the Mauvaise River, a tributary of the Saône. It has a planted area of 1,327 acres (537 ha), twice the size of St-Amour, through the annexation of two neighbouring hamlets: Jullié and Emeringues. The La Bottière, Les Capitans, Les Chers, and Les Paquelets *climats* are particularly renowned.

> **GRAPE VARIETY** Gamay.

> **SOIL** Granite.

> **STYLE** Juliénas wines are more potent and less refined than those of St-Amour. They are at their best two to four years after harvest.

Colour:
Red.

Serving temperature:
57 to 61°F (14 to 16°C).

Ageing potential:
3 to 5 years.

MOULIN-À-VENT AOC

BEAUJOLAIS

Named after a windmill located on a hilltop, this wine is generally considered the best in Beaujolais. Beaune *négociants*, such as Louis Jadot, who own vineyards here, are not mistaken. This is certainly the most suitable Beaujolais for ageing, and the most expensive. Some producers carry out maturation in oak barrels, which is not typical for this appellation, to make the most of the structure of the wines.

> **GRAPE VARIETY** Gamay.

> **SOIL** The granite subsoil, covered with a sandy layer rich in manganese, gives the wine a distinctive character.

> **STYLE** The best wines, which are a dark ruby colour, may retain an impressive structure and density for more than 10 years. Their body and their class are reminiscent of several wines from the Côte d'Or.

Colour: *Red.*

Serving temperature: *57 to 61°F (14 to 16°C).*

Ageing potential: *10 to 15 years.*

ST-AMOUR AOC

BEAUJOLAIS

Located a few miles south of Mâcon, St-Amour is the northernmost of the Beaujolais *crus*, and one of the smallest. Most vineyards are planted on slopes facing east-southeast at an altitude of 787–1,050 ft (240–320 m). With a name like this, it would be surprising if the wine did not sell well, especially since production is limited, the vineyard covering just 746 acres (302 ha). Some producers of Chardonnay here sell their products under the St-Véran appellation.

> **GRAPE VARIETY** Gamay.

> **SOIL** The appellation is located on a granite plateau at the south end of the Saône-et-Loire department.

> **STYLE** Lightweight and subtly fruity, the wines are produced to be consumed while young. They do improve after two or three years in bottle, though.

Colour: *Red.*

Serving temperature: *57 to 61°F (14 to 16°C).*

Ageing potential: *3 to 5 years.*

Selected Beaujolais producers

- **Domaine des Jacques: Moulin-à-Vent AOC.** So what is a *négociant* from the Côte de Beaune doing at Moulin-à-Vent? Quite simply, Louis Jadot is making a top quality Burgundy wine, since buying this excellent estate in 1996. Part of the harvest is aged in oak barrels for 10 months, which adds complexity and durability to the wine.

- **Domaine du Vissoux: Fleurie Poncié, Fleurie AOC.** Pierre-Marie Chermette has become known for his unchaptalized Beaujolais wines, which demonstrate that one can limit yields and harvest at optimal ripeness here for a naturally full-bodied wine. The whole range can be recommended, with special mention for the Fleurie and Moulin-à-Vent wines, firm, precise, fresh and fruity.

- **Domaine Jean Foillard: Morgon Côte du Py, Morgon AOC.** Jean Foillard combines respect for the land and modern techniques to produce a genuine and balanced Morgon, full-bodied and complex, and superb after a few years.

- **Château du Moulin-à-Vent: AOC Moulin-à-Vent** The estate was repurchased by the Parinet family in 2009 and covers 96 acres (39 ha). It has specialized in single vineyard wines and is quickly coming into line with the best estates in the region with its modern and expressive wines.

CHAMPAGNE

Champagne is the wine par excellence *for celebrations. French in origin, it has now conquered the world and inspired its own lifestyle. Everything about Champagne adds to its magic, from its mysterious beginnings to its production, a blending technique jealously guarded by each major house or brand. It is the most famous wine in the world, and also the most copied; but it is made in the Champagne region alone and nowhere else.*

A brief history of Champagne

As is often the case in France, the origins of the Champagne region's vineyards can be traced back to the Roman legions. During the 5th and 6th centuries, it was the Benedictine monks in particular who took over their development. Champagnes were served in the courts of French kings; Louis XIV was very fond of them, but the wines of that era have nothing in common with the versions with tiny bubbles that we know and enjoy today. The wines of old were lively light reds or still whites.

THE FIRST CHAMPAGNES. The Champagne legend only really took off once effervescence had been mastered, a process that began at the end of the 17th century and developed gradually. By tradition, its discovery is attributed to Dom Pérignon (see box on facing page, also p.71), but if the monk didn't exactly 'invent' sparkling Champagne, he nevertheless played a part – notably through the use of blending – in perfecting the production techniques. The first large wine production houses opened for business in the 18th century, and, since then have ensured that Champagne remains famous throughout the world. Back in the 18th century, blending was already being used as a technique to achieve more consistent wines. Then, at the end of the 19th century, phylloxera began destroying the vineyards, and the first decades of the 20th century were marked by economic crises, with the crisis of 1911 being particularly etched in the collective memory. Various advanced production programmes were introduced to re-establish the vineyard region, and these remain in use today.

INFORMED CHOICES. Mindful of its vineyards and their impact on the environment, the Champagne region has rethought its winegrowing practices since 2000. Integrated and organic production have become important considerations for wine houses, cooperatives, and independent producers alike. Today the latter are contributing to a diversification of production, opening up Champagne, with its blends, to wines that can deliver genuine nuances typical of Champagne's many terroirs. Despite a few challenges, the world of sparkling wine is no longer in crisis; indeed it's enjoying great success. Production can barely keep up with demand and there is now talk of an extension of the appellation.

CHAMPAGNE STATISTICS

Vineyard area:
84,015 acres (34,000 ha)

Average production:
309 million bottles /
28 million (9-l) cases

(CIVC, 2015)

Climate and soil

The Champagne region is centred some 90 miles (150 km) northeast of Paris. These are France's most northerly vineyards, and the northernmost limit of commercial wine cultivation. The hillside vine rows are at elevations of between 295 and 1150 ft (90 and 350 m), around 319 villages across five *départements*: Aube, Haute-Marne, Marne, and some villages in Aisne and Seine-et-Marne.

> Winter pruning at the Champagne Roederer estate in France.

Champagne AOCs

- Champagne
- Coteaux Champenois
- Rosé des Riceys

DID YOU KNOW...?

Champagne has often been a female business. *Various widows ran the big houses during eras when it was unusual to see a woman in charge. She may not have been the first (the widow Soyez came before her), but Mrs. Clicquot remains the archetype. Her wine was even called* La Veuve *('The Widow').*

CLIMATE. Characterized partly by continental extremes, with cold winters – and sometimes destructive frosts – as well as sun-drenched summers, and partly by a relatively temperate Atlantic influence with high humidity.

SOIL. Limestone soils are an essential contributor to the quality of Champagne wines. They consist mostly of sand and clay over a chalky subsoil, which regulates moisture and temperature very efficiently and plays a vital role in maturing the grapes. Furthermore, the chalk allows deep caves to be excavated, in which wine can be stored for ageing.

Vineyard landscape

MONTAGNE DE REIMS. This vast plateau, covered with forests, is situated between Épernay and Reims. It is the realm of the Pinot Noir grape (around 70 per cent in some areas), but Chardonnay and Pinot Meunier are also grown. The region boasts the largest number of villages classed as *grand cru*.

CÔTE DES BLANCS. Situated to the south of Épernay, this is a stronghold for Chardonnay, which reigns supreme here – predominantly between Cramant and Le Mesnil-sur-Oger. Some villages, such as Vertus, produce good red wines (AOC Coteaux Champenois).

VALLÉE DE LA MARNE. This area extends from west of Château-Thierry to east of Épernay. It is dominated by red grape varieties, particularly the Pinot Meunier. Various *grands crus* can be found.

VIGNOBLE DE L'AUBE. This area stretches more than 60 miles (100 km) to the southeast of Troyes. The region's subsoils tend to be marl and are mostly planted with Pinot Noir. The appellation Rosé de Riceys lies to the south.

CÔTE DE SÉZANNE. Planted during the 1960s, this region is an extension of the Côte des Blancs southward. This Chardonnay stronghold produces full, rich wines.

Two legendary names, two famous brands

An exact contemporary of Louis XIV (both men lived from 1639–1715), Dom Pérignon was responsible for the vines and cellars at the Hautvillers abbey near Épernay, where he wrote *l'Art de bien traiter la vigne et du Champagne* (How to care for the vine and Champagne). If he wasn't the inventor of sparkling Champagne as we know it, he was a wine expert ahead of his time. He developed the process of blending *crus* and grape varieties, the basis for the preparation of Champagne. Today, Dom Pérignon is also the name of a *prestige cuvée* made by Moët & Chandon, produced since 1936 and always a vintage wine. The other 'Dom', Dom Ruinart (1657–1709), specialized in the study of 'antiquities', specifically the study of monuments and cemetary inscriptions. He met Dom Pérignon in 1696 at Hautvillers abbey. Dom Pérignon is credited with being the inspiration for his nephew Nicolas Ruinart, founder of that renowned house, the oldest in Champagne. Ruinart paid homage to its founder, dedicating its *prestige cuvéet to* Dom Ruinart.

Grape varieties and wine styles

Although seven grape varieties are authorized, just three represent more than 99% of production: Chardonnay for the whites and two Pinot varieties for the reds.

CHARDONNAY. Planted across 30 per cent of regional vineyards, it produces elegant wines that are lively and full of spirit, offering delicate aromas with floral and sometimes mineral notes. It is well suited to ageing.

PINOT NOIR. This red represents 38 per cent of plantings, and brings body, richness, and longevity to the blend.

PINOT MEUNIER. This grape accounts for 32 per cent. It provides flavour and fruitiness. The wines produced from it are supple and fruity, and have an intense bouquet.

A blended wine

Champagne is produced according to a winemaking technique known as the 'Champagne' or traditional method (*see* pp.70–1). Only Champagne may use the title 'Méthode Champenoise'. Champagne is a blended wine *par excellence*. Few *cuvées* come from just one vineyard or one village despite recent developments. The wine producer may choose to blend two or three grape varieties, or simply to use one. Similarly, he or she combines various *crus* and various vintages. The red grape varieties are almost always vinified in the style of white wine. Every year, the cellar master puts together a *cuvée* or blend corresponding to the house or brand quality and image.

TRUE OR FALSE?

Champagne ages better in 750 ml bottles.

FALSE. Experience shows that Champagne is best preserved in a magnum (which holds 1.5 litres). It seems to mature better, and age for longer, in these bigger bottles.

Types of Champagne

There are several different types of Champagne, according to grape varieties, blends, *dosage* (addition of sugar), and ageing.

***BLANC DE BLANCS* CHAMPAGNE.** An exception to the blending rule, this wine is made from the Chardonnay grape variety on its own, and it offers great finesse.

***BLANC DE NOIRS* CHAMPAGNE.** This wine is made from red grapes only, Pinot Noir and/or Pinot Meunier. More rare than blanc de blancs, they give a powerful Champagne with good vinosity, especially if only Pinot Noir is used.

ROSÉ CHAMPAGNE. Champagne is one of the rare AOCs where it is permitted to mix red and white wines to produce rosés. Of course, that red wine (Pinot Noir), which makes up 10 to 20 per cent of the wine, must come from the Champagne region. Other rosé Champagnes may be produced using the *saignée* technique following a short maceration. This elegant type of Champagne is very popular and nearly all the producers today offer 'their' rosé.

Vineyard hierarchy

The name of a *cru* rarely features on Champagne labels, but *crus* represent a rigorous classification system. Called the '*échelle des crus*' or 'ladder of growths' by residents of the Champagne region, it sets percentages that determine the price of grapes. Of the total 319 villages producing Champagne, 17 have the privilege of receiving a 100 per cent *cru* rating. On this basis they may claim the appellation *grande cru*. Some 44 villages are classified between 90 and 99 per cent and have the right to the designation *premier cru*. Far from being just theoretical, this classification determines the wine's quality, and in part reflects the hierarchy of the terroir.

> The *remueurs* or 'riddlers' turn up to 50,000 bottles per day to ensure that the yeast deposits accumulate in the neck.

CHAMPAGNE SANS ANNÉE. Non-vintage, or more precisely, multi-vintage, it is a blend of various years.

VINTAGE CHAMPAGNE. This wine is produced only in great years, and must be aged on the lees for at least three years. It is a great *Champagne*, distinctive and structured, which ages well.

PRESTIGE CUVÉE. Generally produced from a selection of the best base wines, this unique Champagne is usually presented in an original and distinctive bottle. It is often matured for a long or very long time. *The* Champagne for important occasions, some of the most famous examples are: Roederer's Cristal, Pol Roger's Sir Winston Churchill, Laurent-Perrier's Cuvée Grand Siècle, Ruinart's Dom Ruinart.

***GRAND CRU* OR *PREMIER CRU* CHAMPAGNE.** Just 17 villages can claim this first title (*grand cru*) for their wine; and 44 may do so for the second (*see* box on the facing page).

RD (*RÉCEMMENT DÉGORGÉ*) CHAMPAGNE. This Champagne spends a long time resting on its lees before disgorgement. RD is a brand used by Bollinger, its inventor.

BRUT NATURE, DOSAGE ZÉRO OR 'NON-DOSAGE' CHAMPAGNE. This Champagne does not contain added sugar – or at least less than 3 g/l. A dry Champagne, it is honest and fresh.

EXTRA-BRUT CHAMPAGNE. This is similar to Brut Nature, but a little more rounded than that style, with no more than 6 g/l of sugar.

BRUT CHAMPAGNE. This is the most widely produced type of Champagne. It contains less than 15 g/l of residual sugar.

> Champagne bottles tilted in 'A-line' racks, in the Roederer house cellars in Reims.

Selected Grande Marque Champagnes

- **Bollinger (Aÿ).** A Champagne institution. Its inimitable style, instantly recognizable, has long established this house's reputation through three legendary *cuvées*: the Spécial Cuvée (the non-vintage Brut Maison), the Grand Cuvée, and the RD (*Récemment Dégorgé*).
- **Billecart-Salmon (Mareuil-sur-Aÿ).** A style of finesse, harmony, and balance.
- **Duval-Leroy (Vertus).** Known for its extremely rare Rosé de Saignée Champagne.
- **Champagne Gosset (Aÿ).** Its Cuvée Celebris is dense and powerful, and its Grand Rosé is superbly vinous.
- **Jacquesson (Dizy).** Known for its reliable quality.
- **Krug (Reims).** Some people consider this to be the Champagne *par excellence*; others say one of the most sophisticated available. Known for its Grande Cuvée, its Clos du Mesnil, and its Brut rosé.
- **Laurent-Perrier (Tours-sur-Marne).** Acclaimed for its elegant non-vintage Brut, its non-*dosage* Ultra Brut, and its dazzling Cuvée Grand Siècle.
- **Champagne Drappier (Urville).** An excellent Champagne house in Aube offering vibrant and intense Pinot Noirs, including a very good zero dosage example.
- **Louis Roederer (Reims).** A superb range of Champagnes – distinguished, straightforward, and well balanced, including the world-famous prestigious *cuvée* 'Cristal'.
- **Moët & Chandon (Épernay).** The ubiquitous Champagne label. Its Brut Impérial (non-vintage), with its inimitable style, light and fruity, is the most widely sold *cuvée* in the world. The famous brand Dom Pérignon is now under the same ownership.
- **Charles Heidsieck (Reims).** This Champagne house in Reims produces one of the best Brut Champagnes with wonderfully consistent and well-developed notes.
- **Pol Roger (Épernay).** Wines of great finesse. This was Winston Churchill's favourite Champagne.
- **Ruinart (Reims).** This is the oldest house in Champagne and is renowned for its remarkable *cuvée* Dom Ruinart Blanc de Blancs, made from Chardonnay.
- **Salon (Le Mesnil-sur-Oger).** Its Cuvée S is unique: one grape variety, one *cru*, always a vintage wine.
- **Veuve Clicquot Ponsardin (Reims).** Its non-vintage Brut, with the famous sunset-yellow label, is a Champagne of character, as was the 'Grande Dame' to whom this Champagne pays homage.

EXTRA-DRY CHAMPAGNE. This Champagne is charming and supple; with 12 to 20 g/l of residual sugar, it also has an agreeable freshness.
DRY AND MEDIUM-DRY CHAMPAGNE. Despite its name, this variety contains from 17 to 40 g/l of residual sugar, making it an excellent accompaniment for desserts.
SWEET CHAMPAGNE. Very rare, this is particularly high in residual sugar: more than 55 g/l.

Major houses and grower Champagnes

MAJOR HOUSES. These companies shaped the history of Champagne and perpetuate a truly French art and tradition. The most powerful are listed on the stock exchange. At the top is the LVMH group (Dom Pérignon, Moët & Chandon, Veuve Clicquot Ponsardin, Mercier, Krug, Ruinart), an empire producing 57 million bottles. Next in line is the Lanson BCC group (Besserat de Bellefond, Boizel, Chanoine Frères, Philipponnat, De Venoge, Alexandre Bonnet), followed by the Vranken-Pommery Monopole group (Pommery, Vranken, Heidsieck Monopole, Charles Lafitte) and the Laurent-Perrier group (Laurent Perrier, De Castellane, Delamotte, Salon). Others, equally prestigious, have remained within a family: Henriot, Pol Roger, etc. Not all of the more than 300 Champagne houses in existence have their own vineyards. Many buy their grapes from other producers.
GROWER CHAMPAGNES. These wines are often contrasted with the so-called Grand Marques. They are the expression of a particular person, a *cru*, or a *terroir*. The emergence of these *terroir* Champagnes is a recent phenomenon, led by a new generation of wine producers (Selosse, Égly, Vesselle, Fleury, etc.), who make their wines using grapes from their

Selected Grower Champagnes

- **Pierre Gimonnet (Cuis).** Original wines that are remarkably evolved from the Côte des Blancs.
- **Marie-Noëlle Ledru (Ambonnay).** Her Champagnes, matured on the lees for three to five years, are dense.
- **Jacques Selosse (Avize).** The owner is one of the Champagne region's most remarkable characters. His superb and delicious Champagnes, biodynamically cultivated, announce their *terroir* loud and clear.
- **Paul Bara (Bouzy).** Valued *cuvées* full of character, most of which are from Bouzy's Pinot Noir.
- **Égly-Ouriet (Ambonnay).** Champagnes, with little added sugar, and red Bouzy are wines with character that balance vinosity and elegance.
- **Pierre Moncuit (Le Mesnil-sur-Oger).** Champagnes marked by minerality, purity, and the character of their *terroir*.
- **Roses de Jeanne (Celles-sur-Ources).** Its Champagnes play the cards of finesse and elegance.
- **Jean-Pierre Fleury (Courteron).** A pioneer of biodynamics in Champagne, this producer creates wines full of finesse, aromatics, and elegance. Magnificent expressions of the *terroir*.
- **Larmandier-Bernier (Vertus).** Beautiful, well-balanced Champagnes boasting the best *crus* and excellent value for money.
- **De Sousa (Avize).** Distinguished wines, deep and long-lasting to an extent scarcely matched in the Champagne region.
- **Agrapart & Fils (Avize).** Remarkable, fresh, distinguished blancs de blancs, full of depth.
- **Jacques Beaufort (Ambonnay).** Its *cuvées*, blending fruit and *terroir*, produced from grapes given biodynamic treatments, have no equal.
- **Françoise Bedel (Crouttes-sur-Marne).** A remarkable range of Champagnes produced organically.
- **Georges Laval (Cumières).** A small estate of fewer than 7.5 acres (3 ha). which produces distinctive, powerful, vinous wines.

> Vines in the area around Ay, in the Vallée de la Marne.

A few label idiosyncrasies

Champagne promotes its difference, even on its labels. It is not mandatory to state *'appellation contrôlée'* on the label; but, alongside standard information (see p.108), the occupational category of whoever bottled the wine must be stated. This is generally printed at the bottom of the label in very small letters (see *also* p.111).

NM: ***négociant-manipulant.*** The producer or house either harvests or buys its grapes, and then vinifies them in its own cellars.

RM: ***récoltant-manipulant.*** The wine producer makes, vinifies, and markets his or her own wine.

RC: ***récoltant-coopérateur.*** The grower sends grapes to the cooperative to be made into wine, and then reclaims all or some of the completed bottles for sale.

CM: ***cooperative de manipulation.*** The wines are produced and sold by a cooperative.

SR: ***société de récoltants.*** Quite rare, this is an association of independent wine producers who produce and market their wines jointly.

ND: ***négociant-distributeur.*** A wine merchant who buys bottles produced by other producers and redistributes them under his or her own label.

MA: ***marque d'acheteur.*** A label custom-produced for a purchaser, who then markets it under their own name. This is often used for wines sold in supermarkets.

own vineyards. There are several thousand of these innovative, dynamic producers competing in the market with their truly luxurious flagship products. They represent about 25 per cent of total Champagne production. The properties are small (often less than 40 acres, or 15 hectares), many passed down from generation to generation. Their wines are mostly marketed at the property itself.

COOPERATIVES. These collectives have become more widespread in recent years. Among the largest are the Centre Vinicole Champagne Nicolas Feuillatte, the Union Champagne, Alliance Champagne, and the Coopérative Régionale des Vins de Champagne. Their Champagnes are generally blended to a uniform style: light, fruity, well-balanced wines that appeal to all. This does not stop them developing particularly elegant, special *cuvées*, for example, the prestigious wines from Nicolas Feuillatte such as Palmes d'Or, or vintages from Castelnau (CRVC). Smaller groups also exist exist, such as Palmer or Mailly Grand Cru, capable of producing some particularly interesting wines.

Champagne without bubbles

Alongside its famous sparkling wines, the vineyards of the Champagne region also produce still wines under two appellations.

COTEAUX CHAMPENOIS. This appellation covers the entire Champagne region. It produces still, dry wines in white, rosé, and red styles. The whites are cool and light, supported by a beautiful freshness. The rosés are full of elegance and finesse. In good years, the reds can offer the ripe fruit of Pinot and a firm structure. The most famous bears the name of the *village* of Bouzy (Pinot Noir *grand cru*). Like various others (such as Vertus, Ambonnay, Aÿ, Cumières), it is permitted to add its name after that of the appellation.

ROSÉ DES RICEYS. One of France's greatest rosés, this wine is produced in limited quantities in the Aube, at the south end of the Champagne region, grown in limestone soil and Kimmeridgian marls. Produced from Pinot Noir through a short maceration – which must be halted at the precise moment when the famous *'goût de Riceys'* flavours appear – it is a full wine, dense with a pretty nose that is delicately fruity and yet complex.

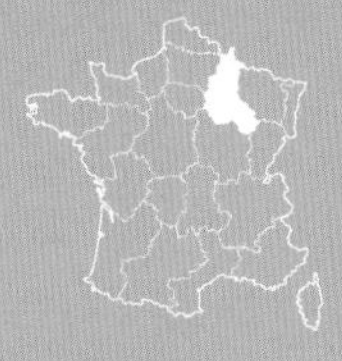

Champagne

CHAMPAGNE *AGRAPART*

Champagnes with a mineral flavour may be an extremely odd prospect, but it is one that makes Champagne Agrapart distinct from the rest. This 'minerality' is the root of the great subtlety of its Champagnes, along with much more. Tireless work on the vines and the soil has created a unique treasure.

CHAMPAGNE AGRAPART

57, avenue Jean-Jaures
51190 Avize

Founded: *end of the 19th century*
Area: *30 acres (12 ha)*
Production: *100,000 bottles p.a.*
Appellation: *Champagne*
Grape varieties: *Chardonnay, Pinot Noir*

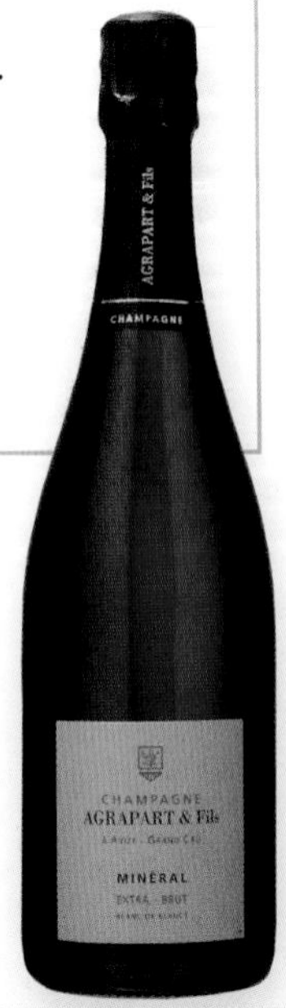

The temple of Chardonnay

The Côte des Blancs is as essential to Champagne as the Eiffel Tower is to Paris. The name derives from the white Chardonnay grape that reigns supreme here, and from its hilly relief, a sharp slope barely nine miles (15 km) long, spread out between Épernay and Bergère-les-Vertus along a northeast/southwest axis. Bounded at its two ends by the hill at Saran and Mount Aimé, the soft and green countryside of the Côte des Blancs stretches out across the plain, where cereals are grown, but vines reign unchallenged on the hills. Of the 17 villages classified as *grands crus* on the Crus de Champagne scale, six are located on the Côte des Blancs: Chouilly, Oiry, Cramant, Avize, Oger, and Mesnil-sur-Oger. The village of Avize is the smallest but among the most famous; situated halfway up the hill in the northern section, Avize lies atop pure limestone that almost reaches the surface, to the delight and benefit of the Chardonnay grapes.

A life to send a message

Agrapart first saw the light of day at Avize. Founded by Arthur Agrapart at the end of the 19th century and made prosperous in the 1950s by his grandson Pierre, it has become an important yardstick under the leadership of Pascal Agrapart. As owner of 30 acres (12 ha) spread across Avize, Oger, Cramant, and Oiry, Pascal Agrapart takes particular care of his vines. He is a fervent advocate of soil tillage, a conviction he acquired when he first started out on his family's land.

The vines had never been treated with herbicides when he took over their management in the 1980s, and the results have been clear: vines cultivated in tilled soils without herbicides produce better wines. Since then, the winemaker's daily duties have included long hours of research, both intellectual and physical. Tilling the soil allows the vines to put down roots, and upon contact with the rock (limestone), the roots pick up signals, made up in part of mineral salts that give the wine particular characteristics. After 30 harvests, Pascal Agrapart is still going strong in his quest for minerality and has indicated that sooner or later he wishes to pass on the secret of the soil to his son and heir.

Mineral – did you say mineral?

'Minerality' is probably the word most commonly used in wine vocabulary, and the term has as many definitions as there are wine-lovers! According to Pascal Agrapart, minerality, acquired the hard way by tilling the soil over the course of years, is the root of the saline, refreshing flavours that characterize all his Champagnes. It is also why he produces vintage wines with every harvest. Tending the soil reduces the effects of the year's climate.

CHAMPAGNE AGRAPART, A WINE TRULY OF ITS TERROIR

An extremely delicate Champagne, with an abundance of aromatic scents and a highly refreshing finish. A reasonably-priced wine for those keen to discover the world of this incomparable wine-maker.

CHAMPAGNE AGRAPART, CUVÉE MINÉRAL

The old vines at Cramant and Avize have given birth to a wine of great magnitude, with omnipresent hints of salinity. No Champagne was ever better named!

CHAMPAGNE AGRAPART, CUVÉE VÉNUS

Named after Vénus, the only horse allowed to plough the old vines at Avize that were planted in 1959, this Champagne has a rare intensity of flavour combined with great delicacy. The pleasure seems to go on forever, to the great delight of Champagne-lovers.

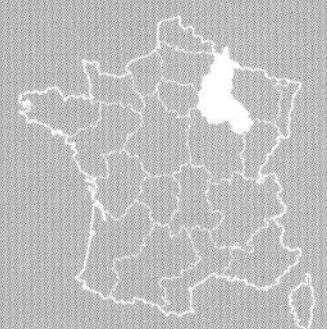

Champagne

CHAMPAGNE
BOLLINGER

The first Champagne brand to receive the prestigious Royal Warrant from Queen Victoria in 1884, recognizing it as official supplier to the Court of St James's, the House of Bollinger owes its universal prestige to skills honed over centuries – and unique in Champagne – that defy the demands of both time and trade.

CHAMPAGNE BOLLINGER

20, boulevard du Maréchal
de Lattre de Tassigny
51160 Aÿ

Founded: *1829*
Area: *405 acres (164 ha)*
Production: *N/A*
Appellation: *Champagne*
Grape varieties: *Pinot Noir Chardonnay, Pinot Meunier*

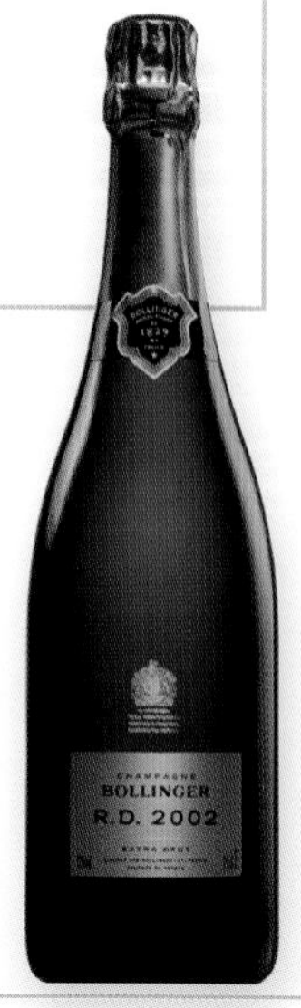

One vineyard, one grape variety, one jewel

Located in the heart of the village of Aÿ, Bollinger is one of the rare Champagne houses to own the majority of its own grape supply. The 405 acres (164 ha), almost exclusively classified as *premier* or *grand cru*, make up the backbone of Bollinger Champagnes. Pinot Noir reigns supreme here, and this noble but capricious grape variety, requiring meticulous cultivation, makes up 60% of the planted area. Pinot Noir is also intrinsic to the jewel of Bollinger: the Chaudes Terres and Clos Saint-Jacques, two vineyards with a total area of less than an acre (36 ares), planted with ungrafted Pinot Noir.

When the rest of Champagne was saved from phylloxera at the end of the 19th century by the systematic use of grafted stock, these vines remained ungrafted and continue to be cultivated by hand using the *provignage* ('tip-layering') method. Even in the best years, they will yield fewer than 5,000 bottles, all made with 100 per cent Pinot Noir grapes: Vieilles Vignes Françaises ('old French vines'). This leafy legacy, steeped in history and underwriting a diversity that is under threat, is now the cornerstone of Bollinger Champagnes. The vineyard has been mostly grassed-over between the rows of vines, and the soils are tilled, a charming, old-fashioned practice that nevertheless provides all the depth needed to create the great wines of the House of Bollinger.

Wood in all its states

As the only Champagne house to have a resident cooper, the House of Bollinger decided early on not to use any stainless steel so that it could continue to ferment the great majority of its wines in oak casks. It owns some 3,500 barrels and uses only the *cuvée*, the first pressing of juice to run from the grapes, which has the greatest potential for ageing and is capable of expressing its full character in active contact with the wood. This meticulous process is the first of many steps on a long journey towards excellence that made no concessions to fashion or the ease offered by technology.

Reserve wines are all stored in magnums, and this immense library of 750,000 bottles, classified by year and wine type, is Bollinger's memory bank. Each bottle is allowed to age under cork, thereby prolonging the wine's privileged association with wood. As each year comes round, its wine is blended using a part of the library, creating the Spécial Cuvée whose style seems to be eternal. The vintage and R.D. wines are also matured under cork, benefiting – after several years of ageing – from the preservative properties of the cork, which protects the Champagnes from the ravages of time.

CHAMPAGNE BOLLINGER, SPÉCIAL CUVÉE

Bollinger's signature wine is typical of the estate as it is made mostly with Pinot Noir. Subtle, delicious, and elegant, with a refreshing finish, it is hard to find a better introduction to the world of Champagne.

CHAMPAGNE BOLLINGER, LA GRAND ANNÉE ROSÉ

A Bollinger Grande Année, ('great year') is special, and when the wine is rosé, it is thanks to the Pinot Noir grapes from the legendary Côte-aux-Enfants where the red wine is created. With its great wealth of aromas, this is Champagne of great quality.

CHAMPAGNE BOLLINGER, R.D.

Since the first vintage in 1952, there have been only 24 further occasions on which an R.D. (Récemment Dégorgé, 'recently disgorged') wine could be made, making it both an exceptional but scarce wine. It is emblematic of the excellent of Champagne and irresistible.

'Madame Jacques'

Scotswoman Elisabeth 'Lily' Bollinger, had a profound effect on the story of this Champagne house. Left as the head of the household at the age of only 42 upon the death of her husband, Jacques Bollinger, 'Madame Jacques' worked miracles for the business. She was also a remarkable visionary, resisting the stainless-steel revolution in the 1950s to save her oak barrels. She also created the first Vieilles Vignes Françaises vintage in 1969, thereby safeguarding a piece of the Champagne region's true heritage. She was also responsible for creating the R.D. vintages, made from an exceptional Grande Année blend that has been aged for at least eight years.

> 'Lily' Bollinger ran the House of Bollinger until 1971.

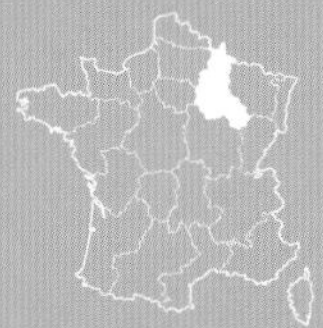

CHAMPAGNE *DOM PÉRIGNON*

The fascinating result of singular blending, Dom Pérignon wines are like a voyage through space and time, with each new universe opening up new realms of aromas and abundant flavour. This Champagne will be enjoyed forever, a precious gift from the celebrated cellar master of Hautvillers.

CHAMPAGNE DOM PÉRIGNON

9, avenue de Champagne
51200 Épernay

Founded: *1921*
Area : *N/A*
Production: *N/A*
Appellation: *Champagne*
Grape varieties: *Pinot Noir, Chardonnay*

An original birth

Dom Pérignon was the first prestige Champagne to be marketed. Although Roederer Cristal was created in 1876, its first vintage was not offered for sale until 1945, nine years after Moët & Chandon brought out the first Dom Pérignon. In the mid 1930s, Moët & Chandon sent 300 bottles of the 1926 vintage to the English wine merchants Simon Brothers & Co, who were celebrating their centenary (1835 to 1935), and the British brokers sent the consignment on to their best customers as a thank you present. These bottles, specially labelled for the 100-year anniversary of the company, had all the features of Dom Pérignon that are known and loved by its admirers: the 18th-century bottle shape and the shield-shaped label, although the name Dom Pérignon itself was missing; for the occasion, the wine has been christened 'Champagne specially shipped for Simon Brothers & Co's Centenary 1835 to 1935'. These 300 bottles were the talk of the town on the other side of the Atlantic as well, generating significant demand, and 100 further cases were sent to New York in November 1936. As he was unable to use the same label, Robert-Jean de Vogüé, Moët head of marketing, decided to create Dom Pérignon, a wholly new brand, and the magnificent 1921 was selected to launch it.

A sculpted wine

In the past, Dom Pérignon wines were produced exclusively from vineyards belonging to the abbey at Hautvillers, where the Benedictine monk Pierre Pérignon worked as cellar master in the 17th century. Pierre Pérignon had a great knowledge and appreciation of wine and said he produced 'the best in the world', an ambition that has no doubt inspired those who have inherited the most famous name in Champagne. Following its purchase by Moët & Chandon in the 1820s, the abbey now makes up just a tiny portion of the vineyards dedicated to the *grand vin*. With the exception of the estate's historic vines, all the grapes are sourced from *grand cru* vineyards with the best exposure.

A classic blend of more or less equal quantities of Chardonnay and Pinot Noir, Dom Pérignon is created in a singular process by the iconic figure of Richard Geoffroy, the Champagne house's cellar master. If the art of blending could be described as playing with the complementary characteristics of grape varieties as a painter would blend harmonious colours, then Richard Geoffroy's take on blending is more like sculpture, shaping his blends from the very dense and rich wines sourced from the most beautiful terroirs. This has the double advantage of reducing the wine's year to no more than a simple historical reference point while creating the perfect balance that gives Dom Pérignon all its fullness, however old it may be.

DOM PÉRIGNON CHAMPAGNE 2002

A delicious Dom Pérignon that lacks for nothing, it boasts an exuberance tempered with subtlety, its power controlled with balance. Enchanting now, it could be easy to forget the great promise it holds for the decades to come.

DOM PÉRIGNON ROSÉ CHAMPAGNE 2004

A definitive rosé in the style of Dom Pérignon; exploding with inspired fruit flavours, it has a simple appearance and yet is so sophisticated, with many levels to its combination of flavours and aromas.

DOM PÉRIGNON CHAMPAGNE 1990 P3 (*PLÉNITUDE TROISIÈME*)

A rare tasting moment of absolute fusion – a sensation of perfect unity and completion. One of the greatest Dom Pérignons and Richard Geoffroy's third vintage.

'Abundance', a journey through time

Dom Pérignon is a contradictory Champagne, delicious when young and splendid when old. This paradox, which goes largely unnoticed by casual wine drinkers, is the result of the inspired notion of *plénitude* ('abundance'), the brainchild of Richard Geoffroy. By releasing the same vintage of Dom Pérignon at regular intervals, Geoffroy enables wine-lovers to experience a journey through a universe of flavours expressed to the full. For example, it is possible to savour a Dom Pérignon 1998 P1 (*Plénitude Première*, the 'first abundance'), which came out in the mid-2000s, followed by a Dom Pérignon 1998 P2, released in the mid-2010s.

> Richard Geoffroy, the cellar master.

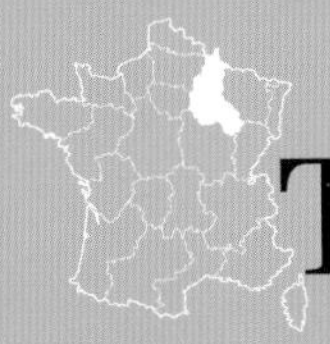

Champagne

THE ART OF CHAMPAGNE *BY KRUG*

The House of Krug made its debut on the Champagne stage in 1843, and over the years it has both achieved and reinforced its unparalleled prestige and excellence, the result of an unwavering insistence on authenticity that was also the mission of Johann-Joseph Krug, founder of the Champagne house.

The sixth generation of the family still maintains the same enthusiasm and passion. A first fermentation in small oak casks (to enrich the complexity of the wine while guaranteeing that it will evolve and develop over time) precedes the great art of the blending process, followed by long ageing in cellar (a minimum of six years). These elements combine to create the wine's excellence and its inimitable signature flavour.

The Grande Cuvée, a symbol of the House of Krug

One of the brand's greatest assets is the immense reserve of old wines made from the best vineyard plots. Ageing serenely in the coolness of the cellars, these still wines are regularly used in the final blending process to create the Grande Cuvée, the emblem of the House of Krug. As a non-vintage wine it is free to include several *crus* from different regions of the Champagne area, to use wines from previous years, and to integrate all three grape varieties (Chardonnay, Pinot Meunier, and Pinot Noir) in appropriate proportions in order to achieve the emblematic style of Krug year after year. Fifty wines (and many more on some occasions) will go into the final composition!

The sparkling Grande Cuvée has a slightly golden appearance, circumscribed by an endless stream of tiny bubbles. Its rich bouquet suggests yellow-fleshed fruit and very ripe citrus fruits, with hints of toasted hazelnuts, brioche, and white flowers. The wine's flavour develops at length on the palate, evolving a rich density that is vinous, aromatic, and flavoursome. Its fine bubbles dissolve into the mellowness of the fruit. The overall experience is flawlessly prolonged thanks to its exceptional freshness and occasional flashes of minerality. The richness and complexity of this Champagne require an expert palate. It is wine for meditation and celebration, capable of holding its own when paired with sophisticated crustacean dishes, meats, and poultry in cream (and with girolle mushrooms) or even roast small game.

Vintage Krug

Vintage Krug is obviously made to different criteria and without recourse to reserve wines. Even though the particular year will inevitably impose its own climatic conditions, the Krug style can be reimposed by playing with the ripeness of the grapes across a whole range of terroirs and through the choice of judicious proportions of the three grape varieties. The development of the wine is closely monitored during its fermentation in small oak casks and the new wine is tasted every day. When the crucial moment of blending comes, the assembled Krug family will have a vast choice of still wines from the same year to make up a wine that is both faithful to its vintage and to its own flavour. Such Champagnes, with their great capacity for ageing, will still retain astonishing freshness after 20 or 30 years in the cellar.

Krug rosé

Krug rosé is now just one of a range of products that demonstrate the family's desire to move towards new types of wine. The first Krug rosé was conceived with the magnificent vintage of 1976 and enjoyed immediate success at the first tastings in 1983. The blend, still as meticulous as ever, includes a small quantity of Pinot Noir, vinified with the skins, delivering the palpable full-bodied feel and flavour that characterize it. Created to pair with great culinary delights, this vinous Champagne consistently embodies the spirit of Krug.

CHAMPAGNE KRUG CLOS DU MESNIL AND CLOS D'AMBONNAY

Two rare wines complete this line up: Clos du Mesnil, a *blanc de blancs*, and Clos d'Ambonnay, *a blanc de noirs*. In 1971, the Krug family acquired the Clos du Mesnil, a 5-acre (1.85-ha) plot planted with Chardonnay with walls unchanged since 1698. This wine is made only in exceptional years and undergoes no blending of any kind – absolutely unheard-of for the Krugs! Nonetheless, it creates one of the most refined and well-rounded of all Champagnes. Rarer still, and an almost extravagant purchase, is Clos d'Ambonnay, the product of a walled plot of fewer than 2 acres (0.68 ha), exclusively planted with Pinot Noir. This wine has a golden-copper colouration and unfolds to reveal a wealth of flavours and scents. What will come next for the House of Krug?

vier Krug, director
House of Krug.

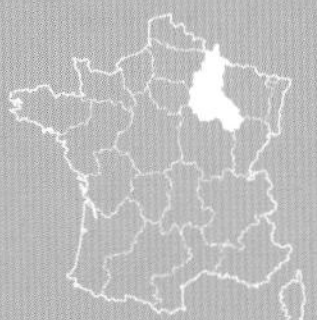

Champagne

CHAMPAGNE *LOUIS ROEDERER*

'An unfathomable clarity that has fallen from the stars'. Corneille rhapsodized eloquently about Cristal Champagne, the beauty and limpidity of the bottle rivalling its superb content. Taking inspiration from the wine made for the Tsars, the appearance of Louis Roederer may be deceptive but will never disappoint. And the distant stars have never been so near to the grapes.

CHAMPAGNE LOUIS ROEDERER

21, boulevard Lundy
51722 Reims

Founded: *1776*
Area: *593 acres (240 ha)*
Production: *N/A*
Appellation: *Champagne*
Grape varieties: *Pinot Noir, Chardonnay, Pinot Meunier*

A visionary

Having inherited the Champagne house in 1833, Louis Roederer was in a position to attack Champagne's practices and customs from the rear. While trading in wine had been the prerogative of wine merchants, vineyards remained in the hands of winemakers, and yet in 1845 Louis Roederer bought 37 acres (15 ha) of *grand cru* vineyard. He wanted to control every stage of the production process and so decided to combine the two professions by becoming a winemaker, a visionary policy that would become a key trump card for the house that was to bear his name. Today, Louis Roederer's vineyards cover 593 acres (240 ha), providing 70% of its grape supply: an exceptional situation that the company exploits to the full for its vintage wines, made exclusively with grapes from the family's vineyards. Despite its largely settled position, the House of Roederer continues to sustain the cutting-edge entrepreneurial dynamism that brought it success by returning to its roots – its vines.

From the vines to the stars

Under the instructions of Jean-Baptiste Lécaillon and Frédéric Rouzaud, the manager and owner of Louis Roederer respectively, the company's vineyards have been turning to biodynamic farming practices since the 2000s. A total of 50 acres (20 ha) are currently certified, and 219 acres (88.6 ha) are in the process of being converted. Biodynamics, an organic farming method that incorporates lunar cycles, marks a return to 'farmer's wisdom', with close attention paid to the land and conditions and a move away from classic farming techniques, outdated symbols of a production-based culture. Taking advantage of this open-air laboratory, Roederer uses massal selection to rejuvenate the vineyard and to preserve the diversity of the rootstock. The effects are imperceptible over the short term but this approach turns out to be essential for coping with the climatic and ecological challenges of tomorrow. By placing its vines at the heart of its strategy, the House of Roederer is opening up new ways in which the quality of its Champagnes can evolve while preparing fertile ground for its successors. It is a timely reminder that Roederer Champagne is an ongoing story of men and women in search of one absolute goal: the best wine possible.

Louis Roederer Cristal

Adored by the very wealthy, Cristal is all about successful product marketing, but one should also be aware of the significance of its history and its characteristics. First created at the request of Alexander II of Russia in 1876, the Tsars' *cuvée spéciale* has stood the test of time and remains an exceptional wine, although the modern bottle is no longer made of lead crystal and the Champagne contains far less sugar. The grapes, some of which are biodynamically farmed, are picked later than average in Champagne in order to ensure a *mousse* of great delicacy. A highly concentrated wine, Cristal spends six years on the lees, and a further six years of bottle ageing are required for it to begin to reveal its potential. Its reserved character, which has unjustifiably earned it a superficial reputation, is necessary to unfold its greatness to those with the wisdom to wait.

LOUIS ROEDERER CHAMPAGNE, VINTAGE CUVÉE BLANC DE BLANCS

Blended from the *grands crus* Mesnil and Avize, this wine gets irresistibly close to Cristal, although without having its depth. While the pure bouquet has delicate hits of Muscat, this *blanc de blancs* really comes into its own in the mouthfeel, coating the palate with an endless and exceptional creamy texture without surrendering to heaviness; a magnificent combination of human inspiration and a great limestone vineyard – Roederer succeeds both in enhancing the terroir and imposing its style.

LOUIS ROEDERER CHAMPAGNE, CUVÉE BRUT PREMIER

Made up of 40% Pinot Noir, 40% Chardonnay and 10% Pinot Meunier, the Brut Premier is a wonderful symbol of Roederer's genius. Rich and yet refreshing, creamy and yet vital, each aspect of the wine finds its counterpart to create a complex, deliciously harmonious whole.

LOUIS ROEDERER CHAMPAGNE, CUVÉE CRISTAL

Picked at full ripeness, Pinot Noir – Cristal's cornerstone – dominates this blended wine, supplying depth and breadth to an immense wine, with Chardonnay (exclusively *grand cru*) lending a counterpoint to the overall effect. Cristal is a great wine for laying down and should be kept for several decades.

> Frédéric Rouzaud, the Champagne house's manager.

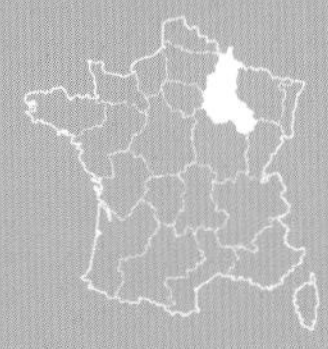

Champagne

CHAMPAGNE
PALMER & CO

Sooner or later, all wine-lovers dream of tasting great wines. Yet the price to be paid often stops even the most passionate in their tracks. Is it possible to obtain exceptional wine for a reasonable sum? The answer is yes. To do so, head to the unassuming Champagne Palmer & Co.

CHAMPAGNE PALMER & CO

67 rue Jacquart, 51100 Reims

Founded: *1947*
Area: *964 acres (390 ha)*
Production: *N/A*
Appellation: *Champagne*
Grape varieties: *Chardonnay, Pinot Noir, Pinot Meunier*

People and vineyards

The story begins in 1947. Seven winemakers, owners of vineyards classified as *premier cru* and *grand cru*, united to buy high-quality grapes and produce wines. A year later, the Palmer & Co brand was created and moved to Avize. Thanks to its success, the young house attracted many winemakers eager to join it. The selection process was ruthless, however, and only the best terroirs were accepted. Some 65 years later and now based in Reims, the Palmer house has grown. It proudly oversees a patchwork of terroirs, covering 964 acres (390 ha), that demonstrate its steadfast commitment to company values. The majority of the vineyards occupy the eastern crescent of the Montagne de Reims, site of the most prestigious *grands crus*.

This area is the main source of supply for Pinot Noir (40 per cent) and Chardonnay (50 per cent), along with the little-known Côte de Sézanne and the magnificent Côte des Bars vineyards. The Vallée de la Marne, the location of choice for Pinot Meunier (10 per cent), completes the tour of the Champagne landscape. These exceptional vineyards form the basis of the Palmer style, developed by years of cellar work, Palmer's secret weapon!

The acclaim of time

Only the best wines are selected. Destined to become great Champagnes, they require many years of ageing to develop. The Brut Réserve can contain up to five different years and vintage wines may be kept for ten years before being sold. This need for patience is perfectly illustrated by the house's very old wines. Stored neck down (*sur pointe*), their maturity seems frozen in time. These rare bottles are disgorged and sold on request, with the years 1959, 1961, 1979, 1989, and many others, ranking among the treasures of the cellar. Champagnes such as these must be given the time to develop in order fully to enhance the drinking experience. They are truly memorable wines, and it is clear that Champagne Palmer, which has enjoyed considerable acclaim over the years, is one of the greatest of the many great wines so produced.

Large bottles

Jeroboam, methuselah, salmanazar, balthazar, nebuchadnezzar – a great deal of care is needed to produce Champagne in these larger size bottles, unlike with the simpler and less risky method of *transvasage*. The latter involves disgorging enough bottles to fill a larger final bottle, say a jeroboam, which will take four 'normal' bottles, into a pressurized vat, then transferring this volume of Champagne to the final container (*i.e.* the jeroboam). Champagne Palmer is one of the very few houses to avoid using this transfer method. The Champagne is actually aged in the large volume bottles in which it is sold. It entails a considerable amount of work: riddling (*remuage*) is done by hand and disgorging is also carried out manually (*à la volée*), but the results are beyond compare, and handsome reward for all the hard work.

CHAMPAGNE PALMER & CO, AMAZON

A blend of the years 1995, 1996, 1998, and 1999, and aged for at least ten years, Champagne Amazon merits careful consideration. It is enhanced in the glass and its great persistence offers an aromatic development of great complexity, where citrus and exotic fruits rub shoulders with sweet spices, honey, and praline. It is a great wine from Champagne.

CHAMPAGNE PALMER & CO, BRUT RÉSERVE

This Champagne is a blend of three grape varieties, and of a rare complexity for a non-vintage. It is drinkable and light, aromatic and delicate, with the different wines that compose it complementing each other perfectly.

CHAMPAGNE PALMER & CO, BLANC DE BLANCS

Produced mainly from the great Chardonnays of the Montagne, this wine deserves admiration for its aromatic exuberance and its lingering palate. Wine-lovers can find this ten-year-old vintage in the 'Palmer Collection'.

> Rémi Vervier, director of Palmer & Co.

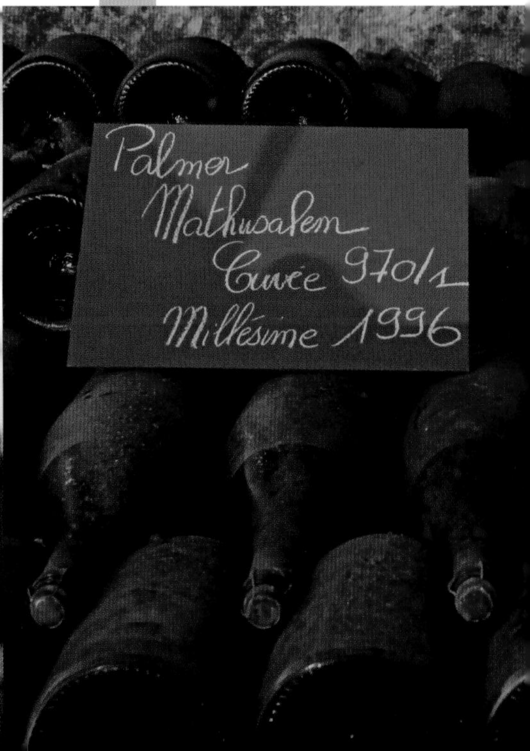

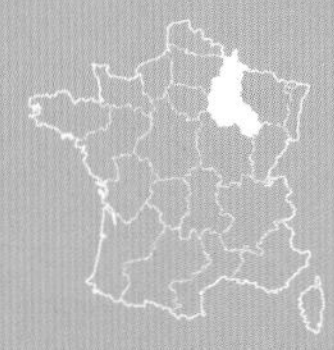

Champagne

CHAMPAGNE
PIERRE GERBAIS

'Understand the past in order to prepare for the future' could be the motto of Champagne Pierre Gerbais, winemakers for four generations and key figures of the Côte des Bar. Heirs to a unique heritage, such as Pinot Blanc Vrai, their Champagnes offer a refreshing taste of history.

CHAMPAGNE PIERRE GERBAIS

13, rue du Pont
10110 Celles-sur-Ource

Founded: *1930*
Area: *46 acres (18.6 ha)*
Production: *N/A*
Appellation: *Champagne*
Grape varieties: *Pinot Noir, Chardonnay, Pinot Blanc*

CHAMPAGNE
PIERRE GERBAIS
Celles-sur-Ource

The most Burgundian of Champagnes

Situated in the southernmost part of Champagne, 106 miles (170 km) south of Reims in the department of Aube, Côte des Bar, at the highest point of the Paris basin, borders the celebrated Burgundy region and is one of the most remarkable vineyards in Champagne. Its steep hillsides from which it derives its name ('bar' is a Celtic word meaning 'summit') are the first distinctive feature of the vineyard. Carved out by numerous streams and rivers, like a piece of crumpled silk, the Côte des Bar has a large number of geographical features that winemakers and their vineyards have made good use of over the years. The other unique feature of the Côte des Bar is its geology. Although it has been adopted by Champagne, its roots lie in Burgundy and consist of Kimmeridgian and Portlandian marls, the same soils that host the famous Chablis vineyard and a characteristic feature that deserves to be as famous for its Champagnes as its still wines, especially reds and rosés.

The Côte des Bar is a varied landscape, with a 'foot' in two regional 'camps', but it is to Champagne that it deservedly owes its name, formalized in 1927 after a lengthy struggle, including the revolt of the Aube wine-growers in 1911, who were aggrieved to see their grapes being used for a Champagne without being able to use the name.

Tradition adapted to the modern world

The rich and fertile heritage of Champagne Pierre Gerbais lies in the small village of Celles-sur-Ource, not far from Bar-sur-Seine. The Gerbais family cultivates 46 acres (18.6 ha) of vineyards on the hills overlooking the Ource valley, varying between Pinot Noir, Chardonnay, noble Champagne grape varieties, and a genuine Pinot Blanc, a rarity and a symbol of the region's Burgundy past, something of which the Gerbais family is extremely proud.

Ulysses is the embodiment of that first pioneering generation. A survivor of both World Wars, he took the first steps on the road towards producing Champagne. A familiar figure in the village, he would say to anyone who met him, 'If you don't drink Champagne, you'll never be a man!' Ulysses' grandson, Pierre, was responsible for choosing the vineyard locations. Thanks to Pierre, the family estate has a patchwork of terroirs providing a range of excellent, high-quality grapes to produce the Champagnes that bear his name. Pierre's son, Pascal, was behind the environmental revolution of the vineyard and put in place natural vine cultivation practices in 1996. This has safeguarded the ongoing traditions of the vineyard. Today, Pascal has in turn passed the baton on to his son Aurélien. With experience in the largest Burgundy estates, Aurélien has made use of his expertize in fine wines using, for example, barrel maturation. Conscious of the family heritage, Aurélien chose to call his son Ulysses.

CHAMPAGNE PIERRE GERBAIS, PRESTIGE

Exclusively based on Chardonnay, this is a stylistic tour de force in a region famous for Pinot Noir. Exotic, fine, and refreshing, it can compete with any of the greatest Côte des Blancs wines!

CHAMPAGNE PIERRE GERBAIS, L'ORIGINALE

This has to be tried. It is unique, original, and pioneering. Such a description scarcely does justice to this superb, high-class wine made from 100% Pinot Blanc. An exceptional Champagne that is universally appreciated by wine-lovers.

CHAMPAGNE PIERRE GERBAIS, RÉSERVE

This blend of 50% Pinot Noir, 25% Chardonnay, 25% Pinot Blanc is the estate's calling card. There is no doubt it represents excellent value, a good balance between easy drinking and creativity. An extra-dry version will please more discerning palates.

A classic grape variety: a genuine Pinot Blanc

The Gerbais family is one of the few to own Pinot Blanc vines (less than 0.3% of the Champagne grape varieties), the oldest of which are over 100 years old. Planted on each side of the Ource valley, Pinot Noir produces grapes that are sometimes rich and exotic, sometimes fresh and lemony, depending on whether they are from the northern or southern slopes. This contrasting combination has enabled Pascal Gerbais to produce an exceptional Champagne, L'Originale, since 1996. It is the first Champagne based exclusively on Pinot Noir. Only 3,000 bottles are produced each year.

ALSACE, JURA, AND SAVOIE

Alsace, Lorraine, Jura, Savoie, Bugey – the vineyards of eastern France are some of the country's smallest. Despite their size, they are nevertheless great and unique in terms of the wide range and originality of their grape varieties, and the typicity of their wines, some of which (such as Château-Chalon) are among the most famous in the world.

ALSACE

A narrow ribbon of valleys and hillsides, the Alsace vineyards extend along some 106 miles (170 km) of a line between Thann in the south and Marlenheim in the north. The region is notable in France for its grape varieties and the style of its wines – and of course for its appellation system, where bottles have always been allowed to display grape varieties: Gewurztraminer, Riesling, Muscat, Pinot Noir, etc. There are only three appellations: one for *vins de cépage*, another for *grands crus*, and the third for *crémants*.

ALSACE STATISTICS (AOC)

Vineyard area: 38,300 acres (15,500 ha)

Production: 12.8 million cases (1.15 million ml)

Whites: 90%

Reds and rosés: 10%

(CIVA, 2015)

Yesterday and today

Established by Roman legions, who introduced their own grape varieties, the vineyards of Alsace reached a peak in the Middle Ages. This period of prosperity – which also saw the arrival of large wine merchants – actually continued until the 17th century, when its dynamism was undermined by war, German annexation, and phylloxera. At the end of the First World War in 1918, though, the vineyards recovered by focusing specifically on quality.

Since the 1970s, Alsace has been committed to organic production, led by wine producers such as Jean-Pierre Frick, a pioneer in the field. The region has 280 wine producers using organic or biodynamic cultivation methods, covering an area of some 5,436 acres (2,200 hectares), representing 14% of the vineyard area. This makes it one of the regions most committed to organic production.

> Vines near the village of Riquewihr.

Vineyard landscape

CLIMATE. Protected by the Vosges mountain range, Alsace benefits from a dry continental climate with warm springs, dry and sunny summers, long and mild autumns, and cold winters, all of which are particularly conducive to growing vines.
SOILS. The vineyards contain no fewer than 13 types of soil – including volcanic, sandstone, granite, gneiss, schist, marly limestone, clay marl, and loess – most of which are closely intermixed. This great diversity allows a single grape variety to produce a huge range of flavours.

Grape varieties and wine styles

Alsace can proudly claim a formidable collection of grape varieties, some of which can be found nowhere else in France.
RIESLING. This is the most prestigious of local grape varieties. Lively and distinguished, it produces wines with a characteristic bouquet of lemon, honeysuckle, citronella, and grapefruit, supported by a pleasant minerality that can take on fascinating notes of petroleum with age.
GEWURZTRAMINER. The name means 'spiced Traminer' in German and Alsatian. Gewurztraminer creates a full-bodied, highly expressive wine offering exceptional aromatic complexity

DID YOU KNOW...?

Alsace and Lorraine are traditionally considered together. *Lorraine is noted for producing Côtes-de-Toul, famous for its vin gris (in fact a rosé made from direct pressing) with its unusual grey colour. It is a fairly lively wine offering aromas marked by flowers and soft fruits.*

End of the single variety?

In Alsace, the rule for most *grands crus* is: one *terroir*, one grape variety. If a wine producer does not respect this rule, the wine loses its appellation. However, Marcel Deiss helped to change the law. He was not content to define his wines as simply varietal expressions of the *terroir* that he manages with great care biodynamically. He instead chose to pursue 'complantation' – the practice of planting different grape varieties in one *terroir* without identifying them – and to produce blends of more than one variety. His Burg and his Grasberg, among others, have met with major success.

dominated by rose and lychee, mingling with white and exotic fruit flavours, as well as spicy notes.

PINOT GRIS. This variety provides rounded, well-structured, rich, complex whites, offering fruity aromas tinged with spice.

MUSCAT. Two varieties are used, often in blends: Muscat d'Alsace (also called Muscat à Petits Grains or Muscat de Frontignan) and Muscat Ottonel. They produce dry wines with an intense nose and palate of fresh grapes.

SYLVANER. This variety yields a pleasant, fresh, light, discreetly fruity wine, with an acacia scent accented by mineral notes. It's often delightfully lively.

PINOT BLANC. This rising star of a grape variety forms a rounded, tender wine. It is fresh and supple, with an aromatic range offering notes of fruit and flowers.

PINOT NOIR. This is Alsace's only red grape variety. It is used to make rosé or red wine. For the latter, it is aged in barrel, and creates reds with a little less depth than their counterparts from Burgundy, but with a typical fruitiness and hints of cherry. These wines can become extraordinary in great years.

KLEVENER DE HEILIGENSTEIN. This is simply Savagnin Rose. Grown in just five villages of Bas-Rhin, it produces original, well-structured wines, with exotic fruits emphasizing spicy notes.

Alsace specialties

GENTIL AND EDELZWICKER. These blended wines are made from various grape varieties, and are pleasant and thirst-quenching. One or other of these terms will therefore follow the appellation AOC Alsace on the label.

***VENDANGE TARDIVE* AND *SÉLECTION DES GRAINS NOBLES*.** These descriptions (not appellations) may be added to AOCs Alsace or Alsace Grand Cru. They are given only to sweet wines made from Riesling, Gewurztraminer, Muscat, and Pinot Gris, which are particularly rich in sugar when harvested. These exceptional wines, capable of competing with the world's greatest sweet wines, are well suited to being aged for long periods, sometimes for more than half a century.

ICE WINE. Some producers are trying their hand at these rare wines, produced from grapes harvested in December and January, at temperatures of between 14 and 19°F (–7 and –10°C). Ignored by French legislation, these sweet wines sell for astronomical prices.

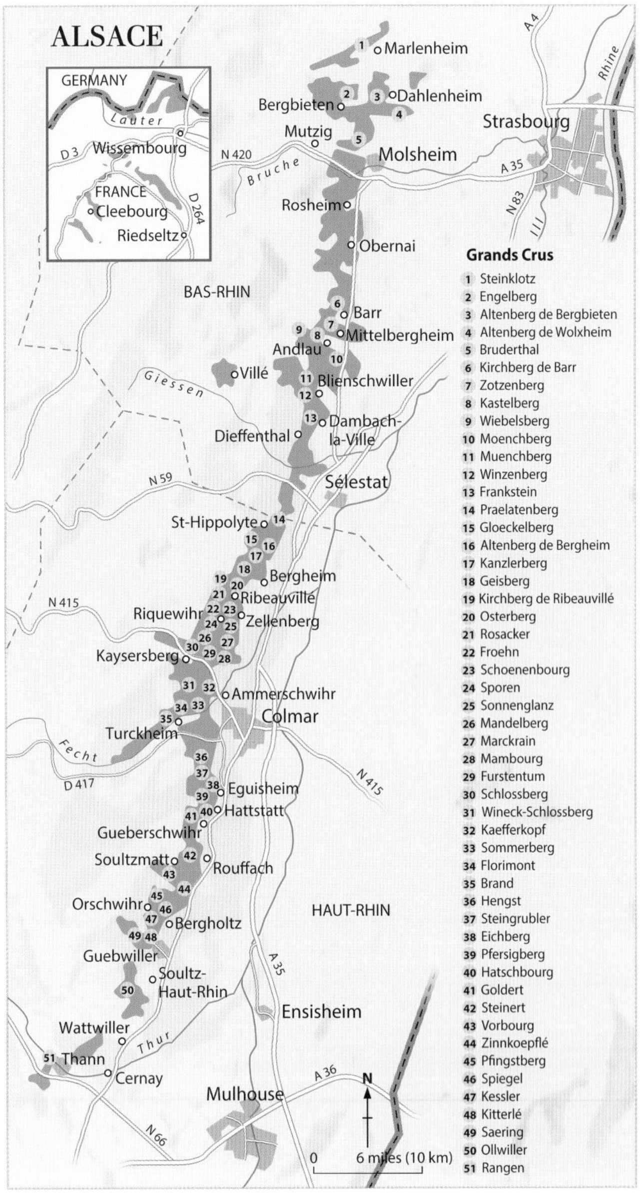

Alsace AOCs

- **Alsace**
- **Crémant d'Alsace**
- **Alsace Grand Cru, followed by the name of one of 51 lieux-dits (named vineyards):**

> *Altenberg de Bergbieten*
> *Altenberg de Bergheim*
> *Altenberg de Wolxheim*
> *Brand*
> *Bruderthal*
> *Eichberg*
> *Engelberg*
> *Florimont*
> *Frankstein*
> *Froehn*
> *Furstentum*
> *Geisberg*
> *Gloeckelberg*
> *Goldert*
> *Hatschbourg*
> *Hengst*
> *Kaefferkopf*
> *Kanzlerberg*
> *Kastelberg*
> *Kessler*
> *Kirchberg de Barr*
> *Kirchberg de Ribeauvillé*
> *Kitterlé*
> *Mambourg*
> *Mandelberg*
> *Marckrain*
> *Moenchberg*
> *Muenchberg*
> *Ollwiller*
> *Osterberg*
> *Pfersigberg*
> *Pfingstberg*
> *Praelatenberg*
> *Rangen*
> *Rosacker*
> *Saering*
> *Schlossberg*
> *Schoenenbourg*
> *Sommerberg*
> *Sonnenglanz*
> *Spiegel*
> *Sporen*
> *Steinert*
> *Steingrubler*
> *Steinklotz*
> *Vorbourg*
> *Wiebelsberg*
> *Wineck-Schlossberg*
> *Winzenberg*
> *Zinnkoepflé*
> *Zotzenberg*

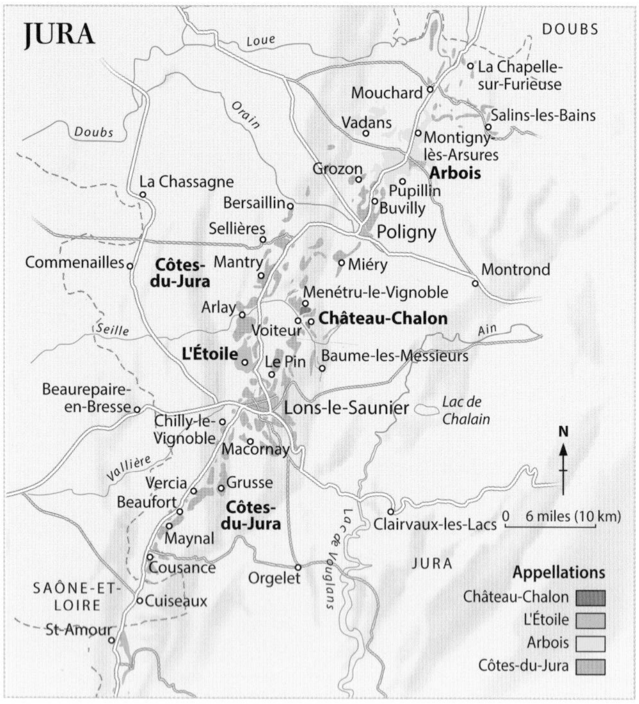

JURA

Facing Burgundy across the Saône River, the Jura wine region occupies a stretch of terrain between plains and mountains. Although particularly famous for its *vins jaunes*, this region still produces an unbeatable range of red, rosé, and white wines (both dry and sweet), and even sparkling styles.

JURA STATISTICS (AOC)

Vineyard area: 4,695 acres (1,900 ha)
Production: 888,000 cases (80,000 hl)
Whites: 41%
Reds and rosés: 25%
***Crémants*:** 25%
Others: 9%

(CIVJ, 2014)

Vineyard landscape

Established during the 1st century BC, Jura's vineyards were really developed by religious communities during the 5th and 6th centuries. At the end of the 19th century, they covered some 49,420 acres (20,000 hectares). Phylloxera ravaged the region, but wine producers decided to pursue quality, and in 1936 received the first French AOC with Arbois.

CLIMATE AND SOIL. Jura enjoys a semi-continental climate, which is favourable to the vine's development and maturation. It is characterized by severe winters, cold and wet springs, hot summers, and sunny autumns. The vines are set in generally west-facing tiers on the hillsides of the Revermont region, at altitudes of between 650 and 1300 ft (200 and 500 m). They benefit from a wide variety of *terroirs* based on various clays and marls, marly limestone soils, limestone scree, and alluvium.

Jura AOCs

- Arbois
- Arbois-Pupillin
- Côtes-du-Jura
- Château-Chalon
- Crémant du Jura
- L'Étoile
- Macvin du Jura

Grape varieties and wine styles

Jura grows five major grape varieties, each highly suited to the *terroir* and each producing original, very distinctive wines.

POULSARD (OR PLOUSSARD). Grown particularly in AOC Arbois, this variety produces a clear, ruby red wine. It's not very tannic, with aromas of small soft fruits that develop into spicy and damp woodland notes.

TROUSSEAU. This wine is characterized by an intense ruby colour and a nose of soft fruits with slightly peppery spices. They are supported by firm tannins, which ensure that the wine has great potential for ageing. Quite often, it is vinified with Pinot Noir or Poulsard.

PINOT NOIR. This grape produces characterful wines profoundly marked by their *terroir* here, with raspberry and cassis aromas enhanced by spicy notes.

SAVAGNIN. This is *the* major white grape variety in Jura, the base for the famous *vin jaune*. Its rich aromatics range from apple to toasted almond, from fresh walnuts to wheat, and from curry to coffee. It is vinified with or without topping up (*see* p.78), alone or as a blend with Chardonnay; and it produces very distinctive, structured wines, suited to a long ageing period.

CHARDONNAY. This is the most widespread grape variety (grown in nearly half of the vineyard area). In this region, it creates wines with their own distinct qualities – including floral, fresh, and well-structured aromas.

Jura specialties

Alongside *vin jaune*, Jura offers two other specialities: Macvin du Jura and *vin de paille*.

MACVIN. This is a *vin de liqueur* produced from two-thirds unfermented grape must and one-third fermented, fortified with Jura brandy. Aged in barrel for 18 months, it provides a superb balance between the sweetness of the fruit and the power of the alcohol.

VIN DE PAILLE. A sweet wine that is produced using a very distinctive production technique (*see* p.66).

VIN JAUNE. This unique wine is made with just one grape variety:

> As *vin jaune* is aged, a film of yeast forms on its surface.

Savignin. Harvested late, it is vinified as dry white wine and then stored in 60-gallon (228-litre) barrels, where its mysterious transformation begins. Aged without topping up, the wine's surface becomes covered with a film of yeast, protecting it from acetification (which would turn it to vinegar) and giving it the inimitable *jaune* taste. After six years and three months, the wine can finally be decanted into its special bottle, the famous 620 ml *clavelin*. Its capacity corresponds to the amount of wine remaining from a litre once the ageing process is complete.

SAVOIE

Savoie is better known for its snow and its glaciers than for its wines, which is a great pity. In this region of lakes and mountains, grain fields and rolling pastures, the Savoie vineyards are set in terraces on hillsides at altitudes of between 980 and 1,970 feet (300 and 600 m), between Lake Geneva and Chambéry. They produce a wide and appealing variety of wines that are mainly consumed locally.

Vineyard landscape

Savoie is blessed with a continental climate, meaning cold winters, hot summers, and sunny late autumns – all tempered by the presence of lakes. The soils are varied, with limestone scree, stony moraines, and sandstone being the most common. Vines have been grown here since the Roman era. The vineyards reached their peak in the 19th century, when they exceeded 19,770 acres (8,000 hectares). But the phylloxera crisis reduced this to less than 4,940 acres (2,000 hectares). They were slow to re-establish themselves, but began to pick up after the 1950s and have continued to increase ever since (5,436 acres/2,200 ha in 2015).

SAVOIE STATISTICS (AOC)

Vineyard area: 5,436 acres (2,200 ha)
Production: 1.35 million cases (122,000 hl)
Whites: 70%
Reds and rosés: 25%
***Crémants*:** 5%

(Syndicat des vins de Savoie, 2015)

Grape varieties and wine styles

Savoie has a wide variety of mostly native, very original, grape varieties. They are largely white and produce very stylish wines.
JACQUÈRE. The most widely planted variety, it creates fresh and light wines, still and sparkling (Crémant de Savoie). This is the principal grape variety in Abymes and Apremont *crus*.
ROUSSETTE (OR ALTESSE). This grape variety, growing in popularity, produces rich and fruity wines with some spicy notes. It forms the base for wines under the AOC Roussette de Savoie.
ROUSSANNE (OR BERGERON). Produced in very small quantities, it creates high quality wines, sometimes even exceptional wines to lay down – notably in Chignin with the AOC Chignon-Bergeron.
CHASSELAS. This variety covers 70 per cent of the vineyards, and is the sole base for Marin, Marignan, Ripaille, and Crépy *crus*.
MOLETTE. This grape produces a clear, light white wine, fairly alcoholic and very fruity, with some herbaceous notes. With high acidity, it is used in Seyssel sparkling wine.
GRINGET. Equivalent to Jura's Savagnin, this produces the famous Ayze sparkling wine.
CHARDONNAY. Introduced in the 1960s, this variety is grown across practically the entire Savoie area. Whether alone or in a blend, it produces lively and fruity wines.
GAMAY. This is the dominant red grape variety, making fresh and light wines. The best examples are to be found in the Chautagne region.
MONDEUSE. This old grape variety traditionally produces well-structured and tannic red wines, notably in Arbin, where it is the only variety used.
PERSAN. This old red grape variety had practically disappeared. Today, it is being grown again by some producers in Combe de Savoie and Maurienne. It makes tannic, rather colourful wines that are well suited to ageing.

The Savoie AOCs

- Vin de Savoie with or without *cru* name
- Crémant de Savoie
- Roussette de Savoie with or without *cru* name
- Roussette de Seyssel

A small neighbouring region

Between Jura and Savoie, Bugey covers some 1,235 acres (500 hectares) and three production areas – Cerdon, Montagnieu, Belley – on sandy-limestone and sandy-clay soils. It primarily produces still and sparkling white wines from Savoie and Burgundy grape varieties. Worthy of note are Bugey-Cerdon, sparkling wines and lightly sparkling wines, whiteor rosé, created using the local ancestral method (see p.70).

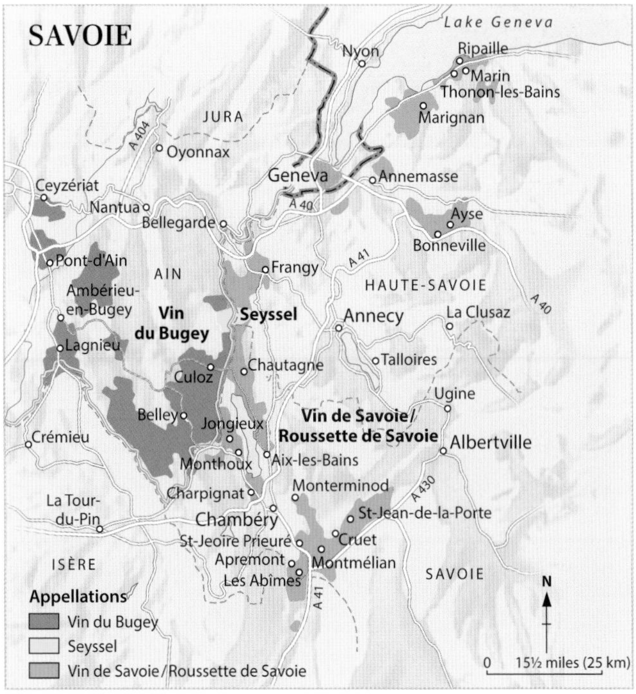

Famous wines from Alsace, Jura, and Savoie

Small vineyards, but great wines. Alsace, Jura, and Savoie can claim to produce several grand vins, *some of which are counted among the best in the world.*

ALSACE

ALSACE AOC

This is the most important of the Alsace AOCs. It covers the entire area, and primarily produces white wines (92 per cent). Where the label mentions the grape variety, this is the only variety used and the wine name follows that of the appellation – such as Alsace Muscat, Alsace Riesling, Alsace Gewurztraminer, Alsace Pinot Noir, Alsace Sylvaner. If the grape variety is not indicated, then the wine is a blend of more than one variety and is sold under the appellations Alsace Edelzwicker or Gentil.

> **GRAPE VARIETIES** Riesling, Sylvaner, Gewurztraminer, Pinot Blanc, Pinot Gris, Muscat, Pinot Noir.

> **SOIL** Schist, granitic, volcanic, marly limestone.

> **STYLE** The whites are generally dry, fruity, and aromatic, with each grape variety having its own specific characters. Gewurztraminer offers powerful, full, structured wines, with notes of rose and lychee. Riesling produces full-bodied and well-structured wines with notes of petroleum (more tactfully known as 'mineral'), and a tang of citrus fruit. Muscat yields winning wines with a nose of fresh grapes, heightened by hints of exotic fruits: you can almost feel the crunch of the fruit. Pinot Blanc produces powerful wine with an intense floral, white fruit nose. Alsace reds, made from Pinot Noir, are slightly tart with aromas of currant and cherry; with age, a crisp palate develops with flavours of ripe soft fruits, from which emerge some gamey notes. Sweet wines in the categories *vendange tardive* (VT) or *sélection des grains nobles* (SGN; *see* p.305) are high-quality wines that produce an exceptional concentration of aromas.

Colour:
White and red.

Serving temperature:
46 to 50°F (8 to 10°C) for whites; 54 to 57°F (12 to 14°C) for reds.

Ageing potential:
Within a year for Muscat; 1 to 3 years for Gewurztraminer, Riesling, Pinot Blanc; 1 to 3 years for reds; 2 to 10 years for VT and SGN whites.

ALSACE

CRÉMANT D'ALSACE AOC

The number one sparkling wine consumed in France (as an AOC), Crémant d'Alsace is very popular. Its method of production includes a second fermentation in bottle (*see* p.71).

> **GRAPE VARIETIES** White: Pinot Blanc, Pinot Gris, Riesling, Chardonnay, either blended or alone (in which case the variety name appears on the label). Rosé: Pinot Noir.

> **SOIL** Granitic, chalky, sandstone, marl.

> **STYLE** Alsace sparkling wines are light, and supple, with notable fruity (white fruit) and floral aromas.

Colour:
White and rosé.

Serving temperature:
43 to 46°F (6 to 8°C), put on ice.

Ageing potential:
Consume within a year.

ALSACE

ALSACE GRAND CRU AOC

Grape variety is less important than the *terroir* here, as this appellation is designed to show off the character of the best sites. For this reason, there are 51 such *terroirs* (*see* p.305) defined according to strict climatic and geologic criteria. They follow stringent rules regarding viticulture, choice of grape varieties, yield, alcohol content, vinification, etc. These wines represent just 4 per cent of production. As well as the vintage and the name of the *cru*, the label must specify the grape variety, unless it is a blend (permitted for the *grands cru* Altenberg de Bergheim Zotzenberg and Kaefferkopf).

> **GRAPE VARIETIES** Gewurztraminer, Riesling, Pinot Gris, Muscat. The Sylvaner variety is granted as an exception for the Alsace Grand Cru Zotzenberg.

> **SOIL** Schist, granitic, volcanic, marly limestone, sandstone.

> **STYLE** It would be impossible to describe the styles of all 51 *grand crus* here; great Alsace whites are so different from each other thanks to each *terroir*. These wines, which reflect and refine their *terroir*, are generally distinguished, powerful, and very well suited to ageing.

Colour:
White.

Serving temperature:
Around 46°F (8°C), fresh but not icy.

Ageing potential:
10 to 15 years for all grands crus.
15 to 20 years for the VT *and* SGNs, *or even more for the greatest vintages.*

JURA

CHÂTEAU-CHALON AOC

Château-Chalon is the cradle of *vin jaune* and the only appellation entirely dedicated to it. The AOC covers four villages and 120 acres (50 hectares), with a production of around 16,700 cases (1,500 hl) depending on the vintage, since wine is only produced in great years. In other years, Château-Chalon is not produced at all.

> **GRAPE VARIETY** Savagnin.

> **SOIL** Blue or gray marl.

> **STYLE** A wine with a unique character, which may sometimes be a little disconcerting, and a complex and rich nose combining the aromas of walnut, apple, curry, and mushrooms. Its palate is both rich and dry, with an extremely long finish (known as the 'peacock tail').

Colour:
White.

Serving temperature:
57 to 61°F (14 to 16°C).

Ageing potential:
50 to 100 years.

Selected Alsace producers

- **Cave des Vignerons de Pfaffenheim.** The most dynamic and award-winning cellar in Alsace, offering a wide range of excellent quality and good value.
- **Domaine Dopff & Irion (Riquewihr).** A wide range of regionally representative wines, notably the Kaefferkopf made with Gewurztraminer, the Rouge d'Ottrott, and the Crémant d'Alsace rosé.
- **Domaine Hugel (Riquewihr).** One of the most famous of the Alsace estates, founded in 1639. The *vendanges tardives* and *sélections des grains nobles* are quite simply remarkable.
- **Domaine Pierre Frick (Pfaffenheim).** This estate producing biodynamically cultivated, extremely pure wines should not be overlooked.
- **Domaine Ostertag (Epfig).** The Vins de Fruit, Vins de Pierre, and Vins de Temps are real success stories.
- **Domaine Seppi Landmann (Riquewihr).** The Gewurztraminers and Rieslings produced as *vendanges tardives* and *sélection des grains nobles* deserve special attention.
- **Maison Trimbach (Ribeauvillé).** Exceptional Gewurztraminers and Rieslings, notably the Clos Sainte-Hune.
- **Domaine Weinbach (Kaysersberg).** Impressive wines, among the greatest sweet wines in the world.
- **Domaine Zind-Humbrecht (Turckheim).** Biodynamically cultivated *grands crus* that clearly emphasize the idea of *terroir*.
- **Marcel Deiss (Bergheim).** One of the biggest estates in Alsace. Biodynamically cultivated *grands crus* that are always exceptional.

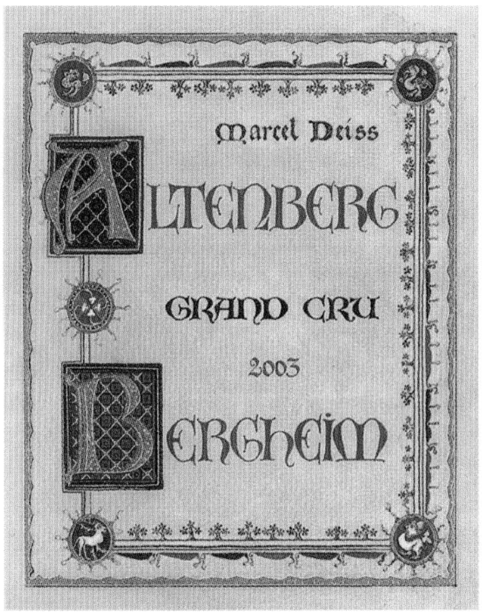

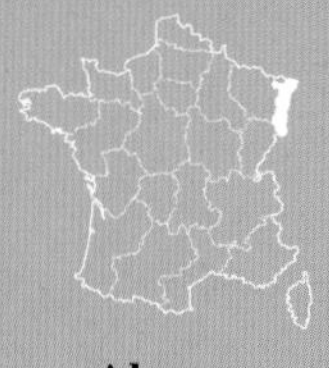

Alsace

DOMAINE *ANDRÉ OSTERTAG*

A winemaker, poet, and rebel, André Ostertag offers his unique interpretation of the Muenchberg Grand Cru, with his A360P wine.

DOMAINE ANDRÉ OSTERTAG

87, rue de Finkwiller
67680 Epfig

Founded: *1966*
Area: *36 acres (14.6 ha)*
Production: *100,000 bottles p.a.*
Appellation: *Alsace*
Red grape variety: *Pinot Noir*
White grape varieties: *Riesling, Gewurztraminer, Pinot Gris, Sylvaner, Pinot Blanc, Muscat*

Muenchberg unveiled

The Bas-Rhin is home to 14 of the 51 Alsace *grands crus*. Although this northern department is adjacent to the large vineyard that extends over most of the Haut-Rhin in the southern part of Alsace, it is just as rich as its southern neighbour in the kind of age-old, sedimentary soil that noble grape varieties love. Just off the main road, not far from Sélestat, lies the Muenchberg Grand Cru, a rich, unique terroir that André Ostertag discovered by chance when uprooting a Sylvaner vine in poor condition. While stripping the vines, André noticed a limestone seam mixed with the pink sandstone subsoil. The area had just been classified as a *grand cru*, nobody really knew what the wines were like, and few wine-growers had any faith in this poor land where yields were naturally capped by the aridity of the soil on the slopes. At the time, many swore by the land at the bottom of the hills, which was more productive and profitable. The winemaker took advantage of this unexpected seam of limestone and planted Pinot Gris.

This grape variety was like a pauper dining at the rich banquet of the noble grape varieties in Alsace, way behind the granite ascetic Riesling, and Gewurztraminer, king of sweetness. At the time Pinot Gris was, in the words of André Ostertag, 'perched on a folding seat between these two stars', hence possessing a soft, sometimes sweet, and bland style.

The first harvest, in 1987, was therefore a leap in the dark. But in 1989 the estate produced an amount of *grains nobles* (nobly rotted grapes) for this Muenchberg Pinot Gris, with a carefully selected *tri* potentially resulting in 28.5 degrees of alcohol. It was obvious that the vines were ripening early and botrytizing from September. At this point the young Pinot Gris became a serious contender.

André Ostertag, a free thinker

Both the wine and its maker have character – André Ostertag matures his wines in oak barrels, unlike other producers, who prefer stainless steel or concrete vats. This preference for barrels came from his old Burgundy friend and specialist in Meursault whites, Dominique Lafon, who sparked his enthusiasm for wines vinified in oak – which makes them refined and complex. But in Alsace the barrel has a bad reputation. André Ostertag defends it for its aromatic contributions (toasted and hazelnut notes) and because it allows oxygen into the wine. Yet his colleagues in Alsace paid no attention and did not rate Muenchberg Pinot Gris, considering it unworthy of *grand cru* status in formal tasting sessions. In 1991 they deemed it 'too woody' and in 2000 'not quite true to type'. The wine was criticized five years in succession. 'A psychoanalyst might call it a phobia,' observed André, 20 years later. 'Alsace has experienced invasion and knows how to preserve its soul, but in this case it did so by curling up on itself and rejecting the barrel as a threat to its identity.'

André Ostertag, cultivating his garden of vines

These formal tasting sessions, which should have been no more than an administrative formality, had nevertheless become a serious commercial obstacle. Yet André put up resistance, naming the forbidden wine after his cadastral plot, A360P, so that it would sell better, describing it poetically as 'a code of survival to resist intolerance'. He went on to add a silhouette of a vine in the form of a crucifix to the label of the 2013 vintage, with the handwritten note: 'Alone but free like an old oak in pink sandstone.' Nowadays, André Ostertag has become synonymous with excellence and his wine no longer suffers such vehement criticism. A sensible man, he now occupies himself with writing, watching the blackbirds nesting in the cosiest parts of his estate, and, echoing Candide, cultivating his own garden. He calls his plots 'vine gardens', small areas all meticulously engaged in organic production on a human scale, where you can see what needs to be done when you start work in the morning. He still has his black notebook, in which he wrote: 'Only the vine goes up to heaven, and poetry allows it to stay living there.'

DOMAINE ANDRÉ OSTERTAG, ALSACE GRAND CRU MUENCHBERG 'A360P' PINOT GRIS

The Ostertag estate owns 5 of the 42 acres (2 ha of the 17 ha) that produce Grand Cru Muenchberg. It is a splendid hillside amphitheatre facing south, in the pink sandstone of the Vosges, with a famous limestone point to the east. The estate produces 4 acres (1.6 ha) of Riesling and just under an acre (36 ares) of Pinot Gris. These grape varieties are the source of this impressively full and balanced wine, with complex floral and white fruit aromas, honeyed with shades of fresh mushroom. A wine with great volume, fullness and depth, and a firm mineral base.

> André Ostertag, head of the estate.

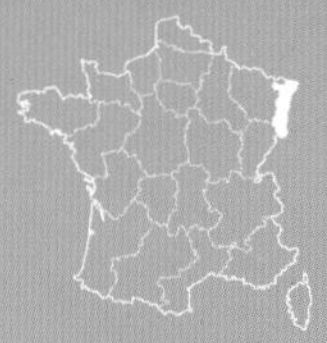

Alsace

TRIMBACH

Pierre Trimbach represents the 12th generation of this old trading house, historically located in Ribeauvillé, at the heart of Alsace's vineyards.And now the 13th generation is asserting itself.

TRIMBACH

15, route de Bergheim
68150 Ribeauvillé

Founded: *1926*
Area: *124 acres (50 ha)*
Production: *one million bottles p.a.*
Appellation: *Alsace*
Red grape variety: *Pinot Noir*
White grape varieties: *Riesling, Pinot Gris, Gewurztraminer, Pinot Blanc, Sylvaner, Muscat*

Pierre Trimbach, proud to be 12th in line

Ribeauvillé and Riquewihr are the focal point of the Alsace wine region: between them, these two wealthy towns have 13 of the region's 51 *grands crus*, which are sheltered from rains from the west by the natural barrier formed by the Vosges, reaching their highest point here and protecting one of the most privileged areas of Alsace. Both towns also possess the most prestigious names in the business, Hugel for one, and Trimbach for another. In fact, the two families have at times become intertwined. The present-day Hugel house once belonged to a now-extinct branch of the Trimbach family, which suffered as a result of the parsimony of its last member, who allowed the place to fall into decline, and fell to his death down a spiral staircase that he was too mean to illuminate with candles. The remaining Trimbachs settled in Ribeauvillé in 1919. Their current location is dominated by an impressive bell tower with a slated, half-timbered turret, perhaps a mark of vanity, or maybe a watchtower to oversee the workers in the vineyards?

Pierre Trimbach enjoys telling the story of the 11 generations preceeding him, who long had had a foothold in vineyards, given that in Alsace, just as in Burgundy, the wine trade has also been a great landowner. However, unlike in Beaune, the classic trade in Alsace was strictly concerned with the purchase of grapes, since the purchase of must or wine in bottles was forbidden, apart from must to make *crémant*. The boundaries were well defined: grapes bought from other growers produced entry-level wines, while fine estate wines could be produced by winemakers who used their own grapes.

Riesling, the Trimbach standard-bearer

The estate now cultivates the Schlossberg vines on granite, the Rosacker Grand Cru on limestone, and, behind the house, the famous Frédéric Émile vines on marl-limestone-sandstone. The entire Trimbach operation is reliant on Riesling, which is planted on more than half of its estate and is an integral part of its brand, as it is in Clos Sainte-Hune, the jewel in its crown, and a widely respected dry wine. When he joined the business in 1979, Pierre Trimbach succeeded his father, Bernard, and his uncle Hubert, who nevertheless still keep an eye on the business.

It was the 11th generation of the family who managed to maintain the independence of the estate in the 1950s, at a time when so many other businesses were being bought by local cooperative wineries. At the time, the vineyards owned by the estate amounted to 30 acres (12 ha) of superb terroirs. Today, it has 111 acres (45 ha), all of which are organically farmed (though this is not indicated on the label, to allow for flexibility in case conventional products are used).

TRIMBACH, ALSACE RIESLING CLOS SAINTE-HUNE

The Trimbach house has owned the 4.1 acres (1.7 ha) of *clos* in Hunawihr that produces the Rosacker Grand Cru for more than 200 years. The vineyard, now about 50 years old, benefits from a south to southeast exposure, on a predominantly limestone subsoil. This terroir brings a distinctive minerality to the Riesling, which achieves a singular intensity in this wine. The aromas are lively and tight, between floral notes, citrus fruits, and the minerality that stretches and develops throughout the tasting. Tight, crystalline, and supported by a magnificent crispness, the palate acquires volume and fullness over time. Although it is never sold before being aged for five years, it needs even more time to reach its best.

Is Pinot Noir the future?

And now the 13th generation has arrived, in the form of Anne, Pierre's daughter and export manager, and Julien, her cousin, who has a BTS diploma in viticulture and oenology. The youngest generation will have to deal with the challenge of global warming, which is already revising the layout of vines on those hills facing south: will Pinot Noir be the future in Alsace? This is what Pierre Trimbach believes anyway; he planted Pinot Noir in Bergheim, on terraces facing west towards Burgundy – the vines were planted close together, which naturally limits their vigour. So the future is red, and involves exports, the only way forward for independent dealers like Trimbach, who are increasingly threatened by mass wine producers who are prepared to buy up the old houses solely to keep their brand names alive.

> A Trimbach family photo: Hubert Trimbach, his nephews Jean and Pierre, and Pierre's daughter Anne.

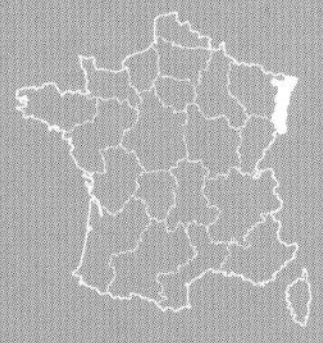

Alsace

RANGEN DE THANN BY *ZIND HUMBRECHT*

Rough, steep, and stony, Rangen de Thann is the southernmost and steepest slope in Alsace. It has given its name to a great wine, of which Léonard Humbrecht is one of the most renowned producers.

DOMAINE ZIND HUMBRECHT

4, route de Colmar
68230 Turckheim

Founded: *1959*
Area: *99 acres (40 ha)*
Production: *N/A*
Appellation: *Alsace*
Red grape variety: *Pinot Noir*
White grape varieties: *Riesling, Gewurztraminer, Pinot Gris, Muscat Blanc à Petits Grains, Muscat Ottonel, Chardonnay, Auxerrois*

Rangen de Thann, from Humbrecht's vertical vines

Of the 51 *grands crus* of Alsace, Rangen is one of the most famous – and one of the most brilliant, too. 'The already vertical slope is still rising,' is how the mountaineer Georges Livanos describes the reddish-brown greywacke rock that falls away sharply down the mountainous slopes for climbers and, sadly also, for wine producers. The Rangen is the southernmost vineyard in Alsace. It is situated where the Thur River valley opens out, overlooking the city of Thann. In the Middle Ages, Rangen was renowned throughout Europe, but the land was very difficult to cultivate, and, producing low yields, sank into a post-phylloxera stupor at the beginning of the 20th century.

Léonard Humbrecht was the only producer to be interested in it in the 1960s, when the slopes lay uncultivated, and to wonder why, after receiving so much praise in medieval chronicles, the vines had become so neglected. Léonard relied solely on old archives to support his belief, and the scant testimony of the only local wine-grower who continued to produce wine there. In Thann, the high wages offered by the chemical plant in the town had stripped the vineyards of their workforce. The greywacke slopes, with their sharp rocks, had once again been overgrown with bushes.

Against the tide

Despite these difficulties, the estate's future saviour, Léonard, cheerfully walked the vineyard with his wife Geneviève pushing son Olivier in his pram, and dreamt how famous the wines of the Rangen would one day become. At the time, Alsace was planted with Gewurztraminer and Sylvaner, and sold great quantities of wine, mass-produced by the litre, from the region's silty plains. To counteract this trend, from 1976 onwards Léonard bought up the finest south-facing plots, some with a 90-degree slope, of the Clos Saint-Urbain in Rangen. This would become the family estate, named after the small chapel at its centre. To reassure himself, Léonard repeated the saying of the great Jean Hugel, the famous merchant of Riquewihr: 'The truth is in the glass.' And in fact, the wine did start to speak, in the Riesling accent of the vines that the Humbrechts planted there. The wine they produced reached the same stratospheric heights as the vines, displaying the fiery soul of the volcanic soil, whose exposure to the sun is tempered by the wind from the valley, which keeps the acidity high. The wine typifies the minerality of Alsace, its concentration on the palate masking its very definite sweetness.

'One hundred small things make something big'

Rangen has since been planted by several other wine producers, but the lion's share belongs to the Humbrecht family, who have restored the legendary reputation it enjoyed in the Middle Ages. Even today, Olivier and Léonard Humbrecht are constantly improving their vines – they now plant them on the slopes rather than on terraces, and use a winch to stop the pickers falling backward. In any case, no horse could possibly climb the slope. 'I choose my grape pickers carefully, and they need to be in good shape,' Léonard jokes. Every basket is balanced and there is meticulous attention to detail.

The estate rarely makes mistakes. The sharp blue eyes of Léonard, a youthful 79, leave nothing to chance. His motto is 'One hundred small things make something big.' So the estate is operated on an organic basis, sources its horse manure compost from far and wide, and has changed its winery four times to finally arrive at the best and least interventionist winemaking process possible. From the 5 acres (2 ha) of Humbrecht and the 10 acres (4 ha) of Zind, the Zind-Humbrecht estate has grown to almost 100 acres (40 ha). Léonard's father was a wine-broker, who sold to the trade, and disregarded a wine's origins, indifferent to whether it came from the mountains, the valleys, or the plain. 'He told me that I was not a good winemaker, because for him, it was necessary to produce grapes to be good. My good fortune was to be supported by my in-laws, who told me, when I hesitated to buy hillsides: "buying land will never lose you money",' Léonard recalls. Today, in Thann, the factories have closed, but the vines above the town are flourishing: the volcanic soil has had its revenge.

DOMAINE ZIND HUMBRECHT, ALSACE GRAND CRU, RIESLING RANGEN DE THANN CLOS SAINT-URBAIN

The estate has 99 acres (40 ha) in total, including around 14 acres (5.5 ha) for Rangen de Thann, in the Clos Saint-Urbain. It cultivates Riesling, Pinot Gris, and some 1.25 acres (51 ares) of Gewurztraminer (at the foot of the slope, near the river) around the chapel of the same name at the side of the Montaigne road. The Rangen Grand Cru covers 46.5 acres (18.82 ha). It is the only *grand cru* produced from volcanic rock in Alsace, and Olivier and Léonard Humbrecht have used this very special subsoil to produce a wine often marked by flinty, smoky, even peaty notes, with an almost iodized sharpness drawn from the mineral content of the soil. Riesling normally produces a good, timely crop, resulting mainly in dry mineral wines. The Pinot Gris, which is harvested earlier, almost always develops *botrytis*. The Gewurztraminer, later for the Rangen than the other grape varieties, frequently develops *botrytis*, too. All the Rangen wines are concentrated, long, age well, and are distinguished by a typically rather crisp, tannic finish.

Selected Jura producers

- **Château d'Arlay (Arlay).** One of Jura's most famous producers. The white wines and *vins jaunes* are quite simply magnificent.
- **Domaine André et Mireille Tissot (Montigny-lès-Arsures).** For the organic wines, and notably for the Cuvée La Mailloche (Arbois Blanc) and the Spirale, a remarkable *vin de paille*.
- **Domaine Berthet-Bondet (Château-Chalon).** Remarkable *vins jaunes* and Côtes-du-Jura whites.
- **Jacques Tissot (Arbois).** Superb Jura *crémants* and *vins jaunes*.
- **Domaine Henri Maire (Arbois).** Symbolic of Jura, Henri Maire has restored his reputation in the region. A beautiful and wide range of wines, and good value.
- **Domaine Pierre Overnoy-Emmanuel Houillon (Pupillin).** Excellent, very pure wines: intense whites, sulphur-free reds, biodynamically cultivated.
- **Frutières Vinicoles (Arbois, Voiteur, Pupillin, Caveau des Byards).** Offering a wide range of wines and excellent value.
- **Michel Gahier (Montigny-lès-Arsures).** Notable for natural wines and the purity of its cuvées.

JURA

ARBOIS AOC

The most important of the Jura AOCs (40 per cent of total production), it covers 13 villages around the town of Arbois; but only the village of Pupillin may couple its name with that of the appellation. A favorite *terroir* for Trousseau and Poulsard, the AOC is most famous for its red wines; but it also produces white wines, *vins jaunes*, *vins de paille*, and *crémants*.

> **GRAPE VARIETIES** White: Chardonnay and Savagnin; red and rosé: Poulsard, Trousseau, Pinot Noir.

> **SOIL** Clay and limestone scree.

> **STYLE** The reds are generous and tannic, with a rich bouquet of soft fruit aromas supported by gamey notes. Great length on the palate. The Chardonnay whites are elegant – their fruity and floral aromas seasoned with spicy, walnut, and honey notes. The Savagnin examples are more opulent with notes of walnut and spices, and a beautiful length on the palate.

Colour: *White and red.*

Serving temperature: *46 to 50°F (8 to 10°C) for whites and rosés; 57 to 61°F (14 to 16°C) for reds; 57 to 61°F (14 to 16°C) for* vin jaune*; 45 to 50°F (7 to 10°C) for* vin de paille*; 43 to 46°F (6 to 8°C) for sparkling wines.*

Ageing potential: *Within a year for* crémants*; 1 to 3 years for whites; 3 to 5 years for reds; more than 10 years for* vin de paille*; 50 to 100 years for* vin jaune.

JURA

CÔTES-DU-JURA AOC

The largest AOC in Jura, this appellation stretches from Salins in the north to St-Amour in the south, across a wide variety of terroirs. It covers 105 villages, the most famous being Voiteur, Poligny, Gevingey, and Arbois. Whites are clearly dominant here, whether dry or sweet, still or sparkling. There is also a wide range of Jura red wines, rosés, *vins jaunes*, and *vins de paille*.

> **GRAPE VARIETIES** White: Chardonnay and Savagnin; red: Poulsard, Trousseau, and Pinot Noir.

> **SOIL** Clay and limestone scree.

> **STYLE** The whites offer a wide variety of styles depending on the terroir, the vinification method, and the blends. Two categories emerge: fresh floral whites, made from Chardonnay; and distinctive whites made from Savagnin. The reds are tannic, rounded, and rich, with soft fruit aromas. *Vins de paille* produce a perfume of exotic and dried fruits.

Colour: *White and red.*

Serving temperature: *46 to 50°F (8 to 10°C) for whites and rosés; 57 to 61°F (14 to 16°C) for reds; 57 to 61°F (14 to 16°C) for* vin jaune*; 45 to 50°F (7 to 10°C) for* vin de paille*; 43 to 46°F (6 to 8°C) for sparkling wines.*

Ageing potential: *Within a year for* crémants*; 1 to 3 years for whites; 3 to 5 years for reds; more than 10 years for* vin de paille*; 50 to 100 years for* vin jaune.

SAVOIE

VIN DE SAVOIE AOC

This is the main Savoie appellation. The name may be used alone or coupled with the names of 16 *villages*, or zones,known as *crus*: Abymes, Apremont, Arbin, Ayze, Chautagne, Chignin, Chignin-Bergeron, Crépy, Cruet, Jongieux, Marignan, Marin, Montmélian, Ripaille, St-Jean-de-la-Porte, St-Jeoire-Prieuré. The wines of this appellation, which covers four *départements*, may be made from more than one grape variety. The AOC Vin de Savoie primarily produces dry whites (70 per cent of production), the rest being shared among reds, rosés, and sparkling wines. With demand being greater than supply, these mountain wines are often consumed locally, and while still young. However, some deserve to be laid down for a few years.

> **GRAPE VARIETIES** White: Jacquère, Altesse or Roussette, Chasselas, Molette, Gringet, Roussanne. Red: Mondeuse, Pinot Noir, Gamay Noir.

> **SOIL** Limestone scree and glacial moraines.

> **STYLE** Generally, the red wines made from Mondeuse have a beautiful purple appearance, with wild aromas of mountain fruits and violet, and highly pronounced spicy notes. Their astringent and persistent tannins become pleasantly rounded with age. The whites are light, very dry, and fruity, especially those made with Jacquère. Roussanne whites, with their floral and exotic fruit scents, are more well-structured and can be aged for longer. Those from Roussette have great finesse.

Colour:
Red, white, and rosé.

Serving temperature:
46 to 50°F (8 to 10°C) for whites and rosés; 54 to 55°F (12 to 13°C) for reds, or 59 to 63°F (15 to 17°C) for Mondeuse reds; 43 to 46°F (6 to 8°C) for sparkling wines.

Ageing potential:
Within a year for sparkling wines; within 2 years for whites and rosés; 2 to 6 years for reds.

SAVOIE

ROUSSETTE DE SAVOIE AOC

The vines of this appellation are grown along the Rhône between Frangy and Jongieux. The four communes Frangy, Marestel, Monterminod, and Monthoux can be attached to Roussette de Savoie. The appellation produces only still white wines using just one grape variety – Roussette.

> **GRAPE VARIETIES** Roussette (also known as Altesse), Chardonnay.

> **SOIL** Limestone scree and glacial moraines.

> **STYLE** These wines have great finesse, and are extremely fresh and lively. Flavours include dried fruit and walnut, and they linger on the palate for some time.

Colour:
White.

Serving temperature:
43 to 46°F (6 to 8°C).

Ageing potential:
Within a year, but can be kept for a few years.

Selected Savoie and Bugey producers

- **Château de Ripaille (Ripaille).** Lively Chasselas wines with fruity and mineral notes, pleasantly long.
- **Château de la Violette (Les Marches).** Very elegant Jacquère whites.
- **Domaine Raphaël Bartucci (Mérignat).** A worthy representative of Bugey wines, the Cerdon rosé produced through organic agriculture contains beautiful small bubbles, merry and lively.
- **Domaine Belluard (Ayze).** Delicate and enchanting sparkling wines, and still Gringet wines, too.
- **Domaine Dupasquier et Fils (Jongieux).** Very well-balanced Roussettes.
- **Domaine Louis Magnin (Arbin).** Wonderful Mondeuses and superb Bergerons, well suited to ageing.
- **Domaine André et Michel Quénard (Chignin).** Remarkable Gamay and Mondeuse reds, and whites from Abymes and Chignin-Bergeron.
- **Domaine de l'Idylle (Cruet).** A very attractive range of specific wines that are vibrant and mineral.

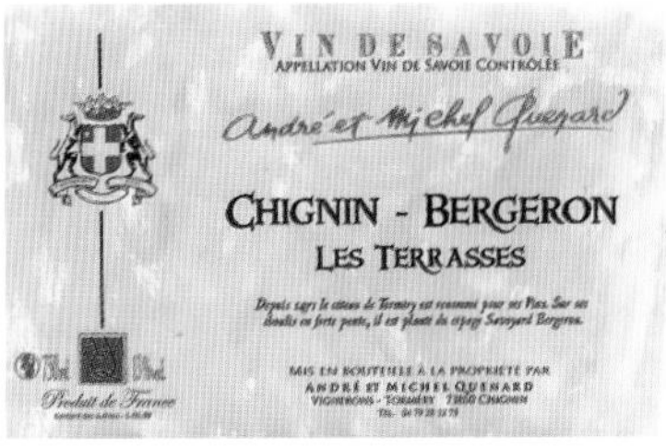

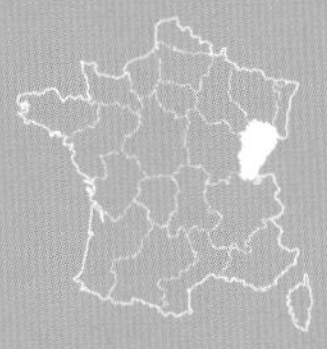

THE KNIGHT IN THE TOUR DE CURON *STÉPHANE TISSOT*

In Arbois, Stéphane Tissot, the renowned wine-maker from Jura, has brought new life to the ancient vines of the Tour de Curon and carefully restored this symbol of the Jura vineyards.

DOMAINE ANDRÉ
AND MIREILLE TISSOT

39600 Montigny-les-Arsures

Area: *124 acres (50 ha)*
Production: *150,000 bottles p.a.*
Appellation: *Arbois*
Red grape varieties: *Pinot Noir, Trousseau, Poulsard*
White grape varieties: *Chardonnay, Savagnin*

The story of the acquisition

The Jura vineyards extend over some 50 miles (80 km), from Salins-les-Bains in the north to Saint-Amour in the south, including Arbois and Poligny, Château-Chalon, and L'Étoile. Established by a decree passed on May 15, 1936, Arbois is the oldest AOC in France. It includes 12 districts and covers 2,360 acres (955 ha), of which approximately 2,100 acres (850 ha) are actually planted with vines. This vast patchwork was long represented by the figure of Henri Maire, who personally owned up to 741 acres (300 ha) of vineyards. The Maire estate then went into decline, until its recent acquisition by Boisset of Burgandy. Vineyards were sold and the library auctioned off. Of this entire historic Arbois estate there remained only La Finette, Henri Maire's tavern, and the Tour Canoz, known as Tour de Curon, which Stéphane Tissot set out to restore. There was nevertheless a cultural and generational gap between the young wine producer, the last in a long line of wine-makers, and the old Parisian merchant and landowner. But, in 2001, Tissot bought Curon's vineyards ('Le Clos') from Maire, who told him, 'I wept, but I am glad you are the one to have them.' Bénédicte and Stéphane Tissot were passionate about this place, which they had known since they were children. As a boy Stéphane used to run beside the drystone walls, heading up the salt road, the dingy path that runs alongside the tower and connects Salins with the precious vineyard. There is even a sentry box built in a recess of the wall.

Twenty years later, the dilapidated tower had become the home of squatters, in the midst of land that by then lay uncultivated. While Henri Maire had had a passion for acquiring land on hilly terrain, which he bought in terraces and as a single unit, the merchant preferred to cultivate more profitable plots, namely those on level ground.

Le Clos restored

In 1992, Stéphane Tissot, who had in turn become a wine-maker, settled on the family estate, which consisted of around 50 acres (20 ha). He once again walked through Le Clos, but this time to compare the maturity of the grapes there with his own. And then came the surprise: Curon's Chardonnay grapes were golden, juicy, and ripe to perfection. He was envious, but held out no hope of acquiring the place. This was the very heart of Henri Maire's estate; there was no chance he could purchase it. However fortune no longer favoured the old merchant, and Stéphane learnt by chance that the Le Clos vines were for sale. His luck was in! He called the manager of the Henri Maire estate and purchased around 5 acres (2 ha) of uncultivated land. He gradually expanded it by buying the hillside in small successive plots. Some had not been cultivated for ten years, others for 50 years. He finally bought the tower itself from the family of Doctor Millet at the end of 2001, thus once more reuniting this ancient estate. In July 2002 he planted Chardonnay, a historic Le Clos grape variety. Today Stéphane Tissot cultivates just over 22 acres (9 ha) in a single plot around the tower, which he has carefully restored.

DOMAINE ANDRÉ AND MIREILLE TISSOT, ARBOIS LE CLOS DE LA TOUR DE CURON

Stéphane Tissot cultivates his 124 acres (50 ha) biodynamically and without a farm manager, he prefers to 'maintain a hands-on approach in the vineyard.' Just under 2 acres (81 ares) of Le Clos de la Tour de Curon, planted at 4,856 feet per acre (12,000 feet per hectare) on a soil of limestone scree, are sold separately. The remainder, covering just over 20 acres (8 ha), is incorporated into Trousseau Singulier wines, as well as the Arbois Les Graviers Chardonnay, and the Sous Curon Pinot Noir. The *en foule* plot, with its closely packed vines, which began production in 2015, produces a unique barrel of wine sold under the name 'Terrasses de Curon.' Among Chardonnays, produced on this mainly limestone soil, Le Clos de la Tour stands out: a clean wine with a striking nose full of floral, citrus, and dried-fruit notes, and a palate lengthened by a magnificent crispness that gives a singular brilliance to this intense and bright wine.

Almost 11,000 vines per acre (27,000 per hectare)

The tower itself rests directly on the purest Bajocian limestone base, and this makes Le Clos de la Tour de Curon: the most Burgundian of the Arbois terroirs. The squatters were evicted and Stéphane repainted it to exactly match the decor of the 1920s, placing the initials B & ST (Bénédicte and Stéphane) on the lintel over the fireplace. The couple spent ten years recreating this splendid heritage, on a hill in the south that dominates the town of Arbois and its golden stone steeples. 'It's my fourth child,' says Stéphane, speaking of this magical place, where he planted a small plot aiming to achieve something that Henri Maire never managed: Savagnin planted *en foule*, the old fashioned-way, with a little under 11,000 vines per acre (27,000 per hectare). You can only enter sideways, with your arms in the air, so as not to damage the clusters! Le Clos is the pride and joy of the Tissot family, who have produced a particular wine from it – and from the very beginning, Bénédicte and Stéphane isolated the characteristics of specific localities (*lieux-dits*). It was also the prototype of what would one day become Arbois, with several future *premiers crus*. Stéphane Tissot, with his 124 acres (50 ha) of vines, his upcoming projects, and his bold approach to vinification, may indeed be the spiritual heir to Henri Maire.

> Bénédicte and Stéphane Tissot, who own the estate.

THE LOIRE VALLEY

The Loire Valley is one of the most versatile wine regions in France. It produces a range of wines with flavours and textures so different that it is difficult to find common characteristics.

Long journey

The vineyards of the Loire have been established in the furrow ploughed by the longest river in France. The Loire rises from the south of the Massif Central, at more than 4,265 ft (1,300 m) in altitude, where vines are rare. Halfway along its passage to the sea, where it begins turning to the west, it reaches the region of Sancerre and Pouilly, where its altitude is no more than 656 ft (200 m). It then runs alongside the forest of Orléans before continuing its course westward through the vast expanses of Touraine, Anjou, and Saumur, at an altitude of only 164 ft (50 m). Finally, it reaches Nantes, which is next to the ocean.

The 629-mile (1,013-km) journey passes through a wide variety of geologic terrains that, together with fluctuations in climate and grape varieties, greatly influence the character of the wines.

LOIRE VALLEY STATISTICS (AOC)

Vineyard area: 113,668 acres (46,000 ha)

Production: 26.6 million cases (2,400,000 hl)

Whites: 47%

Reds: 20%

Rosés: 24%

Sparkling: 9%

(Interloire and B.I.V.C)

From the 10th century, winemaking monks in abbeys and monasteries contributed to the further development of vineyards. In the 12th century, Henry Plantagenet, Count of Anjou, became King of England and served the wines of Anjou to his court.

Later, during the 15th and 16th centuries, the castles of the Loire and their royal owners encouraged the work of wine producers, who sought to improve their wines by carefully selecting grape varieties and improving their cultivation.

Until the middle of the 19th century, Loire wines really flourished, thanks in particular to trade with the Netherlands via the port of Nantes. But the phylloxera epidemic devastated its vineyards, just as it did everywhere else. A fresh start was made in the 20th century, and quality became the watchword. Sancerre, Vouvray, and Quincy were among the first AOC wines here.

Historic inheritance

Regional vineyards date back to Roman times. During the 4th century, St. Martin, the bishop of Tours, encouraged the development of viticulture by reserving the use of wine for the demands of religious worship and the needs of the sick.

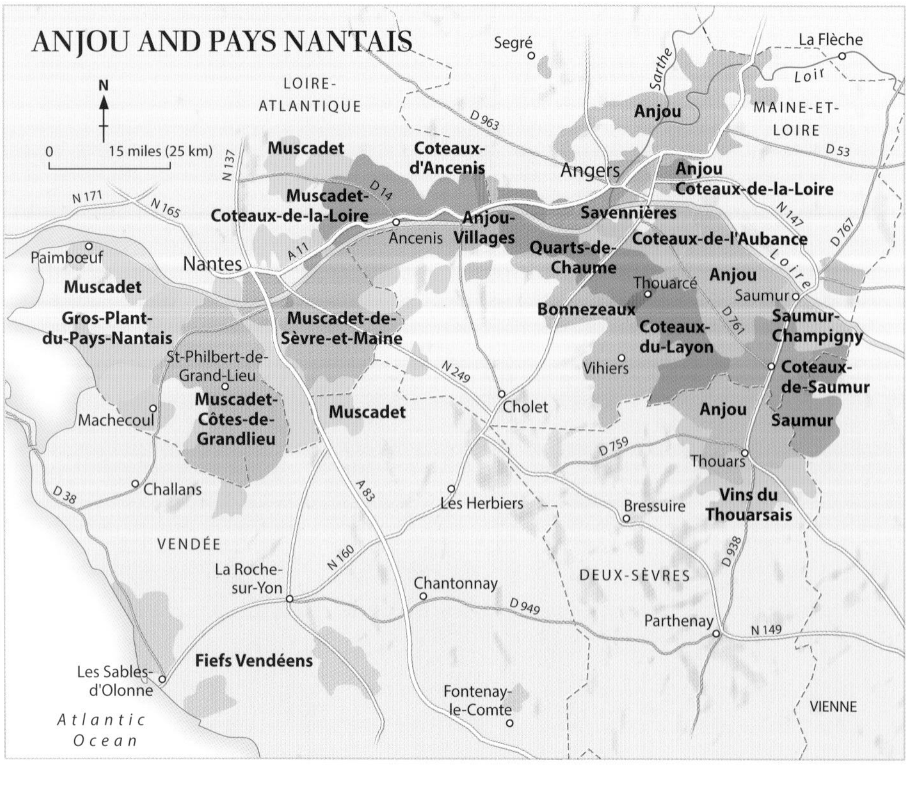

Quality revolution

The Loire Valley now has some 70 wine appellations. They collectively represent the largest producer of white AOC wines in France, and the leading region in the production of sparkling wines (excluding Champagne). For several recent years, there has been a real reawakening about local *terroir*. Lower yields and careful wine growing, winemaking, and ageing are all paying dividends, as demonstrated in the progress made in the average quality of the wines. It has already led to new appellations being created, the latest being those of Orléans and Orléans-Cléry in 2005. This revolution in quality would never have happened without the efforts of many new, young, talented wine producers, who come from diverse backgrounds, often better trained than the previous generation and many of whom have acquired experience abroad.

Sub-regions

The Loire Valley is divided into several sub-regions, each with its own identity and style of wines. The vineyards actually alongside the Loire River, as well as its tributaries – the Cher, Indre,

Allier, and Vienne – are among the most important.

THE CENTRE. This sub-region begins north of the Auvergne Mountains, stretches around the city of Bourges, and then continues to the outskirts of Gien. The white wines of Sauvignon Blanc dominate here, and the leading appellations are Sancerre and Pouilly-Fumé.

TOURAINE. This district starts west of Orléans and reaches Chinon at the outskirts of Saumur. It features a number of important appellations. Along with the different wines of the Touraine AOC, the region is home to two appellations, Chinon and Bourgueil, known for their red wines made with Cabernet Franc. Relatively supple and fruity, they can still excel in the best wines and in the skilful hands of the best producers. Their white counterparts are Vouvray and Montlouis, which lie on opposite sides of the Loire to the east of Tours. The Chenin Blanc grape makes excellent dry or sweet wines, both still and sparkling. It is also from within this sub-region that many of the sparkling wines produced in the Loire Valley originate, including Crémant de Loire and the sparkling and lightly sparkling Vouvray and Montlouis-sur-Loire wines.

ANJOU AND SAUMUR. This vast region extends some 20 miles east of Nantes and along the Loire to Saumur and Angers. The notable appellations here are for white wines made from Chenin Blanc, dry ones such as Savennières, and sweet, rich wines like Coteaux du Layon and Coteaux de l'Aubance. In the area around Saumur, there also are several red and sparkling wines.

PAYS NANTAIS AND VENDÉE. Located close to Nantes and partly in Vendée, these vineyards near the ocean produce mostly white wines, quite refreshing and full of flavours perfect to accompany seafood. The grape variety Melon de Bourgogne finds its finest expression in the Muscadet appellation, producing fresh, light wines, some slightly sparkling when made on their lees, which have a lightness and obvious freshness. Some Muscadets age magnificently. The white wines from the hills of Ancenis are made from the Pinot Gris and Chenin Blanc grapes, whereas Folle Blanche, also grown in southwest France, displays freshness and panache in the Gros Plant du Pays Nantais, a slightly sharp wine that goes well with the local cuisine. Somewhat isolated southwest of the Loire, the appellation Fiefs Vendéens, with its Mareuil, Vix, Brem, and Pissotte *crus*, produces red wines and a few whites that are sometimes very interesting.

DID YOU KNOW...?

Traditionally, the wines of the Auvergne are connected to the wines of the Loire Valley. *The appellations are Côtes d'Auvergne (AOC), Côtes-du-Forez, Côte Roannaise, and Saint-Pourçain (AOC).*

Climate change in the Loire Valley

The year 2003 made its mark in the world of wine because scorching sunshine and high temperatures made life difficult for both grapes and producers. Since then, winemakers have wondered about changes in their *climats*, with a certainty that they will suffer global warming and its consequences in the future. Since 2007, the Loire valley has been one of the test sites involved in a huge programme launched by the CNRS (French National Centre for Scientific Research) to anticipate the effects of global warming. The aim is to simulate the future climate in order to propose changes in cultivation methods to winegrowers or new choices in plant material, including root stocks, clones, and the introduction of new grape varieties capable of adapting to such changes. Surveys have shown that in some vintages, such as that of 2003, Grenache Noir, a decidedly southern grape variety, would have been able to mature in Saumur! In the future, without actually completely changing the identity of appellations, the rules regarding permitted grape varieties can certainly no longer be the same.

> A number of microclimates, soils, and grape varieties are responsible for the variety of wines from the Loire.

Loire Valley soils

The geographic extent of the Loire Valley gives it a wide variety of soils and subsoils. Here is a selection of the most significant.

At the source of the river lie the ancient granite hills of the Massif Central, where several vineyards still remain. They produce some interesting versions of Gamay from their soils.

As it heads north, in the Centre-Loire, the soils are mainly limestone and clay. Sauvignon Blanc (Sancerre, Pouilly-Fumé…) is the predominant grape variety, producing fairly nuanced wines depending on the exposure and type of soil: *caillottes* (chalky stone), *terres blanches* (Kimmeridgian marl), or siliceous clays.

The third region includes the centre of the Loire Valley as well as the small valleys of its tributaries. The terrain here (Touraine and Saumurois) consists of tuffeau, a cream-coloured limestone rock, and the schist that characterizes the soils of Anjou. The area is home to numerous wine cellars. Chenin Blanc and Cabernet are readily cultivated here. The rivers have carved out their beds and formed hillsides with excellent drainage, ideal for the vines that are planted on either bank.

The Pays Nantais sits on the Armorican Massif, with sedimentary, metamorphic, and igneous soils.

Grape varieties

The variety of grapes cultivated in the Loire Valley enables producers to diversify the style of their wines. It is not uncommon for a winery to offer red wine and white wine, still and sparkling. Some grape varieties here produce wines of exquisite quality, such as Chenin Blanc in Vouvray. Also, Sauvignon Blanc in Sancerre displays the outstanding purity of its fruit.

DOMINANT VARIETIES. In the vineyards of the Centre, you will find Sauvignon Blanc and some Chardonnay for white wines, Pinot Noir and Gamay for the reds. From Touraine to Pays Nantais, Chenin Blanc and Melon de Bourgogne (the latter only in the Muscadet AOC) dominate for whites, while the Cabernet Franc stands out as the major red variety.

RARE VARIETIES. Apart from these well-known varieties, there are in places some rare varieties to please the palate. Pinot Gris produces a rosé Reuilly wine with a fresh, sappy texture. Tressalier makes distinctive white wines and Pineau d'Aunis does the same for the reds and rosés of Vendômois.

TRUE OR FALSE?

White Sancerre is best in its early years, very young.

FALSE. The white wines produced from Sauvignon Blanc (as well as Chenin Blanc) are very enjoyable in their youth. But they may also be aged in a cellar for more than 15 years.

> Vines at Sauzay, for the Saumur-Champigny appellation.

DID YOU KNOW...?

The Loire Valley's first official grand cru (2014) is the Quarts-de-Chaume appellation. This small Maine-et-Loire AOC covers 99 acres (40 ha) and is located in the Rochefort-sur-Loire commune. The exposure, gradient, and morning mists emerging from the River Layon combine to create perfect conditions for the development of botrytis. The appellation makes sumptuous white wines that are sweet and complex, with a luminous acidity.

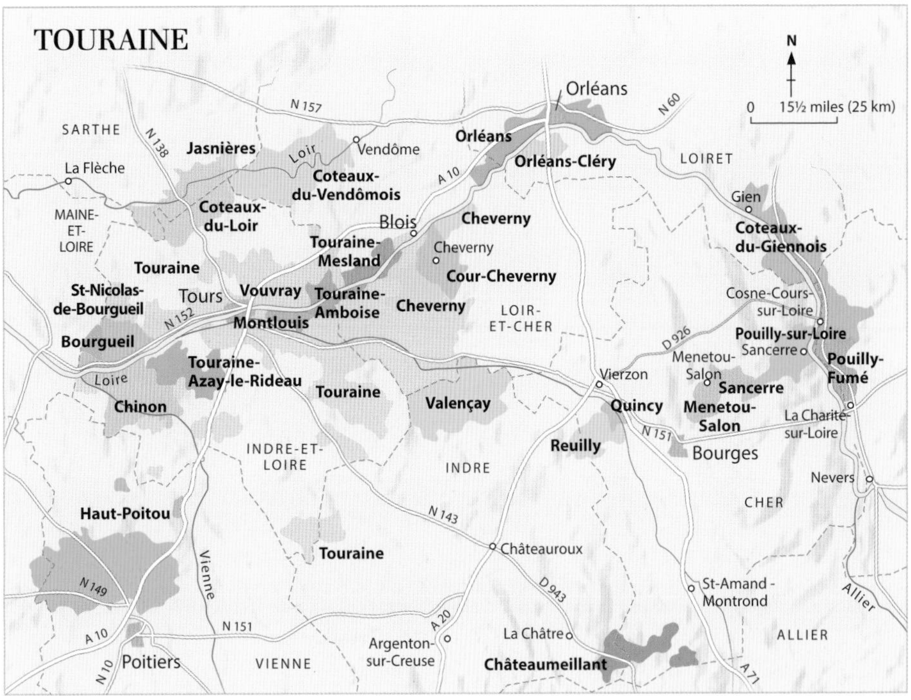

Négociants and estates

The Loire Valley region has small estates that are more similar to the estates of Burgundy than Bordeaux. There are few cooperatives, and the area's wine industry is mainly made up of particular cellars that sell two thirds of production directly. However, the Loire Valley is no Burgundy – its wines do not enjoy the same renown or price. But as a result, it represents an inexhaustible source of good wines and *grands vins*, often very affordable and with a diversity and richness of styles that makes it one of the most attractive wine regions of France. The *négociant* is very important, providing over 50 per cent of the sales of wines from the Loire and playing a key role in some regions such as Muscadet.

Loire Valley AOCs

REGIONAL APPELLATIONS
- Rosé de Loire
- Crémant de Loire

CENTRE
- Châteaumeillant
- Coteaux-du-Giennois
- Menetou-Salon
- Orléans
- Orléans-Cléry
- Pouilly-sur-Loire
- Pouilly Fumé (or Blanc Fumé de Pouilly)
- Quincy
- Reuilly
- Sancerre

TOURAINE
- Bourgueil
- Chinon
- Cour-Cheverny
- Cheverny
- Coteaux-du-Vendômois
- Coteaux-du-Loir
- Jasnières
- Montlouis-sur-Loire
- St-Nicolas-de-Bourgueil
- Touraine
- Touraine-Amboise
- Touraine-Azay-le-Rideau
- Touraine-Mesland
- Touraine-Noble-Joué
- Valençay
- Vouvray

ANJOU AND SAUMUR
- Anjou
- Anjou blanc
- Anjou Coteaux-de-la-Loire
- Anjou Gamay
- Anjou mousseux
- Anjou-Villages
- Anjou-Villages-Brissac
- Bonnezeaux
- Cabernet d'Anjou
- Cabernet de Saumur
- Coteaux-de-l'Aubance
- Coteaux-du-Layon
- Coteaux-du-Layon-Chaume
- Coteaux-de-Saumur
- Quarts-de-Chaume
- Rosé d'Anjou
- Saumur
- Saumur-Champigny
- Saumur mousseux
- Savennières, whether or not followed by the name of the particular site

PAYS NANTAIS, VENDÉE, AND POITEVIN
- Coteaux-d'Ancenis
- Fiefs Vendéens
- Gros-Plant Nantais
- Haut-Poitou
- Muscadet
- Muscadet-Sèvre-et-Maine
- Muscadet-Coteaux-de-la-Loire
- Muscadet-Côtes-de-Grandlieu

AUVERGNE
- Côtes-d'Auvergne
- Côte-Roannaise
- Côtes-du-Forez
- Saint-Pourçain

Famous wines of the Loire Valley

From Centre to Pays Nantais, following the course of river, these are the remarkable wine appellations of the Loire Valley.

CENTRE

REUILLY AOC

This vineyard district was established in the 7th century by the monks of the Abbey of St-Denis. The wines, originally intended only for the city of Bourges, have gradually gained attention throughout France and neighbouring countries. The appellation spans two *départements*, Cher and Indre, southeast of Bourges, with an area of 605 acres (245 ha).

> **GRAPE VARIETIES** Sauvignon Blanc for white wines; Pinot Gris and Pinot Noir for rosés. Pinot Noir is the only variety used for reds.

> **SOIL** Limestone marl and sand on the hills, which provide the wine of this appellation with perfect depth and some slightly sharp notes.

> **STYLE** First, rosé. The significant presence of Pinot Gris always ensures a full and generous palate. The white wines are harmonious and burst with flavour. In the red wines, Pinot Noir seduces with its rich character, freshness, and fruit.

Colour:
White, rosé, and red.

Serving temperature:
46 to 50°F (8 to 10°C) for the whites and rosés; 61°F (16°C) for the reds.

Ageing potential:
2 to 4 years.

CENTRE

QUINCY AOC

Located a few miles east of Bourges, Quincy is the oldest vineyard district in the region. It was also the first vineyard in the Loire Valley to acquire AOC status in 1936. The appellation covers 717 acres (290 ha) and is spread over two areas, Quincy and Brinay. The Sauvignon Blanc grape was first brought to the Notre Dame de Beauvoir Abbey here by monks of the Cistercian order.

> **GRAPE VARIETY** Sauvignon Blanc.

> **SOIL** There are three types of soil, namely sandy-gravelly soils, soils based on formations of red sand, and sandy-silt formations containing various amounts of clay.

> **STYLE** Quincy is a dry, fine, and lively wine. In tasting, it shows a very light colour that is always bright and clear. On the nose there are citrus fruits (pomelo), white flowers, and fresh vegetal notes, while the mouth shows vitality and the frank and direct expression of fruit.

Colour:
White.

Serving temperature:
46 to 50°F (8 to 10°C).

Ageing potential:
2 to 5 years.

Easy-to-drink, good value Loire wines

DRY WHITES

- Coteaux-du-Giennois AOC: Émile Balland (Cosne-sur-Loire).
- Montlouis-sur-Loire AOC: Clos de la Bretonnière, Domaine de la Taille aux Loups (Montlouis-sur-Loire).
- Orléans AOC: L'Excellence, Clos Saint-Fiacre (Mareau-aux-Prés).
- Pouilly Fumé AOC: Domaine Michel Redde (Saint-Andelain).
- Sancerre AOC: Florès et Nuance, Domaine Vincent Pinard (Bué).

SPARKLING WHITES

- Montlouis-sur-Loire AOC: *Brut traditionnel*, Domaine François Chidaine (Montlouis-sur-Loire).
- Vouvray AOC: *Brut* (Traditional method), Domaine du Clos Naudin (Vouvray). Quality sparkling wine: Cuvée Ludwig Hahn, Domaine de l' Écu (Le Landreau).

ROSÉS

- Sancerre AOC: Domaine François Cotat (Chavignol).

REDS

- Chinon AOC: Les Varennes du Grand Clos, Domaine Charles Joguet (Chinon).
- Orléans-Cléry AOC: Clos Saint-Fiacre (Mareau-aux-Prés).
- Sancerre AOC: À Nicolas, Domaine Pascal et Nicolas Reverdy (Maimbray); Domaine François Cotat (Chavignol); Domaine François Crochet (Bué).

SANCERRE AOC

CENTRE

This is the flagship wine appellation from Centre. It covers the slopes and hills around the village of Sancerre, over an area of 7,166 acres (2,900 ha). It also covers the best *terroirs*, traditionally known for the quality of their wines, in Chavignol and Bué.

> **GRAPE VARIETIES** Sauvignon Blanc is the only grape used for white wines; Pinot Noir is the only grape variety for reds and rosés.

> **SOIL** The appellation is spread across a vast array of soils: *caillottes* and *grillottes*, but also white or flinty soils. They combine to produce wines full of flavour with many different characteristics.

> **STYLE** Long considered a fruity, slightly sharp, and refreshing wine, the styles have diversified, between *cuvées parcellaires* and blended wines, and between those made in vats or in barrel. The palette ranges from stimulating wines to be drunk young and enjoyed for their fruitiness to more powerful wines suitable for being laid down.

Colour: *White, rosé, and red.*

Serving temperature: *46 to 50°F (8 to 10°C) for the whites and rosés; 61°F (16°C) for the reds.*

Ageing potential: *2 to 10 years.*

POUILLY FUMÉ AOC (OR BLANC FUMÉ DE POUILLY AOC)

CENTRE

The Pouilly Fumé appellation has long shown Sauvignon Blanc in the best possible light. There is flinty soil on top of the hill at St-Andelain, which is ideal for raising the minerality and crystalline purity of this grape variety.

> **GRAPE VARIETY** Sauvignon Blanc.

> **SOIL** Just like Sancerre, this appellation covers a variety of soils; and they provide evidence of the impact of both time and nature. *Chailloux* (quartz), marl limestone, and flint are the best soils for this wine, as far as wine producers are concerned.

> **STYLE** These wines always match the sites from which they come. The wines from marl limestone are often valued for their fairly straightforward flavours: herbal infusions and fruit; the Chailloux sites convey the expected minerality and some exotic hints; while the flint sites produce a sublime mineral burst, highlighted by stony notes.

Colour: *White.*

Serving temperature: *46 to 50°F (8 to 10°C).*

Ageing potential: *2 to 15 years.*

CENTRE

MENETOU-SALON AOC

To the north of Bourges, this appellation extends the Sancerre appellation towards the south-west. With over a dozen communes and 1,359 acres (550 ha) of vineyard, it produces wines quite close to those from Sancerre, in the three colours and at prices that are often more attractive. It now benefits from a certain notoriety thanks to the presence of some very talented wine producers (Domaine Henri Pellé, Domaine Philippe Gilbert).

> **GRAPE VARIETIES** Sauvignon Blanc for the white wines; Pinot Noir for the reds and rosés.

> **SOIL** Calcareous sediments from the Kimmeridgian.

> **STYLE** The Sauvignon Blancs are fresh, fruity, and floral. Some age very well in barrel. The rosés have the freshness and fruitiness of the Pinot Noir, while the style of the reds fluctuates between simple and crisp to more structured.

Colour:
White, rosé, and red.

Serving temperature:
46 to 50°F (8 to 10°C) for the whites and rosés; 61°F (16°C) for the reds.

Ageing potential:
2 to 10 years.

TOURAINE

JASNIÈRES AOC

This tiny district of 160 acres (65 ha) is one of the oldest Loire appellations. Set slightly back from the river, it has produced wines solely from Chenin Blanc for many ages. They are designed for their minerality and offer great potential for ageing.

> **GRAPE VARIETY** Chenin Blanc.

> **SOIL** The vines face south, and are on a soil that is dotted with flint and tuffeau stones. Consequently, when the warm weather comes, perfect grape ripeness is ensured.

> **STYLE** The appellation creates dry, taut, crystalline white wines that show notes of quince on the palate with a sublime directness. Also, its sweet wines are synonymous with balance and harmony. It is a sweetness that rewards the palate with touches of wax, quince, and acacia honey.

Colour:
White.

Serving temperature:
46 to 50°F (8 to 10°C) for the moelleux*;* *50 to 54°F (10 to 12°C for the secs.*

Ageing potential:
3 to 15 years for the white secs; 10 to 30 years for the moelleux *and* liquoreux.

TOURAINE

VOUVRAY AND MONTLOUIS-SUR-LOIRE AOCs

Vouvray, at 5,436 acres (2,200 ha), and Montlouis-sur-Loire, at 885 acres (358 ha), are twin appellations separated by the Loire River, near Tours. They are the source of great Loire whites. Chenin Blanc, their sole grape variety, offers multiple styles of wine: from the driest and most vigorous, to sparkling wine, all the way through to sweet wines.

> **GRAPE VARIETY** Chenin Blanc.

> **SOIL** Vouvray and Montlouis-sur-Loire are based in a tuffeau *terroir*, a fairly soft limestone and chalk rock. It passes on the most crystalline and mineral elements to the wine. It is the *terroir* of choice for Chenin Blanc.

> **STYLE** The hallmark of these two appellations is variety: dry (*sec*) white wines and lightly sweet *demi-secs*, as well as delightful sweet wines and bubbly sparkling wines. Regarding flavours, there are hints of quince, lime, and bergamot against a background of acacia honey. All are typical features of these two appellations.

Colour:
White.

Serving temperature:
46 to 50°F (8 to 10°C) for the moelleux *and sparkling whites; 50°F (10°C) for the secs.*

Ageing potential:
3 to 10 years for the secs; 7 to 30 years (or more for the best vintages) for the moelleux.

TOURAINE

CHINON AOC

This vast appellation covers 5,930 acres (2,400 ha) on the south bank of the Loire River, across from Bourgueil, around the town of Chinon. This appellation mainly produces red wines in which the Cabernet Franc shows its full potential, offering both significant depth and tannic subtlety.

> **GRAPE VARIETIES** Cabernet Franc and Cabernet Sauvignon for the reds and rosés; Chenin Blanc for white wines.

> **SOIL** Limestone. There are also hillocks of flinty clay and sand in the area.

> **STYLE** The reds require several years of development in the cellar for the Cabernet Franc to reveal its entire character and subtlety. They then release blackberry, blackcurrant, and elderflower fragrances. Their longer development will make them turn smokey and spicy. The whites offer the right balance between a broad texture and chalky or flinty characters. As for the rosés, they show all the richness to be expected from this appellation.

Colour: *White, rosé, and red.*

Serving temperature: *46 to 50°F (8 to 10°C) for the whites and rosés; 61°F (16°C) for the reds.*

Ageing potential: *3 to 5 years for the whites and rosés; 3 to 20 years for the reds.*

TOURAINE

BOURGUEIL AND ST-NICOLAS-DE-BOURGUEIL AOCs

Located on the right bank of the Loire, a few rows of vines upstream from Saumur, these AOCs are appreciated for the structure and depth of their red wines. It is worth pointing out the expansion in quality there in recent years, especially in terms of maturation, and the rise of enthusiastic and committed new wine producers.

> **GRAPE VARIETIES** Cabernet Franc and Cabernet Sauvignon.

> **SOIL** Many of the vineyards in these AOCs are located on hillsides. Soil composition is much more sandy than in other parts of the region, interspersed with patches of clay that have an effect on the power of the wine.

> **STYLE** These reds are a glowing colour, accompanied by scents of blackberry and plum, as well as a firm palate with fine, subtle tannins. In order to fully enjoy these wines, it is best to leave them in the wine cellar for a few years.

Colour: *Red.*

Serving temperature: *61°F (16°C).*

Ageing potential: *3 to 20 years.*

TOURAINE

COTEAUX-DU-LAYON AOC

This represents a major benchmark for sweet wines in the Loire Valley. The vineyard area of 3,460 acres (1,400 ha), located near Angers, extends on each side of the Layon River, a small tributary of the Loire. In the fall, under the cover of mists from the river, botrytis appears on the golden Chenin Blanc berries. The best villages of this appellation, which have *cru* status, are allowed to include their name on the label: Beaulieu-sur-Layon, Faye-d'Anjou, Rablay-sur-Layon, Rochefort-sur-Loire, St-Aubin-de-Luigné, and St-Lambert-du-Lattay. The Coteaux du Layon-Chaume AOC, established in 2007, precisely defines the Chaume *terroir*, situated on a hillside facing south, on schist and sandstone soils. It enjoys the rank of *premier cru*.

> **GRAPE VARIETY** Chenin Blanc.

> **SOIL** This is a real melting pot in which the limestone mingles with the schist and sandstone to provide the Chenin Blanc grape with many different features and flavours.

> **STYLE** Only sweet (*moelleux*) wines are produced, and only the sugar content varies. Each vineyard has its own interpretation of the way to produce Chenin Blanc, and they all show great balance. Alongside the sweetness are perfumes and flavours of crystallized fruit (plum, greengage, and quince) as well as scents of brioche and truffle, showing during the later development of wine.

Colour: *White.*

Serving temperature: *46 to 50°F (8 to 10°C).*

Ageing potential: *5 to 50 years.*

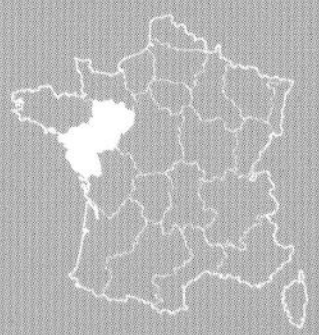

Loire

FRANÇOIS CHIDAINE

It is in Montlouis, the original home of the estate, that François Chidaine and his wife Manuela have produced quality wines of distinction for years, and have also done so more recently on the other side of the Loire, in Vouvray.

FRANÇOIS CHIDAINE

La Cave Insolite
30, quai Albert Baillet
37270 Montlouis-sur-Loire

Founded: *1989*
Area: *91 acres (37 ha)*
Production:
150,000 bottles p.a.
Appellation: *Montlouis*
Red grape varieties: *Côt, Grolleau, Cabernet Franc, Pineau d'Aunis*
White grape varieties:
Chenin Blanc, Sauvignon Blanc

From one bank to the other

François Chidaine admits quite simply and with passion that he never imagined doing anything other than his dream job of working as a wine producer. Over the course of 30 years he set out to achieve this with great determination, initially starting as a farm worker on the family estate in Montlouis, before establishing his own company in 1989. Over the years and with a number of acquisitions, the estate bearing his name has grown, today amounting to 91 acres (37 ha), 49 acres (20 ha) in Montlouis, 25 acres (10 ha) in Vouvray, and 17 acres (7 ha) in the Touraine appellation. In the 2000s he set up on the other side of the mighty Loire River with plots in Vouvray, and his wife Manuela opened the tasting cellar 'La Cave Insolite'. On the banks of the Loire at Montlouis Chidaine was also involved with trading on a small scale for about ten years, buying white and red grapes from Touraine.

A work philosophy

A key figure in the Loire Valley, one of the mainstays of the Montlouis appellation, along with Jacky Blot from the Domaine de la Taille aux Loups, François Chidaine had wanted to switch to organic farming for his plots for about 20 years. So he naturally turned to biodynamics, as 'the aim and desired outcome' for the entire vineyard. This demanding method of cultivation, involving manual working of the soil and harvesting with successive *tries*, produces the best from each of its terroirs, in order to purify the most important grape variety, Chenin Blanc, in all its varied expressions, from dry to sweet. Hence the increasing number of wines from the estate that list a specific terroir. In Montlouis, the vines are mainly located in Husseau, with tuffeau subsoils and flinty clay soils, as exemplified by 'Les Tuffeaux' and 'Les Choisilles', named after the small amount of black flint in the soil, which produces a delightful minerality in the wines.

A never-ending road

François Chidaine has just produced his first vintage. He knows full well that crops succeed one another but no two are ever the same. Along with his fellow wine-makers, he has seen painful evidence of this only recently. The last few years have been particularly challenging for the wine-makers of Montlouis and Vouvray. In 2013 hail struck, hitting the plots on the estate in Vouvray and affecting 40 per cent of the Montlouis vineyard. A charity auction was organized by the Union des Gens du Métier at British auction house Christie's to help his wonderful vineyard, now in peril.

Luckily, the never-ending road down which the wine-maker travels is also scattered with interesting projects and chance encounters. When three of his friends encouraged François to head to Spain, this led to him producing wines in the Murcia region, near the village of Bullas – reds that are a blend of Tempranillo and Monstres (Mourvèdre) and single varietal whites from Macabeu. This large Loire estate still has plenty of life left in it, initially based on Chenin Blanc and now setting down roots in sunny Spain.

SUPERB EXPRESSIONS OF THE GRAPE VARIETY

Chenin Blanc in all its variety is evident across the estate's range: from the vivacious and joyful freshness of Montlouis Les Bournais to the *moelleux*, via the minerality of Clos du Breuil, and lightly sparkling wines, made using the Traditional Method. All the wines of the estate are pure, clean, and endowed not only with a good balance but with a lovely fruity flavour and delightful texture. From a style of salty minerality to full-bodied richness, the wines are beautiful, pure, intense, and excellent. An exceptionally consistent range at this level provides wine-lovers with every nuance and facet of the Chenin Blanc grape.

ınçois Chidaine,
ı of the estate.

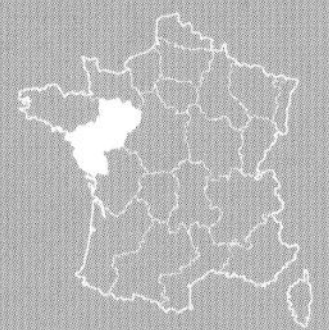

Loire

DOMAINE
DU CLOS NAUDIN

A key representative of the Vouvray appellation, Clos Naudin has now become an unmissable attraction on the banks of the Loire, under the inspired guidance of Philippe Foreau, a great lover of the Chenin Blanc grape variety, and someone who is passionate about wine and food pairings.

DOMAINE DU CLOS NAUDIN

14, rue de la Croix Buisée
37210 Vouvray

Area: *30 acres (12 ha)*
Production: *45,000 bottles p.a.*
Appellation: *Vouvray*
White grape variety: *Chenin Blanc*

The delights of Vouvray

Despite its name, the estate is nothing like a Burgundy or Champagne *clos*, and simply takes its name from the main house of the property. The grandparents of Philippe Foreau established the estate. Since his arrival in 1983, it has maintained a consistent reputation for top-quality wines, following in the footsteps of his ancestors who, unusually at that time, only sold their wines in bottles. Vouvray, on the banks of the mighty Loire River, with a long wine-growing tradition, is rightly proud of being on the Châteaux de la Loire tourist trail, not far from the city of Tours, and of producing the finest grape variety of the Loire, Chenin Blanc. It is at its best here, whether in dry, *demi-sec*, or sweet wines, not to mention in the sparkling wines of Vouvray, which represent more than 60 per cent of the appellation's total production capacity.

High-class wines

Clos Naudin has great respect for the soil, the grapes, and the successive, yet distinct wines produced from them. The cultivation methods are rigorous: working the soil, manual harvesting with no insecticides, and, in terms of vinification, with no chaptalization, nor indeed acidification or malolactic fermentation. Philippe Foreau likes to say that he 'responds to the potential of the crop, not consumer demand.' Depending on the year, the estate produces sparkling wines that are dry, *demi-sec*, *moelleux*, and sweet; not to mention, exceptionally, the famous 'Goutte d'Or' on two occasions, in 1947 and 1990. Located on the superb terroirs of the Perruches, the vineyard combines the effects of clay, which provides texture and silk to the wines, and surface flints, which produce a flinty edge. Balance is the watchword of the estate, and the wines appeal to every palate because of their depth and incomparable purity, with a pleasantly crisp structure and delightful length.

The magic of Chenin Blanc

As is the case elsewhere in the Loire, under the guidance of talented young wine-makers, the vineyard has been transformed, returning to its roots, and now has proper respect for *grand vin*. Clos Naudin is one of the estates to have raised the Vouvray appellation to its peak, along with Noël Pinguet of Domaine Huet, who was one of the pioneers of biodynamics.

All this is undoubtedly the result of an unconditional love for the Chenin Blanc grape variety, which offers lovers of *grand vin* a completely different expression here compared to that in Anjou. The *demi-secs* of the estate or the *moelleux* remain the wines of choice – airy, without any heaviness, finely balanced, but with magnificent power and sensuality. The latter characteristic contributes greatly to successful wine and food pairing, one of the passions of the current owner, who spends hours over his tasting ideas, so that dish and wine complement each other perfectly. Philippe Foreau is a keen wine-taster, with a very good nose, immediately recognizing smells and scents. Looking for the best combination of wine to go with a dish gives him immense pleasure, and a successful pairing makes him a smile, all the more so when it involves matching one of his own wines.

CHENIN BLANC IN A STATE OF GRACE

Perfect balance, a controlled acidity that acts as a perfect backbone, freshness on the palate, and, depending on the wine of course, a sweeping variation between the concentrated, flinty taste of the dry wines and the richness and breadth of the *demi-sec* and sweet wines. The estate's wines linger impressively on the palate, possessing magnificent complexity, and reflecting an expertize that owes nothing to chance. The sparkling wines, as distinctive as they are intense, are a finely-honed part of this masterful range, which is one of the most expressive of the Chenin Blanc grape variety.

> Philippe Foreau, head of the estate.

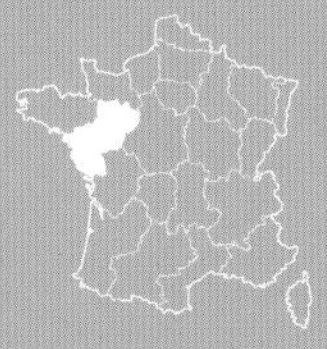
Loire

ALPHONSE MELLOT, *DOMAINE DE LA MOUSSIÈRE*

The Mellots are a very old Sancerre family and deserve credit for the rise to prominence of this appellation, famous for its dry, refreshing white wines. Located in the heart of Sancerre, the estate also makes some high quality reds.

DOMAINE DE LA MOUSSIÈRE

3, rue Porte César
18300 Sancerre

Area: *94 acres (38 ha)*
Production: *300,000 bottles p.a.*
Appellation: *Sancerre*
Red grape variety:
Pinot Noir
White grape variety:
Sauvignon Blanc

Alphonse, the same name for 200 years

Sancerre is the most extensive AOC of Central Loire, and its most famous: with a beautiful citadel overlooking an undulating landscape, with sometimes spectacular slopes, numerous scattered hamlets, and above all a fragrant, refreshing white wine, whose reputation has extended far beyond the borders of the region and the country. This was a wine that was readily available everywhere in the 1980s and moved upmarket by taking its chances, engaging in vigorous promotion, and boasting several outstanding leaders. There is no doubt that the Mellot family played a significant role in this rise. For more than 200 years, the eldest member of each Mellot generation has taken the first name of their founder, Alphonse. In 1881 one family member had the bright idea of setting up a tavern in Sancerre where customers passing through could appreciate the *vins de pays*, and another member, Edmond Alphonse, opened a wine bar in Paris in 1946, which gave a taste of Sancerre to the brewing trade and major restaurants. The tavern no longer exists and the wine bar has been sold, but the Alphonse dynasty still caters for the wine-lover in search of *grands vins* from Sancerre.

Alphonse 'Senior' took over the estate in the 1970s, some 54 acres (22 ha), which has been organically farmed since 1988. His son 'Junior' joined him in the 1990s after working in Burgundy and Chile, and is another talented member of this great dynasty, just like his sister Emmanuelle, who co-manages the estate with him.

Great whites and great reds

The vineyard, which is biodynamically cultivated, covers 89 acres (36 ha) in the heart of the appellation on so-called Kimmeridgian soil. Low yields, maximum maturity, and invigorating soils mean the fruit and the freshness of the Sauvignon grape are always seen at their best, but it is clear that subtle variations can be noted in the individual plots that lie behind the great Génération and Edmond wines. Whatever the vintage, there are no herbaceous Sauvignon aromas because the fruit is always impeccably ripe, readily maturing in wood.

As for the estate's Pinot Noirs, they have few rivals in the appellation: concentrated, ideal for ageing, they almost veer towards Burgundy. In short, the Mellot family produce some of the most definitive and consistent wines of Sancerre, in a delightful range, from splendid reds to straightforward whites. Tempting though their less common wines may be, and these are superbly produced, a wine-maker should be judged by his entry-level wines, and these are exemplary, whether red or white. A few years ago Alphonse Junior teamed up with Vincent Geantet from Burgundy and expanded to the neighbouring, neglected terroirs in the Coteaux Charitois. He proved equally adept there with Chardonnay and Pinot Noir.

LA MOUSSIÈRE, SANCERRE ALPHONSE MELLOT

La Moussière white is a key product of the estate and is produced on a large scale. The consistency and finesse in the expression of the Sauvignon grape is amazing. Fermented in vats and barrels, the wine displays the ripe, fruity, and floral perfume of this grape variety, and is charming and pure, enlivened by a pleasant acidity.

La Moussière red, from Pinot Noir, has the same attractiveness. This wine has the same fruity charm (red fruits, spices, and subtle woody notes) coupled with soft tannins and a pleasant freshness. This is a fruity wine that displays all the attributes of the very best Pinot Noirs.

Refined *terroirs* and patience at Clos Rougeard

For more than a century, Clos Rougeard at Chacé, south of Saumur, has been developing great red wines in the Loire Valley. The Foucault brothers are following the tradition of previous generations, by working on a small scale and crafting the most exquisite wines of the Saumur-Champigny and Coteaux de Saumur appellations. In the vineyard, everything is done to enhance the development of Cabernet Franc, the red grape, and Chenin Blanc, the only white grape variety. Artificial products and chemical treatments are banned, and the land is instead treated much more sensitively. Each individual plot is weeded and ploughed, and yields are deliberately kept low to preserve quality. The grapes are harvested by hand when ready. For the winemakers, it is simple: 'We take our time,' as Nady Foucault says. After lengthy maturation (24 to 36 months), which is rare in French wineries, the wines are ready to last for decades, as is shown by some bottles from 1953, 1937, and 1921.

SAUMUR AND SAUMUR-CHAMPIGNY AOCs

ANJOU-SAUMUR

Both of these appellations are spread around the town of Saumur. Saumur AOC, covering 6,425 acres (2,600 ha), produces dry reds and whites, as well as sparkling wines. Saumur-Champigny AOC, which covers 3,700 acres (1,500 ha), produces only reds and has two styles of wines. The *négociants* make soft wines that should be consumed within the first few years, while the independent wine producers, like Clos Rougeard (see above), aim to make wines that will keep for a much longer period of time.

> **GRAPE VARIETIES** Chenin Blanc, Sauvignon Blanc, and Chardonnay for whites; Cabernet Franc, Cabernet Sauvignon, and Pineau d'Aunis for reds.

> **SOIL** The vineyards of Saumur cover land enriched with chalk. The Saumur-Champigny appellation is based on much richer and deeper soil, as well as tuffeau, limestone clay, and sand-clay.

> **STYLE** The sparkling wines of Saumur impress with the delicacy of their bubbles, subtle flavours, and light texture. It is slightly strange, but this appellation has developed to include a sparkling red made from Cabernet de Franc. Whites, when carefully produced and matured, have juicy fruit flavours and hints of verbena. On the palate, there is a dominant minerality from the limestone. Saumur-Champigny reds are very able to demonstrate depth. They offer an elegant sensation, supplemented by slightly sharp scents of black fruit, wood smoke, and soft spices. Those from Saumur are somewhat more flexible and concentrated.

Colour:
White and red.

Serving temperature:
46 to 50°F (8 to 10°C) for whites (still or sparkling) and rosés; 61°F (16°C) for reds.

Ageing potential:
3 to 10 years for whites; 5 to 20 years for reds.

SAVENNIÈRES AOC

ANJOU-SAUMUR

Curnonsky, the Prince of Gastronomy, rated Savennières is on a par with the legendary Montrachet, Château d'Yquem, and even Château-Chalon. Suffice it to say that Savennières is exceptional in the Anjou wine-production landscape. Ideally located, looking over the course of the Loire River, the 321 acres (130 ha) of vineyards are spread across three communes (Savennières, Bouchemaine, and La Possonnière). The wines are always produced from grapes with high levels of maturity, and tasting each bottle really is a special moment. The La Roche-aux-Moines and Coulée-de-Serrant localities are subject to separate appellations.

> **GRAPE VARIETY** Chenin Blanc.

> **SOIL** The appellation is rooted on slopes perpendicular to the Loire, traversed by schist veins with a sandy base. This soil, which is unique, imbues Chenin Blanc with a noble austerity.

> **STYLE** Savennières need time. Subtle and restrained at first, it must sit for at least 10 years in the cellar before delivering an array of juicy yellow fruit flavours such as plum, quince, and apricot. In the mouth, there is an almosttannic texture that strikes the palate: a Savennières relies on a firm texture and an elegant bitterness with a saline tone.

Colour:
White.

Serving temperature:
50 to 54°F (10 to 12°C).

Ageing potential:
10 to 50 years.

ANJOU-SAUMUR

QUARTS-DE-CHAUME AOC, BONNEZEAUX AOC

If the great wines of the Loire Valley were ranked, these two names would occupy the top positions. Bonnezeaux, comprising 222 acres (90 ha), is located at the heart of the vineyards of the Coteaux du Layon; Quarts de Chaume Grand Cru (99 acres (40 ha) is on the banks of the Loire. Taking advantage of the mesoclimates in the meandering twists and turns of Layon, these appellations, whose origins date back to the Middle Ages, work magic with the Chenin Blanc grape variety from which they are made. As far as wine lovers are concerned, they are the quintessential sweet wines and fully capable of surviving the test of time.

> **GRAPE VARIETY** Chenin Blanc.

> **SOIL** Composed of sandstone and schist, the soil combines with the morning mist of Layon to produce botrytis.

> **STYLE** These wines make a distinct impression with a richness of residual sugar that is refined and developed with evolution in the cellar. If you enjoy them when they are young, notes of bergamot, citrus fruits, pine honey, and quince are apparent. When they are older, after 10 or 20 years, the palate is enriched with aromatic notes of white ground pepper, pear jam, confectionery, and white truffle.

Colour: *White.*

Serving temperature: *50 to 54°F (10 to 12°C).*

Ageing potential: *10 to 50 years.*

PAYS NANTAIS

MUSCADET-SEVRE-ET-MAINE AOC

Close to the city of Nantes the vast vineyards of this Muscadet appellation occupy some 14,826 acres (6,000 ha). The appellation is the most important one in the region and specializes in the method of *sur lie* ageing, which sometimes give wines a slight effervessence but importantly adds volume and aromas. The region offers a wide range that includes simple and lively wines, those for immedite drinking, and other complex wines matured over a long period and offering exceptional value for money.

> **GRAPE VARIETY** Melon de Bourgogne (also known as Muscadet).

> **SOIL** The soil is very diverse. You can find schists, mica schists, gabbros, and, to a lesser extent, granite.

> **STYLE** The best wines are often produced after a very long period of maturation in tank, which gives the wines more palate texture and depth. New work being done in barrels makes it certain that they will be kept for some time in cellars – which is unusual for a wine largely sold and consumed in youth. At tasting, the nose has a floral scent of freshly cut grass and lime, then moves to notes of citrus and white fruit. In the mouth, its freshness invigorates the palate with liveliness and panache.

Colour: *White.*

Serving temperature: *46 to 50°F (8 to 10°C).*

Ageing potential: *3 to 20 years.*

Some great wines

DRY WHITES

- AOC Anjou: Les Rouliers, Richard Leroy (Rablay-sur-Layon).
- AOC Blanc Fumé de Pouilly: Silex, Didier Dagueneau (Saint-Andelain).
- AOC Montlouis-sur-Loire: Stéphane Cossais, Maison Marchandelle (Montlouis-sur-Loire).
- AOC Sancerre: Clos La Néore, Edmond Vatan (Chavignol).

SWEET WHITES

- AOC Coteaux-de-Saumur: Clos Rougeard (Chacé).
- AOC Montlouis-sur-Loire: Domaine François Chidaine (Montlouis-sur-Loire).
- AOC Vouvray moelleux: Romulus, Domaine de la Taille aux Loups (Montlouis-sur-Loire); Domaine du Clos Naudin (Vouvray).
- AOC Quarts-de-Chaume: Château de Suronde (Rochefort-sur-Loire).

REDS

- AOC Chinon: L'Huisserie, Domaine Philippe Alliet (Cravant-les-Coteaux).
- AOC Sancerre: Charlouise, Domaine Vincent Pinard (Bué); Belle Dame, Domaine Vacheron (Sancerre).
- AOC Saumur: Les Arboises, Romain Guiberteau (Mollay).
- AOC Saumur-Champigny: Les Poyeux, Clos Rougeard (Chacé).

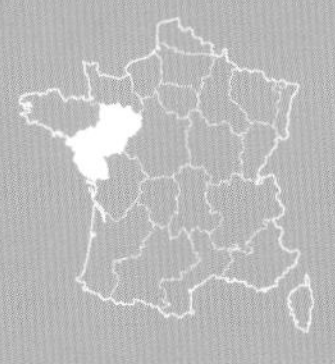

Loire

DOMAINE *PATRICK BAUDOUIN*

Patrick Baudouin is one of the keenest advocates of Chenin Blanc, the Loire's key grape variety. The estate that bears his name, in the heart of the Layon, in Anjou, has steadily improved in quality since its revival in 1990.

DOMAINE PATRICK BAUDOUIN

Princé
49290 Chaudefonds sur Layon

Area: *33 acres (13.4 ha)*
Production: *45,000 bottles p.a.*
Appellation: *Anjou*
Red grape varieties: *Cabernet Franc, Cabernet Sauvignon*
White grape varieties: *Chenin Blanc, Sauvignon Blanc*

Back to his roots

He has the eyes of a dreamer and the sensitivity of a linguistically gifted poet, but Patrick Baudouin is a committed wine producer and a hard grafter, who is constantly active and always working for a new project. In Chaudefonds, near Layon, the 'Canal de Monsieur' (so called because the brother of Louis XVI allowed the river to be made into a canal), lies the estate founded by his great-grandparents, the Juby family. Patrick Baudouin has paid tribute to them by naming one of his wines produced on the Layon hillsides 'Maria Juby'. Born in Angers, Patrick has not always been a wine-maker. Fortunately several careers can be combined into a single life, so he returned to his roots and the comforts of his home region, leaving the book trade to instead set himself up cultivating the hillsides. Returning in 1990, he took over the foundations of a family wine business where everything had to be overhauled. A return to ancestral roots? A desire to return home? The first love is always the strongest. Patrick Baudouin always felt, always knew, that he had made the right choice. He now runs an organically certified 33-acre (13.4-ha) estate, comprising roughly 25 acres (10 ha) of Chenin Blanc and 8 acres (3.3 ha) of Cabernet Franc and Sauvignon. He has produced wines that are much sought-after, under the appellations Anjou, Coteaux du Layon, Quarts de Chaume, and Savennières. In 2008 he also established a small trading company that buys and vinifies certified organic grapes.

Passion for Chenin Blanc

The most important grape variety of the Loire Valley, and a quintessential part of its identity, the *ch'nin*, as it is pronounced locally, cannot be ignored. It is grown by this great gentleman and wine-maker, capable not only of producing great dry whites but also *moelleux* and sweet wines that are balanced and totally fresh, as well as *demi-sec* and sparkling. Patrick Baudouin likes to describe his estate as 'a purveyor of terroirs and a purveyor of exceptional wines'. He is passionate and knowledgeable about this grape variety and, like his fellow wine-makers, its tireless champion, well aware of the danger faced by this wonderful grape. He emphasizes the direction taken by the dry Anjou wines, which are increasingly in the minority, as they are left behind by the rosés and Coteaux-du-Layon. The area dedicated to dry whites is declining and this raises serious questions. In his view, Chenin Blanc should regain its rightful place if given a considered approach to marketing the finest wines, provided that quality is also a prime consideration.

PURITY, FRESHNESS, BALANCE

The dry whites of Anjou are pure, concentrated, and replete with elegance. Depending on the particular wine, they veer between minerality, a beautiful sharpness, and crispness or depth, with a generally fresh and straightforward structure and wonderful fruit purity. The *moelleux* and sweet wines again demonstrate a carefully crafted balance between power, texture, and freshness, without chaptalization. Their flavours are clear and bright. The fruity reds are crisp, with a good balance between structure and liveliness.

Work in depth

Being recognized as one of the best estates in the Loire doesn't happen overnight! Patrick Baudouin has slowly but surely expanded his horizons over more than 20 years, understanding the value of humility, something he greatly appreciates, and trying to get the best from his plots by paying careful attention to each of them. A fan of Anjou Noir, he is happy to explain its pros and cons: it is the product of the schist *terroirs* at the eastern extremity of the Armorican Massif, in contrast to Anjou Blanc that results from the presence of limestone. This respect for specifics is reflected consistently in the range of the estate, which offers *vins de terroirs*, wines that are the product of its carefully nurtured *terroirs*.

> Patrick Baudouin, head of the estate.

THE RHÔNE VALLEY

Situated between Lyon and Marseille, bordered to the west by the Massif Central, to the east by the Alps, and to the south by the Mediterranean, the Rhône Valley has a dual personality. Vineyards grow in granite and are restricted to pretty much one grape variety in the north, while limestone soils and the use of multiple grape varieties frames the south. Commonalities are the sunshine (more generous in the south than in the north), or arid climate, and the wind – as well as a profound belief in regional cohesion. Its current and well-deserved success is due to a combination of the worldwide popularity of its grape varieties and the talents of its producers.

Geographic location

The appellations of the valley are spread over six *départements*. These are, from north to south, Côte-Rôtie in the Rhône *département*; Château-Grillet, Condrieu, and St-Joseph in the Loire; another part of Saint-Joseph, Cornas, and then further south, Côtes-du-Vivarais in Ardèche; plus Hermitage, Crozes-Hermitage, and the appellations of Diois in the Drôme.

The southern part begins in Drôme Provençal, with Vinsobres, Grignan-Les-Adhémar, Châteauneuf-du-Pape, Gigondas, Vacqueyras, Beaumes-de-Venise, Ventoux, and Luberon are in Vaucluse. The eastern Gard contains Lirac, Tavel, and Costières-de-Nîmes.

RHÔNE STATISTICS (AOC)

Vineyard area: 170,503 acres (69,000 ha)
Production: 34.4 million cases (3,100,000 hl)
Reds: 79%
Rosés: 15%
Whites: 6%
(Inter-Rhône, 2014)

> The tiny appellation of Château-Grillet is renowned for producing excellent Viognier whites.

Tumultuous geologic history

The Rhône Valley is the result of the clash of the Massif Central and the Alps, as well as a depression that was filled by the Mediterranean. The granite rock found in the north was produced by volcanic activity in the Massif Central about 300 million years ago. The south was a gulf of a great ocean, where a succession of fluvial and marine deposits assembled – in particular the limestone that would later form peaks such as the Dentelles de Montmirail and Mont Ventoux. So the grape-growing character of the north, with granite, and the south, with limestone, were already being laid down. The actual emergence of the Alps, 40 million years ago, created this valley between two massifs. It was then flooded by the Mediterranean several times: each flood brought new deposits, and with each drainage the river cut its bed several hundred yards deeper – yielding terraces on the sides of its valley, and mixing different elements along the slopes between terraces.

Soil and wine style

The soil of the Rhône Valley is built from three types of rock, which allows us to speak of wine style according to these categories.
GRANITE. Dominant in the northern Rhône Valley as bedrock and deposits (in Côte-Rôtie, Condrieu, Cornas, Château-Grillet,

Recurring drought

Despite some differences in climate – a bit more sun and wind in the south, a little cooler and wetter in the north – the issue of drought affects all the vineyards of the Rhône Valley. Across 2003–08, for example, rainfall numbers dropped (likely evidence of climate change, further supported by earlier and earlier harvest dates). This has resulted in lower yields, the death of some plants, and some imbalances in the wines. While the lack of water requires the grower to pay more attention to the plant, it also can reduce the need for chemical treatments (against mould or rot problems).

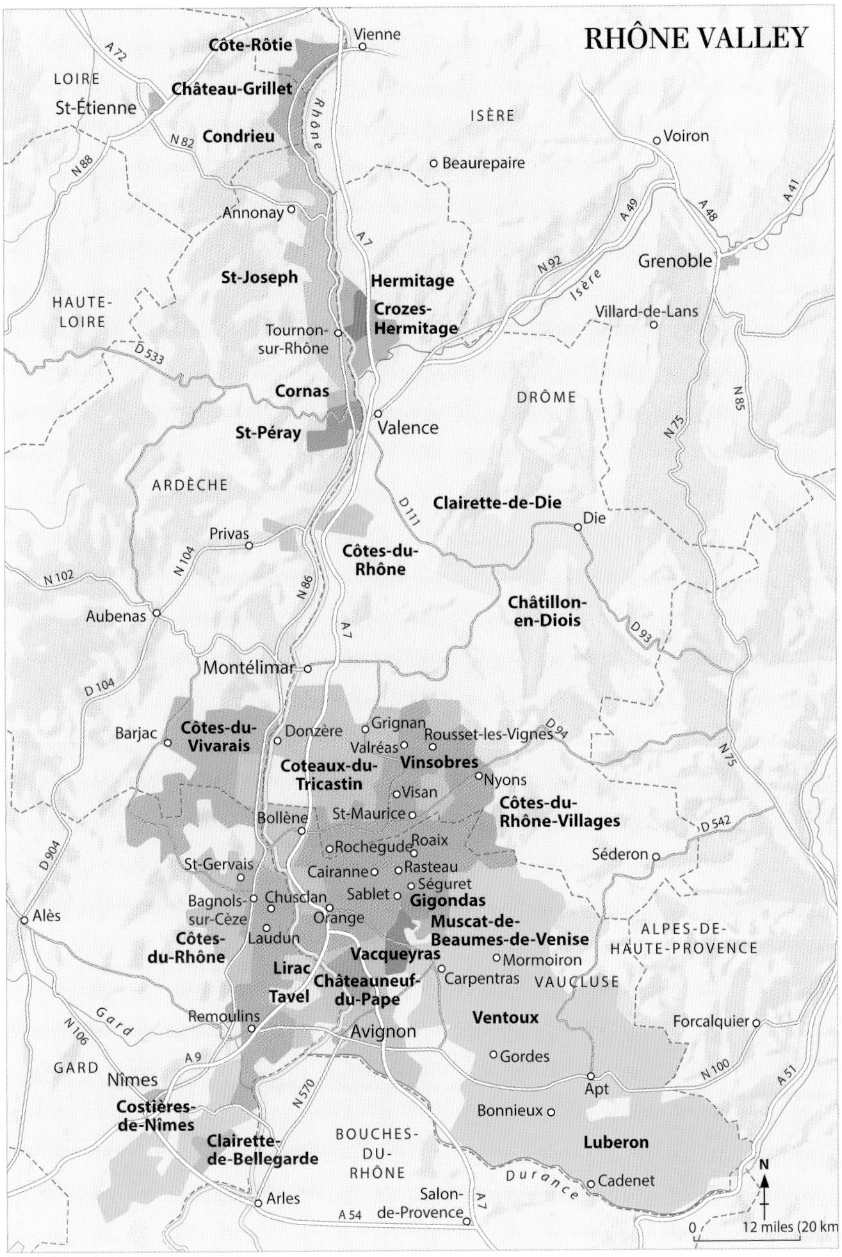

Humble expressions of great wineries

Many of the winemakers crafting the most prestigious Rhône Valley bottles, with prices ranging between €30 and €70 (around $40 to $90/ £25 to £60), are also likely to make affordable wines to demonstrate their style: wines produced from young vines, from less well-known appellations, or *vins de pays* (IGP). For example, in the northern valley, look for Pierre Gaillard, François Villard, Yves Gangloff, Domaine Jamet, and Domaine Chèze; in the south, seek out Clos du Caillou, Domaine de Beaucastel, or even the Domaine du Vieux Télégraphe.

St-Joseph, Hermitage), granite supplies red and white wines with minerality and means that they need to be laid down for a long time.

SILICA (SAND). In the north, silica is the decomposition of the granite (in St-Joseph, Crozes-Hermitage); and in the south, it is marine and river deposits on the terraces and the valley floor (Châteauneuf-du-Pape, Lirac). This type of soil produces light wines with finesse. Sometimes, especially in the south, the silica has reformed into large pebbles (in Châteauneuf-du-Pape, Lirac, Costières-de-Nîmes, Tavel). These help ripen the grapes by a process of retaining and re-radiating the sun's heat. Logically, these types of soil produce powerful and warm red wines with ripe tannins.

CLAY SOILS. In the north of the valley, the clay is the result of the decomposition of the granite (Hermitage, Crozes-Hermitage, Saint-Joseph); in the south it is marine or even glacial marl (south of the appellation Côtes-du-Rhône, Beaumes-de-Venise, Vinsobres, Gigondas, Vacqueyras). The clay in the soil in particular balances the grapes warmed by the pebbles (red Châteauneuf-du-Pape). The white, rosés, and reds wines are full but structured.

LIMESTONE. Found only in traces in the northern valley, as glacial alluvium (in Hermitage, St-Péray), limestone yields white and red wines that are rather fine. But it is most prevalent in the south, as sedimentary deposits that have become bedrock (in Châteauneuf-du-Pape, Coteaux-de-Die, Tavel). The whites and rosés are aromatic and retain good freshness. Also in the south, there are limestone boulders forming the slopes of the Dentelles de Montmirail and Mont Ventoux. The wines here are warm (alcoholic) and red (as Côtes-du-Rhône, Beaumes-de-Venise, Gigondas, Vacqueyras, Côtes-du-Ventoux).

Vineyard history

GRECO-ROMAN ORIGIN. In the south, toward Marseilles, it seems that the vine was flourishing in Ancient Greek times, around the 4th century BC. In the north, in the Vienne region, in the very early years of the 1st century AD, there was a wine said to have the 'taste of pitch' (according to Pliny the Elder), made from a grape variety that was probably local, *Allobrogica*. Its unique feature was its adaptation to colder conditions than the Mediterranean. The fall of the Roman Empire then marked a setback to vineyard development in Rhône because it was deprived of its markets, except for the vineyards near the Mediterranean ports and the vineyards of the far north, which primarily supplied Lyon.

FROM THE POPES TO THE PHYLLOXERA CRISIS. The presence of the papal court in Avignon for the majority of the 14th century encouraged planting in the countryside around Châteauneuf, Tarascon, Avignon, and Arles. The grape varieties were still the ancient ones, originating from Italy or Spain.

> Côte Brune is one of the two slopes forming the famous vineyards of Côte-Rôtie in the northern Rhône Valley.

For centuries, almost all Rhône wines were consumed only locally. Then, in the late 19th century, a profound change took place: phylloxera destroyed the vineyards in much of the valley, especially in Provence. At the same time, the sandy areas of the Gard, Vaucluse, and nearby Languedoc were quickly planted (or overplanted) with vines, since this louse would not thrive on this type of soil. The ensuing crisis of overproduction led to the creation of wine cooperatives.

Collective competition

The Rhône Valley has played an active role in creating the modern structure of French wine production, and it continues to demonstrate faith in the AOC system.

BARON WINEMAKER. Baron Pierre Le Roy Boiseaumarié (1890–1967), a First World War hero and then (by marriage) a winemaker in Châteauneuf-du-Pape, fought for official recognition of that appellation – first through the courts, then by decree in 1933. The model collectively developed there subsequently became the standard for all French AOC decrees: delineation of the area of the appellation, the grape varieties, cultivation methods, harvest dates, production techniques and more. The Baron's work continued to the surrounding Côtes-du-Rhône, turning an old regional name into an official appellation by decree in 1937; he also was president of that association. Finally, he helped found the National Institute of Appellations of Origin (INAO), of which he was president (1947–67), and the International Office of Vine and Wine (OIV) (*see also* p.22).

FAITH IN AOC. Ever since, getting an *appellation d'origine contrôlée* has been a source of motivation to an entire vineyard district, whose villages seek to demonstrate their uniqueness and quality. Consequently, the likes of Gigondas, which had a mere mention appended to Côtes-du-Rhône-Villages, secured its own full AOC in 1970. Many have followed since then: Vacqueyras, Vinsobres, Beaumes-de-Venise, Rasteau, and in 2015 Cairanne.

'Natural' wine

As in all French regions, a minority of Rhône wine producers are becoming known for 'natural' wines, that is to say wines produced from grapes grown organically and vinified with a minimum of intervention and the use of little or no sulphur. These wines can offer a more original and diverse expression of flavour. In the north, these are the Domaines Dard et Ribo, Lucie, Christophe Curtat, La Tache, Texier, Stéphan, and Allemand; in the south, Gramenon, Le Mazel, La Soutéronne, Marcel Richaud, Élodie Balme, La Ferme St-Martin, Chaume-Arnaud, L'Anglore, or even La Cave d'Estézargues.

Reviving the past in Côte-Rôtie

Brigitte Roch and Gilbert Clusel, wine producers in Côte-Rôtie, have always felt limited by the five clones of Syrah available at nurseries. So, in 1990, they began to propagate the 30 indigenous strains present in their oldest vines, belonging to their grandfather. The experiment was extended to the entire appellation; a vine nursery has been created; and a groundswell to replant these old strains is on the move. The wines are more complex and more tannic, but last longer than those from modern clones, and the reintroduction of biodiversity can limit the spread of disease.

Popular grape varieties

Rhône Valley wines have attracted great interest in the English-speaking world because they reflect a global trend. Coming from a warm climate, they possess the popular, concentrated fruit flavours of many New World wines. Three Rhône varieties are particularly noteworthy. Syrah, an indigenous grape variety, is now widely planted in Australia, but also in South Africa and California. Genetic analyses have shown it to be derived from crossing Mondeuse Blanche, a variety of grape from Savoie, and Dureza, a black Ardèche grape, reportedly a distant relative of Pinot Noir. Also a descendant of the Mondeuse Blanche, the white variety Viognier is now grown in the United States, Argentina, and South Africa. Finally, Grenache, the great grape variety of the south, is also widely cultivated in Spain, where it is native, especially in Catalonia, Navarra, and Rioja.

TRUE OR FALSE?

Sweet wines are produced only in the southern Rhône Valley.

FALSE. Besides the Muscats Beaumes-de-Venise and the Rasteau *vins doux naturels*, there is a real collector's item in the *vin de paille* of Hermitage. It is produced in the same way as the wine of that name from Jura, leaving grapes to dry for three months after picking to concentrate the sugars. Produced in very small quantities, and very expensive to manufacture, this wine is unique. Its flavours move between fungi and exotic fruits.

This does not detract from appreciation for the subtlety of other varieties. For red, there is Mourvèdre, with a dark and bitter but appealing character; the delicate Cinsaut, perfect for easy-to-drink wines; and sometimes Carignan, which is delicious when ripe. For white, there is the rich Grenache Blanc, the floral Clairette, the plump Bourboulenc and Marsanne, the aromatic Roussanne and Muscat, and the unctuous Rolle.

Recent vintages

Between 1998 and 2010, the Rhône Valley has enjoyed an impressive series of good vintages. The exceptions are 2002, which was very poor due to the torrential rain at harvest time, and, to a lesser extent, the 2008 vintage. As for the great years, 2005 and 2007, 2009, and 2010 which produced ripe and powerful red wines for laying down. The years that followed were often uneven, notably 2013 and 2014, demonstrating that global warming does not go hand in hand with optimal maturity.

> Châteauneuf-du-Pape: the small stones absorb the sun's heat and release it back to the vines at night.

Rhône Valley AOCs

- Cairanne
- Côtes-du-Rhône
- Côtes-du-Rhône-Villages
- Beaumes-de-Venise
- Château-Grillet
- Châteauneuf-du-Pape
- Châtillon-en-Diois
- Clairette de Die
- Condrieu
- Cornas
- Costières-de-Nîmes
- Coteaux-de-Die
- Côte-Rôtie
- Côtes-du-Vivarais
- Crémant de Die
- Crozes-Hermitage
- Duché d'Uzes
- Gigondas
- Grignan-Les-Adhémar
- Hermitage, *vin de paille*
- Lirac
- Luberon (formerly Côtes-du-Luberon)
- Muscat de Beaumes-de-Venise (VDN)
- Rasteau (VDN), *rancio*
- St-Joseph
- St-Péray
- Tavel
- Tricastin
- Vacqueyras
- Ventoux
- Vinsobres

Leading Rhône Valley wines

The Rhône Valley produces an amazing variety of wines. Its northern zone begins south of the Rhône département *(towards Vienne), reaches the Loire and Isère, then goes as far as the north of Ardèche and Drôme (toward Valence); the southern zone includes Vaucluse and Drôme (toward Montélimar), and reaches east to Gard Vaucluse (around Avignon).*

CÔTES-DU-RHÔNE AND CÔTES-DU-RHÔNE-VILLAGES AOCs

RHÔNE

Côtes-du-Rhône is a regional appellation: any wine produced in the Rhône Valley can claim it, except for wines produced as AOCs for Luberon, Ventoux, Côtes-du-Vivarais, Grignan-Les-Adhémar, and Costières-de-Nîmes, as well as in the Diois. The Côtes-du-Rhône-Villages AOC can be appended with the name of one of the following 17 villages: Chusclan, Laudun, Massif d'Uchaux, Plan de Dieu, Puyméras, Rasteau, Roaix, Rochegude, Rousset-les-Vignes, Sablet, St-Gervais, St-Maurice, St-Pantaléon-les-Vignes, Séguret, Signargues, Valréas, and Visan. The vast majority of Côtes-du-Rhône AOC wines are produced in the southern part of the valley (77 per cent of red and rosé, and 84 per cent of whites are from Gard and Vaucluse).

> **GRAPE VARIETIES** Grenache Noir, Syrah, Mourvèdre, Carignan, Cinsaut, Counoise, Muscardin, Camarèse, Vaccarèse, Picpoul Noir, Terret Noir, Grenache Gris, and Clairette Rosé for the reds and rosés; Grenache Blanc, Clairette, Marsanne, Roussanne, Bourboulenc, Viognier, Ugni Blanc, and Picpoul Blanc for the whites.

> **SOIL** The Rhône Valley is mainly granite to the north and limestone to the south, in both cases with a significant presence of clays and sands. The vineyards are divided between base rock and terraces of varying heights.

> **STYLE** The reds, concentrated and full-bodied, have ripe red fruit and herb flavours. The whites are often rich in flavour, and for a long time were heavy; but they are increasingly enjoyable with improved temperature control techniques. The rosés are often full-bodied and more colourful than in Provence. Côtes-du-Rhône-Villages red wines offer sometimes warm, ripe fruit, with a marked spicy character and supple or more consistent tannins. The style can vary a great deal between the villages.

Colour:
Red, rosé, and white.

Serving temperature:
46 to 54°F (8 to 12°C) for the whites and rosés;
54 to 61°F (12 to 16°C) for the reds.

Ageing potential:
3 years for rosés and whites;
3 to 6 years for the reds.

CÔTE-RÔTIE AOC

NORTHERN RHÔNE

This small appellation – 682 acres (276 ha), on steep slopes – is the northernmost in the valley. It produces red wines for ageing, most of them with time in barrel. After an initial period of bright expression, the wines often close down for three years, before reopening when they are about seven or eight years old.

> **GRAPE VARIETIES** Syrah (here called 'Serine') and Viognier.

> **SOIL** Granite to the south, schist to the north.

> **STYLE** The style is inclined toward concentrated black fruit, mocha, licorice, and chocolate, but also includes specific characteristics from the *terroirs* across this appellation. The wines from Côte Brune in the north are robust (dark mica schist soil) and those from the Côte Blonde in the south more delicate (clayey sand).

Colour:
Red.

Serving temperature:
61°F (16°C).

Ageing potential:
At least 15 years.

CONDRIEU AOC

NORTHERN RHÔNE

With completely granite soils, the 415 acres (168 ha) of this AOC produce white wines exclusively from Viognier. The qualities displayed by this grape variety vary according to the *terroir*; here it can produce wine that demonstrates the minerality of the soil, when the winemaker so chooses. Depending on the year, part of the production can be dedicated to making sweet (*moelleux* or *liquoreux*) wines. Thanks to their aromas and roundness, these wines are pleasant when consumed young. Some are produced in barrels.

> **GRAPE VARIETY** Viognier.

> **SOIL** Biotite granite (white mica), producing wines noted for their minerality; Muscovite granite (black mica), producing more generous wines.

> **STYLE** The grape variety's rich aromatic palette of has notes of white flowers, white pepper, peach, and apricot, with occasional mineral notes. The mouth is supple and round, mouth-filling and perfumed.

Colour: *White.*

Serving temperature: *50 to 54°F (10 to 12°C)*

Ageing potential: *4 or 5 years, if you like a fruitier style, 10 years, if you prefer minerality*

ST-JOSEPH AOC

NORTHERN RHÔNE

This appellation produces red and white wines. Occupying 2,965 acres (1,200 ha), it starts in the north, around the Condrieu district, and ends in the south, across from Hermitage, just above Cornas. The St-Joseph hill, which gives its name to the AOC, is located between the towns of Mauve and Tournon, hence its former name of 'vin de Mauve'. The appellation has a great diversity of soils, which can result in a wide variety of production. Note, however, that larger estates in the northern Rhône region, renowned for production of Cornas, Côte-Rôtie, or Hermitage, are buying more and more vineyards in St-Joseph. The value represented by these wines is often significant. While the centre of the appellation is less prestigious, it still contains many nice surprises.

> **GRAPE VARIETIES** Syrah for the reds; Marsanne and Roussanne for the whites.

> **SOIL** Similar to those of other appellations of the region: partially granite, sometimes broken clay.

> **STYLE** Red wines generally have a nose of red and black fruit with floral elements (violets), becoming a little smoky. They have a striking fruit palate with excellent freshness, and a licorice or peppermint finish. The whites (nine per cent of production) convey some smoothness from the clay soils; but they are rarely heavy, especially when the grape variety blend is mainly Roussanne.

Colour: *Red and white.*

Serving temperature: *50 to 54°F (10 to 12°C) for the whites; 54 to 61°F (12 to 16°C) for the reds.*

Ageing potential: *3 to 10 years.*

Big names in the Rhône

Hermitage, Côte-Rôtie, and Châteauneuf-du-Pape wines have long been recognized by enthusiasts. They represent three of the most prestigious *terroirs* in this region, with bottles priced from €25 to €100 (around $34 to $90+/£20 to £70+), depending on the district and vintage. To the north, the *négociant* Guigal established the reputation of Côte-Rôtie, before developing a whole range of wines in the other *terroirs* of the valley. This producer was later joined by many top estates, such as Mathilde et Yves Gangloff, renowned for magnificent Condrieu wines. In Hermitage, alongside the Jaboulet operation, Michel Chapoutier has produced extraordinary wines over the years, from plots farmed using biodynamics. To the south, the Château Rayas, on sandy *terroirs*, and Château de Beaucastel, on stony soils, are the two of the estates most sought-after for Châteauneuf-du-Pape.

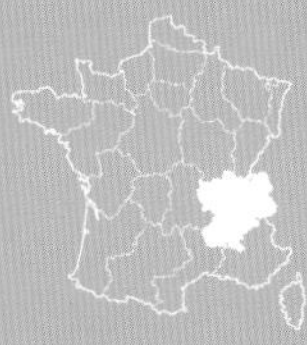

Rhône Valley

E. GUIGAL

The rebirth of this famous Côte-Rôtie vineyard is inseparably linked to the Guigal family, whose fortune has been instructive and fascinating.

E. GUIGAL

Château d'Ampuis
69420 Ampuis

Area: *94 acres (38 ha)*
Production:
5.5 million bottles p.a.
Appellation: *Côte-Rôtie*
Red grape variety: *Syrah*
White grape varieties:
Marsanne, Roussanne, Viognier

A great story

Just like many others in the world of wine, the story of the Guigal company seems like a fairy tale. This one is set on the steep slopes of the Côte-Rôtie, in a castle at Ampuis, with a family called Guigal. In the 1930s, the terrain was desolate, with the sun only ripening a few feet of vines that had survived phylloxera and the economic crisis. A few years earlier, in 1924, the young Étienne Guigal had been employed as an agricultural worker at Vidal-Fleury, a historic merchant of the region. At the age of 16, he made his first harvest on a plot, known as La Turque, carrying it on his back to the cellar. The deep slump extended into the 1940s. A bottle of Côte-Rôtie was worth one franc, or a few pounds of apricots, a paltry price compared to the quality of the wine and the work involved.

Étienne Guigal, who had become cellar master in the meantime, believed firmly in the future of these hills, which had been so famous a century earlier. He founded his own company in 1946, revolutionizing the practices used (small yields, *tries* of grapes, long maturation) and laid the foundations for exceptional progress. In 1962, he became blind and handed over the estate to his son, Marcel, who was only 17 years old. His son was equally visionary, and ensured further development. Excellent business acumen led to the purchase of Vidal Fleury in 1985, the place where his father had started, and the acquisition in 1995 of the Château d'Ampuis, where his mother had previously worked. Under his stewardship Côte-Rôtie has regained its pride, and wine-lovers the world over have once again rediscovered their taste for the *grands vins* of the Northern Rhône.

Plots of land and trading

The company, which is now jointly run by Marcel Guigal and his son Philippe, the current general manager, has acquired other prize assets in Condrieu and Hermitage, as well as the Grippat (Saint-Joseph, Hermitage), Vallouit (Côte-Rôtie, Hermitage, Saint-Joseph, Crozes-Hermitage), and Bonserine (Saint-Joseph) estates, although the last of these remains independent of the parent company. Since 2003, it has had its own cooperage, which produces over 800 new barrels every year to age the fine wines of the estate in the cellars of the Château d'Ampuis, where there are almost 7.5 acres (3 ha) of galleries. The Guigal estate has put its distinctive red badge on a range of wines produced commercially on both sides of the Rhône Valley. Widely distributed and usually very reliable, this is the result of driving hard bargains with wine-growers. The great talent of Guigal is producing legendary wines from the plots La Turque, La Mouline, and La Landonne in Côte-Rôtie and *grands vins* from Condrieu (La Doriane) and Hermitage (Ex Voto), while still offering an extensive range of wines that are generally highly recommended from the terroirs of the Rhône Valley, at affordable prices.

E. GUIGAL, CÔTES DU RHÔNE ROUGE

Any of the legendary wines produced by this estate could have been chosen, but this simple Côtes du Rhône illustrates another aspect of the talent of the Guigal family, namely the ability to produce a truly global product, comprising several million bottles of a very drinkable wine, completely reliable, and typical of the Rhône region. As a Syrah specialist, Guigal uses this grape variety in blending his wine. This Côtes du Rhône offers undried fruit notes, pleasant spices, and a delicate balance, mingled with soft tannins and carefully conserved freshness. It should be drunk young.

cel Guigal, who runs
tate, and his son
pe, an oenologist.

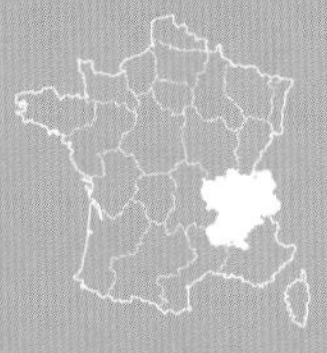

Rhône Valley

CHÂTEAU *D'AQUÉRIA*

Tavel is located on the right bank of the Rhone, not far from Roquemaure. Before the French Revolution its wines were so highly regarded that the barrels had to be marked to avoid counterfeiting. This could be seen as the birth certificate of Côtes du Rhône.

CHÂTEAU D'AQUÉRIA

route de Pujaut
30126 Tavel

Area: *168 acres (68 ha)*
Production: *380,000 bottles p.a.*
Appellation: *Tavel*
Red grape varieties: *Grenache Noir, Syrah, Mourvèdre, Cinsaut*
White grape varieties:
Grenache Blanc, Clairette, Bourboulenc, Roussanne, Picpoul, Viognier

The Premier Rosé de France

The Premier Rosé de France is produced in Tavel, in Le Gard, and, to be more precise, from its unique sandy Pliocene soil, and by its greatest exponent, the Château d'Aquéria. This elegant 18th-century building lies in a park filled with Italian topiary, under the shade of pines and cypresses, and in the middle of the vineyard. The whole place exudes elegance and serenity, a lovely aura skilfully maintained by the same family, who have owned it since 1919.

A structured rosé

The wines are unsurpassed. The 168 acres (68 ha) of vines, have an average age of 35 years and are carefully maintained today by two brothers, Bruno and Vincent de Bez. The former deals with the vineyard, the latter with the cellar. They are the worthy heirs of Paul de Bez, who for 40 years put all his energy into maintaining and restoring this exceptional vineyard. Their Tavel is faithful to the tradition of this appellation. There is no concession to the seductive call for greater paleness and this *rosé de saignée* is a brilliant, deep colour, somewhere between raspberry and cherry. More importantly, it has a structure that allows it to age readily. This is the result of skilfully controlled maceration.

A sophisticated blend

The grape varieties are vinified two by two. The powerful and fruity Grenache Noir makes up 45% of the wine, while the second most important variety is a white grape, Clairette (20%), which provides elegance and floral notes. Next comes Cinsaut for finesse, Mourvèdre and Syrah for structure, rounded off with Bourboulenc and Picpoul. Besides Tavel, the château also makes excellent white and red Lirac, and Côtes du Rhône.

CHÂTEAU D'AQUÉRIA TAVEL ROSÉ

This wine combines seven grape varieties that undergo a 24-hour maceration, allowing colour, scent, and volume to be extracted. The nose offers a combination of currants and *gariguette* strawberries, accompanied by pepper. The lively impression is maintained on the palate. Fruity, rich, powerful, and structured, this rosé generously provides the palate with a wide range of aromas: spices, thyme, oregano, bitter orange, and flint. Long and ample, it is not a rosé merely to quench the thirst, but rather a wine to go with a meal, developing in the glass and becoming more appealing as you engage with it.

CHÂTEAU D'AQUÉRIA, LIRAC ROUGE

This wine is a beautiful ruby colour, with a hint of blood red. The nose evokes Mediterranean spices (thyme, rosemary, and the everlasting flower, cistus) and red fruit compôte. The palate is full, rich, and crisp. The finish is very fresh with hints of citrus. It is fruity, without any hint of wood.

HERMITAGE AOC

NORTHERN RHÔNE

Hermitage – 336 acres (136 ha) located on a hill around the town of Tain – is a large, single swathe of land; yet it has amazingly complex geologic composition. This allows each producer to adopt his own style, whether distinctive wines from single micro-plots or interesting blends. About 25 per cent of the wines from Hermitage are white; they are among the finest in France, and made mostly from Marsanne. Enthusiasts of fruit flavours enjoy Hermitage wines when they are young; those who are more patient wait from 7 to 15 years to enjoy their complexity.

> **GRAPE VARIETIES** Syrah for red; Marsanne and Roussanne for white.

> **SOIL** Hermitage was originally a block of granite that separated the Rhône from the Massif Central. The hill, topped by a small chapel, rises to the east of the AOC and produces great, austere reds. The central and western parts (75 per cent of the land) are covered with multiple alluvial deposits. Areas of limestone and clay, or even sandy deposits, are often planted with white grapes.

> **STYLE** The great complexity of the soil, the south-facing exposure, and the maturation in barrel produces notes of juniper and acacia, butter, white fruit, licorice, nuts, gentian, or even truffle in the whites. The reds are often smooth, with chocolaty black-fruit flavours. They have hints of licorice, pepper, spices, or even violet, and a very long finish.

Colour:
Red and white.

Serving temperature:
54°F (12°C) for the whites; 61 to 63°F (16 to 17°C) for the reds. (Wines younger than 6 years should be decanted for 1 or 2 hours.)

Ageing potential:
More than 10 years, for whites, more than 20 years for reds.

CROZES-HERMITAGE AOC

NORTHERN RHÔNE

Crozes is a large – 3,707-acre (1,500-ha) – AOC in the northern Rhône Valley. While it can be said that the Hermitage is its *grand cru*, it represents an interesting variety of styles. Limited to 1,235 acres (500 ha) in 1937, the AOC was expanded in the 1950s and spreads out on terraces across the hillsides. Despite the extension, the wines are mostly of uniform quality and are a very good value. Note the local cultivation of white wines, often largely from Marsanne, a rich grape variety that requires barrel ageing.

> **GRAPE VARIETIES** Syrah for the reds; Marsanne and Roussanne for the whites.

> **SOIL** The Châssis *terroir* consists, for the most part, of sandy clay alluvial deposits; while in the northern part of the appellation, it is granite, as in Hermitage. There are also some limestone areas, and some rare kaolin (white clay) in the Larnage area.

> **STYLE.** The classic style of wine (in the Châssis area) is fresh and fruity, offering a nice balance between fruit and spice, with a supple body. But there also are wines that have been matured (from the areas of granite and kaolin) for keeping with more marked tannins.

Colour:
Red and white.

Serving temperature:
50 to 54°F (10 to 12°C) for the whites; 54 to 61°F (12 to 16°C) for the reds.

Ageing potential:
3 to 10 years.

Selected Crozes-Hermitage estates

- **Domaine Combier (Pont-de-l'Isère).** Organic farming that develops distinctive whites and reds for ageing.

- **Domaine Les Bruyères (Beaumont-Monteux).** This biodynamic estate produces reds that are full-bodied yet very at ease.
- **Domaine Alain Graillot (Pont-de-l'Isère).** A point of reference for its elegant, structured Syrahs, with real keeping potential.
- **Domaine Pradelle (Chanos-Curson).** Supple and velvety reds and whites in a classic style.
- **Yann Chave (Mercurol).** Wines that strike a perfect balance between conveying elements of the *terroir* and being easy to drink.
- **Cave de Tain (Tain-l'Hermitage).** The largest property on the appellation, this cooperative produces very well-crafted wines, including examples from interesting *cuvées parcellaires*.

CORNAS AOC

NORTHERN RHÔNE

This is a small vineyard district of just 321 acres (130 ha), but one with great character! Unlike Hermitage and Côte-Rôtie, which face directly south, some Cornas vineyards face east – which may explain why some wines are more rustic in style, and always take a little longer to reveal themselves. But style varies by producer, with the most traditional ones not de-stemming the grape clusters and crafting firmer wines, which need to be aged for between 8 and 10 years. Producers who do remove the stems make wines with more supple tannins, but not lacking in character and which also benefit from ageing.

> **GRAPE VARIETY** Syrah.

> **SOIL** The soil in this district is mainly granite, with a few limestone areas (from Vercors) on the hill at Chaillots in St-Joseph.

> **STYLE** Cornas is marked by powerful notes of smoke and black fruits. Plots with more limestone produce wines with a more fruity nose, but they are sometimes firm on the palate. As Cornas ages, very clear notes of menthol, game, and pepper emerge.

Colour: *Red.*

Serving temperature: *61°F (16°C).*

Ageing potential: *More than 20 years.*

CÔTES-DU-VIVARAIS AOC

SOUTHERN RHÔNE

Although located in Ardèche, this is the first southern Rhône appellation, and it uses a majority of Grenache varieties for both red and white wines. Côtes-du-Vivarais is a small appellation, occupying 791 acres (320 ha), but one boasting two major advantages: an unusual character and very reasonable prices.

> **GRAPE VARIETIES** Grenache Noir, Syrah, Carignan, and Cinsaut for the reds and rosés; Grenache Blanc, Marsanne, and Clairette for the whites.

> **SOIL** Limestone pebbles on clays located around the gorges of Ardèche. This soil is warm on the surface and cool as you penetrate to any depth. The area suffers less from drought than much of the valley, while still taking advantage of the sun.

> **STYLE** The wines here are very different from those found throughout the Rhône Valley. They are concentrated like all wines from the south, but also supported by a lovely freshness.

Colour: *Red, rosé and white.*

Serving temperature: *46 to 50°F (8 to 10°C) for the rosés and the whites; 57°F (14°C) for the reds.*

Ageing potential: *3 years for the rosés and the whites; 3 to 8 years for the reds*

Good value wines from the southern Rhône

- **Cave de Rasteau (Rasteau).** This cooperative produces Côtes-du-Rhône in all three colours, notably in the Les Viguiers line.
- **Domaine Boisson (Cairanne).** A range of wines without a single false note, in both red and white.
- **Domaine de la Boisserelle (St-Remèze).** Excellent value white, red, and rosé Côtes-du-Vivarais wines.
- **Domaine Jean David (Séguret).** Very good reds produced from Grenache grown organically.
- **Domaine Coulange (Bourg-St-Andéol).** Distinctive Côtes-du-Rhône produced by an excellent winemaker.
- **Domaine Brusset (Cairanne).** A very good Cairanne wine producer that also makes very affordable Côtes-du-Rhône and Ventoux.
- **Domaine de Durban (Beaumes-de-Venise).** Amazing value for a characteristic Beaumes-de-Venise AOC wine.
- **Domaine de Grange Blanche (Blovac).** A very agreeable Rasteau.
- **Domaine Terre des Chardons (Bellegarde).** Superb Costières-de-Nîmes for as little as €8 ($10/£7).
- **Nicolas Croze (St-Martin-d'Ardèche).** Very good, full-bodied Côtes-du-Rhône.

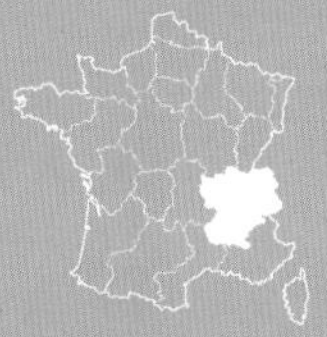

Rhône Valley

CHÂTEAU
SAINT-COSME

In Gigondas, expert winemaker Louis Barruol straddles both past and present, producing superb wines that age well.

CHÂTEAU SAINT-COSME

La Fouille et les Florets
84190 Gigondas

Area: *54 acres (22 ha)*
Production: *90,000 bottles p.a.*
Appellation: *Gigondas*
Red grape varieties: *Grenache Noir, Syrah, Cinsaut, Mourvèdre*
White grape varieties: *Clairette, Viognier, Marsanne, Picpoul*

The taste of tradition

Louis Barruol is always happy to show visitors the Roman remains at the bottom of his cellar, just as he is happy with the perfect results produced by the latest wine-making techniques that he uses, especially when they highlight the qualities of the terroir while maintaining the traditional profile of the estate's wines. The wines are indeed the proof, and are at their peak after a certain amount of ageing. There's no rush at Saint-Cosme, with wine-making based firmly upon tradition and on what produces good results. Louis has taken stock of the situation and made decisions, discarding antiquated procedures and retaining only those that are effective. In the 1970s, before Louis took over, his father Henri introduced organic cultivation. Going much further back in history, it is fascinating to read the scrupulously honest notes penned in 1717 by the Barruol in charge at the time, describing as 'excellent' a wine produced in 1714 but others in the same year as only 'drinkable' or even 'very mediocre'. These descriptions help to illustrate why the current approach at Saint-Cosme – a subtle mix of past and future with a touch of self-deprecation thrown in – is perhaps the best way of keeping everything very firmly rooted in the present.

Two thousand years of winemaking

In 1490, Esprit Vaton, a direct ancestor of the Barruol family, made his home at the foot of the Dentelles de Montmirail. He built his residence on the remains of a Roman villa. Constructed in the 2nd century, little remains of the villa except for the foundations and a section of the cellars that continue to play a part in the estate's production. The ancient vinification vats are still there 15 generations later.

Louis Barruol took over from his parents in 1992 and expanded the cellars in 2007. The vineyard has 54 acres (22 ha) and the vines have an average age of 60 years. The vineyard is based on the main soils of the Gigondas appellation: limestone scree, *safre* (a soft sandstone), marls, and clays. The estate's name comes from the Romanesque chapel erected in the 11th century, dedicated to Saints Cosmas and Damian. It is surrounded by the vineyards of the Le Poste *lieu-dit*, a short distance away, a plot of land on which vines have been cultivated since at least the end of the Middle Ages, as documented in records of the period.

In Saint-Cosme every parcel of land or piece of stone has a story to tell, and the wines play their own part in the narrative. To open any of the Saint-Cosme wines in their first few years would be a waste, they must be aged first. Tasting them too early simply defeats the object. It's a waiting game, as the saying goes. After ten years or so, a wine like Le Claux illustrates this point perfectly.

CHÂTEAU SAINT-COSME, LE CLAUX, GIGONDAS ROUGE

A wine made from old Grenache grapes matured for 12 months in barrel, 30% made from new wood. These old Grenaches are not for immediate consumption. They need to breathe slowly and, once oxygenated, display great finesse and complex aromas: jellied dark fruit, cherry, white pepper, even the hint of a damp cellar. The palate responds with the same fruity vigour, flowing into velvety silk tannins, turning the wine into a refined delicacy. A wine that is definitively 'southern', yet refined and elegant, and one that must age before drinking.

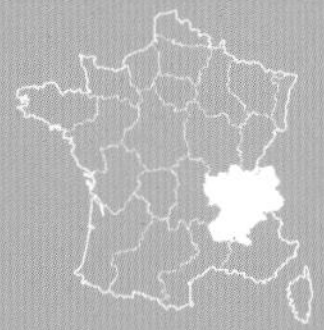

Rhône Valley

DOMAINE *GEORGES VERNAY*

In barely three decades this vineyard has gone from being totally overlooked to gaining an international reputation, raising the Viognier grape variety to new heights in the process. And it has all been the work of just one man, winemaker Georges Vernay, who believed in the estate from the very start.

DOMAINE GEORGES VERNAY

1, route Nationale
69420 Condrieu

Area: *54 acres (22 ha)*
Production:
120,000 bottles p.a.
Appellation: *Condrieu*
Red grape variety: *Syrah*
White grape variety: *Viognier*

The 'Pope of Condrieu'

It's the story of a vineyard that has lived through many changes. Highly regarded in the 18th century, Condrieu had been forgotten by the end of the 19th, only to be revived again in the 20th century. It is also the story of a family, the Vernays, who rescued these steep hillsides from the oblivion into which they had been plunged by phylloxera, wars, and rural depopulation.

After World War II, Georges Vernay took over the Condrieu family estate of just 2.5 acres (1 ha) that had been planted with Viognier by his father. At that time the entire AOC comprised only 10 acres (4 ha) and for many years cherry and apricot trees had relegated the vines to the status of a secondary crop. However, two important clients of Georges – and he had admittedly few – began to order more wine than the tiny estate could provide. It was a small matter relatively speaking but one that would have a significant outcome and Georges began planting again, setting in motion a virtuous circle that would greatly increase the prestige of this great golden white wine, which is rich and perfumed.

The 'Pope of Condrieu' would be widely copied. Today, a green-and-grey patchwork of more than 420 acres (170 ha) covers the hills that make up this revitalized appellation. The Vernay estate owns 22 acres (9 ha) here, along with plots in Côte-Rôtie and Saint-Joseph.

To the rescue of the saviour

Christine Vernay had no intention of being a winemaker, preferring Italian literature instead. But perhaps this plays a part in the way she has combined elegance with passion so successfully, as in the exceptional Maison Rouge Côte-Rôtie. Success did not happen overnight, however. In the mid-1990s, Georges decided to stop working as a winemaker. His sons had left the vineyard and were busy with their own careers, leaving little prospect of their return to the wine business. Of his three children only Christine was left, but she could not resist the call. Condrieu had been her home and all her childhood memories were there, as the famous French author Proust and his *madeleines* in *À La Recherche du Temps Perdu*. Selling up was out of the question, so Christine returned to the family estate in 1996 and was given free rein by her father to learn about every aspect of the vineyard and the cellar. Gradually, the vineyard was transferred to organic cultivation. Christine took great pains to explore every nook and cranny of the terroir of her birth, working tirelessly to take over the whole wine-making process, as demanding and taxing as it is engrossing. She has created new wines, received plaudits from the press, and made her mark definitively. High-quality Côte-Rôtie wines have now been added to Coteau de Vernon and Les Chaillées, the great wines of Condrieu.

DOMAINE VERNAY, COTEAU DE VERNON, CONDRIEU

This beautiful vineyard, planted by Christine Vernay's grandfather before 1940, expanded by her father in the 1960s and a little more by Christine herself more recently, forms a link between the generations. The wine is a pale-golden colour with a hint of green. The mineral nose exudes warm flint-tinged notes with apricot, honeysuckle, and violet. The palate tastes delicate and powerful, carried by a succession of floral, fruity, and toasted flavours, and a fullness that is concentrated and yet restrained.

ristine Vernay,
l of the estate.

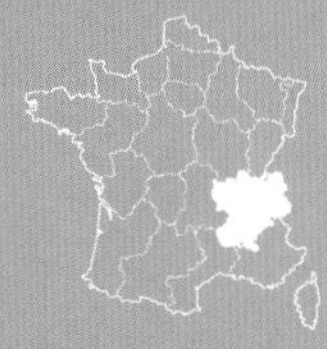

Rhône Valley

CHÂTEAU *DE BEAUCASTEL*

The Perrin family runs this large and beautiful Châteauneuf-du-Pape estate, which enjoys equal renown for its great red wines that can be laid down and for its white wine from vines that are over 100 years old.

CHÂTEAU DE BEAUCASTEL

chemin de Beaucastel
84350 Courthezon

Area: *247 acres (100 ha)*
Production: *300,000 bottles p.a.*
Appellation: *Châteauneuf-du-Pape*
Red grape varieties: *Mourvèdre, Grenache, Syrah, Cinsaut, Vaccarèse, Counoise, Terret Noir, Muscardin, Picpoul*
White grape varieties: *Roussanne, Clairette, Bourboulenc, Picardan, Picpoul*

A Châteauneuf-du-Pape legend

Marc, Pierre, Thomas, Cécile, Charles, Matthieu, and César are the fifth generation to be at the helm of Château de Beaucastel and the Perrin vineyards. Each of them has a particular skill and area of responsibility under the calm but watchful eyes of their respective fathers, François and Jean-Pierre. Pierre Tramier took over the estate in 1909, over 100 years and five generations ago. The Beaucastel coat of arms is significantly older and acts as a reminder of the estate's origins. The plain-and-simple barn purchased by the Beaucastel family in the mid-18th century was transformed a century later into a mansion by Pierre de Beaucastel, who had been appointed governor of Courthézon by Louis XVI in recognition of his conversion to Catholicism.

The vineyard: 247 acres (100 ha) and 13 grape varieties

Since 1950, the vineyard has been cultivated organically, and since 1974, biodynamically. The use of both traditional and new, sometimes even avant-garde, techniques is a family trait. Pierre Perrin, Pierre Tramier's son-in-law, established and built up the cellar. His son Jacques has continued in the same vein, devising new vinification techniques. The two men stick rigidly to the grapes used initially, resisting the urge to move to the more ubiquitous Grenache. Their firm stance that has resulted in the use of 13 authorized grape varieties, including the famous Roussanne, more than 100 years old, as well as an unusually large amount of Mourvèdre, is key to the château's red wines. Although the vineyard covers 247 acres (100 ha), just under a third of the area is always left uncultivated, and each year 5 acres (2 ha) are withdrawn from production while five more are replanted after fallow years. The entire acreage comprises a single plot of bright green vines surrounding the château.

Three-quarters of the wine is labelled Châteauneuf, while the remaining quarter, from geologically similar soil but separated from the rest by the road, is only entitled to the Côtes du Rhône AOC. That said, it is quite clear that this wine, bearing the *lieu-dit* Coudoulet, is of a comparable quality to the Châteauneufs.

CHÂTEAU DE BEAUCASTEL CHÂTEAUNEUF-DU-PAPE ROUGE

This blend, dominated by Grenache and Mourvèdre, is charming even when young but is at its best after a few years of ageing. Dark red with purple tinges, its aromas subtly evoke spices and dried fruit. The fruit keeps its freshness and offers a rich fullness on the palate. The flesh of Bigarreau cherry mingles with the pleasing flavour of jellied red fruit. The spices emphasize the fruit with a mineral resonance that is hidden, like pebbles in the soil.

CHÂTEAU DE BEAUCASTEL CHÂTEAUNEUF-DU-PAPE BLANC, ROUSSANNE VIEILLES VIGNES

An iconic wine produced by Roussanne vines over 100 years old; this great southern white should be kept for ten years, but it possesses a charming spontaneity even when young. A coppery-gold colour, it exudes aromas of honey, beeswax, and white flowers. The rich palate offers ample structure and delicious flavours, with hazelnut, peach, rose jam, saffron, and hints of pepper. An iodine note may recall the distant marine origins of the soil's substrata. There is also the freshness provided by citrus fruits, specifically mandarin, kumquat, and lime, made crisp by a subtle bitterness.

VINSOBRES AOC

SOUTHERN RHÔNE

Vinsobres, which is one of the two most recent appellations in the Rhône (2005), has been a great success. A limited area of 1,087 acres (440 ha) consists of well-drained soils, often located at high altitudes (up to 1,640 ft or 500 m), combined with an environment protected from the Mistral winds to ensure that the wine has good structure. As with all recent appellations, this represents good value. Note that the rules establishing the AOC specifies that young vines can produce Vinsobres only after seven years, which is particularly demanding.

> **GRAPE VARIETIES** Grenache Noir (at least 50 per cent), Mourvèdre, and Syrah, with 5 per cent white grape varieties.

> **SOIL** Clay mixed with pebbles or sand.

> **STYLE** Wine with a nose of red and black fruit, supported by a great mineral depth and a well-structured palate – without heaviness.

Colour: *Red.*

Serving temperature: *57 to 61°F (14 to 16°C).*

Ageing potential: *8 to 10 years.*

GIGONDAS AOC

SOUTHERN RHÔNE

This appellation is located northwest of the Dentelles de Montmirail, and its vineyards are situated between 330 and 1,640 ft (100 and 500 m) in altitude on the side of the massif. The red wines may be enjoyed within three years of the harvest, sometimes five years for firm vintages. It also produces rosés.

> **GRAPE VARIETIES** Grenache Noir (mostly), Syrah, and Mourvèdre, as well as other varieties from the Rhône Valley (except Carignan).

> **SOIL** Red clay dotted with limestone, sand, and pebbles.

> **STYLE** These wines are rather heady, often with nice red fruit notes and good tannic structure.

Colour: *Red and rosé.*

Serving temperature: *46 to 50°F (8 to 10°C) for the rosés; 57 to 61°F (14 to 16°C) for the reds.*

Ageing potential: *8 to 10 years.*

CHÂTEAUNEUF-DU-PAPE AOC

SOUTHERN RHÔNE

This appellation is defined more by the method used to classify AOCs than by the actual extent to which commonalities are found here; but it does follow a certain geologic logic. It is certainly more relevant than any claimed differences attributed to the 13 grape varieties that make Châteauneuf – especially the reds, most of which are dominated by Grenache. Red Châteauneuf wines should be kept from 5 to 10 years depending on the vintage. The white wines are good, mostly aged in barrel, like the reds, but they can be consumed as soon as they go on sale.

> **GRAPE VARIETIES** Grenache Noir, Syrah, Mourvèdre, Terret Noir, Counoise, Muscardin, Vaccarèse, and Cinsaut for the reds; Picpoul Blanc, Clairette, Roussanne, Bourboulenc, and Picardan for the whites.

> **SOIL** On a base of Urgonian limestone (shells), various sands and clays were deposited as sediment. Also pebbles of quartzite and silica from the Alps.

> **STYLE** The limestone *terroir* is well suited for producing white wines that are full of flavour, yet possess a good level of freshness. Clay, which is very common in the southern part of the appellation, produces a structured red wine that is both warm and deep. This represents the classic wines of Châteauneuf-du-Pape. But a current trend is to redevelop the sandy *terroirs*, situated to the northwest of the AOC, which will produce finer, lighter, and spicier wines.

Colour: *Red and white.*

Serving temperature: *50 to 54°F (10 to 12°C) for the whites; 57 to 61°F (14 to 16°C) for the reds. (For young wines, decant for 1 or 2 hours.)*

Ageing potential: *More than 10 years for the whites; More than 20 years for the reds.*

SOUTHERN RHÔNE

BEAUMES-DE-VENISE AOC

This appellation is one of the most recently established (2005). As with the vineyards of Gigondas and Vacqueyras, it lies at the foot of the Dentelles de Montmirail. We also should point out the extremely reliable uniformity of the wines here – a result of the very farsighted set-up of the AOC, both in terms of production regulations and official review of the wines. The vineyards' altitude lends the reds a crispness and freshness that is the local signature.

> **GRAPE VARIETIES** Grenache Noir (at least 50 per cent), Syrah (at most 25 per cent), and all the other Côtes du Rhône grape varieties among reds; white grape varieties are, at most, 5 per cent of production.

> **SOIL** Clays mixed with sand or limestone pebbles that have come down from the Dentelles de Montmirail into this Triassic (200 million years old) *terroir.* It is generally a mixture of gypsum, clay, and limestone.

> **STYLE** Wines have the flavour of very ripe red fruits, with notes of kirsch and often an interesting mineral structure. Depending on the *terroirs*, the wines are either light (clay), concentrated (limestone rocks), or for laying down with a great structure and finesse (Triassic).

Colour:
Red.

Serving temperature:
57 to 61°F (14 to 16°C).

Ageing potential:
2 to 10 years. Wines from (Terres de) Trias 5 years wait and 15 years laying down.

SOUTHERN RHÔNE

VACQUEYRAS AOC

To the west of the Dentelles de Montmirail, this appellation occupies 3,459 acres (1,400 ha), and is close to its neighbour to the north, Gigondas AOC. But it's distinguished by a slightly warmer climate, and hence the style of its wines. The whites are enjoyed immediately; the reds need three to six years to be ready.

> **GRAPE VARIETIES** Grenache Noir (at least 50 per cent), Syrah, and Mourvèdre for the reds and rosés; Grenache Blanc, Clairette, Bourboulenc, Marsanne, Roussanne, and Viognier for the whites.

> **SOIL** Red clay dotted with limestone pebbles and sand.

> **STYLE** These wines have black fruit flavours, with smokey and even gamey notes. The palate finishes marked by licorice and pepper.

Colour:
Red, rosé, and white.

Serving temperature:
46 to 50°F (8 to 10°C) for the whites and rosés; 57 to 61°F (14 to 16°C) for the reds.

Ageing potential:
3 years for the rosés; 7 to 8 years for the whites; 8 to 10 years for the reds.

Château de la Gardine

The style of this Châteauneuf-du-Pape estate is a successful union of finesse and power. Located in the town of Châteauneuf, the property's vineyards combine the three types of soil (limestone, sand, and clay with pebbles) found for the AOC. This enables the development of wines (both white and red) that are very balanced and highly representative of the appellation. The search for balance is also found in the methods of vinification: Patrick, Philippe, and Maxime Brunel are followers of current best practice, such as cold soaking or total de-stalking of some vintages. They cultivate the art of 'Castelneuvois' blending of grapes for winemaking, a practice dating from a time when vines were planted *'en masse'*, regardless of variety. Pursuit of balance does not prevent use of the imagination; in recent years the estate produced a wine made without any addition of sulphur, called 'Peur bleue' (blue fear) in reference to the terror inspired by this risky winemaking procedure! Their Châteauneuf-du-Pape wines are sold at very high prices; but their line includes productions of white, rosé, and red Château St-Roch Lirac and a delicious, low-priced Côtes-du-Rhône.

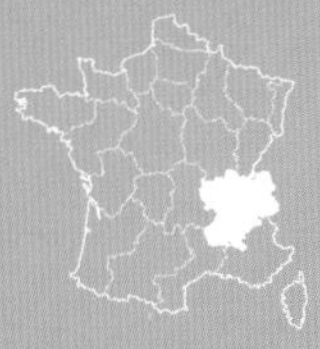

Rhône Valley

CLOS *MONT-OLIVET*

The discreet, family-owned Mont-Olivet produces wines that are both restrained and full-bodied; they are some of the most appealing from Châteauneuf-du-Pape when aged.

CLOS MONT-OLIVET

3, chemin du Bois de la Ville
84 230 Châteauneuf-du-Pape

Area: *79 acres (32 ha)*
Production: *180,000 bottles p.a.*
Appellation: *Châteauneuf-du-Pape*
Red grape varieties: *Grenache, Syrah, Cinsaut, Carignan, Counoise, Vaccarèse, Muscardin, Picpoul Noir, Terret Noir*
White grape varieties: *Bourboulenc, Roussanne, Viognier, Clairette, Grenache Blanc, Picpoul Blanc, Picardan*

A family story

Although the name Mont des Oliviers (Mount of Olives) appears in a 16th-century notarial document, Clos du Mont-Olivet was not established until the beginning of the 20th century. Séraphin Sabon, who lived in the Sérignan-du-Comtat commune, married Marie Jausset, the daughter of a Châteauneuf-du-Pape landowner, and set up the estate in 1932. Three generations later, Céline, Mylène, David, and Thierry, their great-grandchildren, now oversee the family business. Today the estate is a familiar presence on the outskirts of the village of Châteauneuf-du-Pape. This is where Thierry can be found, having abandoned his physics studies to return to the vineyard and cellar, after completing a BTS in Viticulture and Oenology and several courses in South Africa and Australia. He is now the cellar master, but it was a few years before he produced his first wine in his own right, which he did in 2001. Working practices have developed under his guidance, but with caution and without resorting to any drastic change. Each generation leaves its mark with its own innovations: 'I was not going to come back here telling everyone that I knew it all! My great-grandfather was already making wine, but I knew that mine would be different from the wine made by my father and uncle,' explains Thierry. Mutual respect remains a key part of the family tradition and has ensured that the estate develops appropriately.

A patchwork of vineyards

The estate covers around 74 acres (30 ha), two-thirds of which lie in Châteauneuf-du-Pape, with the remainder in Côtes du Rhône and Vin de France, and produces ten wines in total. Very fragmented, the plots include all types of soils, microclimates, and orientations of the appellation. From localities such as Palestor, to the north, to La Crau, to the east via Montalivet, and others, almost all the authorized grape varieties are cultivated, including 100-year-old Grenache, Mourvèdre, and Syrah, along with Muscardin, Counoise, and Vaccarèse.

Harnessing the power of the Mediterranean sun, this extraordinary patchwork of micro-terroirs produces wines with a specific 'Southern' profile, but without sacrificing any of their elegance. The Mont-Olivet wines don't have the overly assertive side that is cultivated elsewhere, and the choices made during vinification always reflect the year's conditions. Time is the best friend of these wines and it makes no sense to drink them young. Instead, they should be laid down and allowed to rest for several years, except perhaps for Le Petit Mont, which, for those wine-lovers with slightly less patience, can be enjoyed a few months after bottling.

CLOS MONT-OLIVET LA CUVÉE DU PAPET, CHÂTEAUNEUF-DU-PAPE ROUGE

Typical of the estate, and created in 1989, this wine is produced from only the finest vintages, and is at its best after a good ten years (or much longer). It then delivers a great complexity of aromas: dried fruits, fig, date, hazelnut, and a hint of caramel. The freshness of the palate is astonishing. Its juiciness overpowers the tannic structure with a velvety veneer. Several spices coat the lingering yet refreshing fruit with a delicate bitterness. A great wine.

CLOS MONT-OLIVET LE PETIT MONT, CHÂTEAUNEUF-DU-PAPE ROUGE

Created in 2005 and the latest Châteauneuf-du-Pape to be produced by the estate, Le Petit Mont consists of 95% young Grenache, supplemented by 5% Syrah, and is matured in barrels and casks, without using new wood. It has a ruby-red colour and is perfumed with ripened cherries and almond paste. The palate is charmingly fresh and has crushed red-fruit flavours, surrounded by silky tannins, with a hint of bitterness making it even more full-bodied.

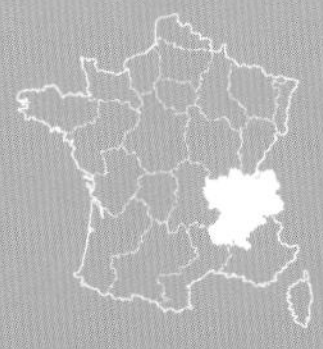

Rhône Valley

M. CHAPOUTIER

The dynamic Michel Chapoutier has revived this old Rhône Valley wine producer and transformed it into a world-famous name.

M. CHAPOUTIER

18, avenue Dr. Paul Durand
26000 Tain

Area (France): *593 acres (240 ha)*
Production: *8 million bottles p.a.*
Appellation: *Hermitage*
Red grape varieties: *Syrah, Grenache (predominantly)*
White grape varieties: *Viognier, Marsanne (predominantly)*

'Fac et spera'

'Do and hope' is the motto on the Chapoutier family coat of arms. Established in 1808, this estate has become a key player in the Rhône Valley under the guidance of Michel Chapoutier, its current owner. Heir to a magnificent vineyard, at the heart of which lies the key property of Hermitage, he has awoken this sleeping giant with self-taught skills: energy combined with passion and deeply held convictions. For Michel, being able to bring out the best of the *terroir's* qualities was of paramount importance and his initial task was to make a careful study of the vineyard, in Hermitage in particular, where he separated out the different plots according to soil configuration. As a result he was able to produce great wines from individual plots at the very top of the range. Meticulous observation of the effect of the *terroir* on the wines led him to review all the vineyard's practices. In the 1990s, well before it became fashionable, the vineyard was transferred to first organic and then biodynamic cultivation.

Since then, Michel has gradually rebuilt and expanded his range adhering to these fundamental principles and one key credo: each wine produced, regardless of quantity, should reflect its origin and vintage.

Conquering the world

It was not long before Michel Chapoutier's appetite for new discoveries and projects had outgrown the Rhône Valley. He acquired vineyards in Roussillon (the Bila-Haut estate) and set out to conquer Australia, where he teamed up with several of the best Australian producers before acquiring the Tournon estate, a vineyard in Victoria. More recently, he has broken new ground in Portugal, and bought Trénel in Mâconnais, while taking on the presidency of the *Union des Maisons de Négoce de la Vallée du Rhône* (the Rhône Valley Wine Merchants' Association) and, since 2014, that of Inter-Rhône (the professional association representing AOC wines in the Rhône Valley).

Michel is certainly a resourceful man. Lauded by the press and financially successful, he has earned a global reputation. There have been a few challenges along the way, yet he has never forgotten the importance of teamwork. His range of wines is broad, and generally exceptionally consistent, whether blended or from his own estate, from the simple Côtes du Rhône Belleruche to the high-end wines from particular plots (Hermitage, Côte-Rôtie, Châteauneuf-du-Pape...), not to mention a delightful version of Crozes-Hermitage. Lovers of Australian Shiraz and fine Portuguese wines will also find much to enjoy. Remarkably, the company doubled its production in four years, while maintaining a very high level of quality.

M. CHAPOUTIER
LE MÉAL, HERMITAGE ROUGE

This is one of the wines from the estate's Méal *lieu-dit*, a south-facing hillside with pebble and clay soils. The old Syrah vines (50 years old on average) produce a deep wine, with a dark colour, and a ripe and smoky nose when young. The palate is powerful, fleshy, and well-structured with surrounding tannins and an underlying freshness. Time loosens this beautiful structure, refines the tannins, and transforms the young fruit into a typical bouquet of fireplace smoke, venison, leather, and ripe fruit.

> Michel Chapoutier, owner of the company.

TAVEL AOC

SOUTHERN RHÔNE

The only Côtes-du-Rhône appellation to produce just rosé wines, the Tavel AOC consists of three types of *terroir*. This allows for a blending of styles: full of flavour or well-structured, deep-coloured or lighter. The resulting wine is quite different from many regional rosés, pale and light, in the Provençal style. These are demonstrably gastronomic rosés, colouful and rich, with aromas of grenadine and spice. Current trends apart, the wine revels in its difference and finds more and more excellent interpretations within the appellation.

> **GRAPE VARIETIES** Grenache, Cinsaut, Clairette, Picpoul, Calitor, Bourboulenc, Mourvèdre, Syrah, and Carignan.

> **SOIL** Limestone rocks or slabs, clay pebbles, sandy soil.

> **STYLE** These are powerful rosés that are boldly coloured, have a long finish, and are ideally suited as table wines.

Colour:
Rosé.

Serving temperature:
46 to 50°F (8 to 10°C).

Ageing potential:
5 years.

LIRAC AOC

SOUTHERN RHÔNE

Lirac has had AOC status since 1947. This appellation sums up the different *terroirs* in the southern Rhône Valley. But whereas Châteauneuf, though five times larger, has found a lucrative market with consistent quality, Lirac is divided between a somewhat diluted, entry-level production and more demanding estates, often from neighbouring Castelneuvois, who want to showcase great *terroirs*. This results in moderate price levels, which are the delight of enthusiasts familiar with the 'big wines from little estates' concept.

> **GRAPE VARIETIES** Grenache Noir (at least 40 per cent), Syrah, Mourvèdre, Cinsaut, and Carignan for the reds and rosés; Clairette, Grenache Blanc, Bourboulenc, Ugni Blanc, Picpoul, Marsanne, Roussanne, and Viognier for the whites.

> **SOIL** Limestone boulders, sand, and clay scree.

> **STYLE** Lirac wines are warm and full of flavour, and structured to a varying extent.

Colour:
Red, rosé, and white.

Serving temperature:
46 to 50°F (8 to 10°C) for the rosés and whites; 57 to 61°F (14 to 16°C) for the reds.

Ageing potential:
3 years for the rosés; 3 to 6 years for the whites; 3 to 10 years for the reds.

VENTOUX OR CÔTES-DU-VENTOUX AOC

SOUTHERN RHÔNE

Since 2008, Ventoux has been the new name of the former Côtes-du-Ventoux AOC. Mount Ventoux has a traditional Mediterranean foothill landscape. The local climate has contrasting summer temperatures 41 to 50°F (5 to 10°C) in the morning up to 86 to 104°F (30 or 40°C) in the afternoon, which allows for optimal ripening of the grape tannins. The result is an original style, also present in the local AOC *vin de table*, the Muscat du Ventoux. But the appellation suffers from its vast scale (14,579 acres or 5,900 ha), more than all of the individual localities of the Côtes-du-Rhône-Villages put together, and a lack of renown, which has the effect of maintaining low prices globally. Nevertheless, it benefits from the presence of some very good wine producers who are able to play a leading and increasingly dynamic cooperative role.

> **GRAPE VARIETIES** Grenache Noir, Syrah, Cinsaut, Mourvèdre, Carignan, Picpoul Noir, Counoise for the reds and rosés; Clairette, Bourboulenc, Grenache Blanc, Roussanne for the whites.

> **SOIL** Mainly limestone.

> **STYLE** Both whites and reds have very ripe fruit flavours and a freshness on the palate.

Colour:
Red, rosé, and white.

Serving temperature:
46 to 50°F (8 to 10°C) for the rosés and whites; 57 to 61°F (14 to 16°C) for the reds.

Ageing potential:
3 years for the rosés; 3 to 5 years for the whites; 3 to 8 years for the reds.

SOUTHERN RHÔNE

LUBERON AOC

Sandwiched between the Rhône and Provence, this vast appellation covers 8,154 acres (3,300 ha). For some years now it has been oriented towards the rosés that form the majority of its production. Without any real unity of *terroir*, it also offers reds of very uneven quality, from characterless wines to luxurious examples matured in wood. The region also has an increasing number of talented producers.

> **GRAPE VARIETIES** For red and rosé: Syrah and Grenache Noir (at least 60 per cent), Mourvèdre, Carignan, Cinsaut. For white: Grenache Blanc, Ugni Blanc, Clairette, Rolle, Bourboulenc, Roussanne, Marsanne.

> **SOIL** Mainly limestone.

> **STYLE** The red wines are warm, with a significant proportion of them receiving barrel ageing. The moderately coloured rosés can have more roundness than those from Provence. The whites are a speciality of the AOC, some have obvious age, while others have successful and interesting results. They are made with some of the classic grape varietys of the Rhône as well as the Rolle.

Colour:
Red, rosé, and white.

Serving temperature:
46 to 50°F (8 to 10°C) for the rosés and whites; 57 to 61°F (14 to 16°C) for the reds.

Ageing potential:
3 years for the rosés; 3 to 8 years for the whites; 3 to 10 years for the reds.

SOUTHERN RHÔNE

COSTIÈRES-DE-NÎMES AOC

Administratively located in Languedoc-Roussillon, this vast AOC of 10,131 acres (4,100 ha) finds its geologic home in the Rhône Valley. It has a number of wines that represent good value, and some estates are increasing production.

> **GRAPE VARIETIES** Syrah, Grenache, Mourvèdre, Carignan, and Cinsaut for the reds and rosés; Grenache Blanc, Marsanne, Roussanne, Clairette, Bourboulenc, Maccabeu, and Rolle for the whites.

> **SOIL** While the surface consists of Castelneuvois silica and quartzite pebbles interspersed with gravel, the clay layer is quite thin and it is sand, which is very porous, that dominates.

> **STYLE** They have the flavour of very ripe concentrated fruit, as can be found throughout the Rhône Valley, but on rather light structures with little tannin, which means the wines need to be consumed fairly quickly. The smoothness of the whites can be significant if the maturation is well handled.

Colour:
Red, rosé, and white.

Serving temperature:
46 to 50°F (8 to 10°C) for the rosés and whites; 57 to 61°F (14 to 16°C) for the reds.

Ageing potential:
3 years for the rosés; 3 to 5 years for the whites; 3 to 8 years for the reds.

SOUTHERN RHÔNE

MUSCAT DE BEAUMES-DE-VENISE AOC

Small in scale (133,000 cases or 12,000 hl) compared to its cousins in the Languedoc-Roussillon, this principally white Muscat is made exclusively from Muscat à Petits Grains. Fortified after fermentation, it is often matured in the vat to preserve the aromatic purity of the grape variety. Some plots still produce red Muscat, allowing the development of red and rosé Muscat de Beaumes de Venise. Producing sweet wines is really popular here, and there are sometimes other interesting versions, such as a late harvest of Mourvèdre and *vin de paille*.

> **GRAPE VARIETIES** Muscat à Petits Grains.

> **SOIL** Clays mixed with sand or limestone pebbles.

> **STYLE** The white wines create a magical world of flowers (acacia, gladiolus, lime, rose, violet) and fruit (apricots, quince, candied orange peel, lemon, pear, mango), with notes of menthol, juniper, licorice and spicy nuances, even sharpness, as well as a crystallized fruit finish. The red wines and rosé wines have beautiful currant flavours.

Colour:
Red, rosé, and white.

Serving temperature:
50°F (10°C).

Ageing potential:
5 to 10 years.

SOUTHWEST FRANCE

Set between the vast expanses of Languedoc-Roussillon to the east and the famous reaches of Bordeaux to the west, the vineyards of the southwest – the most diverse in France – boast a wide variety of soils, grape varieties, and appellations. Scattered over 10 départements*, southwestern French wines maintain a character of their own, concealing a few pearls at value prices – one of the major benefits of the era of wine globalization.*

History

As with many other French wine areas, viticulture was brought here during the Roman occupation. Certain wines, such as Cahors, Madiran, and Gaillac, found great favour with the kings of France during the Middle Ages, and their fame spread throughout Europe (to England and the Netherlands, for example). But this region could not evade the domination and the envy of its prestigious neighbours in Bordeaux, who prevented access to their port until all their own wine had been sold.

The phylloxera crisis at the end of the 19th century brought about the destruction of almost every vineyard here, and winemaking would not be revitalized until the 1970s, under the aegis of dynamic cooperatives and enthusiastic winemakers who emphasized the area's quality and unique character.

SOUTHWEST FRANCE STATISTICS (AOC)

Vineyard area: 64,247 acres (26,000 ha)

Production: 11.1 million cases (1 million hl)

Reds: 56%

Whites: 26%

Rosés: 18%

(IVSO, IVBD France, France AgriMer)

Vineyard districts

Although the hallmark of southwestern France is its variety, there are four key wine-producing areas.

BERGERAC. Following both banks of the Dordogne, the area is famed for Bergerac, of course, but can also lay claim to Monbazillac, Pécharmant, Montravel, and many others.

GARONNE. Set along both banks of the Garonne from Langon to Agen, the vineyards here are upstream from Bordeaux and include the territory of Côtes-de-Duras, Côtes-du-Marmandais, and Buzet wines.

HAUT-PAYS. This zone to the north and northwest of Toulouse includes Gaillac, Frontons, and Cahors.

PYRENEES. Found to the south between the Adour and the Pyrenees, this area includes a number of leading appellations: Madiran, Irouléguy, Pacherenc-du-Vic-Bilh, Jurançon, and others.

> Vines at Château de Haute-Serre, in the Cahors region.

Climate and soils

The climate naturally varies among the banks of the Garonne, the Basque country, and the Pyrenees, but a maritime climate with continental and Alpine influences dominates. There

The Health of South-West IGP Wines

The South-West's many IGP wines form the vast majority of its production. Among them, the Côtes de Gascogne is very healthy indeed and exports more than 70 per cent of its production (7.7 million cases/700,000 hl). The region's white wines, light, lively, and aromatic (85 per cent of the IGP's production), at a very attractive price, have put a smile back on the faces of the wine-producers of the Gers.

> **DID YOU KNOW...?**
>
> ***Tannat, a grape variety from Madiran, has been identified as being particularly effective against some cardiovascular conditions.** It's a claim made in 2006 by a Dr. Corder from a London (UK) medical facility. Tannat has a high concentration of procyanidine, one of the polyphenols with antioxidant properties found in wine. The action of this compound is reinforced by traditional winemaking methods, as these maintain its levels in the wine.*

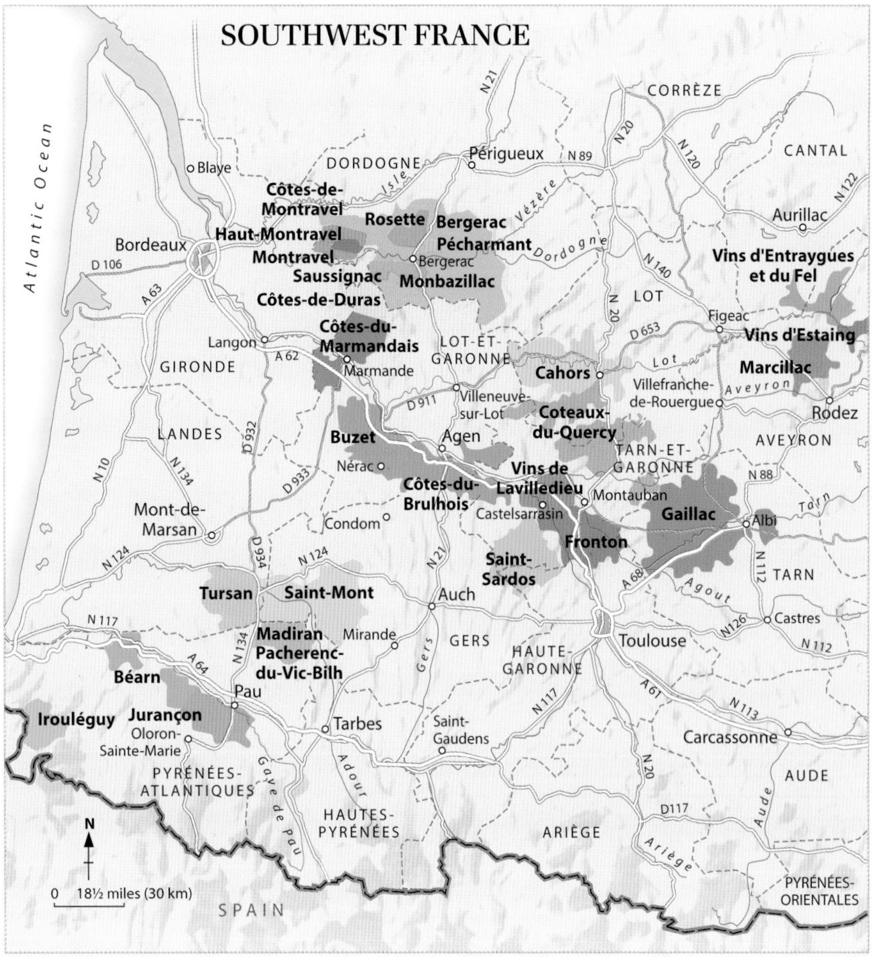

are humid springs and wet winters, as well as hot summers and long, glorious, and sun-drenched autumns. The diversity of the soils supports the plurality of these wines, with a general preponderance of *molasse*, limestone, and alluvial soils on the terraces formed by the many rivers and watercourses.

Grape varieties

Bordeaux varieties grow side by side with local grapes here; and this gives the wines their unique character.

FRENCH COLOMBARD lends dry white wines aromas of grapefruit and exotic fruits.

DURAS is a key to Gaillac, producing light reds with fine tannins and spicy aromas (pepper).

FER SERVADOU Also known as Pinenc and Mansois, this variety originally hails from the Basque country and produces fruity red wines with deep colours and tannins.

GROS MANSENG Another native of the Pyrenees, this grape is used to make dry white wines; but it has also been pressed into service with Courbu and Petit Manseng to make sweet whites.

LEN DE L'EL (also known as Len de l'Eh or Loin de l'Oeil) The grape at the heart of Gaillacs and Gaillac-Premières-Côtes.

MALBEC Also known as Auxerrois and Côt Noir, this grape is the staple variety for Cahors wines – to which it lends characteristic aromas and colour.

MAUZAC A Gaillac grape sought for its power and its aromatic character of apples and pears; it is used to make dry whites and sparkling wines.

NÉGRETTE A Fronton variety that produces very spicy and aromatic reds (violet, licorice).

PETIT MANSENG This Pyrenean grape is the foundation of white wines from Jurançon; when affected by noble rot (botrytized), it produces sweet wines of great subtlety with characteristic aromas of crystallized and exotic fruit, cinnamon, honey, and citrus zest.

TANNAT A native of Béarn, this variety is used for blends in a number of different appellations (including Béarn, Madiran, and Irouléguy). It produces a tannic wine with deep colouration and raspberry aromas (*see also* box above).

Wine styles

Southwestern France produces a great variety of wines – reds, rosés and whites, with a good range of sweet wines. Made with Tannat, Malbec, and Cabernet Sauvignon, the reds are powerful, structured, and tannic. They have an aromatic and spicy nose, and are ideal for laying down. There are also lighter wines that can be enjoyed younger, and these are sometimes reminiscent of certain Bordeaux.

The dry white wines offer much in the way of variety of expression. Most are well balanced with a freshness and aromas that depend on the grape variety and maturation method. The sweet wines are fine and elegant, and some, thanks to their richness, are a match for their neighbours from Sauternes.

Southwestern France's AOCs

- Béarn
- Béarn-Bellocq
- Bergerac
- Brulhois
- Buzet
- Cahors
- Coteaux du Quercy
- Côtes-de-Bergerac
- Côtes-de-Duras
- Côtes de Millau
- Fronton
- Entraygues-Le Fel
- Estaing
- Côtes-du-Marmandais
- Côtes-de-Montravel
- Gaillac
- Gaillac doux
- Gaillac mousseux
- Gaillac-Premières-Côtes
- Haut-Montravel
- Irouléguy
- Jurançon
- Jurançon sec (dry Jurançon)
- Madiran
- Marcillac
- Monbazillac
- Montravel
- Pacherenc-du-Vic-Bilh
- Pécharmant
- Rosette
- Saint-Mont
- Saint-Sardos
- Saussignac
- Tursan

Famous wines of southwestern France

Beyond the leading appellations of Madiran, Jurançon, and Gaillac, this region boasts a multitude of wines worth discovering for their originality, unique character, and easy-drinking quality.

BERGERAC

BERGERAC AND CÔTES-DE-BERGERAC AOCs

At the heart of Périgord, along the border with Bordeaux – from which it has adopted many grape varieties – Bergerac's vineyards extend over some 19,768 acres (8,000 ha). The landscape is one of sunny hills and plateaus on both sides of the Dordogne Valley, forming a strip about 6 to 9 miles (10 to 15 km) long around the town of Bergerac. It is made up of a mosaic of microclimates, and produces both red and white wines. The most sophisticated reds are grouped under the Côtes-de-Bergerac AOC red label, which represents the top flight of the appellation. The Côtes-de-Bergerac AOC white is used to make sweet wine.

> **GRAPE VARIETIES** Cabernet Sauvignon, Cabernet Franc, Merlot, Malbec, Fer, and Merille for reds and rosés; Sémillon, Sauvignon Blanc, Muscadelle, Ondenc, Chenin Blanc, and Trebbiano for whites.

> **SOIL** Clay, limestone, and sand in the northern Dordogne; *molasse*, marl, and limestone in the south.

> **STYLE** The reds are supple, easy to drink, and rather fruity, with notes of strawberries, blackcurrants, and other berry fruits. Often matured in barrel, Côtes-de-Bergerac wines are more tannic with complex aromas (ripe fruits, toasted notes, spices), and further ageing can be beneficial. Made by the *saignée* (draining the vats) technique, the rosés have a salmon-pink colour with crisp fruit flavour (raspberries, wild strawberries) supported by fresh aromas. The dry whites are lively with a charming nose and good length in the mouth. The sweet Côtes-de-Bergerac whites combine freshness, finesse, and full body with a fairly pronounced bouquet.

Colour:
Red, rosé, and white.

Serving temperature:
46°F (8°C) for sweet whites; 50 to 54°F (10 to 12°C) for dry whites and rosés; 59 to 63°F (15 to 17°C) for reds.

Ageing potential:
Rosés within a year; reds and whites within 2 to 3 years; Côtes-de-Bergerac within 5 to 6 years.

BERGERAC

MONBAZILLAC AOC

This appellation is one of the oldest in the region. After falling out of favour for a while, Monbazillac has regained its reputation and is now one of the best-known of all the Dordogne wines. The vineyards are dispersed around five villages located in the steep hills of the Dordogne Valley, south of Bergerac: Pomport, Rouffignac, Colombier, St-Laurent-des-Vignes, and Monbazillac.

The temperate climate is conducive to developing the noble rot necessary to make the finest sweet wines. In good years, Monbazillac is a match for some Sauternes, especially the Monbazillac *Sélection de Grains Nobles.*

> **GRAPE VARIETIES** Sémillon, Sauvignon Blanc, Muscadelle.

> **SOIL** Clay-limestone with high clay content.

> **STYLE** These golden, sweet wines exude a complex bouquet of white flowers, almonds, hazelnuts, honey, and gentle spices. They boast a nice balance of liveliness and power, with a long and aromatic finish.

Colour:
White.

Serving temperature:
43 to 46°F (6 to 8°C)

Ageing potential:
5 to 30 years.

BUZET AOC

GARONNE

Buzet is the oldest and the most famous of the appellations to emerge from the Garonne. It only just avoided falling to the phylloxera crisis, but recovered thanks to the dedication of members of the powerful Vignerons de Buzet growers' association. They never ceased in their efforts to restore it to its former vigour. The AOC now covers 5,000 acres (2,000 ha) situated between the left bank of the Garonne and the edge of the Landes *département*. Buzet produces wine in all three colours, with reds being dominant.

> **GRAPE VARIETIES** Merlot, Cabernet Franc, Cabernet Sauvignon for reds and rosés; Sémillon and Sauvignon Blanc for whites.

> **SOIL** Gravelly, clay-limestone, *boulbène*.

> **STYLE** Reds are powerful and full-bodied, featuring red and black fruit tones with spicy and smokey notes resting on a good framework of tannins. As they age, the tannins grow more supple and the wine gains in aromatic complexity, tending toward forest floor, humus, and game scents. Wines of this calibre are a match for their Bordeaux cousins. The whites are fresh with aromas of fruit and white flowers, and the rosés have a powerfully aromatic nose.

Colour: *Red, rosé, and white.*

Serving temperature: *46 to 50°F (8 to 10°C) for whites and rosés; 59 to 63°F (15 to 17°C) for reds.*

Ageing potential: *1 to 2 years for the whites and rosés; 3 to 6 years for the reds.*

CAHORS AOC

HAUT-PAYS

Nicknamed 'black tie' by the British because of its almost ebony appearance, Cahors wines were a favourite of King Francis I of France and also the Russian court. This is one of the oldest wines in France. The appellation cultivates 9,884 acres (4,000 ha) of land on each side of the Lot Valley south of Quercy. It produces 1.6 million cases (150,000 hl) of exclusively red wine. A number of producers under the aegis of Pascal Verhaeghe (Château du Cèdre) have banded together to set up the 'Cahors Excellence' seal of quality, establishing extremely strict specifications for the production of top wines.

> **GRAPE VARIETIES** Malbec (known here as Auxerrois or Côt Noir), Merlot, Tannat.

> **SOIL** Limestone, alluvial, and *gallet* soils in Lot; clay and limestone elsewhere.

> **STYLE** Cahors is traditionally a powerful and generous wine, with a deep red-garnet hue that can be almost black. The nose shows aromas of macerated red and stone fruits, typical characteristics of the Malbec from which it is made. The tannins soften and the nose becomes more complex with age – with notes of prunes, chocolate, humus, and licorice, and all acquiring good length in the mouth. Today, you also will find Cahors that are predominantly made with Merlot grapes, and these are more supple and easy to drink.

Colour: *Red.*

Serving temperature: *59 to 63°F (15 to 17°C). Best decanted.*

Ageing potential: *3 to 15 years, or more for great vintages.*

FRONTON AOC

HAUT-PAYS

This is the signature wine of Toulouse. Located between the Tarn and the Garonne, the vineyards of Fronton cover 3,954 acres (1,600 ha) of terraces – with soils particularly favourable for Négrette, the local grape that lends the wine its distinct characteristics. Annual production totals 777,000 cases (70,000 hl) of red and rosé.

> **GRAPE VARIETIES** Négrette, Cabernet Franc, Cabernet Sauvignon, Syrah, Gamay, Fer, Malbec, Cinsaut.

> **SOIL** Gravel, iron-rich soils, *boulbène*.

> **STYLE** Reds are supple, elegant, and typical of their variety, the Négrette, with a deep, ruby red colour. The nose mixes aromas of red fruit, flowers (violets and peonies), and spices (licorice and pepper). The rosés are lively, with a charming bouquet that combines white flowers with red and exotic fruits.

Colour: *Red and rosé.*

Serving temperature: *46 to 50°F (8 to 10°C) for rosés; 59 to 63°F (15 to 17°C) for reds. Best decanted.*

Ageing potential: *Rosés should be enjoyed within a year; reds can be kept for 4 to 5 years.*

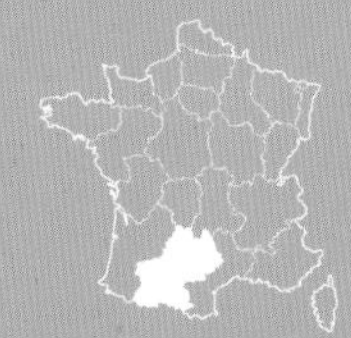

Southwest

DOMAINE
PLAGEOLES

The Gaillac vineyard of Plageoles, which lies on both banks of the Tarn, may be the oldest vineyard in France. It has found a tireless advocate in the Plageoles family.

DOMAINE PLAGEOLES

Très Cantous
81140 Cahuzac-sur-Vere

Area: *67 acres (27 ha)*
Production: *90,000 bottle p.a.*
Appellation: *Gaillac*
Red grape varieties: *Prunelard, Mauzac Noir, Duras, Syrah, Braucol (Fer)*
White grape varieties: *Mauzac, Verdanel, Len de l'El, Ondenc, Muscadelle*

The Plageoles story

The Plageoles family has been in Gaillac for a long time. It was as far back as 1820 that one of their ancestors, Jules, bought 10 acres (4 ha) of land here. Today, the history of the estate revolves around four generations, each contributing in part to the development of this superb wine-making operation. Essential to this story is Marcel Plageoles, who played a vital role in preserving old local grape varieties. His son Robert, a key figure in the region, has built upon this valuable heritage. Robert is the memory, brains, and 'spanner in the works' of the Gaillacois. A keen advocate of massal selection when everyone else swore by cloning, he tirelessly selected cuttings and traversed vineyards throughout Montpellier, scouring the area in search of old vines. He is responsible for the restoration of local grape varieties, including Ondenc and Prunelard, which produce wines that are charming and distinctive. His son, Bernard, and his wife, Myriam, became involved in the 1990s and have been joined recently by their own sons. They have put the finishing touches to the family enterprise by expanding the vineyard to 67 acres (27 ha), switching to organic cultivation, and extending the range of wines.

A pleasing range

A century of development has given wine-lovers a delightful evocation of this AOC, which is truly original, through the autochthonous grape varieties that the Plageoles have chosen to explore as mono-varietals, if necessary under the Vin de France designation. Bernard Plageoles has refined the vinification and the whole range (about 15 wines) is highly recommended. The estate has built its reputation on whites produced in all their forms: dry, *moelleux*, and sparkling, not to mention the original *vin de voile* produced like *vin jaune*, with astonishing longevity. The Mauzac grape variety, or to be more exact grape varieties, since there are several versions, can produce all these variations, including a legendary sweet wine, Vin d'Autan. The others are Verdanel, Len de l'El, Ondenc, and Muscadelle, with special mention for the sweet and *moelleux* wines, which offer remarkable purity and balance.

The red wines now follow a similar pattern. Prunelard, Mauzac Noir, Duras, Syrah, and Braucol (Fer) are always vinified using single grape varieties. The aim is to extract the most clearly defined character, using indigenous yeasts and inert maturation for wines that are unpretentious, easily drinkable, and often fresh and spicy, with added structure in the case of the Prunelard.

DOMAINE PLAGEOLES, MAUZAC NATURE

One of the estate's key wines, this sparkling is made according to the Gaillac method in which the wine is bottled before it has finished fermenting. Pure Mauzac, suitable for any occasion, it bursts with the variety's typical apple and pear notes. It has a charming, fresh palate with a very light sweetness that enhances the appreciation of the fruit.

DOMAINE PLAGEOLES, MUSCADELLE, GAILLAC DOUX

Rarely vinified alone because of its inconsistency, the Muscadelle grape is at its best here, offering crystallized and musky aromas along with a texture that is both rich and light, all supported by a perfect freshness. A delicious sensation of fullness and lightness.

> Bernard Plageoles, head of the estate.

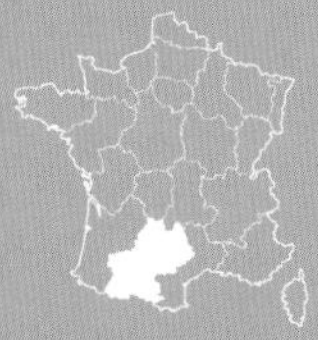

CHÂTEAU *DU CÈDRE*

Located in the Midi-Pyrénées, in the eastern part of a wine region delineated by the Lot Valley, Château du Cèdre is the spearhead of the Cahors appellation. It owes its singular characteristics to the absolute predominance of Malbec, a grape capable of making reds of real class.

CHÂTEAU DU CÈDRE

Bru
41700 Vire-sur-Lot

Area: *67 acres (27 ha)*
[4 acres/1.6 ha to white grapes]
Production: *130,000 bottles p.a.*
Appellation: *Cahors*
Red grape varieties: *Malbec, Merlot, Tannat*
White grape varieties: *Viognier, Muscadelle, Sauvignon, Sémillon*

Bringing a wine region back to life

The reputation of Cahors wine goes back to the Middle Ages, when it was dubbed 'black wine' due to its opaque appearance. Its robust composition meant that it could safely travel from France, via the port of Bordeaux, to dining tables in England and even those of the Court of the Russian Tsars! At the end of the 19th century – and before they were wiped out completely by phylloxera – the vineyards covered some 160,619 acres (65,000 ha), about half the size of the current Bordeaux wine region. As a result, replanting was a laborious task that was nearly halted in its tracks by an exceptional frost in 1956 that once again reduced it to nothing. This new challenge slowed its qualification for AOC status, which was not achieved until 1971. With 11,120 acres (4,500 ha) under cultivation, it is slowly regaining its former brilliance thanks to the estates that have invested so much money into the Malbec cause.

Genesis

Léon Verhaeghe left Belgium for the Lot Valley in the 1950s. His son Charles laid the first stone of what was to become Château du Cèdre by planting a modest 2.5-acre (1-ha) vineyard on the poor-quality, stony soil of a polyculture business. This technique, a mark of quality, had not been common in the days when productivist viticulture predominated but was now to be tried on the fertile parts of the estate's vineyards. The estate had to content itself with modest yields of which only a part was bottled, starting with the 1973 vintage, a legacy passed on in 1988 to his sons Jean-Marc and Pascal.

Terroir and vines

The Cahors wine-making area extends over a series of hills on which terraces rise to gentle heights overlooking the Lot River. Around half of Château du Cèdre's vineyards (35 acres/14 ha) are located on the highest slopes (known as the 'third terraces'), said to be best for producing rich, well-structured wines, while the remainder (32 acres/13 ha) is made up of two plots of cultivated land at the base of the foothills of the Causses, with cones of limestone scree slopes that have the potential to produce fine wines. The majority of the vines on the estate were planted during the 1980s and massal selection was generally used; their meticulous approach to wine-making has also complied with the stipulations of organic agriculture since 2000, although the estate was not officially certified until 2012.

A complementary pairing

There is a perfect division of labour in running the estate, with Jean-Marc taking charge of the vines and Pascal looking after the cellar. The latter trained at Saintsbury, a highly regarded Californian winery, where he learnt how to make and age wine. He put his experience to good use on his return and set Château du Cèdre on course to make quality wines from the outset. The estate has never looked back since, acquiring an enviable reputation as a leading appellation. Its progress has been punctuated by the creation of wines that have revealed new heights of ambition at every turn, and 1996 saw the arrival of Le Cèdre, a wine made exclusively from the plots with the greatest wine-making potential, followed in 2000 by 'GC', conceived and produced to perfectionist standards. Nonetheless, these exceptional, indeed extraordinary, Cahors wines should not be thought of as outliers or extravagant creations. They are the epitome of balance and elegance. Elitism is not the Verhaeghe brothers' only pursuit – they have been at pains since 1995 to produce a more accessible range of wines through a small business supplied by their wine-making partners.

CHÂTEAU DU CÈDRE, LE CÈDRE, CAHORS

The first production year of this wine came in 1996, and its 'Cahors' identity takes centre stage. Made entirely with Malbec grapes, it unites the individual virtues of the two terroirs typical of the estate: robustness from the high terraces and finesse from the lower slopes. In addition, the older vines deliver extra vigour. This wine is the result of patient work, a long vinification process followed by careful maturation in Burgundy casks for nearly two years. It is the logical extension of a philosophy that grants nature its proper place and is the product of carefully considered techniques, with deep concentrations of fruit and a powerful but harmonious texture that guarantees it can be laid down for long periods. It is set to be the ambassador for Cahors' finest wines.

> Pascal and Jean-Marc Verhaeghe, who run the château.

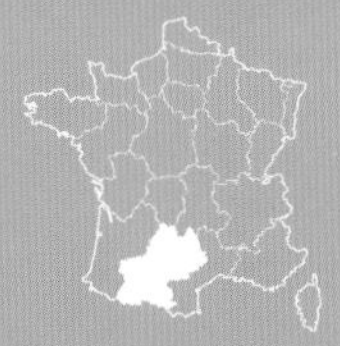

Southwest

THE QUINTESSENCE OF PETIT MANSENG
DOMAINE CAUHAPÉ

Henri Ramonteu, a Jurançon winemaker, is the creator of Cauhapee's Quintessence du Petit Manseng, a signature wine. A delicious, fascinating nectar, it can only be produced if nature is willing and with very exacting methods.

DOMAINE CAUHAPÉ

Quartier Castet
64360 Monein

Area: *106 acres (43 ha)*
Production:
200,000 bottles p.a.
Appellation: *Jurançon*
White grape varieties: *Petit Manseng, Gros Manseng, Courbu, Camaralet, Lauzet*

The golden liquid that flows at the foot of the Pyrenees

'These are the fruits of extreme harvests,' says Henri Ramonteu of the jewel of his estate, a wine that is justly dubbed the Quintessence of Petit Manseng. 'We pick the grapes in several passes during December, until Christmas, and sometimes even in January.' The grapes are 'raisined' – there's no botrytis here – and the result is that the sugar content explodes and the aromas are concentrated in extraordinary ways. The yield is of course very low, around half a ton per acre (8 hl/ha), but the terroir is exceptional – a valley located at an elevation of 1,300 feet (400m), with silica-rich clay soils made up of 40% yellow clay that lends strength and vigour to the Petit Manseng grapes. The valley is open to the south, and the sun shines and the Foehn wind blows with full force. The warm winds that come up the passes from Spain speed up the drying process while the frosts at the end of autumn wither the skin of the grapes and preserve its concentration of acidity.

To achieve such results (which border on the miraculous), much effort is required to help nature along. 'We do lots of work on these plots of land,' explains the wine-maker. 'Meticulous leaf-trimming, removing foliage from each bunch, allows the sun to penetrate and thus harden the skins of the grapes – without which it won't withstand the elements. And we cover the vines in nets so that the birds don't pick the grapes before we do.'

Fabulous richness

However, the harvest is not guaranteed – bad weather can destroy everything or the quality may not live up to expectations. 'We only manage to make Quintessence six years out of ten,' reminds Henri Ramonteu. 'There was none in 2012 or 2013.' Once the grapes have been picked by hand in a series of passes, they are taken away in small baskets and the wine is transferred to new oak casks where it ferments. The wine will then go on to age and mature for two years. The wine's fabulous richness allows it to benefit from this ageing without being tainted by the wood, creating a bewitching texture in the mouth and extraordinary results.

Henri Ramonteu grows eight other sweet and dry wines on the 106 acres (43 ha) of the Cauhapé estate; Canopée, one of the dry wines, has a powerfully aromatic strength that is always harmonious. Harvested at full ripeness and fermented and aged in barrel on the lees, Petit Manseng develops an intense bouquet, taking on hints of yellow-fleshed fruits and spices, with a broad and flavourful mouthfeel and a long, fresh finish with citrus notes: a dry white wine of the very best, both original and enchanting.

DOMAINE CAUHAPÉ, QUINTESSENCE DU PETIT MANSENG, JURANÇON

This wine can look the greatest sweet wines in the world in the eye while retaining the characteristics of its grape variety and local origins. Its astonishing acidity lends it ideal balance, while its sweetness never becomes cloying; its bouquet and scents are explosive, multiplying and spreading endlessly. Opulent and silky it slowly develops and blends flavours of ripe apricots, candied Japanese medlar (loquat), citrus zest, roasted citrus fruits with toasted, even crisped notes, and more. Sensuality of this kind, combined with a length rarely encountered, make this one of those 'wines for meditation' to be enjoyed slowly, with nothing else to accompany it. Of recent vintages, 2011 is highly recommended and can be laid down for a lifetime but it would be a shame not to open it. Its creator maintains that a quarter of a century would be an appropriate length of time to wait.

nri Ramonteu,
ager of the estate.

Cooperatives in the spotlight

Cooperative wineries have played a central role in saving appellations that were on the point of being lost forever, and they continue to this day. Some have set the bar extremely high, such as the Producteurs Plaimont, the largest cooperative in Gascony. It unites the wineries of St-Mont and Crouseilles, and has also awarded its seal of approval to wines from Madiran and Pacherenc-du-Vic-Bilh. Other honourable mentions are due to the Vignerons de Buzet, Cave d'Irouléguy, Vinovalie, (Gaillac, Fronton), Berticot (Côtes-de-Duras), and Cave du Marmandais, all of whom guarantee excellent value.

HAUT-PAYS

GAILLAC AOC

Once famed for its sparkling white wine, this district is one of the oldest in the region and, at 8,154 acres (3,300 ha), also one of the largest in southwest France. Gaillac produces a palette of wines with breadth and depth: reds and rosés, as well as dry, sparkling, and sweet whites – not to mention both red and white *nouveaux* wines. The Gaillac-Premières-Côtes appellation produces a dry white wine.

> **GRAPE VARIETIES** Duras, Braucol (Fer Servadou), Gamay, Syrah, Négrette, and Cabernet Franc for reds; Mauzac, Len de l'El, Muscadelle, Sauvignon Blanc, Ondenc, and Sémillon for whites.

> **SOIL** Gravelly on the left bank of the Tarn, which favours red wines; granite and limestone on the right bank, which is better for whites.

> **STYLE** The dry whites are elegant, lively, and fresh, with a nose of green apples and pears that is characteristic of Mauzac grapes. The palate is light with a slight fizz. A creamier dry white is a Gaillac speciality. It has a very gentle effervescence that reinforces freshness and vivacity, and brings out the natural aromas of the Mauzac and Len de l'El grapes. The sweet white wine reveals notes of stewed apples, honey, figs, and white flowers. The sparkling wine, whether made by the traditional method or the Gaillac method (*see* p.70), is a seductive ensemble of apple aromas and fine bubbles. The rosés are also lively and fresh, with a delightfully aromatic bouquet. The *nouveau* red – which is not supposed to be consumed until the third Thursday in November – has a nose typical of Gamay, the single grape from which it is made. There are aromas of red berries underpinned by a charming freshness. The traditional red has notes of black fruit and spice, and is fairly structured and agreeable, with admirable balance.

Colour:
Red, white, and rosé.

Serving temperature:
43 to 46°F (6 to 8°C) for the sweet whites and the sparkling wines; 46 to 50°F (8 to 10°C) for the dry whites and rosés; 54 to 63°F (12 to 17°C) for the reds.

Ageing potential:
Nouveaux *reds should be consumed during the winter after bottling; sparkling and dry whites and the rosés should be enjoyed within a year; sweet whites can be kept for 2 to 3 years; traditional reds can age for 2 to 5 years.*

PYRENEES

PACHERENC-DU-VIC-BILH AOC

In Gascon dialect, 'pacherenc du vic bihl' means 'marked out with stakes from the old country'. Located in the same wine-producing area as Madiran, a region of hills and dales, this small appellation produces 99,900 cases (9,000 hl) of exclusively white wine. Most are sweet or very sweet, although a few are dry.

> **GRAPE VARIETIES** Arrufiac, Petit Manseng, Petit Courbu, Gros Manseng, Sauvignon Blanc, Sémillon.

> **SOIL** Argilo-siliceous, alluvial soils.

> **STYLE** Made with over ripe grapes that are hand-harvested in multiple passes, Pacherenc is a refreshing, aromatic, and crisp wine of great freshness. It has a charming nose that combines notes of preserved lemons and grapefruit with exotic and dried fruits.

Colour:
White.

Serving temperature:
43 to 46°F (6 to 8°C) for sweet wines; 50 to 54°F (10 to 12°C) for dry.

Ageing potential:
Dry wines should be enjoyed within a year; sweet wines can be kept for 5 to 10 years.

MADIRAN AOC

PYRENEES

Madiran was long the wine of choice for pilgrims to Santiago de Compostela, before becoming a fashionable wine in 1970s Paris. Set northeast of Pau in the middle of Béarn, the appellation covers 3,200 acres (1,300 ha) along terraces at the foot of the Pyrenees. It produces about 721,500 cases (65,000 hl) of exclusively red wine with the distinct character of the Tannat grape, which lends the wine its typical tannic strength.

> **GRAPE VARIETIES** Tannat, Cabernet Franc, Cabernet Sauvignon, Fer Servadou.

> **SOIL** Clay-and-limestone, siliceous, gravel.

> **STYLE** Madiran is concentrated, showing notes of raspberry and black fruits with hints of spices and truffles. It has a framework of robust tannins and a generous helping of alcohol. The tannins soften with age, and the wine's aromas become spicier with hints of black fruits (prunes) and roasted notes, mingling with licorice and mint. Thanks to their rich structure, the wines are prime candidates for laying down.

Colour: *Red.*

Serving temperature: *61 to 63°F (16 to 17°C). Definitely to be decanted.*

Ageing potential: *1 to 5 years for basic wines; 10 to 15 years for fine vintages from larger producers.*

JURANÇON AOC AND JURANÇON SEC

PYRENEES

History has it that Henry IV of France was baptized with a drop of Jurançon and a clove of garlic. Its 2,500 acres (1,000 ha) of terraced vineyards are arranged at an elevation of 980+ feet (300 m) among fields and meadows at the gates of Pau. From these vines, the appellation produces some 422,000 cases (38,000 hl) of exclusively white wine. The sweetest of these are some of the finest in France. The AOC Jurançon produces nothing but sweet wines, and making these with late-harvest grapes has been official since 1996. There is a separate appellation – Jurançon sec – for dry wines.

> **GRAPE VARIETIES** Gros Manseng, Petit Manseng, Courbu.

> **SOIL** Marl and clay-limestone. Also siliceous limestone and conglomerate soil.

> **STYLE** Jurançon wines have a striking bouquet, with notes of slightly crystallized lemon and grapefruit. There is a palate of tropical fruit, and a hint of honey; the finish is long and flavourful. Dry Jurançon is replete with floral scents and exotic fruit notes underpinned with plenty of ebullience.

Colour: *White.*

Serving temperature: *46 to 50°F (8 to 10°C) for Jurançon; 50 to 54°F (10 to 12°C) for dry Jurançon.*

Ageing potential: *2 and 5 years, or up to 15 years for great vintages, for Jurançon; 3 to 4 years for dry Jurançon.*

IROULÉGUY AOC

PYRENEES

Vines once ruled this area nestled in the heart of the Atlantic Pyrenees (Pyrénées-Atlantiques *département*) or Basque country, with vineyards covering more than 2,500 acres (1,000 ha). Today, there remains only a single private estate. Crouching timidly around five villages clustered not far from the Spanish border at the base of the St-Étienne-de-Baïgorry hills, the appellation produces a wide variety of red wines as well as several sought-after whites and rosés.

> **GRAPE VARIETIES** Tannat, Cabernet Franc, and Cabernet Sauvignon for reds and rosés; Gros Manseng, Petit Manseng, and Petit Courbu for whites.

> **SOIL** Clay-and-limestone, siliceous clay, red pebbles.

> **STYLE** The reds have a deep purple colour, with slightly rustic aromas of red fruits and violets. They are heightened by spicy notes against a background of gentle tannins. The finish is long and aromatic. The rosés are lively and fruity, with hints of red fruits lifted by a delightful freshness.

Colour: *Red, rosé, and white.*

Serving temperature: *46 to 50°F (8 to 10°C) for rosés and whites; 59 to 63°F (15 to 17°C) for reds.*

Ageing potential: *Within 2 years for rosés and whites; 5 to 8 years for reds.*

LANGUEDOC-ROUSSILLON

This wine region is one the oldest in France. It has long suffered because of its image as a producer of very ordinary wines. But it accounts for more than a third of national production today, and many of the wines are well worth discovering.

LANGUEDOC

The Languedoc sub-region is almost unique in the French countryside with its patchwork of vineyards and its wide range of wines. After making great strides in the past 30 years, it has become something of hunting-ground, particularly for the amateur wine lover. Three appellations – Corbières, Coteaux du Languedoc, and Minervois – represent three-quarters of sales.

LANGUEDOC-ROUSSILLON STATISTICS (AOC)

Vineyard area: 170,502 acres (69,000 ha)

Production: 15.5 million cases (1,400,000 hl)

Reds: 78% **Whites:** 10%

Rosés: 12%

(CIVL, CIVR, FranceAgriMer)

Yesterday and today

While the Greeks introduced vines to the region during the 6th century BC, it was the Romans who really developed them, under the Emperor Domitian, after the latter had created the vast province of Narbonne. Despite later occupation by the Visigoths, the vine continued to flourish, benefiting from the expansion of monasteries (Lagrasse, Caunes, etc.) during the 9th century. The opening of the Canal du Midi in 1681 and development of railroads during the 19th century further promoted the growth of viticulture. However, by the late 19th century phylloxera had destroyed these vineyards. They reappeared, but quality was sacrificed to productivity. Today, the vineyards here have regained their identity and sense of authenticity, and they are asserting a pivotal role.

> Vineyards near Carcassonne.

Vineyard landscape

Languedoc vineyards cover three *départements*: Gard, Herault, and Aude. It is a region spanning, east to west, from Nîmes to Carcassonne. It is bordered to the north by the foothills of the Massif Central, and to the south by the Mediterranean and the mountains of Corbières. A variety of soils – schist, pebbled terraces, sandstone, marl, limestone, and alluvium – give the wines their distinctive character. The Mediterranean climate, with its high summer temperatures, sporadic rainfall, and strong winds, gives the region a certain unity and allows perfect ripening of its grapes.

Varieties and styles

Key grape varieties are from Bordeaux and the Mediterranean.

RED GRAPES. Carignan, which finds its ideal *terroir* here, gives the wines their structure, appearance, and freshness. Grenache provides warmth and aromatic generosity, while Syrah provides tannins, perfume, and structure. As for Mourvèdre, it produces robust, complex wines that are suitable for ageing. Cinsault is mainly used for making rosés.

WHITE GRAPES. Grenache Blanc produces full-bodied, round, crisp wines with a good finish. Maccabeu produces a dry wine with some Colour, a balance of richness and delicacy, and relatively subtle but ripe fruit on the nose. Picpoul provides a very crisp and fresh wine, and Bourboulenc is used to create floral expressions. Chardonnay (in Limoux) and Marsanne are also grown, along with Roussanne and Rolle.

DRY STYLES AND *VINS DOUX NATURELS*. The red wines of Languedoc are generally a beautiful garnet colour. They are

Languedoc AOCs

- Blanquette de Limoux
- Cabardès
- Clairette du Languedoc
- Corbières
- Corbières-Boutenac
- Crémant de Limoux
- Faugères
- Fitou
- La Clape
- Languedoc
- Languedoc appellations
- Limoux
- Malepère
- Minervois
- Minervois-La Livinière
- Muscat de Frontignan
- Muscat de Lunel
- Muscat de Mireval
- Muscat de St-Jean-de-Minervois
- Picpoul de Pinet
- Saint-Chinian
- Saint-Chinian Berlou
- Saint-Chinian Roquebrun
- Terrasses du Larzac

powerful, generous, and increasingly elegant. Besides *appellation contrôlée* wines, there are very diverse IGP wines, mostly red. Some, like those of Mas de Daumas Gassac, are recognized as truly great wines. The region's white wines are often full and rich, with some sparkling wines (Blanquette de Limoux, Crémant de Limoux), and some *vins doux naturels* (Muscat de Lunel, Muscat de Frontignan) of outstanding quality, but of relatively restricted quantity.

Roussillon AOCs

- Banyuls
- Banyuls Grand Cru
- Collioure
- Côtes-du-Roussillon
- Côtes-du-Roussillon-Les Aspres
- Côtes-du-Roussillon-Villages
- Maury
- Muscat de Rivesaltes
- Rivesaltes

ROUSSILLON

This sub-region is home to exceptional *vins doux naturels*: Banyuls, Maury, and Rivesaltes. The area produces 80 per cent of these wines in France, but also offers a nice range of traditional wines – reds, rosés, and whites.

History

Wine production here dates back to Ancient Greek times. And though the wines of Roussillon have been well known since the Middle Ages, the real development of the vineyards took place from the middle of the 17th century. Then phylloxera devastated plantings, leading to an economic crisis. The industry recovered by focusing on quality, and that work led to AOC status for Rivesaltes, Banyuls, and Maury in 1936.

Vineyard landscape

Vineyards occupy a large amphitheatre facing the Mediterranean between the Massif des Corbières in the north, Canigou in the west, and the Albères to the south. They enjoy a Mediterranean climate with mild winters and hot summers. Soils are very diverse: black and brown schist, sandy granite, and clay-and-limestone.

Varieties and styles

GRAPE VARIETIES. Roussillon cultivates all the Mediterranean varieties – Carignan, Grenache Noir, Mourvèdre, Syrah, and Cinsaut for red and rosé wines; Grenache Blanc, Maccabeu, Roussanne, and Marsanne for whites. There are also some native varieties: Malvasia du Roussillon Blanc produces wines with a golden colour, richness, delicacy, aromatics, and crispness; Lladoner Pelut (also known as Grenache Poilu) produces dry wines with some colour. Muscat of Alexandria and Muscat Blanc à Petits Grains, grapes with very rich flavours, are used in blends for *vins doux naturels*.

VINS DOUX NATURELS. Produced from Grenache (Banyuls, Maury) or Muscat (Muscat de Rivesaltes and Rivesaltes), the wines are at once powerful, elegant, and floral. Very unfairly ignored, they suffer from a negative image as *vins cuits* (overdone, 'cooked') or *vins d'apéritif bon marché* (cheap glugging wine). This is a shame because they deserve to be enjoyed for what they are: great food wines with a remarkable capacity for ageing.

TRADITIONAL STYLES. Reds are fine and light, and should be consumed when young; or they are powerful, concentrated, and suitable for ageing (including Côtes du Roussillon-Villages). The rosés combine finesse and power. The more rare white wines (Côtes du Roussillon) are full of fruit flavour and well balanced.

Top Languedoc-Roussillon wines

This region, one of the world's largest in terms of area, produces many high-quality wines. Some of them, including the vins doux naturels, *are highly sought after for their distinctive character.*

LANGUEDOC-ROUSSILLON

LANGUEDOC AOC

In 2007, the Languedoc regional AOC replaced Coteaux du Languedoc. It covers all the appellation areas in Languedoc and Roussillon and produces red, rosé, and some white wines. The appellation is divided into districts that correspond to particular *terroirs*: Pézenas, Grès de Montpellier, Pic-St-Loup, Sommières, Cabrières, La Méjanelle, Montpeyroux, Quatourze, Saint-Christol, Saint-Drézéry, Saint-Georges-d'Orques, and Saint-Saturnin. These will gradually become AOCs in their own right.

> **GRAPE VARIETIES** Grenache Noir, Syrah, Mourvèdre, Cinsaut, Carignan, and Lladoner for red and rosé wines; Grenache Blanc, Clairette Blanche, Bourboulenc, Picpoul Blanc, Roussanne, Marsanne, Rolle, and Viognier for the white wines.

> **SOIL** Limestone, schist, gravel.

> **STYLE** Whether they are produced in the traditional way or by carbonic maceration, reds can range from soft and light with red fruit flavours embellished with spices, to more elaborate, more concentrated, and with more tannins and notes of leather, dried fruit, and mineral flavours. The rosés are round and soft with a nice floral and fruity nose. As for the whites, they are fresh and have an aromatic bouquet of white and yellow flowers with notes of honey, spice, and garrigue.

Colour:
Red, rosé, and white.

Serving temperature:
46 to 50°F (8 to 10°C) for whites and rosés; 54 to 57°F (12 to 14°C) for light reds; 59 to 63°F (15 to 17°C) for concentrated reds.

Ageing potential:
Within a year for whites; 1 to 2 years for rosés; 2 to 4 years for reds (sometimes up to 8 years).

LANGUEDOC

CORBIÈRES AOC

The vineyards of Corbières are at the heart of the Aude, in a rectangle of 4,250 acres (17,200 ha) between Carcassonne, Narbonne, Perpignan, and Quillan. They mainly produce red wines. The variety of soils is such that there are 11 *terroirs*: Montagne d'Alaric, St-Victor, Fontfroide, Quéribus, Boutenac, Termenès, Lézignan, Lagrasse, Sigean, Durban, and Serviès. Since 2005, Boutenac has had its own AOC.

> **GRAPE VARIETIES** Grenache, Syrah, Mourvèdre, Carignan, and Cinsaut for the reds and rosés; Grenache Blanc, Bourboulenc, Maccabeu, Marsanne, Roussanne, and Vermentino for the white wines.

> **SOIL** Schist, limestone, sandstone, marl.

> **STYLE** It is difficult to describe the Corbières since the *terroirs*, and hence the wines, are varied. The reds are powerful, spicy, and well-structured. They display a complex nose that combines black fruits, spices, and garrigue notes. The palate is long and persistent, with rounded tannins. With age, the flavours develop notes of coffee, cocoa, damp woodland, humus, and game. Carbonic maceration produces light and fruity wines. The rosés are powerful, full of flavour, and fruity. Whites offer a fine, delicate nose of white flowers and exotic fruits, with nice palate roundness.

Colour:
Red, rosé, and white.

Serving temperature:
50 to 54°F (10 to 12°C) for the whites and rosés; 61 to 64°F (16 to 18°C) for the reds (which should be decanted).

Ageing potential:
1 to 2 years for the whites and rosés; 3 to 10 years, or even 15 years, for the reds.

LANGUEDOC

BLANQUETTE DE LIMOUX AOC

This is the oldest sparkling wine in France. Its history dates to the 16th century, when the wine was developed (in 1531) by monks at the Abbey of St-Hilaire, near Limoux. Located in the hills bordering the valley of the Aude, and overlooking the Pyrenees to the south of Carcassonne, the vineyards cover 4,448 acres (1,800 ha) and yield 556,000 cases (50,000 hl) of sparkling white wine. Production is by the traditional method or the ancestral method (*see* p.70), which has its own appellation. These sparkling wines, which are all white, can be *brut*, *demi-sec*, or *sec*.

> **GRAPE VARIETIES** Traditional method: Mauzac, also known as Blanquette (90 per cent at least), Chenin, and Chardonnay. Ancestral method: Mauzac.

> **SOIL** Clay-and-limestone, stones, marl, sandstone.

> **STYLE** With small, fine bubbles and a fruity nose dominated by the scent of ripe apples and a few floral notes (white flowers), the wine fills the palate with a lingering finish.

Colour: *White.*

Serving temperature: *43 to 46°F (6 to 8°C).*

Ageing potential: *1 to 3 years.*

LANGUEDOC

MINERVOIS AOC

This appellation derives its name from the goddess of wisdom, Minerva. The territory of Minervois is an amphitheatre of 12,355 acres (5,000 ha) bounded by the Canal du Midi in the south and the Montagne Noire to the north. It produces very different wines, soft and fruity or structured and meant for ageing. The AOC produces mostly reds, but also white and rosé wines. At the heart of its territory, across six different districts, is the first 'village' appellation of Languedoc to be created: Minervois-La Livinière.

> **GRAPE VARIETIES** For red and rosé: Syrah, Mourvèdre, Grenache, Carignan, Cinsaut, Terret Noir, and Picpoul Noir; for white: Maccabeu, Bourboulenc, Clairette, Grenache, Vermentino, and Muscat.

> **SOIL** Terraces of pebbles, sandstone, schist, and limestone soils.

> **STYLE** The red wines typically display complexity and concentration, with a deep ruby red colour. The nose shows aromas of red and black fruit, hints of garrigue and spice or licorice, as well as delicate violets. The palate has a frame of tannins and a long finish. The rosés are powerful, but fresh. The white wines combine white and exotic fruits in a fine balance.

Colour: *Red, rosé, and white.*

Serving temperature: *50 to 54°F (10 to 12°C) for whites and rosés; 61 to 63°F (16 to 17°C) for reds.*

Ageing potential: *Within a year for whites and rosés; 5 to 8 years for the reds.*

Selected Languedoc producers

BLANQUETTE DE LIMOUX

- **Blanquette Beirieu (Roquetaillade).** Superb *blanquettes* using the ancestral method and respecting tradition absolutely, with no added sulphur.
- **Château Rives-Blanques (Cépie).** An excellent *blanquette* and a superb range of still white wines.

CORBIERES

- **Castelmaure (Embres-et-Castelmaure).** A particularly dynamic cooperative offering a great quality-price ratio.
- **Château Pech-Latt (Lagrasse).** One of the major estates of the appellation.

LANGUEDOC

- **Château Puech-Haut (St-Drézéry).** Superb red wines.
- **Domaine Peyre-Rose (St-Pargoire).** One of the most impressive wines from Languedoc.
- **Clos Marie (Lauret).** An exceptional estate at Pic Saint-Loup.

MINERVOIS

- **Domaine Jean-Baptiste Sénat (Trausse Minervois).** A superb range of wines, from those exploding with fruit to the intense and complex.
- **Domaine Pierre Cros (Badens).** Powerful and generous wines.

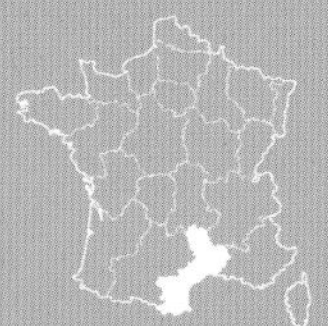

DOMAINE
D'AUPILHAC

The d'Aupilhac estate is a good illustration of the evolution seen in Languedoc over the last 30 years. Sylvain Fadat, the fifth generation of a wine-growing family, is the first to make his own wine himself. His grandfather's wines disappeared into the anonymity of a cooperative wine, but his own are looked after with jealous care.

DOMAINE D'AUPILHAC

28, rue du Plô
34150 Montpeyroux

Area: *69 acres (28 ha)*
Production: *125,000 bottles p.a.*
Appellation: *Languedoc Montpeyroux*
Red grape varieties: *Mourvèdre, Carignan, Syrah, Grenache, Cinsaut*
White grape varieties: *Roussanne, Marsanne, Grenache Blanc, Vermentino*

Spartan beginnings

Sylvain Fadat started his estate in 1989, although its beginnings were rudimentary; he vinified his first wines in tankers while waiting for a roof to be fitted to his cellar. The work he puts into his vines is more important to him than anything else. He harvests by hand to ensure he can properly check the ripeness of the grapes and never introduces any chemicals to the process. Certified organic for only a few years, he has been organic in his heart since the outset. Aupilhac takes its name from that of his first vineyard, 33 acres (13.3 ha) of terraces exposed to the southwest at an elevation of 330 feet (100m) above sea level. Sylvain's vines of Mourvèdre, Carignan, Syrah, Grenache, and Cinsault grapes look out across the ruins of the old Castellas de Montpeyroux castle. Growing wines here means passing on history and a wine-making tradition that goes back a millennium or even further, as far as the Romans and the Gallia Narbonensis era. It involves uncovering the secrets of a particular terroir, where the air of the Mediterranean combines with the freshness of the Cévennes, just as it does in the character of the local Montpeyroux inhabitants.

A quest for freshness

However, Sylvain Fadat's operation is not limited to a single wine or a single terroir; he bought a parcel of 20 acres (8 ha) at

Cocalières in 1998 to complete his range of options, located higher up on the hill at an elevation of 1,150 feet (350m) and in the middle of a natural amphitheatre in the heath. His first job was to remove all the rocks and stones, in order to plant Roussanne, Marsanne, Vermentino, Grenache Blanc, Grenache, Syrah, and Mourvèdre. It is either done the Mediterranean way or not at all. With the elevation and northern exposure here, the wines can achieve a greater balance between acidity and alcohol. 'The bouquet is fresher, without any detraction from the depth and the vigour of the wine', says the wine-maker.

The artist's palette has been enhanced

Sylvain has been able to bring out these new nuances in his creations, and has added a single-vineyard wine, Les Cocalières, to the estate's traditional output, along with a blend from his two terroirs that he has dubbed La Boda (Castilian for 'wedding', a nod to his wife Désirée and her Spanish roots). La Boda has proved a solid marriage, as its wines aged for more than 20 years will attest – there is an impressive brilliance to the wines but it is a carefully considered union, as Sylvain vinifies all of his grape varieties and terroirs separately, whether in steel tanks, barrels, or tuns. Sylvain does not intend to rest on his laurels and has recently rented 6 acres (2.4 ha) of land planted with Cinsaut grapes, located just below the Cocalières site, which, for the moment, he is using for his entry-level wine, Lou Maset, but which one day might well be used in blending the Domaine d'Aupilhac, to add a little more fruit and softness.

DOMAINE D'AUPILHAC, LA BODA, LANGUEDOC MONTPEYROUX

This is a marriage of Mourvèdre and Syrah, of north and south and of high and low; of the blue marl of Aupilhac and the basalts and limestones of Les Cocalières – all of which is left to steep for a long time (30 months) and then aged in 80-gallon (300-litre) barrels for a further two years. It has a pretty classic bouquet for the area: very ripe red fruit, cherries, blackberries, leather, spices, heathland. The mouthfeel is spectacular, with power, concentration, hefty ripe tannins, crisp fruit, and considerable freshness. Sun and coolness, power and crispness, firmness and smoothness – it is breathtaking.

DOMAINE D'AUPILHAC, LES COCALIÈRES, LANGUEDOC MONTPEYROUX

This high-altitude wine uses a trio of southern grapes: Syrah, Mourvèdre, and Grenache. On the nose, black fruits are quite tightly packed but cut through, honed like a good blade. An intense wine, lacking nothing, with great potential for laying down – as has been demonstrated by examples from more than ten years ago.

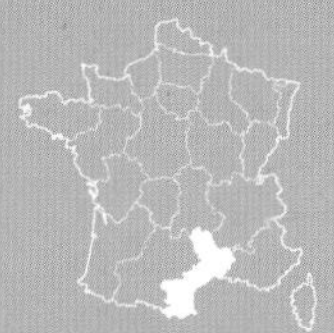

Languedoc

MAS *JULLIEN*

The name Mas Jullien symbolizes the renaissance of Languedoc wines, which it has been helping to revitalize since the 1980s. The estate has long been setting the pace, thanks to Olivier Jullien, a wine-grower whose sensitivity matches his talent.

MAS JULLIEN

route de Saint-André,
34725 Jonquières

Area: *50 acres (20 ha)*
Production: *70,000 bottles p.a.*
Appellation: *Languedoc Terrasses du Larzac*
Red grape varieties: *Carignan, Grenache, Mourvèdre, Syrah*
White grape varieties: *Carignan Blanc, Chenin Blanc, Marsanne, Viognier*

A Languedoc character

Olivier Jullien is, as they say, a Languedoc character. Meticulous, precise, and decent, he doesn't view his business as a competition with his peers, but doggedly pursues a single goal – to refine and improve his wines, in particular through the selection of plots, the management of the vines, biodiversity, blending, and researching perfect ripeness. His cellar, located on the plain at Jonquières, is functional and well equipped but of almost secondary importance, while his vines (about 50 acres/20 ha) are cultivated biodynamically. They are mostly located a little higher and spread out over a number of plots, sometimes several miles apart, across the Terrasses du Larzac area. This is a terroir, or rather a series of micro-terroirs, shaped by the freshness that comes down from the plateau of the same name, with the landmark of the beautiful Mount Baudile rising to more than 2,790 feet (850m). Daily variations in temperature can exceed 20°C (68°F) in summer, encouraging slow, gradual ripening of the grapes, which in turn promotes aromatic complexity and freshness in the wines.

Mediterranean roots

The son of a family of Languedoc winemakers, Olivier Jullien lays claim to his Mediterranean roots, his vines, and to his Mediterranean spirit – one of his wines, États d'Âme, is even named after it. He is open to anything, especially to changing his mind, and his wines are as diverse as the palette of soils here (chalky ground that is more or less rocky, siliceous, or clayey soils) and the exposure of the vines to the sun. In addition, their composition (in terms of grape varieties and choice of vineyard) is evolving over time, when he is not striking one or another from his list. Always looking for a way to express himself, for a broader palette of terroirs, Olivier Jullien has undoubtedly sold more vines than he possesses today. And mention should be made of the contribution made by Jean-Baptiste Granier, Olivier's right-hand man and another fan of southern soils (and of old Carignan vines), with whom he started the joint Vignes Oubliées ('forgotten vines') project. Sophisticated, Mediterranean, ripe and fresh, these red wines deliver a depth and charm that is only enhanced as they age.

MAS JULLIEN, CUVÉE CARLAN, LANGUEDOC TERRASSES DU LARZAC

Fanned by the refreshing winds blowing from the Larzac, the land here – one of the highest plots on the estate – is planted with Grenache, Cinsaut, Syrah, and Carignan grapes. It is located at Saint-Privat, to the north of Montpeyroux and Arboras, where the soils are part sandstone and part schist. The grapes take their time to ripen at altitude and Olivier Jullien has modelled his approach on nature: vinification is gentle, with no overextraction of juice. Aged in small vats, the wine matures for a year on the lees before bottling, producing a wine with smokey aromas and hints of black fruits mingling with black pepper. The mouthfeel is generous, with a very particular texture, almost as solid as it is liquid, with finely grained tannins. Its power is tempered with great freshness.

> Olivier Jullien, director of the estate.

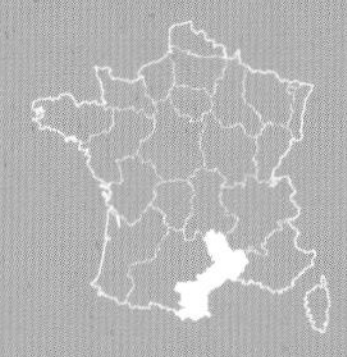

Languedoc

DOMAINE *CLAVEL*

Domaine Clavel celebrated its 30th anniversary in 2015. It was established and has expanded within the Languedoc appellation, and remains one of its finest representatives.

DOMAINE CLAVEL

Mas de Perie
34820 Assas

Area: *82 acres (33 ha)*
Production: *N/A*
Appellation: *Languedoc Pic Saint-Loup, La Méjanelle, Grés de Montpellier*
Red grape varieties: *Syrah, Grenache, Mourvèdre, Carignan*
White grape varieties: *Roussanne, Grenache Blanc, Viognier, Carignan Blanc, Marsanne, Vermentino, Clairette, Muscat*

A pioneering estate

Starting out at the age of 26, Pierre Clavel found himself working in an industry where local initiative was rare. Only a few winemakers like Sylvain Fadat or Olivier Jullien really stood out from the crowd, but these pioneers of the new 'Eldorado' of Languedoc worked together to explore and understand the terroir and to take full advantage of their knowledge of the Mediterranean climate. Pierre Clavel rented some plots at La Méjanelle, on the doorstep of Montpellier, an exceptional piece of land that has long supplied its wines to the neighbouring city.

La Méjanelle's geological make-up explains this in part: its rounded pebbles have the same origin as those at Châteauneuf-du-Pape. However, the climate is different, as the spume from the nearby sea tempers the effect of the nearest uplands, at an altitude of about 160 feet (50m) high. It was to be wine produced from the Copa area (originally known as the 'Copa Santa'), the jewel of the estate, that would put its name up with the greats.

The challenges Pierre experienced along the way found him doing the opposite of what was expected: thinning out the grapes, leaf-trimming, picking at optimum ripeness. But the experiment bore fruit to reveal an incredible Syrah grape, and, with a couple of casks from Château Margaux retrieved from Bordeaux and 18 months of ageing, the trial batch passed the test, the Syrah grapes opening up into generous, velvety, highly aromatic wine.

From La Méjanelle to Pic Saint-Loup

Pierre and his wife Estelle have held on to a part of La Méjanelle – despite Montpellier having spread out and nibbled away at the area, enough remains to ensure that La Copa will survive. The couple set their sights further inland, discovering at the foot of the Pic Saint-Loup a small vineyard just begging to be loved, and having captured their hearts from the start it inspired them to write a new chapter in wine-making history: 'It is a terroir of great generosity, and gives back all the love you pour into it,' confides Pierre. The 35 acres (14 ha) under cultivation at Saint-Jean-de-Cuculles were soon converted to biodynamic farming, following the pattern of the rest of the land farmed by the estate. Surrounded by woods, it is a haven of tranquility in which the vines nestle happily into the chalky colluvium of the soil. Estelle is in charge of the vinification process and helps Pierre keep an eye on the vines. Now, after travelling and completing their own training, sons Martin and Antoine have returned to Assas to write the next chapter in their parents' story.

DOMAINE CLAVEL LA COPA, LANGUEDOC LA MÉJANELLE

The estate's traditional wine is made mostly with Syrah grapes topped off with less than 20% Grenache, followed by ageing in vats and in barrel. Its dark appearance heralds a deep bouquet, somewhere between wild berries, heathland, warm stone, and sea spray. Its compressed tannins are unmistakable but silky, bringing depth, and lending a crispness to the rich texture, which finishes with fruit and floral notes.

DOMAINE CLAVEL BONNE PIOCHE, LANGUEDOC PIC SAINT-LOUP

Largely made up of Syrah and rounded off with Mourvèdre and Grenache, this blend is aged in vats and oval concrete tanks. A beautiful and airy wine with an assertive bouquet of red fruits (cherries and raspberries) and hints of heathland mingled with humus and pine needles. The mouthfeel is inviting and subtle, with silky tannins that are perfectly scented; the finish is crisp, fresh, and spicy.

< > Pierre Clavel, the estate manager.

ROUSSILLON

CÔTES-DU-ROUSSILLON, CÔTES-DU-ROUSSILLON-VILLAGES AOCs

These regional appellations cover 15,320 acres (6,200 ha) right across Roussillon. They mainly produce red wines, but also rosés and occasional white wines from the region. Northern Roussillon, between the Massif des Corbières and Têt, is the stronghold of the Côtes-du-Roussillon-Villages, an appellation consisting entirely of red wines. Four villages, Caramany, Latour-de-France, Lesquerde, and Tautavel, can add their name to the appellation.

> **GRAPE VARIETIES** For red and rosé: Carignan, Grenache, Mourvèdre, Syrah, and Lladoner; for white: Maccabeu, Grenache Blanc, Malvoisie, Marsanne, and Roussanne.

> **SOIL** Granite, schist, limestone.

> **STYLE** Powerful and generous, the reds are distinguished by a nose of wild fruits and mineral notes. Those of the Côtes-du-Roussillon-Villages AOC display a complex nose of crystallized fruit, garrigue, and licorice on a frame of rounded tannins. The palate is intense and resolutely Mediterranean. Produced by the *saignée* method, the roses are full-bodied and fruity. The whites are rounded with aromas of flowers and white fruit.

Colour: *Red, rosé, and white.*

Serving temperature: *50°F (10°C) for the whites and rosés; 59 to 61°F (15 to 16°C) for the reds.*

Ageing potential: *Within a year for whites and rosés; 2 to 5 years for reds.*

ROUSSILLON

RIVESALTES AOC

This appellation derives its name from the town of Rivesaltes (meaning 'high banks' in Catalan). Located mostly in Roussillon, but also in Corbières, it is the largest appellation for *vins doux naturels*. It covers about 6,672 acres (2,700 ha) and produces an average of 3.3 million cases (300,000 hl) of red and white wines. It exists in the categories Grenat, Tuilé, Ambré, and Hors d'Age.

It is important to note that you should not confuse Rivesaltes AOC with Muscat de Rivesaltes AOC, a white *vin doux naturel*, which covers the same territory. Muscat de Rivesaltes is made from the Muscat of Alexandria and Muscat à Petits Grains grapes.

> **GRAPE VARIETIES** Grenache (Noir, Gris, or Blanc), Maccabeu, and Malvoisie du Roussillon.

> **SOIL** Schist, limestone, and silt.

> **STYLE** Young Rivesaltes has aromas of slightly crystallized red fruit, supported by round tannins. 'Tuilé' Rivesaltes has a nose dominated by caramel, mixed with aromas of sweet spices, orange peel, cocoa, quince, coffee, and nuts. 'Hors d'Age' Rivesaltes is aged for a minimum of five years after production. Most are aged for much longer.

Colour: *White and red.*

Serving temperature: *54 to 61°F (12 to 16°C).*

Ageing potential: *10 to 20 years or more.*

Selected *vins doux naturels*

MAURY

- **Domaine de la Coume du Roy (Maury).** Wines of great substance, impressive in their density, concentration, and depth of flavour.
- **Mas Amiel (Maury).** Great Maury wines, beautiful Muscat de Rivesaltes, and a remarkable range of dry wines from Roussillon that are very elegant.

BANYULS

- **Domaine du Mas Blanc (Banyuls-sur-Mer).** An estate famous for its Banyuls and Collioure wines, which are among the best of the appellation.
- **Domaine de la Rectorie (Banyuls-sur-Mer).** Superb and beautiful Banyuls that are stylistic benchmarks, as well as lovely wines from Collioure in the three colours.
- **Domaine du Traginer (Banyuls-sur-Mer).** Full-bodied and powerful wines produced from organic grapes.

RIVESALTES

- **Domaine Cazes (Rivesaltes).** A safe bet. Muscats that are harmonious, rich, and beautifully produced, using biodynamics.

ROUSSILLON

MAURY AOC

At the heart of the Agly Valley, in northwestern Roussillon, these vineyards cover the commune of Maury and three communes at the outer limits forming an enclave within the appellations of the vast Rivesaltes and Côtes-du-Roussillon-Villages. Long identified with its sweet wines, the appellation has been producing dry reds since 2011. Sweet wines include Maury, matured in an airtight environment and bottled rapidly (including Grenat),and and those that have undergone a long oxidative maturing (Tuilé, Hors d'Age, *rancio*), either in wooden casks or in glass demijohns exposed to the elements.

> **GRAPE VARIETIES** Grenache Noir (at least 75 per cent), Grenache Gris, Grenache Blanc, and Maccabeu.

> **SOIL** Schist.

> **STYLE** Red Maury of the Grenat type boasts heady scents of black and red fruits that explode against a chocolate background. The palate is smooth, packed with pulpy tannins, and the finish is long and full of flavour. With its ruby red colour, Maury Rancio has a nose of caramel, smoke, toast, dried and crystallized fruit, tea, nuts, coffee, and cocoa. The palate is rich and fragrant, like the nose, with very good persistence.

Colour:
Red and white.

Serving temperature:
54 to 57°F (12 to 14°C) for young wines; 57 to 61°F (14 to 16°C) for old wines. (Vintage wine should be decanted.)

Ageing potential:
5 to 10 years, or even 20 to 30 years for the very best.

ROUSSILLON

BANYULS AND BANYULS GRAND CRU AOCs

This historic wine region dates to the Carthaginian era, five centuries before Christ. Located on the Mediterranean, along the Spanish border, this *vin doux naturel* appellation spans the towns of Banyuls, Collioure, Port Vendres, and Cerbère. It covers 2,718 acres (1,100 ha) of vines grown in steep terraces, with a yield of around 322,000 cases (29,000 hl). As with Maury wines, there are two kinds of Banyuls: *rimages*, which have been quickly bottled to retain their freshness and fruit; and *rancios*, which have been aged in either tank or demijohn to develop a complex flavour – blending notes of chocolate, coffee, and prunes. Banyuls Grand Cru, which is prepared in the same appellation area, is aged for 30 months (as against 12 months for Banyuls).

> **GRAPE VARIETIES** Grenache Noir (50 per cent for Banyuls, 75 per cent for Banyuls Grand Cru), Grenache Gris, Grenache Blanc, Carignan, and Maccabeu.

> **SOIL** Schist.

> **STYLE** Young *rimage* Banyuls have flavours of stone fruit, blueberry, and blackberry. They are naturally sweet and mellow, even smooth, and have a very long palate. Old *rimages* develop a very balanced mix of leather and roasted notes (coffee, chocolate). The nose is intense and aromatic with a bouquet mingling notes of licorice, coffee, tea, dried fruits, and sweet spices. The palate is soft and gentle. With age, the colour has tinges of bronze and the nose becomes even more complex, revealing lingering hints of toast, nuts, and caramel. Having taken all the time they need to develop their tertiary aromas of stewed fruits, spices, and mocha, Banyuls Grands Crus are powerful wines.

Colour:
Red and white.

Serving temperature:
54 to 57°F (12 to 14°C) for young wines; 57°to 61°F (14 to 16°C) for old wines.

Ageing potential:
10 to 20 years, or more.

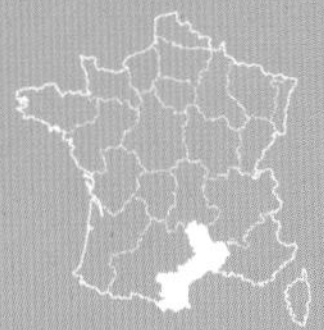

Roussillon

DOMAINE DE *LA RECTORIE*

Having returned to their family's land among the magnificent vineyards of Collioure in 1984, the Parcé brothers have turned La Rectorie into one of the greatest names in Roussillon.

DOMAINE DE LA RECTORIE

65, avenue du Puig del Mas
66650 Banyuls-sur-Mer

Area: *72 acres (29 ha)*
Production: *80,000 bottles p.a.*
Appellation: *Collioure, Banyuls*
Red grape varieties: *Grenache, Carignan, Syrah, Mourvèdre*
White grape varieties: *Grenache Gris, Grenache Blanc*

Between sea and mountain

Nestling between the sea and the mountains, the Parcé family's vineyards seem to have been here forever; spread out across the steep, forbidding schist slopes that surround the Puig del Mas, they waited patiently for their new dawn. Patience was indeed required, at least until 1984, when Marc and Thierry decided to make their own wines rather than take their grapes to the Banyuls cooperative. It heralded the brothers' return after a childhood spent far from the Côte Vermeille, and after having made their wine-making debuts – in 1978 for Marc, and five years later for Thierry. Before they could become fully independent the brothers had to acquire more wine land and so the estate grew from the 17 acres (7 ha) they had inherited to around 75 acres (30 ha). This area is divided between 30 plots of land vinified in groups of micro-terroirs according to orientation, slope, elevation, and grape variety, but with one common factor: the omnipresent schist. However, the proximity of the sea is also essential to these sun-kissed vineyards, as is so successfully demonstrated by the Collioure wines, Côté Mer and Côté Montagne. A majority of old vines are planted here, with relays of Grenache, Grenache Blanc, and Carignan handing on the baton every 50 years. New Grenache, Syrah, and Mourvèdre vines were planted in 1981 and 1990, and all the vines are tended organically and worked by mule or horsepower.

A scale without a single wrong note

Today, the La Rectorie estate is managed by Jean-Emmanuel, Thierry's son; Marc's son Joseph runs La Préceptorie de Centernach in Maury, created independently of La Rectorie in 2001. The latter takes its name from the Roman chapel located a few streets down from the cellar in which 80,000 bottles are filled every year, despite poor yields that never exceed 1 to 1.5 tons/acre (20 to 25 hl/ha). Most of the production process is devoted to Collioure reds but the Parcé family also make excellent white and rosé wines, with a fascinating collection of Banyuls wines in every style, starting with a red that has crisp fruit. There is not a single wrong note in the range, which celebrates the subtleties of the *terroir* with meticulous wine-making and a vineyard worked with great precision.

DOMAINE DE LA RECTORIE, CUVÉE THÉRÈSE REIG, BANYULS

Harvesting at standard ripeness and seven months of ageing in tanks produce a Banyuls *rimage* red (*i.e.* one bottled quickly after tank ageing) with an appealing concentration of fruit. The Grenache and Carignan grapes are picked at normal ripeness. The wine is a dark-ruby colour, with a velvety appearance and a full bouquet of black cherries, figs, and black olives, and a hint of tobacco in the spicy dregs. Its tannins weave together in the mouth, creating powerful notes that are as crisp as they are fruity, with perfectly contained sweetness.

DOMAINE DE LA RECTORIE, L'ARGILE COLLIOURE BLANC

Fermented in barrel and aged on the lees, this wine is made up of 90 per cent Grenache (a grape variety once reserved for fortified wines here) and 10 per cent Grenache Blanc. When young, the wine has a green tint with flashes of yellow. The bouquet has notes of fruit (citrus peel, Mirabelle plums), angelica, green olives, and hints of iodine and rubbed stones, which lend the mouthfeel a touch of minerality. A great southern white wine – refined and fresh with a hint of minerality.

> Thierry and Jean-Emmanuel Parcé, the previous and current estate managers.

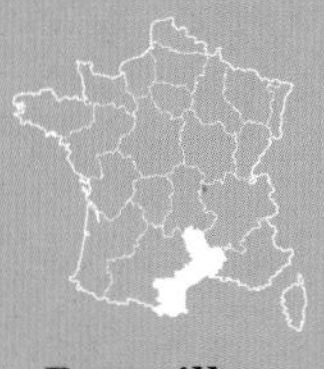

Roussillon

DOMAINE *VAQUER*

The Vaquer estate is one of the greatest exponents of wine in Roussillon's Les Aspres area. Its range showcases the region's specialities with consistent elegance.

DOMAINE VAQUER

1, rue des écoles
66300 Tresserre

Area: *42 acres (17 ha)*
Production: *38,000 bottles p.a.*
Appellation: *Côtes du Roussillon, Rivesaltes*
Red grape varieties: *Grenache, Carignan, Syrah*
White grape varieties: *Grenache Blanc, Grenache Gris, Roussanne Macabeo, Muscat*

Les Aspres

Lying between the Tech and Têt Rivers near the foothills of the Canigou mountain, Les Aspres is home to the Catalan dryness of warm stones, limestone gravel glittering in the sun, and dried-out, sandy clays. This is a landscape of thirsty vineyards coating hilltops and valleys, but its dry and unprepossessing soil is also home to a blend of elegance and subtlety far removed from the stereotypes the region has worked hard to cast off. The Domaine Vaquer estate cultivates Macabeo, Roussanne, Muscat, Carignan, Syrah, and Grenache grapes in the area surrounding Tresserre, and it is from these varieties that Frédérique Vaquer makes her wine. Today, she does so alone, having conceived with her late husband Bernard an ambitious plan to create delicate wines with hints of fruit in Roussillon – heady wines without a doubt, but the freshness and tension of the minerality woven through the fine silk of the tannins balances out its alcoholic aspirations. The idea has progressed a long way and Frédérique can take pride in having achieved that ambition. The results defy comparison.

Flashback to Fernand Vaquer

The estate's story began just before World War I, when Bernard's great-grandfather bought it for his daughter, the wife of Fernand Vaquer, a noted rugby player. Fernand passed on his first name to his son, and Fernand Vaquer junior had just turned 17 at the start of World War II when he decided to join his father in growing wine. They replanted the estate with Carignan, a grape variety still used to this day in the wines known as L'Exception and L'Expression. In 1968, he became one of the first wine-growers in the Roussillon area to bottle his own wine, and concerns about storing the results led him to keep the precious bottles in the mountains, at the family's farm on the slopes of the Cerdagne. If you open one of these old bottles, you will be surprised by its freshness and the presence of fruit, preserved fruit in particular. Before taking over from his father, Bernard studied oenology at Dijon, where he met Frédérique in 1985.

Frédérique Vaquer style

Frédérique Vaquer has been in charge since 2001. A wine expert born in Burgundy, she has charted the course for the estate's powerful and elegant style. The wine's power lies in its assertive character, an echo of the Aspres *terroir* itself, a tough country that yields its best when its needs are heeded. Her Burgundian influence lends a particular nuance to the wines, a mixture of elegance and gourmet pleasure, supplied in no short measure by the gentle touch and sweetness of Muscat and Rivesaltes, the estate's *vin doux naturel* (naturally sweet) wines, as well as its dry varieties.

DOMAINE VAQUER L'EXCEPTION CÔTES DU ROUSSILLON LES ASPRES RED

This wine is a blend of Grenache, Syrah, and Carignan, with 12 months of ageing in concrete tanks or barrel (no new wood), depending on the grape varieties. Made using barrel fermentation, it is overflowing with body and a concentration of flavours, while always maintaining the balance that makes this range of wines so appealing. Powerful and elegant, L'Exception is a perfect illustration of the estate's style: its dark appearance is shot through with a colour of deep purple-garnet, with flecks of mauve. The bouquet is complex, with intense fruits (cherries) and hints of spices, the great outdoors, and the sea. The mouthfeel is full of crisp fruit, licorice, and aromatic plants, with a freshness underscored with citron.

DOMAINE VAQUER RIVESALTES HORS D'ÂGE AMBRÉ

This is a sweet wine made using the *solera* method, an ageing technique that involves topping up wines with an equivalent volume of younger wine. A reddish-ochre colour, the wine leads from the very start with hints of toasted flavours – tobacco, coffee, pine, and roasted pistachios – while the astonishingly fresh mouthfeel prolongs the complexity of a bouquet of dried figs, prunes, white pepper, algae, fenugreek, and dried apricots. Its singular tautness promotes a balance between appealing bitterness and sweetness.

dérique Vaquer,
e manager
2001.

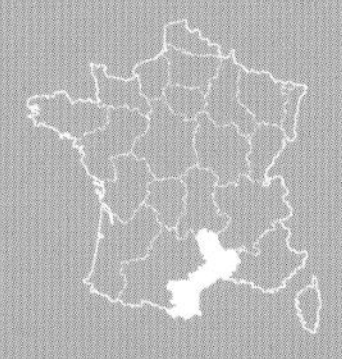

Languedoc-Roussillon

GÉRARD *BERTRAND*

The career of Gérard Bertrand, a charismatic Languedoc-Roussillon wine-grower, is a perfect example of the dynamism that this region has shown for 20 years. From exceptional vintages to branded wine, his range of products is a showcase for every facet of modern Languedoc-Roussillon.

GÉRARD BERTRAND

route de Narbonne Plage
11100 Narbonne

Area: *1,483 acres (600 ha)*
Production: *15 millions bottles p.a.*
Appellation: *Corbières*
Red grape varieties: *Grenache, Syrah, Carignan, Mourvèdre, Merlot, Malbec, Cabernet Franc*
White grape varieties: *Chardonnay, Viognier, Bourboulenc, Roussanne*

Loyalty and modernity

It is not so long ago that Languedoc was a wine factory whose only function was to inundate the world with soulless, characterless table wine. Things have changed with extraordinary speed over the course of a generation. The hillsides are full of vines once more, the majority of the grape variety choices have been revised, and the wine-makers, both local and new to the area, are better trained and more dynamic, extremely so in some cases. They are replenishing their armoury before heading off to conquer the rest of the world from much stronger ground. Gérard Bertrand is a perfect illustration of this trend. While remaining utterly faithful to his region, he has made his name and become an international brand in more than 100 countries with an annual output of 15 million bottles. His athletic stature is a reminder of his former life as a top-flight rugby player who turned out for Narbonne and at the Stade Français. He has retained his competitive spirit from rugby, a mindset that will not contemplate throwing in the towel, and a capacity to weigh people up; he also has an impressive address book. As a young man he would spend his summers in the vineyards at the family's Villemajou estate, working under the burning sun of Corbières with his father, whom he describes as a pioneer in his grasp of the region's potential. His father's accidental death in 1987 led him to return to wine-making, and now, 30 years later, he is the head of an empire in Languedoc and Roussillon. His success has been within the context of a region constantly reinventing itself, and the circle has been squared: a modernized production while keeping the spirit of Languedoc-Roussillon intact.

Every facet of Languedoc

Having begun in a small family business, Gérard Bertrand is now in charge of 1,483 acres (600 ha) of wine country. To the Villemajou estate (Corbières) he has added Château L'Hospitalet (Languedoc), Domaine de Cigalus (IGP Aude), Laville Bertrou (Minervois), Domaine de l'Aigle (Limoux), La Sauvageonne (Terrasses du Larzac), Soujeole (Malepère), and Aigues Vives (Corbières). He has been experimenting with organic agriculture since 2004 and now nearly half of his vineyards are biodynamically farmed. He soon demonstrated a rigour in his winemaking that was absent elsewhere in the region, with a precise approach, sharp fruit flavours, and considered use of barrel ageing. It is this same rigour that has enabled him to offer a wide range of mass-produced wines made without sulphur. Gérard's impressive property portfolio affords him the opportunity to explore every facet of Languedoc-Roussillon, with flamboyant reds, modern whites, and exceptional fortified wines. He has added a large wine merchant's business to cover all his high-volume ranges (which are also a credit to his name.) His particular forte is the provision of both exceptional wines with proven character (Clos d'Ora, Le Viala, La Forge, L'Hospitalitas, old Rivesaltes, etc.) and entry-level wines of admirable reliability that are sold in high volumes. Gérard Bertrand is equally enthusiastic about wine tourism and has turned the Château de l'Hospitalet into a cultural hotspot dedicated to wine, hospitality, and jazz. In short, this former nationally-ranked blindside flanker has become a pillar of international stature in the wine establishment.

GÉRARD BERTRAND, CHÂTEAU LAVILLE BERTROU, CUVÉE DE L'AMIRAL, MINERVOIS LA LIVINIÈRE

This blend of Syrah, Grenache, and Carignan is aged in casks for around 12 months to create a lovely example of a Minervois wine, with a smooth bouquet of wild berries, hot coffee, licorice sweets, and violets. Its rounded texture fills the palate with warm Mediterranean flavours, releasing soft tannins and hints of oak that are never overdone. This is a harmonious and reasonably priced wine that is a prime illustration of Gérard Bertrand's skill, perfectly balanced between its modernity and the expression of its terroirs.

PROVENCE AND CORSICA

Provence and Corsica may be the oldest vineyard regions in France. Their modern production is full of surprises, however, and a far cry from making only easy-drinking wines for the summer, as their reputation sometimes has it.

PROVENCE

Sunshine, vacations, and rosé: this is the image of Provence. And yes, the region's production is 85 per cent rosé. But the vineyards of Provence are not limited solely to the colour pink; they also produce great red wines and quality whites that are well worth a look.

Ancient vines

Vine cultivation was introduced to Provence during the 6th century BC by the Phoenicians or the Phocaeans (Anatolian Greeks) – historians are still uncertain who planted the first vines in Provence and France. Vineyards then prospered under the influence of the great monastic orders. From the 15th century, the industry suffered many disasters, plague, and wars. And it had scarcely recovered when attacked by phylloxera during the 19th century, which destroyed all its work. In the 20th century everything was restored, with just a single watchword for all the appellations: quality.

PROVENCE STATISTICS (AOC)

Vineyard area: 70,425 acres (28,500 ha)

Production: 16.6 million cases (1,500,000 hl)

Rosés: 88%

Reds: 9%

Whites: 3%

(CIVP, FranceAgriMer)

Climate and soils

Given the broad expanse occupied by the vineyards of Provence, between Nice, Marseille, and St-Rémy-de-Provence, they are subject to significant variations in climate. They can be maritime or continental, depending on latitude and topography. However, there is one common: sunshine. Soils are very varied in nature: granite and schist in the Maures, limestone soil in Cassis, and so on.

Varieties

The spectrum of terrain and climate is matched by a wide range of grapes, with traditional varieties coexisting alongside indigenous ones.

PRINCIPAL RED GRAPE VARIETIES. Grenache, which is used as much for reds as for rosés, lends the wines roundness, charm, and elegant red fruit aromas. Cinsaut imbues rosé wines with freshness, finesse, and fruit. Tibouren offers a rich bouquet. Mourvèdre, the star grape of Bandol, provides the latter with power, complexity, and spicy notes. Carignan produces wines that are well-structured, generous, and colourful.

PRINCIPAL WHITE GRAPE VARIETIES. Rolle, especially in the Bellet AOC and in Corsica, produces wines with flavours of citrus and pear; they are rich, balanced, and fine. Clairette lends the wines flavour and bouquet, while Bourboulenc generates finesse and roundness.

Styles

Three appellations, Côtes-de-Provence, Coteaux-d'Aix-en-Provence, and Coteaux-Varois, account for 95 per cent of production. Rosé wines are usually aromatic, fruity, floral, dry, and fresh. But there are more complex rosés, which are structured and full-bodied, with more spicy aromas, capable of accompanying a gourmet meal. Red wines fall into two broad categories. There are lively and fruity wines with aromas of red fruits and flowers, which are consumed

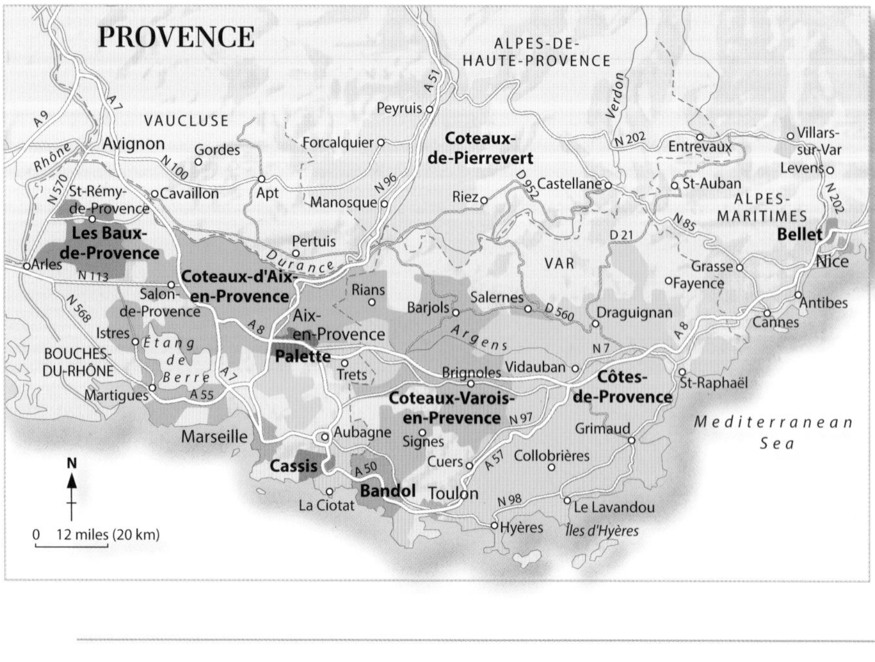

Provence AOCs

- Bandol
- Bellet
- Cassis
- Coteaux-d'Aix-en-Provence
- Coteaux-de-Pierrevert
- Coteaux-Varois-en-Provence
- Côtes-de-Provence (with or without a geographic designation: Fréjus, La Londe, Ste-Victoire)
- Les Baux-de-Provence
- Palette

DID YOU KNOW...?

Six per cent of the world's rosé wines come from Provence. *This is also the leading rosé-producing region in France (40 per cent of national production). The Colour of rosé is the result of the winemaking process (by saignée or direct pressing). It comes in nine shades (according to a classification established by the Center for Research and Experimentation on Rosé in Vidauban, a key resource on this matter): redcurrant, rosewood, raspberry, flesh, pink marble, salmon, onion skin, brick, and coral.*

while young; and there are more elaborate and concentrated wines, with more tannins and a potential for ageing. As for the whites, they generally offer a wonderful aromatic complexity with a pleasant creaminess.

Provence also produces a *vin cuit*: the grapes are extensively heated so as to concentrate flavours and substance. This wine does not come under any appellation.

CORSICA

History

Viticulture in Corsica is more than 2,500 years old. It was developed under Greek and Roman influence. During the 17th century, vineyards occupied much of the territory, and viticulture was the lifeblood of virtually the entire population. But, as elsewhere, phylloxera ravaged the entire region. It was not until the 1960s and the arrival of expatriates from North Africa that the vineyards were reborn. After a period of productivity at all costs, it is now definitely geared toward quality and authenticity.

CORSICA STATISTICS (AOC)

Vineyard area: 6,425 acres (2,600 ha)

Production: 1.2 million cases (110,000 hl)

Reds: 33%

Rosés: 55%

Whites: 12%

(CIV Corse)

Climate and soils

Corsica is more than just an island; it is a mountain massif. It enjoys a Mediterranean climate tempered by the combined influences of the sea and mountains, which is particularly favourable for the maturation of grapes. Across this rugged terrain, there are a wide variety of soils, ranging from schist in the east to granite soil on the west coast and in the south.

Corsica AOCs

- Ajaccio
- Muscat du Cap-Corse
- Patrimonio
- Vin de Corse

Varieties and styles

GRAPE VARIETIES. As well as standard southern French grapes (Grenache and Syrah), Corsica takes pride in its own varieties. Related to Sangiovese (from Tuscany), the Nielluccio grape is the basis of red wines from Patrimonio. It presents flavours of red berries, violets, spices, and apricot. Another red grape variety, the Sciacarello, is grown mainly in the granite soils of southern Corsica; it displays great finesse, combined with an unforgettable peppered bouquet. Among the white grape varieties, the most characteristic is Vermentino, which is also called Malvasia here. It produces a very distinctive wine, which is very rich and has strong floral aromas. It is also used for the development of rosés.

WINES. Corsican rosé and white wines are rich and full of flavour, with a nice balance. They should be consumed young. Red wines are generally light, but those of Patrimonio and Ajaccio have dense tannins with good length on the palate, and may be aged for a few years.

> In northern Corsica, Patrimonio vineyards occupy a privileged position, sheltered from the winds.

Leading wines of Provence and Corsica

Whether large or small, Provençal appellations are widely known for their rosés; but their reds and whites are also worth investigating, as are the sunny wines and Muscats from the island of Corsica.

PROVENCE

CÔTES-DE-PROVENCE AOC

Occupying a vast area, this AOC extends from Gardanne to St-Raphaël over some 48,186 acres (19,500 ha) across three *départements* (Var, Bouches-du-Rhône, and Alpes-Maritimes) and a mosaic of *terroirs* – each with its own distinctive geography, climate, and character. The appellation is made up of five major districts: Mont Ste-Victoire, the Beausset basin, the limestone highlands, the interior valley, and the coastal region. It is especially renowned for its rosé (87 per cent of production, nearly half of the rosés sold in France). It also produces quality reds and several whites. The Côtes-de-Provence AOC includes 18 classified growths: Château Minuty, Château Ste-Roseline, Château Ste-Marguerite, Château de la Clapière, Domaine de l'Aumérade, Clos Cibonne, Domaine de Rimauresq, Château Roubine, Château du Galoupet, Château de St-Martin, Château St-Maur, Clos Mireille, Château de Selle, Château de Brégançon, Château de Mauvanne, Domaine de la Croix, Domaine du Noyer, and Domaine du Jas d'Esclans.

> **GRAPE VARIETIES** Grenache, Syrah, Carignan, Mourvèdre, Tibouren, Cinsaut, and Cabernet for reds and rosés; Clairette, Sémillon, Ugni Blanc, and Rolle for whites.

> **SOIL** Stony.

> **STYLE** The rosés are rather pale and display pleasant, subtle scents of red fruit and citrus fruit mixed with hints of spice and flowers. The reds may be supple and light with a nose of red berries and flowers, or they may be generous, powerful, and elegant with complex flavours of black fruit with touches of damp woodland and spicy notes that linger on the palate. The whites are smooth with a delicate balance between freshness and richness.

Colour: *Red, rosé, and white.*

Serving temperature: *43 to 46°F (6 to 8°C) for whites; 46 to 54°F (8 to 12°C) for rosés; 61 to 63°F (16 to 17°C) for reds (ideally decanted).*

Ageing potential: *Consume rosés the summer after vintage; consume whites within a year; 3 years for reds; 10 to 12 years for classified growths.*

PROVENCE

COTEAUX-VAROIS-EN-PROVENCE AOC

This appellation covers 28 villages in the heart of Provence – around Brignoles, between the massifs of Ste-Baume to the south and Bessillons to the north. It climbs over 1,150 ft (350m) along slopes that are subject to a continental climate. It mainly produces rosé wines, but also reds and whites.

> **GRAPE VARIETIES** Syrah, Grenache, Mourvèdre, Cinsaut, and Cabernet Sauvignon for reds and rosés; Clairette, Grenache, Rolle, Sémillon, and Ugni Blanc for whites.

> **SOIL** Clay-and-limestone.

> **STYLE** With pretty, nuanced colours, the rosés have red fruit flavours (strawberry and raspberry) enhanced by notes of spice and garrigue; and they are highlighted by an attractive freshness and good balance. The well-structured, fleshy, tannic red wines blend floral and red fruit flavours,with herbaceous hints. They need time to soften. The whites have a nose delicately scented with flowers, fruits, and citrus, with good balance between freshness and roundness.

Colour: *Red, rosé, and white.*

Serving temperature: *43 to 46°F (6 to 8°C) for whites; 46 to 54°F (8 to 12°C) for rosés; 61 to 64°F (16 to 18°C) for reds.*

Ageing potential: *Consume rosés within a year; 1 to 2 years for whites; 3 to 8 years for reds.*

PROVENCE

BANDOL AOC

This vineyard region on the edge of Toulon is one of the oldest in France. Limited to eight districts in Var, its terraces cover about 3,707 acres (1,500 ha). Bandol's reputation is primarily for its red wines of great character, but it also produces rosés (the majority of its production) and whites.

> **GRAPE VARIETIES** Mourvèdre (at least 50 per cent), Grenache, Cinsaut, Syrah, and Carignan for reds and rosés; Bourboulenc (at least 60 per cent), Clairette, and Ugni Blanc for whites.

> **SOIL** Sand-and-limestone.

> **STYLE** Stamped with the letter 'B,' the reds, which spend at least 18 months in barrel, are powerful. These wines offer complex black fruit, pine, and garrigue flavours. With age, they develop peony, spice, and licorice characters, with a finish that remains full of flavour. The rosés have a range of red fruit flavours highlighted by spicy notes. Fewer in number, the whites display hints of white and yellow flowers and fruits, and a pleasing finesse.

Colour: *Red, rosé, and white.*

Serving temperature: *46 to 50°F (8 to 10°C) for rosés; 48 to 52°F (9 to 11°C) for whites; 61 to 64°F (16 to 18°C) for reds.*

Ageing potential: *1 to 3 years for whites and rosés; 10 years or more for reds.*

PROVENCE

CASSIS AOC

Located near the charming little port of Cassis, and blown by the Mistral wind, this vineyard area extends over 531 acres (215 ha) between the Calanques and Cap Canaille, the highest cliff in France at 1,312 ft (400 m). It produces highly regarded white wines, as well as some rosés and reds.

> **GRAPE VARIETIES** For red and rosé: Grenache, Carignan, Mourvèdre, and Cinsaut; for white: Clairette, Marsanne, Bourboulenc, Sauvignon Blanc, Terret Blanc, and Ugni Blanc.

> **SOIL** Limestone.

> **STYLE** Young whites offer a refreshing palate with a beguiling nose of white fruits, citrus, and an iodized hint that is reminiscent of the nearby sea. All these flavours have a long finish. With age, the nose becomes complex and releases aromas of honey, and the wine becomes more rounded and softer. The rosés, which are light and supple, present pleasing fruity and floral notes. Fewer in number, the reds offer herbaceous hints of bay leaf and thyme. There also are touches of red fruit (blackcurrant) mixed with some spice and licorice notes.

Colour: *Red, rosé, and white.*

Serving temperature: *46 to 50°F (8 to 10°C) for whites and rosés; 59 to 63°F (16 to 17°C) for reds.*

Ageing potential: *Consume rosés within a year; 3 to 5 years for reds; up to 8 years for whites.*

Selected Provence producers

- **Château de Pibarnon (La Cadière-d'Azur).** A classic of its appellation. Deep and balanced wines from the Bandol AOC.
- **Château du Gros Noré (La Cadière-d'Azur).** Authentic, exquisitely expressive wines that are among the best in the Bandol AOC.
- **Château La Calisse (Pontevès).** Seductive rosés and lovely reds from Coteaux-Varois-en-Provence.
- **Clos Ste-Magdeleine (Cassis).** A key estate for the Cassis appellation, producing wines of character that are tempting and delicious.
- **Domaine Saint André de Figuière (Lalonde).** Good-quality and consistent Côtes-de-Provence in the three colours.
- **Domaine de Garbelle (Garéoult).** Some fantastic Coteaux-Varois-en-Provence reds that are powerful and generous.
- **Domaine Hauvette (St-Rémy-de-Provence).** A great estate of the Coteaux-d'Aix-en-Provence AOC, which produces top quality organic wines.
- **Domaine Rabiega (Draguignan).** One of the best in the Côtes-de-Provence AOC. Its wines are an authentic expression of the *terroir*; its Clos Dière is excellent.
- **Les Maîtres Vignerons de la Presqu'île de Saint-Tropez (Gassin).** A range of superb quality Côtes-de-Provence wines; their red Château de Pampelonne is colourful, rich, dense, and generous.

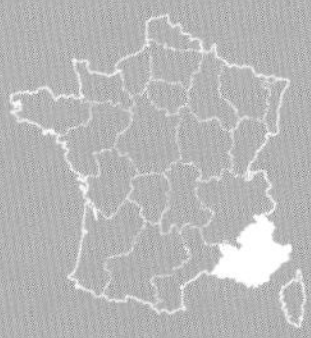

Provence

DOMAINE
DE TRÉVALLON

Situated between Provence and the Camargue, Domaine de Trévallon was founded by Éloi Dürrbach, an exceptional and determined wine-maker, who turned it into the jewel of Les Baux-de-Provence AOCs before striking out on his own. His red continue to be one of the most remarkable expressions of the essential character of the South of France.

DOMAINE DE TRÉVALLON

avenue Notre-Dame du Château
13103 Saint-Étienne-du-Grès

Founded: *1973*
Area: *42 acres (17 ha)*
Production: *60,000 bottles p.a.*
Appellation: *IGP Alpilles*
Red grape varieties:
Cabernet Sauvignon, Syrah
White grape varieties: *Marsanne, Roussanne, Clairette, Grenache Blanc, Chardonnay*

Background

The estate's roots date back to 1955, when painter and sculptor René Dürrbach bought the traditional farmhouse at Trévallon, near the village of Saint-Étienne-du-Grès on the northern slopes of the Alpilles mountains. Extending across 148 acres (60 ha), none of the estate was cultivated, comprising heathland and pine forest. René's son Éloi inherited the estate in 1973 at the age of 23, and although wholly self-taught, decided to plant it with vines. Given the stony, pebbly nature of the land the project seemed foolhardy, but Éloi was determined to go ahead with his plan, resorting to robust measures where necessary to loosen the ground. Dynamite and soil rippers were used to create an initial plantation covering 7 acres (3 ha), which in 1976 produced the first red wine under the VDQS Coteaux des Baux-de-Provence denomination.

Creating the vineyard

To stock his vineyard, Éloi Dürrbach took inspiration from the work of an ambitious and innovative figure who had had the courage to plant (almost) all the Cabernet Sauvignon found in Provence. Georget Brunet was a defector from Bordeaux where he owned Château La Lagune, an Haut-Médoc *cru classé*. Settling, in 1960, to the northeast of Aix-en-Provence, Georget proceeded to create Château Vignelaure, which was to become a beacon estate for the region with an atypical choice of grape varieties largely dominated by this Bordeaux favourite. Following in his footsteps, Éloi also decided to plant Cabernet Sauvignon, with the aim of making a wine to lay down, based on a massal selection taken from the vines cultivated by Brunet (who was also a friend of Dürrbach's). In order to anchor his red wine in a more regional style, Éloi also decided on Syrah, the grape variety best adapted to a terroir with northern exposure, where it ripens slowly and approaches the balance acquired in its homeland the Northern Rhône. He accordingly sourced the Syrah plants from Château Fonsalette, a legendary property in Côtes du Rhône. Hence the Trévallon red wine is made up of equal quantities of these two grape varieties, a blend that allows it to stand out among the gamut of red wines.

DOMAINE DE TRÉVALLON, IGP ALPILLES

The Domaine de Trévallon estate produces a single red that in some ways is the epitome of its kind, but without exaggerated characteristics or contrivance. It is a model of integrity, from the whole grapes that are vinified with their stalks to being free from any of the additives commonly used, such as sulphur or synthetic yeasts. Ageing is carried out in wooden containers, barrels, or vats, and the wine is left to mature for two years, almost without being touched, allowing it to retain its initial essence. The same care is taken to bottle the wine without filtration and with scant clarification through fining. Thanks to all these precautions, the wine has great natural expression, demonstrating vigour and exciting variations in different vintages.

Exclusion from AOC classification

When the Baux-de-Provence area received its own AOC rating in 1995 and separated from the Coteaux d'Aix-en-Provence, Domaine de Trévallon was left in a predicament: its ratio of Cabernet Sauvignon exceeded the 20% authorized by the classification. With 50% of its surface area planted with this grape, the estate clearly broke the regulators' rule, which was based on the belief that the use of Cabernet Sauvignon would compromise the identity of the Baux terroir. And even though Éloi was given a period of grace of 30 years to conform to the AOC's strictures, he refused to submit to a demand that would undermine all his work. As a result he saw his wine relegated to the Vins de Pays category. The downgrading of an estate with a world-class reputation had repercussions of such enormity that the story was even picked up by one of the big national daily papers.

A new destiny

However, the downgrading incident failed to have a major impact on the estate's image or its commercial success, and fans of its wine simply enjoyed the forbidden fruit all the more. Nevertheless, had the opposite been the case, Éloi would not have thrown in the towel, and he continues to make wine as he wishes, such as his white wine, created without reference to the legislation and relying on his own intuition and his knowledge of the terroir. Éloi continues to plough his own furrow and is now working out of a new cellar, the fruit of a project on a more modest scale, unlike the others, taking into account, for the sake of efficiency, ecological and local principles.

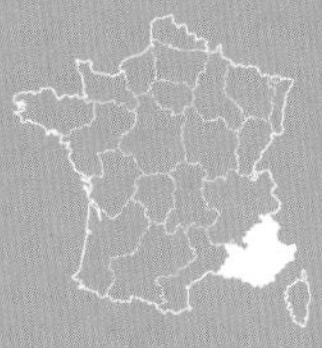

Provence

DOMAINE *TEMPIER*

The success of this estate is bound up with that of the Bandol appellation, which is located on the Var coast to the east of Toulon. Here, the soils work with a gentle and very sunny climate to produce marvellously ripe Mourvèdre grapes for wines that can be laid down for long periods, a unique phenomenon in the South of France.

DOMAINE TEMPIER

1082, chemin des Fanges
83330 Le Plan du Castellet

Founded: *1834*
Area: *99 acres (40 ha)*
Production: *150,000 bottles p.a.*
Appellation: *Bandol*
Red grape varieties: *Mourvèdre, Grenache, Cinsaut, Carignan, Syrah*
White grape varieties: *Clairette, Trebbiano, Bourboulenc, Vermentino, Marsanne*

Mourvèdre, or the soul of Bandol

The Tempier estate was founded by the Peyraud familly in 1834, a time when Bandol enjoyed a thriving cooperage business linked directly with its port and its wine trade. The arrival at the end of the 19th century of the vine disease phylloxera put paid to this prosperity, and the local vineyards, like so many others, were wiped out. They recovered gradually, but were re-established properly only much later, with the creation in 1939 of the *Syndicat des Producteurs de la région historique de Bandol* ('syndicate of wine producers from the historic region of Bandol'). This proved a turning point, and Bandol has enjoyed AOC status since 1941. One of those involved in these developments was Lucien Peyraud, owner of the Tempier estate, who also headed the syndicate between 1945 and 1982 and so influenced the appellation that operated according to strict legislation right from the start to produce reds with the characteristics of wines that could be laid down for years, the equal of the *crus classés* of Bordeaux and the *grands crus* of Burgundy. The principal vehicle for this ambition was Mourvèdre, a Mediterranean grape that would combine with the limestone soils of Bandol to produce powerful, tannic wines with excellent ageing potential. Use of a larger percentage of this grape was thus built into the appellation decree.

A visionary winemaker

Lucien Peyraud was in charge of the Domaine Tempier estate between 1941 and 1982, when his sons Jean-Marie and François took over. During his incumbency, the estate established a style of balance and integrity that was showcased by its Cuvée Spéciale, which contains a very high proportion of Mourvèdre (80 per cent of its content). This wine combines the best aspects of a wine-growing region made up of several sectors, some of which were already being vinified separately. The idea of making wines produced on specific terroirs was never far from their thoughts and came to fruition at the end of the 1970s with the creation of La Migoua, La Tourtine, and Cabassaou, the estate's signature trio, whose names became icons for wine-lovers all over the world. Alongside their intrinsic quality, these wines were fashioned from their terroir and cleverly designed to suit Mourvèdre grapes, which figured heavily in their blend (except in the case of La Migoua), with percentages adjusted each year.

DOMAINE TEMPIER: A LEGENDARY TRIO

The first year of production for La Migoua and La Tourtine, two wines named after their local areas, was in 1979. La Migoua is in fact made in the town of Le Beausset and is atypical of the output of the estate in that it has a relatively low Mourvèdre content (approximately 50 per cent). It is a wine full of vigour and subtlety, echoing the varied make-up of its terroir. With its well-exposed vineyard terraces near the village of Castellet, La Tourtine boasts ideal terrain for Mourvèdre grapes, producing a classy wine that can be laid down for long periods. It is the lower, even sunnier, portion of this area that produces Cabassaou, however, a more select wine with even greater potential for ageing; first made in 1987.

Continuing a great legacy

A turning point in the history of the estate came in 2000, when the Peyraud family ceased to run it directly and handed the reins to Daniel Ravier, an agricultural engineer. With his experience of managing an estate in Bandol and great professionalism, Daniel rose to the challenge of introducing essential innovations, while at the same time fostering a spirit of continuity. Thanks to his training, Daniel was particularly attuned to his wine-making heritage, especially with regard to the preservation of the legendary terroirs. While he doesn't claim to be using organic farming methods, his management of the vines respects organic principles and even goes beyond them where the precepts of biodynamic farming have become the rule. His wine-making methods are otherwise based on long-established techniques, with a fairly long but gentle vinification period followed by traditional ageing in large vats. Under such conditions, the resulting wines continue to reflect a timeless, unaffected style rich in the essence of each *terroir* and providing a wonderful balance between sophistication and artlessness.

> Daniel Ravier, the estate manager.

Dupéré-Barrera, a small négociant of grands vins

Provence is not historically home to large *négociants* but there are some small top-quality companies producing wines with skill and character from its terroirs. Emmanuelle Dupéré and Laurent Barrera are both passionate about wine and in 2000 established a small high-end *négoce*. They own an estate of 12 acres (5 ha) in the Côtes de Provence appellation, cultivated organically, and have formed trusted relationships with excellent winemakers in Provence and the Rhône. They are scrupulous in their choice of grapes or in the wines they purchase and have created a small range of wines that are both full of character and reasonably priced, such the Nowat *cuvée*, which is excellent as a red and white.

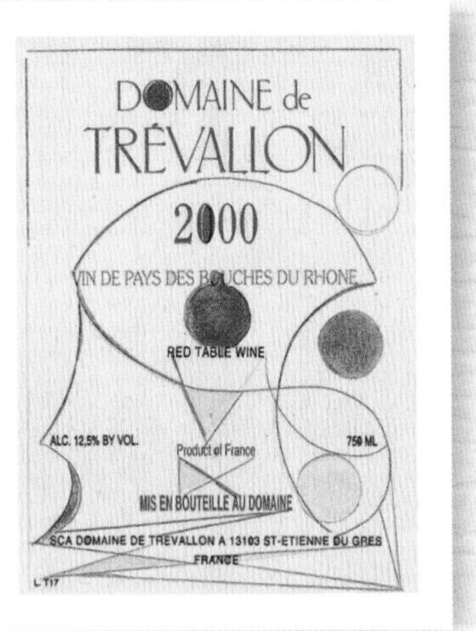

PROVENCE

COTEAUX-D'AIX-EN-PROVENCE AOC

Aix-en-Provence was the city of 15th-century King René, who was both a king and a winemaker. He developed the vineyards; and today, these vast plantings cover the Bouches-du-Rhône *département*. Across sheltered hillsides, woods, and scrubland, they extend over 6,425 acres (2,600 ha). The appellation produces rosé wines, but also some reds and whites.

> **GRAPE VARIETIES** Grenache, Cabernet Sauvignon, Carignan, Mourvèdre, Cinsaut, Syrah, and Counoise for reds and rosés; Clairette, Rolle, Bourboulenc, Ugni Blanc, Grenache, Sémillon, and Sauvignon for whites.

> **SOIL** Sand-and-limestone.

> **STYLE** The rosés are light and soft, with delicate colours. They display a nice variety of fruits (strawberry, peach), flowers (lime), and mineral notes on a fresh palate. The red wines, which are rich and full, combine flowers (violet), herbaceous notes, and hints of spices with persistent palate length. While the white wines are fresh, elegant, and full of flavour, yielding a bouquet of flowers, fruits, and citrus.

Colour:
Red, rosé, and white.

Serving temperature:
43 to 46°F (6 to 8°C) for whites;
46 to 54°F (8 to 12°C) for rosés;
61 to 64°F (16 to 18°C) for reds.

Ageing potential:
1 to 2 years for whites;
2 to 5 years for rosés;
2 to 6 years for reds.

CORSICA

PATRIMONIO AOC

Rising in terraced rows that curve above the Gulf of St-Florent in northwest Corsica, and influenced by both mountains and sea, the vineyards of Patrimonio grow over an area of less than 2,471 acres (1,000 ha). They are best known for their red wines, but also produce rosés and whites in small numbers but of high quality.

> **GRAPE VARIETIES** For reds and rosés: Nielluccio, Sciacarello, and Grenache; for whites: Vermentino and Ugni Blanc.

> **SOIL** Schist covered with limestone.

> **STYLE** The reds, based mainly on Nielluccio, have a powerful nose of macerated red fruits and spices. They are rich and generous with spicy notes. The roses have a savoury nose of spices and fresh fruit (strawberry, cherry), supported by a very full body. The whites are typical of their grape variety, Vermentino. They are dry and crisp, and have a very aromatic bouquet combining notes of white flowers and exotic fruits with a hint of dried grass, all highlighted by a fine freshness.

Colour:
Red, rosé, and white.

Serving temperature:
45 to 46°F (7 to 8°C) for whites;
46 to 50°F (8 to 10°C) for rosés;
59 to 61°F (15 to 16°C) for reds.

Ageing potential:
Consume rosés within a year;
up to 2 years for whites;
3 to 8 years for reds.

VIN DE CORSE AOC

CORSICA

Backing into rocky ridges, these vineyards cover some 4,695 acres (1,900 ha) and produce 999,000 cases (90,000 hl) of mainly reds, but also some whites and rosés. The wines, which can be produced throughout Corsica, come mainly from the east coast, and may add the name of one of these *terroirs*: Sartène, Figari, Porto-Vecchio, and Calvi.

> **GRAPE VARIETIES** Nielluccio, Sciacarello, and Grenache for reds and rosés; Vermentino and Ugni Blanc for whites.

> **SOIL** Granite, schist.

> **STYLE** The red wines have very nice aromas of red fruit, garrigue, and spice that linger on the palate. The whites, produced mostly from Vermentino grapes, have a generous, floral, and fruity nose. They also have hints of citrus and tropical fruit enhanced by a lovely freshness. As for rosés, they are bright and lively, with floral notes punctuated by subdued herbaceous touches.

Colour:
Red, rosé, and white.

Serving temperature:
46 to 50°F (8 to 10°C) for whites and rosés; 59 to 63°F (15 to 17°C) for reds.

Ageing potential:
1 to 2 years for whites and rosés; 4 to 9 years for reds.

MUSCAT DU CAP-CORSE AOC

CORSICA

Muscat is a very old Corsican specialty. The *vin doux naturel* is rare – with only some 22,000 cases (2,000 hl) 1,300 produced – and delicate. It comes from terraced vineyards covering 198 acres (80 ha) at the north end of the island. Production encompasses 17 villages, the area of Patrimonio, and the Vin de Corse-Coteaux-du-Cap-Corse AOC. There is also a local variation called *passito*, a non-fortified wine produced by *passerillage*, the raisining of grapes on the vine.

> **GRAPE VARIETY** Muscat Blanc à Petits Grains.

> **SOIL** Schist at Cap Corse, limestone boulders in Patrimonio.

> **STYLE** Produced by fortification, Muscat du Cap-Corse is a wine of great finesse. It offers a rich and complexbouquet combining notes of dried fruit (figs, currants), tropical fruit, and hints of spices (cinnamon). It all lingers on the palate with a nice balance between freshness and generosity.

Colour:
White.

Serving temperature:
46 to 50°F (8 to 10°C).

Ageing potential:
10 years.

Selected Corsica producers

- **Clos d'Alzeto (Sari-d'Orcino).** Red, rosé, and white wines of great character in the Ajaccio AOC.
- **Domaine Arena (Patrimonio).** Very pure white, red, and rosé wines of the Patrimonio appellation, and a Muscat du Cap-Corse Grotte di Sole.
- **Domaine Comte Peraldi (Mezzavia).** A safe bet from the Ajaccio AOC.
- **Domaine Leccia (Poggio-d'Oletta).** Major estate of the Patrimonio appellation; its dry whites and reds highlight the qualities of its *terroir*.
- **Domaine de Torraccia (Porto-Vecchio).** Powerful, organically produced red Vins de Corse.

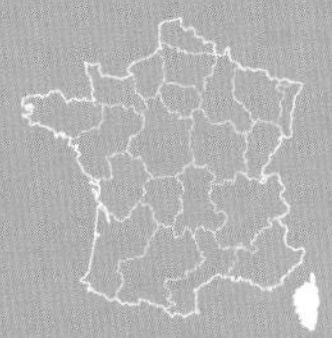

Corsica

DOMAINE *ARENA*

You don't come across Domaine Arena by chance – the road to Patrimonio is long and spectacular whichever way you approach it, and the cliff views from Poggio d'Oletta are breathtaking. It is sometimes said that great locations make great wine-makers, and this old adage has certainly proved true for Antoine Arena, a son of Patrimonio.

DOMAINE ARENA
Morta Maïo
20253 Patrimonio

Area: *35 acres (14 ha)*
Production: *55,000 bottles p.a.*
Appellation: *Patrimonio*
Red grape varieties: *Nielluccio*
White grape varieties: *Vermentinu, Muscat, Biancu Gentile*

An exceptional location and an exceptional family

Although Antoine Arena comes from a wine-growing family, he was not necessarily destined for a wine-making career – it was only on returning from a law degree course on the mainland in 1975 that he decided to follow in the footsteps of his father. At the time, almost everything on the estate needed work and the AOC Patrimonio had only just been established. The wine had enjoyed a good reputation during the Roman period, but a great deal of water had flowed under the bridges over the Nebbio since then! In particular, the productivity of the 1960s had destabilized local output, and even as Antoine took up his post, a drop in table wine consumption was seriously compromising the future of Corsican wine-making.

However, Antoine is one of those people who thinks that where there's a will there's way and rather than engaging in a race to increase yields, he and his wife Maria managed to showcase their small legacy at Patrimonio (7.5 acres/3 ha) by producing select wines – quite a risky gamble at the time.

Grape varieties and vineyards

Naturally, they used the appellation's grape varieties to achieve their goal: Nielluccio (a cousin of Sangiovese) for the reds, and Vermentinu (Vermentino) for the whites. Arena was also the first to replant with Biancu Gentile, an old and highly aromatic white grape from Sartenais that had been identified by the Corsican Wine Research Centre. Antoine soon established himself as the leading exponent of the different characteristics of Patrimonio – a mostly limestone area but much less homogeneous than it appeared, with white chalk, mixed-limestone blocks, and zones of clay. If grape varieties are the base colours on a wine-maker's palette, these micro-terroirs were able to introduce light and shade.

Further land purchases and replanting allowed Antoine to expand the estate from 7.5 acres to 35 (3 ha to 14 ha), including two prime plots: the vineyard at the Grotte di Sole, 7.5 acres (3 ha) of limestone mixed with clay, with direct southern exposure, planted with Nielluccio (5 acres/2 ha) and Vermentinu (2.5 acres/1 ha) grapes; and at Carco, which faces east and has the extremely chalky soils that are particularly well-suited to Vermentinu (5 acres/2 ha), and Nielluccio (2.5 acres/1 ha). These vines date back to the 1950s, with the exception of Carco's Vermentinu, which was planted in 1987 and 2003 (at Haut de Carco). Their Morta Maio wine (a red) is made from Nielluccio vines planted in 2001.

Getting in early with organic farming

For Antoine, another key principle is that the more life there is in the soil, the better the wines, and the estate was already farming organically before the technique was officially introduced to Corsica. Antoine continues to shun treatments that use chemicals, limits sulphur to a minimum, and only uses local yeasts. The vines are ploughed but no synthetics are used, and anything added to the soil must be natural (sheep manure, grape marc). In the last few years, Antoine and Maria have been joined in the running of the estate by their sons Antoine-Marie and Jean-Baptiste. The generations may hand on the baton, but there has been no change in the estate's strictures, and the family adventure continues.

DOMAINE ARENA, PATRIMONIO GROTTE DI SOLE ROUGE

Whatever the year, and almost without exception, this wine exhibits a great melding of tannic power (the signature of its Nielluccio grapes) and elegance, while retaining its astonishing spicy freshness – an iron hand in a velvet glove that offers more than just the characteristics determined by the land on which it was grown. Nielluccio grapes can be tough, and Arena has mastered both the art and skill of taming and getting the best out of them.

DOMAINE ARENA, PATRIMONIO CARCO BLANC

This wine, full of vigour, flowers, and white fruits, is among the most beautiful examples of subtlety to be found on the Mediterranean coast, with a remarkably fleshy mouthfeel along with a slight hint of saline bitterness in the finish.

> Jean-Baptiste Arena returned home to manage the estate.

ITALY

Wine-producing regions
Northern
Central
Southern and islands
Border
Regional border
N
0
125 miles (200 km)
Bolzano
TRENTINO - ALTO-ADIGE
Trento
FRIULI-VENEZIA-GIULIA
VAL D'AOSTA
Como
Adda
LOMBARDY
Lake Garda
Adige
VENETO
Piave
Trieste
PIEDMONT
Milan
Vicenza
Verona
Venice
Turin
Asti
Po
Modène
Reno
Genova
EMILIA-ROMAGNA
Bologna
Ravenna
LIGURIA
SAN MARINO
Ligurian Sea
Pisa
Florence
Arno
Ancona
TUSCANY
Tiber
MARCHE
Montepulciano
Perugia
UMBRIA
Adriatic Sea
Pescara
LAZIO
ABRUZZO
Rome
MOLISE
Foggia
SARDINIA
CAMPANIA
Bari
Naples
PUGLIA
Tyrrhenian Sea
BASILICATA
Tarento
Cagliari
CALABRIA
Ionian Sea
Mediterranean Sea
Reggio di Calábria
Palermo
Messina
SICILY
Catania
PANTELLERIA

ITALY

Italy produces about 15 per cent of the world's wine. In other words, one bottle out of every six on earth is Italian. A land of art and culture, with a vibrant instinct for food and flavour, the Italian peninsula is full of great classics and local surprises, thanks to its many different regions and their rich history.

Wonderful (and confusing) diversity

In an Italian wine cellar, an expert in French wine feels somewhat lost. Each winery follows its own aesthetic inspiration, and the shape of the bottle does not indicate in any way – as it does in France, via the specific bottle shapes for Bordeaux, Burgundy, etc. – the region of production. The only distinctive bottle is the straw-covered flask still occasionally used for basic Chianti, which Tuscany discards for its other wines, preferring instead to adopt the Bordeaux-shaped bottle.

Reading the labels fails to solve the mystery. Except for the most famous names (Chianti Classico, Barolo, and Brunello), the 74 DOCG (*Denominazione di origine controllata e garantita*), the 330 DOC (*Denominazione di origine controllata*), the 120 IGT (*Indicazione geografica tipica*), and the countless references and trademarks of *vino* (table wine) can completely baffle the novice. In terms of the number of appellations for wines and spirits, Italy leads the world. The price ranges are also extensive. So what should we expect when we open the bottle? Is the wine light, full-bodied, dry, sweet, or sparkling? Is it best for simple drinks or for dinner? Which foods will it complement?

To understand and appreciate Italian wines, some key explanatory notes will prove as useful as a corkscrew: the names of key grape varieties, the rich tapestry of soils and climates, and the history of the people and viticulture in the various regions.

ITALY STATISTICS

Vineyard area: 1,705,027 acres (690,000 ha)

Production: 521 million cases (47,000,000 hl) (average 2010–2014)

Whites: 55%

Reds and rosés: 45%

(Assoenologi and Istat, OIV)

A long history of wine

FROM ANCIENT ORIGINS... The vine is an experienced traveller. After beginning its journey in Asia Minor, it moved to Ancient Greece; and the Greeks then taught the Etruscans how to ferment grapes. Many Roman texts detail winemaking methods, classifications of wines (including by the Academy of Medicine in Rome), and the export of its highly priced and very popular nectar to wealthy Gauls: 'a slave or an amphora [of wine]', said Diodorus Siculus. The renowned *terroir* of Campania, between Rome and Naples, suffered from the eruption of Vesuvius at Pompeii in 79 AD. The city was buried under volcanic ash, but even today there are traces of poles that supported vines. So Italian winemakers have refined their know-how for millennia. The Antinori family, as one example, has been making wine since 1385, for 26 generations. But there are countless dynasties of Italian wine entrepreneurs whose names we don't know.

...TO MODERN THREATS... There have been three key threats to the modern Italian wine industry: phylloxera, excessively high yields, and the globalization of style. The first was handled during the late 19th century by planting American vine rootstocks that were resistant to phylloxera – to which any European grape varieties could be grafted as required. But what grape varieties were chosen? Traditional ones with local names unfamiliar to anyone outside the province? Or famous international varieties (Merlot, Chardonnay, etc.), which would often produce higher yields and could be readily exported? Entire regions, such as Veneto, Sicily, and Tuscany, planted international grapes on a large scale. During the 20th century, the second threat was the era of 'bulk wine', with Italy exporting boatloads of cheap wine for blending. These

> Barrels being made in Florio, Sicily.

> Terraced vineyards in Trentino-Alto Adige, northeast Italy.

came from vineyards with very high yields and generous alcohol content and colour; and these still equate to one-third of the volume produced in Italy. Calling them 'pizzeria plonk' would be unfair. They are not very subtle, but they nevertheless can represent a decent house wine. Note that 'bulk' is not necessarily synonymous with poor quality. Many producers sell appealing wine in 3-litre or 5-litre boxes.

...TO THE ERA OF ESTATE BOTTLING. Today, the Italian wine market has matured. Consumption is 'less but better'. So the area occupied by vineyards has decreased from 3,039,396 acres (1,230,000 million ha) in 1980 to 1,705,027 acres (690,000 ha) in 2014. Sources of bulk wine (in order of size: Puglia, Sicily, Emilia-Romagna, and Abruzzo) have reduced their cheap exports to improve quality and sell higher-value bottles. To attract orders, some winemakers are adapting their production to the desires of the international market and accentuating sweeter or oakier flavours. At times, this standardization of such unique varieties is a matter of regret; but other winemakers are reviving local grapes, which provide a fitting response to the more uniform flavours produced by the New World.

Northern regions

On its journey around the world, the vine would have become less attached to Italy if the terrain there been a dreary plain with a uniform climate. But this is one of the few nations in the world where every corner of the country cultivates its own varieties to make the most of its great diversity.

Val d'Aosta, Trentino-Alto Adige, and Friuli have a mountain climate. Vines planted in the snow of Val d'Aosta, at an altitude of more than 3,940 ft (1,200 m), are among the highest in Europe. That climate is reflected in the wines, which have a bracing freshness. But the mosaic of climates and the many varieties found across Italy's northern regions yield some nice discoveries. In Piedmont (literally 'the foot of the mountains'), vines grow on remarkably steep hills, with the rice fields of the Po plain below them. Rich alluvial land, with water from the Alps and warm sunshine, permits the high yields seen in Lombardy and Veneto: up to 8.8 tons/acre (150 hl/ha). By contrast, to create more concentrated wine, appellations like Barolo limit their production to less than 3 tons/acre (52 hl/ha). From a total of 20 Italian regions, the six northern ones (Piedmont, Lombardy, Trentino, Veneto, Friuli, and Emilia-Romagna) provide half the total volume of Italian wine and account for more than half of DOCGs.

TRUE OR FALSE?

Italy is the largest wine producer in the world.

TRUE. In recent years, on average, Italy has been the largest wine producer in the world, although France is hot on its heels in second place. In terms of total planted area, Spain has the largest vineyard area in the world.

Central regions

In the so-called 'green heart' of Italy, the hills of Tuscany produce the world-famous Chianti. This region takes its name from the ancient Etruscans (or Tusci), who learned winemaking from the Greeks before passing this skill on to the Romans. In fact, the Greek word *oinos* became *vinum* in Etruscan and Latin, before becoming *vin* in French and ultimately 'wine' in English. During the 20th century, Tuscany started crafting premium wines created with grape varieties such as Cabernet Sauvignon and Cabernet Franc – and they became known as Super Tuscans. The Marquis Incisa della Rocchetta, a great fan of Bordeaux wines, produced the first bottles of Sassicaia during the 1940s (*see also* pp.368–9). Then other creative winemakers followed, such as the Antinori family with their Solaia. A local appellation, Bolgheri, was even created to formalize this new style of wine. The other aim of this work was to reveal the qualities of Tuscan *terroir* in terms people understood. From the Apennines to the Adriatic, the areas of Lazio, Abruzzo, and Molise benefit from climates and soils of great diversity – from sunny beaches to year-round snow. These zones of ancient viticulture also have the advantages of proximity to Rome, which has been a major wine market for several millennia.

Southern regions

Southern Italy is a land of sunshine. The volcanic soils of Campania and the dry hills of Puglia, Basilicata, and Calabria were appreciated by the Ancient Greeks, who called this part of the Italian peninsula 'Oenotria' (the land of vines). These age-old

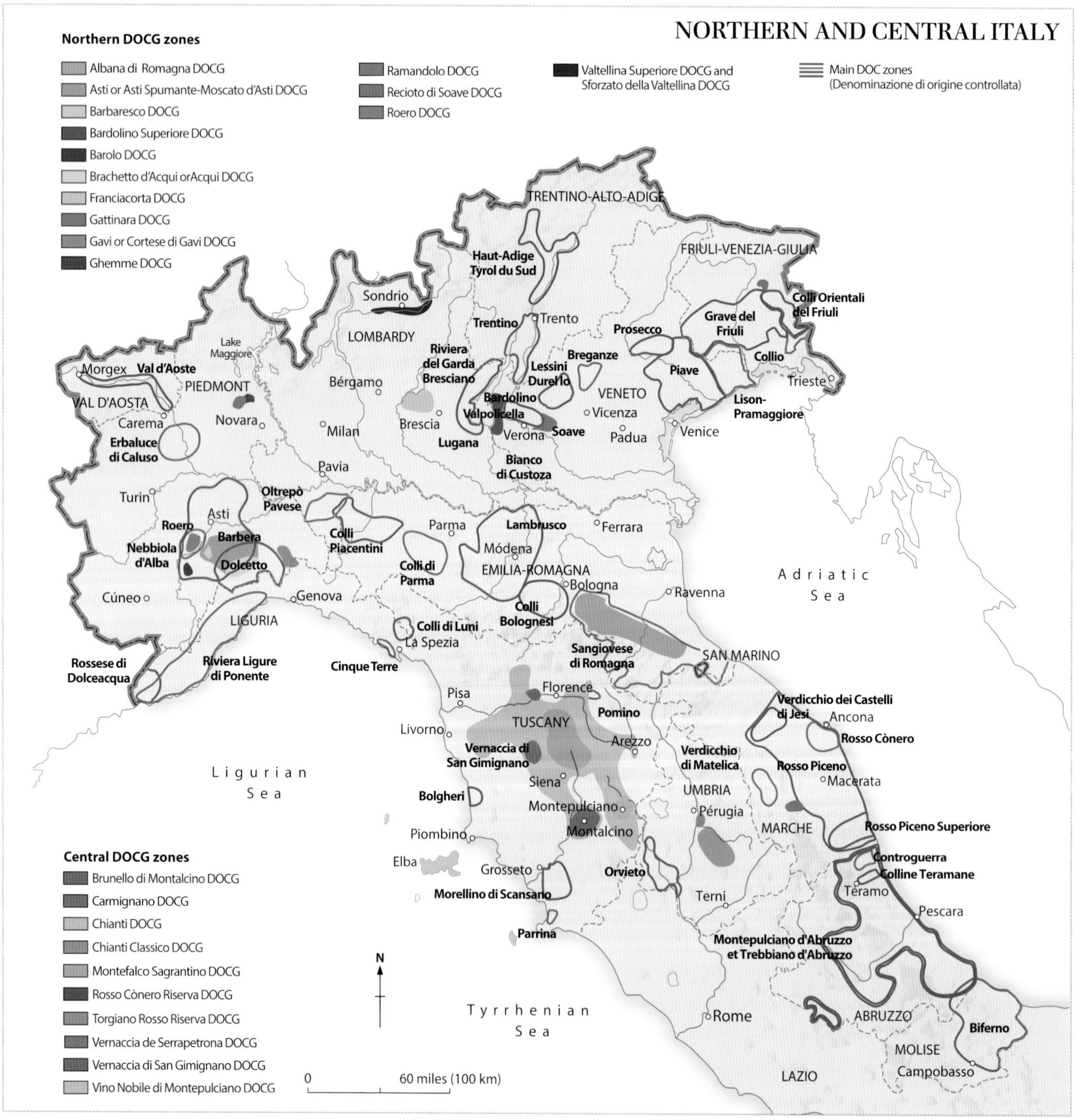

> Tuscan hills around the abbey of Sant'Antimo, near Montalcino.

regions – long dominated by large suppliers of bulk wine – are also changing. Cooperatives and large private cellars still supply the mass market at low prices, but small producers are making niche wines from local varieties.

The islands

With a Mediterranean climate, the islands are a different world from mainland Italy. The mountains of Sardinia have retained grape varieties from the period of Spanish rule. Sicily has a volcano that is still active, and the soils at the foot of snow-capped Mount Etna are unique. At the south end of the island, on the dark sands of Pachino, vineyards are located at a more southerly latitude than Tunis (North Africa). The dry and windy climate limits fungal diseases (such as mildew or powdery mildew) caused by dampness, so chemical plant treatments are less necessary than in northern vineyards – making Sicily the largest region in Europe for organic production. The southernmost Italian vineyard is on Pantelleria, an island between Sicily and Africa, where the grapes are left to dry naturally on the vine.

Key Italian varieties

The broad spectrum of climates and soils, across a distance of 750 miles (1,200 km) from north to south, is the main reason for the diversity of Italian vineyards. The other reason is cultural: until the 19th century, the peninsula was a patchwork of small independent states that were constantly at war. Each one proudly cultivated its local varieties of grape, which had been selected and differentiated by generations of winemakers.

To understand Italian wine, knowing the grape varieties is essential. The front or back label on the bottle often specifies the variety. One-third of the appellations mentioned on pages

Giant vines of Campania

The vine is a creeper that the Greeks left to grow along the ground, but the winemakers of the ancient world invented the *alberello* 'small tree' pruning method that is still used in Italy and France (*gobelet*). To limit any damage to fragile young vines from the wind and their own weight, growers had to find a means of support. The best-known solution was the wooden post. The famous Falerno wine of antiquity, described by Pliny (23–79 AD), even takes its name from the word for 'post'. The 'small tree' concept has been taken one step further in Campania, near Aversa. Here, Asprinio grapevines have been grown against poplar trees for over a century. They intertwine with the branches of the tree about 50 feet (15 metres) up and are harvested using a ladder.

> Sangiovese grapes, the main variety of Chianti.

360–73 are names of grape varieties associated with a particular geographic zone, such as Cannonau di Sardegna DOC (Sardinia) or Montepulciano d'Abruzzo DOC (Abruzzo). But even originally French varieties (Merlot, Chardonnay, etc.) have been adopted by the Italians, and many DOC and DOCG appellations now include them.

TRUE OR FALSE?

Sicily produces mostly red wine.

FALSE. White wine represents 60 per cent of Sicilian production and red 40 per cent. White grapes are not the exclusive preserve of northern vineyards, just as reds are not exclusive to southern *terroirs*.

AGLIANICO. Red, mainly grown in Campania, Basilicata, Molise, and Puglia. Probably brought by Ancient Greek colonists, it derives its name from the word 'Hellenic'. Sometimes vinified as a white (without the skins), as a sparkling or sweet wine, or as a *riserva*.

ARNEIS. White from Piedmont produced both as a dry and sometimes a sweet wine. In the Piedmont dialect, its name means 'little rascal'.

BARBERA. Red from Piedmont, now grown throughout Italy.

BONARDA. Red used in appellations of Piedmont, Lombardy, and Emilia-Romagna, it's transformed into sparkling or still wine and is sometimes cultivated as a dessert grape.

BRACHETTO. Light red from Piedmont that produces a slightly sparkling wine, low in tannins.

CANNONAU. Red grown in Sardinia, also known as Grenache in French, that yields a high level of alcohol. Also vinified as a rosé and *vin doux naturel*.

DOLCETTO. Fresh, fruity, and tannic red from Piedmont.

FALANGHINA. White from Campania. The Romans would have used this in their famous Falerno.

FIANO D'AVELLINO. White used for high quality, full-bodied white that ages well.

FRIULANO. Known for a long time as Tocai Friulano, this white grape variety is grown in Friuli and Veneto.

GLERA. White from Veneto, made in a closed tank as a sparkling 'extra dry', 'brut', or 'dry' wine. This method was developed by Charmat (according to the French) or by Martinotti (according to the Italians). Available in a sweet, *passerillé* version with 16% ABV. Prosecco is made from glera.

GRECO DI TUFO. White grown in Campania. In Italy, several varieties are called 'Greco', probably due to their supposed Greek origins. In danger of extinction, it has been revived for production in line with modern tastes.

INZOLIA. White used to create Marsala, and also used as a blended wine. Wineries now offer a single grape variety version, or blended versions with other whites (Chardonnay, Sauvignon Blanc, Grecanico). It is also known as 'Ansonica' on the island of Elba, in Lazio, and in Tuscany.

LAMBRUSCO. Red grown in Lombardy and Emilia-Romagna. The name is reminiscent of what the Romans called the vines that grew wild on the edge (*labrum*) of cultivated fields (*bruscum*).

MONTEPULCIANO. Intense red from the south (Abruzzo, Puglia, Marche, Lazio).

MOSCATO. White grown throughout all of Italy. It is transformed into still, lightly sparkling, or fully sparkling wines, as well as sweet wines or late-harvest wines. There is also a red variation.

NEBBIOLO. Red from Piedmont and Lombardy. Slow to mature at altitude, it is harvested in mid-October or even November, when there is an autumnal fog (*nebbia*), hence its name. It does best in limestone soils.

NERO D'AVOLA. Red from Sicily, with wild flavours. It is blended with more restrained grape varieties (Cabernet Sauvignon, Merlot, Syrah) or produced on its own for those who like a powerful style. Also available as a sweet red. There are some 20 Sicilian appellations.

PRIMITIVO. Red that is genetically identical to California's Zinfandel. 'These are twin brothers that have been separated for a long time,' claim wine producers from Puglia. It is the first grape to fully ripen each year, hence its name ('early').

SANGIOVESE. Its name comes from the Latin *sanguis Iovis* (Jupiter's blood). An emblematic red from Tuscany, but it's also cultivated in central and southern Italy. There are several clones with very different styles and yields.

Pervasive promotion

In Italy, wine is more than a product: it is a symbol of cultural identity. Tourist brochures mentions it alongside the frescoes in monasteries, an opera by Rossini, a contemporary sculpture, or traditional cheeses, meats, and vegetables. Local agencies (cities,

DID YOU KNOW...?

Italian grape varieties often have colourful names. *Coda di Volpe, an ancient variety from Campania, takes its name from the resemblance of its clusters to a fox tail. In Emilia-Romagna, the Bombino variety, often exported to blend with German wines, is nicknamed* pagadebit *('repaying the debt') as a reference to its efficiency and profitability.*

regions, wine-producing guilds) and national groups (chambers of commerce, the Italian Institute for Foreign Trade [ICE]) publish many brochures, pamphlets, books, guides, educational maps, and websites such as www.enoteca-italiana.it (in Italian and English). The *Strade del Vino* (Wine Routes) indicates tours through vineyards and wineries open to the public.

Deciphering labels

AESTHETIC MESSAGE. Wine is a very mobile agricultural product. When it is a long way from its home region, it needs a means of identifying itself, a kind of passport. Even the Romans attached labels to their amphorae, engraving the name of the manufacturer, the place of origin, and the type of wine. Today, packaging is more diverse. On one hand, electric blue bottles of low-priced whites are aimed at a young audience, with minimal refinement and synthetic corks the same colour as the label. On the other, prestigious wines such as Barolo communicate their message with a restrained or traditional label, or with a chic, contemporary design. On store shelves, the objective remains the same for all wines: stand out or lose out.

QUALITY PYRAMID. There are three levels to note (*see also* p.96): DOCG (*Denominazione di origine controllata e garantita*), identified by a purple numbered collar on the neck of the bottle, and DOC (*Denominazione di origine controllata*); IGT (*Indicazione geografica tipica*); and table wine or *vino*. Each of these three levels (DOC / DOCG, IGT, and *vino*) represents approximately one-third of the total volume produced in Italy every year.

GUARANTEE OF QUALITY? DOC and (especially) DOCG wines, with lower yields than IGT and *vino*, in principle have richer and more concentrated flavours. Generally, a given winemaker will use the most successful expressions of his or her best plots for these wines. The point of the appellation is to define a method of production so that consumers will be able to find, across various producers, a distinct style reflective of that region. Yet many winemakers are creating original, exciting wines that are not part of the appellation system – which is why some IGTs secure higher prices than a DOCG. As always, the market is the ultimate judge. For other wine lovers, the key to quality is respect for the environment through wines produced using organically farmed grapes. Italy also produces kosher certified wines.

> A grocery store in Siena, Tuscany.

GLOSSARY OF ITALIAN WINE TERMS

Some terms found on Italian wine labels:

amabile: medium sweet
amaro: bitter (or very dry)
asciutto: demi-sec
bianco: white
cantina: cellar, winery
cantina sociale: cooperative winery
chiaretto: clairet (light rosé wine)
classico: from the historic centre of an appellation area
cerasuolo: dark rosé wine (cherry-coloured)
consorzio: regional wine producer association
dolce: sweet
frizzante: lightly sparkling
gradi: degrees of alcohol
invecchiato: aged
in purezza: pure, from a single grape variety, not blended
metodo classico: sparkling wine using traditional method (Champagne-style)
nero: dark red
novello: new
passito: dessert wine produced from *passerillage* (clusters are dried in crates or hung to dry)
recioto: sweet wines from *passito* grapes in Veneto
riserva: wine aged for a period defined by the appellation
rosato: rosé
rosso: red
secco: dry
spumante: sparkling
tenuta: estate
vendemmia: harvest, vintage
vendemmia tardiva: late harvest

Leading Italian wines

Tasting Italian wines is like taking a journey through the history and terrain of the peninsula. A real mosaic, the map of Italian appellations reflects a certain alchemy of the terroirs, *the biodiversity of the grape varieties, and the natural and human landscape.*

VALLE D'AOSTA DOC

AOSTA

The smallest of all Italian wine regions is located between Switzerland and France, where they officially speak both Italian and French. Mountain wine producers here cultivate vineyards reputed to be the highest in Europe. The output of this *terroir* represents only a tiny fraction of total Italian wine production, but it nevertheless is divided into 30 categories such as 'Enfer d'Arvier' or 'Petite Arvine'. Wine produced from grapes dried on the vine is both of high quality and small scale.

> **GRAPE VARIETIES** The appellation recognizes 22 varieties: Piedmontese (Nebbiolo, Dolcetto, Moscato, etc.), French (Chardonnay, Pinot, Gamay), German (Müller-Thurgau), and local (Petite Rouge, Petite Arvine, Vien, Malvasia).

> **SOIL** Alpine terraces, some over 3,900 ft (1,200 m) in altitude.

> **STYLE** Valle d'Aosta is the only DOC in the region, and it includes a range of distinctive wines from the mountains. The altitude gives them freshness, a pleasant sharpness, and a reduced alcohol content (at least 9% ABV for white, 9.5% ABV for the basic red).

Colour:
Red (lightly coloured), white, and rosé.

Serving temperature:
46 to 50°F (8 to 10°C) for whites and rosés; 57 to 59°F (14 to 15°C) for reds.

Ageing potential:
1 to 2 years.

ASTI DOCG

PIEDMONT

This popular appellation is for a sparkling version of Muscat. The vines cover the limestone hills and plains of the provinces of Asti, Cuneo, and Alessandria. In winemaking, the tank is cooled to stop fermentation while there is still sugar in the grape must. The alcohol level is stabilized at between 7 and 9.5% ABV; though it would reach 12% ABV if the yeasts transformed all of the sugar. Next, the second fermentation occurs in a closed tank using the Charmat or Martinotti technique (*see box* p.71), though some wines are made in bottle (the traditional method). Poorly produced or stored bottles have damaged the modern reputation of Asti. However, this very affordable sparkling wine is truly modern in terms of its low alcohol content, its sweetness, and its freshness.

> **GRAPE VARIETY** Muscat Blanc, which the Romans called *uva apiana* (a grape popular with bees).

> **SOIL** Limestone hills and plains.

> **STYLE** Its mousse is thin, and the wine is a pale yellow colour. The nose and palate have intense fruit flavours. Asti goes with desserts that are not too sweet, pastries, and Piedmont cookies containing hazelnuts.

Colour:
White.

Serving temperature:
43 to 46°F (6 to 8°C).

Ageing potential:
Less than 2 years.

PIEDMONT

BAROLO DOCG

Barolo is a rare wine and one of the most prestigious in Italy. It is often compared to Burgundy: both are single-variety wines, produced toward the northern edge of a region, on *terroirs* that have been worked for several centuries. Similarly, the wines, whether in a fresh style for early consumption or with potential for ageing, command a premium price. In addition, the Barolo bottle sometimes has the same shape as the Burgundy version. The wine is produced to a 13% ABV minimum and aged in wood for three years (five years if the word *riserva* appears on the label). Finally, something called Barolo Chinato is flavoured with quinine. The six million-bottle production of the 'king of wines and wine of kings' remains a limited amount, just one-thousandth of total Italian output. Barolo has near relatives produced from the same Nebbiolo grape: Barbaresco commands an equally expensive range of prices, but more affordable are Albugnano, Boca, Bramaterra, Carema, Lessona, Gattinara, Ghemme, Nebbiolo d'Alba, and Roero.

> **GRAPE VARIETY** Nebbiolo.

> **SOIL** Clay-and-limestone hills of Langhe.

> **STYLE** Barolo has a moderately intense ruby colour, with orange highlights. Even in a young wine, it has an expressive nose of violets, dried roses, crystallized fruit, and prunes with *eau de vie*. On the palate, there are velvety flavours of cooked fruit, licorice, and spices. It has a slight sharpness, firm tannins, and a long finish. Depending on the winemaking style and length of maturation in barrel, freshness or full-bodied flavours dominate.

Colour: *Red.*

Serving temperature: *61 to 63°F (16 to 17°C).*

Ageing potential: *10 to 30 years.*

LOMBARDY

FRANCIACORTA DOCG

Around 1960, Lombardy producers who were enthusiastic about Champagne decided to produce sparkling wine. However, at that point their region was more famous for its factories than for its wines. They invested in vineyards in Franciacorta, built modern cellars, and financed winemakers and training for technical personnel. Thus Franciacorta wine came into being. Its second fermentation takes place in the traditional manner, in bottle, and not in closed tanks like simple sparkling wines. The minimum alcohol is 11.5%. The *blanc de blancs* or *satèn* (sparkling) is made only from white grapes, and the rosé is with a minimum of 15 per cent Pinot Noir. Vintage Franciacorta contains at least 85 per cent of the wine from that particular year. Today, 6,919 acres (2,800 ha) of vineyards will produce 14 million bottles each year of the most prestigious sparkling wine in Italy. More demanding than Champagne, this appellation limits its yield to 4 tons/acre and needs to be aged on lees for at least 18 months. It should not be confused with the DOC Terre di Franciacorta, which produces still white or red wines.

> **GRAPE VARIETIES** Chardonnay (80 per cent of the area compared to only 26 per cent in Champagne), Pinot Noir (15 per cent), and Pinot Blanc (5 per cent).

> **SOIL** Sub-alpine moraine hills, gravel.

> **STYLE** The wines, which are a straw yellow colour with green or golden glints, have a fresh, floral, or fruity bouquet. On the palate, they show roundness and less acidity than many northern sparkling wines. 'In Franciacorta, lack of ripeness in the grapes is never a problem, quite the contrary!' So say local producers, always quick to make fun of Champagne.

Colour: *White and rosé.*

Serving temperature: *50°F (10°C).*

Ageing potential: *2 to 5 years.*

Piedmont

ROBERTO VOERZIO

Located in the municipality of La Morra, in the heart of the Langhe hills, the fantastic Piedmont estate, Roberto Voerzio, is renowned for its love of Nebbiolo and its expertize in terroirs.

ROBERTO VOERZIO

Località Cerreto, 7
12064 La Morra

Area: *54 acres (21.8 ha)*
Production: *40,000 to 60,000 bottles p.a.*
Appellation: *Barolo*
Red grape varieties: *Nebbiolo, Barbera, Dolcetto, Merlot*

Voerzio, father and son

Roberto Voerzio, the son of a peasant farmer, started from nothing, or very little, in the 1980s: 5 acres (2 ha) of family vines located in La Morra, a village unknown at the time, but now one of the most renowned places for great Italian red wines. A small group of people put Barolo firmly on the map of Italy (and Piedmont) for wine-lovers. The estate was created in 1986, and began to be successful in the early 1990s. Since then, David has joined his father and the pair of them have continued to maintain the excellent reputation of wines from the Voerzio estate. The small volume produced, 40,000 to 60,000 bottles per year, is snapped up quickly and prices have soared, but the Voerzio's have not got carried away, mindful of their modest beginnings. The vineyard has gradually expanded to 54 acres (21.8 ha) and is planted with red grape varieties: Nebbiolo, the highlight of Barolo, Barbera, Dolcetto, and other Piedmont specialities. Plus a smattering of Merlot.

Barolo: an alternative to Burgundy

Northwest Italy has a vast array of vineyards that stretch as far as the eye can see, dotted on the jagged slopes of the Alps, an uninterrupted network of hills of varying steepness, bathed in mists and capped with villages that, like La Morra at 1,800 feet (550 m), offer clearly laid out, panoramic views of the surrounding vineyards.

Barolo is part of this rich tapestry, where everything varies subtly in terms of exposure, altitude, and soils, which are lighter in the west but more compact in the east.

Roberto Voerzio is an interpreter and pioneer of this fascinating mosaic, which, in its complexity and its subtleties, cannot help but bring Burgundy to mind. Like that region, Barolo has a wide variety of wines, with appellation names that appear on the labels. The estate includes plots of land producing some of the most renowned wines from the western part of Barolo, including Brunate, Cerequio, La Serra, and Rocche dell Annunziata, all located south of La Morra, and all variations on a common theme, Nebbiolo.

The essence of Nebbiolo

Like Pinot Noir, Nebbiolo is able to highlight terroir, wines, and talent. And as with Pinot Noir, the relative paleness of its wines conceals a complexity that can be exquisite in the very best wines. Yet this grape is also particularly powerful in terms of tannin, acidity, and alcohol, which can verge on excessive, and it is all credit to Voerzio for managing to keep this in check. From the family, you hear first about vines, high planting density (up to 3,237 feet/acre, 8,000 feet/ha), healthy practices (little or no use of artificial products), drastic green harvesting, and tiny yields: less than 3.3 lb (1.5 kg) grapes per vine on average (barely two bottles), but healthy, ripe, concentrated grapes that are key to the specific intensity and concentration of the Barolos produced here. This exceptional raw material needs a slow transformation in the cellar: long maturation in barrels or casks with some new wood, transfer to vats, and prolonged refining in bottles. In all, the wines wait more than three years before being put on the market, and up to nine years for the rare Riserva.

ROBERTO VOERZIO, BAROLO

An iron fist in a velvet glove. It is not very original but when discussing Voerzio wines we can find fascinating paradoxes between power and elegance, the strength of the tannins and the silky texture. If allowed sufficient time, never less than five years according to its producers and much more if one wants to enjoy it at its absolute best, Nebbiolo will produce a full range of sensations (smokey notes, infused tea, old rose, dried fruit, licorice, leather...) as well as a fresh, refined concentration, common to all the wines in the range. The Fossati Case Nere Riserva, a blend from two plots, which goes on the market after nine years, is a perfect example of this, just like wines from individual plots, such as the Serra, or the rare and much sought-after Brunate, for instance. These are marketed earlier but their quality will please those who cannot bear to wait.

berto Voerzio, tor of the estate.

Piedmont, Tuscany

ANGELO *GAJA*

The most well-known Italian wine producer, the Piedmontese Angelo Gaja has written one of the most beautiful chapters in that old love story linking Italy and its wine.

The commander

Italian viticulture should erect a statue to this Piedmontese wine producer, given how much he has done for his region, and far beyond, for the reputation of Italian wines worldwide. In the 1960s, when he was starting out, Italy did not have much to offer an enthusiast looking for great wines. Angelo Gaja is one of a handful of producers who have given back to the country pride in its superb wines, which have a renown that dates back to ancient Roman times. This tireless and indefatigable defender of the peninsula's wines manages his estates in Tuscany and above all in Piedmont, in Barbaresco, the home of the Gaja family since 1869. Barbaresco, located on a hill, is a peaceful and charming village that exists only for its vineyards. In the 1960s a revolution took place at 36 Via Torino, when, after studying oenology and economics, Angelo joined his father Giovanni on the family estate. The latter had prepared the ground, acquiring decent plots of land in Barbaresco, and passed on to his son a love of good wine and hard work.

The revolutionary

Techniques of pruning, green harvesting, control of malolactic fermentation, thermo-regulation, research on ageing, modern maturation, use of French barrels, etc.: Angelo Gaja has employed all these innovations. But while revolutionizing his methodology, he has been faithful to his Piedmontese roots, which he has fine-tuned and promoted via his wines, thanks to the rigour and precision of his wine production. By extracting the very essence of Nebbiolo, a grape that is variable yet fascinating, he has completely reinvented the style of Barbaresco, through specific wines (Sorì San Lorenzo, Sorì Tildin...) designed like Burgundy. His sleek, modern labels, with names evoking the history of his family and Piedmont, have quickly travelled around the world, making Angelo Gaja one of Italy's leading producers. As an expert on Nebbiolo, he has not remained indifferent to the attraction of Barolo, and has bought vineyards responsible for famous wines such as Sperss, Conteisa, and Dragomis. Gaja has become an haute couture brand. His reputation allows him to act boldly, planting Chardonnay, Cabernet Sauvignon, and Sauvignon in the heart of Nebbiolo.

The appeal of Tuscany

At the same time, the lively Piedmontese producer is pursuing another dream: Tuscany, its landscapes and its Sangiovese grape variety. In 1994, he acquired 62 acres (25 ha) in Montalcino, the source of two 100% Sangiovese wines, Rennina and Sugarille, the former rounded and the latter firm. Two years later, he became interested in the coastal region of Bolgheri, which was then booming. After protracted negotiations, he bought a property that he named Ca' Marcanda, 'the house of negotiation': he planted 272 acres (110 ha) of vines, mainly of Bordeaux varieties, and equipped the property with state-of-the-art facilities. Launched in 2000, the Camarcanda wine, a Merlot/Cabernet blend, has become a standard. Angelo Gaja remains hale and hearty, and with the constant support of his friend, the oenologist Guido Rivella, he continues to promote Italian *terroirs*, albeit with a French twist, employing his particularly deft style and communication skills. His wines are sold in small numbers in more than 80 countries and can be found on the world's finest dining tables. His children are following in his footsteps and carrying on the great work undertaken by their father.

trait of the Gaja family.

OLTREPÒ PAVESE DOC

LOMBARDY

Located, as its name suggests, 'on the other side of the Po' near Pavia, this appellation includes some 20 districts. It comprises white wines, rosés, sparkling whites, reds such as Bonarda, sweet wines, and two amazing specialities: Sangue di Giuda and Buttafuoco. The Sangue di Giuda ('Blood of Judas' is a red that is both sweet and sparkling, hence the humorous name of the wine 'traitor'. It is all too easy to drink, and is just 12% ABV minimum. The Buttafuoco, literally 'fire-breathing', is a deep red, full-bodied, often sparkling wine, though again just 12% ABV.

> **GRAPE VARIETIES** Barbera, Croatina, Pinot Noir, Uva Rara, Vespolina, and Cabernet Sauvignon for the red wines; Chardonnay, Cortese, Malvasia, Moscato, Pinot Gris, Riesling Italico, Riesling Renano, and Sauvignon Blanc for the white wines.

> **SOIL** Sedimentary hills and clay soils.

> **STYLE** The wines come in all kinds of styles. They may be consumed with a meal, or as an appetizer (for the lightly sparkling wines), or as a dessert (for the sweet sparkling wines).

Colour:
White, rosé, and red.

Serving temperature:
46 to 50°F (8 to 10°C) for whites and rosés; 57 to 61°F (14 to 16°C) for reds.

Ageing potential:
2 to 3 years.

VALPOLICELLA DOC

VENETO

Valpolicella is fourth among Italian appellations in terms of production volume, selling more than 20 million bottles per year. Most are exported from Veneto. This is a red wine for dinner, at least 11% ABV. The *superiore*, 12% ABV, is aged for one year. The term 'classico' indicates that the wine is produced in the historic zone. There is also a territorial *denominazione* called Valpantena. Valpolicella should not be confused with the Recioto della Valpolicella dessert wine derived from desiccated grapes, which also exists in a sparkling (*spumante*) style.

> **GRAPE VARIETIES** Corvina Veronese (from 40 to 70 per cent), Rondinella (from 20 to 40 per cent), and Molinara. Other permitted varieties in the blend include Corvinone, Negrara Trentina and/or Rossignola and/or Sangiovese and/or Barbera. Bardolino (*see below*) comes from the same grapes and the same region.

> **SOIL** Fertile alluvial plains and limestone hills.

> **STYLE** The wines have an intense ruby colour and a characteristic bouquet of red fruit (cherry) and bitter almonds. On the palate, they have a dry or velvety texture, as well as a fruity, slightly bitter and spicy sensation.

Colour:
Red.

Serving temperature:
61 to 63°F (16 to 17°C).

Ageing potential:
3 to 5 years.

BARDOLINO DOC

VENETO

With a production of almost 30 million bottles per year, this red wine from the shores of Lake Garda is one of the best known in Italy, particularly through its *novello* (very young) version. Its *Chiaretto*, which is somewhere between red and rosé, is produced after a very short maceration of the must with the grape skins. Bardolino Superiore DOCG is aged for at least one year, with 12% ABV minimum. The *classico* comes from the historic area of the appellation. Until the early 19th century, the must was fermented in cavities in impermeable rock, covered with stone slabs.

> **GRAPE VARIETIES** Corvina Veronese (from 35 to 65 per cent), for body and colour; Rondinella (from 10 to 40 per cent) and Molinara for flavour; also Corvinone, Rossignola, Barbera, Sangiovese, Garganega, Merlot, and Cabernet Sauvignon. These are the same grape varieties as for Valpolicella (*see above*).

> **SOIL** Fertile alluvial plains and moraine hills.

> **STYLE** These wines have a clear ruby colour and cherry flavours. They are easy to drink and light and fruity on the palate.

Colour:
Red and chiaretto.

Serving temperature:
57 to 59°F (14 to 15°C).

Ageing potential:
1 to 3 years.

VENETO

SOAVE DOC, RECIOTO DI SOAVE DOCG

The most famous dry white Italian wine, Soave ranks third in volume after Chianti and Asti. Each year, more than 60 million bottles of Soave leave the region, and 65 per cent are for export. 'If there are Italian wines in a store anywhere on earth, there will be a wine from Veneto!' jokes Luciano Piona, the president of UVIVE (the syndicate of consortia producing DOC wines in Veneto). Soave is the name of a town, but the word also means 'sweet, delicate'. The *classico* is matured for longer, and comes from the historical area of the Colli Scaligeri *terroir*. Soave Superiore DOCG is sometimes aged in barrels, giving it hints of vanilla. It remains at least three months in bottle before being put on the market. Matured for two years from November 1st following the harvest, the DOCG Riserva must reach at least 12.5% ABV. There is also a DOCG 'Riserva Classico'. Within the same appellation, winemakers also produce the Recioto di Soave DOCG, a very sweet wine made from *passerillés* (partially dried) grapes. Before being vinified, they are dried on racks for months. Pressed in February, they yield only about 20 litres per 100 kg of source grapes, hence the high price for 50 cl bottles.

> **GRAPE VARIETIES** Garganega (70 per cent minimum), Trebbiano di Soave and/or Pinot Blanc and/or Chardonnay (25 to 30 per cent), and other local white grape varieties.

> **SOIL** Fertile alluvial plains and volcanic and limestone hills.

> **STYLE** Soave is a straw yellow colour with green and gold glints. Floral notes on the palate are succeeded by flavours of apple, peach, lemon, and grapefruit. It is a fresh, dry, slightly sharp wine. Recioto di Soave suggests dried apricot, crystallized fruit, and lychées, but has an intense sweetness.

Colour of wine:
White.

Serving temperature:
46 to 50°F (8 to 10°C).

Ageing potential:
*1 to 4 years, depending on quality (*superiore, riserva*).*

Which is the best Italian wine?

Assoenologi* lists about 700,000 producers in all regions of Italy – from the large wineries to the small part-time farmers, and even individuals who bring a few baskets from their private garden to a cooperative. Of course, not all actually make wine with their grapes, even if home production is common and deserves further study in terms of both society and wine. But if we limit the choice to bottles sold commercially, which is the best Italian wine? Several rankings (available online) try to answer this question. Every year, *Wine Spectator*'s team tests thousands of products and identifies between 10 and 20 Italian wines in their global Top 100. A Brunello di Montalcino was actually named Best Wine in the World in 2006. Such a designation often comes with prices between $70 and $100, though the *Wine Spectator* has Proseccos and Barberas at $12 and $13. Other ratings are provided by the Festival Grand Tasting, Duemilavini dell'AIS, L'Espresso, Gambero Rosso, and guides by Maroni and Veronelli. The magazine *Civiltà del bere* publishes a wine guide that summarizes all the ratings.

Among top Italian wines, here are some listed according to region.

- **Val d'Aoste:** Crêtes.
- **Piedmont:** Fratelli Cavallotto, Giacomo Conterno, Gaja, Bruno Giacosa, Massolino.
- **Lombardy:** Bellavista.
- **Trentino-Alto Adige:** Cantina Bolzano, Kellerei Kaltern, Tenuta San Leonardo.
- **Tuscany:** Antinori, Castello del Terriccio, Colle Massari-Podere Grattamacco, Montervertine, Ornellaia, Petrolo, Podere Il Carnasciale, Poliziano, San Guido, Tenimenti Luigi D'Alessandro.
- **Umbria:** Arnaldo Caprai, Còlpetrone.
- **Marche:** Ercole Velenosi.
- **Campania:** Galardi, Mastroberardino, Montevetrano.
- **Basilicata:** Basilisco.
- **Sicily:** Abbazia Santa Anastasia, Donnafugata, Palari.

**Associazione Enologi Enotecnici Italiani, www.assoenologi.it*

Veneto

MASI
AGRICOLA

The modern system of appassimento and ripasso was refined, if not invented by Masi, and it is the source of the famous Amarone, the flagship Valpolicella wine produced in Veneto.

MASI AGRICOLA

Via Monteleone, 26
37015 Gargagnago di Valpolicella

Area (region of Verona): *2,372 acres (960 ha)*
Production: *N/A*
Appellation: *Amarone della Valpolicella*
Red grape varieties: *Corvina, Corvinone, Rondinella, Molinara, Oseleta*

A Veronese institution

This Veronese institution has a vast vineyard in Veneto, specifically in the region of Verona, owned by the Masi since the 18th century. It produces a wide range of local wines but is best known for Amarone, of which it is a leading specialist and has a distinguished production history. Masi is a respected producer of several Valpolicella wines, which it often vinifies separately, hence such brilliant wines as the Vaio Armaron, Mazzano, or Campolongo. However, Masi is not the name of a family, but a hamlet in Valpolicella. The owners are a family called Boscaini. It has spent a long time developing and promoting local grape varieties, most notably Corvina, Valpolicella's main grape variety. Masi has planted this as far away as Argentina, where, combined with Malbec, it has produced amazing results. More surprisingly Masi, according to its boss Sandro Boscaini, is completely against the 'forced amaronization' of Valpolicella, so that Amarone remains a rare and prestigious speciality wine, of which the estate is a keen champion.

The subtleties of *appassimento*

Appassimento has been practised in Veneto since Roman times. In this method, the grapes are dried after harvesting (usually on trellises or crates) in ventilated rooms. After several weeks of this treatment, the grape loses one-third of its water, concentrating the sugar and tannins. Next, around January, these grapes are fermented for about 50 days. The wine is then matured in oak barrels. If the wine is dry (and the fermentation of the sugars has been completed), this is Amarone; if there is a lot of sugar, then it is Recioto. Masi excels in the production of both these wines. In the 1980s, the house also reintroduced the technique of *ripasso*, where a dry Valpolicella wine is re-fermented on Amarone skins, resulting in a slightly higher alcoholic content and greater extraction. The wine is then matured for a long period, sometimes for over two years, in barrels that contained Amarone from the previous year. Masi has chosen to replace the skins, or marc, of Amarone, with a proportion of grapes that have undergone the *appassimento* process. The resulting wines are more powerful, deriving more complexity, texture, and richness from this. The technique has ensured the success of its historic Campofiorin.

MASI, SEREGO ALIGHIERI VAIO ARMARON, AMARONE DELLA VALPOLICELLA CLASSICO

The vines grow in terraces at a height of 985 feet (300m) in sandy soil. After desiccation of the berries, the clusters of Corvina, Rondinella, and Molinara grapes are partially scraped, and then delicately pressed. After fermentation, the wine is matured for three years in vats. With a dark ruby colour and a nose of cherry, cinnamon, and nutmeg, even with no residual sugar, the smooth mouthfeel provides a hint of sweetness, with dried apricot and prunes, refreshed with menthol and pine needles. It is a powerful, heady wine that lingers on the palate.

MASI, AMABILE DEGLI ANGELI, RECIOTO DELLA VALPOLICELLA CLASSICO

'Amabile' means 'sweetened'. The clusters spend 150 days on the racks, losing over half of their vegetative water content. At the end of the fermentation, just over 3 oz (90g) of residual sugars per litre remain for 12 degrees of alcohol. It has a beautiful garnet colour and an explosion of spices on the nose: cinnamon, licorice, and cardamom. The palate flows with the concentrated juice of red and black fruits, morello cherry, and blackcurrant. It is full, dense, and lingering. Sugar is present, but harmonizes well with the tannins.

PROSECCO DI CONEGLIANO VALDOBBIADENE DOCG

VENETO

Italians like bubbles in their mineral water, and in their white, rosé, and red wines. Across northern regions in particular, it is common to find wine bars named *proseccheria*, specializing in sparkling wines. Almost all Italian regions produce their own sparkling wines, but the area most famous for its Prosecco is the province of Treviso, specifically around the towns of Conegliano and Valdobbiadene. *Spumante* style generates more bubbles than *frizzante*. Prosecco is produced in 'brut', 'extra dry', and 'dry' versions, with at least 10.5% ABV.

> **GRAPE VARIETIES** Glera, Verdiso, Bianchetta, Perera, Chardonnay, Pinot Blanc, and Pinot Noir.

> **SOIL** Fertile alluvial plains allowing high yields.

> **STYLE** Straw yellow in colour, and bubbly. Despite its fruity flavours, Prosecco remains fresh on the palate. An aperitif wine, also used for celebrations, Prosecco may accompany fish, pasta, or risotto.

Colour: *White.*

Serving temperature: *46 to 50°F (8 to 10°C).*

Ageing potential: *1 to 2 years.*

AMARONE DELLA VALPOLICELLA DOCG

VENETO

Wine producers in the Veneto have retained an instinct for international trade from ancient Venice. Their region, the largest producer of wines in Italy, accounts for 30 per cent of Italian exports by value alone. But the Veneto also produces limited quantities of niche wines, renowned for their individual style, such as Amarone della Valpolicella. Red grapes are handpicked and dried on trays for more than three months, which increases sugar concentration. The vinification of Amarone is allowed to continue until the yeasts convert all of the grape sugars into alcohol. This produces a dry wine at 15 or 16% ABV. It is aged for at least two years.

> **GRAPE VARIETIES** Corvina Veronese (from 40 to 70 per cent), Corvinone, Rondinella (from 20 to 40 per cent), Molinara, Barbera, Negrara Trentina and/or Rossignola and/or Sangiovese, and others.

> **SOIL** Fertile alluvial plains.

> **STYLE** The wine has a garnet colour, and a nose with aromas of ripe red fruits, plums, raisins, cherry jam, and spices (clove, cinnamon, etc.). On the palate it is intense with flavours of *eau-de-vie* fruit.

Colour: *Red.*

Serving temperature: *61 to 63°F (16 to 17°C).*

Ageing potential: *Up to 15 years.*

How to match Italian food and wine

The Sardinian restaurant Fontanarosa is one of the most famous Italian eateries in Paris. It has more than 200 wines on its menu. How does Flavio Mascia guide his customers? Does he advise, as is often done in Italy, choosing wine from the same region as the selected dish? No, because he sells more than just Sardinian wines. How does he match food and wine? Which are his favourite producers? Here is his response.

'Giving you a list of names would be a big mistake. And we must stop the standard clichés that such-and-such a wine goes with polenta, etc. I suggest a light wine for lunch, and a full-bodied one for dinner. I am not talking about alcohol content, but rather its impact on the palate. I observe customers, I ask them a few questions, I try to understand whether they want to focus on and explore the food or the wine, which are two different approaches. Similarly, I ask what they want in terms of price. My advice is this: if you like a wine, write its name down, find the estate on the internet, try to learn more about it. Even better: find the name of the winemaker and the other wines he produces. In three simple words: read the label!'

ALTO ADIGE DOC - SÜDTIROL DOC

TRENTINO-ALTO ADIGE

This *terroir* has a unique history. Until 1919, the region was Austrian – after a brief period of French rule under Napoleon. Today, the autonomous province of Bolzano is home to only 25 per cent native Italian speakers, but the complexity of a DOC label has reached its peak. A bilingual label is required featuring the name of the appellation and grape variety in both German and Italian, hence Alto Adige DOC Pinot Bianco and Südtirol DOC Weissburgunder are the same wine. Then the name of one out of six sub-denominations is added: Colli di Bolzano, Meranese, Santa Maddalena, Terlano, Valle Isarco, or Valle Venosta, along with their German equivalent, given the importance of the German market. An even more precise translation of the label, with references to *vigna*, *gewächs*, or *wachstum*, is possible. But the complications continue: the appellation authorizes some 20 varieties for dual- and single-variety wines (Cabernet-Lagrein, Cabernet-Merlot, and Merlot-Lagrein), and everything is listed bilingually. There are also terms such as 'late-harvest' for sparkling wines and some rosés. The word *riserva* describes wines that are aged for at least two years.

> **GRAPE VARIETIES** There are about 20 German, Italian, and French grape varieties in this area, a living relic of the Napoleonic period.
> **SOIL** Alpine hills and mountain vineyards planted on terraces.
> **STYLE** White wines (55 per cent of production) are fresh and fragrant; reds (45 per cent) are fresh and bright.

Colour:
White, rosé, and red.

Serving temperature:
46 to 50°F (8 to 10°C) for whites, sparkling wines and rosés;
57 to 59°F (14 to 15°C) for reds.

Ageing potential:
1 to 2 years.

COLLI ORIENTALI DEL FRIULI DOC

FRIULI-VENEZIA GIULIA

This appellation includes 30 different sparkling or sweet wines, all produced in the province of Udine. White wines account for 60 per cent of production, reds 40 per cent. The DOC indicates the wine's geographic origin (with two sub-regions, Cialla and Rosazzo) as well as the grape variety, if it amounts to more than 85 per cent. Thus the Colli Orientali del Friuli Rosazzo Ribolla Gialla comes from the Rosazzo area and contains at least 85 per cent of the white grape Ribolla Gialla. Wine producers looking for greater freedom in blends produces a generic Colli Orientali del Friuli Bianco. The reds follow the same principle in terms of appellation.

Colli Orientali del Friuli Dolce is a sweet white wine produced from dried grapes. The word *riserva* on wines indicates those aged for at least two years; in the Cialla area, a minimum of four years is required.

> **GRAPE VARIETIES** For white: Sauvignon Blanc, Traminer Aromatico, Verduzzo Friulano, Chardonnay, Malvasia, Pinot Blanc, Pinot Gris, and Friulano; for red: Cabernet Franc, Cabernet Sauvignon, Merlot, Pinot Noir, Pignolo, Schioppettino, Refosco Nostrano, Refosco dal Peduncolo Rosso, and Tazzelenghe. Wine producers love collecting grape varieties!
> **SOIL** Steep cliffs between the Alps and the Adriatic.
> **STYLE** The Friuli region is characterized by fresh, mineral-laced white wines that are light in alcohol, and produced as a result of excellent technical winemaking. Oysters and oily fish go very well with the dry whites and their hints of white flowers and citrus (lemon and grapefruit). The fresh, light, and mineral-edged red wines are not as well known, despite the undoubted expertise in their production. Some wine producers, however, adopt a more intense and full-bodied style after ageing in barrel.

Colour:
White and red.

Serving temperature:
46 to 50°F (8 to 10°C) for whites;
57 to 59°F (14 to 15°C) for reds.

Ageing potential:
1 to 3 years.

Tuscany

MARCHESI ANTINORI

Founded in 1385, according to records from the city of Florence, Antinori is the oldest currently active winery in the world. But this venerable institution has evolved, as can be seen from the current success of its great wines (Tignanello, Solaia), as well as its entry-level product range.

MARCHESI ANTINORI

Piazza degli Antinori, 3
50123 Florence

Area (Tuscany): *1,507 acres (610 ha)*
Production: *N/A*
Appellations: *Chianti Classico, Brunello di Montalcino, Bolgheri, IGT Toscana*
Red grape varieties: *Sangiovese, Cabernet Sauvignon, Cabernet Franc, Merlot, Syrah, Petit Verdot*
White grape varieties: *Vermentino, Malvasia, Trebbiano*

One family, one estate

Antinori is first of all a story of a family and then of a region: Tuscany. Chianti, Montalcino, San Gimignano, Montepulciano; there is no shortage of great historic *terroirs*, and it is here that Antinori wrote one of the most beautiful chapters in Italy's wine history, with Tignanello. The history of Tenuta Tignanello dates back to the 14th century (founded in 1385). The estate is located in the heart of Chianti Classico, around 19 miles (30 km) southeast of Florence. It has 363 acres (147 ha) of vineyards, including 116 acres (47 ha) dedicated to Tignanello. The vineyard is located on gentle hills, 1,150 to 1,475 feet (350 to 450m) above sea level, and enjoys both good sunshine and a broad temperature range between day and night, which enhances flavour. The plots of Sangiovese are next to those of Cabernet Sauvignon and Cabernet Franc, as well as the local white grape varieties, Malvasia and Trebbiano. The soils are predominantly composed of Pliocene marls.

One man

Tenuta Tignanello has been in the hands of the Antinori family since the mid-19th century. The family invested heavily, buying plot after plot until the turn of the 20th century. It is also of great sentimental value to the Antinori, who took refuge there during the war, after Villa Antinori had been bombed. The introduction of Bordeaux varieties on the property dates from before the war: Marchese Niccòlo was responsible for this 'sacrilege', although it was his son Piero (born in 1939) who would make it famous.

In 1966, when he took control of the company, the world of wine was in turmoil. With the advent of modern oenology, vineyards had set out to conquer new horizons. Everyone dreamed of a place in the sun, and that applied in Italy too. It was at this point Piero decided to give Tuscany a wine to match the great Bordeaux wines, or rather two of them. On the same estate, in 1971, he created a wine, Tignanello, mainly based on Sangiovese (between 80 and 85%), but vinified in barrels, a first in Italy; then another, Solaia, mainly based on Cabernets.

MARCHESI ANTINORI, TIGNANELLO, IGT TOSCANA

The real hallmark of Tignanello is its balance. Here is a wine where, time after time, the elegance of a properly matured wine (12 months in barrel, 12 months in bottle) can be found. The Solaia impresses, while the Tignanello seduces. The Sangiovese has a lovely crisp structure, while the Cabernets, to a lesser extent, have an additional density in their structure. A touch of warmth from the soil. Yet this is merely an external cloak: a velvety woody taste, a palate that is fresh and voluptuous, neither too concentrated nor too subtle. It is like an Italian gentleman, at home in Florence, Paris, or New York.

One philosophy

If the Marchese was convinced of the potential of the Tuscan grape varieties, he also benefited from a vineyard to match his ambitions: well-kept, neat homogeneous plots of land, not scattered like large *latifundia* farms. In terms of tradition, he began by freeing himself from the practice of *governo* (the addition of grapes sweetened in the must to reduce acidity): by generalizing the malolactic fermentation, he was able to manage without it. Likewise, he abandoned the Ricasoli method, which adds white to Chianti wines. He innovated in every aspect: ripening of the grape, vinification, and maturation. He used the best French barrels for the Tenuta, and even vats from Slavonia, to fine-tune the maturation as precisely as possible. To turn his dream into drinking reality, Piero also relied on Giacomo Tachis. A Piedmontese oenologist recruited by his father, he was trained in the art of blending by Émile Peynaud. If a Bordeaux heritage exists in Tignanello, this is where it lies.

CINQUE TERRE DOC

LIGURIA

Set in a crescent around the Gulf of Genoa, the tiny province of Liguria is penultimate in production volume among wine-producing regions. Cinque Terre is a white wine (two-thirds of Ligurian output) developed by versatile wineries. As in Val d'Aosta, vines grow on the sides of cliffs and on terraces, but at a lower altitude and under a more intense sun. Some vineyards are right on the waterfront, others cling high up in the mountains. Five areas produce the wine, hence its name. There is also a Cinque Terre Sciacchetrà, a sweet *passerillé* version.

> **GRAPE VARIETIES** Bosco (at least 40 per cent), Albarola and/or Vermentino (at least 40 per cent), and other local white grapes.

> **SOIL** Steep terraces between the mountains and the Mediterranean.

> **STYLE** The wine is pale yellow in colour, with dry but fruity and floral flavours. Cinque Terre Sciacchetrà wines are sweet and have a golden yellow colour with glints of amber and scents of honey and apricot. This sweet wine goes with strong cheeses and desserts that are not too sweet, as well as slightly sharp fruit.

Colour:
White.

Serving temperature:
46 to 50°F (8 to 10°C) for dry and sweet wines served as an aperitif; 54°F (12°C) for sweet wines served with dessert.

Ageing potential:
1 to 3 years.

LAMBRUSCO DI SORBARA DOC

EMILIA-ROMAGNA

Vast fertile plains in Emilia-Romagna are home to high-yield vineyards that produce an original yet cheap red wine: Lambrusco. Its production is similar to that of Asti (*see* p.360): fermentation is stopped by refrigeration and filtration before the yeast has converted all the grape sugar into alcohol. Instead of reaching 11.5% ABV, the final content is only 8 or 9% ABV and the residual sugars provide its characteristic sweetness. A second fermentation carried out in closed tanks causes *prise de mousse*. This wine, which is widely exported, was mischievously called the 'Italian Coca-Cola™'. It provided young people with an introduction to sweet and sparkling wine. There are other Lambrusco appellations, such as Lambrusco di Grasparossa Castelvetro, produced from 85 per cent of the Grasparossa grape variety, as well as high-end wines crafted with great care by smaller producers.

> **GRAPE VARIETIES** Lambrusco di Sorbara, Lambrusco Grasparossa, and Lambrusco Salamino.

> **SOIL** Alluvial and clay plains and steep hills.

> **STYLE** Lightly sparkling wine with light, fruity, and sweet characters. Suitable as an aperitif, with cold cuts and antipasti, as well as with desserts.

Colour:
Red and rosé.

Serving temperature:
54 to 55°F (12 to 13°C).

Ageing potential:
1 year.

BRUNELLO DI MONTALCINO DOCG

TUSCANY

Unlike the many appellations derived from ancient traditions, this red wine is a recent invention of the Tuscan industry. Around 1870, during the phylloxera crisis, Ferruccio Biondi-Santi replanted his vineyard and gambled on the production of a wine stored for a long time in barrel, and then bottled. At the time, local wines were consumed young, and may have been lightly sparkling. The first vintage of Brunello di Montalcino dates back to 1888. The creation of this wine prefigures the 'Super Tuscans' Sassicaia (*see* pp.468–9) and Solaia – produced a century later by other winemakers in the region. Brunello di Montalcino is released for drinking six years after it is harvested, and its *riserva* only after seven years. Both must be aged for at least two of those years in oak casks, then in bottle.

> **GRAPE VARIETIES** Sangiovese (locally known as Brunello).

> **SOIL** Clay-and-limestone hills.

> **STYLE** The wine is a ruby red colour. On the nose, it has aromas of red fruits and jam, as well as vanilla and spices. It is intense, fleshy, fruity, and tannic on the palate, with a long finish.

Colour:
Red.

Serving temperature:
61 to 63°F (16 to 17°C).

Ageing potential:
10 to 20 years.

CHIANTI DOCG

TUSCANY

The most famous Italian red wine is popularly pictured in the straw flask that used to protect it during shipping.

Today, wine producers more often sell it in Bordeaux-shaped bottles. Chianti comes from a large area of Tuscany, but the label restricts the geographic designation to grapes grown in the following areas: Colli Aretini, Colli Fiorentini (Florence), Colli Senesi (Siena), Colline Pisana (Pisa), Montalbano, Montespertoli, and Rùfina. If aged for at least two years, including three months in bottle, and if it is at least 12% ABV, it is labeled *riserva*. This should not be confused with *classico*, describing wine from the historic heart of the area, and indicated on the bottle by a black rooster surrounded by a red circle. The *classico riserva* is aged for the same length of time, but is a minimum of 12.5% ABV.

> **GRAPE VARIETIES** Sangiovese (at least 75 per cent), Canaiolo Nero, Cabernet Sauvignon, Merlot, Syrah.

> **SOIL** Clay-and-limestone hills.

> **STYLE** Chianti is a bright ruby colour. It displays aromas of violets, and has a dry palate. There are often notes of cherry, vanilla, cinnamon, or even leather. It is slightly tannic and velvety.

Colour: *Red.*

Serving temperature: *59 to 63°F (15 to 17°C), depending on age and complexity.*

Ageing potential: *5 to 7 years.*

VERDICCHIO DEI CASTELLI DI JESI DOC

MARCHE

Verdicchio Bianco is an Italian variety used in nine appellations, including Verdicchio dei Castelli di Jesi DOC. In the area of Jesi, it produces 11.5% ABV wines in both *spumante* and *passito* (made from dried grapes) styles. If aged for at least 24 months, including six in bottle, and at least 12.5% ABV, the term *riserva* is added. The *spumante* can also have this term appended. The wine from the traditional area is called *classico*, and its *superiore* version is at least 12% ABV, with the *classico riserva* containing at least 12.5% ABV. Verdicchio di Matelica, also produced in the Marche, is a close relative.

> **GRAPE VARIETIES** Verdicchio Bianco, along with other white grape varieties, the latter limited to a maximum of 15 per cent.

> **SOIL** Hills between the mountains and sea.

> **STYLE** Shades of green are reflected in the straw-yellow colour. It displays fruity and floral notes; and on the palate, Verdicchio is fresh, dry, and slightly bitter.

Colour: *White.*

Serving temperature: *46 to 50°F (8 to 10°C).*

Ageing potential: *1 to 2 years.*

ORVIETO DOC

UMBRIA AND LAZIO

Produced near Rome, this white wine was popular with popes, princes, and the city's vast middle-class market. The term *classico* describes wine from the historic center of the appellation; *superiore* is a wine of at least 12% ABV, sold after March 1st following the year of harvest. If harvested after October 1st, the Orvieto DOC qualifies for the addition of the term *vendemmia tardiva* (late harvest).

> **GRAPE VARIETIES** Grechetto, Trebbiano Toscano, Canaiolo Nostrano, and other local grape varieties.

> **SOIL** Clay-and-limestone hills.

> **STYLE** On the nose, it has a floral bouquet; but on the palate, the wine is dry, with a slight sharpness. It goes with fish, risotto, or pasta.

Colour: *White.*

Serving temperature: *46 to 50°F (8 to 10°C).*

Ageing potential: *1 to 2 years.*

Tuscany

SASSICAIA, *THE 'SUPER TUSCAN'*

'On these rocks, I will build my vineyard.' Those could have been the words of Marchese Mario Incisa della Rocchetta in 1944. He was a Bordeaux enthusiast, so decided to plant Cabernet, the top Bordeaux grape, because he noted the soils in Graves resembled those in part of his Tuscan property, Tenuta San Guido on the Mediterranean coast near Siena. In Tuscan dialect, Sassicaia means 'stony ground', this would become the wine's name.

Beginnings

The three or four acres he first planted were increased by two or three extra acres after the Baron Philippe de Rothschild offered the Marchese additional Cabernet Sauvignon plants directly from the Château Mouton Rothschild. How encouraging! But for 20 years, from 1948 to 1968, the wine was consumed exclusively by the family of the Marchese, at the estate. Initially, it had little appeal; but the vines grew older, as did the bottles in the cellar – so over time it became both interesting and viable. The idea of a Tuscan wine produced from 100% Bordeaux grape varieties at first unsettled many people. In addition, the wine was entitled to only a modest place in the hierarchy of Italian appellations, as a *vino da tavola* (table wine).

Revelation

In 1977, *Decanter* magazine organized a blind tasting in London of the great Cabernet Sauvignons of the world. The best wine critics participated. Sassicaia 1974 won first place ahead of many world-class wines, including Médocs and Graves. In an instant, this 'new' wine, which was so original as to be almost incongruous, had made its mark in the panoply of legendary wines. When the Marchese died in 1983, his son Nicolò pursued his father's vision with the same enthusiasm. Finally, in 1994, a new DOC (*Denominazione di origine controllata*) was established in Italy under the name Sassicaia Bolgheri, granting formal and unquestionable recognition to the wine.

A model vineyard

The vineyard now covers just under 150 acres (61 ha) and consists of 85 per cent Cabernet Sauvignon and 15 per cent Cabernet Franc. Very fragmented, the various plots extend over stony hills that are well protected from sea winds. The only treatments carried out on the vines use Bordeaux mixture. Numerous nearby groves contain natural predators of any local insects harmful to the vines. Added to these natural advantages is a constant effort, through rigorous pruning and green harvesting techniques, to avoid excessive production, which is harmful to the concentration and quality of the grapes.

Careful production, extended ageing

After harvest and vinification are carefully completed, the new wine is stored in 225-litre (60-gallon) oak barrels. Each year, 40 per cent of the barrels are replaced with new stock. The oak used is from the *département* of Allier in France, and is universally recognized as one of the best materials for ageing fine wines. The wine spends 24 months in barrel. After bottling, the bottles are kept resting for six months before they are shipped around the world.

A great nectar

Sassicaia is treated like great Bordeaux. Despite its humble profile, it has the virtue of Latin elegance and charm. Strictly speaking, it is a wine from two Cabernet varieties – Sauvignon and Franc – and so it could be an austere or rigid wine. Yet the Mediterranean climate makes it undeniably smooth. Time and patience provide the rest, giving the wine a supreme and necessary harmony. Like its distant relatives from Bordeaux, Sassicaia needs to be developed for eight to 12 years before reaching its peak, and therefore must be stored in optimal cellar conditions. Its capacity for ageing means that it can be held for many years, even decades, without any deterioration.

Emotional engagement

It is easy to see how, at that famous blind tasting, Sassicaia was able to make the grade as one of the best wines. But is it really so easy to recognize it among its illustrious rivals? The greatest tasters willingly admit their embarrassment. All truly great wines provide enjoyment and, often, engage the emotions. Now, this great Tuscan wine – showing the cultural richness of the homeland – has entered the pantheon of the best wines in the world.

> Marchese Nicolò Incisa della Rocchetta, son of the creator of Sassicaia.

ABRUZZO

MONTEPULCIANO D'ABRUZZO DOC

The Montepulciano grape (bearing the same name as a town in Tuscany with which the wine has no connection) is grown in many parts of Italy and is included in some 100 appellations. But it has a special place among Abruzzo wines. Montepulciano d'Abruzzo DOC is at least 11.5% ABV and must be aged for at least five months. The *riserva* is at least 12.5% ABV and is aged in tank for at least two years. The finest in the line-up, Montepulciano Colline Teramane DOCG, is produced in the area of Teramo, at 12.5% ABV. It is matured for at least two years, or three years for the *riserva*, including at least one year in oak or chestnut barrels, then six months in bottle.

> **GRAPE VARIETY** Montepulciano. Regulations allow the addition of another variety blended to a 15 per cent maximum, often Sangiovese.

> **SOIL** Ranging from the Apennines (rising 9,560 ft/2914 m) to the Adriatic, there are clay-and-limestone, alluvial, sandy, and stony soils.

> **STYLE** Montepulciano d'Abruzzo has a ruby colour and intense red fruit, licorice, and spice characters. In the mouth, it is robust, fruity, and tannic.

Colour:	Serving temperature:	Ageing potential:
Red and cerasuolo (cherry coloured).	*61 to 63°F (16 to 17°C).*	*10 years or more.*

ABRUZZO

TREBBIANO D'ABRUZZO DOC

As is often the case, the name of this appellation combines both the name of the grape and the name of the region. Trebbiano is a white grape known by many synonyms here, including Bombino Bianco and Pagadebit. The appellation covers the four provinces of Abruzzo: L'Aquila, Chieti, Pescara, and Teramo. The area is renowned for its great geographic diversity, since it extends from the Adriatic coast to the Apennine mountains.

> **GRAPE VARIETIES** Trebbiano d'Abruzzo and/or Trebbiano Toscano (85 per cent minimum), along with other local grape varieties.

> **SOIL** Between the coastal plains and the mountains, there are several types of soil: clay-and-limestone, alluvial, sandy, and stony.

> **STYLE** Trebbiano d'Abruzzo is an easy-to-drink wine. It has a straw-yellow colour with green highlights. The nose is intense, fruity, and floral; but the palate is dry.

Colour:	Serving temperature:	Ageing potential:
White.	*50 to 54°F (10 to 12°C).*	*1 to 2 years.*

CAMPANIA

GRECO DI TUFO DOCG

Along with Fiano, Aglianico, and Falanghina, Greco is one of the endangered local grape varieties that wine producers in Campania, such as Mastroberardino or Francesco Paolo Avallone (Villa Matilde), have worked to revive. Greco di Tufo is a white wine produced near Tufo, northeast of Naples. The name of the grape variety recalls the Greek origins of Italian viticulture. There are also sparkling wines, *brut* or *extra-brut*, employing traditional secondary fermentation in bottle.

> **GRAPE VARIETIES** Greco and Coda di Volpe Bianca at 85 per cent minimum, along with other local white grapes.

> **SOIL** Volcanic and alluvial.

> **STYLE** Greco di Tufo has a golden straw-yellow colour. The nose has fruity aromas of peach and pineapple. Pleasant lemony acidity surprises the palate. It can be enjoyed during a meal, but also as an aperitif due to the freshness and richness of its flavours.

Colour:	Serving temperature:	Ageing potential:
White.	*46 to 50°F (8 to 10°C).*	*2 to 3 years.*

CAMPANIA

TAURASI DOCG

This robust red comes from a single grape variety, Aglianico – though it's possibly combined in the vineyard with other regional varieties. The growing zone is in the province of Avellino, east of Naples. DOCG conditions require the winemaker to age the wine for at least three years (including at least one year in barrel), or four years if the term *riserva* is applied. The minimum alcohol content is 12 and 12.5% ABV, respectively.

> **GRAPE VARIETY** Aglianico.

> **SOIL** Volcanic and alluvial.

> **STYLE** The wine is ruby red in colour, with orange glints typical of old wine, even when the wine is young. The bouquet is intense, with notes of black cherry, cinnamon, vanilla, and nutmeg, supported by a good tannic structure.

Colour: *Red.*

Serving temperature: *61 to 63°F (16 to 17°C).*

Ageing potential: *10 years or more.*

PUGLIA

CASTEL DEL MONTE DOC

An emblematic monument in the province of Bari has given its name to the Puglian appellation. The Riserva and Castel del Monte Bombino Nero versions benefit from their DOCG status. The Castel del Monte Aglianico requires 90 per cent of the blend to be the Aglianico grape variety; the *riserva* is aged for two years, including one year in oak. Using the same production methods, the appellation includes the following other reds and rosés: Castel del Monte Bombino Nero, Castel del Monte Cabernet, Castel del Monte Pinot Nero, and Castel del Monte Uva di Troia. The generic Castel del Monte Rosso (red) is produced from a minimum of 65 per cent Aglianico, Montepulciano, or Uva di Troia, blended with a maximum of 35 per cent of other red grapes. For whites, the methodology is identical. When the appellation lists a Castel del Monte grape variety, it must be greater than 90 per cent of the wine. The generic Castel del Monte Bianco (white) is produced with a minimum of 65 per cent Bombino Bianco or Chardonnay Pampanuto, blended with other local white varieties.

> **GRAPE VARIETIES** For whites: Bombino Bianco, Chardonnay, Pinot Bianco, and Sauvignon Blanc; for reds: Aglianico, Aglianico Rosato, Bombino Nero, Cabernet Sauvignon, Pinot Nero, and Uva di Troia.

> **SOIL** Limestone, gravel, silt deposits.

> **STYLE** This panorama of inexpensive wines offers the chance to discover a spectrum of local grapes and their individual characters.

Colour: *White, rosé, and red.*

Serving temperature: *46 to 50°F (8 to 10°C) for whites and rosés; 57 to 59°F (14 to 15°C) for reds; 61 to 63°F (16 to 17°C) for* riservas.

Ageing potential: *1 year for whites and rosés; 3 years for reds and* riservas.

CALABRIA

CIRÒ DOC

Calabria has a rich history of viticulture. Archaeologists have even found traces of clay pipes for wine, presumably evidence of some kind of 'vinoduct'. It is a rugged region with microclimates ranging from the mountains to the Ionian coast and the shores of the Tyrrhenian Sea. The Cirò DOC spreads over low maritime hills.

In recent years, Calabria has moved forward from its past of only over-ripe oxidized, and very alcoholic wines. Thanks to modern methods of vinification and temperature control, the Cirò DOC now displays fruit and freshness. The term *classico* indicates a provenance of the historic areas of Cirò and Cirò Marina. *Superiore* indicates greater than 13.5% ABV, and *riserva* an ageing period of two years.

> **GRAPE VARIETIES** At least 95 per cent Gaglioppo, sometimes with the addition of whites such as Trebbiano Toscano and Greco Bianco. Nine-tenths of regional production consists of red and rosé wines.

> **SOIL** Apennine limestone, granite, and alluvial deposits.

> **STYLE** The wine is a deep ruby colour. The nose shows aromas of red fruits and berries, and jam. The palate is dry, full bodied, warm, and velvety.

Colour: *Red.*

Serving temperature: *59 to 61°F (15 to 16°C).*

Ageing potential: *3 to 5 years (up to 10 years for* riservas*).*

CANNONAU DI SARDEGNA DOC

SARDINIA

Sardinia was occupied by the Spanish for a long time, and its iconic red wine comes from the Cannonau grape variety, also known as Garnacha in Spain (or Grenache in France). The Cannonau DOC has three sub-regions: Oliena, Capo Ferrato, and Jerzu. The wines are aged for a minimum of seven months and have a minimum of 12.5% ABV. The *riserva* is aged for two years and is at least 13% ABV. The appellation also produces a rosé.

> **GRAPE VARIETIES** Cannonau and other local varieties.

> **SOIL** The soil is complex. There are clay and limestone sediments, granite, Tertiary volcanic rocks, and Quaternary alluvial deposits in the plains.

> **STYLE** The wines have a ruby colour, and ripe fruit and spice characters. On the palate they are dry and tannic, and they confirm jam-like aromas on the nose. They have a long finish.

Colour:	Serving temperature:	Ageing potential:
Red and rosé.	*46 to 50°F (8 to 10°C) for rosé; 61 to 63°F (16 to 17°C) for red.*	*1 to 2 years for rosé; 3 to 5 years for red.*

ALCAMO DOC

SICILY

Located in the provinces of Trapani and Palermo, the Alcamo appellation includes several styles of wine: white, red, rosé, sparkling (white and rosé), as well as late-harvest. The term *classico* refers to wines from the historic heart of the area, and *riserva* applies to wines that are aged for longer than average. When the grape variety is mentioned alongside the DOC, it must constitute at least 85 per cent of the blend. So the Alcamo Grecanico contains at least 85 per cent of the Grecanico grape. Alcamo Bianco DOC is a blend of Catarratto (at least 60 per cent), Inzolia, and other white grapes of the region.

> **GRAPE VARIETIES** Inzolia (also called Ansonica), Catarratto, Chardonnay, Grecanico, Grillo, Müller-Thurgau, and Sauvignon Blanc for the whites; Cabernet Sauvignon, Calabrese or Nero d'Avola, Merlot, and Syrah for the reds.

> **SOIL** Volcanic, limestone, clay, and sand.

> **STYLE** The Alcamo Bianco has a pale straw-yellow colour with green glints, and a fruity nose. On the palate, there is a hint of sharpness and real freshness. The reds are more diverse.

Colour:	Serving temperature:	Ageing potential:
White, rosé, and red.	*46 to 50°F (8 to 10°C) for whites and rosés; 57 to 63°F (14 to 17°C) for reds, depending on complexity.*	*1 to 2 years for whites and rosés; 3 years for reds.*

MARSALA DOC

SICILY

How did early modern merchants transport wine to distant destinations without it spoiling and turning into vinegar? They 'fortified' the wine with additional alcohol, which acted as a preservative. Based on this principle, the British merchant John Woodhouse established the export of Marsala to England and the world at large during the 18th century. This wine, fortified with alcohol, has lost some of its prestige because current fashion runs against overtly sweet wines – and long-term use in cooking never enhances a wine's status. Marsala is classified as 'fine' (1 year old), 'superiore' (2 years old), 'superiore riserva' (4 years old), 'vergine' and/or 'soleras' (5 years old), or 'soleras stravecchio' (10 years old).

> **GRAPE VARIETIES** Grillo, Catarratto, Inzolia, and Damaschino for the whites; Pignatello, Calabrese, Nerello Mascalese, and Nero d'Avola for the reds.

> **SOIL** Volcanic, limestone, clay, and sand.

> **STYLE** The whites are gold and amber, the reds are ruby coloured. The typical flavours of Marsala are crystallized fruits and *eau-de-vie* fruits. Its level of sweetness varies from 'dry' containing the least sugar (less than 40 g/l), 'semi-dry' (41 to 99 g/l), and 'sweet' (more than 100 g/l).

Colour:	Serving temperature:	Ageing potential:
White (amber) and red.	*43 to 46°F (6 to 8°C) served as an aperitif; 57 to 59°F (14 to 15°C) served as a dessert wine.*	*5 to 20 years, depending on the type.*

'Natural' wine at the foot of Mount Etna

Frank Cornelissen is a leading winemaker promoting 'natural' wines. They are most often produced from organic grapes, with minimal intervention from vine to bottle. The wines do not contain added yeast, they are unfiltered, and no sulphur is used in the production process. They can be recognized by their deep colour and a pleasant hint of vinegar scents, known as 'volatile acidity'. In his winery near Etna, Frank fills a glass to the brim, and then dips his finger into it. Wine flows over the sides. 'If we add something, we need to remove something else.' Without fertilizers or treatments, he obtains a very low yield: only 10,000 bottles from the 25 acres (10 ha) of his estate. 'I do not treat the vine, because I want it to stand up for itself. The same goes for my wines. For the wine to be preserved without sulphur, it needs a good concentration, and a certain minerality.' At harvest, fermentation of the grapes (in terracotta jars) does not start with standard, commercially available yeast. 'My yeasts are the air in the cellar.' Frank produces vigorous wines with complex, floral, fruity, and mineral flavours. Cornelissen exports 95 per cent of production at prices between €10 and €150 ($15 to $210/£10 to £130) per bottle.

ETNA DOC

SICILY

In his study *De Naturali Vinorum Historia*, published in 1596, Andrea Bacci, the physician of Pope Sixtus V, indicated the conditions required for agriculture in the volcanic ash of Catania. This mountainous area, still dominated by black sand, is particularly rich in those ashen minerals. Etna, the largest volcano in Europe, and one of the most active in the world, is 10,974 ft (3,345 m) high. It creates a humid climate and provides the fertile soil for viticulture. The Etna appellation produces wines in three styles around the town of Milo (whose name is not derived from the Venus of that same name).

> **GRAPE VARIETIES** Carricante, Catarratto Bianco Comune, and possibly Trebbiano and Minella Bianca for the whites (Etna Bianco Superiore is produced from Carricante); Nerello Mascalese and Nerello Mantellato or Cappuccio for the reds and rosés. (The latter include a small proportion of white grapes.)

> **SOIL** Volcanic.

> **STYLE** The white has a straw-yellow colour, with hints of green or gold. Its palate is dry, fresh, and fruity; and it contains a minimum of 11.5% ABV. The white *superiore* is at least 12% ABV. The red presents ruby colours, and has spice and red fruit (plum, blackberry) flavours. On the palate, it is dry and full-bodied. As for the rosé, it is fruity, light, and refreshing.

Colour:
White, red, and rosé.

Serving temperature:
46 to 50°F (8 to 10°C) for whites and rosés; 57 to 61°F (14 to 16 °C) for reds.

Ageing potential:
2 to 3 years for whites and rosés; 3 to 5 years for reds.

MOSCATO DI PANTELLERIA DOC

ÎLE DE PANTELLERIA

This naturally sweet wine, meaning there is no addition of fortifying alcohol, made the island famous when it was exported to Europe. Located between Sicily and Africa, Pantelleria cultivates vines where the grapes ripen quickly and dry easily on the vine or after harvest. This white Muscat is at least 15% ABV. It should not be confused with the *passito liquoroso* Pantelleria, made from dried grape clusters and fortified with grape spirit during its fermentation.

> **GRAPE VARIETY** Muscat of Alexandria, also called Zibibbo.

> **SOIL** Volcanic.

> **STYLE** This soft white wine has a golden colour and intense aromas, which are typical of Muscat. On the palate, the flavours of dried fruit, apricot, and honey dominate. Moscato may be enjoyed as an aperitif. Those who like foie gras with *vin liquoreux* will enjoy it, too. Still others advise it should be sipped with desserts that are not too sweet or acidic, such as a plum tart. It also goes well with blue cheese.

Colour:
White.

Serving temperature:
46°F (8°C).

Ageing potential:
1 to 2 years.

SPAIN

Txakoli de Bizkaia
Txakoli de Getaria
La Coruña
GALICIA
Oviedo
ASTURIAS
Santander
Bilbao
San Sebastián
Santiago de Compostella
CANTABRIQUE
BASQUE COUNTRY
Rías Baixas
Ribeira Sacra
Biérzo
Vitoria
Pamplona
Ampurdán-Costa Brava
León
NAVARRA
Logroño
Navarra
Vigo
Ribeiro
Miño
Valdeorras
Esla
Burgos
Rioja
Pyrenees
Somontano
Monterrei
CASTILLE AND LEÓN
LA RIOJA
Huesca
CATALONIA
Atlantic Ocean
Cigales
Campo de Borja
Ebro
Costers del Segre
Pla de Bages
Valladolid
Ribera del Duero
Zaragoza
Lleida
Alella
Douro
Barcelona
Toro
Cariñena
Priorat
Rueda
Tarragona
Calatayud
Terra Alta
Mondéjar
Penedès
Salamanca
ARAGON
MADRID
Tajo
Tarragona
Conca de Barberà
Madrid
PORTUGAL
Los Vinos de Madrid
Méntrida
Toledo
Mediterranean Sea
Utiel Requena
VALENCIA
Tajo
La Mancha
EXTREMADURA
Valencia
CASTILLA-LA MANCHA
Xúqueri
Mérida
Guadiana
Almansa
Valencia
Valdepeñas
Ribera del Guadiana
Valdepeñas
Jumilla
Alicante
Yecla
Alicante
Bullas
Cordoba
MURCIA
Murcia
Condada de Huelva
Guadalquivir
Montilla-Moriles
Genil
Binissalem
Huelva
Seville
ANDALUSIA
Palma
Grenada
MAJORCA
Jerez/Xérès
Málaga
Jerez de la Frontera
Málaga
Pla í Llevant
Cádiz
Balearic Islands
Wine-producing regions
Denominación de origen (DO)
Denominación de origen calificada (DOC)
Border of autonomous community
Border
N
0
125 miles (200 km)
Atlantic Ocean
Lanzarote
Valle de la Orotava
Tacoronte-Acentejo
La Palma
Valle de Güímar
Ycoden Daute-Isora
Abona
N
El Hierro
CANARY ISLANDS
0 60 miles (100 km)

SPAIN

After a long period in the doldrums, the Spanish vineyard now ranks among the best in the world. Why such success? Meticulous identification of terroirs, *the targeted use of appropriate native grape varieties, along with a new dynamism and the rapid modernization of production methods have all breathed new life into the Spanish wine industry.*

Then and now

RICH HISTORY. Today's Spanish wine industry has a history encompassing conquest, the crusades, and the successive contributions of individuals who have, little by little, created and enriched the wine-producing landscape. The Phoenicians were the first to bring vines to Spain, in the 7th century BC, particularly to the Malaga and Cádiz regions. Romans arrived in Spain during the 3rd century BC, and they gave the Spanish a better understanding of vine pruning, the process of fermentation, and the maturation of wine which, at that time, took place not in barrels but in amphorae. The grape variety Muscat of Alexandria, with its sumptuously exuberant bouquet, was then brought to Spain by the Arabs from the Maghreb during the 8th century.

SPAIN STATISTICS

Vineyard area: 2,522,945 acres (1,021,000 ha)
Production (av.): 410,700 cases (37 million hl)
Reds: 52%
Whites: 24%
Rosés: 17%
Sparkling wines: 4.5%
Fortified wines: 2.5%
(OI)

PHYLLOXERA ATTACKS. By the time this devastating aphid descended on Spanish vineyards in the late 1800s, a way of dealing with its ravages had already been determined: grafting European varieties onto resistant American rootstocks. Consequently, growers got to work replanting. Many of the most reputable wineries today date from this era.

RECENT DEVELOPMENT. During the second half of the 20th century, Spain started to move from producing just anonymous wines for bulk sale to the creation of real quality. In the 1970s, Rioja wines began significant exports, quickly followed by such estates as Vega Sicilia (*see* pp.384–5), and then by those of Valdepeñas and Catalonia. During the 1980s, Spanish wine underwent a complete quality revolution, and the wine-producing areas were remapped into 17 autonomous regions (*autonomías*), each producing their own distinctive wines.

> Vines planted on terraces in Catalonia.

Climate and geography

> Vines at González Byass, the largest producer of sherry in Andalusia.

Spain is dominated by a vast central plain (*meseta*), with an elevation of 2,150 ft (650 m) above sea level, surrounded on all sides by mountains. So its best wines are made from grape varieties that grow well at altitude – up to 2,625 ft (800 m) in Rioja, for example. Vineyards here benefit from good exposure to the sun without suffering from scorching heat thanks to cooler, fresh nights.

Most great Spanish wines are produced north of Madrid, which is to say, going from west to east, Galicia, the valleys of the Duero and the Ebro, and Catalonia. The best sites are most often found in these mountainous valleys with relatively poor soils based on clay subsoil. On the other hand, much of the valleys of the Ebro and the Douro are rich in alluvial soil.

The climate is similarly diverse: the Atlantic Ocean brings freshness and humidity to the west; the climate in the central and northern zones is of the continental type, with hot summers and cold winters; the eastern and southern coasts enjoy a Mediterranean climate.

Vineyard landscape

Spain has the world's largest area under vine cultivation. There are vineyards in almost every region of the peninsula.

GALICIA AND THE BASQUE COUNTRY. These are Spain's most northerly vineyards. The Atlantic Ocean influences the climate, the economy (based mainly on fishing), and the wines, which are generally light, dry whites that are an excellent accompaniment to seafood.

NAVARRA, RIOJA, AND ARAGÓN. Situated in the north, across the high valley of the Ebro, these regions produce powerful red wines with the potential for long cellaring, as well as robust whites.

DID YOU KNOW...?

Vineyard yields in Spain are among the lowest in the world. *The average yield is just 1.4 tons per acre (25 hl/ha). This figure is remarkably low, especially when compared with that of neighbouring countries (4.2 tons per acre/70 hl/ha on average in France). It can be attributed to the presence of very old vines in the various growing areas, as well as the rigorous climatic conditions that make life quite tough for the vine – but to the benefit of the wine.*

CATALONIA. This north-eastern region which borders the Mediterranean has often been at the forefront of Spanish wine growing. The majority of this dynamic region's vineyard area lies south of Barcelona, on the coastal plain but also in the hills of the interior. Known for its red wines, Catalonia is also the birthplace of Cavas, Spanish sparkling wines.

CASTILE AND LEÓN. Here are the traditional vineyards of the Duero Valley. A continental climate is tempered by proximity to the river. Red wines are fleshy and powerful, and dry whites here are full-bodied. This is home to the legendary Ribera del Duero (*see* p.482) appellation.

ANDALUSIA. In the extreme south, Andalusia forms a single, vast, autonomous region. Its legendary Jerez or sherry wines undergo a lengthy maturation under a veil of *flor* – the beneficial yeast that develops on the surface of the wine there (*see* p.74). Constantly progressing, the Montilla–Moriles and Condado appellations of Huelva make sweet wines, fortified or otherwise, as well as a few dry wines. Finally, after almost disappearing (*see box* p.378), Malaga continues to produce a vast range of sweet wines.

OTHER REGIONS. Most top Spanish wines are produced in northern regions, but vines are very much a force in the centre and the south of the country, too. Cultivation extends across Castile–La Mancha and Vinos de Madrid, on the plateau of the *meseta*, as well as in the Levante, which includes the autonomous regions of Valencia and Murcia, and traditionally produced wines for drinking young. These modernized vineyards are now making good progress and today offer excellent value for money in terms of quality. A small amount of wine is also produced also in the Spanish islands – the Balearics and the Canaries.

Grape varieties: protected heritage

Spain has preserved its native grape varieties, which form a kind of 'memory' of the country's wine heritage. They drive the expression of many appellations to great heights, producing wines with enormous personality.

AIRÈN. This white grape (the most commonly grown white variety in the world) can be found in southern Spain, in Castile–La Mancha. It produces simple, refreshing, aromatic wines.

ALBARIÑO. This white grape variety impresses for the vigour of its fruity aromas and for its notable freshness. Albariño flourishes in Galicia, in northwestern Spain, largely in the Rías Baixas appellation.

CARIÑENA. Known in France as Carignan, this red grape variety is grown on a massive scale in Catalonia, where it produces spicy aromas, tannins, and freshness. It is sometimes used in blends of red wines from Priorat and Rioja (under the name Mazuelo) .

GODELLO. Abandoned for many years, this white grape variety has since made a most convincing comeback. It is valued both for its supple, mineral texture and touches of rubbed stone and pebbles. It forms part of the blend in the Valdeorras and Bierzo appellations, among others.

MENCÍA. Even from its youth, this red grape variety offers up notes of crisp red fruits, and promises an extremely satisfying sweetness on the palate. The appellations where Mencía produces the best results are Monterrei, Valdeorras, Ribeiro, and Ribeira Sacra.

PALOMINO AND PEDRO XIMÉNEZ. This duo of white varieties is cultivated in the Jerez DO (*Denominacion de Origen* – the Spanish equivalent of the French AOC): Palomino brings a natural vivacity and 'PX,' as it is known locally, expresses a range of varied aromas and, most notably, a rich sweetness.

TEMPRANILLO. If only one Spanish variety could be cultivated, it would have to be Tempranillo. The standard bearer of national wine production, it produces dark red wines with a sustained tannic structure. At the same time, it shows freshness and achieves a sumptuous balance. It is expressed to the fullest in the Ribera del Duero appellation, where it works miracles. Tempranillo is also known as: Tinto Fino, Cencibel, Tinto del País, Tinto de Toro, Tinto de Madrid, and so on.

TRUE OR FAL

Most Spanish whites suffer an excess of sunshine and so are very high in alcohol.

FALSE. In northern regions such as Galicia and the Basque country, lively wines like Rías Baixas or Txakoli are low in alcohol with floral and citrus fruit aromas.

Wine styles

Well known for its fortified wines, such as the famous sherries of Jerez, Spain also produces red wines, rosés, white wines, and sparkling wines that range from very modest to highly sophisticated. Almost crunchy reds with sharp tannins are found in the Ribeira Sacra appellation, as well as in Monterrei from Galicia. The best and fleshiest red wines are made principally

> Advertising for Malaga painted on ceramic.

Malaga rescued

Historic Andalusian wine fortified with brandy, Malaga almost disappeared from local wine production – threatened by land development for the vacation property market, and a strong demand for raisins. But since the 1980s, a new generation of wine producers has been flying the flag for this appellation once more. Malaga is a sweet white wine that owes its complex character to the addition of sweet grape syrups or concentrated musts. The wine is aged in *conos* (casks made from chestnut) according to a *solera* system (fractional blending), which can be compared with the technique for making sherry in Jerez (*see* p.74). Its quality depends on a long maturation in those casks. The best wines can be kept in bottle for decades, even centuries. Several categories are recognized, according to the ageing period: Malaga (from 6–24 months), Malaga Noble (2–3 years), Malaga Añejo (3–5 years), and Málaga Trasañejo (more than 5 years). Malaga is also classed according to its colour, from *dorado* (golden) to *negro* (black). Since 1995, it has been officially possible to make dry white wines in this region (*Malaga Blanco Seco*) as well as naturally sweet whites, *i.e.* not fortified, as well as all three colours of dry wines under the Sierras de Malaga DO.

> Barrel cellar for ageing at Señorío de Arinzano, near Estella, in Navarra.

in Priorat (*see* p.488), Toro (*see* p.481), or even in Ribera del Duero (*see* p.484). Spanish white wines have a distinct vivacity, such as Rías Baixas (*see* p.480), Txakoli (*see* p.480), or other wines from Navarra and Rioja (*see* p.485). Several of the best sweet wines – both white and red – are also produced in Penedès, Navarra, and Murcia.

Cava, a sparkling wine with vivacious bubbles, is produced mainly in Catalonia (*see* p.389). The production techniques are the same as those in Champagne (*see* pp.70–1) , but using different grape varieties.

Widely known, Jerez or sherry, a family of fortified white wines, offers a whole range of styles, from the driest to the sweetest. Long popular among the British (who originally called them 'sack'), they owe their delightful flavour to the way they are vinified beneath a film of yeast known as *flor* (*see* pp.74 and 388). The only other place in the world where this develops naturally is the Jura (France), where it plays an essential role in the making of *vin jaune* (*see* p.307).

Pagos wines

The Spanish system of appellations (*see* p.96) is similar to the system that exists in France. *Pagos* wines are at the very top of the quality scale. They each reflect a tiny *terroir*, a specific microclimate, and they are demarcated after long years of observation and tasting. As such, they often are signature wines from a single producer. In France, these wines would correspond to *monopoles* (vineyards that have only one owner) revered by all who have tasted them, such as Romanée-Conti in Burgundy, Château-Grillet in the Rhône Valley, or Coulée-de-Serrant in the Loire Valley. *Pagos* wines are produced mainly in Castile–La Mancha. Marqués de Griñón, Manuel Manzaneque, Dominio de Valdepusa, and Finca Elez are some of the most famous.

Spain's best-known wines

Spain's dynamic vineyards produce a wide range of wines that are winning spectacular popularity on the international market. From north to south, here are the main appellations and their characteristics.

TXAKOLI DO

BASQUE COUNTRY

At the center of Basque Country, nicknamed 'Green Spain', in the provinces of Bilbao and San Sebastián, this appellation includes three geographic denominations: Bizkaia, Getaria, and Alava. Situated close to the Atlantic Ocean, the vines are grown on the slopes of steep hills where typical climatic conditions consist of copious amounts of rain and moderate sunshine.

> **GRAPE VARIETIES** Hondarribi Zuri for white wines and Hondarribi Beltza for reds.

> **SOIL** Vineyards are on soil that is, for the most part, granitic. But there is limestone in some cases.

> **STYLE** Almost the entire appellation produces white wine; though some red wine is made for early consumption, when they are young and fruity. In terms of white wine, a pale, silvery colour is paired with aromas of Granny Smith apples and the zest of citrus fruit. The same is expressed on the palate with a crisp vivacity.

Colour:
White and red.

Serving temperature:
46 to 50°F (8 to 10°C) for whites;
61 to 64°F (16 to 18°C) for reds.

Ageing potential:
3 to 5 years for whites;
3 to 7 years for reds.

RÍAS BAIXAS DO

GALICIA

This DO is located in southern Galicia, very close to the border with Portugal. It contains several production zones, such Valle del Salnés, Condado del Tea, and O Rosal. The region owes its living to the sea and its rich wine-making history.

> **GRAPE VARIETIES** Albariño, Loureiro, Treixadura, Caiño Blanco, Torrontés, and Godello for white wines; Caiño Tinto, Sousón, Espadeiro, Brancellaon, Mencía, and Loureiro for reds.

> **SOIL** The area is strongly influenced by the sea. The soil – limestone, chalk, or even rocky scree – is ideal for making white wines with mineral notes.

> **STYLE** Virtually the entire appellation is given over to making white wines. They are pale yellow or very light in colour, and very aromatic with notes of orchard fruit, such as peach or apricot. As they evolve over time, hints of greengage and Mirabelle plum jam begin to emerge. There is a saline base to the structure of the mouth-feel, enhanced with mineral qualities and a convincing finish.

Colour:
White and red (less than 1 per cent of the latter).

Serving temperature:
50°F (10 °C) for whites;
61°F (16 °C) for reds.

Ageing potential:
3 to 5 years for reds;
5 to 7 years for whites.

GALICIA

VALDEORRAS DO

Valdeorras lies south of the Orense province, between the border with Portugal and the Atlantic Ocean. Home to a number of talented winemakers, this DO has been producing white wines that arouse a great deal of interest due to their mineral character and the mouth-feel they offer. Reds make up only a very small part of total production. The climate, often damp because of its proximity to the sea, is ideal for wine maturation. The vineyards cling tenaciously to the sides of the mountains, but they also extend into the heart of local valleys.

> **GRAPE VARIETIES** Godello, Palomino, Doña Blanca, for white wines; Mencía for the reds.

> **SOIL** Granite and slate soils bring a great deal of tautness to the wines, and honesty to the often fleshy palate.

> **STYLE** The white wines exude aromas of flowers and white fruit, such as pears and Mirabelle plums. On the palate, they have a dense feel with an interesting mineral quality and freshness. For the red wines, the Mencía variety shows a purplish-crimson colour. It goes on to present notes of crisp red fruit and silky tannins offering a welcome richness.

Colour:
White and red.

Serving temperature:
50°F (10 °C) for whites;
61°F (16 °C) for reds.

Ageing potential:
3 to 5 years for reds;
5 to 7 years for whites.

CASTILE AND LEÓN

TORO DO

Established in 1987, this DO became – in just a decade – one of the prime locations in which to make great wines. The average yield is scarcely a ton per acre (15 hl/ha) and the atmospheric temperature range – one of the widest in the country – is ideal for the process of grape development.

> **GRAPE VARIETIES** Malvasia and Verdejo for whites; Tinto de Toro and Garnacha for the reds and rosés.

> **SOIL** The vineyards grow at altitude (between 2,000 and 2,800 ft/600 and 800 m), where the nights are often very cold. The soil – mainly siliceous-clay – provides the vines just the right amount of heat retention, along with the trace elements that they also need.

> **STYLE** It is mainly the red wines that grab attention here. They are generally made from pure Tinto de Toro. The dark red, almost black, colour of the wines is striking. To the nose, they offer warm tones of leather, damp earth, and old varnish around a core of ripe, juicy fruit. On the palate, the concentrated aromas join in a soft and velvety texture. Then comes a series of slightly toasted, spicy flavours, all coupled with great breeding. The white and rosé wines are more classic in character.

Colour:
White, rosé, and red.

Serving temperature:
46 to 50°F (8 to 10°C) for whites and rosés;
61°F (16 °C) for reds.

Ageing potential:
5 to 20 years.

Numanthia, the jewel in Toro's crown

The vineyards here are planted at an altitude of more than 2,100 ft (650 m). The Tinto de Toro grape variety, better known as Tempranillo, produces vigorous wines of great depth – with aromas of juicy black fruit and spices. But one winery in particular stands out in the heart of this region: Numanthia–Termes. Established in 1998, this estate is first and foremost the story of a family, the Egurens, whose talent brings out the best in an exceptional vineyard. The estate (about 100 acres/40 ha) has a remarkable heritage, with old vines that lend great distinction to the wines. Every wine receives special care: very low yields, careful monitoring of fruit ripening, and, above all, meticulous attention to the production process. It all gives these wines a rare persistence and velvetiness. The Cuvée Termanthia, made solely from pre-phylloxera – *i.e.* ungrafted – vines, has become established in recent vintages as one of the greatest Spanish wines.

Castilla y Léon

VEGA *SICILIA*

If any estate in Spain deserves legendary status, it is most definitely Vega Sicilia. The property, close to the town of Valladolid in Castilla y León, extends over 4,900 acres (1,983 ha) and stands some 2,300 feet (700m) above the Duero River.

VEGA SICILIA

47359 Valbuena de Duero
Valladolid

Area: *520 acres (210 ha)*
Production: *250,000 bottles p.a.*
Appellation: *Ribera del Duero*
Red grape varieties: *Temperanillo, Cabernet Sauvignon, Merlot*

The story of a Spanish icon

The tale begins in 1848, when the Marquis of Valbuena, who was in financial difficulties, sold one of his estates to Don Toribio Lecanda. His son Eloy inherited this and planted Cabernet, Carmenère, Malbec, and other grape varieties he had brought back from a trip to Bordeaux. It seemed a strange idea, as the estate made its living from cattle, orchards, and the production of ceramics.

At the end of the 19th century, the Lecanda family also had financial difficulties and sold the *finca* to the Herrero family. The bad luck continued, with the latter in turn forced to rent out the property shortly afterwards to Cosme Palacio, a producer of Rioja affected by phylloxera. This lasted for a further ten years, until the family finally regained its entire property. However, the style created by Txomin Garramiola, director of Cosme, appealed very much to the aristocratic circles in which the Herrero family moved. So it continued to be produced on the estate and resulted in Unico and Valbuena, two wines offered to close relatives and important people. Anyone wanting to buy it had to pay a small fortune. Hence the story arose that it was the most expensive wine in Spain.

Following the death of Garramiola in 1933, the estate was neglected and it was not until its takeover by the Àlvarez family in 1982 that Vega Sicilia and Unico once more regained their place among the world's most prestigious wines. As for the rather curious name for the region, it seems to come from a contraction of the original name of the property, which was too long and complicated to remember or pronounce: 'el pago de la Vega Santa Cecilia y Carrascal', and so it became known as 'Vega Sicilia'.

Unico, an appropriate name

Unico was the first and foremost representative of Spanish wines a few decades ago. At that time Spain was known mainly for its beaches and paella, with only a few varieties of Rioja familiar to a handful of connoisseurs. In the 1970s Unico began to make a name for itself. It was exported and began to appeal to the most discerning palates. The arrival in Vega of the legendary oenologist Mariano Garcia enhanced the reputation of the wine among its new fans. The good work was continued by Javier Ausás López de Castro until 2015.

Without disparaging the *terroir*, 520 acres (210 ha) of vines on limestone slopes and clay terraces, it is above all the production process that makes Unico a unique wine. It is made from 80% Tempranillo, Merlot, and Cabernet Sauvignon. The vines are not treated with herbicides or pesticides; only copper and sulphur are used. After fermentation in conical barrels, which lasts for 15 days, maturation begins in January. The wine is transferred into new barrels made from half-French, half-American oak until the first part of the maturation process is complete. It is the cellar master who decides when the time is right to transfer this back into used barrels. Then, once again, Unico is put back in the conical barrels to complete its maturation. This entire process lasts for seven years, followed by three more years of further refinement in bottles, thus taking ten years in total. Unico is a rare wine similarly priced to Bordeaux *grand crus*, but a second wine, Valbuena, represents a less expensive alternative. Equally affordable, but in a more modern style, the Alión is 100 per cent Tempranillo. The family also own the Castilian appellation Toro, Pintia being a good example of this.

VEGA SICILIA, UNICO, RIBERA DEL DUERO

After ten years of ageing, the wine develops slowly, at first offering a few spices and delicate notes of jellied fruit. It is soft and complex, with an astonishing freshness and an impressive aromatic palette: dried fruits, sweet and gentle spices, scented plants, a touch of citrus, mellow and matured oak. Everything is magically balanced: it is simple and full-bodied, with clear charm, slight tannins, and a light balance conveyed via a sensation of almost paradoxical freshness. The aromatic flavour goes on and on, the true sign of a superb wine.

> Pablo Àlvarez, general manager of the estate.

BIERZO DO

CASTILE AND LEÓN

Situated below the Cantabrian Cordillera, Bierzo vines are grown at more than 1,600 ft (500 m), and so benefit from ideal temperature variation. This is the perfect *terroir* for the Mencía grape variety, which produces some striking red wines here.

> **GRAPE VARIETIES** Godello, Doña Blanca, Malvasia, Palomino, and Chardonnay for whites; Mencía, Garnacha (Grenache), Tempranillo, Cabernet Sauvignon, and Merlot for reds and rosés.

> **SOIL** High elevation together with the proximity of the mountains results in a soil that is made up mostly of alluvial deposits with some limestone. This combination produces slow-maturing wines, with strong mineral notes.

> **STYLE** The white and rosé wines here have been eclipsed in recent years by the progress made with red wines from the Mencía variety. A dark, almost opaque, colour from the very beginning, they offer a concentrated, deep nose with notes of cherry or blackcurrant that become smoky and mineral. There are also rich, intense tannins that require a few years' ageing in order to keep their promise.

Colour:
White, rosé, and red.

Serving temperature:
46 to 50°F (8 to 10 °C) for whites and rosés; 61°F (16 °C) for reds.

Ageing potential:
3 to 5 years for whites and rosés; 5 to 15 years for reds.

RIBERA DEL DUERO DO

CASTILE AND LEÓN

This red wine appellation, which produces primarily red wines, is, along with Rioja, the most famous in Spain. A real standard-bearer for Spanish expertize, Ribera del Duero proves – vintage after vintage – that it is truly the queen of the Iberian peninsula and the cradle of the greatest wines. For example, the legendary estate Vega Sicilia (*see* pp.482–3) was established here in 1864. This appellation is one of the best examples of the Spanish system for classifying wines according to age (*see also* p.96), with a clear vision of the wines it produces. Consequently, 'joven' wines, bottled before 12 months, are drunk young, followed by, in increasing order of age, *crianza* wines, bottled after two years, including 12 months in barrel, which are are for early drinking; the *reservas* are at least three years old, including one year spent in cask; the *gran reservas*, produced in particularly good vintages, are at least five years old, including two years in cask and three in bottle.

> **GRAPE VARIETIES** Tinto Fino, Cabernet Sauvignon, Merlot, Malbec, and Garnacha (Grenache) for reds; Albillo for whites (though the production of white wine is close to non-existent here).

> **SOIL** In this high-altitude *terroir*, the soil is mainly formed from alluvial deposits, chalk, and ancient limestone. This combination produces a wine with unrivalled tactile definition.

> **STYLE** The aromas of the red wines tend toward small black and red fruit, mild spices, and exotic wood passing through hints of smoked meat to finish with essence of dried roses: Ribero del Duero can be intriguing and passionate. The *crianza* wines offer a fair compromise between flavoursome texture and attractive expression of Tinto Fino. The *reservas* and *gran reservas* are wines that are much more profound, rich, complex, and velvety.

Colour:
Red and white.

Serving temperatures:
50°F (10°C) for whites; 64°F (16°C) for reds.

Ageing potential:
10 to 50 years or longer, depending on vintage and the particular winery.

RIOJA

RIOJA DOC

The Rioja region, following the Ebro River in northern Spain, actually derives its name from Rio Oja, a small river that crosses the appellation from west to east. During the 19th century, the producers of Rioja were greatly inspired by the wines of Bordeaux. Enough that, in the midst of the phylloxera crisis, some of them moved to Bordeaux and returned later with new techniques and expertize. As in the Ribera del Duero appellation, the ageing process is very strictly controlled, resulting in a wine of excellent quality. Rioja spends several months in oak barrels: *crianza* is aged for at least two years, including one year in oak; *reserva* is aged for at least three years, including one year in oak; gran *reserva* is aged for at least two years in oak and at least three in bottle.

> **GRAPE VARIETIES** Grenache Blanc, Viura, and Malvasia for whites; Tempranillo, Garnacha, Graciano, and Mazuelo for reds and rosés.

> **SOIL** Most of the soil is a mix of clay and limestone, but specific variations have an impact on wine style. In Rioja Baja, one of the three Rioja *terroirs*, ferruginous clay yields powerful wines; while in Rioja Alavesa, limestone yields more acidity.

> **STYLE** The white wines depend mainly on Grenache Blanc. They are pale in colour and have soothing aromas of white fruit (Japanese pears, peaches) and nuances of damp pebbles. The palate is full and fleshy. During recent years, the reds – dark red with deep purple glints – have gradually been losing their former warmth and generosity. But the aromatics still perfectly express the personality of this great appellation. At maturity, imbued with tertiary notes (venison, game, musk, blackberry jam,

and touches of cocoa powder), the palate is characterized by structure and vigour. The rosés offer a range from fresh to fruity.

Colour:
White, rosé, and red.

Serving temperature:
46 to 50°F (8 to 10°C) for whites and rosés; 61°F (16°C) for reds.

Ageing potential:
3 to 15 years for whites and rosés; 5 to 20 years for reds.

NAVARRA

NAVARRA DO

One of the best-known Spanish appellations, Navarra dates back to the origin of the DO system. Located just 37 miles (60 km) south of the French Pyrenees, the appellation stretches from Pamplona in the north and Logroño in the west to the Sierra de Moncayo in the south. There are several production zones within the DO: Baja Montaña, Tierra Estella, Valdizarbe, Ribera Alta, and Ribera Baja. The immense Navarra terroir covers more than 28,417 acres (11,500 ha) and is immediately adjacent to the Rioja region.

> **GRAPE VARIETIES** Viura, Chardonnay, Moscatel de Grano Menudo, and Malvasia, for white wines; Garnacha (Grenache), Tempranillo, Cabernet Sauvignon, Merlot, Mazuelo, and Graciano for reds and rosés.

> **SOIL** The vineyards are extensive and impressive. Some border the Ebro River, extending north toward the hills and mountains beyond. The soils are as diverse as the vineyard exposures are numerous. There is clay and sand, and a substantial amount of limestone, all providing a noticeable mineral support to the wines.

> **STYLE** The whites are mostly crisp and refreshing, with fruity notes that are extremely well expressed. Worthy of note are the Chardonnays matured 'a la Bourgignonne' – *i.e.* with a period in barrel to give them fleshiness and fullness. Wine lovers on the hunt for rare vintages and new discoveries should try the appellation's sweet wines. For several years now, Muscats have been produced with great success. Made from grapes dried on the vine, these wines offer rich sweetness. The style of the reds is an expression of the diversity of the blends: Tempranillo and Grenache dominate, but Merlot and Cabernet Sauvignon occupy a good third of the vineyard area. Many of the local reds offer a good fruity quality, with supple tannins and spicy, woody notes.

Colour:
White, rosé, and red.

Serving temperature:
46 to 50°F (8 to 10°C) for whites and rosés; 61°F (16°C) for reds.

Ageing potential:
3 to 10 years for whites and rosés; 5 to 15 years for reds.

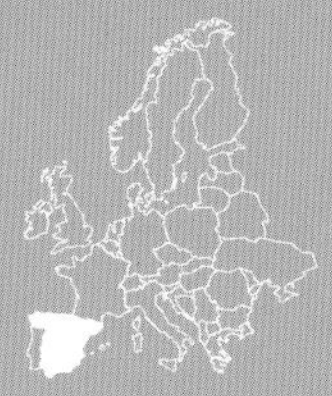

Catalonia

BODEGAS *TORRES*

Bodegas Torres is a leading European wine brand, yet remains a family company on a human scale. The man who initiated the company's global growth, Miguel Torres Senior, initially focused on international grape varieties, before rediscovering local varieties and terroirs.

BODEGAS TORRES

6. 08720 Vilafranca del Penedès
Barcelona

Founded: *1870*
Area: *3,212 acres (1,300 ha)*
Production: *N/A*
Appellation: *Penedès*
White grape varieties: *Chardonnay, Sauvignon Blanc, Riesling, Paralleda*
Red grape varieties: *Cabernet Sauvignon, Grenache, Tempranillo, Merlot, Syrah, Cabernet Franc, Carignan, Querol, Pinot Noir*

International recognition

In the early 1960s young Miguel (born in 1943) began studying oenology in France. After graduating, he returned to Spain. At this point the Torres family decided to buy vines and to replant around Vilafranca del Penedès, in Mas la Plana. They chose to establish the new estate high up for practical reasons: at the time refrigeration was not available, but the altitude meant that the temperature would be sufficiently cool. They tried several international grape varieties, with varying success: Riesling and Pinot were failures, but Cabernet Sauvignon (already made famous in the region by Jean Leon) was a great success. The first wine was produced in 1970 (it was then called Gran Coronas). This wine was successful at the Wine Olympics in 1979. A complete surprise: 'it was our customers who told us about it. We did not really realize, at the time.' Beating the great Bordeaux on their home turf, with a Cabernet made up of young vines, planted in an almost unknown place, you had to pinch yourself to believe it. To those who were surprised that Torres had chosen foreign grape varieties, he replied: 'at the time, our local varieties were poorly managed, not necessarily planted where they should be, and their yield was far too high. It was necessary to make a fresh start, as it were.' Following this, Spain regained its reputation as a leading wine-producing nation.

Rediscovering vines

Over the years, Miguel Torres developed and so did his company. In 1982 he spent a year studying oenology in Montpellier, but this time with an emphasis on viticulture. It represented an opportunity to study in depth something about which he felt passionately, the specific effect of the soil, to learn more about the vine as a plant, and to improve the methods by which it was managed and treated. This seems obvious today, but in 1982 Miguel Torres was a pioneer. Once he returned to Catalonia, he reviewed his vineyard and sought greater understanding of the link between grape varieties, soils, and climate. He reduced pesticide and fungicide treatments. Yields dropped, but this was a necessary price to be paid for improved quality. Torres was a perfectionist and wanted to go further. He was interested in the issues of global warming and water management. He was passionate about the old grape varieties of Catalonia, abandoned after phylloxera, because they are less productive but more resistant to diseases and better adapted to the climate. He appealed to old wine producers to rediscover forgotten plants. He isolated them, multiplied them, and vinified them in miniature batches. If he was satisfied with the results, he incorporated them gradually into his wines, even the finest ones. Thus, Grans Muralles contained more and more Querol, a suitably tannic grape variety named after the village where it was discovered.

Meanwhile, the Torres family also runs vineyards in Chile and California; in Spain it emerged from its Catalan roots to spread to Rioja, Rueda, and Ribera del Duero. The new generation at the helm, Miguel Junior and Mireia Torres, continues to apply the sound principles of their father: a tree only grows well if its roots are sound.

TORRES, MAS LA PLANA, PENEDÈS

A mere 72 acres (29 ha) of limestone and gravel, planted with Cabernet Sauvignon. But what a Cabernet Sauvignon this is! In 1979, under the name of Gran Coronas, the wine finished ahead of Latour, Pichon-Lalande, and Mission Haut Brion at the Wine Olympics in Paris.

MAS LA PLANA

Besides its natural class, this wine has the advantage of being very consistent in terms of its quality. On the nose, it has small fruits from the woods, truffle, and leather. The palate is smokey, and the tannins are elegant, delicate, and refined but still clearly present. A complete, and solid yet versatile performer. A wine to be kept for a long while by those who can bear to wait.

TORRES, GRANS MURALLES, CONCA DE BARBERÀ

It is difficult to find a more historic and more Catalan wine than this: its 79 acres (32 ha) were cleared and planted in the 13th century by Cistercians in the monastery of Poblet, a great symbol of local spirituality. Miguel Torres chose to revive the old traditional grape varieties of Catalonia: Monastrell, Cariñena, and Garnacha, but also Garró, Samsó, and Querol. Unsurprisingly, this results in a wine with Mediterranean notes of garrigue, thyme, spice, and amazing floral notes. The palate is complex and concentrated. Here is a wine that is well structured and full of vigour.

> The Torres family.

ARAGON

CAMPO DE BORJA DO

The region of Aragón is a vast expanse crossed by the Ebro River. The appellation Campo de Borja, situated at the southern edge of the Navarra DO, derives its name from *campo*, which means the area surrounding the old city of Borja. It accurately reflects the quality and nobility of the wines produced from its *terroirs*. The average altitude of most vineyards here is 1,600 ft (500 m). The landscape is made up of long strips of land punctuated by hills with gentle slopes.

> **GRAPE VARIETIES** Garnacha (Grenache), Tempranillo, Mazuelo, Cabernet Sauvignon, Merlot, and Syrah for reds and rosés; Maccabeu, Moscatel, and Chardonnay for whites.

> **SOIL** Limestone, fairly brownish in colour, with touches of ferrous oxide.

> **STYLE** The appellation's reputation is based largely on its red wines, mainly from Grenache. Their colour is suffused with purplish, even opaque, tints. On the nose, the aromas develop notes of macerated black fruit (blackberry, bilberry, fig) over a firm structure that is pleasing to the palate. The tannins progress to a supple, velvety texture. The (far fewer) white wines and the rosés are characterized by fresh aromas and invigorating, crisp textures.

Colour:
White, rosé, and red.

Serving temperature:
46 to 50°F (8 to 10°C) for whites and rosés; 61°F (16°C) for reds.

Ageing potential:
3 to 5 years for dry whites;
7 to 10 years for sweet and 'mellow' whites;
7 to 20 years for reds.

CATALONIA

PRIORAT DOC

This is the queen of Catalan appellations. Twenty years ago, Priorat wines sold in wine-boxes for barely a dollar (equivalent) per litre; the best wines now exceed $500 a bottle. The DOC has undergone a complete transformation and now offers wines of great character. They have 'rewritten' their *terroir*. White and red wines with *crianza* on the label are matured for at least six months in oak barrels; the *gran reservas* spend a minimum of 24 months in barrel and three years in bottle before going on the market.

> **GRAPE VARIETIES** Grenache Blanc, Maccabeu, Parellada, Chenin Blanc, Viognier, and Pedro Ximénez for whites; Cariñena, Garnacha (Grenache), Cabernet Sauvignon, Merlot, Pinot Noir, Syrah, and Tempranillo for reds.

> **SOIL** The landscape is a succession of terraces and plateaus at altitudes of up to almost 3,000 ft (900 m), on soils comprised of shale and granite.

> **STYLE** Dry whites, still produced in limited quantities, are a typical expression of the Grenache Blanc and a true marker of *terroir*. The sweet whites – those in the *rancio* style – are truly irresistible but of lesser importance in terms of production. The reds are purple in colour, with aromas of redcurrant jam, blackberries, and spices. Powerful and fleshy, they rest on a framework of very ripe and generous tannins, offering flavours of black fruit, spice, licorice, and pencil lead.

Colour:
White and red.

Serving temperatures:
50 to 54°F (10 to 12°C) for both dry and sweet whites; 61°F (16°C) for reds.

Ageing potential:
3 to 5 years for dry whites;
7 to 10 years for sweet and rancio *whites;*
7 to 20 years for reds.

Ten top Spanish wineries

- **Agustí Torelló** – Cava DO
- **Bodegas Chivite** – Navarra DO
- **Bodegas Aalto** – Ribera del Duero DO
- **Bodega Álvaro Palacios** – Priorat DOC
- **Bodegas Arzuaga** – Ribera del Duero DO
- **Bodegas Numanthia-Termes** – Toro DO
- **Bodegas San Roman** – Toro DO
- **Bodegas Vega Sicilia** – Ribera del Duero DO
- **Clos Mogador** – Priorat DOC
- **Vall Llach** – Priorat DOC

CATALONIA

PENEDÈS DO

Spread across more than 61,776 acres (25,000 ha), this symbolic appellation covers a large part of Catalonia and includes several subzones: Alt Penedès, Baix Penedès, and Garraf. The vast extent of the area means that several different styles of wine can be produced here.

> **GRAPE VARIETIES** Maccabeu, Parellada, Xarel-lo, Moscatel, Chardonnay, Sauvignon Blanc, Gewurztraminer, Riesling, and Chenin Blanc for white wines; Tempranillo, Grenache, Cariñena, Monastrell, Cabernet Sauvignon, Merlot, Pinot Noir, and Syrah for reds and rosés.

> **SOIL** This large wine-producing area and its different types of landscape include a number of soils: at altitude, the predominant limestone guarantees wines with a remarkable freshness; there are also chalk soils and granite; the plain is dominated by a mixture of sand and clay.

> **STYLE** White wines are based on several grape varieties – the presence of international varieties such as Chardonnay or Sauvignon Blanc means that all styles of wine can be produced here, even the most oaky. On the palate, the aromatic range and the textures will, therefore, all be different. As for the reds, they often go through expertly controlled maturation that gives the wines a deep colour and a bouquet of black fruit (plum, blackcurrant) and spice powder. The tannic composition varies according to the blending of the varieties, but is always relatively supple and velvety.

Colour:
White, rosé, and red.

Serving temperature:
46 to 50°F (8 to 10°C) for whites and rosés; 61°F (16°C) for reds.

Ageing potential:
1 to 3 years for rosés;
3 to 10 years for dry whites;
7 to 10 years for reds.

CASTILE–LA MANCHA

VALDEPEÑAS DO

Sheltered by the Toledo Mountains and the Sierra de Segura, this DO covers more than 69,190 acres (28,000 ha). The wines are made in all three colours, generally using classic techniques that are true to the appellation.

> **GRAPE VARIETIES** Airén and Maccabeu for whites; Cencibel, Grenache, and Cabernet Sauvignon for reds and rosés.

> **SOIL** *Val de peñas* means 'valley of the stones', so it is easy to imagine the arid, barren landscape on which the vines are planted. The most promising plots in this appellation are made up of chalk-and-limestone soils.

> **STYLE** The white wines are based on the duo Airén and Maccabeu. The former brings freshness and vivacity, while the latter is appreciated for its abundant and fleshy mouth-feel, revealing a sumptuous minerality. The red wines are made mostly from the purely Spanish variety Cencibel, the local name for Tempranillo, which serves up some fine surprises for lovers of deep, concentrated, and velvety wines.

Colour:
White, rosé, and red.

Serving temperature:
46 to 50°F (8 to 10°C) for whites and rosés; 61°F (16°C) for reds.

Ageing potential:
3 to 5 years for dry whites and rosés;
8 to 10 years for reds.

MURCIA

JUMILLA DO

Located in southeastern Spain, in the Levant, Jumilla extends over more than 66,718 acres (27,000 ha). The landscape in certain zones looks almost lunar – arid and baked by long hours of intense sun.

> **GRAPE VARIETIES** Airén, Maccabeu, Moscatel, Malvasia, and Pedro Ximénez for white wines; Monastrell, Garnacha (Grenache), Tempranillo, Cabernet Sauvignon, Merlot, and Syrah for the red wines.

> **SOIL** A mix of stones and chalk, it ensures a good supply of trace elements and mineral salts: ideal conditions for the growth of vines.

> **STYLE** The whites and rosés are produced to show off the aromatic qualities of their different grape varieties; they are generous and invigorating on the palate. But the most interesting wines are the reds made from Monastrell (Mourvèdre) grapes, which ripen well in the sun of the Levante, giving powerful, full-bodied wines with spicy flavours. Using the old *passerillage* technique, wine producers can also make rich, sweet wines with aromas of dried fruit (raspberry, plum, figs) allied with a subtle palate, all within an ideally balanced whole. The sweetness remains harmonious, never heavy.

Colour:
White, red, and rosé.

Serving temperature:
46 to 50°F (8 to 10°C) for whites and rosés; 59°F (15°C) for reds.

Ageing potential:
3 to 5 years for dry whites and rosés;
7 to 30 years for reds.

Andalusia

BODEGAS
LUSTAU

How, from a fairly simple terroir and from a non-aromatic grape variety, Palomino, are wines as complex and as varied as those found in Jerez produced? And especially those from Lustau?

BODEGAS LUSTAU

Calle Arcos, 53
11402 Jerez de la Frontera, Cádiz

Founded: *1896*
Area: *161 acres (65 ha)*
Production: *420,000 bottles p.a.*
Appellation: *Jerez, Manzanilla-Sanlúcar de Barrameda*
Grape varieties: *Palomino, Muscat, Pedro Ximénez (PX)*

A complex terroir

The terroir is essentially not as simple as it seems. The south of Andalusia, with its leaden sun and soft hills, seems to be lacking in variation. Yet there is the exposure to the Atlantic winds, in particular, hence the iodine found in Manzanilla. Furthermore, there are three types of soil: limestone *albarizas* (the most highly prized soil), sands, and *barros* or heavy clays. The magic of Jerez lies primarily in the maturation process, and especially in expertize with the *flor*, a yeast veil typical of wines from this region. Not to mention the time factor. Jerez (also known as Xérès or sherry) is one of the earliest great export wines in modern history: London merchants contributed to its spread internationally as early as the 16th century, with Shakespeare one of its most fervent admirers. Spaniards are no different either, and more than any other, Bodegas Lustau has made an effort to preserve this heritage.

'Almanista'

Its founder, Don José Ruiz, was an *almacenista*, a 'warehouse owner' who matured Jerez wines for third parties. These roots live on via a line of Lustau Almacenistas, one of the most traceable of its kind. Numbering eight, these wines, which are not blended, are selected by the oenologist of Lustau, Manuel Lozano, for the producers. They are sold in 50cl bottles, with their label stating the name of the producer, the number of *botas* produced, and the type of wine. Lustau offers many other ranges: the Especialistas, the Soleras, the VORS (more than 30 years old), and the Tres en Rama. Not to mention the brandy and vinegar from Jerez. Lustau is not just a style, it encompasses all the vast diversity of the Jerez range, from the driest to the sweetest, from iodine to fresh almonds, from hazelnut to cocoa, from Fino to Oloroso, from Manzanilla to Amontillado, and PX.

The vastly diverse Jerez range

To simplify, there are two main types of sherries: those that have the *flor* (the yeast veil that protects them from oxidizing too rapidly), namely Fino, Manzanilla, and Amontillado, and those that do not have it (Oloroso and Cream). There is also a precise geographical area, Sanlúcar de Barrameda, which is the source of Manzanilla (a specific appellation), characterized by its cutting edge and iodized flavours. But no description can make the diversity of the vast Jerez range as clear as a visit to the cellars of a Jerez or Sanlúcar bodega.

BODEGAS LUSTAU, LUSTAU MANZANILLA PAPIRUSA

The very pale colour of this sherry gives little indication of the power that follows on the nose. A great oceanic blast conveys the scent of almonds and walnuts, green apples, and raisins, soon joined by bouquets of fenugreek, pepper, and cumin. All of this is both fresh and complex. Then at the end there is a hint of iodine and salt, like a final sea spray.

BODEGAS LUSTAU, EAST INDIA SOLERA

Oloroso mixed with a little of the sweet PX, this wine is 20% ABV and is one of the range of cream (sweet) sherries. Barrels of this type of Jerez once served as ballast for boats en route to the Indies, hence its name. The roll of the ships refined them. The red amber colour is surprisingly dark for a product of white grape varieties. The nose also evokes the Orient: sweet and sour spices, and pepper. The palette is surprisingly smooth: almonds are joined by dried figs and olives, dried orange, coffee, and cedar. The taste lingers long.

YECLA DO

MURCIA

This southern appellation has achieved a real turnaround in quality with its latest vintages. With a much more limited yield – relative to the area cultivated – than neighbouring Jumilla DO, Yecla comprises two zones: Campo Arriba and Campo Abajo. Both produce wines that are greatly appreciated for their maturity.

> **GRAPE VARIETIES** Airén, Maccabeu, Merseguera, and Sauvignon Blanc for the whites; Monastrell (synonymous with Mourvèdre, and with a presence of at least 75 per cent in the blends), Tempranillo, Garnacha (Grenache,) Cabernet Sauvignon, Merlot, and Syrah for the reds and rosés.

> **SOIL** Like several other appellations in southern Spain, Yecla rests on chalk-and-limestone soil, which gives the wines great freshness and balance.

> **STYLE** The whites and rosés are always very expressive, bringing out textures that are crisp, invigorating, and redolent of sunshine. The reds always have an intense colour, underlined by tinges of dark red and crimson. The wines are heavy, powerful, well supported by generous tannins; and the aromas range through spicy, chocolaty, and slightly balsamic.

Colour:
White, rosé, and red.

Serving temperature:
46 to 50°F (8 to 10°C) for whites and rosés; 61°F (16°C) for reds.

Ageing potential:
3 to 5 years for dry whites and rosés; 3 to 10 years for reds.

JEREZ DOC

ANDALUSIA

The southern tip of Spain, and the region of Andalusia, is anchored by the Jerez (or Xérès or Sherry) appellation. A DOC since 1933, it has been famous for centuries – courtesy of the English, who have long enjoyed its character. The Palomino grape variety, which on other *terroirs* produces wine with a narrow aromatic range and little interest, seems to have found ideal conditions here.

> **GRAPE VARIETIES** Two varieties stand out. The first, Palomino Fino, also called Palomino Blanco or Listan, represents well over 90 per cent of the growing area. The second, Pedro Ximénez, called 'PX' for short, is involved mostly in the production of sweet wines.

> **SOIL** Mainly chalky soils and subsoils (a *terroir* known as *albariza*) dominate in this region. Its capacity to retain water is essential over the long and very dry summers.

> **STYLE** The complexity and diversity of this appellation flows from a unique style of production. It creates both the driest and most lively wines, such as *fino*, as well as almost syrupy wines that are rich in tertiary aromas, such as *oloroso* and cream. There are two main families of sherry wines: the dry and light *finos* and the deeper coloured and stronger *olorosos*. The *finos* are dependent on the *flor* process (*see* p.74), but the *olorosos* are not. The rare *palo cortados* are a hybrid of the two.

- Finos. These are very dry and aromatic wines (with notes of walnut, almonds, leather); their alcohol content is lower than that of *olorosos*. They are consumed very young. *Pale cream* indicates a softened fino. *Manzanilla* is a *fino* produced in the small coastal appellation of Sanlúcar de Barrameda.
- Olorosos. These differ from *finos* in their higher alcohol content (between 16 and 18% ABV), and in the length of their oxidative maturation in vats and barrels without *flor* yeast. Their aromatic range includes dried fruit (fig), malt, roasted coffee, and chocolate, but also leather and more balsamic nuances.
– Amontillados. Aged *finos*, which are matured in an oxidative environment, producing an aromatic character somewhere between *finos* and *olorosos*.
– Pedro Ximenez. Used to soften certain sherries (medium, cream), it produces the rare Dulces Naturales sherries, very sweet, rich wines (up to 18 oz sugar per 4.2 cups/500 g sugar per litre).

Colour:
White.

Serving temperature:
46 to 54°F (8 to 12°C) for finos*;*
57°F (14°C) for olorosos.

Ageing potential:
1 to 3 years for finos*;*
7 to 100 years for olorosos.

BALEAREIC ISLANDS

PLA Í LLEVANT DO

This small appellation is located on the island of Majorca. Within its 988 acres (400 ha), a very small area for Spain, there are 13 bodegas producing wine in a fine climate of abundant sunshine and sea air. The result is harvests of great quality. Note that a choice of grapes based on native varieties captures all the richness of the island.

> **GRAPE VARIETIES** Prensal, Moscatel, Maccabeu, Parellada, and Chardonnay for the white wines; Callet, Fogoneu, Tempranillo, Manto Negro, Monastrell, Cabernet Sauvignon, and Merlot for the reds and rosés.

> **SOIL** The vines are planted on limestone terrain strewn with lumps of chalk, ensuring ideal water retention.

> **STYLE** Muscat of Alexandria, with its small grapes, seems to have found the perfect *terroir* in which to grow here. Generally dried before use, this grape variety yields wines with floral scents of lavender and mimosa, going on to deliver a vigorous and aromatic palate. The rosé wines are worth a close look. They catch the eye with pronounced colour, then develop aromatic touches of crystallized orange, new leather, and a hint of smokiness. On the palate, fleshiness and opulence are very evident. All the generosity of wines from the Mediterranean basin can be found in the reds here. Made mostly from Callet and Tempranillo, they attract attention with their dark red colour and offer aromas of blackberry jam on an entrancing chocolate base. The textures on the palate are very apparent thanks to solid and well-ripened tannins.

Colour:
White, rosé, and red.

Serving temperature:
46 to 50°F (8 to 10°C) for whites and rosés; 59°F (15°C) for reds.

Ageing potential:
3 to 5 years for whites, rosés, and reds.

OTHER REGIONS

CAVA DO

The best-known sparkling wines from the Iberian peninsula take their name from the word *cava*, which means 'cave' or 'cellar' in Catalan. Cava's origins are much later than those of Champagne. The first written records date to 1872, when José Raventos – of the famous Cordoníu winery – returned from a journey to Champagne. He decided to produce a local equivalent of the famous sparkling wine using native grape varieties. After much research and many attempts, he finally managed to create a satisfactory version at his San Sadurni d'Anoia winery. Cava is made principally in Catalonia, and especially in the Penedès DO, but it also can be produced in Aragòn, Estremadura, Rioja, Navarra, the Basque country, and in Valencia. It therefore covers an immense, very spread-out area (more than 81,545acres/33,000 ha).

> **GRAPE VARIETIES** Chardonnay, Maccabeu, Malvasia, Parellada, and Xarel-lo for white wines; Garnacha (Grenache), Monastrell, Trepat, and Pinot Noir for rosés.

> **SOIL** The extensive winemaking area means there are many different types of soil. Even so, producers are almost unanimous in the belief that the best wines are produced from limestone or chalky soils that are capable of contributing the necessary minerality and maturity.

> **STYLE** Cavas all show the same pale and scintillating colours, enlivened by strings of bubbles that rise to the surface. On the nose, there are discreet notes of lime tree, yellow fuit, dried fruit, or toast. The palate shows, in general, suppleness and freshness, with an effervescence less marked than with Champagnes. Note that Chardonnay has become increasingly important in blends of the three principal grape varieties (Maccabeu, Parellada, Xarel-lo), bringing its finesse and freshness.

Colour:
White and rosé.

Serving temperature:
46 to 54°F (8 to 12°C) according to the cuvée and the state of the wine's development.

Ageing potential:
3 to 15 years.

Catalonia, Rioja,
Galicia, Tuscany

ÁLVARO
PALACIOS

At the age of 25, Álvaro Palacios left his native Rioja for the hills of Priorat in Catalonia without a penny in his pocket, but with a fierce desire to revive these forgotten vineyards. He is now a famous figure, thanks to his cult wine, L'Ermita, a symbol of the new all-conquering and ambitious Spanish wine production.

A motorbike for old vines

'My life is a love story with wine,' says Álvaro Palacios, the seventh of nine children. His family has had its roots firmly in Rioja for four centuries, but other places have provided him with glory and fame. He remembers how impoverished agriculture in Spain was in the 1980s, along with his hesitation to become a winemaker. Even if he had it in his blood, he was not convinced until several years later during a stay in Bordeaux with the Moueix (Pétrus) family, where he succumbed to 'the magic of great wines' to be tasted again and again each year. When he returned to Spain, he worked trading barrels, travelling the roads, and becoming aware of the tremendous potential of the country's vineyards, in the doldrums after years of isolation. Then, when René Barbier, who was working with his father, offered him the chance to become involved in a forgotten vineyard, Priorat, in the south of Catalonia, he sold his motorbike and started work immediately. In Priorat he was attracted as much by the old, almost abandoned vines as by the ghosts of the wine-making monks who have haunted the place for centuries. 'The Romans created the vineyards, but the monks gave viticulture its nobility and its dignity.' And in all the great classical vineyards of Europe, he saw the decisive influence of monks. The vineyard of Priorat is 31 miles (50 km) west of Tarragona, nestled in an austere hilly landscape far away from the sea. In 1989 these sloping terraces consisted of vineyards that were deserted, because they were too expensive to work.

A monumental vineyard

However, there was no doubt of the potential, if heat could be tempered by altitude, poor schists could regulate the water supply in a region with arid summers, and old Grenache and Carignan vines were available. Álvaro Palacios and his associates, including René Barbier, another key figure in the region, began to make tentative grape purchases and acquire their first vineyards in 1990. Progress continued to be made. In 1993 came the opportunity to buy a small plot of just over 4 acres (1.6 ha) with a small chapel, which he subsequently called L'Ermita. Álvaro Palacios recalls how struck he was by this place: 'captivating' and 'monumental', with spectacular slopes of up to 60 degrees, with an ideal northeast exposure, which would protect the vines from the strong summer heat. With the first vinification, he created a paradoxical wine, both powerful and vibrant, from old Grenache vines, 'the only grape variety capable of transforming heat and aridity into such a refreshing liquid'.

Critics were immediately impressed by the superb wine from this plot, which was lush, concentrated, and with remarkable balance and depth. The charisma of Álvaro Palacios and his marketing ability did the rest: L'Ermita quickly became a Spanish icon and a symbol of the renaissance of Priorat. Through his resolute approach to the identification and development of specific terroirs, he initiated a revolution in Spain, where blending of grapes from several vineyards was the norm. A philosophy that gained him further success in Rioja, where he took over the family estate in 2000, and then in the Atlantic vineyards of Bierzo, in conjunction with his nephew, Ricardo Pérez Palacios, in the Bodega Descendientes de J. Palacios. While in his mind the terroir is more important than the grape variety, he campaigns for the rediscovery of indigenous grape varieties: Grenache, Mencía, Graciano de Alfaro, or old strains of Monastrell (also known as Mourvèdre). In this aspect, too, the child prodigy of Spanish viticulture is a role model, inspiring the new wave of Iberian winemakers.

aro Palacios,
ıger of the estate.

PORTUGAL

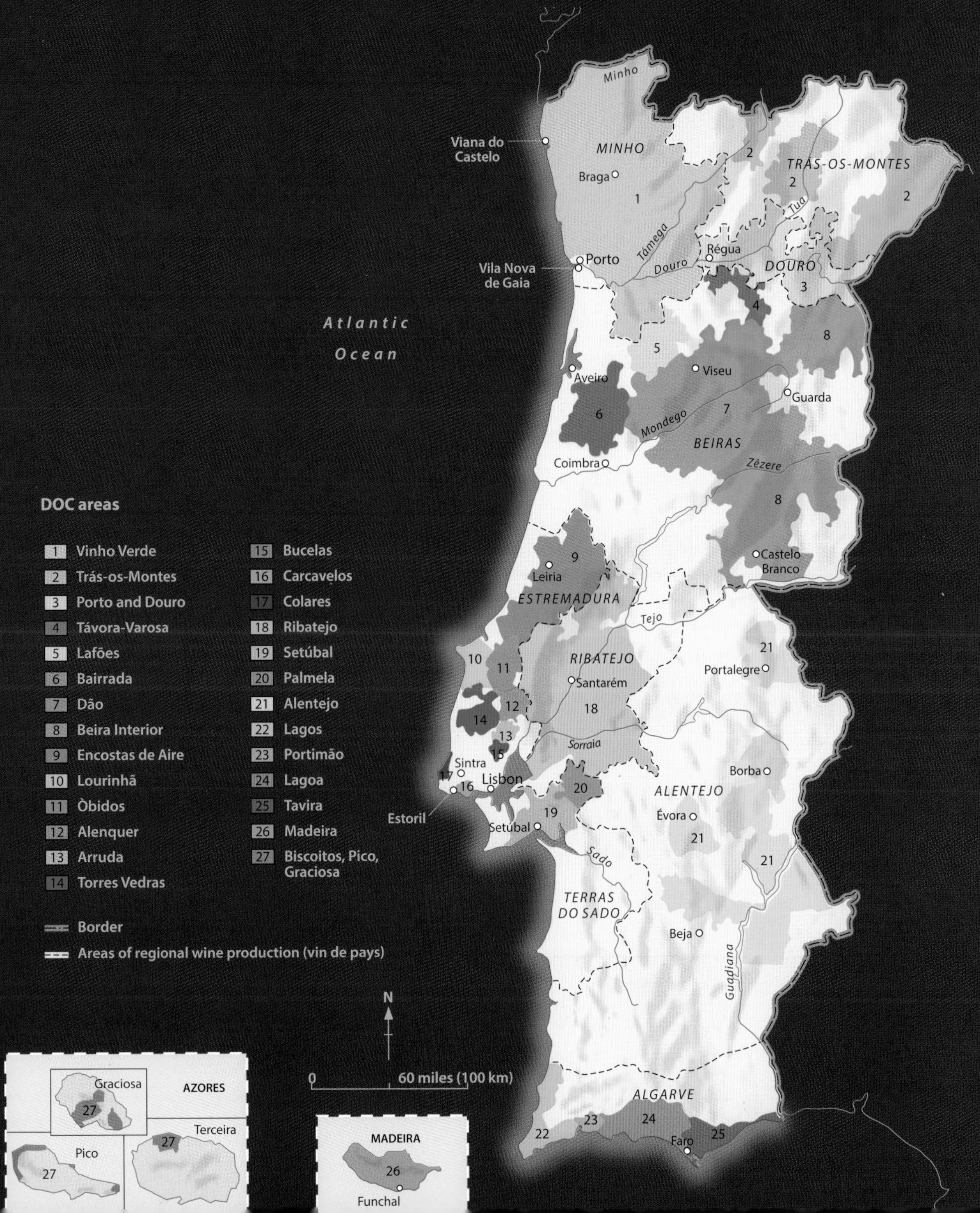

Minho
Viana do Castelo
MINHO
Braga
1
2
TRÁS-OS-MONTES
2
2
Tua
Tâmega
Porto
Vila Nova de Gaia
Douro
Régua
DOURO
3
4
Atlantic Ocean
5
8
Aveiro
Viseu
Guarda
6
7
Mondego
BEIRAS
Coimbra
Zêzere
8
9
Leiria
Castelo Branco
ESTREMADURA
Tejo
10
11
RIBATEJO
21
Portalegre
Santarém
14
12
18
13
15
Sorraia
Sintra
17
Lisbon
16
20
Borba
ALENTEJO
Estoril
19
Évora
Setúbal
21
21
Sado
TERRAS DO SADO
Beja
Guadiana
ALGARVE
22
23
24
25
Faro
DOC areas
1 Vinho Verde
2 Trás-os-Montes
3 Porto and Douro
4 Távora-Varosa
5 Lafões
6 Bairrada
7 Dão
8 Beira Interior
9 Encostas de Aire
10 Lourinhã
11 Òbidos
12 Alenquer
13 Arruda
14 Torres Vedras
15 Bucelas
16 Carcavelos
17 Colares
18 Ribatejo
19 Setúbal
20 Palmela
21 Alentejo
22 Lagos
23 Portimão
24 Lagoa
25 Tavira
26 Madeira
27 Biscoitos, Pico, Graciosa
Border
Areas of regional wine production (vin de pays)
N
0
60 miles (100 km)
Graciosa
AZORES
27
Terceira
27
Pico
27
MADEIRA
26
Funchal

PORTUGAL

Situated on the western edge of Europe, Portugal offers a wide variety of wine styles from its relatively narrow territory. Renowned for centuries for the fortified wines port and Madeira, it now also produces some fine dry reds and increasingly attractive white wines.

Long history

PORT INDUSTRY. Portuguese vineyards date back to antiquity, but it is rather more recently that its wines have acquired a degree of fame. Trade links with England began in the 12th century, and they were the main engine of development for Portugal's wine industry. This long collaboration most famously gave birth to port during the 18th century – a dark red wine from the Douro Valley, fortified to withstand long sea voyages. The Douro region adopted extensive legislation as early as 1756, making it the world's first appellation of origin, 179 years before the introduction of the AOC system in France. But Portugal's slow economic growth and political isolation, until the 1974 revolution, meant that its viticultural practices were virtually frozen in time. This allowed Portugal to retain almost intact its tremendous wealth of local varieties.

RECENT PROGRESS. Since Portugal's admission to the European Union in 1986, an extraordinary energy has been driving many of its producers – from large historic houses, which have always played a leading role, to cooperatives, often fully modernized, to private domains (*quintas*), which have multiplied since the 1990s. Some vineyards have been replanted, and others have been newly established. Some regions previously without a great wine tradition, such as Alentejo, have become places of experimentation. However, there is still a contrast between the old family estates operating according to past practices and domains at the forefront of progress; though the rapid spread of new technology goes a long way to reducing the gap.

PORTUGAL STATISTICS

Vineyard area: 538,690 acres (218,000 ha)

Production: 67.7 million cases (6.1 million hl)

Reds and rosés: 69%

Whites: 31%

(Instituto do Vinho e da Vinha, OIV, 2014)

Topography and climate: a country of contrasts

Portugal is a land of contrasts – some very marked – and they are reflected in the wines. Relative to its total land area, the total Portuguese vineyard area is vast: 538,690 acres (218,000 ha) spread throughout the country, except for the high mountain areas in the centre and northeast.

Relatively narrow from east to west, Portugal has 380 miles (600 km) of coastline. The Atlantic Ocean exerts a strong influence over the coastal regions, with fairly abundant rainfall, temperatures cooled by sea breezes, and lush vegetation, especially in the north. This influence fades rapidly toward

> An estate in the Douro Valley.

the east. In the north, mountain ranges halt the advance of moist sea air and shelter an arid landscape with extreme temperatures in both summer and winter.

South of the Tagus River, which cuts the country in half, the terrain flattens, giving way to vast plains. They are occasionally punctuated by low hills, but all are battered in summer by relentless sun and drought.

> Every year, hundreds of pickers harvest grapes on the sunny slopes overlooking the Douro River.

Northern regions

Portugal's northern vineyards extend from the Douro Valley up to the north and northeast border with Spain. This is where the two largest and most renowned appellations are located: Vinho Verde and port, producing wines in entirely different styles.

VINHO VERDE. The vineyards of Vinho Verde form a vast amphitheatre looking out toward the Atlantic. This densely populated region is wet, with lush vegetation, and is known mainly for its slightly sparkling, dry, light white wines made from a wide variety of local grapes.

PORT AND DOURO. Toward the east, the green countryside slowly gives way to an austere, arid landscape in the central mountains. This is where the Douro and port vineyards are located. Both DOCs share the same area, which follows the Douro River and its tributaries from the Spanish border to the outskirts of the city of Resende, about 60 miles (100 km) inland. The rivers have cut deep canyons into the mountain schist. Vines are planted in hillside plots and are supported either by traditional stone walls or arranged in sloping terraces of more recent construction (*patamares*). Port, fortified by the addition of grape spirit, is a powerful, warm, and spicy wine. It is born out of these spectacular stony vineyards, which are subjected to a harsh, dry climate that is particularly hot in summer. Since the 1990s, this region has also been successfully producing dry red wines bearing the Douro DOC, and made with the same grapes as port.

Four categories

In Portugal, brand loyalty is very strong. The Portuguese consumer will choose a brand name or a trusted producer over that of an appellation of origin. Even so, wine legislation complied with European requirements, and it's now based around four categories: DOC (Denominação de Origem Controlada), IPR (Indicação de Proveniência Regulamentada), although their numbers are dwindling, Vinho Regional (*'vin de pays'*), and Vinho (table wine). This classification structure is intended to be a scale of quality, but many of the best producers prefer to use the Vinho Regional tier, since it allows them greater freedoms, especially in their choice of grape varieties.

TRAS-OS-MONTES. The vineyards of this recent DOC (2006), at the northeastern end of the country, are part of the vast Transmontano Vinho Regional (VR) area. Production is dominated by cooperatives.

Central regions

The wine regions between the Douro and the Setúbal Peninsula account each year for more than 40 per cent of the country's production, half of which is table wine. Including some famous DOCs, this area is divided into four Vinho Regional zones – Beiras in the north, Tejo, Lisbon, and the Setúbal Peninsula – all permitting the planting of international varieties alongside local ones.

BAIRRADA. This humid, rural area is sandwiched between the coast and the granite hills that border the Dão DOC to the east. Famous during the 18th century, the region has rediscovered its potential through the work of some visionary producers including Luis Pato (whose wines sell under the Beiras Vinho Regional appellation). The soils are mostly clay-and-limestone, and the main grape variety, Baga, gives local red wines a powerful and structured character. They often need time to shed the austerity they display in their youth.

DÃO. Set adjacent to Bairrada, this DOC is undergoing a revolution since local cooperatives lost (in 1989) their monopoly on wine production for the entire appellation. Today, it offers some of the country's most successful red wines, along with some generous and compelling whites. The vineyards grow on a granitic plateau, sheltered from the influence of the Atlantic by the Serra do Caramulo mountains. The style of wine ranges from soft to powerful and structured.

TEJO. The Tejo region, crossed by the Tagus River, continues to produce mainly table wines and Vinho Regional (under the appellation Vinho Regional Tejo), including some good Cabernet Sauvignon and Syrah. The Tejo DOC amounts to less than 10 per cent of regional production, but showcases the interesting local varieties.

LISBON. Previously grouped under the name Estremadura, these vineyards extend for about 20 miles (30 km) along the coast north of Lisbon. Most of the area (54,363 acres/22,000 ha) is devoted to ordinary wine production, and the nine DOCs of the region amount to scarcely five per cent of total production. Most are struggling to emerge, and some historic DOCs on the outskirts of Lisbon, like Carcavelos and Colares, are threatened by the capital city's extension. Bucelas, north of Lisbon, could suffer the same fate, but the current fashion for its fresh and fragrant whites from local variety Arinto is protecting it for now.

Southern regions and islands

SETÚBAL PENINSULA. Along with the vineyards on the Setúbal Peninsula itself, this region also includes those situated south of the Sado Estuary. The peninsula enjoys a relatively mild oceanic climate, while the vineyards east of Setúbal, in the fertile plain of the Sado River, are subject to a much more harsh climate. There are only two DOCs: Palmela, planted mainly with Castelão, a red grape known locally as Periquita, yielding soft and fruity wines; and Setúbal, renowned for its sweet white wines from Moscatel de Setúbal. Half of the wines are now labelled Península de Setúbal Vinho Regional, as this appellation allows greater freedom of grape variety choice. The white wines, from local or international varieties, have improved dramatically in the past 10 years. For the red wines, Castelão is still the main variety, but it is becoming increasingly challenged by Cabernet Sauvignon, Syrah, Aragonês, and Touriga Nacional.

ALENTEJO AND THE ALGARVE. The Alentejo is a vast, sparsely populated area covering nearly a third of Portugal. This is a land of vast agricultural estates, and it is subject to a very hot and dry climate with scorching summers. It used to be best known for its cork production, but it is now recognized for its powerful and fleshy red and white wines, made with the modern consumer in mind. The production is divided between Alentejano Vinho Regional and Alentejo DOC – with eight sub-regions, all with their own DOCs. Although local cooperatives still play an important role, the vitality of the Alentejo is due mostly to private investors, large and small, who have contributed to the current success of its wines. The small vineyards of the Algarve (4,201 acres/1,700 ha), on the southern tip of Portugal, are being encroached by the development of new tourism infrastructure, but the domains have been modernized and produce above all soft and fruity red wines from Castelão, Alicante Bouschet, Negra Mole, or Syrah.

ISLAND VINEYARDS. The vineyards of the Azores and Madeira are small in size, but Madeira has given its name to an historic and famous fortified wine, unique in its vinification process and for its extraordinarily long ageing capability (*see box on following page*).

Portuguese grapes: great riches

Long isolated and therefore oblivious to international taste, Portugal has preserved its great range of grape varieties. Portugal's entry into the European Union, along with new international interest in Portuguese wine, was the trigger for a much-needed classification of its varieties. As many as 341 have been documented, including many varieties not found outside

Port vinification

Grapes are first crushed underfoot in traditional stone vats called *lagares*, or by conventional mechanical means. During fermentation, the must is fortified by the addition of about 10 per cent grape spirit to halt the yeast fermentation and to preserve some of the natural grape sugars. Independent producers who make wine only from their own *quinta* (domain) mature the wine at their estate. But the great houses have a very different tradition. In the spring following the harvest, the wines are transported to Vila Nova de Gaia, at the mouth of the Douro, across from Porto, where they will age in wooden containers of different sizes: tuns, the traditional pipes (*pipas*, about 140 gal/ 630 l), or barrels. Here, away from the summer heat of the Douro Valley, the damp cellars of the great port producers age the wine slowly. The length of maturation is quite variable, and depends on the style of wine desired (see p. 396).

> Red ports are classified into two groups, ruby and tawny. The production of white ports remains marginal.

DID YOU KNOW...?

Portugal has more than a third of the world's cork-oak forests. *Seventy per cent are in the Alentejo, the largest cork-producing region on earth.*

> A vineyard in Alentejo, southern Portugal, where the vines grow in arid conditions.

the country. While some international varieties do yield excellent results here (Shiraz, Cabernet Sauvignon, and Chardonnay), it is the native varieties that make Portuguese wines so special.

RED GRAPE VARIETIES. Touriga Nacional is the great red Portuguese grape variety, and it's currently very much in vogue. Originally from Dão, it frequently forms the backbone of port wines and the dry reds of the Douro; but it has proved its worth in other regions, such as the Alentejo and Ribatejo. It presents concentrated, tannic, and intense wines. Spanish Tempranillo (known here as Tinta Roriz or Aragonês) is the most planted variety in the country and makes very powerful wines, though often more supple than those from Touriga Nacional. Baga is the great grape of Bairrada. Hardy and late maturing, it produces very dark, structured, tannic wines with acidity for long ageing. Trincadeira thrives in the hot, dry soils of the Alentejo in the south, and on the hillsides of the Douro (where it is known as Tinta Amarela). When fully ripe, it produces dark and spicy wines for long ageing. Castelão (or Periquita) is one of the most widely planted red varieties, especially in the south, and it's appreciated for its fruity and relatively fresh wines.

WHITE GRAPE VARIETIES. Alvarinho and to a lesser degree Loureiro are highly prized in the region of Vinho Verde, where they make fresh and aromatic wines. Bical offers fresh, intense aromas, and is one of the star varieties in the still and sparkling wines of Bairrada. It is also found in the Dão appellation, alongside the powerful and remarkable Encruzado, one of the most promising white grapes. Arinto grows in most wine regions, but is at its best in the Bucelas DOC, where it is renowned for fresh and lemony wines. Fernão Pires, the most widely planted white variety (especially in the central and southern parts of the country), produces well-rounded, charming, and rather warming wines.

Madeira, unchanged

The wine industry on this Portuguese island, 400 miles (640 km) off the coast of Morocco, had its heyday during the 18th century, when its fortified wines graced the tables of royalty. Powdery mildew and phylloxera in the 19th century, the loss of its traditional markets, and the use of mediocre grape varieties have all gradually tarnished its reputation, and Madeira eventually found its main outlet reduced to the kitchen! Today, just 1,000 acres (400 ha) of vineyards are spread over a patchwork of small plots. But some historic houses still carry on the tradition of the great Madeiras – wines fortified to varying degrees of sweetness, whose unique character reflects their unusual ageing. The wines are heated to 115°F (45°C) in stainless steel tanks for three months (or for two years in sun-baked lofts). The best (vintage or *frasqueira*) wines are from a single harvest and spend a minimum of 20 years ageing in cask. These are powerful wines, both warm and fresh. They have a bouquet of rare complexity – with notes of caramel, leather, candied fruit, dried fruit, iodine, plus balsamic notes – and extraordinary longevity.

The best-known Portuguese wines

Portugal's wine revolution is now in full swing, and great producers are emerging in all regions, whether DOC or Vinho Regional.

NORTH

PORTO DOC

This DOC is reserved for the fortified red and white wines produced within a defined area along the Douro Valley in northern Portugal. It extends over 625,000 acres (250,000 ha), but only 106,255 acres (43,000 ha) are actually planted. There are three sub-regions: Baixa Corgo in the west; Cima Corgo, the historic heart; which was first regulated in 1756; and Douro Superior in the east. The Porto appellation is the world's most strictly controlled – at every stage of production, from a meticulous classification of individual vineyards to particularly demanding certification tastings. The wines take their character both from local geographic conditions – schist soils, a particularly hot and dry climate during the ripening season, well-adapted grape varieties – and the vinification and maturation techniques that ultimately shape the diversity of styles of port.

> **GRAPE VARIETIES** Touriga Nacional, Tinto Cão, Tinta Roriz, Tinta Barroca, and Touriga Franca for reds. Sercial (Esgana Cão), Folgasão, Verdelho, Malvasia, Rabigato, Viosinho, and Gouveio for whites.

> **SOIL** Port can only be produced from the schist soils of the Douro Valley and its tributaries.

> **STYLE** Red ports are sweet, powerful, and intense. They fill the palate with a gentle warmth and provide a rare sensation of fullness. There are two main types of red port.

- Tawny ports. These are aged in barrel for a long period. Under the influence of a controlled oxidation, the colour evolves (tawny means 'reddish' or 'amber') and powerful tertiary aromas (coffee, nuts, dried fruit, fig, cedar) become sharper and increasingly complex over time. Most tawny ports are produced by blending wines of different vintages, whose average age should be the minimum required by law. This category includes, in order of quality: tawny (minimum three years in oak); tawny reserve (seven years); and tawny with an indication of age (10, 20, 30, or 40 years). The *colheitas* (seven years minimum) are vintage tawny ports, meaning from a single year, as shown on the label.
- Ruby ports. These wines are oak-aged, or sometimes aged in the vat, for a much shorter period than the tawny ports, and they keep their youthful 'ruby' colour. Young ruby ports are bright, and intense with aromas of ripe red and black fruit, as well as spicy notes. On the palate, the most ambitious retain a very powerful tannic structure in the best wines. Ruby and ruby reserve are young and exuberant wines, intensely fruity with relatively little tannin. Late bottled vintage (LBV) are from a single vintage, bottled four to six years after harvest. They are more supple than the final category, vintage. Vintage port is a wine from an exceptional year and is bottled two to three years after harvest. Thanks to their intensity and tannic structure, LBVs and, even more so, vintage ports can be kept for several decades. Vintage ports are traded on international markets in the same way as great Bordeaux and Burgundies.
- There is also a very limited production of white port, made solely from white varieties and aged in wood. They may be semi-dry or sweet, and are generally soft and round, but often lacking the complexity of red ports. Rosé ports are a recent innovation.

> **LEADING PRODUCERS** Barros, Burmester, Churchill, Croft, Dow, Fonseca, Gould Campbell, Ferreira, Graham, Niepoort, Quinta do Crasto, Quinta do Noval, Quinta do Vale D. Maria, Ramos Pinto, Andresen, Taylor Fladgate, Warre's.

Colour: *White, rosé, and red.*

Serving temperature: *52 to 57°F (11 to 14°C) for whites; 59 to 63°F (15 to 17°C) for reds.*

Ageing potential: *Whites are best consumed young; up to 50 years for the reds.*

DOURO DOC

NORTH

This appellation covers the same area of production as Porto DOC (see opposite). Red and white table wines have always been produced in the Douro for local consumption, but they were made either from excess crop for port, or from lower-quality grapes. A few port houses, such as Ferreira (from the 1950s with their *cuvée* Barca Velha) or, later, Quinta do Crasto, saw the potential of the area for high quality dry red wines. So the region has rapidly devloped to become a benchmark for this type of wine, which increasingly comes from dedicated vineyards. The wines of Douro DOC can be made with all the grape varieties permitted for port, though certain varieties dominate.

> **GRAPE VARIETIES** Touriga Nacional, Tinto Cão, Tinta Roriz, Tinta Barroca, Touriga Franca, Trincadeira, and Souzão for reds; Malvasia, Rabigato, Viosinho, and Gouveio for whites.

> **SOIL** Schist and granite.

> **STYLE** Red wines (about 80 per cent of production) come in a variety of styles. They are usually deep in colour, with intense aromas of very ripe red and black fruit, plum, and flint or slate-like mineral notes. They are powerful and tannic on the palate, sometimes with a lovely mineral freshness. They are well able to support lengthy ageing in wooden barrels. The white wines are supple and aromatic, the best displaying a remarkable balance with surprising freshness and a very reasonable alcohol level.

> **LEADING PRODUCERS** Alves de Sousa, Barca Velha, Quinta do Côtto, Quinta do Crasto, Quinta do Fojo, Quinta do Passadouro, Quinta de la Rosa, Quinta de Roriz, Quinta do Vale D. Maria, Quinta do Vallado, Niepoort, Sogrape, Ramos Pinto, Wine and Soul, Prats and Symington.

Colour: *White and red.*

Serving temperature: *48 to 54°F (9 to 12°C) for whites; 57 to 61°F (14 to 16°C) for reds.*

Ageing potential: *3 to 5 years for whites; 10 years or more for reds.*

VINHO VERDE DOC

NORTH

This old DOC (1908) in northwest Portugal is one of the largest and best known. Its name immediately evokes fresh and aromatic light white wines, best consumed young (hence the name Verde, meaning 'green' in the sense of young or undeveloped). But the region also produces a similarly fresh red and some sparkling white and rosé. The DOC covers 95,000 acres (38,000 ha), bounded by the Minho River to the north, the Douro River to the south, and mountains in the east. Facing the Atlantic, the region receives about 47 inches (1,200 mm) of rainfall per year. The lush vines are traditionally trained high, on trellises or pergolas, although the most recent plantings are trained low. The appellation has been divided into nine sub-regions according to their geographic and cultural aspects. The region of Moncão in the north is particularly renowned for its whites from the Alvarinho variety (Albariño in Spain).

> **GRAPE VARIETIES** Alvarinho, Arinto, Avesso, Azal, Batocera, Loureiro, and Trajadura for whites; Alvarelhão, Amaral, Borraçal, Espadeiro, Padeiro, Pedral, Rabo de Anho, and Vinhão for reds.

> **SOIL** Shallow, mainly granite, low in nutrients, and fairly acidic.

> **STYLE** The white wines are low in alcohol, vigorous, and aromatic with notes of green apple, citrus fruits, and white flowers. The sensation of freshness they provide is sometimes enhanced by a slight sparkle. The red wines are colourful, lively, and fruity, with mostly soft tannins.

> **LEADING PRODUCERS** Palácio da Brejoeira, Ponte de Lima, Quinta do Ameal, Quintas Melgaço, Reguengo of Melgaço, Sogrape, Casa de Vila Verde, Aveleda, Paço de Teixeiro.

Colour: *White and red.*

Serving temperature: *46 to 54°F (8 to12°C) for whites 57 to 59°F (14 to 15°C) for reds.*

Ageing potential: *2 years for whites; 3 years for reds.*

Bairrada

LUIS PATO

The Luis Pato estate is located in Bairrada, an appellation in northern Portugal, between Lisbon and Porto. Promoting indigenous grape varieties, the wine-maker interprets these brilliantly, marking it as one of the country's most inspired producers.

LUIS PATO

8, rua da Quinta Nova
3780-017 Amoreira da Gândara

Founded: *19th century*
Area: *148 acres (60 ha)*
Production: *350,000 bottles p.a.*
Appellation: *Bairrada*
Red grape varieties: *Baga, Touriga Nacional, Tinto Cão*
White grape varieties: *Maria Gomes, Bical, Cercial, Sercialinho*

Bairrada, the land of Baga

The Bairrada appellation is located in Beira Alta, close to the ocean and the Dão region, which is also rich in vineyards. It has a climate with soft and rainy Atlantic influences and comprises clay-limestone or sandy soils. It produces sparkling wines, particularly from Baga, a native red grape that, under traditional production conditions, results in reds that are unreliable when young and require many years to mature. This inherent characteristic, seen as a handicap by the majority of producers, led to an amendment to the terms of the DOC appellation in 2003 marginalizing the use of the grape variety in favour of other Iberian or international varieties. This is one of the reasons Luis Pato has sidelined the Bairrada DOC and generally speaking now produces Vinho Regional Beiras, a less restrictive appellation, which can be made by a stubborn yet creative producer.

An enterprising and innovative wine producer

In 1986 Luis Pato inherited the Quinta do Ribeirinho, a family estate where wine has been produced since the 18th century. It is located in the small town of Amoreira da Gândara, and is today the focal point of a vineyard spread over several different plots.

As a result of successive expansions, the estate has been carefully managed to maximize the quality of its production, as for example with Vinha Barossa, an old wine that has been lovingly revived and today comes from Baga vines almost 100 years old. That said, the reputation of the estate is mainly due to the progressive attitude of its wine-maker, who carried out a revolution within a region mainly restricted to producing rustic wines. He did so by introducing a series of novel practices in both the vineyard and the cellar.

Nowadays widely accepted and implemented, these techniques had been almost completely ignored in a wine production that was very traditional in its outlook. Applied to long-established grape varieties without any unnecessary attachment to past practice, these techniques showed the grapes' flexibility and their capacity to produce wine of the very finest quality. The biggest winner in this entire process was Baga, with the resulting wines produced by the wine-maker reaching an unquestionably high standard.

Free thinking as a guiding principle

As well as helping local grape varieties gain recognition, Luis Pato also brought to light other little-respected Portuguese varieties such as Maria Gomes, usually used for everyday white wines. However, his creativity was displayed to its fullest extent in 16 distinctive red wines, combining a rare eclecticism and enlightenment. This range can be seen in 'classic' wines that represent the fragmentary nature of the estate: wines to be drunk young or, at the other extreme, kept until they have aged, and also in less familiar variations with distinctively individual sets of characteristics.

One of the most surprising wines is a red developed almost exclusively with white grapes! Others make use of ingenious processes – such as a sparkling and a red from a single vine of Baga but harvested in two stages – to ensure the maturity required for each wine. In addition, a sulphur-free wine addresses current concerns. In the other categories, his talent and deft touch always find the means for him to express himself in an unconventional style – hence, for example, a sparkling obtained without pressing, from just the free-run juice. And even his sweet wines are not produced from the usual late harvests. For these an early harvest is artificially frozen after pressing!

LUIS PATO: GREAT MODERN WINES WITH ANCIENT ROOTS

The modern nature of the wines designed by Luis Pato is at times rooted in the distant past. This is the case with its white Vinha Formal, produced from a clay-limestone soil already famous in the mid-19th century for its colour. In tribute to this glorious past, the estate cultivates a Burgundy grape variety specific to the region, Bical, producing a voluptuous wine that displays mineral notes as it matures. The red wine Quinta do Ribeirinho Pé Franco is reminiscent of times before phylloxera, produced from ungrafted vines, as was the case with all European wine production before this blight. Planted in sandy soils to minimize the risk of this disease, just over 6 acres (2.4 ha) of Baga help to create a deliberately ambitious sensation, concentrated without seeming overly so, and hence well-balanced and delightfully silky.

> Luis Pato, head of the estate, tasting the wines.

QUINTA *DO NOVAL*

First produced in 1715 in Porto, Quinta do Noval is rather like a grand cru classé in Bordeaux. It consistently maintains its high reputation and its exceptional vintage wine, Nacional.

QUINTA DO NOVAL

av. Diogo Leite, 256
4400 111 Vila Nova de Gaia

Founded: *1715*
Area: *358 acres (145 ha)*
Production: *800,000 bottles p.a.*
Appellation: *Porto*
Red grape varieties: *Touriga Nacional, Touriga Franca, Tinta Roriz, Tinto Cão, Tinta Barroca, Tinta Francisca, Sousão*

The 1931 masterstroke

Noval is an estate of 358 acres (145 ha) of vineyards located in a prime position in the Cima Corgo, on slopes with low-walled terraces at 328 to 1148 feet (100 to 350m) altitude. It is a breathtaking setting worthy of an exceptional wine. One of its first owners was the Marquis de Pombal, Prime Minister of Portugal in the 18th century, and, above all, responsible for the Região Demarcada do Porto (officially established in 1756).

Two other great men have made their mark on the history of Noval: Antonio José Da Silva, a merchant, and his son-in-law Vasconzelos Porto. From the turn of the 20th century until the 1960s, these two men gave the estate a new impetus, restructuring the vineyard and rebuilding the cellars. Before the World War I, Noval became the 'model estate' of port and was greatly admired by the mainly English wine enthusiasts of the period. Then came the masterstroke of 1931: in a year when production was being shunned by wine merchants, affected by the crisis of 1929, and very dubious about the possibilities of selling a new vintage when large volumes of 1927 were still on the market, Noval decided to declare its 1931 crop as a vintage. Given the quality of the wine, it was a brilliant decision, and established the reputation of the brand throughout the British Empire and beyond.

The great Nacional, a truly exceptional wine

Today the estate belongs to Axa Millésimes. It is under the watchful care of Christian Seely, the head of this French insurance company subsidiary, who is also manager of Noval. Its acquisition by a large company resulted in huge investment in the cellars and vineyards (a large replanting programme, in particular). Yet they made a point of preserving the identity of the estate, notably through the famous Nacional, a wine produced from ungrafted vines. Old bottles of this wine easily fetch around £3,400 (€3,900) in the big sales. For Christian Seely, Nacional is completely independent from, and does not follow the rules that apply to, the rest of Noval. The vines behave differently, the grapes are distinct, and this is the case 'whatever we do to the vines or in the cellar'. Nacional is not treated differently from the other wines produced but 'when it feels like it', such as in 1963, 1994, 1996, 1997, 2000, 2003, and 2011, it produces a wine that is quite simply extraordinary.

In a more affordable price category, you can find tawny ports of varying ages (the 10-year-old is one of the best quality for the price produced by any of the big houses in Porto), the Colheitas, vintage wines coming from individual vines of the estate, matured in *pipas* for at least seven years before being bottled on demand. The watchword is elegance. As for the vintage ports, their more well-known counterparts, they astonish by their depth, their texture, and their particularly harmonious combination of tannins, sugar, and alcohol.

QUINTA DO NOVAL COLHEITA 1986

Its appearance is fiery with gold reflections. The nose is very expressive, with dried fruits, dried almonds, and figs. On the palate, there are notes of ripe fruit and caramel, all in a fluid and silky texture. The tannins are very soft; slowly, inexorably, a sweet sensation of warmth sweeps across the palate.

QUINTA DO NOVAL VINTAGE 1997

It is dense ruby in colour. The nose is elegant with notes of morello cherry, menthol, violet, minerality, and a touch of blonde tobacco. The palate combines freshness, balance, mineral tension, noble tannins, and minerality, and it is long lasting. A legendary wine that combines fine-quality tannins, aromatic complexity, the minerality of the terroir, and perfect control of the *mutage* process.

ristian Seely,
ger of the estate.

BAIRRADA DOC

CENTRAL

Created in 1979, this DOC is situated in the Beiras region, between the Atlantic coast and the eastern hills that mark the border with Dão. The climate is mild and particularly wet (up to 63 inches/ 1,600 mm of rainfall per year), which unfortunately promotes the development of vine diseases. The vineyard area covers 30,000 acres (12,000 ha) intermingled with other crops. Red wines account for most of the production (70 per cent); the main variety, Baga, must comprise at least 50 per cent of the blend. The quality of the DOC's dry whites has risen sharply recently, and the region has retained a tradition of sparkling winemaking notably using Arinto. Such star producers as Luis Pato choose to produce wines mostly under the Beiras Vinho Regional appellation.

> **GRAPE VARIETIES** Baga, Alfrocheiro, Camarate, Castelão, Jaen, Touriga Nacional, Aragones, Cabernet Sauvignon, and Merlot for reds; Fernão Pires, Arinto, Cercial, and Chardonnay for whites.

> **SOIL** Clay-limestone and sandy; fairly fertile and heavy.

> **STYLE** The red wines are austere in their youth – particularly tannic and crisp; so they need long ageing. When fully mature, the best display great complexity. A more modern style has recently emerged (better grape ripeness, destemming, etc.), and the wines have become more supple and rounded, ready to drink sooner. The white wines are fresh, aromatic (citrus fruit, white flowers, freshly mown grass), and well balanced, especially those from Arinto. Fernão Pires yields more rounded wines.

> **LEADING PRODUCERS** Caves Aliança, Casa de Saima, Caves São João, Luis Pato, Quinta de Baixo, Quinta do Poço do Lobo, Quinta da Rigodeira, Sidónio de Sousa, and Sogrape.

Colour:
White and red.

Serving temperature:
48 to 54°F (9 to12°C) for whites;
59 to 63°F (15 to 17°C) for reds.

Ageing potential:
3 years for the whites;
10 years or more for reds.

DÃO DOC

CENTRAL

This old DOC (1908), set in Beira Alta to the east of Bairrada, is named after the river that runs through it. The region is a granite plateau, with vineyards extending over 50,000 acres (20,000 ha) and planted at altitudes of 1,300 to 2,300 feet (400 to 700 m). The surrounding mountains, especially in the west, protect the area from oceanic influences. The climate is more continental with cold, wet winters and particularly hot, dry summers. Red wines (about 80 per cent of total production) are dominated by Touriga Nacional and Alfrocheiro. They are sometimes vinified as single varietals, but are often blended with other varieties such as Tinta Roriz or Jaen (Mencía in Spain). The dry white wines and a few sparkling wines are mainly Encruzado, often blended with Bical, Cercial, or Malvasia Fina.

> **GRAPE VARIETIES** Alfrocheiro, Alvarelhão, Tinta Roriz, Bastardo, Jaen, Rufete, Tinto Cão, Touriga Nacional, and Trincadeira for reds and rosés; Barcelo, Bical, Cercial, Encruzado, Malvasia Fina, Rabo de Ovelha, Terrantez, Uva Cão, and Verdelho for whites.

> **SOIL** Schist, sand, and granite.

> **STYLE** Today's clean, modern Dão wines have replaced the mediocre wines produced in the days dominated by cooperatives, whose monopoly was abolished in 1989. Among reds, the styles are diverse, but good Dãos display very ripe red and black fruit aromas with spice and vanilla (if aged in barrel), as well as floral notes. On the palate, they are clean, rich, well-structured, tannic, and ready for a few years' cellaring. Encruzado-based whites are aromatic (yellow fruit), substantial, fairly rich, and well-balanced. There also are light and aromatic rosés.

> **LEADING PRODUCERS:** Caves Aliança, Dão Sul, Quinta dos Carvalhais, Quinta das Maias, Quinta da Pellada, Quinta do Perdigão, Quinta dos Roques, and Quinta Saes.

Colour:
White, red, and rosé.

Serving temperature:
48 to 54°F (9 to12°C) for whites;
50 to 54°F (10 to 12°C) for rosés;
57 to 61°F (14 to 16°C) for reds.

Ageing potential:
1 year for rosés;
4 years for whites;
10 years for reds.

CENTRAL AND SOUTH

ALENTEJO DOC AND ALENTEJANO VINHO REGIONAL

Alentejo is a vast region in central and southern Portugal. Its vineyards cover only 56,834 acres (23,000 ha), but the wines have made remarkable progress in the past decade, thanks to the dynamism of its cooperatives and newly established producers. The region is divided into eight sub-regions: Reguengos, Borba, Redondo, Vidigueira, Évora, Granja-Amareleja, Portalegre, and Moura. Each of them can claim a specific DOC, but more than half the wines are labelled Alentejano Vinho Regional. Note that the DOC is Alentejo, but the Vinho Regional is Alentejano (*see* Quinta do Carmo label, right). The climate is particularly hot and dry. Lots of sunlight helps the grapes to ripen fully, but it also means irrigation is necessary and harvesting has to take place earlier than elsewhere, particularly for the whites.

> **GRAPE VARIETIES** Alicante Bouschet, Aragones, Cabernet Sauvignon, Moreto, Periquita, Syrah, Tinta Caiada, Touriga Nacional, and Trincadeira for reds; Antão Vaz, Arinto, Rabo de Ovelha, Roupeiro, and Fernão Pires for whites.

> **SOIL** Clay, sand, granite, and schist.

> **STYLE** In a region where more than 50 grape varieties are authorized (for Vinho Regional), styles necessarily vary. But the reds are characterized by their fullness, the ripeness of their fruit, and their warmth. Very pleasant in their youth, the more tannic reds can be kept for a few years. The whites also have volume, roundness, and power.

> **LEADING PRODUCERS** Adega Cooperativa de Borba, Adega Cooperativa de Portalegre, Adega Cooperativa de Redondo, Cortes de Cima, Quinta do Mouro, Herdade da Malhadinha Nova, Herdade do Mouchão, Sogrape, Quinta do Carmo, and Quinta do Monte d'Oiro.

Colour:
Red and white.

Serving temperature:
48 to 54°F (9 to 12°C) for whites; 59 to 61°F (15 to 16°C) for reds.

Ageing potential:
4 years for whites; 10 years for reds.

Five favourite wines from George Dos Santos

IMPORTER AND WINE MERCHANT (ANTIC WINE, ONLY GEORGES)

- **Maria Gomes, Beiras Vinho Regional (Luis Pato).** A 'quaffer' *par excellence*. A fresh, fruity, pure, and mineral white wine, at a very affordable price. Ideal with Mediterranean cuisine (seafood, shellfish, saffron, olive oil).
- **Docil Loureiro, white Vinho Verde (Niepoort).** All the purity of the Loureiro variety, bursting with soft and fresh citrus fruit, with a well-rounded finish. By one of the best producers in Portugal. A summer wine to share with friends.
- ***Cuvée* Ex æquo (Bento and Chapoutier).** Dense and concentrated wine with aromas of black fruit, smoked bacon, black olives, and elderberry. Grown in the sunshine of Estremadura, it is perfect with grilled meats like the local *porco preto*.
- **Vintage Port 2004 (Quinta do Noval).** A prestigious house at the top of its game with this vintage port that rewrites the rulebook – intense and imposing. Full and rich herb aromas, with a freshness that complements its power.
- **Vintage Port 2006 (Quinta do Vesuvio).** The taste of a legend. A huge wine, from century-old vines grown in an enclosed vineyard, which gives a unique feeling of both fullness and fresh unctuousness.

GERMANY

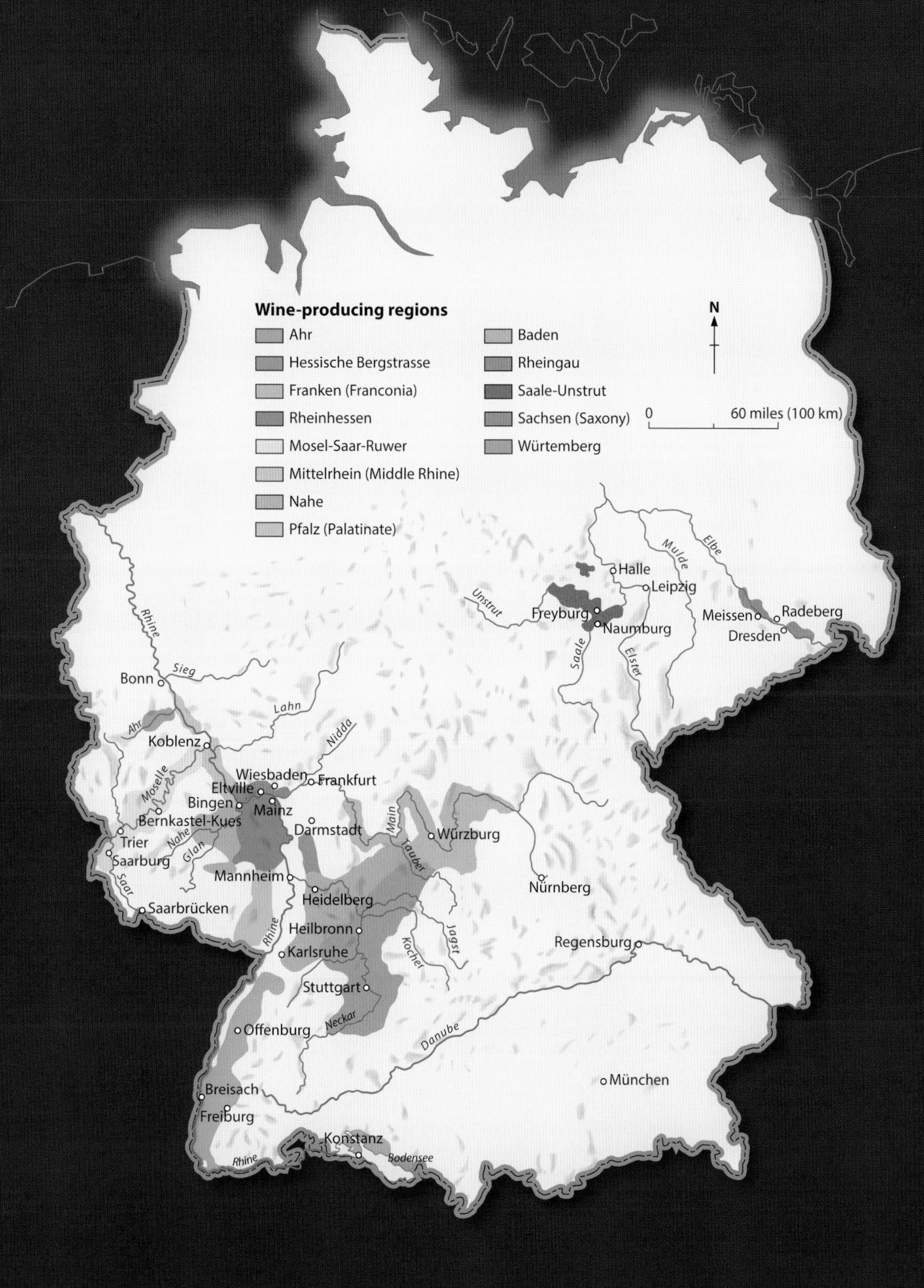
Wine-producing regions
Ahr
Hessische Bergstrasse
Franken (Franconia)
Rheinhessen
Mosel-Saar-Ruwer
Mittelrhein (Middle Rhine)
Nahe
Pfalz (Palatinate)
Baden
Rheingau
Saale-Unstrut
Sachsen (Saxony)
Würtemberg
N
0
60 miles (100 km)
Halle
Leipzig
Unstrut
Freyburg
Naumburg
Saale
Elster
Mulde
Elbe
Meissen
Radeberg
Dresden
Rhine
Bonn
Sieg
Lahn
Ahr
Koblenz
Nidda
Moselle
Wiesbaden
Eltville
Frankfurt
Bingen
Mainz
Bernkastel-Kues
Darmstadt
Main
Würzburg
Trier
Nahe
Saarburg
Glan
Tauber
Saar
Mannheim
Nürnberg
Heidelberg
Saarbrücken
Heilbronn
Jagst
Kocher
Regensburg
Karlsruhe
Stuttgart
Neckar
Offenburg
Danube
München
Breisach
Freiburg
Konstanz
Rhine
Bodensee

GERMANY

The best German wines are among the finest in the world; and even though some very large volume wines may be disappointing, recent efforts by young winemakers are full of promise.

Vine cultivation

The earliest vines here were planted in the 3rd century BC, in the Ahr region; and viticulture had spread along the Rhine and Mosel by the 1st century BC. After the fall of the Roman Empire, no new vines were planted until the emperor Charlemagne came to power; but the foundation of numerous convents and abbeys during the Middle Ages did much to improve the quality of the wines. German wine production expanded between the 11th and the late 16th centuries, peaking at a cultivated area of 740,000 acres (300,000 ha); but war during the 17th century laid waste to a large proportion of the vines. The advent of phylloxera (1874), mildew, and oidium further reduced the area under cultivation to 247,000 acres (100,000 ha), and it is of a similar size today.

GERMANY STATISTICS

Vineyard area: 252,000 acres (102,000 ha)

Production (av.): 96.5 million cases (8,700,000 hl)

Whites: 61%

Reds and rosés: 39%

(Wines of Germany, 2015)

Difficult conditions

German wines are produced in a climate of limited suitability for viticulture, and this may explain their often low alcohol content and acidity levels that at times can be high. Cold weather makes it difficult to achieve good levels of maturity in grapes, and the vagaries of the northern climate can negate the efforts of an entire year. Growers compensate for this handicap by planting vines on the least exposed sites.

With this said, climate change over the past few decades has been good news for German wine growers – a rise in average annual temperatures of nearly 3°F (2°C) has allowed them to achieve riper grapes and to plant red grape varieties, which were previously extremely rare in Germany.

> Hard at work among the vines in Meissen, Sachsen.

GLOSSARY OF GERMAN WINE TERMS

Words you may find on the label:

Grauburgunder: Pinot Gris
Halbtrocken: medium-dry
Eiswein: 'ice wine'
Erzeugerabfüllung: estate-bottled
Grosses/Erstes Gewächs: grand/premier cru (great first growth)
Schwarzriesling: Pinot Meunier
Spätburgunder: Pinot Noir
Spätlese: late harvest (although a wine with this label may be sweet or dry)
Süss: sweet (generally reserved for very sweet wines)
Trocken: dry
Weingut: estate
Weinkellerei: wine merchant/cellar
Weissburgunder: Pinot Blanc
Winzergenossenschaft: wine-producing cooperative

(See also Glossary, pp.614–23, for more German terms)

> Vineyards overlooking the Rhine near the town of Bacharach (Mittelrhein).

Along the rivers

Germany has 13 traditional wine-producing areas (*Anbaugebiete*, as described on pp.516–25), each of which are divided into districts (*Bereiche*). Most of these are located to the west and the south of the country and follow the curves of river valleys – even a glance at the distribution of the main growing areas is enough to demonstrate the importance of a location near a watercourse.

Baden's vineyards are never far from the Rhine. The Neckar and its tributaries wind through the hills of Württemberg before rejoining the Rhine at Mannheim; the Main, another Rhine tributary, shapes the vineyards of Franken as it passes through them. The little region of Hessische-Bergstrasse meets the Rhine Valley north of Heidelberg, and the Pfalz stretches out along the other side of the river. Rheinhessen, lying immediately to the north, is bordered to the east and north by the river, and the vineyards of the Rheingau are found on the east bank here.

The vineyards covering the northwest Rhine Valley combine to form a region known as the Mittelrhein or Middle Rhine. The Nahe, yet another tributary, has also given its name to a growing area. The Mosel, the area that has most gained a name for itself beyond Germany's borders, includes the vineyards along the banks of the Saar and the Ruwer. The beautiful little region of Ahr is not far from the furthest northern reaches of wine production in the west of the country. Then the region of Saale-Unstrut, in the east, takes its name from the two rivers that cross it. Finally, also in the east, Sachsen or Saxony's vineyards lie along the banks of the Elbe.

TRUE OR FALSE?

Most German white wines are sweet.

FALSE. This may have been true at one time, but today Germany produces a multitude of excellent medium-dry and dry wines. Improved selection of varieties and soils, combined with the climate change of the past few years, has allowed the production of riper grapes than in the past. Wine producers are no longer obliged to chaptalize, and fermentation now results in balanced dry and medium-dry wines.

DID YOU KNOW...?

Germany produces some of the best ice wines in the world? *Well-ripened grapes are harvested when vineyard temperatures dip to –10 °C, so the fruit will be at most –7 °C in the press. Cryoextraction (see p.62) is forbidden. The wines have an alcohol content of about 8% by volume, and their fine mineral content lends them great freshness and subtle aromas (dried apricots, citrus fruits, caramelized apples, horseradish, aniseed, candied ginger, honey). They can be laid down for decades.*

Wide range of varieties

German researchers have been cross-breeding classic grape varieties since the end of the 19th century, with the aim of creating new strains more resistant to disease and capable of producing wines of character with better yields and higher sugar levels. However, today these hybrids are less popular than they were. A striking development here over the past 15 years is the growth in red grapes (Pinot Noir, Cabernet Sauvignon), which now occupy 34.6 per cent of the planted land.

> Riesling grapes.

> Trollinger grapes.

CLASSIC WHITE VARIETIES. Riesling is the benchmark for all German wines. Capable of achieving great ripeness during Germany's sunny autumns, it produces wines in a number of different styles. It has been long planted across all the best sites, notably in the central Mosel (Mittelmosel) and the Rheingau. The grape once lost ground as various hybrid varieties were introduced, but its plantings have now stabilized. The decline of Silvaner, another classic grape variety, has been much more significant. This variety is associated mainly with Franken, although the largest vineyards are in Rheinhessen. It produces dry wines that are concentrated and yet lively, with great ageing potential if the vineyards are well situated and the yields reasonable. Other key grapes include Weissburgunder (Pinot Blanc), Grauburgunder (Pinot Gris, sometimes known as Ruländer), and Chardonnay.

HYBRID WHITE GRAPES. Müller-Thurgau, the first hybrid to be created by researchers (*see* p.35), produces quality white wines as long as the yield is low. Scheurebe – the best of the hybrids, judged by wine quality – has been very successful in the Pfalz. This wine is establishing itself thanks to fine bouquet, judicious acidity, and real potential for laying down. Kerner is a variety prized for the consistency of its yields, producing wines of character with fruity and vegetal aromas (elder blossom and mown grass), as well as hints of honey and spices that are reminiscent of Riesling. Due to their sugar content, they are often considered 'late harvest' wines, such as *spätlesen* or *auslesen*.

CLASSIC RED VARIETIES. The main varieties are Spätburgunder (Pinot Noir), which has tripled in acreage over 20 years, and Blauer Portugieser, which produces light wines. Other reds under cultivation include Trollinger, Schwarzriesling (Pinot Meunier), and Samtrot (Pinot Meunier).

HYBRID RED GRAPES. Dornfelder is a recent hybrid that has enjoyed remarkable success and is now the second most planted red grape variety. The wines have a garnet red appearance and aromas of red fruits (blackberries, cherries, prunes) with notes of bitter chocolate on the palate and supple tannins. Acolon, created in 1971, and Domina, in 1927, are planted on nearly 2,224 acres (900 ha). Regent (a hybrid), is capable of producing intense and tannic wines and has enjoyed a degree of success, making it the sixth most planted red grape variety.

Cabernet Cubin, which is reminiscent of Cabernet Sauvignon, is generally used in conjunction with other red varieties; it produces good results when aged in barrels. Domina and Regent produce reds with hints of garnet and fruity aromas.

Private producers and cooperatives

Leaving aside the Baden-Württemberg state, the greatest share of the best wines are made by private domains, state holdings (Rheinland-Pfalz, Hesse, Bavaria), or indeed municipal vineyards. The cooperatives receive grapes from their members and their output accounts for more than a third of national production. This said, the quality and style of wines vary according to each producer's strategy. Generally, a new desire to produce better wines at higher prices seems to be emerging, and these are often estate-bottled (*Erzeugerabfüllung*).

Seeking quality

Climate change, clonally selected vines returning better yields, and training initiatives for young growers have all combined to improve wine quality in Germany. If geographic origin is the principal criterion for classifying German wines, the second is their official tier of quality. This is simply a measure of their sugar or grape juice content. An official hierarchy has been established according to the idea that the riper the grapes, the better the wine. A distinction is thus made between *tafelwein* (table wine), *landwein* (country wine, equivalent to *vin de pays*), QbA (*qualitätswein bestimmter anbaugebiete*, quality wine from a specified area), and prädikatswein (quality wine, with 'distinction'). The *prädikatswein* label may be applied to one of six categories, reflecting the level of maturity at harvest (*see* p.98).

Labels marked 'Classic' and 'Selection'

In 2000, the Deutsches Weininstitut (German Wine Institute) approved two new categories intended to make the available range of wines more transparent. The terms 'Classic' and 'Selection' that now appear on some labels are found only on quality dry white wines made with a single grape variety. The 'Classic' category must feature the name of the grape variety, the producer, the production region, and the year. 'Selection' wine must also name the estate of origin and is subject to certain production regulations (harvest yields, minimum potential alcohol content, etc.).

DID YOU KNOW...?

Sparkling wine is called Sekt in Germany (and in Austria). *Some 800 producers generate an annual total of nearly 400 million bottles of Sekt. If the label features the term 'Deutscher Sekt', the wine was made exclusively with German grapes. This category includes a few wines of considerable quality, but in general almost all Sekt is made with industrial production methods and sold at reasonable prices under a brand name. Only estate Sekt (Winzersekt) conveys a sense of provenance, but sells at higher prices. A vintage Sekt must contain at least 85 per cent of its grapes from the same year declared on the label.*

CULTURAL PRACTICES. This said, some producers are reconsidering their traditions and abandoning sweeter styles in favour of drier wines that satisfy international consumer demand. This trend also encourages growers to limit their yields, with the resulting concentration ensuring an element of balance usually provided by residual sugars. Several estates also have converted to organic and biodynamic production, and that number is growing every year, whether the growers are affiliated to a certifying body (Ecovin, Bioland, Naturland, Demeter) or not.

Quality and awards labels

These are found on the label or directly on the bottle.

An eagle with outstretched wings. This is the emblem of the *Verband Deutscher Prädikatsweingüter* (VDP), an association for top producers of Prädikatswein. The eagle represents wines of great quality, although there are many producers of fine wines who are not members. In 2002, the VDP decided to apply its own classification system to the best vineyard areas: the designation Grosses Gewächs or Erstes Gewächs corresponds to the notion of *grand* or *premier cru* (first growth) wine. Strict production regulations are observed for the grape variety planted, yield, levels of ageing, and vinification techniques.

A roundel or neck label. This represents a medal (gold, silver, or bronze) awarded to the wine by a local jury of the *Deutsche Landwirtschafts-Gesellschaft* (DLG), the Germany agricultural authority.

A coloured *Weinsiegel* (seal). This, too, is awarded by the DLG. A yellow seal denotes *trocken* (dry) wine, green *halbtrocken* (medium-dry), and red all other wines.

> Vats at a Franken estate; on the right, a *Bocksbeutel*, the characteristic bottle of the region, can just be seen.

Leading German wines

Improvements in wine quality have increased demand across Germany's domestic and export markets. Exports rose to 14.4 million cases (1,300,000 million hl) in 2013, principally destined for the USA, the Netherlands, the UK, Sweden, and Norway. From north to south, these are the main wine-producing regions and their wines.

SAALE-UNSTRUT AND SACHSEN (SAXONY)

These two wine-producing areas were part of communist East Germany until 20 years ago. Saale-Unstrut (1,890 acres/765 ha) is located in the valleys of the two rivers after which it is named, and Sachsen's wine district (1,236 acres/500 ha) extends along the banks of the Elbe River north and south of Dresden. These regions mainly produce dry and medium-dry white wines, with red grape varieties representing less than 20 per cent of planted land. The quality of the wine here has improved considerably since reunification.

> **GRAPE VARIETIES** Whites: Müller-Thurgau, Weissburgunder (Pinot Blanc), Riesling, and Silvaner; reds: Portugieser, Dornfelder, and Spätburgunder (Pinot Noir).

> **SOIL** Shell limestone, red sandstone, clay-loess, and copper slate in Saale-Unstrut; schist, granite, sandstone, and strata of loess covered with clay and alluvial sand in Sachsen.

> **STYLE** Saale-Unstrut whites feature fruit aromas (apples, lemon zest, and nuts) with extremely refreshing mineral notes. Red wines made with Portugieser grapes have black fruit aromas (blackberries, cherries) and hints of violets, juniper, and star anise.
Sachsen whites made with Müller-Thurgau feature aromas of apples, peaches, and nuts, while those made with Riesling have scents of apples, apricots, citrus fruits, and little white flowers, all underpinned with agreeable mineral notes. Reds made with Dornfelder reveal aromas of red fruits, violets, and cocoa, whereas Spätburgunders have aromas of red fruits, forest floor, and peppery notes.

> **TOP VINEYARDS** Saale-Unstrut: Freyburg Edelacker, Karsdorf Hohe Gräte, Bad Kösen Saalhäuser, Bad Sulza Sonnenberg, Gosecker Dechantenberg, Höhnstedt Kreisberg, Kaatschen Dachsberg, Naumburg (Sonneneck, Steinmeister), Schulpforte Köppelberg, and Weischütz Nüssenberg. Sachsen: Dresdner Elbhänge, Meissen (Kapitelberg, Rosengründchen), Pesterwitz Jochhöhschlösschen, Pillnitz Königlicher Weinberg, Radebeul (Johannisberg, Steinrücken), Schloss Proschwitz, Seusslitz Heinrichsburg, and Weinböhla Gellertberg.

> **NOTABLE PRODUCERS.** Saale-Unstrut: Günter Born, Gussek, Klaus Böhme, Lützkendorf, Bernard Pawis, Kloster Pforta, Thüringer, and Weingut Bad Sulza. Sachsen: Klaus Zimmerling, Schloss Proschwitz (Prinz zur Lippe), and Vincenz Richter.

AHR

Ahr is a region of just 1,384 acres (560 ha) located very close to the confluence of the Rhine and the river that gives the area its name. Set across steep slopes, the vines grow in soils principally composed of clay and schist, and they can produce excellent Pinot Noir. Only 15 per cent of the area is planted with white grape varieties.

> **GRAPE VARIETIES** Spätburgunder (Pinot Noir), Portugieser, and Domina for reds; Riesling for whites.

> **SOIL** Clay and schist.

> **STYLE** Red wines made with Pinot Noir have pronounced aromas of black fruits and spices. Good vintages can be kept for up to 20 years. Portugieser grapes give wines hints of red and black fruits (cherries, raspberries, blackcurrants, and prunes), as well as spices, leather, and even smoke at the finish. Rieslings, which are usually made medium-dry and sweet, display aromas of bright fruit (apples, apricots, citrus fruits, and wild strawberries), as well as acacia flowers, aniseed, and mineral notes.

> **TOP VINEYARDS** Ahrweiler Rosenthal, Altenahr Eck, Dernau Hardtberg, Heimersheim Burggarten, Neuenahr Schieferlay, and Walporzheim (Gärkammer, Kräuterberg).

> **NOTABLE PRODUCERS** J. J. Adeneuer, Deutzerhof-Cossmann-Hehle, Meyer-Näkel, and Jean Stodden.

MITTELRHEIN (MIDDLE RHINE)

This region of just 1,161 acres (470 ha) begins south of Bonn at the Königswinter estates on the right bank of the Rhine. It takes in Bad Hönningen and Vallendar near Koblenz before arriving at the area around the town of Nassau, which is also the most romantic part of the Rhine. Here we find wine villages of great pedigree, such as Boppard, St Goar, and Bacharach. Vineyards are set on extremely steep slopes, making for hard physical labour. The region is renowned worldwide for its late-harvest wines. Red varieties represent no more than 14 per cent of plantings, although this figure is growing.

> **GRAPE VARIETIES** Riesling (66 per cent) and Müller-Thurgau for whites; Spätburgunder (Pinot Noir) for reds.

> **SOIL** Schist and *Grauwacke* (sedimentary sandstone).

> **STYLE** Riesling produces dry, medium-dry, and sweet wines of very high quality. They feature aromas of citrus fruits, lime, and elderberry blossom, along with very spicy notes, hints of mineral and great potential for ageing. The reds are best consumed young.

> **TOP VINEYARDS** Bacharach Hahn, Boppard Hamm Feuerlay, Engelhöll Bernstein, Oberwesel Ölsberg, and Steeg St. Jost.

> **NOTABLE PRODUCERS** Didinger, Friedrich Bastian, Toni Jost-Hahnenhof, Dr. Randolf Kauer, Lanius-Knab, Helmut Mades, Matthias Müller, August and Thomas Perll, and Ratzenberger.

MOSEL

The region around the Mosel and its tributaries, the Ruwer and the Saar, is one of the most beautiful vineyard areas in Germany. There are 21,498 acres (8,700 ha) of vines, with more than a quarter of them growing on very steep slopes overlooking the river. Wine producers are categorized by the sub-regions of Mosel, Saar, and Ruwer, although only the name Mosel has featured on wine labels since 2009. The cool climate has led growers here to plant exclusively white grape varieties for centuries. And despite many extensively chaptalized wines of mediocre quality, there have always been great Mosel wines: at the turn of the 20th century, prices for late-harvest Rieslings and ice wines here often surpassed those of the great Sauternes. Today, the best Rieslings – which are dry or off-dry – are appreciated when young for their lightness and freshness, but also for their ability to transform themselves with age into fascinating and complex wines. Sweeter Rieslings – *spätlese*, *auslese*, *beerenauslese*, *trockenbeerenauslese*, and *eiswein* – are wines to lay down (some for 30 years and more).

Finally, some attempts have been made in a few locations to grow red varieties such as Pinot Noir and Dornfelder.

> **GRAPE VARIETIES** Riesling and Müller-Thurgau for whites; Dornfelder and Spätburgunder for reds.

> **SOIL** Limestone in the upper Mosel, slate in the central Mosel (Mittelmosel), limestone and sandstone around the Terassenmosel, and slate in the Saar.

> **STYLE** Great Rieslings, whether sweet or dry, have an astonishing range of aromas and flavours. They offer fruits characters (apples, peaches, apricots, and citrus fruits), floral notes (elderberry blossom), and spices (aniseed, cumin). They are fresh, with excellent mineral notes and good length in the mouth.

> **TOP VINEYARDS** Mosel: Bernkastel Doctor, Brauneberg (Juffer and Sonnenuhr), Erden (Prälat and Treppchen), Graacher Himmelreich, Piesporter Goldtröpfchen, Trittenheimer Apotheke, Ürziger Würzgarten, Wehlener Sonnenuhr, and Winningen Uhlen. Saar: Kanzem Altenberg and Hörecker, Scharzhofberg, Oberemmel Hütte, Ockfen Bockstein, Saarburg Rausch, Serrig, and Wiltinger Braune Kuppe. Ruwer: Eitelsbach Karthäuserhofberg, Kasel Nies'chen and Kehrnagel, Maximin Grünhaus Abtsberg and Herrenberg.

> **NOTABLE PRODUCERS** Mosel: Schloss Lieser, Fritz Haag, Reichsgraf von Kesselstatt, Witwe Dr. Thanisch, Erben, Dr. Loosen, Markus Molitor, and Joh. Joseph Prüm. Saar: von Othegraven, von Hövel, Van Volxem, Egon Müller zu Scharzhof, Le Gallais, Reichsgraf von Kesselstatt, Forstmeister Geltz-Zilliken, Dr. Wagner, and Schloss Saarstein. Ruwer: Karthäuserhof and C. von Schubert'sche Schlosskellerei.

Mosel

EGON MÜLLER ZU *SCHARZHOF*

Rarely has a name – Egon Müller – been so closely associated with a wine, in this case Scharzhofberg from Wiltingen, which has been in the family since 1797. This legendary Mosel has also been dubbed the 'Romanée-Conti of Germany'.

EGON MÜLLER

Scharzhof
54459 Wiltingen

Founded: *1797*
Area: *40 acres (16 ha)*
Production: *N/A*
Appellation: *Mosel*
White grape variety: *Riesling*

A page of history

The Scharzhofberg vineyard consists of around 72 acres (29 ha) of steep slope south of Trier, in the German Mosel region, and it has a long history. The vineyard was planted by the Romans before being taken over by the monks of Saint Martin's Abbey, in the 18th century. In Germany, where the notion of the *cru* (or *lage*) is crucial, it has a long-standing reputation, with archives dating from as early as 1340 praising its quality. The estate was withdrawn from the hands of the church during the French Revolution, and part of the vineyard – the Scharzhof, some 20 acres (8 ha – was purchased by a certain Mr Koch, the Müllers' grandfather. The name Egon, which has been in the family over four generations, has become something of a tradition, with the current Egon succeeding his father in 1991. Even more impressive than the vineyard's ancient origin is its location. The vines, facing south, grow on the side of a steep slope that climbs for more than 394 feet (120m), the highest point being at 1,017 feet (310m). Not far away, the River Saar forms a great loop before flowing into the Mosel. The borders of Luxembourg and France are very close. In Scharzhofberg, Riesling is the most important grape. One third of the Müller vines, pre-phylloxera, remain ungrafted, planted at approximately 4,050 feet per acre (10,000 ft/ha). The remainder were replanted at the end of the World War II. In 1945, the vineyard was partially destroyed when an American plane crashed on the site.

Ruthless selection in the vineyard

For decades, successive ranks of Egon Müllers have built up a reputation based on the concentration and exceptional ageing of their wines, including their dry wines. According to Egon IV, this is due to two factors. Firstly, the terroir: quartz slate soils, orientation of the vines, and differences in temperature depending on the slope's altitude, which all produce a good range of maturity. Secondly, the low yields to which the wine-maker is restricted, with no Scharzhofberg above 3.5 tons per acre (60 hl/ha), and much less for the legendary Tyrolean, a Trockenbeerenauslese (TBA) wine, and one of the most expensive in the world. The company does not produce such wines every year (there were none between 1991 and 1994, in 1998, or in 2002, for example), since there is no question of cheapening something so exceptional. Egon Müller makes a *trie* (selection), from the grape harvest. Each picker sets aside the botrytized grapes, and it is just about possible to produce a little over 160 gallons (600 litres) of TBA each year. Given their sugar content, they take their time to ferment: at least six months! It takes about 110 lb (50 kg) of grapes to produce less than a couple of pints (1 litre) of this nectar. Although not organic, the vineyard operates with minimal use of chemicals, including no herbicides, for example. The wines are fermented and allowed to age in old 265-gallon (1,000-litre) casks in the cellar. Nature does the rest.

EGON MÜLLER, SCHARZHOFBERGER TROCKENBEERENAUSLESE RIESLING, MOSEL

This wine achieves a magical balance between sugar and acidity. The complexity of the aromas is astounding: from honey, quince, and lemon to tea, along with hazelnut and linden. The palate is incredibly concentrated. The finish, which is unbelievably long, condenses the aromas of the nose, rounded off by a saline edge. It can be kept without problem: vintages that are 40 years old are still readily enjoyed today. The only downside is that only very few bottles are put up for sale each year, and those are at sky-high prices.

EGON MÜLLER, SCHARZHOFBERGER KABINETT RIESLING, MOSEL

Year after year, this dry Riesling provides superb freshness, with aromas that are polished yet pure, mixed with fruity and mineral notes (perhaps a hint of slate?), and an exceptional tension, in keeping with the style of the estate, a unique combination of purity and intensity. Note that some wines contain a significant proportion of botrytized grapes, which adds to their complexity. The 'entry-level' wine is rather special and best appreciated after ten years.

> Egon Müller III, winemaker.

RHEINGAU

This wine region of 7,660 acres (3,100 ha) has a worldwide reputation for the quality of its Rieslings (both dry and sweet) and its Pinot Noirs.

> **GRAPE VARIETIES** Riesling (78 per cent) for whites; Spätburgunder (Pinot Noir) for reds.
> **SOIL** Marl to a greater or lesser extent, stones with occasional clay-sand, and clay to the east of the region; sandstone, clay-schist, and quartz to the west.
> **STYLE** In the best years, these Rieslings are elegant when young, acquiring complexity and superb balance as they age. They are some of the finest wines in the world. The reds, such as the Spätburgunders, offer aromas of cherries, quince jelly, dried apricots, and cinnamon. They are generally excellent for laying down.
> **TOP VINEYARDS** Assmannshausen Höllenberg, Hallgarten (Hendelberg, Jungfer), Hattenheim Steinberg, Hochheim Hölle, Johannisberg Hölle, Schloss Johannisberg, Lorch Kapellenberg, Kiedrich (Gräfenberg, Turmberg), Rauenthal (Baiken, Nonnenberg), Rüdesheim (Berg Kaisersteinfels, Berg Roseneck, Berg Rottland, Berg Schlossberg), Jesuitengarten Schloss Vollrads, and Winkel Jesuitengarten.
> **NOTABLE PRODUCERS** Staatsweingüter Domaine Assmannshausen, August Eser, J.B. Becker, Georg Breuer, Joachim Flick, August Kesseler, Hessische Kloster Eberbach, Franz Künstler, Johannishof-Johannes Eser, Graf von Kanitz, Josef Leitz, Robert König, Fürst Löwenstein, Peter Jakob Kühn, Querbach, Balthasar Ress, Schloss Johannisberg, and Robert Weil.

Schloss Johannisberg

This Rheingau estate is a jewel among German wineries, with an exceptional location on a hill overlooking the Rhine. No more than 86 acres (35 ha) are turned over to the cultivation of Riesling. Depending on the vintage and the quality (*kabinett, spätlese, auslese*, etc.), these wines display fruit aromas (oranges, lemons, grapefruit, apples, peaches) of great complexity with notes of hazelnut, almonds, and spices (cinnamon, coriander). Their herbaceous side is represented by angelica, hay, and mint. Fine structure affords a nice balance between fruit, crispness, and body. Laying down is generally limited to about 15 years for dry wines, but at least 30 years for sweet wines. Bottles traditionally carry coloured foils according to their level of quality: red (*rotlack*) for *kabinett*, green (*grünlack*) for *spätlese*, rosé (*rosalack*) for *auslese*, silver (*silberlack*) for Erstes Gewächs VDP, yellow (*rosa-goldlack*) for *beerenauslese*, and gold (*goldlack*) for *trockenbeerenauslese*.

NAHE

The Nahe River meets the Rhine at Bingen, and the wine region that surrounds it covers more than 1,0131 acres (4,100 ha), mainly producing whites. Red varieties are making more of an appearance, but they are mainly used to make rosé (*weissherbst*).
> **GRAPE VARIETIES** Riesling, Müller-Thurgau, Silvaner, and Grauburgunder (Pinot Gris) for whites; Dornfelder and Spätburgunder for reds.
> **SOIL** Stony terraces, sandstone, clay, and schist soils.
> **STYLE** Reminiscent of some Mosel and Rheingau whites, these Rieslings have fruity and mineral notes and are generally wines to lay down. The fruity and spicy rosés are at their best when young. The reds, especially the Pinot Noirs, offer a wide range of red and black fruits, with notes of forest floor and spices. The wines have great potential for laying down.
> **TOP VINEYARDS** Bad Kreuznach (Brückes, Kahlenberg), Dorsheim (Pittermännchen, Goldloch), Langenlonsheim Rothenberg, Monzingen (Halenberg), Münster-Sarmshein (Dautenpflänzer), Niederhausen (Hermannsberg), Schlossböckelheim (Felsenberg), and Traisen Bastei.
> **NOTABLE PRODUCERS** Dr. Crusius, Gutsverwaltung Niederhausen-Schlossböckelheim, Dönnhof, Jung, Schlossgut Diel, Tesch, Kruger-Rumpf, Mathern, Göttelmann, Bürgermeister Schweinhardt, von Racknitz, Prinz zu Salm-Dalberg'sches, and Schäfer-Fröhlich.

RHEINHESSEN

German's largest wine-producing region (65,483 acres/26,500 ha), Rheinhessen is located on the west bank of the Rhine and extends from Bingen in the northwest to near Worms in the south. Cultivation of hybrid grape varieties during the 1970s, coupled with high yields and industrial-scale production of mediocre wines for export, did much damage to the region's image. But these days, Rheinhessen produces a wide range of dry, medium-dry, and sweet wines of often excellent quality. The *Rheinterrassen* (Rhine terraces), which occupy just 10 per cent of the eastern part of this region, are some of the best parcels of land. They also are home to a number of famous estates that produce wines of a quality to match those found in the Rheingau.

> **GRAPE VARIETIES** Müller-Thurgau, Riesling, Silvaner, and Grauburgunder (Pinot Gris) for whites; Dornfelder, Portugieser, and Spätburgunder (Pinot Noir) for reds.

> **SOIL** Loess and fine sandy marl to the east; quartzite and porphyrite to the west.

> **STYLE** These vary according to grape variety. Müller-Thurgau, for example, offers fruit (apples, apricots, peaches, citrus) with herbaceous aromas (nettles, elder blossom, basil) and spices (cumin, mustard, aniseed, coriander).

> **TOP VINEYARDS.** Binger Scharlachberg, Flörsheim-Dalsheim (Bürgel and Hubacker), Nackenheim Rothenberg, Nierstein (Brudersberg, Ölberg, Pettenthal), Westhofen Kirchspiel, and Worms Liebfrauenstift-Kirchenstück.

> **NOTABLE PRODUCERS** Klaus Keller, K. F. Groebe, Gunderloch, Kissinger, Kruger-Rumpf, Kühling-Gillot, Manz, Michael-Pfannebecker, Schales, St. Antony, Wagner-Stempel, and Wittmann.

HESSISCHE BERGSTRASSE

Set at the edge of the Odenwald forest, this little wine region (1,112 acres/450 ha) is separated from Worms only by the width of the river (just 650 feet/200 m at this point). The main part of the growing area starts south of Darmstadt, but frosts are exceptional and rains abundant here. A large proportion of the vineyards belong to the state (Domaine Bergstrasse) or to the village of Bensheim. This region produces mainly white wine: good QbA, a large choice of *prädikatswein*, and Eiswein (ice wine). Top local Rieslings are easily a match for those from the Rheingau, but since they are limited in volume, they are rarely encountered far from their point of origin. Müller-Thurgau has been partly replaced by Pinot Noir and Pinot Gris over the past 10 years.

> **GRAPE VARIETIES** Riesling, Grauburgunder (Pinot Gris), and Müller-Thurgau for whites; Spätburgunder (Pinot Noir) and Dornfelder for reds.

> **SOIL** Sand, clay, limestone, loess, and decomposed granite.

> **STYLE** The Grauburgunder is a generally lively wine with aromas of apples, pears, lemon zest, and dried fruits (almond and hazelnuts), as well as notes of lime blossom, celeriac, and cinnamon.

> **TOP VINEYARDS** Bensheim, Kalkgasse, Heppenheim Centgericht, and Steinkopf.

> **NOTABLE PRODUCERS** Domaine Bergstrasse, Weingut der Stadt Bensheim, and Bergsträsser Winzer eG.

FRANKEN (FRANCONIA)

Franken is a region of dense forests located east of the Rhine, at the heart of Germany. Its vineyards (15,074 acres/6,100 ha) are concentrated in valleys along the Main River and its tributaries, and their exposures are to the south and east. Franken's vineyards spread across three sub-regions: Mainviereck, Maindreieck, and Steigerwald. Although the quality of these wines is recognized on the German domestic market, they are less known abroad. More than half are *Fränkisch trocken*, a designation for dry wines with less than 4 g/l of residual sugar content. A small, squat, round bottle called a *Bocksbeutel* is generally used for the best wines from the region.

> **GRAPE VARIETIES** Müller-Thurgau, Silvaner, and Bacchus for whites; Domina and Spätburgunder (Pinot Noir) for reds.

> **SOIL** Red sandstone, limestone, Upper Triassic gypsum.

> **STYLE** The best Franken wines are produced from Silvaner, Domina, and Spätburgunder grapes. Silvaner, first planted in Franken 350 years ago, produces white wines of character that are good for laying down. They are fruity (apples, citrus zest, pears, apricots), floral (elder blossom, hay), and spicy (cumin, mustard flour), with hints of minerals. Domina produces red wines with aromas of dark fruits (blackcurrants, blackberries, prunes), raspberry jam, spices (cinnamon, cloves), and bitter chocolate.

> **TOP VINEYARDS** Bürgstadt Centgrafenberg, Castell Schlossberg, Escherndorfer Lump, Homburger Kallmuth, Iphofen Julius-Echter-Berg, Klingenberg Schlossberg, Randersacker Pfülben, and Würzburg (Innere Leiste and Stein).

> **NOTABLE PRODUCERS** Bickel-Stumpf, Bürgerspital, Fürstlich Castell'sches Domäneamt, Rudolf Fürst, Horst Sauer, Michael Fröhlich, Juliusspital, Fürst Löwenstein, and Schmitt's Kinder.

BADEN

Baden's vineyards cover 39,043 acres (15,800 ha), and stretch for more than 180 miles (300 km) along the Rhine, from Lake Constance in the south to Franken in the north, filling the land between the river and the Black Forest. There are nine sub-regions: Badisches Frankenland (part of the Taubertal), Badische Bergstrasse (located south of Hessische Bergstrasse), Kraichgau (located to the east between Karlsruhe and Pforzheim), Ortenau (from Baden-Baden to south of Offenburg), Breisgau (from south of Offenburg to south of Freiburg), Kaiserstuhl (northwest of Freiburg), Tuniberg (south of Kaisterstuhl and west of Freiburg), Markgräflerland (from south of Freiburg to around Basel), and Bodensee (Lake Constance) in the south. Baden boasts a large number of cooperatives (85 per cent of total production) and has a reputation for making wines of great quality. Breisach's Badischer Winzerkeller is renowned as one of the largest producers in Europe, with a range of 500–600 different wines. There are also a number of beautiful estates with considerable historic pedigrees.

> **GRAPE VARIETIES** Müller-Thurgau, Grauburgunder (Pinot Gris), Riesling, Gutedel and Weissburgunder (Pinot Blanc) for whites; Spätburgunder (Pinot Noir) for reds.

> **SOIL** As many as 15 different kinds of soil.

> **STYLE** Rieslings, especially those from Ortenau, are fruity with enchanting floral notes (hay, elder blossom, lime blossom, mint), spices (aniseed, coriander, ginger). They are one of the most powerful wines of the region.

> **TOP VINEYARDS** Bodensee: Meersburg Rieschen; Breisgau: Bombach Sommerhalde, Hecklingen Schlossberg, amd Malterdingen Bienenberg; Ortenau: Neuweier Mauerberg, Durbach (Ölberg, Plauelrain, Schloss Grohl, Schlossberg, Schloss Staufenberg), Lauf Gut Alsenhof, Neuweier Schlossberg, and Waldulm Pfarrberg; Kaiserstuhl: Blankenhornsberg Doktorgarten, Burkheimer Feuerberg, Ihringen Winklerberg, Oberbergen Bassgeige, and Oberrotweil Henkenberg; Markgräflerland: Efringen-Kirchen Oelberg and Istein Kirchberg.

> **NOTABLE PRODUCERS** Andreas Laible, Bercher, Engist, Graf Wolff Metternich, Gut Nagelförst, Dr. Heger, Heinrich Männle, Jakob Duijn, Schloss Neuweier, Schwarzer Adler, Salwey, Stigler, and WG Durbach.

Bernhard Huber's Wines (Baden)

Working in the Breisgau district of Baden, this family estate of 74 acres (30 ha) is renowned for the fine quality of its white wines and especially for the reds it produces from Spätburgunder (Pinot Noir). The vines, which are divided among the best parcels around the villages of Malterdingen (Bienenberg), Hecklingen (Schlossberg), and Bombach (Sommerhalde), are tended with the greatest respect for nature. Apart from a Muscat, all the white wines are sweet. Pinot Noir accounts for two-thirds of the total plantings, and the wines crafted from this varietal are either from young vines (*junge reben*) or old vines (*alte reben*). The 'R' for reserve, which is visible on the labels, signifies that the wines have spent between six and eight months in barrel in the case of whites, and 18 months for reds. The estate also produces sparkling wines of great quality.

PFALZ

The Pfalz is a region of 58,070 acres (23,500 ha) extending for about 50 miles (80 km) along a north-south axis to the east of the Rhine River. It is divided into three sectors: Mittelhaardt (Central Haardt), Deutsche Weinstrasse (German wine road), and Südliche Weinstrasse (Southern wine road). The best vineyards are arranged across hills to the east of the Palatinate Forest. It is renowned for the quality of its white wines, and for its Rieslings in particular. They have real character and minerality, are usually full-bodied, but also have great refinement. Red wine production has made strong progress, both in terms of volume and quality.

> **GRAPE VARIETIES** Riesling and Müller-Thurgau for whites; Dornfelder, Portugieser, and Spätburgunder for reds.

> **SOIL** Extremely varied: red sandstone and loess, among others.

> **STYLE** Great Rieslings are wines to lay down, and feature aromas of peaches, apples, nuts, apricots, and pineapple. These wines also have fine notes of elder blossom, mint, aniseed, and coriander, and very good minerality.

> **TOP VINEYARDS** Bad Dürkheim Michelsberg, Birkweiler (Kastanienbusch, Mandelberg), Deidesheim Hohenmorgen, Hohenmorgen, Duttweiler, Forst (Jesuitengarten, Kirchenstück, Ungeheuer), Gimmeldingen Mandelgarten, Haardt Bürgergarten 'Breumel in den Mauern', Königsbach Idig, Schweigen Kammerberg, and Siebeldingen im Sonnenschein.

> **NOTABLE PRODUCERS** Acham-Magin, Geheimer Rat Dr. von Bassermann-Jordan, Bergdolt, Friedrich Becker, Josef Biffar, Dr. Bürklin-Wolf, A. Christmann, Dr. Deinhard, Gies-Düppel Knipser, Koehler-Ruprecht, Georg Mosbacher, Müller-Catoir, Pfeffingen-Fuhrmann-Eymael, Ökonomierat Rebholz, Reichsrat von Buhl, Georg Siben Erben, and Dr. Wehrheim.

WÜRTTEMBERG

Württemberg's vineyards (27,923 acres/ 11,300 ha) begin near Bad Mergentheim and continue south to the area around Heilbronn. They reach as far as the environs of Remstal and Stuttgart, and extend toward Tübingen and Reutlingen.

> **GRAPE VARIETIES** Riesling and Kerner for whites; Trollinger, Schwarzriesling (Pinot Meunier), Lemberger (or Limberger), and Spätburgunder (Pinot Noir) for reds.

> **SOIL** Extremely varied, from Upper Triassic to limestone, marl, mixed stones, and clay soil.

> **STYLE** Of the reds, Trollinger has aromas of cherries, prunes, bitter almonds, and redcurrants. It also shows vegetal elements reminiscent of lentils and beets and a note of wood smoke at the finish.

> **TOP VINEYARDS** Bad Cannstatt Zuckerle, Bönnigheim Sonnenberg, Fellbacher Lämmler, Heilbronn Stiftsberg, Hohenbeilstein Schlosswengert, Kleinbottwar Süssmund, Neipperg Schlossberg, Pfaffenhofen Hohenberg, Schnaiter Altenberg, Schwaigern Ruthe, Stettener Brotwasser, Stettener Pulvermächer, Untertürkheim (Gips, Herzogenberg), and Verrenberg Verrenberg.

> **NOTABLE PRODUCERS** Aldinger, Graf Adelmann, Ernst Dautel, Drautz-Able, J. Ellwanger, Karl Haidle, Fürst zu Hohenlohe-Öhringen, Schlossgut Hohenbeilstein, Rainer Schnaitmann, Wachtstetter, Staatsweingut Weinsberg, and Wöhrwag.

CENTRAL AND SOUTHEAST EUROPE TO THE BLACK SEA

CENTRAL AND SOUTHEAST EUROPE TO THE BLACK SEA

Vines first appeared on the slopes of the Caucasus Mountains many centuries ago, and spread throughout Central Europe and the Balkan countries. From Switzerland to the Black Sea, the production of white wines now dominates these wine-growing areas, all influenced by a very continental climate.

SWITZERLAND

Relative economic isolation means that Switzerland has retained a traditional focus for its wine production. It encompasses top quality and everyday wines, most of them consumed locally.

Fragmented vineyards

Dating back to Roman times, Swiss vineyards were, as in the rest of Europe, developed by the church. Precipitous slopes and meticulous reseach to find those locations with the best exposure to the sun explain the extremely small vineyard size – averaging 1 acre (0.4 ha). Historically a white wine country, Switzerland now produces some red wine. Most of the vineyards are located in the French-speaking cantons of Valais, Neuchâtel, Vaud, and Geneva.

SWITZERLAND STATISTICS

Vineyard area: 36,572 acres (14,800 ha)

Production: 1.1 million cases (1 million hl)

Reds: 52%

Whites: 48%

(Office fédéral de l'agriculture, 2015)

Valais

The largest wine-producing region in the country, Valais may also produce the best wines. Located in southern Switzerland, east of Lake Geneva, its 11,108 acres (4,900 ha) follow the Rhône River on what are often very steep slopes. Site elevations rarely exceeding 2,000 ft (600 m) above sea level; but in the Vispertermine, there are plantings at 3,600 ft/1,100 m, among the highest in Europe. Rows of terraces have reshaped the mountain landscape, allowing vines the best possible exposure to the sun. Considerable work is necessary to maintain the dry-stone walls – nestled as they are in mountain hollows with dry microclimates and an ever-present wind that dries the grape clusters. Red wines now dominate at 60% of production. Dôle is a popular light red that is a blend of Pinot Noir and Gamay (the two most planted red grape varieties). It is sometimes vinified as rosé when the grapes are pressed directly. Next in line are Syrah and Humagne, capable of producing powerful, structured wines, while Gamaret has made good progress. The main white grape varieties are Fendant (the local name for Chasselas) and Johannisberg (aka Sylvaner), ahead of Petite Arvine, which is developing well and which gives some of the country's most exciting sweet and dry white wines.

Neuchâtel and the three lakes

The vineyards surrounding Lake Neuchâtel extend as far as Berne. Together with those around lakes Biel and Morat, they cover some 7,41 acres (300 ha), and have been in steep decline for the past 15 years. Red wine is mostly produced here. The Côte Neuchâteloise extends across 18 miles (30 km) on the northern shore of the lake. With an average altitude between 1,400 and 2,000 ft (430

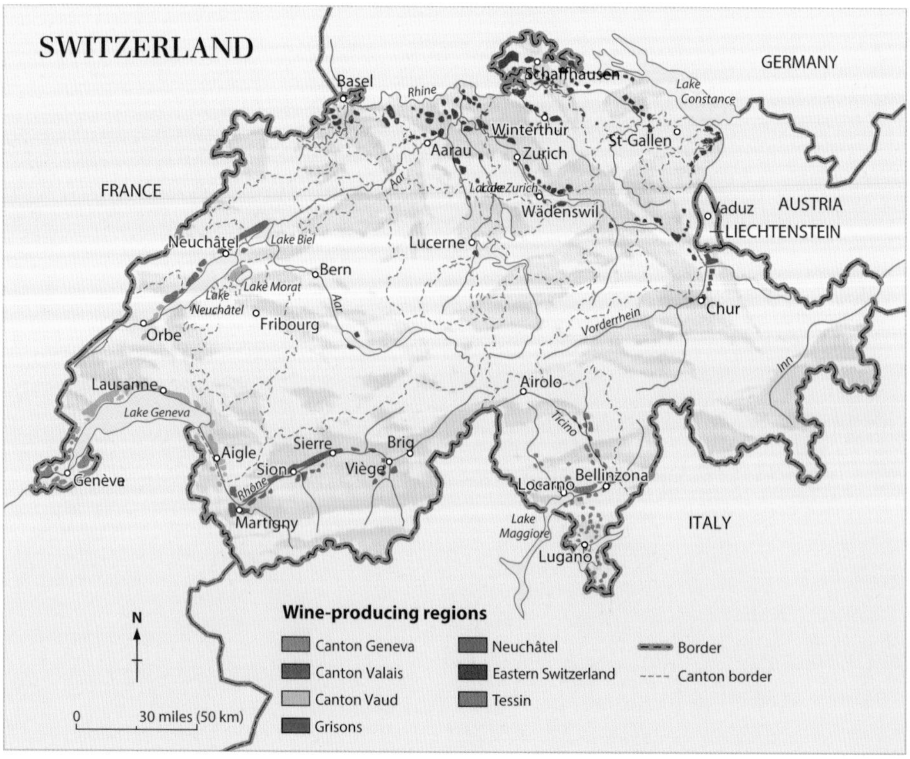

> Vineyards near the town of Sion, in the canton of Valais, Switzerland.

Swiss wine classifications

In Switzerland, appellation legislation is the responsibility of each canton. As a result, there is no unified legislation, which can make deciphering the labels a challenge for the uninitiated. The hierarchy embraces regional and cantonal denominations and, internally, communal appellations that are subject to more demanding production constraints, in particular with regard to blending with wines from outside the zone. Designating wines as a *grand cru* (Vaud et Valais) or *1er grand cru* (Vaud et Genève) is also the purview of the cantons, and their meaning differs according to region.

to 600 m), a cool climate and a drying wind achieve good levels of grape maturity. This is especially so for Pinot Noir, which is vinified into a light rosé called Œil de Perdrix. Apart from the Neuchâtel appellation, there are some 20 communal appellations. There are 18 wine-producing villages here, each claiming their own typicity due to *terroir* or the grape varieties used.

The region is best known for its Chasselas wines, usually consumed locally, unfiltered and therefore a little cloudy. Other wines are produced from Sylvaner, Müller–Thurgau, Chardonnay, Riesling, and Doral, a local crossing.

Vaud

This country's second wine-growing canton, Vaud covers an area of 9,390 acres (3,800 ha), 65% planted with white grape varieties. The vineyards here are cultivated on terraces along the northern shore of Lake Geneva. The landscape is spectacular, especially in the areas of La Côte and Lavaux, which are classed as UNESCO World Heritage sites.

Chasselas has long been the dominant grape variety here, but there are some good red wines from Gamay, Pinot Noir, or local varieties such as Garanoir and Gamarret. Further north, at the southern extremity of Lake Neuchâtel, are the vineyards of Bonvillars and Côte de l'Orbe, which are among the best in the region.

Geneva

The 3,459 acres (1,400 ha) of vineyards here are situated on a plain at the mouth of the Rhône River, along the Arve River and at the southern end of Lake Geneva. It is a dynamic region and home to some of the best Swiss wine producers. Geneva makes most of the red wines (60 per cent) from a rather eclectic planting dominated by traditional grape varieties: Gamay and Pinot Noir ahead of Gamaret, increasingly, and Garanoir and Merlot. The white wines are mostly from Chasselas and Chardonnay grapes.

Ticino

The traditional pergola system of grape growing is becoming rare in this Italian-speaking canton. Also, the character of the reds is similar to their nearby Italian counterparts. Merlot is the main variety, and it thrives on sunny limestone slopes in the sheltered areas of Mendrisiotto, and around Sottoceneri and Bellinzona. Cabernet Sauvignon is also grown in the region, but in more limited quantities. These wines are sometimes blended to produce a 'Swiss Bordeaux' that is enjoyed in affluent Italian circles, meaning often high prices.

TRUE OR FALSE?

Switzerland also produces wines in Jura.

FALSE. The Swiss canton of Jura, southeast of Basel and south of Alsace, has virtually no vineyards. But there are some small producers who craft some 4,500 cases (400 hl) of wine. These are sold under the name of the grape variety, and so don't compete with the French AOC of Jura.

German–Swiss vineyards

Most German-speaking cantons, in northern and eastern Switzerland, have very fragmented vineyards. The wines are usually consumed locally. Due to the cool climate and altitude, the grapes in the vineyards around Zurich, Schaffhausen, St. Gallen, and Grisons reach maturity only late in the season thanks to the *foehn*, a southern wind that keeps the grapes dry. Pinot Noir sometimes produces very good results in Maienfeld, Grisons, or at Stäfa, on the shores of Lake Zurich.

DID YOU KNOW...?

There are 20,000 wine producers in Valais, *if you count all the members of each winemaking family. This large number is due to the small size of individual vineyards. Consequently, most wines are marketed through cooperatives or négociants. The growers who actually sell their wine in bottle are the ones who own the largest domains. (Source: OIV)*

AUSTRIA

Austria boasts a long tradition of winemaking: its vineyards were established more than 2,000 years ago. And modern Austrian wines are generally of very good quality, even if they are largely unknown outside the country. Production is mostly white wine – Grüner Veltliner is the flagship grape variety. The vineyards are situated in eastern and southern Austria, adjacent to the borders with Hungary, Slovakia, the Czech Republic, and Slovenia.

AUSTRIA STATISTICS

Area: 110,000 acres (44,000 ha)

Production (av.): 25.5 million cases (2.3 million hl)

Whites: 67%

Reds: 33%

(austrianwine, 2015)

Lower Austria

Set in the eastern third of the country, and crossed by the Danube River, Lower Austria (Niederösterreich) is the main wine-producing region. It is divided into several wine districts.

WEINVIERTEL. Situated along the Czech and Slovak borders, Weinviertel is an area of some 32,124 acres (13,000 ha) and producing nearly 30 per cent of all Austrian wines. Its white wines are best consumed young; they are light, dry, and fresh. There are also noteworthy sparkling and ice wines. Some excellent red wines are produced on the granite soils around the towns of Retz and Falkenstein, close to the Czech border.

> Welschriesling is a white grape variety that is grown in most regions of Austria.

THERMENREGION. The 'thermal region' to the south of Vienna takes its name from nearby hot springs, where a refreshing glass of white wine is most welcome after a good soak. This is mainly a region of fresh, dry, and aromatic whites: Gumpoldskirchen, a blend of two local varieties, Rotgipfler and Zierfandler, was for long one of Austria's most celebrated wines. There are also some powerful red wines made in the Tattendorf sector, based on Blauer Portugieser and Zweigelt.

WACHAU. In the northwest corner of Lower Austria, this area's 3,114 acres (1,260 ha) vineyards are sited on steep volcanic terraces overlooking the Danube River and a spectacular landscape. Good-quality dry whites are the norm here. Grüner Veltliner and Riesling produce powerful wines for long ageing.

KREMSTAL AND KAMPTAL. The town of Krems, to the northeast of Wachau, is encircled by volcanic and loess terraces – where Riesling and Grüner Veltliner are grown. They also run alongside the Kamp River, a tributary of the Danube. The Grüners here are similar in character to those of Wachau, and there are some fine Rieslings – sometimes late-harvest, renowned as some of Austria's best.

WAGRAM-TRAISENTAL-CARNUNTUM. Between Krems and Vienna, Wagram (formerly Donauland or 'Danube country') is most famous for its white wines made from Grüner Veltliner. Downstream from Vienna, following the course of the Danube, Carnuntum is reputed for its red wines, especially those from Zweigelt. The largest wine-producing domain in Austria is owned by the Capuchin monastery at Klosterneuburg (in Wagram), and is also home to a wine and winemaking school and tasting centre.

Burgenland

Along the Hungarian border, on the land around Lake Neusiedl, is one of Austria's largest vineyard regions (31,629 acres/12,800 ha). It is divided into four sub-zones: Mittelburgenland, Neusiedlersee, Südburgenland, and Neusiedlersee-Hügelland.

DID YOU KNOW...?

The Wachau region has introduced a classification system based on quality for its dry white wines.

It was initiated by Vinea Wachau, an association of small producers. The labels indicate three different levels: the lightest wine is called Steinfeder (11.5% ABV), followed by Federspiel (11.5–12.5% ABV). The richest (the equivalent of a dry spätlese in Germany) is called Smaragd, and must reach a minimum alcohol level of 12.5% ABV. These wines generally come from low-yielding vineyards and late-harvested grapes. When successful, they are superb and age beautifully. The better-known vineyards are mentioned on the label, preceded by the word Ried.

> Harvesting grapes at a Styrian domain.

After a sunny and dry summer, the Neusiedlersee vineyards are bathed in autumn mist rising off the lake. In the Rust area, on the lake's west bank, this encourages the onset of noble rot, and hence the production of Ausbruch, one of the finest sweet wines in the world (*see* p.422). The wines are normally made from Riesling, Welschriesling, Weissburgunder, Müller-Thurgau, or the highly aromatic Muscat Ottonel; although Blaufränkisch makes quality red wine in Mittelburgenland.

TRUE OR FALSE?

Austrian wines are single varietals.

FALSE. While many regions specialize in a particular grape variety, some Austrian white wines are a blend of several varieties, particularly Grüner Veltliner and Riesling.

Styria

Styria (Steiermark) is a vast, rugged region set to the north of the Slovenian border and southwest of Burgenland. Its three sub-regions cover 10,378 acres (4,200 ha). Southern Styria (Südsteiermark) is the largest sub-region and generally produces the best Styrian wines. Many different varieties are cultivated here: Welschriesling, Pinot Blanc, Müller-Thurgau, Riesling, Muskateller, Sauvignon Blanc, Scheurebe, etc. The vineyards are on steep, south-facing slopes at up to 2,000 ft (600 m).

Southeastern Styria (Süd-Oststeiermark) produces mainly light whites, and also some notable wines from Gewurztraminer, Chardonnay (called Morillon), and Sauvignon Blanc. Western Styria (Weststeiermark), between the town of Graz and the Slovenian border, is renowned for Schilcher. This is a slightly tart rosé from Blauer Wildbacher; it's made in very small quantities and is a sought-after local treat, best enjoyed when the wine is young.

Vienna

Some 1,750 acres (700 ha) of vines surround the Austrian capital. Almost all of the wine produced in the region is consumed locally. The wine villages on the edge of the city (Grinzing, Nussdorf...) are full of lively taverns (*heurigen*). There, to the tune of an accordion, winemakers sell their fresh and fruity wines, usually Gemischter Satz, which is a blend of several varieties grown in the same vineyard.

Appellation legislation

Austria has 19 appellations of origin: Kremstal, Kamptal, Wagram, Weinviertel, Wachau, Carnuntum, Traisental, Thermenregion, Weststeiermark, Südsteiermark, Neusiedlersee, Neusiedlersee-Hügelland, Mittelburgenland, Südburgenland, Süd-Oststeiermark, and Wien, plus Niederösterreich, Burgenland, and Styria, these last three being regional appellations.

Austria follows the same rules as the rest of Europe (*see also* p.98). On the label, a named variety is followed by a quality indication similar to that used in Germany, and which focuses on the degree of maturity of the grapes. The DAC (Districtus Austriae Controllatus) category has also been introduced, which applies to wines presenting a strong regional typicity and made with a single grape variety. There are nine DAC regions in Austria.

HUNGARY

It is likely that the Romans planted the first vines in this region, then called Pannonia. The Hungarians, originally a nomadic people who came here from Asia during the 9th and 10th centuries, developed the vineyards over the course of the centuries that followed, even during Turkish rule. It was during the 18th century that Hungary, by then closely allied with Austria, started marketing Tokaji, its most famous wine, throughout Europe.

During the country's 50 years of communist rule, the vineyards were managed by cooperatives, with a guaranteed income for the producers. Since the end of the communist era, the free-market economy has forced many smaller producers to give up, and the vineyard area has been restructured, shrinking by more than 30 per cent. In recent decades several family operations have been established, some of which are making wines of a remarkable quality. Those located in the Villány region, to the south of the country, have enjoyed particular success. In addition, in the Tokaj region several medium-sized companies, often linked with historic estates, benefit from foreign investment. Lastly, there are large concerns that generally buy grapes from small producers: cooperatives, privatized former state-owned farms and new companies created with Hungarian or foreign capital.

HUNGARY STATISTICS

Vineyard area: 16,062 acres (65,000 ha)

Production: 29.9 million cases (2,700,000 million hl)

Whites: 70%

Reds: 30%

(OIV, 2015)

Tokaj-Hegyalja: 'Wine of kings'

The mountain region of Tokaj covers 13,591 acres (5,500 ha) in the northeast of the country, and it produces the most famous of Hungarian wines. It was highly prized during the time of Louis XIV of France for its sumptuous aromas and refreshing character. As the king of wines (or wine of kings), the appellation of Tokaj (*see* p.534) is known first and foremost for its sweet or semi-sweet wine.

The main grape variety is Furmint, which, in the autumn mists of the Bodrog Valley, consistently develops noble rot. On a par with the best sweet wines in the world, Tokaji is astonishingly long-lived – the best vintages can age for 200 years! Confusingly, there also are some traditional dry wines that bear the Tokai appellation.

Other regions

EGER. Northeast of Budapest, the Mátraalja-Egri region boasts many cellars run by small producers. The best-known wine in this region is Egri Bikavér, or 'Bull's Blood of Eger,' a blend of Kékoportó and Cabernet Sauvignon.

> Barrels of wine at the Kovács Borház winery in the village of Hajós, Hungary.

LAKE BALATON. Southwest of the capital, in the volcanic soils of the hills surrounding the 'Hungarian Sea', are vineyards producing mostly white wines from Olaszrizling (Welschriesling), Muscat Ottonel, and Szürkebarát (Pinot Gris). The best wines come from the Badacsony district.

SOPRON. By the Austrian border, from hilly vineyards near the town of Sopron, Kékfrankos, Pinot Noir, and Cabernet Sauvignon produce good quality red wines. The southern shore of Fertö Tó, or Austria's Neusiedlersee, is home to some worthy white wines.

VILLÁNY-SIKLÓS. In the far south of the country, near the town of Pécs, this area is renowned for its full, round, red wines based on Cabernet Sauvignon, Merlot, and Kékoportó.

SZEKSZÁRD. The vineyards around the town of Szekszárd are reputed for their red wines, which also can be labelled 'Bull's Blood', as in the Eger region. The traditional variety has long been the high-yielding Kadarka, but it is being replaced by Merlot, Cabernet Sauvignon, and Kékoportó. The wine village of Leányvár, with three storeys of cellars cut into a hillside, is well worth a visit.

SOUTHEAST EUROPE TO THE BLACK SEA

The fall of the Soviet empire during the early 1990s changed the wine landscape of the countries downstream along the Danube from Austria, as well as in the former republics of the USSR.

Formerly operated as collective farms, the vineyards of Romania and Slovenia have been partly privatized with the help of capital groups from the West. Those from Bulgaria and former Soviet republics are slow to catch up with modern demand.

> Harvest in a Bulgarian vineyard.

Romania

Romania is a large wine producer (474,442 acres/192,000 ha and 44.4 million cases/4 million hl). For a long time, it was one of the main purveyors of the low-quality wine of the Soviet era. The loss of its traditional markets in Eastern Europe has led to a significant restructuring of the sector, with the support of European finance. A large part of the vineyard area has been torn up, with new plantings concentrating on more promising sites. Winery equipment can vary from the most rudimentary to the very latest technology, since some vineyards having benefitted from foreign investment. Some owners whose properties were expropriated in the communist era have been able to repossess their estates, with the ambition and sometimes the capital to develop good-quality production. Among the most successful regions are Dealu Mare in the centre of the country, towards the south, known for its red wines, the small Dragasani area, to the west of Bucharest, Tarnave in Transylvania, famous for its white wines, and Cotnari, in the northeast, known for a sweet wine with a long-standing reputation (see p. 535).

Bulgaria

During the 1970s, Bulgarian Cabernet Sauvignons competed with Bordeaux on the German, British, and Scandinavian markets. Since the end of communism, the country has seen its production drop dramatically due to the modernization that was necessary. The industry has not yet recovered but continues with the restructuring of its vineyard area.

ANCIENT HISTORY. Bulgaria is one of the oldest wine-producing countries in Europe – the Thracians were making wine here 3,000 years ago, as recorded by Homer in the *Iliad*. For a long time, the wine was released only to the internal market; but toward the end of the communist era, there was a surge in Soviet demand and a partnership with the American Pepsi-Cola company that boosted wine sales in Britain and Germany.

GREAT POTENTIAL, FEW RESOURCES. With a Mediterranean climate tempered by altitude and low-nutrient soils, there is great potential for producing quality wine here. But Bulgaria still lacks infrastructure – so there are fewer than 50 significant wine exporters. The hasty privatization of vineyards during the late 1990s, with parcels of land being restored to their pre-1947 owners, has meant that many plots have been abandoned due to lack of resources. Today the wine industry is made up of large producers that sometimes own vineyards or bring together the production of small owners who recognize the advantages to be gained from greater care of the vineyards. Bulgaria is exporting some of its wine to neighbouring countries again, and this Bulgarian renewal also includes the creation of ambitious new estates keen to produce quality wines using local or international varieties. These vineyards, many of which have been recently replanted on high quality *terroirs* will no doubt produce the country's most interesting wines in the future.

Cricova, 'Treasure' of the Republic of Moldova

The former Soviet republic of Moldova, situated between Romania and Ukraine, boasts a unique wine cellar – it's virtually a subterranean town! Cricova's old mines, at a depth of 200–260 ft (60–80 m), have a constant temperature that allows the production of sparkling wines by the traditional method. Placed under the protection of UNESCO, they also store a large number of Moldovan and foreign wines, some of which are very old indeed. A significant tourist destination in Moldova, Cricova even has streets named after grape varieties. About 20–25 ft (6–8 m) wide, their combined length exceeds 60 miles (100 km) over more than 130 acres (53 ha).

> Vineyards in the region of Stajerska in Slovenia.

GRAPE VARIETIES. Pamid, Mavrud, Melnik, Cabernet Sauvignon, Merlot, Gamay, and Pinot Noir for reds; Rkatsiteli, Dimiat, Muscat Ottonel, Misket, Chardonnay, Riesling, Gewurztraminer, Aligoté, and Sylvaner for whites.
PRODUCTION AND LEGISLATION. Some 250,000 acres (100,000 ha) of Bulgarian vines yield 10 million cases/900,000 hl of red wine and 6.7 million cases /600,000 hl of white wine, with a large percentage used for distillation. There are 27 local appellations in Bulgaria. The wine classifications, not yet fully in line with the European Union, include table wines, country wine with an indication of origin and grape variety, wines of controlled geographic origin (DGO), and *Controliran*, a kind of super-DGO.

Ukraine

Crimea enjoys a Mediterranean climate and most of the country's vineyards are located here. This is where 'Krim', a blended, semi-sweet sparkling wine of average quality, has been produced for many years. There are also some red wines known as 'Ruby'. The greatest quality wines are found near Sebastopol, at Massandra. The cellars of the Czars there, established in 1894 and still preserved, hold treasured Black Muscat wines that will soon reach their centennial. Production here is being revived, thanks to the interest it generates among wine lovers in Western Europe.

Slovenia

This former Yugoslav republic is set between Italy, Austria, and Croatia. Its vineyards cover about 39,537 acres (16,000 ha) across 15 wine regions. They face the Adriatic Sea to the west, or are spread through the valleys of the Drava and Sava in the east. The production is usually of high quality, especially white wines from the region of Podravski, due to an ideal climate at altitude. Slovenian winemakers generally produce some fine dry white wines, as well as ice wine and 'late harvest' wine based on Riesling and Pinot Gris. The best red wines come mainly from the Adriatic coast and the Sava valley. They are made from Merlot, Cabernet Franc, Barbera, and local grape varieties such as Refosk (grown near the Italian border) or Cvicek (which is vinified into a pleasant rosé in the region of Sava).

Georgia

It is likely that this former Soviet republic, along the shores of the Black Sea, is the place from which the grapevine first spread to the rest of Europe in the late Neolithic period. This would explain the wealth of Georgia's native grape varieties – amounting to several hundred. Wine growing in Georgia is well established and dynamic. The Russian embargo of 2006 deprived the country of its market but it has been able to respond by accelerating the modernization its wine industry required through state help and the discovery of alternative markets. New legislation designates six main wine zones divided into sub-zones and the law provides for several levels of quality. Georgia has adopted modern processes for wine destined for export while retaining those aspects that have long made it unique: a certain sweetness in a number of its wines and a traditional method of wine-making in large underground earthenware vessels (*kvevri*) on skins, a process that delivers wines rich in tannins, including the whites. Few grape varieties are imported but there are several local ones, most popular among them the Rkatsiteli white grape and the Saperavi red, both planted in the Kakheti region, home to 70 per cent of the country's vineyards.

Croatia

With increasing success Croatia is exploiting the vineyards that lie between continental Croatia, bordered by the Drava and Danube rivers, and coastal Croatia, along the Adriatic. It shows promise with a cultivated area of 72,000 acres (29,000 ha) and dynamic producers already putting that promise into action. The country produces mainly white wines that are dry, sweet or sparkling, particularly in the interior, using grape varieties such as Graševina, Riesling, Pinot Gris and more recently Chardonnay and Sauvignon Blanc. The Adriatic coast produces full-bodied red wines, Mediterranean in style. The most notable wines come from the Dalmatian vineyards where a grape variety with great potential, Plavac Mali, can produce powerful, well-structured wines. Babić, Merlot, Syrah and Grenache are also grown. Istria is home to the Malvasia white grape and Teran, a red grape variety that delivers wines full of character.

Leading wines of Central and Southeast Europe to the Black Sea

Wines from Austria and Switzerland are made according to the production standards of Western Europe. However, except for Slovenia, that's not always the case for former Eastern Bloc countries, whose wine quality remains very mixed.

CHAMOSON GRAND CRU AOC

SWITZERLAND (VALAIS)

Chamoson's vineyards, on steep slopes over the Rhône River, stretch across 1,000 acres (427 ha), and are the largest in Valais. Set within the Valais AOC, Chamoson Grand Cru comprises a wide range of soils and microclimates, where many different varieties (39) thrive. It is also very fragmented, since there are as many as 1,200 vineyard owners. Although Chamoson produces mostly red wines, but owes its reputation especially to its white wines, made from Sylvaner, Chasselas and Petite Arvine. The harvest is entirely by hand and the appellation rules are extremely strict.

> **GRAPE VARIETIES** Sylvaner (known locally as Johannisberg, since its typicity recalls that of the great wines of the Rhine Valley) and Petite-Arvine for whites; Gamay, Pinot Noir, and Syrah for reds.

> **SOIL** Scree and alluvium, though mainly limestone.

> **STYLE** Sylvaner is vinified as a dry white wine. It is light straw in colour with hints of green that turn golden with age. On the palate, there are subtle notes of toasted almonds with a touch of acidity and good minerality. The toasty and fruity notes become more prominent with age. It is also available in sweet versions made from late harvest grapes. The red wines are fairly supple and fruity, except those from Syrah and Humagne, and are generally well structured.

Colour:
Red and white.

Serving temperature:
46 to 50°F (8 to10°C) for whites;
57 to 63°F (14 to 17°C) for reds.

Ageing potential:
5–6 years, and up to 15 years for the best wines of good vintages.

DÉZALEY GRAND CRU AOC

SWITZERLAND (VAUD)

Nestled in the heart of the Lavaux district, within Vaud canton, this appellation covers only 133 acres (53 ha). It is set entirely within the municipality of Puidoux, and produces only white wines from Chasselas. The vineyards are on a very steep slope, warmed by the sun reflected from Lake Geneva below. The vineyards are planted in terraces, the walls of which also help to reflect light and store heat. With the cold, dry winds slowing the ripening of the grapes and helping Chasselas to preserve its aromas, this microclimate is ideal for bringing fruit to full maturity. Local conditions, carefully observed and managed for years by growers, also give the wines their character, with pronounced aromas of ripe fruit supporting a fresh crispness.

> **GRAPE VARIETY** Chasselas.

> **SOIL** Glacial erosion has shaped the Dézaley hillside, leaving behind a moraine with high limestone-clay content, between banks of 'pudding' stones.

> **STYLE** Dézaley Grand Cru is characterized by its depth and power. It offers toasted and smokey aromas, notes of almonds and honey, as well as a fruity or floral character when young, going on to develop smokey, mineral, and honey notes.

Colour:
White.

Serving temperature:
46 to 50°F (8 to 10°C).

Ageing potential:
4 to 8 years, and up 10 years in very good vintages.

RUSTER AUSBRUCH DAC

AUSTRIA (BURGENLAND)

From near the town of Rust, one of the best dessert wines in the world, Ruster Ausbruch, is produced by a method similar to that for Tokaji Aszú (*see below*). Climatic conditions around Lake Neusiedl – hot and dry summers followed by autumn mist from the lake – allow the formation of noble rot with great regularity.

> **GRAPE VARIETIES** Weissburgunder (Pinot Blanc), Welschriesling, Ruländer (Pinot Gris), Muscat Ottonel, Furmint.

> **SOIL** Sandy, on flat or sloping ground by the shores of Lake Neusiedl.

> **STYLE** Sweet wines of great concentration and perfume, with notes of spice and grapey aromas. With age, they take a more pronounced amber colour and a more defined spiciness.

Colour: *White.*

Serving temperature: *46 to 54°F (8 to 12°C).*

Ageing potential: *Up to 100 years for the best vintages.*

KREMSTAL DAC

AUSTRIA (LOWER AUSTRIA)

The 4,942 acres (2,000 ha) of this appellation extend along the central stretch of the Danube in Austria, near the picturesque town of Krems. Although divided into different zones, with individual geologic and climatic characteristics, the vineyards here have a genuine identity. Producing exclusively white wines from Riesling and Grüner Veltliner, Kremstal became an appellation in its own right in 2007. Along with Wachau, it is one of the most highly reputed wine regions of Austria, thanks to the strict legislation to which its producers respond.

> **GRAPE VARIETIES** Riesling and Grüner Veltliner.

> **SOIL** Granite boulders and loess.

> **STYLE** The dry Rieslings are elegant, clean, mineral, and with no botrytis or oak notes. Grüner Veltliner ranges from lively and fruity to powerful, peppery and mineral. The region also produces some sweet wines made from grapes that have been affected by botrytis.

Colour: *White.*

Serving temperature: *46 to 54°F (8 to 12°C).*

Ageing potential: *5 to 20 years, depending on the area and vintage.*

TOKAJ

HUNGARY

The hilly region of Tokaj (Tokaj-Hegyalja) produces sweet, medium-dry, or dry wines, all bearing the appellation Tokaji (meaning 'from Tokaj' in Hungarian), which can be confusing for anyone but experts. The most famous wine is made from Aszú (meaning over-ripe) grapes, affected by noble rot and left to shrivel on the vine. 'Eszencia' is an exceptionally sweet nectar that runs off naturally from the vats. Tokaji Aszú is therefore always vinified as a sweet wine. After pressing, the wine ferments in barrels for many months. Separately, the pressed Aszú grapes are divided into units of 25 kg called *puttonyos*, and multiples of that volume are added to the must or to the finished wine. The number of *puttonyos* added to each barrel (between three and six) determines the sweetness. New legislation in 2014 only authorized Aszú for the most concentrated wines (5 and 6 *puttonyos*). Tokaji Szamorodni ('as is') is also produced, a dry or medium-dry wine that is more simple and can be oxidative. There are also some fresh and luminous dry white wines of great quality bearing the name of the Tokaj appellation.

> **GRAPE VARIETIES** Furmint, Muscat Ottonel, Hárslevelü.

> **SOIL** Loess, clay-limestone, and volcanic.

> **STYLE** Eszencia is very low in alcohol, with a sugar concentration above 250 g/l, while Tokaji Aszú is a minimum of 120 g/l. The latter is a powerful, concentrated wine, with rich and complex aromas and a superb acidity that smoothes the palate and gives vibrance and intensity to the flavours. It can age for several generations, taking on darker shades of amber. The quality of Tokaji Szamorodni is uneven, but the best age very well.

Colour: *White.*

Serving temperature: *46 to 50°F (8 to10°C).*

Ageing potential: *Several decades for the best vintages.*

Reviving East European wines

CONSIDERABLE ROOM TO MANOEUVRE

For more than 20 years, Jean-François Ragot has travelled extensively throughout Eastern Europe in search of rare gems for his Lyon-based company, Dionis. He pioneered the marketing of Hungarian Tokaji in France, and also has the exclusive distribution rights in France of Cotnari Grasă from Romania. 'Tokaj is already established, even if there are still some problems to resolve in vineyard management. Romania has yet to make an impact, but its potential is enormous,' says a very enthusiastic Jean-François Ragot. If he has little trouble sourcing quality grapes for the Tokaj wines that he makes or selects, it is a much more difficult task in Romania. He explains, 'They still have a mentality dating back to the Ceausescu era.' For a good quality Cotnari Grasă, he has to visit the area and make very strict grape selections in the vineyard. 'Bulgaria will be the next major player out of the former Eastern Bloc countries,' he says. As for Slovenia, it is already an established wine country, thanks to its low volume but very high quality wine production.

KARST

SLOVENIA (PRIMORSKY COASTAL REGION)

In southwestern Slovenia, between the Adriatic coast and the Italian border, the Karst region has given its name to the geologic (karst) formation of underground rivers flowing through limestone subsoil. Cultivated since Roman times, the long-neglected vineyards here have now found a new life since the entry of Slovenia into the European Union. This area covers 1,400 acres (560 ha) for a production of 1.7 million cases (150,000 hl). The region is renowned for its red wine made from Teran, also known as Refosk, that is found in Friuli. This grape variety produces dark wines, low in alcohol, and fresh with firm tannins and aromas of red fruit and cherries. There are also some light rosés and dry white wines.

> **GRAPE VARIETIES** Teran or Refosk, Merlot, and Cabernet Franc for reds and rosés; Welschriesling, Sauvignon Blanc, and Pinot Gris for whites.

> **SOIL** Limestone and red clay.

> **STYLE** Red wines are dark, tangy, fruity, and low in alcohol. The rosés are light, and the whites dry and fruity.

Colour:
Red, rosé, and white.

Serving temperature:
46 to 54°F (8 to12°C) for whites and rosés; 57 to 63°F (14 to 17°C) for reds.

Ageing potential:
2 to 10 years for reds; 1 to 3 years for whites and rosés.

COTNARI GRASĂ

ROMANIA

In the northeastern corner of Romania, near the Republic of Moldova, is the small vineyard district of Cotnari. Once very famous for its sweet white wines, it still suffers serious deficiencies from 50 years of communist rule, even if its potential is still there. The grapes are affected by the noble rot that is necessary to produce the best wines; but the strict berry selection that is also essential to this work is not always practiced here, and very different wines can be found under the same appellation.

> **GRAPE VARIETIES** Grasă (similar to the Hungarian Furmint and easily affected by *Botrytis cinerea* or 'noble rot'), Fetească Albă, Francusa, and Tămâioasă Românească.

> **SOIL** Clay-limestone and loess, on often steep hillsides.

> **STYLE** Very uneven. The appellation produces a wide range in quality, from outstanding sweet wines to the very ordinary. The best are characterized by Muscat flavours, taking on spicy notes as they age.

Colour:
White.

Serving temperature:
46 to 50°F (8 to 10°C).

Ageing potential:
Depends on quality (more than 20 years for the best).

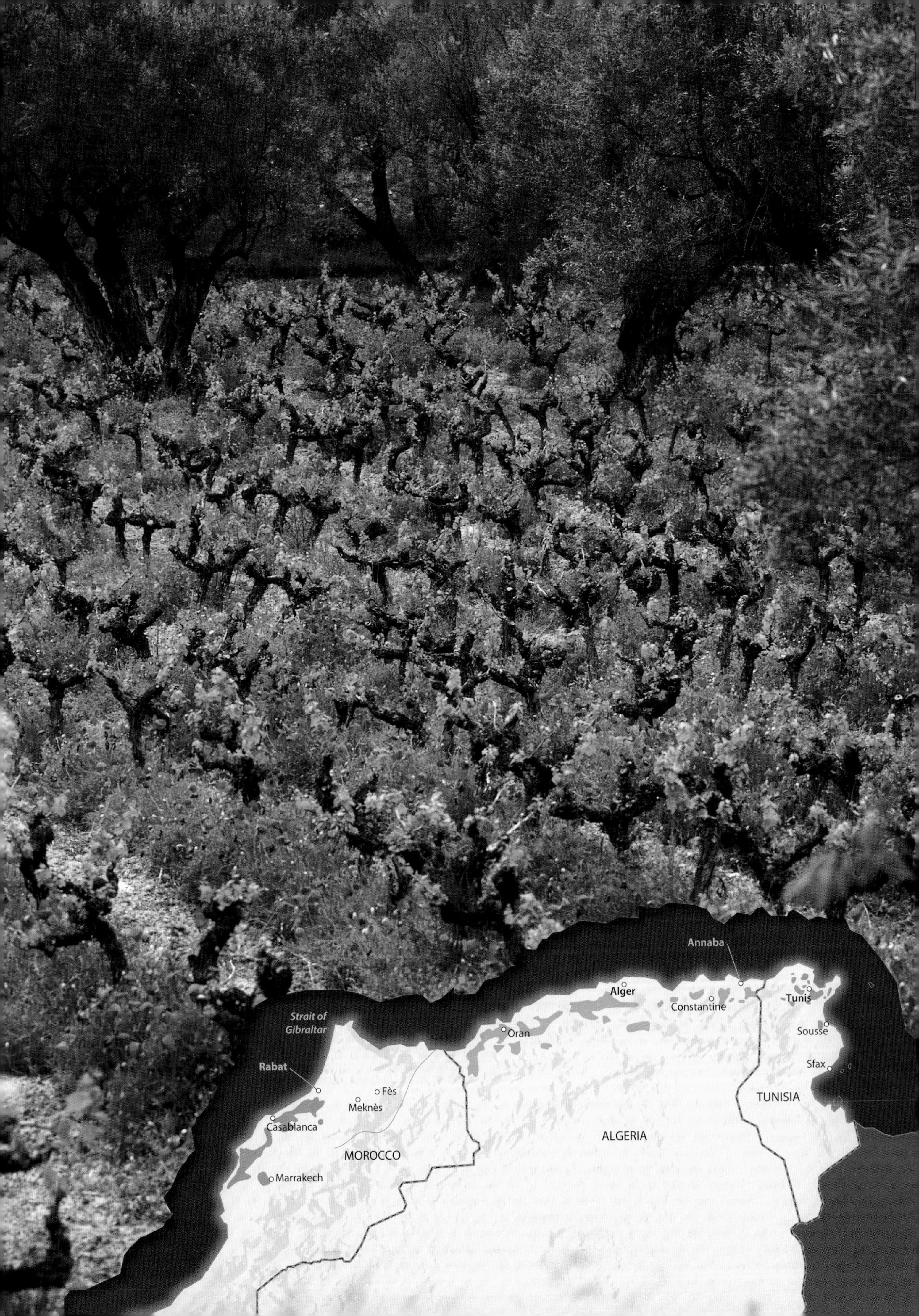
Annaba
Alger
Constantine
Tunis
Strait of Gibraltar
Oran
Sousse
Rabat
Sfax
Fès
Meknès
TUNISIA
Casablanca
ALGERIA
MOROCCO
Marrakech

EASTERN MEDITERRANEAN AND NORTH AFRICA

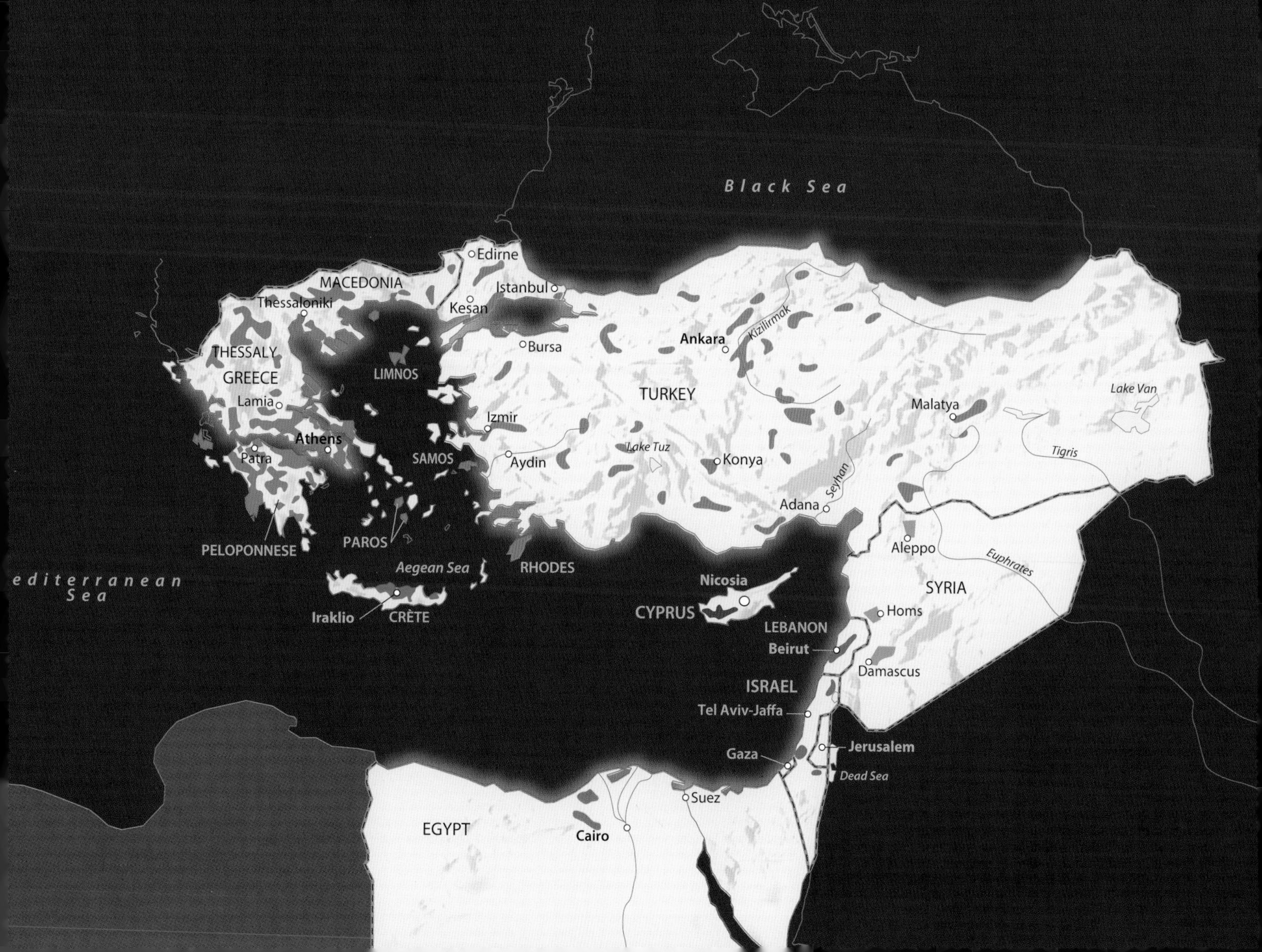

THE VINEYARDS OF THE EASTERN MEDITERRANEAN AND NORTH AFRICA

Vineyards have long been cultivated in the eastern Mediterranean. Those countries with strong Christian traditions, such as Greece and Cyprus, have the most well-established wine culture, although the Lebanon and Israel also produce wines of excellent quality. Some vineyards in North Africa, whose origins hark back to colonial times, also are now achieving high standards.

GREECE

For a long time synonymous with rustic *taverna* wines – particularly Retsina, a white flavoured with pine resin – Greek production has improved significantly in the past 20 years.

Ancient roots

The history of wine in Greece can be traced back to the very beginnings of Greek civilization. Elements of the oldest wine press, from more than 3,000 years ago, have been found in Crete. Greece also was the driving force in the spread of wine culture and the planting of vines across the Mediterranean region. It was from the 13th to the 11th century BC that the development of vineyards hit its peak in the Hellenic world, which included Macedonia. Greek wine production then decreased during the long Ottoman occupation, which ended only shortly before World War I. However, the Greeks never stopped drinking wine, since its preparation was supervised by the Orthodox Church, whose considerable power was always respected by the Turks.

GREECE STATISTICS

Vineyard area: 172,400 acres (69,760 ha) for wine grapes and 162,450 acres (65,740 ha) for table grapes and raisins

Production: 39 million cases (3,500,000 hl)

White: 60%

Red and rosé: 40%
(Greek Ministry of Economy)

Greek wine today

After stagnating across most of the 20th century, Greek wine production has improved markedly in quality since the country's entry into the European Union. Change has been driven by large companies recognizing market potential. The planting of 'international' grape varieties, the training of young Greek oenologists at the best European schools, and a careful study of international demand have resulted in the production of wines of a high standard.

FRAGMENTED VINEYARDS, MODERN METHODS. About 30 per cent of Greek wines are produced and marketed by large producer-merchants, who buy grapes from many small

> In Greece, vines are often grown on pergolas.

DID YOU KNOW...?

Long before its entry into the European Union, Greece was inspired by the French AOC system, *even going as far as to give French-sounding names to certain appellations, such as Muscat de Patras. Today the wines include those with and without a stated geographical origin. The former are then divided into four categories: two IGPs, Topikoi Oenoi (IGP or* vin de pays*) and Oenoi Onomasias Kata Paradosi (an IGP that indicates a style of wine that can be produced throughout Greece, such as Retsina), and two AOPs: Oenoi Onomasias Proelefseos Anoteras. Poiotitas (OPAP) and Oenoi Onomasias Proelefseos Elenhomeni (OPE, the equivalent of the French AOC). The last two make up the best known appellations and wines, with the sweet wines from the Muscat and Mavrodaphne grape varieties, but some Greek* grands vins *are also produced under the Topikoi oenoi banner. Since 2005, wine names and time spent in barrel can be indicated (*réserve *or* grande réserve*).*

estates and often have wineries in various parts of Greece. The main wine regions are, in order of size, the Peloponnese, Crete, Macedonia and Thrace, Thessaly, and the Aegean islands.

GRAPE VARIETIES. Virgil wrote that it was impossible to list all of the varieties. Today, more than 300 are recognized. For red wine, the main varieties are: Agiorgitiko, Limnio, Halkidiki, Xynomavro, Mandilaria, Mavrodaphne, Grenache, Cabernet Sauvignon, Merlot, and Syrah. For white wine: Chardonnay, Muscat à Petits Grains, Roditis, Assyrtiko, Moschofilero, Sauvignon Blanc, and Muscat of Alexandria.

> Carvings on these barrels at a winery in Patras recall the ancient origins of Greek wine.

The Peloponnese

This peninsula in the southern part of the country is the largest wine region. Out of 148,000 acres (60,000 ha) of vines, 54,000 acres (22,000 ha) produce wine grapes, mainly in the northern peninsula around Patras and Corinth. In terms of appellations (*see* box on previous page), the region produces three OPEs: Muscat of Patras, Muscat Rio of Patras, and Patras Mavrodaphne; and three OPAPs: Mantinia, Nemea, and Patras.

The best-known appellation is Nemea. This name also designates the largest and oldest Greek appellation near the Gulf of Corinth. Nemea produces red wines, mostly from the local grape Agiorgitiko (St. George); but international red grape varieties, such as Syrah, Cabernet Sauvignon, and Merlot, are increasingly being planted in the region.

That said, it is mainly white wines that are produced in the Peloponnese, especially from Moschofilero, a Muscat-style grape that yields dry wines. In the prefecture of Achaia, in the area surrounding Patras, wine production is mostly fortified whites made from Muscat grapes and fortified reds made from Mavrodaphne. There are also dry rosés made from Roditis in the Olympia region.

Macedonia and Thrace

These two regions, with a total of 37,000 acres (15,000 ha) of vines, are located in far northern Greece, bordering Albania, the former Yugoslavia, Bulgaria, and Turkey. They are characterized by rugged terrain and a more continental climate than in the rest of the country, with potentially harsh winters. Production is mainly red wines, particularly from the Xynomavro grape, which is used in the wines to lay down of Naoussa, Macedonia's most famous OPAP.

White wines, mainly blends, are found in Thrace and Chalkidiki (or Halkidiki), where the Halkidiki grape, named after the region, is common. Since Thrace does not have an OPE or an OPAP, its wines are primarily known and sold in restaurants under merchants' brand names such as Boutari and Tsantali.

The islands

CRETE. This island has Greece's second largest wine-producing area (approximately 25,000 acres or 10,000 ha). Several thousand years old, the vineyards suffered a relatively late attack of phylloxera in the 1970s, and have gradually been replanted. While, as elsewhere, American rootstock was used, the wine producers were wise enough to graft some native varieties. Crete produces mainly red wines near Heraklion, from the Kotsifali, Mandilaria, and Liatiko grape varieties, and also around Chania, from Romeiko. The most well-known white wines come from the Sitia region in the west.

OTHER ISLANDS. To the north of Crete, the beautiful island of Santorini produces some of Greece's best white wines, mainly from the Assyrtiko grape. The islands of the Aegean Sea are famous for their sweet Muscat wines, especially those from Samos and Lemnos, which are of variable quality. These are either fortified or traditionally produced sweet white wines, meaning grapes that have been dried in the sun.

Retsina

This crisp, white, 'resinated' wine is unique to Greece and has an official European allowance for the addition of small amounts of Aleppo pine resin to the must. Its origin dates back to antiquity, when the earthenware amphorae in which wine was transported were sealed with a mixture of plaster and resin, giving the wine a distinct flavour. Relatively cheap, it is served with mezze, in half bottles or jugs. A few rosé retsinas, that are more refined, are produced in the Peloponnese region from the Roditis grape.

CYPRUS

The ancient vineyards of Cyprus used to extend across the entire island, but they are now concentrated in the southwest – in the Greek part of Cyprus, with very few in the Turkish region.

Vineyards and production

The wine-growing area (over 27,000 acres/11 000 ha) is largely situated in the southwest of the island, a large proportion of which has been uprooted during the last decades, most notably in the lowland vineyards that were producing wines with little character and few commercial outlets. On the other hand, thanks to European Union funds, vines have been replanted in those areas with great potential, in particular on the southern slopes of the Troodos mountains. Cyprus has been known since the time of the Crusades for its sweet red dessert wine, Commandaria, which can be of variable quality. After *mutage* the wines are left to mature in casks for two years, following the Spanish solera system of ageing. At their best the heady wines, black in colour, develop intense and complex aromas.

Grape varieties

The two important local grape varieties, both used to make Commandaria wines, are the red Mavro (meaning 'black') grape and the white Xynisteri. Although the ratio is declining, Mavro represents half of the mix of grape varieties and produces relatively supple red wines. Xynisteri represents a quarter and produces interesting dry white wines when planted at altitude; it is used in various blends with imported varieties. Among the other local varieties of note are Maratheftiko, which delivers deep coloured, tannic wines with a good reputation and the Ofthalmon red grape. Other varieties that are widely grown include Cabernet, Mourvèdre, Syrah, Grenache, Cinsaut, Muscat of Alexandria and Chardonnay.

THE LEVANT

The countries of the Levant – Turkey, Lebanon, Syria, and Israel – have a wine tradition dating back to at least ancient Greco-Roman times and probably even earlier among the Canaanites of Palestine and the peoples of the Tigris and Euphrates. However, across the centuries, Arab and then Turkish conquests prevented vines from flourishing except as a privilege granted to Jewish and Christian minorities. It is therefore most common today to find wine production in Lebanon and Israel.

Turkey

More than a thousand different grape varieties can be found in Turkey, a large producer of grapes, but only a few dozen of these varieties are used to produce wine, and most of the harvest goes to either table grapes or raisins.

Yet wine has always been part of Turkish culture, not only among the Christian (particularly Armenian) and Jewish minorities, but also within the secular Muslim elite, for whom drinking a little wine has always been fashionable. Today, despite a restrictive legal framework, the Turkish wine industy is showing a new dynamism with the production of some very good wines, the advent of modern cellars and the exploration of new local *terroirs*. Production is dominated by a dozen wineries, which use their own grapes but also buy in from private growers; they produce wines in most of the winegrowing areas. Small estates have also appeared, developed by the country's new elite who are quick to use the services of famous consultants. The wine-growing areas of the Aegean, Marmara, and Cappadocia regions are the most dynamic and account for most of the production. Local grape varieties are sometimes blended with imported ones to guarantee the originality of Turkish wines. The most interesting red grapes include Boğazkere, which delivers dark, tannic, very structured wines, and the more supple Öküzgözü and Kalecik Karasi. Sultaniye and Narince are the most popular white varieties. Sauvignon Blanc has found the limestone terroir of Cappadocia to its liking, resulting in some very promising dry white wines.

> In Cappadocia, Turkey, vineyards are exposed to significant variations in temperature with hot, dry summers and cold winters.

Israel

Wine has always been part of Hebrew culture. One of the first modern Jewish settlements even established a vineyard in the sands of Rishon Le

Zion, at the end of the 19th century, although production was mainly of a syrupy red wine sold under the Carmel brand. The Israelis did not begin to make better quality wines until the early 1980s, taking advantage of the soil and the fairly cool climate of the Golan Heights. It is here that the majority of Israel's 13,590 acres (5,500 ha) of vines are located, but irrigation also enables good quality red wines to be produced in the country's central region. There are white and red wines, some of which are kosher. Many Israeli wines are rather neutral in character, but some have justifiably garnered many favourable reviews from international experts. In the wake of the Domaine du Castel, a new generation of small producers are making elegant and personal wines.

Lebanon

This is without doubt the country that produces the best wines in the eastern Mediterranean. Some, particularly those from the Bekaa Valley, are considered by many in the wine world to be exceptionally fine wines. Many estates have been created recently, some of which have significant funds at their disposal. This new generation is taking full advantage the very real potential of Lebanese vines, most of which are located in the Bekaa Valley. The slopes of Mount Lebanon and the Batroun zone have been recently planted recently. The warm and dry climate allows the red grapes to mature fully, in particular Cabernet Sauvignon and Syrah, which give some of the best Lebanese wines their character. Among the other red varieties that are grown are Cinsaut, Merlot, Carignan, Grenache, Mourvèdre, and Pinot Noir. The most widely planted white varieties alongside the local Merwah and Obeidi, the latter often used to make Arak (an anise-flavoured liqueur), are Chardonnay, Muscat, Viognier and Clairette. In 2016 a total of 43 estates covered a winegrowing area of almost 5,000 acres/ 2000 ha (wine-grapes). Some, like Château Musar, have long enjoyed a good reputation while other more recent ones, like Atibaia, a small property, or Baal, are producing wines of excellent quality.

NORTH AFRICA

Vineyards in three North African countries are essentially due to French colonization and the presence of many Maltese, Spanish, and Italian settlers. Today, plantings are steadily shrinking in Algeria, remain constant in Tunisia, and are increasing in Morocco.

Algeria

Until its independence in 1962, Algeria was one of the largest 'French' wine-producing regions. High in alcohol and deep in colour, but lacking in acidity, these wines were made from southern French grape varieties (Cinsaut, Carignan, Grenache) and generously blended into wines from other French regions, including Bordeaux and Burgundy, to give the latter the 'muscle' that they sometimes lacked. Since independence, the Algerian vineyard, with 12 appelation regions including Médéa, Tlemcen, and Mascara, has continued to decline in both quantity and quality

> Vineyard landscape in Tunisia.

Tunisia

Vines have been grown in Tunisia since Carthaginian times and, during the colonial period, the country had beautiful vineyards that were run mostly by settlers from Italy. Today, grapes for wine production are grown mainly in the north and cover fewer than 25,000 acres (10,000 ha). The most popular wines are dry Muscats from the Kelibia region.

Morocco

Among North African countries, it is Morocco that has made the most effort in recent years to produce good quality wines. But only 25 per cent of the 118,611 acres (48,000 ha) of vines there are used to make wine. Production totals nearly 3.3 million cases (300,000 hl), the majority of which is red wine. There are 14 *appellations d'origine garantie* (AOG) and just one *appellation d'origine contrôlée* (AOC).

The heart of the Moroccan wine industry is located in the regions of Casablanca and, importantly, Meknès/Fès, where the vineyards planted at altitude in the foothills of the Atlas mountains produce the country's best red wines. It is divided into several appellations, including Guerrouane, Beni M'tir, and Coteaux de l'Atlas (the only AOC). The traditional mix of varieties (Cinsaut, Grenache, Carignan, Alicante Bouschet, Ugni Blanc, Clairette) has been joined by important international grapes such as Cabernet, Merlot, and Syrah. The best red wines offer all the fullness of the fruit ripened in sun-drenched vineyards. Morocco also produces a rosé with an orange tint, Gris de Boulaouane, which is popular in France and elsewhere.

Wine regions of the Eastern Mediterranean and North Africa

Greece produces most of the wines originating from this part of the world that are known and consumed beyond its borders. Nevertheless, the best Lebanese and Israeli wines are also exported, as are those from Turkey albeit to a lesser degree.

NAOUSSA, AMYNTEON, GOUMENISSA OPAPs

GREECE (MACEDONIA)

These three appellations are considered to be among the best in Greece. The Naoussa production area is located on the southeastern slopes of Mount Velia; the vineyards of Amynteon and Goumenissa are generally planted at higher altitudes, up to 2,100 feet (650 m). The proximity of the sea and the altitude temper the hot summers, and relatively high rainfall gives the wines a certain finesse.

> **GRAPE VARIETIES** Xynomavro for the Naoussa region; Negosca and Xynomavro for Goumenissa and Amynteon.

> **SOIL** Limestone and clay-limestone hills, sometimes with steep slopes.

> **STYLE** Made from the Xinomavro variety, the reds are traditionally dark, structured, and tannic, for long keeping and on maturity offering a complex nose of spice, leather and undergrowth.

Colour: *Red and rosé.*

Serving temperature: *50 to 54°F (10 to 12°C) for rosés; 55 to 61°F (13 to 16°C) for reds.*

Ageing potential: *1 to 2 years for the rosés; 5 to 8 years for the reds.*

CÔTES-DE-MELITON OPAP

GREECE (HALKIDIKI)

One of the most popular Greek OPAPs, the tiny appellation of Côtes-de-Meliton (740 acres/300 ha) lies on slopes over-looking the sea from the centre of Halkidiki's three peninsulas. Red and white, the wines are often of exceptional quality and are prized by the best restaurants. They are also among the most expensive in Greece.

> **GRAPE VARIETIES** Limnio, Cabernet Sauvignon, and Cabernet Franc for the reds; Athiri, Roditis, and Assyrtiko for the whites.

> **SOIL** Steep limestone slopes.

> **STYLE** The dry reds are supple, full-bodied, and very fruity on the palate, developing spicy flavours with age. The dry whites are rich and full-bodied with toasty and citrus flavours, and good length.

Colour: *Red and white.*

Serving temperature: *50 to 54°F (10 to 12°C) for the whites; 55 to 61°F (13 to 16°C) for the reds.*

Ageing potential: *3 to 8 years for the white wines; 6 to 10 years for the reds.*

NEMEA OPAP

GREECE (PELOPONNESE)

The Nemea OPAP is the oldest and largest Greek appellation. It extends over the gentle hills along the Gulf of Corinth and the Saronic Gulf, north of the Peloponnese. Known as the 'blood of Hercules,' the wines are red. Yet there is name confusion with white wines made from Moschofilero, representing the main production of the same region. *Vin de pays* (TO) wine is also produced under the Corinth and Achaia appellations.

> **GRAPE VARIETIES** Agiorgitiko, supplemented with other varieties (15 to 20 per cent).

> **SOIL** Stony limestone hills.

> **STYLE** The wines of Nemea can be dry, medium dry, or sweet. The dry, deeply coloured reds are not very tannic, but they are powerful and full-bodied, with intense aromas of ripe fruit and spice.

Colour: *Red.*

Serving temperature: *59 to 63°F (15 to 17°C).*

Ageing potential: *5 to 10 years.*

Delights of Turkish wines

Only a small percentage of Turkey's grapes are used to make wine; and yet an increasing number of wines are of excellent quality. Doluca, a company based in Thrace, produces several million bottles a year from grapes from all over Turkey. It is known for one of its red wines, Doluca Özel Kav Kirmizi, made from grape varieties grown in the regions of Diyarbakir and Elazig in Kurdistan.The wine won top honours in a tasting organized in 2004 by the *Hürriyet* newspaper. Today, Kavaklidere is the country's top producer, owning an estate of almost 15,000 acres (600 hectares) and using grapes from different regions in Turkey. A modern company with good advisors, it produces a very large range of wines that demonstrate the diversity of Turkish grape varieties. It exports 20 per cent of its production.

LEBANON

BEKAA VALLEY WINES

Most good quality Lebanese wines are produced in the Zahleh region, at the middle of the Bekaa Valley. A number of new estates can be added to the well-known names of Château Ksara, Château Musar, and Château Kefraya. Most of these properties make wines in all three colours.

> **GRAPE VARIETIES** There are nearly 20 varieties in the Zahleh region, including international varieties such as Cabernet Sauvignon, Merlot, and Syrah for the red and rosé wines; Chardonnay, Sauvignon Blanc, and Muscat for the white wines.

> **SOIL** Predominantly loess.

> **STYLE** Powerful, tannic, fruity red wines with an excellent capacity to improve with age. The rosés are fruity and full-bodied. Some white wines develop great expression over many years, with flavours of spice and menthol.

Colour: *Red, white, and rosé.*

Serving temperature: *50 to 54°F (10 to 12°C) for the whites and rosés; 59 to 64°F (15 to 18°C) for the reds. (Decant fine reds 30 minutes before serving.)*

Ageing potential: *Up to 20 years (Château Musar).*

Rebirth of Meknès

French wine merchant Pierre Castel was the driving force in a restructuring of Moroccan vineyards in the area around Meknès during the mid-1990s. Located between the foothills of the Atlas Mountains to the south and Mount Zerhoun to the north, the vines grow in sandy and clay-limestone soil; the hot climate provides the right conditions for the grapes to thoroughly ripen. Beni M'Tir, Zerhoune, and Guerrouane are the three 'appellations of guaranteed origin' in which vast vineyards have been planted with Syrah, Cabernet Sauvignon, and Merlot. The Domaine Sahari and the Domaine Larroque (Beni M'Tir) are modern, supple reds that display a pleasant fruity quality.

UNITED STATES AND CANADA

UNITED STATES AND CANADA

Wine production in North America is concentrated along the west coast. The size of California's industry alone would make it the fourth-largest producer in the world, if it were an independent country. During the past 30 years, several US wines have developed to match the world's best. Canadian wine production is more modest in scale and concentrated in two provinces: Ontario (in the east) and British Columbia (in the west). In fact, 99 per cent of national production takes place in these two regions.

UNITED STATES

The USA is the fourth-largest producer of wine in the world, and it's now the leading wine consumer market. Although wine has been produced here for 300 years, the industry has only really developed since the Second World War. Production is concentrated in four states: California (accounting for about 90 per cent of the national total), Washington State, Oregon, and New York State. A young, modern, and dynamic industry, it has achieved a very high level of quality thanks to huge investment and outstanding research. However, the cultural position of wine in America is still very far from that in Europe: consumption per capita per year stands at just over 3 gallons (11.3 litres), only a quarter of French consumption, for example.

UNITED STATES STATISTICS

Vineyard area: 983,479 acres (398,000 ha)

Production: 213 million cases (19,200,000 hl)

Reds and rosés: 55%

Whites: 45%

(Wine Institute & OIV, 2006)

From the Vikings to the modern era

VINLAND, LAND OF THE WILD VINE. We will never know for sure if the Viking Leif Eriksson really did set foot on the North American east coast around 1000 AD, but his description of a country he called 'Vinland' is preserved in several medieval manuscripts, and it describes a green landscape dotted with wild vines.

EUROPEAN SETTLEMENT AND AN AGE OF EXPERIMENTATION. From the 16th century, when Europeans first colonized North America, they found several varieties of the *vitis* genus (*Vitis labrusca* and *Vitis riparia*), but no *Vitis vinifera*. Along the east coast, despite a damp climate, many attempts were made to produce wine from grapes of these indigenous varieties. The results had a rather gamey or animal character, sometimes described as 'foxy'.

> Napa Valley is the best-known American wine-producing region.

> In the USA, harvest work is most often mechanized.

Later, European settlers introduced different plantings of their own *Vitis vinifera* varieties. Over time, these crossed with local vine strains and resulted in new hybrids up and down the east coast. But all attempts to propagate pure varieties of *Vitis vinifera* failed. The cause of the failures, unknown at the time, was a native insect that would later devastate European vineyards, the aphid *Phylloxera vastatrix*.

VINEYARD EXPANSION. Despite difficulties, vineyards expanded from the central east coast to the southeast and across the south during the 18th and 19th centuries, starting with numerous hybrid varieties.

Early west-coast development was completely separate. During the 18th century, Spanish Franciscan monks had introduced several varieties of *Vitis vinifera* to Mexico and southern California; and the first winery was established near San Diego in 1769. From 1850 onwards, California became the scene of remarkable development. Successful plantings of large numbers of European varieties were coupled with a constant stream of migrants from the east coast. The appearance of *phylloxera*, 30 years later, curtailed this expansion only slightly, since the grafting of *vinifera* onto indigenous vine rootstocks had already been discovered in Europe.

FROM PROHIBITION TO THE MODERN ERA. We can only wonder what American winemaking would be like today if national Prohibition had not ruined a booming business. From 1920 to 1933, 'the manufacture, sale, or transportation of alcoholic beverages' was banned throughout the country, with the exception of wine for religious sacraments. The result was half a century of stagnation, and a shadow that still hangs over industry organization. However, a revival started in the 1960s. California wineries increased in number, and alongside high yields for mass production, a very dynamic sector developed. Driven by winemakers focused on quality, this excellent work has expanded beyond California and producer numbers are growing in almost every state.

American wine labels

Following the name of the producer, or a producer's brand, the grape variety remains the most common way to designate wines in North America. This approach was originally the idea of a wine merchant in New York City, Frank Schoonmaker, during the 1930s. It has gradually replaced the former practice of copying the names of famous European production regions such as Chablis, Burgundy, port, sherry, or Sauternes. For wines blended from several grape varieties, the use of a proprietary name (or that of a vineyard) is becoming increasingly popular – especially among high-end wines.

America's wine market

LEGISLATION. American wine law varies to some extent across the country. Each state sets its own laws regarding the distribution and consumption of alcoholic products. For example, even though Prohibition was repealed in 1933, some places (counties) still maintain a ban on alcohol sales. At the federal level, legislation on wine is governed by the TTB (Alcohol and Tobacco Tax and Trade Bureau). The scope of federal regulation includes approval of labelling, federal taxation, and designation of official production regions–called American Viticultural Areas or AVAs.

AMERICAN VITICULTURAL AREAS (AVAS). To help producers (and consumers) identify a wine's place of production, the government has established a system of certified viticultural areas, AVAs. This constitutes the US appellation system (*see also* p.100). Since recognition of the first AVAs, including the Napa Valley, in 1981, the number of appellations has exploded. Today there are more than 234, and there is a movement to better define more narrow *terroirs*: meaning AVAs within AVAs. With this said, their size is variable – ranging from a single valley to an entire county and sometimes even beyond.

Major wine-producing states

Vineyards exist in most US states, but production is not always significant. With that said, progress in terms of quality is being made everywhere. Three west coast states, California, Oregon, and Washington, produce the vast majority of US wine. California alone produces 90 per cent of the national total. In the east,

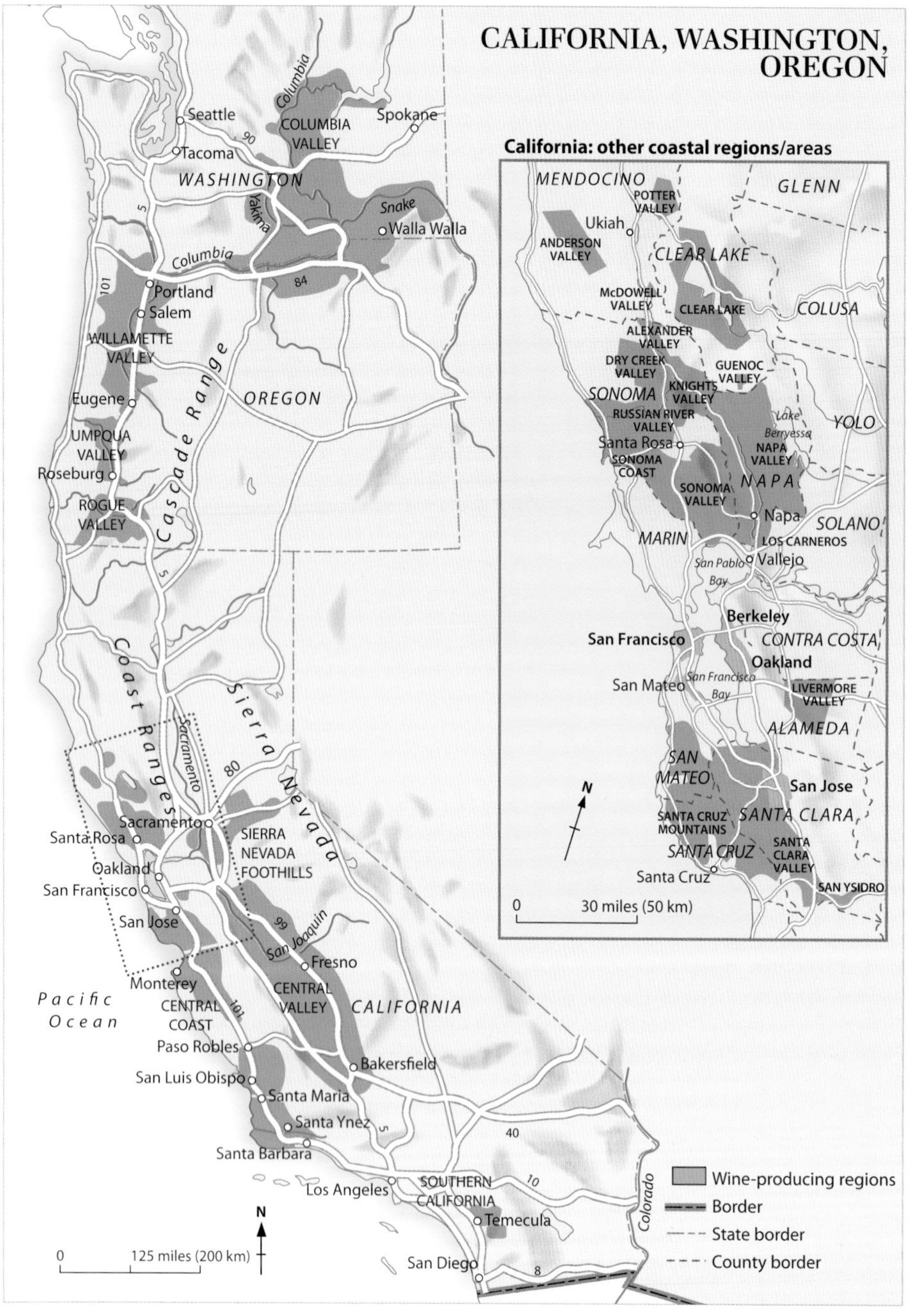

several states have production that deserves consideration, even if their wines are consumed only locally. This is the case for New York, Ohio, and Virginia. These states once cultivated only indigenous grapes, but they have benefited from the introduction of hybrid varieties such as Seyval and Baco, developed in France to resist *phylloxera* and other diseases. To the south, Texas and New Mexico have recently booming industries.

California

According to 2008 figures, there are some 612,821 acres (248,000 ha) planted with vines in California. The vineyards are scattered across more than 600 miles (1,000 km) from north to south. In terms of scale, if California were regarded as a single country, it would be the fourth-largest wine-producing region in the world and the biggest outside of Europe.

California's immense geographic area is matched by great climatic diversity, making it possible to develop all types and styles of wine. The most recognized areas are located in the counties of Sonoma and Napa to the north of San Francisco Bay; but great work is also done around Santa Cruz and Monterey, south of San Francisco, and in locations along the coast down toward Los Angeles.

NORTH OF SAN FRANCISCO. In Napa Valley (*see* p.443), the diversity of local conditions merits its division into districts or sub-appellations. Sonoma County is even larger and more complicated. The AVAs to the north and east, such as Alexander Valley and Dry Creek Valley (*see* p.442), are warmer and produce rich wines from Cabernet Sauvignon, Merlot, and Zinfandel. The Russian River Valley (*see* p.442), in the west, and Carneros (*see* p.446), to the south (straddling Sonoma and Napa), have a cooler climate and produce beautiful Chardonnays and Pinot Noirs. Elsewhere along the coast, wine production is less concentrated. Mendocino County to the north, on the Pacific Ocean, has become a centre for sparkling wines. Many Champagne producers find conditions here ideal for Pinot Noir and Chardonnay, the grapes that produce the base wines. Lake County, which is further inland and drier, is perfect for Cabernet Sauvignon and Sauvignon Blanc.

CENTRAL AND SOUTHERN COAST. The vineyards of central and southern California stretch from San Francisco to Santa Barbara, with a pocket further south toward San Diego. Monterey County produces Chardonnays and Pinot Noir in very dry, breezy conditions. Halfway between San Francisco and Los Angeles, the region of Paso Robles is very popular for its Rhône blends (Syrah, Grenache, and Mourvèdre in particular). In one of the most southerly vineyard areas of California, around

1976: The Judgment of Paris

At the time of America's bicentennial, the British wine merchant Steven Spurrier organized a blind tasting in Paris of some great French and California wines. To everyone's amazement, the California wines won in every category (notably reds from Cabernet Sauvignon, and whites from Chardonnay), beating some of the biggest names from Burgundy and Bordeaux! This now-famous tasting confirmed the quality of California wines to the world. Some felt that the victors would not stand the test of time; but in two 'rematches' in 1986 and 2006, with the same vintages from the same producers, the California wines retained their advantage.

Mexico

Mexico is the oldest wine-producing country in the Americas: from 1521, early settlers were planting vines. Commercially sustainable viticulture has developed since the 1960s. Mexican vineyards total approximately 74,132 acres (30,000 ha), but only 20 per cent are destined for wine production; the rest provide table grapes or go to distillation. The most significant volumes are produced in seven Mexican provinces. The best-known wines come from the north, in Baja California, which accounts for 90 per cent of the country's wine production. This territory is a southern continuation of the US state with the same name, just across the border. Baja's dry climate is very conducive to growing vines, but irrigation is necessary. The varieties planted are the common international ones (Cabernet Sauvignon, Merlot, Malbec, and Syrah for reds; Chardonnay and Sauvignon Blanc for whites); but there are also other varieties such as Zinfandel, Nebbiolo, Barbera, Tempranillo, and Petite Sirah for reds, and Palomino, Colombard, and Chenin Blanc for whites.

> Vineyards and orchards in the Yakima Valley of Washington State.

Santa Barbara and Santa Ynez, the cool ocean air seeps through the mountains, allowing beautiful Pinot Noir and Chardonnay to be produced.

CENTRAL VALLEY AND MASS PRODUCTION. Inland and away from maritime influences, is the vast Central Valley – around the state capital, Sacramento. This hot and dry region produces mainly entry-level wines, except in the areas around Lodi and in the Sierra foothills. There, some of the oldest vineyards in California are capable of producing great wines.

Washington

Anchoring the Pacific Northwest, Washington State is the second-largest wine producer in the country, with 40,000 acres (16,200 ha) of vineyards. Inland valleys (which, in addition to grapes, grow many fruits) are sheltered from the cold, damp weather of the coast by the Cascade Mountains. This protection is complete enough that the skies are largely cloudless and the landscape is semi-desert; so irrigation is drawn from the vast Columbia River system.

The expansion of the wine industry in Washington has been staggering since 1970, and the number of wineries has increased from just a handful to more than 890 today. Officially, 13 AVAs have been defined. The state produces a range of rather fruity white wines (from Chardonnay, Riesling, and Pinot Gris) as well as excellent reds whose style ranges from delicate to powerful, mostly from Bordeaux grape varieties but also from Syrah.

Oregon

Set between Washington and California, the Oregon industry has recently realized its potential for fine wine. The first modern plantings date from the 1960s, with a few pioneers coming from California in search of cooler conditions to produce Chardonnay

> Trimming work in the Rogue Valley of southern Oregon.

Other wine-producing states

While wine is made in almost all US states, production remains limited and intended for local consumption. In addition, legislation in several states bans wine from being shipped beyond their borders, which hardly encourages development. There are a growing number of exceptions, though, especially Texas and Virginia.

Like the state of New York, Texas and Virginia have districts growing *Vitis vinifera*. Texas continues a wine history started by Spanish missionaries from Mexico. It also was a Texan – a botanist called Munson – who helped save the European wine industry from *phylloxera* by shipping native American varieties for grafting during replanting efforts in the 1880s.

There are more than 350 wineries in Texas working about 3,954 acres (1,600 ha) of vineyards. The numbers have been growing at a rapid clip since the beginning of the 21st century, making this the fifth-largest wine-producing state in the country. Most of the vineyards are located in upland areas in the centre and west, where the climate is less humid and the nights cooler. Texas has eight AVAs. As for Virginia, it is the second-largest wine-producing state on the east coast. There are six AVAs and several other districts planted with native varieties, hybrids, and *Vitis vinifera*.

and Pinot Noir. Since then, Pinot Noir has carved a place for itself in the Willamette Valley.

Over 40 years, the region has earned a great reputation for its work with this variety, which thrives in the cooler, coastal weather. The same is true for regional white wines (especially Pinot Gris). There are dozens of other varieties planted Oregon, often on an experimental basis.

Total production here is not large (from 20,000 acres), but there are more than 600 active wineries, and as many as 18 approved AVAs.

New York

The state of New York is the third-largest wine producer in the US (including both *vinifera* or hybrid varieties). Plantings stretch between Long Island and the Great Lakes. This is a region where many native North American varieties and hybrids thrive, some of which are tried and tested: Aurora, Cayuga, and Seyval for white wines, and Baco Noir or Catawba for reds. Total production is even more significant when considering the amount of wine (and juice) produced from *Vitis labrusca* varieties, such as Concord).

New York State's production areas border the Canadian province of Ontario, and the regions share some climatic similarities, especially around the Niagara-on-the-Lake area (*see next page*). The Finger Lakes district is the largest production area in New York; and its temperate climate, the result of these bodies of water, is conducive to vine cultivation, including *Vitis vinifera* varieties such as Riesling. Elsewhere, the ability of vines to withstand harsh winters is the main factor in selection.

DID YOU KNOW...?

In the United States, vineyard regions are classified according to a system developed by scientists Maynard Amerine and A. J. Winkler.
Their work was based on the research of a 19th-century French scientist, A. P. de Candolle, who found that vines begin to grow each spring after the air temperature averages 50°F (10°C). In 1944, Winkler and Amerine, working at the University of California-Davis, drew up a regional climatic classification based on the total number of degrees (above 50°F) accumulated during the seven months that the vine grows. It is sometimes criticized for its oversimplification, but the system is widely used in reference material on the subject. Thus, Level I regions have less than 2,500 'degree-days' per season; those at Level II, between 2,501 and 3,000 degree-days, those at Level III, between 3,001 and 3,500 degree-days, those at Level IV, between 3,501 and 4,000 degree-days; and those at Level V accumulate more than 4,000 degree-days. As a guide, the average Bordeaux climate is considered to be around Levels II or III.

CANADA

Compared with the USA's wine industry, Canada's work is very modest in scale. Two provinces, Ontario and British Columbia, account for 99 per cent of production. A very limited quantity also comes from other provinces, such as Quebec. Wine production on a commercial scale is a recent occurrence here for three main reasons: the difficulty of adapting *Vitis vinifera* varieties to a harsh climate; a puritanical attitude that severely controlled (when it did not entirely prohibit) production and consumption of alcohol; and, as a consequence, a delay in the exploration and development of sites suitable for *Vitis vinifera* or quality hybrids.

CANADA STATISTICS

Vineyard area: 30,147 acres (12,200 ha)

Production: 16.6 million cases (1,500,000 hl)

Whites: 55%

Reds and rosés: 45%

(Canadian Vintners Association 2015)

Recent start and rapid expansion

Modern Canadian viticulture started in Ontario during the 1950s, as a result of experiments by Brights Wines with Riesling and Chardonnay. But it was not until the foundation of Inniskillin Wines in Niagara-on-the-Lake, southern Ontario – in 1974 by Donald Ziraldo and Karl Kaiser – that Canada took its place in world wine production. Using techniques of cultivation and vinification from his native Austria, Kaiser demonstrated the remarkable possibilities for Ontario's production of ice wine, especially from hybrids such as Seyval. Others have followed suit, and ice wine is now a speciality of the region, and widely exported. In 1979, the establishment of Sumac Ridge Winery in the Okanagan Valley marked the starting point for British Columbia's commercial wine industry. Now a quality label, the Vintners Quality Alliance (VQA), brings together the best producers and insists on production from *Vitis vinifera* or the finest hybrids (*see* p.102).

Niagara-on-the-Lake and Okanagan Valley

Separated by thousands of miles, these two regions produce almost all of Canada's wines. While Niagara specializes in ice wine, it also produces good quality dry whites from Riesling, Chardonnay, and hybrid grape varieties. In addition, the local market tends to support Canadian white wines over imported ones. With the gradual development of the Okanagan Valley, it's clear that the warmer, drier climate and rugged terrain are capable of producing fine red wines. Overall, the country's production has increased dramatically – there has some 500 wineries, 10 times more than 20 years ago!

Ice wine: Canada's frozen nectar

Ice wine is a rare and very special product, of which Canada is the world's largest source. The grapes are left on the vine long after the leaves fall, and until bitter cold arrives in December or January. As a result of deep freezing, there is a kind of dehydration that causes a high concentration of all components of the berry: sugars, acids, and other solids. The amount of juice available at the time of harvesting is no more than 5 to 10 per cent of a normal harvest. These precious grapes are picked at night in temperatures around 14°F (–10°C) in order to ensure that the berries are still frozen for the press. After pressing, the thick and very sweet juice is fermented very slowly for several months, producing a white wine or, more rarely, a red, that is relatively low in alcohol (between 10 and 12% ABV), but very rich in sugar and full of flavour. Ice wine is produced in Quebec and British Columbia, but especially in Ontario, in the Niagara-on-the-Lake region. The technique for creating ice wine was introduced for the first time in 1980 by Karl Kaiser, co-founder of the Inniskillin Winery. The importance of this production to Canada is such that the term 'Icewine' has been trademarked.

> In the Okanagan Valley, the vines are sprayed with water to form a layer of ice to protect the plants against frost.

Leading USA and Canada wineries

Although almost every US state produces wine, only four of them – California, Washington, Oregon, and New York – produce any significant volume that is regularly consumed beyond their borders. California, whose most important sub-regions are detailed here, accounts for about 90 per cent of the national total. As for Canada, its production is small, but growing and improving in quality.

WASHINGTON STATE

The second-largest wine region after California, Washington dominates production in the Pacific Northwest. Commercial winemaking is only 45 years old here, but the rapid expansion of vineyard and winery numbers has been unrelenting. All key growing areas are located inland, 150 miles (250 km) from the coast. The Cascade Mountains shelter them from wet weather that comes from the ocean, which means a sunny, dry climate. Irrigation is needed almost everywhere. You might be surprised to discover that the latitude of this region is equivalent to the median between Bordeaux and Burgundy. The continental conditions produce large temperature variations between summer and winter, and even between day and night. The colour and intensity of flavours in the wines are often impressive. Prestigious foreign investors, such as Antinori (Italy) and Loosen (Germany), have been convinced by the potential of this region.

> **PRODUCTION AREAS** (AVAs) Columbia Valley, Horse Heaven Hills, Red Mountain, Wahluke Slope, Walla Walla Valley, Yakima Valley, and others.

> **GRAPE VARIETIES** For red: Merlot, Cabernet Sauvignon, Syrah, Malbec, and others; for white: Chardonnay, Riesling, Sauvignon Blanc, Sémillon, Pinot Gris, and others.

> **SOIL** Loess and sandy, alluvial soil on a bed of volcanic basalt.

> **STYLE** Reds and whites are produced in equal numbers, and both generally display great intensity of flavour. Some may achieve considerable power or finesse (or both).

> **NOTABLE PRODUCERS** Barnard Griffin, Cayuse, Château Ste Michelle, Columbia Crest, DeLille, L'Ecole No41, Hogue Cellars, K Vintners, Leonetti, Milbrandt Vineyards, Quilceda Creek, Andrew Will, and Woodward Canyon.

OREGON

The fourth-largest wine-producing state in America, Oregon is a region of very small producers. Its composition is a reflection of its topography, with numerous valleys divided into artisanal plots. That scale, and the fact that it works with a cooler, wetter climate than its two neighbours, California and Washington, explains why Oregon has developed more slowly. The exact location of plots is often crucial in bringing the grapes to maturity. Despite the cool climate, summer drought is common in inland valleys. Oregon has established its reputation largely with Pinot Noir. In fact, the Burgundy producer Drouhin has established an estate here in the Willamette Valley.

> **PRODUCTION AREAS** (AVAs) Applegate Valley, Rogue Valley, Snake River Valley, Umpqua Valley, Willamette Valley (with six sub-AVAs), as well as several appellations that extend into Washington (including Walla Walla Valley).

> **GRAPE VARIETIES** For red: Pinot Noir and Syrah; for white: Chardonnay, Pinot Gris, and Riesling.

> **SOIL** Mixed sedimentary or fractured volcanic basalt.

> **STYLE** These wines reflect their cool climate. Both whites and reds tend toward finesse rather than power.

> **NOTABLE PRODUCERS** Adelsheim, Amity, Argyle, Beaux Frères, Brick House, Cristom, Domaine Drouhin, Domaine Serene, Eyrie Vineyards, King Estate, Lemelson.

MENDOCINO COUNTY AND LAKE COUNTY

CALIFORNIA

In addition to Anderson Valley, several AVAs cover this vast stretch of northern California. But they sometimes overlap, so that they are not easily differentiated. In Mendocino, the climate varies from maritime to almost continental over a short distance. On the Winkler scale, this climate is generally part of Level III (*see box* p.438). The best vineyards are located on hillsides. The upper part of Lake County is in Level II, that is to say that the climate is much cooler because of the altitude; the lower part, such as Guenoc Valley, enjoys a climate comparable to Mendocino.

> **GRAPE VARIETIES** For red: Pinot Noir, Cabernet Sauvignon, Merlot, and Zinfandel; for white: Chardonnay and Sauvignon Blanc.

> **SOIL** Highly variable. Sometimes volcanic, sometimes schist, as well as alluvial red clay.

> **STYLE** As variable as the exposures and soils, ranging from fresh to powerful.

> **NOTABLE PRODUCERS** Fetzer, Kendall-Jackson, Navarro, McDowell Valley Vineyards, Parducci, and Scharffenberger.

Three Mendocino County estates

- **Fetzer (Mendocino).** With its base and main vineyards in Mendocino, Fetzer is a pioneer of large-scale organic viticulture for the country. It was part of a large corporate spirits group (Brown-Forman) until early 2011, but is now part of Chile's Concho y Toro wine group.
- **Kendall-Jackson (Anderson Valley).** Like many large producers in California, 'K-J' has vineyards in several regions and produces a wide range of wines. Its vineyards in Lake County are the historic home of this company, founded in 1974 by Jess Jackson, a former lawyer from San Francisco. Its wines are well made, highly consistent, and have a very accessible style.
- **Roederer Estate (Anderson Valley).** Working here since 1982, this fine Champagne house focuses on the production of sparkling wines made from Pinot Noir and Chardonnay grown exclusively in its own vineyards. Its sparkling wines are among the finest in the United States.

ANDERSON VALLEY

CALIFORNIA (MENDOCINO COUNTY)

Located in Mendocino County, about 100 miles/160 km north of San Francisco, this narrow valley (rarely more than a mile wide) is sandwiched between two mountain ranges. This produces significant climatic differences between the growing areas at the bottom of the valley (which are cooler and misty), and those at higher altitudes (above the line of mist and sunnier). Visitors to the bottom of the valley would never suspect that red grapes could reach such an excellent level of maturity above them.

> **GRAPE VARIETIES** For red: primarily Pinot Noir; for white: mainly Chardonnay, Gewurztraminer, and Riesling

> **SOIL** Alluvial, clay and gravel soil in the valley; less fertile and more acidic soils on the hillsides.

> **STYLE** Quite fine and fresh, just like the climate; but the precise location of the vineyard may result in large variations in style.

> **NOTABLE PRODUCERS** Greenwood Ridge, Kendall-Jackson, Navarro, Roederer Estate, and Scharffenberger (sparkling wines).

RUSSIAN RIVER VALLEY

CALIFORNIA (SONOMA COUNTY)

This beautiful valley runs east to west, and lies southwest of the fabulous tourist town of Healdsburg. As a result of its orientation to the Pacific, the climate is fresh and cool, especially at the western end, where it is often misty. The area is well suited to Chardonnay and Pinot Noir, which are used to produce high quality sparkling or still wines. Total plantings are about 15,000 acres (6,000 ha), but they are expanding.

> **GRAPE VARIETIES** For red: Pinot Noir (30 per cent of plantings), Zinfandel, Merlot, and Cabernet Sauvignon; for white: Chardonnay (40 per cent of plantings) and Sauvignon Blanc.

> **SOIL** In general, they are Franciscan (a mixture of sandstone and schist) and well drained. But there are variations in certain areas, such as Chalk Hill, where they are sandy and lighter.

> **STYLE** The cool climate enables producers to make fine and intense Chardonnay, as well as notable Pinot Noirs.

> **NOTABLE PRODUCERS** DeLoach, Ferrari-Carano, Gary Farrell, Hartford Family, Iron Horse, J Vineyards, Kistler, Marimar Estate, Rocchioli, Sonoma-Cutrer, and Williams Selyem.

ALEXANDER VALLEY

CALIFORNIA (SONOMA COUNTY)

Located in northern Sonoma County, with the town of Healdsburg at its southern tip, Alexander Valley lies east of Russian River and runs parallel to the coast. The vineyard (just over 15,000 acres/ 6,000 ha) lies between the coastal zone and the Mayacamas Mountains, which separate Napa from Sonoma. The climate is warmer and more diverse than the Russian River Valley. Almost all key varieties can be matured here, and the range is wide. The neighbouring Dry Creek Valley hosts some of the oldest and most sought-after Zinfandel vines in the state of California.

> **GRAPE VARIETIES** For red: Cabernet Sauvignon, Zinfandel, and Merlot; for white: Chardonnay, Sauvignon Blanc, and Viognier.

> **SOIL** Alluvium with a variable amount of gravel, depending on the area; the hillsides have very diverse soils.

> **STYLE** Given the diversity of local climates and grape varieties, it is difficult to identify a dominant style for this region. Cabernet Sauvignon dominates Alexander Valley, but Dry Creek is famous for its Zinfandels, often produced from very old vines.

> **NOTABLE PRODUCERS** Clos du Bois, Coppola, Gallo Family, Hanna, Jordan, Ridge (Lytton Springs and Geyserville), Rodney Strong, Seghesio, Silver Oak, Simi, Trentadue, and Verité.

Two Sonoma County estates

- **Seghesio (Alexander Valley).** This family business could by itself tell the history of Sonoma County wine. The Seghesios came from Italy during the 19th century, and initially practiced cooperative and mixed farming before becoming specialists in wine production. The current generation has changed its focus by concentrating on the production of wines from their own vineyards. Some of them, such as the concentrated and very juicy Zinfandels, are among the best in Sonoma County.

- **Sonoma-Cutrer (Russian River).** Specializing in two grape varieties – Chardonnay and Pinot Noir – this estate has long been responsible for one of the best California Chardonnays, a wine called 'Les Pierres'. All its wines are capable of great longevity.

SONOMA VALLEY

CALIFORNIA (SONOMA COUNTY)

Sonoma Valley is located north of San Francisco Bay and west of Napa. Its topography is very diverse. Unlike Napa, which is almost entirely dedicated to viticulture, Sonoma is fragmented with vineyards alongside other forms of agriculture. Yet its wine production began in the middle of the 19th century (before the first plantings in Napa). The sub-region of Sonoma Mountain is interesting because of the cool air at night and sunshine by day that results from its altitude.

> **GRAPE VARIETIES** For red: Cabernet Sauvignon, Merlot, Pinot Noir, Syrah, and certainly Zinfandel; for white: Chardonnay, Sauvignon Blanc, and Semillon.

> **SOIL** In the valley, Franciscan soils, a mixture of sandstone, schist, and stones that have come down from the mountains; volcanic soils or metamorphic rocks in the hills.

> **STYLE** The Cabernets and Zinfandels from Sonoma Mountain combine power and finesse. Styles in the valley are more variable and depend on their proximity to or distance from San Francisco Bay.

> **NOTABLE PRODUCERS** Cline, Gundlach Bundschu, Hanzell, Kenwood, Matanzas Creek, and Ravenswood.

NAPA VALLEY

CALIFORNIA (NAPA COUNTY)

While Napa accounts for only four per cent of the wine produced in California, this valley – 37 miles (60 km) long and no more than four miles (6 km) wide – is for many a symbol in itself of California wine. It is separated from Sonoma to the west by the Mayacamas Mountains. The only access to the effects of the ocean lies at its southern end, where it opens onto San Francisco Bay. This creates differences in climate between the south (which is cool) and the north end of the valley around Calistoga (which is very warm). Napa is fully enclosed by mountains to the west and east. South of Napa, the Carneros region (*see* p.558), which has its own AVA, extends into Sonoma Valley. Note that Napa Valley encompasses many much smaller AVAs, such as Calistoga, Rutherford, Stag's Leap, Mount Veeder, Howell Mountain, and Oakville. Though if their name appears on the label, it must be overtly associated with Napa.

> **GRAPE VARIETIES** For red: Cabernet Sauvignon, Merlot, Cabernet Franc, Zinfandel, and Sangiovese; for white: Chardonnay and Sauvignon Blanc.

> **SOIL** More than 30 soil types have been identified: alluvium with varying gravel content in the valley; alluvial clays and stony, sometimes volcanic, soils on hillsides and in the northern valley.

> **STYLE** A very full body and rich flavours are the benchmark for Cabernet Sauvignon or Merlot from Napa; though this is of course dependent on the location of the vineyard, the diversity of grape varieties, and the choices of the producer.

> **NOTABLE PRODUCERS** Beringer, Cakebread, Caymus, Château Montelena, Clos Pegase, Clos du Val, Corison, Diamond Creek, Freemark Abbey, Harlan, Heitz, Hess Collection, Joseph Phelps, Newton, Opus One, Robert Mondavi, Rubicon, Schramsberg (sparkling), Shafer, Stag's Leap Wine Cellars, and Storybook Mountain.

Selected Napa Valley wineries

- **Robert Mondavi.** Robert Mondavi died in 2008, but the winery that bears his name remains a tribute to the man who has probably done more than anyone else to make Napa one of the best wine regions in the world (*see also* pp.556-7). The specialities of the estate are Cabernet Sauvignons and a very good Sauvignon Blanc called 'Fumé Blanc'.

- **Clos du Val.** This estate, established by businessman John Goelet during the 1970s, has followed the philosophy of its director, Frenchman Bernard Portet, since its inception. The wines are often lower in alcohol and lighter in extract than the typical Napa style, but age well.

- **Diamond Creek.** This is one of the pioneers of vineyard block-based vinification (which involves producing wines separately from the grapes in each plot). The wines thus bear the names of their parent sites: Red Rock Terrace, Gravelly Meadow, Winery Lake, and Volcanic Hill. Wines of great intensity and power.

- **Joseph Phelps.** This estate is a pioneer in producing Rhône varieties: Syrah, Grenache, Mourvèdre, and Viognier. Its Cabernet Backus and Bordeaux blend Insignia rank it as one of the top producers in Napa.

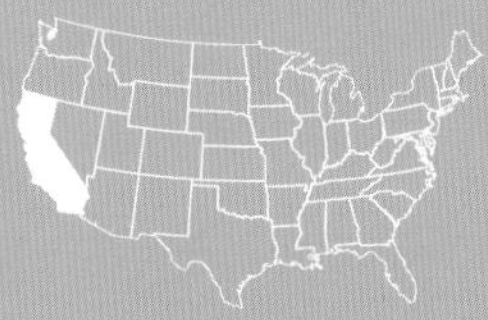

California

OPUS ONE
A GREAT CALIFORNIAN WINE

Opus One is one of the newest legendary wines and is considered one of the best from the New World. It was produced from a magnificent Californian terroir and the alliance of two figures with strong convictions: the Bordeaux baron Philippe de Rothschild and the American Robert Mondavi.

It is now generally accepted that the land to the north of San Francisco, particularly in the Napa Valley, has remarkable *terroirs* for wine production. For decades, many wines produced here have achieved exceptional quality. And this has been confirmed by several blind tastings, the most famous being in 1976, known ever since as the 'Judgment of Paris' (*see* p.548.)

A French Baron and an American winemaker

Philippe de Rothschild will be long remembered as the head of Château Mouton Rothschild. He used his talent and tenacity to ensure that its wine, originally classified as *deuxième cru*, was raised to *premier cru* status in 1973, the only change in the 1855 classification of the Médoc since the beginning. His daughter, Baroness Philippine de Rothschild, took over with the same enthusiasm. For his part, Robert Mondavi had been the leader of California wineries since the mid-1960s. He had proved that it was possible to make great wines in the region, given sufficient determination. He was both obstinate and modest and never gave up on what he called his 'mission'. His sons also followed this same path.

In 1970, these two men met in Hawaii, and they quickly understood each other. So in 1978, Robert Mondavi went to see the baron, and the two men agreed to create a vineyard together in California. In 1979, the cellar master of Mouton went to the Napa Valley and started 'creating' a new wine using the methods from Château Mouton Rothschild.

Birth of an estate

The project was officially announced in 1980, to general amazement. In 1983, sites were chosen in Napa Valley of *terroirs* that met the requirements of both parties. They then thought about a name that would be easy to remember and pronounce on both sides of the Atlantic. The baron, who was a great music lover, suggested 'Opus' and, since this was the first wine of its kind, the name 'Opus One' was finally settled on.

In 1984, two vintages were presented to the public: the 1979 and the 1980. They were an immediate success and were critically acclaimed by the press and by trade experts. Of course, when two such talents work together in a high-quality *terroir* some wonderful bottles of wine are only to be expected.

Since 1991, spectacular new wine cellars have been built to produce and house the wine. And these facilities meet a single criterion: the very best storage for quality wine of this kind.

Bordeaux varieties

As always, it begins with the vine. The majority grape is Cabernet Sauvignon, which produces great results in Napa. Cabernet Franc and Merlot are also represented, and have recently been rounded off with some Petit Verdot and Malbec. All of these varieties originate in Bordeaux and are ultimately blended in varying proportions depending on the vintage. The harvests are handled gently, and are sometimes even carried out at night to take advantage of the cool temperatures. Upon arrival at the estate, the grapes are carefully sorted and all traces of rot or leaves are manually removed.

Careful production

After fermentation, in order to maximize extraction of colour and flavour, the maceration period can last for more than 40 days. The wine is then put into new French oak barrels, where it will spend 17 to 20 months. All of these processes are traditional and lightly handled. For example, when it comes to clarifying the wine, filtration is not used. Instead, the old method of egg white fining is employed: mixed with wine, the egg whites coagulate and carry all fine particles still in suspension to the bottom of the barrel.

Wine for ageing

After three decades of vintages, all successful, Opus One has proven its ability to age. Its development in bottle lasts several years, and its peak can be reached after 20 to 30 years. It's worth decanting this wine two hours before serving. Served at 61°F (16°C), it goes perfectly with red meats and game birds. Rich, dense, and full of flavour, the palate has fine, very ripe tannins, while retaining harmony and genuine nobility.

ert Mondavi
n May 2008.

CARNEROS

CALIFORNIA (NAPA COUNTY)

Carneros is the area overlapping the southern ends of Napa Valley and Sonoma. It occupies the southern foothills of the Mayacamas Mountains, which separate these two valleys. The climate is much cooler than in most of Napa or Sonoma, because it is entirely open to the effect of the ocean via San Francisco Bay. Located in the main corridor that conveys maritime air flows to the east, Carneros is also a very windy area. These conditions have made it a fairly well-defined AVA, and very conducive to producing wines whose character is based mainly on freshness, including white and sparkling wines. Many of the finest Chardonnays come from Carneros.

> **GRAPE VARIETIES** For red: Pinot Noir as well as Merlot, and Syrah; for white: Chardonnay.

> **SOIL** Very shallow, and not particularly fertile. A hard clay subsoil on limestone bedrock. In some places, there are sedimentary pockets rich in manganese.

> **STYLE** The wines are fine and sometimes quite lively. The Chardonnays here have a style that is distinct from those produced elsewhere in California. Fine Pinot Noirs are also produced here.

> **NOTABLE PRODUCERS** For sparkling wines: Domaine Carneros (Taittinger) and Gloria Ferrer (Freixenet); for still wines: Acacia, Buena Vista, Cuvaison, Cline, Saintsbury, and Schug. Note: several good producers located elsewhere include Carneros wines in their line.

Selected Carneros wineries

- **Buena Vista.** This winery was one of the first in California, established in 1857 by Agoston Haraszthy, a Hungarian immigrant. After a bleak period, Buena Vista was re-created in 1979. In recent years, the wines have regained the level required for an estate with such a venerable reputation.

- **Cline Cellars.** In Carneros, which focuses mainly on Chardonnay and Pinot Noir, Cline (based in Sonoma) is an atypical producer. It's known primarily for its pioneering work with Mediterranean grape varieties (Mourvèdre, Barbera, and Carignan), and for wonderful Zinfandel wines.

- **Gloria Ferrer.** This estate, which is owned by the Catalan cava producer Freixenet, is known for its sparkling wines. They are rich but fresh, and among the finest in California. It also produces a range of still wines.

- **Schug.** Originally from Germany, Walter Schug gained professional experiences with well-known California producers (Gallo, Joseph Phelps) and then chose to specialize in artisan wines, produced in a cool climate. His lively and elegant Chardonnays are typical of the style of Carneros.

SANTA CRUZ MOUNTAINS

CALIFORNIA (SAN FRANCISCO BAY)

This mountainous region south of San Francisco can be spectacular. Bisected by the San Andreas Fault (which threatens the entire California coast with earthquakes), it appears to be perched between two worlds: the Pacific is on one side, and on the other is one of the biggest high-tech centres in the world, Silicon Valley. Local climates depend on the altitude and aspect of each vineyard, but overall it is generally cooler than Napa or Sonoma. Most of the vineyards are located above the line of sea mist, which, coupled with cool nights due to altitude, leads to a relatively prolonged ripening of the grapes.

> **GRAPE VARIETIES** For red: Cabernet Sauvignon, Pinot Noir, Merlot, Zinfandel, and Syrah; for white: Chardonnay, Marsanne, and Roussanne.

> **SOIL** Mainly schist, formed by the decomposition of bedrock. The soils are very thin and infertile. They are specific to this region.

> **STYLE** This depends largely on the altitude and exposure of the vines. Some estates, such as Ridge, are among the highest vineyards in California. The alcohol content is lower than for wines from Napa, further north.

> **NOTABLE PRODUCERS** Ahlgren, Bargetto, Bonny Doon, David Bruce, Mount Eden, and Ridge.

Two Santa Cruz estates

- **Bonny Doon.** Few characters in the wine world are as original as Randall Grahm. Philosophical or humorous references abound in the names he gives his wines, and that is just the tip of the iceberg! He has been one of the pioneers of varietal diversification, first using Rhône varieties and then switching to Italian varieties in response to a saturation of Cabernet and Chardonnay. Consequently, the style of its wines mirrors some of those produced in Italy or the Rhône.
- **Ridge.** With its historic base in Montebello, at the top of a mountain, Ridge Vineyards is one of the best wine producers in California and the world. Its Montebello 1973 vintage (a Bordeaux blend) triumphed at the last 'rematch' of the 'Judgment of Paris', after finishing third in the first version in 1976 (*see box* p.548). Ridge wines are often noted for their very reasonable level of alcohol and their ability to age well. This winery, which dates from the 19th century, owes its success to Paul Draper (*see also* p.31), who has been its chief winemaker for 40 years.

> Vineyards in Monterey County.

MONTEREY

CALIFORNIA (CENTRAL COAST)

The Monterey region is a southern extension of the Santa Cruz area. Its climate is cool, and largely influenced by the ocean and nearly constant winds. It includes some smaller AVAs, such as Carmel Valley and Arroyo Seco. At the centre of the region, much of the substantial production of the Salinas Valley is used to make entry-level wines for the broader wine industry. But sheltered areas and those at altitude, like Arroyo, Chalone (an appellation consisting of a single producer!), or the Santa Lucia Highlands, are capable of excellent work with Chardonnay and Pinot Noir.

> **GRAPE VARIETIES** For red: Pinot Noir; for white: Chardonnay, Riesling, Sauvignon Blanc, and Gewurztraminer.

> **SOIL** There are light soils of alluvium in the valley, and more complex soils often consisting of limestone in the hills, such as the Santa Lucia Highlands.

> **STYLE** Interesting, lively, and fresh wines, which have a great deal of flavour, come from higher altitude areas.

> **NOTABLE PRODUCERS** Chalone, Hahn, J Lohr, Jekel, Lockwood, and Morgan.

CALIFORNIA (CENTRAL COAST)

PASO ROBLES TO SANTA YNEZ

This region, stretching from Monterey in the north to Santa Barbara in the south, includes some very promising AVAs. Most of them are only recently established, but plantings are increasing. Not only is land much less expensive than in Napa, but the climate is more varied, and indeed sometimes cooler. Vineyards are generally located in valleys at low altitude and open to the Pacific. Local climatic conditions permit a wide range of grape varieties to be grown.

> **GRAPE VARIETIES** For red: Pinot Noir, Syrah, Mourvèdre, and Grenache; for white: Chardonnay, Marsanne, Viognier, Sauvignon Blanc, and Pinot Blanc.

> **SOIL** Ancient seabeds with varying limestone content and rather neutral (pH 7). Also clay soil, sandy soil, and alluvium.

> **STYLE** Paso Robles specializes in Rhône grape varieties (Syrah, Grenache, Mourvèdre, and so on). In Santa Ynez and Santa Maria, where the climate is similar to Burgundy, some very fine Chardonnays are produced without heaviness of any kind.

> **NOTABLE PRODUCERS** Alban, Au Bon Climat, Byron, Edna Valley Vineyards, Fess Parker, Firestone, Qupé, Sanford, and Tablas Creek.

Two Central Coast estates

- **Au Bon Climat (Santa Barbara).** The name of this estate clearly indicates inspiration from Burgundy. Indeed, Jim Clendenen, its owner, is one of the staunchest defenders of the concept of *terroir* in California. Au Bon Climat is a specialist in Pinot Noir and Chardonnay from vineyards in cool areas, including its own vineyard at Bien Nacido in the Santa Maria AVA.
- **Tablas Creek (Paso Robles).** Tablas Creek is a joint venture between the Perrin family, owners of the famous Château de Beaucastel in Châteauneuf-du-Pape, and its import partner in the United States, Robert Haas. In a beautiful region of undulating terrain, it sits behind the hill that shelters it from the ocean and along a stream that gives it its name. The climate is conducive to Rhône grape varieties, which this estate has made its particular speciality.

CALIFORNIA (CENTRAL VALLEY)

LODI, SIERRA FOOTHILLS, EL DORADO, AND THE REST OF CENTRAL VALLEY

Central Valley extends 400 miles (640 km) from the foothills of Mt Shasta in the north to Bakersfield (around 60 miles/100 km from Los Angeles) in the south. In terms of volume, it is by far the most productive region in California. It is there that future wine giants settled from the 1920s onward, including Gallo (still under family control), which became the largest wine producer in the world. But aside from this industrial-scale production, there has been development of smaller sub-regions in certain parts of the mountains and hills surrounding the valley. The vineyards of Lodi, the Sierra Foothills, and El Dorado, which have their own AVAs, can produce quality wines from some of the oldest vineyards on the continent, mainly Zinfandel.

> **GRAPE VARIETIES** For red: Zinfandel, Syrah, Cabernet Sauvignon, and Sangiovese; for white: Chardonnay, Chenin Blanc, and Sauvignon Blanc.

> **SOIL** Alluvium, or at times sandy, soils in the valley; rather varied and volcanic soils on the slopes.

> **STYLE** A sharp contrast exists between the wines of the valley, which are generally ordinary, and less numerous pockets of vineyards at altitude, which are often concentrated and fine.

> **NOTABLE PRODUCERS** Amador, Gallo, Michael David, and Terre Rouge.

OKANAGAN VALLEY

CANADA (BRITISH COLUMBIA)

British Columbia now has about 9,637 acres (3,900 ha) of vineyards and is the second-largest wine-producing region of Canada, after Ontario and the Niagara-on-the-Lake region. Okanagan Valley is located inland, about 185 miles (300 km) east of Vancouver. In terms of climate, it forms a northern extension of the wine regions of Washington State, just over the border. The southern part of this long valley is semi-desert because the Cascade Mountains shield it from the westerly winds that bring rain off the Pacific. Okanagan Lake, which occupies much of the valley, helps protect the vines from the winter cold. The surrounding mountains cause a very wide temperature variation between day and night.

> **GRAPE VARIETIES** For red: Merlot, Cabernet Sauvignon, Cabernet Franc, Gamay, and Pinot Noir; for white: Chardonnay and Sauvignon Blanc.

> **SOIL** Alluvial deposits produced by glaciers on a very complex background of basalt, limestone, granite, and gneiss.

> **STYLE** Given the temperature range in this region, the wines found here are firm but not heavy. The recent history of the Okanagan Valley and the many grape varieties mean that the wine styles are quite varied.

> **NOTABLE PRODUCERS** Blue Mountain, Cedar Creek, Jackson-Triggs, Mission Hill, Osoyoos Larose (partnered with Château Gruaud-Larose in Bordeaux), Quail's Gate, Sandhill, and Sumac Ridge.

NIAGARA PENINSULA

CANADA (ONTARIO)

It may seem surprising that this area, located along the shores of Lake Ontario, has become the largest wine-producing region in Canada, consisting of 13,591 acres (about 5,500 ha) of vineyards. It can be better understood when we know it is crossed by the 45th parallel; in other words, it is at the same latitude as Bordeaux. The influence of the huge mass of water formed by nearby lakes, and to a lesser degree by the Niagara River, means that some varieties can ripen well in a climate that would otherwise be much harsher. While this peninsula is the largest producer of ice wines in the world, it also produces a number of dry wines, particularly from Riesling as well as a few lighter reds. The region is comparable in size to Napa Valley, and it has established many sub-appellations governed by the Vintners Quality Alliance (VQA).

> **GRAPE VARIETIES** For red: Pinot Noir, Syrah, Gamay, and Cabernet Franc; for white: Seyval, Vidal, Riesling, and Chardonnay.

> **SOIL** Ancient glacier alluvium, with limestone in the hills.

> **STYLE** There is definitely a big difference between the dry wines, which are rather light, and the ice wines, which are very concentrated in both sugar and acidity.

> **NOTABLE PRODUCERS** Cave Spring, Clos Jordanne, Henry of Pelham, Inniskillin, Pillitterri, and Vineland.

Osoyoos Larose

A FRANCO-CANADIAN JOINT VENTURE

Based in the Okanagan Valley of British Columbia, Osoyoos Larose is a joint venture between Château Gruaud-Larose (a St-Julien second growth estate) and the Inniskillin winery. It produces blended wines inspired by Bordeaux (Merlot, Cabernet Franc, Cabernet Sauvignon, Malbec, and Petit Verdot). The small property, whose vineyards overlook Lake Osoyoos, boasts French expertise: (selected vines from a nursery near Bordeaux, French oak barrels, and the assistance of consultant winemakers Michel Rolland and Alain Sutra). Mathieu Mercier is the winemaker at the helm.

CHILE

COQUIMBO
Elqui
Limarí
ACONCAGUA
Choapa
Aconcagua
Valparaíso
Casablanca
Santiago
ARGENTINA
Maipo
San Antonio
et Leyda
Pacific
Ocean
Rancagua
Cachapoal
Colchagua
CENTRAL VALLEY
Curicó
Curicó
Molina
Talca
Maule
Itata
Chillán
Concepción
SOUTHERN REGION
Los Angeles
Bío-Bío
Malleco
N
0
60 miles (100 km)

CHILE

Many of us are familiar with Chile's well-made, single-variety wines: straightforward and very good value for money. But during the past 10 years, the best have broken through to a higher level. The reds are gaining depth and intensity, the whites finesse and freshness. Chile is no longer just a producer of good wines; it also now produces some great wines.

Five centuries of winemaking

At the end of the 1970s, Spain's Miguel Torres was one of the first foreigners to try his luck in Chile, acquiring a small winery in Curicó, in the Chilean Central Valley. He instigated what has become a remarkable economic success. Four centuries earlier, it was another Spaniard, Brother Francisco de Carabantes, who planted the first Chilean vines; and from the 18th century onwards, Chile was a significant wine exporter.

By the 19th century, French grape varieties were being planted in Chile, and the wine industry had become dynamic and modern. In the early 1950s, the region faced a crisis of overproduction, resulting in a massive uprooting of vines. Popularity on the international scene returned a quarter of a century later.

The Chilean wine miracle can be explained by a happy combination of its particularly suitable vine-growing environment, its low production costs, and the dynamism of its producers. Historic estates, investors from abroad, and a new generation of wineries are all increasingly focused on exploring the specificity of Chilean *terroirs*.

CHILE STATISTICS

Vineyard area: 358,302 acres (145,000 ha)

Production: 142 million cases (12,800,000 hl)

Reds: 70%

Whites: 30%

(Ministry of Agriculture, Chile, 2015)

Between mountains and the sea

VINEYARD EXPANSION. Chile occupies a long, narrow strip of land extending over 2,670 miles (4,300 km) from north to south, bordered to the west by the Pacific and to the east by the Andean Cordillera, with desert to the north and glaciers to the south. The wine-producing area is concentrated in the Central Valley, a large sector around the capital, Santiago; but it extends as far as Limarí and Elqui in the north and to Bío Bío in the south. Vines were initially planted on the plains lying between the coastal mountain chains and the Andean Cordillera – on fertile, easily cultivated land. Producers are now going further afield to plant on new land with good potential, such as on the western slopes of Andean foothills, or in the cooler regions close to the Pacific Ocean. Fertile for the most part, the soil is a light mix of sand, clay, and limestone; it is granitic and poorer on the slopes of the Andes.

IDEAL CLIMATE FOR VINES. Chile has an almost ideal climatic situation for ripening grapes. Mediterranean-style weather of sunshine and low rainfall is balanced by cool influences from the west (notably the Humboldt Current that flows along the

Ungrafted vines

Ever since phylloxera invaded the world's vineyards, ungrafted vines have been a rarity. Most vines are now grafted onto rootstocks of American origin, which have a natural resistance to the phylloxera aphid. However, Chile is an exception. This can no doubt be explained by its geographic isolation, but perhaps also by the significant presence of copper in the soil, or by the practice of flooding the vineyards to irrigate them. It is certainly so because of the vigilance of authorities here, who strictly control the importation of all plant matter.

> Cellar on the Errazuriz estate in the Aconcagua Valley.

> Workers among the vines at the Casa Lapostolle estate, in the Colchagua Valley.

coast). Also, nocturnal air from the Andes in the east creates wide temperature variations. A lack of water in summer, when the Central Valley becomes semi-desert, is the only natural deficiency. Irrigation is therefore indispensible in most wine-producing areas.

Varieties and styles

The alternating heat of the sun and the cool of the nights is one of the keys to understanding the style of Chilean wines: rounded and supple with a bright and intense fruitiness that is rarely heavy or oppressive. Chile is a country of principally red wines (75 per cent of production), despite a marked increase in the planting of white grapes. Of the 50 or so varieties now planted (including both reds and whites), just seven make up 85 per cent of the total area. Some grape varieties, such as País (37,500 acres/15,000 ha) or Muscat of Alexandria, are legacies from the Spanish colonial past; but current trends are more than ever skewed toward the big, international grape varieties.

RED GRAPE VARIETIES. Cabernet Sauvignon, which is grown on a total of 108,726 acres (44,000 ha), produces solid wines with supple tannins, marked by notes of black fruit, spices, and menthol. Two other Bordeaux varieties, Merlot and Carmenère, are grown on 30,641 acres (12,400 ha) and 7,922 acres (11,300 ha) respectively. The wines are rounded and velvety, sometimes with marked herbaceous notes. Worthy of mention is new interest in Syrah, Pinot Noir, and Malbec, which are fast gaining ground.

WHITE GRAPE VARIETIES. Most of the white wines for export come from two grape varieties: Chardonnay and Sauvignon Blanc. The first, which is grown on 28,664 acres (11,600 ha), produces supple, rounded, aromatic wines, with more or less pronounced yellow fruit notes. The second has made tremendous progress and is at the point of passing Chardonnay production in numbers; although it seems that a significant proportion could be comprised of related varieties (Sauvignon Vert or Sauvignonasse). In the cooler areas, Sauvignon Blanc produces pleasant, balanced wines, sometimes with dominant herbaceous notes.

Wine regions

Chilean vineyards are divided into four large growing areas, from north to south: Coquimbo, Aconcagua, Central Valley, and the Southern Region. Each is then divided into sub-regions that correspond to valleys running from east to west. Coquimbo is subdivided into Elqui, growing grapes destined to make Pisco, the local brandy, and Limarí, which is potentially more promising, though more sparsely planted. Further south, Aconcagua is now enjoying popularity, thanks to the cool Casablanca and San Antonio valleys, which produce the most convincing of Chilean whites. The vineyards of the Central Valley run from Santiago as far as the Maule Valley in the south on more than 247,105 acres (100,000 ha). This is where the bulk of production takes place and is home to most of the great Chilean wine producers, many of whom are installed in the Maipo and Colchagua valleys. The Southern Region, which includes the Itata and Bío Bío zones, has long been where the traditional varieties such as País are made; but some promising white wines have recently emerged from this sunny, but cool, climate.

Carmenère rediscovered

Argentina has Malbec, Uruguay has Tannat, but Chile long lacked its own 'signature' grape variety. This situation was remedied when two French scientists, Jean-Michel Boursiquot and Claude Valat, formally identified certain Chilean Merlot vines as being Carmenère. A native of Bordeaux, this grape variety from the Cabernet family was ousted from the Gironde region after the phylloxera crisis. Planted in Chile during the 19th century, it has now been reborn under its original name. It produces wines with depth, offering seductive aromas of ripe fruit and licorice, as well as an herbaceous accent (sweet peppers and damp undergrowth).

Key Chilean regions and wines

For a long time, Chilean wine producers concentrated on the production of single-variety wines that were reliable and consistent, and often made by blending wine from more than one region. Today, more wines come from limited geographic zones, from specific valleys (the name of which appears on the label) and sometimes even from individual plots.

MAIPO VALLEY

Maipo is the most famous name in Chilean wine. This valley extends from the Andes to the Coastal Cordillera, with Santiago virtually at its centre. During the 19th century, the proximity of the capital encouraged the creation of vast estates, funded by rich Santiago families. These wine companies, such as Santa Rita and Concha y Toro, have become giant businesses. The vineyards cover 30,888 acres (12,500 ha) and grow predominantly red grape varieties from Bordeaux (Cabernet Sauvignon, Merlot, and Carmenère). The climate is Mediterranean: hot and dry, with sparse rain falling mainly during the winter months. The region is also divided into several zones. Alto Maipo, the highest, is subject to the influence of the Andes. The vineyards on these slopes benefit from wide temperature variation and produce structured red wines. Central Maipo and Pacific Maipo, to the south and southwest of Santiago, experience higher temperatures and produce more supple, fruity, and ripe wines on fertile soil.

> **GRAPE VARIETIES** Cabernet Sauvignon, Merlot, Carmenère, and Syrah for red wines; Chardonnay and Sauvignon Blanc for whites.

> **SOIL** Alluvial (clay-and-limestone) and granite.

> **STYLE** Maipo is known for the quality of its Cabernet Sauvignon. The wines have powerful aromas of well-ripened fruit, spices, menthol, or eucalyptus. Ample structure and firm tannins are found in certain very concentrated wines like Almaviva (*see* below). Other red grape varieties yield fruity wines, ripe and rather supple. In terms of white wine, some of the Chardonnays grab attention with their fruity, very pleasant, roundness.

> **NOTABLE PRODUCERS** Almaviva, Concha y Toro, Cousino Macul, Santa Alicia, Santa Carolina, Santa Rita, Undurraga, Viñedo Chadwick.

Almaviva, a Chilean *grand cru*

In 1997, Concha y Toro – an historic estate, founded in the Maipo Valley in 1883 – partnered with the Bordeaux wine group Baron Philippe de Rothschild with the stated intention of producing a 'great' Chilean wine. Since then, vintage after vintage, the international wine press have been persuaded by this impressive *cuvée*, which combines the ample fruitiness typical of Chilean wines with the refinement of the great wines of Bordeaux. In just over 10 years, the gamble has paid off and Almaviva is now a member of the close-knit circle of the greatest New World wines. This Bordeaux blend, predominantly Cabernet Sauvignon, comes from a 212-acre (85-ha) vineyard in Puente Alto, about 20 miles (30 km) south of Santiago. Produced in a very modern winery, it is subject to long and careful maturation (17 to 18 months) in new oak casks. On the palate, it is a wine of great depth. It is complex, concentrated, warm, and fruity. Modern and seductive, it has a clearly defined structure that makes it good for laying down.

Von Siebenthal

With just 50 acres (20 ha) of vines, this estate is tiny compared with those of many hundreds or even thousands of acres that are the norm in Chile. Based in the beautiful Aconcagua Valley, Von Siebenthal is one of the small, independent estates that, over the past 15 years, have greatly increased the stylistic range of Chilean wines. With a real passion for wine, former Swiss lawyer Mauro von Siebenthal acquired a few plots of land at Panquehue, halfway between the Andes and the Pacific Ocean. Paying careful attention to the characteristics of individual varieties, he matched grapes to soil – planting Cabernet Franc and Merlot in clay-limestone, and Cabernet Sauvignon, Syrah, Carmenère, and Petit Verdot along the stony slopes. The result is a limited but delightful range of wines, dominated by a pure Carmenère (Carmenère Reserva), which is succulent and spicy, as well as an exuberant and delightfully perfumed Syrah (Carabantes).

CENTRAL VALLEY

COLCHAGUA VALLEY

In the Central Valley, the Rapel district is divided into two zones, Cachapoal in the north and Colchagua in the south. The latter has witnessed significant vineyard expansion and they now cover 57,500 acres (23,000 ha) – 95 per cent of which is planted with red varieties. Colchagua enjoys a hot climate that is tempered from the west by the fresh breezes from the ocean. Originally planted in the valleys and foothills, vineyards have now reached the mountain slopes (as high as 3,350 ft/1,000 m). Bordeaux grape varieties have generally proven their worth in Colchagua, giving rise to some of the greatest Chilean *cuvées* (Clos Apalta, Montes Alpha); but Syrah and Malbec are also promising.

> **GRAPE VARIETIES** Cabernet Sauvignon, Merlot, Carmenère, and Syrah for red wines; Chardonnay for white wines.

> **SOIL** Sedimentary (clay and limestone) and granitic.

> **STYLE** Colchagua is well known for its pleasant, ripe, and fleshy red wines. Cabernet Sauvignon, the dominant variety, produces full-bodied wines that are certainly capable of ageing. But the region possesses other specialties, such as concentrated and succulent Merlots, and Malbecs sourced from very old vines, which result in particularly intense and structured wines. The white wines (especially the Chardonnays) are fairly rounded, simple, and warm.

> **NOTABLE PRODUCERS** Casa Lapostolle, Casa Silva, Errazuriz, Guelbenzu, El Araucano (Lurton), Los Vascos, Luis Felipe Edwards, Santa Helena, Siegel, Viña Montes, Viu Manent.

ACONCAGUA

CASABLANCA VALLEY

This area has only relatively recently started producing wine. Development has coincided with the drive to exploit more temperate zones that are capable of producing fresh, fine, and well-balanced white wines. The growing area here now extends over 10,000 acres (4,000 ha), close to the coast between Santiago and the port of Valparaiso. The vineyards are strongly influenced by the Pacific Ocean, thanks to which they are enveloped in morning mist. However, spring frosts, which are an exception elsewhere, prove to be a real menace here. Irrigation is essential, and the cost of drilling wells is one of the reasons why a brake has been put on some new development. Vineyards extend over the Coastal Cordillera, in terraces along the slopes.

> **GRAPE VARIETIES** Pinot Noir, Merlot, and Carmenère for reds; Chardonnay and Sauvignon Blanc for whites.

> **SOIL** Sand, limestone, and granite.

> **STYLE** Casablanca specializes in dry white wines made from Chardonnay and Sauvignon Blanc. The style is elegant and fresh, with fruity and sometimes herbaceous notes for the Sauvignon Blancs. Red grape varieties are in the minority, but Pinot Noir has recently broken through with a style that is fairly full-bodied and fruity, but not lacking in freshness.

> **NOTABLE PRODUCERS** Concha y Toro, Cono Sur, Loma Larga, Quintay, Santa Rita, Veramonte.

ARGENTINA, BRAZIL, AND URUGUAY

ARGENTINA, BRAZIL, AND URUGUAY

During the past 15 years, the wine industry in South America has undergone significant change. Argentina has been successful in securing a place for its wines on the international market, while Brazil and Uruguay are making every effort to modernize and develop high quality production.

ARGENTINA

The profile or perception of a wine-producing country can change radically in the space of a generation, as Argentina has demonstrated. Right up to the end of the 1980s, Argentina was still producing vast quantities of wine lacking in any real appeal. Now, the industry there is producing red wines of great intensity, and Mendoza has become a world-renowned region – unique in part for the altitude at which some of its many vineyards are planted.

ARGENTINA STATISTICS

Vineyard area: 560,929 acres (227,000 ha)

Production: 166.5 million cases (15,000,000 hl)

Reds: 64%

Whites: 33%

Rosés: 3%

(Inst. nacional de vitivinicultura 2015)

Rapid modernization

In 1990, Argentina looked with envy at the success of its neighbour Chile. The two countries had long followed parallel paths, from the very first vine plantings in the mid-16th century, right up to the 1970s, when they both experienced an overproduction crisis linked to a big drop in local wine consumption.

While Chile turned to exporting as a solution, Argentina remained embroiled in economic problems. Then – following the example of many regions and producers before them, such as the French company Moët & Chandon – this South American wine giant finally woke up. Traditional cellars were renovated and new estates appeared, thanks to both local and foreign initiatives. Vineyard area was reduced and the mix of grape varieties completely modified. The wines produced became more focused and fruitier, in response to more demanding global and even local markets. Argentines consume 75 per cent of the wine they produce, but exports have more than doubled in the past five years.

Latin American leader

Argentina is a big country, covering more than a million square miles (2.7 million sq km). The 560,929 acres (227,000 ha) of land growing vines are concentrated in the eastern foothills of the Andean Cordillera. This is a relatively narrow fringe of land, running across 900 miles (1,500 km) from Salta in the north as far as Patagonian vineyards in the south. In Mendoza, the main wine-producing region, the vines stretch farther than the eye can see over high plateaus and on sloping foothills.

VINEYARDS WITH ALTITUDE. Argentina's main advantage can be summed up in a single word: elevation. The vineyards are sited at an average of 2,950 ft (900 m) above sea level, and

> Vines at the Esteco winery in Salta province, Argentina.

Argentina's appellations

For quality wines, Argentina's legislation designates DOCs (*Denominación de origen controlada* /appellation of controlled origin) and IGs (*Indicación geográfica* / indication of geographic location). There are only two of the former, which are Luján de Cuyo and San Rafael in the Mendoza region. The greatest part of wine production comes from more than 180 IGs, which may cover an entire region (Mendoza, for example), a sub-region (Valle de Uco), or a more local zone (Vista Flores).

> The Zuccardi family winery in Mendoza produces a wide range of wines, both red and white.

even reach 9,800 ft (3,000 m) at Salta in the north. Around Mendoza, most are planted at an average of between 1,900 and 3,600 ft (600 and 1,100 m). These altitudes present cool nights, but during the day the temperature range hovers around 68°F (20°C), allowing the grapes to retain all their aromatic potential without being 'burned' by the sun. Thanks to this healthy, dry environment, the fruit ripens well. Argentina's vineyards also are protected against many ailments – including phylloxera, which, although not quite absent, is far from virulent.

Climate and soil

With the exception of some areas in the south, arid conditions are the dominant norm here. Rainfall very often amounts to less than 10 in (250 mm) per year, and is concentrated during the seasonal vine growth phase. Temperatures are moderate, but can reach 104°F (40°C) in the summer. Winters can be cold, and spring frosts are relatively frequent. The same is true of hailstorms, which can be quite dramatic. Vineyards are irrigated with water thawed from mountain snow, and drip irrigation has now largely replaced the old method – where the rows were flooded. Soil is mostly poor in nutritional quality, and alluvial, with a significant amount of sand on a gravelly, limestone, or clay substratum.

Eclectic mix of grapes

Argentina has grown vines for more than 450 years. The origin of the 116 varieties now planted – essentially Spanish, Italian, Portuguese, and French – is a reflection of the different waves of European immigration since the 16th century. While a few varieties are dominant, this abundance of grapes stands in sharp contrast to the simplicity of the grape mix in Chile (*see* p.453) and gives Argentina's producers a great many options. Pink-skinned, traditional grape varieties, such as Criolla, Cereza, and Moscatel Rosada, are still grown in 29 per cent of the vineyards; but they are gradually being replaced, particularly by red varieties.

RED VARIETIES. Malbec, introduced in 1868 by French agronomist Michel Pouget, has become the emblematic grape variety of Argentina. It is planted on 98,842 acres (40,000 ha) and produces a good number of the best wines: opulent, powerful, and ripe in style. Bonarda, originally from Lombardy, is valued for its colourful, supple, and fruity wines. Cabernet Sauvignon produces full-bodied, well-structured wines with generous aromas and capable of ageing. Syrah is very much in vogue, followed by Merlot and Tempranillo.

WHITE VARIETIES. Apart from Pedro Giménez, which is still planted more than any other white, two varieties stand out – each in a very different style: Torrontés, a local grape variety that is back in favour thanks to its supple, tender, and aromatic wines, with notes of flowers and fresh grapes; and Chardonnay, which produces powerful, often warm, wines with exuberant aromas of yellow fruit and spices. Planted at high altitude, Sauvignon Blanc is also arousing a certain amount of interest.

Wine-producing regions

Among three small wine regions in the north – Salta, Jujuy, and Catamarca – only the first produces wines worthy of broad interest (*see* p.574). Further south, La Rioja province specializes in white wines made from Torrontés Riojano and Muscat of Alexandria, but not many of these are exported. With more than 116,140 acres (47,000 ha) of vineyards, San Juan, between La Rioja and Mendoza, is the second-largest wine-producing region in Argentina. Most of the vines are grown in small, irrigated valleys that are subject to a very hot and dry climate. Producing mainly dry white wines and rosés, as well as fortified wines, San Juan is slowly converting to the production of red wines.

The Mendoza region is the powerhouse of Argentina's wine industry, producing most of the best red wines (*see* p.475). In Patagonia, in the far south of the country, the Río Negro and Neuquén regions (totalling just under 10,000 acres/4,000 ha) are influenced by the Atlantic Ocean. The cooler and damper climate, and the limestone soils, form the basis for livelier, very intense wines produced from Malbec, Merlot, and Torrontés. Some zones, like the high valley of Río Negro, are currently attracting investors.

BRAZIL

With almost 219,924 acres (88,000 ha) planted to vines (as of 2014), Brazil is the third-largest wine producer in South America, behind Argentina and Chile. There were a few tentative attempts at planting vines during the 16th century, but Brazil had to wait until the beginning of the 20th century before achieving significant production. And it took until 1970 to see the first high quality wines, with the arrival of big groups such as Moët & Chandon or Martini & Rossi.

BRAZIL STATISTICS

Vineyard area: 219,924 acres (89,000 ha)
Production: 30 million cases (2,700,000 hl)
Reds: 80%
Whites: 18%
Rosés: 2%

(OIV, 2015)

Wine-producing regions

Except for vineyards in the Vale do São Francisco, in the far northeast, most Brazilian wines are produced in the extreme south, in the states of Santa Catarina and Rio Grande do Sul. The latter is by far Brazil's largest and most interesting winemaking region, covering 95,000 acres (38,000 ha). Its vineyards are concentrated in two sub-regions: Serra Gaúcha and Campanha.

Serra Gaúcha produces the bulk of Brazilian wines, and it includes the Vale dos Vinhedos, the country's only appellation of origin. The damp climate (207 in/1,750 mm rainfall per year) and the heavy, badly drained soil impose a limit on the production of quality wines. The Campanha sub-region, along the Uruguayan border, benefits from more favourable conditions with a reasonable amount of rainfall and sandy, well-drained soil.

Varieties and wines

The particularly damp climate, especially in Serra Gaúcha, favours the cultivation of hybrid grape varieties that are resistant to disease, so they are grown in substantial quantities. The most important development, though, is the planting of *Vitis vinifera* varieties in the Campanha region, including Cabernet Sauvignon, Merlot, Tannat, Chardonnay, Sauvignon Blanc, and Pinot Grigio. While Brazil has acquired some reputation thanks to its sparkling wines, made either traditionally or by the sealed tank method (*see box* p.71), the greatest part of its production is made up of dry red wines. These can be very appealing, in a fresh style that is fairly light in alcohol, when the grapes have ripened particularly well.

NOTABLE PRODUCERS. Dal Pizzol, Don Laurindo, Miolo, Mioranza, Pizzato, Salton.

> Hand harvesting at the Vale dos Vinhedos estate in Brazil.

URUGUAY

As perhaps the largest per-capita wine market on the South American continent, Uruguay has a well-established winemaking tradition, which dates back to the 18th century. It is the fourth-largest wine producer in South America in terms of volume, and it consumes most of the wine it produces. However, the quality achieved by its best red wines has opened the doors to the export market, mainly Brazil.

> The Cordon de Royat vine training system (Uruguay).

Wine-producing regions

The Uruguayan climate is maritime with plenty of sunshine, regular rainfall (40 in/1,000 mm per year), and cool nights. The conditions are ideal for the vines as long as vigorous foliage growth is controlled – it can sometimes be excessive due to the humidity and the very fertile nature of the clay-based soils.

The vineyards, which cover 21,250 acres (8,500 ha), are owned and managed by 2,400 growers. They sell their grapes to the country's 272 producers, just over 10 per cent of whom export a part of their production. The large wine-producing regions of Canelones, Montevideo, Colonia, and San José all lie along the south coast, near the capital. But some small vineyards are also set along the left bank of the Río de la Plata as well as in the centre and north of the country, close to the Brazilian border.

Varieties and wines

Though almost 70 grape varieties are grown in Uruguay, only a few varieties are widely cultivated. Tannat is planted in almost a quarter of the vineyards and produces the most highly prized reds. They are made in a firm style, and also yield some interesting rosés. The significant presence of this little-known variety, originally from the southwest of France, is due to Basque immigrants in the 19th century. After Tannat, Merlot, Cabernet Sauvignon, and Cabernet Franc are the most cultivated red grape varieties, and are made into red or rosé. Among the white varieties, Ugni Blanc is by far the most widely grown; but the best white wines, still or sparkling, come from Sauvignon Blanc, Chardonnay, Viognier, or Muscat. The wines are marketed in two categories: VCP (*Viño de calidad preferente* [quality wine]) and VC (*Viño común* [table wine]). These mainly relate to the red wines made from Tannat, sometimes blended with Merlot, Cabernet Sauvignon or Cabernet Franc. The best have an austere but seductive profile with firm tannins, a great deal of freshness, and modest alcohol content. This brings them more in line with European expectations than the more powerful wines of Argentina.

Other Latin American countries

Even though production remains modest, most larger South American countries have maintained a winemaking industry from origins dating back to the Spanish colonization of the 16th century. Ecuador, Columbia, Paraguay, Venezuela, and Bolivia together have a total of several thousand acres of vines. Many of them are planted at altitude (as much as 9,200 ft /2,800 m in Bolivia), in a damp, sub-tropical, or equatorial climate. The wines, both dry and sweet, or wine-based alcohols such as Pisco, are the product of hybrids, traditional grape varieties (Criolla), or varieties of *Vitis vinifera*.

Peru's production of wine has increased considerably in the past 10 years. While the greater part of it is converted into brandy, Peru also makes dry wines that are rapidly improving in quality. The vineyards are concentrated in the coastal province of Ita, which includes the Tacama zone, located 45 miles (70 km) inland. In this semi-desert region, refreshed by the cool air from the Pacific, the vines are planted on poor soil and are irrigated with water from the Andean Cordillera. The Tacama estate, one of the oldest in Peru, has been working with French oenological services and experts since the 1960s and makes good quality wines from the Tannat, Malbec, Petit Verdot, Sauvignon Blanc, Chardonnay, Chenin Blanc, and Albilla grape varieties.

Key wine regions of Argentina, Brazil, and Uruguay

Of Argentina's regions, only Mendoza and, to a lesser extent, Salta (including Cafayate) have any real reputation. Uruguay is known for red wines made from Tannat, but from no specific region. Brazil is slowly emerging from obscurity, thanks to a few model producers.

ARGENTINA

SALTA

Among the small wine-producing regions in northern Argentina, only Salta (7,413 acres/3,000 ha) has created a name for itself. This is thanks to the quality of its dry white wines from the dominant grape variety Torrontés Riojano (a cross, perhaps, between Muscat of Alexandria and Criolla Chica). The most renowned district is in the Calchaquíes Valley, near the town of Cafayate, where vines are perched at an altitude of almost 4,900 ft (1,500 m). Some are planted as high as 9,800 ft (3,000 m), making Calchaquíes the highest vineyard area in the world. The sandy soil and the continental climate are similar to those of Mendoza. The very wide temperature range means that the white grapes ripen while retaining a sufficient amount of acidity. Apart from Torrontés, a few red grape varieties, including Cabernet Sauvignon, Malbec, and Tannat, also produce good results.

> **GRAPE VARIETIES** Cabernet Sauvignon, Malbec, and Tannat for reds; Torrontés Riojano, Chardonnay, and Chenin Blanc for whites.

> **SOIL** Sandy.

> **STYLE** White wines made from Torrontés have a distinct personality, with exuberant or very vivid aromas of fresh grapes (similar to Muscat), flowers, citrus fruits, and spices. On the palate they are supple and mouth-filling, with an alcohol content that can be quite high. Most of them are dry, but some retain a certain amount of residual sugar, which reinforces a typical sense of roundness of this grape variety. They are wines for drinking young, and always between 46 and 50°F (8 and 10°C). The reds are perfumed and intense, with a fruity quality that is typical of most good red Argentine wines.

> **NOTABLE PRODUCERS** La Esperanza Estate, Etchart, Colomé, Trapiche, O. Fournier, Terrazas de los Andes.

François Lurton

Coming from a large wine family in the Bordeaux region, Jacques and François Lurton started a global business in 1988. The idea was to choose the best *terroirs* in the world and produce wines there representing good value. The two brothers arrived in Argentina in 1992, at a time when few people had recognized the potential of the high-altitude vineyards in Mendoza. Three years later, they bought their first plot at Vista Flores, in the Uco Valley. It was at an altitude of 3,600 ft (1,100 m) on poor quality but healthy and well-drained soil, where vines had never been planted before. Today, with a holding of 500 acres (136 ha), Argentina is at the heart of the Lurton empire, and now the property of François since his brother's departure. He produces a very reliable line that is impeccably made, from fruity and intense wines at entry level, under the Piedra Negra label, to the particularly fine Chacayes, an ambitious *cuvée* based on Malbec grown in the best plots of the estate.

ARGENTINA

MENDOZA

Three-quarters of Argentina's vineyards are concentrated in Mendoza. They cover 148,263 acres (60,000 ha), situated mostly to the south and east of the city of the same name. The vines are planted at altitudes between 1,640 and 5,775 ft (500 and 1,700 m), spread over 185 miles (300 km) from north to south. The climate is continental: hot and dry in summer, with a wide temperature variation linked to the altitude, and severe winters. The lower regions – San Rafael to the south, San Martin to the east, and Lavalle to the north – produce everyday wines, white and rosé, from traditional grape varieties. Most of the quality wines come from two sectors: the Central Valley, along each side of the Mendoza River, to the south and southwest of the city of Mendoza; and the Uco Valley, situated more to the south and extending over a distance of nearly 50 miles (80 km).

> **GRAPE VARIETIES** Malbec, Bonarda, Cabernet Sauvignon, Syrah, Merlot, and Tempranillo for red wines; Pedro Giménez, Torrontés, Chardonnay, Muscat of Alexandria, Chenin Blanc, Ugni Blanc, and Sauvignon Blanc for whites.

> **SOIL** Poor, sandy, with gravelly pockets in the Central Valley; thin, mixed sand and alluvium with some limestone zones in the higher reaches of the Uco Valley.

> **STYLE** With warm aromas of very ripe fruit, spices, and licorice, the reds made from Malbec are fleshy and soft. Tannins are more or less powerful according to the level of concentration. The high quality *cuvées* can be aged for five to 10 years. Cabernet Sauvignon offers intense aromas of very ripe black and red fruit, with herbaceous accents (sometimes mentholated) and a generous palate with usually supple tannins. The Chardonnays are pleasant, perfumed, and often warm.

> **NOTABLE PRODUCERS** Alta Vista, Altos Las Hormigas, Fabre Montmayou, Catena Zapata, Cheval des Andes, Clos de Los Siete, Don Cristobal, Etchart, Familia Zuccardi, François Lurton, Monteviejo, Norton, O. Fournier, Terrazas de los Andes, Trapiche.

Miolo, the Brazilian avant-garde

Italian immigrant Guiseppe Miolo established his estate in 1897, near the town of Bento Gonçalves in the Vinhedos Valley. For three generations, his descendants were content to just sell their grapes – until an overproduction crisis drove them to begin making their own wine in the 1990s. A pioneer of planting quality grape varieties and using expert advisors, Miolo set the bar high and was proof of Brazil's potential to produce fine wines. Today, it is one of the country's largest wine businesses, represented in five production regions and offering a very wide range of wines. The Quinta do Seival *cuvée*, from a vineyard in the Campanha region, has done much to establish the reputation of Miolo outside Brazil. But the winery also produces some very attractive *cuvées* based on Cabernet, as well as sparkling white wines with a great deal of finesse.

URUGUAY

TANNAT

Uruguay's wine industry is firmly linked with the dominant red grape variety grown there, Tannat (or Harriague). This variety is grown across 20 per cent of the country's vineyards, planted especially in the two main production regions: Canelones and Montevideo in the south. It adapts well to the rich soil and damp, but mild climate of these coastal zones. Sometimes made into rosé, Tannat is known mainly for its structured red wines. The best have seduced importers in search of more unusual 'niche' wines in a different style from those of Chile or Argentina.

> **GRAPE VARIETY** Tannat, sometimes blended with Cabernet Sauvignon, Merlot, or Cabernet Franc.

> **SOIL** Clay and sand.

> **STYLE** Following in the footsteps of Madiran (*see* p.339), Uruguayan Tannat produces deeply coloured wines with notes of black fruit, licorice, spices, and sometimes damp undergrowth or menthol. Quite austere on the palate when young, with firm tannins, a great deal of freshness, and a modest alcohol level, the wines are closer to European standards than the powerful wines of neighbouring Argentina, for example. Matured in cask or blended with other grape varieties (Merlot, Cabernet Franc), they show a great degree of suppleness. Their rich tannins and acidity make them wines to lay down (10 years). When matured, they can develop a seductive bouquet marked by tobacco, spices, and damp undergrowth.

> **NOTABLE PRODUCERS** Bouza, Carrau, Castillo Viejo, De Lucca, Juanico, Marichal, Leda, Pisano, Pizzorno, Stagniari.

Mendoza

CATENA *ZAPATA*

Italian immigrants reinvigorated Argentinian wine in the late 19th century by creating new vineyards and bringing new techniques, grape varieties, and consumers. Nicolas Catena was one of these pioneers, planting his first Malbec in Mendoza in 1902. Since the 1980s his grandson has developed the family business, now one of Argentina's most renowned vineyards.

CATENA ZAPATA

J. Cobos s/n
Agrelo, Luján de Cuyo, Mendoza

Founded: *1902*
Area: *1,483 acres (600 ha)*
Production: *N/A*
Appellation: *Mendoza*
Red grape varieties: *Malbec, Cabernet Sauvignon, Merlot, Cabernet Franc, Syrah, Pinot Noir*
White grape varieties: *Chardonnay, Semillon, Sauvignon Blanc, Viognier, Gewurztraminer*

Successfully cultivating terroirs at altitude

After selling his wholesale production company, Nicolas Catena put all his effort into the development of fine wines, to the widespread incredulity of his colleagues, for whom the Argentinian market was above all price-driven. But Nicolas saw beyond that. His trips abroad had familiarized him with Californian wines and he was interested both in the development of new areas of cultivation closer to the Andes and in exports.

Despite the fears of his vineyard manager, Nicolas believed in the potential of Malbec in the dry zone and at altitude. He intended to put Argentinian wine on the map. His new plantations proved him right. He tried hard to find the best sites for Chardonnay and Cabernet Sauvignon. In Europe, where everything is clearly laid down and well-established by time and tradition, one can scarcely imagine the challenge that such a tabula rasa can bring: the mastery of new *terroirs*, a dizzying range of choices, contemplation, investigation, unsuccessful efforts, and inevitable failures.

Initial success

In the mid-1990s, the first successes came with the Cabernet Sauvignon of La Pirámide and the Chardonnay of Tupungato (Catena Alta). At the beginning of the 2000s, when Nicolas' daughter, Laura, joined the company, the Malbec produced at altitude attracted the most attention: a selection of the best plants, the 'Zapata vines', named after Nicolas' mother, made it possible to further improve the quality of the grape and produce a variety of wines.

One estate and six vineyards

Today, the Catena Zapata estate is divided into six vineyards from north to south: Angelica Norte, La Pirámide, Domingo, Adrianna, Nicasia, and Angélica Sur. They lie at an altitude of around 3,020 to 4,760 feet (920 to 1,450m).

The range of Catena Zapata includes both blends of different terroirs and wines from individual plots on the estate. The two wines described here illustrate these two different styles.

NICOLAS CATENA ZAPATA, MENDOZA

A blend of 75 per cent Cabernet Sauvignon and 25 per cent Malbec, from four vineyards (La Pirámide, Domingo, Adrianna, and Nicasia). Its production is complex, involving 210 micro-vinifications, and its first production, in 1997, was a revolution for Argentinian wine. During international competitions, it triumphed over other Cabernet Sauvignons, drawing attention to Argentina's potential. A dark colour with a dense nose, combining dark fruits, flowers, and mocha. The palate is ample and firm, with soft tannins bringing a note of suppleness. A surprising finish, with dark fruit, figs, and peppermint.

CATENA ZAPATA ADRIANNA VINEYARD MALBEC, GUALTALLARY, MENDOZA

Adrianna, located in the dry region of Gualtallary (Uco Valley), is one of the best *terroirs* for Malbec in Argentina, according to Nicolas and Laura Catena. At 4,430 feet (1,450m) it is one of the coolest areas of Mendoza, with very poor soil combining sand, gravel, and limestone pebbles. Its almost black colour has some purplish reflections. The nose is full of plum, violets, and ripe cherries. The palate is suave, velvety, and very rich without being too warm. The final cocoa, mocha, and raspberry combination is accompanied by, just beneath the surface, the hallmark of Catena Zapata wines, wonderfully integrated tannins.

...las and Laura Catena, ...ther and daughter ...n the estate.

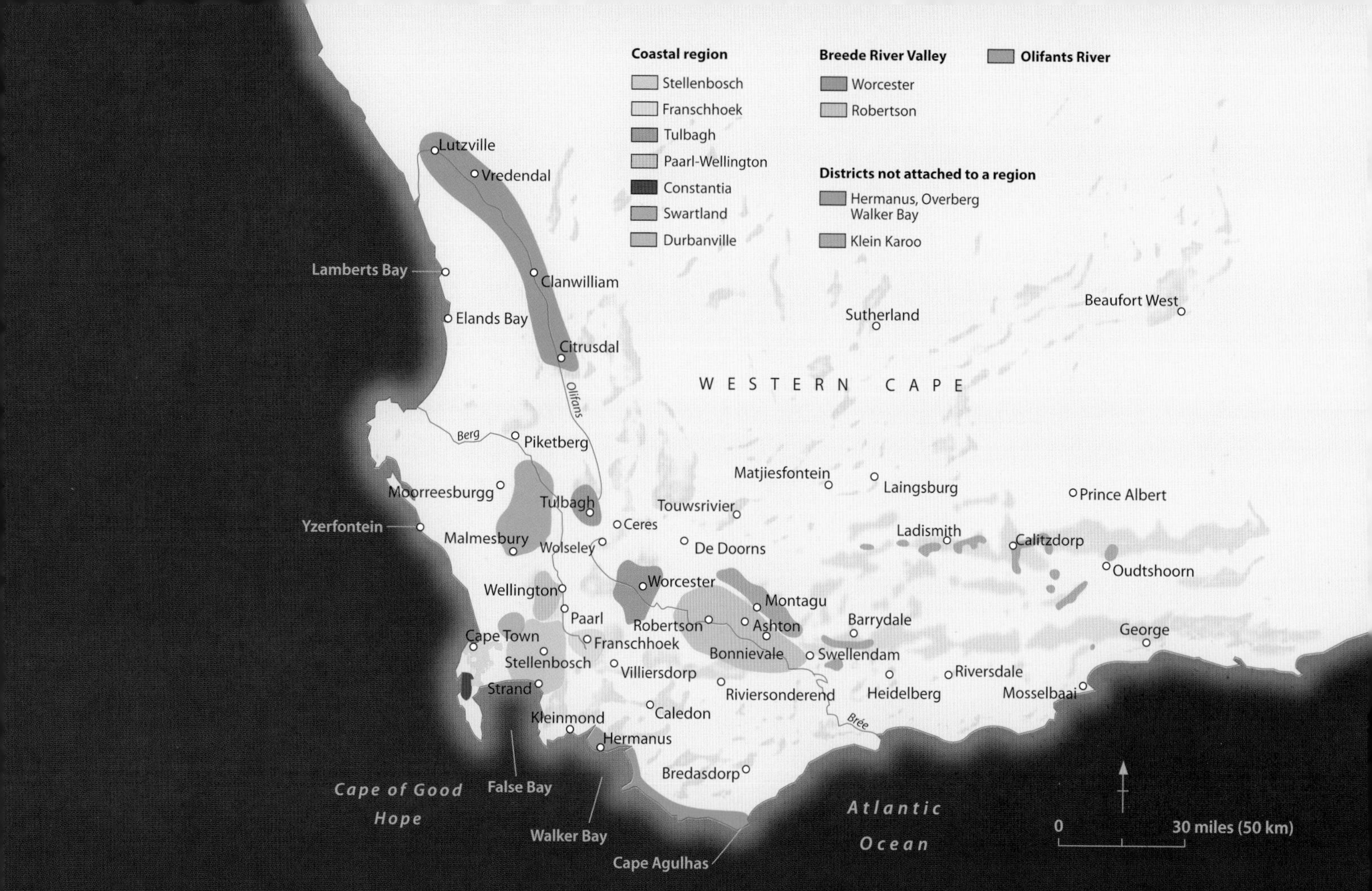

SOUTH AFRICA

SOUTH AFRICA

South Africa is by far the largest wine producer on the African continent. The country's wine tradition dates back to the 17th century, but it wasn't until the end of apartheid that it began to enjoy worldwide success. Since then, and after a long period of political and economic isolation, the country has demonstrated real dynamism in modernizing the industry and making inroads on the international market. Apart from being very good value for money, South African wines are also of high quality.

Long history

The first plantings in the Cape region date from the settlement of Dutch colonies during the 17th century, when this maritime province was a way station for ships en route to Asia. Jan van Riebeeck, the first regional governor, arrived on the Cape in 1652 tasked with exploiting the province's lands and establishing the first vineyards. Reinforced by the arrival of 200 French Huguenot families between 1688 and 1690, South African viticulture prospered thereafter thanks to its principal customer, Great Britain. But the appearance of phylloxera in 1886 led to a long period of crisis, aggravated by conflicts between the British and the Afrikaners.

In the 20th century, serious problems of over-production led to the Kooperatiewe Wijnbouwers Vereniging (KWV, the Cooperative Winemakers Society) being granted, in 1940, almost total control over the South African wine industry. During the period of apartheid, the country's political and economic isolation left South Africa without the benefit of the enormous progress that took place in the wine world during the 1980s. The abolition of the regime in 1991 finally opened the country to the wider world, and producers turned successfully to exporting.

SOUTH AFRICA STATISTICS

Vineyard area (wine grapes): 244,634 acres (99,000 ha)

Production: 122 million cases (11,000,000 hl)

Whites: 56%

Reds: 44%

(SAWIS, OIV, 2015)

> Harvesting grapes at a Paarl district farm in South Africa.

Geography

The Republic of South Africa is situated at the southernmost point of the African continent, at a latitude of about 35° south. The climate is generally hot and dry, but coastal regions are tempered by the cold Benguela Current, which moves along the southwestern coast. The country's 247,105 acres (100,000 ha) of vineyards are largely situated in this coastal region, and it is rare to find a vineyard more than 60 miles (100 km) from the sea. There are two very different seasons: a hot and dry Mediterranean summer, followed by a moderately warm and humid winter season from May to September. Rainfall varies from one region to another, making irrigation essential in many areas.

Grape varieties

Like other New World countries, South Africa has learned to adapt its wines to market forces. Production was largely dominated by white wine, with a significant amount being earmarked for distillation. Chenin Blanc (Steen) remains the most planted variety, capable as much of producing medium-dry wines with little character as fine dry or sweet wines. The other important white varieties are Colombard, Sauvignon Blanc, and Chardonnay. Over the past three decades, red wine has gained significant ground and red varieties are planted in 45% of the vineyard area, mainly Cabernet Sauvignon, Shiraz, Syrah, Pinotage (a Cinsaut/Pinot Noir cross developed in South Africa in 1925), and Merlot. Pinot Noir is little planted but is capable of producing good wines in the country's cooler regions.

Wine regions and districts

Olifants River is the most northerly wine-producing region, and its winelands extend throughout the Olifants River Valley, which borders the Atlantic. Its output remains largely oriented toward bulk production destined for distilling.

Swartland and Tulbagh lie further south; and the Worcester region, adjoining Tulbagh to the southeast, is responsible for a quarter of national wine production. Robertson lies inland to the east, bordering Worcester at its western part; irrigation is essential in this hot, dry climate. White grape varieties flourish in these chalk-rich soils, but in recent years real progress has

> Vines on the Groot Constantia estate.

been made in red wine production. Due to a hot, extremely dry climate, the vast, east-west Klein Karoo region only contributes in a very minor way to national wine output, but it manages to produce good fortified wines.

Turning toward Cape Town, between Swartland to the north and Worcester to the east, the Paarl district is home to 15 per cent of the nation's wine. A long-term producer of fortified wines, it now offers dry white wines and quality reds. The little Franschhoek vineyard area lies southeast of Paarl.

Stellenbosch, although it produces only 10 per cent of the country's output, is the best-known South African wine district. It starts west of Franschhoek and south of Paarl, descending to the ocean at False Bay and extending toward Cape Town to the west. Surrounded by mountains, its topography is varied. It enjoys a moderate climate and an almost ideal level of rainfall, concentrated in the winter months. Many of the best red wines from this country come from the granite soil of its mountain flanks.

Some vineyards in the small Tygerberg region northwest of Stellenbosch are planted on slopes perched along the side of the Dortsberg Mountains, which are cooled by winds blowing from the Atlantic Ocean. Further south, behind Table Mountain, which separates it from Cape Town, the small historic vineyards of Constantia constitute a 'ward', a designation roughly equivalent to a European appellation. Even further south, along the coast toward the east, Walker Bay and Elim have the country's coolest growing climates, favourable to white grape varieties as well as Pinot Noir.

Wine of Origin: Hierarchy of appellations

To understand the structure of South African wine, you need to look at the the hierarchy of regional and local appellations. The introduction of the Wine of Origin system in 1973 established four classifications: the geographical area spanning several regions, including the largest, the Western Cape, then the region, district, and ward, from the largest to the smallest areas (*see also* p.103). At present, there are six official regions: Boberg (fortified wines), Breede River Valley, Klein Karoo, Coastal Region, Olifants River and Cape South Coast, the latter created recently. Each of these regions is divided into several districts, corresponding to the local areas that are the most coherent taking into account both geography and the wine grown. Finally, the ward is a subdivision of these districts. Delineated according to the soil and climate, a ward must be able to produce wines of a certain typicity. The country's best-known appellations, most of which are mentioned in these pages, are generally from districts and sometimes from wards (Stellenbosch, Franschhoek, Constantia). The great majority of quality wines that are exported come from the Coastal Region, which includes many districts, *e.g.* Darling, Paarl, Stellenbosch, and Tygerberg.

Leading South African regions and wines

The best-known regions or districts are those that produce and export the finest wines, led by Stellenbosch. However, the key factor in South African wine production today is the exploration of new regions with cooler climates that are capable of producing even finer wines.

CONSTANTIA

The ward of Constantia is situated on the southeastern slopes of mountains separating the city of Cape Town from False Bay. Although it is quite small, encompassing seven wine domains and around 1,236 acres (500 ha) of vines, it certainly deserves its reputation, as this was where the country's first vineyards were established. The Constantia estate was founded in 1685, taking its name from the daughter of the commissioner of the Dutch Cape Colony, by Simon Van der Stel (who also gave his name to Stellenbosch). In the 18th century, this large property had 1,800 acres (750 ha) of vines under cultivation. It was later subdivided and now several family enterprises work different plots. The relatively cool climate is influenced both by cold air coming from the mountains and by the 'Cape Doctor', a wind blowing from the ocean. This is all very suitable for Bordeaux grape varieties, especially Sauvignon Blanc, a local speciality. Irrigation is unnecessary as the annual rainfall is around 39 inches (1,000 mm).

> **GRAPE VARIETIES** Sauvignon Blanc for white wines; Cabernet Sauvignon and Merlot for reds.

> **SOIL** Ancient, dating from the Precambrian era. Slopes are more or less steep, depending on the altitude, along the southern side of Table Mountain.

> **STYLE** The relatively cool climate and the small size of this ward give the white wines produced from Sauvignon Blanc grapes a distinctive style, full of freshness. The reds may be somewhat 'vegetal'.

> **NOTABLE PRODUCERS** Steenberg, Buitenverwachtig, Groot Constantia, Klein Constantia, Constantia Glen.

STELLENBOSCH

Of all South African wine appellations, Stellenbosch (which is a district) is the best known outside the country; but it is also the most densely planted. This additionally means it has the greatest concentration of top producers in South Africa. The town of the same name, whose architecture is a microcosm of the Cape Dutch style, is home to a viticulture and oenology school and a highly regarded research centre, both at the local university. Given Stellenbosch's diversity of topography and climate, it is difficult to restrict its wines to a single style, all the more so since many grape varieties, both red and white, are cultivated. The wines also differ in relation to the altitude and/or proximity to the ocean.

> **GRAPE VARIETIES** White: Chenin Blanc, Chardonnay, Sauvignon Blanc, Semillon; red: Cabernet Sauvignon, Shiraz, Merlot, Pinotage.

> **SOIL** Varied, with an ancient foundation, since the Cape region is one of the world's oldest geologic structures. The soil ranges from light and sandy to granitic on the mountain foothills, and the topography is often very rugged.

> **STYLE** Stellenbosch's international fame flows from fine, full-bodied Cabernet Sauvignons and blends associated with this grape, although some of the best reds also come from Syrah and Pinotage. The whites are generally rich and aromatic.

> **NOTABLE PRODUCERS** Beyerskloof, Cordoba, De Trafford, Ernie Els, Ingwé, Grangehurst, Kaapzicht, Kanonkop, Meerlust, Morgenster, Raats Family, Rudera, Rupert & Rothschild, Rustenburg, Rust en Vrede, Thelema, Tokara, Waterford, Uitkyk, Vergelegen.

OVERBERG, WALKER BAY, CAPE AGULHAS

During recent years, there has been a significant shift towards production in cooler climates, as in other New World countries. The objective is three-fold: to limit the relatively high alcohol levels that result from a hot climate, to conserve the natural acidity of the grapes, and to cultivate varieties that prosper only in cool climates. Obviously these three factors are interconnected, and this is why plantings are increasingly being developed in high-altitude zones as well as in areas near oceans – the Atlantic meets the Indian Ocean at Cape Agulhas, the southernmost point of the African continent – where the air is cooler, especially at night. Notable among the districts here are Overberg, Walker Bay, and Cape Agulhas, all of which belong to the Cape South Coast region, extending along the coast southeast of Stellenbosch and False Bay.

> **GRAPE VARIETIES** White: Sauvignon Blanc, Chardonnay; red: Pinot Noir.

> **SOIL** Ancient, essentially from the Precambrian era.

> **STYLE** In this appreciably cooler southern area, the wines (largely white) are lively and fresh.

> **NOTABLE PRODUCERS** Agulhas Wines, Bouchard Finlayson, Hamilton Russell, Lomond, Newton Johnson, Raka.

PAARL AND FRANSCHHOEK

Part of the very large Coastal Region, Paarl extends north of Stellenbosch, and its distance from the ocean means that it has a rather warmer climate. For this reason, Paarl specialized for many years in port-type fortified wines, which were appreciated by the home market. Today production is much more diversified, thanks largely to magnificent wines made from Syrah and other Rhône grape varieties. The Franschhoek valley district extends to the southeast and is separated from Stellenbosch by the Simonsberg Mountains. It owes its name ('French corner') to the arrival in the 17th century of Huguenot refugees fleeing religious persecution in France. The names of some farms still testify to this French origin: La Motte, Grande Provence, Mont Rochelle, Chamonix, Cabrière, etc.

> **GRAPE VARIETIES** White: Chenin Blanc, Chardonnay, Sauvignon Blanc, Colombard; red: Cabernet Sauvignon, Shiraz, Merlot, Pinotage, Cinsaut.

> **SOIL** Granite soil at the foot of the mountains, sand and clay elsewhere in the region.

> **STYLE** The wines are often heartier than their Stellenbosch neighbours, but this generalization should be qualified by a given site's geographic situation and its altitude.

> **NOTABLE PRODUCERS** Glen Carlou, Boekenhoutskloof, Fairview, Nederburg, Porcupine Ridge, Veenwouden.

Kanonkop, South African Classicism

Kanonkop ('Canon Hill') is one of Stellenbosch's model estates and one of the best ambassadors for the South African winegrowing industry. It was created in 1910 by the Sauer family, which has also produced several South African ministers. Today, the fourth generation of the family, Johann and Paul Krige, run the 247-acre (100-ha) estate, located on the the lower slopes of Simonsberg Mountain. It has maintained a reputation that was formed well before the end of apartheid by a faithful adherence to a number of constants: control of the yields, harvesting at optimal maturity, fermentation in traditional open concrete vats, and some maturation in new wood. The Bordeaux grape varieties (Cabernet Sauvignon, Merlot, Cabernet Franc) produce wines of a Bordeaux classicism, with extra fullness delivered by the Stellenbosch climate. The estate's excellent wines (Paul Sauer, Cabernet Sauvignon) are built to last, including those made with Pinotage (Black Label), which have a complexity and depth rarely found elsewhere.

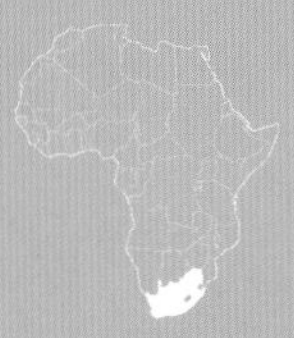

Coastal Region

KLEIN
CONSTANTIA

What do Marie-Antoinette, Napoleon Bonaparte, Jane Austen, and Charles Dickens have in common? All four were great fans of Vin de Constance, the sweet nectar produced at the very tip of South Africa. Nowadays, only modest quantities are mde, but Klein Constantia is reinventing this historic wine.

KLEIN CONSTANTIA

Klein Constantia Rd
7848 Cape Town

Founded: *1685*
Area: *361 acres (146 ha)*
Production: *N/A*
Appellation: *Coastal Region*
Red grape varieties:
Cabernet Sauvignon, Cabernet Franc, Merlot, Syrah, Petit Verdot, Malbec
White grape varieties: *Sauvignon Blanc, Chardonnay, Riesling, Muscat Blanc à Petits Grains*

A renaissance

Napoleon consumed more than 264 gallons (1,200 litres) of Klein Constantia a year during his enforced sojourn on Saint Helena, and Jane Austen recommends its healing powers for heartache in *Sense and Sensibility* – at the turn of the 19th century, a bottle of this sweet ambrosia from the Cape was worth more than a bottle of Chateau d'Yquem. But then phylloxera came and the vines were all ripped out; Vin de Constance did not rise again from these ashes, like a South African phoenix, until 1980.

300 years of history

The Groot Constantia estate was founded by Simon van der Stel, the first governor of the Cape Colony and the man who gave his name to Stellenbosch. It was van der Stel who decided to plant vineyards here, making this the oldest wine-growing area in southern Africa, and the pretty buildings and magnificent gardens surrounding the vineyards are testimony to this Dutch heritage. Since then, this large property has been divided up into several estates, including Groot Constantia, Klein Constantia, and Constantia Uitsig.

Neglect and renaissance

Constantia is also a 'ward', a wine-making district within the Coastal Region, at the base of the Cape Peninsula, where they generally produce white wines that are for the most part dry, using Sauvignon Blanc, Semillon, and Chardonnay grapes, not to mention an excellent Riesling. Although not far from the coast, the elevation of the estate is quite high (985 feet/300m), which guarantees a certain freshness that helps develop the wines' bouquet and promotes a pleasing acidity. Nowadays, however, the proportion of Muscat (Muscat Blanc à Petits Grains and Rose) reserved for the sweet wines that have cemented the reputation of this area for three centuries under the name of Vin de Constance is fairly modest; Klein Constantia deserves credit for reviving this wine after decades of neglect.

'Old style but less sugar'

Klein Constantia has been in the hands of four investors from overseas since 2012, including Bruno Prats and Hubert de Boüard from Bordeaux. The local estate manager is Swedish, but Matthew Day, the resident wine expert, is South African. He took over the job from the charismatic Adam Mason, who is in charge of wine-making, and helped Vin de Constance reconnect with its past.

It is difficult nowadays to get an exact idea of the quality of the wines made in the 19th century, making all comparisons a risky business, but one thing is certain: the *terroirs* (gentle slopes encircling the estate buildings) and the grape varieties are the same (indeed, the vines are clones). And for good measure, today's Vin de Constance uses the original 18th-century bottle.

The vines are irrigated these days, viewed by some as an explanation for a certain 'lack of body' in the modern version of Vin de Constance; it is also no doubt explained by the age of the vines and, in particular, a deliberate desire not to wholly numb the palate of the modern drinker. In short, this Vin de Constance is also a nostalgic wine whose appeal lies as much in its history as in the delightful sensations it can elicit.

KLEIN CONSTANTIA VINE DE CONSTANCE

The finished product is a fairly complex blend of a base wine made from grapes harvested just as they are ripening and a greater part of grapes that are picked once they have withered on the vine. Ageing lasts about 30 months and involves casks made of French and Hungarian oak as well as acacia barrels. This is a highly scented sweet wine (orange zest, dried apricots, citron jam) of surprising balance, with subtlety and lightness despite its high sugar content (between 20 and 24 oz per gallon, or 120 and 150 g/litre). Supple, complex, refined, and with a long finish, it is a distinctive Muscat and an invitation to a journey through time and space.

> Matthew Day, winemaker.

AUSTRALIA

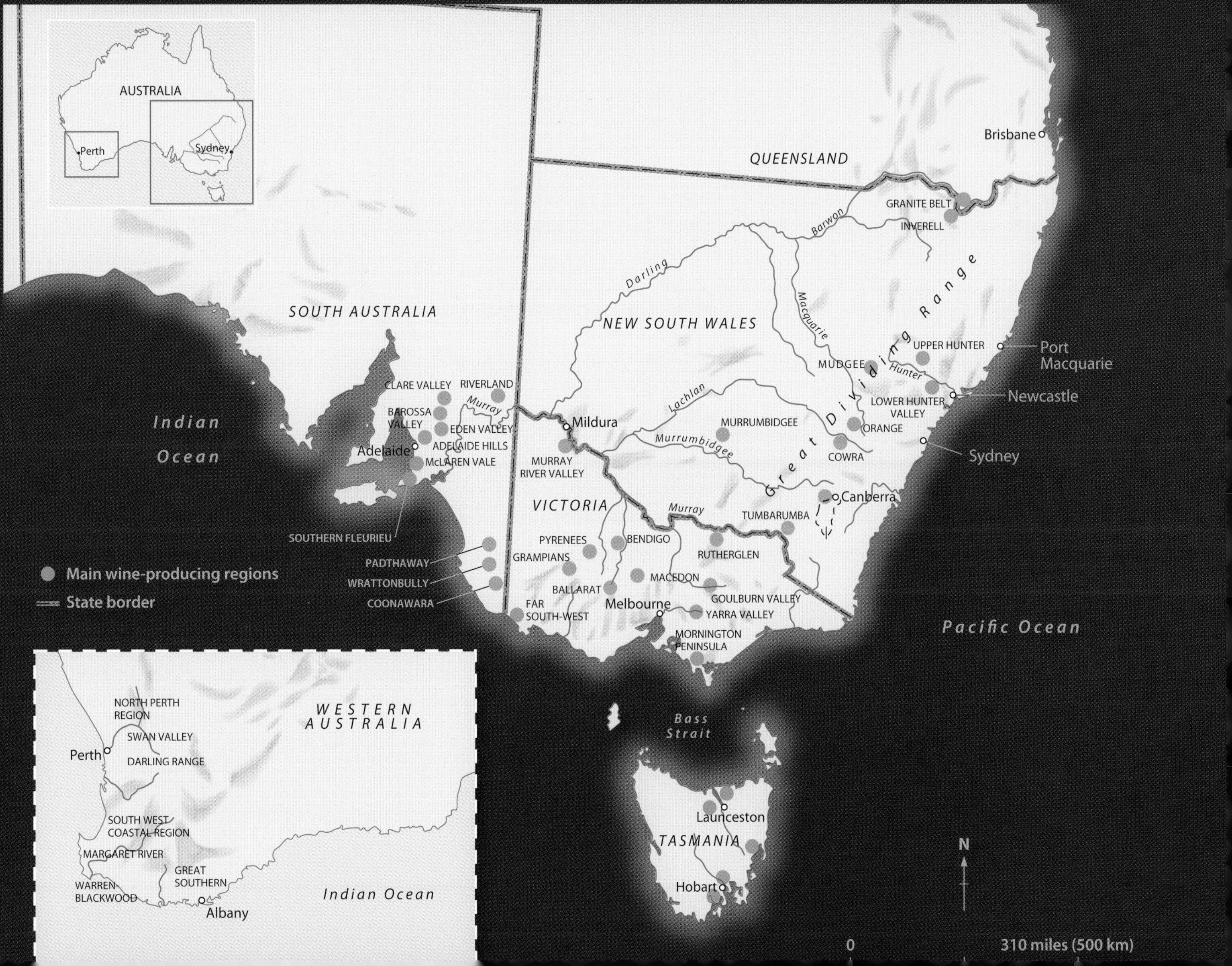

AUSTRALIA
Perth
Sydney
QUEENSLAND
Brisbane
SOUTH AUSTRALIA
NEW SOUTH WALES
VICTORIA
TASMANIA
WESTERN AUSTRALIA
Indian Ocean
Pacific Ocean
Bass Strait
Great Dividing Range
Darling
Barwon
Macquarie
Lachlan
Murrumbidgee
Murray
Hunter
GRANITE BELT
INVERELL
UPPER HUNTER
Port Macquarie
MUDGEE
Newcastle
LOWER HUNTER VALLEY
MURRUMBIDGEE
ORANGE
COWRA
Sydney
Canberra
TUMBARUMBA
Mildura
MURRAY RIVER VALLEY
CLARE VALLEY
RIVERLAND
BAROSSA VALLEY
EDEN VALLEY
Adelaide
ADELAIDE HILLS
McLAREN VALE
SOUTHERN FLEURIEU
PADTHAWAY
WRATTONBULLY
COONAWARA
PYRENEES
BENDIGO
GRAMPIANS
RUTHERGLEN
MACEDON
BALLARAT
Melbourne
GOULBURN VALLEY
YARRA VALLEY
FAR SOUTH-WEST
MORNINGTON PENINSULA
Launceston
Hobart
Main wine-producing regions
State border
NORTH PERTH REGION
SWAN VALLEY
Perth
DARLING RANGE
SOUTH WEST COASTAL REGION
MARGARET RIVER
GREAT SOUTHERN
WARREN-BLACKWOOD
Albany
N
0
310 miles (500 km)

AUSTRALIA

Over the past two decades, Australia's vineyard acreage has almost tripled and Australian wines are now known worldwide. Australian success can be credited to the producers' dynamism, organization, and their skill in developing wines to suit consumer taste. But Australia also produces great wines that owe their character to the terroir *and to an impressive reserve of old vines.*

Early beginnings and modern progress

VINES FROM EUROPE. Between 1820 and 1850, viticulture was a significant agricultural activity in southeastern Australia – the region surrounding the developing townships of Sydney, Melbourne, and Adelaide. Throughout the 19th century, there were many private initiatives to import grape varieties from the Old World as people arrived from Europe with a few cuttings of *Vitis vinifera*.

PRODUCTION FOR THE UK MARKET. Until the outbreak of phylloxera in 1877, the state of Victoria was the country's chief centre of production. After that, the output from New South Wales increased considerably thanks to the production of fortified wines largely destined for the English market, and due to the development of irrigation systems in the Murray Valley. By 1930, 75 per cent of the country's wine output came from this region, and exports flourished thanks to opportunities offered in Commonwealth outlets. In terms of the volume of wine exported to the UK market, Australia had already outstripped France by 1927, a lead France did not recapture until 2005. During the postwar period, the wine industry really began to evolve. The demand for dry wines, especially whites, increased; and producers developed new techniques of vinification, notably the introduction of stainless steel tanks and temperature control systems.

AUSTRALIA STATISTICS

Vineyard area: 370,658 acres (150,000 ha)

Production: 133 million cases (12,000,000 hl)

Reds: 64%

Whites: 44%

(Australian Bureau of Statistics, OIV, 2015)

GROWING HOME MARKET AND QUALITY WINES. Production exploded during the 1980s, chiefly driven by growth of the home market. Faced with new demand, winemakers expanded their output (some of it from unpromising sites), and sales of wine in bulk and in boxes accounted for 80 per cent of production during this period.

Wine quality has come on in leaps and bounds since the 1990s thanks to the rapid spread of technical progress and the improved selection of grape varieties. The wine industry has focused, with great commercial success, on providing reliable, well-made, good-value wines, enabling Australian wines to make great strides in the export markets. Alongside standardized production, a growing number of small, independent estates

> Drought has struck some vineyard areas, prompting the search for cooler climes.

Water problems

In this enormous and arid continent, wine production (like most of the population) is concentrated in the southern and coastal regions, especially in the southeast. Although winter and spring can be rainy, the summers are particularly hot and dry, especially in some parts of western and southern Australia. Lack of water remains a primary concern in many regions, and irrigation is essential.

The Riverland area, bordering the states of Victoria and South Australia, produces nearly 50 per cent of Australia's wine thanks to irrigation, which has transformed a semi-desert region into a sea of vines. However, the limitations of this system are evident, with repeated droughts.

> Vines at the Oliverhill winery in McLaren Vale, South Australia.

are securing a strong regional identity for their wines. Today, Australia is the world's sixth-largest wine producer and the fourth-largest exporter.

Climate and grape varieties

Australia benefits from almost ideal conditions for wine production: plenty of sunshine, low humidity, maritime influences, and local mountain ranges. While Australians originally regarded climate as the essential factor in a vineyard's potential, today the question of soils, orientation, and altitude of plots is taken into account.

The majority of white wines are made using Chardonnay grapes, ahead of Sauvignon Blanc, Semillon, Colombard, and Riesling. Shiraz (Syrah) remains the great national grape variety for red wines. Introduced during the 19th century, it produces several of the country's most successful wines, either as a single grape variety or blended with Cabernet; increasingly it may also be blended with Grenache or Mourvedre (Mataro). Cabernet Sauvignon, Merlot, and Pinot Noir have also gained ground. Beyond these varieties, a certain amount of diversification is in progress: Verdelho, Viognier, and Marsanne being used for white wine; while Mourvèdre, Sangiovese, Barbera, Cabernet Franc, or Petit Verdot are used in reds.

Formerly, producers tried to grow a range of grape varieties whatever the local climate; but now specialization is increasing, especially in relation to regional conditions. Examples include Riesling in the Clare Valley, Cabernet Sauvignon at Coonawarra or Margaret River, and Shiraz in the Barossa Valley.

Moving to appellations

Australian (and now many) consumers rely chiefly on the grape variety and the brand. Until recently, the geographic origin of the wine was a far less important indicator – but that is changing. Following initial efforts in the 1960s, labeling regulations were established in early 1990s under the Label Integrity Program. A particular grape variety may not be cited on a label unless at least 85 per cent of the wine is made from it. If several varieties are named on the label, they must be listed in decreasing order of importance (*see* also p.103). In 1993, the Geographical Indications (GI) system was initiated, comprising several categories: zones, regions, and sub-regions. A zone is the largest area and can include several states, such as South Eastern Australia, which

Cool climate quest

Faced with the difficulties of drought, Australian winegrowers have spent 20 years assiduously searching for cooler climates more favourable to the production of fine wines. As a result, Tasmania and the coastal regions in the extreme south of the country, both in the state of Victoria and in Western Australia, have all seen rapid expansion of their vine plantings.

> Cathcart Ridge estate in the state of Victoria.

applies to blended wines where the grapes come from several south-eastern states (New South Wales, Victoria, Queensland, and South Australia), a single state (for example, Victoria) or a subdivision of a state (for example, Central Victoria). Below these there are some 90 regions or sub-regions. For some of them, such as Coonawarra, boundary disputes have led to prolonged legal battles.

New South Wales

The state of New South Wales, in southeast Australia, is the oldest and one of the largest production areas in the country. It continues to expand, with output growing year on year. The flagship zone is Hunter Valley, 125 miles (200 km) north of Sydney (*see* p.592), famous for its Shiraz and Sémillon wines. Southwest of Hunter Valley, the Mudgee region (*see* p.592) benefits from a drier, warmer climate than its coastal neighbour. Further south, the small Orange region has recently received investment from major groups, attracted by the potential of the cool slopes of Mount Canobolas. Further inland, toward the west, the large Murrumbidgee Irrigation Area produces everyday wines, chiefly from Semillon and Trebbiano (Ugni Blanc) grapes. Finally, in the southeast of the state, and in addition to Canberra District's flourishing boutique wineries, mention should be made of the potential of the Tumbarumba region, which benefits from the altitude of the Snowy Mountains.

DID YOU KNOW...?

Like many countries where wine appreciation is a relatively recent development, Australia places a lot of emphasis on wine challenges and competitions. *These shows are very professionally organized and make a good promotional platform for the winning wines. They may be national or regional, confined to wines from certain grape varieties, or simply encompass all wine categories.*

Victoria

South of New South Wales, the state of Victoria is responsible for 17 per cent of the country's wine vineyard area, spread over a multitude of very different zones and regions.

North East Victoria's particularly hot climate is ideal for Rutherglen's splendid Muscat- or Muscadelle-based dessert wines. Further south, the high-altitude vineyards of King Valley have the advantage of a cool climate and are planted mostly with Riesling, Chardonnay, and Cabernet Sauvignon. In the southeast of the state, the Gippsland zone's vast acreage is sparsely planted as yet, but growing strongly.

In the most southerly regions of Victoria, which benefit from oceanic influences, Pinot Noir and Chardonnay produce rather elegant wines. The area around Port Philip Bay, west of Gippsland, sees similar conditions and is home to several famous regions, such as Mornington (*see* p.594) and Yarra Valley (*see* p.593). Further north, Central Victoria includes the Bendigo region as well as that of Goulburn Valley, which is chiefly devoted to Shiraz (Syrah) and Cabernet Sauvignon. The majority of the grapes grown in the state come from the North West Victoria zone, where the heat can be crushing and irrigation is indispensable. Muscat Gordo Blanco and Sultana grapes are still strongly represented, although their share of the crop is diminishing. In the south of Western Victoria, the climate is cooler and the Grampians region chiefly produces sparkling wines, although the Riesling and Shiraz table wines show promise.

Tasmania

Tasmania is a large island south of Victoria. Until recently, its cool, windy climate was considered suitable only for the production of sparkling wines. But over the past few years (and probably thanks to climate change that has led to rising temperatures) very good still white wines have been made here, as well as promising Pinot Noirs.

South Australia

The state of South Australia produces 50 per cent of the country's wine output. It is largely due to huge volumes of everyday wines made in the Riverland area along the Murray River Valley. However, its true riches are found in the coastal zones that benefit from the cool ocean winds.

In the southeast, several regions of the Limestone Coast zone, such as Padthaway and Wrattonbully, are on the rise; but they are far from reaching the fame of Coonawarra (*see* p.601). Running north along the coast, the zones of Fleurieu, Barossa, and Mount Lofty Ranges are backed by a north-south chain of mountains and are home to several remarkable sites. These include the hills of McLaren Vale (*see* p.600), where a Mediterranean climate produces fine red wines from Shiraz and Cabernet Sauvignon grapes. Further north, the Barossa Valley (*see* p.595) is the stronghold of old Shiraz vines that yield robust, full-bodied wines in a hot climate. Like the Cabernet wines of the Médoc (France), they constitute a kind of stylistic reference point for Australian Shiraz. Bordering Barossa to the east, Eden Valley (*see* p.600) is better known for its Rieslings. Further north, in the Mount Lofty Ranges zone, the coastal influences diminish and the climate becomes more continental. Still further north, Riesling and Cabernet Sauvignon offer good results in Clare Valley (*see also* p.594), where the altitude makes for a cooler climate.

Western Australia

This state produces only seven per cent of the nation's wine, although the volume has tripled since 1997. It is testament to the dynamism of the region, where many sites are being prospected. The climate is varied, ranging from scorching northwestern regions, such as Swan Valley, to the more temperate regions of Margaret River and the appreciably cooler Great Southern region. Margaret River (*see also* p.601) is a very trendy region, and some big companies have recently established themselves there. Further east along the coast, Great Southern (*see* p. 601) is one of the great future hopes for cool-climate grape varieties such as Riesling, Chardonnay, and Pinot Noir. Among other regions of note, Pemberton, situated between Margaret River and Great Southern, stands out for its promising Chardonnays, while Geographe, which extends along the west coast above Margaret River, produces elegant Cabernet Sauvignon and Shiraz wines.

> In the cellar at Campbells Winery in Rutherglen, Victoria.

Leading Australian regions and wines

The precise geographic origins of wines destined for mass consumption are not usually indicated. Most of these wines are made from grapes harvested in several regions. Technology has facilitated this kind of production on an industrial scale, and the result is a remarkable standard of reliability. But Australia also has identified many clearly defined regions that are winning a reputation as distinctive indicators of wine character.

HUNTER VALLEY

NEW SOUTH WALES

North of Sydney and upstream from the port of Newcastle, the Hunter Valley zone sprawls along the river of the same name. It includes Upper Hunter in the north and Lower Hunter in the south, each considered separate regions, although linked by the river. At first glance, the hot and humid climate makes it an unlikely location for the development of great wines. Nevertheless, Hunter Valley is to some extent the cradle of Australian viticulture and remarkable wines are produced there. These include Semillons for laying down; they are some of the country's most distinctive wines.

> **GRAPE VARIETIES** White: Semillon, Chardonnay; red: Cabernet Sauvignon, Shiraz.

> **SOIL** Sandy, well-drained alluvial flats.

> **STYLE** The Semillons are among Australia's best dry whites. Usually fermented in vats, they have remarkable ageing characteristics. Harvested early, the grapes produce light wines, low in alcohol, and with good acidity. They acquire their unique, complex bouquet in maturation, with notes of toasted bread, dried fruit, and honey. The Chardonnays are generally more concentrated and rounder, while the Shiraz style is varied, ranging from round and powerful to relatively fresh and tannic.

> **NOTABLE PRODUCERS** Brokenwood, De Bortoli, Evans Family, Mount View Estate, Rothbury Ridge, Tyrrell's, Wyndham Estate.

MUDGEE

NEW SOUTH WALES

Its Aboriginal name meaning 'nest of hills,' Mudgee is separated from Hunter Valley by the Great Dividing Range, the chain of mountains on its eastern border. It has a hot, dry climate, so irrigation is necessary. The region does not enjoy the same reputation as its neighbour, but much of its harvest is sold to the big Hunter Valley producers.

> **GRAPE VARIETIES** White: Chardonnay, Pinot Gris, Viognier; red: Cabernet Sauvignon, Merlot, Shiraz.

> **SOIL** Sandy loam and clay.

> **STYLE** The most interesting wines are made with Cabernet Sauvignon, sometimes blended with Merlot or Shiraz. They show a rich, warming style with aromas of overripe fruits and cacao with eucalyptus notes. The Shiraz wines are of the same calibre. Chardonnay has long been established here and produces heavy, aromatic wines with good ageing potential – like the Semillon wines made in a style similar to that of Hunter Valley.

> **NOTABLE PRODUCERS** Huntington Estate, Miramar, Poet's Corner.

HEATHCOTE

VICTORIA

This small wine region is situated at the centre of Victoria, between the Goulburn Valley and Bendigo. Although the earliest vine plantings in the area date back to the 1860s, it was not until the 1970s that winemakers took a close look at the region's potential. They remain few in number, but they are often highly reputed and their wines are sought after. The growing area covers less that 4,900 acres (2,000 ha) on moderately elevated slopes (490–1,150 ft/150–350 m). The climate, influenced by the chain of the Mount Camel Range, is cooler, more humid, and windier than surrounding regions. Local production is dominated by red grape varieties, especially Shiraz followed by Cabernet Sauvignon.

> **GRAPE VARIETIES** Red: Cabernet Sauvignon, Merlot, Shiraz.

> **SOIL** Weathered earth (Cambrian greenstone) over chalk and red clay.

> **STYLE** Shiraz expresses itself in a particularly intense way (soft fruits, cherries, prunes); it is powerful and concentrated with supple tannins and, sometimes, menthol notes that bring a touch of freshness. Cabernet Sauvignon, sometimes blended with Merlot, also makes rich, generous wines with mint or eucalyptus notes.

> **NOTABLE PRODUCERS** Coliban Valley Wines, Heathcote Estate, Jasper Hill, M. Chapoutier.

YARRA VALLEY

VICTORIA

Situated less than one hour's drive east of Melbourne, Yarra Valley is Victoria's best-known wine region. With altitudes ranging from 160–1,300 ft (50–400 m), and steep slopes in places, the valley's topography is fairly complex. But the style of its wines is also influenced by the cool, humid climate. Yarra is noted for producing some of Australia's best sparkling wines, and for good Chardonnays and Pinot Noirs.

> **GRAPE VARIETIES** White: Chardonnay, Sauvignon Blanc; red: Pinot Noir, followed by Cabernet Sauvignon and Shiraz.

> **SOIL** Sandy clay-loams in the north, red volcanic soil in the south.

> **STYLE** The best sparkling wines are made by the traditional method and are full of finesse and freshness. The Chardonnays are generally well balanced, perhaps less exuberant than others, but fresh and aromatic (nutty, fig or white peach flavours). The best red wines are made from Pinot Noir, with lots of fruit (cherries), spices, and vivacity; or from Shiraz in a fruity, often juicy style.

> **NOTABLE PRODUCERS** Coldstream Hills, De Bortoli, Domaine Chandon, Giant Steps, TarraWarra, Yarra Yering, Yeringberg, Yering Station.

Giaconda – a small, high quality estate

During the 1970s, Rick Kinzbrunner, a mechanical engineer by training, decided to make a career in wine. For 10 years, he travelled the world honing his skills at the University of California-Davis, at Stag's Leap Wine Cellars and others in the Napa and Sonoma valleys, as well as at the Bordeaux properties of the Moueix family, co-owners of Pétrus, before becoming assistant winemaker at an Australian estate (Brown Brothers, Milawa). In 1982, he planted his first vines in Beechworth, a little regarded region in northeast Victoria, producing his first wine in 1986. Despite its minuscule acreage, Giaconda has become one of Australia's most famous names, and its wines fetch astronomical prices. From a pocket-sized vineyard (10 acres/4 ha), this artisan winemaker draws powerful, complex wines – the result of the most natural vinification possible (local yeasts and no filtration), and of particularly careful viticulture. His Chardonnays (Nantua) and Shiraz (Warmer Vineyard) show a rich, powerful style and are among the best Australia has to offer.

VICTORIA

MORNINGTON PENINSULA

Located at Victoria's southernmost point, the Mornington Peninsula is one of those regions prospected by winegrowers in search of cooler climes. Surrounded by the sea and swept by winds, it enjoys plenty of sunshine and moderate temperatures, and there is no water problem for the vines. A small group of producers have rapidly exploited this fortunate spot to produce fine, fresh wines made from varieties that adapt well to such conditions, notably Chardonnay and Pinot Noir.

> **GRAPE VARIETIES** White: Chardonnay, Pinot Gris, Viognier; red: Cabernet Franc, Cabernet Sauvignon, Merlot, Pinot Noir.

> **SOIL** Compacted, well-drained sandy, clay, and red soils of volcanic origin.

> **STYLE** The Chardonnay produces lively, aromatic wines (citrus and nutty flavours). The Pinot Gris also has recently become much sought-after. As for the red wines, the Pinots Noirs are fresh and fruity (cherries) and are best consumed while young. The Bordeaux varieties are grown in the warmest sectors, such as the Moorooduc Valley, and make relatively light, low-tannin wines.

> **NOTABLE PRODUCERS** Dromana, Kooyong, Montalto, Moorooduc, Paringa, Stonier, Ten Minutes by Tractor, T'Gallant, Yabby Lake.

TASMANIA

The quest for cooler climates than those of Australia's large production zones, which have suffered from global warming and drought, is vividly illustrated in the case of Tasmania. This huge island, just below Australia's southeasternmost point, now harbours a growing number of mostly small-scale producers. The vineyards are all situated on the northern or southeastern sides of the island, where the cool (and sometimes very windy) climate favours the cultivation of white grape varieties and Pinot Noir, as well as the production of sparkling wines. (The latitude is identical to that of New Zealand's South Island.)

> **GRAPE VARIETIES** White: Chardonnay, Riesling, Sauvignon Blanc, Semillon; red: Cabernet Franc, Cabernet Sauvignon, Gamay, Pinot Noir.

> **SOIL** Ancient compacted sandstone and shale; river alluvials and rich volcanic earth in some places.

> **STYLE** Products of a cool climate, most of Tasmania's wines possess great natural freshness. At their peak, the sparkling wines (most frequently Chardonnay and Pinot Noir) offer plenty of vivacity and aromatic finesse. The Rieslings can be sharp and need to be cellared for some time, while the good Sauvignon Blancs are particularly aromatic and firm, close in style to those from Marlborough (*see* p.486). The Pinot Noirs are aromatic (fresh berry fruits, spices) and well structured.

> **NOTABLE PRODUCERS** Bay of Fires, Freycinet, Jansz (sparkling wines), Meadowbank, Pipers Brook, Pirie, Tamar Ridge.

SOUTH AUSTRALIA

CLARE VALLEY

Situated in the northern Mount Lofty Ranges, the Clare Valley's undulating landscape makes it one of Australia's most attractive wine-producing regions. The days are warm to hot and the nights are cool, but local orientation and the altitude within the valley play an important role. Towards the end of the 1990s, local winemakers were the first to adopt the screwcap wine closure. The Clare Valley is particularly renowned for its Rieslings, but red grape varieties (chiefly Cabernet Sauvignon and Shiraz) are also successful.

> **GRAPE VARIETIES** White: Riesling, Semillon; red: Cabernet Sauvignon, Grenache, Malbec, Shiraz.

> **SOIL** Red topsoil over limestone; fertile alluvial soil in the north, sandy loams with degraded quartz to the west.

> **STYLE** Clare Valley's Riesling is a firm, dry wine with fine natural acidity and juicy citrus and mineral aromas; when young it is rather austere, but it has long cellaring potential. In addition to intense white wines, the region also offers well-structured, fruity Shiraz (red berries, spices) and Cabernet Sauvignons that, at their best, are famous for their aromatic complexity (dark berries, menthol, cigar box), balance, and longevity.

> **NOTABLE PRODUCERS** Grosset, Jim Barry, Kilikanoon, Leasingham, Mitchell, Mount Horrocks, Tim Adams.

BAROSSA VALLEY

SOUTH AUSTRALIA

The Barossa Valley is less than 30 miles (50 km) northeast of Adelaide and is the country's most famous wine-producing region. Viticulture dates back to the wave of immigration from Silesia during the 19th century, the influence of which is still evident. Today, it is one of Australia's leading quality winemaking regions and home to producers of varying sizes, ranging from such giants of Australian wine production as Penfolds to many highly regarded smaller estates. Century-old Shiraz vines and some Grenache and Mourvedre sit alongside more recent plantings, notably of Cabernet Sauvignon, Chardonnay, and Riesling. The climate is warm and dry, and the wines exemplify this characteristic.

> **GRAPE VARIETIES** White: Chardonnay, Riesling, Semillon; red: Cabernet Sauvignon, Grenache, Merlot, Mourvedre, Shiraz.

> **SOIL** Clay-loam and sandy soil.

> **STYLE** Powerful, ripe, exuberant reds. They have great depth when made with grapes from old vines. They also have good ageing potential. The Shiraz in particular can achieve rare amplitude, with plenty of fruit. The whites tend to be soft and rounded, although some Rieslings from grapes grown at higher altitude display finesse and elegance. Excellent port-style fortified wines are also produced.

> **NOTABLE PRODUCERS** Charles Melton, Glaetzer, Kaesler, Penfolds, Peter Lehmann, Rockford, St. Hallett, Seppelt, Torbreck, Turkey Flat, Wolf Blass, Yalumba.

Domaine Torbreck in the Barossa Valley

Torbreck is a producer of modest size within the Australian wine industry as a whole, but it is one of the best-known names in the Barossa Valley in South Australia. Although he has now left the estate, it was the founder David Powell who put it very firmly on the region's map. A passionate globetrotter and fascinated by Rhône wines, he worked in the Barossa Valley in the early 1990s for other owners and looked after old, neglected vines at a time when these sleeping gems were being uprooted in large quantities. In 1994, he founded the Torbreck estate, buying grapes from trusted producers, and made his first wines in a modest hangar. His artisan approach, along with his expertise both in terms of taste and knowledge of old vines soon attracted many fans of the powerful and warming Shiraz wines. The estate went from strength to strength, equipped with its Shiraz vines planted back in 1890 and a brand new winery. David Powell left the estate in 2013, but his successors are looking after his legacy and have remained loyal to the Torbreck style: unfiltered, rich, deep, and fleshy reds, made with blends of Shiraz, Grenache, and Mataro (Mourvedre), sometimes enhanced with a touch of Viognier, following the model of Côte-Rôtie.

South Australia

PENFOLDS *GRANGE*

You have no doubt heard of 'garage wines' but what about Grange wines? Nowadays, this Australian producer enjoys a reputation to rival the great châteaux of Bordeaux.

PENFOLDS

Tanunda Road, Nuriootpa
5355 South Australia

Founded: *1844*
Area: *4,942 acres (2,000 ha)*
Production: *N/A*
Appellation: *South Australia*
Red grape varieties: *Shiraz (Syrah), Cabernet Sauvignon, Mourvedre, Pinot Noir, Sangiovese*
White grape varieties: *Chardonnay, Pinot Gris, Sauvignon Blanc, Semillon, Viognier*

Following Schubert

The year is 1951. Max Schubert, Penfolds' new winemaker, was on his way back to Australia after studying in Europe, and Bordeaux in particular. His intention was to diversify Penfolds' production (best-known principally for its fortified wines at this point) by applying the methods of a new science known as oenology. His ambition from the start was to produce a wine matured in barrel that could be laid down for long periods, and by 1952 he had achieved this objective. But Max was still deliberating about the blend and in 1953 he offered two versions: one with 100 per cent Cabernet Sauvignon and one with 87 per cent Shiraz/13 per cent Cabernet Sauvignon; the latter was ultimately chosen for posterity, with a few variant versions depending on the production year. The wine was initially called Grange Hermitage – 'Hermitage' being a synonym for Syrah in Australia – although this reference was dropped in 1990 under pressure from European wine authorities, in order to protect a certain appellation.

The virtues of obstinacy

The experiment very nearly came to an abrupt halt: critical reaction to the first wines was somewhat muted and in 1957, the Penfolds management told Max to stop making the wine –

but he persisted and continued to produce it in secret until 1959, by which time the first years of production were being opened and were showing their true quality. The press did a volte-face and the management followed suit, asking Max to restart production, which in fact had never stopped, as was demonstrated by the sale over the ensuing years of wines from every year between 1957 and 1960.

Despite retiring in 1973, Max Schubert still kept an eye on Grange until his death in 1994. Grange wines started to appear at international competitions from 1962, with the 1955 in particular notching up no fewer than 50 gold medals over the course of the years and the 1971 vintage sweeping all the great Syrahs of the world before it at the *Olympiades du vin* competition in Paris. The wine's reputation had been established beyond all doubt. Every edition of Langton's, the definitive guide to Australian wine, has given it an 'exceptional' classification and it has garnered top marks in the most widely read tasting notes from the UK to the USA – while the National Trust of South Australia has listed it as an item of national heritage.

PENFOLDS GRANGE
SOUTH AUSTRALIAN SHIRAZ
BIN 95

Although mostly made with Shiraz, Penfolds' legendary wine often includes a judicious amount of Cabernet Sauvignon. Ageing takes place over about 20 months in American oak barrels. Its extremely ripe bouquet evokes jammy black fruits and the rich, powerful mouthfeel contains robust tannins that the wine's body has little difficulty in incorporating. It has an enhanced potential for laying down and the 'tasting window' generally begins after about six to eight years, at which point everything has begun to integrate.

A first growth – but what kind of first growth?

It is often said that Grange is Australia's greatest *grand cru*, but in strictest sense of the term, this is not quite true, as it is not a precise wine-making area – the wine is vinified at the Magill estate, near Adelaide, but Penfolds reserves the right to include any other of its vineyards, and the make-up of the wine is reviewed each year depending on the quality of the harvest; the proportion of Shiraz may vary from one year to the next (from 89 to 100 per cent), in the same way that the grape content from the Barossa Valley (100 per cent in 2000, for example) is often topped up with grapes from McLaren Vale or Padthaway. You will nonetheless always find a simple 'South Australian Shiraz' and 'Bin 95' printed on the label.

South Australia

HENSCHKE

These old Syrah vines, a symbol of Australia and the Barossa Valley region, have found formidable ambassadors in the Henschke dynasty. The family have been refining several of country's most legendary wines on the sunlit uplands of the Eden Valley for more than 60 years.

HENSCHKE

Keyneton S.A.
5353 Australia

***Area:** 260 acres (105 ha)*
***Production:** 540,000 bottles p.a.*
***Appellation:** Eden Valley*
***Red grape varieties:** Syrah, Cabernet Sauvignon, Grenache, Pinot Noir, Nebbiolo, Barbera, Mourvedre, Cabernet Franc, Merlot*
***White grape varieties:** Chardonnay, Riesling, Semillon, Sauvignon Blanc, Viognier, Gewurztraminer, Muscat*

Stephen and Prue, the sixth generation

Through the generations of this venerable dynasty of wine-makers there runs the historical watermark of a wine-making region that from a French perspective is often viewed – simplistically – as a spontaneously created generation of monstrous wineries flooding the world with carefully calibrated, soulless wine. But Australian wine-making is far more complex and nuanced, with producers of every shape and size, either newly arrived or with a long family or historical tradition.

The Henschke's story involves emigration in the 19th century, when Johann Christian Henschke left his native Silesia, losing his wife and child during an epic crossing before building a second life in South Australia, in the Barossa Valley region – an area dear to lovers of great wines made with Syrah grapes (or Shiraz, to use its Australian name.) The first in the great dynasty, he laid the foundations with a few vines in the Keyneton region and a small artisan winery dug out of the side of the mountain. Each generation has made its own contribution, buying new land in 1891 (including the future Hill of Grace), acquiring the first fermentation vats in the 1920s, making the first dry wines and single-estate wines in the 1950s, followed by national and international recognition when the Australian wine trade had barely stepped out of the shadows.

Stephen and Prue Henschke, the sixth generation, took up the reins of the estate at the start of the 1980s, and the couple's skills – Prue out in the vineyard, Stephen in the winery – have been honed with the same rigour and scientific curiosity by their various experiences abroad, in Germany (at Geisenheim) and

France (in Bordeaux and Burgundy). Thirty years of experimenting and perfectionism have secured the estate a place at the very pinnacle of Australia's wine hierarchy.

Old vines – and globally unique

The vineyard grew with the purchase of land in the cool part of Adelaide in 1981, but the heart of the estate remains rooted in the Eden Valley, part of the Barossa region, 44 miles (70 km) northeast of Adelaide. The vines grow at altitude, stretching out along the base of Mount Edelstone in rolling countryside of hills, eucalyptus forest, and orchards.

It is here that the Henschke family keep a weather eye on their treasure, a fabulous collection of venerable, ungrafted Shiraz vines more than 100 years old, a legacy that Prue Henschke tends and studies with obsessive attention to detail: practising biodynamic viticulture, tilling the soils, grassing over between the vines, and maintaining humidity by laying straw on the ground instead of using irrigation (the rule rather than the exception in this region of hot dry summers).

In the cellar, Stephen is rewarded with grapes of a rare concentration that, along with the climate, create the character of the estate's great wines, with a little extra depth and texture that only extremely old vines can supply. From a range that includes some 30 wines and a dozen or so grape varieties, the highlights are Hill of Grace and Mount Edelstone, the two single-vineyard wines that established the reputation of the estate and that have had plenty of time since the 1950s to prove their formidable capacity for ageing.

HENSCHKE HILL OF GRACE, EDEN VALLEY

The Hill of Grace is an Australian icon, a vineyard planted with Shiraz vines of a kind that makes them unique in the world. The oldest rootstock is more than 150 years old. Low yields, long ageing periods in vats, and no filtration give this concentrated and silky wine extraordinary depth, and it gradually surrenders all the subtleties of its bouquet: cedar, spices, and aromatic herbs on a base of very ripe fruit. Its velvety texture, meltingly ripe tannins, breadth, and exceptional length make it a wine that can be laid down for very long periods.

Henschke family portrait: hen, Prue, Andreas, ne, and Johann.

EDEN VALLEY

SOUTH AUSTRALIA

At an altitude of 1,200–1,650 ft (370–500 m), Eden Valley enjoys a cooler climate than its famous neighbour. This wooded region is noted for its white wines, with a long tradition in Riesling started by German immigrants during the 19th century. Chardonnay is also cultivated and offers supple, intense wines. In terms of reds, Eden Valley remains largely loyal to Shiraz, which is the basis for Henschke's Hill of Grace.

> **GRAPE VARIETIES** White: Chardonnay, Riesling; red: Cabernet Sauvignon, Shiraz.

> **SOIL** Loamy sand, clay, and silt, sometimes mixed with ironstone gravels and quartz.

> **STYLE** The Rieslings are firm, lively, and aromatic (citrus and flinty notes), with excellent cellaring potential. Shiraz wines have a generous bouquet of candied fruits, spices, and sometimes kirsch or eucalyptus; they are warming on the palate, with a supple, silky structure. The best combine depth and a long finish with good ageing potential, although they are delightful when young.

> **NOTABLE PRODUCERS** Heggies, Henschke, Mountadam, Pewsey Vale.

ADELAIDE HILLS

SOUTH AUSTRALIA

Adelaide Hills is a wine region situated east of the city of Adelaide and north of the McLaren Vale. Its distinction is one of the coolest climates in South Australia, thanks to its proximity to the sea and its altitude, which peaks at above 1,970 ft (600 m). This makes it highly suitable for white grape varieties, notably Chardonnay and Sauvignon Blanc,which are especially dominant in the southern sites of two famous sub-regions: Lenswood and Piccadilly. In the warmer northern sites, Cabernet Sauvignon, sometimes blended with Merlot, achieves a good level of maturity.

> **GRAPE VARIETIES** White: Chardonnay, Riesling, Sauvignon Blanc; red: Cabernet Sauvignon, Merlot, Pinot Noir.

> **SOIL** Sandy loams and clay subsoils.

> **STYLE** Adelaide Hills offers some of Australia's best Sauvignon Blancs. They have a lively, fragrant style (aromas of green fruits, citrus, sometimes exotic fruits), and should be consumed young. The Chardonnays are often used as the basis for sparkling wines, blended with Pinot Noir, which is also widely planted.

> **NOTABLE PRODUCERS** Knappstein, Lenswood, Nepenthe, Petaluma, Shaw & Smith.

MCLAREN VALE

SOUTH AUSTRALIA

Largely open to the ocean and bordered to the east by the Mount Lofty Ranges, McLaren Vale is a small region but one with a longstanding winemaking tradition. Its gently undulating green landscape and its Mediterranean climate have attracted many independent winemakers, often of a high standard. Although there is plenty of sunshine everywhere, local conditions vary significantly depending on aspect, altitude, and the degree of exposure to maritime influences.

> **GRAPE VARIETIES** White: Chardonnay, Sauvignon Blanc; red: Cabernet Sauvignon, Grenache, Shiraz.

> **SOIL** Sandy alluvials, loam, and silt.

> **STYLE** McLaren Vale is known primarily for its instantly seductive, rich, full-bodied red wines with exuberant fruity flavours. The Cabernet Sauvignons evoke ripe dark fruits with spicy, chocolaty notes and rounded tannins. The Shiraz is dark with warming accents, concentrated fruit, and a generous level of alcohol. Grenache from old vines is sometimes blended with Shiraz to make particularly deep, smooth wines with aromas of candied fruit or kirsch.

> **NOTABLE PRODUCERS** Clarendon Hills, D'Arenberg, Gemtree, Hardy's Reynella, Mitolo, Wirra Wirra.

COONAWARRA

SOUTH AUSTRALIA

At the extreme southeast corner of South Australia, this region is one of the temples of great Australian Cabernet Sauvignon. Situated 37 miles (60 km) inland, swept by western winds and cooled by Antarctic currents, it enjoys a temperate maritime climate. Uniquely in Australia, its boundaries are defined – after a long legal battle – by a specific kind of soil called 'terra rossa', composed of a thin layer of reddish earth over a thick bed of limestone. This formation encompasses a narrow strip of vineyards 1.2 miles (2 km) wide by about 9 miles (15 km) long, running north to south. Coonawarra made its reputation with the first plantings of Cabernet Sauvignon in the 1960s, eclipsing Shiraz – although this is still grown, as are Chardonnay and Riesling.

> **GRAPE VARIETIES** White: Chardonnay, Riesling; red: Cabernet Sauvignon, Merlot, Shiraz.

> **SOIL** Friable red clays ('terra rossa') over limestone.

> **STYLE** Cabernet Sauvignon makes intense wines distinguished by flavours of blackcurrant and eucalyptus; they are more structured than most Australian Cabernets, and fresher, with relatively firm tannins. These wines usually have good cellaring potential. The Shiraz shows a similar register, with a more marked fruitiness and freshness than wines from warmer regions.

> **NOTABLE PRODUCERS** Katnook, Parker, Wynns, Zema.

MARGARET RIVER

WESTERN AUSTRALIA

About 165 miles (270 km) south of Perth, this region was hardly planted before the 1980s; but its reputation has grown and grown ever since its potential was highlighted by pioneering estates including Cape Mentelle and Cullen. The climate is Mediterranean – hot and dry – but more tempered and more humid than inland zones, thanks to the ocean that buffers it on three sides. The highly permeable gravelly, sandy soil is excellent for the Cabernet Sauvignon that has given the region its distinction.

> **GRAPE VARIETIES** White: Chardonnay, Sauvignon Blanc, Sémillon; red: Cabernet Sauvignon, Merlot, Shiraz.

> **SOIL** Sandy and gravelly.

> **STYLE** Cabernet Sauvignon, sometimes blended with Merlot, produces particularly distinguished, ripe, and elegant wines, most of which display (with maturity) a refinement and complexity approaching that of top Bordeaux wines. As for the white wines, the Sauvignon Blanc, usually blended with Semillon, produces soft, well-balanced wines, often with herbaceous aromas.

> **NOTABLE PRODUCERS** Cape Mentelle, Cullen, Gralyn, Juniper Estate, Leeuwin, Moss Wood, Pierro, Vasse Felix, Voyager.

GREAT SOUTHERN

WESTERN AUSTRALIA

This vast wine-producing region, with its numerous sub-regions (Albany, Denmark, Frankland River, Mount Barker, and Porongorup), is both Australia's most extensive and most recent wine region, as well as the one least under cultivation. It encompasses a good part of the country's southwest, and is the coolest part of Western Australia. Because of its proximity to the ocean and its southern aspect, the nights are very cool. But the days are sunny; rainfall is lower than at Margaret River, for example. Two sub-regions, Denmark and Albany, are open to strong maritime influences. Many winemakers based elsewhere in Western Australia buy grapes from Great Southern (although 20 years ago, apples were the major crop).

> **GRAPE VARIETIES** White: Chardonnay, Riesling, Sauvignon Blanc, Sémillon; red: Cabernet Sauvignon, Pinot Noir, Shiraz.

> **SOIL** Impoverished gravelly, sandy loams; loams deriving from gneiss or granite bedrocks; rich loams in the Denmark sector.

> **STYLE** The most successful red wines are made with Cabernet Sauvignon, in – for Australia – an unusually firm and structured style; Shiraz produces very fruity, well-balanced wines. In whites, Riesling offers plenty of vigor and intense citrus flavours, while Chardonnay makes fresh and sometimes structured wines.

> **NOTABLE PRODUCERS** Alkoomi, Chatsfield, Howard Park, Mount Trio, Plantagenet, West Cape Howe.

NEW ZEALAND

NORTHLAND
Whangarei
Waiheke Island
AUCKLAND
Auckland
Te Kauwhata
Hamilton
Tauranga
Bay of Plenty
Waihou
Waikato
North Island
WAIKATO
BAIE DE PLENTY
GISBORNE
Gisborne
Rangitaiki
Lake Taupo
Wanganui
TARANAKI
HAWKE'S BAY
Napier
Hastings
Hawke's Bay
MANAWATU WANGANUI
Rangitikei
Wanganui
Palmerston North
Tasman Bay
WELLINGTON
Wairarapa
Martinborough
Wellington
Nelson
Wairau
NELSON
Blenheim
MARLBOROUGH
Clarence
Pacific Ocean
WEST COAST
Southern Alps
Waimakariri
Christchurch
CANTERBURY
South Island
Kawarau
OTAGO
Clutha
Dunedin
SOUTHLAND
Invercargill
Stewart Island
Wine-producing regions
Main wine-producing regions
Other wine-producing regions
Regional borders
N
0
125 miles (200 km)

NEW ZEALAND

Despite relatively small production, this island nation has managed to penetrate the global market with wines of remarkable flavour and freshness. Whether Sauvignon Blanc (the most popular variety), Chardonnay, or Pinot Noir, New Zealand wines occupy a special place in the New World.

Rapid change

The astonishing success of New Zealand wine today had a slow start. Since the establishment of the first vineyards in 1819, the industry has had to overcome vine diseases, which are virulent in such a humid climate, along with puritanical and prohibitionist attitudes that long prohibited, restricted, or supervised the sale and distribution of alcohol. The real turning point was in the 1970s, with the introduction of varieties of *Vitis vinifera* in place of American hybrids, the development of new regions like Marlborough, and the gradual shift of production, once dominated by sweet wines, toward dry wines.

After a realignment in 1986, during which a quarter of old vineyards disappeared, change has continued with expanded plantings of grape varieties such as Chardonnay and Sauvignon Blanc. These permitted the emergence of a fresh style of wine, full of flavour and technically well produced – and this has enhanced the country's reputation. Since 1999, production has quadrupled and been supported by export growth of 600 per cent, and by a significant increase in domestic consumption.

NEW ZEALAND STATISTICS

Vineyard area: 86,487 acres (35,000 ha) 2,340,000

Production: 26 million cases (2,340,000 hl)

Whites: 75%

Reds: 25%

(New Zealand Winegrowers, OIV, 2015)

Climate

The country consists of two parts, North Island and South Island, extending over 930 miles (1,500 km) from north to south. A maritime climate is subject to the influence of moist westerly winds as well as cold southerly winds blowing from the Antarctic. It is more temperate (cooler) and much more humid, especially on the west coast, than its neighbour Australia. The northernmost regions, which saw the very first vineyard plantings, have a semi-tropical (warm and rather humid) climate. South Island, which is closer to Antarctica, has a cooler but sunny climate – perfect for producing lively and aromatic wines.

> Vineyard landscape in the region of Hawke's Bay on North Island.

DID YOU KNOW...?

More than 90 per cent of New Zealand wines are sealed with a screwcap. *Producers started using this closure in 2001 and many are now convinced that it is the best solution for wines renowned for their freshness and aromatic purity. They have even formed an association called the 'New Zealand Screwcap Wine Seal Initiative', designed to promote and explain the virtues of the screwcap.*

> Vines are sometimes protected by nets to prevent birds from pecking the berries.

Soils

Most soils are heavy, such as clay, and impermeable. Combined with the damp climate, this leads vines to develop big leafy expanses and suffer greater exposure to diseases as well as the development of vegetal flavours in a number of wines. However, in some well-drained gravelly areas, such as Marlborough and Hawke's Bay, irrigation may be necessary.

Wine regions

NORTH ISLAND. This area long accounted for the bulk of New Zealand wine production, but it has declined due to the sustained growth of cooler and drier vineyards on South Island. That said, it contains seven of the 11 wine regions in the country. At the northern tip, small parts of Northland and Auckland produce red wines from Bordeaux grape varieties, including magnificent wines from tiny Waiheke Island. The regions of Waikato and Bay of Plenty have been recently converted to Sauvignon Blanc. On the east coast, Gisborne, the third-largest region in terms of volume, is the home of powerful Chardonnays; but there are also some splendid Gewurztraminers. Hawke's Bay, further south on the coast, has a fairly wide range of good quality red and white wines (*see* p.606). The vineyards of the Wellington region are located in the Wairarapa district, which includes the sub-region of Martinborough. It enjoys a reputation disproportionate to its small area (less than 2,200 acres or 900 ha), which has doubled in five years thanks to its Sauvignon Blanc and Pinot Noir in particular.
SOUTH ISLAND. Marlborough, at the north end of the island, produces more than 70 per cent of New Zealand's wines. It is the centre of the country's wine production and the home of the best Sauvignon Blancs (*see* p.486). Nelson, in the northwest, has not escaped the enthusiasm for this grape variety, which covers 50 per cent of its vineyards. Canterbury, with the valley of Waipara (*see details* p.607), is also booming, and produces pleasant Riesling, Chardonnay, and Pinot Noir. In the extreme south, the continental and mountain climate in Central Otago (*see* p.607) is an area full of promise, where some excellent Pinot Noir is already produced.

Grape varieties and wine styles

Of all the New World countries, New Zealand has the coolest climate; and its current grape varieties are well suited to these conditions. Since the 1990s, German grape varieties have almost disappeared (with the notable exception of Riesling) to be replaced by Sauvignon Blanc, Chardonnay, and, more recently, Pinot Noir. Together, they occupy more than 80 per cent of total vineyard area.
WHITE GRAPE VARIETIES. About 75 per cent of the wines produced in New Zealand are white. With 49,421 acres (20,000 ha) planted in 2015, Sauvignon Blanc is the leading grape. It is very often vinified in stainless steel tanks, and is the archetypal New Zealand white wine: fresh, lively, with exuberant flavours, and intended to be consumed young. Chardonnay, although a distant second in terms of planted area, has consolidated its position. It produces wines of great intensity, which can be matured in wood in some cases. Fermented as sparkling wine, often blended with Pinot Noir, it can produce wines of real finesse; and the best of these can compete with good Champagne. Pinot Gris, Riesling, and Gewurztraminer are increasingly produced in the cool regions of Marlborough, Waipara, and Otago. Mainly produced as dry wines, they also provide some very beautiful and rare dessert wines.
RED GRAPE VARIETIES. Only Cabernet Sauvignon has survived from the nation's original plantings (in 1832), but its difficulty in achieving a regularly high level of maturity explains its decline. It has now been widely superseded by Merlot and especially by Pinot Noir – now growing some 13,591 acres (5,500 ha) on South Island. While there are some benchmark wines made from Cabernet and Merlot, produced in an elegant style and close to Bordeaux standards with even ageing capacity, the best red wines come from Pinot Noir. They show an amazing freshness, intensity, and purity of flavour.

Leading New Zealand regions and wines

The New Zealand system of wine nomenclature is based on the grape variety, generally accompanied by the region and sometimes the sub-region on the label. Yet apart from Marlborough and Central Otago, which have a worldwide reputation, it is the producer's name that indicates the most about the wine.

NORTH ISLAND

HAWKE'S BAY

Hawke's Bay is the second-most planted area (11,614 acres or 4,700 ha) in New Zealand. It's located along the east coast of North Island, and the landscape consists of a chain of coastal mountains, protecting the vineyards from westerly winds, and a very fertile coastal plain. Hawke's Bay has excellent sunshine and reasonable rainfall of about 35 inches (890 mm) per year. White and red grape varieties are equally planted. Among whites, Sauvignon Blanc is second only to Chardonnay in terms of area. The region is particularly noted for producing fine reds from Merlot and Cabernet Sauvignon planted on warm, gravelly soils.

> **GRAPE VARIETIES** Chardonnay, Sauvignon Blanc, and Pinot Gris for whites; Merlot, Cabernet Sauvignon, Syrah, and Pinot Noir for reds.

> **SOIL** Varies between rich alluvial soil and poor soils consisting of deep gravel.

> **STYLE** Hawke's Bay is famous for its red wines made from Merlot and Cabernet. They are elegant and structured. Firm tannins are often softened by being matured in wood, and they have good potential for improving with age. The Pinot Noirs and Syrahs are very popular, both fruity and juicy, and should be consumed while they are young. The Sauvignon Blancs and Chardonnays (among the best in the country) are richer and fuller than those of South Island, and some allow the wine to be made in barrel.

> **NOTABLE PRODUCERS** Bilancia, Craggy Range, Esk Valley, Mills Reef, Sacred Hill, Te Mata, Te Awa, and Trinity Hill.

SOUTH ISLAND

MARLBOROUGH

Vineyard planting in this region, on the northeastern tip of South Island, started in 1973. Since then, Marlborough has become both the largest wine area in the country, covering 57,328 acres (23,200 ha), and the most famous. The region includes the long and wide Wairau Valley and its tributaries. Further south, it also includes the Awatere Valley. Apart from frosts in the spring, the weather is an ideal combination of very sunny days and cool nights. Marlborough has developed a global reputation for New Zealand Sauvignon Blanc. Covering 44,479 acres (18,900 ha), it occupies most plantings. But Marlborough also produces good Pinot Noirs and Chardonnays, and some fine Rieslings.

> **GRAPE VARIETIES** Sauvignon Blanc, Chardonnay, Pinot Gris, and Riesling for whites; Pinot Noir for reds.

> **SOIL** Alluvial and gravelly soil. Well drained and rather poor in the north, richer and more impermeable to the south.

> **STYLE** Independent of grape variety, all wines here are characterized by intense flavour and freshness. The Sauvignon Blancs are crisp and fragrant with hints of citrus, green fruit, or fresh grass. They have a bracing sharpness, and sometimes a beautiful volume that gives them great presence on the palate. The best Chardonnays are well balanced and fresh, capable of reaching heights of elegance and intensity. The Pinot Noirs, which should be consumed young, are fruity with a pleasing liveliness.

> **NOTABLE PRODUCERS** Cloudy Bay, Delta, Fromm, Herzog, Jackson Estate, Kim Crawford, Staete Landt, TerraVin, Tohu Wines, Villa Maria, and Wairau River.

CANTERBURY/WAIPARA

SOUTH ISLAND

South of Marlborough on the east coast of South Island, this region has seen vineyard plantings triple (3,707 acres or 1,500 ha) in five years. It consists of two sub-regions (whose names appear on the labels): the Canterbury area, consisting of a large plain surrounding the city of Christchurch; and the hills of Waipara, located about 30 miles (48 km) north of the city. The combination of a cool climate, wind, sun, and little rain, plus light and poor soil is ideal for grape varieties such as Sauvignon Blanc, Riesling, and Pinot Noir. They dominate production, particularly in Waipara, where the current boom has been spectacular.

> **GRAPE VARIETIES** Riesling, Sauvignon Blanc, Pinot Gris, and Chardonnay for whites; Pinot Noir for reds.

> **SOIL** In the south, alluvium, silt, and gravel; to the north, clay, silt, and limestone.

> **STYLE** Many of the wines produced in the region are Rieslings. They are firm, slightly sharp, and straightforward, with mineral (flint) and lemony notes. The best are outstanding. Another regional speciality is Pinot Noir that offers, when properly ripened, fruity, spicy, spirited, fresh, and sometimes very pure wines. It also produces lively and scented Sauvignon Blancs and structured Chardonnays.

> **NOTABLE PRODUCERS** Mountford, Pegasus Bay, Waipara Hills, and Waipara West.

CENTRAL OTAGO

SOUTH ISLAND

Central Otago is the southernmost vineyard region in the world, and also the only inland vineyard region on South Island. This mountainous area, which produces only 5 per cent of New Zealand wine, has become one of the most attractive in recent years because of the quality of its Pinot Noir (80 per cent of production). Its planted area has expanded rapidly (4,942 acres/ 2,000 ha) since 2002, and the number of wineries here has increased sixfold. Vines are planted along valley bottoms and on hillsides with varying exposures. Altitude rarely exceeds 980 feet (300 m) due to the risk of frost. The climate is continental with short, dry, and very sunny summers, plus a wide variation in temperature between day and night. While the growing season is shorter than elsewhere, the exceptionally intense sunshine provides ideal conditions for maturing Pinot Noir.

> **GRAPE VARIETIES** Pinot Gris, Chardonnay, Riesling, and Sauvignon Blanc for whites; Pinot Noir for reds.

> **SOIL** Loess mixed with gravel on a base of schist. There are limestone pockets in the northeast (Waitaki Valley).

> **STYLE** While there are several styles of Pinot Noir from Otago, the wines often present a rich nose (very ripe red fruit), with spicy and toasty notes that vary in power depending on the type and length of ageing. On the palate, they are generous and concentrated wines that impress with their intense fruit flavours. Most are low in tannin but have a fresh structure that gives them a lot of presence and life. Very pleasing when young, the more concentrated may be kept for five to 10 years. The whites are mostly crisp and fragrant.

> **NOTABLE PRODUCERS** Amisfield, Chard Farm, Felton Road, Mount Edward, Maude, Mt Difficulty, Olssens, Quartz Reef, and Rockburn.

Cloudy Bay, Kiwi icon wine

Cloudy Bay is the waterfront at the mouth of the Wairau River in Marlborough. It is also the name of the most famous vineyard in New Zealand, founded by David Hohnen and Kevin Judd from the Australian Cape Mentelle estate. Established in 1985, with a very evocative label featuring a drawing of the surrounding mountains, it has largely driven the popularity of Sauvignon Blanc and its region, Marlborough. It is a wine with great freshness and perfume, and it has become a national and international standard. As it has developed through the years, the wine has gained in finesse and elegance while retaining its exuberant aromas (citrus, green and exotic fruits, and fresh herbs) and its bracing sharpness – all the hallmark of good New Zealand Sauvignon Blancs. Since its inception, the estate has grown dramatically and it has expanded production. It now makes one of the country's finest and most vibrant Chardonnays, vinified in oak barrels, and a pure and refreshing Pinot Noir, as well as a sparkling wine (Pelorus) with impressive finesse.

JAPAN, CHINA, AND INDIA

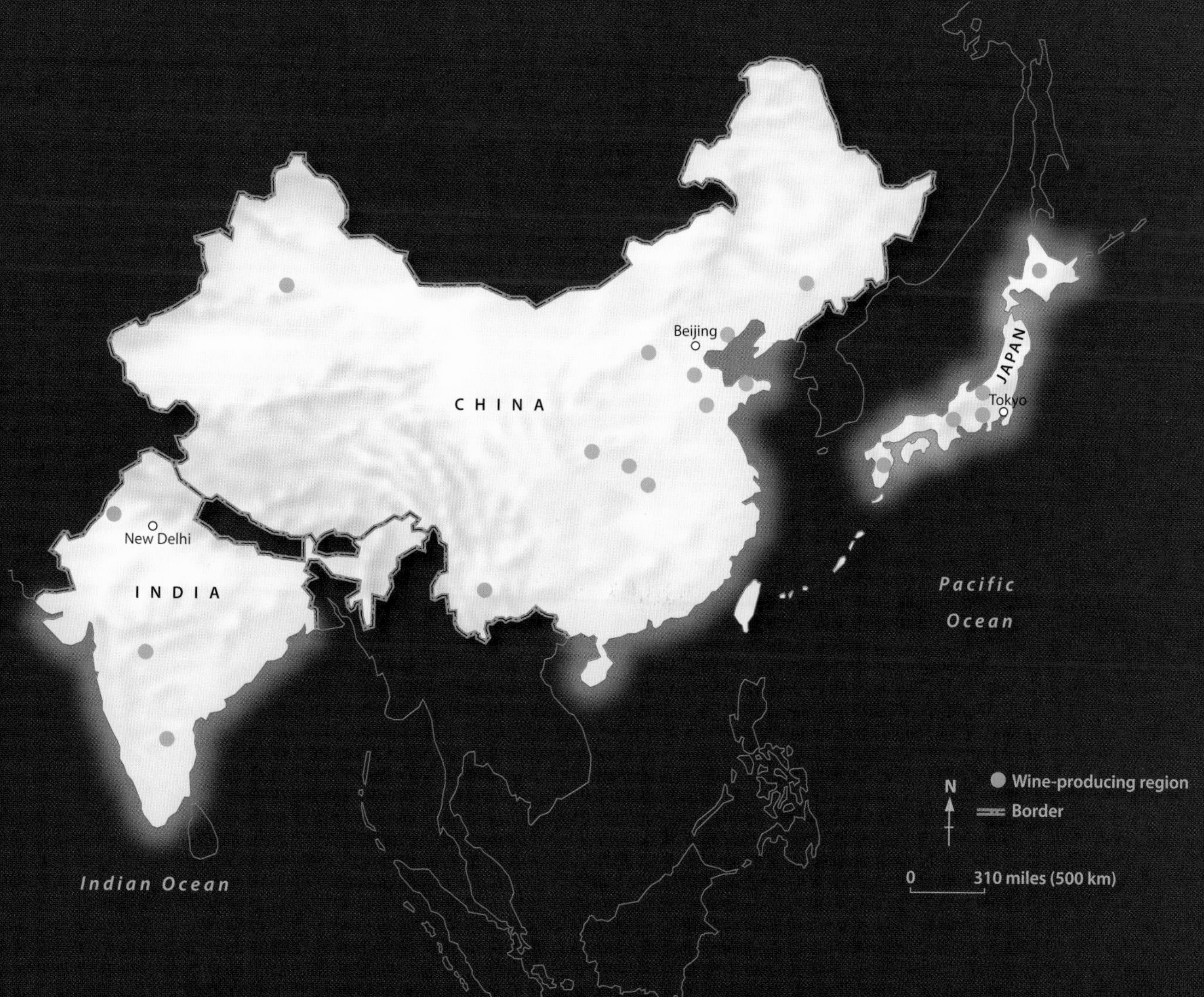

JAPAN, CHINA, AND INDIA

Wine consumption in Asia has risen sharply in recent decades, but only a handful of countries have a significant wine industry. While Japanese and Indian vineyards are small scale, those of China are growing at an impressive rate.

JAPAN

The vine has been cultivated in Japan since the 8th century, but there is little evidence of wine consumption prior to the arrival of Portuguese missionaries during the 16th century. Some 300 years later, in the Yamanashi region, Yamada Hironori and Takuna Norihisa established the first modern wine estate. However, the current craze for wine really dates to the 1980s.

***Japan is the most sophisticated wine market in Asia.* While most wine is imported, there is a small amount of local production from wineries that have learned to cope with a challenging natural environment.**

Vineyard landscape

Only 10 per cent of Japan's 46,950 acres (19,000 ha) of vineyards are intended for the production of wine. Vineyards are cultivated on almost all the islands, but in terms of surface area, the majority are concentrated on the main island, Honshu—especially in the Yamanashi and Nagano regions (40 per cent of production), which lie west of Tokyo. A very wet climate, subject to monsoons and typhoons, as well as rich and acidic soils, represents far from ideal conditions for producing quality grapes. But wine producers have responded with their cultivation methods and the use of suitable varieties.

GRAPE VARIETIES. Hybrids like the Kyoho, the Campbell Early, Muscat Bailey A, and Delaware sit alongside imported varieties (Cabernet, Merlot, Müller-Thurgau, and Chardonnay). But the most prominent wines are made from a local variety of *Vitis vinifera*, the Koshu. At Yamanashi, near Mount Fuji, this pink-skinned variety is capable of producing pleasant, light, and elegant whites. Some of the best wines come from the well-drained hillsides of Katsunuma, where legend has it that the first Koshu vines were planted in the 8th century by Buddhist monks from China.

NOTABLE PRODUCERS. Lumière, Manns, Magrez-Aruga, Château Mercian, Sapporo, Shizen, Suntory.

Bordeaux in Katsunuma

Bernard Magrez, who owns 35 vineyards in France and worldwide, has partnered with Japanese Koshu specialist Yuji Aruga, based in Katsunuma. The wine, which is called Magrez Aruga, is a very pleasant example of this native Japanese grape variety, with a fresh, aromatic, and clean style.

CHINA

About 15 years ago, the per capita consumption of wine in China was almost zero; today that figure is almost half a litre per year. That's very low in terms of Western consumer patterns, but it represents a significant change in a country that has remained culturally impervious to wine for centuries. It also conceals a huge market!

The recent and rapid Westernization of Chinese cities largely explains this development, as can be seen by a significant increase in wine imports. But there also has been a dramatic increase in Chinese wine production, which is now in eighth place in the world rankings following the recent rapid expansion of the vineyard area devoted to growing wine grapes.

> Harvesting near the city of Turpan, in Xinjiang province, China.

> Harvesting grapes on the Grover estate, north of Bangalore, in Karnataka state, India.

Vineyard landscape

The centre of Chinese wine production lies in its eastern regions and includes the vineyards of Beijing, Tianjin, and in particular the provinces of Hebei and Shandong, the locations of the main producers Changyu and Great Wall. The well-exposed slopes of the Shandong Peninsula, overlooking Bohai Bay, offer good potential, with the maritime influence helping to temper the excesses of the climate. The recent development of viticulture has brought new regions to the fore, including Shanxi and Ningxia. Until recently almost desert, Ningxia has been developed by irrigation systems from the Yellow River, financed by local government. The cultivated area is now vast, planted in silty soils, in a very continental, semi-arid climate, which requires the vines to be buried in winter to protect them from damaging frosts. Hot and dry summers make it possible to ripen the grapes in good conditions, especially Cabernet Sauvignon and Merlot, which are extensively planted because of the Bordeaux influence. Chinese and foreign investors have invested heavily in the region, and many of the increasingly competitive Chinese wines come from Ningxia. Other expanding regions include Xinjiang in the far northwest, a large area producing table grapes, but which is now beginning to attract wine-producing companies.

Wines standards

Production is concentrated in the hands of three companies: Changyu, Dynasty, and Great Wall; and some have benefited from joint ventures with foreign partners. This transfer of knowledge is having an impact. Chinese wines, which had been produced using unorthodox procedures only a short time ago, have cleaned up their act and moved closer to international standards of wine production.

Chinese consumers are slowly becoming more demanding and a wine culture is gradually emerging in the country's major cities. This growing sophistication in taste is matched by the emergence of modern estates, some of which are beginning to gain a reputation, such as Silver Heights, a small private estate in Ningxia, or Grace Vineyard in Shanxii. Chinese wine production is booming and attracting many investors. It is at a crossroads.

NOTABLE PRODUCERS. Catai, Changyu, Château Junding, Dragon's Hollow, Grace Vineyard, Great Wall, Huadong.

INDIA

While ancient texts offer evidence that India was producing wine as early as the 4th century BC, religious taboos have long made wine, like other alcoholic beverages, a marginal or suspect drink. With that said, it has been tolerated during different periods of Indian history.

SPECTACULAR PROGRESS. The recent Westernization of urban middle and upper classes has changed the perception of wine in India. A new market has grown dramatically here over the past 10 years. Taxes on imports of foreign wines, and concessions granted to local producers, have meant that domestic production has doubled in recent years. Vineyards cover 155,000 acres (63,000 ha), but only a few thousand are dedicated to wine production.

Key players

Production is concentrated to the east and northeast of Bombay, in the state of Maharashtra (home to 75 of the 93 producers surveyed in 2014), where there are plateaus with acceptable climatic conditions for viticulture, and to a lesser extent in the neighbouring state of Karnataka.

The year 1985 saw the launch of Omar Khayyam, a sparkling white wine produced using the traditional method by the company Indage, which no longer exists. Two other major producers have taken their place: Grover Vineyards, a joint Franco-Indian venture, and Sula, founded in 1997, the most important Indian producer, renowned for the quality of its still wines, including a very successful Sauvignon Blanc. The priority has been to plant mainstream international grape varieties: Sauvignon, Chardonnay, and Chenin for white, and Cabernet Sauvignon, Merlot, Syrah, and Zinfandel for red.

Despite the ban on purchasing vineyards, the promising potential of the Indian market has attracted new investors. LVMH (Chandon India) produces sparkling wines from grapes purchased from vineyards in the Nashik region of Maharashtra. Other companies such as Fratelli (Maharashtra) now produce notable wines from these grape varieties, while Pernod Ricard (Nashik) or United Spirits Limited have also invested, even managing to export a number of wines.

NOTABLE PRODUCERS. Sula Vineyards, Grover Vineyards, Fratelli, Pernod Ricard India, Chandon India, Four Seasons Wines.

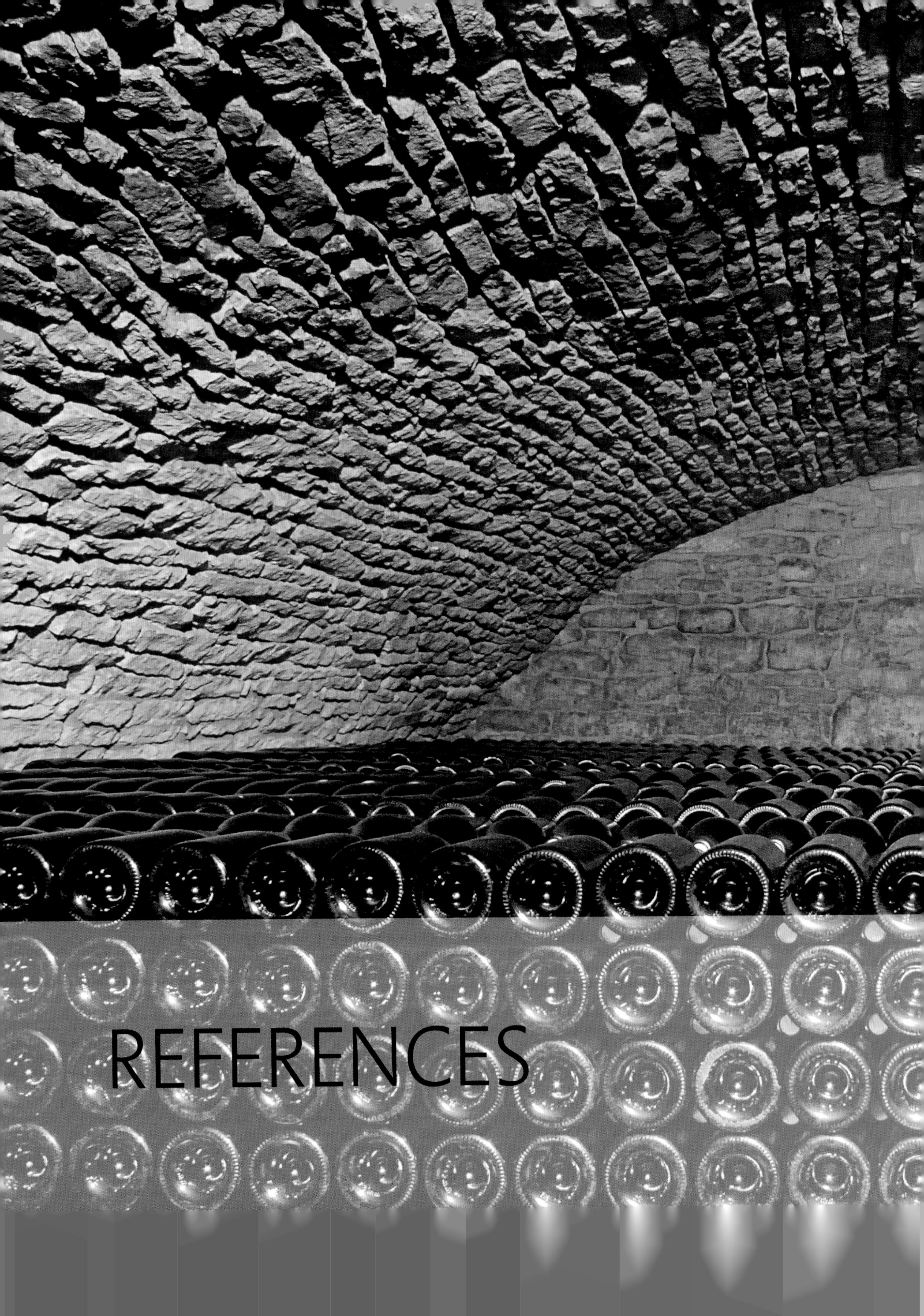

REFERENCES

Glossary

This glossary defines terms used in viticulture and the wine industry – with the exception of tasting vocabulary, which is covered in 'Describing Wine' on pp.228–35. The origins of foreign words are indicated with the following abbreviations: Fr = French; Ger = German; It = Italian; Po = Portuguese; Sp = Spanish.

Words featured as entries in the glossary are marked with an asterisk (*).

A

ABBOCCATO (It) A slightly sweet wine.

ACETIC ACID This acid is found in small quantities in every wine; when quantities grow too large, the wine turns to vinegar.

ACIDITY Wine contains several organic acids (tartaric*, malic*, citric*, lactic*, etc.). Acidity plays an important role in tasting. It augments and partially masks the sweet* elements of a wine (sugar, alcohol, glycerin). Also, in conjunction with tannins*, it creates a synergy that enhances the sensation of crispness or even astringency. Excessive or injudicious acidity can turn a sensation of liveliness into something acrid. By contrast, a lack of acidity, or an imbalance where the acidity is swamped by the wine's sweetness, leads to slackness or heaviness. When acidity is discreetly forthcoming, it creates freshness; when more diffident, it creates suppleness.

ADEGA (Po) A wine cellar or winemaking estate in Portugal.

AGEING The evolution of a wine's components over time.

ALCOHOL Ethyl alcohol, one of the principal ingredients of wine, is produced during alcoholic fermentation*: an enzymatic metabolism by yeasts* transforms sugars in grape juice into alcohol, carbon dioxide, and heat. The alcoholic content* of wine can vary from less than 7% to more than 15% by volume, depending on the natural sugar content of the must* and any added sugar. Contents higher than 15% by volume are often indicative of fortified wines. It should be remembered that obtaining one percentage point of alcohol requires 17 grams of sugar per litre (or 1.7% concentration) for white wines and 18g (1.8%) for red wines. *See also* CHAPTALIZATION*.

ALCOHOL BY VOLUME *See* ALCOHOLIC CONTENT.

ALCOHOLIC CONTENT The amount of alcohol in a wine is calculated as the volume of ethyl alcohol in the liquid (expressed as % by volume [ABV]).

ALCOHOLIC FERMENTATION The primary stage of winemaking: grape juice becomes wine when the sugars contained in the must* are transformed into alcohol, carbon dioxide, and heat by the action of yeast*.

AMABILE (It) A slightly sweeter style of wine than *abboccato**.

AMONTILLADO (Sp) Sherry that develops from a *fino*. It displays an amber colour, and with time develops aromas of dried fruit.

AMPELOGRAPHY The field of botany associated with the identification and classification of grapevines.

ANTHOCYANINS Pigments in grapes that are the source of colour in red wines. The violet colouration of many young red wines is almost exclusively due to mildly reactive anthocyanin molecules (phenolic compounds) that go on to combine with tannins* (which are also phenolic ingredients) as the wine ages. This leads to a ruby red colour, then more brick, then eventually brown.

APPELLATION D'ORIGINE CONTRÔLÉE (AOC) (Fr) A French term meaning 'controlled designation of origin'. It is used for wines made in specific regions and from particular grape varieties* that are strictly defined in regulations laid down by the INAO*. These wines all qualify for the European 'quality wines produced in specified regions' designation. AOC wines must conform to exacting regulations not only with respect to their area of production and their grape variety*, but also minimum sugar content to be obtained in their must*, their alcoholic content*, their yield per hectare, the pruning of their vines, and their method of cultivation and vinification. AOC wines are finally subject to a tasting inspection before they are released to the market.

APPELLATION D'ORIGINE PROTÉGÉE (AOP) (Fr) A European denomination corresponding to the French *appellation d'origine contrôlée* (AOC) and its equivalents in other EU countries.

APPELLATION D'ORIGINE VIN DÉLIMITÉ DE QUALITÉ SUPERIEURE (AOVDQS), (Fr) A wine produced in a specified region to lower qualification requirements than AOC. New European regulations mean that the AOVDQS designation is due to be abolished from the 2011 vintage.

AROMAS A term designating the olfactory characters of a wine. In other words, the sensations perceived more in the nose than in the mouth. A distinction is drawn between aromas resulting from grape variety, from fermentation, and from the maturation period after fermentation.

AUSBRUCH (Aus) An Austrian wine category, sweeter than a Beerenauslese* but less sweet than a Trockenbeerenauslese*.

AUSLESE (Ger) A German wine made with late-harvested grapes, often botrytized but always containing a considerable concentration of sugar. Auslesen may be made dry or sweet.

B

BAG IN BOX (WINEBOX) A soft retractable bag with a tap, enclosed in cardboard packaging. Often used for the sale and storage (for up to nine months after opening) of wine in bulk. Often three litres in capacity.

BAN DES VENDANGES (Fr) Historically, the official date (*ban*) when harvesting (*vendange*) began in a region. The modern term refers to the date after which chaptalization* is authorized; this is proposed by the INAO* in conjunction with the appellation's executive syndicate and decided by the prefect of the region.

BARREL A cask of a size that varies from region to region; in Burgundy, a barrel contains just over 60 gallons (228 litres), while a Bordeaux barrel (barrique) contains 59 gallons (225 litres). A barrel in Touraine-Anjou contains just over 61 gallons (232 litres).

BARRICA (Sp) Spanish barrel containing approximately 59 gallons (225 litres).

BATONNAGE (Fr) *Batonnage* is the process of stirring the fine lees* that have settled at the bottom of a barrel* or vat* of wine after fermentation. It is performed to obtain more complexity, suppleness, and more body.

BEERENAUSLESE (Ger) An Austrian or German wine made with late-harvested, often botrytized, grapes with high sugar content.

BEREICH (Ger) A German winegrowing region.

BIODYNAMICS A form of farming that takes into account the interaction between the movement of the planets and plant growth. It relies on a precise calendar of intervention and preparations based on mineral and organic substances.

BITTERNESS One of the five components of physiological taste.

BLANC DE BLANCS (Fr) A white wine made exclusively with white grapes.

BLANC DE NOIRS (Fr) A white wine made with red or black grapes.

BLENDING The mixing of several wines. The aim of a blend is to produce something better than each element on its own.

BLUSH A US term for a rosé wine.

BODEGA (Sp) The Spanish equivalent of a wine cellar. Also used to mean a winery.

BORDEAUX MIXTURE A vineyard fungicide made from copper (II) sulphate and hydrated lime. It was developed by P.M.A. Millardet during the 19th century to combat mildew*. It is now being increasingly replaced with synthetic copper compounds.

BOTRYTIS Rot caused by the fungus *Botrytis cinerea** . Its growth is promoted by humidity.

BOTRYTIS CINEREA A necrotrophic fungus that attacks grapes. A small amount of botrytis, known as 'grey mould' encourages fermentation agents during *cuvaison**, the period when the seeds, skin, and stalks are left to macerate in the wine. Larger degrees of botrytis will compromise the harvest (more than 10 or 15 per cent for red wines, 20 per cent for whites). The famed 'noble rot*' concentrates the juice in the grapes to a special kind of over-maturity*. Such botrytized grapes produce famous sweet* wines such as Sauternes from France and Tokaji from Hungary.

BOTTLING As the name might suggest, this is the transfer of wine into bottles. Only French AOC* wines may bear the terms *mis en bouteille au château* or *mise d'origine* (estate-bottled); although French country wine (VDP/IGP) may be labelled *mis en bouteilles à la propriété or au domaine* (bottled on the premises). AOC wines that are labelled *mis en bouteille dans la région de production* must be bottled somewhere in the region of their own appellation.

BOUQUET A fairly complex mixture of agreeable aromas* in a wine. Sensed through the nose (rather than the mouth). *See* AROMAS*.

BRANCO (Po) White.

BRANDED WINE Generally wine intended for broad commercial distribution and produced with a consistent flavour and style. Wines in this category may be either: a mix of various basic table wines* topped off with a dash of a superior grape variety to improve it; a judiciously balanced blend of different wines, which, though subordinating their appellation in favour of the brand, will suit the tastes of most consumers; or indeed blends of large volumes of wine with regional or village appellations that are connected with the brand but take a back seat to it.

BREATHING Leaving wine in contact with the air to release aromatic compounds.

BRUT (Fr) A term indicating a very low sugar content in sparkling* wines (from 0 to 12 grams per litre); *brut zéro* and *brut intégral* are completely unsweetened.

BUDDING Point in the vine's growth cycle during which new buds swell and open.

C

CAP A term for the floating mass of solids (skins, pulp, seeds, and stems) that are forced to the surface of the must* during red wine fermentation by the release of carbon dioxide. It is important that maceration* is encouraged to optimize the extraction of colours and aromas* from the cap. For this reason, many production methods agitate, stir, dip, and squeeze this cap in order to increase the interaction of the solid material with the liquid, *i.e.* the wine.

CAPSULE (Fr) Another term for the foil* covering the closure (or cork) of a wine bottle.

CARBONATED A term describing an effervescent* wine produced in a closed vat through the mechanical addition of carbon dioxide – in place of secondary fermentation by yeast*, as would happen in the traditional or Champagne method. High quality wines generally are not carbonated.

CARBONIC MACERATION A method of vinification* whereby red wine grapes are placed in vats* without being pressed. The vat is then sealed and saturated with carbon dioxide, which starts intracellular fermentation or transformation of sugars into alcohol* within berries. This first phase, which may last a matter of hours or days, takes place at relatively high temperatures (between 86 and 90°F/30 and 32°C). The press wine* and the free-run wine* are then subjected to separate second fermentations at lower temperatures (68°F/20°C) for a relatively short period. This method allows the production of a press wine of superior quality to what is typical, and the procedure has proved successful with Gamay wines that are marketed young, such as *Beaujolais nouveau*.

CAUDALIE *See* 'Describing Wine', p.230.

CAVA (Sp) Generic term for Spanish sparkling wines made using traditional methods*.

CELLAR MASTER Person charged with directing the various operations carried out at a winery, from vinification* to maturing*.

CENTRIFUGATION A process to clarify* musts* or wines using centrifugal force to eliminate heavy particles or cloudiness. The procedure can used when 'racking' musts, clarifying wine, and removing deposits of finings*.

CEP The wood section, more than a year old, at the foot of a vine.

CHAPTALIZATION A process first advocated by the chemist J.A. Chaptal, chaptalization consists of adding sugar (cane, beet, or rectified;

or concentrated must*) to grape juice that is insufficiently rich before fermentation. The result obtains a higher alcoholic content* in the wine. Strictly forbidden in a number of countries, the technique is usually very closely regulated in the countries that allow it.

CHARMAT (Fr) A production method for sparkling* wines in which sugar and yeasts* are added to start second fermentation* in closed stainless steel or enamelled tanks.

CHÂTEAU (Fr) Literally a 'castle', but generally a wine-producing estate. There is not always a building that corresponds to the estate *château* mentioned. Many more *châteaux* are listed on wine labels than are actually found in any given area.

CITRIC ACID An acid plentiful in fruit and citrus fruits in particular, but also found in grapes, if only in minute quantities. White grapes contain larger amounts, particularly those affected by the famous 'noble rot*'.

CLAIRET (Fr) A light Bordeaux red or rosé made by the *saignée** (vat 'bleeding') method.

CLARIFICATION A series of operations intended to obtain transparency in a wine. Various procedures may be employed, including centrifugation*, filtration*, and fining*. Clarification must be completed by physical, chemical, and microbiological stabilization of the wine to prevent the later formation of haziness or deposits*.

CLASSICO (It) Wine from the historic heart of a wine region.

CLAVELIN Traditional bottle for Jura wines, especially *vin jaune** ('yellow wine'). Its volume of 21 fl oz (620 ml) represents the sole remains of the wine's original 34 fl oz (1 litre), after considerable evaporation during six years of barrel ageing. This wine matures under a layer of yeasts and is not subject to topping-up*.

CLIMAT (Fr) In Burgundy, this term refers not only to the atmospheric conditions prevailing in the region (climate), but also to specific divisions within each village or commune. Some *climats* have first-growth qualities, while others have remained unclassified. The latter may nonetheless appear on wine labels under the communal appellation, except where this may be confused with an official *premier cru* (first growth) wine.

CLONAL SELECTION The use of exactly identical plants for their resistance to diseases, growing characteristics, or yield.

CLONE A single genetic variant of a vine sub-species, created by asexual reproduction (cuttings and grafts*). *See* CLONAL SELECTION.

CLOS (Fr) A walled vineyard. The term is reserved for those wines to which it applies – the wine must come exclusively from vines within the *clos*. If the designation is of historic standing, the wine may continue to bear the name even if the walls have disappeared over the centuries.

CLOSURE Cylinder of natural cork, a cylinder of plastic, or an aluminum screwcap – used to seal bottles hermetically. The quality of natural cork can vary, and wines of lower quality are sealed with agglomerated cork.

COLOURANTS Phenolic compounds made up of anthocyanins*, tannins*, and anthocyanin or tannin polymers. The colour of young red wine is a result of free anthocyanins; during ageing*, the anthocyanins bond with tannins and precipitate to lend the wine a ruby and then brick-red colour.

COMPLANTATION This is the practice of inter-planting different grape varieties at the same site.

COPPER SULPHATE One ingredient of powdered Bordeaux mixture*, with which vines are treated for cryptogamic* diseases. Bordeaux mixture now refers to a large number of synthetic products that contain no copper sulphate.

CORKED Said of a wine tainted by the odour of cardboard or damp cork; the wine is usually undrinkable. This irreversible phenomenon is quite rare and the result of several specific moulds growing in poorly processed natural cork.

COULURE (Fr) Failure to pollinate the ovaries of grape flowers. It is caused by unfavourable climatic conditions such as cold, rain, or the premature arrival of spring. *Coulure* hampers the redistribution of sugars within the plant; the flowers and the grapes wither and develop either inconsistently or not at all.

COUPAGE (Fr) Blending*.

CRIANZA (Sp) Designation for Spanish wines that have been barrel-aged for a minimum period; con *crianza means* aged.

CROSS The offspring of two varieties of *Vitis vinifera*; the best known is Müller-Thurgau, which is very popular in Germany. *See also* HYBRID.

CRU (Fr) This term generally indicates a specific area recognized for the characteristics of its wine. Similar to the way that *climat** is used in Burgundy. In Bordeaux, however, it refers to a particular winemaking estate, and thus necessarily to the selection of varieties and human expertise as much as to any site. The totality of a *cru* is everything that goes to make up the estate* or *château**. In Champagne, an *échelle des crus** ('ladder of growths') is used to determine grape pricing, and each area is allotted a percentage based on the 100 per cent *crus* that are considered the best. Various designations such as *grand cru*, *premier cru*, and *cru classé* are attached to certain sub-appellations, and these are defined by restrictions to the manner of production (in the case of *grand cru* and *premier cru*) or by classifications set out by the French ministry of agriculture. Such classifications have been laid down for Médoc at Pessac-Léognan, in Sauternes, and St-Émilion wines.

CRU BOURGEOIS (Fr) Bordeaux wines of lesser renown than the *grands crus*. Designation reserved for red wines from the Médoc region, obtained following an eligibility visit by inspectors and a tasting, repeated each year.

CRUSHING Post-harvest procedure, carried out just before fermentation*, whereby grape berries are burst to release their juice.

CRYPTOGAMIC DISEASES Vine ailments carried by spores. The best-known include oidium*, mildew*, black rot, excoriosis (dead-arm disease), and botrytis*.

CUBITAINER (WINE BOX) (Fr) A plastic container protected by a cardboard box, currently used to sell unbottled wine to individual purchasers. Volume may vary between one-and-a-half and nine gallons (5 to 33 litres). As its walls are slightly porous to the air, a cubitainer is only suitable for temporary storage of wine.

CUVAISON (also known as CUVAGE) (Fr) The phase of winemaking that includes leaving the musts* from the harvest to ferment, pumping the grape juice over the cap* (in the case of red winemaking), and running off the resultant young wine. *See* DÉCUVAISON.

CUVÉE (Fr) A term indicating a specific wine, which may or may not be a blend*. In

Champagne, a *cuvée* is a wine made with grape juice from the first pressing.

D

DECANTING A procedure to separate sediment* from clear liquid. A fine wine or a vintage port is decanted by allowing it to flow slowly from its original bottle into a carafe or decanter – leaving the sediment* behind.

DECLASSIFICATION Downgrading a wine from its original appellation. This may be at the request of the producer, or by decree from government inspectors in consultation with experts. Such a decision is made if significant changes are made to the wine; in other cases, a producer may fall back on a more general appellation than the one entitled for commercial or other reasons. This is known in France as *repli*.

DÉCUVAISON (or DÉCUVAGE) (Fr) A term for the process at the end of alcoholic fermentation*, when white wines are transferred into other containers. For red wines, which have often undergone fermentation in the presence of grape skins, seeds, and sometimes stems, the procedure is more complex: first the wine is run off by tapping the lowest part of the vat (thus obtaining so-called 'free-run wine*'); then the upper portion, which is less fluid, is taken to the press to obtain press wine*. The solid material left after this pressing is known as marc*.

DÉGORGEMENT (Fr) An important and delicate phase in sparkling wine production when the deposits of yeast* that have accumulated in the bottle during second fermentation are removed. Called disgorgement in English.

DEMI-SEC (Fr) A category of sparkling* wine conventionally containing between 32 and 50 g/l (3.5 to 5%) [see note in Dosage] of sucrose. This equates 7 to 10 per cent of the total fluid (*see* DOSAGE) that is added after the removal of the yeast (*see* DÉGORGEMENT).

DEPOSIT (*also* SEDIMENT) Solid particles found in wine. In white wines, these often are neutrally coloured flakes or crystals of tartaric acid*; in red wines, they are principally tannins* and pigments*.

DESSERT WINE This category includes fortified wines*, and unfortified wines that may be sweet* very sweet*, or naturally sweet*. These wines may be consumed as an aperitif or at the beginning of a meal, but their most common service is with the dessert.

DESTALKING Procedure to separate grapes from their stems and stalks, whose peduncles contain oils and tannins* that tend to make the wine bitter and sharply pungent.

DESTEMMING *See* DESTALKING.

DO (Sp) The *denominación de origen* is the Spanish equivalent of a French AOC* classification.

DOC (It) Italy's *denominazione di origine controllata* corresponds to France's AOC* classification.

DOC (Po) Portugal's *denominação de origem controlada* corresponds to France's AOC* classification.

DOC (Sp) The *denominación de origen calificada* denotes a Spanish wine of a superior category to a DO. It only applies in two regions (Rioja, Priorat).

DOCG (It) Italy's *denominazione di origine controllata e garantita* is a mark of quality superior to the DOC, and indicates that the wine has been tasted and approved.

DOSAGE After the yeast* is removed from sparkling* wine, a sugary liquid known as *liqueur d'expédition** is added; the sugar content may vary, depending on whether the wine is to be *brut** (a maximum of 12 grams per litre or 1% residual sugar [RS]), *extra dry** (12 to 17 g/up to 1% RS), *sec* (17 to 32 g/l or 3.5% RS), or *demi-sec* (32 to 50 g/3.5 or 5% RS), or *doux* (more than 50 g per litre or 5% RS).

DRY A wine with no perceptible sweetness. In actual fact, the residual sugar content* may not exceed 9 grams per litre (0.9%). For effervescent* wines, this content may rise to between 15 and 35 g/l (3.5%).

E

ÉCHELLE DES CRUS (Fr) ('Ladder of growths') Classification used by villages in Champagne to determine the price of grapes. The best growths are rated 100 per cent, others may drop as low as 80 per cent.

EDELZWICKER Word used in Alsace (France) to denote blended* wines made with various grape varieties.

EFFERVESCENT Denoting a sparkling* wine. A bottle that contains carbon dioxide under pressure, which is released to create bubbles when the bottle is opened. The term 'effervescent' will be the official replacement for the traditional French term *mousseux** ('frothy'). Effervescent wines can be made using a number of methods, including:

- second bottle fermentation, for Champagne and sparkling* wines from traditional appellations;
- fermentation in sealed vats under pressure, for branded products with no appellation;
- injection of carbon dioxide by industrial method, for extremely cheap products. *See* CARBONATED.

One intermediary process between the first two above involves bottle fermentation followed by yeast removal by filtration* under pressure, instead of traditional *dégorgement**. Effervescent wines with a pressure of less than 2.5 bar are not considered *mousseux**. Also, the term *méthode champenoise** is reserved for Champagne wines.

EISWEIN (Ger) Wine made in Austria, Germany, and even Canada, with bunches of late-harvested grapes that have frozen on the vine.

EN PRIMEUR (Fr) A means of purchasing fine Bordeaux wines, generally five or six months after the grape harvest. The wines are kept at the estates until they are bottled some two or three years later. Also called wine futures.

ENCEPAGEMENT (Fr) ('grape selection') Term describing a composition of different grape varieties*; this may refer to a wine, a single estate, or a region. A single variety may be used for many wines, but the use of several varieties can mean more complexity and nuance. Chardonnay is used in Champagne for its finesse and lightness, while Pinot Noir and Pinot Meunier bring body and roundness to the final wines. In regions such as Alsace, planting a wide range of grape varieties produces a varied palette of wines.

ESTATE A legal and geographical entity belonging to a winery. An estate is thus the vineyard, the buildings, and the equipment used to cultivate vines and make wine. Also known as a domain.

EXCISE LABEL Government seal on a wine bottle (marked CRD in France) indicating that the wine may be transported and sold legally.

EXCISE RECEIPT Government document that accompanies alcoholic drinks during shipment. Such documents are not required where tax stamps are used; and some producers and merchants have excise registration supported only by stamps. Other producers and wine merchants use an excise capsule placed over the mouth of each bottle.

EXTRA DRY Term designating an effervescent* wine with a very low dosage* of residual sugar* (from 12 to 17 g/l, or up to 1%). A very dry wine. [See note in Dosage.]

F

FERMENTATION See ALCOHOLIC FERMENTATION, MALOLACTIC FERMENTATION.

FILTRATION A clarification procedure using a physical barrier to trap particles that cloud the wine; this may consist of a layer of *kieselguhr* (diatomaceous earth), cellulose-based plates, or synthetic membranes.

FINING A wine clarification* procedure used before bottling. The method introduces a colloid into the wine that adheres to any residues in suspension (a process known as flocculation) before precipitating to the bottom under the influence of gravity. A number of products are used, including beaten egg whites, isinglass, casein, and bentonite (a clay). The wine is then extracted and usually filtered before bottling.

FLOWERING Phase in the vine's life cycle when pollination is possible. That in turn leads to the formation of grape berries.

FOIL A capsule* or sleeve that surrounds the neck and opening of a bottle. Originally an alloy of tin, the 'foil' is now just as likely to be plastic.

FOUDRE (Fr) A very large vat, with a capacity ranging from 1,320 to 4,000 gallons (50 to 150 hl).

FREE-RUN WINE Wine that runs freely after *cuvasion**, in contrast to press wine*, which results from pressing the *marc** after *décuvaison**.

G

GENERIC In the widest sense, this refers to characteristics relating to any genre of items or products; when referring to appellations of origin, a distinction is generally made between 'generic appellations' and more specific 'regional appellations'.

GLYCEROL or **GLYCERINE** The third key ingredient of wine after water and alcohol*. The presence of 'legs' on the walls of a wine glass is usually attributed to the presence of glycerol.

GRAFTING After the phylloxera* crisis of the 19th century, Europe was obliged to use American vines (*Vitis labrusca*, *Vitis riparia*, *Vitis rupestris*) as rootstock since the latter's roots were resistant to this infestation. The European vine (*Vitis vinifera*) thus largely now exists as just a graft or scion.

GRAN RESERVA (Sp) Spanish red wines from the best vintages, aged for at least 60 months, including a minimum of three years in barrel*.

GRAND VIN (Fr) A term for the premier blended wine from the best vineyards of a Bordeaux *grand cru* estate.

GRAPE VARIETY A variant of the species *Vitis vinifera* (or *labrusca*, *riparia*, *rupestris*). There are several thousand different grape varieties scattered across the world.

GRAVES (Fr) A sub-region of Bordeaux. Also a geographic term indicating areas or specific vineyards with gravel soils. Such a composition often produces wines of great quality.

GREEN HARVEST A practice whereby some grape clusters are removed during the summer (when they are still green), so that the remaining fruit harvested in the fall will be of better quality.

H-I-J-K

HAIL A significant vineyard hazard; hail spoils bunches of grapes by breaking stalks and bursting individual grapes anywhere near maturity*. Such damage is usually followed by rot and mould.

HYBRID The offspring of two different species of vine. After the phylloxera* crisis, cross-breeding American and European vine species resulted in hybrids that are resistant to phylloxera but produce wines of mediocre quality. *See also* CROSS.

INAO (Fr) France's *Institut national de l'origine et de la qualité* is a public body founded on July 30, 1935, to monitor and delimit the production conditions of French wines from a specified region (AOP and IGP).

INDICATION GEOGRAPHIQUE PROTEGÉE (Fr) 'Indication of protected geographic origin' is the official designation (replacing *vin de pays*) for country wine from France or other EU countries. See VIN DE PAYS.

IPR (Po) *Indicação de proveniencia regulamentada*, the second-tier appellation of origin in Portugal.

JOVEN (Sp) Wines matured in vats or in barrel for a short period and bottled in the year following the harvest. In general it indicates supple and fruity wines to drink young.

KABINETT (Ger) Dry white German wines (Prädikatswein) that are never chaptalized.

L

LACTIC ACID A soft acid produced by a wine's malolactic fermentation*.

LEES A mixture of impurities, dead yeast cells, tartaric deposits, and residual matter from harvest, the lees form as a muddy sediment at the bottom of a barrel. The lees are usually removed when the wine is racked.

LEES, ON THE Said of wines (Muscadet, for example) that are aged in contact with lees and theoretically bottled before racking*.

LENGTH *See* 'Describing wine', p.232.

LIQUEUR DE TIRAGE (Fr) Cane sugar syrup added to a base wine to start secondary fermentation. Once fermented by yeast, this sugar produces up to 1.5% more alcohol, as well as carbon dioxide to create effervescence. Approximately 25 g/l (2.5% concentration) is needed to make *mousseux** wines. Some semi-sparkling wines receive only half this amount.

LIQUEUR D'EXPEDITION (Fr) Sugar-based syrup introduced to Champagne or other sparkling* wines after the removal of yeast sediment*. This practice regulates sweetness to produce *extra dry**, *brut**, *sec*, and *demi-sec** wines. It also adds stabilizers, if necessary, including citric acid* and sulphur dioxide*.

LIQUEUR WINE A wine with an elevated alcoholic content*, either natural or added, and a high content of unfermented sugar.

M

MACERATION A phase for vinification* for red wines, and sometimes rosés, whereby grape solids (skins and stems) are left in contact the must* before or during alcoholic fermentation* in order to extract colour, aromas*, tannins*, and other substances. Maceration is a principal area of concern for winemakers, and many technical procedures intended to improve the vinification of red wine revolve around it. *See also* CARBONIC MACERATION.

MADERIZED Referring to a wine that tastes reminiscent of Madeira; most often said of long-aged white wines subject to oxidation*. It can be recognized by the dark amber colour it engenders.

MALIC ACID A strong acid, and an unstable compound found in large quantities in young grapes, but which becomes less concentrated as the grapes ripen. It is recognizable by its sour, green apple taste. Once alcoholic fermentation* is complete, another process converts malic acid to lactic acid*. *See* below.

MALOLACTIC FERMENTATION Chemical conversion that follows alcoholic fermentation*. Malic acid* (which is reminiscent of green apples) is transformed into lactic acid* (which is reminiscent of yogurt) and carbon dioxide under the influence of certain bacteria. Since lactic acid has a less pungent flavour than malic acid, the wine becomes more supple.

MARC (Fr) After pressing grapes, a so-called *gâteau* (or 'cake') of the solid elements remains. This is known as *marc* (or pomace). It can be distilled to make a brandy of the same name.

MAS (Fr) Term sometimes used in southern France to describe the wine estate of an autonomous producer or one with independent means of production.

MASSAL SELECTION Intentional planting of various vine clones (or replanting from a heterogeneous mix) to preserve diversity and quality within a particular parcel of land.

MATURATION A seasonal period in the life cycle of the vine between the onset of fruit ripening and full maturity*, during which grape berries do not grow very much; instead, sugars are accumulated and acids reduced. Physiological maturity is reached once these two processes have stabilized, and grapes passing beyond this stage reach over-maturity*, *passerillage** (drying), or even the noble rot* sought for some wines.

MATURING (WINE) The various procedures between removal of wine from vats* and final bottling*.

MATURITY A physiological stage of the vine's lifecycle. *See* MATURATION.

MEDIUM-SWEET A term applied to a range of sweetness (12 to 45 g/l or up to 4.5% residual sugar) in white wines. A stage between dry* and sweet*.

MERCAPTAN A term derived from a contraction of *mercurium captans*, which denotes a compound arising from the interaction of alcohol and hydrogen sulfide. A faulty condition revealed by very strong and unpleasant odour, reminiscent of rotten eggs.

MERCHANT A buyer and distributor of wine. A merchant-grower will also take over some aspects of the wine's production, notably blending*, clarification*, and bottling*. In the Champagne region, a merchant known as a *négociant-manipulant* is responsible for purchasing grapes, must* or base wine and converting it into Champagne.

MESOCLIMATE Characterizes the specific climate conditions of a specific area of around several hundred square metres.

MÉTHODE CHAMPENOISE (Fr) ('Champagne method') A production method for effervescent* wines with the unique feature that carbonation is effected in bottle. Originally used to make Champagne (after which it is named), but it is also used in other winemaking areas, where it is known as the *méthode traditionnelle**.

MÉTHODE RURALE (Fr) ('rural method') A production method for semi-sparkling wines, which involves bottling before alcoholic fermentation* is completed.

MÉTHODE TRADITIONNELLE (Fr) ('traditional method') A used to describe the use of *méthode champenoise** to make sparkling wines outside the Champagne region. In Italy, this is known as *metodo tradizionale* or *metodo classico*.

MICROCLIMATE In the context of viticulture, this term denotes a collection of climatic conditions in a very small area, corresponding to just a few rows of vines, and which may differ from the local mesoclimate.

MILDEW A fungal condition of North American origin that attacks the green parts of vines. It was once fought with a mixture of copper (II) sulphate and hydrated lime (Bordeaux mixture*), but there are now effective synthetic products.

MISTELLE (FORTIFIED WINE) Known as *mistelle* in French, *sifone* in Italian, and *mistela* in Spanish, this is a blend obtained by the addition of neutral alcohol* to grape juice before any fermentation*.

MUST Grape juice obtained by crushing or pressing, and before it is fermented into wine.

MUTAGE A procedure that halts alcoholic fermentation* through the introduction of neutral alcohol*; this is an essential stage in the production of port and naturally sweet wines known as *vin doux naturel**.

N-O

NATURALLY SWEET WINE *See* VIN DOUX NATUREL.

NECK LABEL Label placed near the bottom of the neck of a bottle, often indicating just the vintage of the wine.

NOBLE (Fr) A term applied to classic, high quality grape varieties* and superior wines to distinguish them from table wines made from ordinary varieties and the hybrids* that flourished after the phylloxera* crisis.

NOBLE ROT When climatic conditions at the end of summer offer a combination of alternating sun and rain or mist, grape berries may be affected by a particular decay caused by the mould known as *Botrytis cinerea**. This fungus can 'rot' grapes to concentrate and alter their juice for the production of great sweet wines.

NOUVEAU (Fr) 'New' wines intended for consumption as soon as possible after harvest. The best-known example is Beaujolais nouveau, which comes to market in mid-November.

NUIT (VIN D'UNE) (Fr) Literally a 'wine of one night'; a deep rosé wine obtained from maceration* of very short duration (between 12 and 24 hours).

OIDIUM A vine disease of North American origin caused by a microscopic fungus that attacks the flowers, leaves, and grape berries; the berries dry out and a whitish powder covers the vine. It can be remedied by application of sulphur.

ORGANIC The cultivation of vines without using any synthetic products.

ORGANOLEPTIC A term referring to sensory properties such as the aroma*, colour, and flavour of a wine.

OVER-MATURITY The physiological state following that of normal maturity* for grape berries. It may reveal itself either through the appearance of noble rot* or through *passerillage**. Over-maturity of white grapes can produce sweet* and very sweet* wines.

OXIDATION Direct contact between wine and air; this may alter its colour, aroma*, and flavour.

P

PASSERILLAGE (Fr) Over-maturity* causing grape berries to dry out, shrivel, and increase their sugar content. This is how so-called 'straw wines*', some Muscats, and sweet Jurançon wines are made. These should not be confused with liqueur wines*.

PASSETOUTGRAINS A wine made in Burgundy from a pre-fermentation vat mixture of Gamay Noir and Pinot Noir grapes; the latter must make up at least one third of the blend.

PASSITO (It) An Italian wine made from dried grapes.

PERLANT (Fr) Term relating to slightly effervescent* wines. In France, the term *perlant* is applied to wines that are less effervescent than *pétillant** wines.

PÉTILLANT (Fr) A category of effervescent* wine made using the second fermentation in bottle method (*méthode traditionnelle**), but resulting in a pressure less than half that of traditional sparkling wines. *Pétillant* wines of this kind are traditional in regions such as the Loire Valley – Montlouis and Vouvray, in particular.

PHYLLOXERA An aphid that attacks vines and their roots. It was accidentally exported from the United States and ravaged Europe's vineyards between 1860 and 1880.

PIGEAGE (Fr) Production method used for red wine*. It involves regularly submerging the cap* of marc* that accumulates on the surface of fermenting wine. *Pigeage* enriches the must* through contact with the grape skins, and promotes the extraction of the anthocyanins* and tannins* responsible for the wine's colour. The procedure also reduces the risk of spoilage that may result from the cap being exposed to the air for too long. Once carried out by hand (or indeed foot), pigeage is now a mechanical process that takes place in specially equipped vats*.

PIGMENTS Vegetable material causing colouration. In the case of grapes, pigments are almost exclusively anthocyanins*.

POLYPHENOLS A range of compounds including tannins*, anthocyanins*, and phenolic acids*. Their combination determines the aromas*, colour, and structure of a wine.

PRÄDIKATSWEIN (Ger) A superior category of quality German wine. Not chapitalized, the wines are divided into 6 sub-categories, which are defined by the grape sugar concentration at harvest. They represent the country's best wines.

PRE-FERMENTATION MACERATION In white winemaking, pressing* takes place before fermentation*. However, there are many aromatic compounds trapped in the grape skins, so pre-fermentation maceration consists of leaving the juice in contact with the grape skins for a few hours to draw out those characters before pressing.

PRESS WINE Red wine* obtained by pressing* any solid matter remaining after fermentation and after the free-run wine* has been collected. *See also* DÉCUVAISON.

PRESSING
1. The act of squeezing grapes in a press to extract their liquid.
2. The product obtained by such a procedure. There are essentially two methods of pressing: with white wines and rosés, fresh grapes are pressed before fermentation and the resultant liquid is known as must* or juice; with red wines, pressing takes places after fermentation using the *marc** obtained during *cuvaison**.

PRUNING Annual or semi-annual elimination of excess growth. Good practice leaves just one or two well-situated branches to provide the buds that will, in turn, produce fruit clusters. (Clusters of grapes grow on buds or 'eyes' that form on wood from previous years.) *Gobelet* or bush pruning makes the vine hardier against the vagaries of a hot climate (wind, drought). *Guyot* pruning (single or double) leaves just a branch or two from the existing vine trunk and is better suited to more temperate climes.

PUMPING OVER A technique in red winemaking whereby the fermenting must* is pumped from the base of the vat* over the top of the cap* of *marc** to aid the extraction of phenolic compounds.

Q-R

QBA (*Qualitätswein bestimmter Anbaugebiete*) Category of German quality wines that have been produced in one of 13 official regions. May be subject to chaptalization*.

QUINTA (Po) The Portuguese term for a wine estate.

RACKING A procedure whereby wine is separated from its lees* and poured into another container.

RAMEAU (Fr) A vine shoot that has grown during the current year.

RANCIO (Fr & Sp) A character (reminiscent of cheese) caused by leaving air in a vat* or barrel* of fortified wine. Rancio is the direct result of oxidation*.

RATAFIA (Fr) An aperitif liqueur made in Champagne and Burgundy by adding approximately one part *marc** brandy to two parts fresh grape juice.

RECIOTO (It) A type of wine made in Italy with grapes that have been left to dry for a certain period. They are thus extremely concentrated, and produce a sweet dessert wine*.

RECOLTANT-MANIPULANT (Fr) A specific term in Champagne for a producer who makes wine from his own grapes.

RED (WINE) A wine produced by maceration of must* with red or black grape skins to extract their colour, as well as aromas* and tannins*. The grapes are most often destemmed*. Maceration* may last from a few days to several weeks, and the colour obtained is dependent on genetic factors (grape variety*), climatic conditions, characteristics of the soil – and winemaking techniques such as the frequency of pumping over, temperature control, etc..

REDUCTION A chemical state that is the opposite or inverse of oxidation*. Wine reduction is caused by prolonged deprivation of oxygen. This presents no danger for wine storage*, quite the contrary. But it does promote the temporary formation of slightly fetid, gamey odours and various hints of sulphur, to the greater or lesser detriment of the wine's bouquet*. These drawbacks can easily be addressed by allowing the wine to breathe* before drinking.

RE-FERMENTATION A faulty re-initiation of alcoholic fermentation*. This phenomenon may occur in poorly stabilized wines containing residual sugar*.

RESERVA (Sp) Red wines matured at a *bodega** for a period of three years, of which at least one is in barrel*. For white wines and rosés, this storage period is reduced to 18 months, of which at least six months must be in barrel.

RESERVE WINE The portion of production held back by wineries for use in later blends*. The final wine is identified with a specific vintage. In Champagne, reserve wines are used to make non-vintage wines. Additionally, producers may use the term reserve simply for their high-end wines.

RESIDUAL SUGAR The amount (grams or percentage) of sugar remaining in the wine after alcoholic fermentation*.

RIDDLING A procedure applied to Champagne-style sparkling* wines, whereby the sediment of spent yeast* is encouraged to settle against the bottom of the bottle closure* before being removed.

RIMAGE (Fr) A vintage Banyuls wine that is bottled quickly to avoid oxidation and preserve the wine's fruit character and freshness. The word means 'age of the grape' in Catalan.

RISERVA (It) Italian DOC* or DOCG* wines that have been aged for official minimum periods in barrel* and in bottle.

ROASTED A term sometimes applied to very sweet* wines with aromas* of grapes affected by noble rot*.

ROOM TEMPERATURE Back in the days when cellars were cold and meals were eaten in rooms that were not continually heated, wines were served at a 'room temperature' that rarely exceeded 64°F (18°C). Today, when 'room temperature' often means 70°F (21°C) or more, it's advisable to serve even red wine as slightly 'cool'.

ROOTSTOCK The underground portion of a vine that has been grafted. Most European vines have been grafted onto phylloxera-resistant North American rootstock since the late 19th century.

ROSADO (Sp) / **ROSATO** (It) Rosé.

ROSÉ (WINE) A wine with a more or less obvious pink colour. It's obtained either by directly pressing* red grapes, by pressing crushed red grapes after several hours of cold maceration*, or by very brief, partial maceration before applying the wine press. Macerated rosés have more intense fruit flavours than directly pressed wines, but lack their finesse.

RUNNING-OFF Part of the vinification* procedure for red wine* during which 'free-run*' wine is removed from the bottom of the vat*, leaving the marc* behind.

S

SABLE (VIN DE) (Fr) Literally 'sand wine', or wine made from vines growing in sandy soil near the sea.

SAIGNÉE (Fr) ('Bleeding the vats'). A procedure during which a fraction of the must is drawn off or 'bled' from a vat* of red wine* – early in its production. Clairet* wine and some rosés* are made this way. It's also a method to concentrate red wines.

SECO (Sp and Po) / **SECCO** (It) Dry.

SECOND WINE A selection or blend* not considered good enough for use in a producer's best wine or *grand vin**. At good estates, the second wine often represents excellent value.

SEDIMENT A small fraction of the must* or wine containing a high concentration of vegetal and organic debris. *See also* RACKING.

SÉLECTION DE GRAINS NOBLES (SGN) (Fr) 'Selection of noble grape berries' – a term used in France to denote wines made with botrytized* or dried grapes.

SINGLE-VARIETY (WINE) A wine made from only one grape variety*. A French single-variety wine must be 100 per cent from the variety in question; but in many other countries there are regulated tolerances (75 or 85 per cent), or indeed no regulation at all. *See also* VARIETAL (WINE).

SOLAR (Po) A *château* or estate in Portugal.

SOLERA (Sp) A system of fractional blending used in Jerez (Spain), whereby several harvests are aged in a succession of barrels* to produce a consistent flavour.

SPARKLING There are several methods to produce effervescent* wine: the *méthode traditionnelle** (also known as *méthode champenoise**); the *méthode rurale** (used in France's Gaillac and Die) among other regions), where effervescence is the result of part-fermentation in bottle; and the Charmat* (closed vat) method, where effervescence is developed in a vat* to avoid the necessity of bottle-by-bottle riddling* and dégorgement (disgorgement)*.

SPÄTLESE (Ger) A QMP* designation for late-harvested German wine.

SPUMANTE (It) An effervescent Italian wine.

STABILIZATION Wines are stabilized during production to prevent in-bottle precipitation of deposits, harmful chemical reactions, and the growth of microorganisms that may arise in the course of transportation and storage*.

STEM The 'skeleton' of a bunch of grapes. Stems are made of woody tissue rich in phenolic compounds, which have a tendency to yield herbaceous flavours.

STILL (WINE) The opposite of effervescent*. The term refers to wines with no discernible carbon dioxide content.

STORAGE Wine is a relatively delicate product, and it may develop unfavourably if not stored correctly. Commonly observed guidelines are intended to protect wine from the action of microbes, particularly acidic bacteria, and against physical and chemical changes that result from exposure to air and heat. Once bottled, the storage period of a wine can of course vary according to the characteristics of the cellar and the wine itself.

STRAW WINE A sweet* wine made from dried grapes. These grapes were traditionally laid on beds of straw or hung up to dehydrate; and their sugars concentrated in greater proportions than their acid content. Principally produced in France, in Jura or Côtes du Rhône, and with an alcoholic content of more than 14% by volume, these wines can be cellared for great lengths of time.

SULPHITING A strictly regulated procedure whereby sulphur dioxide* is added to a wine to assure its microbial and chemical stability.

SULPHUR DIOXIDE (SO_2) Winemakers have adapted sulphur dioxide for a number of uses since time immemorial: it stops premature fermentation* of harvested grapes, inhibits action by various kinds of yeasts*, eliminates microbes and bacteria, protects against oxidation*, acts as a solvent, and can check malolactic fermentation*; it has proved itself a useful ally for sweet* white wines with a tendency toward (faulty) second fermentation in bottle.

SUPERIORE (It) Term for an Italian wine with a higher-than-typical alcohol level (or having undergone a longer period of ageing) than a standard DOC* wine.

SWEET Designation for wine with a sugar content of more than 45 g per litre (or 4.5%).

T

TABLE WINE A wine with no geographic indication of origin or particular quality classification – intended for everyday drinking.

TAFELWEIN (Ger) German table wine.

TANNIN or **TANNINS** The stems*, skins, and seeds of a grape cluster contain chemical compounds (tannins) that are released by pressing and maceration*. These organic chemicals provide the wine's aromas* and flavours, and determine its capacity for ageing.

TARTARIC ACID The most refined acid and the most acidic component of a wine; rarely encountered in the plant kingdom. Its presence in grape berries gradually diminishes with the onset of ripening, and then varies according to climatic conditions.

TARTRATES White crystalline substances that form on the walls of wine vats*, barrels*, and sometimes at the bottom of bottles. They are harmless salts of tartaric acid* and have no taste.

TASTEVIN (Fr) A traditional cellar instrument taking the form of a small, shallow, metallic cup. Used to observe the clarity and colour of a wine, characteristics that are assessed to determine the wine's later treatment. Its use in actually tasting cellared wine from barrels* was originally a secondary function.

TASTING NOTE A systematically documented impression of a wine by a taster. Such notes generally list (in order) visual, olfactory, gustatory, and tactile sensations.

TENUTA (It) Italian wine estate.

TERROIR (Fr) The composite impact of soils, topography, climate, and even cultural practices – all of which determine the final character of a wine.

THINNING Cutting back spring or summer growth so that nutrients necessary to ripen grapes are not lost to unnecessary shoot or leaf development. Too little thinning early in the season many lead to *coulure** and the loss of the harvest.

TINTO (Sp and Po) Red.

TONNEAU Term for a specific type of barrel*. In Bordeaux, the tonneau is a unit of volume equivalent to four standard barrels, or about 240 gallons (900 litres).

TOPPING (or TOPPING UP) A procedure through which wine containers are monitored and refilled so that the wine is not left in (adverse) contact with the air.

TRELLISING Modern vineyards are generally trellised, *i.e.* vines are attached to a structure consisting of stakes and parallel wires.

TRIES or **TRIS** (Fr) This term refers to the succession of very selective harvests used to gather dried or botrytized *grapes.

TROCKEN (Ger) Dry.

TROCKENBEERENAUSLESE (Ger) A German Prädikatswein made from botrytis-affected grapes .

V

VARIETAL (WINE) A wine made from only one grape variety. A French varietal wine must be 100 per cent from the variety in question; but in many other countries there are regulated tolerances (75%, 85%), or indeed no regulation at all. *See also* SINGLE-VARIETY (WINE).

VAT Vats are winemaking receptacles whose capacity may vary between a couple or hundred and several thousand gallons. They are used for vinification*, maturation*, and storage* of wine. A number of materials are used in their construction, including wood, stone, concrete, galvanized steel, stainless steel, fibreglass, and plastic. Vats used for vinification may be equipped with various fixtures to carry out *pigeage** (the submersion of the cap* of grape skins) or *remontage** (pumping of wine over the cap) automatically.

VDN *See* VIN DOUX NATUREL.

VECCHIO (It) An Italian wine that has been aged for longer than average in barrel* or in bottle.

VÉRAISON (Fr) The onset of ripening, or the stage of grape cluster development during which the berries begin to change colour.

VERY SWEET A wine produced with extremely rich must* or a liqueur wine* that has been concentrated by heating; also wine from *mutage** of must with neutral alcohol and without fermentation (naturally sweet* wine).

VIGNA (It) Vineyard.

VIGNETO (It) Winemaker.

VIN DE FRANCE (Fr) Wine sold with no indication of its geographic origin (SIG), previously known as *vin de table*. These French wines may indicate the year and/or grape variety on the label.

VIN DOUX NATUREL (Fr) Naturally sweet wine whose initial sugar content is no less than 252 grams per litre (25%). The alcoholic fermentation* of the wine is halted through the addition of neutral spirit alcohol.

VIN GRIS (Fr) 'Grey wine' is a rosé produced when the pulp and red grape skins come into only brief contact with the must. The slightly pink juice that is run off is then fermented.

VIN JAUNE (Fr) 'Yellow wine', or a white wine from Jura, France, matured in barrel* under a film of yeast*.

VIN SANTO (It) An Italian *passito** wine.

VINE SHOOT The new stems created by the vine each year. Shoots are the year's new growth and not the older wood of the canes or trunk.

VINIFICATION The stages of winemaking between grape-picking and the end of alcoholic fermentation*.

VINTAGE The year of the harvest from which a wine originates. The character of any vintage is a function of many climatic factors, and they determine much of the quality of the wine and its potential for ageing. Differences between vintages are such that a producer may blend wines from different years to obtain a more balanced wine. Multi-vintage blends (non-vintage wines) are the norm in Champagne.

VITIS LABRUSCA A North American species of grape vine.

VITIS VINIFERA The European species of grape vine.

W-Z

WEEDING Vineyards are weeded to eliminate (plant) competition for water and nutrients during the vine-growing season.

WHITE (WINE) A wine made from white grapes (or red grapes with white juice) after immediate extraction of the juice or must* from the skins, followed by alcoholic fermentation*. *See also* VINIFICATION.

WINERY A place where wine is made and/or matured in barrels* or vats*.

YEAST Microscopic single-celled fungi found naturally on grape skins (and such yeasts are known as indigenous yeasts). Yeasts multiply in grape juice and drive alcoholic fermentation*. Research has enabled laboratory cultivation of the most appropriate yeasts for certain kinds of fermentation, and even dried yeast can now be used to make wine.

YIELD The weight of grapes, or equivalent volume in wine, harvested per acre or hectare of vineyard. In Europe, this is a regulated maximum figure for quality wines from a specified region, and is expressed in kilograms of grapes or hectolitres of wine per hectare. In the latter case, the lees* and sediment* are included. In France, the yield of any particular harvest may be reduced by order of the national wine authorities in response to variance in the weather. Depending on the quality of the harvest, the authorities also can set a temporary upper limit for the yield, which will always be lower than the absolute limit prescribed by the definition of each appellation.

207
212

Index

A

D

M

Q

R

T

U

V

Index of grape varieties

Red and rosé grape varieties

P-R

S-U

V-Z

White grape varieties

A-C

D-F

G-I

J-L

M-O

P-R

S-U

V-Z

Acknowledgements

The Editor would like to thank all those who opened their doors to our photographer:

Bouchard Père & Fils, Château de Beaune, 21200 Beaune
Champagne Gosset 69, rue Jules Blondeau, 51160 Ay
Champagne Krug 5, rue Coquebert, 51100 Reims
Champagne Louis Roederer 21, boulevard Lundy, 51100 Reims
Château Climens 33720 Barsac
Château d'Yquem 33210 Sauternes
Château Lascombes 1, cours de Verdun, 33460 Margaux
Château Latour Saint-Lambert 33250 Pauillac
Château Le Bon Pasteur "Maillet," 33500 Pomerol
Château Moncontour 37210 Vouvray
Château de Pommard 15, rue Marrey Monge, 21630 Pommard
Domaine de la Charmoise, Henry et Jean-Sébastien Marionnet, 41230 Soings-en Sologne
Domaine de la Coulée de Serrant, Château de la Roche aux Moines, 49170 Savennières
Domaine Jean-Maurice Raffault 74, rue du Bourg, 37420 Savigny-en-Véron
Domaine Marcel Deiss 15, route du Vin, 68750 Bergheim
Domaine Michel Juillot 59, Grande Rue, 71640 Mercurey
Domaine de La Romanée-Conti 1, rue Derrière-le-Four, 21700 Vosne-Romanée
Domaines Denis Dubourdieu Château Reynon, 33410 Beguey
Domaines Hugel & Fils 3, rue de la Première Armée, 68340 Riquewihr
Domaines Schlumberger 100, rue Théodore Deck, 68501 Guebwiller
Maison Trimbach 15, route de Bergheim, 68150 Ribeauvillé

and Château Lynch-Bages, Château Rayas, Opus One, Ridge Wineyards,
Vignobles Joseph Mellot à Sancerre, le site www.VotreCave.com

and Tonnellerie Vincent Darnajou, Lieu-dit Goujon, 33570 Montagne

The Editor would like to thank the following people for their help :

David Allan (for his collection of corkscrews), Antoine Caron, Etienne Hunyady, Éric Inglessis (for his collection of labels), Yann Lioux (South World Wines), Alain Marnat, Christophe Vidal (Cave de Tolbiac 45, rue de Tolbiac, 75013 Paris) et La Vaissellerie, 85, rue de Rennes, 75006 Paris.

Picture acknowledgements

16 Ph. © Erich Lessing/AKG, 17 Ph. Coll. Archives Larbor, 18 t l Ph. Coll. Archives Larbor, 18 m l Ph. © Heritage Images/Leemage, 18 m r Ph. Coll. Archives Larbor, 18 b Ph. Coll. Archives Larbor, 19 t l Ph. Coll. Archives Larbor, 19 t r Ph. Coll. Archives Larbor, 19 b l Ph. © Photo Josse/Leemage, 19 b r Ph. Coll. Archives Larbor, 20 Ph. © Hervé Lewandowski/RMN, 21 Ph. © Adoc-photos, 22 Ph. © K.J. Historical/Corbis, 23 t Ph. © Library of Congress, Washington, 23 b Ph. © Alamy/Photo12.com, 28 Ph. © Philippe S. Giraud/Terres du Sud/Sygma/Corbis, 30 t l Ph. © J.L. Barde/Scope, 30 m l Ph. © Domaines Denis Dubourdieu, 30 m r Ph. © P. Othoniel/JDD/Gamma/Eyedea Presse, 31 t r Ph. © Charles O'Rear/Corbis, 31 m r Ph. © Josep Lago/AFP, 31 m l Ph. © Ridge Wineyards, 34 Ph. © J. Guillard/Scope, 36 b r Ph. © Jack K. Clark/AgStock Images/Corbis, 37 b l Ph. © J. Guillard/Scope, 37 b r Ph. © S. Matthews/Scope, 38 t Ph. © Alamy/Photo12.com, 38 m Ph. © J. Guillard/Scope, 39 b l Ph. © Alamy/Photo12.com, 39 b m Ph. © Alamy/Photo12.com, 40 b l Ph. © David Gubernick/AgStock Images/Corbis, 40 b m Ph. © J. Guillard/Scope, 40 b r Ph. © J. Guillard/Scope, 41 b l Ph. © J. Guillard/Scope, 41 b m Ph. © J. L. Barde/Scope, 41 b r Ph. © Martin Rugner/Age Fotostock/Hoa-Qui/Eyedea Presse, 42 t Ph. © Alamy/Photo12.com, 44 Ph. © P. Roy/Hemis.fr, 45 t Ph. © J. Guillard/Scope, 45 b Ph. © John Frumm/Hemis.fr, 48 r Ph © Catherine Corbeau-Mellot (Vignobles Joseph Mellot, Sancerre), 55 Ph. © P. Roy/Hoa-Qui/Eyedea Presse, 59 t Ph © Dom. de la Coulée de Serrant, 72 Ph. © Marc Volk/fstop/Corbis, 74 Porto Sandeman. Ph. © D. Bartruff/Encyclopedia/Corbis, 75 t l Ph. © Alamy/Photo12.com, 75 Ph. © Alamy/Photo12.com, 75 Ph. © J.L. Barde/Scope, 96 Ph. © Emilio Suetone/Hemis.fr, 97 Ph. © Alamy/Photo12.com, 98 Ph; © J. Guillard/Scope, 100 Ph. © Alamy/Photo12.com, 101 Ph. © Alamy/Photo12.com, 102 Ph. © S. Matthews/Scope, 103 Ph. © Alamy/Photo12.com, 116 t l Ph. © Hulton Archive/Getty Images, 116 t r Ph. © Costa/Leemage, 125 Ph. © Derrick Ceyrac/AFP, 126 Ph. © Jeff Pachoud/AFP, 127 Ph. © Michael John Kielty/Corbis, 128 l Ph. © Château Lynch-Bages, 129 t r Ph. © J. Guillard/Scope, 129 m r Ph. © Scope, 130 Ph. © Getty Images/AFP, 131 Ph. © Jeff Pachoud/AFP, 134 Ph © VotreCave.com, 136 Ph. © J. Guillard/Scope, 137 Ph. © J.L. Barde/Scope, 141 b r Château l'Angélus barrel cellar, Saint-Emilion. Ph. © P. Roy/Hemis.fr, 142 Ph. © Masterfile-Royalty Free, 143 Ph. © J. Guillard/Scope, 147 Ph. © F. Cateloy/Hoa-Qui/Eyedea Presse, 151 Ph. © Philippe Petit/Paris-Match/Scoop, 152 Ph. © Ryman Cabannes/Corbis, 162 t r Ph. © J.L. Barde/Scope, 163 b r Ph. © Château Rayas, 163 t l Ph. © J. L. Barde/Scope, 163 t r Ph. © J. Guillard/Scope, 163 m l Ph. © J. Guillard/Scope, 169 Ph. © Redcover.com/Getty Images, 170 Ph. © Mallet/Photocuisine/Corbis, 171 Ph. © D. Japy, 173 t Ph. © P. Roy/Hemis.fr, 173 b Ph. © J.-D. Sudres/Hemis.fr, 188–189 b Ph. © Larousse/Diaf Studiaphot/Hervé Geyssels, 195 t Ph. © D. Japy, 196 Ph. © B. Hechler/Fotolia.com, 197 Ph. © J.C. Cuvelier/Fotolia.com, 198–201 l and t r Ph. © D. Japy, 204 Ph. © Sébastien Montier/Fotolia.com, 208 Ph. © Alamy/Photo12.com, 214 Ph. © D. Japy, 226 Ph. © James Jackson/Alamy, 242 Clos de Vougeot. Ph. © C. Boisvieux/Hoa-Qui/Eyedea Presse, 244 Château de Monbadon et son vignoble, AOC Côtes de Castillon. Ph. © P. Roy/Hemis.fr, 252 Ph. © P. Roy/Hemis.fr, 253 Ph. © J.L. Barbe/scope, 254 m Ph. © J.-D. Sudres/Hemis.fr, 255 Cos d'Estournel, Saint-Estèphe. Ph. © Alamy/Photo12.com, 256 t Château Pichon-Longueville. Ph. © A. Chicurel/Hemis.fr, 257 Ph. © P. Roy/Hemis.fr, 260 t Ph. © P. Roy/Hemis.fr, 261 Ph. © P. Roy/Hemis.fr, 263 Ph. © Ph. Roy/Hemis.fr, 267 b Ph. © P. Roy/Hemis.fr, 268 t Ph. © P. Jacques/Hemis.fr, 268 m Ph. © Alamy/Photo12.com, 270 Ph. © P. Roy/Hemis.fr, 272 Ph. © S. Grandadam/Hoa-Qui/Eyedea Presse, 273 Ph. © F. Jalain/Explorer/Hoa-Qui/Eyedea Presse, 275 Ph. © H. Hughes/Hemis.fr, 280 t Ph. © Alamy/Photo12.com, 280 m Maison Deliance, Dracy-le-Fort. Ph. © J.L. Barde/Scope, 281 Ph. © J. Guillard/Scope, 282 Ph. © Alamy/Photo12.com, 283 Ph. © Alamy/Photo12.com, 285 t Domaine du Château Gris, Nuits-Saint-Georges. Ph. © C. Boisvieux/Hoa-Qui/Eyedea Presse, 285 b Ph. © Alamy/Photo12.com, 286 Ph. © J. Guillard/Scope, 287 Ph. © Alamy/Photo12.com, 290 t Château de Meursault. Ph. © Alamy/ Photo12.com, 290 b Ph. © Alamy/Photo12.com, 292 Château de Rully. Ph. © Alamy/Photo12.com, 294 t Ph. © H. Hughes/Hemis.fr, 294 b Ph. © J.L. Barde/Scope, 306 Château d'Arlay. Ph. © J. Guillard/Scope, 310 Domaine Macle, Château-Chalon. Ph. © J. Guillard/Scope, 314 Ph. © M. Guillard/Scope, 316 b Ph. © M. Rougemont/Top/Eyedea Presse, 318 Ph. © P. Blondel/Scope, 319 Ph. © P. Body/Hemis.fr, 321 Ph. © M. Plassart/Scope, 322 Ph. © J. Guillard/Scope, 324 Ph. © E. Labadie, 325 Ph. © J. Guillard/Scope, 326 Ph. © J. Guillard/Scope, 328 Ph. © E. Labadie, 329 Domaine Auguste Clape, Cornas. Ph. © J. Guillard/Scope, 330 Ph. © B. Rieger/Hemis.fr, 332 Ph. © J.-D. Sudres/Top/Eyedea Presse, 334 Ph. © J.L. Barde/Scope, 336 t Clos Uroulat. Ph. © J.L. Barde/Scope, 337 Ph. © Jean-Loius Pieux avec Création, 338 Buzet Cooperative Ph. © J.L. Barde/Scope, 339 Xavier Martin tasting, Irouleguy. Ph. © J. L. Barde/Scope, 340 Ph. © Chris Hellier/Corbis, 342 Abbaye de Lagrasse. Ph. © R. Nourry/Scope, 344 Ph. © Dom. La Coume du Roy, 345 Ph. © Owen Franken/Corbis, 347 Ph. © J. Guillard/Scope, 348 Ph. © C. Moirenc/Hemis.fr, 349 Domaine Ott, Domaine de Trevallon, Château Sainte Roseline and Château d'Esclans. Ph. © J. Guillard/Scope, 350 Ph. © C. Goupi/Scope, 351 Domaine Torracia, Lecci. Ph. © Colonel Mario/Scope, 352 Ph. © Alamy/Photo12.com, 354 Ph. © Cuboimages/Leemage, 355 Ph. © Guenter Rossenbach/Corbis, 357 t Ph. © R. Mattes/Hemis.fr, 357 b DR, 358 Ph. © Alamy/Photo12.com, 359 Ph. © Stefano Amantini/Atlantide Phototravel/Corbis, 360 t Ph. © C. Vaisse/Hoa-qui/Eyedea Presse, 360 m Ph. © Alamy/Photo12.com, 361 t Ph. © Alamy/Photo12.com, 361 b Ph. © Pierrick Bourgault, 362 Ph. © Alamy/Photo12.com, 365 Ph. © Cuboimages/Leemage, 366 Ph. © Stefano Amantini/Atlantide Phototravel/Corbis, 367 Ph. © Alamy/Photo12.com, 368 and 369 r Ph. © Etienne Hunyady, 369 l Mario Incisa della Rochetta. Ph. © Farabola/Leemage, 371 Ph. © Pierrick Bourgault, 372 Ph. © P. Renault/Hemis.fr, 374 Ph. © Jose Barea/Tmn/Hoa-Qui/Eyedea Presse, 376 Ph. © Alamy/Photo12.com, 377 Ph. © Alamy/Photo12.com, 378 Ph. © Alamy/Photo12.com, 379 Ph. © Alamy/Photo12.com, 380 t Ph. © Alamy/Photo12.com, 380 b Ph. © Alamy/Photo12.com, 381 Ph. © Alamy/Photo12.com, 382 Ph. © Alamy/Photo12.com, 383 Ph. © Alamy/Photo12.com, 384 t l Ph. © J. Guillard/Scope, 384 t r Ph. © Charles O'Rear/Corbis, 385 t l Ph. © J. Guillard/Scope, 385 t r Ph. © J. Guillard/Scope, 386 Ph. © Alamy/Photo12.com 388 Ph. © J.L. Barde/Scope, 389 Ph. © Alamy/Photo12.com, 390 Ph. © Alamy/Photo12.com, 392 Ph. © Alamy/Photo12.com, 393 Ph. © J. Guillard/Scope, 394 Ph. © Alamy/Photo12.com, 395 Ph. © J. Guillard/Scope, 396 t Ph. © Alamy/Photo12.com, 396 b Ph. © Alamy/Photo12.com, 397 t Ph. © Alamy/Photo12.com, 398 Ph. © G. Monica/White Star/age Fotostock, 399 t Ph. © R. Mattes/Hemis.fr, 400 Ph. © Alamy/Photo12.com, 402 Ph. © Alamy/Photo12.com, 403 Ph. © Alamy/Photo12.com, 404 t Ph. © M. Rugnier/Age Fotostock/Hoa-Qui/Eyedea Presse, 404 m Ph. © Alamy/Photo12.com, 405 Ph. © Imagebroker/Hemis.fr, 406 t Ph. © Alamy/Photo12.com, 406 b Ph. © Alamy/Photo12.com, 407 Ph. © Alamy/Photo12.com, 408 t Ph. © Doug Pearson/JAI/Corbis, 409 t Ph. © J. Guillard/Scope, 409 b Ph. © Alamy/Photo12.com, 410 Ph. © Alamy/Photo12.com, 411 m Ph. © Alamy/Photo12.com, 412 Ph. © J. Guillard/Scope, 415 Ph. © J. Guillard/Scope, 416 Ph. © J. Guillard/Scope, 417 Ph. © Alamy/Photo12.com, 418 Ph. © Alamy/Photo12.com, 419 Ph. © Anthony Blake/Age Fotostock, 420 Ph. © Richard Nebesky/Lonely Planet Images, 421 Ph. © G. Rigoulet/Hemis.fr, 422 Ph. © J. - D. Sudres/Top/Eyedea Presse, 423 Ph. © Alamy/Photo12.com, 424 Ph. © John Sims/age Fotostock, 426 Ph. © P. De Wilde/Hoa-Qui/Eyedea Presse, 427 Ph. © Yiergos Ventouris-IML/Hemis.fr, 428 Ph. © M. Dozier/Hemis.fr, 429 Ph. © C. Bowman/Scope, 430 Ph. © Alamy/Photo12.com, 431 m Ph. © Alamy/Photo12.com, 432 Ph. © Alamy/Photo12.com, 434 Ph. © Alamy/Photo12.com, 435 Ph. © Alamy/Photo12.com, 437 Ph. © Alamy/Photo12.com, 438 Ph. © Alamy/Photo12.com, 439 Ph. © Alamy/Photo12.com, 440 Ph. © Alamy/Photo12.com, 441 m Ph. © Fetzer Vineyards, 441 b Ph. © Alamy/Photo12.com, 442 Ph. © Alamy/Photo12.com, 443 t Ph. © Alamy/Photo12.com, 443 b Ph. © Clos du Val Winery, 444 t Ph. © Opus One Winery, 444 m Ph. © El Kashi/Corbis, 447 Ph. © David Gubernick/Corbis, 448 Ph. © Alamy/Photo12.com, 449 Ph. © B. Rondel/Corbis, 450 Ph. © Kordcom Kordcom/Age fotostock/Photolibrary.com, 452 Ph. © Kactus/Scope, 453 Ph. © S. Matthews/Scope, 454 t Ph. © S. Matthews/Scope, 455 m r Ph. © Kactus/Scope, 456 Ph. © Eduardo Longoni/Corbis, 458 Ph. © C. Heeb/Hemis.fr, 459 Ph. © Eduardo Longoni/Corbis, 460 Ph. © Jefferson Bernardes/Getty Images, 461 Ph. © Alamy/Photo12.com, 462 t Ph. © C. Heeb/Hemis.fr, 462 m Ph. © Alamy/Photo12.com, 462 b Ph. © Michael Lewis/Corbis, 463 Catena Zapata Winery. Ph. © Michael Lewis/Corbis, 464 Ph. © Alamy/Photo12.com, 466 Ph. © Alamy/Photo12.com, 467 Ph. © Alamy/Photo12.com, 468 t Ph. © Alamy/Photo12.com, 468 b Ph. © P. Narayan/Age Fotostock/Hoa-Qui/Eyedea Presse, 469 Ph. © C. Heeb/Hemis.fr, 470 Ph. © Andrew Watson/Ticket/Photolibrary.com, 472 Ph. © Russell Mountford/Lonely Planet Images, 473 Ph. © Neale Clarke/Robert Harding World Imagery/Corbis, 474 Ph. © Shoot/Age fotostock/Hoa-Qui/Eyedea Presse, 475 Ph. © J. Du Cange/Top/Eyedea Presse, 476 t Ph. © Alamy/Photo12.com, 476 m Ph. © J.L. Barde/Scope, 477 Domaine Chandon, Yarra Valley. Ph. © E. Valentin/Hoa-Qui/Eyedea Presse, 478 Ph. © D. Dutay/Scope, 479 Ph. © B. Gardel/Hemis.fr, 480 Ph. © Alamy/Photo12.com, 481 Ph. © Alamy/Photo12.com, 482 Ph. © Nick Servian/Scope, 484 Ph. © Alamy/Photo12.com, 485 Ph. © Alamy/Photo12.com, 486 t Ph. © Alamy/Photo12.com, 486 b Ph. © Nick Servian/Scope, 488 Ph. © Tony McNicol/Alamy, 490 Ph. © Morales/Age Fotostock, 491 Ph. © Indranil Mukherjee/AFP

Ph. Olivier Ploton © Archives Larousse: 1, 4, 7, 12–13, 14 (Château Reynon), 27, 32, 35, 36 l and m, 37 m, 39 r, 42 b, 43, 46, 48 l and m, 49–54, 56–58, 59 b, 60–61, 62–63, 67–71, 76–81, 82–83 (Tonnellerie Darnajou), 84–89, 90–91 (Bouchard Père & Fils), 92, 94–95, 104–108, 118 (Cave Tolbiac), 120–121, 124 (Cave de Tolbiac), 128 r (Château de Pommard), 129 l, 132 (Château d'Yquem), 135 (Bouchard Père & Fils), 140, 141 (except b r), 142 r, 146 (Bouchard Père & Fils), 150 (Château Latour), 154–161, 164 l, 166–167 (Cave Tolbiac), 172, 177, 181, 186, 189 t, 190 (collection of old corkscrews, coll. David Allan, Paris), 191, 192–194, 195 b, 201 b r, 203–207, 209–213, 217 (Cave Tolbiac), 218–219, 228, 233, 236–237, 241, 247–249, 258–259, 264–266, 267 t, 276, 277 (Bouchard Père & Fils), 279, 288–289, 296, 298–299 (Maison Louis Roederer), 300–305, 308 b, 313, 316 t, 320, 336 b, 479 b, 492–493 (Dom. Michel Juillot).